ZONE HARDINESS OF PLANTS

P9-BJG-415

KEY

0a	4a
0b	4b
1a	5a
1b	5b
2a	6a
2b	6b
3a	7a
3b	7b
	8a

Davis Strait

Foxe Basin

Iqaluit

Hudson Strait

LABRADOR SEA

D

A

Hudson Bay

0a

Caniapiscau

NEWFOUNDLAND & LABRADOR

Churchill

Labrador City

Newfoundland

St.John's

Corner Brook

James Bay

La Grande Rivière

QUEBEC

0b

Gulf of St. Lawrence

TARIO

Albany

Lake pigon

1a

Lac Mistassini

1b

Jonquière Chicoutimi

Saguenay

PRINCE EDWARD ISLAND

Charlottetown

NEW BRUNSWICK

NOVA SCOTIA

Moncton

St. Maurice

2a

Harricana

Fredericton

Saint John

Dartmouth

Halifax

2b Trois-Rivières

3a

Charlesbourg

Québec

St. Lawrence

Ottawa

3b Laval

4a

Sherbrooke

Lake Superior

Sudbury

North Bay

Gatineau

Montréal

Sault Ste.Marie

4b

OTTAWA

5a

Lake Huron

Peterborough

Kingston

Oshawa

Lake Ontario

Toronto

Kitchener

Lake Michigan

Hamilton St.Catharines

London

5b

Sarnia

6a

Windsor

6b

Lake Erie

ATLANTIC OCEAN

Canadian Encyclopedia of
GARDENING

Canadian Encyclopedia of
GARDENING

EDITOR-IN-CHIEF
CHRISTOPHER BRICKELL

EDITOR-IN-CHIEF FOR CANADA
TREVOR COLE

Senior Editors Louise Abbott, Joanna Chisholm, Jill Hamilton
Senior Art Editor Stephen Josland • **US Consulting Editor** Ray Rogers
Editors Lynn Bresler, Candida Frith-Macdonald, Lin Hawthorne, Mary Sutherland
Editorial Assistants Zia Allaway, Christine Dyer, Madeline Farbman,
Jane Perlmutter, Katie Zien
DTP Designers Milos Orlovic, Louise Waller • **Managing Editor** Anna Kruger
Managing Art Editor Lee Griffiths • **Photography** Peter Anderson
Illustrations Karen Cochrane, Rupert Golby, Marian Hill
Picture Research Romaine Werblow, Mariana Sonnenberg, Jane Martin
Production Chris Avgherinos, Bethan Blase • **Design Assistance** Sylvia Figueroa
Index Dorothy Frame • **Project Director** Sharon Lucas
Creative Director Tina Vaughan • **Publisher** Chuck Lang
Editor, Canada Julia Roles • **Project Editor, Canada** Ian Whitelaw

DK Delhi
Editors Dipali Singh, Glenda Fernandes • **DTP** Pankaj Sharma
(DTP Coordinator), Rajesh Chibber, Jessica Subbramanian, Narender Kumar
Index Dipali Singh, Sheema Mookherjee
Managing Editor Ira Pande • **Managing Art Editor** Aparna Sharma

Special thanks to the staff at RHS Wisley and Vincent Square, in particular
Susanne Mitchell, Barbara Haynes, Michael Pollock, Alan Leslie,
Guy Barter, Jim Arbury, Jim England, Andrew Halstead, Chris Prior

Revised Canadian Edition, 2004
04 05 06 07 08 09 10 9 8 7 6 5 4 3 2 1

Previous edition published as
Practical Guide to Gardening in Canada

Copyright © 1992, 2001, 2002, 2004 Dorling Kindersley Limited

Dorling Kindersley is represented in Canada by
Tourmaline Editions Inc.,
662 King Street West, Suite 304,
Toronto, Ontario M5V 1M7

All rights reserved. No part of this publication may be reproduced,
stored in a retrieval system, or transmitted in any form or by any means,
electronic, mechanical, photocopying, recording, or otherwise, without
the prior written permission of the copyright owner.

National Library of Canada Cataloguing in Publication

Canadian encyclopedia of gardening / editor-in-chief, Christopher Brickell;
editor-in-chief for Canada, Trevor Cole. — Rev. Canadian ed.

Includes index.
Previous eds. published under title:
Practical guide to gardening in Canada.
ISBN 1-55363-034-3

1. Gardening—Canada. I. Brickell, Christopher II. Cole, Trevor J.
III. Title: Practical guide to gardening in Canada.

SB453.3.C2C35 2004   635'.0971   C2003-905029-7

Color reproduction by Colourscan, Singapore
Printed and bound in Singapore by Star Standard Industries (Ptc.) Ltd.

Discover more at
www.dk.com

CONTENTS

PART TWO: MAINTAINING THE GARDEN

PRACTICAL ADVICE ON TOOLS AND EQUIPMENT, GREENHOUSES, AND BUILDING MATERIALS AND TECHNIQUES; UNDERSTANDING SOIL TYPE AND CLIMATE, HOW PLANTS GROW AND REPRODUCE, AND HOW BEST TO DEAL WITH PROBLEMS

EDITOR-IN-CHIEF

CHRISTOPHER BRICKELL began his career with the Royal Horticultural Society in 1958, becoming Director of Wisley Garden in 1969. From 1985 until his retirement in 1993 he was Director General of the Society, representing its interests all over the world. Since 1976 he has held the Society's prestigious Victoria Medal of Honour, and in 1991 was made a CBE for his services to horticulture. He is President of the International Society for Horticultural Science and Chairman of the International Commission for the Nomenclature of Cultivated Plants.

EDITOR-IN-CHIEF FOR CANADA

TREVOR COLE graduated from the Royal Botanic Gardens, Kew, in 1960. After immigrating to Canada in 1967, he worked for Agriculture Canada, engaged in the evaluation and cultivation of native plants. He became assistant curator in charge of alpine and herbaceous plants, and was appointed Curator of the Dominion Arboretum in 1972, retiring in 1995. He is listed in *Who's Who in Canada* and has received many awards, including the Canada 125 Medal and an Award of Merit from the Garden Writers' Association of America.

CONTRIBUTORS AND CONSULTANTS

ROGER AYLETT *DAHLIAS* • **SUSAN M. BACHENHEIMER RESNICK** *BONSAI* • **BILL BAKER** *LILIES* • **LARRY BARLOW** (WITH **W.B. WADE**) *CHRYSANTHEMUMS* • **MIKE BENSON** *DISEASES* • **CAROLINE BOISSET** *CLIMBING PLANTS* • **DENI BOWN** *GROWING HERBS* • **ALEC BRISTOW** (WITH **WILMA RITTERSHAUSEN**) *ORCHIDS* • **DR. MARC CATHEY** (WITH **MARK MILLER**) *HEAT AND HARDINESS ZONES* • **ROY CHEEK** (WITH **GRAHAM RICE** AND **ISABELLE VAN GROENINGEN**) *PERENNIALS* • **TREVOR COLE** *VEGETABLES* (WITH **BRENDA COLE** AND **MICHAEL POLLOCK**) *FROST AND WIND PROTECTION* • **KATH DRYDEN** AND **CHRISTOPHER GREY-WILSON** (WITH **JOHN WARWICK**) *ROCK, SCREE, AND GRAVEL GARDENING; ALPINE HOUSES AND FRAMES* • **JACK ELLIOTT** *IRISES; BULBOUS PLANTS; TULIPS AND DAFFODILS* • **COLIN ELLIS** (WITH **MERVYN FEESEY**) *BAMBOOS* • **RAYMOND EVISON** *CLEMATIS* • **ELENA GARCIA** *FRUIT* • **JIM GARDINER** *ORNAMENTAL TREES; DWARF CONIFERS; TOPIARY; HEDGES AND SCREENS; ORNAMENTAL SHRUBS* • **MICHAEL GIBSON** (WITH **PETER HARKNESS**) *ROSES, ROSES FOR DISPLAY AND EXHIBITION* • **GEORGE GILBERT** *GROWING FRUIT* • **RICHARD GILBERT** *HYDROCULTURE* • **WILL GILES** *HARDY PALMS AND THE EXOTIC LOOK* • **DAN GILREIN** *INSECTS* • **RUPERT GOLBY** *GARDEN PLANNING AND DESIGN* • **DEENAGH GOOLD-ADAMS** (WITH **RICHARD GILBERT**) *INDOOR GARDENING* • **DIANA GRENFELL** *HOSTAS* • **JOHN HACKER** (WITH **GEOFF STEBBINGS**) *THE LAWN* • **ANDREW HALSTEAD** AND **PIPPA GREENWOOD** (WITH **CHRIS PRIOR** AND **LUCY HALSALL**) *PLANT PROBLEMS* • **LIN HAWTHORNE** *MEADOW GARDENING* • **ARTHUR HELLYER** (WITH **GRAHAM RICE**) *ANNUALS AND BIENNIALS* • **CLIVE INNES** (WITH **TERRY HEWITT**) *CACTI AND OTHER SUCCULENTS;* (WITH **RICHARD GILBERT**) *BROMELIADS* • **DAVID JOYCE** *CONTAINER GARDENING, BALCONIES AND ROOF GARDENS, WATER GARDENS IN CONTAINERS* • **TONY KENDLE** *SOILS AND FERTILIZERS* • **HAZEL KEY** (WITH **URSULA KEY-DAVIS**) *FERNS, PELARGONIUMS* • **JOY LARKCOM** (WITH **MICHAEL POLLOCK**) *GROWING VEGETABLES* • **KEITH LOACH** (WITH **DAVID HIDE**) *PRINCIPLES OF PROPAGATION;* (WITH **MICHAEL POLLOCK**) *BASIC BOTANY* • **PETER MARSTON** *CONSERVATORY GARDENING* • **PETER MCHOY** (WITH **GEOFF STEBBINGS**) *TOOLS AND EQUIPMENT; GREENHOUSES AND FRAMES; STRUCTURES AND SURFACES* • **KEVIN MORRIS** *LAWNS* • **ANDY PLASZ** *ROSES* • **MICHAEL POLLOCK** *CLIMATE AND THE GARDEN; THE BED SYSTEM* • **DAVID PYCRAFT** *WEEDS* • **PETER ROBINSON** *WATER GARDENING; WATERLILIES; WATER CONSERVATION AND RECYCLING; WATERSIDE DECKING* • **ANDY SENESAC** *WEEDS* • **DON TINDALL** *TENDER VEGETABLES AND FRUITS* • **ISABELLE VAN GROENINGEN** *PERENNIAL GROUNDCOVERS*

TEXT AND PICTURES OF *WILLOW WALLS* COURTESY OF *THE GARDEN* MAGAZINE

PREFACE

GARDENING IS BECOMING the number one hobby in Canada as more and more people discover that they CAN grow plants, and DO have a green thumb. The internet has brought us the availability of on-line shopping so that specialized gardening books and tools can be obtained in even the smallest community, while on-line seed and nursery catalogues give us the ability to browse listings from far-off places at the click of a mouse.

While there are a lot of gardening books describing plants, many gardeners find the need for an authoritative book they can turn to for practical advice – how to actually do something. Whether it is the neophyte gardener wondering how and when to divide a peony, or an experienced gardener looking for information on grafting fruit trees, this book answers their questions. With over 3,400 photographs and more than 360 detailed drawings, DK's *Canadian Encyclopedia of Gardening* offers clear, down-to-earth advice on growing almost any plant.

This guide includes the major groups of plants you are likely to grow, and covers soil preparation, site selection, planting, care, pruning, and propagation. In the first section, ornamentals, vegetables, fruit, and indoor plants are dealt with in a logical sequence. For example, all the leafy vegetables are grouped together, eliminating flipping through the book for information on similar plants.

The second section, Maintaining the Garden, covers soils and climate, pests and diseases, weed control, and tools and equipment – from plant labels to greenhouses. There are step-by-step pictures illustrating the practical aspects of subjects such as laying paths and building fences, while the chapter on climate gives useful ideas on protecting newly planted plants or those of borderline hardiness.

The text was written by a team of experts, while the photographs, taken over the experts' shoulders, make even the most complex task easy to follow. Occasionally, the plant used to illustrate a particular technique may not be hardy in your area, but the method remains the same and can be adapted to other plants.

DK's *Canadian Encyclopedia of Gardening* is a comprehensive ready reference, intended to serve both the beginner and the experienced gardener. It provides the know-how needed to garden successfully, and will help you experience the rewards of this, the most satisfying of leisure activities, whether you have a townhouse courtyard or a country estate.

TREVOR COLE
EDITOR-IN-CHIEF FOR CANADA
OTTAWA, 2004

CREATING THE GARDEN

HOW TO APPLY THE PRINCIPLES OF DESIGN, CHOOSE AND CULTIVATE
EVERY TYPE OF PLANT, AND CREATE AND PLANT GARDEN FEATURES

CHAPTER

1

GARDEN PLANNING AND DESIGN

TO NURTURE a garden over a period of time – seeing it develop and mature through the seasons – is a rewarding experience for its creator. For a garden to be successful, however, it needs careful and considered thought from the very beginning. A garden with simple lines and a natural flow, effortlessly summoning up a relaxed charm, may appear to have received little design input, yet it is almost certainly underpinned by intelligent planning. The design process is conspicuous in a garden of geometric formality, but the same input is required for seemingly artless informal plantings if they are to combine the essential qualities of unity, balance, and proportion, and be in sympathy with their surroundings.

Why do we garden?

WHERE does the motivation come from to cultivate a piece of ground, altering its appearance for our own benefit? Perhaps we still have an instinctive need to grow food to survive, or to mark out a territory that defines a specific area as our own, or to build a defensive boundary around it. Once within the garden gate, we can leave behind our working lives and retreat to the safety of our private space. Whatever the underlying motivation, that first small spark of interest can easily grow into a lifelong passion and a source of real enjoyment.

Climate and surroundings
In the majority of cases a garden will surround a house, creating fundamental practical requirements to tame the environment. The need for entry by foot and by vehicle will mean making clear paths and drives that allow easy access to the house in all weather throughout the year. Similarly basic is the need for light: plant growth near windows and doors must be kept in check.

At a greater distance, planting a windbreak of trees and shrubs can provide invaluable protection against damaging winds, sheltering both buildings and less robust plantings. Such shelterbelts of trees will also prevent snow from drifting into the garden on the prevailing wind. Conversely, in hot climates, trees and shrubs bring shade and coolness to the house and its immediate sur-roundings. Strategic, appropriate plantings of shrubs and trees can also help preserve soil by preventing erosion by wind and water.

The garden setting
The garden should never be viewed in isolation, removed from its context and setting. Garden boundaries define and protect our private space, limiting the influence of the outside world on the place we call home. They make it possible to screen and thus "lose" unsightly features on adjacent land, as well as increasing privacy. Conversely, if your garden backs onto fields, boundaries can be designed to open up the view and bring the countryside into the garden, while still keep grazing animals at bay. Garden hedges and trees can also baffle noise from a neighboring property or busy road.

A garden retreat can be used as an extension to the living areas within the home, making an imperceptible transition from house to garden. Paved terraces, plant-covered structures, and open-fronted verandas all blur the hard interface between inside and outdoors. They create safe outdoor play areas for children – especially welcome in a modestly sized house – as well as providing space for enjoying meals *alfresco*.

Enhancing our environment
Beyond the fulfillment of our basic living requirements, there is of course one obvious role that a garden

DEFINING BOUNDARIES
Land adjoining a garden may not need to be screened for privacy, or for protection. Make the most of an attractive rural view and incorporate it visually to blend with and extend your garden.

performs, and that is to improve the appearance of the house, whether for our own private enjoyment or to enhance the street or neighborhood we live in. Community spirit is not, however, incompatible with a competitive tendency between neighbors, often generating passions and levels of gardening expertise rarely seen in professional horticulture.

To create a beautiful garden around the confines of a house and use the spaces to maximum effect is a challenge that many gardeners relish. Draw inspiration from the period of your house and its construction materials, and let your planting complement the style. The ultimate goal is to achieve a harmonious whole. This may look effortless, but those directly involved can appreciate the hard work, vision, and imagination that went into it.

Planning and designing a garden is a real opportunity to express your creativity and to allow your personality to come through in the concept, design, color, and plant combinations. Unlike interior design or painting a picture, a garden is a living thing that constantly changes, and each passing season will present new rewards and challenges. Although hard work, the practical nature of the majority of the tasks and the visual rewards so readily offered make gardening a great tonic for those who are office-bound in their work.

Homegrown produce

A garden does not need to be large to be productive; even a modest plot can provide vegetables, fruit, and herbs for the kitchen and flowers for

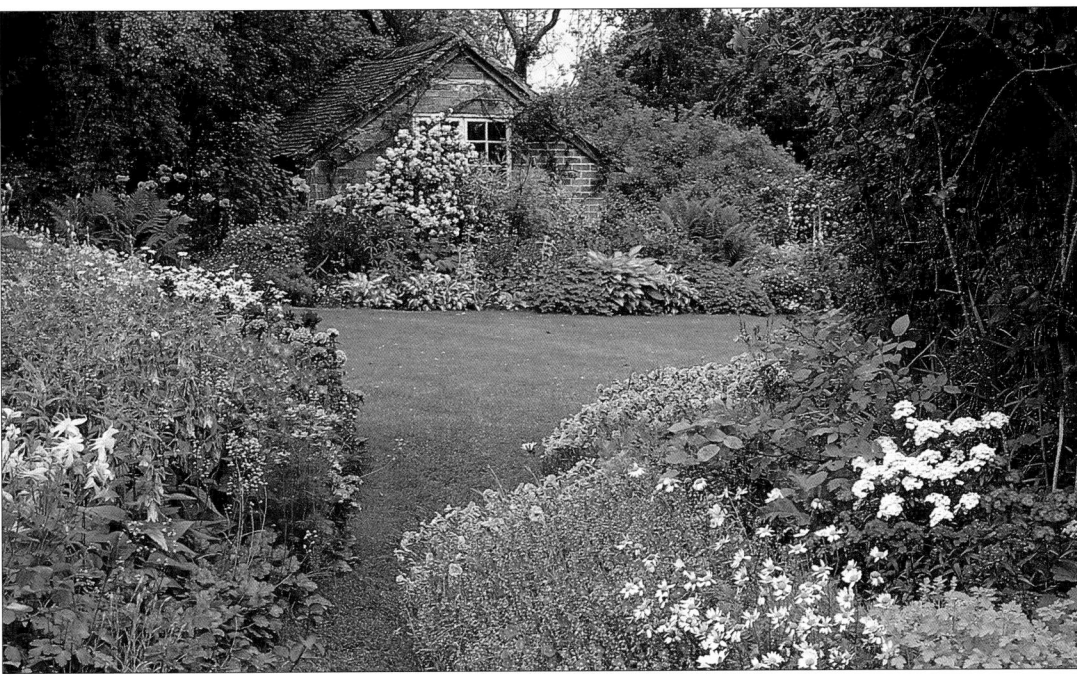

HARMONIOUS SETTING
This beautifully planted cottage garden is perfectly in keeping with the style of the house. Pleasing colors, textures, and shapes blend delightfully, blurring the boundaries between house and garden.

the home. In the past, a home garden often included vegetables for reasons of economy (or even necessity) and to provide a supply of fresh food. Today, despite year-round availability of fruit and vegetables, many people are concerned about the overuse (or even simply the use) of pesticides and inorganic fertilizers and prefer to grow their own produce using organic methods. Although the yield from an organically grown crop may be somewhat blemished and slightly

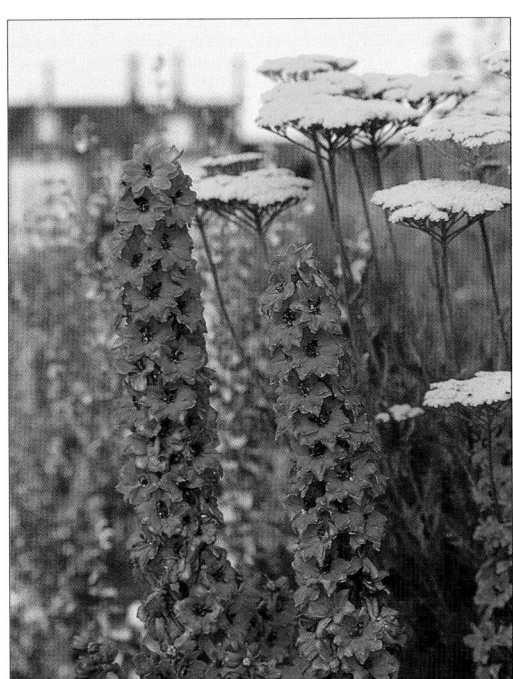

SOFTENING THE LANDSCAPE
Plants, especially flowering herbaceous ones such as this yellow Achillea *and blue* Delphinium*, bring intense colors, natural forms, and seasonal change to the built surroundings. They also provide a valuable haven for wildlife in harsh urban environments.*

lower, many consider the taste and quality to be superior, and there is frequently less waste.

Security and access
The safety and security of your home can be improved by the way the garden is designed and laid out. Open spaces around a house prevent unseen access; they are particularly important if you have security cameras, which require a clear vision around all sides of a building. Footsteps are readily heard on gravel surfaces – a great deterrent to burglars, especially when a dog is alerted by the noise. Impenetrable hedges of prickly and thorny material are also very effective. Climbing plants and wall shrubs that offer easy access to first-floor windows should be avoided. For visitors and deliveries, the everyday accessibility of a house can be greatly improved by the careful planning of the garden, the avoidance of too many level changes, a comfortable width of paths, and the provision of vehicular access.

Environmental concerns
Gardening according to environmentally sound principles is a goal that many today are contemplating. To exclude all harmful chemicals from the garden is a valiant first step toward running a garden in sympathy with the wider natural habitat. There are also many other practices that enhance and protect the environment rather than depleting and destroying

it. Water conservation, recycling organic matter to produce compost, integrated pest management, and buying nursery stock (particularly bulbs) raised in cultivation rather than collected from the wild are all relatively easy measures to adopt. If you wish to develop your garden further along environmentally sound lines, consider a wildlife-friendly

A PLANTED OASIS
The smallest of spaces can play host to a treasured collection of flowering plants and even accommodate a tiny patch of lawn.

garden that includes plants as food sources for birds and insects, shrubs and trees for nesting, and water for aquatic creatures. Avoiding the use of chemicals will also encourage more pollinating insects and improve plant performance and productivity, considerably enriching the entire garden environment.

The importance of garden design

The term "garden design" has connotations of formality and, for many, implies the application of rigid rules and formulas. Fortunately, this is not the case, but there is one overrriding principle – adequate thought and consideration of all the alternatives are needed well ahead of any intended works. Many beautiful gardens have been and are created without the implementation of grand planning designs. They have developed organically from a starting point: a favorite tree planted in an open place; a natural path between road and house; or from a previous owner's layout. Evolving year after year, possibly in a rather haphazard way with much left to chance, a garden of great charm can indeed come about, but opportunities may have been missed, and a lack of cohesion is all too often apparent.

Design awareness
We live in a designed society. There is today a great awareness and appreciation of well-designed products, and gardens have not escaped the attentions of designers or the media. Beautifully illustrated books and magazines as well as informative television programs have created a growing interest in styles, products, and plants, reaching a wider audience than ever before. For the first time, designers have been able to demonstrate visually the advantages

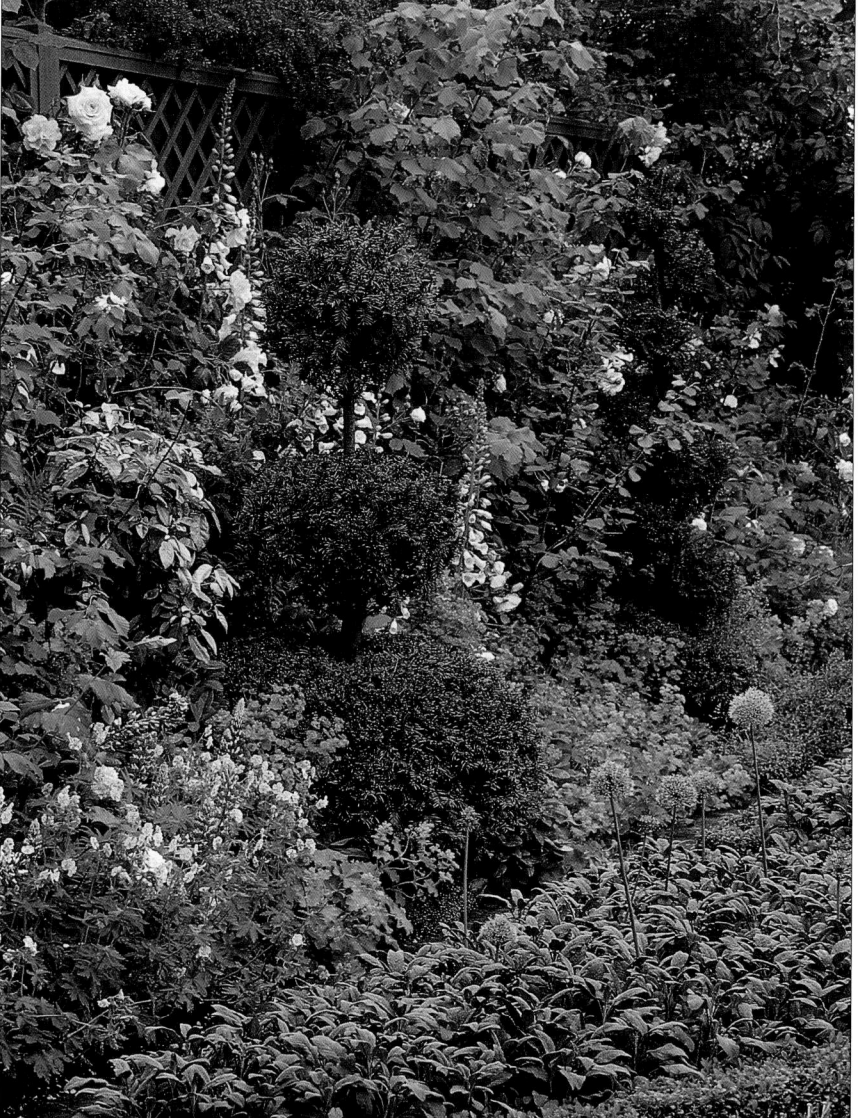

MULTIDIMENSIONAL PLANTING
This planting combination is a rich mix of complementary colors, textures, and forms. Such a dense, opulent design demands a sound knowledge of plants, plus skill and good judgment to restrict the more boisterous specimens and encourage the less robust.

of planning a garden and then to communicate clearly, using photographs of each stage, the development of a design.

A designer's fresh and experienced eye can realize the potential of a plot and draw out its strengths, while respecting and taking inspiration

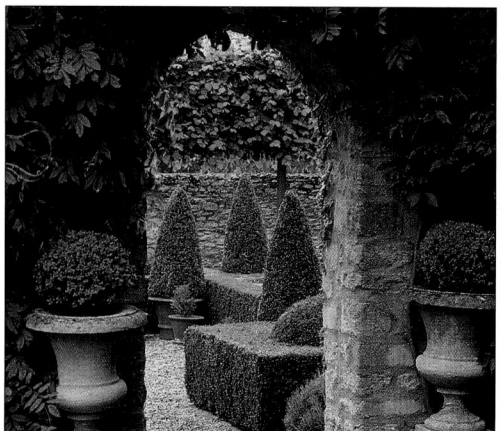

ARCHITECTURAL PLANTS
Clipped evergreens, in the confines of a courtyard, such as this boxwood (Buxus sempervirens), *take on an architectural role. Their structural forms are in perfect sympathy with the shape of the adjacent building.*

from the site. Most important, a good designer will not impose his or her own ideas on the garden without also taking the owner's wishes and lifestyle into consideration.

A professional designer can, of course, be hired to execute the entire project but at some considerable cost. However, even a single visit to offer advice, guidance, and an unbiased opinion can be invaluable and is certainly less expensive, with the option of consultations at a later stage as the project progresses.

Garden types and styles

Categorizing gardens into particular types or styles is fraught with difficulties, because every garden is different. Many gardens consist of a series of disparate themes loosely linked together, while others do not

fit readily into any single category since they incorporate several styles. All divisions, therefore, are somewhat arbitrary and should be regarded only as very general guidelines.

Developing a style
When starting to make a new garden or reshaping an old one a common theme, even if adapted and personalized, is generally adopted. Plucked from a magazine article, a book, or inspired by a visit to a garden, a particular look can reflect a house interior or evolve from the the style of house and its immediate surroundings. A building and its locality have a great deal to communicate to any receptive garden planner, contributing many simple commonsense details to the design.

All gardens should exude a sense of place and of belonging. A garden designed and built in a style that is very alien to the house or landscape may not sit well there, however much

NATURAL SILHOUETTES
A carefully selected combination of trees and shrubs, centered around this fine Cornus controversa *'Variegata' breaking across the lawn edge, gives an impression of elegance and can be maintained with minimum input. A well-tailored lawn and trimmed evergreens flatter beautifully shaped plants, whereas flowering plants might distract the eye.*

not purely decorative; they have an integrity, a personality, and a history, particularly where a botanical collection has been established.

Interestingly, both approaches to gardening can lead to an extended social life. The low-maintenance garden is ideal for outdoor entertaining, while for the plant enthusiast there are opportunities to contact and meet up with like-minded collectors.

Enhancing buildings
The garden presents a wonderful opportunity to manipulate the appearance of a house without running into expensive alterations or major reconstruction. Plants can be used to soften an unsympathetic roof line or to disguise the inappropriate use of ugly and incompatible building materials. An unremarkable structure, too, can be greatly improved by the addition of striking, climbing or architectural plants, which will strengthen the appearance of the building and add character. In both cases, the built structure and planted garden can come together and complement each other. With the exception of very few architecturally significant buildings whose façades are better left unadorned, the majority of houses are greatly improved by allowing plants to stand close by or to clamber partway across a house frontage – by appearing to bring the garden to the house.

it is desired and however great the resources spent on its creation. Developing and refining a design that reflects the sense of place almost invariably gives more harmonious results, especially where relaxation and calm are desired.

Design variations
Within any broad garden style, you can incorporate variations that reflect a personal interest, a lifestyle, or even the age group using the garden. A desire to attract wildlife into the garden or to grow large quantities of culinary herbs will add another dimension to the design. Or you might want to achieve a purely visual effect by introducing a particular flower color or luxuriant foliage that blends with the house colors or surrounding vegetation.

Personal preferences and the way in which you use your garden at various times of the year all have a bearing on what is required. A garden that looks particularly striking in midsummer, for example, may be wanted if the space is used mainly for outdoor entertaining. A garden for relaxation that requires minimum upkeep but has appeal throughout the year may be an attractive idea, or you may wish to shut out the world and create a secluded haven where you can grow plants in peace.

Planting considerations
The choice of plants growing within the framework of the garden will significantly influence its style. Large-leaved, rich-textured foliage gives depth and luxuriance, while a predominance of fine, silver- and gray-leaved plants will provide a lighter

feeling. Of equal influence is the degree of maintenance required in a garden. An efficiently maintained garden with a well-defined layout will look different from a garden of similar design that has been poorly or erratically maintained.

High and low maintenance
Generally speaking, it is possible to make a distinction between two different styles of garden in terms of

their function. A garden may have been designed for visual impact, or the creation of a restful ambience may be a priority. A garden for relaxation should be low maintenance, leaving as much time as possible for enjoying the peaceful setting. In contrast, the pleasure for the plant enthusiast with a specialized collection of plants comes from the hours spent nurturing and maintaining the garden. In a prized collection, plants are

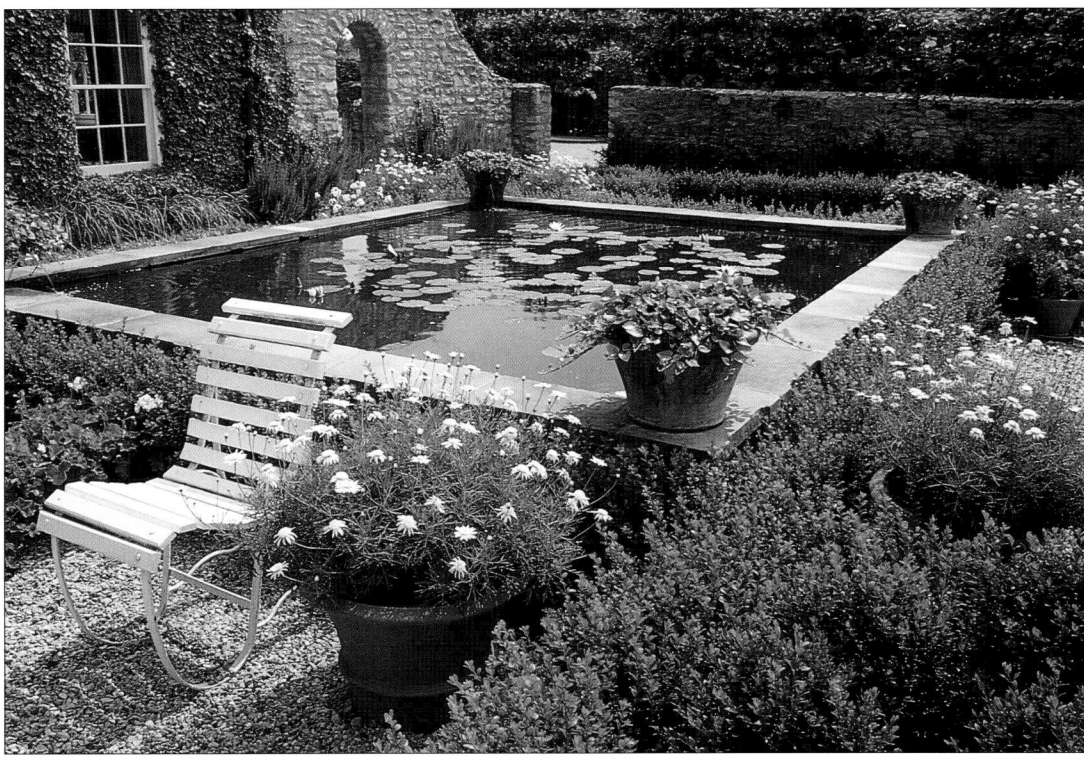

THE GARDEN ROOM
On this sunny terrace, hard landscaping materials play a strong role but are softened by the surrounding planting. In summer, the garden pool will create lively reflections of the surrounding vegetation and buildings.

Formal garden styles

FORMAL gardens are characteristically well proportioned, usually symmetrical and geometrically balanced in layout, and impart a tangible sense of restraint. They usually derive an inherent strength of line from an underlying backbone in the form of walls, paths, or terracing, around which planting is firmly controlled. Formal planting traditionally contains very few different plants, but these are used in quantity to lend a uniformity of texture and color. The entire emphasis is one of an overriding sense of control.

Ordered layouts
The underlying philosophy of the formal garden is to present a strong, simple statement of a very obvious control of nature. Intricately clipped parterres that form a filigree of crisply shaped evergreens when set against fine gravel, or a flat, closely mowed lawn that is framed by neatly trimmed hedges, are good examples of this philosophy in practice.

Historically, the formal style was chosen to convey a sense of power over the wider landscape and, on a large scale, this achieved an intimidating effect that was an intentional expression of wealth and status. A similar impression was conveyed even on a more modest scale, since such layouts required regular, labor-intensive, and costly maintenance.

Ancient inspiration
The grand formal gardens of seventeenth- and eighteenth-century Italy and France, which influenced garden styles throughout Europe, were themselves inspired by the gardens of ancient Greece and Rome. In these, the strongly defined proportions and scale of the buildings were mirrored by the strong, architectural and symmetrical design of the gardens that surrounded them.

These sumptuous but controlled landscapes were frequently laid out as a series of terraces connected by grand flights of steps; they featured water cascades, canals, and fountains among hedged and tree-lined walkways ornamented with classical statuary and potted plants.

Classical gardens
Greek and Roman features that still inspire modern formal gardens include neatly mowed and edged lawns, tightly clipped hedges and topiary, and planted borders framed by low, trimmed hedges. Straight paths and a network of vistas that terminate in a view or focal point may be lined by *allées* and avenues of identical, regularly spaced specimen plants. Ornamentation is added with restraint and, where several decorative items are used, they are either designed to form a matching set or a single design is replicated to form a sequence of repeated incidents.

Plants for formal gardens
Whether clipped and trained as hedging or topiary, shaped plants are an important element in the formal garden. The striking profiles of evergreen topiary lend height, form, and dramatic sculptural interest to an otherwise two-dimensional layout. Slow-growing evergreens, such as yew (*Taxus baccata*), boxwood (*Buxus sempervirens*), and English holly (*Ilex aquifolium*), all withstand the necessary regular trimming over many years. See also TOPIARY, p.118, and HEDGES AND SCREENS, p.82.

Pleached trees and stilt hedges make attractive internal divisions within a formal garden. Their regimented forms and colonnaded trunks provide a sense of rhythm and order when used to flank walkways and *allées*. Lindens (Tilia species) and hornbeam (Carpinus betulus) are the most frequently used species for this type of feature. Such plantings can also be introduced in a highly functional way. Trained lindens, for example, can be used as a boundary to create a living wall that gives privacy and an intimate sense of enclosure. See also "Pleached trees," p.75.

Knots and parterres
Knot gardens and parterres are highly developed types of formal gardening in which control of the planting is absolute. In knot gardens, intricate planting patterns are confined by an edging of dwarf, clipped evergreen shrubs such as boxwood (*Buxus sempervirens*). Traditional knots were inspired by sixteenth-century needlework and decorative plaster ceilings. In parterres, colored gravels or low plantings fill compartments created by low, trimmed hedging. Both knots and parterres offer year-round structure that is of particular value in winter, especially when they are located near the house.

Unity and contrast
Elements of naturalistic plantings among otherwise formal layouts create an element of contrast that can sharpen the underlying formality. The lax and free growth of herbs, for example, planted among clipped lavender (*Lavandula*), rosemary (*Rosmarinus*), bay (*Laurus nobilis*), or boxwood (*Buxus sempervirens*) can be used to create such contrasts. Similarly, containers on a terrace planted with a set of trimmed Portugal laurel (*Prunus lusitanica*) can bring an element of order and uniformity close to the house that could contrast with less structured planting elsewhere in the garden.

Oriental formality
The gardens of China, which can be traced back over 3,000 years, were created as sublimely peaceful places for contemplation and meditation. They drew inspiration from their dramatic surrounding landscapes, which were replicated in miniature within walled enclosures. Plantings were formal and restrained, often clipped or trained and usually highly stylized. Each tree or shrub had a symbolic meaning that was intended to stimulate contemplation.

Traditional Japanese gardens borrowed Chinese design ideas more than 1,200 years ago. With a similarly naturalistic inspiration, they used richer, more diverse plantings, symbolically shaped and sited rocks, and raked gravel or sand. Such a garden was based on formal principles of balance, simplicity, and symbolism.

STRUCTURED LAYOUT
The partitioned squares of this boxwood-edged parterre bring order and year-round structure to an otherwise informal medley of planting. Its strong lines lead the eye to a series of focal points beyond the low wall.

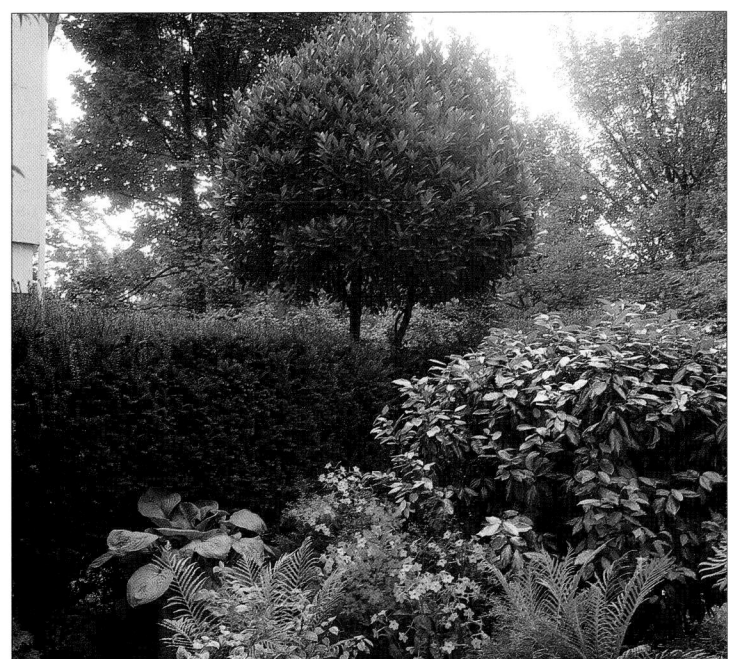

INTEGRATED TOPIARY
The highly stylized shapes of topiary do not necessarily need to be relegated exclusively to formal settings. Here, the head of a standard bay (Laurus nobilis) blends perfectly with the rounded and arching forms of ferns, hostas, and other plants in this border, while its tall, straight trunk lifts the head up and sets it apart from the rest of the planting.

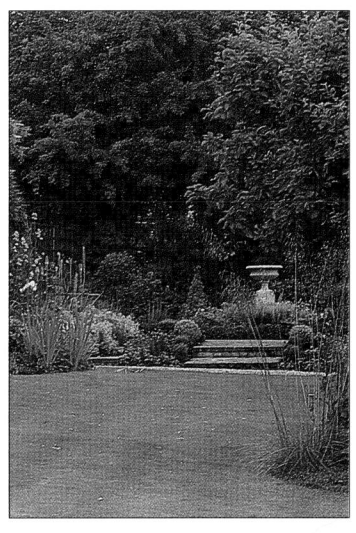

STATUARY
Pleasingly proportioned, well-sited, and framed objects – used with discretion – can often be a great asset to the general garden scene.

PLEACHED LINDENS
High-level screening by a stilted hedge of linden (Tilia) encloses yet does not oppress this small knot garden. After the leaves fall, the skillful training of the branch framework offers yet more to be admired.

FORMAL STILL WATER
Mirrored reflections double the impact of a symmetrical design. The random drifting of floating plants on the surface of the dark water adds interest and movement to the serenity of this formal garden.

Informal garden styles

INFORMAL gardens, at their best, often look as though nature has played a part in their design. There is an irregularity and a softness in their lines that, although manufactured, could conceivably have occurred naturally. Even though informal gardens may appear slightly out of control, their success depends on strong design and on the firm hand of the gardener to retain a degree of order among what might otherwise become chaos.

Elements of informality

A garden with an air of informality offers a relaxed ambience that can provide a sanctuary from the pressures of modern life. In contrast to the hard-edged geometry of the formal style, an informal garden is created with flowing curves and gentle contours. Hard surfaces are softened by plants that spread over their margins, and borders are filled with billowing mounds of plants that mingle together, apparently at random. Climbing plants scramble freely over walls or through trees and shrubs. While shrubs may be pruned to ensure good health and productivity, they are allowed to assume natural shapes and are rarely clipped in a restrictive way, as they are in strictly formal situations.

Informal elements within a garden can produce a sense of maturity in a relatively short time-frame, for example, when plantings are used to disguise unsightly features with a mantle of growth. Great charm can be given to the most unpromising site if softening growth disguises the hard angles or harsh colors of a building. Even the most uniform, rectangular garden acquires an element of mystery when its stark outlines are masked by layer upon layer of informal planting.

Informal garden styles

The style and degree of informality of a garden is influenced partly by the nature of the site and partly by individual preference. At one end of the spectrum, it may be possible to augment an existing woodland or meadow area simply by planting more of the natural flora that already grows there. Alternatively, the creation of an informal garden may entail the remodeling of border edges to form curving, sinuous lines, perhaps with a relaxation of the mowing program and a reduction in border maintenance to permit self-sown plants to thrive. At the other end of the spectrum is a totally new garden,

for which there is a range of informal styles from which to choose.

Cottage gardens

The English cottage garden was essentially a working garden in which to grow ornamental and edible crops. Fruit, vegetables, herbs, and flowers, such as peonies, delphiniums, and columbines, were all combined. The flowers ensured a thriving population of beneficial insects to aid pollination of crop flowers, control harmful insects, and encourage a bird population, all of which helped produce vigorous and healthy crops.

The quaint, homespun appearance of a cottage garden can be created using rustic items such as branchwork arches or woven willow supports for climbers (see WILLOW WALLS, p.85). Brick-patterned or cobblestone paths edged with found or reclaimed materials, such as pebbles, also help define the style.

Wild and woodland gardens

Informal gardens in a more naturalistic style not only provide a beautiful and relaxed type of garden but also offer a lifeline to flora and fauna whose habitats may have become threatened elsewhere.

Areas of grass, for example, where bulbs are naturalized for an early dis-

play, can be left uncut so that grasses and meadow flowers can bloom (see MEADOW GARDENING, p.395). An area of water, however small, attracts a range of wildlife into the garden, particularly if edged with waterside plantings to provide safe shelter for birds and amphibians alike. See also "Wildlife ponds," p.289.

Small trees or an area of woodland, especially if underplanted with shrubs and festooned with climbers, provide nesting places for birds and hibernating sites for insects and small mammals. Even in more controlled areas of the garden, seedheads of herbaceous plants, if retained through winter, will provide excellent food for birds when other sources are low.

Controlled chaos

Plants can be ruthlessly competitive, and the strongest may smother and eventually kill the weakest. They must be controlled to prevent this. It may be necessary, for example, to divide vigorous herbaceous plants regularly to keep them in check, to thin or reduce overly large shrubs, or to remove colonies of self-sown seedlings. These tasks help maintain a balance in wild and informal gardens and will prevent their natural style from degenerating into a wild and unkempt state.

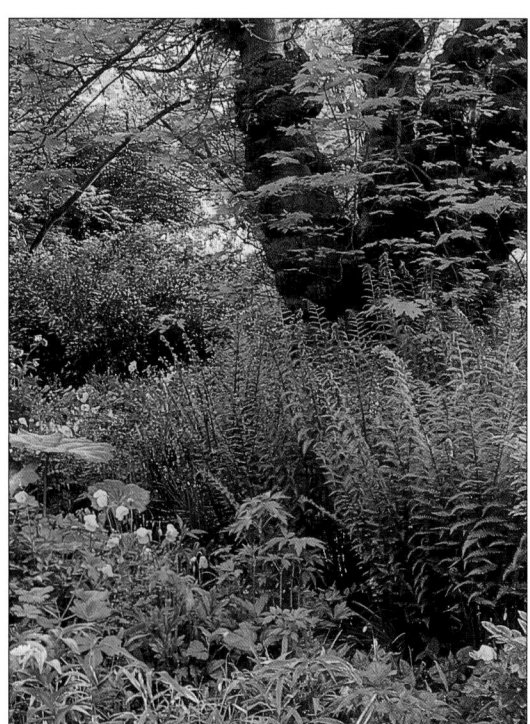

WOODLAND
In the shade of trees, a woodland flora must be selected to tolerate low light levels and the extremes of dry or excessively damp soil conditions.

GRASS BORDER
A shimmering profusion of ornamental grasses makes a dramatic statement in autumn. This planting relies on a variety of heights, colors, and shapes to avoid the monotonous appearance sometimes found in all-grass plantings.

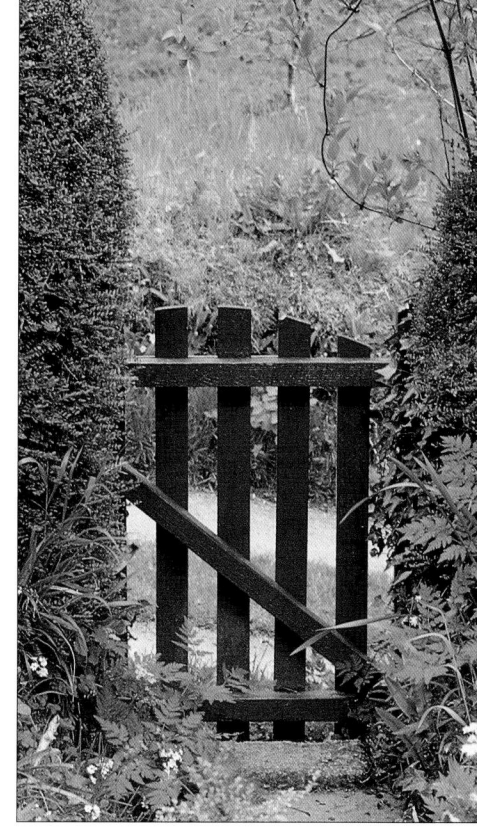

MARGINAL PLANTING (TOP)
Even the smallest pond offers the opportunity to blur the distinction between land and water with a range of garden plants. Native wildlife will benefit greatly from the cool, sheltered conditions.

POTAGER (ABOVE LEFT)
Nasturtiums and calendulas jostle with herbs and ornamental cabbages in cottage-garden tradition, where not even the smallest space is wasted.

SELF-SOWN (ABOVE RIGHT)
Melianthus *and Jacob's rod* (Asphodeline), *planted here at the foot of a wall, simulate a self-sown planting. In a mature garden, such combinations may occur naturally – and to great effect.*

RAMBLING ROSES (RIGHT)
Where space permits, an informal program of pruning and training shrubs and roses allows plants to spill from beds and borders in a generous, relaxed style.

HAND-CRAFTED GATE (ABOVE)
A picket gate and a borrowed view accentuate the theme of a country garden.

MIXED MAINTENANCE (BELOW)
While fruit trees must be well kept for good yields, the relaxation of the mowing routine gives this small orchard a charming air of informality.

People-oriented gardens

A GARDEN to be enjoyed by a family almost certainly needs to be a multipurpose space. To make sure that the design serves the needs of all its potential users, spend some time identifying what these might be. They may include a patio for dining and entertaining, or areas for children to play safely and experiment with growing their own plants. The garden may need to accommodate herb and vegetable patches to provide kitchen produce or borders for cut flowers to decorate the home.

As well as fulfilling its functional requirements, a garden such as this can also be highly decorative. A pergola clothed with scented climbers, for example, is not only ornamental but it could also provide shade for a favorite place for midsummer dining. By installing outdoor lighting, its usefulness can be extended to include evening entertaining, perhaps with a barbecue. It may also display ornaments that are highly individual, perhaps presents from friends or mementoes of anniversaries or vacations abroad.

The style of planting is very much a matter of personal choice, whether highly traditional or more experimental and innovative. Sources of design inspiration have never been more various, from magazines and television programs to the wealth of gardens, both private and public, that are open to visitors.

Gardens for living

Just as the interior of the home is designed to meet the requirements of those living there, so can the garden be tailored to meet the needs and interests of all the household. This often means extending indoor living to outdoors, using the garden as an extra room. If, for example, dining and entertaining are high on the list of priorities, there should be a flat, clean, all-weather surface near enough to the kitchen to make outdoor dining convenient.

To make access safe and easy, avoid steps, slopes, or changes of level between the house and eating area. On a very sunny patio, deciduous (rather than evergreen) climbers trained above head height will provide comfortable shade in midsummer but little or none in spring and autumn, when warmth and light levels are lower.

Where a suitable sheltered, warm site for an outdoor room does not exist, consider creating one by enclosing an area with hedges or scented-leaved shrubs. They will help trap warm air and provide shelter from cool evening breezes.

To maximize use of the space and to create a pleasant ambience, install subtle lighting for the evenings. Bear in mind that the route to and from the dining area should also be well lit.

Special interests

If the garden as a whole is planned with minimal maintenance in mind, this will allow the development of areas for special-interest activities. A simple lawn, for example, surrounded by robust, low-maintenance plantings can offer a playing field and campsite for the children or an oasis of calm for the adults. Around this, areas of more intense activity can evolve. These might include a small kitchen garden to produce unusual vegetables, fruit, and herbs that are difficult to find in stores. If the area is small, tending it will not be a chore; it will give satisfaction to the gardener, and it can even be a learning experience if children are encouraged to participate.

Another special-interest area might be a border for cut flowers to provide material for flower arrangements in the home throughout the year. It might include shrubs such as forsythias and mahonias for early spring and the bright stems of dogwood (*Cornus alba*) for winter decoration. To allow uninhibited cutting during summer and autumn, set aside a patch for perennials, supplementing them with annuals and biennials to supply flowers for many months.

Special needs

For those in the family who are less mobile or who have limited strength, a garden of raised containers or an entire raised bed removes the strain of bending and should satisfy any latent wish to garden. Permanently sited containers can be set at a suitable height and regularly reinvigorated with colorful annuals. A row of outdoor tomatoes planted in pots on top of a sunny wall, or a raised herb garden enjoying a sunny exposure and free-draining soil, will give endless pleasure and produce worthwhile quantities of useful crops.

Looking to the futures

With a little foresight, some areas of the garden can be designed to evolve with a family's changing needs. A wooden playhouse, for example, could in later years become a tool shed or storage bin. An irregularly shaped or formal rectangular sandbox, if positioned carefully when the garden is designed, may be transformed into a small pond once the children are old enough to understand the dangers of water. A climbing frame of smooth lumber could, later on, become an interesting support over which climbing plants may scramble to create a dramatic effect.

WELL-DESIGNED TERRACE
This seating area (right) with its all-weather surface, shelter from wind, and overhead shade encourages maximum use of the terrace over a long season. Ground-level lighting and pots of scented plants, such as lilies (below) that retain their fragrance into the evening, enhance the setting for use later in the day.

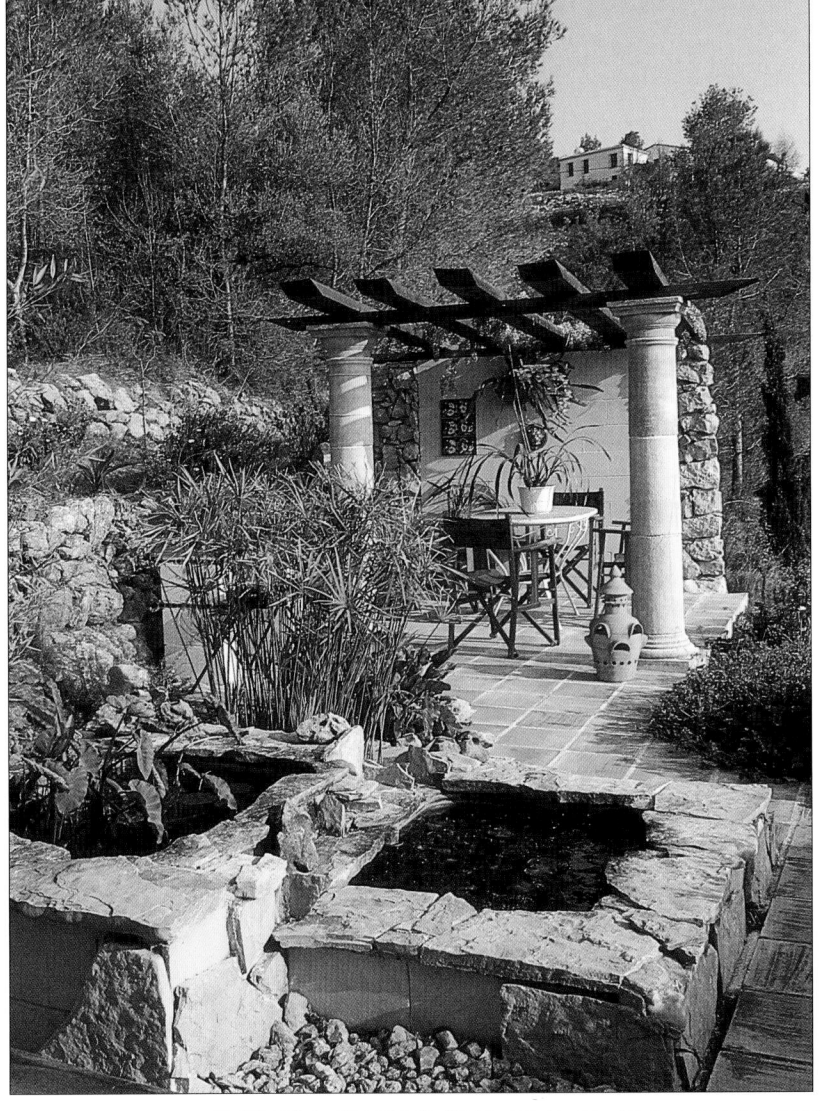

GARDENING INTERESTS (RIGHT)
A garden mirrors the particular hobbies of its occupants, and its design and general layout are unavoidably dictated by these pursuits. A collection of prized alpines, for example, is best displayed in stone troughs and a greenhouse, here connected to the house by a path with an all-weather surface.

SAFE WATER FEATURES (BELOW)
Even the smallest and most shallow of ponds can pose a danger to small children. This small fountain, however, has a strong metal grid over its concealed reservoir.

PLAY AREA (BELOW RIGHT)
A lawn, surrounded by healthy, thorn-free plantings, makes an ideal spot for children to enjoy many types of games.

HIGH-LEVEL GARDENING (ABOVE)
A raised bed makes gardening comfortable for those with limited mobility. An ideal display setting is created where plant detail can be appreciated at close quarters. The use of pots allows those plants in need of attention (here including some developing topiary shapes) to be brought within very easy reach and for seasonal changes to be made.

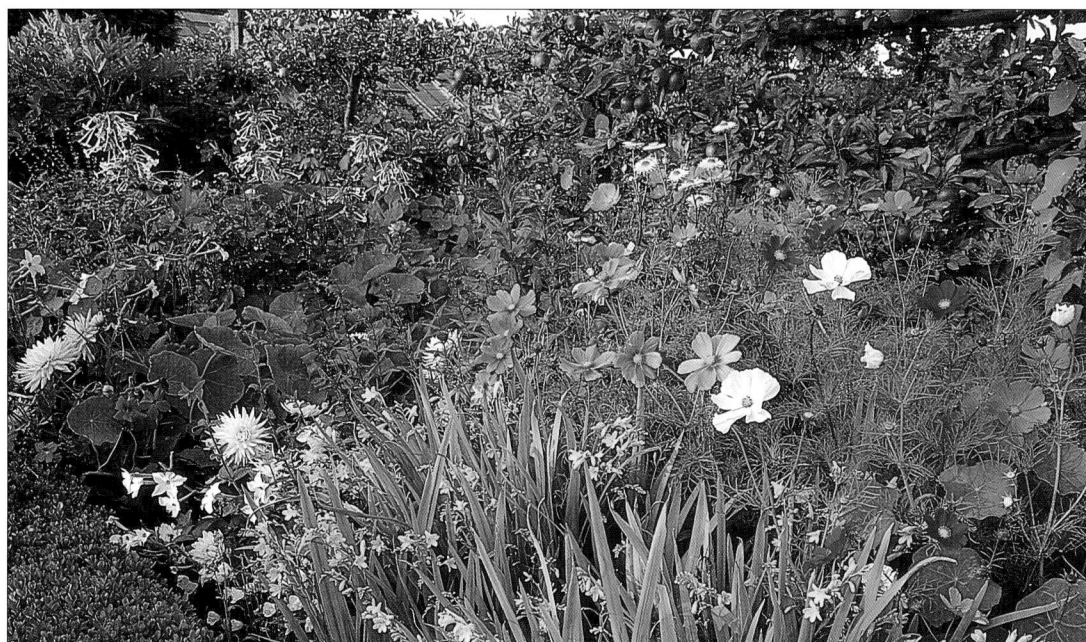

DUAL PURPOSE (LEFT)
Here, in late summer, flowers for indoor decoration are grown alongside plants with ripening fruits to great ornamental effect. This cheerfully haphazard mixture has been planted solely with the needs of the house in mind, yet the result is as decorative as any other type of themed border.

Plant-oriented gardens

IN A PLANT-ORIENTED garden, the plants take center stage, rather than being used simply as "soft" design materials. The owner of such a garden can indulge a fascination in collecting and growing a specific range of botanical or exhibition-quality plants. Some plant groups need much more maintenance than others, since they are extremely fussy about their growing conditions. A garden's soil or microclimate might especially suit one specialized group of plants, although more often additional work will be needed to provide the appropriate soil, light, moisture, and shelter.

Pure gardening
The garden that is inspired by plants first and foremost is perhaps the purest form of gardening. There are many and diverse avenues of interest within this type of garden, but all are led by a love and passion for plants.

It is the fascination of collecting, cultivating to perfection, pollination, and propagation that holds the attention and further develops a gardener's interest in horticulture. The search for rare or newly discovered forms can become a lifelong occupation. In such a "pure" garden, skill and expertise are obvious at every turn and demonstrate the gardener's dedication to a wide range of tasks.

Sources for ideas
The site itself may be the inspiration for the plant-oriented garden. Perhaps a dark and damp, north-facing slope will spark an interest in an extensive collection of ferns.

Alternatively, a dry, stony, south-facing bank may encourage the planting of many different Mediterranean natives, such as a collection of *Cistus* species.

Turning what might appear to be a disadvantage into a positive attribute, an area of overgrown woodland may appear lost to cultivation, yet with careful management it can present a wealth of unusual planting possibilities. A collection of shade-loving, woodland-floor natives that is unique to such a site should thrive beneath a deciduous canopy.

Where the conditions provided are substandard, plants will grow poorly, never realizing their full potential. Such poor conditions, however, can often be rectified. Soil conditions can be modified by adding organic matter or improving drainage; shelter can be increased by the use of windbreaks and shelterbelts (see HEDGES AND SCREENS, p.82, and BAMBOOS, p.94); and light levels can be increased by thinning or lifting the canopies of surrounding trees.

Themed collections
A herbaceous border in matching colors, textures, and forms is one way to display a collection that depends solely on good design skills. Many subtly or dramatically different variations are possible. A historical approach may be taken to re-create an early twentieth-century border, for example. This would contain certain tall herbaceous plants that are very dependent on traditional forms of staking with willow twigs or hazel branches, for example. Color-themed

SPECIALTY PLANTS
The display of a very specific plant collection need not be devoid of all aesthetic qualities. Here, many treasured forms of potted auricula primroses are attractively placed on tiered stands.

borders are another possibility for a collection (see "Planting for color and texture," p.48).

A more modern interpretation might be a mixed border dominated by drifts of shrub roses and self-supporting perennials, self-sown annuals, and swaths of ornamental grasses. Alternatively, such a border, particularly in a sheltered situation, might include lush foliage plants and tender bedding perennials in vibrant colors to give a subtropical flavor (see also HARDY PALMS AND THE EXOTIC LOOK, p.60).

Collections with style
The plant-oriented garden may take a very different course from the refinements of the mixed border. A hobby of growing plants for exhibition may develop, where perhaps dahlias (see p.228) or peppers are grown to perfection to the exclusion of any aesthetic value their arrangement in the garden might offer. Alternatively, such a well-defined collection could be arranged with every possible

attention paid to aesthetics. A fruit garden, for example, with trees trained in particular forms could provide structural boundaries and internal divisions within the garden as a whole (see Growing Fruit, "Trained forms," p.413). Such a display would pay tribute to meticulous, long-term pruning as the trees slowly develop great character, eventually creating an almost timeless ambience.

A collector of trees may be fortunate to have sufficient space to create an arboretum, but this need not be a sterile collection of solitary trees in straight lines. Groupings of trees in clumps and groves create a landscape style that is beautiful in its own right (see also ORNAMENTAL TREES, "Trees as design elements," p.54).

To grow a collection of plants indigenous to a particular region may require the controlled conditions of a greenhouse or alpine house. Plants need not be set on gravel-covered, featureless platforms. With a little imagination, they can be arranged in a simulation of their native terrain.

NATURAL PLANT COLLECTIONS
An extensive specific collection can readily be incorporated into a garden setting. Here snowdrops (Galanthus) flourish in this deciduous woodland.

RESTRICTED COLOR (ABOVE)
A white border, tiered in height and with every shade of green, white, and silver, is a classic, timeless design theme. The dignified purity of the design demands meticulous staking, deadheading, and weeding.

TROPICAL STYLE (BELOW)
A warm, sheltered area with fertile soil provides an opportunity to experiment with tender exotics through the summer months. Many will need careful lifting and storing over winter but will amply repay such attention.

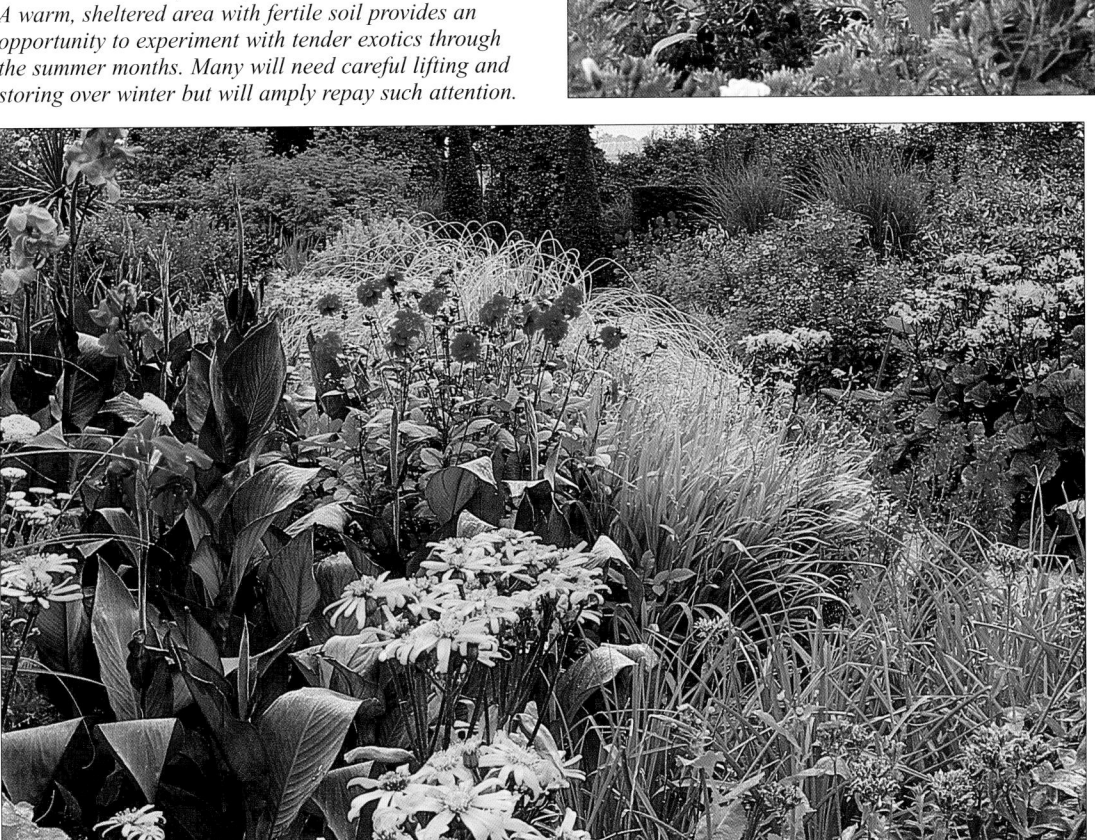

SINGLE-SEASON DISPLAY (ABOVE)
Some garden designers seek to exploit every plant type, shape, form, and color so that they perform and peak at the same time – in this case as a color-coordinated collage.

ALPINE HOUSE (BELOW)
Plants with special needs such as alpines may thrive only in a dedicated greenhouse.

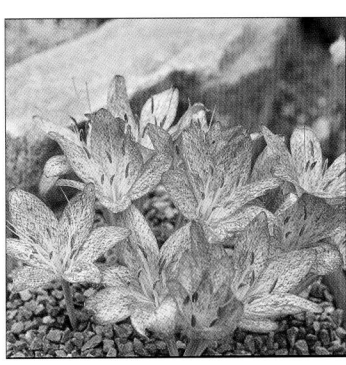

Stylized gardens

A HIGHLY stylized garden can be seen as a refined work of art of purely aesthetic value in which plants fulfill a design function of tight and strictly limited criteria.

Such a garden might serve as a backdrop to a collection of contemporary sculpture, for example, or might form a calm and unobtrusive setting before an architecturally important house. This style of garden demands a high degree of coordination and preplanning to distill the essence of the style required.

The colors, textures, and finishes of all the materials are of utmost importance. Here, plants are used as a furnishing – their qualities being assessed and employed for their utility rather than for their individual beauty as living plants.

Dominant themes

When a designer's sole aim is to create a very stylized image, the approach is very similar to that of an artist when painting a picture, or a designer contriving a theatrical stage set. The result can be breathtaking, because all attention has been focused toward maximum visual impact, undiluted by sentiment or an interest in individual plants. Selecting plants only for their color, form, and texture, and arranging them in an almost abstract, pictorial composition, insures that the finished arrangement forms a cohesive whole of complementary materials.

While this approach is commonly used by landscape architects in large-

MASS BEDDING
Results can be dramatic when plants are used as basic building elements to construct an effect. This softly textured landscape has a sculptural quality that transcends the form of any one individual plant.

scale projects, it might equally well be adapted to smaller, more intimate situations. It avoids the problem of using too many different materials in a confined site, which can prove fussy and distracting. In contrast, minimal materials give an impression of strength and unity. Such essentially sophisticated designs all have at their heart an innate simplicity that is their most telling factor.

Even in gardens of traditional layout, this straightforwardness can underlie the development of an overall concept or theme: for example, a garden based on a restricted color range, made up of plants only in shades of green, with

black or white flowers. A more radical alternative is a garden that is almost free of plants, consisting only of sweeping grass mounds to be mowed in different directions and at varying lengths according to the texture required.

Another alternative that lends style and drama is when a single plant is introduced in great quantity, especially if the plant in question is unusual. Blocks of a hundred or more can be a revelation. A mass planting of peonies, tree poppies (*Romneya coulteri*), or many of the euphorbias can provide a truly spectacular sight. Less radically, gardens of a practical

nature can be given stylistic treatment. A working kitchen garden can be designed as a decorative potager. While still providing edible crops, there is greater emphasis on an attractive display of color and texture within the strict confines of its highly structured layout.

Coordinated designs

In domestic situations, one of the greatest challenges is to match a highly stylized garden with the house or locality. One way of doing this is to use plants and materials from the area, but in a very different form. For example, locally abundant trees and shrubs (if they withstand clipping) can be used to create trimmed hedges and trees that are then arranged in a tightly regimented design within the garden (see ORNAMENTAL TREES, "Pleached trees," p.75, and HEDGES AND SCREENS, p.82). Local stone and gravel could form paving and mulches beneath plantings to create a thoroughly modern reinterpretation of the formal garden.

Small city gardens, especially if framed by boundary walls, are ideal for stylized gardens. Since they are frequently seen from only one viewpoint – the house windows – they present unusual and interesting possibilities. A truly theatrical, almost two-dimensional garden can be created with an odd or false sense of perspective – achieved by the angles of hard surfaces and by the choice of their colors, shapes, and placement relative to each other.

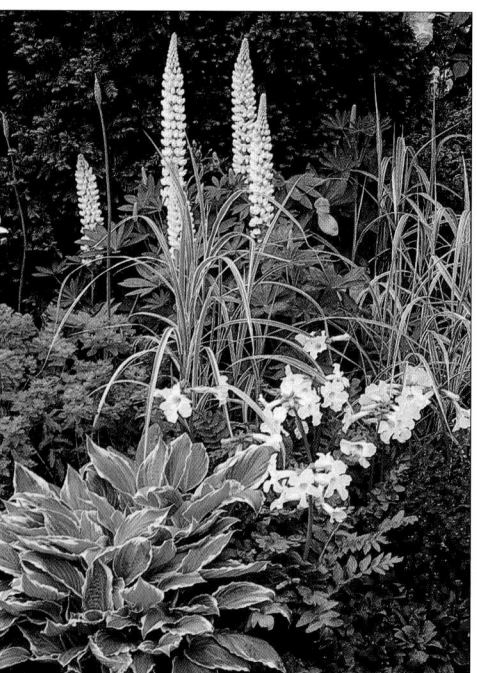

PLANTING ARRANGEMENTS
With skill, knowledge, and care a series of well-planned "vignettes" may be constructed. Harmonious colors and contrasting leaf forms and shapes can be positioned with all the accuracy and poise of a staged flower arrangement.

MODERN STYLE
Even the most ordinary plants in a commonplace setting, here against a picket fence, can be used in a stylized way. Their effect is transformed by the use of unexpected and nontraditional galvanized metal containers, which harmonize beautifully with the silver-leaved plants.

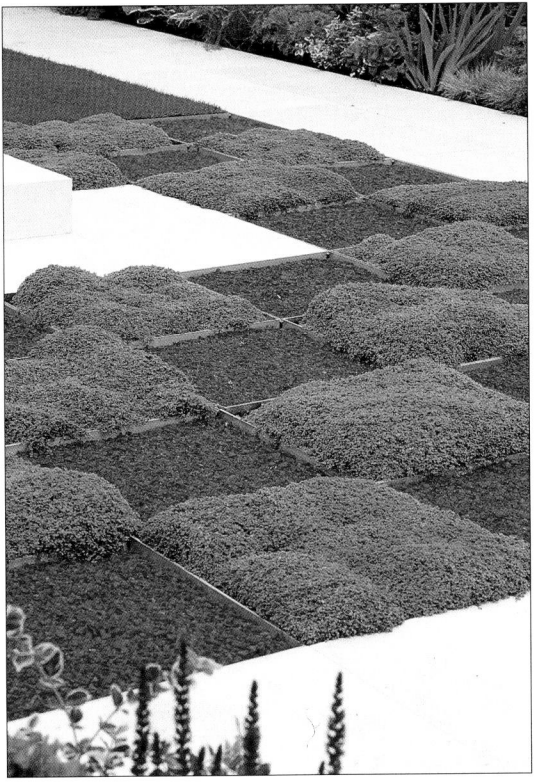

MODERN DESIGN (ABOVE)
Squares of baby's tears (Soleirolia soleirolii), *forming*
tight, ground-hugging cushions of growth, alternate with
blue glass chips in a contemporary design that plays
upon geometry and color blocks.

JAPANESE RAKED GARDEN (LEFT)
In this uncompromisingly simple, abstract arrangement
of rocks and raked gravel, the eye is drawn only to pure
line and the effortless balance of mass and space.

MODERN SCULPTURE
A "habitat" created as a setting for a piece of modern
water sculpture enables an otherwise alien artifact to
appear acceptable within the general garden scene.

SUCCULENTS
Strongly architectural plants, such as Agave *here, form a*
dramatic impression in this sunny, dry, terraced bank,
where the plants thrive in the hot sun.

Assessing the existing garden

WHETHER you are remodeling your own garden or tackling one inherited from a previous owner, one of the most difficult tasks is to envisage how to transfer all one's ideas and aspirations onto what is already there.

Everything that makes up the existing garden must be scrutinized and assessed, determining those components that positively contribute to the overall effect and those that offer least or are farthest removed from your preferred style and taste. No aspect of the garden should escape this scrutiny, for even those factors that might be considered impossible to change can be influenced and modified by skillful design and planting. Nothing can alter the shape and size of a property, for example, yet there are any number of design solutions that can make narrow gardens appear wider, open sites become more sheltered, and awkward shapes flow more freely.

A time for reflection

The inspiration for your new design may be held entirely in your imagination – or be the result of visiting other gardens or poring over books and magazines. Before beginning to make even the roughest preliminary sketch, however, a period of time spent in the garden doing nothing more than simply mulling over possibilities will be well repaid. The earliest

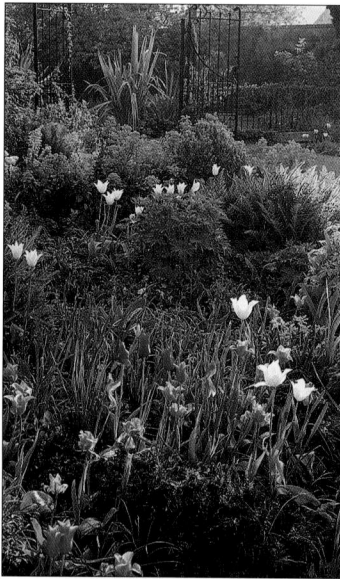

GET TO KNOW THE GARDEN
Useful information can be gathered just by observing a new garden over an extended period of time. Plants new to you may reveal their value in unexpected seasons.

DECIDING ON PRIORITIES
An existing garden may contain many elements that meet your own requirements, such as a seating area or raised beds, even if the materials or finishes used are not exactly to your taste. Just as plants can be judiciously retained or reshaped to preserve the structure of borders, so much can be done to adapt and personalize hard materials.

planning stage of a garden should be a period of calm, cool observation: critical scrutiny of both what exists and what is desired. If insufficient time is given to important decisions, the result will be poor long-term planning.

The garden's development over an extended period of time needs a vision: seeing beyond the clutter of existing features. It should also at this stage be free of the distractions of budgets, labor, and other practical constraints. Defining a goal for the garden, and the means to that goal, can be the realization of a dream that will bestow a style and a personality – your own personality – on the property as a whole. Even if a master plan has to be tackled piecemeal, having such a plan firmly in mind will enable a greater degree of control over the ongoing development of the garden.

Weighing the elements

As you appraise the existing garden, you will begin to form a broad idea of the scale of remodeling that a new design will involve. It is worth considering at this stage whether you intend to implement the new design in a single operation or spread the work and expense over several years.

Carry a notebook with you, in which to enter thoughts and ideas about all of the elements the garden contains, set against what you want. As the wealth of possibilities is distilled into a concept that could work, many ideas will be discarded, refining only those thought appropriate to site and scale, period, and local conditions of soil and weather.

A methodical "audit" of structures, surfaces, features, and plantings – with a view to deciding which ones you will keep, which you will redesign or relocate, and which are superfluous – can be tremendously useful. Examples of the kinds of questions that should be asked and factors that should be considered are detailed in the pages that follow.

SEPARATING MATERIALS FROM THEIR CONTEXT
Even if you do not like a feature, or its design makes it awkward to garden around, consider whether its materials might be used elsewhere. If not, items such as these old, good-quality slabs and sink could be sold.

Taking photographs

Difficult decisions can often be simplified and clarified by the use of photographs. A set of pictures portraying the entire garden will help put all of its features into context and enable carefully considered conclusions to be drawn. Curiously, a photograph has a focusing and simplifying effect, removing the distractions of a live situation within the garden and throwing strengths and weaknesses into high relief. The frozen image is easier to analyze, and it clearly reveals the underlying composition and workings of the garden. This detachment seems to allow decisions to be made with greater freedom. The dominance of an outsized evergreen shrub, the poorly flowing line of the front of a border, or any weak, dull plantings are more vividly displayed in static images, and these can then be rectified in the new design.

Appraising your own garden

Sentimentality can play a significantly negative role in a garden long established by its owners. Plants that really have no place in a well-designed and practical layout are preserved and overlooked; geriatric, diseased, or inappropriately sized plants are retained, particularly when they commemorate an event or were a gift or a reminder of a dear friend or relative. With the passing of a garden to new owners, such anomalies tend to be addressed more objectively – the horse chestnut tree planted as a seed years ago, for example, which now excludes all light from a patio, may be removed without so much as a backward glance.

However, individuality – the lifeblood of interesting gardens – often stems from quirks of personal sentiment. Although unconventional, it may be these features that give the garden a unique character, so, again, deep thought before action is essential. The clean sweep or makeover approach may have unexpectedly negative consequences. The removal of a conifer simply because it is "unfashionable," for example, may also mean the loss of useful screening from neighbors or perhaps a well-placed nesting site, visible from the house, to which birds will no longer return in spring.

Appraising a garden new to you

A new owner will almost certainly wish to make changes to an existing garden. An avid gardener will probably waste little time before introducing personal preferences or old friends in the form of plants or ornaments, but if the garden (or parts of it) is not fundamentally to your taste, then a broader view is required.

In many ways the would-be designer tackling an uncultivated site – for example, in a new housing development – or a completely neglected, featureless yard has an easier task, with a blank canvas on which to project the new vision. To appreciate fully the complexities of an inherited, well-kept garden requires time and patience. The most valuable advice is not to make any hurried changes; an old garden that has evolved over many years may contain features of great worth that have stood the test of time. To retain and perhaps reinterpret some existing plants and structures is greatly preferable to clearing the site and beginning from a sterile piece of ground.

These existing elements in a garden, laid out by the previous owners, may summon up a certain atmosphere, which is important to retain. The overenthusiastic cleaning up of such gardens can suddenly remove any charm or mystery. Such a quality is a rare commodity to be nurtured rather than swept aside. A unique richness may be found within a garden cultivated over several generations, layer upon layer of plantings creating microclimates of mutual benefit,

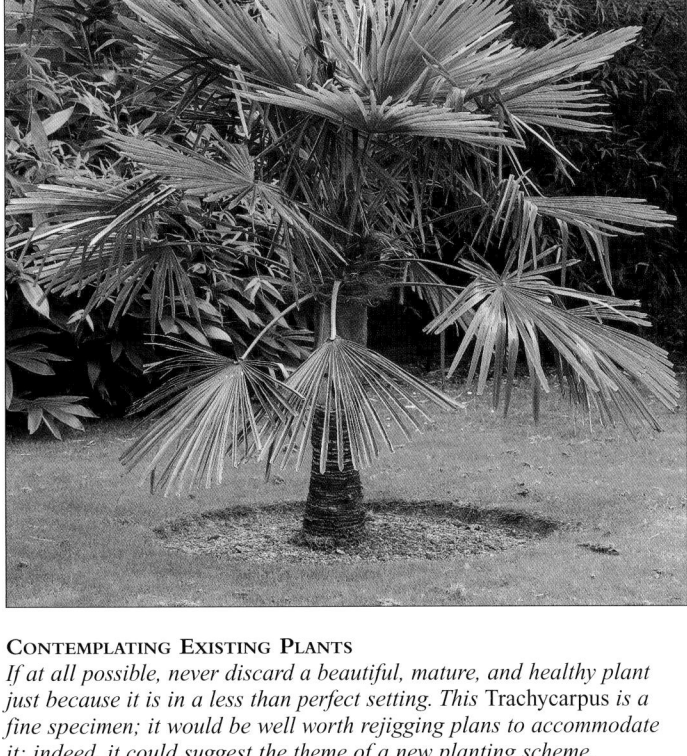

CONTEMPLATING EXISTING PLANTS
If at all possible, never discard a beautiful, mature, and healthy plant just because it is in a less than perfect setting. This Trachycarpus *is a fine specimen; it would be well worth rejigging plans to accommodate it; indeed, it could suggest the theme of a new planting scheme.*

evolving beautifully tiered structures of some complexity. With the passing of time, plants and structures can attain a character that takes them beyond mere furnishings.

Watching the garden unfold
The garden should be monitored during as many seasons as possible (ideally, a full year), during which time observations of factors such as shade, prevailing wind, areas of warmth, and seasonal value of plant-ings can be made. Paths and patios can be used in all seasons, the effectiveness of privacy afforded by screening shrubs can be assessed – summer and winter – and the maintenance requirement of the entire garden and its plantings gauged.

Letting plants show their worth
Only within specific seasons may the reason for certain plantings be revealed: an old cherry tree with low sweeping branches, which bursts into flower in spring in partnership with drifts of bulbs beneath it, will immediately justify its existence and unconventional stature.

All too easily, mistakes can be made: a hastily removed "laurel," for some reason planted up against the south-facing wall of a house, may be cut to the ground and discarded only to discover later that this was a fine *Magnolia grandiflora* of considerable age. If you find plants difficult to identify, advice may be sought from a local nursery, garden club, or botanical garden to avoid the unintentional removal of valuable plants.

Once the identities of all important plants are known, do not be hasty in removing any of them. Retaining some items of obvious age and maturity as a permanent or temporary measure will prevent the complete loss of scale within the reworked garden, offer shelter to young vulnerable plants, and afford privacy while other plantings are establishing.

TAKING INSPIRATION FROM SHAPES
This aging tree cloaked in ivy (far left) may need to be removed, but its overarching low branch creates a pleasing frame for the elements beyond, which might suggest the placement of an arch in its place.

Surfaces, paths, and level changes

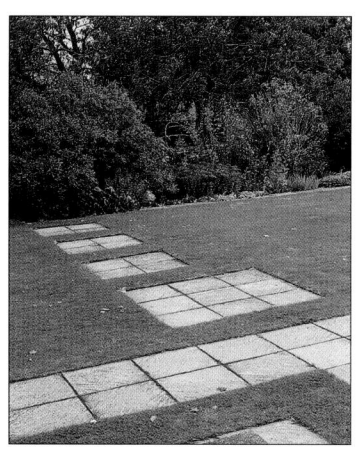

Lawns/Grassed areas

Existing Is the lawn level, composed of good-quality grass, and free from weeds? Or is it in poor condition, perhaps shaded by the house or by trees and becoming patchy because of insufficient light or poor drainage? Will it be large enough to accommodate a tent and be used for games if required? Is it devoid of trees, or should it provide a setting for them? If the lawn is very small, in poor condition, muddy, and essentially more trouble than it is worth, would the area be better paved, grav-eled, or incorporated into a planted bed? Alternatively, if a closely mowed lawn covers an extensive area, then the far periphery could be mowed less frequently to provide a fringe of meadow grass.

Desired A garden without a lawn can seem lacking in serenity. Without a calming area of green it can often feel frenetic and look a little over-worked. Even a broad area of gravel or paving will not have the quietening, soothing effect of grass. There must be adequate access to the lawn for a mower or wheelbarrow, and for pedestrians. Disposal of grass clippings is another consideration. When a lawn is to replace a hard surface that acts as a path through the garden, then it is advisable to retain a hard strip to one side to leave a clear passage for use in bad weather. A lawn, even when relatively small, plays a scene-setting role, providing an open foreground to view a scenic background. This role is important enough to justify the removal or reduction of existing planted borders to give an adequate area of grass. For additional information, see THE LAWN, pp.378–95.

Patios and terraces

Existing Is an existing patio area large enough? Is it sunny, or cold and gloomy? Is it at the junction of paths, making it difficult to position permanent furniture? A patio may be positioned to catch the last rays of the setting sun, but if this is at the far end of the garden, then it may not be practical for outdoor eating and entertainment. Is the surface in good condition, with a slight fall away from the house to remove standing water? Gravel is an uncomfortable surface on which to place chairs and tables. More acceptable is a flat, even surface of paving, or poured concrete with the aggregate exposed to make it nonslip and give texture.

Desired A hard-surfaced area within the garden is invaluable as a working area and for entertaining outdoors. Its position is critical to achieve maximum benefit from its appearance and usefulness. Ideally there should be separate areas of sun and shade for sitting in at various times of the day and in different sea-sons. Even a small paved area with seating for two or three people will enhance the use of the garden if placed so that it has a good view or sunny exposure. Paving materials often look best when sympathetic to surrounding building materials in color and texture. Decide whether the surface should be of one color and uniform texture or decorative in design to make a statement in itself. Always provide clear access between house and patio – without including steps, if possible. This minimizes possible accidents when carrying drinks or food. For further information, see STRUCTURES AND SURFACES, "Patios and terraces," p.579.

Paths

Existing Are paths in good repair and wide enough for easy passage and pushing a wheelbarrow? Broken and uneven surfaces can be haz-ardous and should be repaired or replaced. Do the paths follow natural movement lines through the garden, free of temptations to take short-cuts? Paths should be not only a practical network of hard surfaces but also create visual links from one area to another, giving interest and structure to the garden. If some paths are duplicating routes or appear unnecessary, remove them. Alongside a lawn, paths may also act as mowing edges over which border plants can spill. Grass paths are pleasing yet soft thoroughfares and will survive without damage only on less frequented routes.

Desired Paths should follow the most logical and scenic route. Do not forget that in a private garden beauty should be paramount, so avoid the spaghetti effect of too many paths. Gravel paths are inexpensive and softer on the eye than paved ones, particularly when curves and sweeps are to be negotiated and straight-edged materials are difficult to accommodate. A well-prepared base of compacted stone will insure good drainage and an even surface that will retain its good line over time. Paths should be broad enough for two people to walk abreast. If appro-priate, the width should be sufficient to take a small garden vehicle and a loaded trailer. For further informa-tion, see STRUCTURES AND SURFACES, "Paths and steps," p.587.

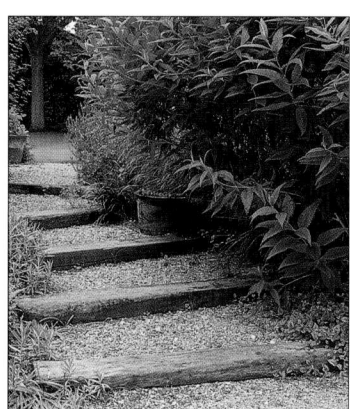

Steps and slopes

Existing Should any sloping sites within the garden be redesigned to form a series of terraces linked by steps to overcome logistical problems of land management? Do existing changes of level divide the garden into workable plots? Within the confines of a small garden, would a slight change in level create a different perspective, adding importance to an area or pro-viding an opportunity for a change in materials or theme? Would a flight of steps add a vital link, physically and visually drawing areas together? Do retaining walls and planted or grass banks contribute horizontal divisions, and do they have the potential to mark a change in style or detail between lev-els?

Desired However cleverly inter-preted, a flat garden will not possess the drama or liveliness of one that exploits a hillside or the moderate undulation of rolling terrain. A very slight variation in land heights can be exaggerated by the use of retaining walls. Changes in height can be exploited to display plants and water to great effect. A series of pools on different levels, linked by waterfalls, makes a lively composition full of interest. Consider whether any changes in level would be appropri-ate, especially for the very young and elderly, who may find steps difficult. Steps should be well built and even in rise and tread width throughout their flight. If the sides are planted, a central area of sufficient width must be left uncluttered. For further infor-mation, see STRUCTURES AND SUR-FACES, "Paths and steps," p.587.

Boundaries and structures

Walls and fences

Existing Are existing walls safe? If in doubt, seek expert advice. If work is needed on old garden walls, it is worth contacting an experienced stonemason or builder familiar with local building techniques in order to effect sympathetic repairs. Check the condition of fencing, in particular inspecting the base of fence posts for rots and fungal growth. Individual panels and posts can often be replaced without renewing the entire structure. The easiest option for an ugly wall or fence is to disguise it with climbers or shrubs. The soil at the base will often be poor and dry; does it need improvement before planting? Where lime has been used in mortars and plasters, especially on an old wall that has shed detritus, note when choosing plants that the soil may have become inhospitable to acidic-soil lovers such as *Camellia*.

Desired Traditional brick or stone walls are among the most challenging and expensive of all garden structures to build. There are cheaper construction options – for example, a block wall rendered in plaster – but workmanship should never be skimped on if the wall is to be of any height. Remember that height restrictions sometimes apply to any wall or fence forming the boundary to a neighboring property. Choose sturdy fencing for garden boundaries; lighter structures such as screens, a trellis, or even woven willow walls (see p.85) make softer, often more pleasing internal garden divisions. For further information, see STRUCTURES AND SURFACES, "Walls," p.590, and "Fences," p.594.

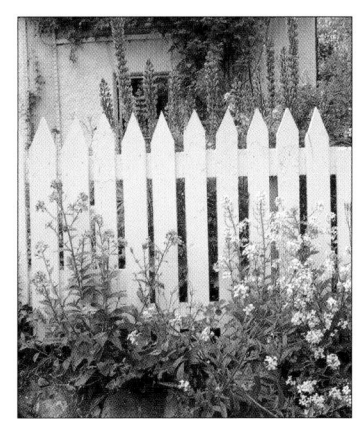

Hedges

Existing Are existing hedges in the right position within the garden, and are they of a suitable type for the site? They may be filtering the wind and sheltering the garden but at the same time creating excessive shade and possibly obscuring distant views.

Have existing hedges grown too wide or too tall for the garden? Evergreen hedges in particular may prove oppressive and too dominant. A deciduous hedge could be more suitable, letting more light into the garden on dark winter days. Old hedges can become thin at their base; reducing the height and width of the upper part of the hedge will encourage regrowth lower down.

Desired A hedge need not have the angular rigid lines associated with walls and fences and can trace a sweeping curve to frame an informal border. The hedging material can also be varied and mixed in different combinations to offer textures and degrees of formality or informality. A hedge of flowering shrubs or those bearing colorful fruits and berries will also give extra interest. Shade cast by overhanging trees will stifle the growth of most hedging plants, a problem that can be overcome by planting a mixed hedge using shade-tolerant species in the reduced light beneath the trees.

A formal hedge can provide structure and definition to a garden design. Closely clipped hedges make living walls for "rooms" containing different garden styles or changes of pace. Windows and archways can also be cut into the hedging to create vistas and entrances from one room to the next. For further information, see HEDGES AND SCREENS, p.82.

Garden buildings

Existing Is the building in good repair? Is it well sited for its purpose? A garden building, whatever its function, should not dominate the garden. If necessary, camouflage it with climbers or shrubs or move the structure to another site. Old garden buildings can be repainted a different color or be refaced with a more sympathetic material. Would a garden building perhaps be more useful if it were refitted for a different role? A shed or summerhouse could be adapted as a storage area for garden furniture, toys, or tools, and a conservatory could double as a greenhouse for plants.

Desired A garden building, however small, can either form part of the general garden scene, adding a modest architectural element to the area, or else be hidden by climbers and shrubs. The siting of the building is critical. A balance must be struck between its practical use and aesthetic quality in any discreet positioning of a building. A summerhouse, conservatory, or greenhouse requires a location with a favorable exposure for its occupants, whether human or plant. Good light, sun, and shelter are all important, with a pleasing outlook essential for a summerhouse, whereas a garden shed or storage bin can be lost in a shady corner. All structures should be readily accessible from a hard surface and have adequate foundations. They should also be constructed from strong, easily maintained materials. For further information, see CONSERVATORY GARDENING, p.350, GREENHOUSES AND FRAMES, pp.560–77, and STRUCTURES AND SURFACES, "Garden sheds," p.599.

Pergolas and arches

Existing A metal or wooden pergola, perhaps with brick or stone supports, must be structurally sound. Can it safely carry the combined weight of plants and overhead structure and withstand the wind resistance offered by the plant canopy? Wood and metalwork structures should be checked and any weaknesses repaired before replanting; sound surfaces should be cleaned and treated with preservative or other paint. It may be advisable to employ a structural engineer or qualified builder to look over large structures. Plantings that threaten to overwhelm should be drastically cut back to allow light and air into the canopy. Old, twisted, and gnarled specimen climbers should be retained for their character and then carefully pruned.

Desired A pergola or series of arches provides a strong architectural element in a garden. It may be used to define the main axis, so directing the flow of the garden, or to mark a transition from one part of the garden to another. Materials and design may be dictated by those already used in the garden or house. A range of weights can be introduced for different effects, from a skeletal metalwork frame to a heavy brick and wooden beam construction. A successfully planted pergola will be draped in plants that obscure most of the construction for much of the year. However, in winter, deciduous plants will reveal their supports, so they do need to be elegant. For further information, see STRUCTURES AND SURFACES, "Pergolas and rustic work," p.597.

Ornamental planting

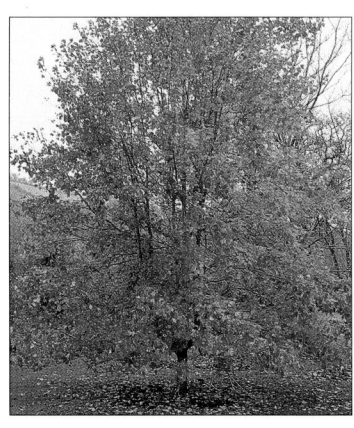

Trees

Existing Mature or semimature trees in a garden are a great asset. Their scale cannot readily be acquired; and the shadows they cast give a special quality to a landscape. Do you wish to add a favorite tree? Small, delicate ones are ideal in confined spaces, while in larger gardens they will, if positioned correctly, enhance the landscape effect of larger specimen trees. Conversely, do existing trees dominate? Often gardens are planted heavily for immedi-

ate results, and this may later require the removal of some trees or at least the reduction of their canopies. If trees have encroached on a view or cut out light, they must be checked with appropriate pruning. The same could apply if leaves from trees near the house are blocking gutters and downspouts, causing moisture problems. It is possible to transplant a tree when it is young.

Desired A single carefully selected tree can fulfill many roles. It may have an elegant form, with flowers,

fruit, good autumn color, and perhaps attractive bark, thus providing almost year-round interest. One species or cultivar used in quantity will give continuity to a garden. A mixture of trees can be planted for short- and longer-term effect; part of the enjoyment is watching a tree develop. Tree roots, especially those of fast-growing species, can damage drains and foundations, so be careful when positioning trees to give adequate clearance around buildings. For more information, see ORNAMENTAL TREES, pp.52–85.

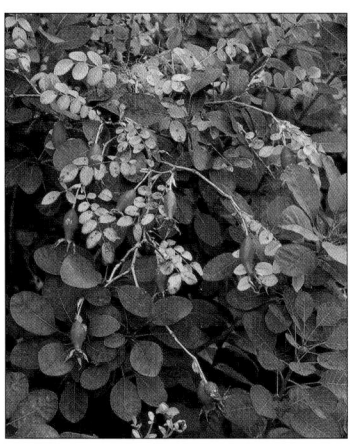

Shrubs

Existing Do existing shrubs give decorative value over a long period of time? Are they performing well, or are they straggly and undernourished or perhaps starved of light? Are they overgrown or too large for the position? Not all shrubs respond well to pruning, and it is important to identify the plants before removing or reducing growth. Shrubs that require regular attention may need to be replaced if a low-maintenance garden is desired. Grafted shrubs may have developed suckers from

their rootstock, which if left in place may overpower the chosen plant. These should be removed cleanly at their source. Similarly, if variegated shrubs have produced green-leaved stems, these should also be cut off.

Desired For every month of the year there is a shrub that can provide color, interest, and scent, even in the darkest days of winter. Their shapes and forms give the garden a soft edge, reducing the predictably angular lines of the average property. Some shrubs are dual-purpose – flowering, then fruiting later in the

year. Shrubs are ideal screening plants since they are usually covered with foliage to ground level, with evergreens retaining their leaves throughout winter. Where a hedge or fence would create too strong a division across the garden, a block of free-form shrubs can be a more sympathetic solution. Shrubs can be chosen to provide habitats for nesting birds or a food source for overwintering creatures. Many shrubs are also suitable for cutting for indoor arrangements. For more information, see ORNAMENTAL SHRUBS, pp.86–119, and ROSES, pp.144–167.

Climbing plants

Existing Do existing climbers enhance the garden, allowing plant growth to flow up, over, and around buildings and walls, uniting the whole? Or are plants too vigorous for supporting structures, whether a tree, wall, arch, or pergola? A plant that has outgrown its allotted space will require considerable pruning, with the result that flowering and fruiting may be much reduced. Large wall-trained shrubs may damage the foundations of buildings if planted too close. They can also create damp

patches if they become too dense, or obscure light from windows if they grow too broad and spreading. Are climbers so overgrown that they are blocking gutters or insinuating their way under roof tiles and clapboards or siding? In all these cases the offending plants must be removed or regularly pruned.

Desired When used with thought and intelligence, well-placed climbing plants can redeem the most mundane or ugly building, gently disguising it with a thin veil of foliage, softening lines and construc-

tion materials. Some climbers will cling tightly to the angles of walls, while others will round and blur the edges, turning corners into curving, flowing forms. The amount of maintenance to which climbing plants are subjected will dictate their appearance. A rampant, trailing climber will, if left unchecked, festoon a building in a few seasons. The same climber, pruned regularly and precisely tied, can offer a neatly tailored, formal layout of well-secured branches. For more information, see "Wall shrubs," p.106, and CLIMBING PLANTS, pp.120–143.

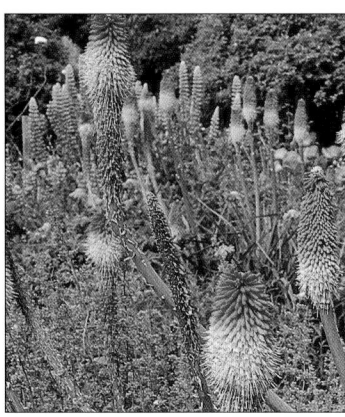

Herbaceous plantings

Existing Is the scale, coloring, and content of an established border to your liking, or does it encompass everything that you dislike? Will the border look spectacular for just one month but boring for the rest of summer? Have some vigorous plants swamped other more delicate species and spoiled the design and balance? Do some plants need to be rejuvenated by lifting and dividing them, replanting only the young vigorous sections? Is the border overrun with

perennial weeds (see p.659) such as goutweed (*Aegopodium podagraria*) or quackgrass (*Elymus repens*)? After taking a year to review the contents, could borders be reduced in size or the planting simplified for easier maintenance?

Desired The main purpose of herbaceous plantings is to provide uplifting color. If borders of herbaceous plants run parallel to the house, they will be critically observed at close quarters and may fail to please for many months of the

year. It is far better to position borders so you look down their length. Then the planting will always appear full and gaps less noticeable. A new border can adopt a special theme – for example, a limited color range, a particular season, a favorite genus, or a form of foliage that will give a specific look, perhaps to harmonize with the color or texture of a hedge or material used as an edging, path, or wall. For more information, see PERENNIALS, pp.168–201, ANNUALS AND BIENNIALS, pp.202–217, and BULBOUS PLANTS, pp.218–245.

Garden features

Kitchen garden

Existing Because of the need for an intensive cultivation program, a vegetable patch demands the best soil in the garden, with a warm, sheltered exposure in good light. Is there a site with more suitable growing conditions than that currently being used? If so, consider relocating vegetable and fruit growing to this area. If you intend to keep an existing kitchen garden area, then before deciding what to grow it is essential that you assess the condition of the soil (see "Soil and its structure," p.610). It may well be in need of improvement or deep cultivation. Are existing fruit trees and bushes productive, or old and neglected? Old specimens may need careful pruning to restore them to productivity, or they may be better replaced. Take into account, too, the requirements of your household and any particular likes and dislikes.

Desired Decide on the main requirement, whether growing salad crops, unusual produce unobtainable at the grocery store, or enough fresh, possibly organically grown vegetables and fruit to supply the kitchen through the year. Growing good vegetables requires a great deal of time and hard work, and this must be considered before embarking on the cultivation of too large a garden. Where smaller crops are wanted, vegetables and fruit can be integrated throughout the entire garden, benefiting the insect population and looking attractive. For further information, see GROWING FRUIT, pp.411–483, and GROWING VEGETABLES, pp.484–542.

Herb garden

Existing Does an inherited herb garden include those plants that are important to you? With such a wide range of possible plants from which to choose, the herb garden and its contents are very much a personal matter. It may be necessary to be ruthless about discarding some of the existing herbs. Replanning and much replanting may be required in order to achieve the desired effect. Have fast-spreading herbs, such as mints, come to dominate and smother less vigorous ones? Such plants should be cut back, but this may not be a permanent solution to the problem; consider growing the more delicate herbs in the safety of containers or confining the rampant growers to pots and planters.

Desired To grow well, herbs require a free-draining soil, which need not be particularly rich, and a very sunny site that receives maximum light and warmth. Ideally a herb garden must be located near the house and within easy reach of the kitchen for use throughout the year. However, it is not necessary to group culinary, aromatic, and medicinal plants together. The herb garden theme may be extended throughout the heart of the cultivated areas of the garden. Flowers, fruit, vegetables, and herbs may be combined, using an extended range of fragrances and color as well as flower and leaf shapes and textures. Larger quantities of herbs required for culinary or other domestic purposes, such as making potpourri, may be grown in specific areas to be harvested and stored for use out of season. For further information, see GROWING HERBS, pp.396–409.

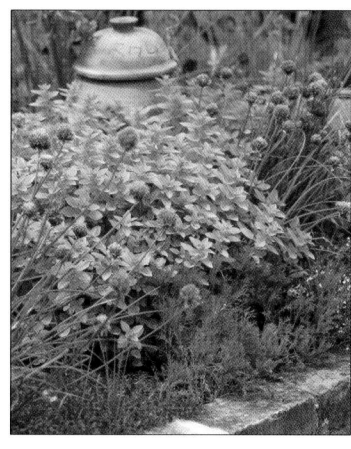

Water features

Existing Are the water features in the garden well maintained or in need of repair or renovation? Before adopting any existing ponds, pools, or canals, their overall condition should be investigated and problems addressed as necessary. Has a pond site become overshadowed by once-small trees, now taking too much light from the water and dropping debris into it? Is the scale of the area of water in relation to the garden as a whole inappropriate, requiring an extension of the water surface and the removal of overly invasive water plants? Ponds and pools require considerable time and effort to keep them in good condition. If this commitment cannot be fulfilled, they may be better removed.

A primary consideration in family gardens must be the safety of the water feature. Is it properly protected? The smallest pond can pose a threat to children – especially those unfamiliar with the garden. The depth of small ponds can be dramatically reduced by filling part of them with rounded pebbles while youngsters are small. Ledges around the sides of pools will help older children to scramble out. Sloping pond margins also allow for escape from deeper water and may save the lives of pets or small garden animals.

Desired The smallest amount of water brings movement, sound, and life into a garden. A patio may host a small spout and basin, a garden of modest nature a pond of indigenous plantings, and a landscape a series of interconnected pools and water courses, each of an appropriate scale to its setting. For further information, see WATER GARDENING, pp.274–97.

Ornaments and pots

Existing Is there a chance of acquiring long-established decorative garden items? If so, such an opportunity should be seized. To inherit statues and large architectural containers with a house and garden is an uncommon occurrence, unless special financial provision for these has been made. In most cases, these objects will be removed along with the house contents or will be sold. A garden that derives strength from well-positioned objects will be weakened by their removal or replacement. Conversely, an over-embellished garden with an excess of decoration, which confuses the eye, needs to be controlled to restore balance and order to the scene.

Desired An extra dimension can be provided by well-placed objects that enhance the style of the garden design. Although seen as a separate entity, the ornament should still comply with local factors, namely scale, style, material, and general appropriateness. Statues and pots can be an indication of, and an outlet for, personal taste and expression, introducing art, whether traditional or contemporary, representational or abstract. They can also act as signs within the garden, encouraging the visitor to move through it or pause to admire a view, enhancing certain points and drawing together otherwise disconnected areas. A distinctive individuality can be achieved with the use of commissioned pieces of sculpture or plant containers. For further information, see CONTAINER GARDENING, pp.298–329.

Sketching out a plan

BEFORE measuring a garden accurately and formulating any new design, a preliminary sketch or sketches will help you assess the overall layout of the existing plot. This will form the basis of a detailed scale plan (see p.36), on which you will be able to mark those features and plants that are to be retained, and the elements to be added (see p.38).

These sketches should consist of rough ground plans on which to note the many practical factors that will affect the final layout and choice of plants. With accompanying notes, they should detail elements particular to the site, such as climate, soil type, views to consider, shade cast, and the orientation of property and house, as well as the shape and size of the area – factors that cannot be changed. They should also include utilities relating to the house as well as to the garden and its maintenance, such as outside faucets and garden sheds. Such items may currently be poorly positioned.

Climate and exposure
The climate of the general locality and that found specifically within the garden are key determining factors, influencing its layout and the choice and placing of plants (see CLIMATE AND THE GARDEN, pp.600–609). Information on the general climatic conditions of the locality, annual rainfall, average temperatures, and quantities of sunlight should be sought and studied. These general conditions will be influenced by the particular terrain within the garden.

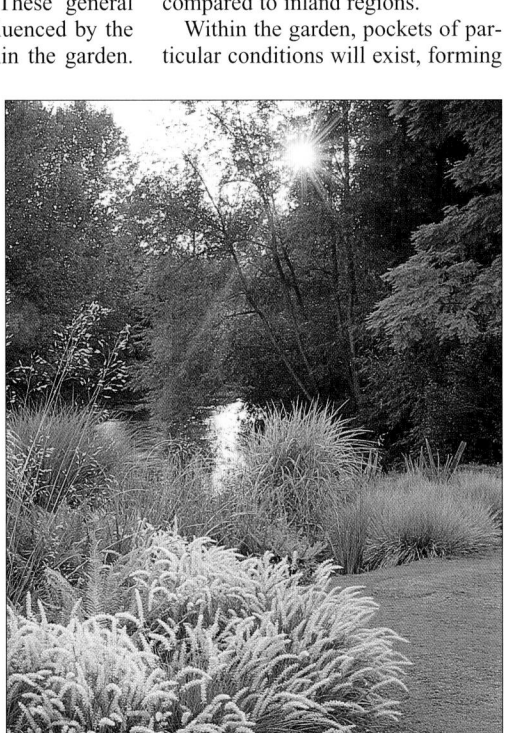

GARDEN TOPOGRAPHY
An area of water not only increases soil moisture but also the humidity of the surrounding air, to the benefit of many plants. However, water often occupies a low-lying spot, which is very likely to be a frost pocket (see p.601). Plants may need to be selected for their hardiness as well as their suitability for the soil and conditions.

GAINING A PERSPECTIVE
An upstairs window may afford a good view when sketching the boundaries and any irregularities in a garden. It is also an ideal vantage point from which to observe and map changing patterns of sun and shade.

A low-lying garden may be sheltered from strong winds but it may also form a frost pocket, whereas a hilltop site may remain several degrees colder than a neighboring, protected, south-facing slope. A garden near the water can also be affected by strong winds, possibly salt laden, but the maritime influence will prevent extreme fluctuations in temperature compared to inland regions.

Within the garden, pockets of particular conditions will exist, forming microclimates of warmth or cold, humidity or dryness, each suiting a different range of plants (see "Microclimate," p.603). The orientation of the garden and the house within it will affect the warmth or coldness of the house walls, and where shadows will create deep or partial shade. These factors will affect not only your choice of plants but also decisions on where seating areas should be positioned.

Assessing your soil type
The soil found within a garden is a crucial factor to take into account. The type, texture, and level of acidity or alkalinity (the pH) of the soil are important to recognize (see "Soil and its structure," p.610). Soils vary greatly from region to region, from a heavy clay to a light sandy loam, or an alkaline or limestone soil to an acidic peat. Each variation in soil will suit a different plant range. Those happily accommodated will thrive, while those planted in an inappropriate soil type will struggle to survive. Moisture retention and drainage will vary with soil type, as will ease of cultivation, which can be severely hindered by poorly drained, heavy soils.

Poor drainage is a factor that may affect more than plant choice. A soft, boggy site will be unsuitable for any substantial building work unless the problem can be alleviated by installing drainage (see "Improving

drainage," p.617). If large areas of rubble or subsoil have been left from building and construction work, it may be simpler to work with them rather than attempt an overhaul. They may be used successfully to form the foundations of a terraced area or perhaps a gravel garden; this type of site provides ideal conditions for plants that prefer fast-draining soil (see "Gravel beds and paving," p.259).

Utilities and access
Other fixed details occurring within the garden should be noted on the plan, including drives and pathways that service the house and important yet irritating features to be worked around, such as utility covers. There may also be meter inspection points and septic tanks to be marked in. An oil tank or propane tank is often an ugly but essential component of the yard, especially in rural areas; it may be possible to relocate it, but screening is obviously an easier option. A rough woodpile, however, can look charming in a garden, and it also makes an attractive wildlife habitat.

Any overhead power or telephone lines need to be entered onto the site plan, because tall-growing trees must not be planted close to overhead wires. It is also inadvisable to plant twining climbers on a house wall where wires enter the building, because the plants will use these as a climbing frame. Such points on the house wall are often inaccessible, too, and attempts to prune or pull away growth can be hazardous.

ELEMENTS TO DISGUISE
Utility covers must be accessible but can be hidden by low, spreading plants or by using recessed lids with paving set into them (see p.581).

A ROUGH SITE PLAN
Sketch the layout of the garden and the position of the house. Then enter in substantial structural planting such as trees and hedges, the outlines of areas of hard standing and lawns, the route of paths, and any internal garden divisions and buildings such as sheds, screens, and walls. At this point, more generally planted borders and areas may be indicated simply by shading. In this northern hemisphere garden, the diagonal hatching represents shade cast by the sun taking its highest, midsummer route across the sky.

Thinking ahead

While your plans may be at an embryonic stage, ideas for major changes may already be germinating; for example, the felling of a large tree or construction of a garden building such as a greenhouse or gazebo. There are certain legal aspects that will repay investigation right from the start, or you may run the risk of unpleasant surprises thwarting your plans later. These include local building and planning codes and regulations, the responsibility for (and delineation between) boundaries separating neighboring properties, and any statutory environmental protection for your area. Any necessary permits should be sought as early as possible, even if you eventually do not follow the ideas through, since agreement and clearance, where forthcoming, can take considerable amounts of time.

Other practicalities

There are certain practicalities that few gardens can be without, and a checklist can be compiled to determine whether the existing garden is equipped to suit your needs. Mark the position of outside faucets, and consider whether these may need to be moved. To inherit a garden with an established compost pile is a boon, but compost can easily be moved elsewhere, as can other potentially useful structures such as cold frames and small sheds. Draw the current position of these onto the plan, together with sheds and storage bins, and consider whether the capacity these offer is adequate, not only for garden tools but also for general family clutter such as folding chairs, toys, and bicycles.

What lies beyond

Elements quite literally beyond your control should still be noted for consideration on the plan. The immediate surroundings of the garden, where views may be taken advantage of or ugly buildings concealed by carefully positioned trees, will enable an enterprising gardener to fully exploit the site. Privacy and security at the boundaries of the area should be examined and noted for their existing effectiveness. Weigh the possible loss of views or sunlight if extra privacy and shelter are required, and make sure that changes will not annoy your neighbors.

Security can often be improved by opening up the garden, rather than reinforcing enclosure; consider whether driveways and sheds might perhaps be better brought into view.

The impact of a busy road passing the property, perhaps with a junction at which point headlights sweep into the garden, can be reduced or lost if the boundary gaps are filled. Dense, clipped hedges can also act as a useful baffle to noise (see also HEDGES AND SCREENS, p.82).

VIEWS TO OBSCURE
An unwelcome reminder of urban life in the form of a distant parking lot intrudes onto this otherwise charming garden. Planting a narrow, upright tree, or perhaps raising the height of the rear wall slightly with trellis panels on which a climber could be trained, would restore seclusion. Consider the viewpoint of neighbors before implementing changes that could block light.

LENGTHENING A VISTA
Reshaping this border and introducing more height in the foreground would open up and lengthen a vista toward the nicely shaped conifer and lead on to views of the countryside beyond. Lowering the hedge would also add distance, but its presence, together with the trees behind it, suggests a windbreak. Prevailing winds should be investigated, since this site could be very exposed.

Making a scale plan

A FINE, dry day is required for compiling a scale plan, with no limitation on time. The assistance of a second person will greatly ease the task, as will a good-sized sketch pad or a clipboard and paper, two 100ft (30m) tape measures, pencil, eraser, a set of compasses, and an ample supply of heavy twine and twist ties with which to pin the twine in place. With a small garden, a single "field plan" can be made of the entire site. Larger gardens can be broken into separate areas, later to be joined on a final plan put together on a larger surface such as a kitchen table or drawing board.

Making a start
The boundaries of the garden should be measured and entered onto the plan with heights of boundary walls, hedges, or fences marked alongside their lengths. Then the house and other buildings must be plotted and fixed within the boundary. This may be achieved by measuring from two known fixed points on the boundary, such as corners, gate posts, or tree trunks, to a corner or fixed point on the house. If three or four points are established around the house, then an accurate location will be found for the building. Surrounding patios can be relatively easily measured from the house to their edges, checking that they run parallel to the house and, if not, gauging the discrepancy.

Plotting positions
When plotting outlying features that cannot be related easily to a nearby boundary or house wall, you must create an artificial line from which measurements can be taken. A long tape measure pulled straight out between known and pinpointed features in the garden, such as a central door in the house and a fence post on the far boundary, provides a "datum line." From this, use a second tape to identify the position of features, such as a tree, sundial, or utility cover, by measuring at a right angle from the first datum-line tape. Note the measurement on the first tape where the second crosses it and the distance from this point to the feature.

Once a datum line has been established, any number of items can be measured using coordinates to the left or right of the line. A number of such datum lines may be necessary to plot all features within a large garden. To pinpoint a single, isolated feature, such as a tree in a lawn, the technique known as triangulation (see p.37) may be used. While

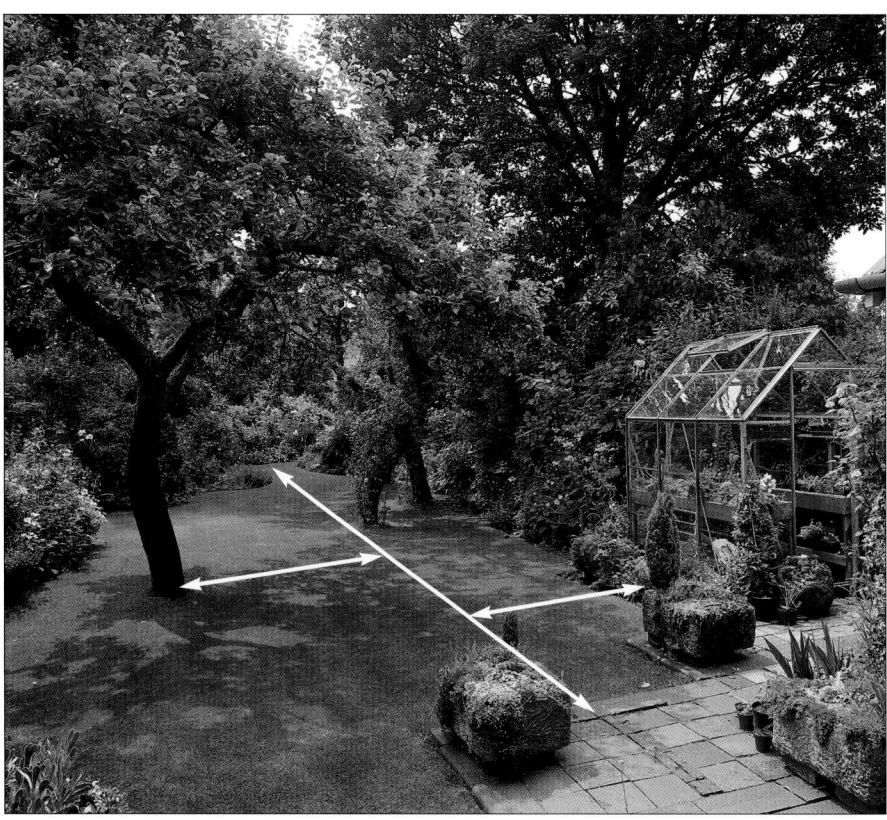

triangulation (see p.37)

MEASURING FROM A DATUM LINE
Except in the tiniest yards, it is almost impossible to position elements such as trees and small buildings on a plan by taking measurements between them and their nearest boundaries. Using a central datum line makes the job much easier. Here, a line in the paving running parallel to the house has provided a useful starting point for a datum line that will run to a fixed, traceable point at far end of the garden.

MEASURING THE EXISTING LAYOUT
Using a datum line, or lines, enables you to build up a plotted plan of the garden by making a series of offset measurements to the right and to the left of the line. The running, or incremental, measurements taken along the datum line are also a valuable way of confirming the site's dimensions.

Tape measure 1 measures down the garden from a fixed point (here, one corner of the house)

START

HOUSE

13ft
14.5ft
16ft
26ft
10ft
30ft
19ft

28ft
25ft
27ft
24ft
33ft
34ft
37ft
17ft

Tape measure 2 is used to make the cross-measurements

10ft
17ft
25ft
50ft

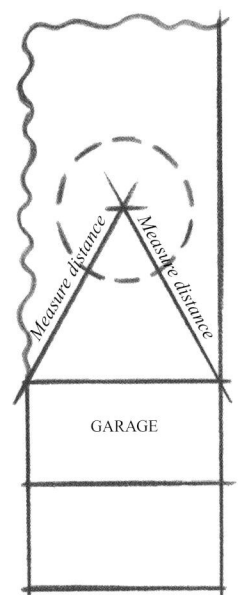

TRIANGULATION
Where a feature such as a tree cannot be directly related to existing straight sight lines, measure against two fixed points to establish its position. To transfer to a plan, scale down the two distances appropriately and use each as the radius of a circle drawn with a compass around the fixed points – here the two corners of the garage. The point at which the circles inter sect will be the location of the feature (here a tree). The compass can also be used to describe the tree's canopy.

GARAGE

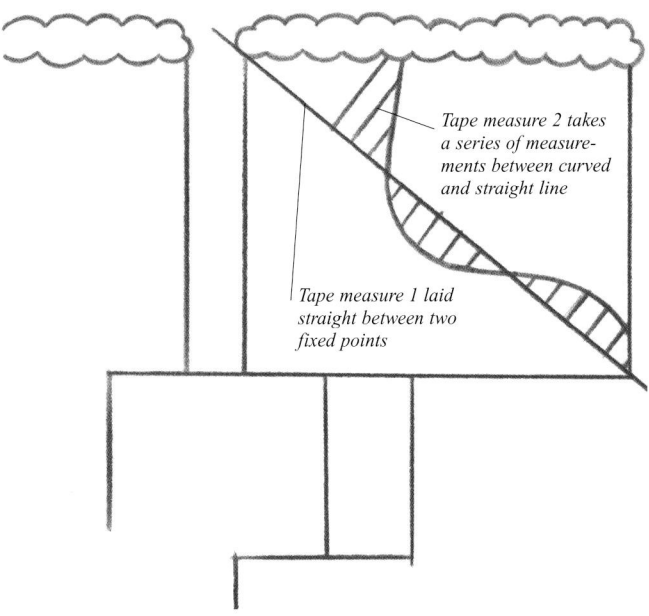

Tape measure 2 takes a series of measure-ments between curved and straight line

Tape measure 1 laid straight between two fixed points

ESTABLISHING AN IRREGULAR CURVE
Two tape measures must be used for this: one to lie straight and flat across the curve (or curves) between two given measured and plotted points, the second to be used to measure the curve at regular intervals from the first tape. For example, at 18in (50cm) intervals along the first tape, the second tape is laid across it at right angles and the distance to the edge of the curve measured and recorded as a series of coordinates.

straight edges are easy to measure and plot, the curved edge of a drive-way or generous sweep of a border may take more time to replicate precisely on paper (see above, right).

Adding more dimensions
As linear measurements are taken, other useful information can be gath-ered. Measure and mark the posi-tions of all gates and entrances on the boundary, and all doors and windows of the house. Heights of internal gar-den divisions such as screens and hedges should be recorded, together with the height and canopy spread of trees, pergolas, or arches.

Changes in level should also be recorded. These are critical factors that may necessitate terracing, retaining walls, steps, and slopes in future plans for the garden where unsatisfactory level changes prevail. Simple slopes and slight changes can be calculated relatively easily, but an undulating site of various levels and cross-falls will be beyond the capa-bilities of the average gardener. For this a professional surveyor must be employed. A large property, which is usually more difficult to plot and coordinate than a small one, may also be better left to a professional.

Transferring the field plan
With the "fieldwork" statistics accu-rately gathered, including a number of extra cross-measurements made as a check to the detail and to verify the overall plan, the information can be put on paper. A plan created at too small a scale will be hard to draw and awkward to read. Where practical, as large a scale as possible should be adopted on which every possible detail can be recorded. Large graph paper will enable the easy transfer of

TRANSFERRING THE FIELD PLAN TO GRAPH PAPER

Establish the scale of the plan using the largest dimensions possible on a sheet of paper that will accommodate them; if necessary, stick several sheets together. A general garden plan such as this showing basic outlines and features can be drawn at a scale of 1:100. Mark everything on the plan, including features you may not want to keep. This plan, together with your visual memory of what already exists in each area, will help in both imagining and deciding on the scale of new outlines and features (see p.38).

measurements from field notes to plan, although designs on blank paper using a scale rule, once mastered, will give greater flexibility. A general garden plan detailing all the items and features may be drawn at a scale of 1:100, but a more detailed one of planting within a border (see also p.45) requires a scale of 1:50 or 1:40 for a comfortable depiction of plantings.

When using graph paper, a decision on how many squares are to represent one square yard (square meter) must be made. The biggest scale that the paper can afford should first be calculated by drawing on the greatest measurement, since if this can be accommodated then the entire drawing will fit. Art and design supply stores stock paper in larger sizes, which may be difficult to find in stationery stores.

Putting pencil to paper

The design novice will almost certainly need several attempts at plotting a scale plan, and even a professional will work only in pencil at this stage. The principal features should be entered onto the plan first, starting with the boundaries and any gateways or openings within them.

From these points, the house with its doorways and windows can be positioned. These openings are important as often a sight line or vista will be revealed from a doorway or window. Once the outer and "inner" perimeters of the garden area are established, small details around the house can be arranged. From here you can draw in paths and driveways, establishing between them areas of lawn, hard surfaces, and borders. These will facilitate the positioning of more isolated features, such as specimen trees, sheds, and greenhouses.

Omit only those features that will definitely not be retained. At this stage all else must appear on the plan, even elements that may be removed later. The drawing can then be made permanent by inking the lines. A thin line should be used to depict all of the existing detail to permit the overlay of new ideas and the blocking in or heightening of old features. Thus you will create a new design that includes worthy existing elements enhanced by proposals, suggestions, and experiments new to the site.

Imposing the new design

The original master copy of the plan should remain unmarked. Either make photocopies on which to work, or use tracing-paper overlays laid across the original. With a known scale and an accurate drawing, there are no limits to the possibilities that can be developed on the plan. Different sizes and positions for patios, driveways, courtyards, and ponds can be considered (see STRUCTURES AND SURFACES, pp.578–99, and WATER GARDENING, pp.274–297). Cutting out shapes representing planting, ornaments, pools or buildings from cardboard to place and move around the drawing helps envisage the impact these features will have on the rest of the site.

This preliminary planning period, although rather abstract and divorced from the physical practicalities of making a garden, is an essential one as all those thoughts, ideas, and dreams of what your personal garden should consist of must be expressed, considered, applied, and then adopted or rejected. Many rough drawings should be made to expose all the design possibilities.

Any working drawings that follow the thought process should be kept; frequently a discarded idea may be resurrected in a different guise. The possibility of two ideas combining and working together when one of the ideas in isolation would be rejected is sufficient reason for retaining every idea and drawing until the project has been completed.

Rounding out the vision

When a design has been rigorously scrutinized, experimented with, and passed such tests as practicality, accessibility, and suitability for the site, then the foundations of a new approach to the garden are beginning to be laid. Areas of the plan could be shaded or colored to give a more powerful representation of the differing elements, aiding final decisions of proportion and scale.

You will also begin to appreciate the proportions of hard landscaping to "soft" – that is, planted areas – in your design and adjust them if needed. You may already have ideas about building materials and the nature of the main planting elements – even the identities of individual structural plants (see also "Principles of planting," pp.42–51). A scrapbook of photographs or pictures from magazines and catalogs will add color and texture to your vision and serve as a reminder of items to order and buy to complete your design.

BUILDING THE NEW DESIGN ON THE EXISTING PLAN

Having created an accurately plotted field plan (see p.37, and above), use copies of it, or tracing paper, to begin experimenting with your new design. The advantage of using tracing paper is that features and outlines that are to be discarded can simply be left out of the drawing to produce a much cleaner and clearer picture. In the overlay on the right, elements to be retained from the existing garden – including some of the fine mature hedging and the most desirable of the trees – have been marked in blue. The driveway has been given a softer profile, more space has been allocated to borders, a potager-style kitchen garden replaces a decrepit orchard, and the \living room of the house now enjoys an attractive view of the patio and the formal pool.

Retain shrubs

Lawn

Retain lawn

Garage

Garage

Retain center of forecourt and remodel sides

Entrance

HOUSE

Rebuild green-house and shed on new site

Pergola

Patio

Seat

KEY

Kitchen garden

Formal pool and sunken garden

What you wish to keep from the existing features

What you wish to add

THE FINISHED DESIGN

This beautifully realized plan has had color, detail, and texture added, not only in planted areas but also in the choice of hard landscaping materials. An existing landscape and house may provide inspiration where materials can be harmoniously linked with those already found on the property. In such a case a seamless flow of materials from the house to the outside will produce a satisfactory design. Even when the identical brick, stone, or concrete cannot be found, a similar color, texture, and scale of material will be perfectly satisfactory.

A garden devoid of existing materials offers the opportunity to introduce new ones. Existing colors and textures should still be respected, yet within the design a particular cobblestone, brick, or block can be selected. Small-scale, intricately patterned materials are appropriate in small, confined spaces but can look overly complicated and busy on a large scale, whereas bigger units offer a calmer feeling.

Lumber for pergolas, gates, or fences, gravel for terraces and paths, and asphalt for the driveway must all be chosen for their suitability for the site, aesthetic appeal, and durability. The color of a fence, whether natural or painted, can alter the appearance of an entire property, as can the color and size of gravel used as loose surfaces.

KEY
1 Long grass with bulbs and woodland herbs
2 Asphalt driveway
3 Closely mowed lawn
4 Mixed shrub planting
5 Specimen tree
6 Planting with year-round interest
7 Border of shade-loving plants
8 Two-car garage
9 Potting/storage shed
10 Greenhouse
11 Asphalt forecourt with enough space for turning
12 Stone-flagged main entrance to house
13 Brick wall with trained fruit
14 Brick paths
15 Vegetables, cut flowers, fruit, and herbs
16 Garden bench
17 Central herb garden
18 Mixed border
19 Stone-flagged patio
20 Pergola with table and chairs
21 Evergreen hedge
22 Tree screening neighboring house
23 Annual color border
24 Axial vista
25 Sculpture
26 Compost and wood piles
27 Formal pool bridged by stepping stones
28 Sunken garden with steps

39

Putting the plan into practice

Iℕ the same way that the existing garden has been recorded on paper, you must now translate your new design onto the site. Often it is during this process of measuring and marking out the proposed plan that problems with the design become apparent. You may have been overly ambitious with the available space, for example, or mistaken about the most practical route for a path. Only by standing at proposed vantage points to contemplate imaginary vistas may an unwelcome eyesore be revealed.

Using props

A design can be laid out *in situ* using whatever is available to simulate temporarily the key elements of the design. You must work around features that are probably destined to be removed – however inconvenient this may be – because the experimental layout may show that these are valuable elements that are worthy of retention after all.

Stakes, containers, hoses, string, pots, cardboard boxes, and trash cans can be used to assume roles such as path and border edges, step treads, specimen trees, ponds, or rows of repeating shrubs across the front of an imaginary terrace. The simplest indicators – heavy wooden tree stakes driven into an open lawn – will readily confirm or reject a suitable location for a broad, spreading tree, where neighboring plantings, buildings, and views may all be important considerations.

TRANSFERRING THE DESIGN
Formal, symmetrical designs can be as simple to mark out on the proposed site as they are to plan on paper. A grid may be created using string guides that correspond with the scale on the plan, enabling the entire design to be transferred onto the ground with relative ease. It is important that all of the measurements and angles are correctly taken and then carefully checked.

Where possible, props should be left in place for their impact to be experienced over a few days and at different times of day. Where string guides and stakes indicating the edges of borders may be disturbed, a line of sand or spray paint from an aerosol can may be used.

Photographs taken of the garden with its props in place may prove invaluable when determining the eventual placement or removal of features. These final decisions should not be hurried; allow enough time to consider and even reconsider. At this point indecision is a strength, as holding onto an original concept doggedly in the light of subsequent modifications is foolhardy. Opportunities available now will not present themselves again, and matters of construction are more easily resolved on the drawing board than on site with an impatient contractor.

Order of work

A carefully orchestrated schedule of work is needed to coordinate and implement a newly designed plan. There are many different elements and skills involved, and each should be undertaken in a logical sequence to provide a smooth running program and keep disruption to an absolute minimum.

A fundamental decision must be made as to whether the garden improvements are to be undertaken as a single operation or in stages over a number of weeks, months, or years. Try to have all hard landscaping work completed in a single phase; this eliminates the need for builders to return and create a second period of dust, noise, and inconvenience (see STRUCTURES AND SURFACES, pp.578–99). Timing the operations is important to allow construction work to be completed in favorable weather in summer or autumn, leaving autumn or spring for planting, sowing, and laying sod.

Remodeling in stages

It is often the case, whether through budgetary constraints, available time, or simply the need to retain a usable outdoor area of some sort at all times, that a reworking of the garden can only be implemented piecemeal. A strategy for change must be drawn up. For some period of time the desired garden will overlay the existing layout, which may perhaps look somewhat odd with permanently retained features, temporarily kept items, and newly established plantings and features all present. The evolving hybrid will require intricate planning to ensure a smooth transition to the new design.

To assist with a phased series of changes, the first practical measure must be to label the contents of the

USING PROPS
By arranging and rearranging items gleaned from the house and garden, you can simulate the key features of the proposed design. Here bamboo tepees indicate the position of obelisks planted with climbers; large inverted pots stand in for shrubs; and the slats and landscape fabric form a terraced area flanked by massed plantings of lavender. To complete the effect, a specimen tree in the lawn and an undulating border edging of boxwood have been added.

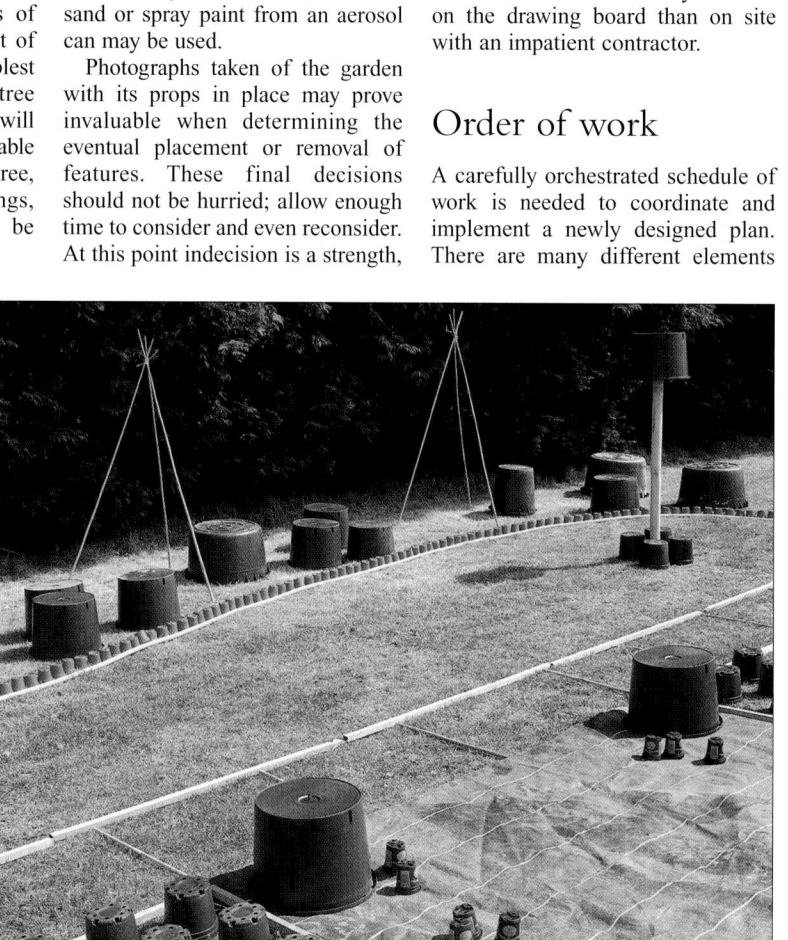

garden with written or color-coded tags indicating plants and materials to stay, to be moved or remain temporarily, or to be removed at once. Although decisions have been made, a period of final deliberation is useful, during which the labeled plants may be reassessed to avoid any later confusion and irrevocable errors.

Hiring professionals

Once the scale of operations has been identified, then the amount of assistance needed to implement the plans can be gauged. It may be possible over a period of time to make all the changes yourself, or some help may be needed to execute construction work or tree felling. On the other hand, a landscape contractor may be hired to create the entire garden. Where assistance is being sought, it is important to state accurately what is needed and to obtain a detailed price quotation. Good references or, ideally, personal recommendations for the firm are also highly desirable.

Professional advice may also be sought to assess the condition of trees, walls, and garden buildings. With their good condition confirmed or otherwise, the appropriate action can be taken. Even if some elements are unaffected by the current work, examine their condition early on; to invite arborists or builders back into the finished garden could be disruptive and damaging.

HARD LANDSCAPING
Because of the inevitable soil compaction involved, built features should always take priority over new planting. Where only part of the garden is being remodeled, as above, clear an area large enough for you to work comfortably. Conduits laid under paving at the construction stage (right) may be useful in the future to carry utilities such as piping and wiring.

Coping with limited access

A house (for example, a row house or townhouse) without direct street access into the garden should ideally have its garden construction scheduled to coincide with house renovation, because materials must be carried through the house itself. Materials can be lifted over adjoining walls, but at some cost and effort. Where large trash containers cannot be brought into the garden, you may have to get permission to place one on the street.

Excavations and refuse

When excavations produce large quantities of soil to be taken offsite, remember to discard subsoil, but keep topsoil. Where levels are being reduced, this will involve taking off and reserving the topsoil, digging out and removing subsoil, and then replacing the topsoil, so that the best soil does not leave the garden. When holes are to be dug, first locate any utilities – water, electricity, or gas pipes – that may be buried in the garden. Carefully excavate to identify their positions precisely before any additional work is carried out.

Clearing the area

The first stage of the garden's refurbishment is the removal of all unwanted materials and built structures. Large trees should be cut down and taken away first. Stumps should also be removed if at all

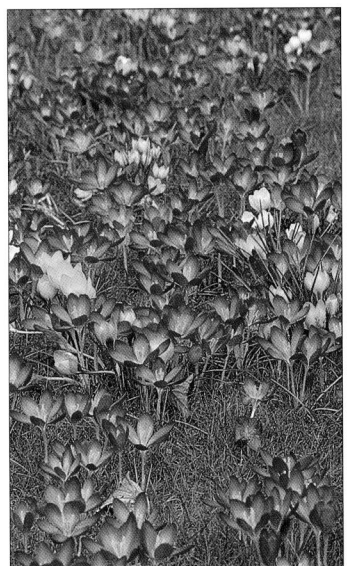

practical. Quality materials in good condition will have a resale value that justifies taking the trouble to find a reputable dealer. Those materials that are eventually to be reused should be cleaned and carefully stacked in a safe place offsite.

In a large garden the area to be worked on should be fenced off, restricting potential damage and spread of materials to one place. Paving and steps to be retained should also be protected by covering with plywood or similar materials while heavy materials are being maneuvered. Sod can be stripped and stacked for a short time (only a few days, particularly in summer) before reuse or cleared for new sod to take its place.

Plants left in place

Plants to be left *in situ* can be carefully wrapped in sheets and tied for a brief period if surrounding walls are being repaired. Large shrubs, too big for their locations yet too interesting and attractive to remove, could be thinned or reduced, or even cut back to the ground to encourage regeneration (see "Renovation," p.108). Before cutting them back, some plants can be propagated as an extra safety measure: in the right season, take cuttings of plants such as roses, hollies, or clematis to make sure the variant survives (see PRINCIPLES OF PROPAGATION, "Cuttings," p.626). Clumps of many perennials will tolerate being lifted, divided, and potted up if kept well watered in a sheltered, shady corner (see PERENNIALS, "Lifting and dividing," p.191). Taking cuttings or collecting seed (see "Gathering and storing seed," p.623) is another way of preserving such plants to incorporate into the new garden.

Laying sod in autumn allows bulbs to be planted simultaneously, to flower in spring.

CORRECT TIMING
Never delay the laying of new sod. The timing of delivery is crucial: if left rolled (as below) for more than a day or two it will swiftly deteriorate. Nothing gives a new lawn an air of maturity like a scattering of bulbs, such as crocuses (left). Laying sod in autumn allows bulbs to be planted simultaneously, to flower in spring.

Creating the landscape

With unwanted materials out of the way, the cleared site should then have any pernicious weeds eradicated (see "Controlling weeds," p.658). At this stage any adjustments to levels can also be made, as well as any excavations for services such as power for garden lighting, or irrigation systems. Wall footings or path bases can now be excavated, and solid foundations built (see "Paths and steps," p.587, and "Walls," p.590). Construction of walls and other structures can then take place (see STRUCTURES AND SURFACES, pp.578–99, and "Erecting the greenhouse," p.565). To add the finishing touches before planting, fences and lumber may be treated or painted, and trellises or support wires put up on walls and fences for climbers.

Ready to plant

Where larger plants are being used in a design, it may be necessary to plant them as the hard landscape is being constructed, since at a later stage it may not be possible to maneuver them into place. However, the task of reintegrating any preserved plant material into new designs and introducing new plants generally begins once the hard construction is completed and services installed.

Before plants are introduced, however, any soil compaction should be remedied and the soil improved by the addition of organic matter (see "Improving soil structure," p.615).

Any protection given to shrubs and hard surfaces can now be removed and surfaces cleaned with a high-pressure hose. With the potentially dirty tasks complete, loose surfaces can have their final layers applied, with clean gravel laid on top. After that, new planting plans (see p.42) can begin to take shape.

Principles of planting

Once the general layout of the garden is in place, the greatest enjoyment comes with selecting plants. The impact plant choice can make on a garden is extraordinary. Plants give a garden style, charm, character, depth, and warmth, to mention but a few of their qualities. An adjacent street may be enhanced by an overhanging tree, which softens rigid lines and brings seasonal color and texture to an urban landscape. A sheltered courtyard with high surrounding walls may look like a prison yard, yet the decorative effect of a climber (such as a wisteria) trained over it will transform the space into a welcoming retreat.

Plants bring calm, clothing severity with flowing form and mellowing tones. As with curtains or drapes in a house, plants will also help deaden harsh sounds. It is increasingly accepted that, allergy sufferers notwithstanding, the presence of plants improves the atmosphere around us, possibly alleviating the effects of pollution and certainly increasing the oxygen and moisture content of the air as well as adding a pleasing fragrance.

Making sure plants succeed

Successful plant choice can quite literally make a garden; it might even be said that until plants and flowers are established and growing well a garden does not really exist. The garden's therapeutic powers, which can soothe the mind and alleviate tension, derive mainly from its thriving plants and perhaps also from the presence of water and the use of sympathetic building materials. The element of quiet combined with charm and style can turn a small patch of planted land into a sanctuary. Even the most elementary of plantings, such as a well-kept lawn that has replaced a hard surface within a built environment, will bring life, color, and softness to an otherwise harsh and alien site.

Selecting plants for success

The wealth of different plants available can be bewildering, but the choice will never be as limitless as it may seem. Within the categories of trees, shrubs, perennials, and so on, many plants can be dismissed immediately as inappropriate on numerous grounds: for example, incompatible soil type, climate, scale, or growth rate. Once the most suitable plants have been identified, personal preference for certain colors and shapes will narrow the choice even more.

The manner and frequency of garden use will dictate the kinds of plants, too: for example, a garden area that is used only in summer will be planted to perform best in that season. Planting immediately around a house and along an driveway will also place greater demands on the choice of plant material, because year-round interest of some description will be expected. A carefully selected combination of plants that will provide a display of flowers in each season is needed. Alternatively, group plants together that combine other attributes – mix evergreens with some fruiting trees or shrubs, add plants with attractive stems or bark, and include bulbs and annuals to inject color and interest at other times of the year.

Defining a style of planting

In every garden there are so many variables that each one is unique. So, to talk about a particular or specific planting style may appear to impose false categories and divisions. However, there are two extremes between which all plantings fall: the formal and the informal styles. Deciding on the degree of formality or informality required will greatly assist the initial selection of plants and the diversity of plant material used. A very formal garden, for example, may have an extremely restricted palette of plants compared to a more informal arrangement.

Formal planting

Great strength and order can be given to a garden by using only a small selection of plants, but in quantity. The planting, however, does not necessarily need to be arranged in an angular and regimented fashion or within precisely designated areas. Some formality can be achieved using sweeps of single plants in broad blocks, creating tranquillity in uniformity. Even relatively informal plants grown *en masse* can assume an orderly role – an expanse of ornamental grasses planted to create a

CONTRASTING PLANTING STYLES
The style of planting within a garden or area of it can be broadly categorized as either formal or informal. Some plants lend themselves more to one style than the other. The labor involved in maintaining the formal garden (far right) is evident, but an informal planting, such as the border (right), does not necessarily involve less work: a great deal of skill and care is needed to maintain a balance between the needs and vigor of different plants when growing in close proximity.

EDITING NATURE
Plant selections, carefully chosen to fit in with their surroundings and compete successfully with less desirable plants, produce a naturalistic scene.

AN ARTIFICIAL ENVIRONMENT
Select plants suitable for the conditions: a roof may not be a natural growing site, but these sun-loving, wind-resistant plants are thriving here.

solid platform of texture can impose order and structure, for example.

The strongly architectural quality of the conventional formal garden conveys a powerful image – one of symmetry and balance, precision and accuracy. Plants may be interpreted as structural elements, more closely aligned to walls and other built elements. The sheared, trimmed, and pruned formal garden owes as much of its visual impact to the selection of appropriate plants as it does to their subsequent control and maintenance. Formal plantings will have an impact on a garden, summer or winter. In winter , with all else bare, their angular simplicity in clear bright sunshine can be very appealing. See also TOPIARY, p.118

Formality often requires restraint, which can pose a dilemma for those who would like to design with the widest possible variety of plants. Faced with a spacious driveway approach flanked by mowed lawns, for example, some gardeners may find it hard to resist the temptation to choose 20 different species of tree. However, far greater formal impact would be achieved by repeating a single species, in regular blocks or in a continuous double line, to form a well-designed avenue.

Softening the effect
Strongly formal plantings in a garden can be varied in a number of ways, all with equal effect. Extreme forms of topiary, knot gardens, and parterres can be planted with or alongside free-flowing informal mixtures of plants to create a marked contrast of styles. This combination changes with the seasons and will reduce the stark impact of the formal plantings. A garden clearly divided into distinct units can also be planted with an area of marked formality to contrast with an adjacent, informal one.

The juxtaposition of styles presents a lively and stimulating garden of surprises at each turn of house corner, hedge, or shrub. Formality can blend with informality when formal features are allowed to relax toward the informal. A precisely clipped hedge of yew (*Taxus*) can be planted in a serpentine line and pruned to simulate clouds; flowering shrubs, planted at regular intervals along the entire length of a broad border, will grow to form large mounds of equally spaced and sized yet irregularly shaped forms. Thus, a degree of formality underpins a broadly informal arrangement.

Informal planting

A planting that appears informal may in fact consist of a wealth of different plants – trees, shrubs, herbaceous perennials, and annuals – their diversity, richness, and profusion all skillfully combined to bring the color, texture, shape, and form of unrelated plants together with dramatic effect.

As with a formal style, there are as many, if not more , variations on the theme of informality. A cottage-style garden of organized chaos, where garden plants are combined in a seemingly haphazard concoction, can rapidly become truly chaotic – an overgrown wilderness in which many plants will not survive the inherent crowding and competition. To preserve and maintain the plant content of such a garden requires expertise and considerable time spent controlling the different plants and keeping their growth restrained.

This informality of planting may be taken a few stages farther by choosing a combination of plants that will grow together in harmony, whose strengths are well matched and whose climate and soil requirements are met. Herbaceous plants that require little or no support provide a good example. Cultivated garden plants can be combined to create the impression of a wild meadow, or indigenous species can be planted to create a "natural" meadow (see MEADOW GARDENING, p.395). Indeed, an entire habitat can be made up of plants that would naturally occur in the locality. Native plants will also attract wildlife to your garden by providing a welcome source of food and nesting sites.

For many people this may be taking informal gardening too far, but by studying the local environment and taking note of which plants thrive in it, the planting plan can be adapted to cultivated garden plants. Planting a light tree canopy allows sufficient daylight to penetrate for an understory of shrubs to be grown. Beneath this, shade-tolerant herbaceous plants will thrive after spring bulbs have faded away. This layered community of plants may appear crowded, yet they will all flourish if the chosen plants are given the appropriate light and conditions at each level of the undergrowth throughout the season.

Making planting plans

To map out plant groups, selections, and numbers accurately, first draw a plan to scale, perhaps using graph paper. A box drawn to represent 1 sq yd (1 sq m) and another to represent 4 sq yd (4 sq m) is a useful guide to the area covered by a clump of herbaceous plants and the area covered by a shrub or small tree, respectively. Always use a scale that is large enough to represent the plants clearly. This may, in fact, require two scales of plan: a large-scale plan to show the general garden area, and a smaller one to detail the composition of a border (see p.36). The simpler the plan the better, both for reading by others and for subsequent alterations. Numbers, symbols, or code initials can be used to indicate individual plants but, where the scale permits, enter full plant names for instant identification.

Making the most of plants

The majority of gardens benefit from areas of calm, so the temptation to crowd them with plants should be resisted. Another common planning mistake is to select as many different plants as possible; using a wide range can weaken the design, whereas the repetition of a few key plants ties the entire plan together.

On the planting plan, shade in any sections where evergreens are to be planted, and work out how much cover will remain during winter. Also indicate where plants with colored foliage or strong, bright flowers are to be planted in a border. This helps assess the proportions of each color, allowing you to maintain an even distribution and also to calculate the number of green-leaved plants to balance the display.

Finalizing the plan

After indicating which plants are to be retained, enter key plants onto the plan. These are plants that frame a view, end a view, give height or weight, and in essence anchor the whole design. In the early stages such plants need not be specified; an idea of the general height and spread of the plant is all that is necessary. Make a list of suitable plants and have photographs from books, catalogs, and magazines available, but try to be flexible and do not attempt to focus too rigidly on a particular plant. A meticulously planned design can lead to an over-designed, predictable garden where heights, colors, and spacings are too accurately determined. A few surprises should be "planned" to add spontaneity and liveliness with height occurring at

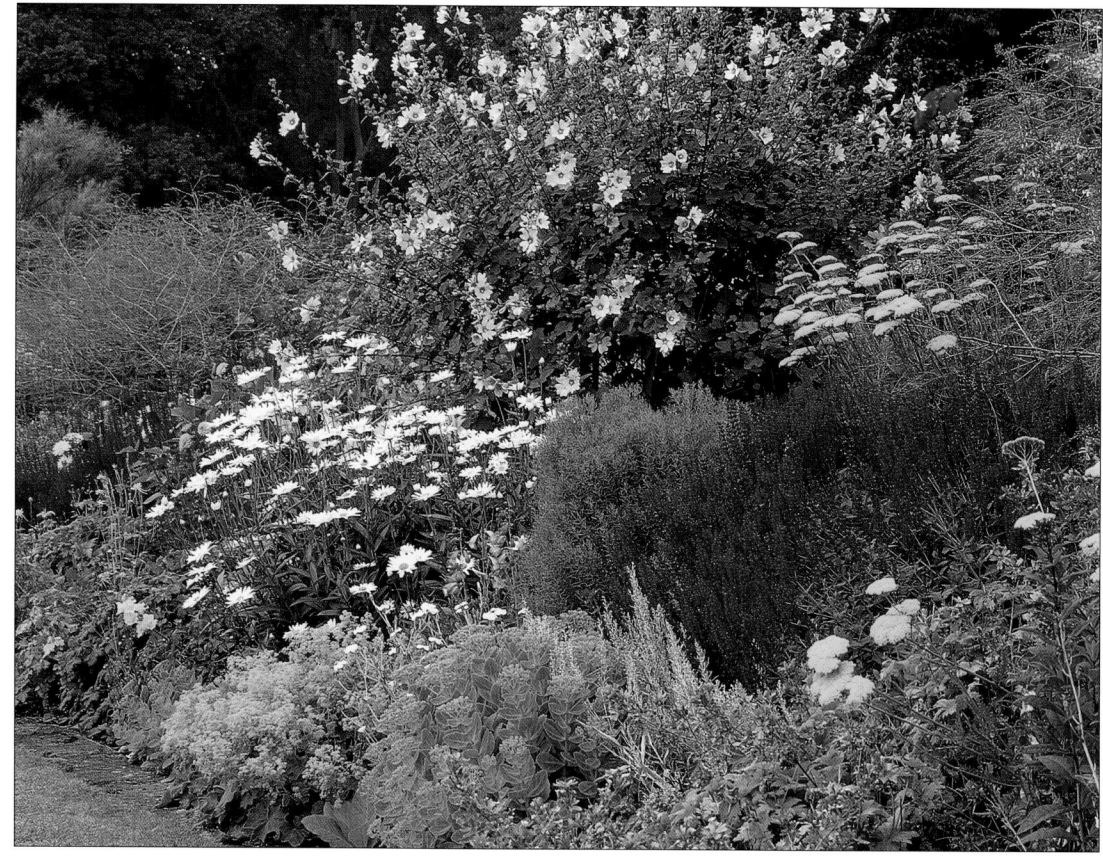

CONTRASTING BORDER STYLES

Two borders of similar proportions and background, consisting largely of herbaceous plants in a similarly tiered array of ascending heights, nevertheless look strikingly different owing to the choice of plant material.

The flower border above faces a mowed lawn, with a strip of bricks (for easier mowing) where plants spill over the edges; the border below, planted thickly with grasses, is complemented by an informal graveled path.

close quarters or a bold color introduced as a sharp contrast.

Grouping and planting distances

Groupings of odd numbers of plants – threes, fives, sevens, or nines – create satisfactory blocks and can be used to produce meandering, shallow drifts. Choosing plants that flower at different times in the drifts will also bring interest to the garden over a long period. Alternatively, a more random planting, repeating single varieties in many small groups of no less than three plants, will produce a lighter, checkerboard effect.

Unlike the interior design of a room, a planting that initially makes little impact can create a spectacular effect in just a few years. When designing and planning a garden, consider your time span. You will need to decide if you wish to thin out the planting in the short or long term,

and whether temporary fillers are to be inserted between permanent plantings to give a little fullness to an otherwise thinly planted area.

A garden planted with semi-mature plants for an instant effect of fullness and scale can, by its very nature, present problems several years later, when those same plants are outgrowing their positions in the garden. If more space is required, valuable plant material may then need to be sacrificed to save the most treasured specimens.

One solution is to purchase a mixture of a few large specimens, which will give some proportion, along with quite a few smaller, less expensive plants. A younger plant will frequently grow more quickly and eventually overtake one that was more mature when originally planted, so you need to have a little patience.

To calculate planting distances, you need to know the mature spread

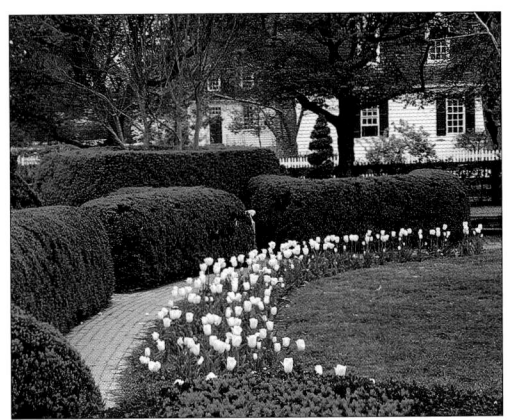

CLOSE SPACING
The exceptions to calculating planting distance based on eventual spread are: when using hedging and edging plants; where a dense effect is needed; and when planting out bedding for a display, since bedding plants have a short life span and so can tolerate cramped conditions.

of the plant or plants. Consult labels, study reference books, or seek advice from a garden center to obtain accurate information. The last source may well be the most reliable, especially if the center is local, because plant performance varies between different regions. Equally valuable is

advice on the time plants take to reach maturity, since this will help you decide whether to include either annual or longer-term perennial "filler" plants.

The distance required between two very similar plants is equal to the spread of one of them. To calculate the space needed between two different plants, simply add their spreads together and divide by two.

If possible, set out all your plants on the ground, *in situ*, before planting according to the plan. Minor adjustments may be necessary to accommodate differing sizes of specimens, and the ground plan may change if you come across buried pipes, for example, or a utility cover that must be concealed by evergreens. Once the plants have been satisfactorily placed, they should be carefully planted out and mulched with a weed-suppressing, moisture-retentive organic medium (see "Organic mulches," p.620). Always be sure that the plants are nurtured carefully during their first all-important year while they are becoming established.

SIZE AND SCALE
In a small area (as right) be careful not to overplant: start with the heights and spreads your plants are likely to achieve when mature, then map out a pattern of overlapping disks that fill, but will not crowd, the available space. With experience, you can estimate how plants will perform in your garden in terms of vigor and size, and, space permitting, begin to sketch in bolder groupings or drifts of plants, as shown in the section of a classic English border (below). To create an annual border requires a slightly different technique: areas are mapped out for sowing, either directly onto the soil (see also p.211) or using a preliminary plan.

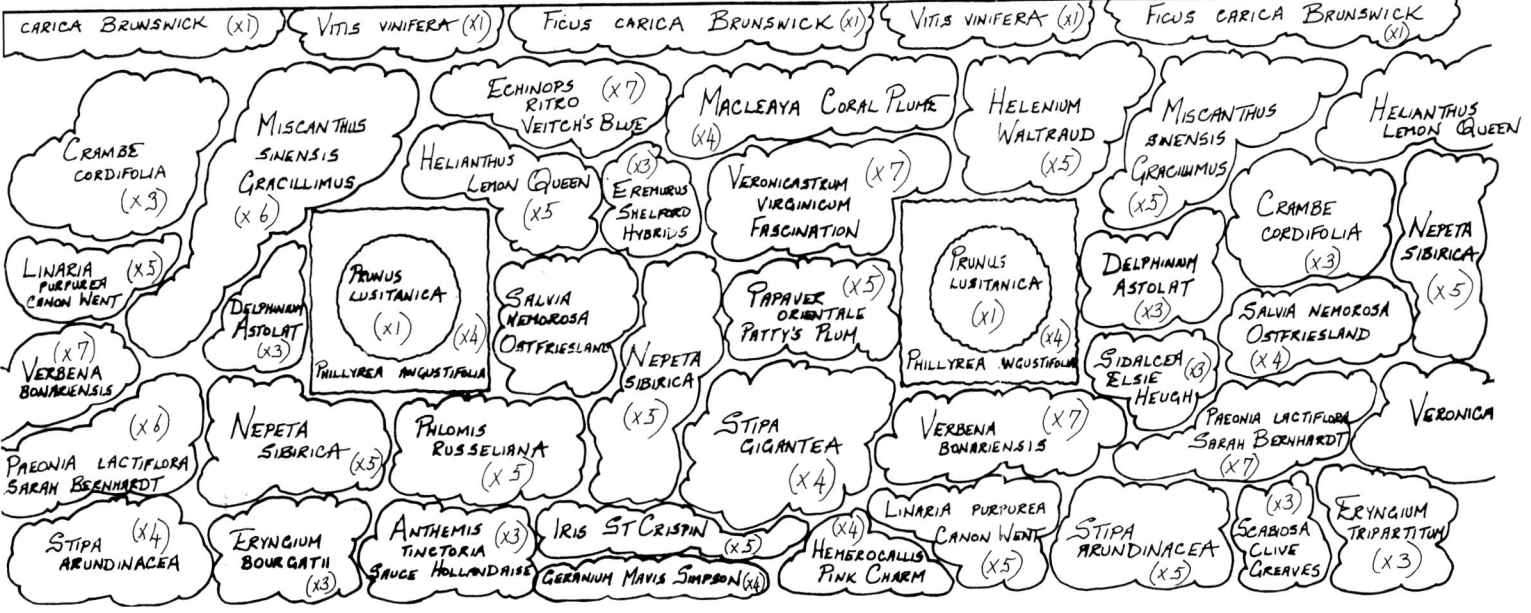

Planting for structure, shape, and form

WHEN selecting a plant for a bed or border, its shape, form, and eventual size are often considered of secondary importance to its flowers, fruits, or autumn hues. Yet these colorful qualities are frequently temporary, lasting just a few weeks, unlike the shape of a tree or shrub.

To create an enduring planting design that will look good throughout the year, select plants that offer beautiful natural forms. The structure of a plant is best appreciated first hand, and visiting gardens where plants have matured and developed is an ideal way to appreciate their more subtle qualities.

Architectural plants

Plants with bold foliage or a dramatic form are described as architectural or accent plants; they make ideal specimens, creating considerable impact when used on their own as focal points or to contrast with their neighbors. The divided, toothed, large leaves of *Melianthus major* or the plumelike flower heads of *Miscanthus sinensis* are examples of such structural plants, while spreading shrubs, such as *Aralia elata,* and the tiered branches of the tree *Cornus controversa* also offer exceptional architectural qualities.

Altering outlooks

Planting can be used to highlight garden features or disguise eyesores. For example, an ugly boxlike building will retain its unsightly silhouette if a clinging creeper, such as *Parthenocissus*, is grown over it; if a more interesting climber, such as wisteria, is used then the outline will be masked beneath its twisted branches and pendulous flowers.

Similarly, a visual barrier, such as a bank that marks a level change, can be lost when a mound-forming or horizontally tiered subject is grown on the lower level. Either *Viburnum plicatum* or *Euonymus alatus* would work well in this situation.

An area of lawn can be enhanced with a specimen tree. When selecting one, the size of lawn and proximity to the house are important factors to consider, as are soil type and local climate. A specimen tree also needs to look appropriate in its setting. One with a rounded canopy will sit well on a lawn, whereas a tall, spirelike form can resemble a rocket on its launch pad in such an open area.

Natural strength

Soothing greens and strong structure can help to create a restful scene. A fernery is a classic example of this style, where beautiful shapes and forms provide interest without the distraction of bright colors (see also FERNS, p.192).

Grasses add a graceful, refined structure, and the sound and movement of their rustling leaves make them indispensable. Even in winter their skeletal forms play an important role in an otherwise bleak landscape. Planted alongside broadleaved *Macleaya cordata*, the elegant grasses *Stipa gigantea* or *Panicum virgatum* are very eye-catching.

A backdrop of large evergreens will provide color and form when all deciduous plants have been left bare in winter. Not only do they present foliage interest and strong shapes throughout the year, but they also protect wildlife in bad weather and can be used to create permanent screens and privacy.

Evergreens that grow into naturally neat shapes resemble topiary, giving the garden a sculptural appearance without the need for trimming. Globes of many dwarf conifers make excellent accent plants along the front of a border, while *Choisya ternata* and *Viburnum dentatum* 'Blue Muffin' both grow into orbs of tight foliage.

Pruning into shapes

A plant's natural structure can be enhanced by pruning. When some willows (*Salix*) and dogwoods (*Cornus*) are pruned to the ground (coppiced) every two years, they produce an explosion of colorful, straight stems. Lindens (*Tilia*) and sycamores (*Platanus*) may be pollarded: if the branches are pruned back to the same point every year or two, they produce swollen "fists" at the pruning points. Both pruning methods create strong architectural forms that can greatly enhance a garden design. See also "Coppicing and pollarding shrubs," p.105.

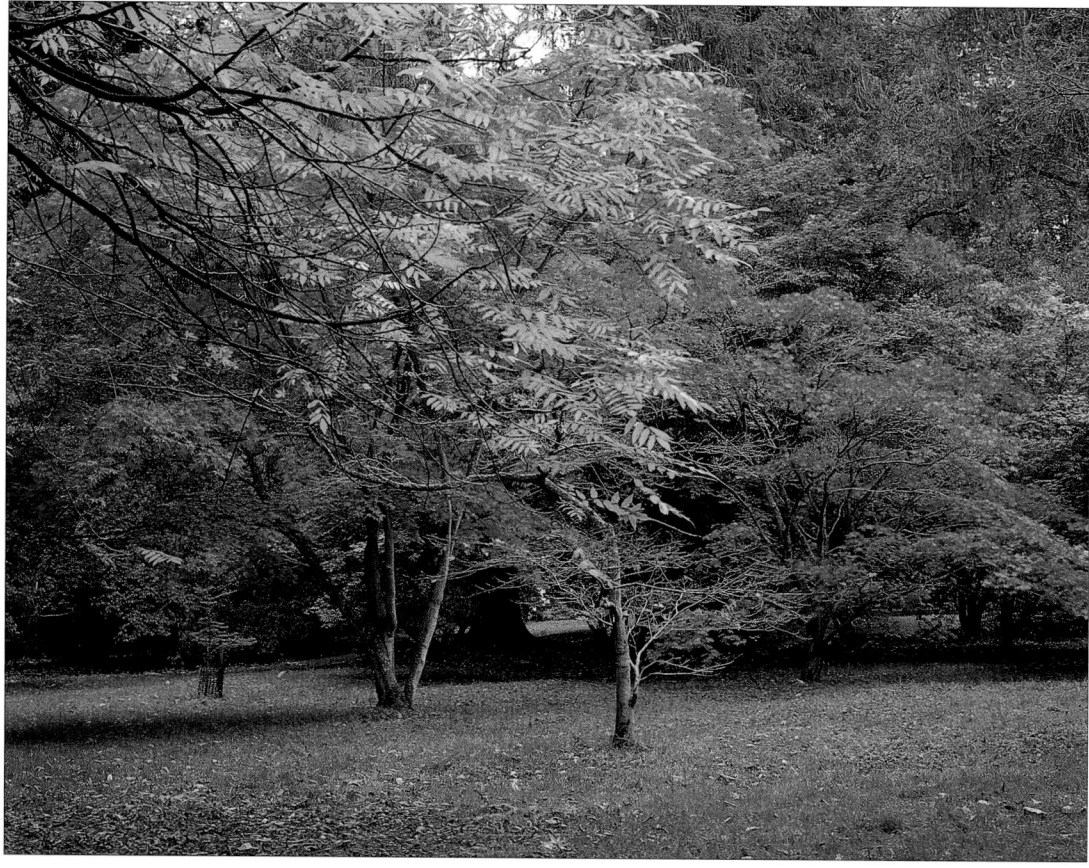

ENDURING FORMS
Trees create permanent structure and form in a garden setting. Look for those with interesting leaf shapes, such as Sorbus, *with its divided foliage, and the deeply lobed leaves of Japanese maple* (Acer palmatum). *Both trees have spectacular autumn colors and beautiful architectural outlines during winter and early spring.*

PLANTS FOR FOCAL POINTS
This variegated Yucca *has striking, spiky foliage in contrast to the solid, rounded outline of the giant urn. The* Tulbaghia *in the foreground accentuates the form of the* Yucca.

TOPIARY-LIKE SHRUBS (RIGHT)
Plants that have a compact shape, such as this golden Choisya ternata SUNDANCE, *blend well with those of a looser habit, such as the purple* Berberis *behind it.*

DRIFTS OF PERENNIALS (BELOW)
Perennials and grasses can produce startling shapes when planted in bold drifts. Their loose stems sway in the breeze, creating the impression of rolling sea waves.

FLOWER FORMS (BOTTOM LEFT)
The shape and structure of stems and foliage can be matched by bold flowers. The flat flower heads of this Achillea filipendulina *'Gold Plate' are here set off by clustered blooms of* Verbena bonariensis.

CREATING CONTRASTS (BOTTOM CENTER)
Using a simple color scheme helps to bring different forms into sharper focus. Here, tall spikes of white lupines are defined by a spreading skirt of Anthemis.

GRACEFUL GRASSES (ABOVE)
A border of mixed ornamental grasses adds structure to the garden throughout the year. Here, fountains of arching flower heads provide the focal point.

SHAPELY BUILDINGS (BELOW)
Growing a structural climber (such as this wisteria) over a dull shed will give it an attractive covering.

Planting for color and texture

THE use of plant colors and textures in all their infinite variations is of central importance in successful garden design, even though many flowers – for it is the flowers that dazzle and entice – offer such a brief display. The tree peony (*Paeonia suffruticosa*) is a classic example that may bloom for only a few days, yet its huge, tissue-paper flowers make it worthy of a prominent place within a border.

When using color in the garden personal taste can be allowed to reign almost unhindered. Yet a totally unlimited palette of colors, where every hue and tone are set against a contrasting shade, may produce an indigestible medley that would challenge even the greatest exponent of color as a tool of garden design. Restraint should be used to limit the range and quantity of color. For example, a backdrop of soft, muted greens will calm a busy foreground of mixed colors and allow the vivid shades to shine.

Color and distance

Bright, light colors such as lemon yellows and whites are better reflectors of sunlight than darker hues, which from a distance may be lost or appear muted. Such light colors used in the foreground will visually jump forward from their positions. These shades introduced at a distance will also appear closer, foreshortening the perceived length of a garden, usually detrimentally.

Traditionally, colors with depth, such as blues, mauves, purples, and silvers, are used to create a sense of distance at the farther reaches of a garden, with paler shades of yellow, white, cream, and pink occupying the foreground. Reds, oranges, and deep yellows are best planted in the middle of a bed; at a distance they are lost, while up close, they dominate.

The influence of light

Location is an important factor to consider when choosing plant color combinations. In strong direct sunlight, the more powerful yellows, oranges and reds become almost luminous and can produce a vibrant picture. If you wish to cool down a seating area in a hot, sunny corner, silver and gray foliage and blue flowers will create a more restful setting.

A combination of pastel colors, such as soft blue, pink, creamy yellow, and silver will create a beautiful composition under low light conditions. A terrace or patio used in the evenings for entertaining and planted with

white flowers and pale or white-variegated foliage will, in minimal light, reflect back atmospheric ghostly hues. Equally effective would be a gloomy courtyard enlivened by the use of bright shades.

Combining colors

One of the most challenging areas of garden design is creating effective color combinations. Blue and white make elegant partners, giving a cool, clean look that is hard to rival, although for sheer purity green and white are unbeatable, especially when on the same flower such as a snowdrop or *Dicentra spectabilis* 'Alba'.

These subtle and refined combinations will be heightened if other plantings display a less restricted palette. Orange and purple, two dominant colors of equal strength, are shockingly brilliant when used together: bright orange calendulas set against the leaden purple foliage of

ornamental cabbages make an eye-catching arrangement. Blue and yellow also create a sharp contrast; the bold intensity of each introduces a lively juxtaposition of colors. When an acid yellow tulip or *Fritillaria imperialis* 'Maxima Lutea' is mixed with the clear blue of forget-me-nots (*Myosotis*) or pansies, the interplay can be truly electric.

Adding texture

Many plants exhibit rich foliage texture, and interesting effects can be achieved when they are planted in broad swaths. A sweep of lavender (*Lavandula*) or rosemary (*Rosmarinus*), clipped annually, will grow into soft mounds of dense aromatic growth, equal in beauty to any herbaceous flower border.

Even plants of little decorative interest individually can be useful in groups. The shrubby honeysuckle, *Lonicera nitida,* or many of the bam-

BLOCKS OF COLOR
Masses of flowers in a single bright color, such as these vermilion 'Sympathie' roses, will dominate a planting design and catch the eyes of all who pass by.

COOL GREENS
There are numerous shades of green within the garden, and each plays an important role calming, cooling, and harmonizing the design.

boos provide masses of textural variations, and make excellent hedging (see BAMBOOS, p.94).

A play of different textures creates subtle interest, even within a single plant. A yew (*Taxus*), for example, clipped neatly below but allowed to spread out at the top to form long, loose stems, provides a wonderful textural contrast. A layered look can be achieved with mixed plantings, such as the feathery fronds of ostrich fern (*Matteuccia struthiopteris*) set off by the vast flat leaves of *Gunnera manicata*, in turn backed by a white-stemmed birch (*Betula*).

Tree stems have tactile qualities that should not be overlooked. Old oaks (*Quercus*) and ashes (*Fraxinus*) develop deep, furrowed bark that contrasts well with smooth, horizontal shapes, while shrubs such as *Hydrangea quercifolia*, *Physocarpus opulifolius*, and *Euonymus alatus* also produce eye-catching bark.

TRADITIONAL PALETTE (ABOVE)
The classic combination of white, pink, and blue is perfect for this romantically planted garden.

FIERY BORDERS (ABOVE RIGHT)
Beds of hot reds, oranges, and rich yellows are energizing and best placed where the sun can illuminate the glowing colors.

SPOT COLOR (FAR RIGHT)
Buttons of dark red Knautia macedonica *are thrown into sharp focus when grown against the pale hues of the sedum and foxgloves in the background.*

SIMPLE COMBINATIONS (RIGHT)
Elegant white daisies and irises edge a tranquil pool, echoing the white window of the house beyond.

PEELING BARK (FAR LEFT)
The beautiful paperbark maple, Acer griseum, *has wonderful chestnut-colored bark that peels to resemble wood shavings. It is particularly noticeable when used as a specimen tree in a winter garden.*

PLEATED LEAVES (CENTER LEFT)
The intricately pleated leaves of Veratrum nigrum *provide a strong architectural accent when sited in a sunny or partially shaded spot.*

TEXTURAL CONTRASTS (LEFT)
Complementary textures and shapes heighten interest here, where the wispy, hairlike spikelets of Hordeum jubatum *fall gracefully behind* Echinops ritro, *with its stiff upright stems of spiny blue flowers.*

Planting for seasonal and year-round interest

THE art of planting the well-planned garden is for each season to bring new richness and interest. All too often, from late spring to midsummer, a garden builds up week after week to a peak, but then it descends rapidly into a flowerless void in autumn and winter. With more than half the year remaining and some late fine weather still to come, it is important to plan for these often-forgotten months.

A garden should contain a well-chosen collection of plants to carry interest throughout these seasons of reduced light and growth. A permanent framework of planting, formed by trees, shrubs, and hedges, will create the basic skeleton onto which a series of overlaying levels – climbers, herbaceous plants, bedding plants, and bulbs – can be used to provide beauty and interest throughout each season.

EXTENDED INTEREST
This garden looks completely different in two very different seasons, yet both views are attractive because plants were chosen for their multiple-season interest. Note how snow accentuates the plant forms and hardscaping.

Spring
Late winter and early spring are not only a time for flowers but also a season for sweet scents. Shrubs, such as Christmas box (*Sarcococca confusa*), winter honeysuckle (*Lonicera* x *purpusii*), wintersweet (*Chimonanthus praecox*), and the many beautiful species of *Daphne* fill the air with their powerful perfumes. Bulbs offer early color, when aconites (*Eranthis hyemalis*) and snowdrops (*Galanthus*) compete to be the first to flower, followed by crocuses, daffodils, and tulips. The bulbs are joined by the earliest flowering perennials, such as hellebores,

and later, as the bulbs die down, other herbaceous plants fill the gaps.

Summer
Early summer heralds an explosion of color from herbaceous perennials, with every shade, shape, and form working together to create a luxuriance unrivaled throughout the rest of the year. Peonies, delphiniums, campanulas, and lupines give a spectacular display, while roses perform alongside deutzias, mallows (*Lavatera*), and mock oranges in the shrub border. As summer peaks, large-flowered clematis can be used to scramble over spring-flowering

shrubs, such as forsythia. Later on, annuals such as *Nicotiana* and *Cosmos* fill gaps between shrubs; tender or marginally hardy perennials, such as penstemons and diascias, brighten bed or border color schemes.

Autumn
The well-maintained garden, where regular deadheading and careful interplanting have been carried out, can often reach a peak in this season. As well as the spillover of summer blooms, late-flowering perennials, such as Japanese anemones, crocosmias, and New England asters (*Aster novae-angliae*) perform through

SEASONAL SUNLIGHT
Not only planting plans alter with the seasons; sunlight can also be used throughout the year to highlight evolving shapes and forms. Here, the weak winter sun casts long shadows that stretch over a colorful carpet of Cyclamen coum, *the flowers of which open throughout mild winter weather.*

autumn. As the light pales, clusters of dark pink blooms open on *Clerodendrum bungei*, scenting the cool air with its rich sweet fragrance.

Foliage tints begin to fire up in autumn, with trees such as maples and *Parrotia persica* slowly turning every shade of yellow, orange, purple, and red. The large leaves of *Vitis coignetiae* also provide spectacular color before they fall. Berries and fruits contribute to the richness of autumn hues, with viburnums, hawthorns, crabapples, and many others decorating the garden with their jeweled displays.

Flowering bulbs and corms, such as cyclamen and colchicums, contribute to the autumn display, too.

Winter
The depths of winter are the most testing times in the garden, when color and interest are most difficult to achieve. It is now that permanent structures take center stage. The stems of deciduous shrubs and trees, such as white birch (*Betula*) and colorful dogwoods (*Cornus*), shine out in the weak winter sunlight.

The texture, form, and shape of evergreens furnish the winter garden when all else is bare. Pines, spruces, firs, junipers, cedars, cypresses, and arborvitaes lend substance to "empty" borders. Some evergreen shrubs, such as *Skimmia japonica* and *Viburnum tinus,* put on displays of beadlike flower buds. These are accompanied by the highly scented flowers of *Viburnum* x *bodnantense,* which will break into bloom at the first hint of milder weather.

EARLY TO MIDSPRING
Among the first flowers to bloom in early spring are the bulbs. Here, bold swaths of daffodils have been planted to brighten up the borders with their nodding heads of golden yellow flowers and straplike foliage. These are accompanied by spikes of spurge (Euphorbia) and emerging perennials, the foliage of which is now pushing its way through the soil.

LATE SPRING
As spring progresses and light levels increase, borders rapidly fill out with lush foliage and early flowers, helping to camouflage the fading blooms and leaves of early bulbs. Here, blue geraniums and wavy-edged, rounded-leaved lady's mantle (Alchemilla mollis) dominate in the foreground, while similarly tinted flowers thrive toward the end of the garden.

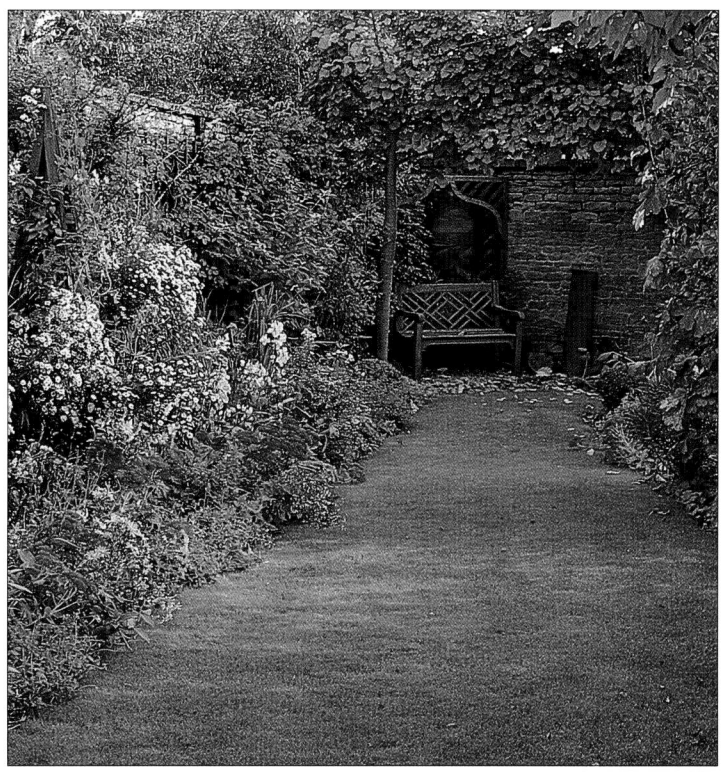

HIGH SUMMER
A profusion of flowers, including the blue geraniums, which are still in bloom, heralds the height of summer. Pastel blues, soft yellows, and creamy whites create a cool border that takes the heat out of the summer sun. These colors also give the illusion of extended perspective, making the border look longer and leading the eye to the seating area at the far end.

SUMMER INTO AUTUMN
The pale pastels have given way to splashes of fiery red designed to mirror tree and shrub foliage, which will soon be taking on vibrant autumn tints. This border design shows how planting can be used to change the color and mood and alter perspectives in the garden as the seasons progress, building up to a crescendo as summer turns into autumn.

CHAPTER

2

ORNAMENTAL TREES

MORE THAN ANY other plants, trees give a sense of permanence and maturity to a garden and link it with the broader landscape. They add height, structure, and focal points to a design, while their large scale and distinctive silhouettes form an attractive contrast with other plantings. There is an enormous variety of trees, differing in shape and form as well as in foliage, flowers, fruit, and bark.

Each has a particular appeal, from the dark, pointing column of a cypress to the blazing fall color of a Japanese maple. Trees may be grown in many ways: in an informal setting, a grouping of redbuds and white birches is highly evocative, while in a formal garden, an avenue of copper beeches is suitably elegant. Some trees, such as magnolias and others with spectacular flowers, are best featured as specimens.

Designing with trees

ORNAMENTAL trees are grown for the beauty of their flowers, bark, or decorative fruits, rather than for edible or wood crops. Many fruit trees, however, are graced by beautiful flowers, and a few ornamental trees such as crabapples (*Malus*) bear rich crops of fruits for preserving. The distinction between trees and shrubs is similarly blurred: trees usually (but not always) have a single trunk; shrubs, for example lilac (*Syringa*), are usually multi-stemmed, although they sometimes reach treelike proportions.

Choosing trees

Trees are generally the largest, most expensive, and longest-lived garden plants, and selecting and siting them are major design decisions. The fewer trees a garden can accommodate, the more important careful choice and siting become; in a one-tree garden these points are crucial to the success of the design. A tree's general appearance and special features obviously matter, but its suitability for a garden's soil, climate, and exposure, and its ultimate height, spread, and growth rate are equally important.

Once a tree is chosen, the design process continues by deciding where to plant it (see "Choosing a planting site," p.63). Garden centers carry a limited range of the most popular ornamental trees. Specialized nurseries, some with mail-order service, offer wider choices.

Heights range from around just 3ft (1m) for some dwarf conifers to the massive 300ft (90m) of a redwood (*Sequoia*). Growth rates vary from 1in (2.5cm) or less a year for dwarf conifers to 3ft (1m) or more for some poplars (*Populus*). A young tree in a garden center gives little or no indication of its potential size; some species, particularly conifers, include both miniature and giant cultivars. Select cultivars with care and, if offered substitutes, make sure that they will be equally appropriate for your specific needs.

Trees as design elements

Trees create a strong visual impact in the same way as hard landscape features. They also help form a garden's permanent framework, around which the more temporary elements come and go.

Trees may be used as living sculptures (see "Specimen trees as focal points," p.55): a simple, contrasting setting is most likely to enhance a tree used in this way. A tree with pale foliage looks striking against a hedge of dark green yew (*Taxus*),

TREES IN THE LARGE GARDEN
The architectural outlines of trees add structure to a garden and form a long-term part of the design framework. In a large garden, several trees may be grouped together to create a strong impact of color and form, as with this informal arrangement of maples (Acer) *and other deciduous trees.*

ENCLOSING SPACE
The arching fronds of palms are used as structural features to enclose and delineate a seating area. They create a lush, cool screen that forms a less rigid division than a wall or fence.

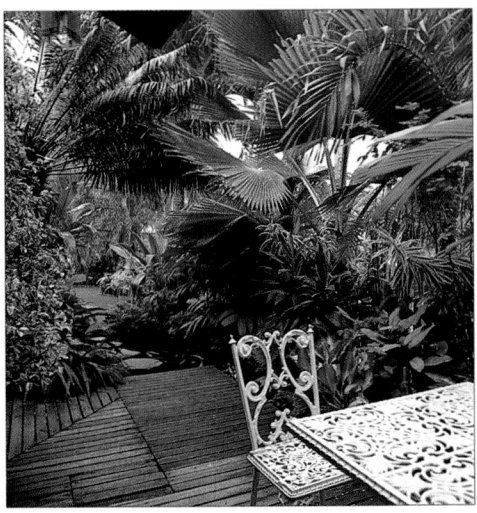

SPECIMEN TREE
Trees that are particularly attractive or well shaped look good sited on their own so that they stand out in a planting. This double pink hawthorn (Crataegus laevigata) has a fine show of blossoms that may be enjoyed from all viewpoints and forms a cornerstone in the design.

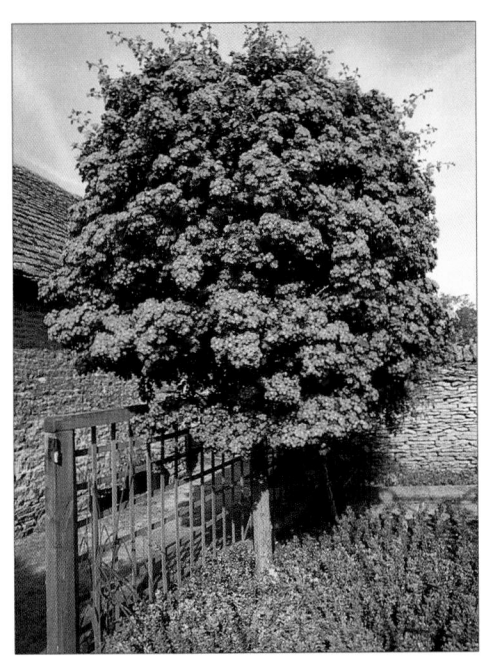

for example, while the bold winter tracery of bare branches stands out dramatically in front of a white-painted wall.

Used structurally, trees can also define or enclose space. A row or informal clump of trees can mark the boundary of a property, separate one part of the garden from another, or emphasize a path. A pair of trees might act as a verdant frame for a distant view or form a living arch through which the garden is entered.

Shape and form
A tree's shape and form are as important as its size, both in regard to setting the mood and style as well as in practical considerations of space. Some trees, such as many ornamental cherries (*Prunus*), are small and charming, while others, such as cedars (*Cedrus*), are grand and monumental. Most can be formal or informal, according to the setting and treatment. Staghorn sumac (*Rhus typhina*) has a striking architectural form, ideal for a modern garden, while the grandly arching fronds of many palms bring lushness to a courtyard or conservatory. Japanese maples (*Acer palmatum*) and the large *Salix matsudana* 'Tortuosa' are suitable for Oriental gardens. Native species are ideal for wild gardens and habitat restorations for attracting wildlife.

Narrow, upright trees such as *Malus tschonoskii* are suitable for small gardens but have a formal, sometimes artificial appearance. Round-headed, widely spreading trees seem more informal but cast much more shade and rain shadow, making underplanting difficult, while those with an irregular, open-branch framework have a naturalistic appeal. Conical and pyramidal trees have a sculptural quality, while weeping trees have a softer silhouette.

Consider how long the tree takes to develop its characteristic shape – in some cases, it can be decades. *Prunus* 'Kanzan', for example, has a stiff growth habit when young, with awkwardly angled branches. After ten years the branches begin to arch, and by 20 years the tree has a graceful, rounded crown.

Where space allows, combining contrasting tree shapes can create a dynamic effect, but planting many differently shaped trees may simply appear fussy and uncoordinated.

Specimen trees as focal points

A specimen tree is grown on its own and so can develop and display its full natural beauty without competition from other trees. Depending on the climate, weeping willow (*Salix x sepulcralis* 'Chrysocoma'), flowering dogwood (*Cornus florida*), various ornamental cherries (*Prunus*), and palms such as *Howea* and *Phoenix* are popular specimen trees. Select a tree that is the right size for its setting; tiny specimen trees look lost in vast gardens, and outsized ones overbearing in confined spaces.

TREE SHAPES

SPREADING
Prunus americana
(American plum)

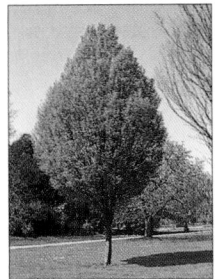

PYRAMIDAL
Carpinus betulus 'Fastigiata'
(European hornbeam)

CONICAL
Pseudotsuga menziesii var. *glauca*
(Blue Douglas fir)

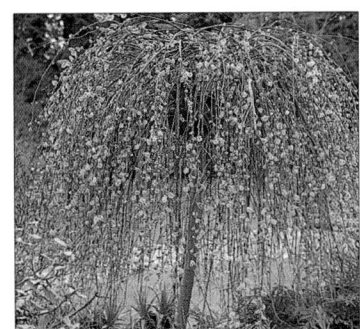

WEEPING
Salix caprea 'Kilmarnock'
(Kilmarnock willow)

ROUND-HEADED
Malus 'Magdeburgensis'
(Crabapple)

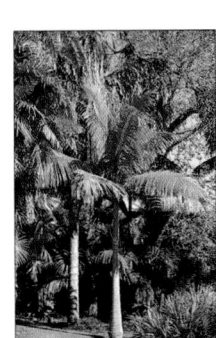

ARCHING
Archontophoenix alexandrae
(King palm)

COLUMNAR
Acer rubrum 'Columnare'
(Red maple)

FOLIAGE COLOR AND TEXTURE
Here, the fall foliage of a deciduous tree is offset by the blue-green mass of a conifer, creating a contrasting tableau of color, texture, and shape.

Specimen trees, particularly in formal gardens, are traditionally placed in the center of a lawn. Siting a specimen tree to one side, however, can add a sense of liveliness and informality to a design as well as allowing a view down the garden. Other options include planting a specimen tree next to a gate or garden entrance, or at the bottom or top of a flight of steps, to mark the transition from one space in the garden to another.

Planting in a swath of gravel or groundcover plants such as ivy (*Hedera*) or periwinkle (*Vinca*) provides a complementary foil for a specimen tree. In a mixed border, use a tree as the keystone around which to build the color and form of the surrounding groups of plants. A specimen tree may be reflected in a garden pond or offset by a statue or white-painted bench beneath it, so that each element enhances the other to make a complete picture.

Grouping trees

If space allows, consider planting three or more trees together in an informal clump of the same or different species. A group of trees also creates a more substantial, curtain-like frame than a single tree for one or both sides of a view. Clumps of large trees such as oaks (*Quercus*) or beeches (*Fagus*) make focal points on a grand scale, as exemplified in the landscapes designed by the great 18th-century English landscape gardener, Capability Brown. In warmer climates, stands of tall, bare-trunked palms can be equally impressive on their own in grass or interplanted with lower-growing or multistemmed species.

On a smaller scale, a modest group of deciduous trees with light foliage, such as poplars (*Populus*) or maples (*Acer*), can form the backbone of an appealing miniature woodland. The dappled shade and leafy soil are perfect for English bluebells (*Hyacinthoides non-scripta*), daffodils, and primroses (*Primula*).

Trees in informal groups can be planted closer than the combined potential spread of their crowns. Relatively tall, narrow, or asymmetrical growth may result but the effect can be pleasantly informal, with intermingled branches forming attractive tracery against the sky.

Features of interest

Although trees are most often valued for their architectural qualities, they also provide interest through particular features such as flowers, foliage, berries, and bark. Site a tree so that its attractive characteristics are shown off to advantage (see also "Successional interest," p.57).

Leaves
For sheer mass and duration of display, leaves are by far the most important feature. Their shape, size, and color offer infinite variation, from the delicate, golden, ferny foliage of *Gleditsia triacanthos* 'Sunburst' to the huge, architectural leaves of palms such as *Phoenix*. Surface texture determines how light is reflected, with glossy leaves adding a bright touch. The density of the canopy ranges from opaque to airy, an important factor if considering underplanting around a tree.

Trees with colored or variegated foliage, such as the reddish purple of *Cercis canadensis* 'Forest Pansy' or the white-edged leaves of *Acer negundo* 'Variegatum', provide a mass of color that contrasts especially well with green-leaved trees.

Some leaves, such as those of eucalyptus, are pleasantly aromatic, while others, such as those of a poplar, quiver in the slightest breeze, adding the extra pleasure of sound.

Flowers
Flowers have a fleeting but memorable presence and range from modest to opulent. Fall, winter, and early spring flowers are especially valuable to provide a display when there may be little interest from other, still-dormant plants.

Flower color should complement the larger design. Pale flowers stand out against dark leaves, while dark flowers show up best in a pale setting. By training climbers such as clematis or roses up mature trees, you can extend the floral display.

Fragrance is a bonus, ranging from the subtle winter perfume of *Acacia dealbata* to the heady summer scent of frangipani (*Plumeria rubra* var. *acutifolia*). For flowers and fragrance a sheltered spot is best, while growing a tree next to a path or patio makes it easy to enjoy its scent.

Fruits, berries, and pods
These can rival or exceed flowers in beauty, ranging from the bright red, strawberry-like fruits of *Arbutus* and

COLOR FROM FLOWERS
The large blooms of Magnolia campbellii *var.* mollicomata *stand out against the bare branches.*

INTEREST FROM BARK AND STEMS
*The striking skeleton of a white birch (*Betula utilis *var.* jacquemontii*) brings bright relief to the garden in the gloom of winter, while its bold silhouette forms a strong focal point in the planting design throughout the year.*

the yellow crabapples of *Malus* 'Golden Hornet', to the sculptural seedpods of magnolias. In warm climates, trees such as lemons and figs may be laden with eye-catching fruits.

Certain trees such as hollies (*Ilex*) need cross-pollination to fruit; others fruit only when mature or when particular climatic conditions are met. Birds find some berries such as those of mountain ashes (*Sorbus*) tempting and may strip them when barely ripe, but you can choose trees with less appealing berries. Ask garden center staff for advice.

Bark and branches

Bark can provide color and textural interest, especially in winter. Options include the mahogany red, silky sheen of *Prunus serrula*, the ghostly white bark of *Betula utilis* var. *jacquemontii*, and the exotic patterning of *Eucalyptus dalrympleana* with its green, gray, and creamy white pythonlike bark.

The young branches of the scarlet willow (*Salix alba* 'Britzensis') are scarlet-orange, brilliant when lit from behind, and the golden willow (*S. a.* var. *vitellina*) has rich yellow shoots. These fast-growing trees are best pruned regularly to produce new shoots since these have the strongest color. Some trees produce showy bark only when mature, while others color well when young.

Successional interest

Plants that change character with the seasons give a garden a lively tempo. Orchestrate their display with careful choice and planning so that foliage, flowers, fruits, berries, and pods come and go against a permanent framework of branches and bark. By planting trees that flower successively, such as a Judas tree (*Cercis siliquastrum*) for spring, *Catalpa bignonioides* for summer, *Eucryphia* x *nymansensis* for early fall, and *Prunus subhirtella* 'Autumnalis' for winter, ongoing interest is maintained, with the focal point altering as the seasons change. Some trees provide interest all year, either from their evergreen foliage or from their fine shape.

Deciduous trees offer the greatest scope to exploit seasonal changes, especially in spring, when many ornamental cherries (*Prunus*) are covered with blossoms, and in fall, when many maples (*Acer*) have brilliant foliage. Evergreen trees, on the other hand, provide a sense of continuity rather than change. Selecting and planting a mixture of deciduous and evergreen trees

TREES WITH ORNAMENTAL BARK

Acer capillipes

Eucalyptus dalrympleana

Betula utilis var. *jacquemontii*

Acer griseum

Acer pensylvanicum

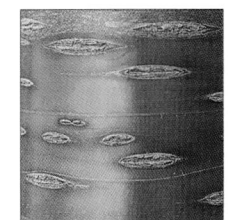

Prunus serrula

provides lasting interest in the garden that changes with the seasons to create a dynamic, rather than a static, composition.

Spring and summer

In spring, emerging leaves and flower buds bring fresh life to the bare branches of deciduous trees. Some – such as the silver-leaved *Sorbus aria* 'Lutescens' – have particularly fine young foliage. As the trees come fully into leaf, they take on their characteristic outlines while the canopies provide striking blocks of color and texture as well as shade.

In late spring and summer, flowers ranging in color and form from the trailing yellow chains of golden-chain tree (*Laburnum*) to the dramatic gold-filled white cups of *Stewartias* add extra color and interest, lightening the dense quality of the massed leaves.

Fall and winter

When most herbaceous plants die down in fall, the color provided by deciduous trees is particularly welcome, whether from leaves turning from green through shades of yellow, orange, and red to brown, or from the bright flecks of color from fruits or berries. Ornamental members of the Rosaceae, especially those from the genera *Cotoneaster*, *Crataegus*, *Malus*, and *Sorbus*, include many species, cultivars, and hybrids that have a handsome display in fall. In some cases, the fruits will remain on the tree right through the winter months.

Winter is often regarded as a bleak time, but this is when many trees truly stand out with little

else in the garden to compete with them. It is in winter that a tree's skeleton or silhouette becomes most noticeable and creates the greatest sculptural impact. The color and texture provided by coniferous and broad-leaved evergreens may be used to complement and soften the architectural, "hard" look of nearby deciduous trees, while patterned, textured, or peeling bark adds an extra point of interest. A few conifers such as forms of Japanese

cedar (*Cryptomeria japonica*) have foliage that takes on attractive russet overtones in winter.

Trees for small gardens

For small gardens, trees that do not reach more than about 20ft (6m) in height are the most suitable. There may be space for only one tree (see "Specimen trees as focal points," p.55), so those that provide more than one season of interest are es-pecially appreciated. A Japanese crabapple (*Malus floribunda*), for example, produces masses of crimson buds, then pale pink or white flowers, and finally small red or yellow fruits on arching branches.

A deciduous tree's appearance when leafless is very important in a small garden, since the tree may be bare for six months each year and visible from every window facing the garden. Good choices include staghorn sumac (*Rhus typhina*) and *Pyrus salicifolia* 'Pendula'. Neither has showy flowers. but both have handsome foliage and winter silhouettes with character.

Heavily thorned or prickly trees such as hawthorns (*Crataegus*) or hollies (*Ilex*) may be unsuitable in a very small garden because they may restrict access on either side. Those such as lindens (*Tilia*) that drip sticky

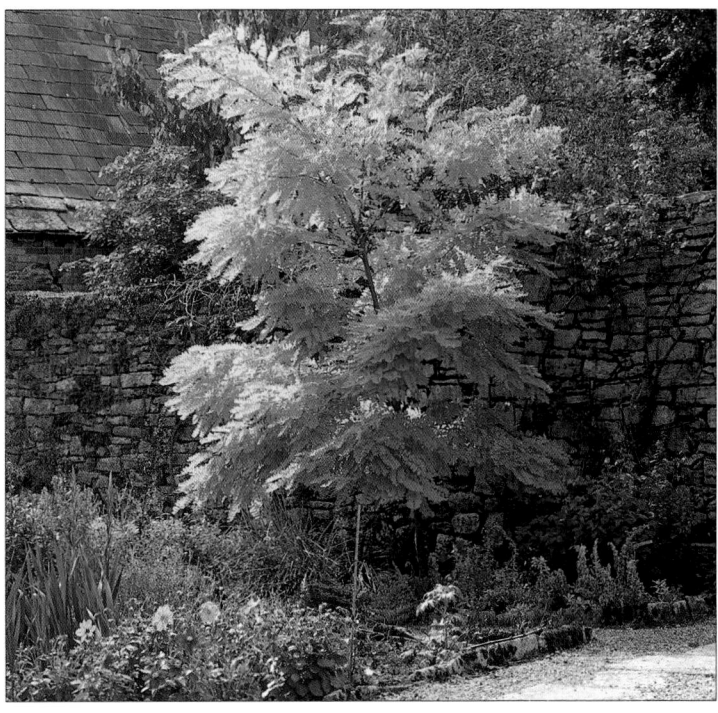

SMALL-GARDEN TREE
The modest stature of this Robinia pseudoacacia 'Frisia' *makes it a suitable choice for a small garden. Its airy foliage brightens up the gray stone wall behind and casts only light shade, allowing other plants to grow beneath it.*

honeydew should not be sited where they will overhang an area for sitting outside. If planning to underplant, choose a light-foliaged, deep-rooted tree, since it is hard for small plants to compete with the shallow, greedy roots of some ornamental cherries (*Prunus*), for example.

Trees for avenues

Primarily used in formal settings, avenues rely on the uniformity of trees and spacing for their grand presence. The longer and straighter the avenue, the more impact the rhythm of the trees and their shadows have on the landscape. Trees should be sited so that they lead the eye to an impressive focal point; large trees are frequently used on both sides of a driveway to line it. Long-lived forest trees such as beeches (*Fagus*) and horse chestnuts (*Aesculus*) are traditionally used for avenues, while the strong shapes of conifers may be more striking in a contemporary design.

Informal avenues may also be created, perhaps with the trees trained to form an arch over a walkway. The spacing may be less rigid than for a formal avenue to avoid a regimented appearance. Trees such as whitebeam (*Sorbus aria*) or the evergreen Chinese privet (*Ligustrum lucidum*) are particularly suitable for smaller gardens.

Training for effect

Trees may be pleached to create an elegant formality. The side branches are trained to meet in horizontal, parallel lines and other growth is

INFORMAL WALKWAY
Flowering cherries arching over a path bring height and structure to a garden with free, informal planting while complementing the character of the setting. The spring display of the arch draws attention up and away from the borders, which will in turn fill out and become the center of interest as the blossoms fade.

FORMAL PLEACHED AVENUE
In this large formal garden, rows of pleached lindens lead the eye to the two arches framing the view beyond, linking the garden with the landscape.

cut back or interwoven to form a vertical screen. Beeches, lindens (*Tilia*), hornbeams (*Carpinus*), and sycamores (*Platanus*) are traditional trees for pleaching and, in the fruit garden, espaliered apples and pears are a variation of this technique.

Pollarding involves regularly lopping back the entire crown to short stumps that produce dense, thin branches and a single, tight ball of foliage. It achieves a formal, if artificial, result and is useful in urban areas where a natural crown would cast too much shade or impede traffic. Some willows (*Salix*) are often pollarded or coppiced (cut back to ground level) for their colorful young shoots. Coppiced trees look appropriate in a naturalistic or informal setting such as a woodland garden or on the banks of a pond.

Trees for screens and windbreaks

Large-scale tree planting can screen buildings and roads, deaden noise, and give shelter from wind and frost. A row of fast-growing Lombardy poplars (*Populus nigra* 'Italica') may be used, but their great height and fingerlike shape tend to highlight

CONTAINER-PLANTED TREES
Small trees grown in containers are valuable for bringing color, vitality, and sculptural interest to a patio, terrace, or balcony. Here, plain paving acts as a stage on which to display a striking Japanese maple (Acer palmatum 'Dissectum Atropurpureum') in an ornamental trough.

what they are intended to conceal. Looser, wider stands of mixed deciduous and evergreen trees look more natural. Hedges are the most compact and densest screening, and their size can be controlled (see HEDGES AND SCREENS, pp.82–84).

Trees *en masse* can filter wind, reducing potential damage more efficiently than solid barriers, which often create wind swirl on the leeward side. A windbreak or group of trees can protect vulnerable plants from frost, especially in spring.

Trees in containers

Growing trees in large pots or tubs greatly extends their design potential. In roof, patio, or courtyard gardens, a collection of containerized trees is the quickest way to create a well-established appearance, adding height and structure to the design.

Use trees in large pots to frame a doorway surrounded by hard paving or to flank steps; these positions are usually appropriate for topiary (see pp.118–19). A group of bonsai, or miniaturized trees in shallow containers, also makes an interesting outdoor feature (see pp.368–9).

Trees too tender to overwinter outside may be grown in containers, displayed outdoors in summer, and moved to a frost-free place as cold weather approaches. Annuals and tender plants such as petunias, fuchsias, or trailing nasturtiums (*Tropeaeolum*) may be included in the container for seasonal color and interest, or ivy (*Hedera*) for permanent groundcover.

Containerized trees are long-term features, so use attractive containers. A wide range of styles and materials is available, such as stone or reconstituted-stone, plain or decorated terracotta pots, wooden half barrels, or wooden Versailles planters. Make sure that the containers are frostproof if they are to be used in an area subject to severe cold.

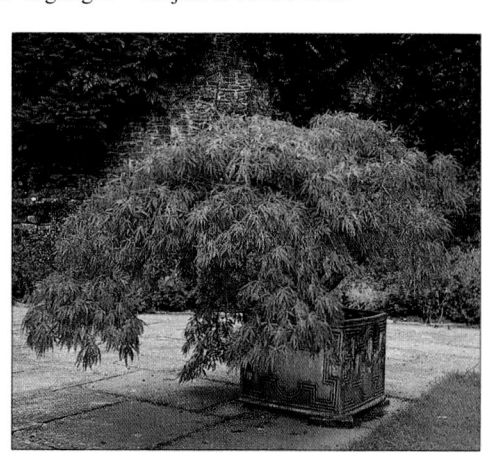

Planter's guide to trees

EXPOSED SITES

Trees that tolerate exposed or windy sites; those marked ✿ are not suitable for coastal sites
Acer pseudoplatanus
Betula pendula ✿, *B. pubescens* ✿
Crataegus x *lavallei*, *C. monogyna*
Fraxinus excelsior
Laburnum (spp. and cvs)
Picea abies ✿, *P. sitchensis* ✿
Pinus contorta, *P. nigra*,
   P. sylvestris
Quercus robur
Salix alba
Sorbus aria, *S. aucuparia* (and cvs)

AIR POLLUTION

Trees that tolerate polluted air
Acer platanoides (and cvs),
   A. pseudoplatanus (and cvs),
   A. saccharinum (and cvs)
Aesculus hippocastanum
Alnus cordata, *A. glutinosa*
Betula pendula
Carpinus betulus (and cvs)
Catalpa bignonioides
Corylus colurna
Crataegus
Fraxinus
Ginkgo biloba
Ilex x *altaclerensis*
Magnolia grandiflora
Malus
Populus
Pyrus
Robinia

Pyrus calleryana
'Chanticleer'

Salix
Sophora japonica
Sorbus aria,
   S. aucuparia, *S. intermedia*
Taxus baccata, *T.* x *media*

SALT TOLERATION

Trees that tolerate salt
Acer platanoides (and cvs)
   A. pseudoplatanus
Aesculus
Ailanthus altissima
Carya ovata
Celtis spp.
Elaeagnus angustifolius
Fraxinus americana
Gleditsia triacanthos var. *inermis*
Nyssa sylvatica
Picea pungens var. *glauca*
Pinus nigra
Populus nigra 'Italica'
Quercus rubra, *Q. virginiana*
Robinia pseudoacacia
Taxodium distichum

WINTER INTEREST

Decorative flowers
Magnolia campbellii (and forms)
Prunus mume, *P. subhirtella*
   'Autumnalis'

Golden foliage
Chamaecyparis lawsoniana
   'Lanei', *C. l.* 'Stewartii',
   x *Cupressocyparis leylandii*
   'Castlewellan Gold'
Cupressus macrocarpa 'Goldcrest'
Juniperus chinensis 'Aurea'

Gray foliage
Cedrus atlantica f. *glauca*
Cupressus glabra 'Pyramidalis'
Eucalyptus pauciflora
Tsuga mertensiana f. *argentea*

Decorative bark
Acer capillipes, *A. davidii*,
   A. griseum, *A. grosseri* var. *hersii*,
   A. palmatum 'Senkaki',
   A. pensylvanicum (and forms)
Arbutus menziesii
Betula albo-sinensis var.
   septentrionalis,
   B. nigra, *B. pendula*,
   B. utilis var. *jacquemontii*
Eucalyptus dalrympleana
Myrtus luma
Pinus bungeana
Prunus maackii 'Amber Beauty',
   P. serrula
Salix acutifolia 'Blue Streak',
   S. alba 'Britzensis',
   S. daphnoides, *S.* x *sepulcralis*
Stewartia pseudocamellia

TWO OR MORE SEASONS OF INTEREST

All year
Acacia dealbata
Arbutus x *andrachnoides*, *A. menziesii*
Betula albo-sinensis var.
   septentrionalis, *B. ermanii*,
   B. 'Jermyns', *B. utilis* var.
   jacquemontii
Ilex x *altaclerensis* 'Golden King'
Magnolia grandiflora

Winter/Spring
Acer negundo

Spring/Fall
Amelanchier lamarckii
Crataegus x *lavallei* 'Carrierei'
Malus, *M.* 'Golden Hornet'
Prunus 'Okame', *P. sargentii*

Summer/Fall
Catalpa bignonioides
Cladrastis kentukea
Cornus kousa, *C. k.* var. *chinensis*
Eucryphia glutinosa

Fagus sylvatica 'Dawyck Gold'
Liriodendron tulipifera
Stewartia pseudocamellia

Fall/Winter
Acer capillipes, *A. davidii*,
   A. griseum, *A. palmatum*
   'Senkaki', *A. pensylvanicum*
Stewartia pseudocamellia

TREES FOR CONTAINERS

Acacia dealbata
Acer palmatum cvs
Chamaedorea
Cupressus macrocarpa
   'Goldcrest',
   C. sempervirens

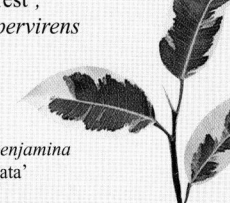

Ficus benjamina
'Variegata'

Ficus benjamina
Howea
Jacaranda mimosifolia
Juniperus scopulorum 'Skyrocket'
Lagerstroemia indica
Laurus nobilis
Olea europaea
Phoenix
Prunus 'Amanogawa',
   P. 'Kiku-shidare'
Rhapis
Sabal
Taxus baccata 'Standishii'
Washingtonia

TREES FOR SMALL GARDENS

Those marked ♠ may grow to 20ft (6m) or more
Acer capillipes, *A. griseum* ♠,
   A. palmatum, *A. p.* 'Senkaki',
   A. 'Silver Vein'
Amelanchier lamarckii
Arbutus x *andrachnoides*
Betula albo-sinensis var.
   septentrionalis ♠, *B. ermanii* ♠,
   B. pendula ♠,
   B. p. 'Dalecarlica' ♠, *B. utilis*
   var. *jacquemontii* ♠
Catalpa bignonioides 'Aurea'
Cercidiphyllum japonicum ♠
Cercis siliquastrum
Cinnamomum
Cornus kousa
Crataegus laevigata 'Paul's
   Scarlet', *C.* x *lavallei* 'Carrierei',
   C. x *mordenensis* 'Toba'
Eucryphia x *nymansensis*
   'Nymansay' ♠
Fagus sylvatica 'Dawyck Gold' ♠
Gleditsia triacanthos 'Sunburst' ♠

Grevillea robusta ♠
Laburnum x *watereri* 'Vossii'
Magnolia 'Elizabeth',
   M. x *loebneri* 'Merrill',
   M. salicifolia
Malus 'Dartmouth', *M. floribunda*,
   M. 'Golden Hornet',
   M. tschonoskii ♠
Melia azedarach
Phoenix dactylifera ♠
Pinus halepensis ♠
Prunus – many, including
   P. 'Okame', *P.* 'Pandora',
   P. 'Spire', *P. subhirtella*,
   P. x *yedoensis*
Pyrus calleryana 'Chanticleer',
   P. salicifolia 'Pendula'
Robinia pseudoacacia 'Frisia' ♠
Sorbus aria (some forms),
   S. aucuparia (some forms),
   S. cashmiriana,
   S. commixta 'Embley',
   S. vilmorinii
Stewartia pseudocamellia
Vitex agnus-castus

SPECIMEN TREES

Abies magnifica, *A. procera*
Acer pseudoplatanus, *A. rubrum*
Aesculus hippocastanum
Alnus cordata
Betula pendula 'Dalecarlica'
Cedrus
Cercidiphyllum japonicum
Eucalyptus coccifera,
   E. dalrympleana
Fraxinus oxycarpa 'Raywood'
Liquidambar styraciflua

*Liriodendron
tulipifera*

*Liriodendron
tulipifera*
Livistona
Magnolia campbellii,
   M. c. 'Charles Raffill'
*Metasequoia
   glyptostroboides*
Nothofagus procera
Nyssa sylvatica
Phoenix
Picea breweriana,
   P. omorika
Pinus nigra, *P. radiata*,
   P. sylvestris, *P. wallichiana*
Platanus x *hispanica*
Roystonea
Salix x *sepulcralis* 'Chrysocoma'
Sequoiadendron giganteum
Tilia 'Petiolaris',
   T. platyphyllos
Tsuga heterophylla
Zelkova carpinifolia

Hardy palms and the exotic look

In the past, in frost-prone regions, many beautiful tropical and sub-tropical plants were grown for their ornamental effect in the protected environment of heated greenhouses. As the costs of maintenance – particularly heating – soared during the twentieth century, the cultivation of these "exotics" declined. Recently, however, a new style of gardening has emerged that re-creates the visual impact of tropical and subtropical plants in sheltered,outdoor gardens in temperate regions. This style makes use of hardy, marginally hardy, and some tender plants with striking shapes, distinctive textures, handsome large foliage, and vivid flowers.

In frost-prone climates, most of the plants used should be hardy enough to survive all year round. Planting designs can then be varied during frost-free months by integrating marginally hardy or tender, container-grown exotics into the design (see also p.61). These can be used as focal points or placed strategically within the overall framework of the planting to create seasonal interest. Such displays require careful planning, of course, as well as the use of a frost-free greenhouse or conservatory in which the plants can be overwintered.

Marginally hardy plants may be attempted permanently outside, although they will need to be wrapped in straw, burlap, or other coverings in winter to protect them from temperature shifts and wind that would otherwise desiccate ever-green foliage. Equally important is to

make sure that such plants are grown in free-draining soil to avoid root decay and crown rot, especially during late fall and early spring.

Exotic planting designs of this type are most likely to succeed in coastal or sheltered city gardens in temperate regions, but variations on this theme may be well worth trying in colder areas.

Key framework plants

Exotic-style plants seldom grow as large in temperate areas as in their native regions, although they can still make handsomely sized, vigorous garden plants for outdoor cultivation in the appropriate situation. Plants to use as treelike, structural elements in the exotic style of gardening can be divided roughly into three groups: palms and palmlike plants, tree ferns, and bananas. Each contains plants with imposing, attractive foliage, and under favorable conditions the palms and bananas may flower. These trop-ical-looking plants can also be blend-ed with more familiar large foliage plants, such as elegant bamboos (see p.94), *Rheum*, and *Gunnera*.

Palms and palmlike plants

Several species of palm are grown successfully outdoors in temperate areas – the most familiar being the Chusan or Chinese windmill palm (*Trachycarpus fortunei*) from the Himalayas. This withstands tempera-tures of 5°F (-15°C) or below, if grown in a reasonably sheltered posi-tion. The closely related *T. wagnerianus* has stiffer, more wind-tolerant leaves. Another suitable palm for a garden setting is the Mediterranean dwarf fan palm (*Chamaerops humilis*). Although it originates in hot, dry regions, it will tolerate 14°F (-10°C) or below when grown in a sheltered spot. Forms with silvery-blue leaves (*C. humilis* var. *argentea*) are particularly attractive.

Blue hesper palm (*Brahea armata*) from Mexico and California is occa-sionally grown in sheltered sites outdoors; in cold areas it is also an excellent container plant for summer garden displays. The jelly palm (*Butia capitata*), although Brazilian and Uruguayan in origin, is also surprisingly tough and of similar stature and hardiness to *Brahea*.

Known to survive outdoors and develop to about 15ft (5m) in mild temperate areas, the Chilean wine palm (*Jubaea chilensis*), with its

BOLD FOLIAGE CONTRAST
Huge, paddle-shaped banana leaves here contrast strikingly with the palmate foliage of a castor bean (Ricinus) *and provide a strong focal point.*

delicate feathery foliage, is another fine candidate for the exotic style, as is the Canary island date palm (*Phoenix canariensis*). Its delightful dwarf relative, *P. roebelenii*, is better grown in a container in the conserva-tory and moved outside in summer.

Unless large specimens are obtained from specialty nurseries, borderline hardy palms should be

grown initially in containers until well established. They can then be planted out in well-drained soil that is reasonably moisture retentive. As the palm stems thicken with age, the plants become more tolerant of lower temperatures, although winter pro-tection is usually advisable.

Palmlike plants, such as cabbage palm (*Cordyline*) and *Yucca* are also

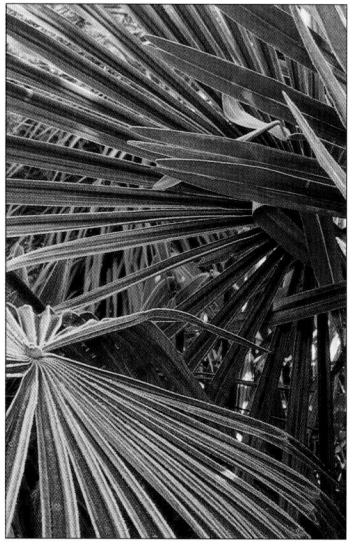

RESISTANCE TO COLD
Frosted fans of a Chusan palm (Trachycarpus fortunei) *demonstrate the surprising hardiness of this plant.*

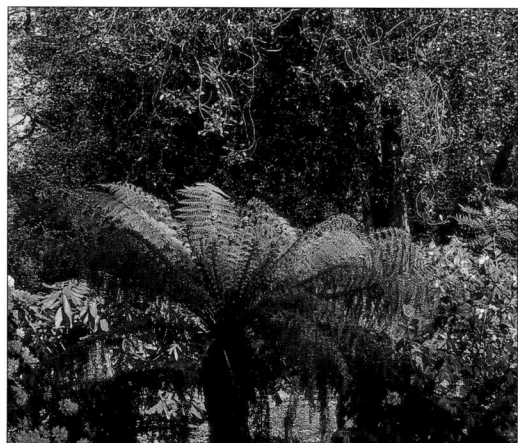

TREE FERN
A nearby tree offers shade and shelter for this tree fern (Dicksonia). *It has been carefully planted just beyond the range of the tree's leafy canopy, beneath which the soil would be too dry for it to flourish.*

OLD PALM FRONDS
As a palm tree increases in height, unsightly dead lower fronds can be removed, but do not cut them back too close to the trunk.

valuable constituents of an exotic-style garden. The New Zealand cabbage or Torbay palm (*C. australis*) can be grown outdoors in mild temperate areas, where it reaches 20–40ft (6–12m) in height. Green-leaved *C. australis* grows well without protection in sheltered gardens but in severe winters may lose some or all of its foliage, although it often recovers in spring. Variants with colored leaves are not always tolerant if the temperature drops below freezing for several days.

Species of *Yucca*, such as Adam's needle (*Y. filamentosa*) and Spanish dagger (*Y. gloriosa*), also provide an exotic feel in a garden and can be used as permanent residents within the planting design, as both will withstand temperatures down to as low as 5°F (-15°C).

Tree ferns
Several species of *Dicksonia* and *Cyathea* are becoming increasingly popular for conservatories and in sheltered gardens. The woolly tree fern (*Dicksonia antarctica*), for example, grows well in humid shade, a habitat that mimics its native temperate rainforests in Australia.

If not already containerized, tree ferns should be planted with the sawed-off "trunk" at least 1ft (30cm) into the ground in a shaded, humid, wind-sheltered site. It is very important, particularly in the first year, to keep the plants moist – they must not be allowed to dry out. A trickle, or drip-feed, system (see p.555) to maintain a high level of humidity around the plants will simulate the natural conditions in which they grow. Sometimes it is better to establish tree ferns in containers, placed in a shaded site, as the developing fronds may burn in bright sun.

Although *D. antarctica* will withstand at least 23°F (-5°C), its crown and trunk should be insulated where more severe cold can be expected (see also "Frost protection," p.605). Slightly more tender are the New Zealand species, *D. fibrosa* and *D. squarrosa*. Both are best grown as container plants that can be given a summer outing. Another tree fern

WINTER COVERING
If banana plants, such as Ensete, are left in situ in winter, some of the foliage can be cut back (above). The plant can then be surrounded by wire netting stuffed with straw and capped with a plastic "hat" (right) to exclude moisture that might promote rot of both the straw and plant.

PROTECTION FOR EXOTICS
Valuable exotics that may be too large to transfer under cover can be given special treatment. Here, a sturdy wooden frame protects a banana plant during the winter. It is filled with dry straw, while a plastic-coated sloping roof guarantees that rain and melting snow do not cause the banana to rot.

that requires similar cultivation and sheltered conditions is the spectacular sago fern (*Cyathea medullaris*).

Bananas
The two main genera of bananas grown as ornamentals are *Musa* (including *Musella*) and *Ensete* – a giant African genus with enormous architectural foliage. Both should be grown in moist, fertile soil and mulched with well-rotted manure. Bananas need sun and a sheltered site to prevent their large, paddlelike leaves from tearing in the wind, as well as plenty of water and fertilizer during the growing season.

A few *Musa* species, including *M. basjoo*, are reasonably cold hardy and will withstand temperatures down to 18°F (-8°C). However, even in sheltered gardens, it is always advisable to provide some winter protection. Young plants should have a deep, straw-filled pot – a tall can is ideal – fitted over the crown after the foliage has been cut off. A board across the pot top will prevent the straw from rotting. Older plants can be protected with a 6in (15cm) mulch of straw placed around each trunk. The old foliage will die off in winter, and new shoots should appear in midspring.

Given suitable over-wintering conditions, *Musa*, *Ensete*, and many other banana genera are among the best of all foliage plants for inclusion in exotic planting designs.

OTHER PLANTS WITH A TROPICAL LOOK
Acanthus mollis
Agave americana
Aralia elata, *A. elata* 'Variegata'
Arundo donax
Astelia chathamica
Beschorneria yuccoides
Blechnum chilense
Brugmansia x *candida*
Canna
Colocasia
Capsicum quitoense
Cycas
Dahlia x *coccinea*,
   D. imperialis
Echium candicans,
   E. pininana
Eryngium agavifolium
Euphorbia characias,
   E. cotinifolia, *E. mellifera*
Fatsia japonica
Gunnera tinctoria
Hedychium
Hibiscus rosa-sinensis
Impatiens tinctoria
Manihot esculenta 'Variegata'
Melianthus major
Passiflora caerulea
Phormium
Phyllostachys
Rheum palmatum (and cvs)
Ricinus communis
Setaria palmifolia 'Rubra'
Solenostemon
Tibouchina urvilleana

Dwarf conifers

DWARF conifers are particularly suited to the small, modern garden, because they can be grown in compact beds or containers and are easy to maintain. Colors range from rich gold through brilliant greens to pale blues and silvers, and shapes include globose, pyramidal, and slender, spire-shaped forms. Habits are diverse, with prostrate, mound-forming, erect, and weeping types; the variation in their foliage texture ranges from soft and feathery to dense and spiky. With careful planning, this rich variety of color, form, and texture can provide interest throughout the year. For details on cultivation, routine care, and propagation, see Ornamental Trees, pp.63–70 and 76–81.

Selecting the plants

When selecting conifers for a small space, it is important to recognize the true dwarf and slow-growing species and cultivars; sometimes so-called dwarf conifers are simply slower-growing variants of large trees. Conifers can be very difficult to identify when young, since their juvenile foliage often differs widely from that when adult. Check that the plants are correctly named when buying to avoid introducing plants that will rapidly outgrow their allotted space. If in any doubt, seek advice from a specialized supplier.

Designing with dwarf conifers

Dwarf conifers are suitable for a wide range of garden situations. They may be planted individually to form a feature or collectively to create a band of colors, and they may be used either to complement other plants or to provide groundcover. Rock gardens, mixed borders, and ornamental containers are also excellent locations for growing many types of dwarf conifer.

ENHANCING CONIFERS
To display dwarf conifers to their best advantage, add other evergreens such as heathers, boxwood, and Vinca *for flower and foliage contrasts.*

Specimen plants
Some of the slow-growing conifers are suitable for use as specimen plants. Spreading forms, for example, may be used to soften the edges of paths and patios, while columnar specimens create a focal point.

Group planting
If space allows, a collection of dwarf conifers can make a very attractive feature. The color spectrum in conifers may also be used to highlight areas at different times of year; blues and silvers, for example, are at their most beautiful in the cool light of winter, while golds and greens appear at their freshest in spring.

Steep slopes and banks, which are often difficult to plant successfully, can make striking landscape features when planted with bold drifts of prostrate conifers. Once the plants are established, these often problematic areas are easy to maintain and are more or less weed-free.

Associating with other plants
Dwarf conifers associate well with other plants that are similar in character. They are often used in heather gardens to extend the season of interest and provide contrast in color and form with the foliage and color variants of *Calluna*, *Daboecia*, and *Erica* cultivars. Other complementary plants include dwarf azaleas (*Rhododendron*), boxwood (*Buxus sempervirens*), and the smaller cotoneaster species and cultivars.

Rock gardens
In the rock garden, dwarf conifers provide an air of permanence and create the framework for other

plants. The complete repertoire of colors, textures, and shapes can be used, but take care to select plants that will not become too large or dominant. The smaller species and cultivars, such as *Juniperus communis* 'Compressa', are ideal for the miniature landscapes of compact, raised beds as well as for troughs, sink gardens, and other containers.

Groundcover
Many dwarf conifers make an excellent weed-smothering groundcover, either by forming dense mats, as with *Juniperus horizontalis* cultivars, or by growing taller and spreading to exclude light beneath them. Some Pfitzer junipers are particularly useful for screening utility meters or for softening paving (see GROUNDCOVERS, p.178).

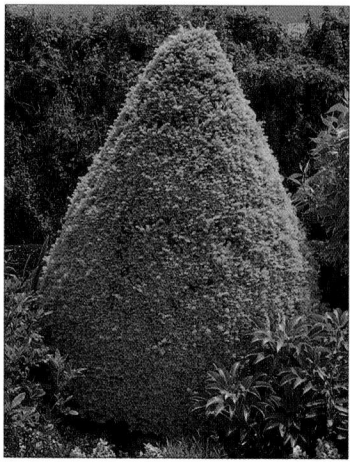

SPECIMEN PLANTING
Ideal for a focal point, the golden yew, Taxus baccata 'Aurea', *has golden foliage all year.*

A SAMPLING OF DWARF CONIFERS

Pinus sylvestris 'Gold Coin'

Juniperus squamata 'Blue Star'

Thuja orientalis 'Aurea Nana'

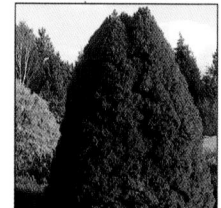

Thuja occidentalis 'Caespitosa'

Picea glauca var. *albertiana* 'Conica'

Picea pungens 'Montgomery'

Chamaecyparis obtusa 'Nana Aurea'

Picea mariana 'Nana'

Soil preparation and planting

Once planted, a tree may remain in place for decades or even centuries, so it is essential to provide it with the best possible growing conditions. Climate, soil type, and the amount of light and shelter available all affect a tree's growth, so take these factors into account when deciding on a planting position. Careful preparation and planting as well as aftercare are vital in helping a tree to establish quickly and grow well.

Climate considerations

Before selecting a tree, check that it will flourish in the temperature range, rainfall, and humidity levels of the site. Special local factors, such as strong winds on exposed hilltop sites, will also influence your choice. Even within a species, different cultivars may be more suited to certain conditions, so one plant may thrive while another may not: various cultivars of *Magnolia grandiflora*, for example, tolerate minimum temperatures ranging from 10°F to 43°F (-12°–6°C).

In areas subject to spring frosts, choose trees that come into leaf late because frost frequently damages young growth. In cold areas, trees that are not fully hardy may be grown outdoors, but they will need protection from cold during winter (see COLD AND WIND PROTECTION, pp.604–5) and should be planted in a sheltered site. If growing tender or tropical species in temperate areas, keep them under cover or grow them in containers so that they may be brought indoors for the winter.

Trees rarely grow well in regions where the annual rainfall is less than 10in (250mm) and most need at least four times this amount. Most trees do not require irrigation, however, except when newly planted, since they obtain enough water from rain and, in some areas, from heavy mists condensing on their foliage.

Choosing a planting site

When planting a tree, choose the best position for it within the garden because the microclimate may vary considerably from one part to another. Make sure that the selected site will provide an appropriate amount of light and shelter: many

large-leaved trees, for example, will thrive in a sheltered, partially shaded position but may not grow well in an exposed site where the foliage would be subjected to strong winds and high light levels.

In coastal areas, choose a planting site that is sheltered since sea spray and salt-laden winds (even a few miles inland) may scorch foliage and cause damage to the growth buds. Some trees, however, tolerate coastal conditions (see "Planter's guide to trees," p.59) and may be planted as windbreaks to help screen other, more vulnerable, plants from strong winds.

Similarly, if trees are being planted on a slope, bear in mind that tender trees are more likely to succeed in a position halfway down where it is usually warmer and more sheltered than at either the top or the bottom (see also "Frost pockets and frost damage," p.601).

It is best not to plant trees very close to walls or buildings; otherwise, when young, the trees may suffer from reduced light and

CHOOSING TREES
CONTAINER-GROWN TREE

GOOD EXAMPLE

Well-balanced branch framework

GOOD EXAMPLE

Well-established root system

POOR EXAMPLE

Tightly wound, congested roots

BARE-ROOT TREE

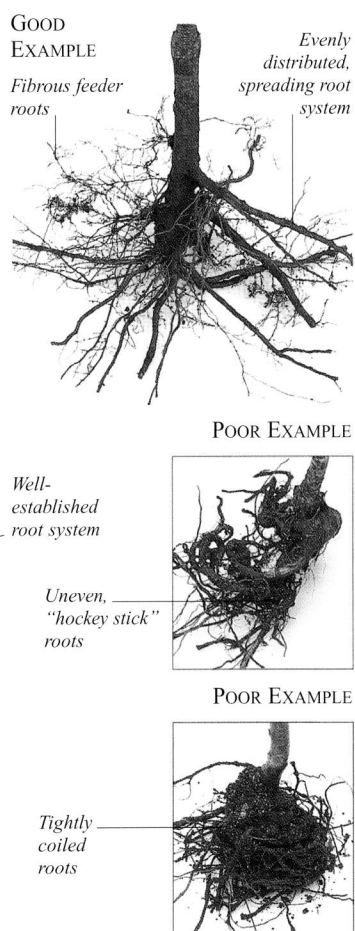

GOOD EXAMPLE

Fibrous feeder roots

Evenly distributed, spreading root system

POOR EXAMPLE

Uneven, "hockey stick" roots

POOR EXAMPLE

Tightly coiled roots

BALLED-AND-BURLAPPED TREE

GOOD EXAMPLE

x CUPRESSOCYPARIS LEYLANDII

Firm root ball with the covering intact

moisture as a result of the "rain shadow" effect. In addition, the strong, fibrous roots of some trees, for example poplars (*Populus*) and willows (*Salix*), may damage drains and the foundations of buildings as they develop. Tender species may be planted near a warm wall, however; there they will benefit from the wall's retained heat and so may be grown in a region where they would fail to survive in more open conditions.

When choosing a site, make sure that the trees will not interfere with overhead wires and underground cables and pipes, which may obstruct trees or be damaged by them.

Selecting a tree

Trees may be bought container-grown, bare-root, or balled-and-burlapped, although conifers and palms are rarely available bare-root. They may be purchased in a variety of sizes and stages of maturity, from seedlings to semimature trees. Young trees tend to become established

more quickly than older trees, while the latter create a strong and immediate impact in the garden but are more expensive. Whichever type you choose, check that the tree has healthy, vigorous top-growth and roots with no sign of pests, disease, or damage. Look for branch and root systems that are well developed and evenly balanced around the stem.

Container-grown trees

These are widely available and may be planted throughout the growing season. Container-grown trees are usually more expensive than bare-root or balled-and-burlapped specimens of comparable size. This is the best method of buying trees that do not establish easily when transplanted, such as magnolias and tupelo, since there is less root disturbance. Exotic and nonnative trees are usually sold this way.

Before buying a tree, remove it from its container, if possible, so that you can see the roots clearly. Do not buy a potbound tree with a mass of congested roots or one with thick roots protruding through the drainage holes. Such trees may not establish well and, because the resulting root system is unstable and not well anchored, the mature tree will be liable to wind-rock. Equally, if the soil mix does not cling to the root ball when the tree is removed from its container, do not buy it since its root system is not sufficiently established. Make sure that the container is large enough in relation to the tree: as a guide, the container's diameter should be at least one-sixth of the tree's height. A tall tree growing in a small container will almost certainly be potbound.

The potting medium is also important: trees that are containerized in soil-based mixes establish more quickly in open ground than those grown in other mixes, since they have less of an adjustment to make to the surrounding soil.

Bare-root trees
Trees sold bare-root, which are almost always deciduous, are grown in open ground, then lifted with virtually no soil around the roots. It is essential to buy them when they are dormant, preferably in fall or early spring; they are unlikely to survive transplanting if bought and planted when in leaf. Ash (*Fraxinus*), poplars (*Populus*), and many rosaceous trees such as crabapples (*Malus*) are often sold bare-root.

Make sure that the tree you choose has well-developed roots spreading evenly in all directions. A number of small roots about 1/16–1/4in (2–5mm) in diameter is a good sign because it indicates that they have been undercut every year or so, a technique that encourages sturdy growth and vigorous root systems. Examine the roots to check that they are not damaged or diseased and that there is no sign of dryness that may have been caused by exposure to wind. Do not buy trees with "hockey stick" roots, where all the growth is on one side; these will not establish well.

Balled-and-burlapped trees
These trees are also grown in open ground, but, when the trees are lifted, the roots and surrounding soil are wrapped in burlap or netting to hold the root ball together and to stop the roots from drying out. Deciduous trees of more than 12ft (4m), and many evergreens, especially conifers and palms of more than 5ft (1.5m), are often sold this way.

Buy and plant a balled-and-burlapped tree when dormant in fall or early spring, following the same criteria as for both container-grown and bare-root trees. Check that the

Staking

Because the root system of a newly planted tree will need one or more growing seasons to anchor it firmly in the soil, staking against strong winds may be necessary at first. Drive the stake in about 24in (60cm) below soil level so that it is completely stable. After two or three years, the tree should be sufficiently established for the stake to be removed. The method of support chosen depends on the tree, the proposed planting site, and personal preference.

Traditionally, a high, vertical stake has been used, placed on the side of the prevailing wind and long enough to reach to just below the crown. A low stake is now often preferred, since it allows the tree to move naturally in the wind.

With flexible-stemmed trees such as crabapples, use a high stake in the first year after planting, cut it down to the lower level in the second year, and remove the stake in the third year.

For container-grown and balled-and-burlapped trees, a low stake angled into the prevailing wind is preferable since it can be driven in clear of the root ball even after the tree has been planted. Alternatively, space two or three vertical low stakes evenly around the tree outside the area of the ball.

In windy sites or for trees more than 12ft (4m) tall, insert two vertical stakes when planting, one on either side of the root ball, to provide support. Large trees are often secured by guy ropes attached to low stakes. Covering the guys with hose lengths or white tape makes them more visible and helps prevent the likelihood of people tripping over them.

HIGH STAKE
Drive in a single, high stake before planting. Secure the tree to the stake using two padded or buckle-and-spacer ties.

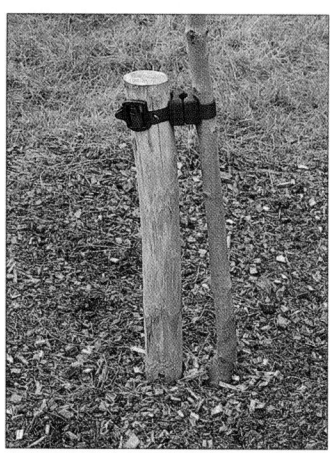

LOW STAKE
A low stake allows the tree's stem some movement; insert it so that only about 20in (50cm) protrudes above ground level.

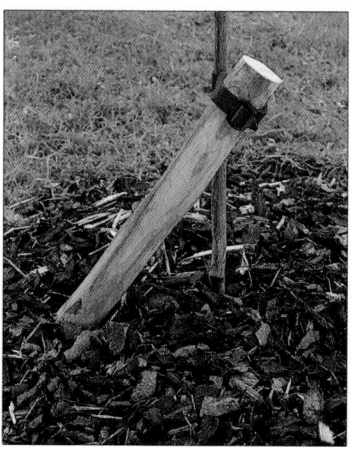

ANGLED STAKE
A low, angled stake may be added after planting. Drive it into the ground at a 45° angle, leaning into the prevailing wind.

TWO STAKES
Insert two stakes so that they are on opposite sides of the tree, and secure them to the tree with heavy-duty rubber ties.

GUY ROPES
For strong support, attach guy ropes to low stakes angled at 45° away from the tree. Space the guys evenly around the tree and secure them to the stakes with long eye bolts or U bolts which you can adjust when necessary (see inset, far right). Cushion the guys with hose lengths where they touch the tree to prevent damage (see inset, right).

Tree ties

Tree ties need to be secure, long-lasting, and able to accommodate the tree's girth as it grows without cutting into the bark. Various commercial ties are available, or you can make them from nylon webbing or rubber tubing. To prevent the stake from chafing the bark, use a spacer or form a padded tie into a figure eight and nail it to the stake. When using two or three stakes, secure the tree to the stakes with heavy-duty rubber or plastic strips. If supporting a large tree with guys, use multistrand wire or nylon rope.

BUCKLE-AND-SPACER TIE
Thread the tie through the spacer, around the tree, and back through the spacer; buckle it so that it is taut but will not damage the bark.

RUBBER TIE
If using a rubber or plastic tie without a buckle, nail it to the stake to prevent bark damage caused by friction.

root ball is firm and its wrapping is intact before purchase: if there is any sign of drying out or root damage, the tree is less likely to establish quickly or well.

Seedlings, transplants, and whips

Seedlings up to one year old are usually available only from specialty nurseries. Transplants are seedlings or cuttings that have been transplanted in the nursery and are up to four years old. They make sturdy, bushy plants and are usually 2–4ft (60cm–1.2m) tall. The age and treatment may be given by the nursery in shorthand: "1 + 1" denotes a seedling left for one year in the seedbed and then transplanted for a further season; "1 u 1" means that it was undercut (see "Bare-root trees," p.64) after the first year and remained *in situ* for a further year.

HEELING IN

If planting is delayed, heel in the tree: first prepare a trench, then set the tree in it. Angle the trunk so that the trunk is supported. Cover the roots and base of the trunk with moist, friable soil and do not allow the roots to dry out.

Whips are single, whiplike shoots sold by height; they are generally 3–6ft (1–2m) tall and will have been transplanted at least once.

Feathered trees

These trees have a single main leader with a spread of lateral branches, or "feathers," down to ground level. They will have been transplanted at least once and are usually 6–8ft (2–2.5m) tall.

Standards and large trees

Standard trees are approximately 10ft (3m) high and have been pruned to create a single main stem without any lateral branches for about 6ft (2m) above ground level. Central-leader standards are similar to feathered trees but have a clear length of stem at the base, while branched-head standards have been pruned so that they have an open

Tree set at an angle

Moist, friable soil

Trench

center. Trees of 6½ft (2.1m) in height with a clear stem of 4–5ft (1.2–1.5m) are half-standards, while trees 11ft (3.5m) tall are selected standards. Larger trees, available from specialized nurseries, include extraheavy standards, which are 15ft (5m) tall, and semimature trees, which are 15–40ft (5–12m).

When to plant

Container-grown trees may be planted at any time of year, except during drought or cold. Deciduous bare-root trees should be planted between midfall and midspring (avoiding periods of severe cold). Hardy evergreens and hardy deciduous trees with fleshy roots should be planted in midfall or mid- to late spring, and marginally hardy trees in midspring. Balled-and-burlapped trees are best planted in early to midfall or mid- to late spring; if deciduous, they may be planted out in winter in mild conditions.

Fall planting allows a tree's roots to become established before the onset of winter. This helps the tree withstand any hot, dry spells the following summer. In cold regions, however, planting in spring may allow trees to establish more successfully. If planting in winter, the ground may be lifted by subsequent cold spells and if so should be refirmed once it has thawed.

Heeling in

It is best to plant trees as soon as possible after purchase, although container-grown and balled-and-burlapped trees may be stored in frost-free conditions for a few weeks if kept moist. If a further delay is unavoidable, heel in the trees in a sheltered place and keep moist.

Soil preparation

Preparing the site in advance allows the soil to settle and minimizes delay between buying and planting a tree. Choose a well-drained site; one that is poorly drained may need to be improved before planting (see "Improving drainage," p.617).Remove all plant growth in the immediate area to eliminate competition for nutrients and water in the soil, then double dig the soil, incorporating organic matter in the lower trench (see "Double digging," p.614).

Most trees require a soil depth of 20in–3ft (50cm–1m) to grow well. Some may grow on soils only 6in (15cm) deep, although they are then less stable and less drought-tolerant.

TREES THAT PREFER ACIDIC SOIL

Abies
Arbutus menziesii
Cercidiphyllum japonicum
Cornus nuttallii
Cryptomeria
Embothrium coccineum
Fagus grandifolia
Magnolia acuminata,
  M. campbellii
  (and cvs)

Magnolia campbellii

Michelia
Oxydendrum arboreum
Picea (most spp.)
Pseudolarix amabilis
Pseudotsuga
Rhodoleia championii
Sciadopitys verticillata
Stewartia
Styrax japonica
Tsuga heterophylla

TREES THAT TOLERATE VERY ALKALINE SOIL

Acer campestre, A. lobelii,
  A. negundo (and cvs),
  A. platanoides (and cvs)
Aesculus
Carpinus betulus
Cedrus libani
Cercis siliquastrum
Chamaecyparis
  lawsoniana (and cvs)
Crataegus
x *Cupressocyparis*
  leylandii (and cvs)
Cupressus glabra
Fagus sylvatica (and cvs)
Fraxinus excelsior,
  F. ornus
Juniperus
Malus
Morus nigra
Ostrya carpinifolia
Phillyrea latifolia
Pinus nigra
Populus alba
Prunus avium
  'Plena'

Prunus sargentii

Prunus sargentii
Pyrus
  (spp. and cvs)
Robinia (spp. and cvs)
Sorbus aria (and cvs)
Taxus baccata (and cvs)
Thuja
Tilia tomentosa

Planting trees

Once the site has been prepared, dig the planting hole between two and four times the width of the tree's root ball, depending on whether the tree is container-grown, bare-root, or balled-and-burlapped. If doing this in advance, backfill it loosely until ready to plant the tree so that the soil remains warm. Do not improve the soil that has been removed since this inhibits the tree roots from growing beyond the planting hole, especially on poor soils. Fork over the sides and base of the hole to break up the soil and allow the tree roots to spread into it more easily; this is particularly important in heavy, sticky soils. If you are using a single stake, drive it into the hole just off-center before planting the tree to make sure that the root ball is not damaged later (see also "Staking," p.64).

Container-grown trees

First thoroughly moisten the soil mix in the container – if it is very dry, stand the container in water for half an hour or until the soil mix is moist throughout. Then remove the container, cutting it away if necessary, taking care not to damage the roots. Gently tease out the roots with your fingers or a hand fork to encourage them to grow into the surrounding soil; this is essential with a potbound plant. If there are any broken or damaged roots, trim them back at this stage with pruners. It is important to check that the planting depth is correct. If a tree is planted too deeply, its roots may not receive enough oxygen and may slow down in growth or even die; if planted too shallowly, the roots may dry out. Place the tree in the hole and locate the soil mark – a dark mark near the base of the stem indicating the soil

TREES THAT PREFER SANDY SOIL

Abies grandis
Acacia dealbata
Acer negundo (and cvs)
Agonis flexuosa
Banksia serrata
Betula pendula (and cvs)
Castanea sativa
Celtis australis
Cercis siliquastrum
Cupressus glabra
Gleditsia triacanthos
Juniperus
Larix decidua
Melia azedarach
Nothofagus obliqua
Phoenix canariensis
Pinus pinaster, P. radiata
Quercus ilex
Robinia
   pseudoacacia 'Frisia'
Schinus molle
Tabebuia
   chrysotricha
Thuja
   occidentalis
   (and cvs)

*Tabebuia
chrysotricha*

TREES THAT TOLERATE CLAY SOIL

Acer platanoides (and cvs)
Aesculus hippocastanum
Crataegus laevigata
   (and cvs)
Fraxinus
Juglans nigra
Malus

*Malus
'Cowichan'*

Metasequoia
   glyptostroboides
Nyssa sylvatica
Pinus strobus
Populus
Pterocarya fraxinifolia
Pyrus calleryana
   'Chanticleer'
Quercus palustris, Q. robur
Salix
Taxodium distichum

PLANTING A CONTAINER-GROWN TREE

1 *Mark out the area of the hole to be dug – about 3 or 4 times the diameter of the tree's root ball. Lift any turf or weeds, then dig out the hole to about 1½ times the depth of the root ball.*

2 *Scarify the sides and bottom of the hole with a fork. There is no need to improve the soil.*

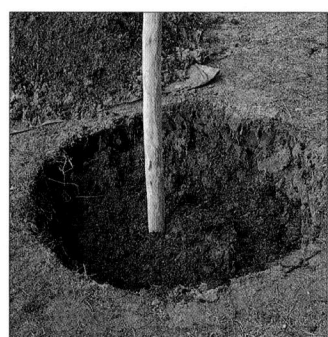

3 *If using one stake, hammer it into the hole, just off-center and on the windward side.*

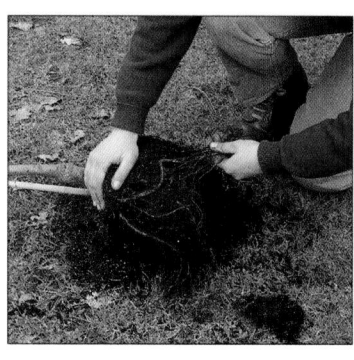

4 *Lay the tree on its side and slide it out of the pot. Gently tease out the roots without breaking up the root ball and remove any weeds from the soil mix.*

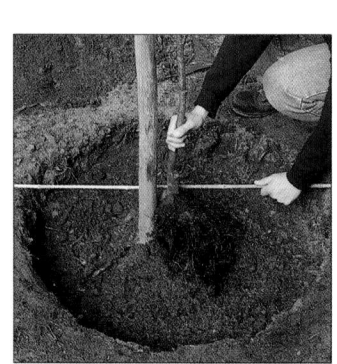

5 *Hold the tree next to the stake and spread out the roots. Lay a stake across the hole to check the planting depth. Adjust this by adding or removing some soil.*

6 *Backfill around the tree with more topsoil, working it down the root ball, then build a ring of soil around the hole to form a water-catching moat.*

7 *Cut back damaged stems, long side shoots, and lower feathers. Mulch 2–3in (5–7cm) deep around the tree.*

level when the tree was growing in the nursery. Place a stake across the hole alongside the stem and add or remove soil from beneath the root ball, if necessary, so that the soil mark is level with the stake.

Backfill the hole, firming the soil in stages to remove any air pockets; take care not to firm too heavily on clay soils since this may compact the ground and impede drainage.

On sandy soils, a shallow moat around the tree helps to channel water to the roots. Conversely, on clay soils, a slight mound around the stem drains water away from the root ball.

Lightly prune the top-growth to balance it with the root system (see "Formative pruning," p.72), then secure the tree to the stake with one or more ties (see "Tree ties," p.65). Water well and apply a thick mulch to conserve moisture in the area where the roots will be developing.

Bare-root trees

Prepare the site in the same way as for container-grown trees, making sure that the planting hole is wide enough for the tree's roots to

PLANTING A BALLED-AND-BURLAPPED TREE

1 Dig a planting hole 2–3 times the diameter of the tree's root ball. Mix the removed soil with well-rotted organic matter, then place the tree in the hole and untie the wrapping.

2 Tilt the tree to one side and roll the material up under the root ball, then tilt the tree the other way and carefully pull out the material. Backfill the hole, firm, and water well.

be spread out fully. Trim back any damaged roots to healthy growth. If using a single stake, drive it in just off-center of the planting hole, and spread out the tree's roots around it in the hole. Adjust the planting depth if necessary, then partly backfill the hole and gently shake the stem up and down to settle the soil around the roots. Firm the

backfilled soil in stages, taking care not to damage the roots. Finally, water the tree well and mulch the area around it.

Balled-and-burlapped trees

The method of planting balled-and-burlapped trees is very similar to that used for container-grown trees. However, the planting hole should be twice the width of the ball, or, in heavy clay soils, three times the width. Place the tree in the hole at the correct depth, then loosen the burlap or netting surrounding the root ball. If using an angled stake or two stakes, one on either side of the root ball, drive them in at this stage; they should rest firmly against the ball without piercing it.

In heavy clay soils, it is possible to improve drainage by planting so that the top of the root ball is slightly above soil level, and covering the exposed part with 2–3in (5–7cm) of friable soil, leaving a gap of 1–2in (2.5–5cm) around the stem. Water thoroughly and mulch.

Aftercare

For the first two or three years after planting, it is important to provide trees with plenty of water, particularly in dry spells and during hot summer weather. Failure to do this may impede establishment, or the tree may even die. Keep the surrounding area clear of grass and weeds, and fertilize and mulch regularly (see "Routine care," pp.68–70).

Some trees need extra protection from cold and wind; evergreens in an exposed site should be protected initially from drying winds with windbreaks, for example (see COLD AND WIND PROTECTION, pp.604–5).

Protecting the stem

In many regions, it is necessary to protect young trees from damage caused by rabbits or other animals that strip bark. Either surround the tree with a barrier of chicken wire or wire netting secured in place with several stakes, or place a commercial tree guard around the tree trunk. There are many types of guard available from garden centers and nurseries, including spiral wraparound guards made of flexible plastic, as

well as those made from wire mesh or heavy-duty plastic. Degradable plastic-net tree guards are also available in a range of heights from 2ft (60cm) up to 6ft (2m).

In exposed sites, such as on hillsides, tree shelters may be used to assist young transplants and whips to become well established; these degradable plastic structures are up to 4ft (1.2m) long, and between 3in (8cm) and 6in (15cm) across.

A   B   C   D

Protect the bark of newly planted trees from animal damage with a barrier of wire mesh or netting secured to the ground with stakes (A), a rigid plastic tree shelter (B), a heavy-duty rubber or plastic stem guard (C), or a spiral, wraparound plastic guard (D).

TREES THAT TOLERATE EXPOSED OR WINDY SITES

Those marked ✿ are not suitable for coastal sites
Acer pseudoplatanus
Aesculus x carnea
Betula pendula✿,
  B. pubescens✿
Crataegus x lavallei,
  C. monogyna
Fraxinus excelsior
Ilex altaclerensis (and cvs)
Laburnum x watereri 'Vossii'
Picea abies✿, P. sitchensis✿
Pinus contorta, P. nigra,
  P. radiata, P. sylvestris
Quercus robur
Salix alba
Sorbus aria, S. aucuparia
  (and cvs)

Sorbus aucuparia

TREES THAT TOLERATE POLLUTED AIR

Acer platanoides (and cvs),
  A. pseudoplatanus (and cvs),
  A. saccharinum (and cvs)
Aesculus hippocastanum
Alnus cordata, A. glutinosa
Betula pendula
Carpinus betulus (and cvs)
Catalpa bignonioides
Corylus colurna
Crataegus
x Cupressocyparis leylandii
Fraxinus
Ginkgo biloba
Gleditsia
Ilex x altaclerensis
Liriodendron
Magnolia grandiflora
Malus
Nyssa
Platanus
Populus

*Populus
x jackii
'Aurora'*

Pyrus
Quercus x hispanica (and cvs),
  Q. ilex, Q. x turneri
Robinia
Salix
Sophora japonica
Sorbus aria, S. aucuparia,
  S. intermedia
Taxus baccata, T. x media
Tilia x euchlora, T. x europaea,
  T. platyphyllos (and cvs)

Routine care

THE amount of maintenance that a tree needs largely depends on the species, microclimate, soil type, and site. Most trees require watering, fertilizing, and a clear, weed-free area during the first few years if they are to establish well. Container-planted trees should also be regularly top-dressed and occasionally repotted. In addition, other procedures such as removing suckers or controlling pests or diseases are sometimes necessary, while in certain circumstances – for example, if a tree is not thriving – the best solution may be either to cut down the tree or to transplant it.

Watering

Most trees need plenty of water to grow well, especially on light, sandy soil or if they have been planted recently. As a general guide, apply 10–15 gallons (50–75 liters) of water for every square yard (square meter) of area beneath the canopy each week in dry weather during the growing season. Once they have become well established, most trees need to be irrigated only during drought.

Fertilizing

All trees benefit from fertilizing, particularly on soils low in nutrients and during the first few years after planting. Older trees usually require fertilizing only occasionally. Trees grown for their flowers and fruit require more potassium and phosphorus than do trees grown for their foliage, which need more nitrogen.

Organic fertilizers such as well-rotted manure or compost are usually applied as a mulch: in fall, or during any frost-free period in the dormant season, spread the material in a layer 2–3in (5–8cm) deep around the tree, keeping a clear area immediately around the trunk. When fertilizing a young tree, extend the

ROOT FEEDING
The root feeder's long nozzle (inset) injects fertilizer deep into the soil.

mulch to the drip line, the ground beneath the outer edge of the canopy. An area 10–12ft (3–4m) in diameter is appropriate for a larger tree.

Inorganic fertilizers are usually applied in spring. Broadcast the fertilizer around the base of the tree, at a rate of 2oz/sq yd (50g/sq m), or

mix it with compost and insert it into small holes dug 6ft (2m) apart around the drip line.

Trees planted in grassed areas may need to be fertilized every year if they are not thriving. Grass between the trunk and the drip line may be removed by hand or sprayed with herbicide and a mulch applied, or use a root feeder (see left) to inject the fertilizer deep into the soil. Push the feeder vertically into the soil at the recommended depth, distributing the total amount of fertilizer among several holes outside the drip line.

Mulching

Mulching around a tree keeps down weeds, reduces harmful temperature extremes around the roots, and cuts down moisture loss from the soil surface. In general, organic materials such as bark chips are used because they are also attractive. Black plastic is also useful, but do not use clear

---

Maintaining trees planted in containers

Container-planted trees generally require watering and fertilizing more frequently than those planted in open ground since the small amount of soil mix in which they are growing can store only limited reserves of water and nutrients. During hot, dry weather, they may need to be watered at least twice a day. Apply an annual mulch of bark chips or similar material on top of the soil mix to help retain moisture. In addition, top-dress the tree each spring before it starts into growth. This involves replacing some of the old soil mix with fresh soil mix enriched with fertilizer. At the same time, prune back

any dead, damaged, weak, or straggly stems to rejuvenate the tree and ensure that it produces healthy, vigorous growth.

Every three to five years, repot the tree completely, either into the same container or, preferably, into a larger one. To do this, first remove the tree carefully from the container, then tease out the roots, cutting back by up to one-third any that are long, large, or coarse. Soak the root system well, if dry, then repot the tree into fresh soil mix (see "Repotting a Container-grown Shrub," p.328). If using the same container, wash it out before adding fresh soil mix and repotting.

TOP-DRESSING

1 *Using a trowel or your hands, remove any mulch and the top 2in (5cm) of soil mix.*

2 *Replenish the container with fresh soil mix combined with a slow-release fertilizer. Water the soil mix well, and mulch.*

REPOTTING

1 *Carefully lay the tree on its side and, with one hand supporting the stem and root ball, knock it out of its pot by sharply tapping the base. Remove any top-dressing or mulch material.*

2 *Using a hand fork, gently tease out the roots, removing some of the old soil mix. Trim any long, large or coarse roots.*

3 *Repot the tree so that the fresh soil mix reaches the soil mark. Firm with your fingers, water well, and mulch.*

REMOVING SUCKERS

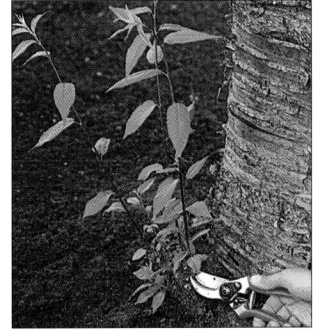

Using pruners, cut off the suckers as close to the trunk as possible, then pare over the cut surface with a knife. Rub off any regrowth as it appears.

plastic since heat is rapidly transferred to the soil and may damage surface roots. Mulches that are rich in nutrients are usually used only if a tree needs fertilizing.

Mulches are best applied in spring but, provided that the soil is moist, they may be spread at any time except during cold or drought. Apply mulch over an area about 12–18in (30–45cm) larger than the tree's root system. Add some fresh mulch every year or two under young trees.

Weeding

The area beneath a tree's canopy should be kept clear of weeds and grass because this guarantees that the tree's feeding roots do not need to compete for water and nutrients. If a tree's growth is too rapid, retaining or establishing grass around it will help to reduce its vigor by competing for fertilizer and water.

Some weedkillers may be used around trees because they do not harm tree roots. Mulching, however, should make weeding largely unnecessary. For treatment of weeds, see "Weeds," pp.658–61.

Suckers and water shoots

Suckers and water shoots will divert nutrients from the main shoots of the tree if they are left to develop unchecked. Remove them as soon as they appear.

Stem and root suckers
A tree may produce both stem and root suckers: a stem sucker is a shoot that appears just beneath the graft

union on the rootstock of a grafted tree; a root sucker is one that develops directly from the roots. Suckers of a grafted plant may quickly grow larger than the top-growth or even replace it within a few years so that the rootstock species predominates rather than the grafted cultivar.

Trees that are particularly vigorous or that have roots near the soil surface, such as poplars (*Populus*) and ornamental cherries (*Prunus*), may form root suckers if the root system is damaged. They may be used for propagation, but are a nuisance if they come up in lawns and paths.

Cut or pull off the suckers as close to the base as possible, digging down to where the sucker joins the root, if necessary. For some genera such as *Prunus*, painting the cuts on the roots with ammonium sulphamate usually prevents regrowth and, in small amounts, does not harm the tree.

Water shoots
Epicormic, or water, shoots may grow directly out of the trunk, often around pruning wounds. Rub them out with your fingers or thumb as soon as they appear, or cut them back to the base and rub them out as they regrow.

Frost and wind

Trees may be broken up by strong winds, and hard frosts may harm young growth, so provide protection such as windbreaks, particularly in exposed sites. Windbreaks may be natural, such as hedges, or constructed, such as fencing (see also "How a windbreak works," p.603).

The soil around newly planted trees may be lifted by frost heaving; if this occurs, refirm it after thawing so that the roots do not dry out. For further information, see COLD AND WIND PROTECTION, pp.604–5.

Tree problems

Lack of vigor is a reliable indicator that there is a problem with a tree. As well as checking for pests and diseases, make sure that the tree has not been planted too deeply or that the roots and stems have not been damaged, since these are possible causes of poor growth and dieback.

The most common pests are aphids (p.639) and spider mites (p.640). A wide range of diseases attacks trees; most are specific to a few species. Some, including fire blight (p.642), may be lethal. To minimize risk, keep trees properly fed and maintained and the surrounding area clear of weeds and debris.

Cutting down a small tree

Tree felling, which may be undertaken at any time of year, is a skilled and potentially dangerous operation; if the tree is taller than 15ft (5m), it should be tackled by an arborist. Ensure that the tree, if on a boundary, legally belongs to you; if not, you should get written permission from your neighbor to remove it.

Make sure that there is space for the tree to fall safely and that there is an escape route at right angles to the proposed fall line, so that you can move out of the way.

A tree is usually taken down in stages. First remove any large branches in sections (see "Removing a branch," p.71), then cut down the rest of the trunk by taking out a wedge of wood on the side where you want the tree to fall

and making another cut on the opposite side of the trunk. The tree can then be pushed over in the required direction. If felling a large tree, tie ropes around the trunk to guide its fall.

It is best to remove the stump, but if this is impractical it may be treated with chemicals. If left to rot it may take many years to disappear. Dig out the stump and any large roots; tough roots should be severed with an ax. If the stump is large, you may need to employ a contractor to grind it up or winch it out with special tools.

Alternatively, cut the stump flush with the ground and treat the cut surface with a commercial solution of ammonium sulphamate. Allow at least 12 weeks before planting in the vicinity.

1 *On the side where you want the tree to fall, make an angled cut. It should be just over one-third of the trunk diameter and about 3ft (1m) from the ground.*

3 *On the opposite side of the trunk, make the final cut just above the base of the wedge cut. As the tree starts to fall, push it in the right direction if necessary.*

2 *Cut out a wedge by sawing horizontally to meet the base of the angled cut. Remove the wedge; this ensures that the tree will fall in the right direction.*

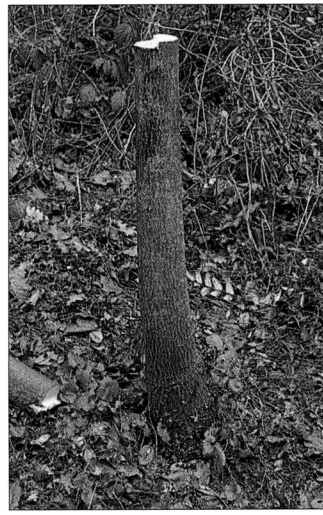

4 *Remove the remaining stump by digging a wide trench around it, loosening the roots with a fork or spade, and then winching or digging it out.*

Transplanting a tree

It is best to prepare the tree a year before transplanting because this will greatly increase its chances of reestablishing. Unless the tree is quite young, it may be difficult to transplant and may not adjust well; if taller than 8ft (2.5m), it may be difficult to establish in its new position. Large trees may need to be transplanted by a specialist.

Preparation

In early fall the year before the planned move, while the soil is still warm and the tree roots are in active growth, mark out the optimum root-ball diameter for the tree – about one-third of its height. Dig a trench about 12in (30cm) wide and 24in (60cm) deep just outside the marked area, and mix the removed soil with large quantities of well-rotted organic matter.

Using a sharp spade, undercut the root ball as far as possible to sever any large, coarse roots. This has the benefit of stimulating the growth of fibrous feeder roots, which will help the tree to develop and grow successfully after transplanting. Then replace the mixture of soil and organic matter in the trench.

Lifting the tree

Transplant the tree the following fall (see "When to plant," p.65), first carefully tying in the branches to the central stem to protect them and to increase the amount of working space around the tree.

Dig a trench just outside the one made the previous year and of similar dimensions, and gradually fork away the excess soil until the root ball is of a manageable size and weight; take care not to damage the fibrous roots. Then cut through any roots underneath the root ball to separate it completely from the surrounding soil. Wrap the root ball securely in some burlap or plastic; this will hold it together and stop the roots from drying out while the tree is removed from the hole and transported to its new position.

Replanting

The tree may then be replanted in its new site (see *Planting a Balled-and-burlapped Tree*, p.67). Until it is well established, support the tree with guy ropes (see "Staking," p.64), and keep it mulched and well watered. If it is impossible to replant the tree immediately, give it the same care as you would a newly purchased tree (see *Heeling In*, p.65).

HOW TO TRANSPLANT A YOUNG TREE

1 *After digging a trench around the tree, carefully fork away the soil from around the root ball.*

2 *Undercut the root ball with a spade, and cut back any awkward roots protruding from the root ball (see inset).*

3 *Tilt the tree to slide a roll of burlap underneath; tilt the other way and pull the burlap through. The root ball should rest on the center of the burlap.*

4 *Pull the burlap up around the root ball so that it is completely covered. Tie it securely with rope to keep the root ball intact while the tree is being moved.*

5 *Tilt the tree and slide two boards beneath. Grasping the rope, slide the tree up the boards. Move the tree to the new site. Lower the tree gently into the prepared hole, then unwrap the root ball, reversing steps 3 and 4. Backfill, attach guy ropes, water, and mulch.*

Changing the grade

If it is necessary to change the grade (soil level) around a large tree, for example to level a slope, precautions must be taken or the tree may die.

If the grade must be raised, build a drystone wall (see "Drystone walls," p.592) around the trunk (leaving room for future growth) and into this set drainage pipes radiating out to the drip line. Cover these with crushed stone and then a layer of gravel. Add a top layer of sandy soil to enable grass to grow. Do not simply cover a tree's entire root area with soil: roots need oxygen to grow, and even a thin layer of additional soil could kill them.

When lowering the grade of the surrounding soil, excavate just outside the tree's drip line (farther out, if possible, where winters are severe) to the depth needed, and build a retaining wall of stone, brick, or wood (see "Retaining walls," p.592) to hold the soil in place.

RAISING THE GRADE

Build a drystone retaining wall to protect the trunk. Lay drainage pipes in a cartwheel configuration around the tree (see inset) and build up the level of the soil using layers of crushed stone, gravel, and sandy soil.

LOWERING THE GRADE

To retain the original grade and prevent erosion, construct a drystone retaining wall just outside the drip line of the tree.

Pruning and training

CORRECT pruning and training help maintain a tree's health and vigor, regulate its shape and size, and, in some instances, improve ornamental qualities. It is important to prune young trees correctly to develop a strong framework of evenly spaced branches; thereafter most trees need minimal pruning.

The degree of pruning and training depends on the type of tree and the desired result. Relatively little is required to produce a well-balanced tree, whereas creating a pleached avenue with interwoven branches demands considerably more work and expertise.

When to prune

Most deciduous trees are best pruned when dormant in fall or winter. They may also be pruned at other times, except in late winter or early spring when many trees bleed (exude sap) if cut. Maples (*Acer*), horse chestnuts (*Aesculus*), birches (*Betula*), walnuts (*Juglans*), and cherries (*Prunus*) all bleed extensively, even toward the end of their dormant season; prune these in midsummer after new growth has matured. Evergreens require little or no pruning except the removal of dead or diseased branches in late summer.

The principles of pruning

The first stage of pruning a tree is to remove any dead, diseased, or damaged wood, and to cut out weak or straggly shoots. Then assess the remaining framework and decide which branches should be pruned back or removed for well-balanced growth. Take care not to impair the natural growth habit of a tree by pruning, unless aiming to produce a certain shape or form, such as an espalier. Hard pruning stimulates vigorous growth; light pruning produces only limited growth.

It is important to make pruning cuts accurately to minimize damage to the tree. If cutting back a stem, cut just above a healthy bud, pair of buds, or side shoot pointing in the required direction of growth. For example, if thinning out congested stems, cut back to a bud or shoot that is growing outward so it will not rub against another stem as it grows. Cut neither too far from the bud, which leaves a stub that provides an entry point for disease, nor too close, which could damage the bud itself.

When pruning trees with opposite buds, make a straight cut with sharp pruners directly above a pair of buds. For trees with alternate buds, make a

WHERE TO CUT

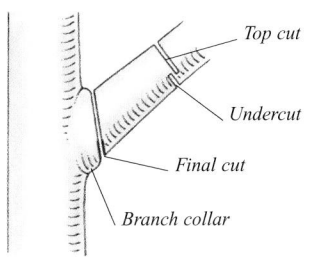

Top cut

Undercut

Final cut

Branch collar

When removing a branch, take care not to damage the branch collar: first remove the bulk of the branch with two cuts, then cut off the stub just outside the collar.

CUTTING BACK A STEM

ALTERNATE BUDS
For trees with alternate buds, make a clean, angled cut just above a healthy, outward-facing bud.

OPPOSITE BUDS
For trees with opposite buds, make a clean, straight cut directly above a strong pair of buds.

sloping cut 1/8–1/4in (3–5mm) above a bud so that the base of the cut is just level with the top of the bud, on the opposite side of the stem.

If pruning back a branch completely, cut just outside the branch collar – the slight swelling on the branch where it joins the trunk. This is where the callus is formed that will eventually cover the wound. Never cut flush with the main stem since this damages the tree's natural protective zone, making it more vulnerable to disease. The branch collar on dead branches may extend some way along the branch, but it is still important to make any cut outside it.

Removing a branch

If removing whole branches of less than 1in (2.5cm) diameter, make a single cut with a pruning saw or pruners. For branches that are thicker than this, first remove the bulk of the weight: partially undercut the branch at least 12in (30cm) from the trunk, then, a little farther out, saw through the branch from above. If no undercut is made, the branch may break off in midcut, ripping the bark back to the trunk and leaving it open to infection.

To remove the remaining stub, undercut it just outside the branch collar, then cut through from above. If you find it difficult to locate the collar, cut through the stub at a short distance from the trunk, making a downward-sloping cut. If the angle between the branch and the trunk is very acute, it may be easier to cut through the stub from beneath.

Do not apply a wound paint or dressing: there is no clear evidence that they speed up the healing process or prevent disease.

CUTTING OFF A BRANCH

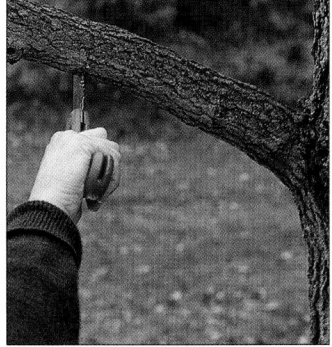

1 *Using a pruning saw, undercut the branch by one-quarter of its diameter, 12in (30cm) from the trunk to keep the bark from tearing back if the branch breaks.*

2 *Make the second cut about 1in (2.5cm) farther away from the trunk, sawing through the branch from above. The undercut will close up, making sawing easier.*

3 *Remove the remaining stub by making 2 further cuts. First make a small undercut just outside the branch collar.*

4 *Make the final cut just outside the branch collar, angling the saw slightly away from the trunk. Saw through cleanly until the top cut meets the undercut.*

Formative pruning

Young trees benefit from formative pruning to make sure that they develop a strong, well-balanced framework of evenly spaced branches. At its simplest, this involves the removal of dead, damaged, and diseased wood, as well as any weak or crossing branches.

Formative pruning may also be used to determine the tree's shape as it grows: for example, a young feathered tree may be pruned over several years to form a standard, or trained against a wall as an espalier. The extent of the pruning depends on both the type of tree selected and the required shape when mature. As with all types of pruning, care should be taken not to spoil the tree's natural growth characteristics.

It is especially important to prune young tropical trees since the growth rate is very rapid and the girth of both main stems and branches develops very quickly. Provided that they have been pruned correctly during the first few years after planting, they may then be left to grow naturally. Most other evergreens, on the other hand, will develop naturally into well-shaped specimens with little or no attention; pruning is usually restricted to the removal of dead, damaged, or crossing stems, and badly placed laterals.

The formative pruning of ornamental garden trees depends on the type of tree bought or required. Feathered trees have a single, central leader and laterals along the whole length of the stem. Central-leader standards have a clear length of stem at the base, while branched-head standards also have a clear stem but have their central leader removed to encourage the formation of vigorous lateral branches – as commonly seen in many Japanese cherries (*Prunus*).

Feathered trees

Feathered trees may be simply pruned to enhance their natural shape or more extensively pruned to train them into standards. This process also sometimes occurs naturally. Although many feathered trees retain their lower branches, these die back in some species and the tree becomes a central-leader standard. Other trees also lose their central-leader dominance and therefore become branched-head standards.

Early training is straightforward, however, regardless of the eventual habit of the tree. First remove any competing shoots to leave a single main leader. Then take out any small, weak, or poorly placed laterals, so

PRUNING AND TRAINING YOUNG TREES

FEATHERED TREE

Remove congested and crossing shoots, then cut out any laterals that are small, spindly, or badly positioned, to achieve a well-balanced framework of branches.

CENTRAL-LEADER STANDARD

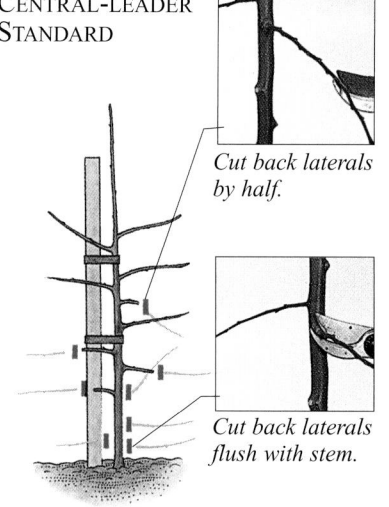

Cut back laterals by half.

Cut back laterals flush with stem.

YEAR 1
On the lowest third of the tree, cut back laterals to the main stem; on the middle third, cut back laterals by half. Remove any weak or competing leaders.

YEARS 2 AND 3
Continue the pruning process, removing the lowest laterals completely and cutting back by about half those laterals that are on the middle third of the tree.

BRANCHED-HEAD STANDARD

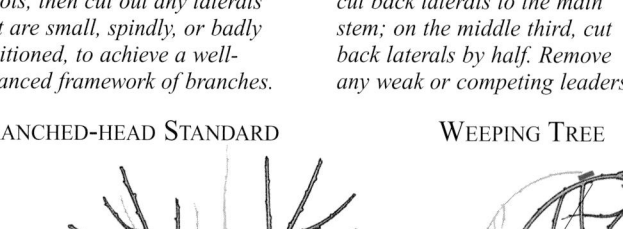

Cut back central leader

Remove crossing branches

Remove lower feathers and water shoots

Remove crossing laterals and any growths on the lower third of the tree. Cut back the leader to a healthy bud or shoot.

WEEPING TREE

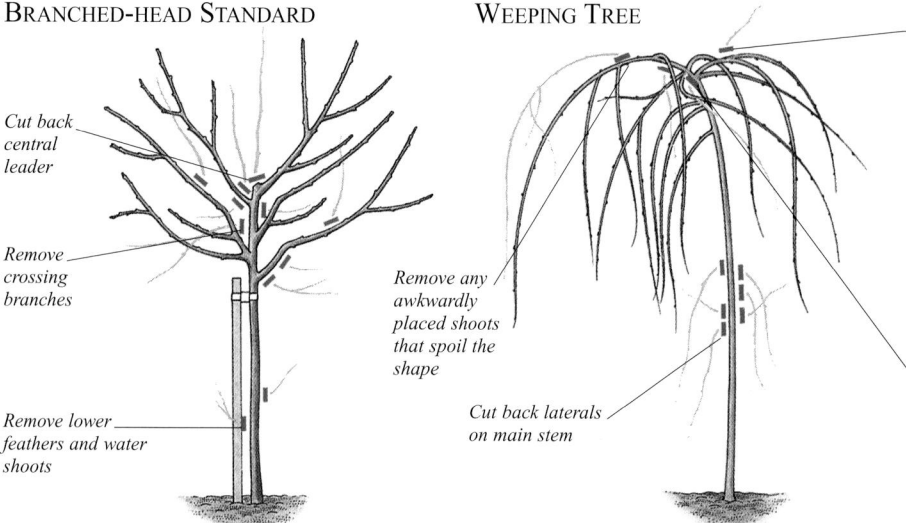

Remove any awkwardly placed shoots that spoil the shape

Cut back laterals on main stem

Cut back crossing or vertical branches that spoil the symmetry of the tree. Remove any growths on the main stem.

Cut upward growing shoots back to a downward pointing bud.

Cut out crossing, rubbing, or congested growth.

that the framework of branches around the main stem is evenly spaced and well balanced.

Central-leader standard trees

Feathered whips may be pruned over two to three years to form a standard. A technique called feathering is often used since it also channels food to the main stem, which thickens and becomes sturdier. Initially, prune a feathered whip to remove any competing leaders or weak laterals. Then, on the lowest third of the tree, cut back all the feathers to the main stem; on the middle third, reduce the feathers by about half;

leave the top third unpruned, but remove any upright shoots that might form a competing leader.

In late fall or early winter, cut back the pruned laterals to the main stem. Repeat the procedure over the next two or three years to form a tree with approximately 6ft (1.8m) of clear stem.

Branched-head standard trees

To form a branched-head standard, train the tree initially as a central-leader standard to achieve the desired length of clear stem. Then, in mid- to late fall, cut back the leader to a strong, healthy bud or shoot to

leave a framework of four or five strong, well-placed lateral branches. At this stage, also remove any crossing or congested laterals and any that spoil the balance of the branch framework.

In subsequent years, prune the tree as much as necessary to keep the crown well balanced and with an open center. Remove any vigorous vertical shoots that may grow into a new leader, and cut back any feathers to the main stem as soon as possible. Some branched-head standards can be formed by top-working (or top-grafting) as for weeping standards (see opposite).

Weeping standards

A weeping standard is formed by grafting one or two scions of a weeping cultivar onto a stock plant with a clear stem of about 6ft (1.8m). This is known as top-working or top-grafting, a technique that is most commonly used for fruit trees (see "Top-working," p.437) but also for weeping ash (*Fraxinus excelsior* 'Pendula'), the Kilmarnock willow (*Salix caprea* 'Kilmarnock'), and a large number of other weeping ornamentals. Young, pendulous branches start to develop once the grafts have taken.

Pruning is best restricted to the removal of crossing and vertical branches and any that spoil the overall symmetry of the framework. Although upward-growing branches are usually removed, leave some semiupright stems to develop naturally since they often grow downward later and produce tiers of weeping branches. If growths appear on the main stem, rub or pinch them out as soon as they appear.

Espalier and fan-trained trees

The aim of both espalier and fan-training is to form a symmetrical, attractive network of branches in a single plane by pruning and training a young tree over several years. These techniques are occasionally used for growing ornamental trees against fences or walls, but they are more commonly associated with growing fruit trees.

Pruning times vary according to the selected species. For example, *Magnolia grandiflora*, which flowers in summer, should be pruned at the start of growth in spring, while the spring-flowering *Acacia dealbata* should be pruned directly after flowering. For further instructions on the pruning techniques, see THE FRUIT GARDEN, "Espalier," p.436, and "Fan," p.435.

Pruning established deciduous trees

Once a deciduous tree is well established, there is little need for further pruning. Major pruning of a mature tree is best carried out by a tree surgeon or arborist, since the work is both skilled and dangerous and, if poorly executed, may ruin the tree.

Many branched-head trees become overcrowded in the center as they mature, restricting the amounts of air and light that reach the central branches. Cut out inward-growing shoots and any branches that spoil the balance of the framework.

REMOVING A COMPETING LEADER

Prune out a competing leader by making a clean cut at the base with pruners or loppers, taking care not to damage the remaining leader.

If a tree is too large for its situation, do not attempt to restrict its size by heading back all new growth each year. This "haircut" pruning produces an unsightly, congested cluster of shoots each season which spoils the tree's natural appearance and reduces flower and fruit production. The correct treatment is as for the renovation of old trees (see p.74).

As a result of hard pruning or the removal of large branches, a tree may produce a mass of epicormic or water shoots; rub or cut these out immediately (see p.69).

If the central leader is damaged, select a strong shoot close to the top of the main stem and train it vertically as a replacement leader. Tie the selected shoot to a stake secured high on the main stem, and prune out any potential competing shoots. Once the shoot has developed into a strong, dominant growth, the stake may be removed.

If a tree develops two or more competing leaders, remove all but the strongest shoot. The very narrow crotch angle between rival leaders is a source of structural weakness, and the tree could split open at this point in a high wind.

Vigorous, upright shoots may develop on young, branched-head trees. If left, these will quickly grow into competing leaders and so it is important to remove them entirely as soon as possible.

Pruning established evergreen trees

Broad-leaved evergreens need minimal pruning. Provided that the trees have an established leader and that any badly placed laterals have been cut out when young, it is only necessary to remove any dead, damaged, or diseased wood.

Conifers require only basic pruning once established, except when they

are grown as a hedge (see HEDGES AND SCREENS, pp.82–4). On some pines (*Pinus*), firs (*Abies*), and spruces (*Picea*), the terminal bud on the leader may die; if this occurs, train in the best placed lateral as a replacement leader (see above) and cut out any competing, upright shoots. Established palms require no pruning apart from the removal of dead leaves, which should be cut back to the main stem.

Root pruning

If an established tree is growing vigorously but producing very few flowers or fruit, pruning the roots will help slow down growth and stimulate better flowering or fruiting performance.

In early spring, dig a trench just outside the extent of the tree canopy. Then prune back any thick roots to the inner edge of the trench, using a pruning saw, pruners, or loppers. Retain any fibrous roots at the inner edge of the trench, backfill the soil, and firm. For further details, see THE FRUIT GARDEN, "Root pruning," p.424. In some instances, it may be necessary to support the tree with stakes or guy ropes if it seems unstable afterward (see "Staking," p.64).

HOW TO COPPICE A TREE

Coppicing may be used to restrict a tree's size, to enlarge leaves, or to enhance stem color.

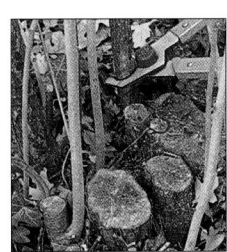

Use loppers to cut back all stems to 3in (7cm); do not cut into the swollen, woody base of the tree.

TRAINING IN A NEW LEADER

Replace a damaged leader by training in a strong shoot vertically. Attach a stake to the top of the main stem and tie the shoot to the stake. Prune out the old, damaged leader. Remove the stake once the new leader is dominant and growing strongly.

For root pruning of trees in containers, see "Maintaining trees planted in containers," p.68.

Pruning container-planted trees

Container-planted trees should be pruned annually, following the same principles as for other trees, to regulate their shape and size and maintain a strong, balanced framework of evenly spaced branches.

Coppicing and pollarding

Coppicing is the regular pruning of a tree close to the ground to encourage strong basal shoots. Pollarding is the pruning of a tree back to the main stem or branch framework to stimulate new shoots. Both techniques were traditionally used to give a supply of firewood or pliable stems for basketwork and fencing. Now they are used in gardens to enhance leaf color and size or the color of ornamental stems, or to restrict tree size.

Coppicing

Trees should be coppiced in late winter or early spring; some willows, when grown for their colored stems, may be left until midspring, however, and pruned just before or very shortly after the buds break into new growth. Cut back all stems to the base, leaving the swollen basal wood unpruned because all new growth forms from here.

Pollarding

To form a pollard, plant a young branched-head standard (see p.48). When its trunk has reached 6ft (2m) or the desired height, prune back the branches to 1–2in (2.5–5cm) from the main stem in late winter or early spring. This results in a mass of shoots developing from the top of the cut stem. Prune back these shoots annually (or every second year) to stimulate growth of further young shoots from the enlarged head of the stem. Thin them if they become congested. Remove shoots that grow on the trunk as soon as they appear.

To produce a pollard with a main branch framework, allow the tree to develop a well-balanced branch system at the desired height. In late winter or early spring, prune back the branches to about 6ft (2m). Cut back the resulting secondary shoots every two to five years, depending on the species, until the pollard is established. Thereafter, prune every year or two, and thin the shoots as required. If too many enlarged heads develop

TREES FOR COPPICING AND POLLARDING
Acer pensylvanicum
  'Erythrocladum'
Corylus avellana
  'Contorta' ∨
Eucalyptus
  dalrympleana,
  E. gunnii ∨,
  E. pauciflora

Populus candicans
  'Aurora'

Populus x *canadensis*
  'Serotina Aurea',
  P. candicans 'Aurora'
Salix acutifolia 'Blue Streak',
  S. alba 'Britzensis',
  S. a. var. *sericea,*
  S. a. var. *vitellina,*
  S. daphnoides 'Aglaia',
  S. x *sepulcralis*
    'Erythroflexuosa'
Tilia platyphyllos
Toona sinensis 'Flamingo'

KEY
∨ Coppice only

PRUNING AN ESTABLISHED POLLARDED TREE

Prune back the shoots every 1–2 years in late winter or early spring to 1/2–3/4in (1–2cm) from the pollarded head of the main stem. This will stimulate new shoot production the following spring. The new wood of trees such as this Salix alba *var.* vitellina, *grown for its ornamental stems, is particularly highly colored.*

Using pruners or loppers, cut back the old stems to the base, taking care not to damage the enlarged head.

close together, cut out some of them entirely.

Renovating old trees

Trees that have outgrown their situation or that have been neglected should be either removed and replaced, or renovated to return them to full health and vigor. Renovation requires considerable care and expertise, and it is advisable to consult an experienced arborist. In some cases, a tree may be too old and potentially dangerous to renovate, so it may be better to replace it.

Renovation may be undertaken at any time except the start of growth in spring. For most trees, however, and particularly those that produce a lot of sap, such as horse chestnuts (*Aesculus*) and birches (*Betula*), late

fall or early winter is the best time. Prune flowering cherries in early summer to reduce the production of overvigorous new growth which might favor leaf diseases.

The first stage is to remove all dead, diseased, and damaged wood. Then prune out any crossing or congested branches and those that spoil the balance of the framework. It is best to carry out extensive renovation over two or three years to allow gradual recovery – drastic pruning may severely weaken or even kill a tree in poor health. If you need to remove any large branches, cut them off in sections (see "Removing a branch," p.71).

After renovating the tree, mulch it with well-rotted manure and apply fertilizer to the ground beneath the tree canopy in spring for two to three years. Hard pruning may stimulate

the growth of a mass of side shoots; if congested, thin some of them out to leave a well-balanced framework. Any suckers and water shoots should be removed as soon as they are noticed (see p.69).

Renovating "haircut" pruned trees

Trees that have had all their new growth trimmed back annually produce a congested cluster of shoots every season on knobby branches, but without the balanced framework of a true pollard. Such "haircut" pruning is unsightly and reduces flowers and fruit. To correct it, first thin out the knobby stumps at the ends of the main branches. Cut out most of the young shoots on the remaining stumps to leave just one or two and cut these back by about one-third; repeat this procedure in the following three or four seasons to develop a more natural growth habit.

Arborists

For pruning, renovation, or removal of large trees, it is advisable to consult a qualified arborist (often referred to as a "tree surgeon"). The International Society of Arboriculture has branches across the US and Canada as well as in many other parts of the world. They can advise you of registered arborists in your area. Also check your telephone directory. Before inviting contractors to give estimates, decide exactly what work is required, including the disposal of any debris. Get several estimates: they may be provided free, but a fee may be charged if advisory work is involved.

RENOVATING A TREE

YEAR 1
Cut out any dead, diseased, and damaged wood, and remove any branches that cross or rub against others and that spoil the balance of the framework.

YEARS 2 AND 3
The following year, thin out the new growth that results from the initial pruning and remove any water shoots. Repeat the next year if necessary.

Pleached trees

Pleached trees are clear-stemmed trees planted in one or more rows with their branches trained horizontally to intertwine, creating a formal, raised wall of foliage when in leaf (see "Trees for avenues," p.58). Hornbeams (*Carpinus*) and lindens such as *Tilia platyphyllos* and *T.* 'Euchlora' make excellent pleached avenues, since they can be clipped precisely and, within four or five years, develop an attractive, boxed appearance. It is best to use young trees with pliable stems; attempts to pleach mature trees are generally unsatisfactory.

Constructing the framework

Until the trees are established, they should be trained in to a framework. First, using one stake for each tree to be planted, set up a row of sturdy, 8–10ft (2.5–3m) high stakes an equal distance apart. Once driven into the ground to a depth of approximately 2–3ft (60cm–1m), they should be at the required height of the lowest branches – about 6ft (2m) or more for people to be able to walk underneath comfortably. Attach a secondary framework of thinner posts to these stakes to create the desired overall height.

Initial training

Plant a young tree next to each stake in late fall or early winter. Choose trees that are sufficiently tall so that their laterals may be trained in to the framework. Cut back any lower feathers below the lowest horizontal rail, and prune out any sublaterals that cannot be tied in easily. The leader may either be bent horizontally and tied in, if tall enough, or left to grow for another season before being trained.

Further training

Late the next summer, intertwine any untrained branches into the framework and cut back any long laterals to stimulate new growth. Sublaterals growing at right angles to the branches may be tied in along the stakes. Continue to develop a boxed appearance in subsequent seasons by tying in branches and cutting back the laterals to stimulate new shoots and dense growth.

Once the pleached trees are fully established and the branches have intertwined, the framework may be dismantled. Maintain healthy, dense growth by removing any dead, damaged, or diseased wood, and strongly outward-growing laterals; rub out young shoots on main stems as soon as you notice them.

ESTABLISHING THE FRAMEWORK

YEAR 1

Drive a row of stakes into the ground about 7–9ft (2.2–2.7m) apart. Secure strong, vertical posts to the stakes, then fix horizontal rails about 24in (60cm) apart to these to form the framework. Plant a young standard or feathered tree next to each stake.

Bend over any laterals adjacent to the horizontal rails and tie them in without straining them excessively.

Prune back laterals that cannot be tied in easily. Cut back to the main stem any feathers that are growing below the bottom horizontal rail.

YEAR 2

Late in the following summer, tie in any untrained branches to the framework to fill in spaces, and prune back long laterals to two or three buds to encourage the growth of new side shoots.

Once the leader is tall enough, bend it over onto the top horizontal of the framework, and tie it in.

Prune back laterals to a strong side shoot to encourage further branches to grow.

ANNUAL MAINTENANCE

Tie in all unruly and awkward branches to maintain the pleached effect, and prune back laterals to encourage new growth and a dense branch framework.

Cut back awkward stems growing away from the framework to maintain a neat, well-trained shape.

Continue to tie in new stems to the framework; check old ties and replace them where necessary.

Prune any long laterals pointing away from the desired shape to encourage further side shoots to grow along the framework.

Propagation

TREES may be propagated from cuttings, seed, layering, or grafting. Taking cuttings is probably the most common method of propagation; it is fairly simple and provides new plants fairly quickly, while raising trees from seed or layering is easy but very slow. Grafting is rarely used by amateur gardeners because it requires considerable expertise to grow new plants successfully this way.

Tree species may be propagated from seed, but seeds from hybrids and cultivars rarely produce plants that are true to type. Vegetative methods of propagation, such as taking cuttings, layering, and grafting, may be used for hybrids and cultivars as well as species. However, some care in the selection of plant material is required for success.

Hardwood cuttings

Many deciduous trees may be propagated from hardwood or dormant cuttings. In early fall, prepare the ground for the cuttings while it is still warm. Where winters are long and harsh, the cuttings usually die if left outside: they can be rooted in deep boxes in a basement or frost-free root cellar.

Cuttings of trees that root easily, such as willows (*Salix*), may be inserted directly into a trench, while those that are more difficult to root, such as *Metasequoia*, should be inserted in a sand bed and then transplanted into a trench early the next spring. In either case, make the trench narrow and with one side vertical so that the cuttings are held upright while they root. The depth of the trench will depend on the type of plant to be rooted. For multistemmed trees, it should be 1in (2.5cm) shallower than the length of the cuttings; for single-stemmed trees, it should be the same depth as the cuttings so that the top bud is barely covered and the lack of light inhibits the growth of all other buds.

For best results, dig the trench in friable, well-drained soil; in heavy clay soil, add some coarse sand to the base. If preparing a few trenches, space them 12–15in (30–38cm) apart in open ground, or about 4in (10cm) apart in a cold frame.

1 *For species that do not root easily (here* Metasequoia)*, tie cuttings into bundles. Dip the ends in hormone rooting powder.*

2 *Insert the bundles of cuttings in a sand bed and leave in a cold frame over winter. In spring, insert them individually in a trench in a prepared site outside.*

Preparing and inserting the cuttings

Select the cuttings just after leaf fall. Choose strong, vigorous shoots of the current season's growth and remove them by cutting just above a bud or pair of buds at the junction between the current and the previous season's growth. Trim down the cuttings as shown and dip the basal cuts in hormone rooting powder to encourage them to root. Place the cuttings against the vertical side of the trench at the correct depth, and backfill with soil. Then firm in gently and water well.

For species that do not root easily, tie cuttings into small bundles and then plunge them into a sand bed (see p.632) in a cold frame for the winter, where they should callus or root before being transplanted.

FAST-ROOTING HARDWOOD CUTTINGS

1 *To prepare the trench, push the spade vertically into the soil, then press it forward slightly to form a flat-backed trench about 7in (19cm) deep.*

2 *Select strong, straight stems with healthy buds (right); avoid old, soft, spindly, or damaged stems (left). Remove about 12in (30cm) of the stem, cutting just above a bud.*

3 *Remove any leaves. Trim the cuttings to about 8in (20cm); make an angled cut just above the proposed top bud and a horizontal cut below the bottom one.*

4 *Insert the cuttings in the trench 4–6in (10–15cm) apart, and at the correct depth depending on whether a multi- or single-stemmed tree is required.*

PLANTING DEPTHS

MULTISTEMMED TREES

For multistemmed trees, insert cuttings with the top 1–1¹/₂in (2.5–3cm) above the soil surface.

SINGLE-STEMMED TREES

The top bud of each cutting should be just below the soil surface.

5 *Firm the soil around the cuttings, rake the surface, and label. Space any additional rows 12–15in (30–38cm) apart.*

6 *Lift the rooted cuttings the following fall. Then pot them up individually or transplant them into open ground in their final positions.*

Aftercare

Label the cuttings and leave them until the following fall. During the winter, the ground may be lifted by frost; refirm the soil around the cuttings if this occurs. By fall, they should be well rooted and may then be transplanted individually into open ground or into containers, as required. If they have been kept in a cold frame, harden them off the first spring, then transplant outside; the following spring, pot them up or move them to their final positions in open ground.

Semiripe cuttings

Many conifers, as well as certain broad-leaved evergreens such as *Magnolia grandiflora* and *Prunus lusitanica*, may be propagated readily from semiripe cuttings. These cuttings are taken in late summer or fall from stems that have virtually ripened; that is, when they have thickened and become harder (see also ORNAMENTAL SHRUBS, "Semiripe cuttings," p.110).

Selecting the cuttings

In a closed case, at 70°F (21°C), or in a cold frame, prepare a suitable rooting medium for the cuttings. This should consist of equal parts of grit and compost or peat (see also "Standard rooting media," p.622). Using a sharp knife, take heel cuttings from healthy sideshoots, including a sliver of hardened wood from the main stem. Alternatively, take 4–6in (10–15cm) long cuttings from leaders or sideshoots and trim immediately below a node with pruners or with a sharp knife.

For cuttings from conifers, choose leaders or sideshoots that are characteristic of the parent, since conifer shoots vary considerably in their growth patterns. It is particularly important to select cutting material carefully from slow-growing and dwarf conifers: since some may produce reverted or uncharacteristic growth, use only shoots that typify what you want to propagate.

Preparing and inserting the cuttings

For all semiripe cuttings, cut off the lower pair of leaves with a sharp knife and reduce the remaining leaves by one-third or a half to minimize the loss of moisture; if the cutting tips are soft, pinch them out. To encourage the cuttings to root, use the tip of the knife to make two shallow, vertical wounds, about 1in (2.5cm) long, on opposite sides of each cutting down to the base. Alternatively, make a longer wound along the side of each cutting with a knife, and remove a sliver of bark as well. In either case, dip the basal cut, including the wound, in hormone rooting powder.

Use a dibber to make a hole in the rooting medium and insert the bottom third of each cutting, taking care to leave enough space between the cuttings so that they do not overlap; this allows air to circulate freely around them. Then firm the medium, water thoroughly with a solution containing fungicide, and label.

Aftercare

Check the cuttings periodically, watering them only to keep them from drying out. Remove any fallen leaves as soon as they appear since these may rot and spread disease to the cuttings. During cold spells, cold frames should be insulated with burlap or a similar covering.

If the cuttings are being kept in a closed case with bottom heat, they should root by early spring. Cuttings in a cold frame are usually left until the following fall, although it is preferable to leave them in the frame for a second winter and pot them up the following spring.

During the summer, mist-spray the cuttings often to stop them from drying out and control any pest or dis-ease infestations that might develop. If the cuttings are in strong, direct sunlight they risk being scorched, so it may be necessary to shade them. Apply a greenhouse shading paint or place shading material over the frame (see p.570). Once the cuttings root, lift them out carefully with a hand fork and transplant them into individual pots, then harden them off (see p.631) before potting them on further or planting them out in open ground. Rooted cuttings in a cold frame may be hardened off while still in the frame by raising the frame cover for short then longer periods. Give the cuttings a liquid fertilizer and pot them up or transplant them outside.

Softwood cuttings

This method of propagation is suitable for some ornamental cherries (*Prunus*) and a few other tree species, although it is more commonly used for shrubs. Softwood cuttings are taken in spring from the fast-growing tips of new shoots and usually root very easily. They wilt rapidly, however, so it is vital to prepare and insert them as quickly as possible after removing them from the parent plant.

Preparing and inserting the cuttings

In spring, before taking the cuttings, prepare containers by filling them with an appropriate medium and then firming to just below the rim. Take the cuttings by removing the new growth from stem tips, cutting just above a bud or leaf joint with pruners or a sharp knife. To reduce any moisture loss, immerse the cuttings in water immediately or place them in an opaque plastic bag and seal it. Even a small loss of water will hinder the development of new roots.

Prepare the cuttings by trimming them with a sharp knife to about 2½in (6cm), cutting just below a leaf joint. Remove the lower leaves and dip the base of each cutting in hormone rooting powder to encourage rooting. Insert the cuttings into the prepared pots of medium, label them, and water them with a dilute solution of fungicide.

To encourage rapid rooting, place the containers in a mist unit or closed case at 70–75°F (21–24°C), preferably with bottom heat, and water with a fungicide once a week to protect against rotting and disease. Once they are rooted, the cuttings may be hardened off gradually before they are transplanted carefully into individual pots.

PREPARING A SEMIRIPE CUTTING

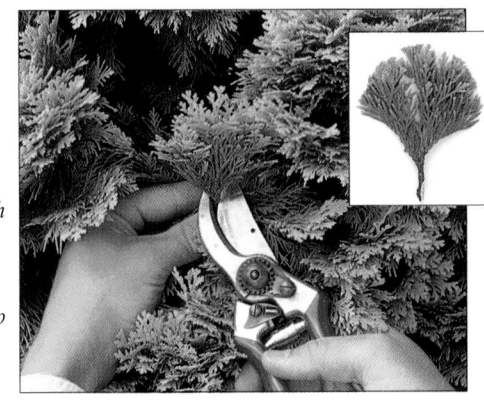

Cut a shoot 4–6in (10–15cm) long from a leader or sideshoot and trim immediately below a node. Strip off the lower leaves (here of Chamaecyparis obtusa *'Nana Aurea') and pinch out the tip if it is soft. Make a shallow wound, about 1in (2.5cm) long, down the cutting and dip it in rooting hormone.*

TREES THAT MAY BE PROPAGATED BY CUTTINGS

Hardwood
Cordyline
Ficus
Metasequoia glyptostroboides
Morus
Platanus
Populus
Salix

Morus alba 'Laciniata'

Semiripe
Austrocedrus▽
Calocedrus▽
Chamaecyparis▽
Cinnamomum▽
x *Cupressocyparis*▽
Cupressus▽
Distylium racemosum▽
Drimys winteri
Eucryphia

Eucryphia x *nymansensis* 'Nymansay'

Grevillea
Ilex
Juniperus▽
Ligustrum lucidum
Magnolia grandiflora▽
Metrosideros excelsa,
  M. robusta,
  M. umbellata
Michelia▽
Nothofagus dombeyi
Podocarpus,▽
Prunus lusitanica
Quercus ilex▽,
  Q. myrsinifolia▽,
  Q. semecarpifolia▽
Thuja▽
Thujopsis▽
Trochodendron araliodies▽
Tsuga▽
Weinmannia

Softwood
Acer cappadocicum
Betula
Catalpa
Celtis occidentalis
Cotinus coggygria
Eucryphia lucida
Ginkgo biloba
Halesia
Koelreuteria paniculata
Lagerstroemia
Liquidambar styraciflua
Metasequoia glyptostroboides
Prunus
Ulmus

KEY
▽ *Take cuttings with a heel*

Raising trees from seed

Tree species may be propagated from seed since their seedlings usually retain the characteristics of the parent plant. Hybrids and cultivars rarely come true to type. Raising a tree from seed is a relatively simple process; it is, however, a slow method if a tree is being grown mainly for its flowers, because it will take a number of years to reach flowering size.

Extracting seed

The protective covering of some seeds should be removed first. The method for this varies, depending on the type of seed coat. The coating on winged seed may be removed by rubbing it between finger and thumb. Some cones disintegrate naturally, and the scales may then be separated. Place pine and spruce cones in a paper bag and keep them in a warm, dry place until the cone scales open and shed the seed into the bag. Immerse cedar cones in hot water and allow them to soak until the scales open.

The method of extracting seed from fruits or berries depends on the seed size and type of flesh. Large fruits, such as those of crabapples (*Malus*), may be cut open and the seeds extracted. Soak smaller fruits, such as those of *Sorbus*, in warm water for several days; viable seed will sink. Discard the pulp and soak again until the seed can be removed and any remaining flesh picked off.

Storing

Once the seed has been extracted, dry it if necessary and place it in a sealed and labeled plastic bag. If planning to sow the seed within a few days, store it at room temperature; for longer-term storage, keep it on the top shelf of a refrigerator so that it is cool but not frozen.

CLEANING FLESHY SEED

1 *Remove the fleshy seed with your fingers. Immerse it in warm water, and soak for 1–2 days. Once the fleshy coating has softened and split, drain off the water.*

2 *Pick off the remaining coating and dry the seed with tissue. Sow the seed fresh or store it in a plastic bag in a refrigerator for no more than a few weeks.*

Breaking seed dormancy

Some seeds have a natural period of dormancy to prevent germination in adverse climatic conditions that would threaten the survival of the seedlings; this has to be overcome before the seed will germinate. Several kinds of dormancy occur, sometimes combined, which vary according to the species. Most commonly, dormancy is achieved either by a hard, thick seed coat, which prevents water from being taken up, or by a chemical inhibitor, which delays germination until there is a significant temperature change. In most cases, dormancy can be broken artificially by wearing away the seed coat or by chilling the seed.

Scarification

Before sowing seeds with an impermeable coating, scarify them to allow germination to occur. Large seeds with a particularly hard covering, such as oaks (*Quercus*), may be nicked with a sharp knife or a section of the seed coat filed away to let in moisture. Smaller seeds that are not easily nicked, such as those of pines, may be shaken in a jar that has been lined with sandpaper or partly filled with sharp grit, or they may be filed individually with an emery board. Seed from legumes (for example *Acacia* and *Robinia*) should simply be left to soak in a container of hot water for approximately 24 hours in a ratio of 3 parts hot water to 1 part seed.

Stratification

Dormancy in seed of trees from temperate climates is commonly overcome by chilling (stratification). Seed may either be sown outside so that it is chilled naturally during winter or, more reliably, stratified artificially by being stored in a refrigerator.

If refrigerating seed, first mix it with moistened vermiculite, or peat and sand. Place it in a clear plastic bag, then seal the bag and put it in a refrigerator. Check the seed regularly through the unopened bag – it should be sown as soon as there are signs of germination.

The length of chilling time required varies considerably: as a guideline, many deciduous species require about six to eight weeks of chilling at below 41°F (5°C), while conifers need only about three weeks. Some seeds germinate only after they have been sown and once chilling has ceased. Sow batches of such seed at intervals – for example after four, eight, and twelve weeks of chilling – since this should guarantee that at least some seeds germinate.

Sowing seed in containers

This is a simple way of raising a small number of seedlings. Thoroughly clean any work surfaces and containers to be used before sowing the seed to avoid contamination from soilborne pests and diseases. First fill the pots, pans, or seed trays up to the rim with sowing medium.

Large seeds or those that produce seedlings with long taproots, such as oaks (*Quercus*), should be sown about 3in (8cm) apart in deep seed trays or packs, or in individual pots that are about 4in (10cm) deep. Using a presser board, press the seeds into unfirmed medium, then cover them to their own depth with the medium and firm to about ¼in (5mm) below the rim (see opposite).

Sow very large seeds, for example those of horse chestnut (*Aesculus*), singly in 4–6in (10–15cm) pots. Insert the seed in firmed sowing medium, so that just the top of the seed is exposed above the surface.

Small seeds, for example those of *Sorbus*, may be either scattered evenly or, if sufficiently large, individually pressed into prepared pots or trays of firmed medium. They should then be barely covered with sieved medium followed by a layer of fine grit ¼in (5mm) deep.

After sowing, thoroughly water all seeds from above and label. Place the containers in a cold frame or in a

SOWING IN CONTAINERS

1 *Sow fine seed (here* Sorbus) *onto firmed sowing medium, making sure it is scattered evenly; keep your hand low to stop the seeds from bouncing.*

2 *Hold a sieve containing sowing medium over the tray, then tap the side of the sieve until the seeds are just covered to their own depth with sieved soil mix.*

3 *Cover the sown seeds with a ¼in (5mm) deep layer of horticultural grit. Label the seeds and water with a fine spray.*

4 *Once the seedlings are large enough to handle, gently prick them out into individual pots, taking care not to crush the delicate stems or roots.*

SOWING LARGE SEED

1 *Press large seeds and those of trees with long taproots into unfirmed medium in individual pots. Cover with medium.*

2 *Sowing in deep pots allows the taproot (see inset) of each seedling (here* Quercus*) to develop without any restriction to root growth.*

greenhouse, either in a closed propagation case or under a pane of glass. Temperate species are best kept at 54–9°F (12–15°C), and warm-temperate and tropical species at 70°F (21°C) to stimulate germination. Once the seeds have successfully germinated, spray them periodically with a fungicide to discourage damping off (see p.651).

Pricking out
When the seedlings are large enough to be handled by their seed leaves, prick them out so that they have more space to grow. This may be done by knocking the container sides to loosen the medium, and then lifting and transplanting the seedlings into individual pots. Alternatively, remove all the seedlings and medium together from the container so that the seedlings may be separated with minimal root disturbance. After transplanting, firm the medium gently around the seedlings, then level it by gently tapping the pot on the work surface.

Aftercare
Water and label the seedlings, and keep them out of direct sunlight in a temperature similar to that needed for germination until established. Gradually harden them off over a few weeks, fertilizing them regularly, and spraying them with fungicide. Do not overwater, but make sure that the medium does not dry out. Once hardened off, they may be planted out if there is no danger of frost.

Sowing seed outdoors
If raising a large number of seedlings, seed may be sown in an outdoor seedbed. With this method, the seedlings require less regular attention and their growth is less restricted than if sown in containers, but a special bed must be prepared. If possible, do this a few months before sowing by thoroughly digging the area to a spit deep (see "Single digging," p.613), incorporating organic matter and some coarse grit. Keep the ground clear of weeds.

When ready to sow, rake the soil down to a fine tilth, then broadcast small seeds or sow larger ones singly. (For depth of sowing, see "Sowing seed in containers," opposite.) Lightly rake over the seeds, cover the bed with a ¼–½in (0.5–1cm) layer of grit, and firm with a presser. If the soil is at all dry, water thoroughly; then label with the plant name and sowing date.

In exposed sites, young seedlings may need to be protected with windbreak netting (see p.605) or with a floating row cover (see p.576). If the seeds are well spaced, disease should not be a problem and the seedlings may be grown on in situ for 12 months before being pricked out. Water the seedlings as necessary and check them regularly in case treatment is needed for pests such as aphids (p.639) and spider mites (p.640).

Layering

Layering may be used to propagate hybrids and cultivars as well as species. This method of propagation occurs naturally in some plants, when a low-growing stem roots itself in the ground; once this happens, the stem may be removed from the parent plant and grown on. Air layering, where the shoot remains above ground, may be used for trees without low-growing stems.

The advantage of layering is that the layered stem needs very little attention while the roots become established. It is a slow method, however, because in order to obtain

SIMPLE LAYERING

Cut a 2in (5cm) tongue 12–18in (30–45cm) behind the tip of a vigorous shoot, or remove a narrow ring of bark at this point. Brush the wound with hormone rooting powder and peg the shoot into a shallow hole. Tie the shoot to a supporting stake and backfill the hole.

Vigorous shoot

Friable soil

Peg

Tongue

suitable material the plant must be prepared a year in advance, and the layered stem may take a year or more to root.

Simple layering
In this method, a shoot is pegged down into the ground until it has rooted and is then cut off from the parent plant (see also Propagating a Shrub by Simple Layering, p.114).

Prepare the parent plant a year before layering is to take place. In late winter or early spring, prune a low branch to stimulate new, young shoots that will root easily. In early spring the following year, select a vigorous shoot and make a small wound 12–18in (30–45cm) from the tip. Brush this with hormone rooting powder to encourage rooting. Add plenty of leaf mold or similar organic matter and sharp grit to the soil where the shoot touches it and peg the shoot down into a shallow hole, tying it to a vertical stake.

Backfill the hole and firm the soil well, leaving the shoot tip exposed, then water thoroughly and, if necessary, protect the shoot from rabbits and other animals with wire netting. About 12 months later, check to see whether the shoot has rooted. If it has, sever it from the parent and either plant it in open ground or pot it up; if it has not rooted, leave it in place and check a month later.

Air layering
The principle of air layering is the same as simple layering, except that the layered shoot roots above the ground rather than in it (see also *Air Layering a Shrub*, p.115). In spring, select a strong stem that has ripened in the previous year, and remove any leaves 12–18in (30–45cm) behind the growing tip. Prepare the stem either by cutting a tongue 2in (5cm) long in the bark, 9–12in (22–30cm) behind its tip, or by removing a ¼–⅜in (6–8mm) wide ring of bark from the stem at this point. In either case, brush the wound with hormone rooting powder.

Surround the cut stem with a moist rooting medium and seal it in. To do this, first make a plastic sleeve by cutting off the sealed end of a plastic bag, then slide it along the stem until it surrounds the cut, and secure the lower end with string. Moisten some well-aerated rooting medium (such as sphagnum moss or a mix of equal parts of peat and perlite), then use it to wedge open the tongue. Add more medium around the stem inside the sleeve and seal the top.

If the layer has rooted by the next spring, carefully sever the stem from the parent plant, remove the sleeve, and pot up; if the layer has not rooted, however, it should be left in place for another year.

TREE SEED BENEFITING FROM STRATIFICATION
Acer (some)
Aesculus
Betula
Carya
Celtis
Fagus
Sorbus

TREES THAT MAY BE LAYERED
Simple layering
Cercidiphyllum
Chionanthus retusus
Corylus
Davidia
Dipteronia
Eucryphia
Halesia
Hoheria lyallii
Laurus
Magnolia campbellii,

M. grandiflora

Magnolia hypoleuca

Air layering
Ficus
Magnolia campbellii,
M. grandiflora

Grafting

Grafted plants, unlike cuttings, have the benefit of a developed root system so they establish relatively quickly. Part of a stem (the scion), taken from the plant to be propagated, is joined to a compatible rootstock of another plant, usually of the same genus. In some cases, the rootstock may confer a desirable characteristic, such as a particular growth habit or high resistance to disease, on the resulting plant.

Grafting methods include side-veneer, chip-budding, apical-wedge, whip-and-tongue, and basal-whip (or splice). For details of basal-whip and whip-and-tongue grafting, see PRINCIPLES OF PROPAGATION, p.630. Check that the rootstocks and scions are compatible; if necessary, seek advice from a specialty nursery.

Side-veneer grafting

This is the most common grafting technique for ornamental trees; a one-year-old stem is used for the scion and is grafted onto the side of the prepared rootstock. It is usually carried out just before leaf break, in mid- to late winter, although for maples (*Acer*) summer grafting is sometimes more successful.

Prepare the rootstocks a year in advance by potting up one- or two-year-old seedlings in the fall and establishing them in an open frame. About three weeks before grafting, bring them into a cool greenhouse to force them gently into growth. Keep the rootstocks dry, particularly those from trees that bleed sap, such as birches (*Betula*) and conifers, since excessive sap may prevent successful union with the scions.

For the scions, collect strong, one-year-old stems from the tree to be propagated; the diameter should be similar to that of the rootstock stems, if possible. Trim scions down to 6–10in (15–25cm), cutting just above a bud or pair of buds, and place them in a plastic bag in a refrigerator until ready to graft. Either cut back the top-growth of the rootstocks to about 2–3in (5–7cm) or leave some top-growth above the graft and cut this back in stages later (see "Aftercare," opposite).

Prepare the rootstocks and scions, one pair at a time, with compatible cuts. It is important to unite the rootstock and scion immediately; even slight drying out is likely to impede successful union. If the scion is narrower than the rootstock, align one edge to make sure that at

TREES THAT MAY BE GRAFTED

Chip-budding
Crataegus
Laburnum
Magnolia
Malus
Prunus
Pyrus
Sorbus

Aesculus indica 'Sydney Pearce'

Apical-wedge
Aesculus
Catalpa
Cercis
Fagus

Side-veneer
Abies
Acer
Betula
Carpinus
Cedrus
Cupressus
Fagus
Fraxinus
Ginkgo
Gleditsia
Larix
Magnolia
Picea
Pinus
Prunus
Robinia
Sorbus

Robinia pseudoacacia 'Frisia'

Whip-and-tongue
Fraxinus
Gleditsia
Robinia

PROPAGATING TREES BY SIDE-VENEER GRAFTING

1 Trim the scion to a length of 6–10in (15–25cm), cutting just above a bud or pair of buds. Place it in a plastic bag and refrigerate until ready to graft.

2 Using a sharp knife, make a short, downward, inward nick about 1in (2.5cm) from the top of the rootstock.

3 Starting near the top of the rootstock, make a sloping, slightly inward cut down to the inner point of the first cut. Remove the sliver of wood.

4 Make the final cut on the rootstock by slicing straight up from the first cut below. This leaves a flat cut on one side of the rootstock (see inset).

5 Now prepare the scion: make a shallow, sloping cut about 1in (2.5cm) long down to the base; then make a short, angled cut at the base, on the opposite side (see inset).

Growth visible from buds

6 Fit the base of the scion into the cut in the rootstock (see inset). Starting at the top, wrap a length of grafting tape around the union to secure it.

7 Brush grafting wax over the external cut surfaces on both the rootstock and the scion. In addition, wax the top of the scion if it has been trimmed back.

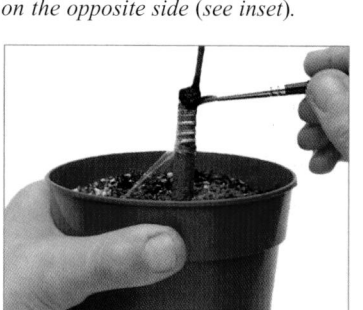

8 A few weeks later, if the graft has taken, the buds of the scion will show signs of growth. Remove any suckers that may have appeared on the rootstock or they will divert growth away from the scion.

least one side of the cambium layer unites. Tie the scion in position with clear plastic, grafting tape, raffia, or a rubberized strip, then wax over all external cut surfaces to reduce moisture loss. For aftercare, see right.

Chip-budding

Used mainly for fruit trees, this is also a good way to propagate plants of the Rosaceae family, for example crabapples (*Malus*). In this method, the scion includes a single bud from which the new growth develops, and the grafted plant remains outdoors rather than being potted up.

During fall, establish one- or two-year-old seedlings or hardwood cuttings in open ground for the rootstocks. In midsummer, remove any lateral branches from the bottom

18in (45cm) of the stem. For the scions (or budsticks), select vegetative (nonflowering) shoots that are of similar diameters to those of the rootstocks from well-ripened, current season's growth.

The rootstocks and budsticks are then prepared and united (see below). If successful, the graft should take within a few weeks; the tape or tie may then be removed, and the bud should start to swell. For aftercare, see right.

Apical-wedge grafting

This grafting method is similar to side-veneer grafting, except that the scion is placed directly on top of the rootstock. In late winter, collect some stems of the previous season's growth from the plant to be propagated, and heel them into the ground.

In late winter or early spring, lift and wash one-year-old seedlings or vigorous plants for the rootstocks, then cut them back to 2in (5cm) above the roots. Make a vertical cut 1–1¼in (2.5–3cm) down the center of each rootstock. Cut the base of each scion into a wedge, and insert them into the tops of the rootstocks; leave the top of the cut on the scion exposed. Bind and pot up the grafted plants, then follow the aftercare guidance given below (see also ORNAMENTAL SHRUBS, "Apical-wedge grafting," p.117).

Aftercare

Deciduous trees should be kept in the greenhouse at 50°F (10°C), while conifers, broad-leaved evergreens, and summer-grafted trees should be kept in an enclosed, humid

environment at 59°F (15°C). The graft should take in a few weeks, and new growth will be seen on the scion. Pinch off any suckers appearing below the union, since these are growing from the rootstock. After six to ten weeks, harden off the grafted plants. If not, cut back at grafting, reduce top-growth of the rootstock to within 4in (10cm) of the union.

Tie the growing bud to the remaining top of the rootstock to make sure that the new shoot grows straight. In midsummer, cut back the rootstock to just above the union and tie in the new shoot to a supporting stake. Alternatively, the rootstock may be cut back to just above the union in late spring. Once they are beginning to grow vigorously, pot on the grafted trees or transplant them into open ground.

PROPAGATING TREES BY CHIP-BUDDING

1 *Select and cut the budstick (here Malus), choosing a long, vigorous shoot of the current season's ripened wood. It should have well-developed buds and be roughly the thickness of a pencil.*

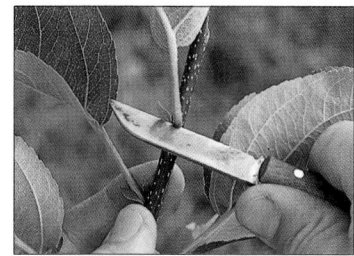

2 *Cut off the soft wood and strip away any leaves at the tip of the shoot.*

3 *Using a sharp knife, make the first cut ¾in (2cm) below a healthy bud, inserting the blade about ¼in (5mm) deep at an angle of approximately 45°.*

4 *Start making a second cut about 1½in (4cm) above the first. Cut down through the wood to meet the first cut, taking care not to damage the bud.*

5 *Remove the budchip, holding it by the bud between finger and thumb to keep the cambium layer clean. Place it in a clean plastic bag to prevent it from drying out.*

6 *To prepare the rootstock, cut off all the shoots and leaves from the bottom 12in (30cm) of the stem; it is easiest to do this while standing astride the stock.*

7 *Make two cuts in the rootstock to correspond with those on the budchip so that the stock can be united with the chip. Remove the resulting sliver of wood, taking care not to touch the stem's cut surface (see inset).*

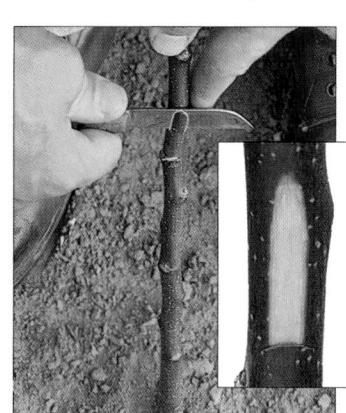

8 *Place the budchip into the lip of the cut rootstock, so that the cambium layers of the chip and stock match as closely as possible (see inset). Bind the join tightly with grafting tape. If the graft takes, the bud will start to swell and develop; the tape can then be removed.*

9 *Next spring, cut back the stock just above the union; the bud will develop as the leader.*

Hedges and screens

HEDGES and screens, both formal and informal, can play an important role in the structure and character of a garden as well as having a variety of practical uses.

Practical uses

Most hedges, whether informal, open hedges or formal, solid, clipped ones, are planted for utilitarian purposes: to delineate boundaries, to provide shelter and shade, and to screen the garden or yard. It is possible, however, to combine use with beauty.

Living barriers
As living barriers, hedges may take some years to establish but, if properly maintained, they are often preferable to fences because they provide changing textures, colors, and shapes. Most plants used for hedging are long-lived; if correctly maintained, they will provide dense and sometimes virtually impenetrable barriers for many years.

Shelter
Hedges make excellent windbreaks, filtering fast-moving air and reducing the impact caused by turbulence when wind hits a solid object such as a wall or fence. The porosity of a hedge varies between species and times of year; a close-clipped, evergreen yew hedge (*Taxus*) will be considerably less porous than a deciduous beech hedge (*Fagus sylvatica*) during winter. At the ideal of 50 percent porosity, it has been calculated that with a 5ft (1.5m) hedge, wind speed is reduced by 50

percent at a distance of 24ft (7.5m) from the hedge; by 25 percent at a distance of 50ft (15m); and by 10 percent at a distance of 100ft (30m). The shelter provided by hedges is invaluable, particularly in windswept gardens, where even hardy plants may suffer damage as a result of heavy storms and strong winds.

Noise barriers
Hedges may contribute to noise reduction by screening out unwelcome sounds. One of the most efficient types is a green "environmental barrier." A horizontal weave of pussy willow (*Salix caprea*) is threaded through two rows of vertical stakes and the core is packed with soil to form a solid wall. The willow roots into the soil core, and the top and side growth are pruned back to the woven wall at regular intervals.

Ornamental hedges

A wealth of plants of diverse shape, size, texture, and color can be used for hedges, deciduous or evergreen, formal or informal, or with flowers and fruit. Mixing two or more species selected for flower and foliage creates a living mosaic.

Formal
Arborvitae (*Thuja*) makes an excellent hedge, provided that four to six years are allowed for establishment. A hedge of x *Cupressocyparis leylandii* grows extremely rapidly and needs to be clipped at least twice

a year to keep it neat and within bounds. Low formal hedges are frequently seen in parterres as well as knot gardens. Various forms of boxwood (*Buxus sempervirens*), especially 'Suffruticosa', are commonly used, as are *Santolina* and

YEAR-ROUND COLOR
x Cupressocyparis leylandii *cultivars produce contrasting shades of foliage in a mixed conifer hedge.*

PLANTS FOR INFORMAL HEDGES

Pyracantha 'Golden Charmer'

Hibiscus syriacus 'Red Heart'

Escallonia 'Langleyensis'

Ilex aquifolium 'Madame Briot'

Rosa 'Roseraie de l'Haÿ'

Forsythia ovata 'Ottawa'

FORMAL, CLIPPED HEDGES

HEDGING PLANTS	PLANTING DISTANCE	APPROPRIATE HEIGHT	CLIPPING TIMES	RESPONDS TO RENOVATION
EVERGREEN				
Buxus sempervirens (boxwood)	12in (30cm)	1–2ft (30–60cm)	Twice/3 times, in growing season	Yes
Chamaecyparis lawsoniana (Lawson cypress) – most cultivars except dwarf types	24in (60cm)	4–8ft (1.2–2.5m), but may be larger	Twice, in spring and early fall	No
x *Cupressocyparis leylandii* (Leyland cypress)	30in (75cm)	6–12ft (2–4m), but up to 20ft (6m)	Twice/3 times, in growing season	No
Ilex aquifolium (holly) and cultivars	18in (45cm)	6–12ft (2–4m)	In late summer	Yes
Lavandula (lavender)	12in (30cm)	18–36in (45–90cm)	In spring and after flowering	No
Ligustrum (privet)	12in (30cm)	5–10ft (1.5–3m)	Twice/3 times, in growing season	Yes
Lonicera nitida	12in (30cm)	3–4ft (1–1.2m)	Twice/3 times, in growing season	Yes
Pinus strobus (white pine)	30in (75cm)	6–12ft (2–4m), but up to 20ft (6m)	Once as candles extend	No
Taxus x *media* (yew)	24in (60cm)	4–12ft (1.2–4m), but up to 20ft (6m)	Twice/3 times in summer and fall	Yes
Thuja (arborvitae)	24in (60cm)	5–10ft (1.5–3m)	In spring and early fall	No
DECIDUOUS				
Caragana aurantiaca	18in (45cm)	2–4ft (60cm–1.2m)	Once, in summer	Yes
Carpinus betulus (hornbeam)	18–24in (45–60cm)	5–20ft (1.5–6m)	Once, in mid- to late summer	Yes
Crataegus monogyna (hawthorn)	12–18in (30–45cm)	5–10ft (1.5–3m)	Twice, in summer and fall	Yes
Fagus sylvatica (beech)	12–24in (30–60cm)	4–20ft (1.2–6m)	Once, in late summer	Yes

Lonicera nitida. Tapestry or mosaic hedges combine a number of compatible plants within the same hedge line to provide changing visual impact throughout the year. Useful species include *Taxus* x *media, Ilex aquifolium, Carpinus betulus,* and *Fagus sylvatica.*

Mixing evergreen and deciduous species provides an interesting and colorful background throughout the year. Species used must have similar rates of growth if overvigorous species are not to dominate.

Informal

Informal hedges combine practical and ornamental qualities. Although not suitable for strictly formal designs, they can be very decorative and still provide useful screening and shelter. Many of the plants used in these informal boundaries produce flowers and fruit, or both, contributing form and color to the garden.

Integrate the different color backgrounds carefully into the overall design. *Berberis julianae, Chaenomeles speciosa,* or forsythia are often used; hybrid shrub roses and species also make fine informal hedges. Most strong-growing bamboos are suitable for areas where soil moisture is high and a wind filter is needed.

FORMAL ELEGANCE
The symmetrical use of dwarf hedges in shades of green frames the brick path and draws attention to the ornamental sculpture.

Choosing plants

Before selecting species for hedging, consider their eventual height, spread, and speed of development, and make sure that species chosen are hardy within the climatic zone and are suited to the soil type of the garden. Plants for formal hedges must have a dense habit of growth and be tolerant of close clipping. For informal hedges grown for their flowers or berries, choose plants that need pruning only once a year. The timing of pruning is critical; otherwise, the next season's display of flowers or fruit may be spoiled.

The choice of evergreens or deciduous species is partly a matter of taste, but bear in mind that evergreens and conifers provide a dense, windproof screen throughout the year, offering protection that may be critical in severe winters.

Soil preparation and planting

Hedges are a permanent feature of the garden. It is therefore important to prepare the site thoroughly before planting, and to top-dress each spring with a well-balanced fertilizer and mulch. Soil preparation and planting techniques are the same as for trees and shrubs (see pp.63–7 and pp.95–7). The width of ground preparation required will be between 24–36in (60–90cm).

Spacing for most hedging plants is 12–24in (30–60cm) – see the charts below. If a hedge 36in (90cm) thick or more is needed, plant a double, staggered row with spacing of 36in (90cm) between plants, and 18in (45cm) between rows. Plants for all dwarf hedges, parterres, and knot gardens should be spaced about 4–6in (10–15cm) apart.

Pruning and training

The initial training of a formal hedge is crucial to promote even growth from the base of the hedge to the top. Careful attention to pruning in the first two to three years is essential.

Early pruning and shaping

Most deciduous plants, especially those with a naturally bushy, low-branching habit, need to be cut back by one-third on planting, with strong laterals also cut back by one-third of their length. In the second winter, cut back again by about one-third.

INFORMAL AND FLOWERING HEDGES

HEDGING PLANT	ORNAMENTAL QUALITIES	PLANTING DISTANCE	APPROPRIATE HEIGHT	WHEN TO PRUNE
EVERGREEN				
Berberis julianae	Yellow flowers, blue-black fruits	24in (60cm)	5–7ft (1.5–2.2m)	In summer
Berberis verruculosa	Yellow flowers, blue-black fruits	18in (45cm)	2–3ft (0.6–1m)	In summer
Escallonia	White, red, or pink flowers	18in (45cm)	4–8ft (1.2–2.5m)	Immediately after flowering
Garrya elliptica	Gray, green, red, or yellow catkins	18in (45cm)	5–7ft (1.5–2.2m)	Immediately after flowering
Ilex aquifolium	White flowers, berries	18–24in (45–60cm)	6–20ft (2–6m)	In late summer
Lavandula	Purple flowers, gray foliage	12in (30cm)	2–3ft (0.6–1m)	After flowering
Pyracantha	White flowers, red berries	24in (60cm)	6–10ft (2–3m)	For pruning, see p.107
DECIDUOUS				
Chaenomeles speciosa	White, pink, red flowers	24in (60cm)	8ft (2.5m)	Immediately after flowering
Crataegus monogyna	Fragrant white flowers, red berries	18–24in (45–60cm)	10ft+ (3m+)	In winter, remove selected vigorous shoots
Euonymus alatus 'Compactus'	Pink to plum fall color	18in (45cm)	3–5ft (1–1.5m)	Remove older shoots occasionally in spring
Forsythia ovata 'Ottawa'	Yellow flowers	18in (45cm)	5–7ft (1.5–2.2m)	After flowering, remove old stems
Hibiscus syriacus	White, pink, blue flowers	18in (45cm)	5–7ft (1.5–2.2m)	In spring
Potentilla fruticosa	Bright yellow flowers	12–18in (30–45cm)	2–4ft (0.6–1.2m)	In spring
Prunus tomentosa	White flowers, edible red fruit	18in (45cm)	5ft (1.5m)	In winter, remove selected vigorous shoots
Rosa 'Champlain'	Bright red flowers all summer	18in (45cm)	2ft (0.6m)	In spring
Rosa 'Roseraie de l'Haÿ'	Fragrant crimson flowers	18in (45cm)	5ft (1.5m)	In spring, remove thin twigs
Spiraea x *bumalda* 'Goldflame'	New foliage is red, turning yellow, then green	12–18in (30–45cm)	3ft (1m)	Very occasionally in spring

PLANTING IN SINGLE AND DOUBLE ROWS

SINGLE PLANTING
Hedging plants are usually planted in a single row about 12–24in (30–60cm) apart.

DOUBLE PLANTING
For a denser, wider hedge space the plants 36in (90cm) apart in a double, staggered row.

FORMATIVE PRUNING

BEFORE PRUNING
*Leaders and laterals have grown unrestricted; the hedge (*Lonicera nitida*) needs formative pruning.*

AFTER PRUNING
Cut back the laterals by half and prune the leaders to the required height to encourage bushy growth. Water, fertilize, and mulch.

HOW TO SHAPE A HEDGE

1 *Stretch a taut, level string between two upright posts to act as a guideline for the highest point of the hedge, then cut the top of the hedge along this line.*

2 *Cut a template of the shape required. Place the template on the hedge and cut following the line of the template, moving it along as you proceed, then cut the sides.*

3 *Once you reach the end of the hedge, remove the template, posts, and lines of string. Clip the end of the hedge neatly.*

To shape strong-growing plants and those with an upright habit of growth, such as privet (*Ligustrum*) and hawthorn (*Crataegus*), cut them back to within 6–12in (15–30cm) above ground level in late spring, followed by additional clipping back of laterals in late summer. During the second winter or early spring, cut back hard, removing at least half of the previous season's growth.

Even from this early stage the hedge sides should be cut at a more or less oblique angle (referred to as the slope), with the base as the widest point. Hedges with a flat-topped A shape or a gently curved,

pointed top are less vulnerable to snow and strong winds. Snow will quickly fall away down the sides of a tapered hedge; high winds or storms will be deflected by its sloping sides, causing minimal plant damage.

A level top is achieved by cutting to a straightedge or to a garden line stretched between stakes. It is important to use a guide when clipping low hedges, too, since discrepancies are just as likely to occur when looking down as when viewing the hedge from eye level. Once the size and slope have been achieved, clipping to keep the hedge in shape is all that is required in subsequent seasons.

Conifers and many evergreens are used extensively as hedges. In most cases, laterals only are pruned during the early years, particularly in the formative second year, allowing the apical shoot to grow to the desired height before trimming back.

Maintaining a hedge
A formal hedge needs to be clipped regularly to maintain its shape: in most cases the hedge should be

SHAPING HEDGES
Make hedges narrower at the top to deflect strong winds and snow. In heavy snowfall areas, hedges should have pointed tops to prevent snow from settling and causing damage.

HORNBEAM   YEW

trimmed twice annually, in spring and late summer (see *Formal, Clipped Hedges*, p.82). Most formal hedges are cut with shears or an electric trimmer. Use a straightedge or a garden line as a guide when trimming the hedge to shape.

Informal hedges also need regular pruning to shape. Remove misplaced growths, and cut back within the required bounds. Flowering or fruiting hedges must be pruned only at the appropriate season (see *Informal and Flowering Hedges*, p.83). Informal hedges and those with large evergreen leaves should, where practical, be trimmed with pruners to avoid unsightly damage to the leaves.

Renovation
A number of hedging species, notably hornbeam (*Carpinus*), honeysuckle (*Lonicera*), and yew (*Taxus*), respond well to renovation even where hedges have been neglected and have become overgrown. For best results, deciduous hedges should be renovated in winter and evergreen ones in midspring.

If drastic pruning is required, alternate sides should be cut back in subsequent seasons. If the renovation is to be successful, it is important to fertilize and mulch the plants in the season before pruning, and then again after cutting back to encourage healthy new growth.

TRIMMING HEDGES

TRIMMING WITH SHEARS
To make sure that the top of the hedge is cut level and flat, keep the blades of the shears parallel to the line of the hedge at all times.

CUTTING WITH HEDGE TRIMMERS
When using an electric trimmer, keep the blade parallel to the hedge and use a wide, sweeping action.

HOW TO RENOVATE AN OVERGROWN HEDGE

Cut back growth to the main stems on only one side of a neglected, deciduous hedge, trimming the other side as usual (right). A year later, if growth has been vigorous, cut back growth on the other side to the main stems (far right).

Willow walls

WEAVING with willow (*Salix*) stems has a long and distinguished history. Woven barriers have been used for fencing since prehistoric times, and, when coated with thick layers of mud, clay, and dung, were a major building material in many parts of the world: wattle and daub.

Living willow, used as sculpture, is a new form of horticultural art. The contrast between the lines of the stems and exuberant, fresh young growth gives even functional items such as seats, screens, arbors, and arches an inherent sculptural quality, which many gardeners are becoming eager to incorporate into their own personal landscapes.

Suitable choices

The species or cultivar of willow must be matched to the size and nature of the proposed living structure. Vigor, physical strength, and aesthetic qualities are the main considerations. Most willows are flexible enough for weaving, with the exception of the brittle *Salix fragilis*. Cultivars of *S. alba* are especially suitable, since their brightly colored stems look spectacular in winter.

Preparation

Planting and weaving should be carried out in winter, when the plants are dormant. Willow can be inserted as normal hardwood cuttings of the current year's growth, about 15in (38cm) long and set 12in (30cm) deep, which are then allowed to grow on site, or as long rods that can be woven together immediately. Rods can establish just as successfully as cuttings provided the ground is well prepared, they are freshly cut, and they are kept well watered. Another option is to use multistemmed plants, which are easy to develop from nursery-grown stock, pruned hard to encourage the growth of two or more stems.

Plan the shape and height of the screen; it can follow a straight or curved baseline. Mark out the outline before planting, bearing in mind that willows need bright light to thrive.

Work out how many rods of what length will be needed. Rods should be planted at least 6in (15cm) apart and should be more widely spaced for tall screens using more vigorous cultivars. At 6in (15cm) apart, a 40ft (12m) screen would need 80 rods.

Weaving and tying

Once a row of evenly spaced rods has been planted, weaving can begin so an attractive diamond pattern is created. It is best to try to weave to the desired height in one go to keep the main lines straight. New shoots can be used to continue the structure upward but will not follow the original

rods exactly. The weaving itself will hold the stems together to some extent, but crossing points should be tied firmly with twine. For simple screens, tie only every third or fourth crossing point.

The twine will biodegrade over about two years, but grafts may form more quickly than this. Check the tied crossing points regularly and, if the stems have united, remove the tie.

Where long rods have been planted, remove sideshoots as they appear, so growth is restricted to the stem tips. This will encourage extension growth and the formation of the pressure grafts. Once the stems have united, allow sideshoots to develop and use them to fill in as required, again weaving them over and under the main stems. When structures are established, trim back or weave in new shoots regularly.

Weaving horizontal and vertical stems to form a screen of squares is more difficult. Horizontal living stems cannot be established initially, because they would need to be bent through 90 degrees. Dead stems can be woven in as horizontals until the verticals produce sideshoots which can take their place, but the screen will take longer to establish. Training shoots horizontally also lowers their sap flow and reduces vigor.

More complex structures

The other main weaving technique, which is used to form arches and tunnels, is to bend and twist the stems around each other. The twisted stems need to be tied to hold them together. Extra stability is also provided by planting large rods deeper than 12in (30cm); this does not affect their ability to root successfully.

REGULAR MAINTENANCE
Although different willow cultivars vary in vigor, all living willow structures need pruning every winter and new shoots woven in. In summer shoots should be trimmed but weaving should be avoided, because soft, new shoots are easily broken.

HOW TO SHAPE A LIVING WILLOW WALL

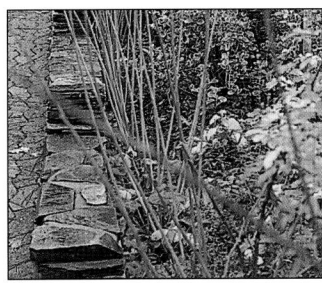

1 *Plant a row of evenly spaced rods. Then weave together by angling them at 45 degrees from the vertical and alternately crisscrossing over and under each rod.*

2 *Tie the crossing points securely with twine. This will force the stems together as they expand and so unite their cambium layers, forming pressure grafts to hold the structure.*

3 *At the top of a screen, join the last row of crossing points with rubber plant ties. These allow the rods to move slightly in the wind and prevent their tops from breaking.*

LIVING TRELLIS
Screens of living willow make excellent garden sculptures. They have even been employed on a scale large enough to shield English villages from the sights and sounds of heavy traffic.

CHAPTER

3

ORNAMENTAL SHRUBS

VALUED BY GARDENERS for their architectural quality and long-term interest, shrubs are unequaled for forming the skeleton of a planting design. In a mixed border, they provide welcome solidity and substance, balancing the more transitory pleasures of herbaceous plants. Grouping evergreen and deciduous shrubs together allows you to create an attractive year-round display that is also relatively low in maintenance. As well as a diversity of shapes and forms, shrubs possess a magnificent variety of features: from the glossy, exotic leaves of *Fatsia japonica* or the heavily perfumed plumes of lilac to the beadlike berries of pyracanthas or the spectral white stems of *Rubus biflorus*, there is a shrub to fit every size of garden in every location and climate.

Designing with shrubs

SHRUBS are woody-stemmed plants that typically produce a framework of branches from the base, unlike the single trunk characteristic of most trees. The division between shrubs and trees is not a rigid one, however, because some shrubs (such as fuchsias) can be trained as standards with a single trunk, and a number of trees are multistemmed. Similarly, the difference in scale is not a clear one, since some shrubs grow larger than some trees.

Whether the term "shrub" is used very strictly or more loosely, it covers an enormous choice of plants suitable for gardens of any size and style. Species have been collected from many parts of the world, and these have given rise to numerous cultivars and hybrids of ornamental value.

Choosing shrubs

Shrubs are invaluable in the garden for many reasons. Perhaps most important of all, they impart shape, structure, and substance to a design and provide a framework. They are far from being purely functional keystones, however. They are also endowed with a variety of ornamental qualities, including fragrant and colorful flowers, evergreen or variegated foliage, attractive fruits, and colored or shapely stems.

These decorative attributes exert great influence on your choice of plants. There are, however, important practical considerations to take into account when deciding which shrubs to grow.

INFORMAL PLANTING
A grouping of shrubs, including yellow-variegated English holly (Ilex aquifolium)*, fiery* Euonymus alatus*, and tall* Aesculus parviflora*, provide an ever-changing display of contrasting colors and shapes.*

Compatibility with the given or adapted growing conditions is essential (see "Suiting plants to site conditions," p.89), while a shrub's growth rate, habit, and eventual height and spread also determine whether it is suitable for a garden or not and where it is best sited.

Form and size
Shrubs range in size from dwarfs, such as the mat-forming *Penstemon newberryi* at only 6–8in (15–20cm) high, that are suitable for the rock garden, to much more substantial plants that are 15–20ft (5–6m) in height, such as some of the handsome evergreen rhododendrons.

Shrubs have many different forms and habits, including rounded, arching, and vertical. Some – for example *Yucca glauca*, with its explosive spray of swordlike leaves and erect panicles of flowers – are worth growing for their form alone. Others, such as *Chaenomeles japonica*, have a sprawling habit that often looks better if wall-trained.

Shrubs as design features

When selecting shrubs, consider how they will associate with the other planting as well as any structural elements nearby, such as the house or patio. If they are to form part of the design framework, shrubs with distinctive, sculptural silhouettes are usually most suitable – for example the spreading, wavelike form of *Juniperus squamata* 'Blue Carpet' or the bold, upright mass of *Mahonia bealei*. Think of them as abstract shapes that may be used singly or in combination to create a balanced planting of contrasting and complementary forms.

Foundation planting
Shrubs are often used as foundation planting to link the house with the garden, forming a transition between the rigid lines of the building and the softer shapes and textures of border plants and lawn.

This type of planting is effective when used to mark the entrance to the house. For example, symmetrical groups or rows of shrubs could flank the driveway or the door, or an informal curved bed might border a winding path to the door.

Design the planting so that it complements the style, color, and scale of the building. Evergreen shrubs are often chosen because of their continuous display but, especially in an informal setting, including deciduous plants as well creates a greater variety of interest while still providing mass and structure.

Suiting plants to site conditions

To make sure that shrubs flourish and give pleasure for a long time, it is essential to invest in plants that are suited to the particular conditions of your garden. Even within a small garden, these growing conditions often vary considerably. Since there are so many shrubs from which to make a selection, there is no need to grow plants that are unsuitable for the chosen site.

Soil types

The character of the soil should be the first consideration; in many cases, it can be improved to widen the range of plants that can be grown satisfactorily. It is particularly important to make heavy soils more open and free-draining and light soils more moisture-retentive, as well as to moderate any excessive acidity or alkalinity that may be a problem.

Successful planting must take into account the soil's underlying character, however. Even for relatively extreme conditions, there are a number of plants from which to choose: dogwoods (*Cornus*) and

willows (*Salix*) like moist soils, while broom (*Cytisus/Genista*), lavender (*Lavandula*), and *Phlomis* thrive on well-drained soils. Rhododendrons and other ericaceous plants generally require acidic conditions, but many shrubs do well on alkaline soils, including *Deutzia*, *Hypericum*, and *Philadelphus*.

Exposure and microclimate

A plant's preference for sun or shade should also be borne in mind. Sun-lovers such as *Cistus* will become drawn and straggly if not planted in full sun, but many shrubs tolerate or even prefer some shade. Shade-loving shrubs are often ideal for city gardens, where instead of dappled light filtering through the tree canopy there tend to be sharp contrasts between full sun and deep shade cast by surrounding buildings.

The hardiness of shrubs is another factor to consider. The temperature range, altitude, degree of shelter, exposure, and length of growing season all affect the range that may be grown. The ocean has a moderating influence on temperature, but salt-laden winds can damage many plants in gardens near the coast. There are, however, shrubs (such as most

GROWING PLANTS IN THE RIGHT CONDITIONS
Light shade from the tree canopy and acidic soil are ideal for these impressive banks of rhododendrons lining an informal grass path. Contrasting shades have been boldly mixed to create a spectacular avenue of color.

Escallonia and *Genista*) that benefit from the milder conditions and tolerate salt spray. Plants of borderline hardiness for the area that might well succumb if grown in the open garden are more likely to thrive as wall-trained specimens in a sheltered position.

Successional interest

When selecting shrubs, take account of the seasonal interest that they provide and whether it is continuous, as from evergreen foliage, or transitory, as from a burst of summer blooms. A shrub with a brief period of splendor is often best sited near one that reaches its peak shortly afterward to create a changing but unbroken display.

Spring

Shrubs bearing spring flowers in addition to their newly emerging leaves are valued for the color and vitality that they bring early in the year. Combine them to provide interest throughout the season – from the early *Salix melanostachys*, with its black catkins borne on dark red twigs, to *Jasminum nudiflorum*, treasured for its cheerful yellow flowers on arching, slender green stems, to the fragrant white and pink flower clusters of *Daphne* x *burkwoodii* 'Somerset' in late spring.

Summer

The choice of summer-flowering shrubs is immense and, again, they are best combined to form a continuous display. Invaluable shrubs such as *Potentilla* 'Elizabeth' and *Syringa microphylla* 'Superba' deserve to be

widely grown, since their flowering period extends from spring until early fall. Cultivars of *Buddleja davidii*, if deadheaded routinely, will continue to bloom until frost.

Fall

This is the season when many deciduous shrubs really come to the fore, with colorful foliage providing an eye-catching spectacle. Shrubs for fall interest include *Euonymus alatus*, with its intense red leaves, and the various cultivars of *Cotinus coggygria*, with yellow, red, or purple foliage. Colorful berries, such as the orange clusters of *Pyracantha* 'Mohave', the shiny red fruits of *Cotoneaster divaricatus*, and the wide range of attractive fruit provided by *Viburnum* (especially *V. dilatatum* and its hybrids and cultivars), are very valuable, often lasting into winter and providing food for birds.

Winter

Shrubs are vital elements in the winter garden, with a rich variety of features. Evergreen foliage probably makes the greatest contribution, providing bold masses of color and texture. Flowers also play their part, with a choice ranging from the sculptural *Mahonia japonica*, with its spreading yellow sprays, to the spiderlike red flowers of *Hamamelis* x *intermedia* 'Diane'. Other fragrant shrubs such as *Viburnum* x *bodnantense* are equally welcome. Less common are shrubs with ornamental stems such as *Cornus stolonifera* 'Flaviramea', which has vivid lime green shoots, and *C. sanguinea*. 'Winter Flame', with yellow stems appropriately grading into orange and tipped with red.

RECOMMENDED SHRUBS FOR ACIDIC SOIL

***Rhododendron* 'Homebush'**

***Camellia* x *williamsii* 'Donation'**

***Erica* x *williamsii* 'P.D. Williams'**

Eucryphia milliganii

Gaultheria shallon

Vaccinium parvifolium

Rhododendron wardii

***Pernettya mucronata* 'Wintertime'**

Zenobia pulverulenta

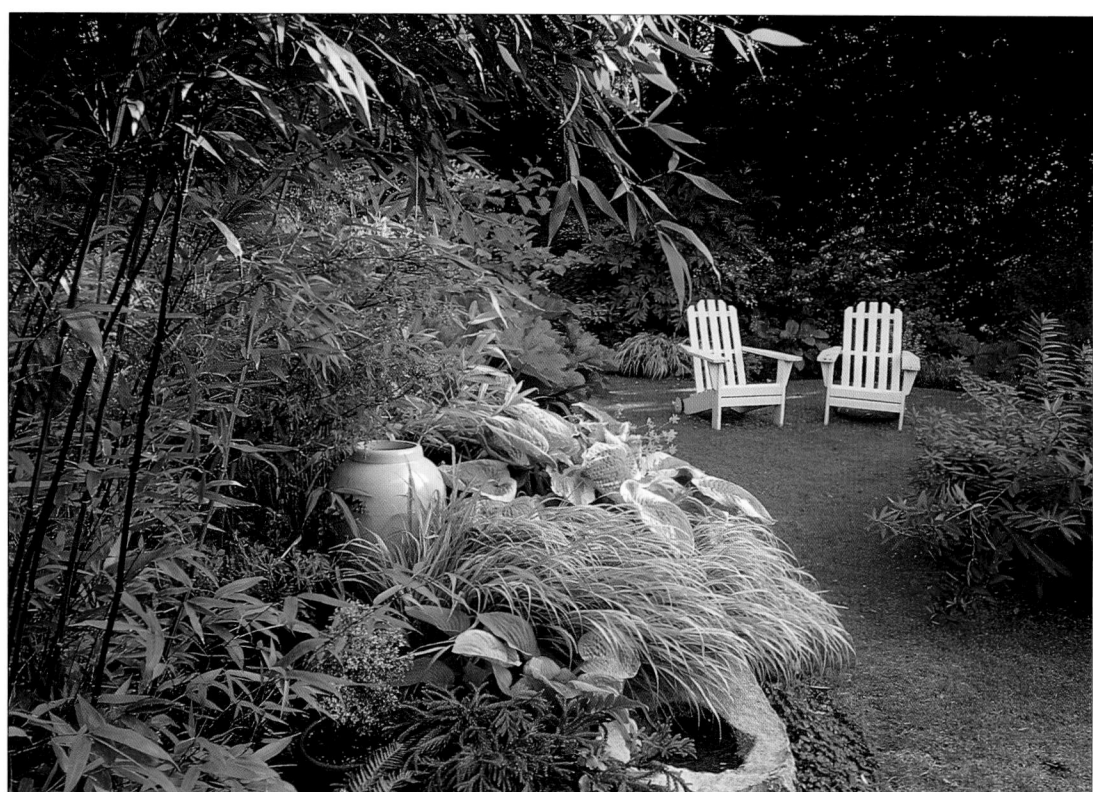

COOLING GREENS
Bamboos help create a softly textured partition around this quiet garden "sitting room." The wide variety of leaf color and size of these evergreens provide invaluable sources of plant shape and height and fit with many types of landscape and climate.

Shrub borders

One of the most satisfactory ways of using shrubs in the garden is to grow them in a border on their own. From the large range available that will suit the soil, climate, and site, a selection may be made that will give a succession of flowers, foliage, fruits, and other attributes throughout the year. The aim is to create a balanced design, taking into account the shape, form, height, and spread of each shrub, as well as its ornamental qualities and any seasonal changes in its appearance.

The planting may rely almost entirely on a blend of foliage textures and colors, but other features may also play their part. Include shrubs with interesting shapes, for example, and others with colorful berries or stems to maintain interest throughout the year. Resist the temptation to rely on flowers, since their display may be impressive but transitory. By care-ful selection, however, it is possible to sustain a long succession of flowers in the shrub border.

Some shrubs may be regarded as long-term plants, while others tend to mature and fade quickly. When planning a border, space out the long-term shrubs so that they will not need thinning or drastic pruning to keep them in check once mature. Fast-growing shrubs can also be included, but they should be thinned as soon as they threaten to crowd out the core planting of shrubs. Herbaceous perennials, annuals, and other plants may be interplanted initially, so that in the short term the shrub border might have the same components as a mixed border. Dense planting, including ground-covers, may help keep down weeds, although mulching is advisable to reduce weeds and water loss while the plants are becoming established.

Mixed borders

The idea of a mixed border is to combine a framework planting of shrubs with a variety of herbaceous plants to reap the benefits of both. Its main advantage is that the shrubs provide long-term, sometimes year-round, interest and a background to a succession of other plants. As the shrubs provide height and structure, there is less need to grow tall perennials that require staking than in a traditional herbaceous border.

The mixed border can be designed to suit various settings. If it is situated next to a wall, the planting may include a combination of wall-trained and other shrubs at the back as well as climbers. Other plants may be introduced in loosely shaped niches between shrubs in the foreground. In an island bed, shrubs are normally used to form an irregular core at the center, surrounded by other plants in clumps or drifts.

Managing a mixed border is sometimes more complex than managing a shrub border, because the various plants have different requirements. It is, however, one of the most attractive ways of bringing together the wide-ranging qualities of many different groups of plants.

Specimen shrubs

Shrubs that are particularly beautiful, perhaps because of their fine shape or a characteristic such as exquisite flowers or striking foliage, may be best planted as individual specimens, sited so that they can be seen from a number of viewpoints.

Suitable shrubs

Since a shrub grown in this way clearly stands out in the garden, it is important that its appearance warrants its prominent position. Shrubs with very shapely silhouettes are especially suitable, such as the dense, symmetrical cone of *Picea*

RESTRICTED-COLOR BORDER
Here, a restricted color scheme with a predominance of yellow, gold, and bright green creates a sunny, cheerful feeling with evergreen and deciduous shrubs including elders (Sambucus), *golden conifers, and* Euphorbia.

glauca var. *albertiana* 'Conica'. A flowering shrub such as *Camellia japonica* 'Mathotiana' would also be an impressive focal point.

When selecting a plant to be grown as a specimen, its long-term interest is an important consideration. In a large garden, a relatively short but magnificent display may be sufficient. A shrub occupying a prime spot in a small garden, however, needs to justify itself by contributing color and form throughout the year or by having more than one season of interest – spring flowers and good fall foliage, or attractive summer fruit and flaky winter bark, for example.

Siting a specimen shrub

When deciding where to site a specimen shrub, make sure its size will be in keeping with its position in the garden and that it relates attractively to neighboring plants and to the overall design. Often the best location is as the focal point of a view from a main window of the house or at the meeting point of two vistas. The background is as important as the shrub itself; preferably, a uniform texture and color as provided by a dense, evergreen hedge or the green carpet of a lawn forms the most complementary foil. There is, however, opportunity for experimenting with the positioning of specimen shrubs, particularly in combination with other garden features, such as a pond that creates appealing reflections. Before planting, roughly assess the effect of the shrub's scale and position in the design by substituting stakes or a similar prop of the same or similar height and width.

SPECIMEN SHRUB
In late spring and early summer, the spreading tiers of Viburnum plicatum 'Mariesii' *are richly clothed with* blooms, but its unusual shape guarantees its value as a strong feature throughout the year.*

Wall shrubs

A border at the foot of a warm, sheltered wall is a prime site, although it often tends to be rather dry. If the plants are adequately watered, the conditions suit many shrubs that might otherwise be too tender.

Training shrubs against a wall is often the best option for lax types such as *Forsythia suspensa* that make tangled growth unless supported. For a number of shrubs, it is the best way of displaying their ornamental features, such as the orange or red berries of pyracanthas. Some shrubs that can also be grown free-standing, such as *Chaenomeles*, look very attractive when trained against a wall.

Sometimes no training is needed: shrubs such as myrtle (*Myrtus*) may simply be planted close to the foot of a wall for them to benefit from the warmth and shelter. Other shrubs such as *Buddleja crispa* do need training to flower well.

Dwarf and ground-cover shrubs

Planting low shrubs (such as many *Hebe* or *Daphne blagayana*) in raised beds or containers makes it easy to enjoy them at close quarters, as well as providing structure and long-term interest in the overall planting. On a large scale, use low-growing and spreading shrubs to balance contrasting rounded or upright forms in beds and borders.

These shrubs are also excellent where interest is needed at ground level; *Helianthemum* cultivars and a vast array of colorful heathers (*Calluna*, *Daboecia*, and *Erica*) brighten up the front of a mixed border or soften the sometime hard edges of a path.

Some spread into an attractive carpet that forms a fine foil for other planting. Those that are relatively fast-growing can be used as groundcovers (see p.99). Groundcover shrubs present one of the best solutions for sites such as steep banks that are difficult to cultivate. Even in the unpromising, shady areas directly beneath trees, shrubs such as *Mahonia repens* and cultivars of *Euonymus fortunei* grow well.

Foliage

The substance and seasonal continuity of a garden depend to a large extent on foliage. Evergreen shrubs, in particular, hold the garden together all through the year. The leaves of deciduous shrubs – from spring growth to fall leaf – also give a much longer period of interest than most flowers.

WALL-TRAINED SHRUBS
Growing a shrub such as this Pyracantha *against a wall enhances its display of highly ornamental berries.*

COLORFUL GROUNDCOVER
To create a colorful patchwork pattern, use harmonizing and contrasting low-growing shrubs. Here, massed heathers make an exciting display.

Color

Much may be made of foliage color, which includes not only every shade of green but also silvers and grays, reds, and purples, as well as yellow, gold, and variegated forms. The boldest leaf colors, such as the gold and red of *Spiraea japonica* 'Goldflame', the red of the young growth of some *Pieris*, or the white-splashed green of *Euonymus fortunei* 'Silver Queen', may be used in much the same way as flower color.

Shape and texture

There are many other attributes of shrub foliage that are worth exploiting in an ornamental display. Large or distinctively shaped leaves such as those of Japanese aralia (*Fatsia japonica*) are particularly striking, and changes of texture, from smooth and glossy to matte and felted, also provide satisfying contrasts.

Flowers

There is an impressive diversity of shrub flowers, ranging from the tiny, pealike flowers of many brooms (*Cytisus/Genista*) to the large, heavy panicles of lilacs (*Syringa*).

Color and form

Shrubs have flowers in every color, with endless variations of each: for example, shades of pink range from the pale pinkish white of *Syringa yunnanensis* to the crimson of *Rhododendron* 'Hinodegiri'.

Sometimes it is the sheer mass of flowers that appeals, as with the dense blue clusters of *Ceanothus* or the sprays of starlike yellow flowers of forsythias, while other shrubs, such as the exquisite but short-lived flowers of *Paeonia suffruticosa*, seduce by the sumptuous beauty of their individual blooms.

In a large garden it does not much matter that a plant's star turn is only brief, but in a small garden, this can

ORNAMENTAL STEMS
An informal group of redtwig dogwoods (Cornus alba) *forms a striking blaze of color rising from a spreading mass of variegated* Euonymus fortunei.

FLOWERS FOR SCENT
Fragrant shrubs are often best grown next to a path or patio so that their scent may be easily enjoyed. This sweetly perfumed Carpenteria californica (*with white flowers*) *also benefits from the warmth and shelter of the wall behind it.*

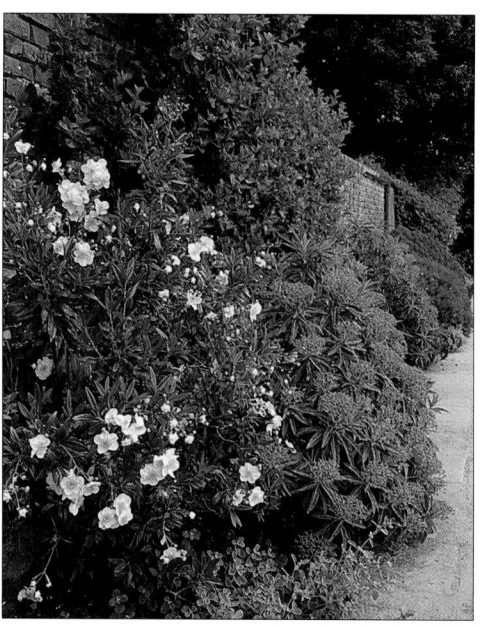

be a serious drawback. Consider a plant's form and foliage if its floral display is very short.

Scent

While the appeal of some flowers lies largely in their color and form, scented ones give the garden another dimension. The flowers may be showy and also deliciously fragrant, as are many mock oranges (*Philadelphus*), or, like the minute flowers of *Sarcococca*, more muted in appearance but casting their fragrance through the garden.

Berries

Berrying shrubs are valuable for continuing color from summer into winter, and also for attracting birds. On evergreens such as pyracanthas, bright berries framed by green foliage make an attractive contrast, while those on deciduous shrubs such as *Viburnum opulus* are seen against a changing backdrop of fall foliage and winter stems.

Orange and red berries are common, but there are other colors – from the yellow of *Viburnum dilatatum* 'Xanthocarpum' to the pink of *Pernettya mucronata* 'Seashell'.

Bear in mind that with some species of shrubs, male and female flowers are borne on separate plants. Satisfactory fruiting is possible only when male and female plants are grown near each other.

Bark and stems

In winter, the silhouettes of bare stems can be very striking. Some, in their sculptural simplicity, are strongly colored, such as dogwoods (*Cornus*), while others, for example *Salix irrorata*, are overlaid with an attractive glaucous bloom.

Group a few shrubs of the same type together to reap the benefit of their massed stems, or site a single fine specimen against a simple background. Imagine the brilliant red stems of *Cornus alba* 'Sibirica' offset by a plain white wall, or the chalky white skeleton of *Rubus biflorus* by a dark one.

The delicate tracery of fine stems is often overlooked unless it is highlighted by vivid coloring, but unusual shapes and heavily thorned or contorted shoots provide added interest. The bizarrely twisted stems of *Corylus avellana* 'Contorta' and *Salix* x *erythroflexuosa* make them interesting curiosities to set against a plain wall or plants of more familiar growth pattern.

Many shrubs grown for their stems require regular pruning, because it is the new wood that is most eye-catching (see "Coppicing and pollarding shrubs," p.105).

Shrubs in containers

Provided that they are watered regularly, many shrubs adapt happily to life in containers. Grown in this way, they make versatile as well as ornamental features. Use them as living sculptures to provide strong shapes and a framework to offset other planting. An evergreen shrub or dwarf conifer forms a year-round centerpiece in a pot or planter, which may be complemented by bulbs in spring and colorful, trailing annuals in summer.

A container-grown shrub is particularly valuable in a small paved garden. It can be used alone as an isolated specimen or combined with a changing display of other plants in containers. In a larger garden, a single, handsomely potted shrub can make a more striking focal point than a piece of statuary. Container-grown shrubs may introduce a formal note simply, such as a pair flanking a flight of steps or an archway, or, more elaborately, making a symmetrical framework or an avenue in grander designs.

Selecting plants

The most suitable shrubs are those with a long season of interest. Good examples for containers include evergreen camellias and rhododendrons, which remain attractive even after their flowers have faded. For a striking foliage display, consider the tender *Chamaerops humilis*, which has huge, palmlike, glossy fans, and conifers with their wide range of colors and textures.

Deciduous foliage can change from spring to fall and, in the case of Japanese maples (*Acer palmatum*), an intricate pattern of delicate stems remains when all the leaves have fallen. Shrubs such as *Spiraea japonica* 'Goldflame', with its strikingly colored leaves and rose pink flowers, often look particularly attractive growing in a complementary ornamental container.

Practical advantages

An advantage of growing shrubs in containers is that tender plants, such as *Nerium oleander* and palms, may be used to give the garden a Mediterranean or subtropical look in the summer, and then be moved to a protected site, such as a greenhouse, conservatory, or even a slightly heated shed, for winter. It is also an excellent way of including shrubs that would not otherwise tolerate the soil of the open garden. For example, given alkalinity-free water and acidic soil mix, camellias and rhododendrons can be grown in pots or other containers even in limestone areas.

Planter's guide to shrubs

EXPOSED SITES

Shrubs that tolerate exposed or windy sites; those marked ✿ are not suitable for coastal sites

Acer tataricum subsp. *ginnala*
Amorpha fruticosa
Arctostaphylos uva-ursi
Calluna vulgaris (and cvs)
Caragana
Cistus
Cornus stolonifera
Cotoneaster (dwarf spp.),
　C. horizontalis
Elaeagnus commutata
Erica carnea (and cvs)✿
Escallonia
Euonymus alatus
Euonymus fortunei
　(and cvs)
Fuchsia magellanica
　(and cvs)

*Fuchsia
magellanica*

Gaultheria shallon✿
Genista
Halimodendron
　halodendron
Hebe
Hippophäe rhamnoides
Ilex aquifolium
Lavatera
Myrica
Phormium
Potentilla
Prunus tomentosa
Pyracantha
Rhamnus alaternus
Rhododendron ponticum✿
Salix
Spartium
Spiraea
Tamarix
Ulex
Yucca

SHELTERED SITES

Shrubs that prefer sheltered sites

Abelia grandiflora
Abutilon
Acer palmatum (cvs)
Aucuba japonica
Buxus microphylla
Camellia
Citrus
Coprosma
Cornus florida
Datura
Dendromecon rigida
Euryops pectinatus
Musa basjoo
Pieris
Rhododendron maddenii (and
　subsection), R. vireya (sections)
Taxus
Vibernum plicatum

WALL SHRUBS

Abelia
Abutilon
Acacia dealbata
Azara
Buddleia crispa
Callistemon
Camellia
Ceanothus
Cestrum
Chaenomeles
Daphne bholua
Euonymus fortunei (and cvs)
Fremontodendron
Itea ilicifolia
Pyracantha
Solanum crispum 'Glasnevin',
　S. jasminoides

AIR POLLUTION

Shrubs that tolerate polluted air

Aucuba
Berberis
Buddleja davidii
Camellia japonica (and cvs)
Cornus stolonifera
Cotoneaster
Elaeagnus
Euonymus japonicus
Fatsia japonica
Fuchsia magellanica (and cvs)
Garrya
Ilex x altaclerensis, I. aquifolium
Ligustrum
Lonicera pileata
Magnolia grandiflora
Mahonia aquifolium
Philadelphus
Salix
Spiraea
Viburnum

DRY SHADE

Shrubs that tolerate dry shade

Aucuba
Cornus canadensis
Daphne laureola
Euonymus fortunei, E. japonicus
Fatsia japonica
Hedera
Ilex aquifolium
Pachysandra

MOIST SHADE

Shrubs that prefer moist shade

Aucuba
Buxus sempervirens
Camellia japonica
Cornus canadensis
Daphne laureola
Euonymus fortunei, E. japonicus
Fatsia japonica
Ilex aquifolium
Lonicera pileata

*Sarcococca
hookeriana
var. digyna*

*Mahonia
　aquifolium*
Osmanthus
Sarcococca
Skimmia
Vinca
Xanthorhiza simplicissima

TWO OR MORE SEASONS OF INTEREST

All year

Ardisia japonica
Elaeagnus x ebbingei 'Gilt Edge'
Euryops acraeus
Lavandula stoechas

Winter/Spring

Berberis temolaica
Corylus avellana 'Contorta'
Salix irrorata

Spring/Summer

Calycanthus occidentalis
Pieris 'Forest Flame'

Spring/Fall

Cornus 'Eddie's White Wonder'

Summer/Fall

Aesculus parviflora
Cornus mas 'Variegata'
Cotinus coggygria 'Flame'
Cotoneaster conspicuus
Hydrangea quercifolia
　'Snowflake'
Lonicera korolkowii
Myrtus communis
　var. tarentina
Pyracantha
Rosa 'Frau Dagmar Hartopp',
　R. moyesii 'Geranium'

*Myrtus
communis*

Fall/Winter

Arbutus unedo
Berberis temolaica
Cornus mas 'Variegata'

AROMATIC FOLIAGE

Calycanthus
Caryopteris
Perovskia
Santolina

FRAGRANT FLOWERS

Abeliophyllum distichum
Buddleia alternifolia
Camellia sasanqua
Choisya 'Aztec Pearl', C. ternata
Clethra alnifolia 'Paniculata'
Cytisus battandieri
Daphne (many)
Elaeagnus
Erica lusitanica
Hamamelis mollis 'Pallida'
　H. vernalis, H. virginiana
Lonicera x purpusii 'Winter
　Beauty', L. standishii
Magnolia sieboldii,
　M. x thompsoniana
Mahonia japonica
Osmanthus fragrans
Philadelphus (many)
Pittosporum tobira
Rhododendron auriculatum,
　R. edgeworthii,
　R. 'Fragrantissima', R., Ghent
　Hybrids, R., Loderi Group,
　R. luteum, R. occidentale (and
　Hybrids), R. 'Polar Bear',
　R., Rustica Hybrids, R. viscosum
Rosa (many)
Sarcococca
Syringa (many)
Viburnum (many)

*Rhododendron
luteum*

ARCHITECTURAL SHRUBS

Agave
Aralia elata 'Aureo-variegata'
Fatsia japonica
Hydrangea quercifolia
Phormium
Sabal
Yucca

COLORED FOLIAGE

Purple and red

Acer palmatum 'Atrupurpureum'
Cotinus coggygria 'Royal Purple'
Prunus x cistena

Yellow

Cornus alba 'Spaethii'
Philadelphus coronarius 'Aureus'
Spiraea japonica 'Goldmound'

Gray

Elaeagnus (most)
Shepherdia argentea

Variegated

Euonymus fortunei cultivars
Kerria japonica 'Picta'

Bamboos

BAMBOOS are evergreen, woody members of the grass family and have delicately handsome foliage and a graceful habit. They store their food in underground stems (rhizomes), from which both woody stems (culms or canes) and roots develop. The culms grow to their full height in one season but usually take three years to mature fully. Culms produce new leaves each growing season, thus maintaining a fresh look. Most species grow without flowering for 20 years or more. After they have eventually flowered, however, they may be so weakened that they need replacing or cutting back to ground level.

Many bamboos are tropical but a considerable number are hardy in temperate regions. Some will grow 22ft (7m) tall, while others reach less than 20in (50cm). Their great diversity makes them invaluable in the garden: some bamboos make good specimen plants, others useful screens, hedges, or windbreaks; most will grow happily in containers. Some bamboos are reasonably docile and clump-forming, others invasive.

General cultivation

Most bamboos will grow in sun or shade, and prefer organic, moist but well-drained soil. The pH is not important. As bamboos are shallow rooted, their planting hole should be no deeper than 16in (40cm). Dig the site thoroughly and add bone meal and well-rotted manure, before planting the bamboo.

Never let bamboos dry out, especially when young, nor allow their roots to freeze. Container-grown ones should be kept frost free. Even hardy bamboos may occasionally be slightly cold-damaged but they usually recover quickly in spring, provided there is sufficient water.

In spring, give an annual application of balanced fertilizer at a rate of 2oz/sq yd (50g/sq m), a mulch of well-rotted manure, and a dressing of calcium silicate.

Restricting bamboo growth
Some of the best-looking bamboos are highly invasive. To keep them in their allotted space, insert a physical barrier into the soil, at least 16in (40cm) deep, around the root ball, and seal well at the join(s); then keep a careful watch and cut off any rhizomes that spread across the top of the barrier. Alternatively, a couple of times a year, insert a sharp spade around the clump, then pull out any rhizomes that have strayed outside the cut line.

To reduce the vigor of low-growing bamboos, cut them to the ground in early spring. Such pruning will also make the plants look even more attractive as they will display only fresh new culms each summer.

Pests and diseases

Bamboos are particularly vulnerable to the bamboo spider mite – a sap-sucking insect that lives on the underside of leaves covered by a fine web. New plants should be inspected for dots and dashes (like Morse code) of longitudinal, yellow variegations on the leaves. To eradicate bamboo spider mite, remove and discard infected leaves; if necessary, spray with an acaricide that will kill these mites. Whiteflies (p.639) and spider mite (p.640) will attack bamboo under cover but are not a problem outdoors. Aphids (p.639) are a nuisance on some species, and rabbits (p.656) and squirrels (p.651) may eat the new growth.

Pruning

Dead, damaged, or spindly culms and all those more than five years old should be removed at or very close to the base, in spring. Never partially shorten culms as this ruins their appearance. Loppers or a saw, and heavy protective clothing, are often essential when pruning.

If a clump has become too dense and overwhelming for its position, it can be thinned in spring or late summer to let air and light into the centre. Thinning also displays well those species that have colored stems or those in which the young culms are the most attractive.

Propagation

Bamboo roots are sensitive to drought, so choose a cool, overcast day for propagation to stop the roots from drying out.

Tightly clumped bamboos can be increased by simple division in spring, when new growth is visible (see "Division," p.116). Spray water on divided plants regularly and liberally until they are established.

All bamboos can be propagated in spring by dividing their rhizomes. Lift a clump or part of one, and cut one or more rhizomes into pieces, making sure that each has at least one growing shoot. Take care not to damage the fine roots. Insert the pieces into individual pots of a free-draining soil mix and cover the rhizomes to their original depth. Keep them cool and moist, and in good but not strong light until the plants are established.

PROPAGATING BAMBOOS BY DIVIDING RHIZOMES

1 *Dig around the clump to expose the outer rhizomes with new shoots. Separate these from the parent plant.*

2 *Cut the rhizomes, each with at least one shoot, into pieces. Dust the cut surfaces with fungicidal powder (see inset).*

3 *Pot up each piece with the rhizome just below the surface of the soil mix and the shoots exposed. Firm in and water.*

RESTRICTING THE SPREAD OF BAMBOO

1 *Dig a narrow trench, deeper than the plant's roots, all around the clump. Chop through and remove peripheral roots.*

2 *Insert a barrier made of nonperishable material such as stone slabs or rigid plastic. Fill the trench; firm the ground well.*

THINNING ESTABLISHED CLUMPS OF BAMBOO

Wearing thick gloves and using loppers, remove weak, dead, and damaged culms, then cut out the oldest ones at the base until the desired effect is achieved. Then, without damaging new shoots, clear away debris at the base to relieve congestion, let in light and air, and allow young culms to grow unchecked.

Soil preparation and planting

MOST gardens allow you to grow a wide range of shrubs even though the soil falls short of ideal – a fertile loam that is well drained but moisture-retentive. Improving the drainage of wet soils and, by the addition of organic matter, the structure and moisture-holding properties of dry soils will greatly increase the range of shrubs that may be grown satisfactorily. The level of acidity or alkalinity, another factor limiting the range of plants that can be grown, can also be modified.

Important though these improvements may be, garden soil will still naturally tend toward being moist or dry, heavy or light, and acidic or alkaline. The best shrubs for your garden are those suited to the growing conditions available.

Selecting shrubs

Shrubs may be bought from garden centers, nurseries, and from non-specialized outlets such as supermarkets. They are sold in containers, balled-and-burlapped, or bare-root. Shrubs for sale should be accurately labeled, healthy, undamaged, and free of pests and diseases. Inspect the plants thoroughly and select a specimen with evenly distributed branches close to ground level or, with standard shrubs, at the head of a clear stem of the desired height.

Shrubs sold in the warm, dry atmosphere of a supermarket have a short shelf life. Reliable suppliers will give a year's guarantee to replace the shrub if it is not true to name or if it dies within its first year, provided that it has been given reasonable care. Many nurseries also sell shrubs by mail order; plants are normally shipped during their dormant period.

Shrubs in containers

Shrubs are most commonly sold as container-grown specimens, the containers ranging from rigid pots to heavy paper. Most shrubs sold in this way have been container-grown throughout their lives. Others are field-grown and potted up (containerized) in the season before sale to prolong their sale life. Look through the drainage holes to see whether there is a well-developed root system. If so, the shrub is most probably container-grown and not containerized. If possible, slide the shrub out of its container; the roots should show healthy, white tips. Reject plants with poorly developed root systems, and those that are potbound (with roots protruding from the container), since these rarely grow well.

A major advantage of container-grown shrubs is that they can be bought and planted out at anytime, except when there are extremes of temperature or drought. Containerized shrubs can be safely planted at the same times, but before buying and planting in the active growing season, check that they have a well-developed root system (if so, they will retain all or most of the soil mix around the roots when removed from the pot).

Bare-root shrubs

Deciduous shrubs that are easily propagated are sometimes lifted from the open ground during their dormant season and sold with their roots bare of soil. The buying season for these bare-root shrubs is from fall to spring. To prevent them from drying out, the roots are normally wrapped in plastic. Before purchasing, check that bare-root shrubs have an evenly developed, fibrous root system.

Balled-and-burlapped shrubs

Some shrubs, especially conifers, are sold with their roots and soil wrapped in burlap or netting. The buying season for these balled-and-burlapped shrubs is fall or early spring. Always check that the wrapping is intact, so that the roots have not been exposed to drying wind, and that the root ball is firm.

SELECTING A SHRUB

CONTAINER-GROWN SHRUB

GOOD EXAMPLE

Vigorous, well-balanced top-growth

POOR EXAMPLE

Twiggy, sparse stems showing little new growth

Potbound roots

PROSTANTHERA CUNEATA

Well-established, fibrous root system

PRUNING CONGESTED ROOTS

Tease out potbound roots and cut back any that are very long or damaged

CONTAINER-GROWN SHRUB

GOOD EXAMPLE

Well-developed, even branch framework

VIBURNUM FARRERI

Healthy, vigorous growth, free from damage and disease

BALLED-AND-BURLAPPED SHRUB

Wrapping is intact, not split or damaged

Check that the root ball is firm

SHRUBS THAT PREFER SANDY SOIL

Berberis empetrifolia
*Calluna vulgaris (*and cvs)
Ceanothus thyrsiflorus (and forms)
Cistus x *cyprius*

Cistus x *cyprius*

Cytisus scoparius (and forms)
Erica arborea var. *alpina*,
  E. cinerea (and cvs)
Fuchsia magellanica (and cvs)
Genista tinctoria
Hakea lissosperma
Halimodendron halodendron
Helianthemum
Helichrysum
Hibiscus syriacus
Lavandula
Olearia
Phlomis
Phormium
Rosa pimpinellifolia
Spartium junceum
Tamarix
Ulex europaeus

SHRUBS THAT TOLERATE CLAY SOIL

Amelanchier
Aralia ♦
Aronia arbutifolia ♦
Aucuba
Berberis ♦

Chaenomeles x *superba* 'Nicoline'

Chaenomeles x *superba* ♦
Citrus
Clethra alnifolia ♦
Cornus alba 'Sibirica' ♦
Cotoneaster ♦
Forsythia
Garrya
Hippophäe
Kalmia latifolia
Ligustrum
Lonicera
Mahonia x *media* group ♦
Philadelphus
Pyracantha
Rosa
Salix caprea ♦
Sambucus racemosa
Taxus
Viburnum opulus ♦

KEY
♦ *Tolerates waterlogged soil*

When to plant

Fall to spring is the planting season for balled-and-burlapped and bare-root shrubs, and the optimum time for container-grown and container-ized shrubs. Planting in fall allows the roots to establish while the ground is still warm, so the shrub should be growing vigorously before dry weather the next summer.

In some areas, planting can be carried out during mild weather in winter but not when the ground is frozen. Roots will not begin growth in very cold soil, and there is a risk that they may freeze.

The major disadvantage of spring planting is that top-growth is likely to develop before the roots establish and, if there is an long spell of dry weather, watering may be required to help the plants to survive.

Soil preparation

Many shrubs are potentially long-lived, so the ground needs to be thoroughly prepared before planting. The aim should be to cultivate an area well beyond the planting site for an individual shrub and, preferably, the entire bed.

The best seasons for cultivation are late summer and fall. Remove or kill all weeds first, taking particular care to eradicate perennials (see "Weeds," pp.658–61). Double dig (see p.614), incorporating a 3–4in (8–10cm) layer of well-rotted organic matter into the lower trench. If this is impractical, work large quantities of organic matter into the top 12–18in (30–45cm) of soil. Add fertilizer if appropriate (see "Soil nutrients and fertilizers," pp.618–19).

How to plant

The planting hole for a shrub must be wide enough to accommodate the root ball. For container-grown or balled-and-burlapped plants, make the hole twice the width of the con-tained root mass, or as much as three times the width if planting in clay soils. For bare-root shrubs, the hole must be large enough to allow the roots to be spread out fully, as well as sufficiently deep to allow the shrub to be planted at the same level as it was in its container or in the open ground. This is indicated by the soil mark, a dark mark near the base of the stem. A stake laid across the top of the planting hole provides a useful guide to the depth of planting. Treatment of a containerized shrub depends on how developed the root system is when removed from the pot. If the soil mix falls away, plant as for a bare-root shrub; if it does not, treat as if container-grown. Remove or untie and spread out the burlap or netting surrounding a balled-and-burlapped shrub after it is in the hole. When backfilling the hole, shake a bare-root plant gently to settle the soil. Gently firm the soil in stages.

To improve drainage around a shrub planted in clay soil, plant the

PLANTING A WALL SHRUB

1 Dig a hole at least 9in (22cm) away from the wall. Plant the shrub (here a firethorn) and tie in the supporting stake to a wire.

2 Replace the soil. Secure lateral stakes to the central stake and both wires, so that the sideshoots can be supported and tied in (see inset).

PLANTING A CONTAINER-GROWN SHRUB

1 Dig a hole about twice the width of the shrub's root ball (here a Viburnum). Fork over the base and sides of the hole.

2 Placing one hand on top of the soil mix and around the shrub to support it, carefully ease the plant out of its container. Place the shrub in the prepared hole.

3 Lay a stake alongside to check that the soil level is the same as before. Adjust the planting depth, if necessary, by adding or removing topsoil beneath the shrub.

4 Backfill around the shrub with the removed soil, firming in stages to prevent air pockets from forming.

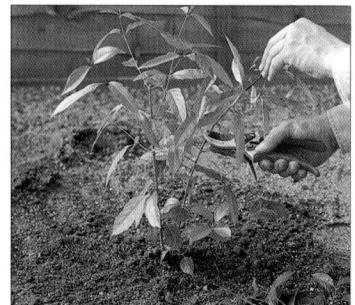

5 Once the hole has been filled with soil, carefully firm around the shrub with your heel or hands.

6 Prune any diseased, damaged, or weak wood, and cut back any inward-growing or crossing stems to an outward-growing shoot or bud.

USING A WATERING RING

To help retain water, create a shallow depression with a low wall of soil around the shrub. After several waterings, push the wall into the depression, then mulch.

shrub slightly above soil level and mound soil around the exposed section of the root ball up to the level of the soil mark. On sandy soil, plant the shrub in a slight dip to channel water around the plant's roots. Water the shrub, then mulch it.

Planting wall shrubs

Some shrubs may be trained on wires attached to a wall or fence. Plant these as for free-standing shrubs, at least 9in (22cm) from the wall so that the roots are not in its rain shadow, and lean the plant in toward the wall. Support the main stem and laterals of the shrub with stakes, which are then tied into the wires (see also "Wall shrubs," p.106).

Staking

Shrubs do not normally need staking, except for large, rootbound specimens and standards. The former, which ideally should not be selected, will almost certainly need some support in their first year or two at least, until their roots begin to spread out and they become stable.

The best method for any shrub that branches from near ground level is to brace the shrub with guys fixed to three stakes spaced evenly around a circle with a radius of about 3ft (1m) centered on the shrub. To prevent bark damage, cover the guys where they touch the branches with rubber or similar material (see also ORNAMENTAL TREES, "Staking," p.64).

For a standard, insert the stake in the planting hole before planting to avoid damaging the root system. The top of the stake should be just below the first branches. Secure the stem to the stake, using a commercial tie with a spacer or a homemade figure-eight tie to prevent chafing.

STAKING A STANDARD SHRUB

1 *Drive a stake into the hole just off center. The stake should reach to just below the head of the shrub after planting. Plant the shrub next to the stake.*

2 *If the depth is correct, backfill and firm in, then create a watering ring around the shrub to retain water. Secure the stem with a suitable tie (see inset).*

Protecting newly planted shrubs

Newly planted shrubs may suffer from drying out or cold if not protected. Broad-leaved evergreens and conifers in exposed positions are particularly vulnerable.

A screen of burlap or mesh significantly reduces the drying force of cold winds. Erect a strong, wooden framework 12in (30cm) away from the windward side of the shrub needing protection. Tack the burlap or the mesh to the frame, which should extend at least 12in (30cm) above and to either side of the shrub. More complete protection is given by surrounding individual plants with a four-sided framework to which burlap or mesh is tacked.

Another measure, which may be used either alone or in addition to screening, is to spray the plants with an antidesiccant to reduce drying out. Apply a thin film of spray to both sides of the leaves.

A mulch spread around the base of the shrub will help protect the roots from ground frost. It is best to spread the mulch during mild weather, preferably when the ground is reasonably warm and damp.

In areas of heavy snow, particularly vulnerable evergreen shrubs may need additional protection. This is best provided by placing a wooden A-frame over them. Dislodge any heavy accumulations of snow promptly. More extreme measures may be needed to protect less hardy and tender shrubs (see COLD AND WIND PROTECTION, pp. 604–5).

When removing the insulation in spring, check for pests and diseases that may have benefited from the winter protection.

Planting shrubs in containers

Late summer to fall is the main period for planting shrubs in containers, although container-grown shrubs can be planted in an ornamental pot at most times.

Select a container that is the right size for the shrub. When transplanting a shrub, the new container should be about 2in (5cm) larger in depth and diameter than the previous one. If it has already been used, scrub its inside surface thoroughly.

Heavy containers should be placed in position before planting. Stand the container on bricks, blocks, or pot feet to allow free drainage. Place a piece of screen-ing over the drainage holes to keep the soil mix from falling out before the roots grow into it.

A soil-based potting mix, which is rich in nutrients, is preferable to a peat-based mix, which contains only limited added nutrients. Shrubs are likely to remain in their containers for years, and any grown in peat-based soil mixes will require frequent fertilizing. Additionally, peat-based soil mixes dry out more rapidly than soil-based ones. Use an acidic soil mix for rhododendrons and other acidic-soil lovers, or to obtain blue flowers on hydrangeas. Make sure that the soil mark is level with the surface of the soil mix.

With container planting, be sure that the soil mix is at least 1¹/₂in (4cm) below the rim to allow room for mulching and watering.

SHRUBS THAT REQUIRE ACIDIC SOIL

Andromeda
Arbutus (most spp.)
Arctostaphylos (some spp.)
Calluna
Camellia

Camellia x *williamsii*
'Wilber Foss'

Clethra
Cornus canadensis
Corylopsis (most spp.)
Desfontainia spinosa
Enkianthus
Erica (most spp.)
Fothergilla
Hakea
Hamamelis
Kalmia
Leucothoë
Magnolia (some spp.)
Menziesia
Pernettya
Philesia magellanica
Pieris
Rhododendron (most spp.)
Styrax officinalis
Telopea speciosissima
Vaccinium
Zenobia pulverulenta

SHRUBS THAT TOLERATE VERY ALKALINE SOIL

Aucuba japonica (and cvs)
Berberis darwinii
Buddleia davidii (and cvs)
Buxus
Ceanothus impressus
Chamaerops
Choisya ternata
Cistus
Cotoneaster (all)
Cytisus
Deutzia
Euonymus
Forsythia
Hebe
Hibiscus
Hypericum
Ligustrum
Lonicera
Nerium oleander

Philadelphus
'Dame Blanche'

Philadelphus
Phlomis fruticosa
Potentilla (all shrubby spp.)
Rosa rugosa
Rosmarinus
Rubus 'Benenden'
Spiraea canescens
Syringa
Viburnum tinus
Vitex agnus-castus
Xanthoceras sorbifolium
Yucca aloifolia

Routine care

THE following guidelines for maintenance are generally applicable, although not all shrubs have the same requirements. Newly planted shrubs usually need watering, while those planted in contain-ers should also be periodically top-dressed or repotted. In addition, fertilizing, deadheading, removing suckers, weeding, and controlling pests and diseases may all be necessary.

Watering

Established shrubs need watering only in periods of prolonged drought, but young specimens may need regular watering. Apply the water to the ground around the shrub, soaking the soil. Do not water often and lightly, since this encourages root growth close to the surface. Shallow roots make shrubs vulnerable in drought conditions. The best time to water is in the early evening, when evaporation is minimal.

Fertilizing and mulching

Most shrubs benefit from regular applications of organic or inorganic fertilizers. These are available in a variety of forms.

Mulching with well-rotted, bulky manures helps soil conserve moisture and, if nutrient-rich, improves soil fertility. It also moderates extremes of temperature around the roots and inhibits weeds.

Fertilizers

Shrubs, especially if pruned regularly, are usually given slow-release fertilizers, which are best applied in early spring. Some of these fertilizers release their nutrients only when temperatures are high enough for plants to use them. A standard rate of application is 2oz/sq yd (60g/sq m).

Quick-release powder fertilizers are useful to boost growth as it commences in spring. Liquid fertilizers work even faster than powders, and these should be applied once the shrub is growing.

Fertilizers in granular or powder form should be worked into the soil over an area slightly wider than the spread of the top-growth of the shrub. With surface-rooting shrubs, allow the fertilizer to leach in naturally or water it in to avoid the risk of the roots being injured by forking. The application of fertilizers may alter the soil's pH level; most inorganic, nitrogenous fertilizers, for example, make the soil more acidic (see also "Soil nutrients and fertilizers," pp.618–19).

Mulches

Apply the mulch around newly planted shrubs over an area about 18in (45cm) wider in diameter than the plant's root system. The mulch around established shrubs should extend beyond the area of top-growth by 6–12in (15–30cm). A mulch of bark chips, wood chips, well-rotted-manure, or similar material should be 2–4in (5–10cm) deep but kept clear of the stems of the shrub. Do not apply any mulch in freezing weather or when the soil is dry.

Weeding

Weeds compete for nutrients and moisture, so it is essential to clear the ground of all weeds before planting.

The area around newly planted groundcover shrubs needs weeding until the plants form dense growth that suppresses competition. For treatment, see "Weeds," pp.658–59.

Removing suckers

Some grafted shrubs, especially roses, are prone to producing growths, or suckers, beneath the graft union, from either stems or roots. Rub out suckers between finger and thumb as soon as they are noticed; if too large to treat in this way, cut them off as close as possible to the stems or roots from which they are growing. Pulling them off helps remove any dormant growth buds, but take care not to damage the stem or root. Watch for further growth.

Reversion and mutation

Many variegated shrubs are propagated from green-leaved plants that have produced mutated branches, known as sports. From time to time, branches of variegated shrubs revert to the original foliage of the parent plant or mutate to plain cream or yellow leaves. Since these branches are usually more vigorous, they eventually crowd out those showing variegation and should be cut out.

DEADHEADING A RHODODENDRON

Before new buds have fully developed, snap each dead flower head off at the base of its stem. Take care not to damage any young growth.

Deadheading

Some shrubs, including rhododendrons, lilacs (*Syringa*), and *Kalmia*, benefit if their faded flower heads are promptly removed, where possible, before seed sets. Removing old flowers diverts energy into growth, improving the flowering potential for the following season, but it is not essential to the health of a shrub.

To avoid damage to new growth buds, deadhead as soon as the flowers fade, using fingers and thumb to pick off each one where it joins the stem. Most flower heads come away cleanly, but any snags should be trimmed with pruners.

HOW TO REMOVE SUCKERS

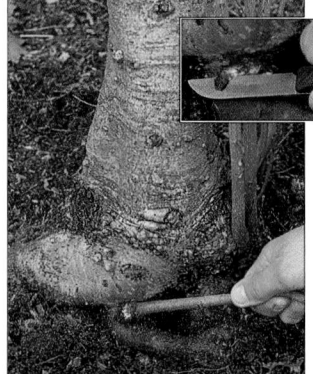

SUCKER REMOVAL
Pull or cut off the sucker (here on a Hamamelis) *at the base. If it is pulled off, pare back the wound to leave a clean cut (see inset).*

RECOGNIZING SUCKERS
A sucker can usually be distinguished by its leaves: a normal stem from the top-growth, left; a sucker from the root, right.

REMOVING NONVARIEGATED AND REVERTED SHOOTS

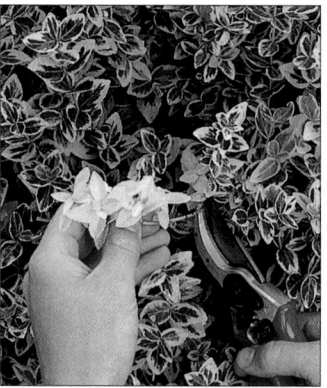

NONVARIEGATED SHOOT
With variegated shrubs (here Euonymus fortunei 'Emerald 'n' Gold'), *cut any plain shoots back to the variegated growth.*

REVERTED SHOOT
Cut back reverted shoots (here on E. f. 'Emerald Gaiety') *to the main stem. If necessary, remove the entire stem.*

Groundcover shrubs

COVERING the ground with a dense carpet of flowering or foliage plants is a planting technique designed primarily to minimize weeding among ornamental plants. Groundcovers can also reduce evaporation from exposed, freely draining soils. A dense planting of drought-resistant evergreens, such as *Cistus* x *hybridus* or the pink-flowered *C.* x *skanbergii*, and most cultivars of rosemary (*Rosmarinus*) and lavender (*Lavandula*), will shade the soil and keep it cool, and their slowly decomposing leaf litter also acts as a mulch.

Steep banks, subject to erosion by rain and wind, may be planted with groundcover shrubs such as *Juniperus squamata* 'Blue Carpet' or *Cotoneaster dammeri*. Their low, spreading habit, evergreen foliage, and vigorous rooted layers combine to form a stable cover that prevents erosion of topsoil.

In a wildlife garden, groundcovers can be used to attract bees and butterflies: the low, creeping thymes, such as *Thymus praecox* and its cultivars, for example, are extremely attractive to bees.

Once established, groundcover plants will smother most weed seedlings that attempt to grow beneath their canopy, by depriving them of light, as well as by competing with them for water and nutrients. In the wild, this is frequently a natural

TEXTURAL CARPET
A vigorous dwarf juniper, Juniperus squamata *'Blue Carpet' provides a spreading mat of color and texture up to 10ft (3m) wide.*

process; nature may be imitated in the garden to create attractive, integrated plantings that require very little aftercare.

In open gardens, evergreen groundcover shrubs can act as low boundary markers. They also trap wind-blown rubbish beneath their branches; it should be raked out routinely and removed.

Selecting plants

Choose attractive, vigorous plants that will quickly cover their allotted space with close, dense growth. Low-growing shrubs with a spreading habit are among the most useful. Evergreens are a good choice for year-round visual interest, especially if, like *Euonymus fortunei* 'Gold Spot' with its golden-variegated, dark green leaves, they will brighten a dark corner.

Plants should be selected for the location, for example, wet or dry, shady, or hot and sunny situations. They should be easy to care for, routinely requiring either no pruning or perhaps an annual clipping and fertilizing. Choose long-term plants that should remain healthy for five to ten years or more. Finally, look for species, cultivars, and forms that will provide attractive foliage and habit, with flowers and fruits as a bonus.

Combining plants

Massed groupings of a single plant give a unified "carpeting" effect, but plants can be combined provided that they are of similar vigor. Ground-cover plants with various colors, textures, and forms may be mixed to make garden features in their own right, or may provide an attractive linking element in a design. A low carpet of shrubs can also make an excellent, low-maintenance background for naturalized bulbs such as daffodils, and, unlike grass, will not need mowing as the bulb foliage fades.

Some shrubs are particularly useful in providing medium-height cover, or as an undercanopy below trees. *Cotoneaster conspicuus*, with bright scarlet berries, dense and spreading *Prunus laurocerasus* 'Otto Luyken', and *Viburnum davidii* and *V tinus*, with their glossy, dark green leaves and showy winter buds, cover the ground well and provide interest, even in winter.

General cultivation

Once the ground has been thoroughly prepared, there are several ways of planting groundcover shrubs to provide quick cover: plant them at spacings recommended for the species or cultivar concerned and cover the soil with a loose mulch; plant them at recommended spacings through a weed-resistant, black plastic sheet mulch; or plant them more densely than would be usual to provide cover more quickly.

The choice of method will depend on the type and cost of plants used, the climate and soil conditions, and how long you are willing to wait for the final effect. Fast-growing plants in favorable conditions and at recommended spacings will generally fill in within two to three years.

Once established, many shrubby plants benefit from an occasional trim, to keep them compact, as well as the removal of dead or damaged shoots. A few need more intrusive, annual pruning: for example, shrubs such as *Vinca* and *Hypericum calycinum* that, after a few years, become rather straggly, and those such as *Santolina* that tend to open out, revealing their center.

PRUNING GROUNDCOVERS

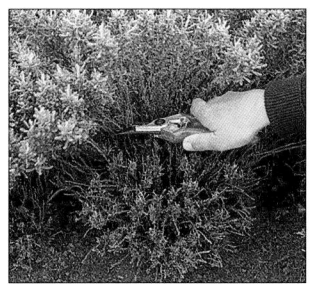

SANTOLINA
Some bushy plants need hard pruning. In spring, cut back to just above where new growth is breaking on the main stems.

HYPERICUM CALYCINUM
In spring, cut the previous season's shoots back hard.

Mulching groundcovers

When groundcover plants have been newly planted at the correct distance, the ground between them will still be bare. Until the plants have begun to spread over the surrounding area, it is advisable to apply a mulch in the gaps around them. This will help retain moisture in the soil and will also discourage the growth of weeds. A loose mulch, for example bark chips, is ideal for the purpose, and should be applied to a depth of about 2in (5cm).

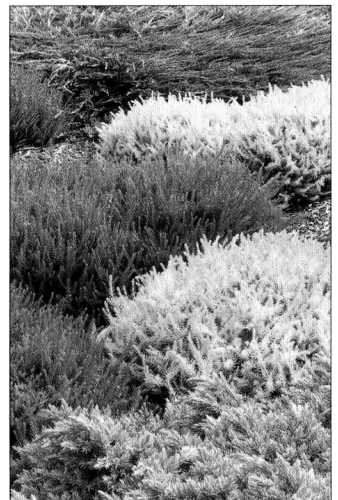

To preserve moisture between new plants (here Erica carnea*), apply a loose mulch 2in (5cm) deep. Every spring, renew the mulch around established plants.*

Moving an established shrub

Careful selection and siting of a shrub should make transplanting unnecessary, although sometimes it may be desirable or unavoidable. In general, the younger the shrub, the more likely it is to reestablish after being moved.

When to transplant

Most young shrubs may be lifted bare-root when dormant. Established shrubs that have large root systems should be lifted with a ball of soil around the roots before being moved. Fall is the best time to do this.

Balling-and-burlapping a shrub

Most often, it is best to ball-and-burlap a shrub so that root damage is kept to a minimum. Prepare the new position before lifting the shrub.

Dig a trench around the shrub just beyond the spread of its branches. Cut through woody roots but leave fibrous ones intact. Use a fork to loosen the soil around the root ball and reduce its size. Then undercut it with a spade and use pruners to sever any woody taproots.

Once the root ball is free, work a sheet of burlap or similar material underneath it, tipping the shrub from side to side carefully so that the soil is not disturbed. Tie the burlap firmly around the ball, lift the shrub from the hole, and transplant it. Untie the burlap before replanting.

The shrub needs the same treatment as one that has been planted for the first time, but it may take longer to reestablish (see p.97).

Shrub problems

Plants are less likely to succumb to pest attack or disease if they are given good growing conditions and care. Many problems originate from poor drainage, lack of moisture, planting too deeply, compaction of the soil, or exposure to temperature extremes in an unsuitable site.

Physical damage

Wounds caused by a jagged pruning cut, a badly placed cut, or pruning at the wrong time may allow disease organisms to establish. This may also cause dieback. Mechanical wounding of bark, stems, or roots by lawn mowers, for example, also provides an entry point for disease.

Pests and diseases

As shrubs age, they lose vigor and become more prone to pests and diseases. Old or diseased shrubs that have lost their vigor are rarely worth saving and should be replaced.

Pests and diseases most likely to affect shrubs are aphids (p.639), spider mites (p.640), black vine weevils (p.638), *Phytophthora* stem rots (see "*Phytophthora* root rots," p.646), and powdery mildew (p.640). Be alert to the signs of a problem, which include streaking and changes in the color of foliage, drooping leaves, loss of leaves, distorted growth, and the development of mushrooms.

Maintaining good garden hygiene minimizes the chance of pests and diseases establishing a foothold. Dispose of dead and diseased wood, and keep the ground around a shrub free of debris such as old fruit.

Cold and wind

When selecting and siting shrubs, it is vital to take account of the general weather pattern of the area as well as the garden's own individual microclimate. It is almost impossible, however, to take precautions against freak extremes of temperature or exceptional winds.

There is a wide range of hardy shrubs available, and many gardeners choose to rely on these rather than risk the loss of more tender specimens. If growing shrubs that are of marginal hardiness for your area, then it is worth using the appropriate cold and wind protection methods (see pp.604–5).

Container-grown shrubs are more vulnerable to extremes of weather than those grown in the open garden. In areas where temperatures only occasionally fall below freezing, most container-grown hardy shrubs can be overwintered outdoors (except those that are root-tender, such as camellias). In colder areas, however, move shrubs indoors to where the ambient daytime temperature is about 45–55°F (7–13°C) or higher, according to the species.

TRANSPLANTING A SHRUB

1 *Using a spade, mark out a circle around the extent of the shrub's branches (here* Ilex aquifolium *'Golden Milkboy'). If necessary, tie in any trailing stems or wrap the shrub in burlap to prevent the stems from being damaged.*

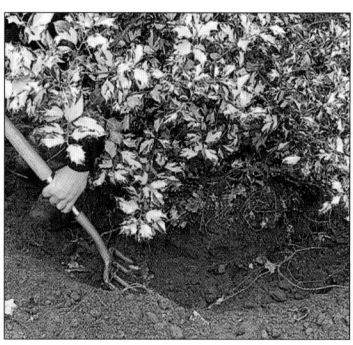

2 *Dig a trench around the circle, then use a fork to loosen the soil around the root ball. Take care not to damage too many fibrous roots.*

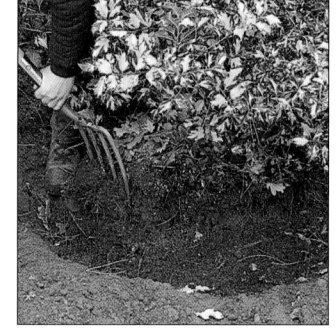

3 *Continue carefully to fork away soil from around the shrub's root ball to reduce its size and weight.*

4 *Undercut the root ball with a spade, cutting through woody roots if necessary to separate them from the surrounding soil.*

5 *Roll up a length of burlap. Tilt the shrub to one side and unroll the burlap beneath the root ball. Tilt the root ball the other way, and unroll the rest of the burlap.*

6 *Pull the burlap up around the root ball and tie it securely. Remove the shrub from its hole and transport it to its new position.*

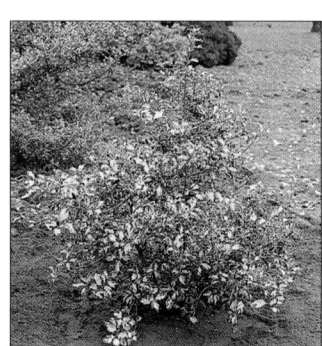

7 *Remove or untie the burlap when replanting in the newly prepared hole. Plant with the soil mark at the same level as before. Firm, water well, and mulch.*

Pruning and training

Some shrubs, particularly ever-greens of naturally compact habit such as *Sarcococca*, make attractive plants with little or no pruning or training. They may require no more than the removal of dead, damaged, and diseased wood. If left untreated, this will be unsightly and, more seriously, may put the health of the whole shrub in jeopardy. Many shrubs, however, need pruning or a combination of pruning and training in order to realize their full ornamental potential.

Aims and results of pruning and training

The most common requirement is for formative pruning that creates a vigorous and well-shaped shrub. Many shrubs also require a regular schedule of pruning to maintain or enhance the ornamental quality of their flowers, fruit, foliage, or stems. The timing of this pruning, which may often be critical, varies depending on the growth pattern of the shrub and the result desired.

Pruning can also be a way of bringing neglected and overgrown plants back to healthy, manageable growth. It is a matter of judgment whether a shrub warrants being rescued. Replacement is often the best course when a shrub requires regular cutting back because it is too large for the space available.

Shrubs grown as topiary or hedges require specialized pruning from their formative stage. For further information see TOPIARY, pp.118–19, and HEDGES AND SCREENS, pp.82–4.

In training, the gardener plays an active role in directing the growth of plants. Most shrubs grown in the open require no training at all. Shrubs grown against supports, however, normally need a combination of pruning and training to form a well-spaced framework of branches.

Principles of pruning and training

Pruning normally stimulates growth. The terminal shoot or growth bud of a stem is often dominant, inhibiting by chemical means the growth of buds or shoots below it. Pruning that removes the ends of stems affects the control mechanism, resulting in more vigorous development of lower shoots or growth buds.

WHERE TO CUT

OPPOSITE SHOOTS
Prune stems with opposite buds to just above a strong pair of buds or shoots, using a clean, straight cut.

ALTERNATE SHOOTS
For shrubs with alternate buds, prune to just above a bud or shoot, using a clean, angled cut.

MAKING AN ANGLED CUT
Angle the cut so that its lowest point is opposite the base of the bud and the top just clears the bud.

Hard or light pruning
Hard pruning promotes more vigorous growth than light pruning. This needs to be borne in mind when correcting the shape of an unbalanced shrub. Hard cutting back of vigorous growth often encourages even stronger growth. Prune weak growth hard, but strong growth only lightly.

How to prune
Pruning wounds, like other injuries that a shrub might suffer, are possible entry points for disease. The risk is reduced by making well-placed, clean cuts with sharp tools.

Stems with alternate or whorled arrangements of growth buds should be cut just above a bud pointing in the desired direction of growth – for example, an outward-facing bud that will not cross another shoot as its growth develops. Use an angled cut, starting opposite a healthy growth bud, and slant the cut so that it finishes slightly above the bud. If the cut is too close, the bud may die; if too far, the stem itself may die back.

With shrubs that have buds in opposite pairs, cut straight across the shoot just above a pair of healthy buds. Both buds will develop, resulting in a forked branch system.

In the past, gardeners have often been advised to use a wound paint on pruning cuts, but research now suggests that wound paints are not generally an effective way of controlling diseases and in some cases may even encourage them.

Pruning alone will not promote vigorous new growth. Shrubs that are renovated or regularly cut back benefit from feeding and mulching. Apply a general-purpose fertilizer at the beginning of the growing season at a rate of 4oz/sq yd (120g/sq m) and mulch to a depth of 2–4in (5–10cm) with well-rotted organic material in spring, when the ground has warmed up a little.

Training
The growth of lower buds or shoots on a stem may also be modified by training. When a stem is allowed to grow upright, the lower shoots on the stem usually grow weakly. With stems that are trained more horizontally, however, the lower shoots and buds grow more vigorously. Training branches near the horizontal can substantially increase the amount of flower and fruit that a shrub is able to carry. Wall-trained shrubs should be tied in to supports as growth develops. As stems ripen and turn woody they become far less flexible and are therefore more difficult to train successfully.

Formative pruning

The aim of formative pruning is to make sure that a shrub has a framework of well-spaced branches so that it will develop according to its natural habit. The amount of formative pruning required depends very much on the type of shrub and on the quality of the plants available. When

FORMATIVE PRUNING

After planting a young shrub (here a Philadelphus*), cut out any dead, damaged, and weak stems, and remove crossing and congested stems to form a well-balanced framework with an open center.*

Prune back crossing or congested shoots to an outward-facing bud or, if necessary, cut right back to the base.

Prune out any very weak and spindly, or long and straggly stems, cutting them right back to the base.

Also remove any very awkward stems that spoil the shape of the shrub to leave an evenly branching framework.

DECIDUOUS SHRUBS THAT NEED MINIMAL PRUNING

Amelanchier
Aronia
Buddleia globosa
Caragana
Chimonanthus
Clethra (deciduous spp.)
Cornus alternifolia 'Argentea'
Corokia
Corylopsis

Daphne mezereum

Daphne (deciduous spp.)
Decaisnea
Disanthus
Enkianthus
Eucryphia (deciduous spp.)
Fothergilla
Hamamelis
Hoheria (deciduous spp.)
Lindera
Poncirus
Ptelea
Pterostyrax
Rhamnus (deciduous spp.)
Viburnum (deciduous spp.)

DECIDUOUS SHRUBS THAT SHOULD BE PRUNED IN SPRING

Abelia x *grandiflora*
Abutilon
Aloysia
Buddleja davidii
Caryopteris x *clandonensis*
Ceanothus 'Autumnal Blue',
  C. 'Gloire de Versailles'
Ceratostigma willmottianum
Colquhounia
Cornus (for winter stems)
Cotinus
Datura
Fuchsia (hardy cvs)
Hibiscus syriacus
Hydrangea
Hypericum
Indigofera
Lavatera

Lavatera assurgentiflora

Leycesteria
Perovskia
Potentilla
Prunus triloba
Salvia
Sorbaria
Spiraea douglasii,
  S. japonica
Tamarix ramossissima
Vitex
Zauschneria

buying shrubs, look for sturdy specimens with a well-balanced branch formation.

Evergreen shrubs generally need little formative pruning. Excessive growth resulting in a lopsided, unbalanced shape should be lightly pruned in midspring, after the shrub has been planted.

Deciduous shrubs are much more likely to require formative pruning than evergreen shrubs. This should be carried out in the dormant season, between midfall and midspring, at or after planting.

The following guidelines apply to most deciduous shrubs. If a particularly vigorous shoot distorts the framework, cut it back lightly rather than severely. If the shrub does not have a well-spaced branch framework, cut it back hard to promote strong growth.

In the case of most shrubs, remove completely any spindly and crossing branches that clutter the framework. An exception is made for a handful of slow-growing deciduous shrubs, in particular Japanese maples (*Acer japonicum* and *A. palmatum*). The numerous maple cultivars have a complex growth pattern that can be easily spoiled by this type of pruning.

Sometimes an apparently good specimen will make too much top-growth in relation to the size of its roots. Reducing the number of stems by up to one-third, and then shortening those stems that remain, also by one-third, will help to create a more stable plant.

MINIMAL PRUNING OF DECIDUOUS SHRUBS

Immediately after flowering, prune out any dead wood, weak stems, and congested growth to maintain a balanced, open-centered framework on shrubs such as Hamamelis.

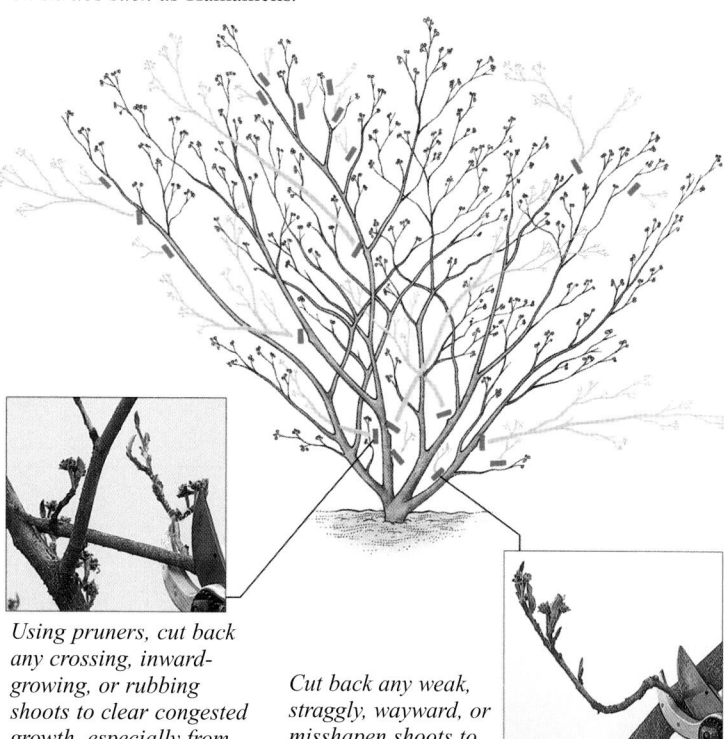

Using pruners, cut back any crossing, inward-growing, or rubbing shoots to clear congested growth, especially from the center of the shrub.

Cut back any weak, straggly, wayward, or misshapen shoots to the main stems.

Deciduous shrubs

These can be divided into four groups: those that require minimal pruning; those that are pruned in spring and usually flower on the current season's growth; those that are pruned after flowering in summer, and usually flower on the previous season's wood; and those of suckering habit. Two important factors are the degree to which shrubs produce replacement growths and the age of the flower-bearing wood.

SHRUBS THAT ARE PRUNED IN SPRING

*Shrubs (*here* Spiraea*) that flower on wood produced during the current growing season should be pruned in spring in order to encourage the growth of new flowering stems.*

Prune out any dead or damaged stems back to healthy growth or, if necessary, cut them right back to the base of the shrub.

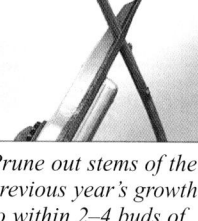

Prune out stems of the previous year's growth to within 2–4 buds of the older wood to stimulate new flowering shoots.

Using loppers, cut back some of the main stems to the base to retain an open framework.

Using pruners, cut back any weak, twiggy, or spindly growth right to the shrub's base.

Minimal pruning

Shrubs that do not regularly produce vigorous growths from the base or lower branches need little pruning. The chief need is to remove dead, diseased, and damaged wood and to cut out crossing or weak growth just after flowering. Many may require formative pruning. Fertilize and mulch in spring. Japanese maples (*Acer* spp.) and other shrubs prone to heavy bleeding if pruned in spring should be pruned in mid- to late summer, when their sap is least active.

Pruning in spring

Left unpruned, deciduous shrubs that bear flowers on the current season's growth tend to become congested, and flower quality deteriorates. When pruned in spring, these shrubs generally produce vigorous shoots that carry flowers in summer or early fall. To minimize the risk of wind-rock, shorten flowered stems in fall as well.

Some large shrubs, such as deciduous *Ceanothus*, develop a woody framework. In their first spring, lightly prune the main stems of less vigorous shrubs and, in the second spring, reduce the previous season's growth by half. In late winter or early spring of subsequent years, prune hard to leave only one to three pairs of buds of the previous season's growth. Prune framework branches to different heights to encourage flower production at all levels. On mature specimens, cut out some of the oldest wood as part of the annual pruning operation to prevent congestion. For pruning *Buddleja davidii*, see above.

Some subshrubs, for example *Perovskia*, may form a woody base that allows them to be pruned back hard to a 6–12in (15–30cm) high framework. Cut back the previous season's growth annually in spring, leaving one or two buds.

A few shrubs (such as *Prunus triloba*) that flower in late winter or early spring on wood produced in the previous season are best pruned hard in spring after flowering, and so may be treated as other shrubs in this group. In the first spring after planting, shorten the main stems by about half to form a basal framework. After flowering in subsequent years, cut back all growth to two or three buds of the framework stems. Where annual growth is limited by cool summers, cut back only one-third of shoots near to ground level, and the others to 6–12in (15–30cm).

For all shrubs in this group, apply fertilizer just after pruning. In midspring, mulch the area matching the spread of the shrub before pruning.

Pruning *Buddleja davidii*

Because it is very vigorous, *Buddleja davidii* needs more drastic formative pruning than most shrubs that flower on new wood. At the back of a border, where a tall plant is required, prune to leave a woody framework 3–4ft (90–120cm) high. In another position, however, this may be no more than 2ft (60cm) high.

In the first spring after planting, shorten main stems by a half to three-quarters, pruning to pairs of shoots or buds. Cut out growths other than main stems. In early to midspring of subsequent years, cut back the previous season's growth and shorten new growth from the base. To avoid congestion, cut out one or two of the oldest branches each year.

Using loppers, cut back some of the woody spurs to clear congested growth and produce an open, balanced framework.

Using pruners, cut back all the main shoots that flowered the previous year to within 1–3 buds of the old wood.

Hydrangeas

For pruning purposes, hydrangeas (excluding climbing species such as *Hydrangea anomala* subsp. *petiolaris*) fall into three groups.

The first group (for example *H. paniculata*) flowers from midsummer onward on the current season's growth, and these plants should be treated in the same way as other shrubs that require hard pruning in spring (see opposite).

In early spring of the first year after planting, cut out all but two or three strong stems, pruning these back to a healthy pair of buds about 18in (45cm) from ground level. If the shrub is planted in an exposed position, and where summer temperatures will not ripen the stems sufficiently to withstand very cold winters, prune to just above ground level. Apply a quick-release fertilizer at a rate of about 4oz/sq yd (120g/sq m) and a 4in (10cm) deep mulch in a 24in (60cm) circle around the shrub. In early spring of subsequent years, cut back the previous year's growth to leave one or two strong pairs of growth buds. Then fertilize and mulch.

The second group, consisting of mophead and lacecap hydrangeas (*H. macrophylla*), also flowers from midsummer but on shoots made during the previous growing season.

Lightly prune young plants in early spring, cutting out thin, twiggy growth and any old flowerheads. Once the plant is established and about three or four years old, remove some of the oldest wood annually in early spring. Cut out stems that are more than three years old and shorten the other stems that flowered in the previous season, cutting back to a strong pair of buds 6–12in (15–30cm) from the base. Then fertilize and mulch.

Other species such as *H. aspera* and related forms constitute a third group and need only minimal pruning in spring.

In spring, prune back all flowered stems and all damaged and weak growth, and cut back some older wood to the base.

H. MACROPHYLLA

Cut back any dead wood to healthy growth or right back to the base, if necessary.

Prune out all flowered stems, making a straight cut above a strong pair of growth buds.

Shrubs pruned in summer after flowering

Many deciduous shrubs that flower in spring or early summer carry their flowers on wood produced in the previous growing season. Sometimes the flowers are formed on last year's wood, as with *Chaenomeles* and forsythias, for example. Other shrubs bear their flowers on short lateral growths produced from last year's wood, for example *Deutzia*, *Philadelphus*, and *Weigela*.

Without regular pruning to encourage development of vigorous, young growth from close to ground level, many shrubs in this group tend to become densely twiggy, often top-heavy, and the quantity and quality of flower deteriorate. The removal of spent flower heads also prevents shrubs from expending energy in seed production.

When planting any shrub in this group, cut out all weak or damaged growth and trim back the main shoots to a healthy bud or pair of buds, to encourage the development of a strong framework. If any flowers are produced in the first year, prune again immediately after flowering. Cut back flowered shoots to a strong bud or pair of buds and remove any

spindly growth. After pruning, lightly work in fertilizer and apply a mulch around the shrub.

Carry out the same procedure immediately after flowering in subsequent years. Although it is desirable to cut back flowered wood to the strongest buds, do not adhere to this rigidly because it is also important to maintain a well-balanced shape. Fertilize and mulch as a matter of course after pruning.

As plants mature, more drastic pruning may be required to encourage growth. After the third year, up to one-fifth of the oldest stems may be cut back annually to within 2–3in (5–8cm) of the ground.

Use your discretion when following these guidelines, since harsh pruning of young specimens of some shrubs in this group, for example forsythias, can result in an awkward and unnatural shape.

Other shrubs in this group, especially when grown as free-standing rather than as wall shrubs, require very little pruning. *Chaenomeles*, for example, has a naturally twiggy habit, with numerous crossing branches, and mature specimens need little pruning. Spur pruning will, however, encourage heavier flowering (see THE FRUIT GARDEN, "Spur pruning," p.432); shorten spurs and sideshoots to three to five leaves in midsummer.

Particular care must be taken in pruning shrubs, such as lilacs (*Syringa*), that come into growth during flowering. The new shoots that form below the flowers can be easily damaged when the old flower heads are cut, and this reduces flowering in the next year.

Flowering shrubs of suckering habit

A few shrubs that are grown for their flowers produce them on wood of the previous year. Most of the new growth is made from ground level. These shrubs spread by suckers and need to be pruned in a different way from those that form a permanent woody framework.

After planting, prune suckering shrubs by cutting out weak growth but retain vigorous stems and their sideshoots. The following year, immediately after flowering, remove any weak, dead, or damaged stems, then cut back flowered stems hard to a strong bud or pair of buds.

From the third year, annually cut back one-quarter to a half of all flowered stems to 2–3in (5–8cm) above ground level. Prune back others by about half to vigorous replacement shoots. After pruning the shrubs, fertilize, and mulch.

SHRUBS THAT SHOULD BE PRUNED IN SUMMER AFTER FLOWERING

Buddleia alternifolia
Calycanthus
Chaenomeles
Corylopsis
Cotoneaster (deciduous spp.)
Deutzia
Exochorda
Forsythia
Jasminum humile
Kolkwitzia
Magnolia
    x *soulangiana*,
    M. stellata

Neillia thibetica

Neillia
Philadelphus
Photinia villosa
Rhododendron (deciduous spp.)
Ribes sanguineum
Rubus deliciosus, *R.* 'Tridel'
Spiraea x *arguta*,
    S. prunifolia,
    S. thunbergii
Stephanandra
Syringa
Weigela

PRUNING SHRUBS IN SUMMER

After shrubs such as Weigela *have flowered, cut back flowered shoots and remove dead and spindly stems. Also prune out some old main stems.*

Using pruners, cut any dead wood back to healthy growth.

BEFORE

AFTER

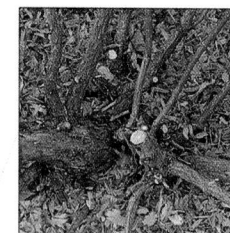

Cut out up to one-fifth of the oldest wood to within 2–3in (5–8 cm) of the ground.

Cut out any very weak, twiggy, or straggly stems back to the base just above soil level.

Continue cutting out weak or crossing stems to form a well-balanced, open-centered shrub.

PRUNING A DECIDUOUS SUCKERING SHRUB

After flowering, prune back all flowered stems on deciduous suckering shrubs (here Kerria*), most by about half, the remainder almost to the ground. Cut out any weak, dead, or damaged growth.*

Prune the flowered stems by about half their length, cutting back to strongly growing new shoots.

Cut back up to half of the flowered stems to within 2–3in (5–8cm) of the ground. Also cut to the ground any dead or damaged shoots.

Coppicing and pollarding shrubs

A number of deciduous shrubs grown for the ornamental value of their stems or leaves require severe pruning in spring. Most of them flower on shoots formed the previous season but, when grown for their stems or leaves, their flowers are sacrificed. The method of hard pruning used on these shrubs is essentially an adaptation of traditional methods of managing trees and shrubs to give a constant and renewable supply of wood for stakes, firewood, and fencing materials. In coppicing, shrubs and trees are cut back regularly to near ground level. In pollarding, growth is cut back each year to a permanent framework of a single stem or several stems.

Coppicing shrubs such as *Cornus alba* guarantees a regular supply of young growths, which are more strikingly colored than older wood and showier in winter. On shrubs such as *Sambucus racemosa* 'Plumosa Aurea' that are grown for their foliage, hard pruning generally results in larger leaves. Just before growth commences in early to midspring, coppice vigorous shrubs such as *Salix alba* 'Britzensis' (syn. *S. a.* 'Chermesina') by pruning all shoots to within about 2–3in (5–8cm) of ground level. It may be preferable to vary the height to which stems are cut back to avoid a rigid, uniform outline. Weaker shrubs such as *Cornus alba* 'Sibirica' may be cut back less severely by coppicing only about one-third to one-half of the stems. Then apply a quick-release fertilizer and mulch liberally, covering a circle of 24in (60cm) radius around the shrub.

Shrubs that have been trained so that they have one or more clean, main stems are pruned back – or pollarded – to this stem framework each

POLLARDING A EUCALYPTUS

Establish a framework by cutting back a young shrub to one or more main stems (below). Each subsequent spring, cut the previous year's growth back hard, either to within 2–3in (5–8cm) of the framework or to the base, since eucalyptus can regenerate from ground level (right).

season. The aim of pruning in the first year is to establish the framework. After planting, before growth commences in spring, cut back a young plant to form a standard with a single stem of 1–3ft (30–90cm). Alternatively, leave three, five, or seven stems, depending on the size of plant required and the space available in the garden. Apply a quick-release fertilizer and mulch around the stem (or stems), as for shrubs that are coppiced.

During the plant's first growing season, restrict the number of shoots growing from below the cut to only four or five, rubbing out all others that are superfluous and any that develop low down on the main stem. Continue this process for the next year or two; this will allow the main stem to thicken so that it will be able to support heavier top-growth. In

spring of the second and subsequent years, reduce the previous season's growths to above a bud within 2–3in (5–8cm) of the framework (see also *Pollarding a Eucalyptus*, above). If a larger specimen is needed, prune only a half or one-third of the stems. Fertilize and mulch.

Evergreen shrubs

The appropriate method for pruning and training most evergreen shrubs depends on the size they are expected to reach when mature. All evergreens that show signs of dieback after a particularly hard winter, however, should be treated in the same way, regardless of size.

In midspring, prune out all dead wood to where the shrub has started to regenerate, and thin out the new shoots if they are overcrowded or crossing. If a shrub shows no sign of life by midspring, nick the bark to see if there is any live green wood beneath. Some shrubs may remain dormant for an entire growing season.

Small shrubs up to 3ft (90cm)
Low-growing evergreen shrubs can be divided into two main groups, each requiring a different pruning technique. The first group includes a number of relatively short-lived shrubs that flower profusely, provided that they are trimmed each year and are not too old. Examples of these shrubs include lavender (*Lavandula*), lavender cotton (*Santolina chamaecyparissus*), and most heathers (*Calluna, Daboecia,*

SHRUBS FOR COPPICING AND POLLARDING

Coppicing
Cornus alba 'Aurea',
   C. a. 'Elegantissima',
   C. a. 'Flaviramea',
   C. a. 'Kesselringii',
   C. a. 'Sibirica',
   C. a. 'Spaethii',
   C. a. 'Variegata'

Corylus maxima 'Purpurea'
Cotinus coggygria,
   C. 'Grace'
Hydrangea paniculata
   'Floribunda',
   H. p. 'Grandiflora',
   H. p. 'Unique'
Rubus biflorus,
   R. cockburnianus,
   R. thibetanus
Salix alba 'Britzensis',
   S. daphnoides,
   S. irrorata
Sambucus racemosa 'Plumosa
   Aurea'

Pollarding
Cornus stolonifera
Cotinus coggygria
Eucalyptus
Euonymus alatus
Hydrangea paniculata
Salix acutifolia

and *Erica*, but not tree heaths). These shrubs are generally best replaced about every ten years or so. Also replace plants that have been left unpruned for several years since they become weak and leggy and seldom flower or regenerate successfully.

In midspring, use pruners or garden shears to cut out any weak growth or flowering shoots on newly planted shrubs. This makes sure that new growth is generated from basal shoots in the center of the plant. Each subsequent year in midspring, remove the old flower heads, as well as any dead, diseased, or damaged shoots. Some heathers have attractive winter foliage and these, as well as other evergreens, are sometimes deadheaded in fall. In very cold areas, however, there is a risk of dieback after fall deadheading, and for this reason pruning is normally delayed until midspring. After pruning, apply slow-release fertilizer at a rate of 2oz/sq yd (60g/sq m) and apply a mulch to a depth of 2in (5cm). The second group consists of slow-growing shrubs such as dwarf cotoneasters and *Hebe*. These require

COPPICING A SHRUB FOR WINTER STEM COLOR

With shrubs that have colored stems (here a Cornus stolonifera *cultivar), cut back hard all the shrub's stems to about 2–3in (5–8cm) from the base before growth begins in spring (see inset). Apply fertilizer around the shrub to promote new growth, and then mulch. Coppicing stimulates the growth of new, vigorous stems whose color is especially strong.*

less pruning than those in the first group, the main purpose in pruning being to remove dead, diseased, damaged, or severely congested shoots in midspring. Deadheading, however, is not necessary.

Medium-sized evergreen shrubs up to 10ft (3m) tall

Most medium-sized evergreen shrubs require little pruning once a well-balanced framework has been established. This principle applies to *Berberis darwinii*, camellias, *Escallonia*, *Hibiscus rosasinensis*, and many rhododendrons.

In midspring, just before growth is about to commence, remove any weak or crossing shoots as well as any that may upset the overall symmetry and balance of the shrub. Fertilize and mulch. Subsequent pruning is normally limited to cutting out straggly growth, restricting size, and shaping the plant to suit its position in the garden. Use pruners or long-handled loppers to remove all or part of selected branches.

Winter- or spring-flowering shrubs, such as *Berberis darwinii* and *Viburnum tinus*, should be pruned immediately after flowering. Prune *Escallonia* and others that flower from midsummer onward by removing older wood at the start of growth in midspring or by cutting out flowered stems in late summer. *Hibiscus rosa-sinensis*, with a flowering season from spring to fall,

is best pruned in midspring. Fertilize and mulch spring-pruned shrubs after pruning. Shrubs pruned in late summer should not be fertilized or mulched until the following spring, since any new, soft growth produced would be highly vulnerable to damage from winter cold.

Large, evergreen shrubs more than 10ft (3m) tall

Large rhododendrons and other tall evergreens require little pruning but may need shaping as young plants to create a well-balanced framework. Prune young plants in midspring or wait until the flowers have faded.

The aim of pruning here is to encourage an open-centered bush with well-spaced branches. Cut out all weak and crossing branches, and fertilize and mulch after pruning. Regular pruning is generally limited to the removal of dead, damaged, and diseased wood. Some large evergreens such as cherry laurels (*Prunus laurocerasus*) may also be used for hedging (see pp.82–4).

Palms and *Cordyline*

These require little or no pruning apart from the removal of dead leaves. Certain rhizomatous palms, for example *Chamaedorea*, can be invasive, however, in which case unwanted stems should be removed at ground level in spring.

The palmlike *Cordyline* needs pruning only if it has suffered frost damage or if a bushy, multistemmed specimen is required. Once new growth has started to appear, cut damaged branches back to just above newly formed shoots. Fertilize and apply a mulch. To create a multibranched specimen, remove the growing point before growth commences in spring, then fertilize and mulch.

Wall shrubs

There are three reasons for growing shrubs against walls. First, some are too tender for the open garden in frost-prone areas, but will thrive if sheltered against a warm wall. Second, training shrubs against a wall (including hardy shrubs such as firethorns) makes it possible to accommodate plants for which there might not otherwise be space. Third, some shrubs are natural scramblers (for example *Cestrum elegans*) and therefore need to have support of some kind.

It is important to train and prune all wall shrubs from an early stage so that they present a compact and well-tailored appearance and produce plenty of flowering shoots. When

training wall shrubs, provide a framework to which growth can be tied. A trellis, netting, or regularly spaced horizontal wires employed for wall-trained fruit trees (see p.413) may be used. Plant hardy shrubs in fall, marginally hardy or tender ones in spring.

Recommendations for pruning free-standing shrubs also apply to wall-trained specimens, but more care is needed for formative training and pruning. It is vital to tie in shoots as they grow and cut back sublaterals growing strongly away from the wall.

Formative training and pruning

During the first growing season, train in the leader and main laterals to form a framework. Prune back any outward-growing laterals to encourage short sideshoots to develop close to the framework. Remove completely any laterals growing toward the wall or fence, and any shoots that are growing outward in the wrong direction. The aim should be to create a neat, vertical carpet of foliage to cover the allotted space.

Routine pruning

In the second and subsequent seasons, flowering laterals should be formed. After flowering, cut back the flowered shoots to within 3–4in (7–10cm) of the main framework. This encourages new flowering laterals to develop, which will provide next season's display. Continue tying in framework shoots; trim outward-pointing laterals and remove inward-growing and other wrongly aligned shoots. Do not trim wall shrubs after midsummer since this may reduce the next year's flowering shoots. It may also induce *Ceanothus* and marginally hardy evergreen shrubs to produce soft growth liable to frost damage. Fertilize and mulch wall-trained shrubs annually in spring to maintain healthy growth.

Shrubs such as pyracanthas that are grown both for flowers and fruits or berries need slightly modified pruning. The shoots that have flowered are not cut back but are left to develop fruits. Trim back any laterals to two to three leaves

PRUNING EVERGREEN SHRUBS

After flowering, prune evergreen shrubs (here Prunus lusitanica) *by removing damaged or dead wood and cutting back flowered stems and any awkward or straggly stems that mar the shape.*

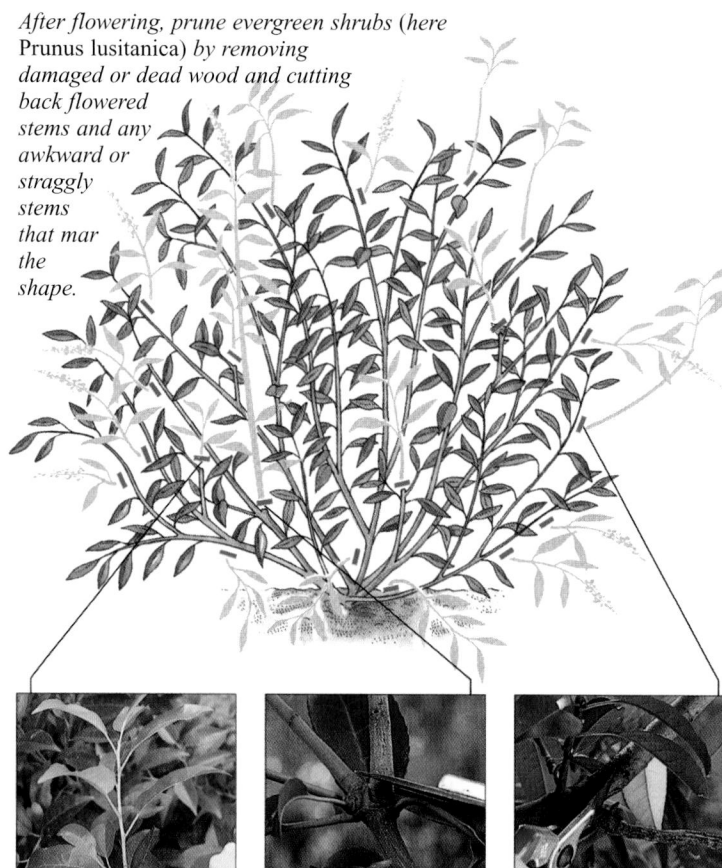

Cut back flowered stems to a main stem. Cut out thickly congested and crossing stems.

Cut back awkwardly growing stems to well-placed, healthy, outward-growing shoots.

Cut out any dead or damaged wood back to healthy growth or, if necessary, to the base.

EVERGREEN SHRUBS THAT TOLERATE SEVERE PRUNING
Aucuba
Berberis darwinii
Buxus
Choisya ternata
Citrus
Elaeagnus pungens
Escallonia 'Donard Seedling'
Euonymus fortunei, E. japonicus
Hibiscus rosa-sinensis
Ilex x *altaclerensis,* I. aquifolium
Ligustrum japonicum
Lonicera nitida, L. pileata
Nerium oleander
Phillyrea
Prunus laurocerasus, P. lusitanica
Rhododendron ponticum, R. Subsection Triflora (incl. R. augustinii)
Rosmarinus officinalis
Santolina
Sarcococca humilis
Taxus
Viburnum tinus

PRUNING AND TRAINING A YOUNG WALL SHRUB

In the first year, prune the shrub (here a Pyracantha) to build up a balanced framework, tying in main stems. In subsequent years, tie in new growth in spring; in midsummer, cut back inward- and outward-growing shoots to form a vertical "carpet," and remove dead, damaged, or spindly growth entirely.

Using pruners, cut back any weak, spindly stems as well as any dead or damaged wood.

Trim back any outward-growing stems to 3–4in (7–10cm) from the framework in midsummer.

Check and replace any broken ties, using garden twine tied in a figure eight to resecure the stem to the wire.

PRUNING AN ESTABLISHED WALL SHRUB

Prune mature plants to maintain a well-balanced framework of stems and, on berrying shrubs, to expose the berries. In late summer, remove outward-growing shoots and, with the exception of shrubs grown for their fruits or berries, cut back flowered shoots to promote dense growth. The shrub shown here is a Pyracantha.

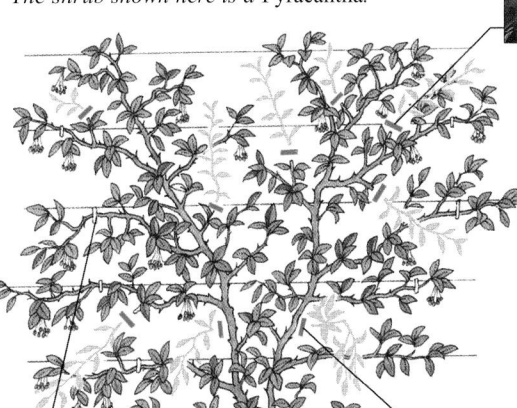

Cut back young shoots to 2–3 leaves from their base to expose the ripening berries.

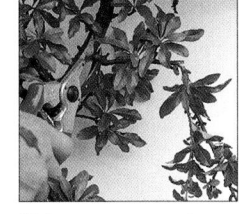

Using pruners, cut back any damaged or dead wood to healthy growth.

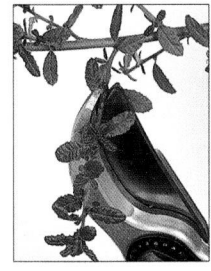

In late summer, check and replace ties where necessary; in spring, tie in new shoots.

from their base as the fruits swell, so that they are exposed to more light and ripen well. Old fruit clusters may be cut out in spring as young growths develop.

Summer- and fall-flowering wall shrubs, including some *Ceanothus*, should be trained as described earlier but pruned according to whether they flower on the previous season's wood (see "Shrubs pruned in summer after flowering," p.104) or that of the current season (see "Pruning in spring," p.103). Some less hardy or tender shrubs, particularly *Ceanothus*, do not grow readily from old wood and are difficult to renovate once neglected.

Scrambling shrubs

These also require careful training to contain their flexuous, often floppy and wayward shoots. On some (such as *Cestrum elegans*) that produce flowers in late summer on terminal shoots or short laterals, the flowered shoots may be cut out entirely or cut back to strong, low, lateral growths in spring. Others flower in summer mainly on lateral growths, which should be cut back after flowering to 3–4in (7–10cm) and will often produce further sublaterals that flower the same season. In spring, these laterals are pruned back again to 3–4in (7–10cm) and will flower in summer.

Fan-training ornamental shrubs

A few shrubs, such as ornamental peaches (for example *Prunus persica* 'Klara Meyer'), are suitable for fan-training like fruit trees. In the first spring after planting, cut back the plant 15–18in (38–45cm) above the graft union, retaining three or four strong shoots. Train the shoots on stakes tied to horizontal wires. Toward the end of the growing season, remove the central shoot if three strong shoots were retained; if four shoots were kept, space these out to form a fan. In winter, reduce all shoots by half their length.

The following growing season, select two or four new shoots on each stem. Attach each of these to a stake tied to the wires. Then, in midsummer, remove all other shoots. In the third year, immediately after flowering, cut back all framework shoots by a quarter to one-third. Tie in two or three new shoots on each framework stem. Remove unwanted shoots in midsummer. If there are gaps in the fan, prune back adjacent shoots by one-third after flowering has finished to encourage new growth. Cut back all other extension growths to 2–3in (5–7cm) to encourage flowering on one-year-old spurs. For full details, see THE FRUIT GARDEN, "Fan," p.447.

PRUNING CEANOTHUS

Immediately after flowering, cut back new shoots of spring-flowering Ceanothus *to 2–3 leaves. Tie in new shoots and trim back outward-growing shoots to keep growth trained close to the wall or fence.*

FAN-TRAINING A SHRUB

This fan (Prunus mume 'Beni-shi-dare') *has been trained to develop an evenly spaced branch framework, in the same way as pruning fan-trained fruit trees.*

Training and pruning standard shrubs

Some shrubs, for example fuchsias and *Buddleja alternifolia*, can be grown as standards. The height of the stem varies according to the vigor of the plant and the result wanted. For details on pruning a standard rose, see p.160.

To train a shrub such as *Buddleja alternifolia* as a standard, tie a strong stem to a stake in the first growing season. Pinch all sideshoots back to two or three leaves, leaving a few growing near the stem tip. As the stem grows, continue to pinch back. When the clear stem is at the desired height, pinch the terminal shoot to encourage shoots to form the head. In early spring of the following year, shorten the branches of the head to about 6in (15cm). Retain two or three of the shoots that each produces. Fertilize and mulch. Prune subsequently as for other shrubs pruned in summer after flowering (see p.104).

Some pendulous cultivars are grafted onto the clear stem of a rootstock. Remove any suckers (see p.98) from the stock and treat as for roses (see "Suckers and how to deal with them," p.157).

Root pruning

Root pruning is sometimes used to control the top-growth of vigorous shrubs and to make them flower more freely. Grafted specimens that are making prolific leaf growth but producing few flowers or fruits usually benefit from root pruning.

In early spring, dig a trench around the shrub to a depth of 12–24in (30–60cm) with a circumference just beyond the spread of the top-growth. Use loppers or a saw to cut back the thick, woody roots; as a guideline, shorten them to about half the radius of the trench. Leave the fine, fibrous feeder roots unpruned. Control further spreading of the roots by inserting a barrier of rigid plastic or heavy-gauge plastic sheeting around the circumference of the trench to a depth of at least 2ft (60cm). After backfilling, mulch the area within the trench to a depth of 3in (8cm).

Root pruning is often used to control container-grown shrubs. This is best carried out when repotting the shrub. Shorten up to one-fifth of woody roots by a quarter and cut back others so that they fit comfortably in the container. Repot, using fresh soil mix with a slow-release fertilizer added, and water thoroughly.

Renovation

Old, tangled, or overgrown shrubs can sometimes be renovated by extensive pruning. Shrubs that respond well usually produce young growth from the base. It is not worth trying to salvage a shrub that is badly diseased. Some shrubs do not tolerate drastic pruning; if in any doubt about a particular shrub, stagger a program of heavy pruning over a period of two or three years.

Renovate deciduous shrubs such as lilacs after flowering or when dormant; for evergreens such as *Viburnum tinus*, delay renovation until midspring.

Renovating old or overgrown shrubs

Cut out all weak and crossing stems and shorten main stems to 12–18in (30–45cm) above ground level, ensuring that a balanced framework is left. Apply a slow-release fertilizer at 4oz/sq yd (120g/sq m), and mulch the area around the shrub to a depth of 2–4in (5–10cm). Keep the shrub well watered throughout summer.

During the following growing season, a mass of shoots should grow from below the cuts on the main stems. Retain only two to four of the strongest on each stem to provide the new branch framework. On deciduous shrubs, cut out superfluous shoots during the dormant season. On evergreen shrubs, do this in midspring.

In the following growing season, some secondary growth may occur where shoots have been cut. Rub out these growths.

Staggered renovation

An alternative, less drastic method is to spread the pruning over two or three years. Prune deciduous shrubs after flowering, evergreens in midspring. Prune half of the oldest stems to 2–3in (5–8cm) from the ground. Where possible cut back the remaining stems by about half to new, vigorous shoots. Apply a slow-release fertilizer, water well, and mulch. At the same time the following year, repeat the process on the remaining old stems. Thereafter, prune the shrub according to its growth and flowering characteristics.

DRASTIC RENOVATION

A shrub that produces new growth from the base (here a lilac) can be renovated when dormant if it is deciduous or in midspring if evergreen. Cut back all main stems to within 12–18in (30–45cm) of the ground. Remove suckers by cutting them off at the base.

GRADUAL RENOVATION

Renovate deciduous shrubs after flowering and evergreens in midspring. Cut back a third to a half of the oldest main stems (here on a Philadelphus) *almost to the ground and remove dead, twiggy stems. Over the next year or two cut back remaining old main stems.*

Cut back about half of the stems to within 2–3in (5–8cm) of the base. Remove the oldest stems and any that spoil the shrub's shape.

Cut back older stems by half to new, vigorous shoots, and remove any weak, twiggy growth or dead wood.

Prune back any crossing, rubbing, or congested stems to a bud or stem that will not cause another crossing shoot to develop.

Propagation

THERE are many ways to propagate shrubs to raise new plants, including taking cuttings, sowing seed, layering, division, and grafting.

Taking cuttings is a simple way of propagating many shrubs and, unlike seed, which may produce variable offspring, it may be used for cultivars, hybrids, and sports.

Sowing seed is simple and inexpensive but it is relatively slow to produce plants of flowering size. Some shrubs can be divided, while others can be layered, a method of stimulating stems to root while still attached to the parent plant.

Grafting involves uniting a stem from the plant to be propagated with the rootstock of a compatible plant. It is not commonly used since it requires more expertise and skill than other methods, but it is the most suitable method for some shrubs.

Softwood cuttings

This technique is suitable for raising several (mainly deciduous) shrubs, for example *Fuchsia* and *Perovskia*.

Softwood cuttings are taken in spring from fast-growing stem tips. They have a soft base and a higher capacity to root than cuttings of maturer wood.

Preparing the cuttings

Take the cuttings early in the morning. Select healthy, pliable, single-stemmed shoots and seal them in an opaque plastic bag. Prepare the cuttings as soon as possible after collection. Trim the cuttings to 3–4in (8–10cm), just below a node, and remove the lower leaves. Use a rooting medium of equal parts peat and either perlite or sharp sand. Insert the cuttings into the soil mix. Water them in, applying a fungicide to minimize rot, and label.

Aftercare

Softwood cuttings wilt quickly if not kept in a humid atmosphere, so aftercare is very important.

Cover the pots with a clear plastic bag or, alternatively, place them in a mist box. A mist box, or fogging chamber, is a simple way to control humidity for softwood cuttings. Construct mist boxes by covering a

USING A MIST BOX

A mist box may be used to maintain the high humidity needed for softwood cuttings. Attach plastic sheets to a homemade frame and place a cool-mist humidifier inside. Do not run the humidifier constantly, or moisture levels will rise too high.

homemade wood frame with sturdy clear plastic. Use pieces of plastic long enough to be tucked underneath the edges of the frame. A cool-mist humidifier designed for household use is ideal for maintaining the humidity inside the box, but it should not be used constantly or moisture levels will get too high. A humidistat can be a useful addition. Air the box every few days to provide good air

circulation, or leave one side open. Remove fallen leaves daily and apply a fungicidal spray weekly. Harden off the rooted cuttings and transplant into individual pots. Water, label, and keep them in a shaded position. Alternatively, grow on the rooted cuttings in the original container, giving supplementary fertilizer every two weeks and planting out individually the next spring.

PROPAGATING SHRUBS BY SOFTWOOD CUTTINGS

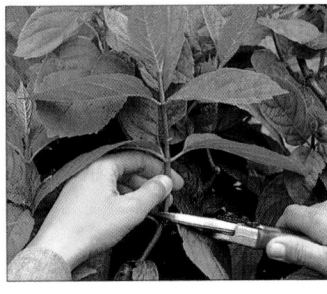

1 *In spring, cut off young, non-flowering shoots (here from* Hydrangea paniculata) *with 3–5 pairs of leaves. Seal them in an opaque plastic bag and keep shaded until they can be prepared.*

2 *Reduce each cutting to 3–4in (8–10cm) in length, making a straight cut just below a node (see inset). Trim off the lower leaves.*

3 *Insert the cuttings into prepared pots of rooting medium, making sure that the leaves do not touch each other.*

4 *Water the cuttings with a fungicidal solution, then label and place them in a propagator. Maintain a temperature of 64–70°F (18–21°C).*

5 *Once the cuttings have rooted, harden them off, then remove them from the pot and carefully tease them apart.*

6 *Transplant the separated cuttings into individual pots and firm in. Water, label, and keep the cuttings in a shaded position until well established.*

SHRUBS THAT MAY BE PROPAGATED BY SOFTWOOD CUTTINGS

Abelia
Abutilon
Buddleia
Calluna
Caryopteris
Ceanothus (deciduous spp.)
Ceratostigma
Cotoneaster (deciduous spp.)
Cytisus
Daboecia
Daphne x *burkwoodii*
Enkianthus
Erica
Forsythia
Fuchsia
Genista
Halesia
Hydrangea
Kolkwitzia
Lagerstroemia
Lantana
Lavatera
Lonicera
Nandina
Perovskia
Philadelphus
Potentilla
Rosa
Spiraea
Syringa
Viburnum (deciduous spp.)
Vitex

PROPAGATING BY SEMIRIPE CUTTINGS

1 *In mid- to late summer, select healthy shoots of the current season's growth for the cuttings. Sever them from the parent plant (here Ilex x altaclerensis 'Golden King') just above a node. They should be semiripe – still soft at the top but firm at the base.*

2 *Remove the side shoots from the main stem. Trim each side shoot to 4–6in (10–15cm) long, cutting just below a node.*

3 *Trim off the soft tip of each cutting and then remove the lowest pair of leaves, cutting flush with the stem.*

4 *Stimulate rooting by wounding the cutting: carefully cut away a piece of bark about 1–1½in (2.5–4cm) long from one side of the base.*

5 *Dip the base of each cutting in hormone rooting powder, then insert it into rooting medium in a propagator or in pots in a cold frame.*

6 *Once they are well rooted, carefully lift the cuttings and plant them individually. Gradually harden them off before growing them on in their pots or transplanting them outside.*

Semiripe cuttings

Many evergreen as well as some deciduous shrubs may be propagated from semiripe cuttings, including some that are difficult to propagate from hardwood cuttings such as *Aucuba* and *Choisya*.

Suitable cuttings

The cuttings are normally taken from mid- to late summer and sometimes into the early fall. Select shoots from the current season's growth that are firm and woody near the base but still soft at the tip. Unlike softwood cuttings, they should offer some resistance when bent. Some shrubs are propagated by variations of this semiripe cuttings technique, such as mallet cuttings (see opposite) or leaf-bud cuttings (see opposite).

Preparing the rooting medium

Before gathering the cutting material from the parent shrub, fill sufficient containers of appropriate size or a propagator (equipped with basal heating) with a suitable rooting medium: use fine-grade pine bark or a mixture of equal parts of peat and either grit, sharp sand, vermiculite, or perlite.

Preparing the cuttings

Cuttings may be taken with a heel (see opposite) or as nodal cuttings. Heel cuttings should be 2–3in (5–7cm) long, trimmed to a short heel at the base. Nodal cuttings should be 4–6in (10–15cm) long, taken from leaders or side shoots, and cut with a sharp knife just below a node.

Remove the soft tips of nodal and heel cuttings. In both cases, remove the lowest pair of leaves, and with large-leaved plants reduce the size of the remaining leaves by about a half to minimize moisture loss.

An optional step is to prepare the base of the cuttings by making a shallow wound at one side. On plants that are difficult to root, such as *Daphne sericea*, this cut should be made deeper so that a sliver of bark is also removed.

Potting up

Dip the bases of the cuttings, including the entire wound on wounded cuttings, in a rooting hormone before using a dibber to insert them in the prepared medium, either directly in a propagator or in containers.

Space the cuttings approximately 3–4in (8–10cm) apart, and make certain that their leaves do not overlap, since this may create stagnant conditions in which rot fungi thrive. Gently firm the medium around the cuttings. Label each container

and water the cuttings thoroughly with a fungicidal solution to protect them against damping-off diseases (see p.655).

Correct temperature

Overwinter cuttings in containers in a cold frame or greenhouse. Those that have been inserted directly in a propagator should have basal heat maintained at 70°F (21°C).

Aftercare

Inspect the cuttings periodically during the winter, removing any fallen leaves promptly. Water the containers if the medium shows any signs of drying out, such as slight shrinking toward the edges of the container. If the cuttings are being overwintered in a cold frame, it may need some form of insulation, such as a burlap cover or a piece of old carpet, to protect the cuttings from damage by cold.

Cuttings kept in a cold frame or unheated greenhouse will almost certainly need a further growing season in their containers before rooting satisfactorily. Keep the frame closed, except on very mild days. The glass should be kept clean and free of any condensation, since the high moisture content of the air inside the frame provides ideal conditions for fungal infection to occur. In late spring and early summer, gradually open the cover for longer and longer periods to harden off the rooted cuttings. If necessary, protect the cuttings from strong, direct sunlight by covering the glass with suitable shading material.

Throughout the growing season, apply liquid fertilizer every two weeks to all semiripe cuttings. Check them regularly, and remove any that are weak or showing signs of disease.

Transplanting

Cuttings overwintered in a propagator should have rooted by early spring, since the basal heat helps to speed up root development. Check that there is strong root growth before transplanting the cuttings. Ease them from their containers, separate each cutting carefully, and either pot up individually or plant, clearly labeled, in the open ground. If some cuttings have not rooted but have formed a callus, scrape off some of the callus to stimulate rooting and reinsert the cuttings in the medium until roots have formed.

Cuttings grown in a cold frame may be planted out in fall, if well developed, or kept in a sheltered position outside or in the cold frame until spring. They are then potted up individually or planted out.

Heel cuttings

Heel cuttings, which may be taken from greenwood, semiripe, or hardwood stems, are vigorous side shoots of the current season's growth. Each cutting is taken with a "heel" of old wood at its base, in which the growth hormones that assist the rooting process are concentrated.

Heel cuttings are particularly suitable for a number of evergreen shrubs such as *Pieris* and some azaleas (*Rhododendron*), deciduous shrubs that have pithy or hollow stems such as barberry (*Berberis*) and elder (*Sambucus*), and those

shrubs that have greenwood stems such as broom (*Cytisus* and *Genista*).

Select as cuttings healthy sideshoots that are characteristic of the parent. Carefully pull the shoot from the main stem so that a small strip of bark from the parent comes away with it. Avoid excessively tearing the bark of the main shoot since this may expose it to infection. Trim the heel and follow the technique for greenwood (see p.626), semiripe (opposite), or hardwood cuttings (see right), according to the stem's maturity.

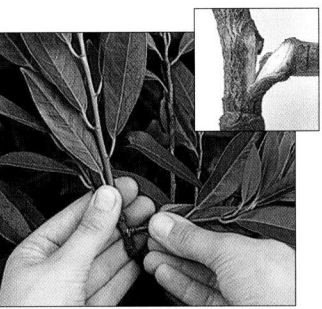

1 *Pull away healthy sideshoots of the current season's growth (here on* Prunus laurocerasus *'Schipkaensis') with a heel of bark.*

2 *Using a sharp knife, trim off the tail at the base of the cutting before inserting it in rooting medium.*

Mallet cuttings

A mallet cutting, which is taken from semiripe stems, is a ripened shoot of the current season's growth attached to a piece of wood from the previous season, forming a mallet-shaped plug at its base. These cuttings are often used to propagate shrubs with pithy or hollow stems, because rot fungi are less likely to affect older wood. It is particularly

suitable for many *Spiraea* and deciduous *Berberis*, which produce short sideshoots on main branches.

In late summer, remove a stem of the last season's growth from the parent and cut it into sections, each containing a vigorous sideshoot of new growth. If the mallet is more than ¼in (5mm) in diameter, slit it lengthwise. Then treat as for semiripe cuttings (see opposite).

MALLET CUTTINGS

Remove a stem produced the previous year, and cut it above each sideshoot and about 1in (2.5cm) below. Reduce it to 4–5in (10–13cm), and trim off lower leaves.

Leaf-bud cuttings

A leaf-bud cutting is taken from a semiripe stem and consists of a short piece of stem bearing a leaf and a leaf bud. In comparison with stem cuttings, leaf-bud cuttings make much more economical use of the material that is taken from the parent plant. This method of propagation is most commonly used for camellias.

In late summer or early fall, select a vigorous shoot of the current season's growth bearing healthy leaves and well-developed buds. Using a sharp knife or pruners, cut the stem just above each leaf, then make a cut about ¾in (2cm) below the petiole so that the shoot is divided into several sections.

Leaf-bud cuttings do not need to be treated with hormone rooting powder before potting up, but may be wounded at the base to hasten rooting. Insert them in containers of rooting medium and treat as for semiripe cuttings (see opposite).

To save space, roll up any large leaves and secure them with rubber bands. A stake inserted down the middle of a rolled-up leaf will give extra support by helping to anchor it firmly in the soil mix. Trim compound leaves on shrubs such as *Mahonia* by a half.

Hardwood cuttings

Where the soil does not freeze deeply, an easy way to raise many shrubs is from hardwood cuttings. Use ripe, vigorous growths of the current season, taken from midfall to early winter. Take cuttings of deciduous shrubs just after leaf fall.

Preparing the ground
Cuttings are best rooted in a prepared bed or containers kept in a

PROPAGATING BY LEAF-BUD CUTTINGS

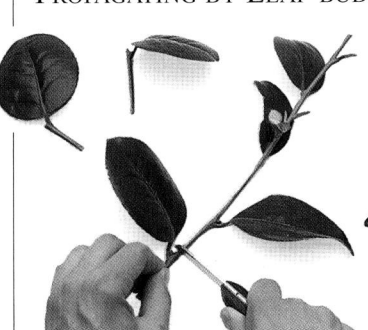

1 *Select semiripe shoots (here of* Camellia japonica*). Make a straight cut ¾in (2cm) below each leaf and a further cut just above.*

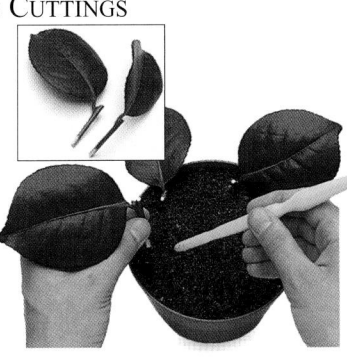

2 *Remove a ¼in (5mm) sliver of bark at the base of each cutting (see inset). Insert the cuttings in the medium so that the leaf axils are just visible above the surface.*

SHRUBS THAT MAY BE PROPAGATED BY SEMIRIPE CUTTINGS

Andromeda
Arctostaphylos
Aucuba▽
Azara ▽
Berberis ▽
Boronia ▽
Brachyglottis
Bruckenthalia
Bupleurume
Callistemon ▽
Camellia
Cantua ▽
Carmichaelia ▽
Carpenteria▽
Cassinia▽
Cassiope▽
Ceanothus ▽
Colletia▽
Coprosma ▽
Corokia▽

Cotoneaster 'Firebird'

Cotoneaster▽
Cytisus ▽
Daphne
Deutzia
Drimys
Elaeagnus▽
Escallonia▽
Garrya▽
Gordonia ▽
Grevillea ▽
Hibiscus rosa-sinensis
Ilex
Itea ilicifolia▽
Lavandula
Leptospermum ▽
Leucothoë▽
Magnolia grandiflora▽
Mahonia
Nerium ▽

Olearia phlogopappa

Olearia ▽
Philadelphus
Photinia▽
Pieris▽
Pittosporum
Prunus (evergreen spp.)▽
Pyracantha
Rhododendron▽
Skimmia▽
Spiraea
Viburnum
Weigela

KEY
▽ *With a heel*

111

SHRUBS THAT MAY BE PROPAGATED BY HARDWOOD CUTTINGS

Atriplex halimus
Aucuba japonica
Buddleia
Buxus
Cornus alba, C. stolonifera
Cotoneaster x *watereri*
Deutzia x *elegantissima*
  'Rosealind', *D. longifolia,*
  D. x *rosea, D. scabra*
Forsythia
Hypericum x *moserianum*
Ligustrum ovalifolium
Philadelphus

Deutzia longifolia 'Veitchii'

Ribes
Rosa rugosa
Rubus
Ruta graveolens
Salix
Sambucus
Spiraea
Symphoricarpos
Tamarix
Viburnum (deciduous spp.)
Weigela

cold frame, but they may also be inserted in a bed in open ground.

Prepare the bed in late summer or early fall, first working the soil until it is friable, and then digging out a flat-backed trench 5–6in (12–15cm) deep. To encourage rooting, put a 1–2in (2.5–5cm) layer of coarse sand in the base of the trench; this is essential on heavy soils. Space the trenches 15in (38cm) apart.

Preparing the cuttings
Take cuttings that are about pencil thickness, cutting at the junction of the current and the previous season's growth.

Trim the cuttings into 6in (15cm) lengths, cutting at the top just above a bud or pair of buds and, at the bottom, below a bud or pair of buds; on evergreens, make the cuts above and below leaves. Take heel cuttings of pithy stems (see p.111). Remove all leaves on the bottom two-thirds of evergreen cuttings, and cut large leaves in half. Treat the basal cut with a rooting hormone. Removing a sliver of bark near the base may encourage difficult cuttings to root.

Insert the cuttings in containers of rooting medium. Alternatively, place them against the vertical side of the prepared trench, 6in (15cm) apart in open ground or, in a cold frame, 4in (10cm) apart. Leave

1–2in (2.5–5cm) of the cuttings above ground. Backfill the trench and firm in the cuttings.

Aftercare
If the ground is lifted by frost, firm it down around the cuttings. Keep the bed weed-free and well watered during the growing season. Cuttings in a cold frame will normally root by the following spring. Harden them off before potting up or planting out. Those in the open ground should be left in place until the following fall and then transplanted to their permanent position.

Root cuttings

Shrubs that may be propagated from root cuttings include *Aesculus parviflora, Aralia, Clerodendrum, Myrica, Rhus,* and *Xanthorhiza simplicissima*. Lift a young plant when dormant and tease the soil from its roots. If this is not practical, expose part of the shrub's root system. Cut off young roots – 1/4in (5mm) in diameter or more – close to the main stem. Keep them in moist burlap or a plastic bag until they can be prepared.

Preparing the cuttings
First remove and discard fibrous lateral roots. Then make a straight cut on an undamaged root at the end where it was severed from the plant. At the opposite end of the root, make a slanting cut. Cuttings should be 2–6in (5–15cm) long, so several cuttings may be prepared from the same root. The colder the rooting environment and the thinner the root, the longer the cutting needs to be; cuttings to be rooted outdoors need to be at least 4in (10cm) long. Dust each cutting with fungicide but do not treat with a rooting powder, since this will tend to discourage the production of shoots.

Inserting the cuttings
Aralia and other shrubs that reproduce readily from root cuttings may be inserted in open ground. For shrubs that root less readily, a controlled environment is preferable. Prepare containers of rooting medium large enough for several cuttings. Firm the medium lightly and insert each cutting vertically 2in (5cm) apart with the slanted end down. Firm the medium so that the flat end of each cutting is just visible. Cover with 1/8in (3mm) of sand, and water. This watering may be sufficient to last until the shoots develop; excessive moisture may lead to rot.

Aftercare
Cuttings will root in ten weeks outdoors, eight weeks in a cold frame or cool greenhouse. Under cover, cuttings will produce shoots in four to six weeks if they are kept at 64–75°F (18–24°C). Cuttings from shrubs that make rapid growth should be repotted as soon as they have rooted. Other root cuttings may be left in their containers for 12 additional months; apply liquid fertilizer once or twice a month. Then pot up singly or plant out in nursery beds.

Raising shrubs from seed

Growing shrubs from seed is simple and economical. In genera whose species hybridize readily, only use seed produced by controlled pollination.

Gathering and cleaning seed
Gather the seed capsules or fruits when ripe. Extract the seed, then clean and dry it before sowing or storing. Soak fleshy fruits in warm water or squash them so that the

EXTRACTING SEED FROM BERRIES

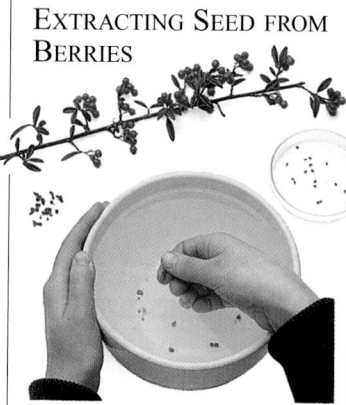

1 *Mash the berries (here Pyracantha) between finger and thumb, removing most of the outer flesh. Wash the seeds by rubbing in warm water.*

2 *Dry the seeds and place them in a clear plastic bag with a little sphagnum moss or coarse sand, then refrigerate them until ready to sow.*

PROPAGATING SHRUBS BY HARDWOOD CUTTINGS

1 *Select strong, healthy, ripened shoots from this year's growth for the cuttings (see inset, left); avoid weak, thin stems (center) and older wood (right).*

Healthy   Weak   Old wood

2 *Remove any deciduous leaves and trim off the soft wood at the tip. Cut the stem into 6in (15cm) lengths. Then dip the bases into hormone rooting powder.*

3 *Insert the cuttings into prepared pots of rooting medium so that approximately 1–2in (2.5–5cm) of each is visible. Label the pots and place in a cold frame.*

seed may be picked out more easily. Gather fine seed by gathering whole capsules, preferably when they have already turned brown. Place the capsules in a paper bag and keep at room temperature until they split open.

Storing seed
The length of time seed is viable depends on the species and the storage conditions. Oily seeds do not store well and should be sown soon after harvesting. The viability of seed may be prolonged if it is stored at a temperature of 37–41°F (3–5°C) in low humidity.

Breaking seed dormancy
The seeds of some shrubs have a form of dormancy to prevent germination in adverse conditions. This dormancy may be broken artificially by scarification or stratification (see also PRINCIPLES OF PROPAGATION, "How to overcome dormancy," p.623).

To allow air and moisture to penetrate large seeds with hard coats, such as peonies (*Paeonia*), scarify them by nicking the seed coat with a knife or filing away a small section before sowing. Hard-coated seeds that are too small to be nicked may be rubbed with sandpaper. Germination of some seeds may be aided by soaking the seed in either cold water (for example *Camellia* and *Pittosporum*) or hot but not boiling water (for example *Caragana* and *Coronilla*) for a few hours. This softens the hard seed coat, allowing water to enter and the germination process to begin.

Some seeds need a period of chilling, or stratification. As soon as the seed is gathered, put it in a plastic zip-locking bag and add a mix of equal parts of barely moist peat and sand. Store in the refrigerator below 41°F (5°C), put the container in the open garden, or place it in a cold frame. After about 90 days (or in spring for seeds kept outside during winter), the mix should be spread on the surface of a pot of sowing medium and placed in a warm location to germinate.

Some seeds may not require 90 days' stratification, so inspect the bags from time to time and, if germination is occurring, remove and sow. Other seeds may need more than the 90-day period; if in doubt, sow portions of the seed at two-week intervals thereafter.

Sowing seed in containers
Most seed should be sown in fall; however, seeds of tender shrubs that in temperate regions are germinated under cover should be sown in spring. Clean all containers, implements, and surfaces. Use a standard sowing medium, but for alkalinity-intolerant plants, use an acidic medium.

Station sow large seeds. Overfill a pot or tray with medium and gently firm before scraping off the surplus. Firm again with a presser board so that the level is ½in (1cm) below the rim of the pot or tray. Sow the seeds 2in (5cm) apart, then firm them evenly into the medium. Cover with a ¼in (5mm) layer of sieved medium and a ¼in (5mm) layer of clean sand. Label and date, then water the seeds. Many medium-sized seeds may also be sown in this way, but the gap between the rim and medium should be ¼–⅜in (5–8mm). Cover seeds with sieved medium and then ¼in (5mm) of clean sand. Place wire netting over the container to protect the seedlings from small animals. When sowing fine seed, firm the medium to within ¼in (5mm) of the container rim. Water and allow the medium to drain before sowing, carefully shaking the seed out over the surface. Do not cover the seed or water it from above.

Aftercare for seedlings in containers
After sowing, place the containers in a propagator, greenhouse, or cold frame. Temperate species need a temperature of 54–59°F (12–15°C); warm-temperate and tropical species prefer 70°F (21°C). For seed sown in spring under cover, a temperature of 54–59°F (12–15°C) should be maintained. Inspect containers of seed regularly and water as necessary. Never water fine seed from above; place the container in a shallow pan of water for a short time so that water is taken up by capillary action. When the seeds have germinated, spray occasionally with fungicide.

Pricking out
Once large enough to handle, prick out the seedlings. Either knock the sides of the container to loosen the medium, or remove the seedlings and medium together and separate the seedlings, disturbing their roots as little as possible.

Transfer the seedlings into clean pots or seed trays of soil mix, leveled but not firmed. Make a hole in the soil mix and insert the seedling. Level the soil mix by tapping the top of the container and firm in, then label and water. Until the seedlings are established, the pots should be placed out of direct sunlight in a temperature similar to that needed for germination.

Sowing seed outdoors
Open-ground seedbeds are useful for sowing large batches of seed that do not require daily attention. Prepare the bed between six months and a year before sowing the seeds, and get rid of weed seedlings as they appear.

In fall, rake the soil to a fine tilth. Sow the seed in rows 18in (45cm) apart, station sowing medium or large seeds 4–6in (10–15cm) apart and sowing fine seed thinly.

Cover large and medium seeds to a depth of ¼–½in (0.5–1cm) but leave fine seed uncovered. Then place a ¼–½in (0.5–1cm) layer of sand over the seedbed. Firm the sand with a presser board, and label the rows.

Aftercare for seedlings outdoors
Protect seedlings from wind with a burlap screen. If the seeds are well spaced, they should not be troubled by disease, but spider mites (p.640), aphids (p.639), and mice, rats, and voles (p.653) may be a problem.

If the spacing is adequate, the seedlings may be left in the seedbed until the following fall, at which time they should then be either potted up or transplanted into a separate nursery bed.

SOWING SEED IN CONTAINERS

1 Sow seeds evenly onto a prepared tray of sieved sowing medium by tapping them from a folded piece of paper.

2 Cover the seeds with a fine layer of sowing medium a ¼in (5mm) layer of sand. Label and place in a cold frame until the seeds have germinated.

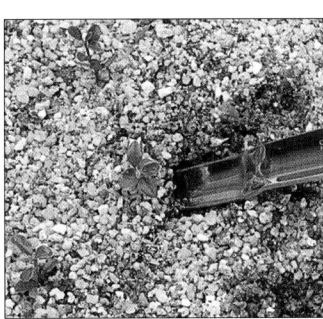

3 When the seedlings are large enough to handle, prick them out, lifting them carefully with a widger and holding them gently by their leaves.

4 Transfer the seedlings into individual pots or insert 3 into a 5in (13cm) pot. After the second pair of leaves has formed, pot them up individually.

SHRUB SEED THAT REQUIRES SPECIAL TREATMENT
Stratification
Amelanchier
Cornus
Cotoneaster
Euonymus
Hippophäe
Ilex
Lindera
Viburnum (some spp.)

Scarification
Camellia
Paeonia

Soaking
Arbutus
Callicarpa
Camellia
Caragana
Coronilla
Cytisus
Pittosporum

Sown when fresh
Acer palmatum
Daphne
Kalmia
Rhododendron

Kalmia latifolia

Propagation by layering

Layering is a method of propagating shrubs whereby a stem is encouraged to develop roots before being removed from the parent plant. Dropping and stooling, techniques often used commercially, are variations of layering.

Simple layering

Many deciduous and evergreen shrubs may be propagated by this method. In fall or spring, about 12 months before layering is to take place, prune a low branch on the parent plant to encourage vigorous shoots, which have a greater capacity to root. Between the following late fall and early spring, prepare the soil around the stem to be layered so that it is friable. Add sand and compost if the ground is heavy.

Retain any leaves at the tip of the selected shoot, but strip off others and any sideshoots. Bring the stem down to ground level and mark the ground about 9–12in (22–30cm) behind its tip. Dig a shallow hole or trench at this point for the stem. Wound the stem at the point where it will be pegged into the hole, which is about 12in (30cm) behind its tip, either with an angled cut or by removing a ring of bark. Dust the cut with rooting hormone, then peg the stem in the hole with bent wire, turning up the tip and securing it to a stake. Fill in the trench and firm the soil, leaving the tip exposed.

Throughout the growing season keep the area around the layer moist. The layer should have rooted by fall. In the following spring, check that there is a good root system before severing the layer from the parent plant and potting it up or planting it out in the open garden. If it has not rooted or there are only a few roots, keep it attached and in place for another growing season.

Air layering

This technique is particularly suitable for shrubs with branches that are difficult to lower to ground level.

In spring, choose a strong, healthy one-year-old stem that has ripened. Trim the sideshoots or leaves to produce a clear length of stem behind the tip. Wound the stem with an angled cut, then dust the cut surface with a rooting hormone.

Cut off the sealed end of a black or opaque plastic bag, about 7 x 9in (18 x 22cm). Slip it over the stem like a sleeve and secure the end farthest from the growing tip by tying the bag tightly around the stem using insulating tape, raffia, or string.

Moisten a well-aerated rooting medium of sphagnum moss or equal parts of perlite and peat so that it is wet but not sodden. Pack the moist medium into the bag around the stem's cut surface and seal the top end. Keep the bag in position for a complete season.

The following spring, check that the layer has rooted. If so, sever it immediately below the point of layering. Remove the bag and tease out the roots. Prune back any new growth on the layered stem to a leaf or bud close to the old wood. Pot up using a standard or acidic potting soil mix, as appropriate. Label and place the layer in a cool greenhouse or cold frame until the young plant is well established. If only a few (or no) roots have developed when the bag is removed, reseal it and leave it in place for several months more. Then again carry out the process described above.

Tip layering

A few shrubs, mainly species and hybrids of the genus *Rubus*, root readily from the tips of stems and may be propagated in this way. In spring, select a vigorous one-year-old shoot and pinch out the growing point to promote sideshoots. In late spring, cultivate the soil around the shoot. Work in organic matter and sand if the soil is heavy.

In midsummer, when the tip growth has firmed slightly, bring the stem down to ground level and mark the position of the tip. At that point, dig a trench about 3–4in (7–10cm) deep, with one side vertical and the other sloping toward the parent plant. Using inverted U-shaped wire staples, peg the growing tip at the bottom of the trench close to the vertical side. Fill in the trench, firm lightly, and water.

By late fall, well-rooted plants should have developed. Sever these at the point where the arched stem enters the trench. Lift the rooted layers and pot on or replant outdoors. (See also *Tip Layering*, p.465.)

Dropping

With this technique a plant is almost buried. It is used to raise dwarf shrubs such as low-growing rhododendrons and heathers (*Erica*, *Daboecia*, *Calluna*) from parent plants that have become straggly.

In the dormant season, thin out branches of plants that have a mass of congested stems, to allow the remaining stems sufficient contact with the soil to develop roots once

PROPAGATING A SHRUB BY SIMPLE LAYERING

1 Select a young, pliable, low-growing stem. Bring it down to the soil and mark its position with a stake about 9–12in (22–30cm) behind the tip.

2 At the marked point, dig a hole in the prepared soil about 3in (8cm) deep, with a shallow slope on the side where the stem joins the parent plant.

3 Trim off sideshoots and leaves on the selected stem. On the underside of the stem, at a point where it touches the ground, cut a tongue of bark.

4 Apply a rooting hormone to the wound on the stem. Peg down the stem with bent wire so that the stem's cut surface is held in contact with the soil.

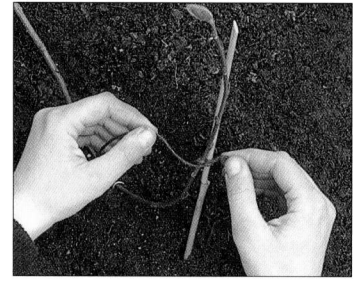

5 Gently bend up the stem's tip vertically and secure it to the stake with a tie. Fill in the hole with more soil. Lightly firm with your fingers and water in.

6 Once rooted (see inset), lift the layered stem and cut it off the parent plant, severing it close to the new roots. Pot up the layer or plant it out.

AIR LAYERING A SHRUB

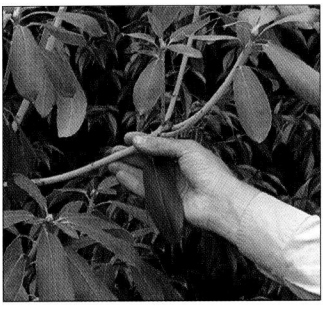

1 Select a healthy, horizontal stem from the previous year's growth. Trim off any leaves and sideshoots to provide a 9–12in (22–30cm) section of clear stem.

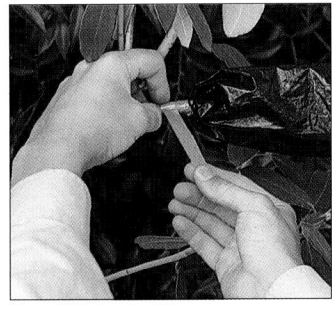

2 Slide a plastic sleeve over and along the stem; seal and secure the lower end of the sleeve to the stem with adhesive tape.

3 Fold back the plastic. Make a 1½in (4cm) diagonal cut ¼in (5mm) into the stem in the direction of growth, away from the shrub. Apply rooting hormone.

4 Soak about 2 handfuls of sphagnum moss in water, then gently squeeze it out. With the back of the knife, pack the cut with moss, wedging it open.

5 Pull back the plastic sleeve over the cut. Carefully pack the sleeve with more moistened moss so that the moss is all around the stem.

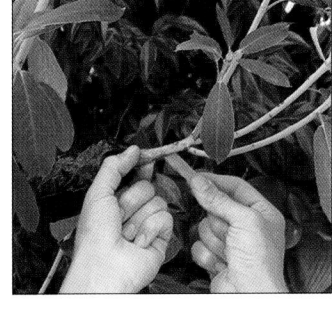

6 Continue to pack the sleeve until the moss is about 2in (5cm) from the open end. Close the end and secure it firmly in place with adhesive tape.

7 The sealed sleeve encourages rooting by retaining moisture. Leave it in place for at least a growing season to allow new roots to develop.

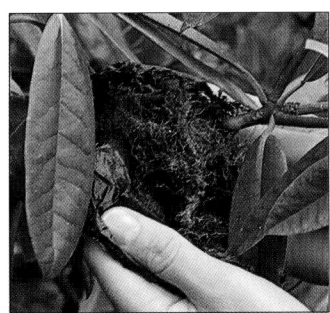

8 Once the layer has rooted, remove the sleeve and cut off the layer below the roots. Pot up or plant out the new shrub (here a rhododendron) in the open ground.

STOOLING

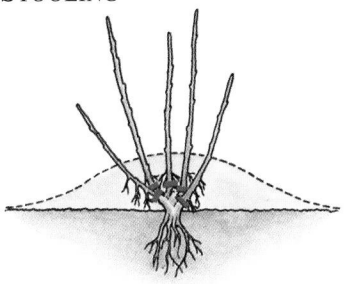

Cover shoots with freely draining soil, adding more as they grow. The shoots will root down and can be separated in fall and potted on.

buried. Before growth starts, but after the risk of penetrating frosts has passed, dig a pit large enough to bury the plant with only the branch tips visible. If the soil is heavy, add sand and organic material.

Lift the parent plant with the root ball as complete as possible and "drop" it into the prepared hole. Work the soil around each stem, leaving 1–2in (2.5–5cm) of each tip exposed. Firm the soil and label the plant. In summer, keep the soil moist and, in fall, carefully tease away the soil around the plant to check for rooting. Sever any rooted shoots from the parent plant, and pot up or plant out, clearly labeled. If rooting has not occurred, replace the soil and leave for 12 more months.

Stooling

Although primarily used to raise fruit tree rootstocks, stooling may also be used to propagate deciduous ornamental shrubs such as dogwoods (*Cornus*) and lilacs (*Syringa*) from ungrafted plants.

Plant a rooted layer or other young plant in spring, label, and grow on for a season. The next spring, cut back the stem to within 3in (8cm) of the ground and apply a balanced fertilizer at 4oz/sq yd (110g/sq m). When the resulting shoots from this stem (or stool) are 6in (15cm) long, work friable soil enriched with organic matter between the shoots and bury them. Add sand if the ground is heavy. As the shoots grow, continue mounding up soil until about 9in (22cm) of each shoot is buried. Keep the soil moist in dry weather.

In fall, gently fork away the soil to ground level straight after leaf fall, leaving the rooted shoots exposed. Cut them off and pot them up or plant them out. Provided that the stools are kept fertilized, the process may be repeated annually and the same stool used for propagation in subsequent years.

SHRUBS THAT MAY BE PROPAGATED BY AIR LAYERING

Citrus
Ficus
Hamamelis
Kalmia latifolia
Magnolia
Rhododendron

SHRUBS THAT MAY BE PROPAGATED BY STOOLING

Amelanchier
Cotinus coggygria (and cvs)
Hydrangea arborescens,
*   H. paniculata*
Prunus glandulosa

Ribes sanguineum

Ribes
Salix
Spiraea
Stephanandra
Thymus

French layering

This method of propagating shrubs is a form of stooling and is suitable for increasing the stock of deciduous shrubs such as dogwoods (*Cornus alba, C. stolonifera*) and *Cotinus coggygria*.

In spring, plant a rooted layer or young plant, label it, and grow it on for a season. Then, in the dormant season, cut back the stool to within 3in (8cm) of the ground. In the following spring, apply a balanced fertilizer at the rate of 2–4oz/sq yd (60–110g/sq m).

The following fall, cut out all but about the ten best stems; shorten the tips of these so that they are all about the same length. With U-shaped wire staples, pin each stem to the ground, spreading the stems evenly around the parent stool. Each bud along the length of the stem should break evenly in spring.

When the new shoots on the pegged-down stems are approximately 2–3in (5–8cm) long, take out the pegs and cultivate the ground around the parent stool, incorporating a balanced fertilizer at a rate of 2–4oz/sq yd (60–110g/sq m). Space the stems evenly again, dropping each one into a 2in (5cm) deep trench. Peg down each stem and cover with soil, leaving the shoot tips exposed. Hill up all but 2–3in (5–8cm) of the new shoots as they develop, until the mound is 15cm (6in) high. Water in hot, dry weather.

After leaf fall, carefully fork away the soil from around the new shoots until the stems that were laid horizontally are exposed. Cut these flush with the central stool. Then cut the stems to separate the rooted sections. Pot these up or plant them out in the open garden, and label them. The same stool may be used to produce further layers.

Division

Division is an easy way of increasing shrubs that produce suckers. Suitable shrubs include *Ruscus*, *Kerria*, *Gaultheria*, and *Sarcococca*. Shrubs must be grown on their own roots, not grafted onto another rootstock.

Before growth starts in spring, lift the plant. Break the clump into sections, retaining those with vigorous shoots and well-developed roots. Prune any damaged roots, and cut back the top-growth by one-third to a half to reduce water loss. Replant the divisions in the open, and water in dry weather. Alternatively, simply lift a suckering root, severing it from the parent plant, and then replant it in the open.

With a few shrubs, including *Rhus*, suckering may be encouraged by digging deeply around the parent plant in summer or fall. This damages the roots and stimulates adventitious buds to develop suckers in spring. These rooted suckers may then be lifted and potted up or planted out.

Grafting

This technique is used to unite two plants so that they grow together as one. One part, known as the scion, is taken from the plant to be propagated and provides the top-growth of the new plant, while the other part, known as the rootstock or stock, provides the root system. The rootstock and scion must be compatible, so they are normally of the same or closely related species.

Grafting is an important way of propagating shrubs that are difficult to root or that are unlikely to come true from seed. By using selected rootstocks, it is possible to improve a plant's vigor, disease resistance, or tolerance to specific growing conditions, or sometimes to control its basic growth pattern.

Among the many variations of this technique, three that are widely used are saddle, side-veneer, and apical-wedge grafting. In all cases, the stocks and scions should be joined immediately after they have been cut, and the cut surfaces of each should be kept clean.

Saddle grafting

This grafting technique is predominantly used to propagate evergreen rhododendron species and hybrids, with *Rhododendron* seedlings generally serving as rootstocks. About one month before grafting is to commence, in late winter or early spring, bring the rootstock into a greenhouse maintained at a temperature of 50–54°F (10–12°C).

In late winter or very early spring, select the scion material so that it is ready for grafting. The scions selected should be about 2–5in (5–13cm) long, and taken from vigorous, non-flowering, one-year-old shoots on the plant to be propagated. If only shoots with flower buds are available, pinch these out. The scions should be labeled and stored in a plastic bag in a refrigerator.

Select a straight-stemmed rootstock of about pencil thickness and cut it back to within 2in (5cm) of the base, making a straight cut across the stem with pruners. Then, using a knife, make two slanting cuts to make an upside-down V wound on the top of the stock. Prepare the scion by making two corresponding angled cuts so that its base – the saddle – will fit snugly onto the apex of the rootstock.

Make sure that the two sections of the graft fit well together, then bind the stock and scion together with a length of clear grafting tape. Cut back any very large leaves by half to reduce moisture loss. Label clearly, and then place the grafted plant in a propagator and shade it from direct sunlight. Check the plant daily for watering and hygiene, and spray it once a week with a fungicide solution. Union normally takes place within four to five weeks.

Once the scion starts to grow, remove the tape and gradually harden off the grafted plant – opening the propagator for longer periods each day. If the grafted plant is kept in the original pot for a season, give it a liquid fertilizer once a month.

Side-veneer grafting

This grafting technique is used to propagate a variety of both evergreen and deciduous shrubs. Most side-veneer grafting is carried out in midwinter, but deciduous shrubs such as *Hamamelis* may also be grafted during the summer.

For the appropriate rootstocks, choose one- to three-year-old seedlings that are compatible with the plant to be propagated. The stems should be of pencil thickness. About three weeks before grafting, bring the rootstock into the greenhouse. Water it sparingly so that the rootstock does not break dormancy too quickly, since vigorous sap movement may prevent successful grafting. If grafting in summer, use two-year-old seedlings for the rootstocks and keep them fairly dry for a month in advance.

For both summer and winter grafting, prepare and unite the stocks and scions in the same way.

Just before grafting takes place, select vigorous one-year-old shoots that have some mature wood to be used as scions. They should be of a similar thickness to the rootstocks onto which they will be grafted. If there will be any delay, label the scions and place them in a plastic bag in a refrigerator.

When grafting, first trim the scion to a length of 5–8in (12–20cm), or 4–5in (10–12cm) for magnolias. Make a sloping cut at the base of the scion 1–1½in (2.5–4cm) long, turn it over, and make a small wedge-shaped cut on the other side.

Reduce the rootstock stem to about 12in (30cm). Make two cuts in

SUCKERING SHRUBS THAT MAY BE DIVIDED

Amelanchier canadensis
Andromeda
Aronia
Aster albescens
Berberis buxifolia
Buxus sempervirens
Cassiope hypnoides
Ceratostigma plumbaginoides
Clerodendrum bungei
Cornus alba,
    C. canadensis,
    C. stolonifera

Cornus canadensis

Danäe racemosa
Diervilla lonicera
Erica
Euonymus fortunei
Gaultheria
Itea virginica
Kerria
Mahonia repens
Menziesia ciliicalyx
Paxistima
Pernettya
Polygala
Rhus
Rosa (nongrafted plants)
Ruscus aculeatus
Sarcococca
Spiraea japonica (cvs)

PROPAGATING SUCKERING SHRUBS BY DIVISION

1 Lift a root with suckers on it, without disturbing the parent plant. Check that there are fibrous roots at the base of the suckers.

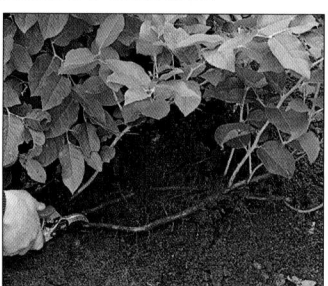

2 Remove the suckering root by cutting it off close to the parent plant. Firm back the soil around the parent plant.

3 Cut the main root back to the fibrous roots, then divide the suckers so that each has its own roots. Cut back the top-growth by about half.

4 Replant the suckers in open ground in prepared planting holes. Firm the soil around the suckers and water in. (*The plant used here is* Gaultheria shallon.)

SADDLE GRAFTING

1 Select vigorous, nonflowering shoots of the previous year's growth from the plant to be propagated (here a rhododendron) as scions.

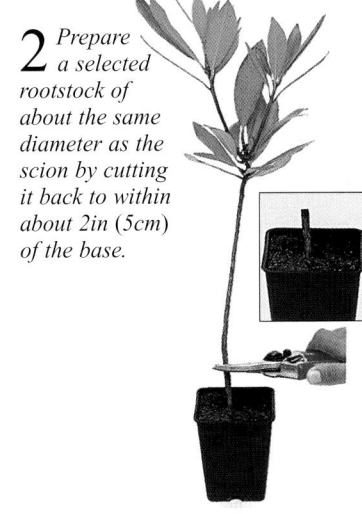

2 Prepare a selected rootstock of about the same diameter as the scion by cutting it back to within about 2in (5cm) of the base.

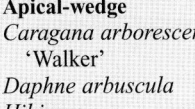

3 Using a sharp knife, cut the stock with 2 upward angled cuts so that its apex is shaped like a slightly rounded, upside-down V.

4 Make compatible, angled cuts on the scion (see inset), trimming its length to about 2–5in (5–13cm).

5 Place the cut scion (see inset) on top of the stock so that they fit together. If the scion is too narrow, place it so one side of the cambium layer meets that of the stock.

6 Bind the scion in place with plastic grafting tape or raffia. Cut back very large leaves by half. Leave the grafted plant in a propagator until union occurs.

SHRUBS THAT MAY BE GRAFTED

Saddle
Rhododendron (many hybrids and species)

Side-veneer
Acer palmatum (cvs)
Aralia elata 'Aureovariegata' and 'Argenteovariegata'
Arbutus unedo (cvs)
Camellia reticulata,
 C. sasanqua
Caragana arborescens
Cotoneaster
 'Hybridus Pendulus'
Daphne bholua,
 D. petraea
Hamamelis
Magnolia
Pittosporum eugenioides
 'Variegatum'
Prunus glandulosa
Rhaphiolepis

Hibiscus sinosyriacus 'Lilac Queen'

Apical-wedge
Caragana arborescens
 'Walker'
Daphne arbuscula
Hibiscus
Syringa

---

the stock, starting 3in (8cm) above soil level, to take out a sliver of wood, leaving a cut that roughly matches that on the scion.

Place the rootstock and scion together so that the cambium layers match as closely as possible, and if necessary on one side only for stocks and scions of differing widths; tie them securely in position with grafting tape. Label the grafted plant and place it in a propagator at an even temperature of 50–59°F (10–15°C). Water the plant regularly and spray with a fungicide once a week.

Union should occur in four to five weeks. Harden off the grafted plant over the next four weeks, then remove it from the propagator and grow it on in a cool greenhouse.

As the scion starts to grow, gradually cut back the stem of the stock; by the end of the first growing season, all the stock above the graft union should have been cut back. During the first season, remove the initial tie and, if growth is rapid, replace it with a single raffia tie.

On plants that have been grafted in the summer, cut back the stock just above the union before growth starts in spring. Replace the original tie with a small one around the union, since there is a tendency for the scion to be pushed off the stock. Support the leader with a stake after repotting. For further details, see *Propagating Trees by Side-veneer Grafting,* p.80.

Apical-wedge grafting

Apical-wedge grafting, or cleft grafting, is a comparatively straight-forward technique and is suitable for the propagation of a number of shrubs, including *Caragana, Hibiscus,* and lilac (*Syringa*).

During midwinter, collect vigorous one-year-old stems for use as scions. Place these in a clearly labeled plastic bag and store them in a refrigerator in order to retard their development.

Also in midwinter, select one-year-old seedlings of compatible shrubs as rootstocks. Stock and scion should both be about the thickness of a pencil. Immediately prior to grafting, lift the rootstock and wash it. Cut its stem horizontally, about

1in (2.5cm) above the roots. With a sharp knife, make a 1in (2.5cm) vertical cut down the center of the rootstock stem.

Remove the scions from the refrigerator and select one with healthy buds that is of similar diameter to the rootstock. Trim it down by making a horizontal cut just above a healthy bud or buds and a similar cut 6in (15cm) below. To form the wedge, make a 1–1½in (2.5–4cm) long, sloping cut down toward the middle of the scion base, and a similar cut on the other side.

Push the scion into the prepared cut on the stock. If the scion is narrower than the stock, align one edge of the scion so that it is flush with one edge of the stock. Bind them with grafting tape or moist raffia. If raffia is used, coat the union edges with grafting wax to stop moisture loss and to seal the top of the scion.

Either pot up the grafted plants or insert them in potting mix in a seed tray. Label and then place them in a propagator at 50–59°F (10–15°C), the higher temperature inducing a faster union.

The union of the stock and scion should take place within about five to six weeks. Remove the tape or raffia when there is a firm union. Pot up the plants that are in seed trays and harden them off gradually. Grow the plants on for another year in a cold frame before planting them out.

APICAL-WEDGE GRAFTING

Make a simple vertical cut down into the stock. Cut the base of the scion with 2 downward cuts into a V, then push the base into the stock. Bind them together, pot up, and place in a propagator.

Topiary

A FORM of training and pruning trees and shrubs to create attractive, boldly artificial shapes, topiary is a garden art that has been popular since Roman times. Traditionally used to produce strongly architectural and geometric shapes in formal gardens, it has been developed to include birds, animals, and unusual, even whimsical features such as giant chess-pieces and full-size trains.

Designing with topiary

Different styles of topiary may be used to create a variety of effects. Imaginative, living sculptures express personal style and add a humorous or bizarre touch. Using topiary for geometric shapes such as cones, obelisks, and columns provides a strong, structural element in a design. This type of topiary may be valuable both in formal gardens, perhaps to frame a vista or form an avenue, and in informal gardens, as a contrasting foil for less structured planting.

In some gardens, it may be appropriate to treat part of the hedge top as topiary, clipping it into one or more birds, spheres, or cubes, for example. Topiary may also be effective in containers; use a single container plant as a centerpiece, a pair to flank a doorway, or several to line a path. It can also be adopted to create eye-catching stem effects, such as twists and spirals, with one or more stems.

HOW TO CREATE A SIMPLE DESIGN

1 *If using a young plant (here boxwood) to form a geometric shape, first cut to shape by eye.*

2 *The following year, make a cutting guide from stakes and wire, place over the plant, and cut the plant to shape.*

3 *When the plant is the desired shape, clip each year with pruners to retain a crisp outline.*

Plants for topiary

Plants to be used for topiary require dense, pliable growth, small leaves, and the ability to recover quickly from clipping. Evergreens such as boxwood (*Buxus sempervirens*), privet (*Ligustrum ovalifolium*), yew (*Taxus*), *Osmanthus delavayi*, and *Lonicera nitida* are ideal in a temperate climate. *Cupressus sempervirens* can be trained into geometric designs, but it thrives only in warmer climates. Bay (*Laurus nobilis*), holly (such as nonspiny clones of *Ilex* x *altaclerensis*), and many other evergreens may be used but are more difficult to train.

Ivies (such as *Hedera helix* 'Ivalace') are very adaptable and may easily be trained to grow up a frame; alternatively, several cuttings can be taken from an existing plant to grow up a moss-padded structure.

Creating a shape

Most topiary designs are best formed with the aid of a guiding framework, although some simple shapes may also be cut freehand.

Simple designs

Using young plants, select the stem or stems that will form the core of the design. The simplest shape to produce is a cone, which needs only guiding stakes. For other shapes, attach a framework made from chicken wire or single wires attached to stakes placed in the ground next to the main group of shoots. Tie in the stems to the wire framework and then pinch back the shoots to encourage them to branch and cover the form.

Train new shoots into the framework to fill in any gaps, until they meet around its perimeter. Growth will vary around the plant, depending on the aspect. Shoots trained downward always grow slowly.

Complex designs

Frameworks for complex designs are now generally available, although you may decide to make your own basic framework from sturdy materials such as heavy-duty fencing wire. Chicken wire or thin-gauge wire may then be intertwined to form a more precise shape. Garden stakes are also useful as a temporary aid in developing and shaping a framework. Coated twine is good for tying shoots onto a framework, since it eventually decays.

SHAPING A TOPIARY BIRD

1 *In year 1, insert a fan-shaped stake support at an angle to form the bird tail. Select and tie in well-placed shoots to the stakes using soft twine. Tip back weaker shoots to stimulate branching.*

2 *During the growing season, shorten the trained-in shoots by up to one third of their length, cutting just above a node. This will encourage dense, compact growth and a solid mass of foliage.*

3 *In year 2, insert a supporting stake for the bird head and tie three strong shoots to this stake. Trim the tail and tip back shoots on the body. Remove unwanted shoots or wire them to bulk out the tail.*

4 *In year 3, tie down the strongest shoot at the head to form the beak. Continue trimming to shape the body more precisely; keep the tail growth dense. Once the shape is formed, clip regularly.*

CLIPPED BIRD
Traditional shapes are still the most popular for topiary. This delightful bird sits on top of its nest surveying the surrounding gardens.

Training stems

Young stems being trained onto a frame grow quickly, and considerable work is thus required to tie in new shoots throughout the growing season. Tie in the shoots while they are young and pliable and check previous ties to make sure that they are not broken, rubbing, or in any way restricting the shoots.

If stakes have been used in the framework, make sure that they are still firm and have not cracked, snapped, or bent. If they are defective, replace them with new ones.

Clipping

Topiary involves much more precise clipping than is required for normal hedge cutting. Take time, particularly when initially forming topiary pieces, to cut the branchlets carefully to the required shape. Do not cut too much in one place as it may spoil the symmetry of a topiary design for an entire season until new replacement growth appears.

Even if you have a good eye for shaping plants, it is sensible to use levels, plumb lines, and any other aids available to check the accuracy of a cut. Always work from the top of the plant downward and from the center outward, cutting both sides together in order to retain a balanced symmetry.

Rounded topiary pieces are easier to produce and maintain than angular, geometric shapes and may often be cut freehand. To produce a spherical shape, first trim the top of the plant and then cut a channel downward around the circumference to leave a ring. Another ring at 90° should then be cut, leaving four distinct quarters to be trimmed.

Geometric topiary that has precise, flat surfaces and angled or squared edges is difficult to form and maintain successfully and needs to be tackled with confident, accurate clipping for a well-defined shape. Such geometric designs are best cut using guidelines attached to stakes to maintain symmetry.

When to clip

Once a topiary feature is established, it will need frequent routine clipping during the growing season. The time between cuts will depend on the rate of growth. An intricate, geometric design in boxwood may need to be cut at four- to six-week intervals. Trim as soon as any new growth begins to appear uneven.

ARCHITECTURAL DESIGNS
Two spiral shapes eye-catchingly enhance the central, cone-shaped topiary along this path as well as complement the two dome-shaped side pieces.

If a perfect finish is not required throughout the year, two cuts during the growing season are usually sufficient for a reasonable effect, depending on the plant used. Yew, for example, need be cut only once a year, boxwood (depending on the cultivar) usually needs to be cut twice, and *Lonicera nitida* three times.

Clip plants at the appropriate time of year. Do not clip bushes after early autumn, since the young shoots produced after the first clip need to ripen sufficiently to withstand low winter temperatures. In warm climates where growth may be almost continuous, regular trimming will be required throughout the year.

Routine care

Weeding, watering, and mulching is essential in the same way as for free-growing shrubs (see p.100). It is important, however, to apply two or three doses of a balanced fertilizer at a rate of 2oz/sq yd (60g/sq m) during the growing season.

Winter care

In regions where regular snowfalls occur, netting topiary pieces will help prevent the branches from breaking under the weight of snow. Knock snow off any flat surfaces since it may damage the framework.

Repairs and renovation

If a leader, a section, or a branch of topiary has been damaged or broken, cut it back cleanly with pruners. Manipulate nearby shoots by tying them in to fill the gap.

If topiary plants have been left unclipped for one or two years, regular clipping should restore the original form within the season. If the topiary has been neglected for years, and the shape has been lost, severe pruning to restore the outline should be carried out the first spring followed by two or three seasons of more precise clipping.

Scorch and dieback

The foliage of some evergreens may be scorched in hard winters and can die. The damaged foliage will soon be covered by new growth in spring, but cut it back where it is unsightly, taking care to follow the shape of the topiary piece. If shoots do not fill the gap, there may be a root problem, which will need to be treated.

HOW TO MAKE A COMPLEX DESIGN

1 *Make frameworks for large topiary pieces from strong materials; they will be in place for several years. Clip a young plant (here yew) as necessary to keep it within the framework.*

2 *As the plant grows and fills the frame, clip it over once a year, following the outline of the framework and pinching out shoots to encourage bushy growth.*

3 *When mature, the plant will form a dense bush and cover the framework. It needs regular clipping to maintain the precise outline of the design.*

CHAPTER
4

CLIMBING PLANTS

WOODY AND HERBACEOUS climbers make up one of the most versatile of plant groups, providing great opportunity for imaginative garden design. Climbers introduce a strong vertical element when grown with support, whether against a wall, fence, or pergola. If unsupported, some climbers sprawl luxuriantly, adding a horizontal line as well as color and texture; others perform a lowly task as weed-smothering groundcovers. When allowed to scramble upward through other tall plants, climbers can prolong the season of interest. One of their greatest assets is their potential for covering unsightly garden features – tree stumps, toolsheds, or other garden buildings. Many of the most popular climbers have heavily scented flowers on their high and far-reaching stems, casting their perfume over the garden.

Designing with climbers

GARDENS of every size and situation can be enhanced by climbing plants. Some, such as clematis and *Passiflora* species, are grown primarily for the exquisite beauty of their flowers. Others – *Lonicera periclymenum*, for example – are equally valued for their fragrance. Many are appreciated for their handsome evergreen foliage or their rich and spectacular fall color, as with *Parthenocissus* species and *Vitis coignetiae*. Even when leafless, their elegant habit and often strong architectural form enhance the stark winter outlines of fences, archways, and other hard landscape features. Some climbers produce fruits or berries that are attractive both to gardeners and to wildlife.

In their natural habitats, climbers use various techniques to climb through host plants to gain access to the light. Plants, walls, and other features can be used to provide support for the wide range of growth habits among climbers.

A FLORAL ENTRANCE
Bougainvillea *gracefully links a series of archways in this elegant courtyard setting. The brilliant spectacle of its showy magenta bracts harmonizes well with the sun-baked supporting wall. In frost-free gardens it is one of the most vigorous and luxuriant of all climbers.*

Climbing methods and supports

Some climbers are self-clinging, attaching themselves to their supports either by aerial roots (adventitious rootlets), as do ivies (*Hedera* spp.), or by adhesive tendril tips, as does Virginia creeper (*Parthenocissus quinquefolia*). These cling to any surface offering sufficient foothold, including walls and tree trunks. They need no additional support except during the early stages, when they need the guidance of a stake, string, or wire until they are able to establish secure contact. Climbers with aerial roots are also particularly well suited for use as groundcovers.

Twining species coil their stems in a spiral habit around their support, clockwise or counterclockwise, depending on their anatomical and morphological characteristics. Both *Lonicera periclymenum* and *Humulus lupulus*, for example, twine clockwise, whereas *Ceropegia sandersonii* and *Wisteria sinensis* twine counterclockwise. All twining species need some form of permanent support, usually provided by a trellis or wire attached to an overhead support. The plants may also be grown up the stems of a sturdy host plant (see also "Growing climbers through other plants," p.124).

A few climbers, such as clematis and some nasturtiums (*Tropaeolum*), attach themselves to supports by means of curling leaf stalks. Many others are tendril climbers that twine around their supports by means of contact-sensitive tendrils. These tendrils are often modified leaves

GARDEN DESIGN
Framing a formal piece of statuary, the fresh lime green leaves of Humulus lupulus 'Aureus' *help reinforce a striking focal point in this garden.*

or leaflets, as in *Bignonia capreolata* and sweet peas (*Lathyrus odoratus*); terminal shoots, as in grapes; or axillary shoots, as in *Passiflora*. In *Parthenocissus*, the tendrils develop adhesive disks at the tips once they come into contact with a support.

Scandent, scrambling, and trailing climbers, such as *Bougainvillea* species, *Quisqualis indica*, and winter jasmine (*Jasminum nudiflorum*), produce long, arching stems that attach themselves only loosely, if at all, to their supports. These plants need to be tied in to a wire framework or trellis with plastic twist-ties or vine ties. Alternatively, they may be left to sprawl over walls and banks for a less formal look. Plants in this group are also sometimes used as groundcovers.

Some species, including climbing roses and certain *Rubus* species, are equipped with hooked thorns that help them to scramble naturally through host plants. If not grown through other plants, these need to be tied in to sturdy supports.

Site and exposure

To achieve their full potential, a number of climbers prefer a sunny position with their roots in shade, although some need a cooler spot. Many others, including *Parthenocissus* and *Schizophragma,* are less demanding and, while preferring a sunny exposure, tolerate shade.

Less hardy climbers will require protection, such as a south-facing wall, in colder climates. There are numerous hardy climbers, however, that will perform perfectly well without any protection at all.

Sunny or sheltered sites
A sheltered wall can provide a suitable microclimate for growing marginally hardy or tender flowering climbers. *Lapageria rosea* and blue passionflower (*Passiflora caerulea*), among many others, should thrive in such a position if given some winter protection; the heat reflected by the wall helps ripen the wood so that the plants are better able to withstand cold winter temperatures.

The wall also gives protection against temperatures slightly below freezing. If frost is likely at flowering time, avoid planting climbers in positions where the flower buds are exposed to early-morning sun, because the buds often will be damaged as a result of rapid thawing. Sun-loving herbaceous plants and bulbs may be planted at the base of the climbers to help keep their roots cool.

Cool or exposed sites
For shady, north-facing walls and those exposed to cold winds, vigorous, hardy climbers – Virginia creeper (*Parthenocissus quinquefolia*) and some honeysuckles, in particular – are the most suitable plants. In very cold climates, using annuals will extend the range of suitable climbers; scarlet runner beans (*Phaseolus coccineus*) and canary creeper (*Tropaeolum peregrinum*) are good choices.

Climbers on walls, buildings, and fences

Whether complementing or camouflaging their support, climbing plants make an immediate visual impact.

Most buildings can be enhanced by the softening appearance of a climber, and garden walls and fences become decorative features when clothed with plants bearing blossoms and foliage.

Enhancing a building
Before planting, assess the architectural merits of a building, using the plants to emphasize its good points. A well-designed building may be complemented by climbers that have a strong visual impact, with, for example, distinctively shaped or colored foliage or outstanding flowers. *Actinidia kolomikta*, with its pink- or white-tipped leaves and cup-shaped white flowers in summer, is one of the most spectacular climbers for this purpose.

A less visually pleasing building can also be made more attractive by using climbers. Regular panels of plants may be used to break up long stretches of blank wall, and may also serve to exaggerate or lessen strong vertical or horizontal lines. Narrow panels of foliage that extend upward can make a building seem taller than it actually is. On the other hand, wider panels of plants allowed to grow only as high as the second floor will make a tall, narrow building appear broader. The most suitable plants for this purpose include most species of ivy (*Hedera*) and other self-clinging root climbers, such as *Schizophragma hydrangeoides* and *Hydrangea anomala* subsp. *petiolaris*. Their rich panels of foliage may be pruned into the desired shape.

In a more relaxed, informal setting, vigorous climbing plants can be combined for a profusion of flowers and fragrance. The dark green foliage and white flowers of *Clematis paniculata*, together with the strongly fragrant red and yellow flowers of *Lonicera* x *americana*, combine well with many species of climbing rose, perhaps with annual sweet peas (*Lathyrus odoratus*) grown through them. This combination can be particularly attractive around a window or doorway, where the flowers and scents of the plants are best appreciated.

Screening with climbers
The more vigorous climbing plants can be relied upon to camouflage an unattractive toolshed, wall, or fence

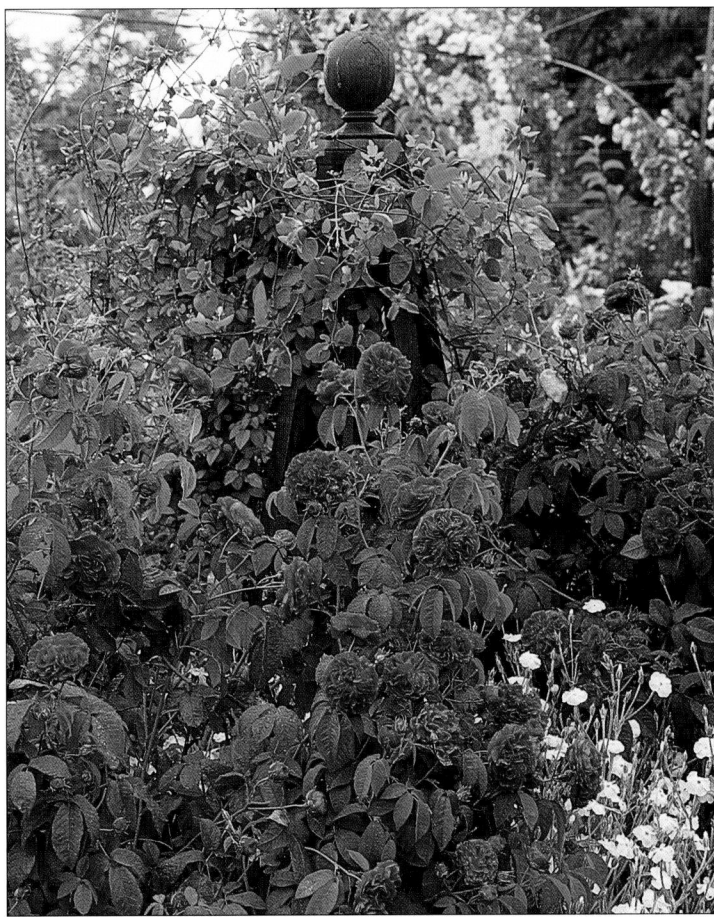

AN INFORMAL SCREEN
These clematis and climbing roses weave through wires to provide an attractive mix of color and a long season of interest.

remarkably quickly. Use plants such as *Clematis montana*, for its profusion of creamy white flowers in late spring, or the silver lace vine *Fallopia baldschuanica* (syn. *F. aubertii*), which soon produces dense cover combined with clusters of tiny flowers in late summer. *Fallopia baldschuanica* is also known as mile-a-minute vine, a name it fully deserves: it is extremely rampant and must therefore be sited with great care, since it will quickly outcompete even reasonably vigorous neighbors. It also needs regular and severe pruning to keep it within bounds.

Where year-round cover is desired, ivies may be more appropriate. Alternatively, use a combination of evergreen and deciduous plants; the bluish green, evergreen leaves of *Lonicera sempervirens*, for instance, provide the perfect foil in summer for the soft pink blooms of the climbing rose 'New Dawn'.

Climbers on pergolas and pillars

Pergolas, pillars, and other man-made structures enable climbers to be viewed from all sides and, in addition, contribute strong stylistic elements to the garden design. They can be used to add height to an otherwise flat garden. Depending on materials used, they may be formal and elegant, or informal and rustic. If designed well, they can be at their most attractive when only partially covered with plants. They must, however, be strong enough to

carry the often considerable weight of stems and foliage and should also be durable, since the plants will need their support for many years.

Pergolas

Pergolas or arbors festooned with climbers provide a cool, shady sitting area in the garden and bring a sense of seclusion and privacy to an otherwise open site. The most suitable plants are those that put on their best display at the time of day or during the particular season when the structure is most often used.

If an arbor is to be used often on summer evenings, suitable plants might include common white jasmine (*Jasminum officinale*), *Lonicera periclymenum* 'Graham Thomas', or the climbing rose 'Mme. Alfred Carrière', all with beautifully fragrant blooms in pale colors that show up well in the fading light. For summer shade, use large-leaved climbers such as *Vitis coignetiae* (which also gives splendid fall color) or *V. vinifera* 'Purpurea', whose claret-colored young leaves turn dusky purple as they mature. Alternatively, use the massed floral display of *Wisteria sinensis* 'Alba' as a spring canopy. The flowers of this plant look beautiful if grown up pergolas flanking walkways. Be sure that the crossbeams are high enough, however, so there is no need to stoop to avoid the flowers.

For winter interest, plant evergreens such as ivy or, in mild areas, tender *Lardizabala biternata*. Alternatively, use deciduous plants such as *Celastrus* or *Wisteria* species, whose bare stems take on beautiful sculptural qualities in winter.

GROWING ON PERGOLAS
Wisteria sinensis 'Alba' is an ideal choice for a pergola over a walkway. It produces a mass of fragrant white blooms that hang down in garlands in spring, releasing their welcome scent at just the right height to be appreciated.

Pillars

To add a strong vertical element to a mixed or herbaceous border, climbers such as clematis or *Passiflora* species may be grown up and around pillars. Also consider using pillars to mark an axis or focal point, perhaps at the corner of a border or at a point where the garden level changes. A series of pillars at the back of a flower bed or along a path can also be linked by rope or chain swags and climbers trained along them.

For an evergreen climber, or as a temporary feature, a sturdy post with mesh panels wrapped around it will provide adequate support. If growing a deciduous plant, which means that the pillar will be visible in winter, buy a ready-made trellis obelisk or column, which will be attractive when it is bare.

Growing climbers through other plants

In the wild, many climbers grow naturally through other plants, which is a habit that may be copied successfully in the garden, although

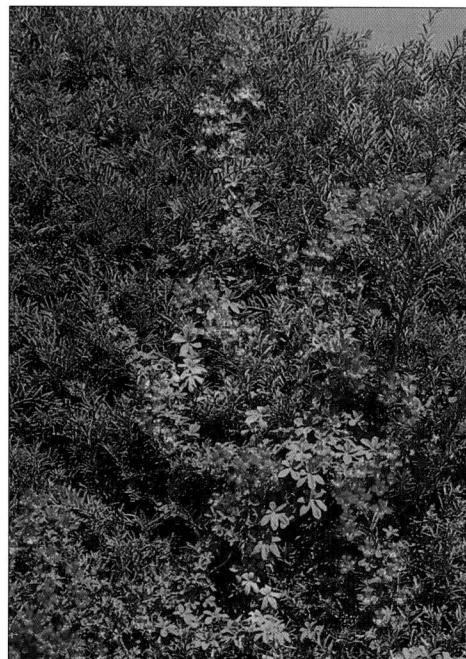

NATURAL SUPPORT
The scarlet flowers of Tropaeolum speciosum *are made even more intense by the deep green backdrop of a hedge of English yew* (Taxus baccata).

PLANT ASSOCIATION
The heart-shaped leaves of Vitis coignetiae *make a striking contrast of shape and texture with those of* Euonymus fortunei *'Silver Queen'.*

the climbers should not be too vigorous for the hosts. Always plan color combinations before planting, taking flowers, foliage, and fruit into consideration. The climber may either complement or contrast with its host when the latter is putting on its best display, or it may extend the season of interest.

Climbers that are suitable for growing through shrubs include *Clematis viticella* hybrids and those large-flowered clematis that are cut back each year. It is also a useful method for growing most annual climbing plants and *Tropaeolum speciosum*, whose stems and fiery red flowers are best supported by another plant.

For growing through trees, vigorous species such as *Ampelopsis brevipedunculata* var. *maximowiczii* or *Schizophragma hydrangeoides* produce beautiful combinations of foliage, fruit, and flower. Alternatively, try mingling the cascading blooms of *Rosa filipes* 'Kiftsgate' with the white or pink sprays of *Clematis montana*. Both produce strong, twining stems that quickly scramble into the branches of a tree.

Climbers as groundcovers

Some climbers, particularly those with aerial roots or those with a scandent, trailing, or scrambling habit, may be grown without support to produce swaths of groundcovers. They are particularly useful when allowed to sprawl over a sloping bank or when trailing over a wall, where they will often root in the soil beneath.

Climbers that attach themselves by means of adhesive tendrils, such as *Parthenocissus* species, and root climbers are extremely effective at suppressing weeds when grown as groundcovers. Take care when siting these plants, however, because if there is any other plant nearby that could serve as a support, it may be swamped. To reduce the risk of this, choose less vigorous climbing species or relocate other plants so that the climber has a free run.

Twining climbers may also be used as groundcovers, provided that their shoots are spread evenly across the ground; if needed, wire hooks can be used to keep the shoots in place. The large, deeply colored flowers of *Clematis* 'Ernest Markham' and *C.* 'Jackmanii' are very eye-catching at ground level, as are the blue-green leaves and scarlet flowers of *Tropaeolum speciosum*.

GROUNDCOVER
Clematis viticella *cultivars* 'Etoile Violette' *and* 'Abundance' *make a carpet of color, using winter-flowering heathers* (Erica) *as host plants.*

Colorful climbers

Color impact varies according to light levels in different parts of the garden. In a sunny spot, bright or deep colors, which absorb light, show up more strongly than paler ones, which reflect light. The latter, on the other hand, may look washed out in bright light but may successfully illuminate a dull, dark space. They can be used to great advantage in gardens that are most often viewed in the fading light of evening.

Before planting climbing plants, consider the color of the garden's permanent features. If the wall or support is already bright, use plants with more subtle coloring, unless you wish to create a particularly vibrant combination.

Color combinations
Growing different climbers together or in combination with other plants adds another dimension to color schemes. Climbers can be particularly useful for interweaving the different color components of a planting design, creating brilliant combinations with complementary colors or more subtle harmonies with closely related tones.

Flowers for color
The flowers of climbers occur in colors across the spectrum, from the deep violet of *Clematis viticella* 'Etoile Violette' through the brilliant scarlet of *Campsis radicans* to the soft, creamy white of *Araujia sericofera*. A large number of the

most vividly colored climbers are tropical in origin and are not hardy in temperate zones, however.

Climbers with strongly colored flowers have a bold and exuberant appearance, but these usually need thoughtful placement if they are not to be overwhelming. Those that offer softer colors, such as the pink

of *Clematis montana* 'Tetrarose' or the pale violet-blue of *Codonopsis convolvulacea*, are more suitable for subtle-hued plantings.

Foliage and fruits for color
Make use of the leaves of climbers as well as their flowers in a planting design. Leaf tone can provide soothing contrasts and balance vivid flower color. *Humulus lupulus* 'Aureus' has yellow leaves that appear almost gold if placed against a dark background. Even more striking is *Actinidia kolomikta*, which has leaves tipped with creamy white and pink. The variegated ivies are almost as showy and, being evergreen, give a year-round display.

Other climbers bear fruits that are at least as colorful as their flowers: outstanding among these are the fruits of *Akebia quinata* (purplish), the slightly frost-tender *Billardiera longiflora* (purple-blue or white), and *Celastrus orbiculatus* (green, then tan, splitting to show yellow insides with red seeds).

Interest through the seasons

For continuity of interest throughout the year, devise a planting plan in which different climbers succeed each other as the seasons progress.

COMPLEMENTARY COLORS
An old stone wall provides a natural setting for climbing plants. This one has an unobtrusive wire framework supporting clematis and the golden-leaved Humulus lupulus 'Aureus' *twining around it.*

FOLIAGE PATTERNS
Actinidia kolomikta *is
a deciduous climber
with highly unusual
and decorative foliage:
many of the leaves are
tipped with bold
splashes of pink or
white. Small, cup-
shaped, scented white
flowers appear in
the summer.*

CLIMBING ANNUALS
Hyacinth bean (Lablab
purpureus) *is a
deciduous plant often
grown as an annual for
quick cover in summer.
This huge and gnarled
old tree trunk lends its
support to the twining
stems and pealike pink
and purple flowers.*

This technique may be applied to climbers that are being grown together or in separate parts of the garden, so that there is always something to catch your eye.

Spring and summer
Numerous climbers put on their best show in spring and summer. The early-flowering *Clematis macropetala* and *Lonicera periclymenum* 'Serotina', which reaches its peak in midsummer, make an extremely attractive combination. The flowers of the clematis also leave behind fluffy seedheads to augment the beauty of the honeysuckle's scented

FALL FOLIAGE
This striking display combines the crimson leaves of Parthenocissus
tricuspidata *with the reddening foliage of* Vitis coignetiae.

tubular blooms, and often continue the display throughout fall and sometimes even into winter.

Fall color
Some climbers produce glorious fall leaf color. The deeply cut, sometimes crinkled, leaves of *Parthenocissus tricuspidata* may be the most spectacular of all, turning scarlet, crimson, and burgundy before they fall.

Winter interest
Climbers that flower in winter are few, and most do not tolerate much cold, but winter jasmine (*Jasminum nudiflorum*), hardy to 0°F (-18°C),

produces delicate yellow blooms even on a north-facing wall. The tender *J. polyanthum* produces a profusion of flowers in warmer areas, and *Clematis cirrhosa* blooms during frost-free weather.

Evergreens with unusual foliage provide interest in winter, too. Ivies are the most versatile, since many are quite hardy and are widely adaptable. The bold variegation of some ivies, such as *Hedera helix* 'Buttercup' and 'Goldheart', is especially attractive. Other ivies are grown for their leaf shape – good examples include the bird's-foot ivy (*H. h.* 'Pedata'), with leaves shaped like a bird's foot, and 'Parsley Crested', with crinkly edged leaves.

Scented climbers

Fragrant climbers, such as the tropical *Beaumontia grandiflora* and the sweet pea (*Lathyrus odoratus*), have special appeal. To appreciate the fragrance fully, plant sweet peas near doorways or windows. If planted in a border, place them close to the outer edge.

Some release their fragrance at a particular time of day. Jasmine species (*Jasminum*) are more heavily scented at night, so place them over an arbor or near a terrace or patio that is used in the evening.

Annual climbers

Annual climbers and those that are treated as annuals in cool-temperate climates, such as *Eccremocarpus scaber* and kudzu (*Pueraria lobata*),

are particularly useful for short-term enjoyment. Annuals provide an excellent way of introducing variety into planting designs, since they can be changed every year, if desired. They may also be used to fill gaps in the border until more permanent plants become well established.

Climbers in containers

Climbers grown in containers may be trained over walls and pillars in the same way as those in open ground; if the support is attached to the container, the plant can be moved around as desired. Some lower-growing climbers, such as *Clematis macropetala*, may also be grown without support. Plant them in tall containers so that their stems trail gracefully to the ground. Ivies are well suited to being grown in this way but need regular pruning once established.

In gardens where space is limited, it is still possible to grow more rampant climbers, such as *Bougainvillea* and *Wisteria* species, in containers. Their growth will be checked, and winter protection may be required. Regular repotting will also be needed to keep them healthy.

Containers are especially suitable for less hardy climbing species that may need winter protection, such as *Hardenbergia comptoniana* and *Senecio macroglossus* 'Variegatus'. Simply take the containers indoors or into a heated greenhouse at the onset of fall frosts, putting them outside again the following spring.

Planter's guide to climbers

NORTH-FACING WALLS

Climbers that may be grown against north-facing walls
Agapetes (some spp.)
Akebia quinata
Allamanda cathartica
Aristolochia elegans
Berberidopsis corallina
Cissus
Clematis
Clerodendrum thomsoniae
Clytostoma callistegioides
Codonopsis convolvulacea
Dioscorea discolor
Epipremnum
Hardenbergia
Hedera
Hoya
Humulus lupulus
Hydrangea anomala subsp.
  petiolaris
Kadsura japonica
Lapageria rosea
Lathyrus latifolius
Lonicera x americana,
  L. x brownii, L. x heckrottii,
  L. sempervirens,
  L. x tellmanniana
Mitraria coccinea
Monstera deliciosa
Parthenocissus
Philodendron
Pileostegia viburnoides
Schizophragma hydrangeoides
Stigmaphyllon ciliatum
Syngonium podophyllum
Tropaeolum speciosum
Vitis coignetiae

AIR POLLUTION

Climbers that tolerate polluted air
Campsis radicans
Clematis
Fallopia
Hedera

Clematis
'Elsa Spath'

Hydrangea anomala
  subsp. petiolaris
Parthenocissus
Vitis

SHADE

Climbers that tolerate shade
Actinidia
Asteranthera ovata
Euonymus fortunei and variants
Fallopia
Humulus lupulus
Parthenocissus tricuspidata

FRAGRANT FLOWERS

Anredera cordifolia
Beaumontia grandiflora
Clematis armandii, C. montana
Hoya australis, H. carnosa
Jasminum
Lathyrus odoratus
Lonicera spp. (not L. sempervirens
  or L. x tellmanniana)
Quisqualis indica
Schisandra
Solandra maxima

Stephanotis
floribunda

Stephanotis floribunda
Trachelospermum
Wisteria

CLIMBERS FOR CONTAINERS

Asarina erubescens
Bougainvillea (prune very hard)
Cissus (some spp.)
Clematis alpina, C. macropetala
Dioscorea discolor
Epipremnum
Gynura aurantiaca
Hardenbergia
Hedera helix
Jasminum officinale,
  J. polyanthum
Lapageria rosea
Monstera deliciosa
Philodendron (some spp.)
Senecio macroglossus
  'Variegatus'
Stephanotis floribunda
Streptosolen jamesonii
Syngonium (some spp.)
Tetrastigma voinierianum
Thunbergia alata
Wisteria (prune very hard)

EVERGREEN CLIMBERS

Allamanda
Anemopaegma
Anredera
Araujia
Argyreia
Asteranthera ovata
Beaumontia
Berberidopsis
Calceolaria pavonii
Calochone
Cissus
Clerodendrum splendens,
  C. thomsoniae
Clytostoma
Combretum grandiflorum
Decumaria sinensis
Dioscorea discolor
Distictis

Epipremnum
Gelsemium sempervirens
Hardenbergia
Hibbertia scandens
Holboellia
Hoya
Jacquemontia
Kennedia
Lapageria
Lardizabala
Macfadyena
Mandevilla
Merremia
Monstera
Mucuna
Mussaenda
Mutisia
Pandorea
Pileostegia
Podranea
Pyrostegia
Rhoicissus
Semele
Senecio confusus,
  S. macroglossus,
  S. mikanioides , S. tamoides
Solandra
Stauntonia
Stephanotis
Stigmaphyllon
Strongylodon
Syngonium
Tecomanthe
Tecomaria
Tetrastigma
Trachelospermum
Wattakaka

CLIMBERS THAT MAY BE GROWN THROUGH OR OVER OTHER PLANTS

Bomarea caldasii
Bougainvillea

Bomarea
caldasii

Celastrus
Clematis
Codonopsis convolvulacea
Humulus lupulus
Lonicera
Mutisia
Tropaeolum peregrinum,
  T. speciosum
Vitis coignetiae
Wisteria sinensis

FAST-GROWING CLIMBERS

Allamanda cathartica
Ampelopsis
Anredera cordifolia

Antigonon leptopus
Aristolochia elegans
Clematis
Clitoria ternatea
Clytostoma callistegioides

Cobaea
scandens
f. alba

Cobaea scandens
Epipremnum aureum
Fallopia
Humulus lupulus
Kennedia rubicunda
Parthenocissus
Passiflora
Phaseolus coccineus
Philodendron scandens
Plumbago auriculata
Pyrostegia venusta
Solanum
Stigmaphyllon ciliatum
Strongylodon macrobotrys
Vitis vinifera

ANNUAL CLIMBERS

Asarina erubescens
Convolvulus tricolor
Eccremocarpus scaber
Ipomoea (some spp.)
Lablab purpureus
Lathyrus odoratus
Mikania scandens
Phaseolus coccineus
Quisqualis indica
Thunbergia alata
Tropaeolum peregrinum

HERBACEOUS CLIMBERS

Bomarea caldasii
Codonopsis
  convolvulacea
Humulus lupulus
Lathyrus grandiflorus,
  L. latifolius
Pueraria lobata
Tropaeolum speciosum,
  T. tricolorum,
  T. tuberosum

CLIMBERS TO USE AS GROUNDCOVERS

Clematis
Hedera
Mitraria
Parthenocissus
Pileostegia
Plumbago auriculata
Senecio
Tecomaria
Trachelospermum
Tropaeolum

Soil preparation and planting

G IVEN ideal growing conditions, climbing plants bring enduring rewards, so always make sure they are appropriate for the type of soil in which they are planted. Climbers seldom thrive in excessively damp or dry conditions. A few, such as *Agapetes* and *Mitraria*, do not tolerate alkaline conditions; others, such as clematis, thrive on alkaline soils but also grow well on all but the most acidic soils. Many climbers are vigorous and require ample nutrients, so dig and fertilize the soil well before planting (see also "Soil nutrients and fertilizers," pp.618–19).

When planting climbers, it is important to use the correct support. Choose one that will easily accommodate the eventual height, spread, and vigor of the plant.

Types of support

The three main types of support used for climbers are wooden or plastic trellis panels, wire or plastic mesh, and wires (usually plastic-covered) stretched between vine eyes or rustproof nails. Horticultural string or reinforcing wire may be adequate for annuals or for herbaceous climbers if the supports are replaced each year. Make sure that the supports are securely in the correct position before planting. Do not use U-shaped metal staples to attach stems to a support. Plants rapidly outgrow these staples, and the stems may become constricted and die back.

Choose a support that will match the size and strength of the climber. One that is not sufficiently sturdy for a vigorous climber may quickly become engulfed and will eventually collapse. A trellis is the most reliable support for all twining climbers, and it may also be used for scramblers if they are tied in. Wires or mesh are appropriate supports for tendril climbers.

If the support is not to be a permanent structure, use climbers that are either herbaceous (*Lathyrus grandiflorus* and *L. latifolius*, for example) or cut to ground level each year (late-flowering *Clematis viticella* hybrids and cultivars), or annual climbers such as *Ipomoea hederacea*. When growing plants against a flat, free-standing trellis or over a pillar, bear in mind that climbers grow toward the light and flower on one side of the support only, so plants should always be positioned to provide their display where it will be most prominent.

Trellises and mesh
To allow air to circulate freely, mount a trellis panel or mesh so that it is held slightly away from the wall or fence; make sure that the base of the framework is approximately 12in (30cm) above soil level.

Walls are likely to need maintenance (repointing, painting, or repairing) at some time, so wherever possible, attach a trellis or mesh with hooks at the top and hinges at the base, or hooks at the top and bottom. The entire plant and its support can then be lowered from the wall or, if hooks only are used, taken down and laid flat on the ground while the wall is repaired.

Wires
Wires can be stretched horizontally or vertically between vine eyes or rustproof nails. As with trellis panels, the wires should be held 2in (5cm) from the surface of the wall or fence and must be kept taut to prevent sagging. Either tighten the vine eyes with pliers or attach tensioners at approximately 6ft (2m) intervals. Space the wires 12–18in (30–45cm) apart, with the lowest horizontal wire (or the base of vertical wires) 12in (30cm) above soil level.

VIGOROUS CLIMBERS

Actinidia chinensis
Akebia quinata
Beaumontia grandiflora
Bougainvillea
Campsis
Cissus
Clematis montana
Distictis buccinatoria
Fallopia
　baldschuanica

Distictis
buccinatoria

Ipomoea horsfalliae
Lonicera japonica
　var. *halliana*
Mandevilla
Parthenocissus quinquefolia,
　P. tricuspidata
Passiflora
Petrea volubilis
Pueraria lobata
Solandra maxima
Solanum wendlandii
Tetrastigma voinierianum
Vitis coignetiae
Wisteria sinensis

Climbing methods

Climbers attach themselves to supports by various means. Many climbers have aerial roots that readily attach to vertical surfaces without support. Other methods, all of which require some support, include twining stems and leaf stalks, and coiling tendrils. Scandent and scrambling climbers, such as *Bougainvillea*, produce long stems that need to be tied in at regular intervals.

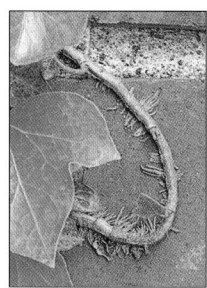

AERIAL ROOTS
Ivy (Hedera) *is a self-clinging plant.*

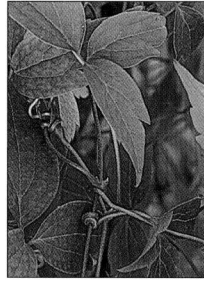

LEAF STALKS
Clematis climbs using its leaf stalks.

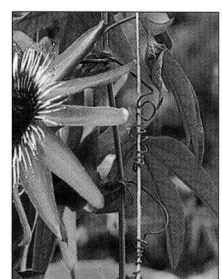

COILING TENDRILS
Passiflora *attaches itself with tendrils.*

TWINING STEMS
Akebia *weaves its stems in a spiral around the support.*

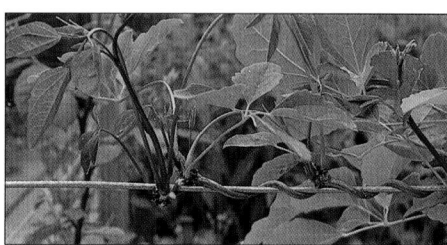

Attaching a trellis panel to a wall

To mount a trellis support, first securely attach vertical wooden laths at least 2in (5cm) thick to the wall and trellis. This allows the trellis to be suspended away from the wall and enables air to circulate freely. The trellis can then be permanently attached to the laths with screws (right); however, this restricts access to the wall. Using hooks and hinges enables the plant and support to be lowered, if required. Hooking the trellis to the laths at top and bottom allows it to be removed from the wall altogether.

USING LATHS
Screw the trellis to thick wooden laths.

Trellis attached at top with hook and vine eye

Hinge fitting at base

USING HOOKS AND HINGES
To allow access to the wall for maintenance, attach laths to both the wall and the trellis. Use hinges along the bottom of the panel with hooks at the top to hold it in place.

HOW TO SELECT CLIMBERS

GOOD EXAMPLE

Label

Vigorous, sturdy stems

Healthy buds

HONEYSUCKLE (LONICERA)

GOOD EXAMPLE

Roots are visible and healthy but not coiled

POOR EXAMPLE

Spindly, weak growth with damaged buds

POOR EXAMPLE

Roots coiled tightly around the root ball

Buying climbers

Climbing plants are usually sold container-grown, although a few (including climbing roses) may be sold bare-root. Choose a healthy plant with a well-balanced framework of strong shoots, and reject any that show signs of pest infestation or disease. Bare-root plants should have plenty of healthy, well-developed fibrous roots that are in proportion to the amount of top-growth. For pot-grown plants, turn the pot over and check that the tips of the young roots are just showing; if so, the plant is well rooted. Reject potbound plants – those that have tightly coiled roots or a mass of roots protruding through the drainage holes – since they seldom grow satisfactorily.

Planting outdoors

If you choose to include marginally hardy climbers in your garden, plant them in spring so that they are well established before their first winter, and provide some protection. Evergreen and herbaceous climbers are more quickly established if planted in spring when the soil is warming up, but they may also be planted in fall in a protected situation. All other container-grown climbers can be planted at any time of year as long as the ground is not frozen or waterlogged. Planting during dry spells in summer is not recommended, but if this is unavoidable, cover the newly planted climber with a paper bag or a piece of burlap for the first few days, and make sure the plant is watered daily while dry conditions persist.

Positioning the plant
Walls and solid fences create their own rain shadow, so plants that are to be trained against them should be planted at least 18in (45cm) fromthe foot of the support. In this way, once

Planting a climber in a container

Select a container large enough to accommodate the climber for at least two seasons. Concrete, stone, or terracotta pots are more stable than plastic ones. Shallow pots are not suitable. Choose a frost-proof pot if the climber is to remain outdoors in winter.

The soil mix should be moisture-retentive but also freely draining. Use a mixture of two parts of regular soilless potting mix and one part of sharp sand. Supplement this with a slow-release fertilizer, and combine it with the soil mix according to the manufacturer's instructions.

Trellis panels specially made for containers are available, with two legs at the base. Anchor these into the soil mix before planting rather than after, to avoid damaging the plant's roots. Tie the top of the trellis to a wall or fence to keep it steady.

1 *Put stones or pieces of broken pots at the base to help support the trellis and to help steady the pot in wind. Add soil mix.*

2 *Plant the climber at the same level as in the original pot. Fill in with soil mix, leaving 2in (5cm) below the rim to allow for watering.*

3 *Tie the main shoots carefully to the support, then water thoroughly to settle the roots.*

CLIMBERS THAT TOLERATE SANDY SOIL

Adlumia fungosa
Anredera cordifolia
Asarina
Bomarea andimarcana
Ceropegia
Clianthus puniceus
Ercilla volubilis
Gloriosa superba
Humulus
Ipomoea

Kennedia rubicunda

Kennedia rubicunda
Merremia tuberosa
Mutisia oligodon
Parthenocissus
Passiflora
Petrea volubilis
Solanum wendlandii
Streptosolen jamesonii
Thunbergia alata

CLIMBERS THAT TOLERATE CLAY SOIL

Akebia
Aristolochia durior
Campsis
Celastrus scandens
Clematis
Distictis
Euonymus fortunei
  'Silver Queen'
Hedera
Humulus lupulus 'Aureus'
Hydrangea anomala
  subsp. *petiolaris*
Lathyrus latifolius
Lonicera
  (some spp.)

Parthenocissus tricuspidata 'Lowii'

Parthenocissus
Passiflora
Schisandra
Vitis coignetiae,
  V. vinifera
Wisteria

CLIMBERS THAT REQUIRE ACIDIC SOIL

Agapetes
Asteranthera ovata
Beaumontia grandiflora
Berberidopsis corallina
Billardiera
Lapageria rosea
Lardizabala biternata
Mitraria coccinea
Mutisia

established they normally receive sufficient rain to grow without additional water. A pillar or free-standing trellis does not produce the same density of rain shadow, and so the planting distance need be only 8–12in (20–30cm).

When grown through another plant, the climber will compete with the host plant for food and moisture. To minimize this, plant the climber so that its roots stay as far away as possible from those of its host. If the host plant has deep roots, and a sufficient depth of soil is available, plant the climber fairly close to the host's main stem. If the host has a mass of rhizomatous or shallow roots, however, plant the climber about 18in (45cm) from the root spread. A stake tied to the host, inserted just behind the climber's main stems, can be used to train the climber toward it at an angle.

Preparing the soil

Remove all weeds from the planting area, using a systemic weedkiller to kill perennial weeds, if necessary. Then dig in coarse organic matter;

CLIMBERS THAT TOLERATE VERY ALKALINE SOIL

Actinidia kolomikta
Akebia quinata
Ampelopsis brevipedunculata
Asarina antirrhiniflora
Campsis x *tagliabuana*
 'Mme. Galen'
Celastrus scandens
Clematis
Eccremocarpus scaber
Fallopia baldschuanica
Hedera
Hydrangea anomala
 subsp. *petiolaris*

Lathyrus grandiflorus

Jasminum officinale,
 J. polyanthum
Lathyrus grandiflorus,
 L. latifolius
Lonicera
Parthenocissus
 tricuspidata
Passiflora caerulea
Schizophragma
 integrifolium
Solanum crispum
Trachelospermum
 jasminoides
Vitis
Wisteria sinensis

this will improve the water retentiveness and fertility of sandy soils, and also lighten the texture of heavy clay soils. Carefully fork in a dressing of slow-release fertilizer at a rate of 2–3oz/sq yd (50–85g/sq m).

The planting hole should be at least twice the diameter of the container in which the climber was grown in order to allow the roots ample room to spread in the prepared soil. This may not be possible, however, if the climber is to be encouraged to grow through a tree or shrub. In these cases, dig a hole large enough to accommodate the root ball, and leave plenty of room for the roots to spread.

How to plant

Before removing the plant from its pot, make sure that the soil mix is moist. Water the plant well so that the root ball is thoroughly wet and then allow it to drain for at least an hour. Remove the surface layer of soil mix to eliminate weed seeds, and then invert the pot, taking care to support the plant as it slides out. If the roots have begun to curl around inside the pot, gently tease them out. Any dead, damaged, or protruding roots should be cut back to the perimeter of the root ball.

Position the plant so that the top of the root ball is just level with the surrounding soil. It is advisable to plant clematis more deeply, however (see *Planting a Clematis*, p.137). Climbers that have been grafted (as is the case with most wisterias) should be planted with the graft union 2½in (6cm) below soil level. This encourages the scion itself to root and reduces the incidence of sucker growths from the stock. For information on planting bare-root climbers, see "Planting a bush rose," p.155. Fill the planting hole with soil, then firm the plant in and water well. Insert stakes at the base of the plant and secure them to the support. Fan out the main shoots and tie them individually to the stakes and to the support itself (if they will reach) to train them in. Do not damage the stems by attaching them too tightly. Remove dead or damaged growth, and cut back wayward shoots.

Tendril climbers readily attach themselves to a support, but the shoots may require gentle guidance and some tying in until they become firmly established. Twining climbers soon fasten their shoots to a support in their natural direction of growth (clockwise or counterclockwise) but may also need tying in initially. Scramblers that do not support themselves should have their shoots care-

fully fastened to the support at regular intervals with appropriate ties. For additional information, see "Training established climbers," p.134.

Watering and mulching

Water the newly planted climber thoroughly, then cover the surface of the soil surrounding the plant with a 2–3in (5–7cm) layer of mulch to a radius of about 2ft (60cm). This is beneficial to the roots because it retains moisture throughout the area, giving the roots a chance to establish themselves. In addition, the mulch discourages the germination of weeds that would otherwise compete with the newly planted climber for nutrients and moisture.

PLANTING A CLIMBER AGAINST A WALL

1 *Attach a support 12in (30cm) above the soil and 2in (5cm) from the wall. Dig a hole 18in (45cm) from the wall. Loosen the soil at the base and add compost.*

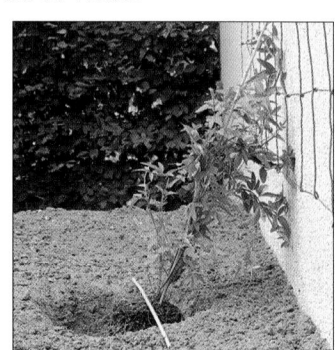

2 *Soak the climber's root ball well. Position it in the hole at a 45° angle, placing a stake across to check the planting level. Spread the roots away from the wall.*

3 *Fill in around the plant and firm and level the soil, making sure no air pockets remain between the roots and that the plant is fully supported.*

4 *Untie the stems from the central stake and select 4 or 5 strong shoots. Insert a stake for each shoot and attach it to the lowest wire. Tie in the shoots.*

5 *Using pruners, trim back any weak, damaged, or wayward shoots to the central stem. This establishes the initial framework for the climber.*

6 *Water the plant thoroughly (here Jasminum mesnyi). Cover the surrounding soil with a deep mulch to retain moisture and discourage weeds.*

Routine care

CLIMBERS need fertilizing annually to maintain healthy growth, and the soil around their base should be kept moist. Climbers grown in containers need top-dressing or repotting regularly, and adequate watering is essential. Regular deadheading helps prolong flowering. Plants also need protection from pests, diseases, and (if tender) cold.

Fertilizing

Fertilize climbers in spring during their first two seasons with a dressing of 2–3oz (50–85g) of a balanced fertilizer. Thereafter, apply a slow-release fertilizer annually at the manufacturer's recommended rate.

Watering

During dry periods, water climbers weekly. Soak thoroughly around the base of the plant. Apply a 2–3in (5–7cm) mulch over the root area to prevent the soil from drying out.

Deadheading and tying in

Where practical, deadhead climbers as the flowers fade. This enables the plant to concentrate its energies on producing more flowers, rather than fruits or seedheads. However, if fruits or seedheads are desired for ornamental purposes, deadhead only a quarter to one-third of the flowered shoots. This will be enough to encourage a continuing display.

Tie in new shoots as they develop, while still flexible, and cut back overgrown plants as needed (see "Pruning and training," pp.132–35).

Pests and diseases

Check carefully for signs of pests and diseases and treat any affected plants as recommended in PLANT PROBLEMS, pp.633–61.

Protecting tender climbers

Protect the top-growth and base of marginally hardy and newly planted climbers with some sort of cover to block wind and sun and to moderate temperatures (see COLD AND WIND PROTECTION, pp.604–5).

CUTTING BACK CLIMBERS

*Where a climber (*here Hedera colchica 'Sulphur Heart'*) has outgrown its allotted space, cut it back with pruners. Trim the stems irregularly for a natural look.*

Maintaining container–grown climbers

Container-grown climbers may need to be watered once or twice a day in dry weather. When cold is likely, they may be moved indoors or plunged in the ground in a sheltered part of the garden. During the year, a climber grown in a container uses up most of the nutrients in the soil mix. The top-dressing (the top layer of the soil mix and any mulch) should therefore be renewed annually. When the plant is watered, the fresh nutrients will gradually permeate and replenish the soil mix below. All but the most slow-growing climbers need to be moved into a larger container, using fresh soil mix, every two to four years. Spring-flowering plants should be repotted in fall, all others in fall or spring.

RENEWING THE TOP-DRESSING OF A CONTAINER-GROWN CLIMBER

1 *In spring or early summer, scrape away and discard the top 1–2in (2.5–5cm) of soil mix in the container. Take care not to disturb any surface roots of the climber and any companion planting.*

2 *Replace the discarded soil mix with a layer of fresh soil mix mixed with a little slow-release fertilizer. Firm gently to eliminate air pockets. Make sure that the level of the soil mix is the same as before. Water well.*

3 *To aid moisture retention during the summer months, cover the soil mix in the container with a light, decorative mulch such as cocoa shells or bark chips.*

REPOTTING A CONTAINER-GROWN CLIMBER

1 *Every 2 to 4 years, repot container-grown climbers (such as this variegated ivy) to prevent them from becoming potbound (see inset). Soak the soil mix well, then carefully slide the root ball out of the container.*

2 *Tease out the roots and trim back the thicker roots by about one-third. Leave fibrous roots intact, and retain as much soil mix as possible around them.*

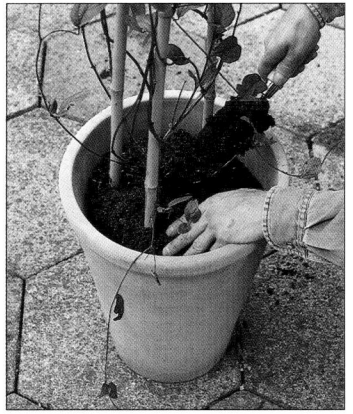

3 *Prune the top-growth by a third, and remove dead or damaged stems. Repot the plant in fresh, moist soil mix, adding slow-release fertilizer to the top 1–2in (2.5–5cm).*

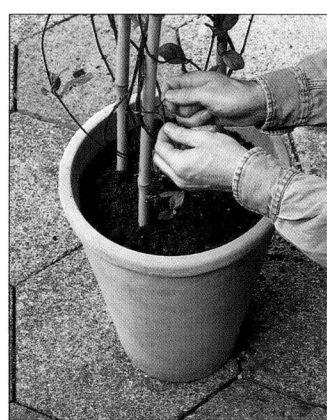

4 *Be sure that the final planting level is the same as before. Insert a triangle of stakes, then tie in the main shoots securely but not too tightly.*

Pruning and training

DURING the early years, pruning is carried out to build a strong framework for a plant; to promote vigorous growth of healthy, productive wood; and to facilitate training over the support. Training should be aimed at guiding a selected number of strong, major stems over and across a support while they are flexible, to create a pleasing shape.

Some climbers, such as the fast-growing silver lace vine (*Fallopia baldschuanica*), send out a mass of small shoots in addition to main stems, and these need to be regularly tied in during initial training to retain the required shape. Frequently, however, vigorous climbers are difficult to train after the first year and are best left to grow freely. Restrict them only when they grow beyond their allotted space.

Basic principles

Routine pruning is essential to the successful cultivation of almost all established climbers. Without this control, the plants may fail to

flower well, and, equally importantly, some of the more vigorous climbers may swamp nearby plants or damage roofs, gutters, and masonry. Training can be combined with pruning to achieve the most desirable structure and appearance for the plant.

Where to cut
The stems should be cut ¹/₁₆–¹/₈in (2–3mm) above a plump bud. Select an appropriately placed bud that faces the direction in which a new shoot is required. Then, as the shoot develops, it can be tied in either to fill the framework or to replace an old shoot.

Make each pruning cut cleanly with sharp pruners, at an angle slanting slightly away from the bud. This ensures that rainwater does not gather around the bud and encourage possible disease infection. The position of the cut is important: a cut that is made too close to the bud may damage it, while one made too far away from the bud will leave a stub that dies back and may provide an entry point for disease.

Using the correct tools
A pair of sharp pruners is the best tool for most types of pruning. Long-handled loppers may also be useful, especially for thicker stems, and shears can be used where a great deal of dead or weak growth needs to be removed (see "How to prune honeysuckle," p.135).

Formative pruning and training

At planting time, and as the plant starts to grow, training consists of tying in the strongest shoots to the support to achieve a balanced framework. During the growing season, a little guidance will be needed to make sure that the soft, twining stems or tendrils attach themselves to their support while they are still pliable and before the wood becomes

too mature. Hardened stems cannot be bent into the required position without damaging them.

In late winter or early spring following initial planting, once all danger of severe frost has passed, cut back each sideshoot to an appropriately placed bud that is near the central or main stem, tying the pruned shoots to the support. Several strong stems will grow from these pruned shoots during the following season, from which the framework of the plant develops. These should be trained in as they develop, as before.

The following year, cut back each stem, and possibly the leader, to a bud that is pointing in the direction in which the stem is to be trained. This results in the growth of vigorous shoots with which to extend the main framework. Carefully tie in all the stems, and cut back any other shoots to within two buds of the nearest stem.

SPRING PRUNING

Climbers that flower on the current season's shoots, such as Solanum crispum *shown here, should be pruned in late winter or early spring.*

FORMATIVE PRUNING AND TRAINING

In order to establish a healthy, strong framework for a climbing plant, begin pruning and training as soon as possible after planting, in late winter or early spring. The plant here is Jasminum nudiflorum.

Remove any crossing shoots. Use sharp pruners to cut just above a healthy bud.

Cut out all congested growth, removing crossing shoots and the weaker of any shoots that are competing.

Remove dead or cold-damaged shoots and stems, cutting back to live, healthy wood.

To encourage flowering, cut back sideshoots to 5 or 6 strong, healthy buds, making an angled cut just above a bud.

Pruning established climbers

The time of year to prune established climbers depends on their flowering habit. Some flower on the current season's shoots or, occasionally, on shoots that are produced late in the previous growing season. These are usually pruned in late winter or early spring, before new buds begin to develop. They will flower later in the same season on new shoots.

Other climbers flower on the previous year's ripened shoots or on older shoots. These should be pruned immediately after flowering to allow new shoots time to ripen before winter. These are the shoots that will bear the next season's flowers. Some early-flowering climbers may well produce a second crop later in the season if pruned immediately after flowering.

Distinguishing between first- and second-year shoots is not normally difficult. First-year shoots are still pliable and usually green, whereas second-year ones are usually gray or brown. Shoots more than two years old have a distinct, usually dark bark and are tough and woody.

When pruning, always remove all dead or damaged wood and any congested, twiggy growth. Cut back stems that have grown beyond the plant's allotted space, both to maintain the shape of the climber and to control excessive growth.

For methods of pruning clematis, see pp.136–37.

EARLY SUMMER PRUNING

Climbers that flower on the previous year's ripened shoots, such as Jasminum beesianum, *should be pruned immediately after flowering to allow new shoots to develop before the onset of winter.*

Cut back shoots that have flowered, pruning to a vigorous shoot lower down.

Remove all dead or damaged wood, cutting cleanly, close to a healthy shoot or stem.

Where there is congested growth, weak shoots should be removed.

Pruning Wisteria

Wisteria may be reluctant to flower unless the vigorous, leafy summer shoots are severely curtailed and the plant's energies diverted into producing flower buds. Flowering is also improved if the main stems are trained horizontally rather than vertically. The flower buds are produced on short spurs, so the aim of pruning is to encourage these spurs to develop along the framework branches of an established plant. The simplest method is to carry out a two-stage pruning schedule. In summer, cut back long growths and shorter lateral growths. Leave stems unpruned only if they are needed to extend the framework, and train them in. In late winter cut back summer-pruned spur shoots to two or three buds. At the same time, reduce to 6in (15cm) any long growths that developed after summer pruning.

1 *In summer, restrict the growth of vigorous, stringy shoots to encourage more new buds to grow next year.*

2 *Cut back long shoots to about 6in (15cm), leaving 4–6 leaves. Make the cut clear of the last bud, since the buds are easily damaged.*

WINTER
Prune shoots shortened in summer. Reduce them to 3–4in (8–10cm), leaving only 2–3 buds.

CLIMBERS THAT FLOWER ON CURRENT SEASON'S GROWTH

Anredera cordifolia
Antigonon leptopus
Bignonia
Billardiera longiflora
Campsis
Clematis
  (large-flowered cvs)
Clerodendrum thomsoniae
Clianthus
Clytostoma
Distictis
Fallopia baldschuanica
Ipomoea
Lapageria
Lonicera
Mandevilla
Mikania
Mutisia decurrens
Parthenocissus
Passiflora
Pileostegia viburnoides
Plumbago
Podranea
Pyrostegia venusta

Solanum crispum

Solanum crispum,
  S. jasminoides
Stephanotis
Streptosolen
Thladiantha
Thunbergia gregorii
Vigna caracalla
Vitis

CLIMBERS THAT FLOWER ON PREVIOUS SEASON'S GROWTH

Actinidia
Allamanda cathartica
Aristolochia
Beaumontia
Bougainvillea

Bougainvillea 'Miss Manila'

Clematis alpina
  and cvs, *C. armandii,*
  C. cirrhosa, C. macropetala
  and cvs, *C. montana* and cvs
Decumaria sinensis
Gelsemium sempervirens
Hoya
Hydrangea
Jasminum
Pileostegia
Schizophragma
Solandra maxima
Streptosolen jamesonii
Strongylodon
Wisteria

WINTER PRUNING

When pruning climbers in winter, it is easy to assess the framework of the plant and train in any new growth. The climber shown here is Schisandra glaucescens.

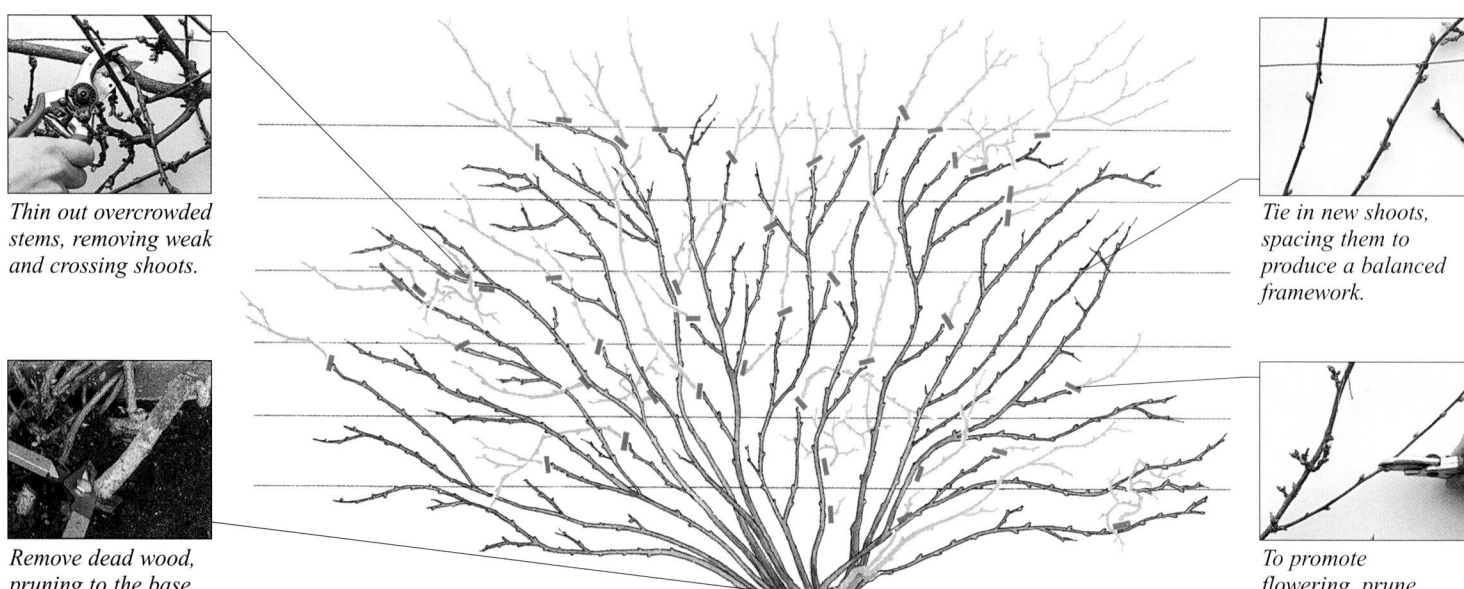

Thin out overcrowded stems, removing weak and crossing shoots.

Remove dead wood, pruning to the base of the stem if this is necessary.

Tie in new shoots, spacing them to produce a balanced framework.

To promote flowering, prune all sideshoots to about 5 buds.

Evergreen climbers

Prune evergreen climbers in spring, after all danger of frost has passed and as the plants are about to begin fresh growth. Evergreen climbers that are grown for their flowers as well as their foliage produce flowers on the previous season's wood, so delay pruning these until after flowering. In both cases, simply remove dead or damaged wood and trim stray shoots to shape.

Winter pruning

Climbers that have already had at least one pruning during the previous growing season may be pruned again in winter to neaten their appearance (see illustrations above). This is particularly useful for deciduous plants, whose frameworks can be assessed more easily when the branches are bare. Do not remove ripened wood, which will carry the next season's flowers. If in mild spells winter-pruned plants are stimulated into new growth, the new young shoots may later be damaged by cold. Prune these back in spring.

Ornamental grapevines (*Vitis*) should be pruned in early winter, when the plants are dormant and pruning cuts may be made without the risk of bleeding, or loss of sap, occurring.

If the stems are cut in spring when the sap is rising, they bleed profusely; this is difficult to stop and weakens the plants. (For information on how to prune grapevines, see pp.456–60.)

Training established climbers

Climbers that attach themselves by means of aerial roots need very little training, except in the first few years until enough aerial roots have formed to support the plant. All other climbing plants need their new shoots trained in each year to maintain the desired shape.

Each year during the growing season, select the strongest new stems, before they become hard and woody, and train them in to continue the basic framework. Follow the shape of the allocated space, and allow the leading stem to extend in a straight line until it has reached the required height. Tie all stems securely to the

Pruning Bougainvillea

Bougainvillea is rampant and normally flowers reliably whether pruned or not. Prune between midwinter and early spring to keep the plant in check. Shorten sideshoots to within a few inches of the main stems, but leave any needed to extend the main framework.

1 *Trim wayward sideshoots to within 1–2in (2.5–5cm) of the main framework stems.*

2 *Cut cleanly, close to a healthy bud. The buds will soon produce new growth.*

Training climbers on pergolas and pillars

To produce an even distribution of growth over a pergola or pillar, tie in the main stems throughout the growing season, spreading them out as required to fill any gaps. To promote flowering lower down a plant's stem, regularly train sideshoots of twining species around their support, making sure that the shoots are following their natural direction of growth: clockwise or counterclockwise.

After the flowering season, remove any dead or diseased shoots and prune the main stem and any leaders. This will encourage the plant to produce strong lateral growth in the following year.

1 *Guide stray sideshoots onto the support in their natural direction of growth, then tie in.*

2 *After flowering, cut back all the leading stems by one-third to promote lateral growth.*

support at regular intervals using plastic twist-ties or twine. Make sure that the ties are tight enough to prevent the stems from being blown about in strong winds and rubbing against the support; however, they should not restrict the stem's development. The ties will need to be loosened periodically as the stems thicken with age.

Renovating an old or neglected climber

Unpruned climbers, and those that have not been trained, often become a mass of tangled, woody stems and produce a poor display of flowers. Such plants can be pruned hard to rejuvenate them. Most climbers withstand pruning close to the base or to main framework stems, but an unhealthy plant may not survive this treatment. In this case, it is preferable to reduce the size of the plant gradually over a period of two or three years, in conjunction with annual fertilizing.

For a plant that is to be pruned to the base, cut back all growth in early spring to within 1–2ft (30–60cm) of the ground. To promote rapid new growth, apply a dressing of quick-

How to prune honeysuckle

Climbing honeysuckles (*Lonicera*) require little pruning to flower profusely but tend, if neglected, to develop into a mass of thin, tangled stems that bear foliage and flowers only at the top of the shoots. To renovate a honeysuckle in this condition, prune it severely in early to midspring at the beginning of the growing season. New shoots will soon begin to develop, and these should be trained in to provide an evenly balanced framework of stems.

If such severe pruning is not required, it is still possible to renovate the plant by removing dead or damaged shoots and stems from beneath new, young growth. Use a pair of shears, rather than pruners, for speed.

RENOVATION PRUNING
If the plant is badly overgrown, cut back all the stems with long-handled loppers to within 1–2ft (30–60cm) of ground level.

ALTERNATIVE METHOD
If it is undesirable or unnecessary to prune so severely, cut away all dead material from underneath the new, fresh growth.

acting, balanced fertilizer at a rate of 2–3oz/sq yd (50–85g/sq m). Soak the root area with water, and mulch. Train in all new growth as for newly planted climbers.

Renovation over a two- to three-year period (see below) is more difficult, since the stems frequently become entangled. In spring, remove

as much congested growth as possible, then cut to the base one in every two (or three) main stems. Gently unravel the top-growth of the severed stems. If any shoots are damaged, cut them out after the pruned main stems and their top-growth have been removed. Cut out the weak, spindly shoots, which will not flower

satisfactorily, and any dead wood. Fertilize, water, and mulch, as when pruning to the base, to encourage healthy new growth. Train in fresh basal shoots to fill gaps, making sure they do not become entangled with old shoots. The following spring, repeat the process and fertilize, water, and mulch the plant.

RENOVATING A NEGLECTED CLIMBER

A neglected climber (here Celastrus orbiculatus*) can be renovated gradually over 2 or 3 seasons by pruning hard each spring.*

Remove as much congested growth as possible.

Remove weak, twiggy, or damaged shoots so that only strong shoots remain.

Using long-handled loppers, cut back to the base one-third to one-half of the old stems, retaining the more vigorous ones.

All dead or diseased wood should also be removed. Prune to a healthy bud, using sharp pruners.

CLIMBERS THAT MAY BE CUT TO THE GROUND

Allamanda cathartica
Anredera cordifolia
Antigonon leptopus
Aristolochia
Campsis x *tagliabuana*
Clematis (most spp.)
Clerodendrum thomsoniae
Clytostoma callistegioides
Distictis buccinatoria
Fallopia baldschuanica
Lonicera (most spp.)
Macfadyena unguis-cati
Manettia cordifolia,
  M. inflata

Passiflora x *caponii*
'John Innes'

Parthenocissus
Passiflora
Petrea volubilis
Pyrostegia venusta
Quisqualis indica
Solandra maxima
Solanum
Stigmaphyllon ciliatum
Strongylodon macrobotrys
Thunbergia
Vitis
Wisteria

Clematis

CLEMATIS are suited to almost any situation and climate. Of all the climbers, they offer the longest flowering period, with species or hybrids that bloom in almost every month of the year, many with the additional interest of silvery clustered seedheads appearing flowering. Their diverse habits range from herbaceous plants, for example *C. integrifolia* and the clump-forming *C. recta*, to sprawling subshrubs such as *C. x jouiniana*, as well as the better-known climbers.

Clematis also present a huge range of flower color and flower forms, ranging from the attractive sprays of delicate, ivory-colored bells of *C. rehderiana* and exotic-looking, fleshy, golden lanterns in *C. tangutica* to the simple but richly colored blooms of *C. viticella* and its many hybrids, or the more complex forms of large-flowered double clematis such as *C.* 'Proteus' and *C.* 'Vyvyan Pennell'.

Where to grow clematis

Clematis can be chosen for almost any garden setting. The vigorous spring-flowering species and cultivars are ideal for covering and camouflaging unsightly buildings, fences, and walls, or for scrambling over old trees, tree stumps, and arbors, adding color and interest to otherwise dull features.

Less rampant types may be wall-trained on trellises and pergolas or allowed to cascade over terraces; at ground level, more delicate species will sprawl where their blooms can be best appreciated.

Some clematis are suitable for container cultivation, on patios, or, for tender species, under glass. Others have great potential for being grown through host plants – trees, climbers, and sturdy shrubs, for example – to provide an extended season of interest, a splash of color, or to create unusual and unexpected plant associations.

Clematis groups

Clematis may be divided into three main groups, based on their flowering time and habit.

Group 1 is made up of the early-flowering species and their cultivars, and the Alpina, Macropetala, and Montana groups, which flower directly from the previous season's ripened stems. In Group 2 are the early, large-flowered cultivars, blooming on the current season's short stems, which arise from the previous season's mature wood. Groups 1 and 2 are sometimes called old-wood-flowering clematis. Group 3 includes the late-flowering species, late, large-flowered cultivars, and herbaceous types, which flower on the current season's growth.

Early-flowering species and cultivars

The early-flowering evergreen species and their forms are mostly from warm climates and must be grown, therefore, with protection in areas where marginally hardy. The hardiest evergreens are the vigorous *C. armandii* and smaller *C. cirrhosa*. Both grow best in a south- or southwest-facing site and are lovely when growing through other wall-trained plants.

The Alpina and Macropetala groups withstand low winter temperatures and are ideal for growing through shrubs and wall-trained trees in any exposure. Do not grow them through climbing roses or other shrubs that need annual pruning, since these clematis need little or no cutting back. They are suitable in exposed sites such as northeast corners of buildings, but also make superb container plants for the patio and can be trained to any support.

The members of the Montana group are hardy and vigorous, climbing 22–40ft (7–12m). These plants will cover walls and arbors and are dramatic growing through conifers or old fruit trees past their productive best, but they may damage the evergreens with their rampant growth.

Early, large-flowered cultivars

These are generally hardy, growing to 8–12ft (2.5–4m). The more compact cultivars such as *C.* 'Edith', which are normally the first to flower, are ideal for containers. The double and semidouble cultivars, and the midsummer-flowering types with very large flowers are best grown through the branches of other wall-trained trees or shrubs, where their flowers are protected from severe wind or heavy rain. Paler-flowered cultivars with pink or mauve-striped flowers are best planted in the shade where their flowers may be used to lighten a dark wall and will not be bleached out by the sun. The deep reds and purples are better for sunny situations because they develop better color in strong light.

Late-flowering species and cultivars

This group of clematis includes the late, large-flowered cultivars such as *C.* 'Jackmanii', small-flowered *C. viticella* and its hybrids, and a wide range of species and their forms, including the herbaceous clematis. The Jackmanii types are superb when grown through climbing roses, shrub roses, or most medium-sized shrubs, both evergreen and deciduous, whether free-standing or wall-trained. The *C. viticella* hybrids in particular are excellent for growing through groundcovers, especially the summer- or winter-flowering heathers (*Calluna*, *Daboecia*, and *Erica*).

Of other members in this group, *C. x jouiniana* makes an ideal groundcover, and the tiny, tuliplike flowers of *C. texensis* and its hybrids are dramatic against a background of low-growing evergreens. The vigorous *C. orientalis* and *C. tangutica* need a large wall or tree where they can grow unconfined and display their abundant flowers and fluffy seedheads. *C. heracleifolia* var. *davidiana* and other herbaceous species do not climb and should be grown in mixed or herbaceous borders; *C. integrifolia*, for example, associates very well with cluster-flowered bush roses.

Soil preparation and planting

When using vigorous clematis to clothe trellises or pergolas, be sure that the support structure is strong and sound before planting. Similarly, when growing clematis through old trees, the branches must be strong enough to bear the often considerable weight. For clematis

CLEMATIS GROUPS

GROUP 1

C. montana var. rubens

C. alpina 'Frances Rivis'

C. macropetala 'Markham's Pink'

GROUP 2

C. 'The President'

C. 'Henryi'

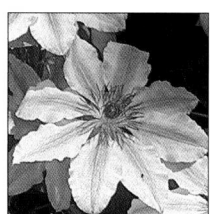

C. 'Nelly Moser'

GROUP 3

C. 'Ernest Markham'

C. 'Jackmanii'

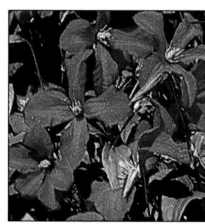

C. viticella 'Mme. Julia Correvon'

grown through other host plants, it is essential to match the vigor of the clematis with that of its host, if the host is not to be overcome. Also be sure that the pruning requirements of host and clematis are compatible.

Most climbing species can be sited in part shade or in sun, provided that the roots are cool and shaded. Either underplant them with low shrubs or plant on the shaded side of the host tree or wall. The herbaceous species thrive in a sunny situation. To grow clematis on a patio, use a container with dimensions of 18in diameter x 18in deep (45 x 45cm).

Most clematis will thrive in any rich, fertile, and well-drained soil, especially if it is neutral or slightly alkaline. Evergreens and species such as *C. tangutica* and *C. orientalis* should not be grown in soil that remains wet during the winter months because they have fine, fibrous root systems that quickly rot. Planting details are the same as for other climbers (see "Soil preparation and planting," pp.128–130), except that clematis should be planted about 2in (5cm) deeper than normal to encourage basal buds to develop below soil level. If the stems are damaged, the plant may then grow again from below soil level.

Routine care

Keep newly planted specimens well watered until established, and mulch climbing and herbaceous species annually in spring with compost or well-rotted manure.

Fresh young growth is very susceptible to slug damage (p.638) in early spring. Clematis may be prone to attack from aphids (p.639), and the later-flowering, large-flowered cultivars may be afflicted by

COLOR CONTRAST
Clematis are excellent as companion plants and can be grown through a variety of host plants to create an unusual display. Here, the bright petals of
C. viticella
'Venosa Violacea'
present an attractive contrast to the green of
Juniperus sabina
var. tamariscifolia,
over which it is scrambling.

PLANTING A CLEMATIS

Plant clematis 2in (5cm) deeper than the nursery planting level. This helps buds develop below soil level, which helps overcome clematis wilt.

powdery mildew (p.640). Clematis wilt, a condition that is caused by a fungus, can attack newly planted, large-flowered clematis.

Pruning and training

Pruning requirements vary for each group, so always check before cutting back. If pruned incorrectly, the flowering wood may be cut out.

Initial pruning and training for all groups

Clematis climb by means of leaf-stalk tendrils that attach themselves to their support. They need to be trained to reach their support, and new growth will need tying in during spring and summer. Tie just below a node (or leaf axil buds), and space stems evenly on the support, leaving enough room for further growth to develop.

Clematis require special care in initial training and pruning. If they are left untrained, vigorous clematis may produce one or two stems that

can grow to as much as 50–60ft (15–18m) long. producing a top-heavy tangle of growth and a bare base. To avoid this, all newly planted clematis should be pruned hard the first spring after planting.

Unless the plant already has three or four stems growing from the base, cut back all the stems just above a strong, healthy pair of leaf buds about 12in (30cm) above soil level. If this hard pruning does not produce three or four extra stems in early spring, any new stems should be pruned to about 6in (15cm), just above a strong pair of leaf buds.

Group 1

Many of these vigorous clematis require little, if any, regular pruning, especially if cut back hard when first planted. If restricting the size or neatening tangled growth is necessary, pruning should be done after flowering. Any dead, weak, or damaged stems can also be removed at this time. New growth will ripen during late summer and fall and provide flowers the following spring. Any excess growth may be reduced during the fall and tied into its support, but bear in mind that this will reduce the flowering display. *C. armandii*, which produces a mass of flowers on trailing stems, may be thinned annually to avoid congestion; cut back to well-placed young shoots immediately after flowering.

PRUNING GROUP 1 CLEMATIS

Mature stems of Group 1 clematis produce flower stems for the next season, so prune after flowering only if the plant has become overgrown.

Cut back any damaged shoots to a healthy pair of buds or to the main stem.

Thin or remove stems that are growing densely or that have outgrown the available space, cutting them back to their point of origin.

GROUP 1, EARLY-
FLOWERING SPECIES

C. alpina and cvs
C. armandii and cvs
C. cirrhosa

*Clematis
armandii*

C. macropetala and cvs
C. montana and cvs
C. montana
  var. *grandiflora*
C. montana
  var. *rubens*

Flower stem growing directly from last season's growth

Group 2

The solitary, large flowers are produced on stems of lengths varying from 6in to 24in (15–60cm) and arise from the previous season's growth. Prune these plants in early spring, just before the new growth commences.

Remove any dead, weak, or damaged stems, and cut back healthy stems to just above a strong pair of leaf buds. These buds will produce the first crop of flowers. This group may also produce a second, but smaller, flush of blooms on new shoots in late summer.

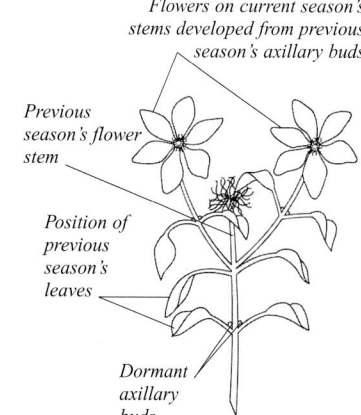

Flowers on current season's stems developed from previous season's axillary buds

Previous season's flower stem

Position of previous season's leaves

Dormant axillary buds

brittle, new stems. Space them evenly and tie in at regular intervals.

Clematis growing over host or groundcover plants, such as heathers, should also be pruned. In late fall remove excessive growth to keep the plant and host neat and less prone to wind damage. When clematis are grown over winter-flowering heathers, all clematis top-growth should be removed down to 12in (30cm) in late fall, before the heathers come into flower.

Propagation

Clematis species can be propagated by seed sown in fall and overwintered in a cold greenhouse or frame (cultivars do not come true from seed). Cultivars are usually increased by softwood or semiripe cuttings (see pp.626–27) or layering (see p.625); division (see p.372) or basal stem cuttings (see p.198) are used for herbaceous types.

Internodal cuttings of softwood and semiripe wood are preferred to nodal cuttings. Take them in spring just above a node, and trim the stem to 1–2in (2.5–5cm) below the node. Remove one of the pair of leaves 1/4in (1cm) away from the node. Reduce the remaining leaf area by half, and cut the stem above the node back to approximately 1/4in (1cm). Treat the base with hormone rooting powder. Root in a closed propagating case with bottom heat. Harden off the new plants gradually (see p.631) before planting out the young clematis after frost danger has passed in spring.

INTERNODAL CUTTINGS

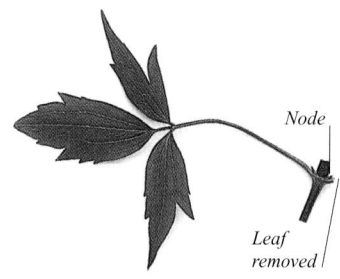

Node

Leaf removed

Make cuttings 2in (5cm) long by trimming just above a node and 1½in (3.5cm) below the node. Remove one leaf from each cutting.

PRUNING GROUP 2 CLEMATIS

Group 2 clematis flower on the current season's stems, so prune in early spring before growth starts.

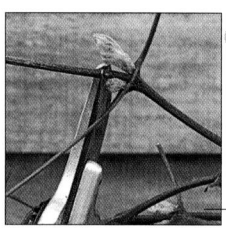

Cut back old stems to a strong pair of buds. Growth from these will produce this season's flowers.

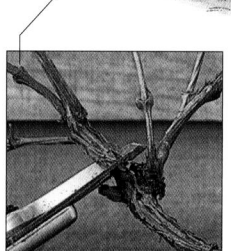

Before new growth starts, cut out any damaged stems to their point of origin or to ground level.

Group 3

Flowers produced by this group are on stems of the current season's growth. Prune in early spring before new growth commences. Remove all the previous season's stems down to a strong pair of leaf buds just above the base of the previous season's growth, 6–12in (15–30cm) above soil level. As new growth appears, tie it to its support or host. Take care with the soft, and often

PRUNING GROUP 3 CLEMATIS

Group 3 clematis produce flowers on the current season's growth, so prune in early spring before new growth begins.

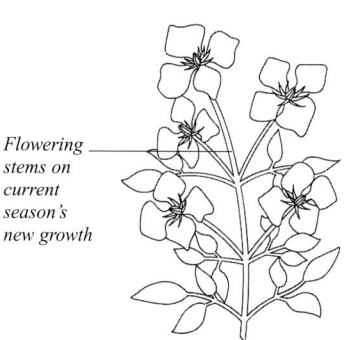

Flowering stems on current season's new growth

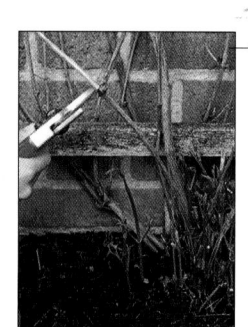

Cut just above the lowest pair of strong buds on each stem – this will be 6–12in (15–30cm) above soil level. Make a straight cut with sharp pruners, ensuring that the buds are not damaged.

GROUP 2 – EARLY, LARGE-FLOWERED CULTIVARS

C. 'Barbara Jackman'
C. 'Carnaby'
C. 'Daniel Deronda'

Clematis 'Vyvyan Pennell'

C. 'Duchess of Edinburgh'
C. 'Elsa Spath'
C. 'General Sikorski'
C. 'Henryi'
C. 'Lasurstern'
C. 'Marie Boisselot', syn.
    C. 'Mme. Le Coultre'
C. 'Mrs. N. Thompson'
C. 'Nelly Moser'
C. 'Niobe'
C. 'The President'
C. 'Vyvyan Pennell'

GROUP 3 – LATE-FLOWERING SPECIES AND CULTIVARS

C. 'Comtesse de Bouchaud'
C. 'Duchess of Albany'
C. 'Ernest Markham'

Clematis 'Perle d'Azure'

C. florida and cvs
C. 'Hagley Hybrid'
C. 'Jackmanii'
C. 'Lady Betty Balfour'
C. paniculata
C. 'Perle d'Azure'
C. tangutica and cvs
C. 'Ville de Lyon'
C. viticella and cvs

Propagation

CLIMBING plants may be propagated from seed, from stem or root cuttings, or by layering. *Wisteria* is also often propagated by grafting (for further information on this technique, see ORNAMENTAL TREES, "Grafting," p.80).

Propagation from seed is the most cost-effective way of producing large quantities of plants. It is also the only practical method for increasing annuals and the easiest method for propagating herbaceous climbers. Hybrids and cultivars, however, seldom reproduce true from seed, so it is therefore advisable to propagate these by vegetative methods, such as cuttings. Also, woody plants may take several years to reach flowering size if they are raised from seed.

Propagation from stem cuttings that are taken from soft or semiripe wood can be carried out successfully for almost all climbers and is the best method for selected cultivars. Propagation from hardwood cuttings is normally used only for grapevines (*Vitis*). Root cuttings can be used for a small number of

plants, such as *Celastrus*. Some climbers produce new plants naturally by self-layering. If only a few plants are required, simple and serpentine layering are both straightforward methods of propagating climbers that are difficult to raise successfully from cuttings.

Propagating climbers from seed

Many species produce viable seed without any difficulty. In the case of some marginally hardy plants, however, a long, hot summer may be necessary for the seed to ripen fully. To obtain seed from unisexual plants, such as *Actinidia deliciosa* and *Celastrus* species, plants of both sexes must be grown reasonably close together to make sure that they pollinate each other.

The sex of any seedling is unknown until the time that it reaches flowering size. Named, vegetatively propagated male and female clones are available for some plants,

such as *Actinidia deliciosa*. For sowing and planting annual climbers, see ANNUALS AND BIENNIALS, pp.202–17.

Preparing the seed
For certain climbers it may be necessary to soak the seeds in water before sowing them: *Hardenbergia* seeds should be left in the water for 24 hours, and *Lapageria* for 48 hours. Seeds with a hard outer coating may need to have their dormancy broken by a period of cold, which is best achieved by putting them in a refrigerator for at least six to eight weeks (for further information, see PRINCIPLES OF PROPAGATION, "Cold stratification," p.624.)

Sowing
If sowing seed in a pot, first cover the drainage holes with a piece of screen (this is not necessary when plastic pots, seed trays, or pans are used). Then fill the pot, pan, or tray with sowing medium. Firm with a presser board to be sure that there are no air spaces or hollows. Large seeds should be evenly spaced; press them

gently into the medium and then cover them to their own depth with a layer of sifted medium that has been mixed with a small amount of fine grit. Combine tiny seeds with a little fine, dry sand so that they may be sown evenly and thinly; no extra covering of medium is needed.

Label the pot and water the soil mix with a fine spray. Add a thin layer of fine grit or place clear plastic film or glass over the container to stop the soil mix from drying out.

The seeds of certain climbers such as *Eccremocarpus* and *Tropaeolum peregrinum* require supplemental heat to germinate when grown in a cool climate and so should be placed in a propagator at 55–60°F (13–16°C). Sow *Cobaea*, if grown as an annual, in late winter with heat so that young plants are well developed by the time they are planted out. Most other seeds should be kept in a warm place out of direct sunlight. Cold-hardy climbers, such as most clematis, however, germinate best in cold conditions: plunge the containers into a protected place such as a cold frame.

Pricking out
As soon as the seedlings emerge, remove the glass or plastic film, if used. When the first pair of true leaves has formed (the seedling's first leaves may differ significantly from the leaves of the adult plant), prick out the seedlings singly into small pots. If they are very small, however, it is best to use a tray, pricking out into rows separated by the space of about one leaf's width.

Inspect the base of the pots or tray at frequent intervals. As soon as the roots are visible through the drainage holes, pot on the seedlings. Seedlings that were germinated in a cold environment should be grown on in warmer conditions under cover.

Planting out
Plant out the seedlings when they are well established. Fast-growing climbers, both annual and perennial, can be planted where they are to flower. If frosts are likely and the climbers are not fully hardy, either plant them under some sort of cover or delay planting out until all danger of frost has passed.

Slow-growing climbers should be potted on each time the roots begin to appear through the base of the pot. In their first season, grow them on in a sheltered position or in a nursery bed. Provide stakes to support the plants in all cases, and keep the soil mix of potgrown plants moist.

SOWING SEED

1 *Harvest seed (here clematis) from the plant when ripe – it should pull away from the seedhead easily. There is no need to remove the fluffy "tails."*

2 *Sow thinly in a prepared pan or other container of firmed, moist, gritty sowing medium.*

3 *Cover the seeds with a thin layer of gritty medium, add a shallow layer of fine grit, and label. Plunge in a sand bed or cold frame outdoors.*

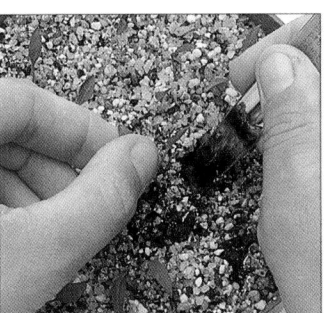

4 *After germination, prick out the seedlings. Loosen a clump with a widger, then lift and replant the seedlings singly, holding each gently by the leaves.*

5 *When the seedlings have developed their first pair of true leaves, pot them on individually in moist soil mix. Label and place in a cold frame.*

6 *Grow on the seedlings until well established. They are then ready for planting out in their permanent positions.*

Propagation from softwood cuttings

Softwood is the youngest and greenest part of a stem resulting from the spring flush of growth. Take the cuttings in late spring or early summer, after new growth has started but before the stems have begun to harden. Prepare a pot, pan, or tray by filling it almost to the brim with moist rooting medium, and firm.

Taking the cuttings

Cut lengths of stem approximately 6in (15cm) long, making cuts above leaf joints or nodes on the parent plant. Then trim the base of each cutting immediately below a node. (Clematis is an exception to this rule: cuttings should be internodal, with a small piece of stem below the node – see "Propagation," p.139.)

Softwood cuttings are particularly vulnerable to water loss, so place them immediately in a clear plastic bag to retain moisture.

Preparing and inserting the cuttings

Remove the leaves from the bottom third of the softwood stems with a clean, sharp knife. Dip the bottom ¼in (½cm) of each cutting in a softwood-strength hormone rooting powder that contains fungicide, and tap off the excess. Insert each cutting into the medium so that the lowest leaf (or pair of leaves) rests just barely above the surface.

Label the cuttings, then moisten them with a fine spray. Place them in a propagator, cover trays with sheets of glass, or place clear plastic bags over pots with a rubber band. Keep the cuttings in good light, checking them daily to make sure that they do not dry out.

Potting up

The cuttings generally take four to eight weeks to root, although honeysuckles (*Lonicera*) may take longer. Pot them up in standard, soil-based mix. Alternatively, use a mixture of two parts soilless mix to one part sand; since this contains no nutrients, apply a liquid or foliar fertilizer every two weeks.

Cuttings taken in early spring should be ready to plant out in fall. Any taken later should be overwintered under cover and planted out the following spring once there is no danger of frost. In cold areas, all tender cuttings must be overwintered in a frost-free place, gradually hardened off the following spring, and then planted out when all danger of frost has passed.

Propagation from semiripe cuttings

From midsummer to early fall, take semiripe cuttings from healthy shoots. Prepare a pot or pan of moist rooting medium, as for softwood cuttings. Select lengths of about 4–6in (10–15cm) from wood that has not fully hardened, making the cuts above leaf joints or nodes.

PROPAGATION FROM SOFTWOOD CUTTINGS

1 *Fill a 5in (13cm) pot with moist, standard rooting medium. Remove any surplus with a straightedge to level the surface, then firm lightly.*

2 *Select 6in (15cm) lengths from the soft growing tips of healthy shoots (here Solanum crispum). Place the cutting material in a clear plastic bag to prevent drying out.*

3 *Trim the stem of each cutting to approximately 4in (10cm), straight across just below a leaf joint. Remove the lower leaves, cutting flush with the stems.*

4 *Dip each cutting in hormone powder. Insert two or three to a pot, with the lowest leaves just above the medium. The cuttings must not touch each other.*

5 *Water the cuttings with a fine mist, label, and place the pot or pots in a propagator or in clear plastic bags filled with air so that they do not touch the cuttings.*

6 *After they have rooted, pot on the cuttings into individual pots. Keep the cuttings moist by misting lightly.*

PROPAGATION FROM SEMIRIPE CUTTINGS

GOOD
EXAMPLE

POOR
EXAMPLES

HONEYSUCKLE
(LONICERA)

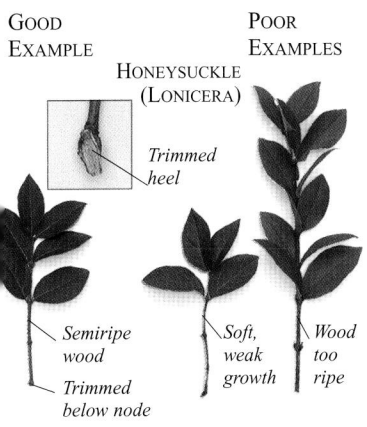

Trimmed heel

Semiripe wood

Trimmed below node

Soft, weak growth

Wood too ripe

Select 4–6in (10–15cm) lengths from healthy new wood and trim just below a node. Some cuttings are taken with a small heel of bark at the base (see inset). These should be trimmed before use.

Then trim the bases to just below a node, as for softwood cuttings.

Alternatively, make a clean cut through the base of the selected shoot where it is attached to the parent plant. Some cuttings root more readily if taken with a heel, by gently tugging a shoot away from the parent plant; the shoot peels away with a small triangular section of bark, or heel, at its base. Trim the heel of each cutting and treat with hormone rooting powder, then insert it into the medium, and label. The pot or pan should then be placed in a propagator. Semiripe cuttings generally take eight to twelve weeks, sometimes longer, to root.

When the cuttings have rooted, pot them on, using a standard potting soil mix and grow on in a cold frame once reestablished. The rooted cuttings should be ready for planting out into their permanent positions the following spring, after they have been hardened off.

Propagation from hardwood cuttings

Take hardwood cuttings in fall and early winter from healthy shoots that have become woody during the growing season. Using pruners, remove a length of stem, cutting just above a bud. Trim off any sideshoots, then divide the stem into pieces 2–3in (5–8cm) long, using a sloping cut above a bud at the top and a straight cut at the bottom. Longer cuttings, with two or more buds, may also be taken. To encourage

PROPAGATION FROM HARDWOOD CUTTINGS

Soft, under-ripe wood

Overripe wood

Healthy, woody shoot

1 *Remove a healthy stem from the current year's growth, cutting just above a bud. Do not use overripe and soft, new growth.*

2 *Trim off tendrils and side shoots. Cut the stem into pieces, with an angled cut above a bud and a straight cut at the base.*

3 *Pare away the outer bark of each cutting, making a clean, downward cut, to reveal the cambium layer (see inset).*

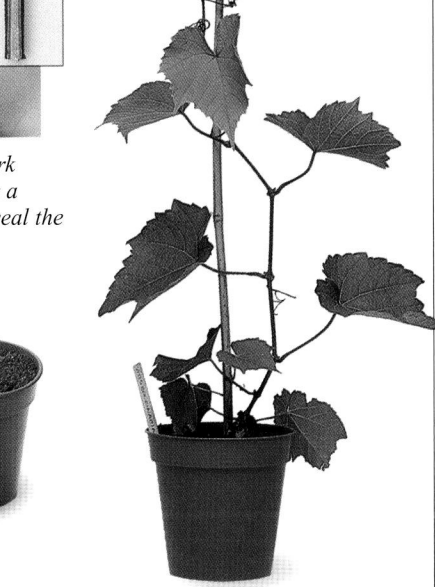

4 *Insert the cuttings into gritty rooting medium so that the top buds just show above the surface. Label, water, and place in a cold frame.*

5 *When the cuttings are well rooted, pot on into a larger pot. Stake, as required, and grow on before planting out.*

rooting, wound each cutting at the base by removing a thin sliver of bark with a sharp knife. An application of hormone rooting powder to the wounded section may speed up rooting for climbers that are difficult to root, but it is not always needed if suitable stems are taken at the appropriate season.

Inserting the cuttings
Prepare a pot or pan of free-draining rooting medium (add a little extra sand or grit to the soil mix), filling the pot almost to the brim, and moisten the soil mix well. Insert the cuttings around the edge of the pot, approximately 2in (5cm) apart. Gently insert the cuttings by up to two-thirds of their length, so that just

the top buds are visible. Firm the medium, then water the cuttings, label the pot, and place it in a cold frame to overwinter. Alternatively, insert the cuttings directly into a cold frame or in a trench in a sheltered part of the garden (see ORNAMENTAL TREES, "Hardwood cuttings," p.76). Hardwood cuttings of plants that are not fully hardy must be overwintered in a frost-free place.

Hardwood cuttings may take several months to root, but most should be ready for potting up or transplanting by midspring of the following year. Either pot them into a standard soil mix, or grow them on in a sheltered place before planting them out in their permanent positions the following fall.

(see ORNAMENTAL TREES, "Hardwood cuttings," p.76)

CLIMBERS THAT MAY BE PROPAGATED BY SEMIRIPE CUTTINGS
(CONTINUED)

Clytostoma
Decumaria
Dioscorea
Distictis
Ercilla
Euonymus
Fallopia
Gelsemium sempervirens
Hardenbergia
Hedera
Hoya
Jacquemontia
Jasminum
Kennedia
Lonicera
Macfadyena

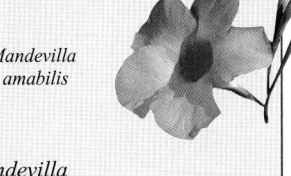

Mandevilla x amabilis

Mandevilla
Manettia
Mitraria
Mutisia
Paederia
Pandorea
Passiflora
Petrea
Pileostegia
Plumbago
Podranea
Pyrostegia
Quisqualis
Sarmienta
Schisandra
Schizophragma
Senecio
Solandra
Solanum
Stauntonia
Stephanotis
Stigmaphyllon
Strongylodon
Tecoma
Tecomanthe
Tecomaria
Thunbergia
Trachelospermum
Wattakaka

CLIMBERS THAT MAY BE PROPAGATED BY HARDWOOD CUTTINGS

Actinidia kolomikta
Bougainvillea
Lonicera
Parthenocissus
Vitis

Actinidia kolomikta

Root cuttings

A few climbers, notably *Celastrus* and *Solanum*, may be propagated from root cuttings taken from late winter to early spring.

Taking the cuttings

Dig a hole 18–24in (45–60cm) away from the base of the plant to expose roots that are about ½in (1cm) thick; these provide the best cutting material. Remove sections of root up to 8–12in (20–30cm) long, depending on how many cuttings are required. Cut straight across the top of the root (nearest the plant) and cut the base of the root at an angle. Place the cutting material in a clear plastic bag to prevent it from drying out.

Preparing and inserting the cuttings

Wash the sections of root to remove any soil, then cut them into smaller pieces and remove the fibrous laterals. Make a horizontal cut at the top and a slanted cut at the base. Insert the cuttings, with the slanted cut downward, in a pot filled with a rooting medium of equal parts peat and sand. Space them approximately 3in (7cm) apart, with the tips protruding slightly. Cover them with a ½in (1cm) layer of sand. Moisten the soil mix thoroughly, label the pot, and place it in a cold frame or propagator, or plunge it in a trench. Keep the soil mix moist.

Hardening off and potting on

Buds will appear near the top of the cuttings in spring. Pot up the cuttings individually during early summer, and harden them off gradually, occasionally applying a liquid or foliar fertilizer. Stake the cuttings as they develop. The new plants can be planted in their permanent positions the following fall.

PROPAGATION FROM ROOT CUTTINGS

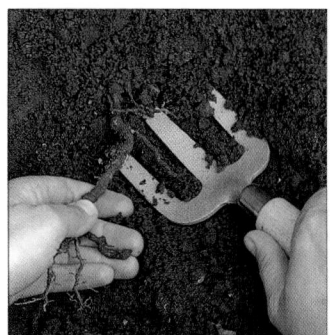

1 *Dig a hole well away from the base of the plant to expose some of the roots.*

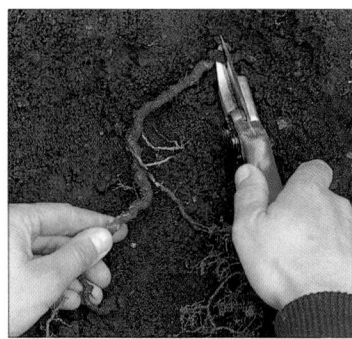

2 *Cut off sections of root with pruners. The pieces should be about ½in (1cm) thick and at least 4in (10cm) long.*

3 *Wash the roots and divide into pieces 1½–2in (4–5cm) long, cutting horizontally at the top and obliquely at the base (see inset).*

4 *Insert each cutting vertically into a pot of rooting medium so that the tips are just protruding above the surface of the medium.*

5 *Cover with a ½in (1cm) layer of sand. Water, label, and place in a cold frame or protected spot.*

6 *Pot on into individual pots once the cuttings are well rooted and young shoots are 1–2in (2.5–5cm) high.*

Self-layering climbers

Many climbers have trailing shoots that root naturally where they come into contact with the surrounding soil. A shoot that has self-layered can be lifted and severed from the parent plant in fall or early spring. Choose a healthy-looking, well-rooted layer that has fresh new growth. Lift it carefully and cut it off. Trim back the layered shoot, retaining only the piece or pieces of stem that have produced new roots and that have healthy new buds forming. Strip off any leaves growing near the roots. Pot up the rooted layers individually into standard rooting medium consisting of half peat and half sand, and water them in well. Alternatively, if the layer is well developed with strong, vigorous roots and shoots, it can be planted immediately in its permanent position.

PROPAGATION OF SELF-LAYERING PLANTS

1 *Select a low-growing shoot that has rooted into the ground, then lift the rooted section with a hand fork.*

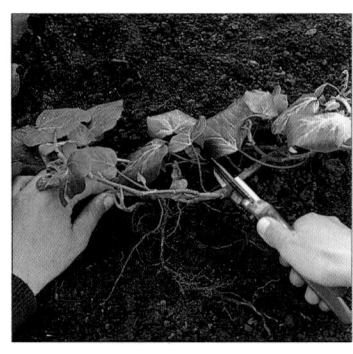

2 *Sever the shoot from the parent plant (here an ivy, Hedera helix), cutting between two nodes with pruners.*

3 *Cut the shoot into sections, each with a healthy root system and vigorous new growth. Remove the lower leaves.*

4 *Replant each section of rooted shoot either into a pot of rooting medium or in its permanent position.*

Simple layering

The long, trailing shoots of climbers may often be propagated by simple layering if they do not root naturally. A shoot is wounded and pegged down into the surrounding soil. This induces it to root at a node to provide a young plant that is later separated from the parent.

Layers of many climbers that have been pegged down in spring will develop strong root systems by fall, at which time they can be separated from the parent plant. *Akebia*, *Campsis*, and *Vitis* should be layered in late fall or winter, however, because if the stems are wounded in spring, the layers bleed sap and are less likely to root.

Soil preparation
If the surrounding soil is poor, fork in some organic matter at least a month before layering takes place. Alternatively, fill a pot with soil mix and plunge it into the ground at the place where the layer is to be pegged down.

Making the layer
Choose a healthy, vigorous, non-flowering shoot or stem that is long enough to trail along the ground. Trim the leaves and any sideshoots from the section of stem to be layered to provide a clear length of stem for about 12in (30cm) behind the tip of the shoot.

Gently bend the stem down to the ground and, to encourage root formation, wound the underside of the stem close to a node, making an angled cut halfway through with a sharp knife. For most climbers, apply hormone rooting powder to the wound and shake off any surplus powder. Vigorous climbers such as *Wisteria*, however, do not need it.

Peg the stem firmly to the ground with one or more U-shaped pieces of wire, and cover with not more than 3in (8cm) of soil. Attach the tip of the layered stem to a stake so that it is kept upright.

Separating the rooted layer
In fall, when new shoots and roots have grown from the buried part of the stem, sever the rooted layer from the parent plant and pot it up or plant it out. Trim back the old stem before replanting and stake the new plant. If the layer is planted in a pot, it should be overwintered in a cold frame or plunged into a protected spot, and mulched lightly. Pot on, as necessary, before gradually hardening off and planting out into its permanent position the following year if the plant is big enough.

PROPAGATION BY SIMPLE LAYERING

1 *Select a young, low-growing shoot (here* Akebia quinata*). Trim off the leaves to provide a clear length of stem behind the tip.*

2 *Make an angled cut on the underside of the shoot to form a tongue in the center of the trimmed length of stem.*

3 *Using a clean brush, dust the incision with fresh hormone rooting powder (see inset) and gently shake off any surplus.*

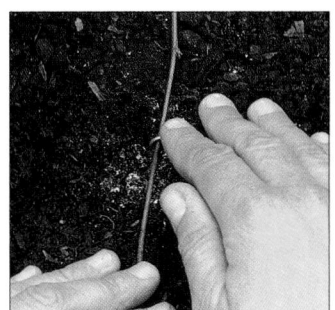

4 *Peg down the shoot firmly in the prepared area, using wire pegs. Cover with up to 3in (8cm) of soil.*

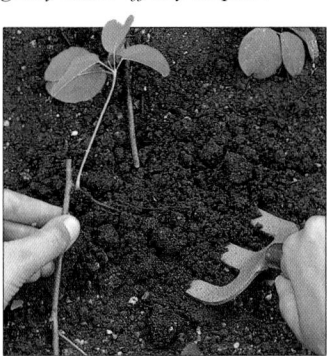

5 *The following fall, sever the layered shoot close to the parent plant. Lift with a hand fork and trim back the old stem.*

6 *Plant the layer in a 5in (13cm) pot of standard potting mix or into its permanent position. Then water and label.*

Propagation by serpentine layering

Carefully bend a trailing shoot down to the prepared soil and trim off leaves and sideshoots. Make several wounds close to nodes, leaving at least one bud between each incision. Apply hormone rooting powder and peg down the wounded sections, as for simple layering. Separate plantlets in fall, when roots will have formed from each of the wounds. Trim the old stem from the new plants before replanting and staking.

Several new plants may be produced by serpentine layering. Peg down layers with wire pegs (see inset).

CLIMBERS THAT MAY BE LAYERED

Self-layering
Asteranthera
Celastrus
Euonymus
Ficus pumila

Hedera helix 'Atropurpurea'

Hedera
Hoya
Hydrangea
Mitraria
Monstera deliciosa
Parthenocissus
Philodendron
Scindapsus
Tecomaria
Trachelospermum
Tripterygium
Vigna

Simple layering
Actinidia
Akebia
Beaumontia
Campsis
Cissus
Humulus
Lapageria

Lonicera x *americana*

Lonicera
Mandevilla
Monstera
Mucuna
Mutisia
Passiflora
Pileostegia
Podranea
Schizophragma
Solanum
Strongylodon
Tecomanthe
Thunbergia
Vitis amurensis, *V. coignetiae*
Wisteria

Serpentine layering
Akebia
Ampelopsis
Campsis
Celastrus
Clematis
Fallopia
Hedera
Holboellia
Kennedia

Parthenocissus tricuspidata

Parthenocissus
Sarmienta
Schisandra

CHAPTER

5

THE ROSE GARDEN

GARDENERS AND POETS since well before Roman times have revered the rose as the queen of flowering plants. Roses offer an enormous range of flower color, shape, and scent, whether it be the simplicity of a wild rose, the pastel charm of an old garden rose, or the jewel-like brilliance of many modern hybrids. Few plants are so varied or versatile as the rose in its growth habit, height, foliage, and form. It is possible to fill your entire garden with rose blooms, from the delicacy of a tiny pot rose to the foaming mass of a huge climber. Whether grown alone in the splendor of a formal garden, or bringing a touch of class to the profusion of a mixed planting, roses epitomize the glory of the garden.

Designing with roses

WHETHER you choose to grow old garden roses for their grace of habit, foliage, and scent; miniatures in a pot; or modern roses for their long flowering season and showy blooms, the diversity among roses makes it possible to find a plant for almost every part of the garden. Use them to create many styles and moods of planting, from restrained classicism to luxuriant informality.

Roses are adaptable plants that grow well in almost all parts of the world. They are most vigorous in warm-temperate regions, although some adapt well to subtropical or cold regions. In hot climates, some may flower most of the year.

Choosing roses

The number of rose cultivars available is bewildering, with many new ones added to the lists each year. Before making a final choice, it is well worth making a visit to some established gardens to observe as many different roses as possible growing in garden conditions. Do this over a period of time to assess the plants' habits, eventual heights, health, vigor, fragrance, fastness of flower color in strong sun, continuity of flowering, and all the other desirable features of a good rose.

Many rose societies publish listings that give details of where species roses and cultivars offered by member and other nurseries may be purchased; these listings are often invaluable in locating suppliers of more unusual roses.

Fragrance

Roses have long been prized for their scent. Most old garden cultivars and species, plus many modern roses, possess enchanting and diverse perfumes with hints of clove, musk, honey, lemon, spice, and even tea, as well as the "true" rose fragrance. It is not easy to be specific about rose scent, since its character and intensity may vary greatly with the time of day, the humidity, the age of the bloom, and the nose of individual gardeners; some will find a particular cultivar fragrant, while others will not.

With some roses one must be quite close to smell them; they are best enjoyed by planting them near a door or a window where their scent may drift into the house on summer evenings, around the patio or along a path, or in a sheltered position in the garden. Other roses, particularly many vigorous old garden roses, are so freely scented that they can perfume the entire garden.

Flower color

Modern roses embrace virtually every color of the spectrum, from pale pastels to bold, bright reds and yellows. The blue rose remains the stuff of legend, despite the use of the word "blue" in such cultivars as 'Blue Moon', which is actually pale lilac. Old garden roses range in hue from white through the palest of blush pinks, deep pink, crimson, and violet to purple; many are striped pink and white or purple and white.

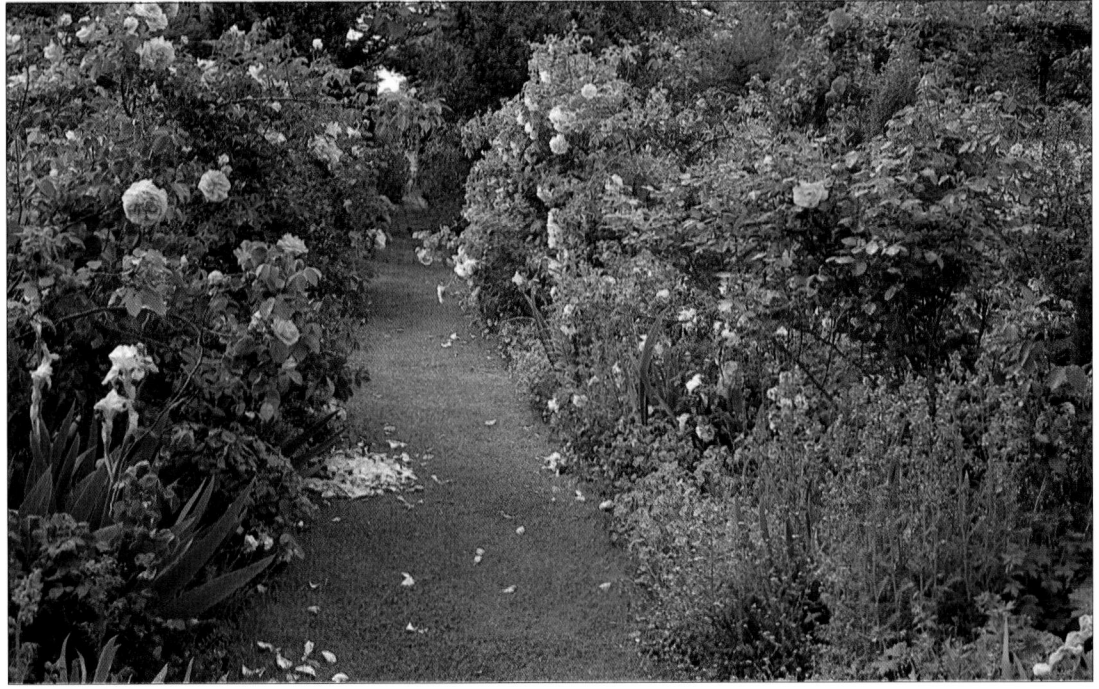

OLD WORLD CHARM
The open blooms and sprawling habit of shrub roses, including 'Constance Spry', 'Céleste', and 'Cerise Bouquet', blend with perennials in a subtle color theme to create a mood of informal and restful abundance. The proximity of the beds and the grass walk provide a secluded setting in which to enjoy the heady rose scents.

FLOWER SHAPES

Flat *Open, usually single or semidouble, with petals that are almost flat.*

Cupped *Open, single to fully double, with petals curving outward from the center.*

Pointed *Semi-double to fully double Hybrid Tea type, with high, tight centers.*

Urn-shaped *Classic, curved, and flat-topped, semi- to fully double Hybrid Tea type.*

Rounded *Double or fully double, with overlapping, even-sized petals forming a bowl-shaped outline.*

Rosette *Flattish, double or fully double, with many irregular, slightly overlapping petals of uneven size.*

Quartered-rosette *Flattish, double or fully double, with irregular, uneven petals in a quartered pattern.*

Pompon *Small, rounded, double or fully double, with masses of small petals; blooms are usually borne in clusters.*

Rose classification

There are about 250 naturally occurring species roses, as well as many natural hybrids, growing in the wild. After 2,000 years of being grown as ornamentals, rose cultivars now number in the thousands. The ancestry of almost all of them is so mixed (after many centuries of casual and indiscriminate breeding before cross-pollination was understood and proper records of parentage kept) that it is impossible to classify them precisely.

The borderlines between established groups have become blurred; for example, the flower size of the Floribundas has been increased by crosses with Hybrid Tea roses. Similarly, the hybridizing of miniature roses with Floribundas has led to recently developed Patio roses, intermediate in stature between the parents.

Naming rose categories

In 1979, the World Federation of Rose Societies decided that long-established terms such as "Hybrid Tea" and "Floribunda" had lost their original meaning because of the results of hybridization and agreed to adopt a new rose classification to clarify the groups so that they could be understood readily.

The new classification keeps most of the traditional rose group names; two differences most likely to affect gardeners are the changes of the names "Large-flowered bush" for "Hybrid Tea," and "Cluster-flowered bush" for "Floribunda." In 1987, the World Federation adopted the category "Dwarf cluster-flowered bush" for "Patio" roses.

However, although this system is regarded as the official classification by most rose-growing bodies, the Canadian Rose Society (CRS) has not chosen to adopt it.

The World Federation terminology is included here for reference. The CRS groupings are as follows, with synonymous classification names in parentheses.

Modern garden roses

Hybrid Tea and Grandiflora (Large-flowered bush) Upright, remontant (repeat-flowering) shrubs with large flowers carried one to a stem, or in small clusters.

Floribunda (Cluster-flowered bush) Upright, remontant shrubs with better continuity of bloom than Hybrid Teas; the smaller flowers are borne on large sprays.

Patio (Dwarf cluster-flowered bush) Similar to Floribundas, but with a smaller, neat habit.

Miniature Tiny counterparts of Hybrid Teas and Floribundas.

Groundcover Low-growing, trailing or spreading roses. Some flower once a year; others are remontant.

Climbing Climbing roses with long, strong shoots and large flowers borne singly or in small clusters. Some flower once a year; most are remontant. Climbing roses include a small group of roses, such as 'Albertine', which in habit are between a climber and a rambler. They were once classed as ramblers, but culturally they should be treated as climbers.

Rambler Vigorous, climbing roses with long, flexible shoots that bear small blooms in large clusters, flowering once a year.

Shrub A widely varying group impossible to classify further, ranging from low, mound-forming cultivars to wide-spreading shrubs and giant cluster-flowered bushes. Some bloom once a year; many are remontant.

Old garden roses

Alba Large, freely branching roses with flower clusters borne once in the season among abundant, gray-green foliage.

Bourbon Very vigorous, open, fully or partly remontant roses that bear double, fragrant flowers, often three to a cluster. Many grow tall and open.

Centifolia (Provence) Rather lax, thorny shrubs bearing fragrant flowers once a year. Commonly called cabbage roses.

China Small to medium remontant shrubs of twiggy, airy growth, bearing small, mainly double flowers singly or in clusters.

Damask Open shrubs bearing loose clusters of very fragrant flowers, mainly once a year.

Gallica Fairly dense shrubs that produce richly colored flowers, often three to a cluster, once a year.

Hybrid Musk Vigorous, remontant shrubs with abundant foliage and fragrant, primarily double blooms borne in clusters.

Hybrid Perpetual Vigorous, sometimes remontant, shrubs with flowers borne singly or in threes.

Moss Often lax shrubs with a furry, mosslike growth on stems and calyx. Most bloom once a year, but some are remontant.

Noisette Remontant climbing roses that bear large clusters of flowers with a slightly spicy fragrance.

Portland Upright, dense, and less vigorous (but more remontant) version of the Damask rose.

Tea Remontant shrubs and climbers bearing loose, usually double flowers that have a spicy fragrance.

Species roses

Wild, or species, roses and species hybrids (which share most characteristics of both parent species) are mainly large, arching shrubs bearing one flush of single, five-petaled flowers in spring or summer and decorative hips in fall.

Notable among the species is *Rosa rugosa*, the remontant parent of a diverse group of dense, very hardy and disease-resistant, vigorous shrubs bearing extremely fragrant, single to semidouble blooms. A few are more open in habit, less hardy, and not as fragrant as some.

Consult local rose experts for further information suited to specific regional and garden conditions.

THE SWEETBRIAR ROSE
The foliage of Rosa eglanteria, *a species rose, smells like cooking apples, especially on a misty or humid day.*

DESIGN FOR A FORMAL ROSE GARDEN

Here, all is symmetry and order, with clean lines and color laid out in patterns of geometric simplicity. This design creates a restrained setting in which to enjoy the classic beauty of roses. Formal yew hedges enclose

beds of massed bush roses in pale and deep golds and white, which in turn focus on a graceful trailing rose in the center. Red standard roses lift the planting with a bold contrast of color and form.

1 Yew (*Taxus*)
2 *Rosa* 'Golden Showers'
3 *R.* 'Europeana'
4 *R.* 'Summer Fashion'
5 *R.* 'Amber Queen'
6 *R.* 'Sunsprite'
7 *R.* 'Margaret Merril'
8 *R.* 'Swany'

Many roses coordinate beautifully together and with other plants, but combining too many brilliant colors, for instance bright vermilion with cerise pink and golden yellow, may create a discordant clash. Plant white roses or those with softer, pastel hues between groups of strongly toned roses to cool them down and to prevent them from clashing.

Flower shapes

Roses offer a great variety of forms of flower, from the simple, single flowers of the species rose to the elegantly furled blooms of the modern rose and the cabbagelike complexity of many old rose flowers.

The main flower shapes illustrated on the previous page page give a general indication of the shape of the flower when it is in its perfect state (which in some cases may be before it has fully opened). The flowers may be single (4–7 petals), semidouble (8–14 petals), double (15–20 petals), or fully double (over 30 petals).

Foliage color

As well as producing a fine flowering display, some groups of roses provide color in other ways to extend the season of interest. The Alba roses and many of the species (see below) have pleasing foliage, from a soft gray-green to a deep, glossy blue-green, making them attractive even when the bush is not in flower. The rich green foliage of Rugosa roses has an interesting wrinkled (rugose) texture and, if the roses are planted as a hedge, it makes a good background for other

plantings. The leaves of some species are a dusky plum-purple, as in *R. glauca*, while the foliage of some, such as *R. virginiana* and *R. nitida*, turns to vivid sunset tints in fall.

Ornamental rose hips or thorns
Rugosa roses with single or semidouble flowers also develop bright red, decorative hips at the end of the flowering season. Some of the species, such as *R. moyesii* and its hybrids, display ornamental hips in fall that range from yellow and orange, through all the shades of red to a blackish purple.

R. sericea subsp. *omeiensis* (syn. *R. omeiensis pteracantha*) has huge, flat thorns which, when young, glow ruby red if the sun is behind them.

The garden setting

One of the best settings for the beds of a rose garden is a smooth, green lawn, but the subtle gray and mellow tones of stone paving can be just as attractive. A subtle brick path may complement a rose planting alongside it, especially one of soft, pale tones. Whatever the material, avoid multicolored patterns that may compete with the roses. Gravel, although pleasant in appearance and texture, can be troublesome to look after because weeds soon appear and the stones may gradually spread or disappear into the soil.

Edging plants may be used to frame a rosebed. A traditional boxwood hedge makes a formal boundary, but many other plants may be used more

informally, particularly those that provide gray-green or silver-gray foliage. Pearly everlasting (*Anaphalis*) and pussytoes (*Antennaria*), with their woolly leaves, or the more dwarf forms of lavender are suitable, as is catmint (*Nepeta*) if there is room for it to sprawl over the path.

Many of the more restrained species and hybrids of *Geranium*, in particular those with blue flowers, are similarly appealing. Even miniature roses, in contrasting or complementary colors, may be grown on the sunny side of a bed.

Formal rose gardens

A popular way to grow roses is in a formal rose garden devoted to displaying the glories of the rose in beds shaped to reflect the plant's classic elegance. Generally, modern cultivars grown as bushes and standards are used as permanent bedding plants, grouped in blocks of color. The rather stiff and upright growth of many such bushes lends itself to the formality of bedding and tends not to blend so well with other plants, although roses may be attractively underplanted (see opposite).

Rosebeds may be designed in any shape or size – square, oblong, triangular, or round; at the edges of paths or drives they may be narrow and ribbonlike. Before creating new rosebeds, draw a plan on paper and experiment with different shapes and layouts of beds in order to decide which is the best design for the site

that has been chosen. Do not make the beds so wide that access to the roses for spraying, mulching, and pruning becomes difficult.

Not all cultivars reach their peak of flowering at exactly the same time. If mixing cultivars in the same bed, plant no less than five or six plants of the same cultivar together in a regular formation for substantial clumps of color. A garden planted with variations on a color theme, for instance pale and deep pinks with a touch of blush-apricot or white, creates a harmonious picture that is more pleasing than a busy crowd of color.

When planting, bear in mind the variations in eventual height of different cultivars. For a bed in an open area, choose cultivars of a more or less uniform height. A rosebed that is backed by a wall or hedge is more attractive if the roses at the front are shorter than those behind.

Standard roses may be used to give height to any bedding design. Placing a single standard in the center of a round bed that echoes the shape of the rose creates a graceful symmetry, while several standards placed at intervals of about 5ft (1.5m) along the middle of a long bed help break up its uniformity.

Informal plantings

The charm of roses may be enjoyed in a wide range of informal planting designs, particularly with herbaceous plants or many shrubs. Roses suitable for virtually any garden site may be chosen from the multitude of shrub, miniature, climbing, and groundcover roses of varied stature and habit now available.

Roses combine well with other plantings. For instance, miniature roses give both summer color and height to a planting of rock plants that are mainly spring-flowering, and a groundcover rose may clothe a bank with fragrant flowers.

The belief that roses do not mix with other plants probably dates from the days when many commonly used cultivars were large and ungainly and did not fit into Edwardian and Victorian bedding designs. They were grown in separate walled gardens simply to provide cut blooms for the house. It has, however, long been recognized that roses need not be grown in isolation.

INFORMAL STYLE
Large roses, including 'Penelope' in the foreground, clothe the background walls with a fragrant mass of summer color. They provide a magnificent foil for the tall spikes of plants such as Campanula *and delphiniums and the low mounds of the other perennial plants in an informal mixed border of cool blues and whites.*

Roses with herbaceous plants

Growing roses in beds or borders with herbaceous plants both highlights the beauties of the rose in flower and provides interest when the rose itself is dormant. The growth habit of many shrub roses, such as the light and airy China roses or the lax and open Damasks, perfectly suits the casual profusion of an informal planting while bringing it height and structure.

Muted drifts of flower or foliage, for example the haze of tiny white *Crambe cordifolia* flowers, best complement the showy flowers of roses in the summer. At other times of the year, use more flamboyant flowering plants or some with evergreen foliage to extend the season and to conceal the bare rose stems.

Many plants may enhance an area dominated by roses. For example, the tall spikes of purple foxgloves (*Digitalis purpurea*), white *Lilium regale*, or other white and pink lilies pushing up through a planting of lush, old garden roses make for a striking contrast, both in growth habit and flower form.

Roses with other shrubs

Both shrub and species roses combine well with other shrubs, as long as they receive enough sunlight. They provide abundant, beautiful, often fragrant flowers to set against the foliage of other spring-flowering shrubs, sometimes right through the summer. Many such roses have almost evergreen foliage and colored hips in the fall (see "Ornamental rose

hips or thorns," p.148). Smaller shrub roses as well as the Gallicas, most of the Damasks, the Portland roses, and many modern cultivars of similar stature make an excellent ornamental foreground to any planting of shrubs.

Roses that have long, questing branches, such as the freely flowering 'Sea Foam' or 'Complicata' with its deep pink blooms, may scramble through and enliven a dull, evergreen shrub. Ramblers may adorn a tree's foliage with their blooms or transform a dead tree into a spectacular feature.

Underplanting a rosebed

The display in a rosebed may be enhanced and extended beyond the rose flowering season by growing low, shallow-rooted plants between the roses. A wide range of plants may cover the ground and provide the roses with a background of contrasting color, texture, and form. Violets (*Viola*) are a favorite choice: the white, soft blue, and mauve cultivars complement roses well. All such groundcover plants make mulching difficult, however. Take care not to step on the groundcover planting when spraying the roses in a particularly wide bed.

When planting between roses, take account of the eventual heights of the various companion plants, and place them so that they will not obscure each other or the roses when they are mature.

The yellow-green of *Alchemilla mollis*, pink and white heads of *Armeria maritima*, and spreading, hardy *Geranium* species also make a fine display under roses.

Use spring bulbs to brighten up bare rosebeds early in the year: try planting blue or white *Chionodoxa*, daffodils, snowdrops (*Galanthus*), and starry white *Tulipa turkestanica* to create a bright patchwork of color. Their only drawback is their dying foliage, which looks messy until it is removed and may make it difficult to maintain the bed.

A number of fragrant herbs are good companion plants for roses: use lavender cotton (*Santolina chamaecyparissus*), various thymes (*Thymus*), or sages (*Salvia*) – either the culinary kind or any that have attractive, variegated leaves. Roses always look well when they are contrasted with the silver foliage of perennial plants, such as the fern-leaved *Artemisia* 'Powis Castle' and *A. frigida*, or the gray, woolly-leaved, mat-forming *Stachys byzantina* (syn. *S. lanata*).

FLOWERS AND FOLIAGE
Richly colored rose blooms are set like jewels against the elegant gray-green foliage of underplanted herbs and the golden tones of gravel.

SINGULAR SPLENDOR
A standard rose, 'Little White Pet', provides a handsome focal point.

Terraces

On a steep hillside, terraces may be used to transform a difficult site into a striking showcase for roses. They provide areas sufficiently level for planting and retain moisture, which the roses need, while creating eye-catching gradations of height and perspective. The terrace walls look best if made of weathered brick or mellow stone. Bush roses may be grown in the terrace beds, and ramblers or groundcover roses may be planted to tumble over the retaining walls, creating curtains of bloom.

Smaller terraced beds are ideal for growing miniature roses. It is much easier to savor the beauty and scent of their tiny, individual flowers if they are raised some way above ground level. Each bed for miniature roses should be approximately 1½–2ft (45–60cm) wide. Place miniature standards along the top bed of the terrace to draw the eye, and use some of the smaller and more dainty groundcover roses to tumble over the walls.

Terraced beds are not a good idea in areas where winter temperatures may drop to -20°F (-30°C).

Specimen planting

A rose planted on its own makes a handsome specimen plant, perhaps in a lawn or to mark a focal point

SUMMER RETREAT
A mature rambler rose in full, glorious bloom transforms this trelliswork arbor into an eye-catching feature that is at once intimate and airy. The floral canopy fills the air within the arbor with its delicious perfume and provides a cool, leafy shelter from which to enjoy the views of the surrounding garden.

in a garden, as long as it is an outstanding rose of its type; any defects in a specimen are immediately obvious. Used in this way, weeping standard roses can be especially striking. These are formed by grafting rambler cultivars onto a 5ft or 6ft (1.5m or 2m) stem, so that their long, flexible shoots, laden with blossoms in summer, hang down all around the stem and right down to the ground. They usually flower for a rather limited period unless a standard grafted from a remontant groundcover rose is chosen.

Climbing roses grown as standards may provide a profusion of blooms throughout the entire summer, but their stiff growth does not produce the same dramatic waterfall effect as weeping standards.

Many of the larger shrub roses are natural choices for planting as specimens in larger gardens. 'Nevada', for example, which can reach 6 x 6ft (2 x 2m) or even more, is smothered with large, cream blooms in early summer and again in late summer. Other roses, particularly most species roses and many of their hybrids, such as 'Frühlingsgold', have no second period of bloom.

For a small garden where space for flowering plants is limited, use remontant roses such as the strongly scented 'Frau Dagmar Hartopp'. Smaller shrub roses, such as 'Sally Holmes' with large, white flowers clustered above the foliage, and 'Champlain', which has masses of bright red, slightly fragrant blooms, are not quite large enough to justify being planted on their own but are very handsome if planted in specimen groups of three.

Walls, arbors, and pergolas

Most ramblers and climbing roses are very vigorous and produce exuberant bloom from summer until the first frosts. They may drape structures such as arbors, walls, and fences; disguise unsightly features; or give height to the summer display in the garden. Be sure to choose a rose with an eventual height that will cover the intended area well without outgrowing it.

Ramblers and climbing roses may be trained on a wide range of plastic-

coated metal bowers, tunnels, arches, and tripod pillars now on the market. Although metal supports may not look so attractive initially as ones made from rustic poles, they have a much longer life and are soon concealed once the roses trained on them become well established. Rustic arches, even if treated, eventually rot at soil level.

Other climbing plants, such as clematis or honeysuckle, may be planted to grow through the rose to complement the rose blooms as well as to extend the flowering season; climbers with blue flowers are particularly suitable. Some of the more vigorous shrub roses, particularly Bourbons, also make excellent short climbers for a pillar or small wall.

Ramblers
Ramblers have more flexible shoots than climbers and are easier to train along complex structures such as pergolas, arches, and trellises to form a great mass of flowering shoots. When grown against walls, however, they may become mildewed as a result of the poor air circulation.

To cover a long pergola, use one of the vigorous, small-flowered, white ramblers such as 'Trier' or 'Seagull', but remember that they can grow to 30ft (10m) or more and will, therefore, overwhelm a small structure.

For a picturesque effect, try training roses along chains or ropes that are suspended between uprights to create great swags of bloom.

Climbers
The stiffer shoots of climbing roses are less easy to prune than those of ramblers but still may grace walls and fences. Many of the less robust modern climbers may be grown on

FALL TINTS
The brilliant scarlet hips of this species rose contrast vividly with its yellowing foliage.

AN ORNAMENTAL ARCH
The old-fashioned, rich pink flowers of Rosa 'Bantry Bay' *festoon this rustic arch to form an enticing and decorative frame to the view beyond.*

DECORATIVE HEDGING
Rosa gallica
'Versicolor' (*often more
commonly known as
'Rosa Mundi') is one
of the oldest roses
available and has
unusually striped
petals. It forms an
attractive informal
hedge that bursts into
a riot of bloom to
create an enchanting
ribbon of color. Here,
the line of the rose
hedge provides a
pleasing contrast of
height and perspective
with the tall spikes of
mulleins* (Verbascum). *
The deep pink flowers
in the rose hedge betray
reversion to its parent,
R. gallica var.
officinalis.*

pillars or as free-standing shrubs with great results. 'John Davis' is pleasantly scented but is too stiff and upright in habit for an arch, although it would suit the pillar supports of a tall pergola.

The Bourbon rose 'Zéphirine Drouhin', which has medium pink flowers, is an old favorite for growing on arches, trellises, and pergolas because it is one of the few climbers that is both thornless and fragrant. It is, however, prone to mildew.

Rose hedges and screens

Roses may, if carefully chosen, provide some of the most colorful and attractive plants for an informal hedge or screen. A few, such as *R. rugosa* and its hybrids, may be shaped to some extent by gentle clipping in winter to make dense hedges while maintaining the natural outline of the shrub. No rose is fully evergreen – few provide a screen that gives privacy all year, although the thorns make the hedge virtually impenetrable. For further details, see HEDGES AND SCREENS, pp.82–4.

The Hybrid Musk roses, such as the apricot 'Buff Beauty', grow into a thick, thorny screen up to 6ft (2m) in height covered in fragrant flowers all summer long, provided their natural unpredictability of growth is curbed by training on hori-

zontal wires or chain link fencing. If a rose hedge is intended to line a path, use upright cultivars for this purpose, since those of unpredictable growth may impede the pathway.

For a small garden, a hedge of taller Floribunda roses is preferable. These are generally upright plants with little spread and, if planted in two staggered rows (see *Planting Distances for a Rose Hedge*, p.155), cultivars such as the apricot-yellow 'Apricot Nectar' rapidly form a pretty screen about 4ft (1.2m) tall. Some shorter-growing old garden roses, such as *Rosa gallica*

A CARPET OF BLOOM
This groundcover rose, 'Max Graf'*, attractively masks an expanse of bare soil with its delightful profusion of dainty flowers.*

'Versicolor' ('Rosa Mundi'), have attractive foliage and form hedges of similar height, but they flower only once. Their natural vulnerability to mildew is, however, increased by close planting.

A delightful way of dividing one part of a garden from another is to train climbing roses or ramblers on decorative screens formed by constructing open, wooden frameworks of the desired height. Ready-made wooden trellises are available, but make sure that they are sturdy, since they must support a considerable weight and last for years.

Groundcover roses

Some low-growing roses readily spread along the ground to form a dense and floriferous carpet. These may be used to continue the theme of a rosebed, or as a prettily sprawling edging to a cottage border. They may also disguise an unsightly feature such as a utility meter, or scramble down a steep bank that would otherwise be difficult to plant.

Some more recently introduced cultivars, such as 'J.P. Connell', cover the soil very well and bloom profusely although, growing to 3–4ft (1–1.2m), they are too tall for true groundcover. Others suitable for a small space are 'Rosy Cushion', 'Ralph's Creeper', or 'Red Cascade'.

Ramblers such as 'Grouse' and 'Pheasant', which both have small, pink flowers and glossy foliage, make marvelous groundcover roses, but their vigor makes them unsuitable for a small garden. They grow naturally along the ground, rooting as they go and covering the soil very

closely, but they need strict control to prevent them from spreading too far.

If you have a sunken rose garden with fairly low walls, roses such as 'Nozomi' or 'Raubritter' are suitable for planting along the top, since they have the right kind of low, spreading growth to form waterfalls of flowers over the walls.

Some cultivars sold as groundcovers are simply low-growing but fairly wide-spreading bushes. They are seldom dense enough in growth to be very efficient weed-smotherers, and in winter they shed their leaves, thus allowing in air and light, which enable weeds to germinate.

Roses in containers

Roses are invaluable for their summer color and fragrance in patio gardens where the surface is mostly paved and there are few or no beds. Containers of many sorts are suitable as long as they are big enough to accommodate the root system of the fully grown rose, and are located in a spot that receives sun for at least half a day. Choose species and cultivars that are bushy and compact, since leggy roses with bare basal stems look unsightly. If grouping a number of roses in a container, make sure it is large enough for the roses to be spaced out to allow for future growth.

Even quite vigorous climbers may, given the support of a wall, be grown in large tubs or half barrels. They should be planted and trained as other climbing roses, but since the nutrients in the containers will be quickly exhausted (and the roses difficult to repot), they will require regular applications of fertilizer. They will also benefit from a yearly application of an organic mulch.

Miniature roses are ideal plants to use in containers, whether on their own or with other plants. Try cultivars such as 'Baby Masquerade' (whose abundant blooms change from yellow to pink and finally to rose-red), the brilliant orange 'New Beginning', or Patio roses such as the pointed, white 'Stardance'. They look especially good in a planting trough built into a low wall bordering one or two sides of a patio or terrace. Even an old washtub may be used to display miniature roses as long as it is at least 8–10in (20–25cm) deep to allow sufficient space for the root growth of the roses.

Roses grown in containers do not need to be confined to a patio garden. They may bring color to other paved areas, such as the center of an herb garden, the area around a pool, or along a broad walkway.

Planter's guide to roses

MOST FRAGRANT FLOWERS

Combining excellent scent with reliable garden performance
Rosa ALEC'S RED ('Cored')
Rosa 'Arthur Bell'
Rosa x centifolia cultivars
Rosa 'Climbing Etoile de Hollande'
Rosa 'Compassion'
Rosa DOUBLE DELIGHT ('Andeli')
Rosa FRAGRANT CLOUD ('Tanellis')
Rosa GERTRUDE JEKYLL ('Ausbord')
Rosa 'Korresia'

Rosa FRAGRANT CLOUD

Rosa L'AIMANT ('Harzola')
Rosa 'Madame Hardy'
Rosa 'Madame Isaac Pereire'
Rosa MARGARET MERRIL ('Harkuly')
Rosa NEW ZEALAND ('Macgenev')
Rosa PERCEPTION ('Harzippee')
Rosa 'Prima Ballerina'
Rosa 'Rose de Resht'
Rosa ROSEMARY HARKNESS ('Harrowbond')
Rosa 'Roseraie de l'Haÿ'
Rosa SCEPTRE'D ISLE ('Ausland')
Rosa 'Wendy Cussons'

DECORATIVE HIPS

Rosa 'Fru Dagmar Hastrup'
Rosa 'Geranium'
Rosa glauca
Rosa rugosa 'Charles Albanel', R. rugosa 'Jens Munk'
Rosa 'Scabrosa'
Rosa 'Sealing Wax'

HEALTHIER ROSES

Garden roses with good resistance to and/or tolerance of disease
Rosa 'Alexander MacKenzie'
Rosa ANNE HARKNESS ('Harkaramel')
Rosa ARMADA ('Haruseful')
Rosa 'Arthur Bell'
Rosa 'Ballerina'
Rosa CHATSWORTH ('Tanotax')
Rosa 'Cuthbert Grant'
Rosa 'Dortmund'
Rosa ELINA ('Dicjana')
Rosa ESCAPADE ('Harpade')
Rosa GORDON'S COLLEGE ('Cocjabby')
Rosa HERTFORDSHIRE ('Kortenay')
Rosa 'John Davis'

Rosa LOVELY LADY ('Dicjubell')
Rosa MARJORIE FAIR ('Harhero')
Rosa MISTRESS QUICKLY ('Ausky')
Rosa PINK FLOWER CARPET ('Noatraum')
Rosa 'Prairie Joy'
Rosa PRETTY LADY ('Scrivo')
Rosa QUEEN MOTHER ('Korquemu')
Rosa ROSE GAUJARD ('Gaumo')
Rosa rugosa hybrids
Rosa SAVOY HOTEL ('Harvintage')
Rosa SURREY ('Korlanum')
Rosa 'The Fairy'

MIXED FLOWER BORDERS

Front of border
Rosa AVON ('Poulmulti')
Rosa BERKSHIRE ('Korpinka')
Rosa 'Champlain'
Rosa 'Henry Hudson'
Rosa KENT ('Poulcov')
Rosa 'Morden Amorette'
Rosa PRINCESS OF WALES ('Hardinkum')
Rosa 'The Fairy'
Rosa VALENTINE HEART ('Dicogle')
Rosa 'Winnipeg Parks'

Middle ground
Rosa ARMADA ('Haruseful')
Rosa 'Ballerina'
Rosa BETTY HARKNESS ('Harette')
Rosa BONICA ('Meidomonac')
Rosa 'Buff Beauty'
Rosa 'David Thompson'
Rosa ESCAPADE ('Harpade')
Rosa 'Frontenac'
Rosa 'Fru Dagmar Hastrup'
Rosa gallica 'Versicolor'
Rosa ICEBERG ('Korbin')
Rosa JACQUELINE DU PRÉ ('Harwanna')
Rosa MARJORIE FAIR ('Harhero')
Rosa 'Morden Ruby'
Rosa 'Penelope'
Rosa ROSY CUSHION ('Interall')

Rosa GERTRUDE JEKYLL

Middle to rear
Rosa 'Captain Samuel Holland'
Rosa 'Cornelia'
Rosa 'Fantin-Latour'
Rosa 'Felicia'
Rosa GERTRUDE JEKYLL ('Ausbord')
Rosa 'Golden Wings'
Rosa GRAHAM THOMAS ('Ausmas')
Rosa 'Louis Jolliet'

Rosa 'Marguerite Hilling'
Rosa 'Roseraie de l'Haÿ'
Rosa WESTERLAND ('Korwest')

SOUTH- AND WEST-FACING WALLS AND FENCES

Rosa ALTISSIMO ('Delmur')
Rosa ANTIQUE ('Kordalen')
Rosa BREATH OF LIFE ('Harquanne')
Rosa CLAIR MATIN ('Meimont')
Rosa 'Compassion'
Rosa CRIMSON CASCADE ('Fryclimbdown')
Rosa 'Danse du Feu'
Rosa 'Dreaming Spires'
Rosa DUBLIN BAY ('Macdub')
Rosa GOOD AS GOLD ('Chewsunbeam')
Rosa HIGH HOPES ('Haryup')
Rosa 'Madame Alfred Carrière'
Rosa 'New Dawn'
Rosa PENNY LANE ('Hardwell')
Rosa SUMMER WINE ('Korizont')
Rosa 'White Cockade'

NORTH- AND EAST-FACING FENCES AND WALLS

For structures over 6ft (2m)
Rosa 'Albéric Barbier'
Rosa 'Compassion'
Rosa 'Dortmund'
Rosa 'Morning Jewel'
Rosa 'New Dawn'

For areas up to 6ft (2m)
Rosa ARMADA ('Haruseful')
Rosa 'Chinatown'
Rosa 'Cornelia'
Rosa 'Penelope'
Rosa 'Prosperity'

ATTRACTIVE FOLIAGE

Rosa fedtschenkoana
Rosa glauca
Rosa gymnocarpa var. willmottiae
Rosa nitida
Rosa primula
Rosa sericea subsp. omeiensis f. pteracantha
Rosa virginiana

GROUND-COVER ROSES

Rosa AVON ('Poulmulti')
Rosa BERKSHIRE ('Korpinka')
Rosa 'Morden Cardinette'
Rosa RED BLANKET ('Intercell')
Rosa ROSY CUSHION ('Interall')
Rosa 'Simon Fraser'
Rosa SURREY ('Korlanum')

SPECIMEN SHRUB ROSES

Rosa 'Cerise Bouquet'
Rosa 'Complicata'
Rosa 'Felicia'
Rosa 'Fritz Nobis'

Rosa 'Marguerite Hilling'
Rosa 'Nevada'
Rosa 'Scabrosa'
Rosa xanthina 'Canary Bird'

ARCHES AND PILLARS

Rosa ALOHA ('Kormarcus')
Rosa ALTISSIMO ('Delmur')
Rosa 'Bantry Bay'
Rosa BRIDGE OF SIGHS ('Harglow')
Rosa CITY GIRL ('Harzorba')
Rosa 'Compassion'
Rosa 'Dortmund'
Rosa 'Dreaming Spires'
Rosa DUBLIN BAY ('Macdub')
Rosa 'Golden Showers'
Rosa 'Goldfinch'
Rosa LAURA FORD ('Chewarvel')

Rosa CITY GIRL

Rosa 'Leverkusen'
Rosa 'New Dawn'
Rosa 'Phyllis Bide'
Rosa ROSALIE CORAL ('Chewallop')
Rosa 'Veilchenblau'
Rosa WARM WELCOME ('Chewizz')

PERGOLAS

Rosa 'Albéric Barbier'
Rosa 'Albertine'
Rosa 'Alister Stella Gray'
Rosa 'Climbing Cécile Brunner'
Rosa 'Easlea's Golden Rambler'
Rosa 'Emily Gray'
Rosa 'Félicité Perpétue'
Rosa 'François Juranville'
Rosa HIGH HOPES ('Haryup')
Rosa 'Madame Alfred Carrière'
Rosa 'Madame Grégoire Staechelin'
Rosa 'Maigold'
Rosa 'Sander's White Rambler'
Rosa 'Sympathie'

ROSES TO GROW INTO TREES

Rosa 'Bobbie James'
Rosa 'Blush Rambler'
Rosa 'Emily Gray'
Rosa filipes 'Kiftsgate'
Rosa mulliganii
Rosa 'Paul's Himalayan Musk'
Rosa 'Rambling Rector'
Rosa 'Seagull'
Rosa soulieana
Rosa 'Treasure Trove'

Roses for exhibition

ENTERING cut roses in a local rose society show and, with time, in a regional or national rose society show can be very rewarding. Higher levels of competition, however, do require more dedication and time than the average gardener can give.

Rules for exhibiting roses vary from country to country, depending on the requirements of local and national rose societies. It is as important for serious exhibitors as it is for judges to be familiar with the details of such rules, so always check with your local society before thinking about entering a show.

Cultivating roses for exhibition

Grow several bushes of the same cultivar to ensure a wide choice of blooms. Some cultivars are as good in the garden as on the show table, provided that they are well looked after and the foliage is kept free

DISBUDDING ROSES

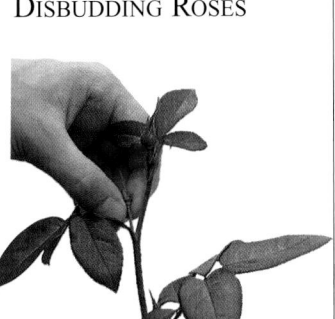

HYBRID TEA ROSES
As soon as they are large enough to handle easily, pinch out all the side buds, leaving the central bud to grow on.

FLORIBUNDA ROSES
Pinch out the young central bud of each spray for more uniform development.

CHINESE HATS

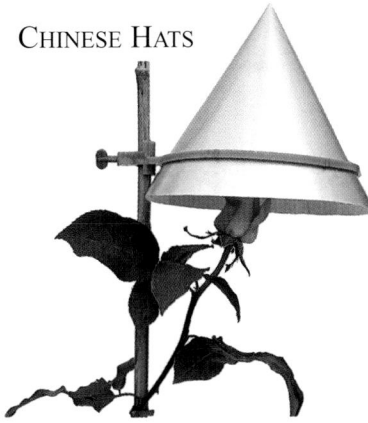

To protect a show bloom from rain damage, insert a stake with a "Chinese hat" by the rose stem, then tie the stem in to the stake.

from pests and disease. Prune severely to produce a limited number of strong shoots per season from which to choose exhibition blooms. Maintain vigorous growth with extra water and fertilizer. Roses are often disbudded to produce exhibition quality blooms: remove the newly formed side buds from Hybrid Tea roses so that the main bud develops strongly. Removing the central bud of Floribunda roses ensures that all the other buds develop at roughly the same time.

Some blooms are easily damaged by rain, so some exhibitors create individual bloom protectors, or "Chinese hats," in the form of plastic cones attached to stakes. They are by no means essential, however. Aluminum pie plates are easier to use over the sprays of Floribundas.

Selecting blooms

Timing is crucial in exhibiting. A Hybrid Tea bloom should, at the moment of judging, be only two-thirds open. A Floribunda spray should have the maximum number of flowers open in various stages from bud to fully open bloom. Blooms should be of typical size for the cultivar. Good, healthy foliage is also important.

Preparing for a show

The novice exhibitor should restrict entries in any one show to a manageable number at first. Cut more than the number of roses to be entered, with stems at least 16in (40cm) long, on the day before the

show, and label them. Remove the lowest leaves and plunge the stems into buckets of tepid water, right up to the necks of the flowers. Recut them underwater, and keep them overnight in a cool place.

Do not be put off if some of your blooms suffer weather damage. Other people may be in the same position, so bring in your blooms and take your chances. If the roses must be transported any distance, keep each bloom or spray separated, so that they are not damaged.

Staging the blooms

Once at the show, obtain some entry cards from the show secretary and carry your roses to the staging table. The show committee usually supplies containers for roses. Staging the blooms always takes longer than expected, but greater speed will come with experience.

Recut the stem of every rose before putting it into the container. To keep the roses as straight as possible, you may stuff foil, foam or plastic wrap into the neck of the container around the stem, but be neat. Cut out faded blooms, but do not leave obvious cut stems or gaps. Use a watercolor brush to remove insects or dust specks, and sponge off any insecticide residues with a cotton ball. If needed, "dress" blooms by gently teasing into the correct position any petals that are slightly out of place. Do not reposition the petals too much, because over-dressed blooms may lose points. Carefully remove any outer petals that are damaged.

EXHIBITION-QUALITY BLOOMS

HYBRID TEA ROSE
'VALERIE MARGARET'

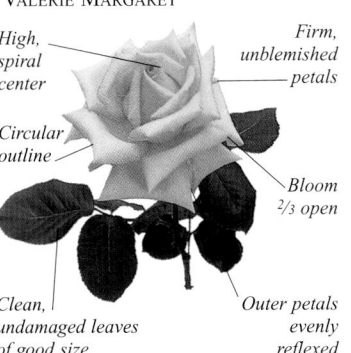

High, spiral center

Circular outline

Firm, unblemished petals

Bloom 2/3 open

Clean, undamaged leaves of good size

Outer petals evenly reflexed

FLORIBUNDA ROSE
'HANNAH GORDON'

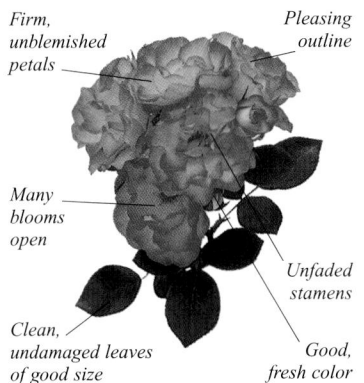

Firm, unblemished petals

Pleasing outline

Many blooms open

Clean, undamaged leaves of good size

Unfaded stamens

Good, fresh color

When arranging the blooms, check that they conform to the schedule, for example "medium pink Hybrid Tea, one bloom per stem without side buds." If there is any deviation, the entry may be disqualified and removed from competition. Place the entry card with the exhibit, and carry on with the entry process.

EQUIPMENT FOR EXHIBITING ROSES

Soft cloth to clean leaves

Mounted tube for showing miniatures

Clear bottle to hold rose

Plastic wrap for righting stem in bottle (floral foam and aluminum foil may also be used)

Pruners to recut stems

Scissors for trimming leaves

Entry cards

Tweezers to remove imperfections

Show schedule

Soft brush to clean petals

Swabs to clean and arrange petals

Cotton balls to wedge tight petals into a more open position

Toothpicks for rearranging petals and other grooming

Handbook for selecting roses (gives color classification)

Soil preparation and planting

Growing roses in the garden is not difficult if their basic needs are satisfied. They are relatively long-lived flowering plants, so it is worth investing time and effort in choosing a suitable site, properly preparing the soil, selecting cultivars appropriate to the conditions, and planting the roses correctly.

Site and exposure

All roses need a site that is open to the sun and sheltered from strong winds, with good air circulation and a fertile soil. They do not thrive in deep shade, under trees, if crowded by deep-rooted plants, or in excessively dry or waterlogged soil. Most sites may be improved to meet these needs, for example by erecting wind-breaks or by draining heavy, wet soils (see SOILS AND FERTILIZERS, "Improving drainage," p.617). Planting roses in an appropriate soil mix in raised beds or containers may solve the problem of unsuitable soil.

Evaluate the planting site carefully before choosing a cultivar: the enormous variety among roses provides plants that tolerate a range of conditions. Most modern roses do not flourish in very alkaline soil, but almost all the old garden roses grow well in it if given large quantities of organic material when being planted

and mulched. *Rosa rugosa* and *R. pimpinellifolia* groups do well on sandy soil. These are generalizations, since even among modern roses there may be great differences between cultivars: for example, on poor soils 'Gold Medal' and 'Maid of Honor' suffer, but 'Elina', 'Crimson Glory', and others thrive if given extra nutrients and moisture. Certain rootstocks may help in some circumstances: for example, *R. multiflora* often grows well in heavy, cold soils.

Soil quality

Roses grow in most types of soil but prefer slightly acidic conditions, about pH 6.5. If in doubt, use a commercial soil-testing kit to gauge the acidity of the soil. A water-retentive yet well-drained soil is ideal. Always clear weeds when preparing the soil so the young roses will not need to compete with them for light, moisture, and nutrients.

Improving the soil
The drainage of clay soils, the water-retentiveness of light, sandy soils, and the pH level of alkaline soils may be improved by incorporating plenty of organic matter. Excavate very shallow topsoil to about 24in (60cm) when planting, and replace some of the subsoil with

extra organic matter. For further information on how to influence the acidity of the soil, and on general soil preparation, see "Soil cultivation," pp.612–15. If possible, prepare the soil approximately three months before planting to allow it to settle.

Choosing roses

Where and how you buy roses will depend to some extent on the particular cultivars that you wish to buy. Many old roses are obtainable only from specialty nurseries by mail order if they are not located locally. Bear in mind that catalog photographs may not always accurately represent the flower color, nor is it possible to assess the quality of the plant before it arrives, although with a reputable nursery this should not be a problem. Beware of special "bargains," often advertised in the press, that offer bedding or shrub roses cheaply, since the plants may be of poor quality.

Nurseries in North America use a variety of rose species as rootstocks, depending on the climate of the region where the mature plants will be grown. Rootstocks may be purchased by gardeners wishing to bud their own roses (see also "Hybridizing," p.166).

Bare-root roses
Mail-order suppliers, stores, and supermarkets sell roses bare-root; local retailers usually sell them in sleeves or boxes filled with peat. The roses are in a semidormant or dormant state, and their roots are essentially clean of soil. Provided that they have not dried out in transit and are planted as soon as possible after arrival, they should establish quite satisfactorily.

When buying a bare-root rose in a store, examine it carefully. If the environment in which the rose has been kept is too warm, the rose either dries out or starts growing prematurely, producing blanched, thin shoots that usually die after planting. Do not purchase any roses that display such symptoms.

Container-grown roses
Roses grown in containers may be planted at any time, except during periods of prolonged drought or when the ground is frozen. Some garden centers and suppliers trim the roots of unsold bare-root roses and pot them into containers for convenience, so before buying a rose in a container, check that it has not been recently potted up – hold the plant by its main shoot and gently shake it. If the rose is not firmly rooted and moves about in the soil mix, it probably has been in its container for a short time. However, these roses may be acceptable, provided that they are in general good health and do not have spindly, weak growth. Treat them as bare-root roses where storage and planting are concerned. If any roots are growing through the drainage holes in the container, knock the plant out of its pot and make sure that its roots are not thickly coiled around the root ball – a sign that the rose is potbound and has been in the container for too long.

Selecting a healthy rose
Whether bare-root or container-grown, the plant should have at least two or three strong, firm main canes and a healthy network of roots in good proportion to the top-growth. Any foliage on container-grown roses should be vigorous, abundant, and free from pests and diseases. If buying a climbing rose, check that the shoots are healthy and at least 12in (30cm) long. Choose a standard rose with a balanced head, since it is likely to be viewed from all sides; a straight stem on a standard is best, although a slightly crooked stem is acceptable.

SELECTING HEALTHY ROSES

A BARE-ROOT BUSH ROSE
GOOD EXAMPLE

A CONTAINER-GROWN ROSE
GOOD EXAMPLE

A STANDARD ROSE
GOOD EXAMPLE

Strong bud union

Good network of fibrous roots

Vigorous foliage of a good color

Healthy root system

BAD EXAMPLE

Sturdy, well-balanced top-growth

Moist soil mix

BAD EXAMPLE

Strong, healthy shoots, evenly distributed

Stake

Straight stem

BAD EXAMPLE

Spindly, damaged shoots

Stunted root system

Spindly shoots

Blackspot

Leaf drop

Weeds

Dead wood

Unbalanced, one-sided head

PLANTING DISTANCES FOR A ROSE HEDGE

TALL SHRUB ROSES
Plant the roses in a line 3–4ft (1–1.2m) apart, so that when mature, the branches intermingle to form a dense, effective screen.

MODERN BUSH ROSES
For a denser hedge, plant roses in a staggered formation in 2 rows that are 18–24in (45–60cm) apart.

Preparing to plant

Following a few simple principles at the planting stage, such as observing correct planting distances and depths, handling the roots carefully, and providing proper support where necessary, avoids problems with routine care later on. Delay planting for a few days if the ground is frozen, too wet, or too dry for roots to adjust easily to the soil.

When to plant bare-root roses
Bare-root roses are best planted just before or at the beginning of their dormant period, in fall or early winter, to lessen the shock of transplanting. Early spring may be better in areas that have bad winters. Plant the roses as soon as possible after purchase. If there is any delay, perhaps because of unsuitable weather, it is best to heel them into a spare piece of ground, with the roots buried in a shallow trench (see ORNAMENTAL TREES, *Heeling In*, p.65). Alternatively, store the roses in a cool and frost-free place, and keep the roots moist.

When to plant container-grown roses
These may be planted at any time of the year in suitable weather conditions. Container-grown roses, unlike bare-root roses, may be left outdoors in their containers for three weeks or more while awaiting planting, as long as they are kept properly watered. Even though most roses are quite hardy, do not expose them to prolonged cold, since the roots in the containers may suffer some damage in very cold conditions.

Spacing bedding roses
The growth habit determines the planting distances between bedding roses. A narrow, upright cultivar needs less space for healthy growth than a lax, sprawling one and so tolerates closer planting. As a general rule, plant the bushes 18–24in (45–60cm) apart and about 12in (30cm) from the edge of the rosebed.

If underplanting large shrub or species roses, allow more space, about 2½–4ft (75–120cm) or more, depending on their ultimate size and growth habit. Space miniature roses roughly 12in (30cm) apart.

Another factor to consider when spacing your plants is the length of your growing season. A longer growing season allows the plants to grow larger, so it makes sense to allow for this by spacing your plants farther apart than would be done in an area with a shorter growing season. Generally, the farther north the garden, the closer you need to plant to fill the space adequately.

However, be aware that overly close planting makes mulching, spraying, and pruning more difficult and may create stagnant air conditions, which allow rapid spread of mildew and blackspot.

Spacing roses for a hedge
The size and growth habit of the chosen cultivar govern the position of roses in forming a hedge. To gain uniformly dense growth, plant tall shrub roses such as 'Penelope' and 'Golden Wings', which reach 4ft (1.2m) or more across, in a single line, and modern bush roses such as 'Tropicana' in two rows in a staggered formation.

Planting a bush rose

The first stage in planting a rose is to prepare the plant. If the roots of a bare-root rose look dry, soak the plant in a bucket of water for an hour or two until thoroughly moist. Place a container-grown rose in a bucket of water until the soil mix surface appears moist. If the root ball is wrapped in plastic or burlap, cut away the wrapping very carefully. Remove any loose soil mix, gently tease out the roots, and prune any damaged or diseased parts.

Make a planting hole that is wide enough to accommodate the roots or root ball, and deep enough so that, when planted, the bud union is at the correct level for your region. The bud union is easily recognizable as a bulge at the base of the shoots. As a general guide, in hardiness Zones 4–5, plant so that the union is about 1in (2.5cm) below ground level, or ½in (1cm) for budded miniatures. Place the bud union more or less level with the ground in Zones 6–7, and position the bud union as much as 1in (2.5cm) above the soil surface in Zone 8.

Position the rose in the center of the hole, then check that the planting depth is correct. If the roots of a bare-root rose all point in one direction, place the rose close to one side of the hole and fan the roots out.

Water and backfill the hole in stages, shaking the rose a little to allow the soil to settle around the roots. Do not compact the wet soil around the rose, especially if the soil is heavy.

Carefully mound soil over the crown of a newly planted bare-root bush to protect the new shoots while the roots become established. The mound should then be removed in stages over the course of two to three weeks; use a gentle stream from a hose for a few minutes each day. After reducing the mound of soil, create a watering ring from the remaining soil to retain water when irrigating, then cover the entire area beneath the rose bush with an organic mulch (such as bark chips or leaf mold) to help retain moisture, to moderate soil temperatures, and to suppress weeds.

To lessen stress on a newly planted container-grown rose, you could remove flowers and larger buds or spray with an antidesiccant, but this is usually unnecessary unless the weather is quite hot and dry.

HOW TO PLANT A BARE-ROOT BUSH ROSE

1 *Remove diseased or damaged growth, crossing shoots, and thin or straggly stems; trim thick roots by one-third. Dig a hole and fork in compost mixed with bone meal or balanced fertilizer.*

2 *Center the rose in the hole and spread out the roots evenly. Lay a stake across the hole to check that the bud union will be at the correct depth for the type of rose and your climate zone.*

3 *In 2 or 3 stages, water the hole and backfill with soil after the water has drained out. Do not walk on the backfilled soil to avoid compacting the soil and breaking the roots.*

4 *Loosely mound the rose with soil to protect it from the sun, cold, and wind. If spring-planted, gradually remove the soil mound; retain the mound if planted in fall.*

HOW TO PLANT A CLIMBING ROSE

1 *Place the rose in the planting hole, leaning it toward the wall at an angle of about 45° so that the shoots reach the lowest support wire. Place a stake across the hole to check the planting depth.*

2 *Use stakes to guide the shorter shoots toward the wires. Tie all the shoots to the stakes or wires with plastic straps (see inset).*

Planting a climbing rose or a rambler

Train climbers grown against a wall or fence along horizontal wires that are about 18in (45cm) apart and held in place by tapered vine eyes or strong nails driven into the surface. If the brickwork or masonry of a wall is very hard, drill holes for the vine eyes with a ³⁄₁₆in (4.7mm) bit. Keep the wires 3in (7cm) away from the wall to allow air circulation and discourage diseases. A rambler has more flexible stems than a climber and may be trained on a hinged trellis that folds away from the wall so that the wall may be maintained without harming the rose.

The ground next to a wall is likely to be dry, since it is in a rain shadow and the masonry absorbs moisture from the soil. Plant about 18in (45cm) from the wall, where the soil is less dry and water from any eaves will not constantly drip on the rose.

Prepare the soil and planting hole, and trim the rose as for bush roses. Position the plant, leaning it toward the wall at 45°, and fan out its roots toward moist ground. If necessary, train the shoots along stakes pushed into the ground, but keep each stake far enough from the roots to avoid damaging them.

After planting as for a bush rose, attach the shoots to the support wires with plastic, string, or burlap ties or with plastic straps designed for tying in roses. Take care not to tighten the straps too much around the rose's stems, since room must be left for the shoots to grow. Check the ties frequently, and loosen and retie them when necessary.

Prune the main shoots of a climber or a rambler at this stage. For further pruning instructions, see "Climbing roses and ramblers," p.162. Keep the roots thoroughly watered and uncrowded by other plants to help them establish.

Planting a rambler by a tree
Choose a rose that will not overwhelm the host tree while scrambling up it. Plant it on the windward side of the tree so that the rose's young, flexible shoots blow toward and around it, rather than away from it. Dig a planting hole at least 3ft (1m) away from the trunk to increase the amount of rain that reaches the roots of the rose. Train all the new shoots toward the tree along sloping stakes, tied at their upper ends to the trunk and inserted just behind the rose. If planting in this way on a boundary, bear in mind that the blooms grow toward, and are visible from, the direction of the strongest sunlight.

Planting a standard rose

Some nurseries bud their standard roses onto stocks that have a tendency to sucker, although some are experimenting with better rootstocks. To keep suckering to a minimum, plant the rose no deeper than the recommended depth for your area (see "Planting a bush rose," p.155). Deeper planting will encourage increased sucker growth.

A standard rose needs a stake, placed on the side of the prevailing wind, to support it. Paint the entire stake with a preservative that is not toxic to plants, then allow it to dry. Insert the stake very firmly near the center of the planting hole before positioning the rose to avoid damaging the roots and, as a result, encouraging suckers. Position the rose next to the stake and check that it just reaches the base of the lowest branches; if necessary, adjust the height of the stake. Use a stake or rake handle to make sure that the bud union is at the correct level.

Fill in the soil and water as for a bush rose. Secure the stem to the stake with two ties. These need to incorporate a buffer (such as in a figure-eight tie) to prevent the stake from rubbing the stem. Do not tighten the ties fully until the rose has settled in the soil. They will need to be loosened at least once during the growing season as the diameter of the stem increases.

HOW TO PLANT A STANDARD ROSE

1 *Position the stake in the hole so that the rose stem will be in the center. Drive the stake into the ground, then check that the top is just below the head of the rose.*

2 *Place a stake across the hole to check the planting depth. Use the old soil mark on the stem as a guide and plant at the correct depth. Fill in the hole, then water.*

3 *Use a tie (see inset) just below the head of the rose, and another halfway up the stem, to attach the rose to the stake. Cut out weak or crossing shoots.*

Planting roses in containers

The container should be at least 12–18in (30–45cm) deep for bush roses or 9–14in (23–35cm) deep for miniatures to allow for root growth. Place a piece of screening over the drainage hole(s) in the base of the container, then fill it with a standard soil-based potting mix. Plant the roses in the same way, and at the correct depth, as bush roses (see p.155). Take care to space them correctly.

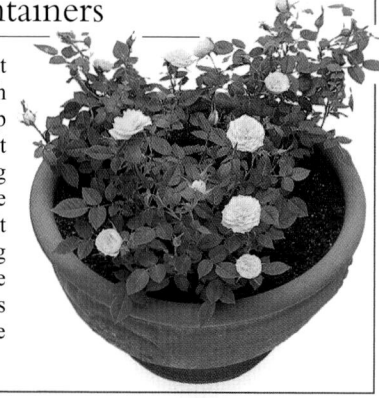

Routine care

Roses need regular care to produce healthy, vigorous plants that are resistant to pests and diseases. Attention paid to fertilizing, watering, mulching, and general maintenance will be rewarded with a fine display throughout the season.

Fertilizing

Roses are gross feeders and quickly exhaust even a well-prepared rose-bed that is rich in nutrients. Many essential mineral salts rapidly leach out in the rain, especially from light soils. If the roses are to flourish, they require regular fertilizing in a balanced formulation of essential nutrients (nitrogen, phosphorus, and potassium) and other elements. Many suitable commercial rose fertilizers are available, mostly in powder or granular form. For information on how to deal with particular nutrient deficiencies, see PLANT PROBLEMS, pp.633–61.

After pruning in the spring, and when the soil is moist, sprinkle a small handful, 1–2oz (25–50g), of fertilizer around each rose. Hoe or rake it in lightly and evenly, keeping it clear of the stems. Repeat this application about a month after the first bloom flush, before a second crop of bloom develops. Fertilize at least monthly throughout summer, but do not apply a general fertilizer once temperatures cool down in fall, because this encourages soft growth in fall that may suffer frost damage. A dressing of potassium sulfate, however, applied at a rate of 2oz/sq yd (75g/sq m) in early fall, protects late shoots by helping them mature before the first frosts.

Foliar fertilizing (spraying a liquid on the leaves and bypassing the roots) is recommended for producing larger blooms and leaves, especially on exhibition roses. Before doing so, water thoroughly with plain water to help avoid scorching the foliage.

Fertilizing roses in containers

Roses in containers soon use up the soil mix nutrients. Compensate for this loss by top-dressing annually with a balanced fertilizer and foliar fertilizing every week or two in the growing season to maintain vigor.

Watering

Roses need plenty of water for healthy growth, especially if they are newly planted. Watering too little and too often can be counterproductive, because it encourages the roots to grow toward the surface. Give the roses enough water to soak the soil thoroughly around their roots instead. Try not to wet the foliage, because this spreads some diseases.

Roses are deep-rooted plants and can flourish even in long, dry summers and near-drought conditions, particularly if they are well established. In such conditions, the flowers may be smaller than usual and may open very quickly. The petals may also be vulnerable to scorching by the sun. In hot, dry climates, avoid wetting the flowers in strong sun, because the blooms may spoil. Water roses in containers every other day, or even daily if the weather is exceptionally hot and dry.

Suckers and how to deal with them

Suckers are shoots that grow below the bud union, directly from the rootstock onto which a cultivar has been grafted. They are usually narrower and a much lighter green than those of the cultivar, often with thorns of a different shape or color, and the leaves may have seven or more leaflets.

Remove any suckering shoots as soon as they appear. This prevents the rootstock from wasting energy on the sucker's growth at the expense of the cultivar. Some rootstocks produce suckers more readily than others, especially if they have been planted at the wrong depth. Damage to the roots, caused by severe cold or any accidental nicks from hoes, other implements, or a stake, may also stimulate the production of suckers.

Pull the sucker to detach it from the rootstock: this removes any dormant buds that may be present at the point where it joins the roots. Do not cut it, since this is the equivalent of pruning it and only encourages more vigorous growth. It may, however, sometimes be necessary to cut a sucker if it originates from beneath the rose and if pulling it off would mean damaging or lifting the rose.

Shoots on the stem of a standard rose are also suckers, since the stem is part of the rootstock. As with other grafted roses, any suckers will look different from the cultivar. Snap them off or pare them cleanly from the stem with a sharp knife.

REMOVING A SUCKER FROM A STANDARD ROSE
Pull away any suckers growing from the rose stem (see inset), taking care not to rip the bark.

REMOVING A SUCKER FROM A BUSH ROSE

1 *With a trowel, carefully scrape away the soil to expose the top of the rootstock. Check that the suspect shoot arises from below the bud union.*

2 *Using a glove to protect your hand, pull the sucker away from the rootstock. Refill the hole and gently firm the soil.*

HOW A SUCKER GROWS

Sucker

The sucker (right) grows directly from the rootstock. If cut back only at ground level it will grow again and divert further energy from the rose.

Eradicating weeds

To avoid damaging the roots of roses when weeding around them, do not disturb the soil too deeply. Control annual weeds by hand or with light use of a hoe. Use weed-killers carefully, because they may severely damage roses. Mulching roses (see right) or underplanting them with shallow-rooted ground covers also suppresses weeds.

Hygiene

The uncollected fallen leaves, prunings, and any other debris from infected plants can spread diseases among roses. Gather up and dispose of such material regularly, but never put it on a compost pile, because any disease organisms present may survive to infect other roses in your garden (and those of your neighbors).

Mulching roses

A 3in (8cm) layer of mulch, if applied in early spring after pruning and fertilizing, helps smother any weed seeds and maintain high moisture levels and even temperatures in the soil. Well-rotted stable manure is an ideal mulch, providing many of the nutrients that roses need, but if this proves difficult to obtain, bark chips or shredded leaves are both satisfactory. For further details, see also SOILS AND FERTILIZERS, "Top-dressings and mulches," p.620.

Deadheading

The purpose of deadheading (removing faded flowers) is to stimulate the earliest possible development of new, young shoots and additional blooms throughout the flowering season. Once a rose flower has been pollinated, it starts to fade. If left on the plant, it may delay the production of new flowering shoots below the old flower cluster.

In some roses, a seedpod (hip) forms, and this diverts energy from further flower production; remove the dead flowers regularly unless you desire the hips for ornamental purposes. In late summer, even if some roses continue to bloom, stop deadheading to avoid encouraging new, soft growth, which would be damaged by the first frosts.

Moving roses

A rose may be moved at almost any age, but the older it is, the greater the risk that it may resettle badly. It is not difficult to move roses that are up to three or four years old; older plants may be moved but will require much more careful effort. The roots of older roses are thick and spread deeply; they also have fewer of the fine feeding roots that are essential for reestablishing the plant.

If circumstances allow, move a rose only when it is dormant and always into a well-prepared bed. First loosen the soil by cutting down on all sides with a spade at least 10in (25cm) out from the root ball. Insert a fork well

Blind shoots

These are shoots that develop without a terminal flower bud. They divert the plant's energy in the same way as a sucker (see "Suckers and how to deal with them," p.157) so prune out any as soon as they appear.

Cut the blind shoot by about a half to an outward-facing bud to encourage it to grow and flower. If no bud is visible, cut back to the main stem.

HOW TO DEADHEAD ROSES

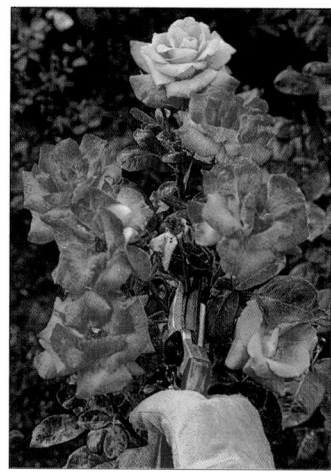

1 The central bloom of a spray fades first and should be cut out to maintain the display.

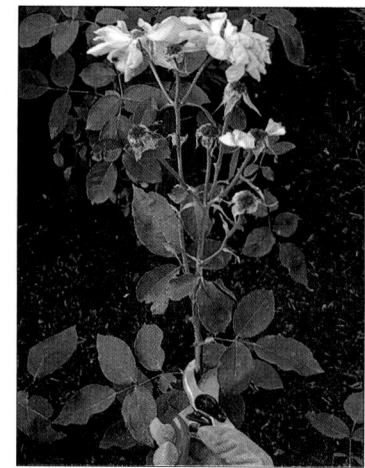

2 When all the flowers have faded, remove the entire spray by cutting back to an emerging bud or a fully formed shoot.

HYBRID TEA ROSES
Cut back stems bearing faded flowers to an outward-facing bud (see inset) or fully formed shoot.

---

away from the center of the plant and lift it, taking some soil with it and disturbing the roots as little as possible; on light soils use a spade, since the soil is likely to fall away from the roots. Trim off any coarse roots and wrap the root ball in plastic or burlap to prevent the roots from drying out before transferring the plant to its new position. Water immediately after replanting and regularly until the rose is established.

Fall cutback

Strong winter winds may rock taller roses and loosen their roots, making them vulnerable to cold damage. To help prevent this, shorten any overly long shoots in fall.

Winter protection

In temperate climates, roses need protection in a cold winter. In heavy and poorly drained soils, any accumulated water will later freeze. The expansion of the water as it freezes lifts and breaks the roots, and it may damage the bud union – the most vulnerable part of the rose. Mound soil, brought from another part of the garden, 6–8in (15–20cm) above the bud union. Loosely packed leaves or straw, held in place by a staked ring of chicken wire, gives an added measure of protection.

Roses that are hardy between -4°F and -10°F (-20°C to -23°C) include Centifolias, *Rosa californica*, and *R. wichuraiana*. At colder temperatures, provide protection, or choose

roses that tolerate extreme cold. Hybrid Teas, Grandifloras, and Floribundas may tolerate temperatures as low as -20°F (-29°C) for a week or so if soil is mounded over the crown. Pack the crowns of standard roses with straw or leaves, loosely tied in place with twine. Grow Alba, Damask, and Gallica roses, and some of the species roses, such as *R. multiflora* and *R. palustris*, in areas where the temperature falls to -22°F (-30°C). A few roses, such as *R. virginiana*, *R. blanda*, *R. canina*, *R. glauca*, and *R. rugosa*, survive cold as severe as -35°F (-37°C). For full instructions

CUTTING BACK IN FALL

on protecting roses during the winter, see COLD AND WIND PROTECTION, pp.604–5.

Pests and diseases

Aphids (p.639), blackspot (see "Fungal leaf spots and blotches," p.641), rose dieback, powdery mildew (p.640), and rusts (p.641) are common problems. Inspect regularly and control diseases or pests at once. As a general rule, modern roses are more prone to pests and diseases than are species and most old garden roses.

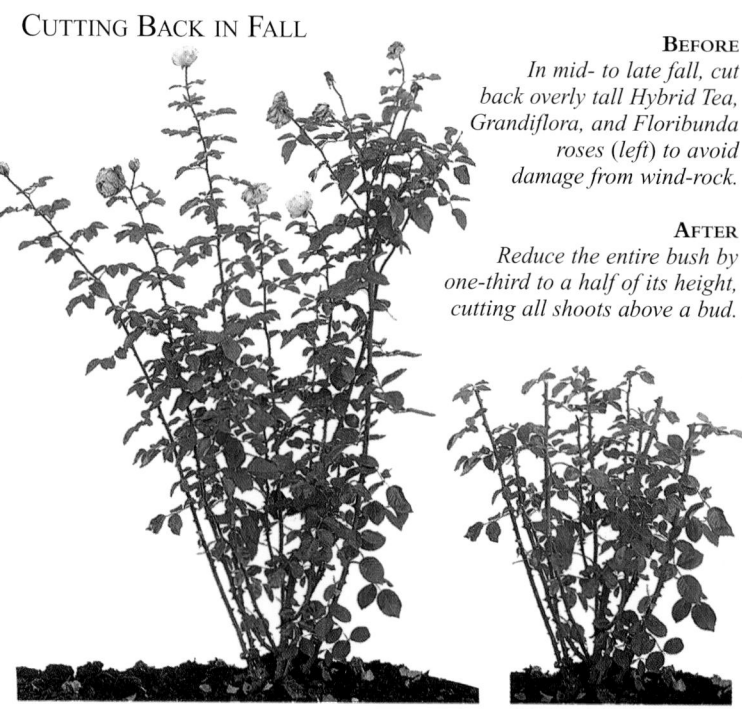

BEFORE
In mid- to late fall, cut back overly tall Hybrid Tea, Grandiflora, and Floribunda roses (left) to avoid damage from wind-rock.

AFTER
Reduce the entire bush by one-third to a half of its height, cutting all shoots above a bud.

Pruning and training

THE purpose of pruning is to speed up the natural process of new, vigorous, disease-free shoots developing to replace the old, weakened ones and so produce an attractive shape and the optimum display of blooms. Training a plant on supports stimulates the production of flowering sideshoots and directs new growth into the given space. The severity of pruning depends on the rose type; certain principles of pruning, however, apply to all roses.

Basic principles of pruning roses

A pair of sharp, high-quality pruners is essential; loppers and a fine-toothed pruning saw are also useful for removing gnarled, woody stumps and thicker shoots. Wear strong, protective, comfortable gloves for all pruning tasks.

How to prune

Always make a clean, angled cut above a bud that faces in the direction in which the resultant new shoot should develop. This is usually an outward-facing bud, but it may face inward on a lax, sprawling rose if the center of the bush needs filling out. Cut to the appropriate height if a dormant bud is not visible, and cut out any stubs that develop later.

Always remove dead and dying shoots, cutting back to disease-free, usually white pith, even if this means pruning almost to ground level. Remove any crossing growth that might impede the main shoots, or twiggy growth, such as the matchstick-thin twigs that bear only a leaf or two. This concentrates energy in the more vigorous and productive shoots and allows good air circulation, which helps prevent disease.

Applying wound paint to large cuts after pruning is often recommended for modern hybrids to prevent entry of disease spores or pith-boring insects. While some growers do not use wound paint or other sealants against diseases, many rose enthusiasts routinely use them to exclude cane borers.

When to prune

Prune roses when they are dormant or semidormant, between leaf drop in fall and when the buds are just beginning to break in the spring. Heavily pruning a rose in active growth is sometimes necessary, but it severely checks growth. Do not prune in cold conditions, because the growth bud below the cut may be damaged and the shoot may die back. Following a very severe winter, cut back cold-damaged shoots in spring to a healthy bud; if the winters are always severe, prune roses in spring, immediately after removing any winter protection material. Conversely, in a climate so warm that the roses flower almost continuously, prune them in the cooler months to induce dormancy and give them an artificial period of rest.

MAKING A PRUNING CUT

Position the thin blade of the pruners just above the bud. Take care not to make the cut too far from the bud or leave a snag, because disease may enter the stem and cause dieback. If this happens, cut back the shoot as far as necessary to reach good, healthy wood.

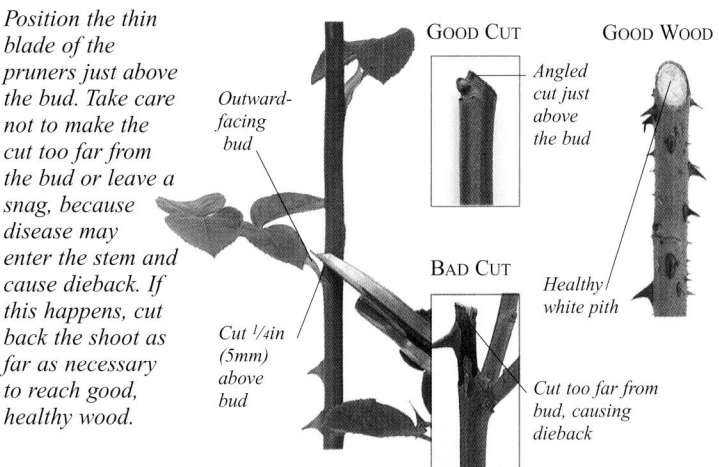

Outward-facing bud

GOOD CUT

GOOD WOOD

Angled cut just above the bud

Cut 1/4in (5mm) above bud

BAD CUT

Healthy white pith

Cut too far from bud, causing dieback

Pruning roses after planting

Almost all newly planted roses should be pruned hard to encourage the development of vigorous shoot and root systems. Fully leafed-out, containerized roses are an exception to this rule – give them only a light pruning to remove any weak, dead, or damaged shoots. Remove any weak, dead, or crossing growth from standard roses. Less severe pruning

HOW TO PRUNE A HYBRID TEA OR GRANDIFLORA ROSE

Prune the rose fairly hard, in fall or spring, by trimming off any unproductive growth and then reducing the main shoots to form a strong, balanced framework

Cut out crossing, congested, and twiggy or spindly growth.

Remove dead wood and any that shows signs of damage or disease.

Prune main shoots to within about 8–10in (20–25cm) of ground level.

PRUNING A NEWLY PLANTED BUSH ROSE

Prune a newly planted bush rose to about 3in (8cm) above ground level. Cut back to outward-facing buds, and remove any cold-damaged growth.

and regular fertilizing are preferable for roses grown in soils that are deficient in nutrients.

Pruning modern garden bush roses

Modern roses flower best on new or the current season's growth, so they are pruned fairly severely to stimulate vigorous new shoots and to produce a good display of blooms.

Hybrid Teas and Grandifloras (Large-flowered bush roses)

Remove completely any dead, diseased, thin, or twiggy shoots. Using long-handled pruners or loppers, cut out stumps from previous years that, although healthy, have not produced any worthwhile new growth in recent years.

Thin out any weak or crossing shoots from the center of the bush to leave a well-balanced framework and allow free air circulation around the plant. It is not as important to produce a balanced framework for closely planted bedding roses as for one grown as a specimen, which will be seen from all sides.

Depending on the extent of winter kill and on the differences among cultivars, in temperate climates the main shoots should then be pruned back to between 8–10in (20–25cm). In extremely mild areas, the shoots may be cut down less severely, to about 18–24in (45–60cm). To achieve blooms that are of exhibition quality, cut the main shoots back hard to leave only two or three buds.

Floribundas (Cluster-flowered bush roses)

When pruning this type of rose, cut out any unproductive wood as for Hybrid Teas (see p.159). Reduce any sideshoots by about one-third on smaller cultivars and by two-thirds on taller-growing cultivars such as 'Fred Loads'. Cut back the main shoots to 12–15in (30–38cm), but reduce the shoots of taller cultivars by about one-third of their length. Do not prune them any harder unless growing the roses for exhibition, because this reduces the number of blooms that will be produced in the upcoming season.

Patio roses (Dwarf cluster-flowered bush roses)

These are smaller versions of Floribunda roses and should be pruned in fall or spring following the same principles as above.

Miniature roses

There are two distinct methods of pruning miniature roses. The simpler of the two is to give them only the minimum of attention: remove shoots that have died back, thin out occasionally the shoots of those cultivars that produce a dense tangle of twiggy growth, and shorten any overvigorous shoots that may throw the whole plant out of balance.

The second method is to treat them as if they were miniature Hybrid Teas or Floribundas. Remove all growth except the strongest shoots, and then cut them back by about one-third. This method is used satisfactorily for cultivars introduced from distant areas that do not adapt easily to their new conditions. Such plants benefit from the extra stimulus of a severe pruning and produce strong new growth.

HOW TO PRUNE A FLORIBUNDA ROSE

In fall or spring, cut out unproductive growth and prune the sideshoots. Reduce the main shoots by a proportion suitable to the eventual height of the cultivar.

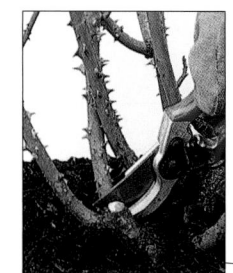

Remove crossing or congested wood and twiggy, spindly growth.

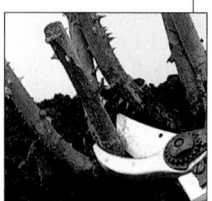

Prune out all dead, damaged, or diseased wood to a healthy bud.

Prune main shoots to 12–15in (30–38cm) from ground level.

Reduce sideshoots by one- to two-thirds, cutting to a bud.

Pruning standard roses

The majority of standards are formed from Hybrid Teas or Floribundas or from small shrub roses budded onto a straight, unbranched stem, usually 3½–4ft (1.1–1.2m) high. Prune as for bush or shrub rose equivalents, but cut back the main shoots by about one-third so that they are all roughly equal in length. It is especially important to achieve a balanced head that will look pleasing from all sides. If the head is unbalanced, prune the shoots on the denser side less hard so that they do not produce as much new growth as those on the thinner side.

Weeping standards

These roses are usually formed from cultivars of small-flowered ramblers grafted onto especially tall standard stems of about 5ft (1.5m). The flexible shoots are pendent and require only limited pruning: remove the old flowered wood when the blooms have faded, leaving growth from the current season intact.

Pruning shrub and old garden roses

Although these vary enormously in their growth habit, most modern and old garden shrub roses, and all the species roses, flower on wood that is two or more years old. They should be pruned fairly lightly to leave the flowering wood intact. Many flower freely for years without any formal pruning if allowed to develop naturally. It is necessary to cut out only any dead, damaged, diseased, or weak wood to keep the roses really healthy. Despite this, some pruning may help to increase the number and quality of the blooms.

Give a mature remontant shrub rose a light renewal pruning each winter by cutting down some of the older main stems to the base. This encourages the production of vigorous new basal shoots that will flower the following summer. Over a four-year period of renewal pruning, all the shoots are replaced and, with regular fertilizing, the bushes will remain free-flowering and healthy for many years. Treat nonremontant roses similarly, but prune them immediately after flowering.

Rugosa, China, and Hybrid Musk roses may be given a similar annual renewal pruning.

HOW TO PRUNE A MINIATURE ROSE

BEFORE
Miniature roses often produce a mass of twiggy growth (left). The shape of this plant is unbalanced by overly vigorous shoots growing from the base.

AFTER
Twiggy growth and damaged wood have been removed, and vigorous shoots cut back by half (below).

HOW TO PRUNE A STANDARD ROSE

BEFORE
In the spring, prune a standard rose to prevent the plant from becoming too top-heavy and to retain an evenly shaped, floriferous head.

AFTER
All dead and damaged wood and any crossing stems have been removed to leave healthy shoots. The main shoots have been reduced to 8–10in (20–25cm), and the sideshoots by about one-third.

PRUNING A GALLICA ROSE

Throughout the growing season, thin out the rose to keep it healthy. The annual pruning after flowering involves cutting back side-shoots, unproductive wood, and some older shoots to encourage new growth.

Thin out twiggy growth regularly, and remove spent blooms by cutting back to the main shoot.

On mature roses, cut out up to one-quarter of old main shoots at the base.

Shorten sideshoots, but not the main shoots, by about two-thirds. Cut out any dead, diseased, or weak wood.

PRUNING ALBA, CENTIFOLIA, DAMASK, AND MOSS ROSES

Prune after flowering, cutting back both main shoots and sideshoots. If necessary, prune again in late summer to remove any overly long shoots that have developed.

Reduce main shoots that are old and woody by one-quarter to one-third.

LATE SUMMER

Cut back any overly long, whippy shoots by about one-third.

Prune side-shoots to about two-thirds of their length.

Gallica roses

Many of these produce a twiggy tangle of shoots that should be regularly thinned out to improve air circulation. After flowering, shorten the sideshoots only and remove any dead or diseased wood. Gently clip over Gallica roses used for hedging to maintain a neat shape. Follow their natural outline and do not attempt to shape them into a formal hedge, since this would remove many of the sideshoots on which flowers are produced in the following year.

Species roses

Much of the charm of these roses lies in their arching shoots which, in the second and subsequent years, carry flowers all along their length, often on short sideshoots. Formative pruning is needed to establish a balanced framework of strong, new growth. Thereafter, these roses need no further pruning other than the removal of dead and diseased wood, unless they become too dense or produce few flowers, in which case renewal prune them in the same way as non-remontant shrub roses.

Severe pruning encourages strong vegetative growth but produces few, if any, flowers until the second year. If the bush becomes lopsided, reshape it after flowering and trim back all the overly long shoots.

Alba, Centifolia, Damask, and Moss roses

After flowering, reduce both main shoots and sideshoots. At the end of the summer, cut back any vigorous,

Pruning ground-cover roses

The majority are low-growing, spreading, modern shrub roses, so renewal prune them as for shrub roses. Some, mostly related to *Rosa wichuraiana*, creep over the ground, rooting as they go. Prune these only to stop them from spreading beyond the available space.

Prune shoots to well within the intended area of spread, cutting to an upward-facing bud.

overly long shoots that might whip about in the wind and cause wind-rock damage to the roots.

Bourbon and Hybrid Perpetual roses

These are usually remontant, so prune them, and all hybrids partly derived from *Rosa rugosa*, in early spring as you would Hybrid Teas (see p.159), but much more lightly.

Pegging down roses

This technique is an effective, although time-consuming, way of increasing flower production on Bourbon and Hybrid Perpetual roses that tend to send up long, ungainly shoots with flowers only at the tips. Instead of pruning the shoots in late summer or fall, bend them over gently, taking great care not to snap them. Peg the shoots firmly into the ground. Alternatively, tie the tips to pegs in the ground, to wires strung between pegs, or to a low wire frame placed around the plant. Shorten sideshoots on the pegged shoots to 4–6in (10–15cm).

This has much the same result as horizontally training the shoots of climbing and rambler roses (see p.162) and produces an arching mound covered with a large number of flowering sideshoots in the following season.

Select long, nonflowering shoots and prune the soft tips. Gently bend each shoot over and fasten it to the soil with sturdy wire hoops (see inset).

Climbing roses and ramblers

These roses require minor pruning but regular annual training. Neither climbing roses nor ramblers are self-supporting; if trained incorrectly, they may not flower freely and may become bare at their base. Some bush roses that send out large shoots at awkward angles, such as a few of the Hybrid Musks, may also be trained against walls, fences, or other supports for an attractive display.

Climbing roses

In their first year (and in their second unless they have made exceptional growth) do not prune climbing roses except to remove any dead, diseased, or weak, twiggy growth. Never prune climbing sports of bush roses (roses with the word "climbing" before the cultivar name, for example 'Climbing Shot Silk') in the first two years, since they may revert to the bush form if cut back hard too soon.

Begin training as soon as the new shoots are long enough to reach the supports; train them sideways along horizontal supports to encourage flowering. Where this is not possible, such as on a narrow area between a door and a window, choose a cultivar that is halfway between a tall shrub and a climbing rose. Many of these flower well from the plant base without special training: examples are 'Golden Showers', 'Joseph's Coat', and some of the more vigorous Bourbon roses.

Many climbing roses flower well for years with little pruning, except the removal of dead, diseased, or

HOW TO PRUNE AND TRAIN A CLIMBING ROSE

In the first two years after planting, restrict pruning to cutting out unproductive growth. From the third year, prune in fall after flowering.

Reduce the sideshoots by about two-thirds or about 6in (15cm), cutting above an outward-facing bud.

Tie all new shoots into horizontal wires 6–8in (15–20cm) apart. The shoots should not cross each other.

Remove any diseased, dead, or twiggy growth, cutting back to healthy wood or the main shoot.

twiggy growth. Prune them in fall, after flowering. Leave the strong main shoots unpruned unless they are exceeding their allotted space, in which case shorten them as appropriate. Otherwise, simply shorten the sideshoots. Train in all the new season's growth to the supports while it is still flexible.

Occasional renewal pruning may be necessary if the base of a climbing rose becomes very bare. Cut back one or two of the older main shoots to within 12in (30cm) or so above ground level to encourage vigorous new shoots to develop and replace the older growths. Repeat this as required in subsequent years.

Rambler roses

Like climbing roses, ramblers flower satisfactorily for a good many years without any routine pruning. However, they produce much more growth from the base than most climbers and, if not carefully trained, grow into a tangle of unmanageable shoots. This results in poor air circulation, which encourages disease, and makes it extremely difficult to spray the plants thoroughly.

Prune ramblers in summer, after they flower. In the first two years, restrict pruning to cutting back all the sideshoots by about 3in (7.5cm) to a vigorous shoot; also remove dead or diseased wood. In later years,

prune more heavily to maintain the framework. Untie all the shoots from their supports and, if possible, lay them on the ground. Cut no more than one-third of the oldest, spent shoots to ground level, leaving the new shoots and some older, but still vigorous, shoots for tying in to form a well-balanced framework.

Remove any immature wood from the tips of the main shoots and cut back any sideshoots. Cut back any wayward shoots that are outgrowing the available space or spoiling the overall shape of the rose. Train in the shoots, as close to the horizontal as possible, to encourage flowering on new, short sideshoots that will develop all along the main shoots.

Training on arches, pergolas, pillars, and trees

Climbing roses or ramblers may be trained up pillars, arches, or pergolas. Twist the main shoots around the uprights to encourage flowering shoots to form low down. Carefully train the shoots in the direction of their natural growth before they have matured and hardened. This is vital for climbers that have stiff, semirigid shoots. Tie them in using twine or other rose ties; these are easy to undo when pruning or to loosen as the shoots develop. Once the main shoots reach the top of the support, regularly prune them to keep the rose within bounds.

Too many overly long sideshoots may spoil the appearance of a pillar rose, but a little additional pruning soon remedies this. Cut sideshoots back to three or four buds or by about 6in (15cm) in spring.

HOW TO PRUNE AND TRAIN A MATURE RAMBLER ROSE

After the first two years, prune as soon as flowering is over, cutting out any dead, diseased, or weak wood. Then train in the new shoots.

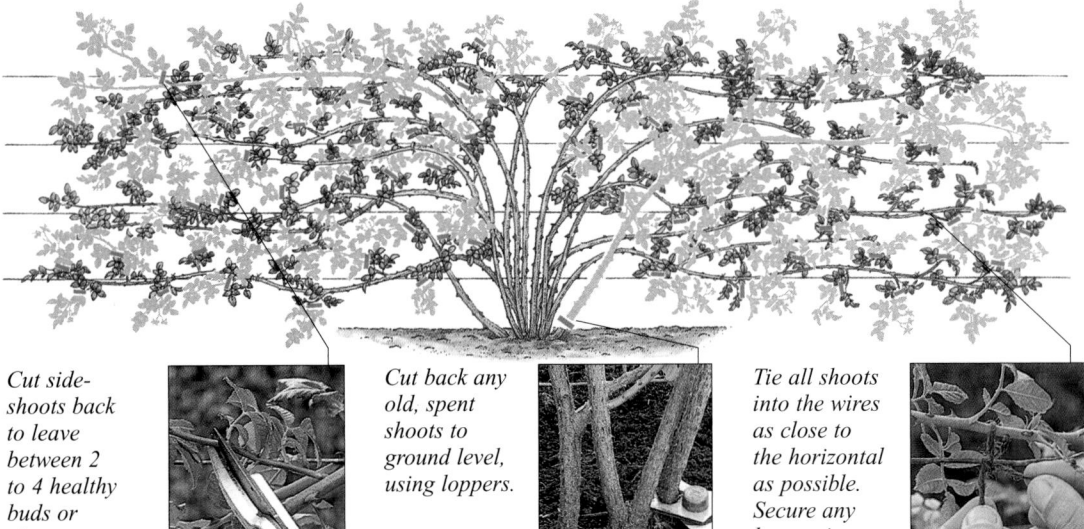

Cut sideshoots back to leave between 2 to 4 healthy buds or shoots.

Cut back any old, spent shoots to ground level, using loppers.

Tie all shoots into the wires as close to the horizontal as possible. Secure any loose wires.

Propagation

Roses may be propagated in three main ways: by taking cuttings, budding onto a rootstock, or from seed. Taking cuttings is the easiest method but it involves the longest wait: it takes about three years for the new plant to become established, except for miniature roses. Budding requires rootstocks that have grown on in advance but usually produces stronger and more vigorous plants. Many species roses (*Rosa glauca*, for example) readily breed true from seed. Cross hybrid roses with other hybrids, or sometimes with species, to produce new cultivars.

Hardwood cuttings

Most roses may be propagated from hardwood cuttings, particularly some cultivars that are related quite closely to wild species, such as rambler roses. Cuttings taken from miniature roses root so easily and develop so quickly that they are propagated this way commercially. Hybrid Teas and others of complex parentage do not root so readily and, consequently, may not be of sufficient size to sell commercially for two or three years, so they are less available on their own roots.

One advantage of roses grown from cuttings is that they do not have a different rootstock and so do not produce suckers. The disadvantages include a loss of vigor with some cultivars (although this may be useful with miniatures), and a tendency toward vigorous but nonflowering growth in the first few years, particularly with species.

In many climates, roses from hardwood cuttings are the most reliable, but success in rooting them is variable. It is therefore sensible to take a good number of cuttings to allow for possible failures.

Preparing the cuttings

In early fall, select the material for cuttings from the current season's healthy growth. Trim any old flower heads from the chosen shoots, and put the cuttings into a transparent plastic bag to prevent them from drying out. Cut them into 9in (23cm) lengths, and remove their leaves. Carefully breaking off the thorns will make the cuttings easier to handle. Moisten the base of each cutting, dip it into hormone rooting powder, and shake off the surplus.

Take shorter lengths of stem for miniature rose cuttings, which need be only 2–4in (5–10cm) long.

Preparing the cutting bed

Choose an open site for the cutting bed, preferably one that is sheltered from the midday sun. Single dig the area required, firm, and rake it to produce an even surface.

Inserting the cuttings

Make a series of deep planting holes with a stake or dibber, then trickle a little coarse sand into the bottom of each one to improve the drainage. Alternatively, dig a narrow, slitlike trench to the same depth and trickle sand along the base. On light, sandy soil, it is sufficient to push a spade vertically into the soil along a center line, working it backward and forward to widen the slit.

Insert the cuttings vertically into the holes or trench, leaving about one-third of their length above ground. They should be inserted far enough apart so that, once rooted, they may be lifted individually without disturbing adjacent cuttings. Firm and water the soil around the cuttings. In any dry spells that follow, water them again. After frost, which may loosen the roots in the ground, refirm the soil.

Another option is to root hardwood cuttings in deep pots of light, sandy soil. Plunge the pots in soil or sand in a shady outdoor site, and water them as needed. Growing miniature rose cuttings in bags or pots in a cold frame or cool greenhouse may be more convenient.

Development of the cuttings

During fall a callus should develop at the base of each cutting, from which the roots will be produced in spring. Once rooted, the young plants should develop strongly, but if flower buds form during the summer, remove them so that the plants can concentrate their energy on the production of new, strong, vegetative growth. The following fall, provided they are large enough, that is, about 9–12in (23–30cm), transplant the young roses to their permanent positions; if they are not yet large enough, allow them to grow on for another year.

Semiripe cuttings

Semiripe cuttings may be more successful than hardwood cuttings in areas that experience severe winters. In the late summer after flowering, select mature sideshoots that are still green. Take 6in (15cm) lengths, cutting above a bud where the shoot is beginning to turn woody, and trim off the soft tips. Prepare cuttings about 4in (10cm) long, following the same procedure as for hardwood cuttings.

Insert them into deep pots of sandy rooting medium (equal parts peat and sand). Cover the pots with plastic bags or put them in a propagator to prevent the cuttings from losing moisture. Keep in a cool, frost-free place. In spring, plant out the rooted cuttings in a nursery bed.

HOW TO PROPAGATE ROSES FROM HARDWOOD CUTTINGS

1 *Select a healthy, well-ripened shoot of roughly pencil thickness that has flowered in the summer and is about 12–24in (30–60cm) long. Remove it, cutting at an angle, just above an outward-facing bud. Prepare the cuttings by removing the leaves and soft tips.*

2 *Cut into 9in (23cm) lengths, making an angled cut above each top bud and a straight cut below the bottom bud. Dust the base with hormone rooting powder.*

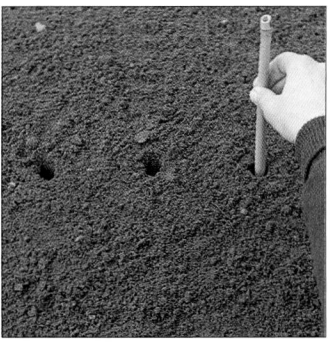

3 *Make a row of planting holes 6in (15cm) deep and the same distance apart. In heavy soil, put a little coarse sand to a depth of about 1in (2.5cm) in each hole.*

4 *Insert a cutting into each hole. Make sure that it reaches the bottom and that about 6in (15cm) of the cutting is buried. Firm the soil, water, and label the cuttings.*

5 *A year later, lift each rooted cutting with a hand fork, taking care not to damage the roots. Plant them in a bed or put them in a cold frame to grow on.*

HOW TO BUD-GRAFT A ROSE

1 *Select a flowered shoot about 12in (30cm) long, with 3–4 growth buds. Remove it, making an angled cut above an outward-facing bud on the parent plant.*

2 *Hold the budwood so that the buds point downward. Insert the knife ¼in (5mm) from a bud. With a scooping action, remove the bud with a 1in (2.5cm) long tail.*

3 *Holding the scion by the tail between thumb and forefinger (see inset), carefully remove the coarse, woody material from behind the bud by pulling it away.*

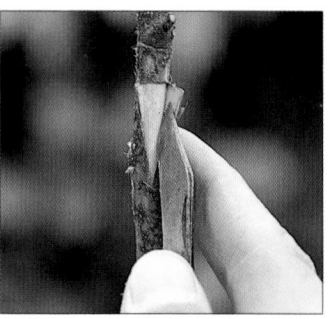

4 *Use the blunt side of the knife to remove the thorns from the stem of the rootstock, cleaning a section about 1½in (4cm) long.*

5 *Cutting just deeply enough to pierce the bark, make a T-shaped incision, with the horizontal cut about ¼in (5mm) long and the vertical cut ¾in (2cm) long.*

6 *Insert the tapered end of the budding knife under the flaps of the T, then ease them outward to reveal the inner, white cambium layer.*

7 *Hold the scion by its tail and insert it behind the bark flaps of the rootstock, sliding it well down so that the bud is held firmly in place, just below the cross-stroke of the T.*

8 *Using the knife, carefully trim away the surplus tail protruding above the T, following the line of the horizontal cut. Try to do this without damaging the wood beneath the bark. Discard the tail.*

9 *Attach a rubber binding tie tightly around the grafted area, pinning it on the side opposite the bud. This binds the stock and scion tightly together.*

STANDARD ROSES
Graft 3 buds around the stem (left). Cut back the stock in spring just above the new shoots (right).

BUSH ROSES
If grafting a bush rose, insert only 1 bud (or 2, equally spaced on the stem) onto the rootstock (see inset). In spring, cut back the rootstock just above the new shoots.

Bud-grafting

The budding process involves uniting plant material taken from two different roses in order to combine the virtues of both. A dormant bud (the scion) from the top-growth of one plant, usually chosen for its display, is inserted under the bark and just above the roots of a rootstock, normally a rose species or a specific clone that is selected for its vigor and hardiness. Different rootstocks may be used to suit the soil conditions or climate or to promote the vigorous growth of the scion.

Choosing a suitable rootstock

Many rootstocks are used to suit varying conditions: the hardy and vigorous *Rosa multiflora* is widely used as a rootstock, particularly where the winters are cold; it is also suitable for use on poor soils, although plants budded onto this rootstock are not long-lived. *Rosa canina* produces hardy plants and is popular on heavy soils or where winters are severe, but it suckers freely; the crimson climber 'Dr. Huey' (at one time known as 'Shafter' when used as a stock) is more frequently used where the dormant period is shorter. The selected clone 'Laxa' has now largely replaced most other commercial rootstocks, since it performs reliably in most soils and climatic conditions, is almost thornless, is easy to use for budding, and rarely produces suckers. Any commercial supplier of rootstocks, or a local nursery, should be able to advise on the best rootstock to use for local growing conditions.

Stocks may be obtained from wild roses growing in fields and on roadsides, but their quality is unreliable. It is better to use proven rootstocks.

Planting the rootstocks

Plant the rootstocks in fall in a nursery bed, about 12in (30cm) apart and with 30in (75cm) between the rows. For bush roses, the scions are inserted at the point where the shoots and roots join (the "neck"), so for ease of budding, plant the rootstocks at an angle of 45°, with the top of the root just at soil level. Mound soil up to the base of the shoots to keep the bark moist and supple at the point where the scion is to be inserted. Standard rootstocks must be grown on to about 6–7ft (2–2.2m), and any buds rubbed off before they develop to create a straight, bare stem.

When to bud-graft

Budding should be carried out from mid- to late summer, preferably in cool, showery weather, when the air is not too dry. If the weather is very dry in the months that precede budding, water the rootstocks regularly and thoroughly. This ensures a free flow of sap that prevents the wood from drying out, so that it is possible to lift the bark from the wood without bruising the wood underneath. Speed is also important to prevent the wood of both bud and rootstock from drying out before they have been grafted together.

A budding knife, with a single, specially formed blade and a sharp, tapered end (see "Garden knives," p.549), may be used, but an ordinary horticultural knife is also suitable. Any knife used for budding must be kept scrupulously clean and sharp.

Selecting the budwood
Prepare scions from well-ripened shoots that have well-formed, dormant growth buds in their leaf axils. These shoots are known as the budwood. Cut off the leaves and leaf stalks; alternatively, leave the stalks as handles for inserting the buds later. Place the budwood (wrapped in wet newspaper or paper towels) in a plastic bag to prevent it from drying out before it is used.

Preparing the scion
Hold a piece of budwood upside down and, from just above the base of a bud, use the budding knife to scoop out the bud together with a thin tail. This shieldlike piece of bark, about 1in (2.5cm) long, within which the growth bud is contained, is known as the scion. Remove the small sliver of pith behind the bud: if retained, it will prevent the bud from uniting with the rootstock ("taking"). It is difficult to do this without damaging the bud if the shield has been cut too deeply from the shoot. The base of the bud should then be visible as a small, circular growth.

Preparing the rootstock
For a bush rose, clear the soil from the rootstock neck, take off the thorns, and wipe the neck clean. With the budding knife blade, make a T-shaped cut in the neck, penetrating the bark without cutting into the wood, since this causes damage.

Grafting the bud onto the rootstock
Carefully peel back the cut bark of the rootstock with the blunt side of the knife blade, taking care not to tear the bark or the wood beneath. Gently push the scion into position in the T so that the bud faces upward. Trim off any of the tail that may still be visible and, if necessary, the leaf stalk. Use damp raffia, knotted well

clear of the bud, or a special rubber binding tie to hold the bud securely in place and keep the flaps of bark tightly closed to avoid moisture loss. The rubber tie is easily pinned in place and does not inhibit the growth of the bud, because it soon rots away. Inserting two scions opposite one another on the rootstock is sometimes recommended to produce balanced shoot growth more rapidly. This is seldom practiced commercially, except on standard roses.

Cutting back the rootstock
If the scion takes successfully, the bud will quickly swell and will then produce a shoot, generally by the following spring. Once the shoot develops, cut off the growth of the rootstock above the scion. If the shoot needs support, stake it; this is not usually necessary, however.

Bud-grafting a standard rose
Budding onto a standard rootstock is performed near the top of the stem at the desired height, usually about 3½–4ft (1.1–1.2m); weeping standards are usually budded a little higher, at about 5ft (1.5m). Insert two or three buds around the stem to achieve an evenly balanced head. If using *Rosa canina* rootstocks, insert the buds into equally spaced lateral growths, close to the main stem. It is more usual to place three buds around the main stem of *R. rugosa* stock, staggered vertically.

Layering roses

Any rose that possesses shoots that are long and flexible enough to be bent over and pegged into the ground may be successfully propagated by simple layering.

In late summer after flowering, choose a shoot of healthy, mature wood, then trim some of the leaves to create a clear length of stem. Work some compost or peat into the soil where the shoot is to be layered, then peg the shoot down into the prepared ground to encourage it to root. The next spring, separate the rooted layer from the parent by cutting the shoot just behind the roots, and plant it out into its destined position to grow on.

Ramblers and climbing roses are ideal for layering, although if they are planted in narrow beds along the base of a wall there may not be a large enough area of exposed soil to peg down the shoots, particularly if other plants are growing around the base of the rose. Many shrub roses, such as Damask, Centifolia, Bourbon, and most Alba and species roses, are suitable for layering,

HOW TO LAYER ROSES

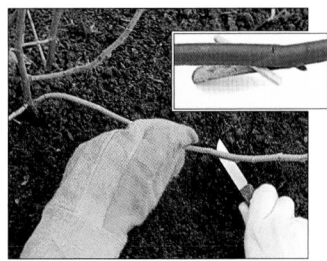

1 *Make a 1in (2.5cm) slit on the lower side of a long, mature, but flexible shoot. Dust the cut with hormone rooting powder, and then wedge it open with a twig or matchstick (see inset).*

2 *Position the shoot in a small depression in prepared soil, then peg it down firmly with a wire hoop. Cover it with soil, firm, and tie in the tip of the layered shoot to a short stake.*

because they have a lax growth habit and are likely to have more exposed soil around the base into which the selected shoots may be inserted.

Modern shrub roses, such as 'Chinatown', which are in fact very tall-growing Floribunda roses, have fairly stiff shoots, so train these shoots horizontally while still young and flexible to prepare for layering. Cultivars of groundcover roses lend themselves to this method of propagation. The shoots of some, such as 'Pheasant' or 'Grouse' or 'Nozomi' root naturally into the soil; simply separate them from the parent and plant them out.

The modern Hybrid Tea and other roses found in the majority of gardens are almost without exception too stiff and upright in their habit of growth for successful layering; they should be increased by grafting or taking cuttings. Only a few cultivars that are lax, wide-spreading growers, such as 'Europeana', are easily increased by layering.

Propagation by division

If a rose is growing on its own roots, taking rooted suckers and planting them out is an easy method of propagation. Most roses from nurseries are grafted onto rootstocks, so suckers will be from the stock and not the cultivar budded onto it.

Some species grown from seed, and some roses grown from cuttings, sucker naturally. In the dormant period, detach the rooted suckers or shoots from the parent and plant them out, either in a nursery bed or into permanent positions. Deep planting of budded shrub roses sometimes stimulates the cultivar shoots to produce roots (in effect, a form of layering). Treat such rooted shoots as rooted suckers.

Roses that sucker freely, such as the cultivars of *Rosa pimpinellifolia*, *R. rugosa*, and some Gallica roses, are readily propagated in this way.

PROPAGATING ROSES BY DIVISION

1 *In late fall or early spring, select a well-developed sucker. Scrape away the soil to expose its base. Sever it from the rootstock, with as many roots as possible.*

2 *Prepare a hole, wide and deep enough for the roots. Plant the sucker immediately, then water and firm the soil (see inset). Trim shoots to 9–12in (23–30cm).*

RAISING ROSES FROM SEED

1 *Slit open a ripe hip (see inset), taken from the parent plant, with a clean, sharp knife. Take out individual seeds carefully with the back of the knife blade.*

2 *Place the seeds in a plastic bag of moist soil mix or peat, then keep it for 2–3 days at room temperature. Then put it in a refrigerator for 3–4 weeks.*

3 *Sow the seeds singly onto the surface of a sandy medium (1 part sand:1 part peat). Cover with grit, label, and put in a cold frame or other protected spot.*

4 *When the seedlings have their first pairs of true leaves, prick them out singly into 2in (5cm) pots filled with soil-based potting mix.*

Propagating roses from seed

Species roses, unlike cultivars, are self-fertile and may be raised from seed in the same way as other shrubs. Although seeds are not generally available from commercial sources, it is easy to extract them from mature roses in the garden. Hybrid roses do not breed true to type from seed, so they are usually propagated by bud-grafting (see p.164).

Extracting and sowing seed

In the fall, when the rose hips are swollen and ripe, extract the seeds and stratify them before sowing. Stratification, which is the simulation of natural temperature changes to induce the seeds to germinate evenly, is considered necessary for all seed of species roses.

Sow the rose seeds into seed trays, packs, or individual pots, which should be at least 3in (8cm) deep. If using a seed tray, place the seeds on the medium about 2in (5cm) apart, and cover them to their own depth with sand or grit. Then leave the tray or pack in a cold frame to protect it from mice and other animals. The seeds may take up to a year to germinate. Prick out the seedlings into individual containers as soon as the first true rose leaves have formed; the first pair (the seed leaves) are oval, unlike typical rose leaves. Care is needed in handling the seedlings, since they are very fragile at this stage in their development.

Grow on the young seedlings in the cold frame until they have become established in their pots. Then harden them off by moving them out of the cold frame during the day. Once acclimatized, the seedlings may be kept in the open. Pot them on as necessary until they are large enough to be planted out.

Hybridizing

New rose cultivars are created by hybridizing, a process by which one cultivar or species is cross-pollinated with another and the new seed sown and grown on. The aim is to create a new rose that inherits the best characteristics of both parents.

Selecting the parents

Most roses are of mixed ancestry, so it is impossible to predict the results of hybridization, and the chances of producing a quality cultivar with distinct characteristics are small. Knowledge of the parent roses' genetic characteristics, in particular

their chromosomal number and structure, is important in breeding.

The chromosomes are the parts of plant cells that control the inheritance of characteristics through the genes. Roses may have different chromosome numbers, although the total number per cell in each case is always a multiple of seven. Most of the species roses have 14 (diploid),

28 (tetraploid), 42 (hexaploid), or 56 (octoploid) chromosome numbers. When two roses have been cross-pollinated, equivalent chromosomes from the parents arrange themselves in pairs, which then join and count as one in the chromosome number of the new cultivar. Most garden roses are tetraploids, and two tetraploids brought together in this

HOW TO HYBRIDIZE ROSES
PREPARING THE SEED PARENT

1 *Select an unblemished bloom (here 'Sun Flare') that has not fully unfolded its petals and should therefore not yet have been pollinated.*

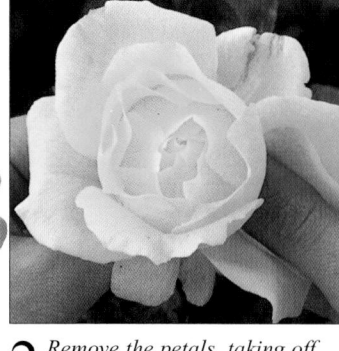

2 *Remove the petals, taking off the outer ones first. Work gradually toward the center, taking care not to damage the stigmas as they become exposed.*

3 *Using tweezers or a small pair of scissors, remove the stamens around the stigmas and all fragments of stamens or petals.*

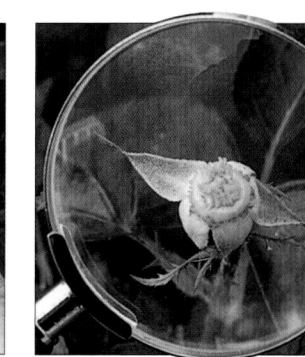

4 *Use a magnifying glass to inspect the rose and make sure that no fragments remain. If left, they may decay and allow rot fungi to enter the rose hip.*

5 *Make a paper cone, twisting its point firmly closed (see inset). Holding back the sepals, cover the flower with the cone, and tie securely around the stem.*

ALTERNATIVE STEP
Place a clean, dry plastic bag over the flower, then secure it with a firm tie. The flower is thus protected from pollinating insects.

fusion produce another tetraploid rose. A diploid (14) crossed with a tetraploid (28), however, results in 7 + 14 chromosomes, or a total of 21 (triploid) in the new rose. Since this is not an even number, there are seven chromosomes left without comparable chromosomes with which to pair. Triploids are often sterile and of little or no use in breeding.

Where the chromosome count is known, it is given in the most recent edition of *Modern Roses* (published by the American Rose Society on behalf of the International Registration Authority for Roses). This also gives detailed pedigrees of many roses.

Heredity is not the only factor influencing the selection of parent plants. Some hybrid roses make good pollen (male) parents, but poor seed (female) parents, and vice versa. Some are completely infertile, and others almost so. In a rose with a very large number of petals, such as a Centifolia, a proportion of these may have taken the place of the stamens, so that little pollen is available for hybridizing. Crossing a nonremontant rose with a remontant one may be a problem if remontancy is one of the desired characteristics, since the first generation from such a cross is always nonremontant. At least one more cross is needed before remontancy reappears in the offspring.

This is a simplification of a very complex subject, and there is a good deal of chance involved in rose breeding. However scientific an approach is taken, the result is still somewhat unpredictable. As a general principle, choose the healthiest cultivars available as parents and start with what is perhaps the easiest cross of all, that between two different cultivars of Floribunda roses.

Controlling the growing environment

Except in a frost-free climate, use potgrown roses in a greenhouse, since this allows greater control of temperature, humidity, insect pests, and diseases and gives the hips a better chance of ripening properly. Precise record-keeping is essential: after crosses have been made, carefully identify all the flower stems with a dated label on which is written the names of both parent plants, giving the seed parent first, for example 'Europeana' x 'Showbiz'.

Preparing the seed parent

First select a bloom of the rose you have chosen for the seed parent, at the stage when it is starting to unfold but before insects could have reached the stamens in the center and contaminated them with alien pollen. Carefully remove the petals and the stamens (a process called emasculation), and make sure that no tissue is left that could later lead to rot in the hip. Tie a paper cone or plastic bag over the emasculated flower, then leave it for one or two days to allow the stigmas to mature.

Preparing the pollen parent

Cut the flower that is to be the pollen parent, which should be at about the same stage as the seed parent. Stand the pollen parent in a vase of water and protect it from insects until the anthers release tiny orange pollen grains, usually on the day after being cut. The stigmas of the seed parent should begin to exude a sticky secretion, indicating that they are ready to receive the pollen. Pull off the petals from the pollen parent, leaving the anthers intact.

Pollinating the seed parent

Remove the protective covers and brush the stamens of the pollen parent against the stigmas of the seed parent; their sticky secretion helps the pollen adhere to the stigmas. Replace the cover on the pollinated flower, then label the stem.

An alternative method is to cut off the pollen parent's anthers, place them in a small, clean container (such as a plastic pillbox labeled with the name of the rose), and store it in cool, dry conditions until the released pollen grains are visible in the box. Using a fine brush, dust pollen from the box onto the stigmas of the seed parent. If carrying out more than one cross with different roses, make sure that the brush has been thoroughly cleaned between each operation, preferably with rubbing (isopropyl) alcohol.

If the cross has not taken successfully, the newly forming hip will shrivel quickly. If it has been successful, the sepals will begin to lift and the hip to swell; once this is evident, remove the protective cone or bag to allow the hip to grow.

The hip will continue to swell; it normally takes about two and a half months to ripen, depending on the climate. As it ripens, the hip changes color from green to red, to yellow, or possibly maroon, depending on the individual rose.

Harvesting and sowing

Remove the ripened hip from the plant and carefully extract the seeds. Sow and raise the seed (see "Extracting and sowing seed," p.166). Seed resulting from hybridization, however, may be sown fresh without a stratification period.

Selection

The seedlings are likely to flower in the first year – often within a few weeks of germination in a greenhouse – but it is only in the second year that the blooms will be more or less typical of the new hybrid and it is possible to judge whether it should be kept and developed or discarded.

Promising new seedlings can be budded onto rootstocks (see "Budgrafting," p.164) when they have stems of sufficient thickness, that is about ¼in (5mm). Even experienced hybridizers, however, find this stage challenging, because it is often not easy to detect faults until a selection has been grown in trials for several years.

PREPARING THE POLLEN PARENT

6 *Select an unblemished bloom that is not yet fully open (here 'Elina'). Cut the stem of the flower at an angle just above a bud.*

7 *Place the chosen flower in water and keep it indoors, free from insects, until it opens fully (usually overnight).*

8 *When the flower is open and the anthers split, revealing the pollen, gently remove all the petals.*

9 *The exposed anthers are now ready to release their tiny pollen grains.*

POLLINATING THE SEED PARENT

10 *Uncover the seed parent, then brush the anthers of the pollinator across its stigmas. The pollen grains will adhere to the sticky stigmas of the seed parent.*

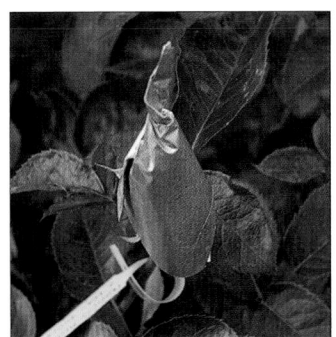

11 *Replace the protective cone over the seed parent, and tie securely. Label the rose with the names of the seed parent and pollen parent, then allow it to ripen.*

CHAPTER

6

PERENNIALS

WITH FLOWERS IN every color of the rainbow, a breathtaking range of shapes and textures, and often fine scents, perennials richly deserve their popularity. Their diversity makes them suitable for most gardens, while their reliability makes them a lasting source of pleasure. For many people, a traditional herbaceous border is the epitome of garden beauty, but perennials can be equally effective in mixed borders, interplanted with shrubs, annuals, bulbs, and vegetables, or grown in containers or as groundcover. Foliage ranges from lacy fern fronds to the straplike leaves of crocosmias; and there are flowers to suit all tastes, from delicate *Gypsophila* to sumptuous peonies. Some, like many sedums, are followed by pretty seedheads. Against a more static background of woody plants, perennials provide an almost unlimited, changing planting palette.

Designing with perennials

ALTHOUGH botanically speaking these plants should be referred to as herbaceous perennials, they are usually known as just "perennials." "Herbaceous" explains the fact that the part above ground dies down each year, while "perennial" refers to the fact that the root system lives for three or more years. A few perennials, such as *Helleborus foetidus*, are evergreen and so have a valuable winter presence.

Most perennials will flower, set seed, and then die back to ground level by autumn, going dormant for the winter season. Some retain a woody base, such as *Achillea filipendulina*, or fleshy shoots, such as *Sedum telephium*, while others disappear completely underground. Some perennials, such as *Doronicum orientale*, go completely dormant during the heat of summer, instead of during the cold of winter. Most perennials flower during the warm months, though some, such as *Iris unguicularis*, enliven the garden in winter, while *Helleborus orientalis* and *Pulmonaria* brighten the scene in early spring.

Choosing perennials

More than any other group of plants, perennials have an immense variety of shape, form, color, texture, and scent. Mostly valued for their flowers, many also have attractive foliage – from ribbed, unfurling hosta leaves, or swordlike straps of iris, to transparent tracery of fennel (*Foeniculum*

vulgare). Particularly in a small garden, some perennials should have ornamental leaves, to extend the season of interest – the foliage usually outlasting the flowers.

Perennials range in height from the *Acaena* at just 2in (5cm) tall to the statuesque *Helianthus salicifolius*, whose feathery stems reach 8ft (2.5m) or more. Low-growing perennials are ideal for the front of borders or in between shrubs, while tall, plants belong at the back of a border to give height and structure to the planting design. Perennials with an attractive structure, such as the African blue lily (*Agapanthus*) or some grasses such as *Chionochloa rubra* and *Carex comans* 'Frosted Curls', are good specimen plants in a border or container.

Some perennials, such as many carnations and pinks (*Dianthus*) and highly perfumed lily-of-the-valley (*Convallaria majalis*), are worth growing for their fragrance alone. Carnations and pinks are ideal for raised beds or windowboxes, while ground-covering lily-of-the-valley thrives in shady woodlands. Other perennials, such as *Sedum spectabile* and many of the daisy and carrot family, such as asters and *Angelica*, bear flowers that attract beneficial insects such as bees and butterflies.

It is also possible to prolong the season of interest into autumn and winter by selecting plants with unusual seedheads and winter silhouettes. Fennels, *Iris sibirica*, and *Achillea* are a few examples of flowers that will surprise you at a time of

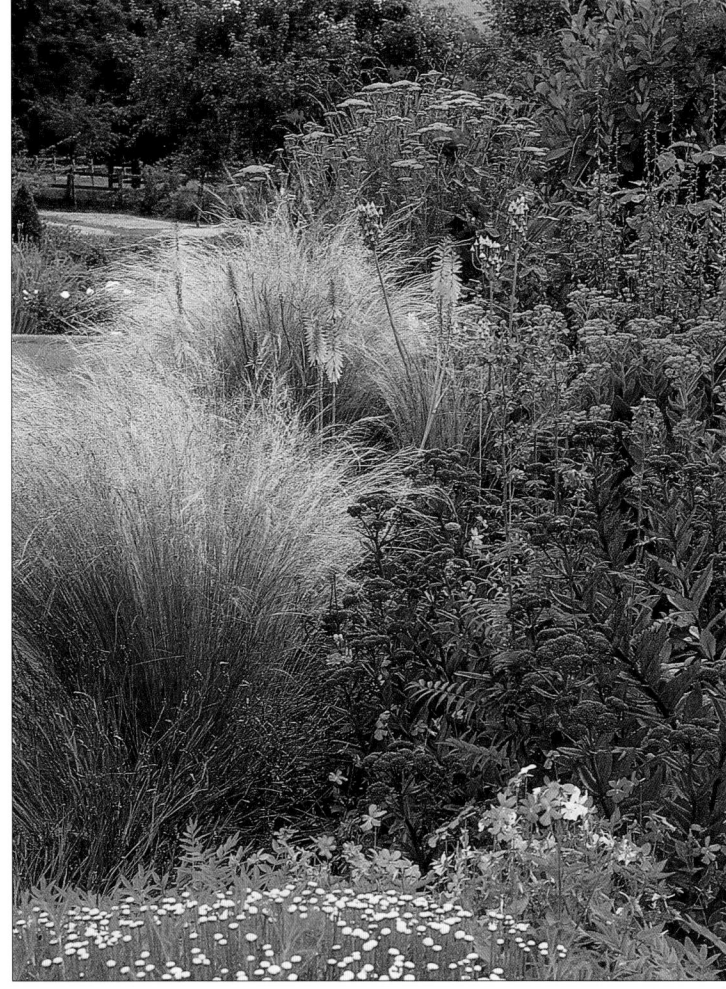

PERENNIAL BORDER
The addition of the elegant ornamental grasses and Achillea *'Terracotta' gives this planting a contemporary feel that fits well with the traditional, hot-colored flowers, such as* Crocosmia *and the spearlike* Kniphofia.

FORMAL BORDERS
In this formal garden, a traditional grass path divides a pair of wide, straight borders. The plants are arranged by height, with low plants such as Sedum spectabile *at the front so that all can be clearly seen. While the planting in each border is not a rigid mirror-image of the other, a number of plants are repeated on both sides to provide a balanced, harmonious effect.*

year when you least expect it. Birds will gain twofold from these seedheads: they enjoy eating the seeds, and benefit from the insects that overwinter in the cavities created by hollow stems and seedheads.

As with all plants, when choosing perennials for a planting plan, make sure that they are appropriate for the growing conditions, such as soil, microclimate, and exposure of the bed or border. Given the correct environment, plants are much more likely to flourish and require less maintenance than those struggling in an unsuitable position (see also "Site and exposure," p.183).

Herbaceous and mixed borders

Perennials are traditionally used in borders: these are long, rectangular beds, fronted by lawn or a path and backed by a hedge or wall, either as a single border or as double facing borders. Popularized in the late 19th century, herbaceous borders were planted only with perennials, in groups or drifts, the shortest plants at the front, grading up with lupines, phlox, and the like, to the taller ones such as delphiniums at the rear. Their season of interest was restricted to the summer months, because in many gardens the borders were one of many areas of interest, each with a different seasonal highlight. As gardens reduced in size during the 20th century and space became more restricted, the flowering season and plant range of borders were forced to extend. As a result, mixed borders have become increasingly popular; they now contain a variety of plants including bedding plants, shrubs, climbers, and even small flowering trees as well as perennials. The

advantage of a mixed border is that it can be less labor-intensive than a herbaceous one, because larger areas may be filled with less-demanding woody plants (see "Designing beds and borders," p.172)

A successful border requires regular maintenance. Careful staking is needed, since the perennials may grow long and lanky as they compete for the somewhat reduced light levels caused by either the close planting or the presence of a wall or hedge in the background. Water and nutrient levels also need monitoring regularly in any such dense planting plan.

Additional chores generated by a mixed border involve bedding out early bulbs and annuals, followed by dahlias, cannas, and other tender plants, in order to extend the length of interest into early spring and autumn. Plants also need to be deadheaded and kept neat over the longer flowering period.

Island beds

Surrounded by lawn or paving, island beds can be seen and accessed from all sides, so the planting design should

be effective from all viewpoints. As with borders, beds that are dedicated solely to herbaceous plants are at their most impressive in summer. For a more enduring display, interplant the perennials with a variety of bulbs and perhaps one or two shrubs.

Because access to the center of the bed may be difficult, plants should be sturdy, dwarf, or compact to reduce the need for staking, although generally there will be less need for support as higher light levels and better air circulation promote sturdier plant growth there than within the borders.

Geometrical, round, square, or rectangular island beds suit a formal setting; in an informal garden or one with gently undulating ground, loosely curved island beds are more appropriate. Avoid intricate shapes and tight curves, since they are awkward to maintain and may detract from the planting itself. To gain space, small gardens can be filled with island beds.

Raised island beds can provide improved growing conditions for demanding perennials, tougher alpines, and Mediterranean plants in gardens where the soil is poor or waterlogged. The increased bed height also enables plants to be tended with minimal stooping – which is an important factor for less able or elderly gardeners.

RAISED PLANTING
Easily accessible beds such as this raised wooden one are not only at a convenient height for watering, deadheading, and other maintenance but can also be used to provide different soil conditions from those in the rest of the garden. Acidic soil-loving plants, for example, can be grown or those that prefer very well-drained soil.

MIXED BORDERS
Colorful tulips provide spring interest, while shrubs such as a golden-leaved Spiraea japonica *'Goldflame' and the sculptural mass of* Euphorbia characias *subsp.* wulfenii *add color and form from spring to autumn, extending the period of interest beyond the summer burst of color offered by the* Geranium *species and other perennials.*

CONTRASTING SHAPES
The pointed swords of red Crocosmia *here create a strong vertical accent behind the rounded* Ligularia *leaves in this large border.*

Designing beds and borders

When designing a planting plan, the principles are broadly similar whether planning a herbaceous or mixed border or an island bed. Considerations of height, mass, scale, texture, sequential interest, form, and color are all variable factors that influence the design. Planting is a very individual issue.

Everybody has favorite plants and colors as well as set ideas as to which plants look good together.

Imagination and personal taste will inevitably influence your planting plans, but there are a few basic guidelines to follow.

General principles
Herbaceous borders may be designed and planted in various styles so that they set or strengthen the character and tone of the garden. Crisply edged, straight-lined borders backed by well-trimmed hedges create a dominant structure, which will be attractive in winter but can be softened by planting during summer. Irregularly shaped island beds, weaving their ways through the garden, are much more relaxed but will do little for the garden during winter. Self-contained, stately plants such as lupines, delphiniums, and veronicas, arranged according to a restricted color combination and planted in a rhythmical pattern look somewhat formal. For a more relaxed approach, introduce plants with a loose, less ordered habit, such as baby's breath (*Gypsophila*) and lady's mantle (*Alchemilla mollis*), and then add key feature plants such as *Sedum* 'Herbstfreude' at random rather than at strict intervals.

Before starting a planting plan, prepare a comprehensive list of plants you want to use. This should contain any existing plants you would like to keep, as well as a thoroughly researched list of others that will cover all seasons and are well suited to your garden. It may be easier to compile this list with the help of a good local nursery catalog, because you will know where to obtain the plants.

Allow sufficient room for the plants to spread as they mature, taking account of the different rates at which they develop. Slow-growing plants can be surrounded by shade-tolerant groundcover (see PERENNIAL GROUNDCOVERS, p.178) to fill the area while waiting for the main plant to reach its desired size. Start by placing the key plants, such as shrubs, roses, and any imposing perennials and grasses as well as the important feature plants, which you may wish to repeat at regular intervals to create a symmetric rhythm to the border. Position the smaller plants last. Set out the plants according to your planting design and make any adjustments at this stage – before planting. However carefully the design has been planned, minor

MASSED FORM AND COLOR
Large drifts of perennials and grasses create a generous sense of space within a garden. The vertical spires distract the eye from the horizontal bands of color created by the wide-scale plantings. Even after flowering is over, such a display will look effective until the flowerheads are cut off in late winter.

HARMONIZING TEXTURES
A mixture of moisture-loving plants with airy and feathery flowers, such as Astilbe, Filipendula palmata, *and tall yellow* Ligularia stenocephala *forms a satisfying pattern of textures. The fluffy outline of the* Filipendula *flower heads successfully breaks up the general mass of vertical heads on the other plants.*

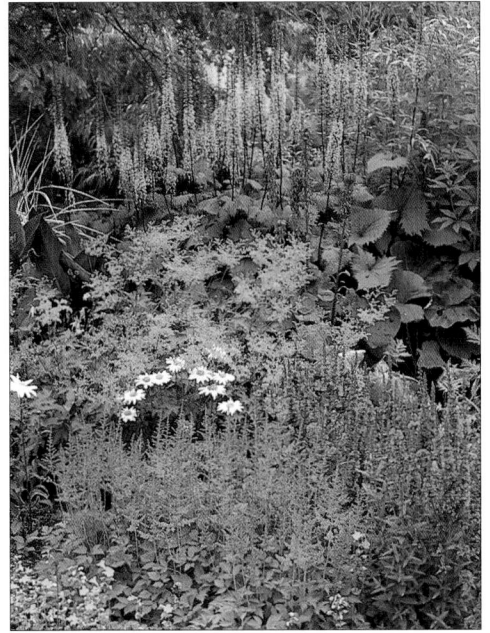

CONTRASTING FORMS
This grouping of foliage plants gives prominence to differences in form and texture. The huge, jagged leaves of Rheum palmatum *at the rear contrasts with the heart-shaped leaves of* Ligularia dentata *and the softly arching straps of an ornamental grass. The* Rodgersia *adds a distinct color and texture accent with its large, ribbed, dark red foliage.*

adjustments are inevitable, since no two gardens are alike, and plants react differently, however well you may know them.

Scale of planting

Although the size of beds and borders is usually dictated by the surrounding space, the scale of planting should take account of the scale of the garden and adjacent buildings.

The extent of a border or bed will vary but, as a rough guide, the larger the garden setting, the more generous the border or bed can be. Two large beds are better than three or four little ones; they will enhance the

feeling of space and will prevent the garden from looking too disjointed.

A border should be no less than 5ft (1.5m) deep, and preferably 10ft–15ft (3–5m), depending on a path's length and width. This will give a good planting width and create a layered, well-balanced effect.

Large borders, seen from a great distance and flanked by a wide path, should be planted with bold groups of plants to create sufficient visual impact. The smaller the viewing distance, the smaller the planting scale should be, so that the border remains interesting as you walk along it (see also "Planting in groups," right).

Varying plant height

Traditionally, tall plants are placed at the back of a front-facing border, grading down the heights as they approach the front to create a tiered effect in which no flowering plant is hidden behind another. In an island bed, the tallest plants are placed in the center, with the smallest around the outer edge. This planting rule will create quite a formal, rigid scheme. Mystery and contrast can be added by introducing the occasional taller but "transparent" plant near the front; this will give a stronger undulation to the overall design. Particularly transparent plants such as

Verbena bonariensis or many grasses such as *Stipa gigantea* provide extra height, while allowing the eye to wander past them. Plant textural perennials, such as *Molinia caerulea* subsp. *arundinacea* 'Transparent' with its soft flower panicles, so they are close enough to touch from the edge of the bed.

As a rule, later-flowering perennials tend to be the tallest, since they have the longest growing period. This can result in late summer flowers towering over the dead flower stalks of earlier plants. To hide gaps where earlier flowerers such as Oriental poppies have vanished, plant some of the lower late flowers such as *Aster* x *pringlei* 'Monte Cassino' near the front of the bed.

Generally, the wider the bed or border, the taller the plants may be; very tall plants in narrow borders may look awkward and the angle from the tallest to the shortest, uncomfortably steep.

Planting in groups

Several plants of the same cultivar can successfully be massed together to create larger groups. Particularly toward the rear of a border, or the center of a bed, large clumps of one plant will create a good impact, whereas near the front smaller clumps will increase variety and interest. Depending on the scale of the plan, always aim to plant in groups of three or more, up to a dozen or so. For a fluid, informal style, plant in odd numbers – even numbers creating a formal rigidity to a bed or border.

Groups of varying sizes should also be introduced. If in doubt, create an "outline" of the plants – using

ISLAND BED
A flower bed often looks best when shaped to reflect the contours of its surroundings. It should also have most of the tallest plants in the middle of the bed and the lowest ones at the edge. Here eye-catching height is provided by Astilbe, Lobelia, *and* Filipendula, *which are planted with lower-growing variegated Solomon's seal (*Polygonatum*), *Blechnum, and hellebores among other perennials.*

bamboo stakes, brooms, or other more bulky props – to see what would fit the space.

Small-leaved perennials are more impressive when planted in large groups: small-leaved London pride (*Saxifraga* x *urbium*), for example, is best planted in groups of seven or more, while large-leaved *Bergenia* species and hybrids look effective in threes. The huge *Gunnera manicata*, however, is striking enough to be planted singly (see "Specimen planting," p.177).

Plants that have strong outlines, such as *Kniphofia caulescens* with its upright, spearlike flowers, are more dramatic when planted in smaller groups than those of less distinct forms such as the loose-flowered *Geranium phaeum*.

Forms and outlines

Perennials have widely differing forms and silhouettes, including upright, rounded, arching as well as horizontally spreading outlines. Juxtapose groups of plants with contrasting forms to create a series of vignettes, which build up within a bed or border. The slim spikes of delphiniums or *Eremurus*, for example, act like giant, colorful exclamation marks, when seen against the foaming, cloudlike cushions of *Gypsophila paniculata* or *Crambe cordifolia*. Contrast is introduced when the vertical lines of irises and other strap-leaved plants contrast with the horizontal planes of the flower heads of *Achillea* 'Moonshine' or *Sedum telephium* 'Matrona'.

Some plants are two tiered and have their own contrasting form: a fine example is *Rheum palmatum* 'Atrosanguineum', which makes a lower layer of reddish purple leaves 3ft (1m) tall, over which tower smoky pink plumes of tiny flowers.

Understanding plant textures

Although flowers, and to a lesser extent stems, contribute to the overall texture of a planting plan, it is

LONG-LASTING DISPLAY
The rich brown seedheads of Sedum spectabile *may be left uncut to provide interest in late autumn and winter long after the succulent leaves have died back.*

foliage that provides the strongest impact, because it is present for a much longer period of time during the year. Even when seen from a distance, it can create striking contrasts and subtle harmonies. The dainty leaves of *Coreopsis verticillata* or the filigree fronds of fennel (*Foeniculum vulgare*) are very delicate, whereas large, individual leaves such as those of *Hosta sieboldiana* var. *elegans* create a bold, textural effect.

Grasses, particularly, can add a wide range of textural variety to a garden. The narrow flowering stems and strap-shaped leaves tend to be very supple yet strong, waving in the wind, bringing flowing movement into a garden as well as a gentle rustling sound of the foliage. Many, such as *Miscanthus sinensis* 'Malepartus' or *Calamagrostis* x *acutiflora* 'Karl Foerster', are so strong that their dried flower stems will remain standing well into autumn, or even throughout winter.

Texture is also affected by a leaf's surface, whether it is the matte, waxy foliage of *Sedum spectabile*, the glossy, leathery leaves of *Bergenia purpurascens*, or the woolly texture of *Lychnis coronaria*. It is important to understand how a leaf's texture will affect your planting plan: glossy surfaces, for example, reflect light, adding sparkle on a sunny day, while matte ones absorb light, creating a more somber effect.

As with form, juxtaposing groups of plants with contrasting textures increases interest; for example, the downy, pleated leaves of lady's mantle (*Alchemilla mollis*) contrast well with the spiny stems and jagged foliage of sea holly (*Eryngium*). Groundcover perennials such as *Geranium* species and cultivars and *Ajuga reptans* are especially useful to grow as a low foil for other plants and to fill a gap in a planting plan, and thus complete the textural tapestry (see also PERENNIAL GROUND COVERS, p.178).

AN "ALL-GREEN" PLANTING
A monochromatic garden composed primarily of shades of green provides a restful contrast to more colorful areas of a garden. To avoid boredom, choose plants with contrasting textures, and include bits of color.

Color blends and contrasts

Choosing colors is a very personal affair. Everyone has preferences as well as dislikes. It is important to select hues that you feel comfortable with, regardless of their current fashion status or your best friend's opinion. A restricted color palette can be wonderful but may be hard to adhere to in a small garden.

For the widest plant choice, choose an extensive range of colors that will either appear at the same time or follow in a seasonal succession. If you are concerned about creating too dramatic clashes, try using all but one of the colors. The most awkward ones to combine are oranges and pinks. Using one or other with yellows, violets, blues, and reds can look very attractive. Alternatively, you could choose complementary colors – those opposite each other in the color wheel – such as oranges and blues, yellows and violets, or greens and reds. Another possibility is to use adjacent hues,

combining all the hot colors such as yellows, oranges, and reds, or the cool pinks, blues, purples, and mauves. Such combinations were frequently used by the doyenne of color schemes, Gertrude Jekyll.

In a monochrome planting design, foliage plays as important a role as flowers. Such a one-color design, however, not only restricts the plant range but can also prove visually boring unless there is considerable contrast and variety within the design. When creating a white garden, for example, it is important to include different types of white, such as cream, pinkish white, and blue-white as well as shades of green. Introducing contrasting leaf tones, shapes, and textures help to bring tension to a design. Thus, in a white garden, use silver, gray, and glaucous leaves as well as light, mid-, and dark green ones.

Unusually tinted foliage plants will emphasize a color scheme, particularly in a mixed border, where golden, silver-, or red-leaved shrubs can help to enhance flowers. They should be used as small accents and not become the main features.

Color intensities can also play an important part in garden design. Light colors such as white, pale pink, and pale yellow reflect higher levels of light than do darker shades – blue, red, and violet – and will be seen from farther away. They also start shimmering at dusk when light levels have dropped – causing some flowers seemingly to disappear, while others develop an almost luminous character. These luminous plants can be used near an area where you may sit in the evenings. Light colors also help enliven dark corners or can be used to draw attention to a focal point. Dark colors, on the other hand, are better used in the foreground, nearest the viewpoint.

Seasonal interest

Although in a mixed border it is possible to plan a succession of color schemes that change with the course of the seasons, to do so involves coordinating the timing of each plant's display, so that one feature smoothly follows another and fading flowers pass unnoticed, eclipsed by nearby plants coming into bloom. A plan that manages to maintain a succession of interest requires forethought, yet mistakes are easily corrected by re-siting the offenders in spring or autumn.

The spring season may be announced as early as midwinter, when the first snowdrops (*Galanthus*) and winter aconites (*Eranthis hyemalis*) reveal their petals, soon followed by hellebores. Some winter-flowering shrubs and climbers, such as wintersweet (*Chimonanthus praecox*) and honeysuckle (*Lonicera x purpusii*) at the rear of mixed borders will help increase the early show. Later in the season such woody plants can support not-too-vigorous herbaceous climbers such as the flame creeper (*Tropaeolum speciosum*) or *Clematis viticella* hybrids. In late winter and early spring, yellow is predominant, from primroses (*Primula vulgaris*), daffodils, and *Doronicum*, and pale blue, from irises and *Pulmonaria*, interspersed with grape hyacinths (*Muscari*). With tulips, spring comes to an end.

By early summer, most of the bulbs have finished their performance, and the real season for perennials starts. There are showstoppers such as Oriental poppies, with their short-lived but showy flowers, and the wonderfully baroque peonies as well as dainty, long-spurred *Aquilegia chrysantha* and the numerous hardy

RIMED IN FROST
By retaining attractive seedheads, such as those of Cynara *and* roses *(here) and other eye-catching plants, the season of interest in the garden can be extended well into winter. After a heavy frost, this border, with its columnar conifers and yew hedge in the foreground, is transformed into a glimmering wonderland.*

geraniums. Once there is little risk of frost, the remainder of the tender plants will gradually vie for attention, including dahlias, argyranthemums, osteospermums, and cannas. These all flower over a long period and are invaluable for providing color until the first frosts arrive in autumn. There are hundreds of plants to choose from, including lupines, old-fashioned scabious, fluffy meadow rue (*Thalictrum*), strongly scented phlox, red-hot pokers (*Kniphofia*), and numerous daisy family members such as fleabanes (*Erigeron*), *Helenium*, coneflowers (*Echinacea purpurea*), sunflowers (*Helianthus*), *Rudbeckia*, chrysanthemums, and

asters – the last two being vital for autumn flowers.

It is sometimes possible to extend the effect of a particular plant or group by growing next to it a plant that gives a similar impression. The deep blue flower spikes of *Delphinium* 'Blue Nile', for example, could be followed by those of *Aconitum carmichaelii*, and if the latter is planted in front the yellowing delphinium foliage will be hidden. Plant perennials such as lupines (*Lupinus*) that die back early in front of plants, such as *Physostegia* that develop later in the season, to hide awkward gaps or fading leaves.

In mixed borders, bulbs are particularly useful for providing color in late winter and spring when perennials are starting into growth. Similarly, the new growth of the latter masks the fading foliage of the bulbs once their flowers have finished. For example, the black purple leaves of the evergreen *Ophiopogon planiscapus* 'Nigrescens', the soft gray blue foliage of *Acaena saccaticupula* 'Blue Haze', or the copper variants of *A. microphylla* make excellent foils for white snowdrops (*Galanthus*) and continue to provide interest after the snowdrops are past their best. Daffodils and tulips, planted toward the rear of a border, will have finished flowering by the time perennials come into growth, and so hide the dying foliage.

Particularly in small gardens, shrubs are invaluable to maintain the shape and structure of the design in

NATURALISTIC PLANTING
The bronze inflorescences of reed grass Calamagrostis x acutiflora *'Karl Foerster' provide vertical interest behind a sizable, horizontal drift of* Helenium *'Moerheim Beauty' and* Hordeum jubatum. *The dark evergreen background brings the ornamental grasses and other perennials more into focus.*

late autumn and winter, as well as contributing color and texture. The inclusion of deciduous shrubs with attractive autumn foliage (such as *Cotinus coggygria* 'Royal Purple') and those with bright fruits (such as many shrub viburnums) will also help to distract attention from perennials with dying foliage.

Naturalistic planting styles

Particularly in a large area, sizable drifts of perennials look good when planted in naturalistic settings. Plants should be chosen to match the given habitat – such as woodland plants for woodland conditions, and waterside plants for boggy margins – and the planting pattern should reflect each plant's natural regeneration habits. Such planting plans should be allowed to evolve gradually. Plants that increase by self-seeding in the immediate vicinity should be placed singly, while those with spreading rootstocks, such as asters, are best planted in drifts. All soil should be covered, either by plants or with an appropriate mulch.

In creating a matrix of vegetation, a much more natural and relaxed effect is obtained, one in which plants can evolve and change. Looking after such a design becomes more an issue of vegetation management than gardening in the conventional way, since you need to control vegetation groups, occasionally reducing a species or cultivar if it is getting out of hand. Ideally such a plan is looked after by somebody who understands its aims and who knows which seedlings to leave and

MOIST WOODLAND
Where there is a permanent source of water from a pond or stream, a wide range of moisture-loving perennials such as candelabra primroses and skunk cabbage (Lysichiton) *can be grown for a prolonged spring and early summer display. The fresh green fronds on the ferns here add a luxuriant touch to this wooded setting.*

which ones are likely to become a threat. Maintenance is minimal because there is little or no need for staking or deadheading; plants are usually selected with their autumn and winter appearance in mind and are allowed to retain their seedheads. Grasses play an important part in naturalistic plantings. They bring movement and are likely to remain looking good into autumn and winter, especially when dusted with snow.

Cottage gardens

Traditional cottage gardens are a glorious mixture of herbs, roses, climbers, annuals, fruits, and vegetables as well as perennials. They are noted for their simplicity in form, maximizing the space for production, with little money invested in elaborate structures. Planting areas are intersected by narrow paths and adorned with such simple structures

as arches supporting climbers. In the past, gardeners bred plants themselves and produced enchanting perennials such as pansies (*Viola* x *wittrockiana)*, auricula primroses (*Primula auricula*), and scented pinks (*Dianthus*). Plants were exchanged or passed on to other gardeners necause there were few plant nurseries until the late 19th century. Many of these old cultivars have now been lost or have been superseded by stronger or more reliable ones.

Other typical cottage plants are irises, peonies (*Paeonia*), lupines (*Lupinus*), Madonna lilies (*Lilium candidum*), Oriental poppies, delphiniums, and phlox, while wild flowers with fragrant, double, extra-large, or unusually colored blooms, such as primroses and daisies (*Bellis perennis*), are also appropriate.

Perennials in woodland gardens

Deciduous woodland provides conditions of shelter, light shade, and organic soil suitable for many perennials. A small grove of birches (*Betula*) and other light-foliaged, deciduous trees may provide a suitable setting for a number of shade-loving plants; site the perennials where they

SPRING SHOW
Most woodland perennials, such as columbines and peonies here, flower early in the growing season, while light levels are still relatively high. Many become dormant once the trees burst into foliage, and remain so until leaf fall. In summer in a woodland garden, attention switches to foliage shape and colors such as on Bowles' golden grass (Milium effusum 'Aureum') *here.*

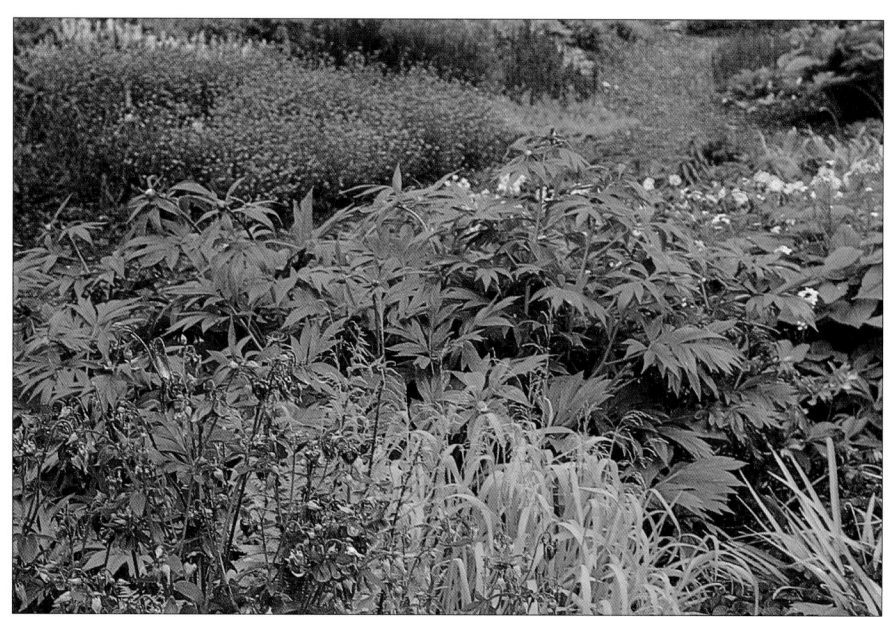

will not face too much competition from tree roots. If such roots are unavoidable, make sure the planting area is generously mulched with a medium- to low-fertility mulch, such as leaf mold, each year, to give the shallow-rooted perennials a moist rooting zone.

Woodland gardens are normally rather informal, imitating nature in their layout, structure, and planting. Therefore straight lines and sharply defined planting groups should be avoided by intermingling plant communities at the edges and scattering individual plants such as foxgloves through the area. Many ferns thrive in the low light levels of a woodland setting and add architectural interest, whether planted in bold swaths or scattered through other planting.

Some of the most enchanting perennials are the small woodland plants that usher in spring. In order to grow, they make use of the light and rain that penetrate through to the woodland floor during autumn, winter, and spring, and then lie dormant during dry, dark summer, having adapted to the low light levels and dry conditions that prevail in the summer months. For color and interest in spring, while the overhead canopy is still leafless, feature perennials such as cyclamen, snowdrops (*Galanthus*), primroses (*Primula*), wood anemones (*Anemone nemorosa*), and dogtooth violet (*Erythronium*). Combine them with woodland bulbs and shade-loving shrubs. In cool, dry woodland shade, grow groundcover perennials such as lily-of-the-valley (*Convallaria majalis*), Solomon's seal (*Polygonatum*) with its pearly white flowers, and *Pulmonaria*, some of which have attractively marked foliage.

Among the few shade-tolerant, summer-flowering perennials are *Kirengeshoma palmata*, with its waxy, soft yellow, tubular bells, and *Aster divaricatus*, which bears white, starry flowers on lax, wiry stems.

Specimen planting

In large areas of lawn or gravel, stately perennials with an architectural form or sculptural foliage, such as *Acanthus spinosus*, may be sited on their own as specimen plants to create a striking effect. In smaller gardens, a specimen perennial, surrounded by low groundcover, could be used to provide a focal point where a border projects onto a lawn or driveway, or in a corner of a garden where two borders meet. The jutting, sword-shaped leaves and arching, fiery red flower stems of *Crocosmia* 'Lucifer', for example, look spectacular rising above the frothy, lime green mass of lady's mantle (*Alchemilla mollis*) or a neatly cropped blanket of *Acaena microphylla* 'Kupferteppich'.

For year-round interest, evergreen perennials such as *Phormium tenax* and *Euphorbia characias* subsp. *wulfenii* are excellent. In sheltered areas, try *Melianthus major* with its neatly serrated, gray-green foliage. Many of the grasses will provide a long show. Especially well behaved and elegant are *Molinia caerulea* subsp. *arundinacea* 'Karl Foerster', with its slender flower spikes that arch elegantly in the rain, the tall, light panicles of *Stipa gigantea*, and the airy, silky plumes of *Miscanthus sinensis* 'Grosse Fontäne', which will be especially eye-catching through autumn and well into winter, if left uncut.

Other perennials that provide a briefer display may also make spectacular accent plants because of their form, flowers, or foliage. These range from the towering, felty stems of *Verbascum olympicum* to the massive leaves of the moisture-loving *Gunnera manicata* or the glorious, pink blooms of *Paeonia lactiflora* 'Sarah Bernhardt'. Since these are all plants that die down in winter, it may be desirable to place another feature, such as a pot-grown plant, nearby to create interest during their dormant period.

Specimen plants are best offset by a plain backdrop, such as a hedge, wall, or stretch of lawn, so that nothing detracts from their impact.

Growing perennials in containers

Perennials are as welcome in containers on a paved patio, courtyard, balcony, or roof garden as they are in open beds and borders (see also CONTAINER GARDENING, p.309). Growing them in this way also makes it possible to include plants that must be brought under cover for winter, as well as those that require a different soil type or moisture levels from the garden soil, such as the ornamental rhubarb *Rheum palmatum* 'Atrosanguineum', which does best when it has its feet moist. Pots are also ideal for plants that might otherwise invade a garden, such as variegated goutweed (*Aegopodium podagraria* 'Variegatum') or *Houttuynia cordata* 'Chameleon'.

Container-grown evergreen perennials such as *Bergenia purpurascens* and *Liriope muscari* can be on display all year round, while herbaceous perennials may be better planted with an evergreen shrub or winter-flowering bulbs such as winter aconites (*Eranthis hyemalis*), to extend the season of interest.

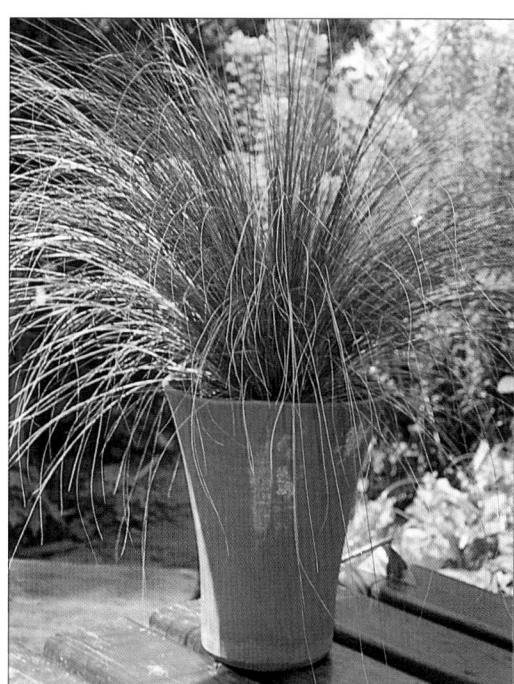

PERENNIALS IN CONTAINERS
A clump of one type of perennial in a large pot can perform the role of a specimen plant in a paved area. Those with fine flowers or foliage, for example Chionochloa rubra, left, *are particularly attractive in appropriate containers and may be left for years to increase in size.*

ACCENT PLANTING
A few well-chosen plants with particularly eye-catching texture, shape, or size of leaves or flowers, such as this mullein (Verbascum bombyciferum 'Polarsommer'), *look stunning when introduced selectively in a planting.*

Perennial groundcovers

GROUNDCOVER plantings are particularly suitable for areas of minimal maintenance, such as woodlands and shrub plantings, or on embankments, which need stabilizing with plants. It is also important in areas that would otherwise have bare soil, since groundcovers not only prevent topsoil erosion and nutrients leaching out but also reduce evaporation and weed growth.

Many groundcover perennials will cope with shady conditions, because their natural habitat is the understory in woodlands. They are therefore ideal when planted among taller perennials, shrub roses, or other shrubs, especially when such plants are young and will take several years to bulk out. The ground can be covered with some shade-tolerant, early-flowering perennials such as *Viola odorata*, *Pulmonaria* 'Sissinghurst White', or *Doronicum orientale*. These can be removed and planted elsewhere when the shade becomes too dense for healthy growth.

Plants to use

A variety of perennials can be used as groundcover. Some, such as the daylily (*Hemerocallis*) or the mousetail plant (*Arisarum proboscideum*), develop through underground tuberous growths, which form large, dense

clumps. Some of these die back quite early, so they are suitable under spreading, late perennials or deciduous shrubs and trees.

Carpeting plants produce surface runners that root where they touch the soil. Alpine strawberries, the purple-leaved *Ajuga reptans* 'Catlins Giant', or the silver-variegated *Lamium maculatum* 'Beacon Silver' are good colonizers, often covering large areas within a few years.

The most effective type of groundcover plants produce underground roots, which send up new shoots. Good examples of these are the stately *Acanthus mollis*, goosenecked *Lysimachia clethroides*, or *Euphorbia cyparissias* 'Fens Ruby' with its fine, needle-like, glaucous foliage and dark red buds in spring. Such persistent spreaders can become problematic if they are too invasive.

Some groundcover perennials are better weed suppressants than others. The most valuable establish quickly, have dense foliage that blocks out light to prevent weed germination, and retain their leaves during the dormant season. Good examples are *Bergenia cordifolia* and *B*. 'Abendglut', with its red foliage in winter, *Epimedium*, and some of the geraniums, particularly *Geranium* 'Tiny Monster' and *G. macrorrhizum* cultivars, which flower over a long period, have scented foliage and provide

LEAFY CARPET
Many perennials make excellent woodland groundcovers; they carpet the floor with dense foliage that excludes sunlight and prevents weed growth.

some autumn color. Clump-forming plants that bear low, spreading stems, such as *Euphorbia myrsinites*, also quickly and extensively cover the surrounding soil.

Mixing plants

To create a more naturalistic effect and extend the season of interest, drifts of one plant can be interspersed with key specimens of another species, flowering at a different time. A groundcover that flowers later in summer can be interplanted with bulbs: medium-height perennials can be mixed with daffodils and tulips, while low-growing ones look good interspersed with crocus and snowdrops. Low-growing, early-flowering species that are not too rampant can be planted with summer- and autumn-flowering sturdy perennials, such as *Persicaria polymorpha* or *Kirengeshoma palmata*, as well as a wide variety of ferns.

General cultivation

Particularly in areas where established trees and shrubs create competition for light and moisture, it is important to plant in early autumn, soon after leaf fall, giving the groundcover plenty of time to become established before the trees produce new growth and leaves.

Plant groundcover perennials in well-prepared soil and water them

well, especially in areas where there is considerable competition from tree roots. Additional mulching will help to keep the area weed-free, increase fertility, and retain moisture.

Most groundcover perennials need only minimum routine care (see pp.189–91). *Epimedium* foliage, however, should be cut back in late winter, enabling flowering stems to come up before the new leaves.

ORNAMENTAL GROUNDCOVERS

Hosta fortunei var. ***aureomarginata***
Plant 12–18in (30–45cm) apart.

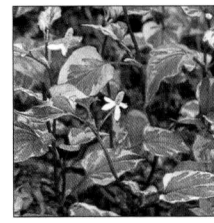

Houttuynia cordata **'Chameleon'**
Plant 12–18in (30–45cm) apart.

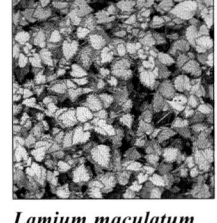

Lamium maculatum **'Beacon Silver'**
Plant 8–12in (20–30cm) apart.

Tanacetum densum
Plant 6–8in (15–20cm) apart.

Tiarella cordifolia
Plant 12in (30cm) apart.

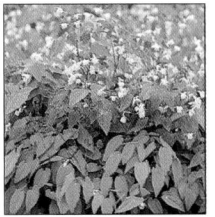

Epimedium x ***youngianum*** **'Niveum'**
Plant 12in (30cm) apart.

MORE PERENNIAL GROUNDCOVERS
Ajuga reptans
Anaphalis triplinervis
Asarum europaeum
Cornus canadensis
Duchesnea indica
Epilobium angustifolium
   var. *album*
Epimedium
Fragaria vesca
Galium odoratum
Geranium
Heuchera
Luzula sylvatica
Lysimachia clethroides
Persicaria
Prunella
Pulmonaria
Sedum cauticola, S. spathulifolium, S. spurium
Stachys
Symphytum
Tellima
Tiarella
Viola odorata, V. riviniana
   'Purpurea'

Planter's guide to perennials

EXPOSED SITES

Perennials that tolerate exposed or windy sites.

Agapanthus
Anaphalis
Anemone hupehensis
Artemisia absinthium
Centaurea dealbata, C. hypoleuca
Centranthus ruber
Eryngium variifolium
Euphorbia characias
Festuca glauca
Kniphofia caulescens
Lavatera maritima, L. thuringiaca
Limonium latifolium
Phlomis russeliana
Phormium cookianum, P. tenax
Sedum spectabile, S. telephium
Stachys byzantina
Yucca filamentosa, Y. flaccida

AIR POLLUTION

Perennials that tolerate polluted air

Aconitum napellus
Aquilegia vulgaris
Bergenia cordifolia
Dicentra eximia,
    D. formosa
Euphorbia
    amygdaloides
Geranium endressii
Helleborus niger,
    H. orientalis
Hemerocallis
Heuchera
Hosta
Iris
Lamium
Leucanthemum x superbum
Libertia grandiflora
Polemonium
Polygonatum
Pulmonaria

Rudbeckia laciniata 'Goldquelle'

Rudbeckia
Sedum spectabile,
    S. telephium
Sisyrinchium striatum
Smilacina racemosa
Symphytum
Thalictrum
Tiarella
Veronica gentianoides, V. spicata

DRY SHADE

Perennials that tolerate dry shade

Acanthus mollis
Aconitum carmichaelii, A. napellus
Anemone hupehensis, A. x hybrida
Aquilegia vulgaris
Dicentra

Digitalis grandiflora, D. lutea
Epimedium
Euphorbia amygdaloides
Geranium
Helleborus foetidus, H. orientalis
Iris foetidissima
Luzula sylvatica 'Marginata'
Ophiopogon
Saxifraga umbrosa, S. x urbium
Symphytum grandiflorum
Tellima grandiflora 'Purpurea'
Vinca minor
Viola labradorica, V. odorata

MOIST SHADE

Perennials that prefer moist shade

Astilbe simplicifolia
Astrantia major
Bergenia
Brunnera macrophylla
Convallaria majalis
Gentiana
    asclepiadea

Hemerocallis 'Marion Vaughn'

Hemerocallis
Hosta
Kirengeshoma palmata
Ligularia przewalskii
Peltiphyllum peltatum
Persicaria bistorta 'Superba'
Phlox stolonifera
Primula bulleyana, P. florindae,
    P. japonica, P. pulverulenta
Rodgersia aesculifolia, R. pinnata
Thalictrum
Trillium grandiflorum, T. sessile

WINTER INTEREST

Decorative flowers
Bergenia 'Ballawley', B. cordifolia
Doronicum
Euphorbia amygdaloides
    subsp. robbiae, E. characias
Helleborus argutifolius, H. niger
Iris unguicularis
Pulmonaria
Ranunculus ficaria

Decorative leaves
Arum italicum 'Marmoratum'
Bergenia 'Ballawley', B. cordifolia
Euphorbia amygdaloides
    subsp. robbiae, E. characias
Festuca glauca
Helleborus argutifolius
Heuchera 'Palace Purple'
Hosta (many)
Iris foetidissima 'Variegata'
Lamium maculatum 'Chequers'
Liriope muscari 'Variegata'
Ophiopogon planiscapus 'Nigrescens'
Phormium (cvs)
Stachys byzantina 'Silver Carpet'
Tiarella polyphylla

FRAGRANT FLOWERS

Centranthus ruber
Convallaria majalis
Cosmos atrosanguineus
Dianthus 'Brympton Red',
    D. 'Old Clove Red'
Dictamnus albus
Dracocephalum moldavicum
Filipendula ulmaria
Galium odoratum
Hosta plantaginea var. grandiflora
Iris graminea
Oenothera odorata
Paeonia lactiflora
Petasites fragrans
Phlox paniculata
Viola odorata 'Czar'

FLOWERS FOR CUTTING

Alstroemeria
Aquilegia
Aster
Astrantia
Centaurea
Cephalaria
Delphinium
Dicentra
Doronicum
Erigeron
Gypsophila
Helenium
Helleborus
Kniphofia
Monarda
Paeonia
Phlox
Primula
Rudbeckia
Scabiosa
Solidago
Stokesia
Veronica

FLOWERS FOR DRYING

Acanthus spinosus
Achillea
Alchemilla mollis
Anaphalis
Aruncus dioicus
Astilbe
Catananche
Cynara
Echinops bannaticus, E. ritro
Limonium
Phlomis russeliana
Rodgersia
Sedum spectabile, S. telephium
Solidago

DECORATIVE SEEDHEADS

Acanthus
Belamcanda chinensis
Dictamnus albus
Eryngium
Eupatorium
Festuca glauca

Iris foetidissima
Lunaria rediviva
Papaver orientale
Physalis alkekengi

ARCHITECTURAL PLANTS

Acanthus hungaricus, A. mollis
Angelica archangelica
Arundo donax 'Variegata'
Bergenia 'Ballawley'
Cortaderia selloana
Crambe cordifolia
Cynara cardunculus, C. scolymus
Foeniculum vulgare
Gunnera manicata
Helleborus argutifolius
Heracleum (can be invasive)
Hosta sieboldiana var. elegans
Ligularia dentata 'Othello'
Lysichiton americanus
Melianthus major
Miscanthus sinensis
Phormium tenax
Rheum palmatum 'Atrosanguineum'
Rodgersia

FAST-GROWING PERENNIALS

Artemisia lactiflora
Aruncus sylvester
Arundo donax 'Macrophylla'
Campanula lactiflora
Centaurea macrocepha
Cephalaria gigantea
Crambe cordifolia

Cynara cardunculus

Cynara cardunculus, C. scolymus
Euphorbia characias
Ferula communis
Filipendula rubra
Galega x hartlandii
Gunnera manicata
Helianthus
Kniphofia caulescens,
    K. uvaria
Lavatera cachemiriana,
    L. maritima
Ligularia stenocephala
Macleaya cordata
Malva alcea var. fastigiata,
    M. moschata, M. sylvestris
Miscanthus
Phormium tenax
Rheum palmatum
    'Atrosanguineum'
Romneya coulteri
Rudbeckia laciniata 'Goldquelle'
Salvia confertiflora, S. sclarea
    var. turkestanica,
    S. uliginosa
Silphium perfoliatum
Solidago canadensis
Thalictrum flavum

Irises

THE genus *Iris* includes some of the loveliest of flowering plants. Their intricate blooms offer a rich spectrum of colors as well as satin or velvet textures. Species can be selected for diverse situations, ranging from woodland and rock garden, waterside and bog, to herbaceous border. Botanically, Iris is divided into subgenera, sections, and series; these divisions vary in their cultural needs and form a convenient horticultural classification.

Routine care and propagation
Species may be propagated in the fall or spring by division of offsets or rhizomes, or by seed in fall (named cultivars by division only). For further information, see PERENNIALS, "Routine care," pp.189–91; BULBOUS PLANTS, "Routine care," pp.236–8, and also "Propagation," pp.239–44.

Rhizomatous irises

Irises in this group have rhizomes as rootstocks, and their sword-shaped leaves are arranged in a basal fan. Botanically, they are divided into several subgenera and series, but for horticultural purposes the main groups are bearded, crested, and beardless irises.

Bearded irises
Characterized by a "beard" along the centerline of the falls (the hanging or horizontal petals), this group includes iris species and thousands of their cultivars and hybrids, most flowering in spring and early summer. Suitable for herbaceous and mixed borders, they are easy to grow

in fertile, well-drained soil in sun; many also tolerate partial shade and poorer soils.

Based on bloom height and bloom time, bearded irises are divided into six groups: miniature dwarf bearded (MDB), standard dwarf bearded (SDB), intermediate bearded (IB), miniature tall bearded (MTB), border bearded (BB), and tall bearded (TB). Within these groups are some that rebloom in summer or fall. Rebloomers generally benefit from extra fertilizer and water in summer.
Oncocyclus irises are natives of areas with little summer rainfall and need the protection of an alpine house or frame in climates that are subject to summer rains. They have large, beautiful, and arguably bizarre blooms but are exacting in their requirements and are not easy to grow. They need a fertile, sharply drained soil and full sun, with a dry dormant period after flowering. If they are grown in pots, the soil mix must be nutrient-rich, well drained, and preferably alkaline.
Regelia irises are related to the Oncocyclus irises and have similar cultural requirements, although they are easier to grow. Some species may be grown outside if they are given good drainage and a hot, dry site in the summer.

Crested irises
These have ridges, or cockscomblike crests, instead of beards.
Evansia irises are usually found in damp woodlands. Larger species, such as *I. confusa* and *I. japonica*, benefit from a sheltered position in organic soils, with some shade provided in warm climates. Most of

the smaller crested species, such as *I. cristata* and *I. gracilipes*, are ideal for planting in peaty pockets in a shaded rock garden.

Beardless irises
Irises in this group do not have bearded falls, but usually have marks called signals. Most have similar cultural requirements to bearded irises, but some prefer heavier soil.
Siberian irises have slender leaves and beautifully formed, delicately marked flowers. This group includes *I. chrysographes* and *I. sibirica*, plus many cultivars. They are easily grown in borders in rich soil that does not dry out, and are particularly suited to moist, waterside soil. The flowers last well when cut.
Spuria irises have narrow, reedlike foliage and elegant blooms. Spuria species, including *I. orientalis* and *I.graminea*, and their cultivars do well in sunny herbaceous borders in well-drained soil; they tolerate drier conditions than the Siberian irises.
Pacific Coast irises, a group that includes *I. innominata* and *I. tenax*, are useful for cutting. Many good, free-flowering hybrids have been produced that are excellent for organic, acidic soils in sun in cool regions or in shade in warmer climates. Others from groups that need similar conditions include *I. missouriensis*, which is more tolerant of alkaline soils; *I. verna* and *I. prismatica*; and *I. setosa*, which is more tolerant of sun.

Water irises are a group of elegant, moisture-loving plants that thrive in pond margins, bog gardens, or rich, permanently damp soils. They include *I. laevigata*, *I. pseudacorus*, *I. ensata* (syn. *I. kaempferi*), *I. versicolor*, and the Japanese and Louisiana irises. They are sometimes slow to establish.

Bulbous irises

The storage organs of these irises are bulbs, sometimes with thick, fleshy roots. Subgenera include Reticulata, Juno, and Xiphium irises.

Reticulata irises
These are dwarf, hardy bulbs that flower early. They prefer a sunny position in well-drained, acidic or alkaline soil, or may be grown in pots in the bulb frame.

Juno irises
Junos need similar conditions to the Oncocyclus irises and are often difficult to grow. Vigorous species such as *I. bucharica* and *I. magnifica* grow well in warm, outdoor sites.

Xiphium irises
These include the brightly colored Dutch, English, and Spanish irises, often grown for cut flowers. Any well-drained soil in full sun is suitable. In very cold areas, lift the bulbs in fall to overwinter in a frost-free place. Replant in spring.

A SAMPLING OF IRISES

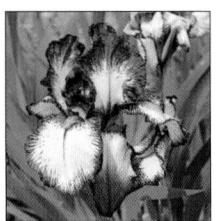
I. 'Bold Print'
(Intermediate bearded)

I. 'Carnaby'
(Tall bearded)

I. innominata
(Pacific Coast)

I. 'Geisha Gown'
(Japanese)

I. bucharica
(Juno)

I. 'Joyce'
(Reticulata)

INFORMAL ELEGANCE
The colorful blooms of Siberian irises (blue and white) and I. pseudacorus (*yellow*) *provide a focal point by a garden pond.*

Daylilies

ALTHOUGH they belong to the lily family (Liliaceae), daylilies (*Hemerocallis*) are not true lilies; their common name comes from the lily-shaped flowers that, in the older selections, open in the morning and fade before sunset. Many modern cultivars stay open into the evening, whereas others open in the evening and last through the following day, especially if the weather is overcast.

Types of daylily

There are three growth types of daylily: dormant, semievergreen, and evergreen. Daylilies range in size from compact plants that grow to only 12–15in (30–38cm) tall, to large plants that can reach heights of 5ft (1.5m) or more. Tetraploid daylilies, which have four sets of chromosomes in their cells, are larger overall than the diploids (with two sets) and produce sturdier growth. However, some enthusiasts consider them to be less graceful than the diploids.

Modern hybrids are available in a wide range of colors, from near white through shades of yellow, orange, red, pink, and purple to almost black. Many cultivars have contrasting eye zones, washes, bands, and other markings of varied colors on the petals. The flowers may be from 1½in (4cm) to more than 9in (22cm) in diameter, and they come in a variety of forms, including single, double, spider (with long petals, often referred to as tepals) and polytepal (with more than 6 tepals).

Daylilies bloom throughout late spring into fall. Good modern cultivars flower for three to four weeks. Extended-flowering cultivars bloom longer, and there are some repeat-flowering varieties, such as 'Pardon Me'. Some species, such as *H. liliosphodelus* and the night-blooming *H. citrina*, are strongly fragrant.

Using daylilies

With their long period of flowering, daylilies are good for a wide variety of situations. In the mixed border, daylilies make good accent plants; you might choose tall cultivars, such as 'Autumn Minaret', or *H. altissima*. Their abundant leaves may be used to hide the dying foliage of *Papaver orientale*. Daylilies are also useful as a groundcover on gentle slopes or simply to cover large areas. For containers, use fast-growing, upright cultivars, such as 'Janice Brown', 'Always Afternoon', and 'Strawberry Candy'. After flowering, container-grown daylilies featured on a patio, for example, can be moved to a less prominent position.

Cultivation

Evergreen daylilies are generally best suited to warmer climates and dormant ones to colder, whereas semievergreen types are usually suitable for both. Local nurseries should sell appropriate cultivars for your climate. All have the same cultural needs.

DAYLILY FLOWERS AND GROWTH TYPES

Hemerocallis 'Ice Carnival' (dormant)

H. 'Cream Drop' (semievergreen)

H. 'Circle Round' (dormant)

H. 'Leebea Orange Crush' (evergreen)

H. 'Milk Chocolate' (dormant)

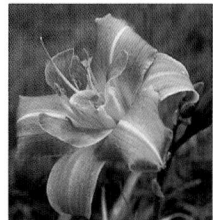

H. 'Louise Mercer' (dormant)

Site and planting

Daylilies will survive in almost any soil, except wet clay. They thrive in sun or shade but bloom best if they are in sunlight for at least half the day. When grown in shade, the blooms will be fewer and the plants taller. For details of how to plant, see "Planting perennials," p.184.

Routine care

For the greatest number of flowers, fertilize daylilies in early spring and again in summer, using a balanced fertilizer at a rate of 2oz (50g) per established plant. Water daylilies well, especially during bloom. In cold climates, lightly mulch for winter to protect the crowns.

An established clump needs dividing to maintain vigor once its flower size becomes smaller and the clump becomes congested. Division is usually necessary every three to five years in rich soil, especially for repeat-flowering cultivars, but less often in poorer soil. Divide in spring or four to six weeks after bloom.

Pests and diseases

Thrips (p.648) may feed on flower buds, causing pale streaks on the petals. Earwigs (p. 649), Japanese beetles (p.649), and spotted cucumber beetles (p.649) eat the buds, flowers, and leaves. Crown rot can cause problems in wet soils during hot, humid weather.

Propagation

The easiest method is by division (see "Fibrous-rooted plants," p.196). To make the clump easier to handle, cut the foliage down to about 8in (20cm) and trim and wash the roots before dividing the clump. Aim for plants with at least two shoots ("fans") each, although most will reestablish from a single fan.

Daylilies are also easy to raise from seed (see p.194); they should come into flower from one to three years after sowing.

DAYLILIES IN A MIXED BORDER
Daylilies blend with other herbaceous perennials, including hostas, asters, and delphiniums. Here, they grow with shrubs along a meandering stream.

REPEAT-FLOWERING DAYLILIES
Cultivars such as 'Stella de Oro' offer an extended flowering season.

Peonies

THE exotic, often fragrant blooms of peonies are one of the delights of the garden in spring. After flowering, they maintain their attractive, deeply divided leaves into the fall, and some species, such as *Paeonia mlokosewitschii*, bear colorful seedpods.

The genus includes herbaceous perennials (common garden peonies), which often reach a height of 3ft (1m), and deciduous shrubs (tree peonies) up to 6ft (2m). Their cup-shaped or globular flowers are classified as single, double, semidouble, or anemone-form. Colors range from pure white through pink to crimson and purple, plus shades of yellow and salmon. Peonies combine easily with other perennials and woody plants. They prefer sun but tolerate light shade.

Herbaceous peonies

The spectacular blooms of some herbaceous peonies have traditionally mingled well in cottage gardens (see p.176). They may be planted as a hedge, lasting from the bronze-red shoots in spring until the foliage is cut down by fall frosts. Once established, herbaceous peonies can also be cut freely for indoor decoration.

Herbaceous peonies need 30–60 days with night temperatures around freezing in order to flower.

Planting

Herbaceous peonies should be planted bare-root in early fall (see p.185); if planted in spring, they may not bloom for a year or two. Space them at least 18in (45cm) apart with 2in (5cm) of soil over the buds or "eyes"; if planted too deeply, the peony may not flower, and if too shallowly, the buds may dry out. Maintain a loose, 1in (2.5cm) mulch throughout the year.

Routine care and propagation

Apply a high-phosphorus fertilizer in early spring. Support herbaceous peonies when the new shoots are ankle-high (see "Staking," p.190). For extra-large or exhibition blooms, disbud in spring when the lateral buds are pea sized.

TYPES OF PEONY

Paeonia mlokosewitschii (single; herbaceous)

P. 'Auguste Dessert' (semidouble; herbaceous)

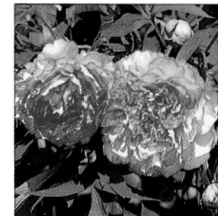

P. 'Souvenir de Maxime Cornu' (double; tree)

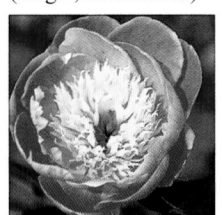

P. 'Bowl of Beauty' (anemone; herbaceous)

P. 'Krinkled White' (single; herbaceous)

P. 'Coral Supreme' (double; herbaceous)

After a hard frost in fall, cut the stems to the ground. Peony wilt and gray mold/Botrytis (p.646) may be troublesome.

Propagate by division in late summer or fall (see "Dividing peonies," p.197); peonies are slow to reestablish. Alternatively, sow seed in fall after cold stratification (see p.194); it may take three years to germinate.

Tree peonies

Tree peonies are often planted in front of evergreens, such as yew (*Taxus*), *Euonymus*, or holly (*Ilex*), which show off the peony blooms. They may also be used as accent shrubs in herbaceous borders and mixed borders where their flowering time coincides with *Dicentra*, candytuft (*Iberis*), irises, tulips, crabapples (*Malus*), azaleas (*Rhododendron*), and *Wisteria*. Tree peonies make perfect cut flowers if the blooms are cut as the flower buds show color and start to open.

Tree peonies are usually bought container-grown and grafted onto a readily available rootstock so that the cultivar comes into flower more quickly. Tree peonies prefer a slightly alkaline pH; prepare the soil for and plant as for other shrubs in fall (see "Soil preparation" and "How to plant," p.96). Space them at least 4ft (1.2m) from nearby plants. Bury the rootstock 4in (10cm) below soil level so that the grafted cultivar develops its own roots.

Routine care and pruning

Apply a high-phosphorus fertilizer in spring. Protect from small animals (p.639) in the first few years, and from spring frosts.

Prune tree peonies to improve their shape and, occasionally, to maintain or reduce size. In spring, cut out dead and crossing branches and any frost-damaged shoots. After flowering, cut back new growth that is straggly or unbalanced to a shoot or bud facing in the required direction.

Propagation

Propagate by semiripe cuttings in late summer (see p.110) or by apical-wedge grafting in winter (see p.117). Species may also be propagated by seed in fall (see p.112).

PRUNING A TREE PEONY

In spring, prune tree peonies to remove any dead or frost-damaged wood and crossing branches.

Remove any branches that overlap or cross each other.

Cut out dead wood at the base, using loppers if necessary.

Cut back frost-damaged shoots to where new growth starts.

DISBUDDING

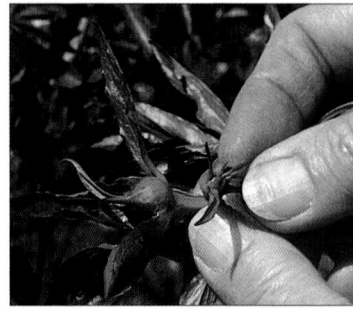

When the lateral buds below the top bud of each shoot are about $^{1}/_{2}$in (1cm) in diameter, pinch them out to concentrate growth into the central bloom.

Soil preparation and planting

Herbaceous perennials originate from many regions that have widely varying climatic and soil conditions, so whether the proposed site is sheltered or exposed, fertile or stony, there is always a number of plants that will thrive. It is better to select plants that will flourish in the given growing conditions rather than struggle against nature.

Site and exposure

When deciding which plants to grow, take into account climate, exposure, and soil, as well as the amount of sun, shade, and shelter the site receives at different times of day and from season to season. For example, shade cast by deciduous trees is densest in late spring and summer when the trees are in full leaf.

Different areas of the garden may provide varying growing conditions: for example, a south-facing border would be ideal for plants that thrive in sun, such as sedums, while a north-facing site or a position beneath a tree would be better for shade-loving species such as hostas, if they can be kept moist.

The ground next to a wall, fence, or hedge is usually fairly dry due to the effect of rain shadow, but since it also tends to be warm and sheltered, it may be a good position for plants that are not fully hardy.

Altering conditions

Especially in small gardens, it may be necessary to adapt some elements to create growing conditions that suit a wide range of plants. Heavy, waterlogged soils may be drained or the plants grown in raised beds or containers, while lighter soils may benefit from the addition of organic matter. Shade from trees may be reduced by judicious pruning or shelter provided by shrubs, hedges, or windbreaks (see also COLD AND WIND PROTECTION, pp.604–5, and HEDGES AND SCREENS, pp.82–4).

Soil preparation

The ideal soil for the majority of perennial plants is a fertile loam that is well drained but retains adequate moisture. Use a commercial soil-testing kit to find out the degree of acidity or alkalinity of the soil because this partly determines which plants will thrive there.

It is also important to check soil drainage; if much of the ground remains waterlogged in wet weather, then tile or French drains must be installed (see SOILS AND FERTILIZERS, "Installing drains," p.617).

Clearing the site

All weeds should be cleared from the site prior to planting since once other plants are established, perennial weeds, in particular, are difficult to eradicate. If the ground is infested with weeds, treat the whole area with an appropriate weedkiller during the season before planting. If there are only a few perennial weeds, however, fork them out when you prepare the soil before planting.

During the first growing season, any remaining perennial weeds should be carefully removed with a hand fork as soon as they are noticed. They can also be treated with a systemic weedkiller, being very careful not to harm the newly planted perennials. Annual weeds can be either sprayed or forked out before the site is planted.

Improving the soil structure and fertility

All soils may be improved by the addition of well-rotted organic matter such as manure or compost; this not only increases the water retention of light, free-draining soils and helps to open up the texture of heavy clay soils but also improves the soil's fertility. Before planting (preferably a few weeks in advance), apply a 2–4in (5–10cm) layer of well-rotted organic matter over the site, then fork or rototill it into the top spit of the soil. Allow the soil to settle before planting. Provided that the soil is fertile and organic, it is usually unnecessary to use fertilizer when planting perennials, although they may require fertilizing in subsequent seasons (see "Fertilizing," p.189).

CHOOSING PERENNIALS

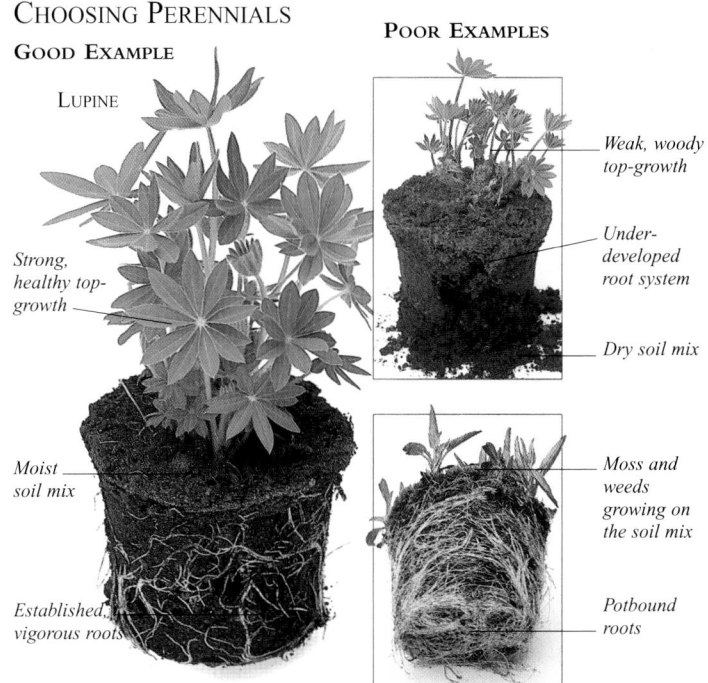

GOOD EXAMPLE

LUPINE

Strong, healthy top-growth

Moist soil mix

Established, vigorous roots

POOR EXAMPLES

Weak, woody top-growth

Under-developed root system

Dry soil mix

Moss and weeds growing on the soil mix

Potbound roots

Selecting plants

Most perennials are sold container-grown, but bare-root plants are also sometimes available from fall to early spring, when they are dormant. When selecting plants, look for healthy, vigorous specimens with no sign of dieback or abnormally colored leaves that may indicate a lack of nutrients. If buying herbaceous plants at the beginning of the growing season, check that there are strong, emerging shoots. Plants that have a few fat, healthy looking buds are better than those that have a large number of weaker ones.

One or two annual weeds growing in the soil mix may be removed easily enough, but do not buy any container-grown plants that have perennial weeds, moss, or liverworts.

These often indicate that the plant has been in its container for too long and may be starved of nutrients or that the soil mix is poorly drained, in which case the plant's roots may have rotted or died back.

When possible, remove the plant from its container and inspect the roots. Do not choose a plant with a mass of tightly coiling roots or one that has large roots pushing through the drainage holes. The roots should, however, be sufficiently established to retain most of the soil when the plant is removed from its container. Look for withered tips on the shoots: this can indicate a plant that has been allowed to dry excessively.

If buying bare-root plants, make sure that the root systems are strong and have not dried out, and that the young shoots are not wilting. Plant them as soon as possible after purchase, or protect them against moisture loss by wrapping them in plastic or wet newspaper until they are ready to plant.

Dividing large plants

When buying fibrous-rooted plants, choose large examples with a number of healthy shoots that may be divided before planting, rather than a few smaller, less expensive specimens. Divide the plant by pulling it apart with your hands or two hand forks used back to back, taking care that each division has its own root system and retains as much soil around the roots as possible (see also "Dividing perennials," p.196).

DIVIDING LARGE PLANTS

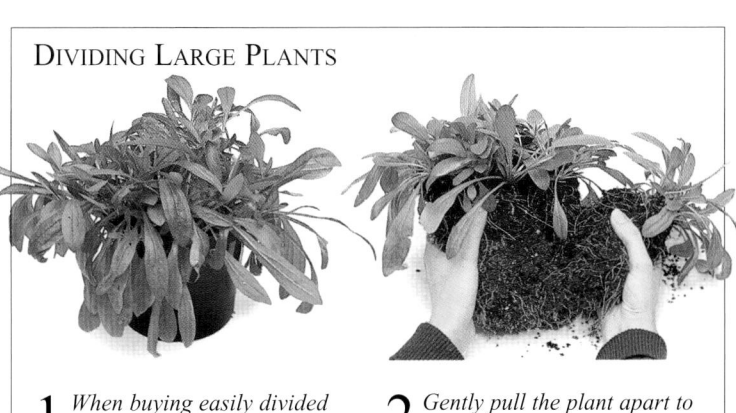

1 *When buying easily divided perennials, look for a large plant with several strong shoots (here Aster tongolensis).*

2 *Gently pull the plant apart to make several small sections, each with its own roots. Keep plenty of soil around the roots.*

PERENNIALS THAT PREFER SANDY SOIL

Acanthus spinosus
Achillea
Alchemilla
Armeria
Asphodeline lutea
Centranthus ruber
Dianthus

*Echinops ritro
'Veitch's Blue'*

Echinops
Eryngium tripartitum
Gaillardia x grandiflora (cvs)
Globularia
Limonium latifolium
Nepeta x faassenii
Origanum vulgare 'Aureum'
Papaver orientale
Romneya coulteri
Sedum
Sempervivum
Sisyrinchium

PERENNIALS THAT TOLERATE CLAY SOIL

Aruncus dioicus
Astilbe
Butomus◆
Caltha◆
Cardamine pratensis
Dodecatheon
Eomecon
Filipendula ulmaria 'Aurea'
Gunnera manicata◆
Hemerocallis
Hosta
Houttuynia
Lobelia cardinalis, L. fulgens
Lysichiton◆
Lysimachia
Lythrum
Mimulus guttatus◆
Myosotis scorpioides◆
Peltiphyllum peltatum
Persicaria
Phormium
Pontederia◆

*Primula
bulleyana*

Primula bulleyana,
  P. florindae, P. rosea
Ranunculus ficaria,
  R. flammula◆
Rheum
Rodgersia
Sagittaria
Scrophularia
  auriculata
Trollius

KEY
◆ *Tolerates waterlogged soil*

When to plant

Perennials grown in containers may be planted out at any time of year when the soil is workable, but the best seasons are spring and fall. Planting in fall helps the plants to establish quickly before the onset of winter because the soil is still warm enough to promote root growth, yet it is unlikely to dry out.

In cold areas, however, spring planting is better for perennials that are not entirely hardy or that dislike wet conditions, such as *Kniphofia*, *Schizostylis*, *Lobelia cardinalis*, and *Scabiosa caucasica*. This ensures that they are fully established before their first winter.

Bare-root specimens should generally be planted in spring or fall, although a few, such as hostas, may be transplanted successfully during the growing season.

Planting perennials

Plant perennials in prepared ground, taking care to position them at the right depth (see below): for example, those prone to basal rot are best planted slightly above ground level so that excess water may drain away.

Container-grown plants
First dig a planting hole, then water the plant thoroughly and remove it from its container, taking care not to

HOW TO PLANT A CONTAINER-GROWN PERENNIAL

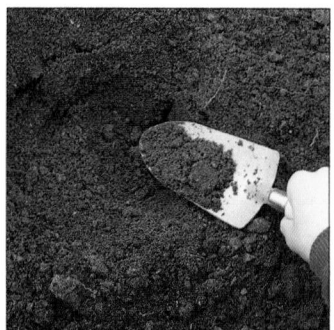

1 *In a prepared bed, dig a hole 1½ times wider and deeper than the plant's root ball.*

2 *Soak the soil mix in the pot before sliding out the plant (here an* Aster*).*

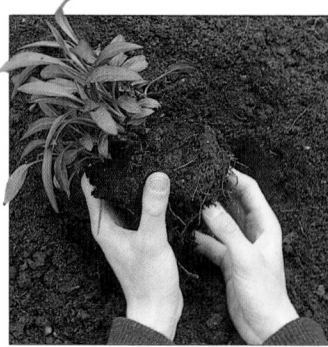

3 *Gently scrape off the top 1½in (3cm) of soil to remove weeds and weed seeds. Carefully tease out the roots around the sides and base of the root ball.*

4 *Check that the plant crown is at the correct depth when planted and fill in around the root ball. Firm in around the plant and water thoroughly.*

Planting depths

SISYRINCHIUM STRIATUM 'AUNT MAY'

ASTER

HOSTA

POLYGONATUM

While most perennials are best planted out at the same soil level as they were in their pots, a number grow better if planted higher or deeper, depending on their individual requirements. Some prefer a raised, well-drained site, while others thrive in deeper, moist conditions.

GROUND-LEVEL PLANTING
The majority of perennials should be planted so that the crown of the plant is level with the surrounding soil.

RAISED PLANTING
Set plants that are prone to rot at the base, and variegated plants that tend to revert, with their crowns slightly above soil level.

SHALLOW PLANTING
Plant perennials that require a moist environment with their crowns about 1in (2cm) below ground level.

DEEP PLANTING
Plant perennials with tuberous root systems so that their crowns are about 4in (10cm) below the soil surface.

damage the roots. To help the plant establish quickly, carefully loosen the sides and base of the root ball, particularly if rootbound, by teasing out the roots with your fingers or a hand fork. Place the plant at the appropriate depth in the prepared hole, backfill with soil, and firm. Loosen the surface of the soil with a hand fork and water in thoroughly.

Bare-root plants

To prevent dehydration, plant bare-root perennials as soon as possible after purchase. Prepare a hole as for container-grown plants, spread out the roots evenly, check the planting depth, and work in soil between the roots as you firm. Water well.

Transplanting self-sown seedlings

A number of perennials, for example *Aquilegia* and foxgloves (*Digitalis*), regularly produce self-sown seedlings that can be transplanted to a nursery bed or moved to another position in the garden.

Before lifting the seedlings, prepare suitable planting holes, spacing them to allow room for the plants to develop. Then gently lift each seedling with a trowel, taking care to retain as much soil around the roots as possible, and replant it immediately. Firm it in well and water it thoroughly. Shade the plants in sunny weather and water them regularly until they are established.

Raised and peat beds

These beds are often used for growing acidic soil-loving plants in a garden with alkaline soil or for providing a free-draining bed on heavy, clay soil. Plants that thrive in acidic soil alone are best planted in a raised bed filled with an acidic soil mix (see also THE ROCK GARDEN, "Raised beds," p.251, and "Peat beds," p.250).

Raised beds may be constructed from a variety of materials including wood, bricks, or stone (see also STRUCTURES AND SURFACES, "Raised beds," p.593). Include a deep layer of coarse drainage material (such as broken bricks) in the base; about one-third of the bed depth is ideal. Cover this with a layer of fibrous material, then fill with good topsoil.

Containers

As well as being a highly attractive way of displaying a number of plants, growing perennials in containers provides an opportunity to include plants that would not flourish in the open garden, either because they are too tender or because the soil type is not suitable. If growing different plants together in one container, take care to choose those that thrive in similar conditions.

When choosing a container, make sure that it is sufficiently deep and wide to allow room for the plants' roots to develop properly. Consider how the selected plants will look when in full growth in relation to the container to achieve a pleasing balance between them. Tall plants in deep, narrow containers and small plants in large, wide ones may seem out of proportion.

TRANSPLANTING SEEDLINGS

Lift seedlings with soil around their roots to avoid breaking up the root ball. Plant out and water well.

Planting in containers

If using a heavy container such as a stone urn, lead trough, wooden half barrel, or large terracotta pot, place it in position before filling and planting, since it will be very cumbersome to move afterward. Plastic containers are, of course, considerably lighter, but they are less stable and may be blown over in strong winds. Set the container on a support of blocks or bricks to allow free drainage.

Make sure that the container has drainage holes in the base or low on the sides to prevent waterlogging. Cover the holes with pieces of screening (either metal or plastic window screening, or a similar open-weave plastic or nylon mesh will do); this allows water to filter through freely yet prevents soil mix from being washed out or blocking the drainage holes.

Most potting mixes are suitable, although acidic-soil-loving plants must be planted in an acidic soil mix. A prepared general soil mix containing a slow-release fertilizer will be suitable for most plants; those that need extra drainage (such as *Sedum* or *Achillea*), prefer a soil mix containing additional grit or very coarse sand.

Before planting, arrange the plants on the soil mix to make sure that they have enough room to develop freely. Plant as for perennials in open ground, and keep well watered until established.

Heuchera 'Palace Purple'

Artemisia 'Powis Castle'

Penstemon 'Rich Ruby'

Geranium sanguineum var. striatum

1 *When planting in a container, group the plants while still in their pots to determine the spacing and arrangement. Then plant, firm in, and water well.*

2 *A few months later, the plants will have grown and developed to form a well-balanced, attractive combination suitable for display on a patio or other showcase location.*

PERENNIALS THAT REQUIRE ACIDIC SOIL

Anigozanthos manglesii
Cypripedium reginae
Darlingtonia

Anigozanthos manglesii

Drosera
Gentiana, many
Nepenthes
Pinguicula
Sarracenia flava
Shortia galacifolia
Trillium
Uvularia

PERENNIALS THAT TOLERATE ALKALINE SOIL

Acanthus spinosus
Achillea filipendulina 'Gold Plate'
Aconitum
Anchusa
Anemone hupehensis, *A.* x *hybrida*
Anthyllis
Bergenia
Berkheya
Brunnera
Campanula lactiflora
Catananche
Centranthus
Clematis heracleifolia, *C. recta*
Coronilla varia
Corydalis lutea
Dianthus
Doronicum
Eremurus
Eryngium
Galega
Geranium pratense
Gypsophila paniculata
Helenium
Helleborus
Heuchera
Kniphofia
Lathyrus vernus
Linaria purpurea
Linum narbonense
Lychnis chalcedonica
Paeonia
Salvia nemorosa
Saponaria
Scabiosa

Scabiosa caucasica 'Clive Greaves'

Sidalcea
Stachys
Verbascum
Veronica spicata

Hostas

Grown primarily for their bold, sculptural foliage, many hosta species and cultivars also produce attractive white, lilac, or purple flowers. Easy to maintain and long-lived, hostas make a valuable addition to any garden.

Using hostas in the garden

Hostas are highly sought after as foliage plants for shaded areas, and make eye-catching displays in pots or beside ponds. The range of colors, textures, and shapes of their foliage is stunning: modern hybrids may have leaves patterned in shades of green, white, and gold, or edged in a contrasting color. Their texture may be rich and glossy or soft and velvety. Leaves may be narrow and ribbonlike, heart-shaped, or almost circular. There are hostas suitable for any degree of shade, from light or dappled, to deep. In general, the blue-leaved hostas flourish in deep shade, while yellow-leaved cultivars prefer some sun.

Hostas for shady places
Hostas make excellent companion plants for other shade-loving perennials. They act as a foil for bright flowers such as those of *Astilbe*, while their large leaves make a counterpoint to the finer foliage of other plants, including Japanese painted fern (*Athyrium niponicum* 'Pictum') and sedges (*Carex*). For shady locations in the rock garden, choose miniature hostas such as *H. venusta* and *H.* 'Kabitan'.

Consider planting a hosta to enliven a shady entrance. Fragrant hostas ideal for planting close to the house include *H.* 'Sugar and Cream', *H.* 'So Sweet', and *H. plantaginea*, which is one of the last to flower.

On a shaded patio, grow hostas in containers to contrast with more flamboyant annuals. The bright green *H.* 'Sum and Substance' or delicately mottled *H. tokudama* 'Aureo-nebulosa' are excellent plants for containers.

Groundcover
Hostas make a particularly striking groundcover when planted as a mass. Choose cultivars carefully for continuous interest from both foliage and flowers. For example, a combination of the bold *H.* 'Green Piecrust', *H.* 'Krossa Regal', *H.* 'Honeybells', and *H. plantaginea* makes an exotic planting that will flower for several months in succession. A more subtle effect is achieved by restricting the design to a few hostas within a limited spectrum of leaf colors. For a fast-growing, lower groundcover, choose cultivars such as *H.* 'Blue Cadet' and *H.* 'Ground Master'.

MIXED BORDER
Hostas blend well with other shade plants, acting as a foil for summer flowers and providing interest after the flowers have finished.

Cultivation

Hostas tolerate a wide range of soils, except for heavy clay or pure sand. They grow best in a good, moist loam, rich in organic matter, with a pH from 6.5 to 7.3. Prepare the soil well before planting, particularly if it is lacking in nutrients (see "Soil preparation," p.183).

Planting hostas
Bare-root hostas can be planted in spring or fall. Container-grown hostas can be planted at any time, but do not disturb the roots if planting while they are in active growth (see "Planting perennials," p.184). In spring or fall, however, unless the container is full of roots, it is better to shake off much of the soil and treat as a bare-root hosta.

Plant with the crown slightly buried so that it remains moist (see "Planting depths," p.184), but on heavy soils, plant with the crown at ground level. Do not allow any manure to come into contact with the roots at planting, since it may cause discolored foliage in the first year. Leave a slight depression around the plant at first so that when you water, the moisture soaks directly down to the roots.

Routine care
Hostas can take about five years to reach maturity and can then be left undisturbed for many years. Water only in prolonged periods of drought.

To produce lush foliage of a good color, apply well-rotted manure or compost, since these increase the soil organic content. In spring, apply an all-purpose inorganic fertilizer to hostas in poor soil.

Mulching
Apply a spring mulch while the soil is moist. Use only well-rotted materials, in order to discourage slugs. In regions with very cold winters, apply a mulch of straw or leaves around each hosta after the ground is frozen; take care not to cover the crown of the plant too thickly. On new, shallow-rooted plants the mulch prevents them from lifting after a severe frost, while on established plants it often reduces crown rot. If very coarse material is used as a mulch, it should be removed in the spring.

Pests and diseases
Slugs and snails may devastate hostas, sometimes reducing leaves to tatters by the end of the season (p.638). Earwigs (p.638) also chew holes in leaves. Crown rot may cause problems, especially on heavy soils.

Propagation

Hostas are easily increased by division (see "Dividing hostas," p.196); it is also possible simply to cut a slice out of a crown with a sharp spade. Hostas may be raised from seed gathered when the pods turn brown. Sow the seeds outside in fall or inside in the winter (see p.194), then grow on as usual for perennials.

HOSTAS FOR DIFFERENT SITUATIONS

Hosta tokudama 'Aureo-nebulosa'
Medium-size, for moderate to deep shade

H. 'Gold Standard'
Medium, prefers light shade

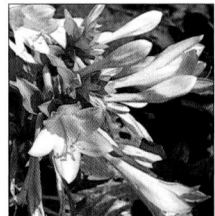

H. 'Halcyon'
Medium, for quite heavy shade

H. lancifolia
Small to medium, tolerating full sun

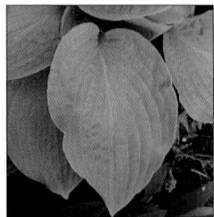

H. 'August Moon'
Large hosta, for dappled shade

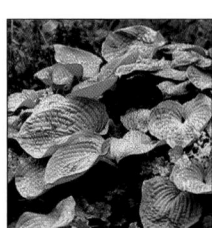

H. sieboldiana var. elegans
Medium, for light shade

Grasses, sedges, and rushes

These plants have a variety of elegant and architectural forms that, combined with arching or upright stems, feathery inflorescences, and subtly colored seedheads, make an outstanding display. Grow them in masses, as specimen plants, or in borders.

Grasses are often confused with other grasslike plants, particularly sedges and rushes, but each of them belongs to a separate family.

The grass family

True grasses (those of the Poaceae, or Gramineae, family) almost always have hollow, round stems, with solid nodes at regular intervals. The woody-stemmed, perennial bamboos (subfamily Bambusoideae, see page 94) are good examples, with the obvious hollowness of their canes. Grass blades extend in two ranks from a sheath that can be split or peeled back. Grass flowers are borne in panicles, racemes, or spikes.

True grasses
These vary widely in color and habit. The architectural qualities of the taller grasses make them a striking feature in the herbaceous border, while low-growing grasses provide a contrast at the front of the bed. Do not choose vigorous, creeping grasses such as *Phalaris arundinacea* var. *picta* for this purpose, however, because they are likely to engulf adjacent weaker plants. More easily managed are the tufted grasses, which slowly build up and out from a central crown.

Some are suitable for paved areas, such as *Molinia caerulea* subsp. *caerulea* 'Variegata'. For a warm, sunny pocket on the patio, use the taller *Helictotrichon sempervirens*, with slender blue leaves that are upright and stiffly radiating. For a lawn specimen, good choices include pampas grass (*Cortaderia*), with tall, nodding plumes in late summer, or the many selections of *Miscanthus*, with more delicate inflorescences. For the water's edge, species such as *Glyceria maxima* 'Variegata' display attractive form and variegation and provide interesting reflections.

Most grasses prefer full sun to very light shade, an open position, and well-drained but moisture-retentive soil. Very fertile soil encourages lush, often floppy foliage at the expense of flowers. A few species need moist soil, growing well alongside stream banks.

Sedges and rushes

Sedges (Cyperaceae family) have three-sided stems that are solid and pithy throughout. The leaf blades tightly encase the stem, arising from each side in threes: in cross section they are concertina-like and cannot readily be split or rolled back.

The family Juncaceae contains two cultivated genera, *Juncus* and *Luzula*, both known commonly as rushes. In *Juncus*, the leaves are cylindrical in cross section and have a solid pith; in *Luzula*, the leaves are flat and usually edged with hairs. Woodrushes (*Luzula* spp.) are most appealing when used to provide a spreading groundcover in areas of shady woodland. A number of sedges, such as *Carex elata* 'Aurea' and *C. oshimensis* 'Evergold', with their attractive golden or variegated foliage, also offer fine color contrasts in the border.

The woodrushes thrive in semishade, but they will also tolerate open conditions. The sedges, although most often found in damp habitats, are usually very tolerant of drier sites, with the exception of moisture-loving species such as *Carex acuta* and *C. riparia*.

Routine cultivation

In general, most ornamental grasses require little care, as long as they are grown in an appropriate, correctly prepared site. Sedges and rushes are generally treated as grasses.

Preparing the soil
On dry soils, incorporate plenty of organic or fibrous matter to provide adequate moisture retention; this should not be rich in nutrients, however. In mild areas with high rainfall, grasses from the subtropics and very dry regions need a deep, gritty soil with excellent drainage. A topdressing of stone chips around the crown in winter helps disperse surface moisture, which, in combination with cold, can kill many plants from warm zones and high altitudes; this is not necessary in regions where the ground remains frozen.

Cutting back
Deadhead annual grasses after flowering to prevent self-seeding, but do not deadhead perennials, since the parchment colors of the fading inflorescences are often an essential part of their winter appeal.

As grasses begin to wither and become unsightly, trim off the old, messy growth. In early spring, cut back the plant to ground level to encourage vigorous foliage to develop. Grasses from warm climates should be cut back in spring, because the old foliage helps protect the crown from winter cold.

LAWN SPECIMEN
*The strong shape and tall, graceful plumes of pampas grass (*Cortaderia selloana*) are ideally suited to specimen planting.*

When handling grasses, wear thick gloves; the sawlike leaf edges are razor sharp and may cause injury.

Propagation

Perennial grasses may be propagated from seed (see PERENNIALS, "Seed," p.194) or by division. Annuals are usually increased by seed sown in spring (sometimes in fall).

Seed
Gather the seeds when they are fully ripe; that is, when the inflorescence is dry and fluffy and the seeds can be easily pulled away from the spike. Sowing seeds in small pots or cell packs allows you to pot on without disturbing the young plants. If sown as soon as the seeds are ripe, germination is quick, but the young seedlings will need protection from winter cold.

Division
Clump-forming grasses are easily increased by simple division in spring or fall. Many gardeners prefer division in spring, when new growth is visible, because the plants establish more successfully.

To increase rhizomatous species, lift the clump and cut it into sections, ensuring that each has at least one growing point. Do not damage the fine roots. Insert the sections into individual pots of a freely draining soil mix, then cover them to their original depth. Keep them cool and moist and in good light, but shaded from strong sun, until the plants are established. For further information, see "Dividing perennials," p.196.

LIGHT AND MOVEMENT
The subtle colors and feathery heads of many grasses (here mostly forms of Cortaderia selloana *and* Miscanthus) *make an animated, informal display.*

Chrysanthemums

THE rich colors and luxuriant shapes of their long-lasting flower heads make chrysanthemums (*C. morifolium* hybrids) ideal for garden displays and cutting. The flower types are classified by the type and arrangement of the florets.

Chrysanthemums form a number of flower heads on sideshoots (called sprays). Disbuds are produced by removing the side buds of sprays to leave one terminal bud that forms a larger flower head. Early-flowering chrysanthemums flower from late summer to early fall. Late-flowering types bloom from mid- to late fall.

Early-flowering chrysanthemums

These need a sunny site with well-drained, slightly acidic soil. Set out small plants in spring (see "Soil preparation and planting," p.183–5).

TYPES OF CHRYSANTHEMUM FLOWER HEAD

INCURVED
C. 'Alison Kirk'
Fully double flower heads with incurved florets closing tightly over the crown.

REFLEXED
C. 'Rose Yvonne Arnaud'
Fully double flower heads with partly reflexed florets and a spiky outline.

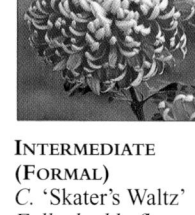

INTERMEDIATE (FORMAL)
C. 'Skater's Waltz'
Fully double flower heads with loosely incurving florets and a regular shape.

POMPON
C. 'Maria'
Fully double, dense flower heads bearing tubular florets with flat, rounded petals.

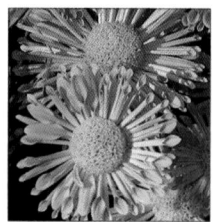

SINGLE
C. 'Rytorch'
Flower heads with prominent central disks and 5 rows of flat-petaled florets.

SPOON
C. 'Pennine Jewel'
Single flower heads with tubular florets. Florets open at the tips to form a spoon shape.

C. 'Morning Star'
Dwarf plant bearing a mass of single flowers, each with a diameter of 1in (2.5cm). The blooms densely cover the plant to form a rounded head.

Pinching and disbudding

Soon after planting, pinch central growing tips of chrysanthemums grown as sprays or disbuds to encourage lateral displays.

For sprays, when laterals are 3in (8cm) long, reduce to four per stem and pinch again. Another pinch may be made in long growing seasons, but allow six weeks from the last pinch to flowering. For small, even-sized flower heads, pinch the terminal bud to encourage sideshoots.

For disbuds, reduce laterals to four to six well-spaced shoots. To produce one flower per lateral, snap off all the sideshoots and remove the side buds.

Routine care

A month after the final pinch, apply a balanced fertilizer at a rate of 2oz/sq yd (70g/sq m). Repeat this one month later. Give a weekly liquid fertilizer until the buds show color.

In frost-free climates, overwinter early-flowering types in the ground, cutting down stems in spring. In temperate climates, lift plants and trim to 9in (22cm). Shake off surplus soil, then store the rootstocks in a shallow box of slightly moist to almost dry soil-based mix in a frost-free place. Do not bury too deeply. In early spring provide light, heat, and water to encourage shoots.

Taking cuttings

Take cuttings four to six weeks after new shoots appear (see *How to Propagate by Basal Stem Cuttings*, p.198). Pot up the rooted cuttings and grow on. Harden them off, then plant out when danger of frost is past.

DISBUDDING

For disbuds, once the side buds around each terminal bud have tiny stalks, pinch them out so that only the central bud will develop.

Late-flowering chrysanthemums

Usually grown in pots so that they may be easily moved, these are unsuitable for planting out in the North.

Pot up young plants in late spring into soil-based potting mix with a slow-release fertilizer. In summer, place the pots outside in a sunny, sheltered place and water well. Pinch and disbud in midsummer as above.

Move the pots to a cool greenhouse in early fall; keep them at 50°F (10°C). Cut back the plants after flowering to about 9in (22cm). Overwinter at 40°F (5°C), in a cool greenhouse. Bring them back into growth in spring at about 45°F (7°C). Take cuttings as above.

PINCHING AND REMOVING LATERALS

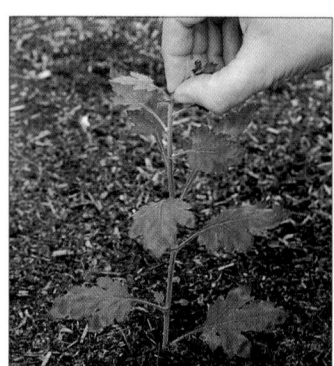

PINCHING
When the cutting is 6–8in (15–20cm) high, pinch out 1/2 in (1cm) at the tip to encourage new laterals.

REMOVING EXCESS LATERALS
About 2 months later, select 3 or 4 healthy, evenly spaced laterals and remove any others.

Routine care

Although most perennials will thrive with only little maintenance, certain routine tasks help keep them looking attractive and in the peak of health through the growing season. Occasional watering and feeding is necessary, and the surrounding ground should be kept clear of competing weeds. In addition to this, many perennials produce further growth and flowers if deadheaded or cut back, while dividing the plants from time to time renews vigor. Tall, fragile perennials, or those with top-heavy flower heads, may also require staking, particularly in exposed gardens.

Watering

The amount of water that plants require depends on the site, climate, and the individual species. Provided that they are grown in appropriate conditions, established perennials generally need little or no additional irrigation. If there are prolonged dry spells during the growing season, give extra water to the plants to keep them turgid. If they wilt or die back from lack of water, they will normally recover fully after heavy rainfall or will become dormant until the following season.

Young plants need to have sufficient water to become established, but they should not be watered once they are growing satisfactorily, except in very dry weather. In regions where summer drought is normal, such as the Southwest, installing irrigation tubing around the plants, with individual emitters for each plant, may be required.

Fertilizing

In soil that has been thoroughly prepared before planting, few perennials require more than an annual top-dressing of a balanced slow-release fertilizer, preferably applied in early spring after rain.

If conditions are dry, first water the soil thoroughly, then work the fertilizer into the soil surface with a hand fork. Do not let the fertilizer touch the leaves since it may scorch them. Plants that are grown primarily for their ornamental foliage, for example *Rheum* and hostas, benefit from an occasional liquid fertilizer during the growing season.

If a plant is not growing well, in spite of being in a suitable site, look carefully to see if it has been attacked by pests or disease, and treat accordingly. Foliage that is yellowing prematurely may indicate problems with soil drainage or a lack of certain nutrients. If appropriate drainage or fertilizng does not seem to improve the condition of the plant, send a soil sample for analysis by a laboratory to determine which elements are lacking (see also "Soil nutrients and fertilizers," pp.618–19).

Mulching

An annual mulch of organic matter such as spent mushroom compost or bark chips helps to suppress weed growth, reduce soil moisture loss, and improve the soil structure. Apply when the ground is moist during spring or fall by spreading a 1–2in (2.5–5cm) layer around the crowns of the plants (see also Soils and Fertilizers, "Mulches," p.620).

Weeding

Keep beds and borders free from weeds at all times, if practical, because they compete with the ornamental plants for moisture and nutrients in the soil. Underplanting with suitable groundcover plants (see Groundcovers, p.170) or mulching in spring helps to reduce problems with annual weeds. Any weed seedlings that do appear from windblown seed or seeds that have been dormant in the soil should be removed by hand before they become established.

If perennial weeds appear in the ground after initial cultivation, carefully dig them out with a hand fork. It is usually impractical to apply systemic weedkillers at this time because, to be effective, they must be applied when the weeds are in full growth, usually as they reach the flowering stage. At this point it is virtually impossible to avoid accidentally spraying the ornamental plants at the same time.

If the roots of a perennial weed have grown into those of a border plant, dig up the plant in early spring, wash the roots, and carefully pull out the weed. Then replant the border plant, making sure that no part of the weed is left in the original site. Do not hoe around perennials since this may cause damage to any surface roots and emerging shoots. For further information on controlling weed growth, see Plant Problems, "Weeds," pp.658–61.

Applying Mulch

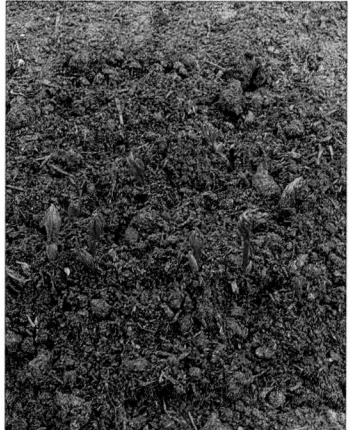

Clear any weeds, and apply a 1–2in (2.5–5cm) layer of mulch to moist soil; do not damage the young shoots of the plant (here a peony).

Improving flowering

Certain perennial plants may be cut back during growth in one of three ways to improve the number or size of their flowers or to extend the flowering season.

Thinning

Although most herbaceous plants produce numerous vigorous shoots in spring, some of these may be spindly and thin. If these weak shoots are removed at an early stage of growth, the plant then goes on to develop fewer, sturdier shoots that usually produce larger flowers. When the plant is about a quarter to one-third of its eventual height, pinch out or cut back the weakest shoots. This thinning technique may be used successfully with, for example, delphiniums, phlox, goldenrod (*Solidago*) and asters.

Pinching

It is possible to increase the number of flowers on perennial plants that readily produce sideshoots, such as *Helenium* and *Rudbeckia* species and cultivars, by removing (pinching) the growing tip of each stem. This technique also produces sturdier growth and prevents plants from becoming too tall and straggly. Pinching should be carried out when the plant is about one-third of its ultimate height. Pinch off 1–2in (2.5–5cm) of each shoot using your fingers or cut back with pruners just above a node. This encourages the buds in the uppermost leaf axils of the shoot to develop.

Individual plants in a group may be pinched a few days apart; this has the added benefit of producing a longer flowering season overall. For further information on how to produce fewer but larger blooms, see Dahlias, "Pinching and disbudding," p.228.

Deadheading

Unless decorative seedheads are desired or the seed is to be collected to raise additional plants, remove the

How to Thin and Pinch Perennials

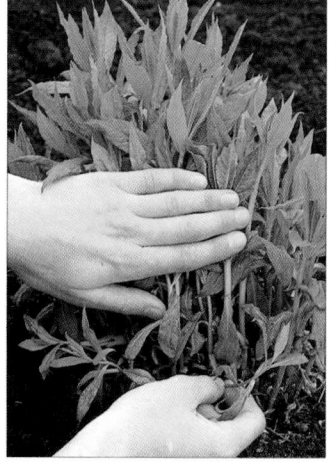

Thinning
Thin young shoots (here of a phlox) when no more than one-third of their final height. Remove about 1 shoot in 3 by pinching or cutting weaker shoots at the base.

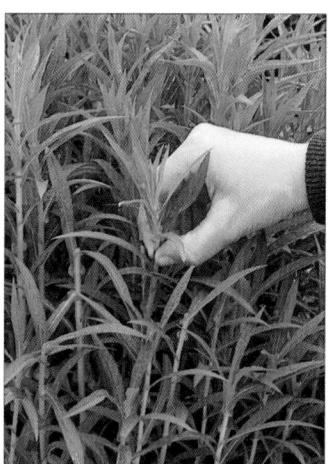

Pinching
When the shoots (here of an Aster) have reached one-third of their final height, pinch out the top 1–2in (2.5–5cm) to promote bushier growth.

CUTTING BACK TO EXTEND FLOWERING

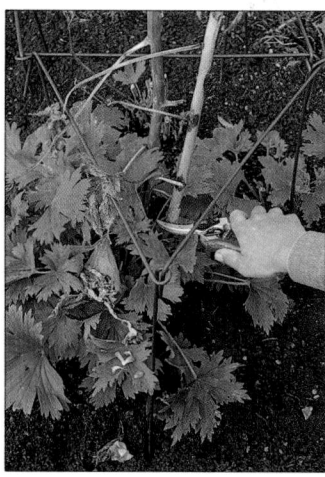

DELPHINIUM
After flowering, cut back old stems to ground level. In colder climates, remove only partway.

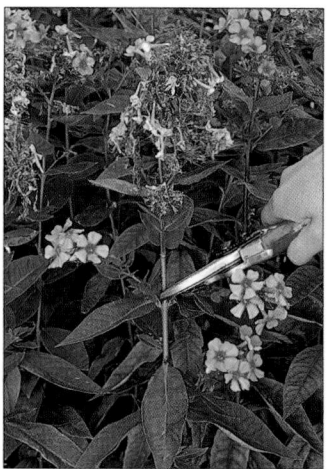

PHLOX
Cut back the central part of the flower head as the blooms fade to encourage the sideshoots to flower.

flowers as they begin to fade. Additional flowering sideshoots may then develop on the plant and extend the flowering season.

With a number of perennials, for example delphiniums and lupines (*Lupinus*), cutting back the old flowering stems partway when the first flowers have faded may encourage new shoots to develop that will produce a second display of flowers later in the season.

Cutting back

Shrubby perennials, for example the Nippon daisy (*Nipponanthemum nipponicum,* syn. *Chrysanthemum nipponicum*), should be pruned annually in early spring. Cut back the main stems with pruners to reduce the plant to less than half its former size. Also remove all twiggy, unproductive shoots. This encourages the growth of more compact plants that will better support the blooms throughout the flowering season.

Fall cleanup

Once perennial plants have finished flowering in fall, cut down the shoots to the base and remove them. In cold climates, leave about 6in (15cm) of stem to trap insulating snow, and cut this back later in spring. For marginally hardy plants, the entire top-growth should be left to protect the crown from frost heave; the dead top-growth is then removed in spring. Some perennial plants, such as *Sedum spectabile* and many grasses, have foliage or flower heads that remain attractive even when brown,

and these may be left on the plant to provide winter decoration, if desired, until early spring.

Transplanting established perennials

Most perennials may be transplanted easily if you wish to change the planting design. If possible, move them when dormant in fall or when just coming into growth in spring. Plants that dislike cold, wet conditions, such as *Kniphofia*, and those that are marginally hardy, should be moved in spring once the soil has warmed to encourage rapid growth.

A few long-lived plants, notably peonies (*Paeonia*) and hellebores

CUTTING DOWN IN FALL

In fall or early winter, cut dead stems (here of Rudbeckia) *to ground level, or to just above new growth.*

Staking

Tall and fragile perennials may need stakes to support them, particularly in windy situations. Insert stakes early in the season, since staking is harder to do and more likely to cause damage when growth is more developed. Push the stakes deeply into the ground so that they can be raised in stages as the plant grows.

For delphiniums and other tall, single-stemmed perennials, use sturdy stakes that are two-thirds of the stem's eventual height. Push a stake firmly into the ground near the base of each shoot, taking care not to damage the roots. Secure the stem to the stake with figure-eight twine ties as it grows.

To support plants with many stems, it may be easier to use a number of stakes placed at intervals in a circle around the plant.

Loop twine around the stakes at about one-third and two-thirds of the plant's height. Clump-forming plants, such as peonies (*Paeonia*), may also be supported with commercial devices such as ring stakes and link stakes, or similar homemade supports constructed from large-gauge wire mesh fixed to stakes. Stems grow through the support and eventually hide it.

There are two other fairly unobtrusive methods of staking. Push several twiggy stems, or peasticks, into the soil next to the young shoots and bend them toward the center of the clump to form a sturdy cage that will soon be covered by the plant as it grows. Alternatively, insert one sturdy stake in the center of a small group of plants or stems and radiate ties out to each stem.

RING STAKE
Stake low, clump-forming plants (here peony) early in the season. Raise the stake as the plant grows.

LINK STAKES
For taller plants such as this Aster, *push link stakes deep into the soil, then raise them as the plant grows.*

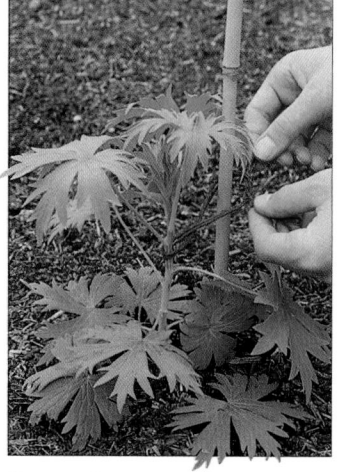

SINGLE STAKE
Stake single-stemmed plants (here delphinium) when 8–10in (20–25cm) high. Tie in the stem loosely.

RING OF STAKES
Encircle weak-stemmed plants (here Centaurea) *with twine, looped around thin stakes.*

(*Helleborus*), resent disturbance and may take two or more years to establish after transplanting. Normally they should be lifted only if it is necessary to propagate them.

Prepare the new site as for planting, and dig a hole of suitable size. Lift the plant, keeping as much soil around the root ball as possible. It is best to divide the plant at this stage (see "Lifting and dividing," right). Remove any weeds from the clump by hand, then replant the divisions as for container-grown perennials (p.184), firming the plant in and watering it well.

Moving plants during the growing season

Occasionally, it may be necessary to move a plant while in full growth; however, mature plants may not transplant successfully and should be treated carefully if transplanting is essential at this time. To minimize the stress caused to the plant, soak it in a bucket of water for several hours after lifting it. Then cut back the topgrowth to 3–5in (8–12cm) above the base and pot up the plant into a good potting mix. Keep the plant in a cool, shaded position, spraying daily but lightly until there are signs of

healthy, fresh growth, then replant it in its new, prepared position, and keep it watered.

Storing plants

Perennials may be lifted and stored over winter or if replanting is to be delayed, such as when transplanting them to a new garden during a house move. The plants should be lifted when they are dormant and carefully packed in boxes or crates of moist bark or peat so that they do not dry out; they should then be stored in a cool place.

Lifting and dividing

Where practical, perennials in a bed or border should be lifted, divided, and replanted every three to five years. Fast-growing, vigorous species, particularly those with a mat-forming habit such as *Ajuga* and *Stachys*, may need to be divided every other year. Plants that become woody, with signs of dieback at the center, or that look congested and flower less freely than in previous years, need to be divided. Some plants, such as peonies, must be

divided with particular care (see p.197).

Lifting plants makes it possible to clear the site of any weeds and to dig over and incorporate well-rotted organic matter or fertilizer as required. Dividing a plant rejuvenates it, keeps it healthy, and checks overvigorous growth.

In late fall or early spring, lift the plant, taking care not to damage its roots, and divide it into several portions by gently pulling them away from the main plant. Discard the old, woody center. Each division should contain a number of healthy, young shoots and its own root system (see also "Dividing perennials," p.196). Then dig over and lightly fertilize the original site as necessary and replant the divisions, leaving enough space between each for the plants to develop. Alternatively, replant the divisions in prepared ground in a new position as required.

Pests and diseases

Perennial plants, if grown in fertile soil, are not usually seriously troubled by fungal diseases, insects, or

> **PREPARING PLANTS FOR TEMPORARY STORAGE**
>
> *Lift the plants when dormant and place them in a box half-filled with moist bark or peat. Cover the roots with more bark or peat to keep them from drying out.*

other pests. Slugs, snails (p.638), aphids (p.639), thrips (p.640), mildews (p.640), and viruses (p.642) may attack a wide range of perennials but seldom give cause for concern. Check plants regularly during the growing season and treat them with an appropriate control if necessary. To help prevent problems, use clean tools and keep the garden neat.

Maintaining perennials in containers

Perennials planted in containers require more care than those in open ground since they have limited reserves of food and water. Make sure that the soil mix does not dry out during the growing season: daily watering may be necessary in hot, dry weather. Plant roots should always remain moist but not wet. Be sure that water can drain through the container.

Mulching helps reduce soil water evaporation and suppresses weeds. If using an organic mulch, replace it periodically when dividing or repotting the plants.

Every year or two in spring or fall, divide the plants and replant the most vigorous portions using fresh soil mix; otherwise, they soon exhaust the available nutrients and become too large for the container. If using the same container, wash the inside well before replanting, or repot into a larger container (see "Planting in containers," p.185). Cut back the roots of shrubby perennials by about one-quarter before repotting.

Where needed, bring in marginally hardy and tender plants in fall, keeping them protected until all danger of frost has passed (see COLD AND WIND PROTECTION, pp.604–5).

1 *In early spring or fall, rejuvenate perennials in containers by thinning out plants and renewing the soil mix.*

2 *Lift out the plants, separating them carefully, and shake the old soil mix from their roots. Discard half of the old soil mix.*

3 *Refill the container with fresh soil mix to within 4in (10cm) of its rim. Divide overgrown plants and arrange as required.*

4 *Plant up the container, fill in with more fresh soil mix around the plants, and firm them in with your fingers.*

5 *Finally, top-dress with mulch and water well until the soil mix is thoroughly wet and water runs through the drainage holes at the base. The plants grown here are* Bergenia *cultivars,* Pachysandra terminalis, *and a hosta (now dormant).*

Ferns

AMONG the most popular of the foliage plants, ferns add texture and atmosphere to the house or garden; here they are particularly appropriate in settings by streams or in damp, shady corners.

Cultivation

Hardy ferns are suitable for growing in the open garden, whereas tender tropical ferns are best cultivated indoors in a greenhouse or conservatory, or as houseplants.

Hardy ferns

Most hardy ferns are easily grown and are suitable for shaded, moist conditions. Being very tough, they require the minimum of cultivation and upkeep once they have become established. With the exception of *Thelypteris oreopteris* and all the *Blechnum* and *Cryptogramma* species, which require very acidic soil, ferns grow best in neutral soils (pH of 6.5 to 7.5). Garden soil with added organic material suits most species.

Planting may be carried out at any time if container-grown plants are used. Water them regularly in dry weather until established. Always plant in full or dappled shade. Some genera, such as *Dryopteris*, will tolerate dry conditions if they are well shaded, but almost all require damp conditions to thrive.

Many ferns, such as *Athyrium*, *Cryptogramma*, and *Osmunda*, die down at the first touch of frost, but some *Dryopteris* retain their fronds well into winter. Leaving the old fronds on the plant until early spring protects the crowns, but these should be removed as the young ones start to uncurl. Many species and cultivars of *Asplenium*, *Cyrtomium*, *Polystichum*, and *Polypodium* make good plants for the cool greenhouse, flourishing in a minimum daytime temperature of 41–50°F (5–10°C), and a nighttime temperature of no less than 35°F (2°C).

Tender tropical ferns

Ferns that will not withstand cold make excellent greenhouse or conservatory foliage plants, grown in pots or hanging baskets. Some also make good houseplants. Most require a winter minimum temperature of 50–59°F (10–15°C) but do not like hot, dry conditions and should be shaded from direct sunlight. A north-facing position on a bed of gravel that can be damped down in hot weather is ideal.

Tender ferns are usually sold in small pots and should then be potted up into 5in (13cm) or 6in (15cm) pots using a soilless potting mix. For this, use 3 parts peat-based potting mixture to 2 parts coarse sand or medium-grade perlite or vermiculite.

WATER SETTING
Matteuccia *thrives in damp conditions by a stream and provides a striking contrast of form and texture with the* Rodgersia *in the foreground.*

Add a cupful of charcoal granules to every 1¾ pints (1 liter) of mixture and, following the package instructions, a balanced granular or powdered fertilizer.

The root ball should not dry out completely; keep the plant in its pot inside a watertight outer container with about 1in (2.5cm) of sand or gravel permanently kept damp at its base. Ferns, particularly *Adiantum* species, should not be sprayed or overwatered, and *Nephrolepis*, probably the easiest to keep as houseplants, should be almost dry before watering. Fertilize occasionally with a liquid houseplant fertilizer.

Propagation

Ferns are raised mainly from spores but may be propagated by division or, in some species, by bulbils.

ROCK CREVICE
The lance-shaped fronds of the semi-evergreen Ceterach officinarum *contrast well with the rock behind that provides shade and shelter.*

PROPAGATION BY BULBILS

1 *Select a frond that is drooping under the weight of bulbils. The bulbils may have tiny green fronds emerging from them. Cut off the parent frond close to the base. The plant shown here is* Asplenium bulbiferum.

2 *Peg down the frond onto prepared soil mix. Make sure the frond's ribs are flat.*

3 *Water thoroughly, label the tray, and put it in a plastic bag. Seal the bag and leave the tray in a warm, light place until the bulbils have rooted.*

4 *Remove the wire pegs and lift each rooted bulbil with a widger or knife; if necessary, cut it away from the parent frond.*

5 *Put each rooted bulbil into a 3in (6cm) pot of moist, soilless potting mix. Keep moist in a warm, light place until the plants are large enough to transplant.*

Bulbils

Asplenium bulbiferum and some of the hardy *Polystichum* species produce bulbils or small plantlets along the fronds. These can be used for propagation by pegging down that part of the frond with bulbils onto a tray of seed or rooting medium. The bulbils soon produce rooted plantlets, which can then be separated and potted up. The bulbils root fastest when the parent plant is actively growing during the dormant season; rooting may take six months.

Spores

Ferns produce neither flowers nor seeds and have a unique way of reproducing. Fronds carry on their undersurfaces very small capsules (sporangia) that release large numbers of powdery spores; when sown on damp soil mix, these spores produce small growths (prothalli). Each prothallus carries both the male and female organs: the male organ (antheridium) produces spermatozoids, which swim across the surface moisture of the prothallus to fertilize the egg cell lying within the female organ (archegonium). After fertilization, a zygote is formed, which eventually develops into a tiny new fern. In this way the normal cycle of growth is continued.

Growing ferns from spores may take 18 to 24 months from sowing the spores to planting out the new ferns. Collect the spores by removing mature fronds that are almost ready to shed their spores. Ripe sporangia are plump and vary in color between species; many are dark brown, some blue gray, others are orange. Immature sporangia are flat and green or pale yellow. If the sporangia are dark brown and rough,

they will probably already have shed their spores. Lay the fronds on a sheet of clean paper and leave them in a warm room. In a day or so the spores will be shed onto the paper, looking like brown dust. Transfer them to a labeled seed envelope.

Fill a 3in (6cm) pot with standard sowing medium; firm and smooth the surface. Sterilize the medium by carefully pouring boiling water through a piece of paper towel laid on the surface until water comes through the drainage holes. When the medium has cooled, remove the paper towel and sow spores very thinly over the surface. Cover the pot, or put it in a propagator, and leave it in a warm, light place out of direct sunlight. To keep the surface constantly moist, mist-spray it regularly with previously boiled, lukewarm water. Remove the cover when the top of the pot is covered with a green, velvetlike "moss"; if the soil mix seems dry, moisten it by standing the pot in a saucer of boiled water for a short time.

Depending on the species, it takes from six to 12 weeks for the young prothalli to cover the medium surface. Prick them out by lifting small pieces of the "moss." Space them evenly, green side up, on the surface of other pots of sterilized sowing medium, press them down, and spray with lukewarm water that has been boiled. Cover the pots with plastic wrap or return them to the propagator. As the prothalli develop, spray them daily with lukewarm water until tiny plantlets appear. When they are large enough to handle, transplant them separately into pots of soilless mix and grow them on, potting on as necessary, until they are large enough to plant out.

FORMAL PLANTINGS
The clean, horizontal line of the golden boxwood (foreground) provides a perfect foundation for the shuttlecock shapes of Matteuccia struthiopteris.

PROPAGATION BY SPORES

1 *Examine the undersides of the fronds to find one with sporangia that are ready to release their spores. Cut off the selected frond with a clean, sharp knife, then place it carefully on clean, white paper to gather the spores. The plant shown here is* Adiantum fritzluthii.

NOT READY

READY

TOO LATE

2 *Sow a few of the spores onto a pot of prepared sterile sowing medium by tapping them from a piece of folded paper. Cover with some plastic wrap or place the pot in a propagator.*

3 *Mist-spray twice a week until the surface is covered with a bumpy green "moss." Lift small clumps with a widger or a knife.*

4 *Divide the clumps into small pieces, then gently firm them down onto sterile sowing medium. Spray with water and return them to the propagator.*

5 *When leaflike plantlets appear, lift them carefully. Firm into packs or small pots of moist soil mix. Pot on when they have developed small fronds.*

Propagation

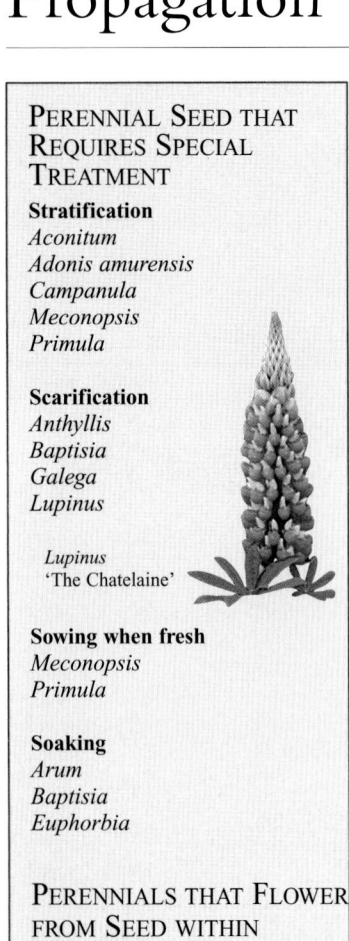

PERENNIAL SEED THAT REQUIRES SPECIAL TREATMENT

Stratification
Aconitum
Adonis amurensis
Campanula
Meconopsis
Primula

Scarification
Anthyllis
Baptisia
Galega
Lupinus

Lupinus
'The Chatelaine'

Sowing when fresh
Meconopsis
Primula

Soaking
Arum
Baptisia
Euphorbia

PERENNIALS THAT FLOWER FROM SEED WITHIN TWO YEARS

Alchemilla
Anemone
Aquilegia
Aster
Astrantia
Campanula
Catananche
Centaurea
Cuphea
Delphinium
Dianthus
Gaura
Hemerocallis
Iris
Linaria
Lobelia
Lychnis
Malva

Meconopsis
grandis
'Branklyn'

Meconopsis
Osteospermum
Papaver
Polemonium
Primula
Rudbeckia
Salvia (not shrubby spp.)
Scabiosa
Sidalcea
Silene
Verbascum

THERE are several ways of propagating herbaceous perennials. Growing them from seed is ideal where a large number of new plants is desired. Little experience or expertise is needed to raise the seedlings successfully, but this method is generally suitable for propagating species rather than cultivars.

For many perennials, the simplest and most common method of propagation is to lift them and divide clumps into separate plants. Others are better raised from seed or by vegetative means such as cuttings or, more rarely, grafting. Vegetative methods should be used for propagating almost all named cultivars.

Seed

Raising plants from seed is a simple and inexpensive way to propagate many perennials but, apart from a few named cultivars (for example, *Aquilegia* 'Crimson Star'), most cultivars do not come true from seed. Most species also show some variation in habit and flower color so, if collecting seed yourself, always gather it from plants with the best flower and growth characteristics.

Seed of early-flowering perennials, which ripens on the plant in early to midsummer, usually germinates quickly if sown as soon as it is ripe, producing young plants that may be overwintered successfully in open ground or in a cold frame. For most perennials, however, sow the seed immediately after it has been gathered in fall so that it germinates early the following spring. If stored in cool, dry conditions, most seed also germinates well when sown in spring.

Seed of herbaceous plants such as peonies (*Paeonia*) and hellebores (*Helleborus*) usually remains dormant for a considerable period unless suitable conditions are provided or occur naturally to break dormancy and induce germination. Some require a period of exposure to cold or light, while others have hard seed coats that should be weakened by scarification or softened by soaking before sowing (see also PRINCIPLES OF PROPAGATION, "How to overcome dormancy," p.623).

Pregermination treatment of seeds
Seeds that need to be subjected to a cold period to break dormancy may be either sown outside in fall or winter (see also *Sowing Seed that Requires Chilling*, opposite) or chilled in a refrigerator for a few months before sowing in spring. This method of breaking dormancy is suitable for many genera, including *Aconitum*, *Adonis*, *Campanula*, and *Primula*. Seeds of a few plants, such as those of *Gentiana asclepiadea*, require a period of exposure to light for successful germination.

Scarifying and soaking
A number of perennials, particularly those of the pea family, have seeds with thick, hard coats that preclude rapid and uniform germination. Just before sowing the seeds, scarify them either by rubbing with coarse sandpaper or by chipping each one slightly with a sharp blade to allow water to be taken up and then germination to occur.

Alternatively, many seeds may have their hard coats softened by being soaked in initially hot, but not boiling, water for 12–24 hours; this allows the seed to absorb water and germination to take place. Soaking is suitable for a number of perennials, for example *Baptisia* and *Euphorbia*. Once soaked, the seed should be sown immediately.

Double dormancy
Peony and *Trillium* seeds usually require two periods of cold to trigger germination of both roots and shoots. Root development from the germinating seed occurs during the first season, but the shoots do not normally start to appear until the seeds have received a second period of cold, usually during the following winter. Sow the seeds in containers in fall in the normal way.

Sowing seed in containers

Unless a very large number of plants is desired, it is easiest to sow seed in containers. A plastic half tray accommodates as many as two or three hundred seeds, while even a large square pot is adequate for sowing up to 50 seeds, depending on their size. Square pots fit closely in rows and provide a greater area of soil mix than round pots of the same width.

Whether using trays or pots, place a piece of window screening over any drainage hole(s), then fill them with an appropriate sowing medium. Soil-based mixes are often preferred to peat-based ones if the young seedlings are to be kept in them for more than a short period after germination. Gently press the medium around the edges of the container, then roughly level the surface and firm it with a presser so that it is about ½in (1cm) below the container rim.

Sowing
The seeds should always be sown thinly – about ¼in (0.5cm) apart; sowing too densely may result in thin, spindly plants that are prone to damping off (see p.651). Fine seeds, and those that require light to germinate, for example some gentians

Collecting seed

Gather the seed as it ripens: shake it from the pods or tie the seedheads into small bunches, enclosed in paper bags, and hang them upside down so that the seeds fall into the bags. Make sure that the seed is completely dry before storing it in clean paper bags or envelopes labeled with the plant name and harvesting date.

Gather ripened seedpods (here of Meconopsis) *when they have turned brown. Shake the seeds out of each pod onto a piece of paper and store in a cool, dry place until ready to sow.*

(*Gentiana*), may be left uncovered or sprinkled with a shallow layer of fine, sieved medium and then gently firmed with a presser. Larger seeds, such as those of peonies (*Paeonia*), should be covered with a ¼in (0.5cm) layer of sieved medium.

Aftercare

Label the containers with the seed name and sowing date, then water them with a fine spray, taking care not to dislodge the seeds. Alternatively, if small seeds are being sown, stand the containers in a bowl or tray of water for a short time until they have absorbed enough to moisten the medium throughout; this method prevents the seeds from being washed away. Minimize evaporation by covering the containers with glass, a plastic sheet, or plastic film, and place them in a cold frame, greenhouse, or windowsill. In sunny weather, provide some shade with newspaper or netting. Once the seeds have started to germinate, remove the cover and reduce any shading.

Plunging the containers in an outdoor bed

If the containers are to be placed outside, unprotected from the weather during fall and winter to break seed dormancy, add a covering of sand over the sown seeds. This prevents them from being washed out of the containers by heavy rain and, to some extent, deters mosses and liverworts from growing on the medium surface. Cover the containers with fine-mesh chicken wire to protect the seed if rodents or birds are likely to be a problem.

Plunge the pots in an open sand bed since this provides stable, even conditions for germination. Once the seed has germinated and the seedlings are visible, place the containers in a cold frame or other protected spot and care for the seedlings as for those raised under cover.

Pricking out

Once the seedlings are large enough to handle, that is when the first or second pair of true leaves has formed, they may be pricked out. Either space them evenly in seed trays with about 30–40 in each tray or prick them out into individual containers. The latter is advisable for seedlings that do not tolerate much root disturbance. Alternatively, prick out the seedlings into cell packs (compartmentalized trays). In all cases, use a good, soil-based potting mix.

Water the seedlings thoroughly, label them, and then place them in a cold frame or cool greenhouse until they are established. They may then

RAISING PLANTS FROM SEED

1 *Fill a 5in (13cm) pot with moist sowing medium. Firm the medium to about ½in (1cm) below the rim, using a presser.*

2 *Using a clean, folded piece of paper, scatter the seeds (here* Leucanthemum x superbum) *sparingly over the medium.*

3 *Cover the seeds with a shallow layer of fine, sieved medium. Label and then water without displacing the seeds.*

4 *Cover with glass or a clear plastic sheet to retain moisture. Place the pot in a cold frame until the seedlings develop 2 to 4 true leaves.*

5 *Prick out the seedlings into pots; peat pots (inset) allow planting out direct. Handle the seedlings by the leaves because the stems are easily damaged.*

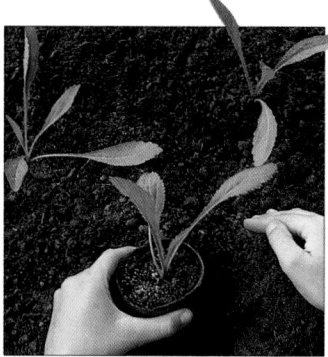

6 *When the seedlings have developed into small plants with a good root system, plant them out or pot them up, as appropriate.*

SOWING SEED THAT REQUIRES CHILLING

1 *In fall, sow the seed thinly in pots of sowing medium, then cover with a thin layer of medium and top-dress with fine sand.*

2 *Label the pots with the seed name and date of sowing, and water thoroughly. Then plunge the pots in an open sand bed outside to encourage the seeds to germinate.*

be potted on individually or planted out in their permanent site in open ground when they are large enough.

Sowing outside in open ground

If large numbers of plants are needed, it may be more convenient to sow seed outside. Prepare an area in fertile, well-drained soil by clearing any weeds and cultivating the soil to a fine tilth. Using a line or a straight-edged board as a guide, make a seed drill using a draw hoe, onion hoe, or the point of a large label.

The depth of the drill depends on the size of the seed to be sown: about ¼in (0.5cm) deep is adequate for small seeds, while large seeds require a drill at least ½in (1cm) deep. If the seedlings are to be transplanted when young, set the drills 4–6in (10–15cm) apart; if, however, they are to be grown on in rows, allow about 6–9in (15–22cm) between them. Sow small seeds thinly so that they are about ¼in (0.5cm) apart, large seeds such as peonies at intervals of 1in (2.5cm) or more.

After sowing, cover the drills by raking soil lightly over them, then label each drill with the name of the seed and the date. Water carefully, without washing away the soil. For further details, see ANNUALS AND BIENNIALS, *Sowing in Drills*, p.211.

Dividing perennials

This method is suitable for propagating many perennials that have a spreading rootstock and produce plenty of shoots from the base. As well as being a way of increasing stocks, in many cases division rejuvenates the plants and keeps them vigorous, since old or unproductive parts may be discarded (see also "Lifting and dividing," p.191).

Some perennial plants can be divided simply by pulling sections apart by hand, or by using two forks back to back; other plants that have fleshy roots are best split apart by using a spade or knife.

When to divide

Most plants should be divided when they are dormant, from late fall to early spring, but not in extremely cold, wet, or dry weather because these conditions may make it difficult for the divided plants to reestablish successfully.

Fleshy-rooted perennials are usually best moved in late summer in order to give them time to make new roots before winter sets in. Irises, peonies (*Paeonia*), and poppies (*Papaver*) are the most common fleshy-rooted perennials. Potted plants may be planted in spring.

Preparation

First lift the plant to be divided by loosening the surrounding soil, taking care not to damage the roots, then levering it up gently with a fork. Shake off as much loose soil from the roots as possible and remove any dead leaves and stems to make it easier to see the best points for division. This also enables you to see which are the healthy parts of the plant to be retained and which are the old, unproductive parts that can be discarded.

Wash most of the soil off the roots and crowns of fleshy-rooted plants, so that all the buds are clearly visible and therefore do not become damaged inadvertently when you are dividing the plant.

Fibrous-rooted plants

Insert two hand forks back to back near the center of each plant so that the tines are close together and the handles apart. Push the handles gently backward and forward so that the prongs gradually tease the plant apart, then separate the clumps into two smaller portions. Repeat this process with each portion to divide the plant into more sections, each with some new shoots.

Plants that tend to form woody clumps or that have thick, solid roots should be cut into portions with a spade or sharp knife. Make sure that there are at least two growth buds or shoots on each piece. The sections containing vigorous young shoots and healthy roots tend to grow at the perimeter of the plant. Discard the old, weak, and often woody growth from the center of the plant.

Perennial plants that have loose, spreading crowns and numerous shoots, such as phlox and asters, are easy to pull apart by hand or with two hand forks. Simply separate off single stems growing at the edges of the crown so that each has its own root system.

Fleshy-rooted plants

Plants that have bulky, almost solid, fleshy roots, such as *Rheum*, may need to be divided with a spade since it would be difficult to separate the crowns using back-to-back forks. After cleaning the plant so that the developing buds are clearly visible, slice through between them with a spade, taking care to leave two or more buds on each piece. Then trim each division neatly with a knife, discarding any old, woody material and any damaged or rotting roots.

Plants with numerous, intertwined crowns, such as *Kniphofia* and tufted ornamental grasses, may also be divided with two forks.

Replanting and aftercare

After dividing a plant, dust any cut surfaces with an appropriate fungicide (see PRINCIPLES OF PROPAGATION, "How roots form," p.626). Replant the divisions as soon

---

Dividing hostas

Large hostas with tough rootstocks should be divided using a spade. Include several buds on each division and trim any damaged parts with a knife. Hostas that have looser, fleshy rootstocks may be separated by hand or with back-to-back forks; each division should have at least one eye (shoot).

TOUGH, FIBROUS ROOTS
Divide the crown with a spade; each section should include several developing buds.

LOOSE, FLESHY ROOTS
Divide small plants and those with a loose rootstock by pulling the clump apart by hand.

HOW TO PROPAGATE PERENNIALS BY DIVISION

1 *Lift the plant to be divided, taking care to insert the fork far enough away from the plant so that the roots are not damaged. Shake off surplus soil. The plant shown here is a* Helianthus.

2 *Separate plants with a woody center by chopping through the crown with a spade.*

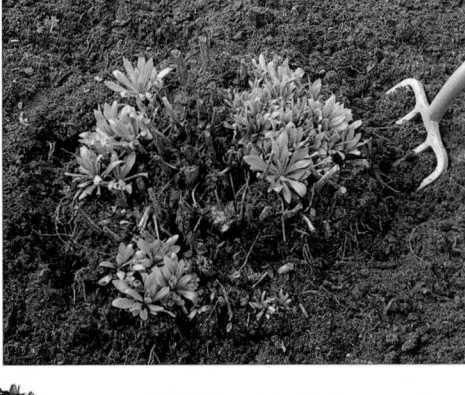

3 *Divide the plant into smaller pieces by hand, retaining only healthy, vigorous sections, each with several new shoots.*

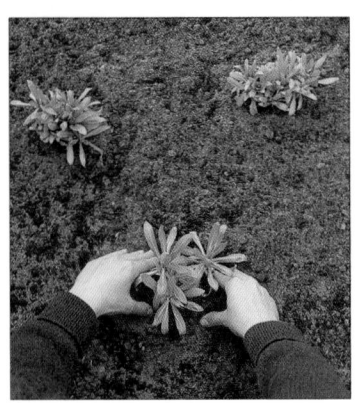

4 *Cut back the old top-growth and replant the divided sections to the same depth as before. Firm in and water thoroughly.*

ALTERNATIVE METHOD

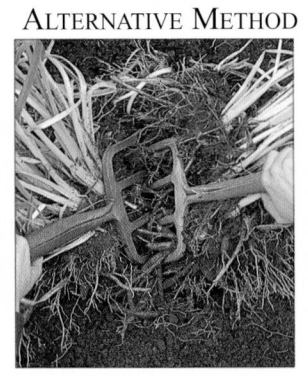

Divide fibrous-rooted, herbaceous plants (here Hemerocallis) *using 2 forks back to back.*

as possible. It is important that they do not dry out, so if replanting is unavoidably delayed for a couple of hours, dip the plants briefly in water and keep them in a sealed plastic bag in a cool, shady place until you are ready to replant them.

Large divisions, if replanted immediately in spring, may still provide a good show of flowers in the same season, although the stems are often slightly shorter than those of more established plants. Very small divisions, however, are best grown on for a season in a nursery bed or in pots in order to become established. In general, the divisions should be replanted at the same depth as the original plant, but those plants that are prone to rotting at the base are best set slightly above the surrounding soil level to keep their crowns free of excess water (see also "Planting depths," p.184).

When replanting, make sure that the roots are well spread out in the plant-ing hole and the plant firmed in. Water newly planted divisions thoroughly; take care not to expose the roots by washing away any soil.

Dividing peonies

Peonies should be divided with particular care because they tend to reestablish slowly after being transplanted. For best results, lift and divide the plants toward the end of summer, when the swelling red growth buds are clearly visible. The crown should be cut into sections, each with a few buds. Take care not to damage the thick, fleshy roots. See also PEONIES, p.182.

See also PEONIES, p.182.

PERENNIALS THAT MAY BE DIVIDED

Achillea
Aconitum
Adenophora
Anemone hupehensis
Arum
Aster
Astilbe
Astrantia
Bergenia

Aster novae-angliae
'Harrington's Pink'

Buphthalmum
Campanula
Centaurea dealbata
Clematis (herbaceous)
Coreopsis verticillata
Crambe cordifolia
Doronicum
Epilobium
Galega
Geranium
Helenium
Helianthus
Helleborus orientalis

Helleborus orientalis

Hemerocallis
Heuchera
Hosta
Iris (rhizomatous)
Kniphofia
Liatris
Lobelia cardinalis, L. fulgens
Lychnis
Lysimachia
Lythrum
Nepeta
Oenothera fruticosa
Ophiopogon
Paeonia
Phlox
Phormium
Physostegia
Polemonium
Pulmonaria
Rheum
Rudbeckia
Salvia nemorosa, S. pratensis
Saponaria
Scabiosa caucasica
Schizostylis
Sedum spectabile
Sidalcea
Silphium
Smilacina
Solidago
Stachys byzantina
Symphytum
Tanacetum coccineum
Thalictrum
Tradescantia x *andersoniana*
Trollius
Veronica

Division of rhizomatous plants

Divide plants with thick rhizomes, such as *Bergenia* and rhizomatous irises, by splitting the clump into pieces by hand, then cutting the rhizomes into sections, each with one or more buds (see right). Bamboos have tough rootstocks that either form dense clumps with short rhizomes or have long, spreading rhizomes. Divide the former with a spade or two back-to-back forks; cut the latter into sections (each of which should have three nodes or joints) with pruners (see also GRASSES, SEDGES, AND RUSHES, p.187).

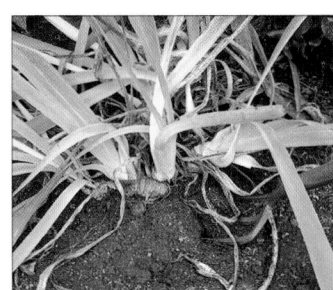

1 *Lift the plant to be divided (here an iris), inserting the fork well away from the rhizomes to avoid damaging them.*

2 *Shake the clump to remove any loose soil. Using your hands or a hand fork, split the clump into manageable pieces.*

3 *Discard any old rhizomes, then detach the new, young rhizomes from the clump and neatly trim off their ends.*

4 *Dust the cut areas with fungicide. Trim long roots by one-third. For irises, cut the leaves to a miter about 6in (15cm) long to prevent wind-rock.*

5 *Plant the rhizomes at least 6in (15cm) apart. The rhizomes should be half buried, with their leaves and buds upright. Firm in well and water.*

1 *Lift the plant in late summer, when healthy growth buds are visible. Remove old stems, then cut the plant into sections, each one with several buds.*

2 *Dust all the cut surfaces of the divided sections with fungicide to discourage infection and rot.*

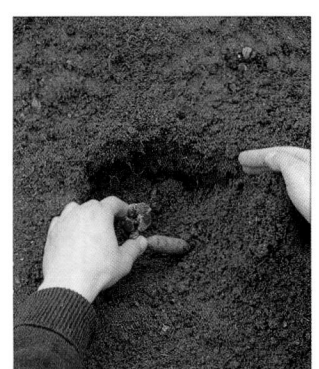

3 *Plant the divided sections approximately 8in (20cm) apart. The buds should be 1 to 3in (2.5–8cm) deep. Firm the soil well and water.*

PROPAGATING PERENNIALS BY STEM TIP CUTTINGS

1 Select short lengths of soft wood about 3–5in (7–12cm) long from the tips of strong, healthy shoots. The plant shown here is a Penstemon cultivar.

2 Trim the lower end of each cutting just below a node, with a straight cut, reducing the length to 2–3in (5–7cm). Carefully remove the lower leaves.

3 Insert the cuttings around the edge of a 6in (15cm) pot of rooting medium and water in. Cover with a plastic bag, held away from the cuttings by stakes.

4 When the cuttings have rooted, gently lift them and pot them up individually into 4in (10cm) pots.

PERENNIALS THAT MAY BE PROPAGATED BY STEM CUTTINGS

Tip
Anisodontea
Arctotis
Argyranthemum
Calceolaria integrifolia
Cuphea
Dianthus
Diascia
Epilobium canum
Erysimum
Euryops
Felicia
Gazania
Helichrysum petiolare
Lavatera
Lotus berthelotii
Malvastrum
Mimulus aurantiacus
Oenothera missouriensis
Osteospermum

Osteospermum 'Buttermilk'

Parahebe
Pelargonium
Penstemon
Phygelius
Salvia
Scrophularia auriculata
Sphaeralcea
Trifolium pratense
Verbena
Viola

Basal
Anthemis tinctoria
Chrysanthemum
Delphinium
Lupinus
Monarda

Anthemis tinctoria 'E.C. Buxton'

Stem tip cuttings

This method of propagation is used most commonly for herbaceous perennials that are difficult to divide successfully and for cultivars that do not come true from seed. Cuttings may be taken at any time during the growing season provided that suitable shoots are available.

Select strong growing tips without flower buds, rejecting any that are thin, weak and leggy, or damaged. If there is likely to be any delay before inserting the cuttings, place them in a sealed plastic bag to protect them from dehydration.

Preparing and inserting the cuttings

Take cuttings with pruners or a sharp knife, cutting across the stem immediately above a node. Trim the cuttings to just below a node, then remove the leaves from the lowest third of each cutting. Insert the cuttings into prepared pots or trays of an appropriate rooting medium and firm in with your fingers. Leave sufficient space between the cuttings so that the leaves do not touch each other and air can circulate freely. This inhibits the spread of damping-off diseases (see p.651).

Aftercare

Water the cuttings carefully with a fine spray and treat them with a fungicide to reduce the risk of infection and rot. It is important that the cuttings are maintained at a high humidity level; otherwise, they will wilt. If possible, keep them in a mist unit or propagator. Alternatively, cover the cuttings with a plastic tent or bag. This should be supported on stakes or hooped wires to prevent the plastic from touching the leaves, since any condensation forming on the foliage could encourage fungal infection and rot.

In hot weather, shade the cuttings with newspaper, commercial shade netting, or other semitranslucent material to prevent the leaves from scorching or wilting. Take off the shading as soon as possible after the hot weather to allow the cuttings plenty of light. Inspect them daily, removing any fallen and dead leaves and any material that is infected. Water the medium as necessary so that it remains moist but not wet.

After about two to three weeks, the cuttings should produce roots and may be potted on into individual pots. Any healthy cuttings that have not developed roots by this stage should be reinserted and cared for as before until they have rooted.

Basal stem cuttings

This type of cutting is suitable for taking from a wide range of herbaceous plants that produce clusters of new shoots at the base in spring. Short, basal cuttings may also be taken in midspring from sturdy shoots of plants, such as lupines

HOW TO PROPAGATE BY BASAL STEM CUTTINGS

1 Take cuttings when the shoots (here of Chrysanthemum) are 1½–2in (3.5–5cm) high, each with a small piece of basal wood.

2 Remove the basal leaves from each cutting and trim the lower end, making a straight cut.

3 Insert the cuttings into a prepared pot of moist rooting medium. Place the pots in a propagator or plastic bag to encourage rooting.

4 When the cuttings have rooted, separate them, retaining as much medium as possible around the roots. Pot up the cuttings individually.

(*Lupinus*) and delphiniums, that later develop hollow or pithy stems, as well as those that have soft tissue.

If required, the plants to be propagated may be lifted and grown in pots or trays in a warm greenhouse to encourage the production of basal shoots earlier than if the plants were growing in the open ground. The cuttings may then be rooted and young plants established earlier in the season. The plants from which cuttings have been taken may then be replanted in the garden.

Preparing and inserting the cuttings

Select strong, sturdy shoots whose first leaves have just unfolded and, using a sharp knife, remove them as close to the base as possible. Include part of the woody basal tissue in the cutting. Do not use any shoots that are damaged or hollow.

Trim off the lower leaves of the cuttings, dip them in hormone rooting powder, and insert them in rooting medium, either individually or several to a pot, or in trays. Firm in the cuttings, water thoroughly, and allow the containers to drain before placing them in a cold frame or propagator. Alternatively, cover each of the containers with a clear plastic bag supported on wire hoops firmly inserted into the medium. Shade the cuttings from direct sunlight to prevent the leaves from scorching or wilting.

Aftercare

Check the cuttings every few days, removing any dead or decaying foliage as soon as possible to prevent the spread of rot. Be sure that the medium is moist, but not wet, at all times, and wipe or shake away excess water and condensation from the glass or plastic covers. The cuttings should be well rooted within a month; they may then be potted on into individual pots filled with equal parts of soil, sand, and peat, or use a standard soil mix.

Root cuttings

This is a useful method of propagating perennials that have fairly thick, fleshy roots, such as *Verbascum* and *Papaver orientale* cultivars. It is also the only way of raising new, healthy plants from border phlox cultivars that are affected by nematodes. Because the nematodes occur in the top-growth of affected phlox, but not in the roots, taking root cuttings makes it possible to produce healthy, nematode-free plants. This method is not used for those phlox cultivars with variegated foliage, however, because the resulting plants produce only plain green leaves.

Take care to minimize damage to the parent plant when cutting its roots, and replant it immediately after taking the cuttings. Root cuttings are most successful when they are taken during the plant's dormant period, usually in winter.

Preparation

Lift a strong, healthy plant and wash off the soil so that all the roots can be clearly seen. Select roots that are young, vigorous, and fairly thick, since these are more likely to produce successful new plants than those that are weak and thin or old, gnarled, and woody. Cut off the young roots close to the crown and replant the parent plant.

When propagating plants with thick roots, for example *Acanthus*, *Anchusa*, *Romneya*, and *Verbascum*, choose roots that are about the thickness of a pencil and cut them into sections 2–4in (5–10cm) long. With thin-rooted perennials, cut the roots into 3–5in (7–12cm) lengths so there is sufficient food storage for the developing cuttings.

Trim each section so that the top end (that nearest the plant's stem) is cut straight across and the bottom end (nearest the root tip) is cut at an angle; this makes it easy to insert the cuttings the correct way up. Shoots will develop from the top end of the cutting and roots from the lower end. Trim off any fibrous roots before inserting the cuttings.

Inserting the cuttings

After preparing the cuttings, dust them with fungicide to protect against rot. Then insert them vertically, straight ends at the top, in prepared pots or trays of rooting medium about one and a half times their depth. The tops of the cuttings should be level with the surface. Cover the pots with a thin layer of fine sand or grit; label, and place them in a propagator or cold frame. Do not water the cuttings until they begin to root. Once young shoots have developed, pot them up singly into an appropriate soil mix.

Plants with thinner roots, such as *Anemone hupehensis*, *A. x hybrida*, *Campanula*, phlox, and *Primula denticulata*, are often treated slightly differently because their roots may be too fine to insert vertically. Lay the root cuttings flat on the surface of pots or trays of firmed medium, then cover with more medium. Then treat as for standard root cuttings.

HOW TO PROPAGATE PERENNIALS BY ROOT CUTTINGS

1 *Lift the plant (here* Acanthus*) when nearly dormant, then wash the roots. Select roots of pencil thickness and cut them off close to the crown.*

2 *Trim the roots and cut each into lengths of 2–4in (5–10cm). Make a straight cut at the upper end of each cutting and an angled cut at the lower end (see inset).*

3 *Insert the cuttings into holes made in pots of moist rooting medium, then firm. The top end of each cutting should be flush with the medium surface.*

4 *Top-dress the pots of cuttings with coarse sand, label them, and place them in a cold frame until the cuttings root.*

5 *When the cuttings have developed young shoots, pot them up into individual pots filled with soil-based potting mix. Water and label the pots (see inset).*

ALTERNATIVE METHOD FOR THIN ROOTS

Place the trimmed cuttings horizontally on moist, firmed medium. Cover with medium and firm lightly.

PERENNIALS THAT MAY BE PROPAGATED BY ROOT CUTTINGS

Acanthus
Anchusa azurea
Anemone hupehensis,
　A. x hybrida
Arnebia
Campanula
Catananche caerulea
Dodecatheon
Echinops

Catananche caerulea 'Major'

Erodium
Eryngium
Gaillardia
Geranium
Gypsophila
Limonium latifolium
Linum
Mertensia
Morisia
Papaver orientale
Phlox decussata,
　P. subulata
Primula denticulata
Pulsatilla vulgaris
Romneya
Stokesia
Trollius
Verbascum
Viola

Pelargoniums ("geraniums")

PELARGONIUMS are almost all tender, evergreen, perennial plants of South African origin. When introduced to Britain, they were given the common name "geranium" because of their botanical similarity to the hardy, herbaceous species of the genus *Geranium*, which was commonly cultivated in Europe at that time. The common name "geranium" is widely used in North America today; for purposes of precision, the term "pelargonium" is used in this discussion.

Types of pelargonium

Pelargoniums may be divided into five broad groups, according to the main characteristics of the plants. The groups are: zonal, dwarf and miniature zonal, regal, ivy-leaved, and scented-leaved.

Zonal

These pelargoniums have rounded leaves, usually marked with a distinct, dark zone and single, semi-double, or double flowers. Some cultivars, however, do not have a zone, and others have golden, white-variegated, or tricolored leaves.

In temperate climates, they grow well in the open garden and are ideal for summer bedding since they bloom continuously from early summer until the first frosts. They also thrive in windowboxes, hanging baskets, and containers. Zonals will readily adapt to the growing conditions in a greenhouse or conservatory.

TYPES OF PELARGONIUM

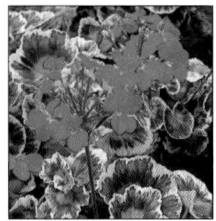

ZONAL
P. 'Dolly Varden'
Rounded leaves with a darker zone, and single to double flowers.

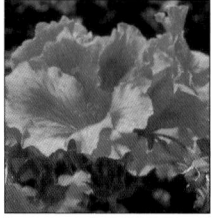

REGAL
P. 'Purple Emperor'
Deeply cut leaves and broadly trumpet-shaped flowers.

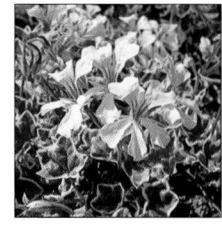

IVY-LEAVED
P. peltatum 'Amethyst'
Trailing plants with lobed leaves and single to double flowers.

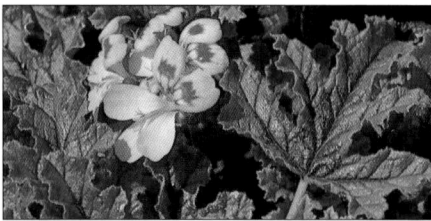

SCENTED-LEAVED
P. 'Royal Oak'
Plants with small, often irregularly star-shaped flowers, grown for their fragrant leaves.

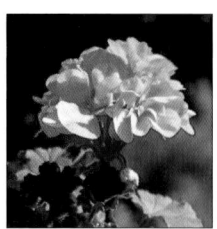

DWARF ZONAL
P. 'Timothy Clifford'
Bushy, free-flowering plants, similar to zonals, up to 8in (20cm) tall.

Dwarf and miniature zonal

Dwarf zonal pelargoniums are 5–8in (13–20cm) tall, bushy, and very free-flowering. They make excellent windowbox plants and pot plants for displaying in greenhouses and conservatories. Miniature zonals have smaller leaves and flowers than the dwarf zonals and are no higher than 5in (13cm). Many are very floriferous plants, with double and single blooms in a wide range of colors, and green to greenish black leaves.

In recent years, F1 and F2 hybrid zonal pelargoniums have been developed. These are grown from seed and are used mainly for bedding. They are single-flowered and are available in many of the same colors and combinations as the cultivars that are propagated vegetatively.

Regal

These pelargoniums (also known as Martha Washington geraniums) are small, shrubby plants with rounded, deeply cut leaves and wide, trumpet-shaped flowers, often in bright, exotic colors.

They may be grown in the open garden but, in temperate regions, are much more extensively used as greenhouse, conservatory, and houseplants, since the flowers are easily spoiled by rain. In frost-free climates, where they may be planted out permanently, they make splendid flowering shrubs, almost continuously in bloom year-round.

Ivy-leaved

These trailing pelargoniums have rounded, lobed, ivylike leaves, and flowers similar to those of zonals, available in a rich assortment of colors. They are used mainly in hanging baskets and other containers, where their flowers on trailing stems can be displayed to best advantage. They may also be planted so that they spill over the edge of a raised bed or a wall.

Scented-leaved

Scented-leaved pelargoniums have small, delicate flowers with five petals, and fragrant foliage for which they are chiefly grown. They make good house- and greenhouse plants, and in temperate climates may be grown outside in the summer and fall, in containers or beds.

Fertilizing/watering

All pelargoniums, especially when they are grown in containers, need weekly fertilizing throughout summer with a high-potassium liquid fertilizer, such as tomato fertilizer. This helps the plants continue to produce a mass of good-quality blooms without becoming too leafy. Nitrogen-rich fertilizers will produce too much leaf at the expense of flower production and should not be used. Pelargoniums in containers should be watered as soon as the top of the soil mix dries out.

Overwintering

Pelargoniums must be kept frost-free, except for *P. endlicherianum*, a rare, hardier species from Turkey. In temperate climates, plants grown outside may be saved for replanting the following season by moving them under cover before frost occurs. Lift the plants before the first frosts are expected, shake as much soil as possible off the roots, trim back the roots and stems, and remove any remaining leaves.

For storing, use a wooden or strong cardboard box with deep sides, and make a few small drainage holes in the bottom. Half fill the box with a soilless potting mix, which should keep the plants alive but contains insufficient food for them to grow vigorously during storage. Place the prepared stock plants in the box, so that they are close together but not touching. Fill in with more soil mix around each plant and firm it in stages until the soil is level with the top of the box.

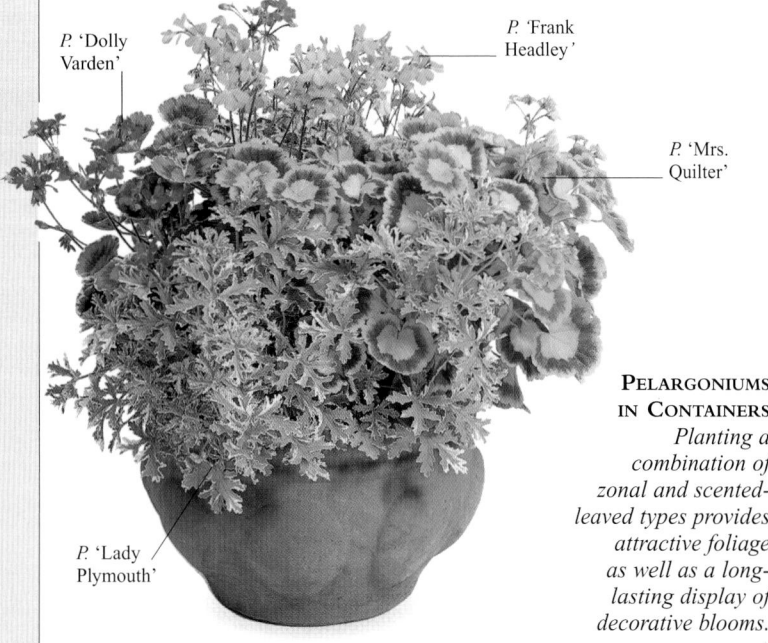

P. 'Dolly Varden'

P. 'Frank Headley'

P. 'Mrs. Quilter'

P. 'Lady Plymouth'

PELARGONIUMS IN CONTAINERS
Planting a combination of zonal and scented-leaved types provides attractive foliage as well as a long-lasting display of decorative blooms.

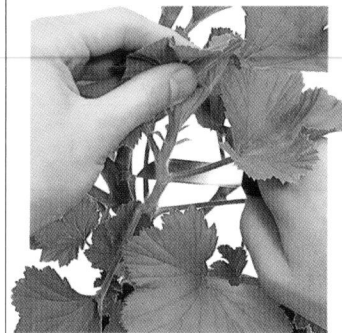

CONTRASTING HABITS
Use trailing ivy-leaved pelargoniums to spill over the edge of a container. These will make an attractive contrast with upright forms in the center.

Water the soil mix thoroughly and leave the box outside for a day to drain. The plants should be watered again during the winter only if they become very dry. Store the box where it will receive plenty of light and remain frost-free; if the temperature remains just above freezing, the plants will not grow much but should survive.

By midwinter, new shoots will begin to appear on the stock plants; these may be used as cuttings in early spring. Alternatively, the stock plants may be potted up separately and grown on for planting out in the early part of the summer.

Propagation from cuttings

Pelargoniums are easily propagated from cuttings, and the method used is the same for all types. Taking cuttings is an inexpensive way of producing new plants and allows the parent plant to remain outside in the garden until the first frosts, thus prolonging the display.

Selecting the cuttings
Although it is possible to take cuttings from spring onward, the best time is in late summer, when light conditions are good and the weather is still warm. Select strong, healthy shoots (nonflowering ones if from a regal or scented-leaved pelargonium), cutting just above the third joint below the growing tip. Trim each cutting just below the lowest joint and remove the lower leaves.

Inserting the cuttings
Choose the pot size according to the number of cuttings: a 5in (13cm) pot will take up to five cuttings. Fill the pot with a standard rooting medium, press down firmly, and place the pot in a container of water until the surface of the medium becomes moist. Remove the pot and allow it to drain. Insert the cuttings, pressing them down gently to eliminate any air pockets beneath the bases of the cuttings. Do not water them yet.

Aftercare
Place the pot in a light, warm position, but not in full sun. A week after insertion, water the cuttings from below (see above) and again about a week later, by which time the cuttings should be rooting. If watered from above, the cuttings may suffer from gray mold/*Botrytis* (see p.646) or other damping-off diseases (p.655). Do not use propagators or cover them with plastic sheeting for the same reason. Allow free air circulation around them. As soon as the cuttings have rooted (when they resist being pulled up and fresh leaves appear) pot them up singly into 3in (6cm) pots.

Growing F1 and F2 hybrids from seed

Seed-sown F1 and F2 hybrids are quite easy to grow, and given good light, they will flower in as little as three months. Start the seeds in late winter. Sow them on a moistened piece of coffee filter or paper towel in a covered glass dish. They often germinate erratically. After germination, transfer the sprouted seeds to individual cell packs or to 2in (5cm) pots. Be careful not to overwater the seedlings; a slightly dry soil mix is best to promote healthy growth.

When the seedlings are 6in (15cm) high, pinch out the growing tips to encourage bushy growth. Grow the seedlings on as cool greenhouse plants throughout the winter and spring, to enable them to flower throughout summer and fall. Particularly good-quality plants may be overwintered as for other pelargoniums (see left).

TAKING CUTTINGS

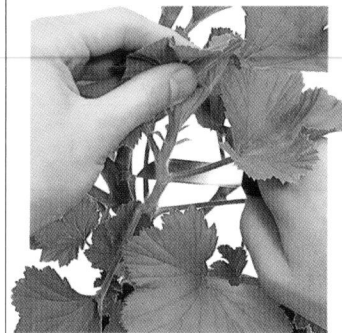

1 *Choose a healthy shoot and cut straight across the stem just above the third joint below the growing tip.*

2 *Using a sharp knife, remove leaves from each cutting, leaving two at the top. Pinch out any flowers or buds.*

3 *Carefully trim the base of each cutting to just below the lowest joint with a straight cut.*

4 *Make holes 1in (2.5cm) deep in pots of moist, firmed rooting medium. Insert the cuttings, then firm.*

OVERWINTERING

1 *Lift the plants before the first frosts and shake off any loose soil. Cut down the stems to about 4in (10cm) and remove the leaves. Trim back roots to about 2in (5cm).*

2 *Half fill a box at least 6in (15cm) deep with soilless mix. Put in the plants so that they do not touch each other. Fill in with mix, then water and drain.*

3 *Store in a frost-free place until new shoots start to appear, then pot up the plants. Use the new shoots to take cuttings from, as necessary, later in spring.*

CHAPTER
7

ANNUALS AND BIENNIALS

ANNUALS AND BIENNIALS are traditionally regarded as a quick and inexpensive means of providing color. To restrict their use in this way, however, is to overlook their vast range of attributes. They can bring to life any garden within just a few months or, as cut flowers, transform the home. They also provide opportunities to experiment by changing color schemes from one year to the next. Although short-lived, a large number flower freely for weeks or even months. The gardener can use this profusion of color to create infinite patterns of bedding with plants that are planned to flower in succession. While annuals and biennials are most often used to adorn beds and containers, some varieties with a trailing or climbing habit are particularly striking grown up a support or allowed to sprawl luxuriantly over a bank.

Designing with annuals and biennials

THE term "annual" describes a plant whose entire life cycle, from germination to seed production to death, takes place within one year. Those that can withstand some cold are known as hardy annuals; those that are not are termed half-hardy and must be raised under cover and planted out after all danger of frost has passed.

Biennials, however, require two growing seasons. During their first season after sowing they produce leaf growth; they then overwinter and flower in the following year.

Many plants grown as annuals are actually tender perennials and will survive outdoors only where frosts do not occur.

Annual borders

Whole borders or beds devoted to annuals produce colorful displays. Ideal in a new garden where they quickly provide a vibrant show, annuals may also be used as features in established gardens. The plants can be changed several times in a season to create different displays.

Color

The most attractive annual borders are often those that rely on a limited range of colors: dazzling oranges and reds, muted pinks and purples, soft blues and mauves. Plan the planting with a broad sweep of color, selecting tones that blend together harmoniously. Grays, greens, and whites are particularly useful for providing a respite from some of the more vibrant reds and blues. Many annuals, such as snapdragons *(Antirrhinum)*, pansies *(Viola x wittrockiana)*, and petunias, are available in a range of colors, making it possible to select a plant whatever the color range. A bed devoted to pure white flowers looks fresh and crisp, but green-foliaged plants prevent the planting from looking cold. Creams should not be substituted for cleaner whites here.

Form and texture

Border compositions are often enhanced by the leaf texture or the overall plant shape as much as by color alone. Place plants with contrasting leaf or flower textures in adjacent groupings. Their differing characteristics will then be better appreciated. Form and texture of annuals are often overlooked, but they add greatly to the character of a planting, whether it be with the wispy flowers of *Nigella*, the bold spikes of *Salvia*, or the sprawling informality of the poached-egg flower *(Limnanthes douglasii)*. A particularly valuable plant is the ornamental corn *(Zea mays* 'Japonica Multicolor'), with its variegated leaves, plumelike flower tassels, and

SUMMER-FLOWERING ANNUALS AND BEDDING PLANTS
Frost-tender perennials grown as annuals bring exotic color to gardens in temperate climate zones. Although they last only one season, high-impact designs like these can be achieved in a matter of a few weeks.

A TAPESTRY OF SUMMER COLOR
This beautiful display of annuals has an artistic quality that could be changed the following season for a totally different effect.

ears of variously colored kernels. Including a variety of shapes and sizes also adds interest to the planting. For example, select the daisy-like shapes of *Gaillardia*, the golden disks of sunflowers (*Helianthus annuus*), the large bells of petunias, the feathery plumes of *Celosia cristata*, or the tiny pompons of English daisies (*Bellis perennis*) or double-flowered feverfew (*Tanacetum parthenium*).

Grouping the plants
Many annuals look their best when planted in large groups of one cultivar to give a bold block of color. Single plants can otherwise easily become isolated and weaken the structure of the planting. Sow in irregular patches so that the impact as the plants mature is similar to the interlocking drifts of flowers made by perennials in a traditional herbaceous border. The shapes and sizes of the groups should be varied to create a natural, free-flowing look.

When a border is to be viewed mainly from one direction, perhaps from a path or lawn, or is backed by a fence or hedge, graduate plants according to height. Plant the tallest plants, such as hollyhocks (*Alcea*), *Amaranthus*, and sunflowers, at the back. Place naturally low-growing species such as *Ageratum*, sweet alyssum (*Lobularia maritima*), and annual phlox at the front of the border. Between them, juxtapose groups of intermediate, but slightly different, heights to achieve variation. This produces a billowing, undulating informality.

Combine plants that flourish in similar conditions. For instance, species or cultivars of *Nicotiana*,

which have loose clusters of tubular flowers on short to tall stems, combine well with the low-growing, flower-covered, compact shapes of *Impatiens* cultivars, since both generally prefer cool and shady sites.

Foliage plants
There are several annuals grown chiefly for their foliage to harmonize or contrast with bright flower color, and to add to the range of textures in a bed or border.

The silver-gray *Senecio maritima* is easily grown from seed. Although often treated as a half-hardy annual, it is in fact a perennial, and it may be kept for years if protected from cold where marginally hardy. A clump of castor beans (*Ricinus communis*), another perennial that flourishes in cooler climates when treated as a half-hardy annual, provides a striking accent with its green or purplish bronze leaves.

The curious bright green, cuplike flowers of the annual bells-of-Ireland (*Moluccella laevis*) contrast well with colorful planting designs. Selected cultivars of *Solenostemon* (coleus) have a range of foliage color in reds, purples, yellows, and greens.

Other colorful foliage plants include 'Ruby' chard (a cultivar of *Beta vulgaris*), with its vivid red, upright stalks, and ornamental cabbages (*Brassica oleracea* forms), which have low-growing, muted foliage in pinks, greens, and white.

Seasonal display
Plan the planting so that the flowering periods of the annuals coincide as much as possible to avoid gaps in the design. To provide interest over a long period, use annuals that bloom in succession; for specific color combinations, make sure that the chosen plants all bloom at the same time.

For a spring display choose wallflowers (*Cheiranthus*), forget-me-nots (*Myosotis*), pansies (*Viola* x *wittrockiana*), and primroses (*Primula vulgaris* and *P.* x *polyanthus*). For summer and early fall, the selection of plants coming into flower is much greater, and the scope for creating pleasing combinations is essentially limitless.

Petunias have been diversified so greatly that elaborate color schemes may be created using them alone. Choose from the boldly contrasting,

striped blooms, the bright, single colors, or the subtly shaded ones, using them either singly or in combinations. Both the multiflora and grandiflora types are excellent for use in large or small bedding designs.

Marigolds also offer a wide range of colors, from cream to deep orange to mahogany-red, and the flower heads vary from the single daisies of *Tagetes signata* to the great globes of the splendid African cultivars. French marigolds (*Tagetes patula*), with single and double flower heads, display rich crimson or mahogany-red coloring. Many other marigolds, intermediate between the African and French types, are also available.

Formal bedding designs
The wide variation of color, shape, and size, as well as the uniformity of growth obtainable in many modern cultivars of annuals, provides opportunities to create long-lasting displays from spring to fall. One of the glories of annuals is the intensity of color achieved when a single cultivar of one of the low-growing, floriferous kinds is massed in a bed so that individual plants merge together. A scarlet carpet of geraniums

AN ANNUAL BORDER
A complete border may be devoted to annuals, biennials, and other short-lived plants. In this design, good use has been made of the different heights and growth habits of a wide variety of plants. Newer cultivars of sunflower (Helianthus), of medium height and with sturdy, self-supporting stems, lend valuable stature and focus.

FORMAL BEDDING
*Perfect for coloring in a preexisting pattern of boxwood, lavender, and santolina, here forget-me-nots (*Myosotis*) make vivid monochrome panels*

A MIXED BORDER
Annuals and biennials create a rich tapestry when planted among perennials. Tall yellow spires of biennial Verbascum, *golden sunflowers, and pot marigolds are interwoven with blue cornflowers and pink* Cosmos.

or of *Salvia splendens*, for example, makes a vivid display when set into a fresh, green lawn. Patterned designs, using annuals of different colors, can produce similarly dramatic eye-catching effects.

The dense growth habit and continuous flowering of many annuals make them ideal candidates for these complex, formal patterns. There is a wide range of dwarf and intermediate cultivars available. Plants may be used to add color to designs that have been delineated with bricks, gravel, or other architectural materials.

Annuals are excellent for knot gardens and parterres where small evergreen plants such as boxwood (*Buxus*), thyme (*Thymus*), or lavender (*Lavandula*) are clipped to create permanent outlines. Vary color schemes with the seasons: a spring planting of pansies can be followed by a summer one of dwarf zinnias, for example.

Alternatively, various annuals, biennials, and other temporary plants can be used alone to create designs that make the most of their contrasting colors and form. An outline of low, mounded plants in a single color will help define the pattern and contain filler plants. White always makes a crisp, clear edging – English daisies (*Bellis perennis*) can be used in spring, and sweet alyssum (*Lobularia maritima*) or *Lobelia* do well in summer. The fillers can be flowers with a looser, more irregular shape, such as snapdragons.

Mixed borders

A mixed border containing shrubs, perennials, bulbs, and annuals is one of the delights of the garden.

With such a diversity of plants, it offers the greatest possible variety of color, contour, texture, season of interest, and design. Annuals and biennials warrant a place in any permanent planting plan, in which they can be sown each year or left to self-seed. If allowed to self-sow they will produce a random profusion of flowers reminiscent of the traditional English cottage garden, where all kinds of plants, including fruit, salad vegetables, and crops, jostle for space in the same informal plot.

ANNUALS IN MIXED BORDERS

Used as color highlights among perennials and shrubs, both annuals and biennials bring life to established borders. Possibilities range from cheerful mixtures of *Clarkia* (syn. *Godetia*), *Cosmos*, and California poppies (*Eschscholzia californica*), to carefully coordinated one-color schemes. For instance, flowering annuals, such as crimson

Amaranthus caudatus and *Nicotiana alata*, or scarlet begonias, geraniums, and *Verbena* cultivars, will add highlights to a red border that has a framework of purpletoned foliage.

Self-sown annuals and biennials may soon become a permanent feature in a mixed border, helping unify the planting and introducing a pleasing

1 *Onopordum acanthium*
2 *Papaver orientale*
3 *Paeonia* 'Sarah Bernhardt'
4 *Papaver somniferum*
5 *Digitalis purpurea* cvs
6 *Bergenia cordifolia* 'Purpurea'
7 *Thalictrum aquilegiifolium*
8 *Ornithogalum narbonense*
9 *Dianthus* 'Mrs. Sinkins'
10 *Allium giganteum*
11 *Dicentra formosa*
12 *Viola tricolor*

In this bed, annuals (represented by gray areas on the diagram) have been planted between the perennials and bulbs to fill the gaps and to provide extra interest as well as wonderful splashes of bright color throughout the summer months. The sculptural, silvery gray Scotch thistle and the tall purple and white spikes of foxgloves appear majestically above the interlocking clumps of

perennials. Bright red opium poppies punctuate the planting and, at the front of the border, the delicate Viola tricolor *sprawls out over the path. The pinkish purple of the* Viola *complements the pink of the peony* 'Sarah Bernhardt'. *The rich purple foxgloves and the profuse blooms of* Thalictrum aquilegiifolium *help create an integrated and attractive planting design.*

unpredictability. In early summer, delicate love-in-a-mist (*Nigella damascena*) makes a hazy web of color, filling any gaps and weaving together neighboring blooms and the young leaves of later-flowering plants. The spirelike stems of certain biennials such as *Verbascum* and foxgloves (*Digitalis*) add an air of cottage garden informality to an otherwise structured border.

Architectural plants

Handsome leaves, eye-catching flower shapes, and striking habits of growth make certain plants stand out from their companions. Annuals or biennials with such architectural qualities can be key features in a mixed border, enhancing the composition. These plants have the greatest impact when they complement (rather than dominate) the other plants in the vicinity. The large, spiny gray leaves and tall, widely branched flower stems of the Scotch thistle (*Onopordum acanthium*), for instance, make a statuesque centerpiece in a border that features other types of silver-foliaged plants. The flower spikes of the Excelsior Series foxgloves and larkspur (*Consolida*) rise gracefully above all the neighboring plants. Shapely or unusual blooms, such as the large and complex flower heads of spider flower (*Cleome*), never fail to command attention.

Plants grown primarily for their foliage also play an architectural role. In large borders the green or purple-red palmate leaves of castor beans (*Ricinus communis*) add a strong textural quality, as do the bold leaves of the ornamental cabbages (*Brassica oleracea* forms).

Annuals and biennials as fillers

Since they grow rapidly and are relatively cheap to raise, use annuals and biennials to fill gaps in both herbaceous and mixed borders. Place them where a plant has failed, or in the spaces between immature perennials or recently planted shrubs in a new border. Make the effort to select species that provide a pleasing contrast in form or texture, choosing cultivars in a height and color range that complement (not detract from) the permanent plantings.

In warmer areas, at the end of the season, plant wallflowers (*Cheiranthus*) for their winter foliage and spring flowers. Multicolored carpets of winter-flowering pansies (*Viola* x *wittrockiana*) and primroses (such as *Primula vulgaris*) may be interplanted with spring-flowering bulbs, such as daffodils, hyacinths, or late-flowering tulips.

Until alpines become established, gaps in the rock garden may be filled by sun-loving annuals that enjoy the same conditions. To avoid overwhelming the delicate colors and modest stature of the alpines, however, choose annuals that are on a similar scale, such as *Viola tricolor, Lobelia erinus, Thymophylla tenuiloba*, and *Portulaca*.

ANNUALS TO TRAIL
With its tumbling form, shapely leaves, and long-lasting, attractive double flowers, this annual nasturtium, Tropaeolum 'Hermine Grasshof'*, needs no companion plants to make a vivid and striking focal point in a decorative terracotta pot.*

Annuals and biennials as groundcovers

Some annuals and biennials may be used as temporary groundcovers, creating pools of color in an otherwise bare space. There are annuals for shade as well as sun, poor soil as well as rich. Single-color cultivars of sweet alyssum (*Lobularia maritima*) or annual candytufts (*Iberis*) may be used to provide dense cover in a sunny spot. Use *Impatiens* cultivars in shade, where their spreading growth and colorful, continuous blooms will quickly cover bare ground. For a more textured quality as well as lively color, sow corn poppies (*Papaver rhoeas*) or California poppies; both spread quickly. An attractive groundcover is also swiftly created by using cultivars of *Catharanthus roseus* in white or rose, or nasturtiums (*Tropaeolum*) in red, orange, and yellow.

Climbers and trailers

Vigorous annuals and biennials that climb and trail may quickly transform an expanse of wall or fence with a colorful curtain of foliage and flower, weaving a screen to provide privacy, or embellishing an existing structure. Many annuals have attractive leaves as well as beautiful flowers, and quite a few, such as high-climbing or low-growing bush sweet peas (*Lathyrus odoratus*), mignonette (*Reseda odorata*), heliotrope, sweet alyssum (*Lobularia maritima*), flowering tobacco (*Nicotiana*), sweet sultan (*Centaurea moschata*), some petunias, and stocks (*Matthiola*) offer the added pleasure of scent.

Plants with a climbing or trailing habit are particularly valuable in restricted spaces such as patios and balconies, where they make use of the vertical space as well as the ground area. Moreover, many annual climbers can be grown in pots. They are ideal for furnishing new gardens, softening bleak surfaces, and disguising or distracting from an unsightly view.

Exuberant annuals that twine around and clothe architectural features may be used to provide an abundance of summer flowers in company with more permanent perennial climbers. Try morning glories (*Ipomoea*), twining cultivars of nasturtium (*Tropaeolum*), or cup-and-saucer vine (*Cobaea scandens*) with its large bell-shaped flowers in purple or greenish white. For quick results, grow *Thunbergia alata* or *Rhodochiton atrosanguineum*, which is a fascinating plant with curious, deep purple, tubular flowers in dusky maroon calyces. You might even consider using gourds and their relatives, including pumpkins and squash, for this purpose

Climbing annuals are intriguing when grown through host plants such as ivy (*Hedera*) or conifers. Use the twining canary creeper (*Tropaeolum peregrinum*), which has broadly lobed leaves and bright yellow, fringed flowers. Another choice is *Eccremocarpus scaber*, which climbs by means of tendrils and has a long flowering season, with clusters of tubular flowers that glow yellow, orange, or red among its small, tooth-shaped, pinnate leaves. For a dense, leafy screen, plant scarlet runner beans (*Phaseolus coccineus*), which bear delicate, scarlet flowers and a useful and practical bonus of edible pods.

GROUNDCOVER ANNUALS
Low-growing Impatiens *cultivars form a carpet of intense color in the cool shade under trees or shrubs.*

Annuals in containers

Whether it is a relatively small terracotta pot, wooden Versailles tub, or plastic windowbox, any container is a potential focal point in the garden, and the plants grown in it can make an eye-catching feature. F1 hybrid annuals, with their uniform growth habit and consistent flower colors, are specifically bred to provide reliable, long-lasting displays. However, most annuals may be used in containers, either on their own or to complement other plants.

The shape, style, and material of the container may be chosen to play a major part in the display, or it may be completely subordinate to the planting. A shapely urn or a handsome stone trough can be veiled by wisps of foliage, while a more functional container can be disguised with trailing leaves and flowers.

Increasing the choices

The choices of annuals suitable for containers or patio beds close to the house may be greater than that for the open garden, since the protection of adjacent buildings often enables plants to be grown that are normally too tender for more exposed sites in the same area. Consider how sunny, shady, or windy the site is before deciding which plants to grow.

Annuals are available for an all-season display. In late spring and early summer, some cultivars of pansies and primroses continue to provide color when growing in sheltered spots away from blazing sun and heat. Protected but sunny sites on patios, for example, are also ideal for gazanias, *Solenostemon* (coleus), New Guinea *Impatiens* cultivars, and seed-raised dahlias, all of which maintain their vibrant color throughout summer and well into fall.

WINDOWBOX COMPOSITIONS
This restrained cream, blue, and green combination mixes begonias and pansies with trailing Lobelia, ivy, Helichrysum, *and* Lysimachia.

Selecting cultivars

Compact cultivars are particularly useful, since they will better withstand windy sites and will not need support. Choose dwarf and intermediate snapdragon cultivars rather than tall ones, and dwarf bedding geraniums. Some ivy-leaved geraniums, which have a long flowering season, can be raised from seed and grown as half-hardy annuals, then particularly good specimens can be brought back under cover for winter for propagation and planting the following season. New hybrid geraniums, intermediate in habit between the trailing and the bushy types, include, among many others, the Sensation, Breakaway, and Multibloom Series. They have been specially bred for production from seed and are ideal for growing in containers. For further details see PELARGONIUMS, pp.200–1.

Gazanias grow well in hanging baskets and containers positioned in sunny spots, where they open their brightly colored flower heads. Heliotrope is valuable around the house in containers near a window or doorway, where its perfume can be appreciated. Stocks (*Matthiola*) have similar qualities of beauty and scent, particularly the Ten-week Series in summer and the East Lothian and Brompton Series in both fall and spring.

Hanging baskets and windowboxes

Plants with a trailing habit are ideal for growing in windowboxes and hanging baskets, and appealing displays can be created by a mass of foliage and flower. Reliable performers include trailing petunias,

Lobelia erinus such as the Cascade Series, blue fan flower (*Scaevola aemula*) and *Verbena* x *hybrida* cultivars, available in a wide range of colors, including pure reds and scarlets, deep purples, crimsons, and whites. Trailing and spreading F1 geraniums, renewed annually from seed, are also a good choice (see PELARGONIUMS, pp.200–201).

Annuals for cutting and drying

Many annuals provide excellent cut flowers. If space is available in your garden, it is worth growing a number of flowers especially for cutting. They may be either integrated into borders or sown in a separate area. Taller cultivars may be particularly suitable; choose cornflowers (*Centaurea cyanus*), snapdragons (*Antirrhinum*), stocks, and *Gypsophila*. Sweet peas (*Lathyrus odoratus*) are particularly good as cut flowers and fill the house with their heady fragrance; if the flowers are cut regularly, the plants will bloom for many weeks. Larkspur (*Consolida*) is also useful for cutting and is equally attractive whether fresh or dried.

Many annuals may be grown to dry as everlasting flowers for indoor display throughout the year, including *Helichrysum*, *Limonium*, and *Amaranthus caudatus*. Others, such as honesty (*Lunaria*) and *Nigella*, are grown for their decorative seedheads. Annual grasses, such as hare's tail (*Lagurus ovatus*), are also worth growing because their feathery seed-heads make a fine display.

PLANTING IN THE VERTICAL PLANE
Hanging baskets and windowboxes transform a bare wall. Trailing plants such as ivy-leaved geraniums contrast with bright yellow and rust marigolds, creating a continuous curtain of color.

Planter's guide to annuals and biennials

EXPOSED SITES

Annuals and biennials that tolerate exposed or windy sites

Borago officinalis
Calendula
Catharanthus roseus
Centaurea cyanus
Cheiranthus
Chrysanthemum carinatum,
    C. coronarium, C. segetum
Clarkia
Dianthus barbatus, D. chinensis
Echium vulgare
Eschscholzia
Glaucium flavum
Iberis amara, I. umbellata
Lavatera trimestris
Limnanthes
Linum grandiflorum
Lobularia maritima
Lunaria
Malcolmia
Oenothera biennis
Papaver rhoeas, P. somniferum
Petunia
Rudbeckia hirta (hybrids)

Rudbeckia
hirta

Salvia horminum
Tagetes signata
Vaccaria hispanica

DRY SHADE

Annuals and biennials that tolerate dry shade

Digitalis purpurea
Matthiola bicornis

MOIST SHADE

Annuals and biennials that prefer moist shade

Impatiens walleriana
Matthiola bicornis
Mimulus – seed selections including:
    M., Calypso Series
    M., Malibu Series
Oenothera biennis
Primula vulgaris
Viola x wittrockiana

FRAGRANT FLOWERS

Centaurea moschata
Dianthus, Chabaud Series,
    D. chinensis
Exacum affine
Heliotropium
Humea elegans
Lathyrus odoratus
Lobularia maritima
Matthiola bicornis

M., Brompton Series,
M., East Lothian Series,
M., Ten-week Series
Nicotiana alata, N. x sanderae
    (some cvs), N. sylvestris
Primula
Reseda odorata
Viola x wittrockiana

FLOWERS FOR CUTTING

Agrostemma githago 'Milas'
Antirrhinum (tall cvs)
Calendula
Callistephus (tall cvs)
Centaurea cyanus
Cheiranthus cheiri
Chrysanthemum carinatum,
    C. coronarium, C. segetum
Consolida ambigua
Coreopsis
Cosmos
Dianthus barbatus,
    D., Giant Chabaud Series,
    D., Knight Series
Gaillardia pulchella
Gilia capitata
Gomphrena globosa
Gypsophila elegans
Helianthus annuus,
    H., Color Fashion Series
Helipterum
Lathyrus odoratus
Limonium sinuatum
Lunaria annua
Matthiola, Brompton Series,
    M., East Lothian Series,
    M. incana, M., Ten-week Series
Moluccella laevis
Nigella damascena
Papaver nudicaule
Psylliostachys suworowii
Rudbeckia hirta (hybrids)
Salvia horminum
Xeranthemum annuum
Zinnia

FLOWERS FOR DRYING

Ageratum
Amaranthus
Avena sterilis
Bracteantha bracteata
Briza maxima, B. minor
Calendula
Celosia
Centaurea cyanus
Clarkia
Consolida ambigua
Gomphrena globosa
Helipterum
Hordeum jubatum
Lagurus ovatus
Limonium sinuatum
Lonas
Moluccella laevis
Nigella
Panicum violaceum

Pennisetum villosum
Rhodanthe manglesii
Salvia horminum
Setaria glauca
Stipa pennata

ARCHITECTURAL PLANTS

Alcea rosea, syn. Althaea rosea
Amaranthus caudatus,
    A. tricolor
Brassica oleracea 'Cabbage
    Cherry Sundae', B. o. 'Kale
    Red and White Peacock'
Cleome hassleriana
Digitalis purpurea
Helianthus annuus
Kochia scoparia f. trichophylla

Helianthus
annuus

Onopordum acanthium
Ricinus communis
Salvia sclarea var. turkestanica
Silybum marianum
Verbascum bombyciferum,
    V. densiflorum
Zea mays 'Gracillima Variegata',
    Z. m. 'Japonica Multicolor'

TRAILING PLANTS FOR CONTAINERS

Ageratum
Arctotis stoechadifolia
Begonia semperflorens
Bidens ferulifolia
Brachycome iberidifolia
Convolvulus tricolor
Gazania
Helichrysum bracteatum
Heliotropium
Impatiens walleriana
Lobelia erinus
Osteospermum 'Starshine' (and
    other seed selections)
Pelargonium 'Breakaway',
    P. 'Multibloom',
    P. 'Sensation', P. 'Summer
    Showers'
Petunia
Scaevola aemula
Senecio
Sutera cordata
Thymophylla tenuiloba
Tropaeolum majus (semitrailing
    cvs), T. m. 'Empress of India',
    T. m., Whirlybird Series
Verbena x hybrida
Viola x wittrockiana

ANNUAL CLIMBERS

See list on p.127.

CONTAINER PLANTS

Annuals suitable for growing from seed as (greenhouse) container plants

Antirrhinum
Begonia semperflorens
Campanula pyramidalis
Capsicum (ornamental fruit cvs)
Centaurea moschata
Coleus
Exacum affine
Humea elegans
Impatiens walleriana (tall cvs)
Osteospermum
Pelargonium (F1 and F2 hybrids)
Petunia
Primula malacoides,
    P. obconica, P. sinensis
Psylliostachys suworowii
Salpiglossis
Schizanthus
Senecio x hybridus (cvs)
Thunbergia alata
Torenia fournieri
Trachelium caeruleum
Trachymene coerulea, syn.
    Didiscus coeruleus

PERENNIALS THAT MAY BE GROWN AS ANNUALS

Alternanthera
Antirrhinum

Antirrhinum majus,
Princess Series

Argemone mexicana
Begonia semperflorens
Browallia speciosa
Cobaea scandens
Coreopsis, Early Sunrise Series
Eccremocarpus scaber
Gazania
Gomphrena globosa
Heliotropium arborescens
Impatiens walleriana
Lotus berthelotii
Mimulus, Malibu Series (and other
    seed selections)
Mirabilis jalapa
Nierembergia rivularis
Pelargonium (all F1 and F2 seed
    selections)
Ricinus communis
Salvia farinacea, S. splendens
Senecio cineraria
Solenostemon
Sutera (Bacopa)
Verbena x hybrida

Sowing and planting

ANNUALS and biennials are among the easiest of plants to raise from seed. They can also be obtained as seedlings or young plants from nurseries or garden centers, and will provide an instant display of color in a garden border or container placed indoors or outside.

Buying seeds

Always buy fresh seeds that have been stored in cool conditions. Their viability varies greatly; some, such as members of the pea family, may remain viable for a few years if kept cool and dry, but most start to deteriorate after a year, especially if they are stored in damp, warm conditions. Seeds in sealed foil packets should last for several years; however, once the packets are opened, the seeds deteriorate.

F1 hybrid seeds are available for many annuals and some biennials; these produce plants that are vigorous and true to type with even growth and flower characteristics. These seeds are ideal for the gardener who is seeking uniformity, but for most ordinary garden purposes the well-produced, open-pollinated seeds are equally satisfactory and provide some variation in the plants.

Pelleted seeds
Seeds may be individually coated with a paste, or pelleted, to form a small, smooth ball. This enables them to be handled separately, so that

they can be more easily spaced in containers or the open ground. If pelleted seeds are space-sown at the correct distance they do not need to be thinned, so, although they cost more, fewer are required. The seeds should be watered thoroughly after sowing to make sure that the moisture needed for germination penetrates the seed coat as quickly as possible. Pelleted seeds are normally available only for F1 hybrids.

Seed tapes and gels
Seed tapes are tissuelike, soluble strips with evenly spaced seeds embedded within them. The tapes are laid at the base of a drill, then covered with a thin layer of soil. Gel kits can be purchased for fluid sowing – seeds are added to a paste that suspends and thereby evenly spaces the seeds throughout it. The mixture is then squeezed along a prepared drill. It is important not to allow the

Growing perennials as annuals

Many tender and marginally hardy perennials can be difficult to overwinter and often do not flower as well in subsequent years. To be grown as true perennials they need to be overwintered under some sort of cover, but it is often easier to propagate the plants from cuttings each year or to grow them afresh from seed. Tender perennials grown in this way often produce a much better display, particularly in cold areas.

Those that are best propagated by tip cuttings include *Acalypha, Alternanthera*, marguerites (*Argyranthemum frutescens*), *Iresine, Justicia, Lantana, Pachystachys*, and *Tibouchina*. Take the cuttings in late summer or early fall (see PERENNIALS, "Stem tip cuttings," p.198) and then overwinter them in a frost-free place such as a

greenhouse, sun porch, or heated cold frame, or indoors under fluorescent lights. By late spring, after the last frosts, the young plants can be planted out.

Tender perennials usually propagated from seed (see "Sowing," right) include snapdragons (*Antirrhinum*), wax begonias (*Begonia semperflorens*), gazanias, *Gerbera*, flowering tobacco (*Nicotiana*), castor bean (*Ricinus*), petunias, and scarlet sage (*Salvia splendens*).

Some plants can be raised either from cuttings or seed; they include *Browallia, Catharanthus roseus* (syn. *Vinca rosea*), *Coleus, Felicia*, heliotrope (*Heliotropum*), *Hypoestes, Impatiens, Nierembergia*, bedding geraniums (*Pelargonium hortorum* cultivars), and *Pentas*.

Hardy and half-hardy annuals and biennials

Annuals complete their life cycle in a year, while biennials require two years. Horticulturally, annuals and biennials are termed hardy or half hardy. Hardy annuals are resistant to cold and so may be sown early in open ground and will be established before more tender annuals. Half-hardy annuals withstand only a limited amount of cold and are killed or badly damaged at freezing temperatures; they need to be maintained in frost-free conditions of 55–70°F (13–21°C) to germinate and become established.

Hardy biennials should be sown by midsummer to allow the plants to become well established by the winter. Overwinter half-hardy biennials in a cool greenhouse or insulated cold frame.

mixture to dry out. Both methods distribute the seeds evenly so that less thinning is required than for hand-sown seeds.

Small seedlings already well established in wedges or plugs of soil mix are also available, ready for potting up individually in small pots or for planting in compartmentalized trays. They should be grown on in an unheated greenhouse or frame, or on a sunny windowsill, until they are at the planting-out stage. They are much cheaper than bedding plants.

Sowing

When and where to sow annuals and biennials depends on when they are required to flower and on the temperature they need for germination.

Hardy annuals
When the soil has warmed up to at least 45°F (7°C) in the spring, sow hardy annuals where they are to flower. If sown in successive batches until midsummer, hardy annuals provide a long summer display.

Some hardy annuals, if sown in situ in the fall, germinate to produce small plants that overwinter satisfactorily outdoors and flower in late spring or early summer the following year. Candytufts (*Iberis*), pot marigolds (*Calendula*), and poppies (*Papaver*) are some examples.

Seeds of hardy annuals can also be sown in pots or seed trays and either planted out in their final positions in late fall or overwintered in a cold frame to be planted out in spring. This technique is particularly useful in gardens with clay soil that is slow to warm up in spring.

Hardy biennials
Most hardy biennials can be sown outdoors from late spring until midsummer. The optimum time varies according to what is being grown.

ANNUALS THAT ARE BEST
SOWN IN SITU

Agrostemma
Anchusa capensis
Borago officinalis
Centaurea cyanus, C. moschata
Clarkia
Collinsia bicolor
Consolida ambigua
Cynoglossum amabile
Eschscholzia californica

Eschscholzia
californica

Gilia capitata
Gypsophila elegans
Limnanthes douglasii
Linaria maroccana
Linum grandiflorum
Malcolmia maritima
Malope trifida
Mentzelia lindleyi
Papaver rhoeas, P. somniferum
Phacelia campanularia
Scabiosa atropurpurea
Silene coeli-rosa

forget-me-nots (*Myosotis*) grow rapidly so should not be sown until midsummer, while Canterbury bells (*Campanula medium*) need longer to develop and should be sown in late spring or early summer.

The young plants may be transplanted to their final flowering position in fall or, if they are not crowded, the following spring. Premature flowering before winter reduces the spring display, so pinch out any flower buds that form during the first season.

Half-hardy annuals and biennials
In cold regions, sow seed of half-hardy annuals in containers during spring, at a temperature of 55–70°F (13–21°C), according to the particular genus. Half-hardy biennials may be sown in containers under cover in midsummer. In warmer climates, sow half-hardy annuals and biennials directly outside once the soil temperature reaches the optimum for germination.

Tender perennials such as *Impatiens* cultivars and gazanias can be raised from seed in the same way as half-hardy annuals. Other tender perennials, such as marguerites (*Argyranthemum frutescens*) and *Osteospermum*, and annuals that do not produce seeds, such as some double nasturtiums (*Tropaeolum*), can be treated as half-hardy biennials. Propagate by taking cuttings in fall, overwinter them in frost-free conditions, then plant them out in late spring (see PERENNIALS, "Stem tip cuttings," p.198).

Sowing in open ground

There are two main methods of sowing outdoors *in situ*: broadcast and in drills. For both, a seedbed should be prepared first. Dig over the soil to one spade's depth, then rake over the area and firm. Do not sow in soil that is too rich, since this encourages leaf growth at the expense of flower production. In soils lacking nutrients, however, a dressing of 2oz/sq yd (70g/sq m) of a balanced fertilizer should be forked in prior to sowing (see "Soil nutrients and fertilizers," p.618–19).

It's a good idea to prepare a plan showing the position of each cultivar, using any areas likely to be shaded to grow shade tolerant plants. Before sowing the seed, mark the outline of the area for each cultivar with grit, sand, or a stake so that it is easy to check the balance of colors, heights, and habits of each of the different plants to be used.

MARKING OUT ANNUAL BORDERS

1 Sprinkle grit or sand on the soil, or score the soil with a stick, to mark out interlocking areas for sowing seeds.

2 The seedlings may appear too sparse at first, but they will blend together as they grow.

Broadcast sowing
This method is particularly suitable for annuals that produce deep taproots, such as *Clarkia*, *Gypsophila*, and poppies (*Papaver*). They are best sown where they are to flower since they do not transplant readily. Sprinkle seeds thinly and evenly on the surface of the prepared seedbed and rake them in lightly. Label, then water the area gently but thoroughly with a fine spray.

Sowing in drills
Seeds sown in drills produce seedlings growing in straight rows at regular intervals, so they are readily distinguished from weed seedlings, which are randomly distributed. The seedlings initially look regimented but, once thinned, will form a dense and informal planting.

Using either a trowel tip or the corner of a hoe, mark out shallow drills 3–6in (8–15cm) apart, depending on

SOWING IN DRILLS

1 Using a line of string as a guide, make a furrow about 1in (2.5cm) deep with a hoe.

2 Carefully dribble the seeds from your hand to make sure that they are scattered evenly along the drill.

ALTERNATIVE STEP

If the seeds are pelleted, place them individually in the base of the drill.

3 Rake the soil back over the drill without dislodging the seeds. After labeling the row, water the soil using a fine spray.

BROADCAST SOWING

1 Prepare the soil by raking to produce a fine tilth. Scatter the seeds thinly over the prepared area by hand or from the packet.

2 Rake over the area lightly at right angles to cover the seeds so that they are disturbed as little as possible.

SELF-SEEDING ANNUALS AND BIENNIALS

Annuals and biennials that self-seed either true to type or with minor variations

Agrostemma
Angelica archangelica
Antirrhinum majus
Borago officinalis
Calendula officinalis
Centaurea cyanus
Chrysanthemum segetum
Clarkia amoena
Collinsia bicolor
Digitalis purpurea
Eschscholzia californica
Hesperis matronalis
Limnanthes douglasii
Linaria maroccana
Lobularia maritima
Lunaria annua
Malcolmia
Myosotis
Nigella damascena
Oenothera biennis
Omphalodes linifolia
*Onopordum acanthium,
 O. arabicum*
Papaver rhoeas, P. somniferum
Platystemon californicus
Silene armeria
Silybum marianum

*Tanacetum
parthenium*

Tanacetum parthenium
Tropaeolum majus
Vaccaria hispanica
Verbascum
Viola (many spp.)

THINNING SEEDLINGS

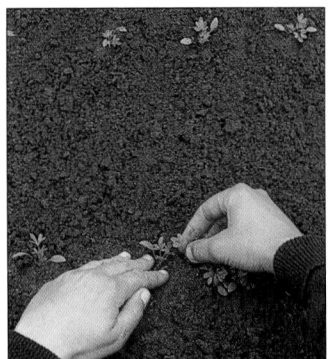

INDIVIDUAL SEEDLINGS
Press on either side of the seedling to be retained (here larkspur, Consolida ambigua) while pulling out the unwanted ones around it. Refirm and water.

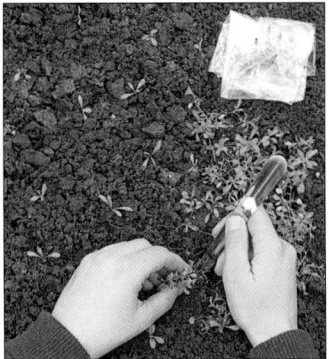

SEEDLING GROUPS
Gently lift groups of seedlings (here sweet William, Dianthus barbatus) with plenty of soil around the roots if they are to be replanted. Firm in the remaining seedlings.

the ultimate size of the plants. Sow seeds thinly and evenly by sprinkling or placing them along each drill at the appropriate depth for the annuals being sown, then carefully draw back the displaced soil with a rake or hoe to cover them. Label each row, and water gently but thoroughly with a fine spray.

Thinning

To prevent overcrowding, the seedlings usually need to be thinned. Do this when the soil is moist and the weather mild, taking care to retain the sturdier seedlings where possible and to achieve even spacing. To minimize disturbance to a seedling being retained, press the soil around it with your fingers as the surplus seedlings are extracted.

If seedlings are very dense, dig them up in clumps, retaining plenty of soil around the roots; do not disturb the other seedlings in the area more than is necessary. Some biennials such as forget-me-nots (*Myosotis*) and honesty (*Lunaria*) germinate readily, and if sown where they are to flower should be thinned appropriately – forget-me-nots to 6in (15cm) and honesty to 12in (30cm), for example.

The thinnings may be used to fill sparse areas caused by uneven sowing or irregular germination, or they may be transplanted for use elsewhere. Select the strongest and healthiest of the thinned seedlings for transplanting, then replant them where needed at the appropriate spacings and water them lightly to settle their roots.

Many annuals and biennials scatter their seeds freely, often producing dense clumps of seedlings. These need to be thinned to the appropriate distances to enable the young plants to develop without competition.

Sowing in pots or trays

Half-hardy annuals are usually sown in containers so that they can develop under cover and then be planted out as young plants when conditions are favorable. Hardy annuals may also be sown in containers left outside. Transplant the seedlings to their flowering positions when there is sufficient room.

Pots, seed pans, seed trays, and packs are all suitable containers, depending on the number of seeds to be sown and the space they require. Peat pots are also useful for seedlings that do not transplant well since the whole pot may be planted out without disturbing the roots.

Sowing the seeds

Fill the chosen container to its rim with standard sowing medium and press in lightly around the edges with your fingertips to make sure that there are no air pockets. To settle the medium, tap the container against a hard surface, then gently firm it so that the top of the medium is slightly below the rim of the container. Water with a fine spray, then leave it for an hour or so to drain.

Sow the seeds thinly on the surface of the medium, tapping them from the seed packet or from a fold of paper to achieve an even spread. Large or pelleted seeds can be sown individually in compartmentalized packs or spaced out in trays or pans. Very small seeds are easier to sow if they are mixed first with a small amount of fine sand; this produces a more even distribution.

Cover the seeds to about their own depth with sieved medium, then water lightly, to avoid disturbing the seeds or the surface of the medium. Dustlike seeds, such as those of begonia, should be left uncovered and watered from below: place each container up to its rim in water until the surface of the medium is moist. Do not leave them soaking for too long, since waterlogging may cause the seeds to rot before germination or encourage seedling diseases (see "Damping off," p.651).

To maintain even humidity, place a piece of glass or clear plastic sheeting over the container; do not let it touch the medium surface

Supporting and protecting seedlings

Support is required for slender-stemmed or tall annuals. Carefully insert peasticks or thin twigs into the soil around young plants; the supports should be slightly shorter than the ultimate height of the plants so that they will be concealed when the plants reach their mature size. These supports will also help protect the seedlings from possible rodent and bird damage.

Alternatively, stretch wire netting, with a mesh no greater than 1in (2.5cm), over the seedbed, bending it down at the edges so it does not touch the seedlings. Secure it firmly in the soil, using a stick or wire pin. The plants grow up through the mesh and cover the netting when fully grown.

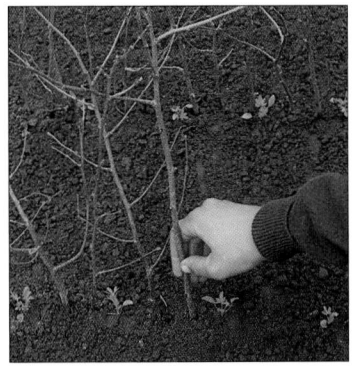

SUPPORTING WITH TWIGS
Peasticks or thin twigs may be pushed into the soil among the seedlings. Tall annuals (here larkspur, Consolida ambigua) grow to hide the support.

WIRE PROTECTION AND SUPPORT
Protect seedlings (shown here is ere Eschscholzia) with mesh wire netting bent to form a cage. The netting will support the seedlings as they grow through it.

SOWING IN A TRAY

1 Fill the seed tray with a standard sowing medium, then level with a presser board to 1/2in (1cm) below the rim.

2 Sprinkle the seeds thinly over the surface of the medium to achieve an even distribution.

3 Cover the seeds with a layer of sieved, moist soil mix to about the same thickness as the seeds themselves. Water the seeds in lightly.

4 Place a piece of glass or clear plastic sheeting over the tray to maintain even humidity.

5 Shade the tray with netting if the tray is in direct sunlight. Remove both glass and netting as soon as germination starts.

Seeds with special requirements

A few seeds need special conditions in order to germinate successfully. Begonia, *Impatiens*, and coleus seeds require light and prefer a constant temperature of 70°F (21°C). Pansies (*Viola* x *wittrockiana*), and other *Viola* should be germinated in darkness. Seeds of *Thunbergia alata* and geraniums require 70–75°F (21–4°C) to germinate. Scarify (break down by scratching) geranium seed before sowing (see "Scarifying and soaking," p.194). Seeds of bells-of-Ireland (*Moluccella laevis*) are difficult to germinate unless they have been stratified: set the seed pan in a refrigerator for a couple of weeks before bringing it into a temperature of 65–70°F (18–21°C) for two or three weeks more.

because this may disturb the seeds. Place the container on a windowsill or a greenhouse bench, and shade it with fine netting or newspaper if it receives direct sunlight. As soon as the first seedlings germinate, the cover should be removed. Grow them in good light and keep the medium moist until they are sufficiently large to prick out.

Pricking out

Seedlings raised in trays or pans need to be transplanted into larger containers before they become overcrowded, because they may quickly become weak and spindly if deprived of sufficient space or light. This process is known as pricking out. It enables the seedlings to continue to develop properly until they are ready for planting out in the open garden.

Fill the new containers with a soil-based mix and firm gently to eliminate any air pockets. Small pots, no more than 3in (6cm) in diameter, or compartmentalized plastic packs are ideal for individual seedlings; larger pots, pans, or trays can be used for several plants.

To prick out, first knock the container of seedlings against a table-top or bench to loosen the medium slightly and remove it intact from the container. Then hold each plant gently by the small seed leaves to avoid bruising the foliage, stems, or growing tips, and loosen it with a widger or other small implement. Take care not to damage the roots. Carefully lift each plant from the medium, retaining some of the medium around the roots to make sure that there will be little check to growth when the seedlings are replanted.

Use a dibber to make holes in the soil mix 1½–2in (4–5cm) apart, and insert a seedling into each hole. Make sure that all the roots are covered with soil mix, then gently firm in each seedling using fingers or a dibber, and level the mix. As each container is filled, water with a fine spray to settle the mix. Increase the humidity around the seedlings by covering the containers with clear plastic for a few days while the seedlings reestablish themselves. Make sure that the plastic does not touch the leaves, because this may encourage rot. Return the seedlings to their previous growing conditions to develop further.

If seedlings are ready for planting out, but this is delayed because of a late frost, pot them on into a larger container. This guarantees that growth is not checked, so the long-term success of the plants is not jeopardized.

Seeds that have been sown singly in packs or space-sown will not need pricking out but must be hardened off before planting out.

Hardening off

All half-hardy annuals that have been raised either under cover or in any other controlled environment need to be acclimatized gradually to the outdoor conditions before being planted out. The aim of this is to harden the plants, reducing their dependence on artificial heat and protection without exposing them to sudden environmental changes that might cause damage.

PRICKING OUT INTO A PACK

1 When the seedlings (here marigolds) are large enough to handle, tap the tray on a hard surface to loosen the medium.

2 Carefully separate the seedlings, handling them by their seed leaves. Keep plenty of medium around the roots.

3 Transplant each seedling into a separate section of a pack. Firm the soil mix around each one with fingers or a dibber, and water.

Annuals in pots

Many annuals make excellent pot plants. Prick out young seedlings into divided trays or individual pots and, when the roots have just filled the container, transfer each seedling to a larger pot prepared with soil-based potting mix. The pot size will vary according to the species or cultivar and time of sowing. Shift plants sown in late summer into 3½in (9cm) pots over the winter when growth is slow, then transfer them later to their final pots – either 5in (13cm) or 7in (19cm), or much larger pots for groups of three or five plants per container. Transplant spring-sown annuals directly into their final pots or containers.

Many annuals (here Schizanthus*) are very useful for providing an early, colorful display in a cool greenhouse in spring.*

When raising bedding plants in an unheated greenhouse, it may be sufficient to leave the ventilation open for progressively longer periods until, just before planting out, the vents are permanently open. If a cold frame is available, move the plants out into it in sequence, starting with the most frost-resistant, such as snapdragons and gazanias, to give more growing space. In the North, provide heating cables to warm the frame; in the rest of the country, lay old blankets over the cold frames at night if necessary to supply additional insulation. Acclimatize the plants in the frame by leaving the sashes open for increasingly longer periods once the danger of severe frost has passed.

When cold weather is forecast, the frames or greenhouse must be shut earlier than on a night when the minimum expected temperature is not close to freezing.

If a cold frame is not available, a few trays can be started on a sunny windowsill and moved outdoors when the weather permits. Take the trays outside during warm days for increasing lengths of time, and move them back indoors at night before the temperature drops to or below freezing. When nighttime temperatures are expected to be only a degree or so above freezing, move the plants against the house wall and cover them with an old blanket. Eventually they may be left out overnight unprotected, against a house wall at first, but finally out in the open. They are then ready to plant out.

Plants purchased from a garden center are likely not to be hardened off. Buy them early, while the selection is good, but harden them off as above before planting them out.

Planting out
Plant out half-hardy seedlings once all danger of frost has passed. This is particularly important in the case of more tender plants such as begonias and *Salvia splendens*. Provided that

they have been hardened off, some half-hardy annuals will tolerate cool, but not frosty, conditions for short periods.

Before you plant out seedlings, first prepare the bed (see "Sowing in open ground," p.211), water the young plants thoroughly, and then allow them to drain for an hour or so. To remove a plant from its pot, invert it, supporting the stem with a finger on either side. Then tap the rim against a hard surface to loosen the root ball from the pot. Break apart cell packs or divided trays to remove each seedling individually with its root ball undisturbed.

If plants are in trays without divisions, hold the tray firmly with both hands, and tap one side sharply on the ground to loosen the medium. Gently slide out the contents in one piece. Separate plants carefully with your fingers, keeping as much medium as possible around the roots. Alternatively, remove each plant gently using a widger or other small tool.

Make a hole sufficiently large to accommodate the root ball readily. Space the plants so that the leaves will just touch when the plants are fully developed. Normal planting distances range from 6 to 18in (15 to 45cm), depending on the habit of the species or cultivar being grown.

Check that the plants are at the same depth as in the container, then firm the soil around the base of the stem, without compacting the soil too much. After planting, gently break up the soil surface between the plants with a hand fork. To settle them in, water the plants thoroughly using a high-phosphorus soluble fertilizer (such as 10-52-10) to stimulate root production.

Pinching out
As young annuals develop, some, such as snapdragons (*Antirrhinum*), may need to be pinched out to

FIRST-YEAR GROWTH

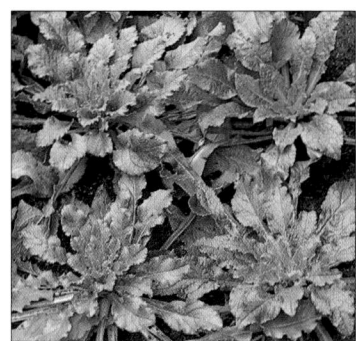

Biennials such as Canterbury bells make only vegetative (leafy) growth in their first year. Flowers develop the following summer.

encourage the plants to produce side-shoots and to develop a bushy habit. Do not pinch out plants such as *Celosia* or stocks (*Matthiola*) that have strong terminal shoots, because these develop the main flower spikes and also produce lateral growths during the summer.

Pinching is done by nipping the growing tip off a young plant. This may be necessary even with annuals that branch naturally, especially when a few plants in a bed produce stronger shoots than others. If a uniform growth habit is required, pinch

PLANTING OUT INTO OPEN GROUND

1 *Break the pack apart and carefully remove each seedling (here* Tagetes*) with its root ball intact.*

2 *Place each plant in a hole large enough to take its root ball, making sure that the plant is slightly lower in the soil than it was in its container.*

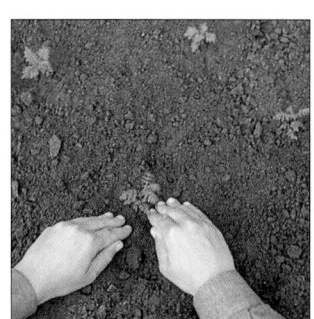

3 *Gently firm the soil in the well around the plant so that there are no air pockets. Water the area.*

HARDENING OFF

POLYTUNNEL
Place half-hardy annuals (here Tagetes*) in a polytunnel. Lift the sides for ventilation, as required.*

COLD FRAME
Seedlings may also be placed in a cold frame left open for progressively longer intervals.

HOW TO BUY PLANTS

BEDDING PLANTS

GOOD
EXAMPLE

*Compact,
vigorous
growth*

POOR
EXAMPLE

*Healthy,
green
foliage*

PETUNIAS

*Leggy,
bare stems* SALVIAS *Dead leaves*

POT-GROWN ANNUALS

GOOD
EXAMPLE

POOR
EXAMPLE

*Bushy, sturdy
growth*

*Healthy
buds
developing*

IMPATIENS CULTIVAR

*Moist soil
mix*

*Yellowing,
discolored leaves*

tall plants at five or six joints by removing the tip of each long shoot back to the required height.

Pinching delays flower production, so it should not be carried out if an early display is preferred.

Bedding plants

Buying more mature annuals and biennials to plant out directly into containers, beds, or borders can save time and effort. However, most growers routinely offer only varieties that have been proven to grow well in their area. When planning to grow something unusual, you may need to start the plants yourself.

Judging the quality of bedding plants

Sturdy young plants with evenly balanced, short-noded shoots and healthy foliage are most likely to give the best results. The plants should have well-developed root systems but must not be potbound. Do not buy plants with yellowing or discolored foliage or those in dry medium.

If you buy half-hardy bedding plants ahead of the safe time to plant them outdoors, make sure you have the right conditions to grow them under cover properly.

Planting and supporting annual climbers

Plant climbing annuals where they can climb naturally through a shrub or small tree or be trained against a wall or other support. If a twining annual is to be grown through a shrub, position the plant at the perimeter of the shrub, on the side where it will receive the most sunlight, with a stake leading the shoots into the host plant if necessary.

If the climber will be grown up a wall or fence, provide a support to suit its habit of growth (see CLIMBING PLANTS, "Types of support," p.128).

Twining climbers may also be grown up a tepee constructed out of of several stakes tied securely near the top. Push the stakes well into the soil first and plant just outside the tepee then tie in the young seedlings to the stakes.

Planting annuals to a design

Before starting to plant up a bed or border, assemble all the bedding plants to be used and check them off against the plan. Place the plants, still in their containers, roughly in position on the prepared soil to be sure that the bed will be neither too crowded nor too sparsely planted. Now is the time to make any final adjustments to plant positioning – it will be too late once they are in the ground. Keep a few plants in reserve to replace any that may die.

1 *Mark out the design of the entire bed before starting to plant. Work from the center outward, or from the back of the bed to the front. Use a board or kneeler for kneeling on so that the soil does not become compacted, making it difficult to work and inhibiting drainage.*

2 *Plant the seedlings carefully, handling the plants as little as possible. Firm the soil around each. Complete one section of planting before moving on to the next.*

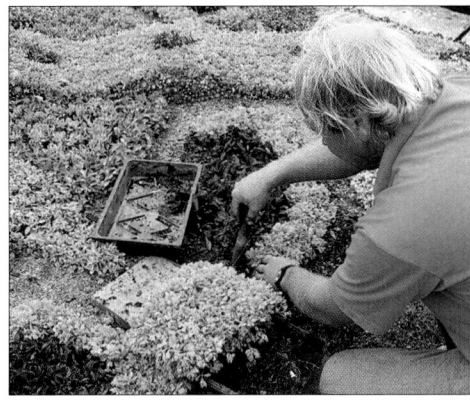

3 *As each section of planting is completed, trim off any damaged, uneven, or straggly shoots to make the patches of plants more compact.Water thoroughly section by section so that the seedlings planted first do not dry out while the others are being planted.*

Routine care

ANNUALS generally require little maintenance since they have a relatively short life. They do need to be watered regularly during drought, however, especially if they are grown in containers, and should be deadheaded to prolong flowering. Tall annuals may require staking during or soon after planting to prevent them from blowing over or toppling under their own weight. When the foliage starts to die down after flowering or at the end of the season, the plants should be cleared away.

Watering, fertilizing, and weeding

Young annuals and biennials that are planted in open ground should be watered regularly with a sprinkler or hose, soaking the bed thoroughly. Once the plants have become established, water only during prolonged dry weather.

Most annuals rarely need extra fertilizing if the soil has been well prepared. A liquid fertilizer may be applied on very poor soils as flower buds develop. Biennials may benefit from a little fertilizer, but only those grown for show purposes need regular fertilizing. Rich conditions produce vigorous vegetative growth at the expense of flowers, which is beneficial for foliage annuals such as coleus and some *Amaranthus*.

Keep annuals and biennials nearly free from weeds, since these compete for light, water, and nutrients and are unsightly. Pull out any weeds by hand while they are still small or hoe them if space permits, and remove self-sown seedlings in the same way if they are not required or are too numerous.

Providing supports

Many annuals and biennials have rather slender stems that benefit from some support. Use small, bushy branches (peasticks) gathered from trees or shrubs (hazel and willow are traditional, but most anything will do) for plants with a mature height of up to 3ft (1m). When the plants are an inch or so high, insert the sticks in the soil around them so that they can grow up through the sticks, which will quickly be covered and hidden.

Tall annuals in containers may be supported by inserting a few stakes around the edge of the pot and tying soft string around the stakes – the supports are hidden by the plants as they develop. Very tall plants, such as hollyhocks (*Alcea*), Mexican sunflower (*Tithonia*), or sunflowers (*Helianthus*), may need to be individually staked. Push the stake into the soil where it will be least visible and, as the plant develops, carefully tie in the stem at intervals as required.

Some scrambling annuals that lack tendrils or do not twine will need to be tied in to their support. Attach the leading shoots with soft string and continue to tie as needed. Twining annuals and those that have tendrils may need occasional guidance as well.

Annuals as dried or cut flowers

Dried or fresh flowers of many annuals and biennials are decorative indoors. Harvest everlasting flowers such as *Xeranthemum*, *Helipterum*, and *Limonium* when they are about half open, then hang them upside down in a warm, well-ventilated area. Cut *Helichrysum* flower heads before they show color to help keep their shape when dried. Cut fresh flowers as the buds show color. Dip the ends of Iceland poppies (*Papaver nudicaule*) into boiling water to seal them and avoid air locks that prevent water uptake.

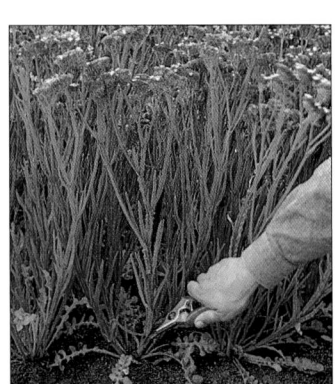

1 *Cut flowers for drying (here statice,* Limonium sinuatum*) as the heads start to open. Use a slightly angled cut as near as possible to the base of the stem.*

2 *Many everlasting flowers may be dried upside down in bunches fastened with soft string or raffia. Once they have dried, any excess stem may be cut off to suit the flower arrangement.*

Supporting tall and climbing annuals

Many annual climbers reach 6–10ft (2–3m) during their short life, and these are best guided to their support with plastic ties or soft twine until they take hold. The twine should be tied loosely around the stem and support using a figure-eight knot to prevent chafing against any hard surfaces and to allow for stem expansion.

Very tall plants, such as hollyhocks (*Alcea*) or sunflowers (*Helianthus*), may need to be individually staked. Push the stake into the soil where it will be least visible and, as the plant develops, tie in the stem at intervals.

Tall annuals in containers may be supported by inserting a few stakes around the edge of the pot and tying soft string around the stakes – the supports are hidden by the plants as they develop.

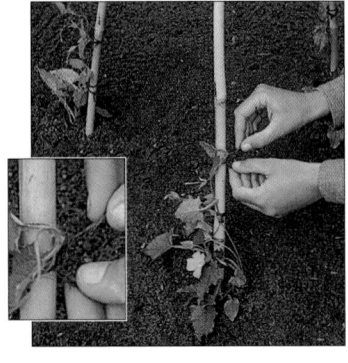

SUPPORTING WITH STAKES
A tripod, or tepee of 3 stakes tied together at the top and securely inserted into the ground, provides support for twining annuals (here Thunbergia alata*). Tie a seedling loosely to each of the stakes, while its stem is still young and supple.*

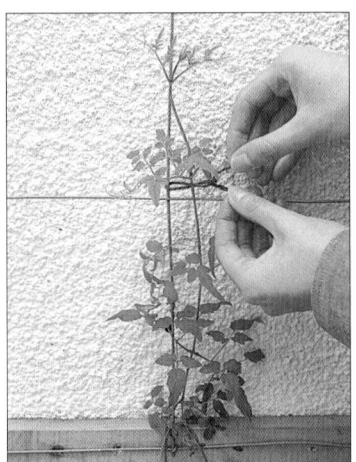

SUPPORTING CLIMBING ANNUALS
When planting climbers (here Eccremocarpus scaber*) near a wall or fence, support them on wire or a trellis. Tie the stems to the support while still supple.*

SUPPORTING TALL ANNUALS
Support tall annuals such as Salpiglossis *by pushing stakes into the soil around the pot and twining string around the stakes. As the plants develop they hide the stakes.*

DEADHEADING

To prolong the flowering period, remove flower heads as they fade, cutting near the base of the stalk. The plants (here violas) will produce new blooms for some time.

Deadheading

In many cases, the flowering season of plants may be extended and their appearance improved by promptly removing any flower heads that are fading or dead. This prevents a plant from setting seed, and its energy is used to produce additional flowers. Snap off any faded flowers between your fingers and thumb, breaking the stems cleanly. Use a pair of sharp scissors or pruners for tougher stems or where there is a danger of disturbing the plant as the dead flower heads are removed.

Do not deadhead if the seeds or fruits form part of the ornamental characteristic of the annual or biennial, as they do with honesty (*Lunaria*), *Hibiscus trionum*, and ornamental corn (*Zea mays*), for example. Nor should plants be completely deadheaded if their seeds are required for growing the plant during the following season.

A few annuals and biennials, such as poppies (*Papaver*), do not produce more flowers after deadheading.

SAVING SEEDS

1 *Seeds may be gathered when the capsules or seedheads (here* Nigella) *have been dried on blotting paper or newspaper and release their seeds.*

2 *Once the seedhead has dried, shake the seeds out and separate them from any other debris. Store them in a labeled envelope in a dry place at a cool temperature.*

Saving seeds

Seeds can easily be gathered from many annuals for sowing the following year. However, the seeds saved from most garden-grown cultivars will not produce plants that possess flowers or habit characteristics similar to those of their parents. It is often worth saving seeds only from those annuals and biennials that stay true to type, such as *Nigella* or honesty (*Lunaria*).

Deadhead those plants that have poor flowers so that no seeds are formed and later collected for sowing the following season. Such seeds are unlikely to produce plants with good-quality flowers.

Self-sown seedlings are likely to vary to some extent in character and quality but may nevertheless produce quite acceptable plants. Distinct cultivars of *Eschscholzia*, Excelsior Series foxgloves (*Digitalis*), sweet alyssum (*Lobularia maritima*), pot marigolds (*Calendula*), forget-me-nots (*Myosotis*), and many other annuals and biennials usually vary in flower color and other characteristics from the original plant.

When seed capsules turn brown and begin to split, cut them off and spread them on paper-lined trays in a warm, sunny place until they are fully dry. Extract the seeds and clean away any debris. Package, label, and store them in dry, cool conditions until they are required for sowing.

Clearing the bed

In fall, once the flower display is over, lift and compost all dead and dying plants after any seeds required have been gathered. Discard any diseased plants that might spread infection. Perennials grown as annuals or

FALL CLEANUP

When annuals have finished flowering, carefully loosen the soil around their roots with a fork and then rake up and compost or discard the old plants.

biennials, such as pansies (*Viola* x *wittrockiana*) and primroses, can be lifted and replanted elsewhere, where they may grow and flower satisfactorily for several years. Others, for example wallflowers (*Cheiranthus*), where winter hardy, and snapdragons (*Antirrhinum*), seldom grow as well after their first year, so they are usually not worth retaining.

Tender perennials such as begonias and *Impatiens* cultivars can be lifted and potted up in late summer to continue flowering in the house, conservatory, or greenhouse. Short-lived perennials, such as hollyhocks (*Alcea*), should be cut down in fall and retained since they sometimes survive for several seasons, although the quality and vigor of the plants will deteriorate. It is not worth keeping plants of the new F1 strains of geranium since they are quite easy to raise from seed, and you eliminate the risk of overwintering diseases. Where hardy, *Eccremocarpus scaber* will survive for years in protected positions outside.

Pests and diseases

The pests most likely to affect annuals and biennials, both when they are seedlings and when they are more mature, are slugs and snails (p.638), cutworms (p.647), fungus gnats (p.656), caterpillars (p.639), and aphids (p.639); plants may also be attacked by gray mold/*Botrytis* (p.646) and other fungal problems (see "Fungal leaf spots," p.641). Fungicides may prevent or check these diseases, but often little can be done beyond pulling out and discarding badly infected plants. Any young seedlings under cover may suffer from damping off (p.655), a group of soilborne diseases, which cause the plants to rot and collapse.

CUTTING DOWN SHORT-LIVED PERENNIALS

1 *Not all seedheads ripen at the same time. To prevent self-seeding, remove flowered stems before any seedheads ripen fully.*

2 *Short-lived perennials such as hollyhocks may flower for 3–4 seasons if cut down immediately after flowering.*

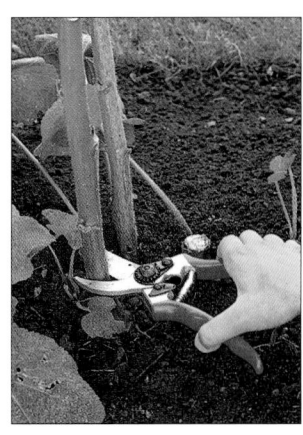

3 *Carefully cut each stem at its base, making sure that the new growth that has been produced during the growing season is not damaged in the process.*

CHAPT

8

BULBOUS PLANTS

FROM THE CHEERFUL daffodil trumpeting the arrival of spring to *Colchicum*, herald of fall, bulbous plants mark the seasons with glorious flower displays. Some possess handsome foliage and others are valued for their fragrance, but it is their blooms that make bulbs essential in a well-planned garden. They offer a wide variety of form and color, from the grandeur of the gladiolus spike to the tiny cups of the smallest crocus, and from bright primary shades to delicate pastel hues. Whether they form bold patterns in a formal bed, fill in the detail of a mixed border, provide a splash of color in a container, or create sweeping highlights beneath trees or in grass, bulbs bring vitality to the more permanent plantings of the garden.

Designing with bulbs

GROWING bulbs is an easy way to brighten up the garden with decorative, often flamboyant, and sometimes fragrant displays. The bulbs that are grown in the garden are dominated by cold-hardy favorites, for example crocuses, irises, daffodils, hyacinths, and tulips, of which there is an immense variety of both species and cultivars. Many less hardy to tender bulbs also deserve a place in the garden, including dahlias, begonias, fragrant *Crinum*, gladioli with their colorful spikes, fiery *Tigridia*, and stately *Galtonia*.

The key characteristic of bulbs is that they generally provide visual interest for only one season, remaining dormant and unnoticed for the remainder of the year. This can be an asset with careful planning, making bulbs invaluable as border plants as well as ideal for naturalizing in grass or for growing in containers.

In many gardens, bulbs may be left to increase naturally from year to year while their dying foliage is hidden by the developing growth of herbaceous plants or shrubs that provide a succession of interest. Many bulbs, including the popular crocuses, daffodils, and snowdrops (*Galanthus*), increase very rapidly in most sites. Bulbs may also be lifted after flowering and replanted each year to create room for other seasonal plants, making them especially convenient for small gardens or restricted areas.

Seasons of interest
The main bulb season is from early spring to early summer, but many other bulbs flower outdoors or under cover at other times of the year. For

USING BULBS IN A MIXED BORDER
The dusky, purple-pink globes of Allium sphaero-cephalon *pick up the color theme of this mixed border,* *providing a strong accent of color and form amid herbaceous perennials in various shades of pink.*

color in late winter when most of the garden is dormant, early bulbs such as pink *Cyclamen coum*, deep blue *Iris histrioides* 'Major', and white snowdrops may be grown outdoors, and other bulbs forced indoors. Bulbs that flower in summer or fall are often larger and of more exotic shapes and hues than spring bulbs.

Where to grow bulbs
If given the well-drained soil that they need to grow and flower well, bulbs are among the easiest of all garden plants to cultivate. There are numerous cultivars and species now available that thrive in all exposures except deep, constant shade.

Many bulbs in cultivation come from areas with a Mediterranean climate, so they need to be grown in sunny sites and prefer hot, dry summers, although a huge range of bulbs flourishes in the open garden in regions with summer rainfall.

Bulbs that would normally grow in woodland thrive in moist, light shade. Many others, including some described as sun-loving, do best in the light shade cast by nearby shrubs, walls, or trellises. Even dry shade is tolerated by most hardy cyclamen. Bulbs with white or pale flowers appear almost luminous in dusky light and look ethereal when planted in a shaded site.

Whatever the setting, bulbs usually look best planted in groups of the same species or cultivar, whether jostling shoulders with other plants or forming a single, swaying sea of color in a formal bed or in grass.

The different types of bulbous plant

BULB (*Hyacinthoides hispanica*)

CORM (*Gladiolus murieliae*)

In this book, the term "bulb" refers to all bulbous plants, including corms, tubers, and rhizomes as well as true bulbs. The terms "corm," "tuber," and "rhizome" are used only in their specific sense throughout. With all bulbous plants, a portion of the plant is swollen into a food storage organ that enables the plant to survive when dormant or when conditions are unsuitable for growth.

Bulbs
True bulbs are formed from fleshy leaves or leaf bases and frequently consist of concentric rings of scales attached to a basal plate. The outer scales often form a dry, protective skin or tunic, as found in daffodils, Reticulata irises, and tulips. With some lilies (*Lilium*) and *Fritillaria* species, the scales are separate and no tunic is formed. Juno irises are unusual in having swollen storage roots beneath the bulbs.

Corms
Corms are formed from the swollen bases of stems and are replaced by new corms every year. They are common in the family Iridaceae, which

TUBER (*Dahlia* 'Monk Marc')

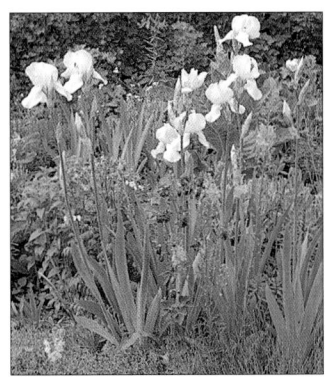

RHIZOME (*Iris* 'White City')

includes crocuses, gladioli, *Romulea*, and *Watsonia*; usually they have a tunic that has been formed from the previous year's leaf bases. In the Liliaceae and related families, they are found in such genera as *Brodiaea* and *Colchicum*.

Tubers
"Tuberous" is a term applied to many plants with swollen, often irregularly shaped stems or roots used for food storage. It is often misapplied, for example, to the tuberlike roots (actually rhizomes) of *Anemone blanda* and the long, thin rhizomes of *A. nemorosa* (for convenience, both are included here as bulbous plants). True tubers of various kinds are found in *Corydalis*, in some orchids such as *Dactylorrhiza*, in cyclamen species (although these are often called corms), and in plants such as *Ranunculus asiaticus*,where they are lobed or clustered together.

Rhizomes
Rhizomes are swollen, usually more or less horizontal, underground stems, found in the Iridaceae, notably in irises, and in the Liliaceae.

Formal beds

Bulbs make a valuable contribution to formal bedding displays. Spring-flowering bulbs are excellent for planting *en masse* in a bed to be occupied by bedding annuals later in summer, since they may be lifted and stored during their dormant season. Hyacinths and tulips are

A PAGEANT OF COLOR
Ranks of tulips parade along these formal beds in bold, bright blocks of contrasting color, creating an energetic counterpoint to the quiet orderliness of the formal garden. White tulips are interspersed among those of stronger hue to prevent the color combinations from appearing too strident.

classic bedding bulbs because of their strong, sculptural forms; in general, the larger, showy flowers of hybrids look best in a formal position in the garden. Plant in blocks of color, each of one type of bulb, or in mixed groups that flower at different times to provide a long display of color during the spring. Bulbs may completely fill the bed or be combined with companion plants having flowers in complementary or contrasting colors, such as deep blue forget-me-nots (*Myosotis*) and fiery wallflowers (*Cheiranthus*).

There is also opportunity for formal planting with summer- or fall-flowering bulbs: *Galtonia*, with its elegant white or green spikes, or the more compact cultivars of gladioli (especially the Primulinus and Butterfly groups) look impressive when planted in large blocks bordered by purple or white sweet alyssum (*Lobularia maritima*) or any similar, low-growing groundcover. *Agapanthus* Headbourne Hybrids, with their large, round flower heads of blue or white, combine well with the graceful pink blooms of *Nerine bowdenii*.

Mixed herbaceous and shrub borders

Bulbs fill in the permanent planting of a border with a lively variety of seasonal color. Loose drifts may blend in with the general design or draw the eye with splashes of bright color. Architectural bulbs, such as *Crinum* x *powellii* with its huge pink or white trumpets, punctuate borders with an arresting contrast of height and form. Grow some bulbs through low groundcover plants so that their blooms appear to float above the mat of foliage. For a more informal cottage border, consider using species bulbs, since fancy hybrids may look out of place.

Mixed plantings for spring flowering
Planting bulbs in a mixed border extends the flowering season and provides an array of fresh, bright color from late winter to early summer. Before the herbaceous perennials and deciduous shrubs in the border begin to grow and spread, bring the front to life with the smaller daffodil species, pale or dark blue Reticulata irises, snowdrops, (*Galanthus*), and the golden cups of winter aconites (*Eranthis hyemalis*).

Plant starry carpets of pink and blue *Anemone blanda*, *Chionodoxa*, and *Scilla bifolia* beneath such early-flowering shrubs as *Corylopsis*, *Forsythia*, and witch hazel (*Hamamelis*) to complement their display, or grow pale yellow drifts of the more freely increasing dwarf daffodil species and hybrids.

For later in spring, a much wider range of bulbs is available. Larger plants, such as the tall daffodils, *Fritillaria* species (for example the purple-black *F. persica* and the regal *F. imperialis*), or tulips may be used in casual groups to give height among the shrubs and perennials.

Mixed plantings for summer and fall flowering

A number of bulbs add greatly to the beauty of the garden in summer. Although often regarded as only of secondary importance, in fact many summer- and fall-flowering bulbs are quite tall and robust enough to hold their own among the surrounding flowering perennials, and they offer a dazzling range of colors and flower forms.

Early in the season, try *Camassia leichtlinii* 'Alba' with its creamy white flower plumes; the large, purple globes of *Allium aflatunense; Triteleia laxa* (syn. *Brodiaea laxa*) for its loose, purple-blue clusters of bloom; and the bold scarlet goblets of *Tulipa sprengeri*.

Follow them with vivid or pastel gladioli, sun-loving lilies (*Lilium*) in a huge range of colors and forms, arching sprays of blazing red or yellow *Crocosmia*, and, later, the slim pink, red, or white spires of *Schizostylis*. The tender greenish white *Eucomis* with its pineapple-like flower heads brings an exotic touch to the border planting.

In fall, continue the display with fragrant, pink trumpets of *Amaryllis belladonna*, brilliant yellow funnels of *Sternbergia lutea,* and blue to white forms of fall-flowering crocuses.

Naturalizing bulbs

When left undisturbed, many bulbs readily increase to form flowing drifts of color. Allowing them to naturalize in this way gives interest

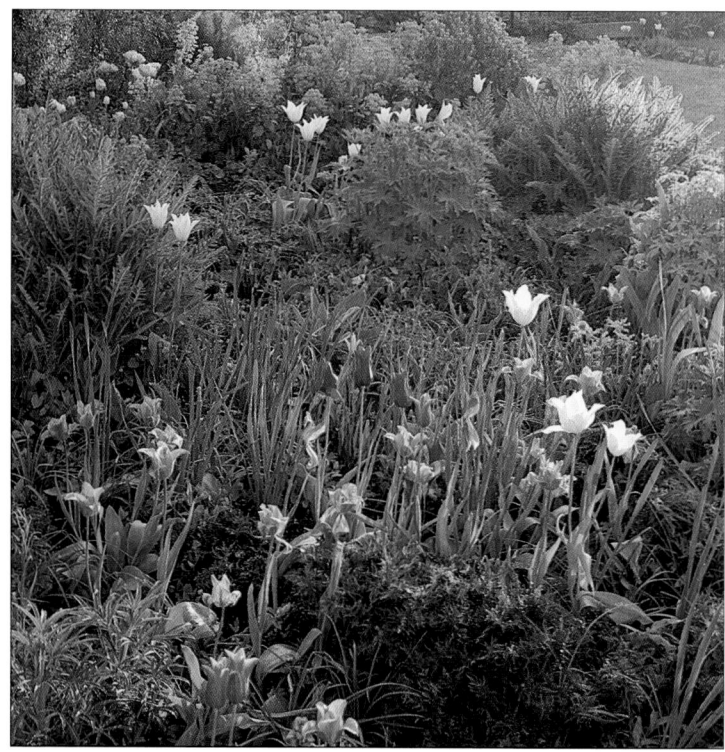

BULBS FOR BRIGHT HIGHLIGHTS
Loose drifts of slender tulips bring brilliant color to this mixed border and contrast with the soft, mounded foliage of the perennials.

to areas of the garden that otherwise might not be given over to flowering plants. Species, which are more delicate in hue and form than most cultivars, create a natural appearance when planted in large, informal groups.

Planting with specimen trees

Bulbs make perfect partners for specimen trees with deep roots and light, deciduous canopies. Use bulbs that flower mostly in spring and fall to form a decorative groundcover

when the tree has few leaves to deepen the shade. In spring, the soil beneath the tree is moist and sunlit, ideal for anemones, crocuses, daffodils, or *Scilla*. Hardy fall-flowering cyclamen, with mottled, silvery foliage and softly folded petals, tolerate the dry summer conditions and enjoy partial shade.

Plant bulbs whose flowers complement a tree's habit. White-flowered bulbs, for example, mirror the white blossoms of ornamental cherries (*Prunus*); the goblet-shaped flowers of crocuses echo the chalice form of magnolia blooms; and bulbs with pendent flowers imitate the habit of a weeping tree.

Use dwarf cultivars to naturalize the area around a newly planted tree or shrub, since rapidly increasing bulbs such as large daffodils can greatly reduce the available food.

Woodland settings

Bulbs are invaluable grown as large, informal pools of color to enhance the beauty of a deciduous woodland. Many do best in woodland conditions, blending well with other woodland plants such as ferns, hellebores (*Helleborus*), primroses (*Primula*), and foamflower (*Tiarella*).

The succession of bloom and contrast of form and height among bulbs can create the subtle variations and tranquil mood of a woodland. White snowdrops (*Galanthus*) and

cyclamen species in pinks and purples make a striking combination, while drifts of *Scilla* and *Chionodoxa* add shades of blue. Spanish bluebells (*Hyacinthoides hispanica*, syn. *Scilla campanulata*) or many of the more rampant grape hyacinths (*Muscari*), together with the delicate white sprays of lily-of-the-valley (*Convallaria majalis*), provide swaths of blue and white. These can all colonize considerable areas once established. English bluebells (*Hyacinthoides non-scripta*) should be planted on their own, since they rapidly invade other plantings.

Planting in grass

Bulbs can transform grass, whether a bank, a section of a lawn, or an entire meadow, into a bright carpet of spring or fall color that spreads more thickly each year. The bulbs must be robust species that can withstand competition from grass roots. Many of the larger bulbs look best in tall grass where, after flowering, their fading foliage is less obtrusive.

Plant early-flowering bulbs in grass that is mowed from spring onward: their leaves will have time to die down before the grass is cut. Later-flowering bulbs, such as *Camassia* and species lilies, may be grown with grass and wildflowers in meadows that are not cut until late summer. Bulbs that bloom in fall start into growth and flower before the end of the usual mowing season, so the grass must be left unmowed after late summer. Alternatively, plant bulbs in irregular but defined areas so that it is possible to mow around them.

Daffodils are the classic choice for grass, and a remarkable range – especially the more robust species and hybrids – can be grown in this way. Many crocuses grow well in grass where they are protected to some extent from mice and squirrels. A more delicate feeling may be achieved with the pendent bells of the summer snowflake (*Leucojum aestivum*) and the snake's-head fritillary (*Fritillaria meleagris*), which shiver softly in the breeze.

Some of the dwarf bulbs do well where the grass is less vigorous, particularly in partly shaded areas. *Chionodoxa* species, the purple *Crocus tommasinianus*, *Scilla* species, some daffodil species (e.g. *Narcissus cyclamineus*), and snowdrops all do well in these conditions.

Bulbs planted on the grassy outskirts of a formal garden soften the rigidity of formal beds, but the informal frame also provides a contrast that strengthens the focus on the formal plantings (see "Naturalizing in grass," p.232).

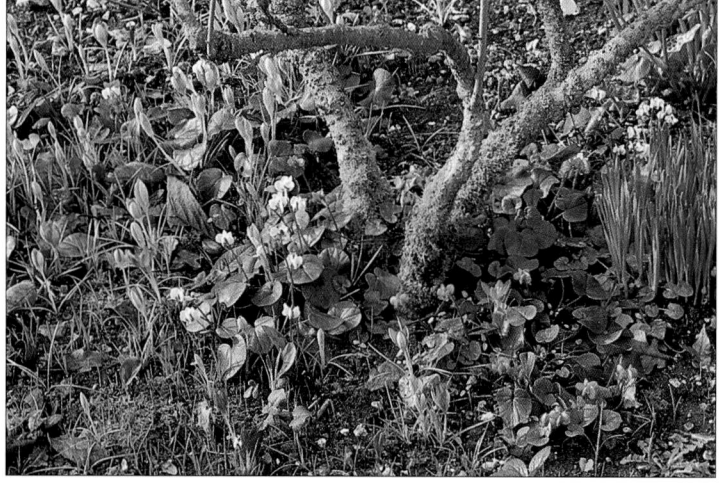

WOODLAND CHARM
Cyclamen coum *and crocuses in deep and pale shades of pink, lilac, and violet colonize woodlands, clustering prettily around the base of the trees to provide a show of color when the trees are bare.*

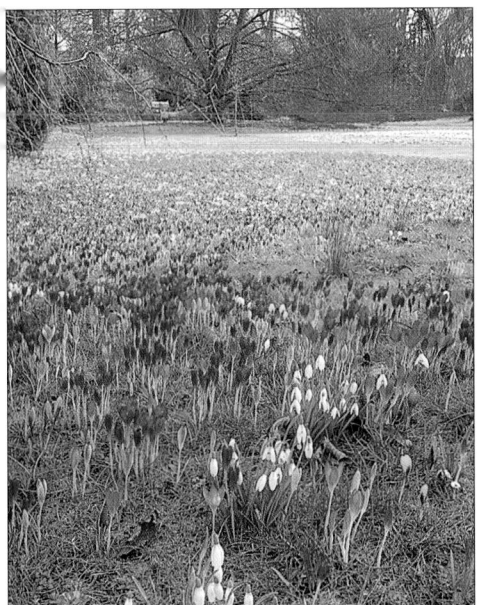

SPRING SPECTACLE
*Naturalized crocuses cover this lawn with vivid purple, magenta, and yellow. The bulbs are planted in great swaths of a single hue that merge with each other to create a sea of color. Snowdrops (*Galanthus*) planted among the crocuses provide highlights of white.*

Bulbs with alpines

Using bulbs with alpines in the rock garden, trough, or peat bed can prolong the season, because most alpines flower only in late spring. The erect habit, upright flowers, and spearlike leaves of bulbs contrast well with the low, mounded, or spreading habit of most alpine plants. Choose dwarf bulbs with dainty blooms to complement the character of the alpines, and plant some bulbs to grow through and brighten the alpine planting. Avoid mat-forming alpines that exhaust the soil around the bulbs, thus depriving them of food.

In the rock garden
Many smaller bulbs, especially the more exacting species for which fast draining is essential, thrive in sunny or partially shaded rock gardens. Dwarf

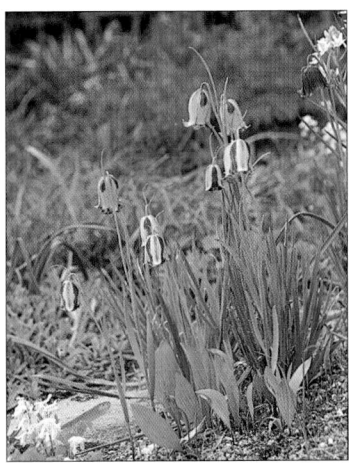

AN ALPINE SETTING
The unusual beauty of the bell-like flowers of Fritillaria acmopetala *is best shown off in the small-scale planting of an alpine garden.*

bulbs look attractive when planted in pockets of rock or offset against the grit top-dressing of the bed, which also stops their delicate flowers from being muddied during wet weather. If planting very small alpines in the bed, do not use the taller bulb species, which would appear out of proportion to their neighbors.

In troughs
Old stone troughs make an attractive setting for a collection of dwarf bulbs and smaller alpine plants, since their tiny charms may be appreciated close at hand. The bulbs benefit from the gritty, well-drained soil, and may easily be given the careful watering that they need.

To keep the display in proportion, grow the smallest species and their less robust hybrids; rapidly increasing bulbs may swamp neighboring alpines. Many of the smaller species offer intriguing flowers, such as purplish brown and yellow *Fritillaria michailovskyi* and several *Narcissus* species in white and yellow.

Rhodohypoxis are excellent for troughs, producing pink, red, or white starry flowers through most of the summer. Keep the bulbs moist during the growing season, and give them an occasional liquid fertilizer. *Cyclamen* includes species that are suitable for troughs in spring and fall, ranging in hue from pure white to deepest purple-pink.

In a peat bed
A peat garden, with its terraced beds, peat-block walls, and a soil mix consisting mainly of leaf mold and peat or compost, provides perfect conditions for the dwarf woodland bulbs, whether planted on their own or with ericaceous shrubs or alpines. Try

Corydalis solida, with purplish gray flowers, or the lady's slipper (*Cypripedium calceolus* var. *pubescens*), yellow with chocolate-maroon wings, among many others. The plant choice is determined to an extent by the degree of shade.

Bulbs to associate with water gardens

A few bulbs do well in damp, poorly drained conditions and provide some of the most striking flowering plants to grow around water. Their strong shapes and colors create pleasing reflections; plant them in clumps to contrast with the flat, open surface of the water. Several handsome rhizomatous irises and the calla lily (*Zantedeschia aethiopica*), with large, white spathes above broad, arrow-shaped leaves, thrive in pond margins. Both the snake's-head fritillary and summer snowflake (*Leucojum aestivum*) grow naturally in wet meadows and thrive in moist sites or damp beds around ponds.

Other bulbs that enhance water gardens are the magnificent purple-red *Iris ensata* (syn. *I. kaempferi*, one of the Japanese irises), and *Dierama pendulum,* with its wand-like flower sprays. Both of these require a soil that is well drained as well as moist.

BULBS IN POTS
Larger bulbs are naturals for use in containers. Here, Lilium regale *provides the focus of interest in this grouping of pots, which have been arranged on different levels and in gradations of size to draw the eye upward. The huge white lily trumpets combine with white geraniums and terracotta tones to form an attractive composition that is in harmony with the natural stone wall and greenery behind it.*

Bulbs in containers

Growing bulbs in ornamental pots, windowboxes, and other suitable containers can provide a varied and spectacular display throughout virtually the entire growing season. Well-considered choices of bulbs may extend the season to include late winter as well as spring and summer. Plant a single species or cultivar in each container to provide a uniform display, and then group the containers together for a mass of color.

Place pots of bulbs with fragrant flowers (especially hyacinths and Tazetta narcissus, also known as paperwhites) near the house entrance, where they may be fully appreciated. Pots used for spring bulbs may be used for summer-flowering plants later: when the bulbs die down, lift and replant them in the garden (or store them) and replace them with annuals or tender perennials.

Some larger bulbs are sufficiently commanding to be planted on their own in containers. Tall lilies (*Lilium*) or *Crinum* x *powellii*, in pink or white forms, are particularly suitable. Any *Agapanthus* species or hybrid provides a long season of showy flowers. Alternatively, group several bulbs of varying heights and colors in a large container such as a half barrel to provide a feature on a patio.

Windowboxes

When planting in windowboxes, choose smaller bulbs (such as irises, crocuses, miniature daffodils, and Kaufmanniana tulips) that are in proportion to the size of the container. They are excellent for planting in layers below other plants to make best use of limited space; the bulbs thrust through the surface planting to create a pleasing contrast of height and form. Blending the plants with early-flowering pansies (*Viola* x *wittrockiana*) and ivy (*Hedera*), followed by trailing tender perennials and annuals, gives a prolonged display of color.

Bulbs under cover

Growing bulbs under cover extends the possibilities that may be cultivated to include many rare species that need particular care. In temperate or cold regions, tender bulbs may be grown that would not survive unprotected in the open garden. In regions with summer rainfall, it is the most practical way of growing many of the species bulbs currently in cultivation that need a dry, summer resting period. Bulbs may be planted in pots or in a greenhouse bed or bulb frame. This allows easier control of the local environment to accommodate the individual needs of a wide range of bulbs, be it a long summer drying-off period or protection from excessive winter moisture, cold, or frost.

Bulbs in pots

Growing bulbs in pots allows each plant to be grown in conditions that best meet its individual requirements, especially when cultivating small quantities of uncommon or challenging bulbs. The pots are easily transferred from outdoor conditions to the shelter of frames or greenhouses when required, or from the greenhouse to the living room, kitchen, or conservatory to enjoy them when in full flower.

Pot cultivation in a cool greenhouse enables many bulb species that are otherwise of borderline hardiness in temperate climates to be grown. Many are South African and South American bulbs with a variety of richly colored blooms, such as *Watsonia* with its dense spikes of deep pink and red. The shelter of a cool greenhouse is often needed for tender bulbs such as *Gloriosa* and winter-flowering *Veltheimia*. Tender species or cultivars of such genera as begonias, *Canna*, or *Crinum* should also be overwintered in a cool greenhouse, then brought out when in bloom to enhance the summer display in the open garden.

If desired, bulbs may be grown in shade and the soil mix adjusted accordingly to grow small woodland bulbs. These include *Trillium rivale*, which has finely spotted petals in pink or white, and tender terrestrial orchids such as the free-flowering *Calanthe* species.

Gardeners with an alpine house may add a little height and splashes of color to the display by interspersing the plants with pots of dwarf spring bulbs. The alpine house environment is especially suitable for rare or tender bulbs (e.g. ice-white *Narcissus cantabricus* or bright blue *Tecophilaea cyanocrocus*).

Greenhouse beds

Tender bulbs may be planted directly in prepared greenhouse beds, rather than in pots, for a more natural and vigorous display. The bulbs may be combined in a mixed bed with other plants that flower in summer when the bulbs are dormant. Choose companion plants that tolerate a dry period coinciding with that needed by the bulbs, or those that can be plunged in plastic pots and watered without the moisture reaching the bulbs around them.

Spreading, heat-loving plants such as *Osteospermum*, gazanias, and many silver-foliaged plants could be used in this way and then removed or cut back hard at the end of summer when the bulbs start into growth. Late-flowering *Brodiaea*, *Calochortus*, and *Triteleia* prolong the flowering season still further: group them together but water them separately. Summer-growing bulbs such as the tender *Nerine* species, *Eucomis*, and some *Gladiolus* species do not need interplanting.

Bulb frames and raised beds

The term "bulb frame" usually refers to a raised bed devoted solely to bulbs; it is covered with a cold frame or sashes during the natural resting period of the bulbs in summer, and also in winter to protect them from excessive moisture, which could cause them to rot. Alternatively, a frame may simply cover bulbs in pots plunged in a sand bed. Such frames may be made more attractive by using stone for the sides. Bulb frames are the best alternative to the alpine house as a place to grow tender or exacting bulb species without the root restriction of pots, and are used mainly by enthusiasts or collectors. This method of cultivation is suitable for most bulbs, other than

Bulbs for cut flowers

Many bulbs have flowers that can be cut for the house since their shapely, often solitary, flowers on long stems make them especially suitable for flower arrangements. A few have powerful scents that can fill a room, and most are long-lasting if picked before the blooms reach maturity. Some, such as daffodils, are so vigorous and prolific that they may be cut without leaving a gap in the garden display. Alternatively, set aside a separate area to grow bulbs especially for cutting.

Gladioli make fine cut flowers and are often used in this way, since the taller cultivars are difficult to place satisfactorily in the open garden.

Wonderfully fragrant freesias, related to irises, are tender corms commonly grown under cover to provide cut flowers. They have a long flowering season during the winter but make somewhat straggly pot plants that need staking, so they are best cut for display indoors, where they will last well. They also grow outside in milder areas.

Schizostylis coccinea '**Sunrise**'

Crocosmia '**Lucifer**'

Narcissus '**Cheerfulness**'

Dahlia '**Early Bird**'

Freesia '**Everett**'

Gladiolus '**Tesoro**'

Zantedeschia aethiopica '**Crowborough**'

Nerine bowdenii

Alstroemeria **Ligtu Hybrids**

Tulipa '**Clara Butt**'

Allium giganteum

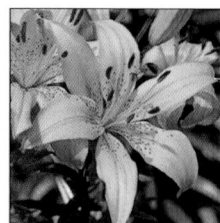
Lilium '**Enchantment**'

those accustomed to some summer rainfall (such as woodland and high mountain species). Some of the crocus, daffodil, *Fritillaria*, and tulip species, Juno and Reticulata irises, and the more difficult *Brodiaea* and *Zigadenus* species tend to be less successful in temperate climates as open garden plants. These bulbs may not survive excess moisture –

whether in winter or in summer – unless they are protected in bulb frames or seasonally covered raised beds during the dormant season.

Forcing bulbs

An excellent way of bringing color and fragrance indoors during winter

and early spring is to force hardy and tender bulbs in pots. The bulbs are kept in a cool to cold (slightly above freezing), dark place, depending on the species, for a few months before bringing them into warmth, moisture, and light to encourage them to flower earlier than they otherwise would do naturally. Hyacinths, tulips, daffodils (including the paper-

whites), irises, crocuses, and amaryllis (*Hippeastrum*) are all suitable. Some hardy bulbs such as crocuses may abort their flowers if forced too quickly. A gentler method is to grow bulbs under cover in pots, bringing them indoors a week or two before they would normally bloom in the open garden, so that the warmth stimulates them into bloom.

Planter's guide to bulbous plants

EXPOSED SITES

Bulbs that tolerate exposed or windy sites

Anemone
Chionodoxa
Colchicum
Crocus
Cyclamen
Fritillaria (dwarf spp.)
Galanthus
Ipheion
Iris reticulata
Muscari
Narcissus (dwarf spp. and cvs)
Ornithogalum
Oxalis

Oxalis
depressa

Scilla
Sternbergia lutea
Triteleia
Tulipa (dwarf spp.)

WALL PROTECTION

Bulbs that benefit from the protection of a wall

Agapanthus (most spp.)
Alstroemeria
Bloomeria crocea
Eucomis
Fritillaria persica
Gladiolus (tender spp.)
Gynandriris sisyrinchium
Habranthus (some spp.)
Hippeastrum advenum
Hymenocallis
Ixia
Moraea spathulata
Nerine bowdenii
Schizostylis coccinea
Scilla peruviana
Sparaxis
Sternbergia lutea, S. sicula
Tigridia
Tulbaghia
Watsonia
Zephyranthes candida

DRY SHADE

Bulbs that tolerate dry shade

Anemone nemorosa
Arum italicum 'Pictum'
Cyclamen coum,
  C. hederifolium, C. repandum
Galanthus nivalis (forms)
Hyacinthoides non-scripta
Ranunculus ficaria

MOIST SHADE

Bulbs that do best in moist shade

Anemone apennina, A. blanda,
A. ranunculoides
Arisaema (most spp.)
Arum italicum
Cardiocrinum
Corydalis (some spp.)
Eranthis
Erythronium
Fritillaria camschatcensis,
  F. cirrhosa, F. roylei
Galanthus
Ipheion uniflorum
Leucojum aestivum, L. vernum
Lilium (some spp.)

Lilium
hansonii

Narcissus cyclamineus,
  N. triandrus
Nomocharis
Notholirion
Scilla bifolia
Trillium
Tulipa sylvestris

FLOWERS FOR CUTTING

Agapanthus
Allium (some spp.)
Alstroemeria (taller spp. and cvs)
Amaryllis belladonna
Anemone De Caen Series,
  A. St. Brigid Series
Camassia
Clivia
Crinum
Crocosmia

Dahlia
Dierama
Freesia
Galtonia
Gladiolus
Gloriosa
Iris, Dutch Hybrids
Ixia
Lilium
Narcissus
Nerine
Ornithogalum (tall spp.)
Polianthes
Ranunculus asiaticus (forms)
Schizostylis coccinea
Sparaxis
Tulipa
Watsonia
Zantedeschia

ARCHITECTURAL PLANTS

Allium christophii,
  A. giganteum
Canna
Cardiocrinum giganteum
Crinum x *powellii*
Eucomis
Fritillaria imperialis
Lilium (most spp. and cvs)
Veltheimia

ROCK GARDENS

Bulbs suitable for planting in rock gardens

Albuca humilis
Allium (dwarf spp.)
Anemone (some spp.)
Bellevalia (some spp.)
Brodiaea (smallest spp.)
Bulbocodium vernum
Colchicum (small spp.)
Corydalis (some spp.)
Crocus
Cyclamen (hardy spp.)
Fritillaria (many spp.)
Galanthus
Ipheion
Iris (dwarf spp.)
Leucojum (some spp.)
Muscari (noninvasive spp.)
Narcissus (dwarf spp. and hybrids)
Ornithogalum (dwarf spp.)

Oxalis (some spp.)
Puschkinia
Rhodohypoxis
Romulea (some spp.)
Scilla
Sternbergia lutea, S. sicula
Tulipa (dwarf spp.)
Zephyranthes candida

BULBS FOR ALPINE HOUSES

Albuca
Anemone (some spp.)
Anomatheca
Arum (some spp.)
Babiana
Bellevalia
Bongardia chrysogonum
Bulbocodium vernum
Calochortus
Colchicum (small spp.)
Crocus
Cyclamen
Ferraria
Fritillaria (most spp.)
Gagea
Galanthus
Habranthus
Hippeastrum (dwarf spp.)

Moraea huttonii

Iris (dwarf spp.)
Lachenalia
Leontice
Leucocoryne
Leucojum (some spp.)
Merendera
Moraea (some spp.)
Muscari (some spp.)
Narcissus (dwarf spp.)
Ornithogalum (dwarf spp.)
Oxalis (some spp.)
Pancratium
Pinellia
Puschkinia
Rhodohypoxis
Romulea
Scilla
Sternbergia
Tecophilaea
Tulipa (dwarf spp.)
Zephyranthes
Zigadenus

Tulips and daffodils

TULIPS and daffodils are highly valued for the bold splashes of color they bring to the garden in spring. Grow them together to extend the flowering season in a mixed border: some daffodils bloom quite early in the year, while many tulips last well into late spring. Tulips are excellent for beds or borders, and many daffodils are especially suitable for naturalizing in grass. Dwarf forms are ideal for rock gardens, alpine houses, or containers, where they may be seen at close range.

Tulips

This diverse, versatile genus is horticulturally classified in 15 divisions based on flower form, but it may conveniently be grouped by flowering season and garden use.

Early tulips

Single early tulips have classic, goblet-shaped blooms, some with striped, flushed, or margined petals. Early doubles have long-lasting, open bowl-shaped flowers, often flecked or margined in contrasting colors. Traditionally used for cutting, in formal bedding, or as border edgings, many may also be grown in pots indoors. In informal designs, their elegant outlines contrast well with spreading or prostrate plants.

Midseason tulips

This grouping includes Triumph tulips, with their simple, conical blooms, and the Darwin hybrids, with rich and intensely colored flowers, often with a satiny, basal blotch and dark, velvety anthers. Both types are sturdy, robust, and noted for their weather resistance.

Late tulips

Some of the most vibrant colors and intricate forms are seen in late-flowering tulips. They include the graceful lily-flowered types, vivid and extravagant Parrot tulips, green-tinged Viridifloras, and exuberantly striped and feathered Rembrandts. Peony-flowered forms are suited to informal cottage gardens. All are attractive used informally with dark green or gray groundcover plants or in formal bedding designs.

Dwarf species and hybrids

Compact Kaufmanniana hybrids produce brightly colored blooms early in the spring, while the taller Fosteriana and Greigii tulips usually flower a little later. Many have very attractively marked foliage. The dwarf species are ideal for containers, raised beds, or rock gardens. *Tulipa sprengeri* and *T. sylvestris* tolerate light shade and will naturalize in thin grass.

Cultivation and propagation

Most tulips thrive in fertile, well-drained, organic soils, in sun and with shelter. In ideal conditions, some robust cultivars persist from year to year. Many, however, are best regarded as short-lived perennials, to be lifted after a few years and discarded. Where soils warm up rapidly, unless planted deeply at 10–12in (25–30cm), the

GROWING IN CONTAINERS
The lily-flowered tulips 'West Point' here display their pointed blooms.

TULIPS IN A SPRING BORDER
The strong, vertical stems and distinctive cups of tulips provide height, structure, and vivid color to an informal spring border.

Types of tulip

Tulips include an impressive range of flower forms, from the simple, upright goblets of single-flowered tulips to the frilled and twisted petals of Parrot tulips and the open, double blooms of peony-flowered forms. They are available in most colors except true blue, from the purest white to the deepest purple, with many glorious shades of yellow, red, and crimson in between. Many of the dwarf tulips also have attractively marked leaves.

SINGLE

***Tulipa* 'Dawnglow'**
Darwin hybrid

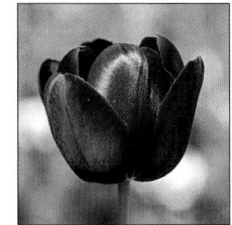
***T.* 'Queen of Night'**
Single late

***T.* 'Spring Green'**
Viridiflora

DOUBLE AND PARROT

***T.* 'Peach Blossom'**
Double early

***T.* 'Estella Rijnveld'**
Parrot

DWARF SPECIES AND HYBRIDS

T. tarda
Dwarf species

***T.* 'Dreamboat'**
Greigii hybrid

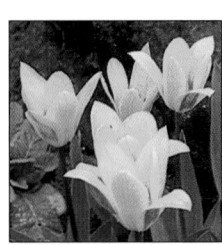
***T.* 'Giuseppe Verdi'**
Kaufmanniana hybrid

***T.* 'Greuze'**
Single late

EXTENDING THE FLOWERING SEASON
Growing tulips and daffodils together provides a continuous display of color for many weeks throughout spring.

Daffodils

Daffodils (*Narcissus*) are among the easiest and most rewarding bulbs to grow. They are horticulturally divided into 12 groups, based on the form of the flowers and on the species originally used in breeding them.

Daffodils in containers
Most daffodils can be grown in pots, if they are deep enough to allow at least 2in (5cm) of rooting medium beneath the bottom of the bulbs. Tazettas, with clusters of up to 12 scented blooms, are often grown under cover or as potted plants to bloom from late fall to spring. The richly fragrant jonquil hybrids are also useful for house decoration. Small species such as *N. cantabricus* and *N. romieuxii* produce blooms early in the year in the alpine house; they may also then be brought indoors.

Daffodils in the garden
Valuable for formal spring bedding and to give early color in the mixed border, daffodils are among the most reliable of bulbs for naturalizing: they rarely need lifting in borders or grass. Even tiny species such as *N. cyclamineus* and *N. minor* will thrive in thin grass. Dwarf daffodils are ideal for rock gardens and raised beds; some, such as *N. asturiensis*, *N.* 'Tête-à-tête', and *N.* 'Little Gem', flower early in the year.

Cultivation and propagation
Daffodils will grow in almost any soil type, but prefer well-drained, moist, slightly alkaline conditions. They

NATURALIZING DAFFODILS IN GRASS
In an informal or wild garden, daffodils may be grown in grass, bringing welcome color to a shady corner or the ground beneath a tree.

bulbs usually divide into several smaller ones, which after a few years are too small to produce flowers.

Dwarf tulips generally require open, gritty soils in full sun; lift and replant only when overcrowded. Propagate by offsets (see p.239) or, for species, by seed (see p.240). Tulips are prone to tulip fire/blight and other problems (see p.238).

thrive in sun or lightly dappled shade. Plant the bulbs two to three times their depth in late summer or early fall. When bulbs are naturalized in grass, do not cut the old foliage until at least six weeks after flowering. Bulbs in containers must be grown in cool conditions, with plenty of fresh air. Temperatures above 45°F (7°C) while rooting is taking place may cause flowers to abort. Place the pots in a cold place such as a cold frame after

planting, and bring them into a cool room about 12–16 weeks later. Once flower buds appear, blooming can be advanced by raising the temperature gently, although not exceeding 63°F (17°C).

Propagate by offsets (see p.239) or by chipping (see p.243); plants may also be raised from seed (see p.240). Daffodils may be infested by narcissus basal rot (p.654), narcissus nematodes, and bulb flies.

Types of daffodil

Daffodils provide a wide variety of shapes and forms, from the tiny, exquisite Cyclamineus hybrids with their swept-back petals to the tall trumpet daffodils and the more showy double forms. Modern developments include the split-corona and collarette types. In addition to the characteristic bright golden flowers, cultivars display a wide range of shades of white, yellow, pink, and orange, some with touches of red and green and often in combination.

DWARF SPECIES AND HYBRIDS

Narcissus triandrus
Dwarf species

N. romieuxii
Dwarf species

***N.* 'Jumblie'**
Cyclamineus hybrid

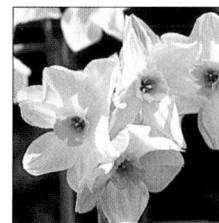
***N.* 'Pride of Cornwall'**
Tazetta

SINGLE

***N.* 'Passionale'**
Large-cupped

***N.* 'Fortune'**
Large-cupped

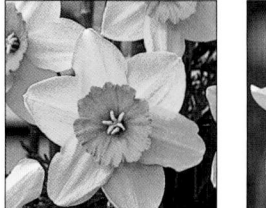
***N.* 'Ambergate'**
Large-cupped

DOUBLE

***N.* 'Irene Copeland'**
Double

***N.* 'Tahiti'**
Double

Dahlias

DAHLIAS flower from the middle of summer to the first frosts in fall, providing bright color in the garden for several months. The top-growth is very frost tender, but the tubers will survive outdoors in USDA hardiness zone 8 and warmer, and they may survive in colder areas if planted deeply and given a thick but loose winter mulch. They are excellent sunny border plants and can be grown in various soil types, providing that the soil is fertile and well drained.

If grown for exhibition or for cut flowers, dahlias are best planted in rows in specially prepared beds. The dwarf bedding dahlias, usually grown annually from seed (see ANNUALS AND BIENNIALS, "Sowing in pots or trays," p.212), are suitable for planting in containers. Dahlia flower heads have a diversity of petal forms in a wide color range, from white to rich yellow through pinks and reds to purples; many cultivars offer at least two colors in subtle to dazzling combinations.

Dahlias are classified according to the size and form of their flower heads. Several types are subdivided by the size of their blooms: miniature, 2–4in (5–10cm); small, also termed BB, 4–6in (10–15cm); medium (B), 6–8in (15–20cm); large (A) 8–10in (20–25cm); and giant (AA) over 10in (25m) and at least 5in (13cm) in depth.

DAHLIA FLOWER TYPES

SINGLE
D. 'Yellow Hammer'
Flower heads with 8–10 broad florets that surround an open, central disk.

ANEMONE
D. 'Comet'
Fully double flowers with one or more rings of flattened ray florets surrounding a group of shorter, tubular florets.

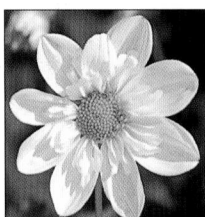

COLLARETTE
D. 'Easter Sunday'
A yellow disk in the center, with a collar of small florets lying between the disk and the larger florets.

WATERLILY
D. 'Vicky Crutchfield'
As their name implies, these flower heads look like waterlilies and have broad, flat florets.

DECORATIVE
D. 'Frank Hornsey'
Fully double. Florets have broad petals rounded at the ends, usually curling inward along their length, flat, and slightly twisted.

BALL
D. 'Wootton Cupid'
Rounded flower heads with spirally arranged florets. The petals are rolled for over half their length.

POMPON
D. 'Small World'
Similar to ball dahlias but smaller, to a maximum diameter of 2in (5cm) and more globular; florets are rolled for the whole of their length.

CACTUS
D. 'Majestic Kerkrade'
Fully double, with narrow, pointed petals curled backward or quilled, which are either straight or incurving.

SEMICACTUS
D. 'So Dainty'
Fully double. The ray florets have curled edges for up to one-half their length and are straight or curved in or out.

Cultivation

Dahlias thrive in well-drained, fertile soils of pH 6–7. They are heavy feeders, so dig in plenty of manure or compost in spring, then add bone meal at 4oz/sq yd (125g/sq m), allowing the soil to settle a few weeks before planting. Another way is to prepare the bed in late fall, leaving it roughly dug so that frost action can break up the soil. Many exhibition growers fertilize routinely throughout summer.

When and where to plant

Dahlias may be planted as potgrown plants, as dormant or just-sprouting tubers or clumps, or as rooted cuttings from tubers. Plants in leaf may be preferable to tubers, because they are often more vigorous. Tubers and clumps may be planted directly, about three weeks before the last frosts, whereas plants in leaf should not be planted until all danger of frost has passed.

Choose an open, preferably sheltered site in full sun. Immediately before planting, top-dress with a balanced fertilizer at 4oz/sq yd (125g/sq m) worked well into the soil. Tie young plants into stakes to support them as they develop.

Planting potgrown dahlias

When planting potgrown dahlias, stakes should be positioned at the appropriate spacings. Plants that will grow 4–5ft (120–50cm) tall are best planted 2–3ft (60–90cm) apart, and those that will grow 3–4ft (90–120cm) tall, 2ft (60cm) apart. Water the plants in their pots and allow to drain. Plant with care to avoid disturbing the root ball, and firm gently, leaving a slight depression at the base of the stem. Water thoroughly. The plants will make a clump by late fall; this may be lifted and stored for replanting in spring.

Insert a 3ft (1m) stake in a planting hole. Place soil around the clump so that the base of the new shoots is 1–2in (2.5–5cm) below soil level.

Planting tubers and clumps

Plant out tubers and clumps about three weeks before the last frost date, preparing the ground as for potgrown plants. Prepare a planting hole at least 9in (22cm) across and about 6in (15cm) deep, place the tuber or clump in the hole, and cover. Mark the position of the plant with a stake placed just to the side; this will indicate the plant's exact position when inserting its sturdier support stake.

Planting rooted cuttings

Tubers may be grown on in the cold frame or greenhouse to provide cuttings (see opposite). Plant out the rooted cuttings after all danger of frost has passed.

As growth develops, water the plants moderately; to retain moisture, mulch with well-rotted compost or manure when the plants are 12–15in (30–38cm) high. Do not place the mulch directly against the base of the plants, since this may encourage stem rot.

Pinching and disbudding

When the dahlias have grown to about 15in (38cm), remove the growing points to encourage side-shoots. Insert two more stakes to make a triangular support then tie the shoots in, with about 6in (15cm) between ties.

The number of shoots allowed to develop should depend on the size of the blooms required. For giant or large blooms, restrict each plant to 4–6 shoots; for medium and small blooms, allow 7–10 shoots. To produce high-quality blooms, remove (disbud) pairs of buds developing below the terminal bud. Disbud at least two pairs of these side (wing)

PINCHING

1 *When the plant is about 15in (38cm) high, pinch out the central shoot to encourage the development of sideshoots.*

2 *When the plant has 6–8 sideshoots, pinch out the top pair of buds. Tie in the stems to stakes.*

buds; for giant blooms, take out three pairs. Remove them carefully before they grow large; if removed too late, ugly scars will appear.

Summer fertilizing

Six weeks after planting, fertilize with a high nitrogen and potassium fertilizer, either in granular form, or by weekly applications of liquid fertilizer to the roots or leaves. As flower buds develop, extra potassium in the liquid fertilizer gives strong stems and good flower color, especially for pink shades. If interested in

DISBUDDING

Pinch out the side (wing) buds growing below the terminal bud on each young plant so that the bud that remains will develop into a larger bloom.

growing dahlias for exhibition, local enthusiasts will be happy to suggest supplemental fertilizer schedules.

The tuber's development during late summer and early fall is stimulated by the shortening day length. During this period, apply a split application of tomato fertilizer and superphosphate at the manufacturer's recommended rate. Avoid contact with leaves or stems, since this may cause scorch.

Pests and diseases

Dahlias are attacked particularly by aphids (p.639), thrips (p.640), spider mites (p.640), and earwigs (p.649). These may be controlled by spraying regularly. Immediately discard any plants showing symptoms of virus infection (p.642).

Lifting and storing clumps

When the foliage has been blackened by the first frosts in fall, trim back the stems to about 6in (15cm). Lift and clean the clumps of soil, trim off any fine roots, and treat the clumps with fungicide. Place them upside down for a few weeks in a frost-free place to dry out.

Label the clumps and pack them in boxes in vermiculite, perlite, fine turface, peat, or a similar medium. Store in a cool, frostproof place. Inspect the clumps regularly in winter: if any mildew or rot develops, scrape it out and dust the wound with sulfur. Mist-spray very lightly if needed to prevent shriveling.

Tubers of seed-grown dahlias (if they form) may be lifted as for the cultivars, but the tubers may be very small and delicate. They may need extra attention paid to their moisture requirements to prevent them from being lost over winter.

LIFTING AND STORING

1 *Cut the stems to about 6in (15cm) above ground level. Loosen the soil and ease the clumps out. Remove excess soil.*

2 *Store the clumps upside down for about 3 weeks in a frost-free place so that the stems dry out thoroughly.*

3 *When the stems have dried out, place the clumps in a cool, frost-free place and cover them with a layer of peat or vermiculite. Keep them almost dry until spring.*

Propagation

Divide established clumps in spring. First bring them into growth in a cold frame or greenhouse. Place the clumps gently into a tray of soil mix, spray with water, and keep them warm and damp, but not waterlogged. As soon as shoots develop, divide the clump into sections with a sharp knife, making sure that each piece has at least one growing shoot. Pot up each section separately using a general-purpose soil mix.

Alternatively, in late winter, force clumps at 60–65°F (15–18°C). When shoots are 3in (7.5cm) long, take basal cuttings, trim at a node, and root in a propagating case with bottom heat. Grow on under cover and harden off before planting out.

Showing dahlias

Cut blooms in the morning or evening, making sure that the length of the stem is in proportion to the bloom. When exhibiting, blooms should be well developed with undamaged florets. Read the schedule and present the correct number of stems staged in the container, with the blooms facing the front.

HOW TO PROPAGATE BY BASAL CUTTINGS

1 *In late winter, force the clumps under cover. Take cuttings when the young shoots each have 2 or 3 pairs of leaves.*

2 *With a knife, remove each shoot with a thin segment, or heel, from the parent clump. Trim the basal leaves from each cutting.*

3 *Insert the cuttings in a pot of moist soil mix. Place in a propagator or plastic bag to root. Then pot up singly to grow on.*

Soil preparation and planting

Most bulbous plants have long dormant periods underground after flowering and need relatively little attention for much of the year. However, the initial stages of selecting good stock, preparing the soil, and planting bulbs correctly contribute significantly to long-term success in cultivating bulbs.

Buying bulbs

There is considerable variation in the quality and size of bulbs available commercially, so examine any bulbs carefully before buying them. Different types of bulb are sold at various times of the year; always buy them when they are as fresh as possible. Select bulbs that are appropriate to the planting site: most need sun, some require shade, and others will naturalize in grass.

Conservation

Conserving bulbs in the wild is of the utmost importance, and strict rules govern their importation. Before purchasing bulbs, check (wherever possible) that the stocks on sale at nurseries and garden centers have been obtained from sources of cultivated bulbs, rather than from stocks that have been collected in the wild.

Dry bulbs

Most bulbs are sold in a dry state during their dormant period. Buy these as early as possible before they start into growth; most daffodils, for example, normally start producing roots in late summer, and most other spring-flowering bulbs will begin to grow by early fall. Fall-flowering crocuses and *Colchicum* species and hybrids especially benefit from early planting: specialized nurseries sell them in midsummer.

All fall-flowering bulbs are best bought and planted by late summer. Bulbs tend to deteriorate if kept dry too long; they have a shorter growing period and take some time to recover and flower satisfactorily, so buy and plant them as soon as they are available. Many bulbs, usually those that have a summer growing season, including *Galtonia*, gladioli, and *Tigridia*, are available for purchase in spring.

When buying bulbs, make sure that they are healthy and firm with strong growing points. Avoid those with soft or diseased areas or insect damage. Bulbs that are much smaller than average for their type, and bulb offsets, will not produce flowers in their first season.

Juno irises are unusual in having permanent storage roots beneath the bulb; if these have broken off, do not buy the bulb since it will not develop satisfactorily. Tulips should have intact skins or tunics; otherwise, they may be vulnerable to disease.

Moist bulbs

Although most bulbs may be stored dry, a few are better kept in slightly moist bark, peat, shredded wood, or some similar material. This particularly applies to some of the shade-loving bulb species such as *Erythronium*, *Anemone nemorosa*, and *Trillium* that are normally found growing in damp woodlands.

When buying cyclamen tubers, look for those with fibrous roots that are stored in moist bark or that are in root growth in pots. Cyclamen with healthy roots establish much more successfully than dry tubers and so, although more expensive, are a much better buy.

Potgrown bulbs

Pots of bulbs in active growth, and frequently in flower, are often sold in nurseries and garden centers. These are usually bulbs that were not sold when dormant and have been potted up. They grow satisfactorily and may be planted at once without disturbing the roots. Alternatively, they may be kept in pots until they have flowered and planted as dry bulbs after they have died down. They are more expensive, however, than dry bulbs.

The influence of different soil types

Bulbs grow in a range of soil types, habitats, and climates throughout the world; the conditions in which they occur naturally indicate their needs in cultivation. Most hardy bulbs are from Mediterranean-type climates and thrive in a warm, sunny site, in the freely draining soils that warm

How to Select Bulbs

GOOD EXAMPLES

TULIP

HYACINTH

DAFFODIL (SINGLE-NOSED)

DAFFODIL (TWIN-NOSED)

POOR EXAMPLES

Split tunic

Signs of disease

Diseased tissue

Damaged outer scales

No tunic

Deterioration of bulb tissue

Soft nose

Offset too small to flower

Choosing Corms, Tubers, and other Bulbous Plants

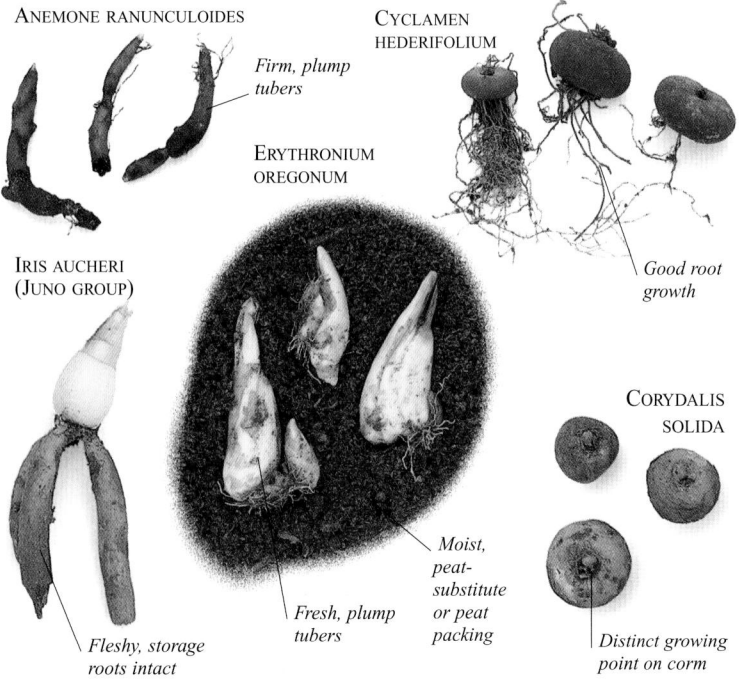

ANEMONE RANUNCULOIDES

Firm, plump tubers

CYCLAMEN HEDERIFOLIUM

ERYTHRONIUM OREGONUM

Good root growth

IRIS AUCHERI (JUNO GROUP)

CORYDALIS SOLIDA

Moist, peat-substitute or peat packing

Fresh, plump tubers

Distinct growing point on corm

Fleshy, storage roots intact

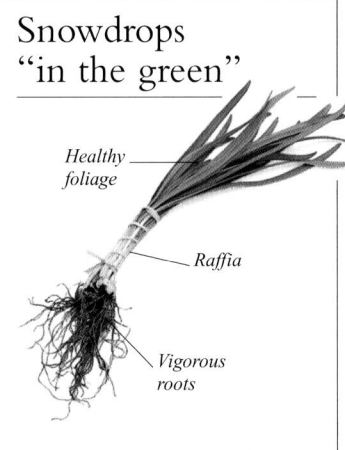

Snowdrops "in the green"

Healthy foliage

Raffia

Vigorous roots

If possible, obtain snowdrops in the green (i.e., still in leaf) after flowering, preferably just as the leaves begin to yellow at the tips. Fall-planted dry bulbs, although much cheaper, often fail to establish well. Although rarely obtainable, a few specialized nurseries do supply snowdrops in the green.

up quickly in spring and become dry in summer. Some bulbs tolerate heavy soils that are moist during the growing season, as long as they are baked dry in summer. If the soil is moderately fertile and organic, many bulbs increase steadily from year to year by seed or vegetative means. Most do best in a near-neutral or slightly alkaline soil.

Good drainage is vital; most bulbs are prone to rot while dormant if the soil is wet and poorly aerated. A few occur in the wild in riverside or swampland habitats. These thrive in moist (or even permanently wet) soils that do not dry out in summer.

Light soils

Sandy or light soils usually warm up rapidly in spring and provide the good drainage that most bulbs need, although they are often deficient in organic matter and nutrients. Dig in plenty of well-rotted compost or manure before planting and, in early spring, top-dress with a balanced fertilizer applied at the manufacturer's recommended rate. Always incorporate manure below the level at which the bulbs are planted to avoid the risk of disease or chemical damage. If using fresh manure, dig it in at least three months before planting. More fertile, sandy, and loamy soils benefit from extra organic matter, although fertilizer dressing is unnecessary in the first year. In rock gardens, dig in coarse sand to make up at least one-third of the top 12in (30cm) of soil for the extra drainage that most dwarf bulbs need.

Heavy soils

Heavy clay soils often need a lot of work to improve their drainage; on very poorly drained soils, a drainage system must first be installed to grow bulbs successfully. Coarse sand or grit at a rate of at least $1\frac{1}{2}$–2 buckets/sq yd (sq m) dug into the whole planting area will be required to make a significant difference. Heavy applications of well-rotted organic matter also improve the soil structure and therefore the drainage. For further information, see "Soil structure and water content," p.614.

Shady areas

Shade-loving bulbs most often occur naturally in woodland habitats but grow well in any shady situation, as long as the soil is properly prepared: it should be rich in nutrients and organic matter and also retain moisture. Incorporate plenty of leaf mold or other organic matter, such as well-rotted manure or compost, before planting. Acidic soil-loving woodland bulbs thrive where at least half the soil is leaf mold, peat, or compost.

Planting time

Dry bulbs should be planted as soon as possible after purchase. If the bulbs have been stored over winter (see "Lifting, drying, and storing," p.237), plant them at the end of their dormant period before they start growing. Potgrown bulbs may be planted after purchase throughout the season, or kept in their pots until after they die down and treated as dry bulbs. Plant summer-flowering bulbs, including those that bloom in late summer under cover, and bulbs "in the green," in early to midspring.

Planting in the open

Bulbs are usually best planted several to a large hole dug out with a spade, but they may also be planted singly. Do not make the outline of the planting area or the spacing of the bulbs symmetrical: this looks unnatural, and if one or two bulbs fail they leave unsightly gaps.

Bulbs may also be planted together in layers for a succession of blooms (see right).

Planting depths and spacing

Plant bulbs with three to five times their own depth of soil above them (deeper in light than in heavy soils) and two to three bulb widths apart. Remove soil to the correct depth, fork some bone meal into the bottom of the hole, and insert the bulbs.

It may be difficult to identify the top of a bulb, especially with rootless cyclamen or *Arisaema* tubers. The upper surface is usually flatter than the lower, or sometimes concave.

Corydalis tubers can be almost globular, but usually have some sign of shoot growth on the top. If it is impossible to be sure which end should be up, plant the bulb on its side.

Replace the soil, breaking down any clods and removing any large stones. Firm gently so that there are no air spaces around the bulbs. Give fall-planted bulbs an occasional deep watering until winter sets in. Lightly mulch areas of spring-planted bulbs to conserve moisture.

CORRECT PLANTING DEPTHS

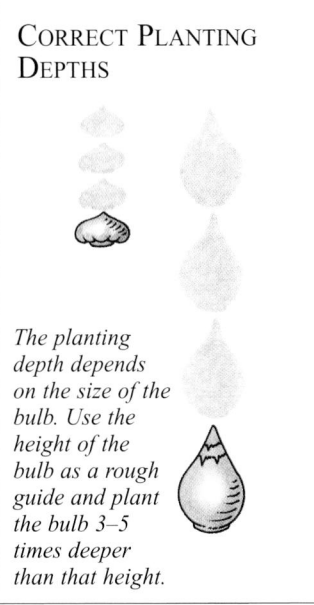

The planting depth depends on the size of the bulb. Use the height of the bulb as a rough guide and plant the bulb 3–5 times deeper than that height.

PLANTING BULBS IN THE OPEN

1 *Dig out a large hole in well-prepared ground. Plant the bulbs (here tulips), at least 3 times their own depth, and 2–3 widths apart.*

2 *For a natural effect, space the bulbs randomly. Once they are in position, gently draw the soil over them with your hand to avoid displacing or damaging them.*

3 *Tamp down the soil over the planted area with the back of a rake. Avoid walking heavily on the soil surface, because this may compact the soil excessively.*

PLANTING BULBS
SINGLY

Plant each bulb in a separate hole at the appropriate depth. Draw back the prepared soil with a trowel, then firm it down gently.

Potgrown bulbs

Bulbs that have been purchased as potgrown plants may be planted in the open ground once the tops have died down. Keep watering them until the foliage turns yellow; this allows the bulbs to produce strength for flowering the next year. When planting the bulbs outdoors, make a hole large enough to accommodate the whole pot, so that the contents may be planted without disturbance.

PLANTING BULBS IN LAYERS

Two or more kinds of bulb may be planted in the same space. Plant each kind at its correct depth, carefully covering each layer before planting the next type of bulb.

HOW TO PLANT CYCLAMEN IN ROOT GROWTH

1 *Select a planting site where the soil is rich in leaf mold or organic matter, or prepare the soil as necessary, working in organic matter well below the depth of the planting hole to encourage the roots to grow into the soil after planting. Allow it to settle for a day or two, then make a hole that is deep enough to plant the tuber with its roots spread out below it.*

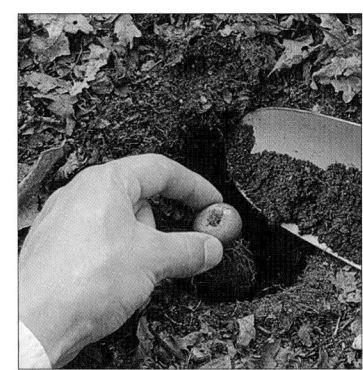

2 *Plant the tuber so that it will lie with its upper surface just visible at soil level. Fill in around the roots with soil, taking care not to damage the roots.*

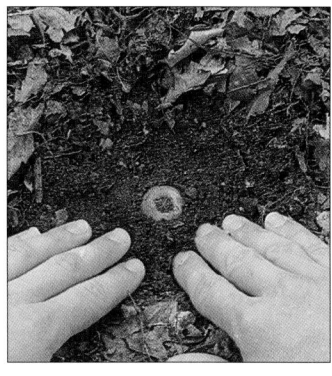

3 *Gently firm the soil around the tuber with your fingers, leaving the growing point just exposed. Lightly cover it with a loose mulch.*

If the bulbs are potbound, gently tease out the roots at the base before planting to encourage them to grow out into the soil. If they are growing in a peat-based soil mix, keep the bulbs under cover in winter; otherwise, the peat acts as a sponge and the dormant bulbs rot in the waterlogged soil mix.

Planting tubers and corms in root growth

A number of woodland species, such as cyclamen, are best planted when they are in root growth, rather than as dry bulbs, since they will become established more quickly. They are also more likely to flower in their first season after planting; dry corms or tubers are much less reliable in this respect. Planting in root growth also eliminates any problems in distinguishing between the bottoms and tops of tubers or corms. Work plenty of leaf mold or well-rotted organic matter into the soil before planting to create the moist, organic conditions that woodland bulbs require; otherwise, the bulbs will not thrive.

Planting depth and spacing
Calculate the spacing and planting depth for corms and tubers in the same way as for dry bulbs (see "Planting in the open" and *Correct Planting Depths*, p.231), but allow extra space for the roots.

Cyclamen are unusual in that they grow near the soil surface in the wild, so do not plant the tubers too deeply or they may not flower. Make sure that their tops are at about the same level as the surrounding soil. They may be planted more closely than other bulbs, but they should be spaced at least their own width apart.

Planting
Plant the corms or tubers singly or as a group. It is important for the planting hole to be sufficiently deep and wide to properly accommodate the roots. Spread them out in the hole to help the plants establish more quickly. Fill in the hole and firm well to remove any air spaces.

The tops of cyclamen tubers may be left exposed or, if preferred, lightly covered with a loose mulch. Use leaf mold or, if the bed already has a top-dressing, coarse grit.

PLANTING LARGE BULBS IN GRASS

1 *Clean the bulbs (here daffodils), removing any loose outer coatings and old roots. Scatter the bulbs randomly over the planting area, then make sure that they are at least their own width apart.*

2 *Make an individual hole for each bulb, using a bulb planter to remove a circle of sod and a core of soil to a depth of about 4–6in (10–15cm).*

3 *Place a pinch of bone meal, mixed with a little of the soil from the core, into each hole and put in a bulb, making sure that the growing point is uppermost.*

4 *Break up the underside of the core over the bulb, so that it is completely covered with loose soil. Then replace the remains of the core on top of it.*

5 *Replace the lid of sod, and firm it in gently, taking care not to damage the growing point of the bulb. Fill in any gaps in the grass with more soil.*

Naturalizing in grass

When planting bulbs that are to be naturalized in grass, first cut the grass as short as possible. Random rather than regimented planting achieves a more natural effect; scatter the bulbs gently by hand over the area and plant them where they have fallen, making sure that they are

PLANTING SMALL BULBS IN GRASS

1 *Using a half-moon edger (or spade), cut an H shape in the sod. Cut to the full depth of the half-moon blade to make sure that it penetrates the soil below.*

2 *Undercut the sod and fold back the flaps to expose the area of bare soil beneath. Take care not to crack or tear the sod too much.*

3 *Using a hand fork, loosen the soil beneath to a depth of at least 3in (7cm), mixing in a little bone meal at a rate of about $^1/_2$oz/sq yd (15g/sq m).*

4 *Press the bulbs (here crocuses) gently but firmly into the soil, taking care not to damage the growing points. Space the bulbs randomly at least 1in (2.5cm) apart.*

5 *Score the underneath of the sod with a hand fork to loosen the soil, so that the bulbs will be able to grow up through the sod easily.*

6 *Roll the sod flaps back into position, taking care not to dislodge the bulbs or damage the sod. Firm down the sod, particularly along the seams.*

USING A FORK TO PLANT SMALL BULBS

1 *Push a garden fork into the grass to the appropriate depth and rock it back and forth. Repeat at random over the rest of the planting area.*

2 *Thoroughly mix a little bone meal with some garden soil. Trickle a small amount of this mix into the bottom of each hole, using a widger or a small spoon.*

3 *Place a single bulb in each hole, growing point upper-most, making sure that it is buried at twice its own depth. Then cover all the planted bulbs with soil.*

NATURALIZING IN GRASS

Allium moly
Anemone apennina,
  A. blanda (and cvs),
  A. pavonina
Camassia
Chionodoxa
Colchicum autumnale,
  C. speciosum

Crocus pulchellus

Crocus biflorus,
  C. chrysanthus,
  C., Dutch Hybrids,
  C. flavus, C. nudiflorus,
  C. ochroleucus,
  C. pulchellus, C. speciosus,
  C. tommasinianus
Dactylorrhiza fuchsii,
  D. maculata
Eranthis hyemalis
Erythronium dens-canis,
  E. revolutum,
  E. 'White Beauty'
Fritillaria meleagris,
  F. pyrenaica
Galanthus caucasicus,
  G. elwesii, G. nivalis
Gladiolus communis subsp.
  byzantinus
Hyacinthoides hispanica
Leucojum aestivum,
  L. vernum
Muscari

Narcissus 'Fortune'

Narcissus (some
  dwarf and most large spp.),
  N. bulbocodium,
  N. cyclamineus, N. nanus,
  N. obvallaris, N. poeticus,
  N. pseudonarcissus,
  N. pumilus, N. triandrus
Ornithogalum nutans
Puschkinia scilloides
Scilla bifolia,
  S. siberica
Tulipa sprengeri,
  T. sylvestris,
  T. tarda

at least one bulb's width apart. Dig holes with a trowel or use a bulb planter, which cuts out plugs of sod and soil to a depth of about 4–6in (10–15cm); dig deeper if necessary for larger bulbs.

Check that all the holes are at the correct depth and that the bulbs are the right way up before inserting them and replacing the sod; then give them a good watering.

Planting large groups of small bulbs in grass

It is easier and less time-consuming to plant large numbers of very small bulbs, such as crocuses, by lifting a section of sod and planting a whole group of bulbs in the soil beneath, rather than planting each bulb individually. Loosen the soil beneath the sod since it may be compacted; fork in a little balanced fertilizer or some

bone meal. Position the bulbs randomly, at least their own width apart. Replace the sod over the bulbs, and firm it by hand or tamp it down gently with the back of a rake.

Alternatively, in lighter soils, use a broad-tined garden fork to make a series of holes in the sod, and rock the fork back and forth in the ground to enlarge the holes slightly so that they easily accommodate the bulbs.

The tines should be inserted to three times the depth of the bulb, for example 3in (7cm) for crocuses. Repeat this at random for the entire planting area, so that the final arrangement of holes is in straight but crisscrossing lines. Mix a little bone meal with soil and place some in each hole before planting the bulbs singly, then top-dress the entire area with more prepared soil.

HARDY BULBS FOR FORCING

Allium neapolitanum,
    A. oreophilum
Arisaema
Camassia
Chionodoxa
Crocus

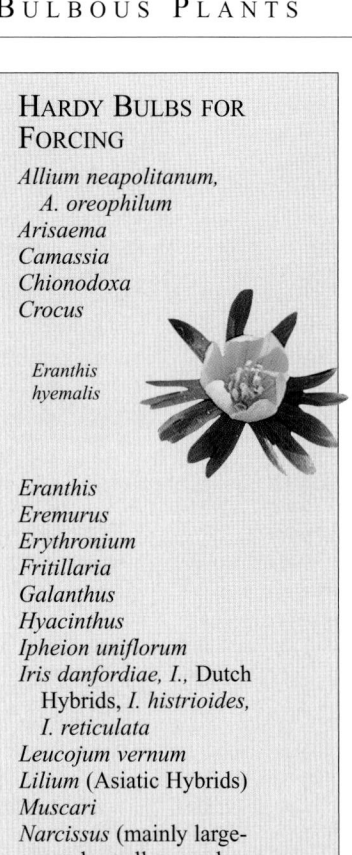

*Eranthis
hyemalis*

Eranthis
Eremurus
Erythronium
Fritillaria
Galanthus
Hyacinthus
Ipheion uniflorum
Iris danfordiae, I., Dutch
    Hybrids, *I. histrioides,*
    I. reticulata
Leucojum vernum
Lilium (Asiatic Hybrids)
Muscari
Narcissus (mainly large-
    cupped, small-cupped,
    and trumpet hybrids)
Ornithogalum
Oxalis adenophylla
Puschkinia
Scilla
Tulipa (many early-
    blooming spp.
    and cvs,
    Triumphs and
    Darwin Hybrids)

Tulipa
'Prinses Irene'

Planting in ornamental containers

Bulbs may be planted in troughs, tubs, patio pots, or any ornamental container that is clean and has sufficient drainage holes in the base to allow water to drain away quickly. Place a piece of window screening or similar sort of rot-resistant netting over the hole(s) of the container. Raise the pot off the ground with bricks or pot feet to stop water from gathering in the base and, if the pot is made of ceramic or terracotta, help protect it against cold damage.

Vary the soil mix, whether it be soil-based, rich in leaf mold, or very gritty, to suit the requirements of different types of bulb. The soil mix must be free draining or it may become waterlogged, and the bulbs may rot. Insert them at the same depths and spacing as for standard pots (see *How to Plant Bulbs in Pots*, above).

HOW TO PLANT BULBS IN POTS

Growing tip uppermost

1 *Plant the bulbs (here daffodils) at twice their own depth, and one bulb's width apart.*

2 *Cover the bulbs with soil mix to ¹/₂in (1cm) below the rim. Top-dress with grit (see inset), and label.*

Soil mixes for pots, beds, and frames

A good general soil mix, containing the required organic content and drainage may be prepared as follows: mix together 2 parts peat, 3 parts coarse sand, and 4 parts soil; then add a base fertilizer or some bone meal at a rate of 1oz/1 gallon (25g/5 liters) and (except for acid-loving plants) garden lime at a rate of 1oz/4 gallons (25g/18 liters).

For bulb beds make up sufficient soil mix for a layer that is at least 12in (30cm) in depth, with a layer about 2in (5cm) deep, of well-rotted compost or manure beneath it.

A similar mix is suitable for most bulbs, in pots or other containers both indoors and outside. If using a commercial potting mix, add some grit or coarse sand – at least one-third by bulk – because these soil mixes are often not sufficiently well drained for use with most bulbs.

Woodland bulbs grown in pots or containers require a well-drained mix with additional organic matter that is rich in nutrients, for example a mixture of 3 parts leaf mold or compost, 2 parts good garden soil, and 1 part sharp sand or grit.

Forcing hardy bulbs

Forcing is the process of bringing a plant into flower out of season. It is easy to force most bulbs in containers both indoors and outdoors, because the growing conditions can be tailored to the particular needs of the plant. Suitable soil mixes may be used for different types of bulb, and plants can be given the correct seasonal care, from planting in fall, encouraging roots to form in winter, and bringing into bloom in early spring.

Similar control is possible when cultivating bulbs that are planted directly into a greenhouse bed or bulb frame; the planting method is the same under cover as for bulbs grown in the open (see "Planting in the open," p.231).

Choosing clay or plastic pots

Bulbs may be planted in either clay or plastic pots. Clay pots are not as readily available, but they are more suitable for bulbs that are unable to tolerate excessive moisture, because the soil mix dries out more quickly after watering than in plastic pots. Plastic pots are now extensively used and are perfectly satisfactory as long as they are filled with a freely draining soil mix; water the soil mix less frequently than with clay pots. For plants that need moist conditions, such as woodland bulbs, the greater water retentiveness available in plastic pots is particularly valuable.

If using clay pots, a piece of screening or similar netting placed over the drainage hole(s) keeps the soil mix from washing out and prevents worms and other small creatures from entering the pot.

Planting in pots

Ideally, bulbs should be planted in pots at the same depths as bulbs grown outdoors (see "Planting depths and spacing," p.231). However, this is often not possible with larger bulbs, in which case make sure the pot is deep enough to allow at least 1in (2.5cm) of moist soil mix beneath the bulb. When filling the pot with soil mix, allow ¹/₂in (1cm) of space below the rim of the pot to allow for adequate watering. A standard 6in (15cm) pot provides room for these requirements for many bulbs and will take at least three daffodils or five to six tulips.

Select similar-sized bulbs of the same variety for forcing; otherwise, flowering may be irregular. For crocuses and other small bulbs, a 6in (15cm) pan or azalea pot holds at least ten to 12 bulbs.

Place a layer of soil mix at least 1in (2.5cm) deep in the pot and space the bulbs evenly on this. Do not press the bulbs into the soil mix too firmly; this may compress the soil just beneath the roots of the bulbs and impede their growth. Leave about one finger-width between each bulb. Position tulip bulbs with the flat side facing out: the first leaf will then grow over the edge of the pot. Work more

THE PRACTICE OF "CROCKING" A POT

Placing a layer of stones or a piece of broken pot (called a "crock") at the base of a pot takes up space that could otherwise usefully be filled with soil mix. Instead, cover the hole with a piece of screen.

BULBS IN A PLUNGE BED

Plunge the labeled pots up to their rims in a sand bed or cold frame. Check the pots regularly to be sure that the soil mix does not dry out.

soil mix down between the bulbs and firm gently. Small bulbs should be covered completely, but tulips and daffodils may be left with the tip of the bulbs showing. Top-dress the pot with a generous layer of horticultural grit, which helps to retain moisture and improves the appearance of the pot. Label with the plant name, the date of planting, and source. Do not allow the soil mix to dry out completely. Check regularly; as bulbs begin to root and grow, more frequent watering will be necessary.

Cold storage of pots

After planting, keep the pots in a cold frame or cold greenhouse. Bulbs in pots are particularly susceptible to cold damage; in severe winters, pots in a cold frame or unheated greenhouse may freeze solid. Protect them by sinking the pots in a plunge bed of coarse sand, perlite, or grit, mixed with enough peat to stop the insulating material from collapsing into the hole when the pots are taken out. The pots may also be plunged in a straw-lined trench in the garden and covered with an insulating layer of straw, loosely packed leaves, or perlite. The lining and covering should be thick enough to prevent the pots from freezing in midwinter.

If only a few pots are being forced, they may be placed in a refrigerator, a root cellar, or a cool corner of a basement. The temperature should remain between 35–40°F (2–4°C). Do not store the pots with apples, which produce ethylene gas that can cause flowers to abort.

Check periodically in winter for watering needs. After about ten weeks, begin checking for pots ready to bring into gentle warmth. Early-flowering varieties need less cold treatment than later-flowering ones, which may need up to 16 weeks. When ready, new

BULBS IN A STRAW-LINED TRENCH

After planting in pots, give hardy bulbs their necessary cold period by storing outdoors. Store deeply and cover thickly with straw to prevent the soil mix from freezing solid. Water if necessary during unfrozen spells.

shoots are visible and roots show at the base of the container. Move the containers into a cool room or greenhouse, between 50–55°F (10–12°C), and keep them out of direct sunlight initially. Once the shoots turn green and elongate, move them into more light and warmer conditions, and keep moist but not wet. In the home, flowers will last longer if the pots are moved into a cool room at night. (For care after flowering, see "Bulbs in containers outdoors," p.237).

Bulbs that have been forced into bloom should be planted in the garden once spring arrives or allowed to go dormant in their pots and then planted out in fall. They will rarely force well for a second year.

Popular bulbs for forcing indoors

Some bulbs can be planted in pots and bowls and kept indoors in the dark to induce them to flower early. The bulbs are best grown and displayed in a 60°F (16°C) room. In warmer conditions, the flower stems grow very quickly and look out of character, and the flowers do not last as long as in cool conditions.

Hyacinths

The fragrant hyacinth is a popular bulb for indoor forcing. Specially prepared bulbs are available; if they are given suitable treatment, they will come into flower by midwinter.

Buy the hyacinth bulbs in early fall and plant them in bowls filled with bulb fiber or moistened soil mix. Plant the bulbs close together, so they are not quite touching one another, with their growing tips protruding just above the top of the fiber or soil mix. Put the newly planted bulbs in a cool, dark place: a closed cupboard in a cool room is suitable. This encourages the flowering stems to develop before the leaves and allows the root systems to become well established. Keep the fiber or mix just moist by carefully watering between the bulbs.

Leave the bowls in the dark for about eight weeks, or until the pale new shoots are about 1½–2in (4–5cm) high and the flower buds are just visible. Once they have reached this stage, bring the bulbs into the daylight, but do not expose them to bright sunlight. Do not remove the bowls of bulbs from the dark earlier than this, because the leaves will grow very rapidly and obscure the flowers. Once exposed to the light, the leaves will gradually acquire their natural green color.

Tender daffodils

Some tender daffodils, including *Narcissus* 'Paper White' and 'Soleil d'Or', may be grown in bulb fiber in the same way as hyacinths. They do require more light, however, and should be placed on a sunny windowsill as soon as the shoots appear. If the light is inadequate, daffodils may become pale and excessively tall, and they will need staking for support.

Amaryllis

The large-flowered *Hippeastrum* hybrids and a few species, commonly known as amaryllis (true *Amaryllis* are not forced), are popular as indoor plants. Garden centers and stores supply them complete with a suitable soil mix, ready to be planted in pots and grown to flowering in a warm, light room.

After flowering, remove the dead flowers, but do not cut down the stalks until they shrivel. Keep the plants in a well-lit room or in a greenhouse, and water regularly. Fertilize once a month with a flowering house plant fertilizer. When danger of frost is past, plunge the pot outside in light shade (or keep the pot inside; this will keep creatures out of the soil mix, help guard against bulb rot, and will give better control over watering. Reduce watering in late summer to induce dormancy. When the leaves turn yellow, gently pull or cut them off and then store the pot in a cool to cold (but frost-free), dark, and dry location. After about one to three months the bulb may start to grow, so check regularly for the emerging tips. If growth does not start naturally, watering begun in mid-November should produce flowers before the end of the year.

FORCING HYACINTHS IN A CONTAINER INDOORS

1 *Place some moist bulb fiber or soil mix in the bottom of a container. Position the bulbs and fill with fiber, leaving the bulb crowns just visible at the surface. Leave them in a cool, dark place.*

2 *When the flower spikes are visible between the pale leaves, bring the container into bright, indirect light.*

Growing hyacinths in water

Hyacinth bulbs may be forced in water in special glasses designed to hold one bulb with its base just at water level. Place a bulb in its glass in a cool room away from sunlight, and keep the water level filled to just below the base of the bulb. It rapidly produces roots that grow down into the water.

Wait until the flower buds begin to show color before moving the rooted hyacinth into a warm, brightly lit room. The flowering shoots then develop and produce blooms. After flowering, discard the exhausted bulb, since it is unlikely to provide a good display the following year.

Fill the glass with water up to the neck and place the bulb in the top so it sits just above the water. Leave in a cool place. As the roots grow, keep the water filled up.

Routine care

Bulbs do not require a great deal of maintenance if the correct environment is provided. If they flower poorly, the most likely cause is overcrowding: this is easily remedied by dividing them and replanting in a fresh site. Bulbs are not prone to pests or diseases, but any present must be controlled promptly.

Bulbs in grass

Bulbs left to naturalize in grass do not need as much attention as those planted in other sites in the garden, but correct timing in mowing is very important. Deadhead regularly and fertilize occasionally; this will help the bulbs stay healthy and able to multiply steadily over the years.

Fertilizing
Bulbs in grass should not be given fertilizers high in nitrogen, since these increase the vigor of the surrounding grass at the bulbs' expense. If fertilizer is needed (such as. for daffodils that fail to flower freely), use a high-potassium fertilizer to encourage the production of blooms.

Deadheading
Prompt removal of faded blooms improves vigor in bulbs by preventing them from wasting energy on unwanted seed production. After flowering, pinch through the stems below the seedpods. If the seed capsules will be harvested later or left to seed naturally, leave some to ripen on the plant, then cut the stems to the ground after harvesting the seed.

CUTTING DOWN BULBS IN GRASS AFTER FLOWERING

Leave clumps of bulbs (here daffodils) planted in grass until the leaves start to turn yellow. Then cut them down to ground level with shears before mowing the grass.

When to mow
If cultivating early-flowering bulbs such as daffodils, do not cut the grass until at least six weeks after they have flowered, or until the foliage is turning yellow. If growing bulbs that increase by self-seeding, do not mow the grass until the seed capsules have been able to shed all their seed, usually about three weeks after the leaves begin to die down.

Fall-flowering bulbs such as *Colchicum* start into growth before the end of the lawn-mowing season. When the first leaves or tips of the flowering shoots appear, mow with the blades set high enough to avoid them. Stop mowing when the shoots are too tall to escape the blades.

In a wildflower meadow that includes late-flowering spring bulbs, delay mowing until mid- to late summer, when all the foliage has died down completely.

DEADHEADING

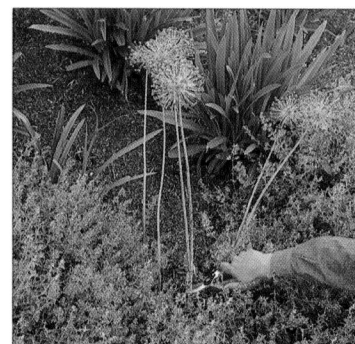

Unless the seeds are to be used for propagation, cut down all dead flower stems of bulbs in the border (here Allium*) with pruners to ground level.*

Bulbs in borders and woodlands

The level of maintenance required for bulbs in herbaceous or mixed borders, or in woodlands, depends on whether they are intended to be temporary or permanent fillers. Permanent bulb plantings need little maintenance until the bulbs become overcrowded, when they should be lifted and divided (see opposite).

If the ground is well prepared, no fertilizing is necessary the first year. An application once or twice in a season of a low-nitrogen, high-potassium fertilizer, which promotes flowering rather than leafy growth (see SOILS AND FERTILIZERS, "Types of fertilizer," p.618), will encourage a fine display in subsequent years.

Bulbs need adequate moisture during the growing season, especially in woodlands, and it may be necessary to water them if there is a prolonged early drought. Deadhead them at regular intervals in the same way as for bulbs in grass.

Care of temporary plantings is the same as for the first-year care of bulbs that are permanently planted. Lift the bulbs for storing at the end of the growing season (see opposite).

Removing dead leaves
After the bulbs in the border have finished flowering, allow the leaves to die down completely before removing them. Do not neaten the leaves by tying them together while still green, because this reduces their capacity to photosynthesize and store energy in the bulb for the next growing season, and therefore the bulb loses vigor. It also makes them die down prematurely.

WHEN TO HARVEST SEEDS

If seeds are desired, do not deadhead until the seed capsule (here Fritillaria*) is brown and begins to split. The ripe seeds are then ready to harvest for sowing or storing.*

Staking

A few tall bulbs with slender stems need staking. Stake these plants as soon as they are tall enough for a tie to be put around them; tie in the stems again when the plants are near their full height and are about to flower. Where the bulbs are planted in groups, place bamboo stakes on the inward-facing side of the stems so that they are concealed by the growing plants. Insert the stakes well away from the base of the stems so that the bulbs are not damaged.

1 *Support a tall, single-stemmed plant such as a gladiolus with a bamboo stake when the plant is 6in (15cm) tall. Attach the stem to the stake with string or raffia.*

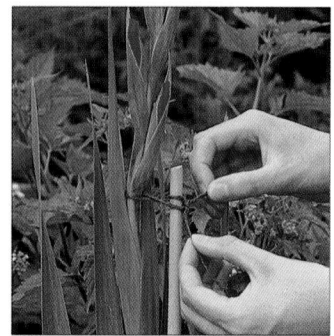

2 *When the flower buds are forming, tie in the stem to the stake just below the buds to prevent the stem from breaking when the buds open.*

STAKING BULBS IN GROUPS

For plants such as lilies that grow in clumps, place one or more stakes in the center of the clump. Tie in surrounding stems to each stake with a figure-eight loop so that the stems do not rub against the stakes.

Lifting and dividing overcrowded bulbs

If mature bulbs flower less freely than in previous years, the deterioration is usually due to overcrowding. This may not be obvious unless the bulbs are readily visible near the soil surface, as is often the case with *Nerine*.

Lift crowded clumps during the dormant season, before root growth starts. Separate the clumps into individual bulbs and replant them in irregular groups. Insert separately at three to five times their own depth and two to three bulb widths apart. Plant small offsets or bulblets between bulbs of flowering size. Alternatively, grow them in pots, in a nursery bed, in a frame, or in the garden in the same way as for two-year-old seedlings (see "Care of seedlings," p.240).

If, on lifting, the bulbs are found not to be overcrowded but are deteriorating or no longer thriving, inspect them for pests and diseases (see p.238). If there is no obvious explanation for their failure, replant them in a different site that is well drained and has sufficient light and nutrients. Alternatively, grow the bulbs in pots in a cold frame or greenhouse until they recover.

Lifting, drying, and storing

Bulbs planted temporarily in beds or borders should be left *in situ* until the foliage has begun to yellow. Then lift and clean them, lay them out on a tray to dry, and store them in paper (not plastic) bags in a dry place until the next planting season. If there is any sign of fungal disease, dust them with fungicide. You can also lift them in full growth soon after flowering or as the foliage dies down, and then replant them immediately in another part of the garden so that they may die down naturally.

Dwarf bulbs in the rock garden or raised bed

The principles of routine care of bulbs in borders also apply to dwarf species in raised beds or in the rock garden. Many of the rarer bulbs are slow to increase, however, and do not become overcrowded for several years. Keep them reasonably moist during the growing season, particularly in drought conditions, and fertilize them regularly with a high-potassium, low-nitrogen fertilizer.

If seed is required, harvest the seed capsules when ripe; then clear away the dead leaves to improve the appearance of the bed and reduce the likelihood of disease.

HOW TO DIVIDE AN OVERCROWDED CLUMP

1 *When bulbs planted in the open become overcrowded, use a garden fork to lift the entire clump as the leaves die down. Take care not to damage them.*

2 *Divide the clump of bulbs (here* Nerine*) by hand, separating it first into smaller clumps and then into individual bulbs. Remove any dead or diseased material.*

3 *Discard any unhealthy bulbs. Clean the good bulbs with care, removing the loose tunics, in preparation for replanting them singly in freshly prepared soil.*

Bulbs in containers outdoors

Bulbs in containers should not be allowed to dry out when in growth and should regularly be given a high-potassium fertilizer to boost flower production. Wait until the foliage of spring-flowering bulbs has died back naturally, then lift and clean them, and store them in a cool, dry place during summer. Replant the bulbs in a container of fresh soil mix in early fall for a display in the following spring. Alternatively, if the container is needed for a summer display, transfer the bulbs while still in the green to a spare bed, and allow them to die back before lifting, cleaning, and drying them in the normal way.

Spring-flowering species such as crocuses, daffodils, and hyacinths may be transplanted directly into the garden for naturalizing. Store summer-flowering bulbs in a cool, dry place over winter and replant them in spring.

Some bulbs, such as lilies (*Lilium*), do not grow well if allowed to dry out completely after flowering. Keep them moist by plunging them in their pots in a shaded place or in a cold frame to rest. Repot the lilies every year in the spring.

Bulbs in frames and covered raised beds

Bulbs that are grown in frames or under cover need similar treatment after planting to those in borders (see opposite), but they require special care with watering and feeding.

Remove the covers of the raised beds or frames during the growing season, but replace them temporarily during excessively cold or wet weather. Keep the bulbs watered in dry periods. When most of the bulbs are beginning to die down, replace the covers until the beginning of the next growing season. Improve

HOW TO LIFT, DRY, AND STORE BULBS

1 *When the leaves are turning yellow about a month after flowering, gently lift the bulbs (here tulips) with a fork. Put them in labeled containers to avoid confusing different bulbs.*

2 *Clean the soil off the bulbs and rub off any loose, flaking tunic tissue. Cut or carefully pull off the dying foliage. Discard any bulbs that show signs of damage or disease.*

3 *Place the bulbs on a wire tray, spaced so that they do not touch, and allow them to dry overnight. Then dust them with fungicide and store them in clean, clearly labeled paper bags.*

the vigor of the bulbs by fertilizing them once the nutrients in the original soil mix are exhausted. Use a granular fertilizer sprinkled on the soil mix surface as the bulbs come into growth, or apply a liquid fertilizer every two or three weeks. In the latter part of the season, use a high-potassium, low-nitrogen fertilizer to produce a good display of blooms.

Bulbs in pots under cover

In coastal regions where winters are mild and summers rainy, bulbs that need a warm, dry summer and a winter and spring growing period grow well in an unheated or cool greenhouse. Keep such bulbs dry from the time their leaves die down until their natural growing period begins again either in late summer or early fall.

During the growing season, give the pots a good soaking when they are nearly dry, but take care not to overwater them, especially in winter. Give them extra water in the growing season up to flowering time, after which gradually reduce watering until the leaves die down. Do not allow some hardy bulbs, such as crocuses from mountainous areas and woodland bulbs, to dry out completely; keep the soil mix slightly moist during the summer.

Bulbs such as *Galtonia* from areas with summer rainfall, such as parts of South Africa and South America, must be watered regularly so that they keep growing during the summer; they should then be allowed to dry out during their natural dormancy in winter.

Renewing soil mix
Changing the top layer of soil mix in a pot of bulbs supplies them with enough nutrients for a further year. Before they start to grow, gently scrape away the old soil mix to expose the tops of the bulbs. If they are healthy and not overcrowded, cover them with fresh, moist soil mix of the same type that is in the pot. Separate and repot overcrowded bulbs or, if hardy, plant them out.

Repotting
Bulbs may sometimes be kept in the same pot for several years, but they eventually become overcrowded and need repotting, usually indicated by a failure to flower well and by undersized or unhealthy foliage. At the end of dormancy, repot the bulbs to encourage them to start into growth. Pot up larger bulbs singly, as for the initial potting up and in a similar soil mix (see "Planting in pots," p.234). Plant small bulbs or bulblets between the adult ones or pot them up separately (see "Care of seedlings," p.240).

In early spring, repot tender bulbs that are dormant in winter when the new growth is about to begin.

Fertilizing
If the bulbs are kept in the same pot for several years, fertilize them regularly throughout the growing season at alternate waterings with a liquid formulation high in potassium and low in nitrogen. Extra fertilizer is unnecessary if the bulbs are repotted or the top layer of soil mix in the pot is replaced each year.

Care of forced bulbs
When they are ready to be brought into the light, place forced bulbs, according to their needs, on a shady windowsill or in a cool, bright room (see "Cold storage of pots," p.235). The bulbs tolerate slightly warmer conditions when their flower buds are well formed. Rotate the bowl periodically and keep the soil mix moist. Forced bulbs are generally in poor condition after flowering. Discard them or plant them out in the garden where they will eventually, perhaps after two years or more, flower again in their normal season.

Amaryllis (*Hippeastrum*) may be kept in good condition from year to year by renewing the top layer of soil mix with a fairly rich, well-drained mix before growth resumes. Do not water them for at least a month during dormancy, and repot them if they are overcrowded.

Bulb problems

Bulbs that occasionally fail to flower are referred to as blind bulbs. In a long-established clump this problem is often due to overcrowding, so the bulbs should be lifted and replanted separately in fresh soil (see "Lifting and dividing overcrowded bulbs," p.237). A severe shortage of water during the active growing season is another possible cause.

Newly planted bulbs that are blind may not have been stored correctly, or they may not yet be fully mature.

Iris danfordiae, *Fritillaria* species such as *F. recurva* and *F. thunbergii*, and some other bulbs do not flower regularly even in nature, and so are described as shy-flowering. Do not dig up such bulbs unless they look unhealthy or seem crowded, since they may eventually flower if left undisturbed. It may be helpful to plant the bulbs especially deeply, because this discourages them from dividing into bulblets.

Pests and diseases
During the growing season, keep a careful watch for the symptoms of diseases and pests, and control any problems as soon as they arise. When planting, repotting, or propagating dormant bulbs, inspect them and destroy any badly damaged bulbs.

Bulbs may suffer from rot or fungal diseases, including ink spot, which infects bulbous irises, and iris soft rot (p.654), which damages all irises. Iris borers (p.652) primarily affect rhizomatous irises. Aphids (p.639) can cause the spread of viruses (p.642). Spider mites (p.640) occasionally affect bulbs grown under cover.

REPOTTING OVERCROWDED BULBS

1 *Remove some soil mix from the pot to inspect the bulbs (here daffodils). If they have become overcrowded in the pot, they should be repotted.*

2 *Carefully tip out the contents of the pot, and remove the bulbs from the soil mix. Discard any dead material or any bulbs that show signs of pests or disease.*

3 *Separate any pairs or clumps of bulbs with large offsets into individual bulbs by gently pulling them apart.*

4 *Select only healthy bulbs and clean them, rubbing with your finger and thumb to remove any loose outer tunics. Dust the bulbs with fungicidal powder.*

5 *Replant the bulbs in a pot of fresh, moist soil mix. Insert them at twice their own depth, and space them at least their own width apart.*

Propagation

MANY bulbs increase naturally by forming offsets or bulblets around the bulb and may be propagated by separating these from the parent bulbs. Those that do not divide freely may be increased by cutting them into sections and treating these as new bulbs. Some are propagated by other vegetative means such as scaling or scooping. Seed propagation yields larger stocks, but bulbs may take several years to flower.

Dividing bulbs

During the growing season, many bulbs increase by forming offsets from the parent bulb, usually within the bulb tunic. Separate them every year or two, and plant them out or pot them up individually. If left, they may become seriously overcrowded and take longer to develop to flowering size. The offsets may be small and numerous, as with some *Allium* species, or larger and fewer, as with daffodils and tulips.

Other bulbs may form bulbils in the leaf axils, as with lilies (*Lilium*) and some *Calochortus* species, or bulblets around the base of the bulb; both may be used for propagation. (Some lilies, such as some American species and hybrids, produce small rhizomes. Pot these up, placing them horizontally, to grow on for one or two years before planting out in the open garden.)

Propagation from offsets

Some bulbs, for example *Crinum*, may be increased by lifting and dividing a clump. Pull the offsets gently from the parent plant, or cut the basal plate at the point at which they are attached to the larger bulb. Clean off any loose material or soil, and dust cut surfaces with fungicide.

Replant the larger bulbs in the garden in a well-spaced group. Pot up smaller offsets separately, or insert several in a larger pot or deep tray. Keep them for one or two seasons in a cool greenhouse to grow on; then plant out in the open.

Propagation from bulblets and bulbils

Bulbs raised from bulblets will generally flower a year or two earlier than those grown from seed. When repotting bulbs, remove the bulblets from around the base of the parent bulb, and insert them in rows in trays. Use well-drained soil mix with a little slow-release fertilizer added. Space the bulblets in the tray as when sowing

HOW TO PROPAGATE BULBS FROM OFFSETS

1 *In the spring, before active growth begins, lift a clump of bulbs (here* Crinum*) with a garden fork. Shake excess soil from the roots and pull the clump apart.*

2 *Select a large bulb with several well-developed offsets. Clean off the soil from the offsets and pull them away from the parent bulb, taking care to preserve any roots.*

3 *Prepare 6in (15cm) pots with a moist, sandy soil mix. Insert a single offset into each pot, and cover it with about 1in (2.5cm) of soil mix. Label and water.*

seed (see "Sowing the seeds," p.240) and cover them with a 1in (2.5cm) layer of soil mix. Label, and grow them on in a shaded part of the garden. Keep the soil mix moist; if using clay pots, plunge them in beds to keep them damp. Treat the bulblets thereafter as for seed (see p.240).

Bulbils may be removed and treated similarly (see LILIES, *Propagating from Stem Bulbils*, p.245).

Gladiolus cormels

Gladioli often form small cormels at the base of the corm. Remove these from the parent and treat them

as bulblets (see left). Alternatively, plant them in rows at three to five times their own depth in fertile, well-drained soil, either in a bulb frame or in a nursery bed. They may be left in place to flower two to three years later. In cold regions, they must be lifted and stored for winter.

HOW TO PROPAGATE GLADIOLUS BY CORMELS

1 *When the plant has finished flowering and the foliage is dying back, use a handfork to lift the corm. Cormels should have developed all around the basal plate of the corm. Store all the corms over winter in a cool, dry place.*

2 *In late winter or early spring, pull off cormels; they should readily come away from the parent corm. The cormels may vary in size, but all may be used.*

3 *Half fill a tray with moist, gritty soil mix. Insert cormels, growing points upward, in rows 1in (2.5cm) apart. Fill the tray with more soil mix; level, firm, and label.*

BULBOUS PLANTS THAT MAY BE DIVIDED

Offsets
Allium (some spp.)
Alstroemeria
Arum
Crinum
Crocus
Galanthus
Iris, Juno group,
   I., Reticulata group (some spp.)
Leucojum
Lachenalia
Lilium
Muscari
   (some spp.)
Narcissus
Nerine
Ornithogalum
Tulipa

Gladiolus 'Deliverance'

Bulblets
Allium (some spp.)
Fritillaria acmopetala,
   F. crassifolia, F. pudica,
   F. recurva, F. thunbergii
Iris, Reticulata group (some spp.)
Lilium (some spp.)
Muscari (some spp.)

Cormels
Crocus
Gladiolus

Bulbs from seed

This method of propagation produces a large number of bulbs that initially are free from any viruses (except those specifically transmitted by seed), unlike division, which passes on any disease present in the parent bulb to the young plants.

Most bulbs take from three to five years to reach mature flowering size from seed. A few bulbs, such as *Cardiocrinum*, die after flowering, but their seeds may be gathered and sown regularly every year to ensure a steady succession of healthy plants that will mature and provide flowers in each growing season.

Gathering seeds

The seed capsules of bulbs are carried on the old flowering stems, but some plants, mainly crocuses and Reticulata irises, have capsules formed at or just above ground level and are difficult to see.

Watch the ripening capsules carefully for signs of splitting, because the seeds may be shed quickly. Remove the capsules as they begin to turn brown and start to split. Extract the seeds as soon as possible. A few bulbs, such as *Corydalis*, shed seeds when the capsules are still green; cut off and store the capsules in paper bags until the seeds are shed. Let the seeds dry without extra heat, and store them until sown in labeled paper packets in a cool, dry, and airy place. Do not use plastic bags, since they seal in the moisture and the seeds may rot.

When to sow seeds

The following method is suitable for most spring-flowering, hardy bulbs such as *Fritillaria*, daffodils, and tulips. The best time to sow is early fall, but if seed is available earlier (such as seed you may have gathered from your own plants), sow immediately. Germination should follow in early spring.

Sowing media for bulbs

Use a commercial soil-based sowing medium, with one-quarter part coarse sand added if the mixture does not have a sandy appearance. A suitable soil-based medium may be made from 2 parts sterile soil, 1 part peat or compost, and 1½ parts very coarse sand or seed-grade perlite with superphosphate and lime, each added at a rate of 1oz/4 gallons (25g/18 liters). Some commercial media containing only peat may also be used, but they contain only enough nutrients for a few months, and peat-only media are difficult to rewet once they have dried out.

Sowing the seeds

Clay or plastic pots may be used, but it is usually easier to maintain adequate moisture levels in plastic pots. Whatever sort of pot you are using, be sure to place a piece of screening over the drainage hole(s). Fill the pot with medium and firm it before sowing the seeds thinly on the surface. Space large, flat seeds of bulbs such as *Fritillaria* or tulips approximately one seed's width apart, and smaller, rounded seeds about ¼ in (5mm) apart. Sieve a light covering of the medium over the seeds so that they are no longer visible, and then cover with a generous layer of grit or aquarium gravel. Label the pots with the plant name, source, and date. Stand them in a shady place in the open garden, or plunge them in a sand frame, and keep them moist.

Care of seedlings

When the seedlings have germinated, bring the pots into full light in a cold frame or greenhouse. Keep them moist until they show definite signs of dying down, and then stop watering them. Seedlings of bulbs that are not naturally dry in summer even in their dormant period, such as certain *Crocus* species from mountainous areas, should be kept slightly moist. Start watering again in early fall, or as soon as there is new growth, and keep the pots watered until the growth dies down.

Leave most bulbs for two growing seasons before repotting, unless they grow very vigorously. It is not essential to fertilize seedlings in the first growing season, but larger bulbs form if they are fertilized regularly in the second. Use a commercial liquid formulation as used for tomatoes, but at half the manufacturer's recommended strength.

Removing seedlings from pots

After the seedling bulbs have completed two seasons of growth, or one in the case of very vigorous bulbs, pot them up into the soil mix recommended for use with mature bulbs (see "Soil mixes for pots, beds, and frames," p.234). After the foliage has completely died back (toward the end of the dormant period), empty out the pot. Separate out the young bulbs, clean, and repot them in fresh, moist soil mix to start them into growth. It is better to grow them in pots for two or three years until they are large enough to establish successfully outdoors.

Keeping seedlings in pots

Seedling bulbs may be grown on in pots and planted out together with the soil mix to avoid handling the bulbs and disturbing their root growth. Pot on a complete potful of one-year-old seedlings into a slightly larger pot, and fertilize them regularly while they are in growth in the second year. If they are large enough by the end of the season, plant the entire potful of young bulbs in the open garden when they are dormant or just starting into growth. Give them extra fertilizer after planting to avoid any delay in flowering. If they are too small, keep them in the pot, and fertilize them regularly for another year.

Woodland species

Many shade-loving bulbs grow best in a medium that contains some leaf mold. For seed sowing, use a mix of 1 part sterilized leaf mold, 1 part peat or compost, and 1 part sterilized soil, with a further 1½ parts of coarse horticultural sand or seed-grade perlite.

The growth of many of these bulbs, for example *Erythronium* and *Trillium*, is slow. Planting the entire panful of seedlings after two or three years' growth into a well-prepared bed is better than regular re-potting over several years, which disturbs the roots. Others, such as *Arisaema*, grow surprisingly quickly and tolerate disturbance.

HOW TO PROPAGATE BULBS FROM SEED

1 *Prepare the pot: fill it to within ½in (1cm) of the brim with commercial sowing medium mixed with a quarter part coarse sand. Firm it well with a tamper.*

2 *Sow the seeds evenly over the medium by tapping the open packet, holding it near the surface so that the seeds (here* Fritillaria meleagris) *do not bounce out.*

3 *Use a sieve to scatter a thin layer of fine soil mix evenly over the seeds. There should be just sufficient soil mix to conceal the seeds.*

4 *Top-dress the pot with at least ½in (1cm) of coarse grit, adding it carefully to avoid disturbing the medium or seeds.*

5 *Label the pot. Place it in a shady situation in the open. Plunge the pot in damp sand and water, as required, to keep the medium moist.*

POTTING UP SEEDLINGS

1 *Carefully knock out the entire pot contents; some of the bulbs (here* Fritillaria raddeana) *will be visible among the medium. Remove all the bulbs carefully.*

2 *Replant the young bulbs in a pot of fresh, gritty soil mix, placing them at twice their own depth and spaced their own width apart.*

Cyclamen

Seeds of hardy cyclamen germinate most readily if sown as soon as they are ripe, usually in midsummer. If using dry seeds, soak for about 24 hours before sowing to aid germination. Sow as described opposite.

The seedlings generally grow well in their first year, and the young tubers may then be repotted in sowing medium, preferably while they are still in

TWO-YEAR-OLD BULB SEEDLINGS

After 2 years, seedling bulbs (here Calochortus tolmiei) *may vary noticeably in size, but all should develop satisfactorily.*

growth. Add 1 part leaf mold to 3 parts of the medium to encourage vigorous growth. The tubers usually develop well if planted several to a pan, rather than singly. Insert them with their roots spaced out, and cover the tops with grit or sharp sand.

Place the pans in a shaded cold frame to grow on for a second year. In spring of the third year, repot the tubers singly using the same soil mix, then leave them until the tubers are approaching flowering size. Plant them out in the open garden in late summer or early fall.

Growing lilies from seed

Sow the seeds in pots about 4in (10cm) deep filled with peat, compost, or sowing medium based on soil or peat, preferably as soon as they are ripe (in late summer or early fall). Sow the seeds thinly to avoid the need for pricking out, cover them with fine grit, and place the pots in a cold frame or cold greenhouse.

In some lilies, the seedlings germinate two to six weeks after sowing. Others may take several months to germinate. Lily seeds differ in the way they germinate. With hypogeal lilies, root formation occurs initially; a cold period is then needed to stimulate leaf production. Seeds of epigeal lilies usually (but not always) germinate fairly rapidly with both root and shoot development occurring almost together (see also PRINCIPLES OF PROPAGATION, *How a Seed Germinates*, p.624).

Overwinter the pots in a cold frame or sheltered place outdoors, then bring the pots into a cold greenhouse in spring. Do not discard the containers even if no seedlings appear after the first year; germination can take two or occasionally more years, depending on the species.

Leave the germinated seedlings in their pots for their first growing season and regularly give them a liquid

EXTRACTING CYCLAMEN SEEDS

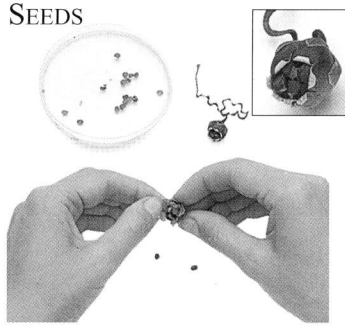

Harvest the seed capsules in early summer when they are beginning to split. Shake out the seeds and soak them in a bowl of tepid water overnight to assist germination.

PLANTING OUT WOODLAND BULBS

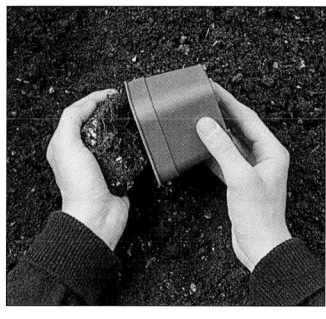

1 *Plant out woodland species without separating the young bulbs. Invert a pot of 2-year-old bulbs (here* Erythronium). *Slide out the mass of bulbs and medium.*

2 *Plant the entire potful of medium and bulbs, so that the top of the bulb mass is at least 1in (2.5cm) below the surface. Firm, label, and water lightly.*

fertilizer. Alternatively, prick them out when they have two true leaves into a soil-based potting mix. Repot them regularly or transfer them to nursery beds until they are large enough to plant out in the garden. This process takes from one to three years, depending on the species.

Tender bulbs

Sow the seeds of tender bulbs as described above, but keep the pots at a temperature above freezing during winter, plunged in bulb frames or beds under cover. Seeds of many tender species, for example amaryllis (*Hippeastrum*), germinate more quickly if bottom heat is used (this is usually supplied by heating cables; see GREENHOUSES AND FRAMES, p.574) and a minimum temperature of about 70°F (21°C) is maintained.

If the germination characteristics of a particular plant are uncertain and there is plenty of seed available, sow half with bottom heat and half in normal greenhouse temperatures. If germination has not taken place within six to eight weeks in heat, move the pots to a cooler place. Some genera, notably *Alstroemeria*, germinate rapidly when a warm period is followed by a cool period.

Sow fleshy seeds of bulbs such as *Clivia* fresh, directly from the seed capsule while it is still green. If left in the capsule, the seeds may germinate *in situ*, and they should then be removed and sown in the normal way. Grow on the seedlings (see "Care of seedlings," opposite). Seedlings of some genera, such as *Hippeastrum*, remain in active growth for more than one entire growing season; if so, keep the soil mix moist (less so in winter), and the plants may grow until they flower without going completely dormant

Large, flat seeds of such tender genera as *Hippeastrum* can also be germinated easily by floating the seed on water in a container, placed in a warm (70°F/21°C) greenhouse or on a windowsill Germination takes three to six weeks, after which the seedlings can be potted up in sowing medium in a 3in (7cm) pot.

Seeds with erratic germination

Seeds of certain bulbs, for example Juno irises, germinate very erratically, sometimes over several years. If, after two seasons, only a few seedlings have appeared, repot the entire potful without disturbing the soil mix; late-germinating seedlings often appear a year or so later.

Germination in plastic bags

Seeds of some genera may be germinated in plastic bags rather than pots; this is most frequently done with lilies (*Lilium*), but is applicable to most bulbs with large seeds, for example *Fritillaria*, tulips, and tender genera such as *Hippeastrum*.

Mix the seeds with three or four times their bulk of moist peat, vermiculite, or perlite. The medium used should not exude water when squeezed. Add a little fungicide, place the mixture in small plastic bags, then seal and label them.

For seeds that benefit from an initial warm period, such as those of the smaller *Hippeastrum* species, keep the bags at approximately 70°F (21°C), for example on top of a refrigerator. When the seeds have germinated, prick out the seedlings into pots or trays of well-drained rooting medium and keep them in cooler conditions. If the seeds have not germinated after six to eight weeks, transfer the bags to a cold frame or cool greenhouse until germination occurs, and grow on.

HOW TO SCALE LILIES

1 Clean the lily bulb; remove and discard any damaged, outer scales. Gently snap off about 6 good scales as close as possible to the base of the bulb.

2 Place some fungicidal powder in a plastic bag and add the scales. Shake the bag gently so that all the scales are thoroughly coated with the fungicide.

3 Remove any surplus fungicide from the bag. Place the coated scales into a second bag containing a 50:50 mix of peat and perlite, or peat and vermiculite.

4 Inflate the bag, then seal and label it. Store at about 70°F (21°C) in a warm, dark place.

5 When small bulblets have developed on the scales, remove the scales if they are soft. If they are fleshy and firm, leave them attached to the bulblets.

6 Plant the groups of bulblets either singly in small pots or several in a pan. Top-dress the pots with grit, label them, and leave them in a warm, light place.

7 The following spring, harden off the young bulbs by placing the pots in a cold frame.

8 In the fall, when the bulbs have grown on, remove them from the pots and separate them. Pot them up individually or plant them in their permanent positions.

Scaling

Scaling is an important method of propagating lilies (*Lilium*), but it may also be used for other genera that have bulbs consisting of scales, for example some species of *Fritillaria*. The bulbs of most lilies are composed of concentric rings of scales attached at their lower ends to a basal plate. If these scales are detached from the parent bulb close to the base, so that they retain a small piece of basal tissue, they may develop bulblets, normally near the base of the scale. Portions of scales that lack this tissue seldom form bulblets. Remove lily scales for propagation in late summer or early fall before root growth starts. Lift the dormant bulbs, then remove a few of the scales. Usually only a few are needed, and the parent bulb may be replanted to flower the following season. If many new plants are required, scale the whole bulb. Alternatively, without lifting the parent bulbs, remove the soil from around them and snap off a few scales.

Select only disease-free, plump, unblemished scales. If using only a few scales for propagation, coat them with fungicide, then mix them together with some damp peat and perlite or peat and vermiculite in a plastic bag. Seal the bag and place it in a warm, dark place at about 70°F (21°C) for approximately three months. Then place the bag in a cold place, such as a refrigerator (but not a freezer), for six to eight weeks to encourage bulblets to develop. When these form, fill some pots with a free-draining soil mix. Insert one or more scales, with their small bulblets attached, so that the tops of the scales are just below the surface of the soil mix.

Keep the pots in a shaded cold frame or cool greenhouse in hot weather. During the summer, plunge the pots of hardy bulbs in a frame or sheltered position in the open garden. At the end of the first growing season, separate the bulblets and repot them individually in a freely draining soil mix suitable for mature bulbs (see "Soil mixes for pots, beds, and frames," p.234). Grow them on in a cold frame or a cool greenhouse until the following spring when they may

HOW TO PROPAGATE BULBS BY TWIN-SCALING

1 Remove the brown outer scales of a bulb (here a daffodil). With a sharp knife, trim off the roots without damaging the basal plate, and slice off the nose.

2 Place the bulb upside down on its cut end. Cut downward through the basal plate to divide it into small sections, each piece having a section of basal plate.

3 Divide the sections into pairs of scales by peeling back the layers. Use a scalpel to cut each pair away with a piece of the basal plate attached (see inset).

be repotted into a container or planted in their flowering position in the garden.

Alternatively, after dusting with fungicide, insert the scales in trays filled with 2 parts damp vermiculite, perlite, or peat mixed with 1 part coarse sand. Keep them moist and shaded, preferably in a warm greenhouse at about 70°F (21°C), for two months. In spring, move them to a cool place to promote good leaf growth; the bulblets may then be repotted singly and grown on for a year before being planted out.

Twin-scaling

This is used to build up stocks of genera such as daffodils, hyacinths, and snowdrops (*Galanthus*). Cut up the bulbs into pairs of scales, with each pair retaining a small section of the bulb's basal plate. Be sure to keep your hands, the knife, and the cutting surface scrupulously clean so that no disease has the opportunity to infect the cut scales. After dusting the twin-scales with fungicide, treat them in the same way as single scales (see opposite).

Cutting bulbs into sections

Sectioning bulbs is not widely used by amateur growers, but it is useful for plants that do not divide freely or set seed. Bulbs may be sectioned near the end of the dormant period: parts of the basal plate may be cut through, or the entire bulb may be cut into pieces.

Chipping

Many bulbs may be propagated at the end of the dormant period, for example in the early fall, by cutting them into several segments (chips).

HOW TO PROPAGATE BULBS BY CHIPPING

1 *When the foliage has died down, lift the dormant bulbs and select a healthy, undamaged specimen (here* Hippeastrum*). Trim off the growing tip and the roots, taking care not to cut into the basal plate.*

2 *Place the bulb on a clean cutting surface, with its basal plate uppermost. With a clean, sharp knife, carefully cut down into the bulb, dividing it into halves.*

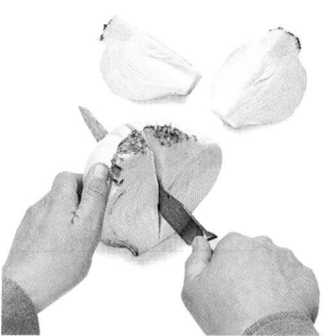

3 *Cut each half of the bulb again in the same way, making sure that the basal plate is divided equally between the individual segments.*

4 *Repeat until the bulb has been cut into about 16 chips. Soak them in fungicide for 10–15 minutes, occasionally agitating the container. Drain off any excess moisture.*

5 *Half-fill some plastic bags with moistened vermiculite. Put several chips in each bag. Seal the bags with rubber bands or plastic twist-ties. Store in a warm, dark, airy place, and check occasionally.*

6 *When bulblets appear around the basal plate of the chips, plant the chips individually into 3in (6cm) pots filled with a well-drained soil mix. Place in a sheltered position to grow on.*

Chipping allows more rapid propagation of bulbs that do not increase rapidly by offsets; it also serves to build up stocks of new cultivars. Large bulbs, such as daffodils or amaryllis, may be cut into as many as 16 chips; smaller daffodils and others, for example snowdrops (*Galanthus*), are usually chipped into four or eight segments.

Good hygiene is essential to avoid disease infecting the chips through their exposed cut surfaces. Wear gloves for cleanliness and protection because some people are allergic to the sap the bulbs release when cut. Clean and sterilize the bulbs with rubbing alcohol to help prevent rot. Use a knife or scalpel that has been sterilized in rubbing alcohol to cut the bulbs on a clean, disinfected surface. Soak the chips in a suitable fungicide after cutting. Alternatively, dust the cut surfaces with some flowers of sulfur.

Store the chips in the dark for 12–15 weeks in plastic bags of vermiculite that contain plenty of air. A temperature of 68–77°F (20–25°C) gives good results for most genera. Separate the young bulblets that develop on the chips, and pot them on into pans of freely draining soil mix. They generally reach flowering size in two or three years.

Cutting up bulbs that have growing points

Some cyclamen species, particularly *C. hederifolium* and *C. rohlfsianum*, form multiple growing

BULBS THAT MAY BE PROPAGATED BY CHIPPING

Allium
Amaryllis
Crinum
Galanthus
Hippeastrum
Hyacinthus
Iris
Leucojum
Lycoris
Muscari
Narcissus
Scilla
Sternbergia
Zephyranthes

Hippeastrum

points on the surface of the tubers. as do the corms of several genera, such as *Crocosmia* and *Gladiolus*. Such tubers and corms may be propagated by cutting them up, as long as each section has a growing point.

Almost fill 2–3in (5–6cm) pots with well-drained soil mix. Dust the pieces with fungicide, insert them singly with their growing points

CUTTING UP *CYCLAMEN* FOR PROPAGATION

1 *Take a large, healthy tuber (here* Cyclamen hederifolium*) and cut it into pieces with a clean knife. Each piece must have at least one growing point. Dust the cut surfaces with fungicide.*

2 *Leave the pieces (see inset) on a wire tray in a warm, dry place for 48 hours, until the cut surfaces form a callus. Pot them up individually into pots containing fast-draining soil mix.*

243

uppermost in the soil mix, and cover the tubers with some more soil mix. Top-dress the pots with grit, label, and leave in a cool greenhouse until they begin to grow. Keep the soil mix moist enough to sustain the sections until growth starts.

Grow them on in well-lit conditions in a cold frame, and shade them from the hot summer sun. Water with care; do not let young plants dry out when in growth. Plant them out the next fall.

Simple cutting

Make cuts ¼in (0.5cm) deep with a sharp knife through a bulb's basal plate; the number of cuts depends on the bulb's size. Dust the cuts with fungicide. Keep the bulb in a plastic bag of damp perlite or vermiculite, and some fungicide, in a warm place.

The damage to the basal plate induces bulblets to form along the cuts. When these have formed, insert the bulb upside down in a gritty soil mix made of 1 part peat to 1 part perlite or coarse sand. The bulblets will develop above the old bulb. A year later, carefully separate the bulblets, then plant them in trays in a cool greenhouse to grow on.

HOW TO PROPAGATE HYACINTHS BY SCOOPING

1 *Use a clean, sharpened teaspoon or a knife to scoop out the inner part of the bulb's basal plate, leaving the outer rim intact. Discard the basal plate.*

2 *Dip the cut surfaces in fungicide, then lay the bulbs, with their scooped areas uppermost, on a tray of sand. Place the tray in a warm place.*

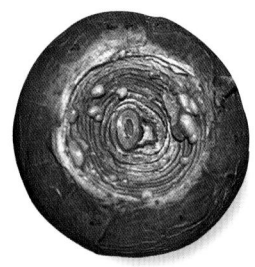

3 *Water the sand lightly as needed to keep it moist. When bulblets form around the edge of the scooped base, separate them from the parent, then pot them up.*

Scooping hyacinths

Scooping is a technique used for the commercial propagation of hyacinths. The center of the basal plate of the bulb is scooped out and discarded, the exposed surface dusted with fungicide, and the bulb kept upside down in warm, dark conditions. Numerous small bulblets eventually form on and around the cut surface. They may then be separated from the parent bulb and grown on in the same way as bulblets (see "Propagation from bulblets and bulbils," p.239) in individual pots.

Basal cuttings

The sprouting tubers of a few bulbs may be used in late winter for basal cuttings – young shoots that retain a piece of the parent tuber from which new roots develop. Place the cuttings in a pan of moist soil mix until they root, and then pot up. For details of the technique, see DAHLIAS, *How to Propagate by Basal Cuttings*, p.229. Grow on the rooted cuttings in a warm greenhouse until danger of frost is past. Harden them off in a cold frame and plant out in early summer. Propagate tuberous begonias and gloxinias (*Sinningia speciosa*) in this way in spring.

Scoring and scooping trillium

Various cutting techniques may be used to propagate *Trillium* rhizomes in late summer, after the leaves have died down.

One method that avoids lifting the parent plant is to remove sufficient soil to expose the top of a rhizome and to score lightly a shallow cut around the growing point of the rhizome. Dust the cut with a fungicide and cover the rhizome with a top-dressing of peat and coarse sand in equal parts, or cover with soil if it is light and well draining. Small rhizomes should form along the cut, and in time they should become large enough to separate.

Lift the rhizomes and scoop out their growing points. Make concave scoops, rather than cutting across the base of the growing points, to make sure that no soft tissue remains that could rot. Dust the cut surfaces with fungicide and replant the rhizomes. Small rhizomes should then form around the excised growing tip.

One year later, expose the rhizomes, remove the young ones, and grow them on in pots as described for young seedlings (see "Care of seedlings," p.240).

HOW TO PROPAGATE TRILLIUMS BY SCORING

1 *Carefully scrape away the topsoil to expose the rhizome. Score a shallow incision around it with a sharp, clean knife, just below the growing point (see inset).*

2 *Use a clean, soft brush to dust the cut surface of the rhizome with fungicidal powder.*

3 *Carefully cover the scored rhizome with a mix of peat and coarse sand in equal parts to the same level as before. Gently firm it with your fingers.*

4 *A year later, remove the topsoil to expose the rhizomes and remove any young ones that have formed. Pot them up individually and grow them on.*

CUTTING OUT GROWING POINTS

1 *Remove the growing point of the rhizome entirely by making a cut in the form of a concave scoop with the tip of a clean, sharp knife.*

2 *Dust the cut surfaces of the parent rhizomes with fungicide. Cover them up again with soil and firm the soil down lightly.*

Lilies

LILIES are among the most graceful of summer-flowering plants. Their tall, slim stems bear flowers with an enormous variety of dazzling colors and exotic shapes. There are a great many to choose from – more than 80 species of lilies and thousands of hybrids, which are more tolerant of different conditions and so are often easier to grow.

Lily classification

Lilies are classified according to their origins, parentage, and flowers:
Div.I Hybrids of Asiatic species such as *L. cernuum* and *L. davidii*.
Div.II Hybrids of *L. martagon* and *L. hansonii*.
Div.III Hybrids of *L. candidum* and *L. chalcedonicum*.
Div.IV Hybrids of American species lilies.
Div.V Hybrids of *L. longiflorum* and *L. formosanum*.
Div.VI (Aurelian hybrids): Trumpet lilies and *L. henryi* crosses.
Div.VII (Oriental hybrids): From Japanese species.
Div.VIII All other hybrids.
Div.IX All other species and their cultivars.

Where to grow lilies

Lilies are excellent border and woodland plants and make superb companion plants for shrub roses. A few of the smaller lilies may be used to add summer color to the rock garden when most alpine plants have already finished flowering. Lilies look splendid planted in containers, especially on terraces and patios. Where not hardy, Div.V lilies make excellent potted plants for the cold greenhouse and conservatory .

Planting and care

Always buy fresh bulbs and plant them immediately. Do not buy dried or shriveled bulbs. Most lilies grow well in a range of soils. Div.III lilies prefer alkaline soils and full sun; Div.VII hybrids must be grown in acidic soil (or acidic soil mix in containers); Div.IV hybrids are best suited to damp, woodland conditions. Plant lilies in fall or spring at two to three times the depth of the bulb in well-prepared, free-draining soil; *L. candidum* needs only 1in (2.5cm) of soil above the bulb and should be planted in late summer. The routine care of lilies is similar to that of most bulbs (see pp.236–8). Stake the plants well so that their flowering stems do not snap.

Propagation

Lilies may be propagated easily by stem bulbils, scaling, or seed. Use simple division for *L. pardalinum* and Div.IV hybrids. Always propagate from healthy stock.

Bulbils and bulblets

Species such as *L. lancifolium* (syn. *L. tigrinum*), *L. bulbiferum*, and their hybrids produce stem bulbils in the leaf axils and bulblets at the base of the old flowering stem. Remove these and pot them up to grow on. The following fall, either plant out the whole pan of young bulbs or pot them up individually.

Seed, scaling, and division

Sowing seed produces vigorous, virus-free bulbs (see "Growing lilies from seed," p.241), but is slow; Div.V lilies are easy to propagate in this way. For details of division and scaling, see pp.239 and 242.

Pests and diseases

Lilies are particularly vulnerable to several viruses (p.642) transmitted by aphids. Visible symptoms are mottled or twisted leaves. *L. lancifolium* and some of its hybrids are carriers but show no symptoms; keep them away from other lilies to minimize infection. Gray mold/*Botrytis* (p.646) may cause problems in damp, windless conditions. Red lily beetles destroy leaves and flowers.

A SELECTION OF LILIES

L. martagon (turkscap flowers; good in shady areas)

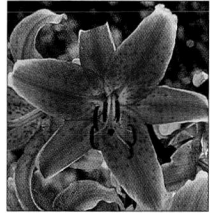
L. Oriental cultivar (highly scented; good in light shade)

L. 'Bright Star' (an Aurelian hybrid; tolerates alkaline soil)

L. 'Connecticut King' (one of many Div. 1, or Asiatic, cultivars)

L. regale (fragrant trumpets; easy to grow)

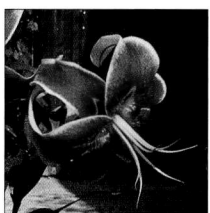
L. 'Scheherazade' (hybrid from cross of Aurelian x Oriental)

PROPAGATING FROM STEM BULBILS

1 Throughout summer, as soon as the bulbils loosen and are ripe, gather them from the leaf axils of the lily stems by carefully picking them off.

2 Insert the bulbils in pans of moist soil-based potting mix, pressing them gently into the surface. Cover with grit, then label (see inset). Place in a cold frame until young bulbs develop.

RAISING LILIES FROM BULBLETS

1 After flowering, lift the bulb and dead stem, pick off the bulblets, and replant the main bulb. Alternatively, leave the bulb in the ground, cutting the stem above it to remove the bulblets.

2 Plant the bulblets at twice their depth in pots of soil-based potting mix, then place in a protected spot until spring. You may also plant them in a line in the garden to grow on.

CHAPTER

9

THE ROCK GARDEN

SOME OF THE loveliest garden plants come from mountain ranges around the world, where they are adapted to survive in a surprising diversity of specialized habitats. These range from rock face niches and sparse alpine pastures to the rich meadows of lower altitudes. With alpines and rock garden plants, you can enjoy a wealth of beautiful species that retain the charm of wildflowers unembellished by hybridizers.

Because some alpine and rock plants are adapted to specific environments, which may be difficult to reproduce in a garden, they often present a challenge to even the most experienced gardeners. Happily, many more are amenable and undemanding plants that will grow readily in a suitably prepared site in the open garden. They will richly reward a little extra time and attention paid to their requirements.

Designing a rock garden

ALPINES are plants that grow at high altitudes, above the tree line, although the term is often loosely used to include a vast range of low-growing rock garden plants, including many bulbs, that may be grown at relatively low altitudes. Their diminutive form and graceful habit make them well suited for grouping together in fascinating, brilliantly colored collections.

True alpines
Alpines may be deciduous or evergreen woody plants, or they may be herbaceous, or grow from bulbs, corms, or tubers – there are very few annual alpines. They are characteristically hardy, adapted to survive in extremes of climate, and compact, with few over 6in (15cm) tall. In their native mountain habitat, the dwarf or creeping habit of alpines reduces their wind resistance and helps them withstand the heavy weight of snow in winter.

In alpine regions, plants experience brilliant sunshine and fresh, constantly moving air during the growing season. Their cushion- or mat-forming habit and their small, fleshy, hairy, or leathery leaves protect them from water loss in high winds and hot sun. Edelweiss (*Leontopodium alpinum*), for example, has its entire surface covered in woolly hairs that help to conserve moisture, while the leaves of hen and chickens (*Sempervivum*) have fleshy, water-retaining tissue.

Although most alpines are adapted to extremes of temperature, few withstand constant wetness at the roots in winter or warm, humid, summer conditions. In their native habitats, they often grow in thin, poor soil that lacks nutrients and has a low organic content but allows rapid drainage. Most develop extensive, spreading root systems to seek out nutrients and moisture.

Rock garden plants
Rock plants are simply those slow-growing plants of relatively small stature that are suitable in scale for growing in rock gardens. They include dwarf trees and shrubs, which are particularly useful for framework, or background, plantings, and many other plants that do not necessarily come from alpine regions. Some, such as *Armeria maritima*, originate in coastal habitats, while many miniature bulbs are native to sunny, Mediterranean hillsides. In common with true alpines, they share the need for a freely draining soil and are therefore suitable for planting among alpines.

Since many true alpines bloom in the spring and early summer, rock garden plants are especially valuable if they are late blooming, since they may be used to extend the season of interest.

A WELL-FURNISHED ROCK GARDEN
This gently sloping rock garden is studded with a diverse range of alpine plants, including herbaceous plants, shrubs, and conifers. Seen here in late spring, it will continue to provide color and interest well into fall.

Alpines and rock plants in the garden

The usually restricted size of alpines and rock garden plants fits particularly well into the confines of the small, modern garden. Few other types of plant are so characteristically neat and compact, allowing a substantial collection of species and hybrids to be grown in a relatively small space.

Garden-tolerant plants

Many alpine species, and their more showy cultivars, are undemanding in their cultural requirements and may be grown easily in the open garden. They present a wealth of habit and form, ranging from tiny, cushion-forming plants to spreading mound- and mat-formers. Some of the easier alpines bloom well into summer and almost invariably produce a profusion of flowers. The low-growing cultivars of *Aubrieta*, phlox, and *Veronica* form dense mats of clear, bright color when in bloom and can be used to edge beds; their informal, spreading habit gently softens straight lines.

Specialized alpines

Other alpine genera, such as some *Androsace* and the tight cushion-forming saxifrages, have special

PLANTING IN THE OPEN GARDEN
Daphne x burkwoodii 'Somerset' has a profusion of pale pink flowers that spill over the edge of a mixed border and drift into the plants on either side.

requirements, in particular a need for extremely freely draining soil and protection from excessive winter moisture. Most also require plenty of sun, but their roots need to be cool. Lower-altitude, woodland species often prefer dappled shade and may need moist, acidic soil.

The rich and varied colors and diverse forms of many specialist plants may still be enjoyed in the garden, however, as long as well-drained conditions and a suitable exposure

are provided. The best way to fulfill these requirements is to raise the plants in some way from the underlying garden soil. Plant them in specially constructed or carefully controlled environments and use prepared, gritty, freely draining soil or soil mixes.

Some alpine plants need a cool root run and shelter. Rock gardens and pockets within stone or brick walls are an ideal way to grow such plants and to display them to their

best advantage in natural-looking surroundings. In more formal garden settings or where space is limited, raised beds or troughs and sinks are attractive alternatives, especially when they are constructed from materials that complement any existing hard landscape features. Free-standing troughs and sinks also allow color to be introduced at a variety of heights and on hard surfaces such as patios and paths.

The rock garden

A sunny south- or southwest-facing slope makes an ideal site for the stony outcrops of a rock garden. Well-constructed rock gardens emu-late natural rock formations and make strikingly beautiful features. They replicate, as nearly as possible, the natural habitat of alpine plants, re-creating the conditions in which they thrive: the soil beneath the rocks provides the cool, moist, but freely draining root run that they particularly enjoy.

Planning a rock garden

For the greatest visual impact, a rock garden should be constructed on as generous a scale as the site allows. Where possible, choose a naturally sloping, open site that will provide good drainage. A series of rocky outcrops with gullies running in between is highly attractive, especially if streams and pools are also included in the design.

A sunny exposure will meet the needs of most rock plants, although those that require shade may be grown in cooler, shady pockets on the north side of large rocks. Thoughtful placing of the rocks during construction (see p.257) will provide a wide range of planting areas and niches to meet the needs of many alpine plants.

Choosing plants

Several alpine species, such as *Gentiana verna* with its flowers of intense blue in spring, do best in deep pockets of well-drained, gritty soil, while the mat-forming *Persicaria affinis* 'Donald Lowndes', for example, thrives in broader terraces between rock strata. Both *Lewisia* Cotyledon Hybrids and *Saxifraga* 'Tumbling Waters', which has cascades of white flowers over rosettes of alkaline-encrusted foliage, are most at home in the narrow crevices between vertical stone faces.

Plan the planting design to include as much seasonal variation as possible. Alpine bulbs such as *Crocus laevigatus* 'Fontenayi' bring

A BLAZE OF SUMMER COLOR
The brilliant red flowers of Sedum spurium *and* Helianthemum *cascading down the rocky outcrop make a pleasing contrast with the gray-green stems and leaves of the* Dianthus *and* Hebe pinguifolia *'Pagei' just behind them. The fresh green foliage of the surrounding plants provides a bright but cool counterpoint.*

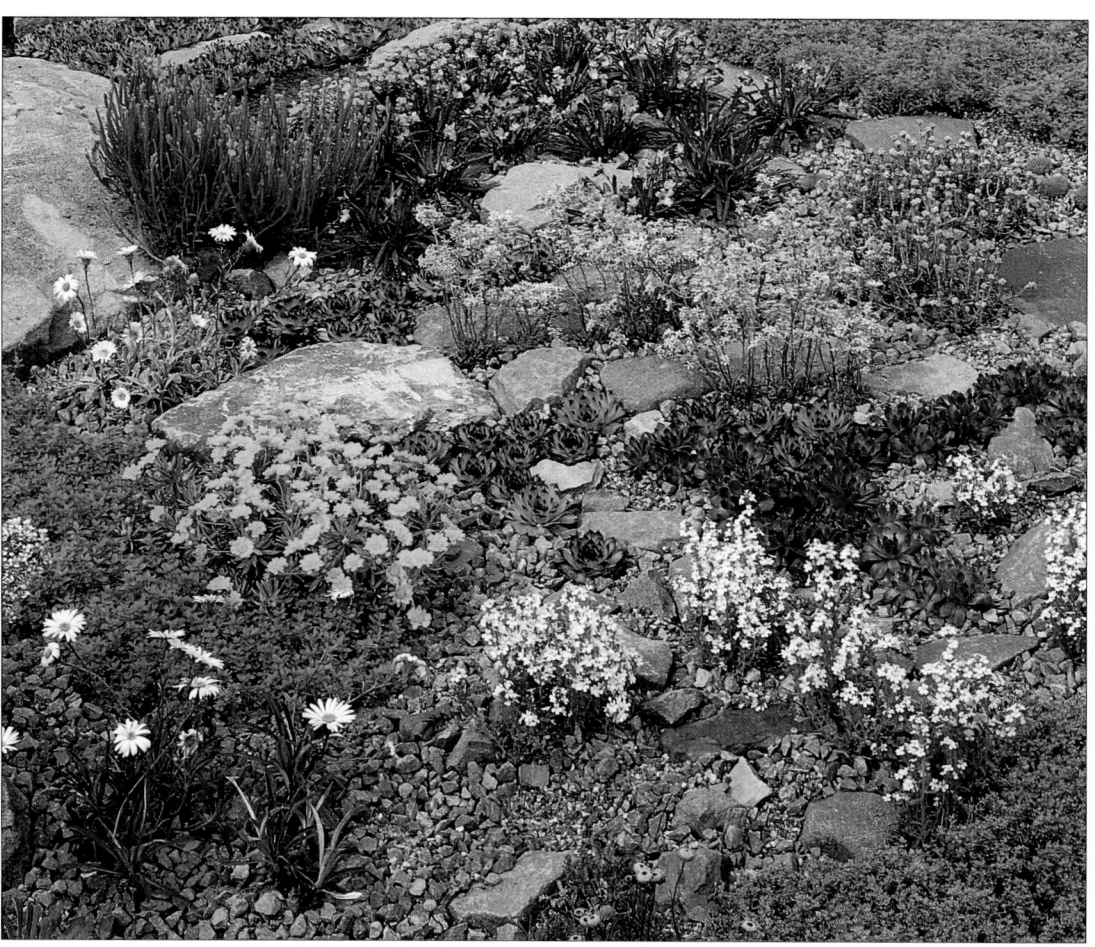

SCREE ROCK GARDEN
Many rock plants retain the charm of wildflowers, but selected forms and hybrids often display greater numbers of attractive, sometimes larger flowers in a range of clear colors. Some need a specialized environment, such as this scree bed, but many more are amenable plants that grow in any well-prepared site.

the garden to life in late winter or early spring, and *Cyclamen hederifolium* and *Sternbergia lutea* add interest in fall. For year-round color, include evergreens, such as the dwarf *Chamaecyparis obtusa* 'Nana Pyramidalis' and *Juniperus communis* 'Compressa', and dwarf shrubs such as *Genista lydia*.

Add texture and structure to the planting by using species with unusual leaves or stems and variation in height and form. Contrasting leaf textures can be particularly striking: bold, fleshy, rosette-forming plants may be used to offset the delicate, feathery leaves and flowers of *Pulsatilla* species, for instance. A combination of spreading, cushion-forming, and trailing alpines with dwarf shrubs or trees, provides great visual interest. The sword-shaped silver leaves of *Celmisia coriacea* contrast well with mat-forming plants such as *Polygala calcarea* 'Bulley's Variety', with deep blue flowers in late spring and early summer, and *Campanula cochleariifolia*, with clusters of pale blue or white bells in summer.

Scree formations

In mountainous areas, the natural weathering of rock outcrops produces variously sized masses of small, broken rocks and stones at the base of the slopes. These loose, stony formations, known as screes, are home to many plants that need plenty of moisture at their roots (water flows freely under a scree during a portion of the growing season, especially as snow melts in spring), but at the same time grow best through an apparently dry 6in (15cm) surface layer of stones. Scree dwellers are among the most beautiful and jewel-like of alpine plants and are well worth the extra attention needed to grow them well.

The scree bed

The scree bed attempts to re-create the highly specialized habitat of natural scree dwellers. A scree is a deep, preferably gently sloping bed of loose rock fragments of varying size, into which is added a suitable soil mix (see p.257). Screes may also be constructed on flat sites, raised from

ground level to assist drainage, becoming, in effect, a specialized form of raised bed (see opposite).

Scree dwellers usually form low mats or cushions of dense foliage; many bear their small, brilliantly colored blooms in such profusion that the flowers almost completely obscure the leaves. The neutral background of small stones offers an ideal foil for the rich textures and colors of this type of planting.

Specialized plants that are difficult to grow in the open garden, for example *Vitaliana primuliflora*, *Anchusa caespitosa*, and *Myosotis alpestris*, thrive in screes. Other rock garden plants that are easier to grow also appreciate the unique conditions created in a scree bed. Some species, such as *Achillea clavennae* and *Artemisia glacialis*, are grown primarily for their silver foliage, which provides a cool contrast for stronger colors. A number of species, including *Androsace carnea* subsp. *laggeri*, which bears a mass of pink blooms in early summer, naturally self-seed. The tiny, blue, bell-shaped flowers of *Campanula cochleariifolia* also

spring up around the garden but may become a nuisance if the plants compete with less robust species.

Integrating the scree bed

Where space is available, one or more scree beds may be integrated with a rock garden to form a bold, unified design and provide a broad range of habitats. A central, visually anchoring formation of large rocks (or boulders) skirted by scree beds is particularly effective.

Alternatively, pockets of scree mixture can be included in a rock garden to accommodate specialized scree dwellers that need particularly good drainage around their crowns. *Dianthus haematocalyx*, for example, is a tightly tufted pink whose deep rose petals have an unusual buff underside; it benefits from a collar of loose, dry stones.

The visual impact of a scree bed is enhanced by incorporating just a few carefully positioned, larger rocks. Plants can then be allowed to skirt their base or to grow over them to soften their outlines.

Peat beds

Alpine plants that require an acidic soil or a woodland environment are not always easily accommodated in a rock garden. Acidic-soil-loving plants such as *Arctostaphylos*, *Cassiope*, gentians, and most *Vaccinium* species will thrive only in soil with a low pH; woodland plants do best in moist, shady conditions and leafy, organic soil. Specially constructed peat beds are an excellent way of providing a moist, acidic growing medium and, when sited in dappled shade, closely imitate woodland conditions, extending the range of species that may be grown.

Site and materials

Peat beds may be constructed either as individual garden features or as extensions to a rock garden. The shady, north-facing side of a rock garden provides ideal conditions. Do not place a peat bed beneath trees, since water dripping from the leaves after rain may rot the plants. For best results, the site should be in sun for part of the day.

Traditionally, the acidic medium of the peat bed is based on sphagnum moss, which has a naturally low pH, good aeration, and excellent water retention. Depending on the source of the moss, the pH may vary considerably; it may even be slightly alkaline. Before purchasing large quantities, determine the pH of a single bale to be sure it is acidic enough.

Raised beds

In small gardens, raised beds make highly economical use of limited space. In larger gardens, narrow raised beds can make a useful and attractive boundary feature. The formal appearance of raised beds often blends in well with the design and layout of many modern gardens. In areas where appropriate types of rock is not easily available or is prohibitively expensive, a raised bed provides a satisfactory substitute for a conventional rock garden situated in the open garden.

Since drainage in raised beds is entirely independent of the underlying soil, these structures are especially useful in gardens with poorly drained soils (such as wet, heavy clay) that are otherwise unsuitable for the cultivation of alpines. In addition, the dimensions of a raised bed may be planned so that a suitable bed will accommodate a cold frame sash (or multiple sashes) put over the bed in winter to allow cultivation of choice species that require protection from too much winter moisture, without restricting airflow around the plants.

Various materials may be used for the construction of a suitable raised bed, including traditional bricks or drystone wall construction, pressure-treated lumber, and well-weathered railroad ties. For further information, see STRUCTURES AND SURFACES, "Raised beds," p.593.

Planting in raised beds

Large raised beds can be divided into separate areas or compartments, and different soil mixes used in each to suit the specific requirements of different plant groups. Rocks can be introduced to the surface of the soil mix and bedded in to provide textural contrast as well as vertical niches and crevices for those plants that demand them.

Rectangular raised beds present several exposures, so that plants with different requirements may be planted in niches on their sunny or shady side, if required. In addition to growing plants in the bed itself, the walls of the bed may be designed to incorporate planting niches, in the same way as walls that are used for trailing species.

Choose plants that will flower in succession as the seasons progress. The dense, evergreen rosettes of *Haberlea rhodopensis* send up sprays of funnel-shaped flowers in spring; they may be succeeded in summer by *Aquilegia flabellata* 'Nana', a clump-forming alpine that produces bell-shaped, soft blue flowers, each with fluted petals and a short spur. Both of these plants thrive in semishade and are small enough to be planted in a raised bed without overcrowding it.

For a sunnier exposure, choose compact species of *Dianthus*, such as *D. alpinus* and *D.* 'Bombadier', with *Erinus alpinus* 'Dr. Hähnle' trailing from the retaining wall.

A LOW RAISED BED
Here, a raised alpine bed flanks one side of a narrow stone path. The plants draw the eye along the path and entice the visitor to the open lawn beyond.

Walls

Garden walls may be modified, if required, to provide appropriate sites for alpines and rock garden plants. The walls of raised beds and those used to retain banks of soil on a terraced slope can be modified in the same way. If possible, however, leave spaces, crevices, or cracks between the stones or brickwork during the construction of such walls so that these may be planted up when building is complete without needing to deconstruct part of the structure.

Choosing plants

The most suitable plants to choose are cushion- or mat-forming plants such as *Acantholimon glumaceum*, which forms evergreen cushions that are clothed in pink flowers during summer, or *Dianthus deltoides* and other alpine pinks. Plants that are prone to rotting at the collar, such as *Lewisia* and *Ramonda* species, are well suited to being grown in walls, since the roots will benefit from the cool conditions within the wall as well as from the extra drainage provided by the crevices. The trailing, semievergreen *Asarina procumbens*, with its creamy white, snapdragon-like flowers borne over a very long season, and the shrubby *Penstemon newberryi* f. *humilior*, bearing a profusion of flowers on gently arching branches, are also ideal for walls.

Drystone walls

These provide ample room for the root systems of many rock garden plants to penetrate and also allow sharp drainage. Free-standing, single or double drystone walls may be used to form boundaries or dividers in the garden and, with careful choice of suitable plants, make extremely attractive features.

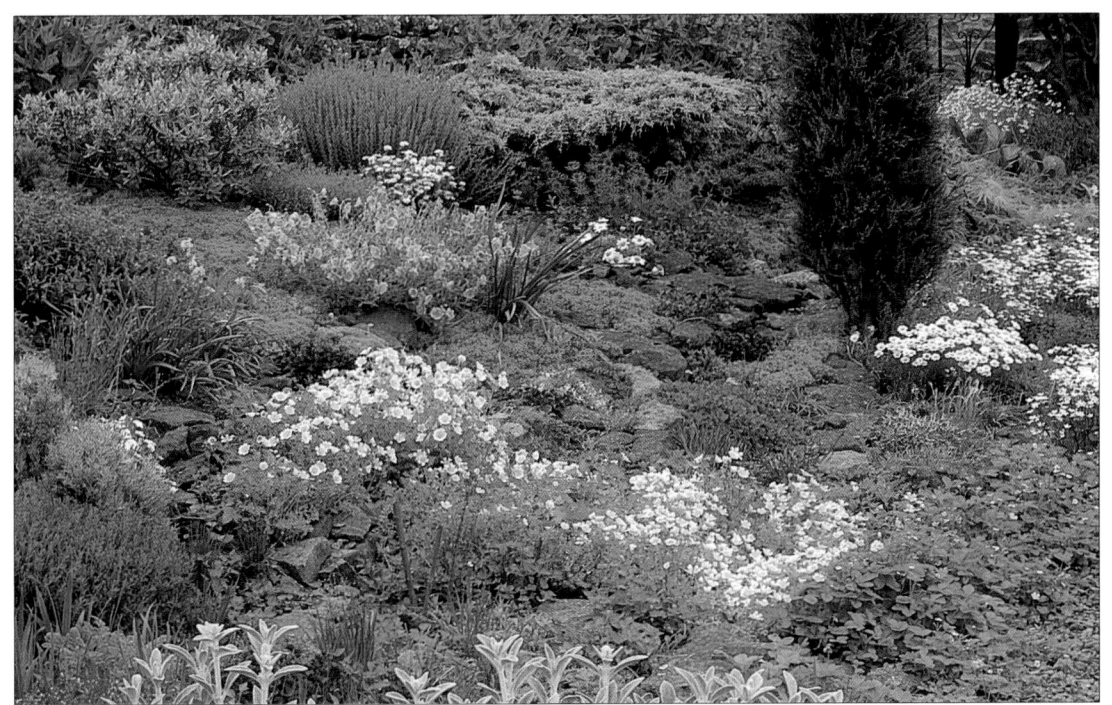

A TAPESTRY OF COLOR
A vivid display in which the rich colors and varied forms of the alpines blend with the evergreen shrubs and dwarf conifers, which form the framework of this attractive rock garden.

The well-drained tops of drystone walls provide an ideal home for mat-forming plants such as *Gypsophila repens* or *Saponaria ocymoides*, both of which cascade attractively over the edge of the wall. The neat, spreading rosettes of alkaline-encrusted saxifrages and hen and chickens (*Sempervivum*) can be dotted at intervals across the surface. Using both vertical faces of a wall will allow both sun- and shade-loving plants to be grown.

Troughs and sinks

Old stone sinks and troughs once used for feeding and watering animals make handsome containers for rock plants; unfortunately, they are both scarce and expensive. However, troughs made of reconstituted stone or hypertufa, and glazed sinks coated with this material (see p.260) are ideal, inexpensive alternatives. Troughs and sinks may be used as features in patios and courtyards, or on terraces and graveled areas in larger gardens.

Planting in troughs
By carefully selecting dwarf and slow-growing species you can create a miniature rock garden in a trough. The smallest alpine plants are often the most intricate and beautiful; their beauty can be appreciated much more easily when grown in a container placed at or near eye level. Use *Antennaria dioica* 'Minima' and other compact alpines and rock plants for trough planting.

Introduce a few small conifers, such as *Chamaecyparis obtusa* 'Nana Pyramidalis' or *Juniperus communis* 'Compressa', and dwarf trees such as *Ulmus parvifolia* 'Geisha' as framework plants. For the middle and foreground of the trough, showy flowering plants such as *Campanula zoysii*, *Dianthus alpinus*, or *Bolax gummifera* may be used. Miniature shrubs may be added to provide contrasting form and color throughout the year.

Growing plants in other containers

Where containers are selected to complement other hard landscape features of the garden, such as walls and paths, they bring a cohesive element to the overall design of the garden. Containers provide an opportunity to grow alpines in a small garden, and they may also be used to flank pathways or steps.

AN ALPINE TROUGH COLLECTION
A collection of troughs makes an appealing feature. Large troughs accommodate dwarf trees and shrubs as well as smaller alpine plants.

Choosing plants
Containers are especially suitable for cultivating miniature species, and they allow plants such as the tiny *Primula scotica*, with its golden-eyed purple flowers, to be appreciated and grown in a situation where they will not be swamped by larger and more vigorous neighbors. Grouping several containers together provides a good opportunity to build up collections devoted to plants of one genus that flourish under similar environmental conditions, and a collection of such containers can become an attractive landscape feature in its own right if sensitively arranged and placed within the context of the garden as a whole.

A long season of interest can be achieved by underplanting low-growing, mat-forming plants such as *Raoulia australis* and *Globularia cordifolia* with late-winter flowering dwarf bulbs, for example *Narcissus watieri* or *Iris reticulata* and its many cultivars.

Choosing a container
The range of decorative containers suitable for alpines and rock garden plants is enormous. Make sure that the container can provide the appropriate level of drainage required for the plants to thrive. If a suitable soil mix is used and the plants are watered according to their needs and otherwise well maintained in general, almost any container may be used to good effect.

Large flower pots and terracotta tubs are suitable for small collections of the tiniest alpines, and particularly for those that trail over the edges of the pot, such as *Silene schafta*. Small containers are ideal for compact, slow-growing alpines such as *Androsace chamaejasme* and *Sempervivum arachnoideum*, which will provide a display over several years before they start to outgrow their situation.

Where winters are cold, move unglazed terracotta pots indoors, (especially strawberry jars and pots with rolled rims or more elaborate ornamentation) to stop them from flaking and disintegrating.

The alpine house

In the wild, many alpines spend their very long winter dormancy insulated by a deep snow blanket that shields them from cold drying winds, brilliant sun, the heaving and settling of the soil from ice forming and melting in the soil, and severe cold. Temperatures under the snow normally hover at, or just below, the freezing point. In gardens at lower altitudes, where conditions are very different, the more exacting alpines need protection from fluctuating temperatures and frost in spring and fall, and from potentially fatal high temperatures and humidity in summer. They also benefit from the protection given from extreme weather (such as wind and hail) and from the depredations of insects and larger animals.

A simple, open cloche may be sufficient protection for some plants. However, a specially designed greenhouse, or alpine house, (see GREENHOUSES AND FRAMES, "Alpine house," p.563) greatly extends the range that may be grown and allows the enthusiastic gardener to grow some of the most challenging plants.

Using an alpine house
An alpine house will accommodate a huge range of the choicest alpines in carefully controlled conditions. The season of interest in the alpine house can be maintained throughout the early winter months, when color in the open garden is scarce. Interest increases rapidly in early spring, when the majority of true alpines flower. Where dwarf shrubs, bulbs, conifers, and ferns are also included in the collection, there will be something to attract attention throughout the year.

Alpine houses are generally used for plants unsuited to growing in the open. But many less demanding alpines, and even robust plants that are strong enough to withstand the vagaries of weather, may be grown to perfection in an alpine house (see also ALPINE HOUSES AND FRAMES, pp.271–3).

AN UNUSUAL CONTAINER
Many different types of container can be used for rock plants and alpine species. Here, part of a hollowed-out tree trunk has been planted with Sedum spathulifolium 'Cape Blanco', *valued for its small clusters of tiny yellow flowers above the rosettes of silvery green leaves.*

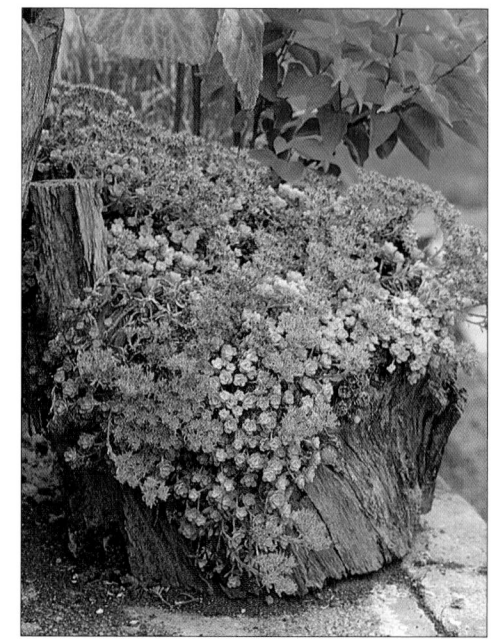

Planter's guide to rock plants

EXPOSED SITES

Rock plants that tolerate exposed or windy sites

Antennaria dioica
Campanula portenschlagiana
Carlina acaulis
Chiastophyllum oppositifolium
Crepis incana
Dryas octopetala
Erigeron karvinskianus
Eryngium ▲
Euphorbia myrsinites
Hebe ▲
Helianthemum
Limonium bellidifolium
Pterocephalus perennis
Sedum ▲
Sempervivum
Silene vulgaris subsp. maritima
Veronica spicata

AIR POLLUTION

Rock plants that tolerate polluted air

Aubrieta
Aurinia saxatilis
Campanula garganica,
    C. poscharskyana
Erinus alpinus
Euphorbia ▲
Sedum ▲
Sempervivum

DRY SHADE

Rock plants that tolerate dry shade

Ajuga pyramidalis, A. reptans
Dianthus carthusianorum,
    D. deltoides
Diascia cordata, D. 'Ruby Field'
Erodium guttatum
Genista sagittalis
Gypsophila dubia, G. repens
Helleborus
Lamium maculatum
Saponaria ocymoides
Waldsteinia ternata

Waldsteinia
ternata

MOIST SHADE

Rock plants that do best in moist shade

Adonis amurensis
Cassiope
Cyclamen hederifolium,
    C. purpurascens
Daphne blagayana
Galax aphylla

Hepatica nobilis,
    H. transsilvanica
Hylomecon japonicum
Iris cristata
Meconopsis cambrica
Primula (many spp.
    and cvs)
Sanguinaria canadensis
Shortia uniflora
Stylophorum diphyllum
Trillium

SCREE GARDENS

Acantholimon glumaceum
Aethionema pulchellum,
    A. 'Warley Rose'
Alyssum montanum

Androsace
lanuginosa

Androsace lanuginosa,
    A. sarmentosa,
    A. sempervivoides
Dianthus alpinus, D. anatolicus,
    D. echinacea
Erinus alpinus
Gypsophila aretioides
Hutchinsia alpina
Linaria alpina
Papaver burseri,
    P. miyabeanum,
    P. rhaeticum
Sempervivum
Silene acaulis
Viola cornuta 'Minor', V. jooi

CREVICES AND PAVING

Aubrieta deltoidea (many cvs)
Aurinia saxatilis
Campanula cochleariifolia,
    C. portenschlagiana
Erinus alpinus
Erodium chamaedryoides
Geranium sanguineum var. striatum
Globularia cordifolia
Mentha requienii
Onosma albo-roseum, O. echioides
Pratia pedunculata
Scabiosa graminifolia
Thymus

WALL CREVICES

Antirrhinum glutinosum, A. molle
Aurinia saxatilis 'Citrina'
Campanula portenschlagiana
Erinus alpinus
Globularia cordifolia

Haberlea rhodopensis (shade)
Lewisia, Cotyledon Hybrids,
    L. tweedyi
Onosma taurica
Polemonium pulcherrimum
Ramonda myconi (shade)
Saxifraga callosa, S. cochlearis,
    S. longifolia, S. paniculata
Silene vulgaris subsp. maritima
    'Flore Pleno'

PLANTING IN TROUGHS

Anchusa caespitosa
Androsace (small spp. and cvs)
Antennaria dioica 'Minima'
Arenaria purpurascens
Asperula suberosa
Dianthus alpinus, D. freynii,
    D. glacialis
Dryas octopetala 'Minor'
Edraianthus pumilio
Gentiana saxosa, G. verna
    var. angulosa
Helianthemum oelandicum
Linum suffruticosum subsp.
    salsoloides 'Nanum'
Myosotis rupicola
Omphalodes luciliae
Oxalis enneaphylla
Paraquilegia anemonoides
Petrophytum hendersonii
Phlox subulata
Primula farinosa,
    P. marginata

Saxifraga
sancta

Saxifraga (many
    spp. and cvs)
Sedum cauticola
Soldanella alpina, S. montana
Thymus serpyllum 'Minus'
Vitaliana primuliflora

PLANTING IN TUFA

Androsace (small spp. and cvs)
Campanula piperi, C. zoysii
Draba mollissima, D. polytricha
Edraianthus pumilio
Paraquilegia anemonoides
Physoplexis comosa
Potentilla nitida
Saxifraga (many types,
    especially the Kabschias)
Viola cazorlensis, V. delphinantha

RAISED BEDS

Aethionema 'Warley Rose'
Androsace
Antirrhinum molle, A. sempervirens
Aquilegia discolor, A. flabellata

Armeria juniperifolia
Bolax gummifera
Callianthemum anemonoides
Campanula raineri, C. zoysii
Daphne arbuscula, D. cneorum,
    D. petraea 'Grandiflora'
Dianthus
Draba bryoides, D. polytricha
Edraianthus dinaricus,
    E. graminifolius
Erinacea anthyllis
Gentiana acaulis,
    G. verna var. angulosa
Globularia meridionalis, G. repens
Haberlea rhodopensis
Leontopodium alpinum, L. nivale
Lewisia (some spp. and hybrids)
Origanum (some spp. and hybrids)
Oxalis adenophylla,
    O. enneaphylla, O. 'Ione Hecker'
Papaver burseri, P. miyabeanum
Paraquilegia anemonoides
Primula auricula, P. marginata
Ramonda myconi
Saxifraga cotyledon, S. longifolia,
    S. paniculata,
    S. 'Tumbling Waters'
Sempervivum
Silene acaulis
Verbascum 'Letitia'

DWARF SHRUBS

Berberis x stenophylla 'Corallina
    Compacta'
Betula nana
Chamaecyparis obtusa 'Intermedia'
Cryptomeria japonica
    'Vilmoriniana'
Daphne cneorum, D. retusa,
    D. sericea
Dorycnium hirsutum
Erinacea anthyllis
Euryops acraeus
Genista delphinensis
Hebe buchananii 'Minor'
Helichrysum coralloides

Helichrysum
coralloides

Ilex crenata 'Mariesii'
Juniperus communis
    'Compressa'
Picea abies 'Clanbrassiliana',
    P. a. 'Gregoryana', P. a. 'Nidiformis',
    P. glauca var. albertiana 'Conica'
Potentilla 'Nana Argentea'
Salix x boydii
Sorbus reducta
Thymus membranaceus

KEY
▲ Rock garden species only

Construction, soil preparation, and planting

VARIOUS methods may be used to grow alpine plants in gardens. Planting them in a rock garden is perhaps the best-known method, although this can take up a great deal of space. For a smaller display, screes, raised and peat beds, and the crevices of walls can make very attractive features. Where space is more limited, troughs, sinks, and other containers can also be used for a fine alpine display.

ROCK PLANTS THAT REQUIRE ACIDIC SOIL

Arctostaphylos alpina
Cassiope
Corydalis cashmeriana,
   C. flexuosa
Cyananthus
Epigaea gaultherioides,
   E. repens
Galax urceolata
Gentiana sino-ornata
Glaucidium palmatum
Haberlea rhodopensis
Kalmia angustifolia,
   K. polifolia 'Microphylla'
Leiophyllum buxifolium
Leucopogon fraseri
Leucothoë keiskei
Linnaea borealis
Lithodora diffusa
Menziesia ciliicalyx
Mitchella repens
Ourisia caespitosa,
   O. coccinea, O. 'Loch Ewe'
Paris polyphylla
Pernettya

*Phyllodoce
caerulea*

Phyllodoce caerulea
   P. glanduliflora,
   P. nipponica
Pieris nana
Polygala chamaebuxus,
   P. vayredae
Primula boothii,
   P. edgeworthii,
   P. gracilipes,
   P. sonchifolia
Pyrola rotundifolia
Rhododendron
   (dwarf spp. and cvs)
Shortia soldanelloides
Soldanella villosa
Tanakaea radicans
Vaccinium delavayi,
   V. myrtillus,
   V. uliginosum

Buying plants

The rock garden should be regarded as a feature that, with careful choice of plants, will provide much interest throughout the year.

Before buying any plants, refer to standard texts to find out the likely plant choices that are suitable for a particular type of locality in terms of climate, soil, and general situation. Visit established rock gardens in parks and botanic gardens, as well as specialty nurseries, to assess the relative merits of various plants for your own requirements. The shape, form, and color of foliage, fruits, stems, and the overall growth habit are often as important as flowers.

Where to buy plants

Plants are available from a wide range of sources, including garden centers and specialty nurseries. Nonspecialty outlets often sell a limited range of colorful cultivars and easily grown species; these may form large, spreading clumps that quickly overwhelm more delicate plants in the rock garden.

The experienced nurseryman is able to advise on the most suitable choice of plants for a particular situation, and often has display beds of mature plants. These give a good indication of the ultimate size, spread, and habit of different plants, and are invaluable at the planning stage. Local rock garden societies can also advise on suitable plants, sources, and general information.

A much wider selection of plants will be offered by the specialty grower, who is also able to provide detailed advice on cultivation – this is particularly useful for the beginner. Demand for rare or unfamiliar plants sometimes means that general suppliers may carry plants that are best left to the specialist, since they are often unsuitable for the average rock garden. Such plants may be attractive but are often expensive and may be difficult to cultivate. They offer a rewarding challenge, but purchase them only after obtaining advice on growing them.

Selecting alpine plants

Choose plants that have healthy, compact foliage, and no sign of pests and diseases or water deprivation. Do not buy plants with yellowing or weak growth, since this indicates that they have been kept in low light. Labels should bear the name of the plant as well as details of flowering times and brief cultivation require-

HOW TO SELECT ALPINE PLANTS

GOOD EXAMPLE

SAXIFRAGA

Healthy-looking, compact growth

Weed-free soil mix

POOR EXAMPLE

Unbalanced, weak growth

Weeds in soil mix

Roots curled around inside of pot

ments. Plants should not be potbound, and the roots should be barely visible, if at all, through the hole in the base of the pot. Do not purchase any plants that have rooted into the material on the surface of the display area, since these are almost certain to be potbound.

The top-growth of a plant may remain healthy for some time after the root system has been damaged or has actually died, so check that the plant has a healthy root system by sliding it out of its pot and inspecting the root ball carefully.

Large specimens are sometimes available, but unless they are grown on correctly, with careful attention to watering, they may take much longer to become established than smaller, vigorous ones.

Select plants that are as weed-free as possible. Before planting, gently scrape off the grit or surface soil mix so that any weed seeds are removed. Introducing weeds such as pearlwort (*Sagina procumbens*) and several

kinds of oxalis cause problems because, once established, they are difficult to eradicate.

A number of plants that are sold for growing in the rock garden, such as some of the ornamental onions (*Allium*), are overly prolific seeders. Choose carefully to avoid introducing such problem plants.

Siting a rock garden or scree bed

Good siting is critical for a rock garden or scree bed because alpine plants require good light and well-drained conditions to thrive. The rock garden or scree should also blend in with the rest of the garden. Before starting construction, draw a rough plan on paper showing the rock garden or scree bed in relation to other garden features. A scree may be integrated into a rock garden or built as a separate feature.

SITING A ROCK GARDEN

Limit of afternoon shade from near-by plants

Sloping ground

Limit of morning shade from hedge

Build a rock garden on sloping ground, if possible, to provide excellent drainage. Choose an open site that receives full sun, away from the roots and overhanging branches of trees and large shrubs.

Choosing the site

Choose an open, sunny site away from the shade of overhanging trees. Trees drip water onto the plants beneath and shed their leaves in fall, which could smother plants or create a damp atmosphere leading to rot. Their roots may also compete with the plants for moisture and nutrients. Do not site a rock garden or scree in a frost pocket or on a site exposed to cold, drying winds.

A sloping site is ideal for a rock garden: it will have good drainage, and the artificial outcrops of rock can be made to look more natural, providing different pockets and exposures for a variety of plants. Level sites present more problems than sloping ones; scree beds (see p.250) or raised beds (see p.251) are usually better for such sites.

It is best to preserve a feeling of space by siting the rock garden or scree so that a distant view is visible beyond it. In small, enclosed gardens, boundary fences or walls that rise behind the rock garden can be concealed with suitable climbers. Plan any water features, such as a pond or stream, into the design at an early stage. In large rock gardens, paths or stepping-stones are essential to provide access and to facilitate garden maintenance.

Making a natural-looking feature

A rock garden or scree is best sited where it will blend into an informally planted area of the garden, such as on a slope, by a terrace, or as a natural-looking outcrop from an area of shrubs. If the rock garden or scree is to be next to a lawn, position it so that it does not interfere with cutting and edging the lawn. It is unlikely to

Natural strata

Sedimentary rock, such as limestone, occurs naturally in distinct layers, or stratum lines, that are clearly visible to the eye. Rocks of this type can easily be split along the stratum lines for use in rock gardens.

Sedimentary rocks that occur in nature always have stratum lines following the same direction; it is important to place the stones in a rock garden to simulate their natural orientation; otherwise, they will look too obviously artificial.

NATURAL STRATUM LINES

look natural if placed next to such features as herbaceous borders, bedding displays, or any other formally planted areas such as the vegetable or fruit garden. If the main garden is rather formal, it may be better to grow alpines in a rectangular raised bed (see p.263) rather than trying to integrate the informality of a rock garden into the otherwise formal design.

Choosing stone

Use locally available stone for rock garden construction, wherever possible, to harmonize with the local landscape and to reduce transportation costs. However, this may not be possible in regions where supplies of natural rock are limited or where the local stone is unsuitable.

Do not use soft, quick-weathering rock, such as shale, or hard, featureless, igneous rocks without strata, such as granite and basalt. Hard stone with no clear strata may be

inexpensive, but it is difficult to use, takes several years to acquire a weathered appearance, and seldom looks natural. Other materials, such as slate, are also used, but they are sometimes difficult to blend in.

Buying stone

If possible, visit local quarries to inspect the rock and choose suitable pieces, making sure that the rocks are not too large to handle after being delivered. Choose stone in a range of different sizes, since this makes it easier to construct a natural-looking outcrop. Garden centers may offer a range of stone, although there is sometimes a limited choice of size and shape.

Sandstone

The most suitable rocks are the various sandstones, in which the natural strata or layers are clearly visible. One great advantage of using rocks with stratum lines is that they may be split easily, making it relatively easy to create planting pockets and natural-looking fissures in the rock.

Limestone

Limestone is useful for creating gardens for plants that prefer alkaline soil. Where it occurs locally, try to get weathered rock from fields or woods. These will be slightly rounded and will have a patina of moss or lichens. New rock, for example from building sites or road cuts, takes several years to mellow.

Tufa

Tufa is a porous, alkaline rock that is formed as deposits around mineral springs. It is filled with numerous air pockets, and its light weight makes it easy to transport and handle. Cavities for plants may be dug or drilled out of its relatively soft surface. It provides ideal conditions for many plants that require free drainage, but it is scarce and expensive.

Types of stone

Tufa is an excellent choice for the rock garden because its soft, porous nature means that plants may be grown in cavities on the surface as well as in crevices between the stones. Natural-looking, weather-worn sandstone is also a good choice, as is limestone (if growing alkaline-tolerant plants).

TUFA

SANDSTONE

LIMESTONE

ROCK PLANTS THAT PREFER SANDY SOIL

Acaena caesiiglauca,
    A. microphylla
Achillea x *kellereri*
Aethionema 'Warley Rose'
Arabis ferdinandi-coburgi
    'Variegata'
Arenaria montana
Armeria juniperifolia
Artemisia schmidtiana 'Nana'
Ballota pseudodictamnus
Cytisus x *beanii*
Dianthus carthusianorum,
    D. deltoides
Erodium guttatum
Gypsophila repens
Helianthemum
Iberis saxatilis

Lewisia,
Cotyledon
Hybrids

Lewisia, Cotyledon
    Hybrids
Linum suffruticosum
Onosma echioides, O. taurica
Phlox bifida
Saponaria ocymoides
Sedum
Sempervivum

ROCK PLANTS THAT TOLERATE VERY ALKALINE SOIL

Achillea
Aethionema
Alyssum
Anemone magellanica
Aubrieta
Campanula
Chrysanthemum hosmariense
Dianthus
Draba
Erysimum helveticum
Geranium farreri
Gypsophila repens
Helianthemum
Leontopodium alpinum

Origanum
'Kent Beauty'

Origanum
Papaver burseri,
    P. miyabeanum
Pulsatilla
Saponaria ocymoides
Saxifraga
Sedum
Sempervivum
Silene schafta
Thymus caespititius

HOW TO PREPARE THE SITE AND PLACE THE STONE

1 *Place a 6in (15cm) layer of coarse rubble, such as broken bricks, on the proposed site to form a mound and improve drainage in the rock garden.*

2 *Cover the mound with inverted sod to prevent soil from being washed down to the layer of rubble at the base.*

3 *Cover the inverted sod with 9–12in (22–30cm) of well-drained top-soil. Before beginning to lay the stones, use pegs and a length of rope to mark out roughly the shape of each main rock outcrop.*

4 *Using a spade, dig out a hollow for each large piece of stone to make it more stable when placed in position.*

5 *Use a crowbar to maneuver large stones into their final positions. Be sure that the stones are well supported by wedging smaller stones or bricks underneath.*

6 *Fill in underneath and in between the stones with garden soil, making sure that each stone is firmly in place.*

7 *Build each out-crop of the rock garden in the same way. Firm down the soil gen-tly around the stones (see inset) to eliminate air pock-ets and to make sure that each stone is firmly seated.*

8 *When all the stones are in place, fill in around them with more garden soil so they are buried by one-third of their depth to ensure complete stability. Loosen the soil between the rocks so that it is not compacted.*

Preparing the site for a rock garden

Never attempt to construct rock gardens when the soil is wet, since heavy rocks may compact the soil and severely damage its structure; this interferes with drainage and causes problems with the establishment and growth of the plants. If the site is grassy, cut the sod carefully and remove it for later use.

Clearing weeds
Remove all perennial weeds from the site and, if siting the rock garden near trees or shrubs, remove any suckers that these may have produced. Perennial weeds are very difficult to eradicate from an established rock garden, so it is essential to dig them out or kill them with a weedkiller at this stage. Spray the whole area with a systemic weedkiller several weeks before construction begins, to kill the deep roots of perennial weeds and clear the site of vegetation.

Drainage
Make sure that the site, particularly if level, is well drained. If necessary, install a French drain or some other drainage system (see SOILS AND FERTILIZERS, "Improving drainage," p.617). This is important on heavy clay soils. Do not simply dig deep holes – these act as sumps in which the water remains, unless they are connected to a drainage ditch. Raising the rock garden above the level of the surrounding ground – by as little as 6in (15cm) – helps improve drainage. Drainage is not usually a problem on naturally sloping sites, although a ditch or other drain may be needed at the lowest point.

If the underlying drainage is good, just dig the soil over and remove any perennial weeds. Then settle the soil by compacting it gently to avoid subse-quent sinking. Fork over the surface of the soil to maintain good soil structure.

Constructing a rock garden

To visualize the finished rock garden, make a miniature rough scale model, using plastic foam bits or small stones to simulate rock outcrops. Use different sizes of stone and place them at various levels, linking them, if required, by groups of outlying rocks and small scree areas. On large sites, construct several outcrops, linked by gullies or scree beds, and incorporate water features, if desired. Outlining the proposed shape on site with a hose may help. Aim for a natural look, with miniature cliffs and valleys, along natural stratum lines. Plan the planting, bearing in mind the relative vigor and ultimate spread of the plants. Once the design is satisfactory, construction of the rock garden may begin.

Building the base

Put down a 6in (15cm) layer of coarse rock, broken bricks, stones, or pea gravel. Spread over this a layer of inverted pieces of sod, if they are available; these prevent the rock garden soil mix from clogging the free-draining layer at the base without inhibiting normal drainage. If sod is not available, use landscape fabric or a few layers of burlap.

Purchase topsoil or bring in good soil from elsewhere in the garden, ensuring that it is as weed-free as possible. Use this for the top layer of the rock garden. Specially prepared, well-drained soil mix (see "Special mix," p.258) should be used for filling in between rocks where plants are to be grown.

Placing the stone

Rock is heavy and rough on the hands, so wear gloves and protective footwear. Use rollers to move large rocks, and arrange for the load to be delivered as close to the site of the rock garden as possible. To maneuver large rocks into their final positions, it may be necessary to use a block and tackle, with a steel crowbar as a lever for final adjustments. Mark the approximate positions of larger rocks first, to avoid unnecessary labor.

Select first the large stones that will act as keystones – the dominant rocks from which each outcrop is developed. Place the largest of the keystones first, and position the remaining ones so that the strata flow naturally from them to form the outcrops in the required directions. Additional large stones acting as subsidiary keystones may then be used to extend the outcrops. Use enough rock to make the outcrops realistic, while leaving sufficient room for planting. Check progress visually as construction proceeds. If the rocks being used have stratum lines, make sure that these all run in the same direction and at the same angle.

The rocks should be placed to provide the widest range of opportunities for planting. For example, butting rocks together serves to create the narrow crevices in which a variety of plants may thrive. Where space allows, a carefully planned, tiered rock garden may produce a number of useful, broad planting pockets between the rocks.

Bury the rocks to a third of their volume and tip them backward slightly. This provides stability and allows water to run back off the rock into the bed rather than onto the plants beneath. Stand on the rocks to make sure that they are stable.

As rocks are positioned, fill in planting spaces with prepared soil mix and firm it in. Any obvious unconformities in the rocks may then be masked by careful planting.

Soils for rock gardens and scree beds

In nature, many alpines and rock garden plants grow in soil that is largely made up of rock fragments and gravel, usually with some accumulations of organic detritus, which retains moisture. Such a growing medium is extremely well drained, and it is important to simulate this as closely as possible in a rock garden or scree bed.

Ordinary garden soils may be adapted, to some extent, for cultivating most rock garden plants and alpines by adding peat, compost, and/or sand. Large quantities of sand are required to provide the rapid drainage that is needed for the more moisture-sensitive species, such as those grown in scree beds.

HOW TO PLANT A ROCK GARDEN

1 *Before starting to plant, water all the plants and allow them to drain. To check the planting arrangement, set out the pots on the surface of the bed, taking account of the eventual height and spread of the plants.*

2 *Carefully remove each plant from its pot and loosen the root ball a little to encourage the roots to spread. Remove any moss and weeds before planting.*

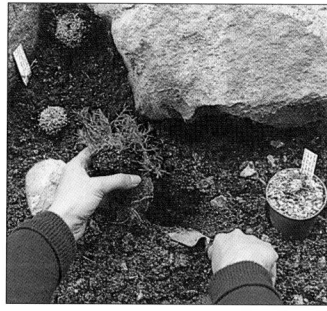

3 *Using a trowel, dig a hole large enough to accommodate the root ball. Ease the plant into the hole, and label.*

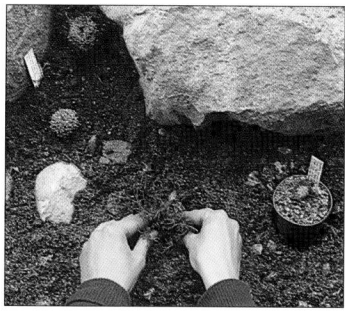

4 *Fill in around the plant with soil mix and firm gently, making sure that there are no air pockets between the root ball and the soil mix.*

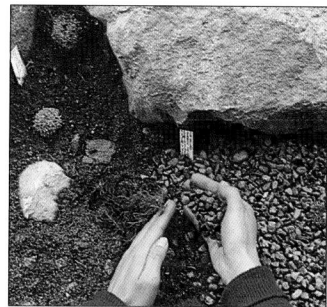

5 *Top-dress the soil mix with a layer of sand or gravel, easing a little around the collars of the plants.*

6 *Continue to plant in the same way until the rock garden is complete. Check that the entire area is properly top-dressed, then water in the plants well.*

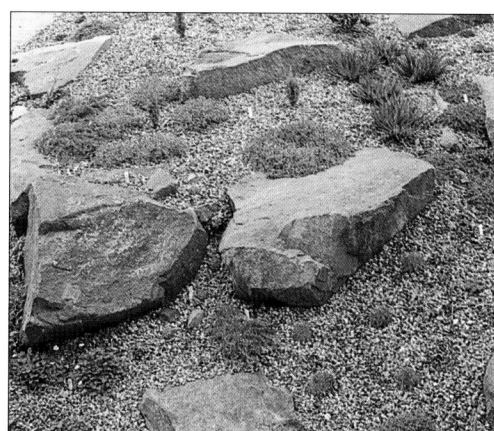

THE FINISHED ROCK GARDEN *The plants will soon grow to produce an attractive and natural-looking rock garden.*

Standard mix

A mix of 1 part clean garden soil, 1 part peat or compost, and 1 part sharp sand or coarse grit is suitable for most rock garden plants. The organic materials provide moisture retention, while the sand or grit maintains good drainage.

Scree mixture

Scree plants require a freely draining soil mix. Make up a mixture using the same ingredients as for the standard mix, but in different proportions: 3 parts coarse grit or stone chips (not sand) instead of 1 part. In order to produce an even more freely draining soil mix, increase the proportion of stony material included in the mix. In dry areas, this proportion may have to be reduced to 2 parts. Alternatively, use a more retentive mix of 2 parts soil, 2 parts leaf mold or peat, 1 part sharp sand, and 4 parts stone chips.

Special mix

Some choice alpines, such as the tiny, cushion-forming *Androsace*

species and saxifrages, need very freely draining soil mix. These plants usually come from high altitudes where soil nutrient levels are low. Use a mix of 2 or 3 parts stone chips or gravel to 1 part soil, leaf mold, peat, or compost.

Acidic soil-loving plants

For these, use a mix of 4 parts non alkaline leaf mold, peat, composted bark, or compost with 1 part coarse sand. On a naturally alkaline soil, however, growing plants in pockets of acidic mixture is practical only in the short term, due to the inevitable percolation of lime into the soil, which soon kills them. A better solution is to grow these plants in peat beds (see p.263).

Planting a rock garden

Alpines and rock garden plants are almost always purchased as potted plants and may be planted at any

time of the year. However, it is better not to plant them when the ground is either wet or frozen, or during very warm or dry periods.

Water all the plants thoroughly before planting and allow them to drain. Set the plants out in the planned positions while still in their pots to give an idea of the finished design. Make any rearrangements at this stage and adjust planting distances, allowing for the vigorous and rapid growth of some types. Slide each plant carefully out of its pot and remove any weeds from the soil mix. Inspect the roots and top-growth for pests and diseases and treat, as necessary, before planting (see PLANT PROBLEMS, pp.633–61).

Make a planting hole with a trowel or hand fork, making sure that the hole is big enough to accommodate the roots. Loosen the root ball, position the plant in the hole, and firm in the soil mix. The plant should sit with the collar slightly above the surface of the soil mix to leave room for a top-dressing of gravel or chips.

When all the plants are in place, water them in thoroughly. Keep them moist until they are established and starting to make new growth. If planting is followed by a dry period, water the plants at approximately weekly intervals until the roots have penetrated the surrounding soil mix. Thereafter, there should be no need to water except during a drought.

Planting in crevices

Alpines and rock garden plants may be difficult to establish in crevices and need extra care when planting. It is preferable to plant them at the construction stage, although this is not always possible. If planting in the crevices of an established rock garden, use a small tool such as a widger to make a planting hole.

Use young, rooted cuttings with vigorous root systems. If only pot-grown plants are available, trim the root balls and top-growth to the appropriate size before planting. Put a small stone in the crevice and place a little soil mix on top, then ease in the roots with a widger so that the plant faces outward. Add more soil mix around the plant and firm in. Place a small stone on top of the root ball for extra support.

Aftercare

Use netting or other deterrents to protect newly planted alpines from birds. Periodically refirm any plants that may have worked loose, adding new soil mix if necessary. Label the plants or maintain a planting plan to record their names at the time of planting; update planting plans and labeling as plants are added, replaced, or relocated.

Constructing a scree bed

Prepare the site in a similar way to a rock garden, installing artificial drainage, if necessary (see SOILS AND FERTILIZERS, "Improving drainage," p.617). Sloping sites have naturally good drainage, but on flat ground screes are best raised slightly above the ground to assist drainage, and retained within low walls, logs, or old railroad ties in the same way as raised beds (see p.263).

Scree beds should be 12–16in (30–40cm) deep. About half of the depth should be composed of coarse stones, as for rock gardens, and the upper layer of scree mixture (see opposite). Mark out the site with a rope or hose, and remove the soil from grassy areas. Lay the stone

---

MEDITERRANEAN-STYLE PLANTING ON AN INCLINE

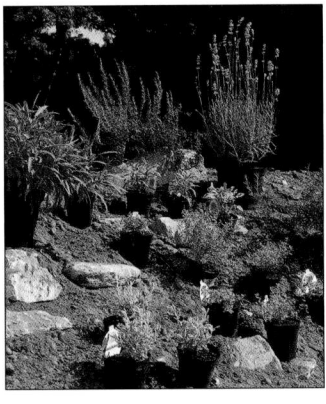

1 *If necessary, work sharp sand or grit into the soil to improve drainage. Dig and firm in larger stones. Arrange the plants in their pots (here a selection of herbs).*

2 *Plant the large and then the small plants at the same depth as they were in their containers, and water well. Let the soil surface dry a little before top-dressing.*

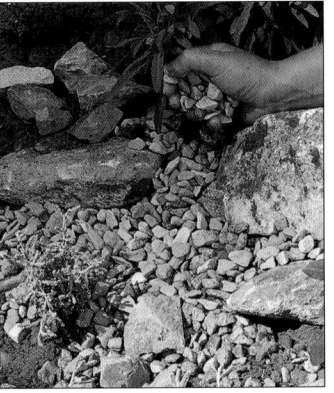

3 *Add smaller stones and then a thick layer of stone chips or pea gravel. Use a trowel or your hands to spread it carefully between and around the plants.*

THE FINISHED "MEDITERRANEAN" BANK
Such a drought-tolerant garden provides an attractive low-maintenance area that should need little watering once the plants are established. The surface layer of chips or pea gravel will help conserve moisture in the soil, reflect heat onto the sun-loving plants, and keep down weeds. Remove any weeds that do appear by hand as soon as you spot them.

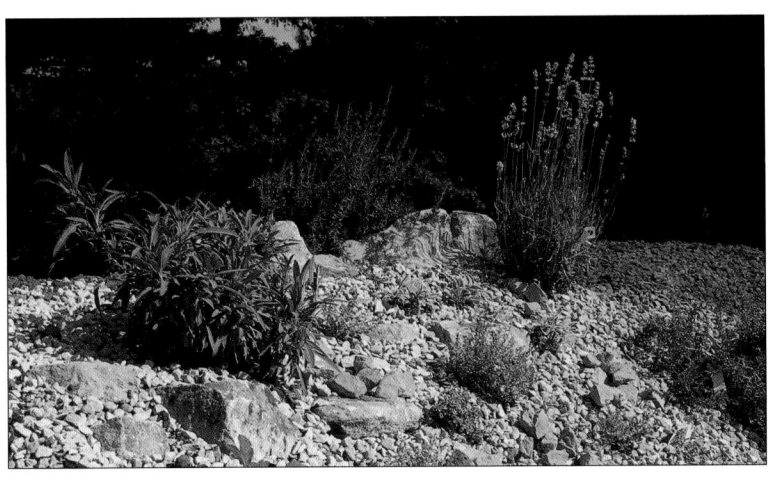

IMPROVING SOIL DRAINAGE BENEATH A GRAVEL BED

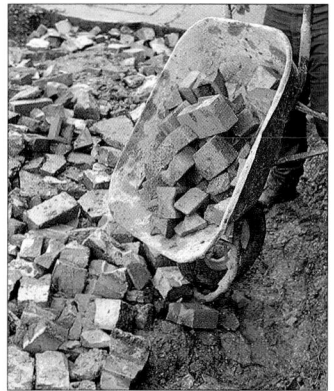

1 *On heavy soil, remove and reserve the top layer of soil to a depth of 24in (60cm), fork the ground, and spread a 6in (15cm) layer of bricks or crushed stone.*

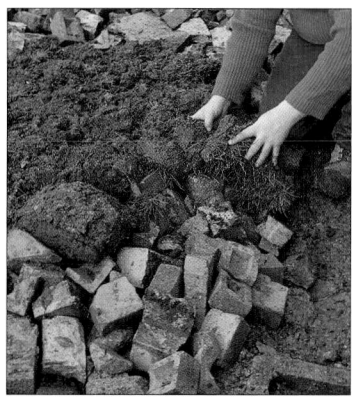

2 *Cap the base with a layer of inverted sod, in order to prevent the top layer of lighter soil from being washed down into the base.*

3 *Mix the reserved soil with plenty of sharp sand or gravel, and spread it over the sod layer. Tamp the soil with the head of a rake or walk on it lightly to firm.*

4 *After firming, water the area to settle the soil, and fill any depressions. Top-dress with a 4in (10cm) layer of coarse grit or pea gravel, then rake it level.*

---

foundation, then line the entire planting area with thinly cut, inverted pieces of sod or landscape fabric cut roughly to shape.

Finish off the bed with a 6–8in (15–20cm) layer of scree mixture, and firm by gently treading over the entire area. Water the bed and allow it to settle, then fill with scree mixture any areas that may have sunk before loosening the surface with a hand fork.

Planting in a scree bed

It may be more difficult to establish plants in a scree bed than in a rock garden, since the freely draining soil mix tends to dry out before the plants are established. Proper care during planting and conscientious watering are the keys to success.

The well-developed root systems of potgrown alpines do not readily penetrate the gritty scree soil mix, so gently shake off most of the soil mix (especially if peat-based) from the roots. Keep the bare roots moist. Place the plant in a planting hole with its roots spread out, and fill in carefully with scree mixture. Top-dress with stone chips and water immediately and thoroughly.

Scree mixes drain quickly, so water young plants regularly until they are established. In their natural habitats, scree dwellers have deep and extensive root systems to seek out water and nutrients, so when established they will survive for long periods without watering.

PLANTING IN A GRAVEL BED
Large plants are more conveniently planted before the gravel is spread, but small plants can be added later. Draw the gravel aside and scoop out a hole; if necessary, mound the soil on a plastic sheet to keep the gravel clean. Water well.

Top-dressing rock gardens and screes

After planting is completed, the rock garden or scree bed may then be top-dressed with stone chips, grit, or gravel. This material should match as closely as possible the rock used at the construction stage.

Top-dressing has a number of advantages: it provides an attractive and natural setting for the plants and blends in better with the rocks than bare soil, creates especially good drainage around the collars of the plants, inhibits weed growth, conserves moisture, and protects the soil surface from compaction during heavy rain or watering.

The layer of top-dressing on a rock garden should be at least 1in (2.5cm) deep, while on a scree bed it may be ¾–6in (2–15cm) deep, depending on the plants grown; for most screes, a ¾–1¼in (2–3cm) layer is sufficient.

On gravel beds and gardens, a water-premeable geotextile fabric may be used beneath a layer of grav-

el to further assist in weed suppression and to extend the life of the top-dressing by preventing it from gradually working into the soil (see "Using weed-suppressant geotextile fabric," left). Such fabrics also largely prevent ornamental plants from self-seeding and are ideal where a very low-maintenance feature is desired, although they do prevent plants from spreading naturally.

Various grades of stones and gravels are offered by garden centers and builders' supply stores. Choose a size and color that complements the stonework and the plantings. If the surface is to be walked upon regularly, a fine grade of gravel (pea gravel) is recommended for providing a smooth, more easily negotiable surface. Small pavers may be set unobtrusively in the gravel to provide spots for walking on.

Never gather any quantity of stones or gravels from natural areas, such as beaches or rivers. Doing so would probably damage the area, and in many cases it is illegal as well. Reputable suppliers offer responsibly obtained materials.

Using weed-suppressant geotextile fabric

These fabrics, now widely available, may also be referred to as mulching membranes or landscape fabric. They are easily pegged down using wire hoops. Soak plant root balls thoroughly before planting them through cross-cuts in the fabric (see WATER CONSERVATION AND RECYCLING, p.606). Water them regularly until they are established. The fabric should help retain more moisture in the soil than a surface layer of grit or pea gravel alone.

HIDING THE FABRIC
Once the fabric is secured over the entire area, the top layer of grit or pea gravel can be added. Since black or white are the only colors generally available, the layer must be thick enough to prevent any fabric from being visible.

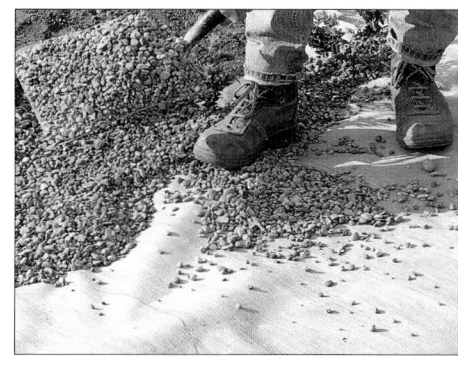

Troughs, sinks, and other containers

Alpines and rock garden plants look particularly attractive when grown in troughs and sinks, although most containers are suitable, provided that they allow good drainage and are frostproof. Choose the correct site at the outset since, once filled, they are heavy and difficult to move. Rocks may be placed in the containers, if desired, to create the look of a miniature rock garden; this should be done before planting up the container. Select a soil mix to suit the plants to be grown, and choose plants that have similar growth rates.

Types of container

Old stone sinks and animal troughs have traditionally been used to grow alpines and rock garden plants, but they are very scarce and expensive. Glazed sinks coated in hypertufa, or troughs made entirely of hypertufa or of reconstituted stone, are now often used, as are large terracotta pots and tubs. All should have drainage holes to make sure that there is a free flow of water through the soil mix. If extra drainage holes are needed, they should be at least 1in (2.5cm) in diameter. If the base of the container is not flat, make the drainage holes at the lowest point.

Covering glazed sinks

Deep, glazed, flat-bottomed sinks can easily be made to resemble stone containers by coating them with hypertufa. Be sure that the sink is clean and dry before coating it, then score the surface with a tile- or glass-cutter to form a rough surface to help the hypertufa adhere to the sink. To aid adhesion further, paint the surface with a bonding agent before applying the hypertufa.

Make hypertufa from 1–2 parts sifted peat, 1 part coarse sand or fine grit, and 1 part cement. Add sufficient water to form a thick but still workable paste. Apply this to the outside of the sink and also inside, down to well below the final level of the soil mix. Put the hypertufa on by hand (wear gloves); it should be ½–¾in (1–2cm) thick. Roughen the

COVERING A GLAZED SINK WITH HYPERTUFA

Glazed sinks covered with hypertufa make fine containers for alpines.

surface so that it resembles stone. When the hypertufa is fully dry, after about a week, scrub the surface with a wire brush and coat with liquid manure, buttermilk, or mossy soil to encourage the growth of mosses and lichens for a more natural look.

Hypertufa troughs

Troughs may be made entirely from hypertufa, if required. The mixture should be prepared as for covering glazed sinks, but the proportion of sand and grit increased to 3 parts to make a stiffer mix.

Use two wooden boxes that fit inside one another, with a cavity of 2–3in (5–7cm) between them. Stand the larger box on blocks so that it may be lifted once finished. Pour a thin layer of the hypertufa mix into the base. Cover the mix and the sides of the box with wire netting (such as chicken wire or pig wire), then pour in another layer of hypertufa mix. Press thick dowels or pegs through the hypertufa to make drainage holes. Fit the smaller box inside the larger, and fill the space with the mix, tamping it down to remove air pockets.

When the cavity is full, cover the trough with a sheet of plastic for at least a week while the mix sets, and protect the trough from cold, if necessary. When the mix has set hard, remove the boxes and dowels. If the boxes do not slide off easily, ease them off carefully with a fine chisel and a small hammer. Roughen the surface of the trough with a wire brush and paint on a coat of liquid manure to encourage algal growth.

HOW TO MAKE A HYPERTUFA TROUGH

1 *You will need two boxes to make the trough, one slightly larger than the other. Coat the boxes with oil to prevent the hypertufa from sticking.*

2 *Place a 1in (2.5cm) layer of hypertufa mix in the base of the larger box. Put wire netting on top of this layer and around the sides to reinforce the trough. Then add another layer of hypertufa.*

3 *Press several thick wooden dowels into the wire and hypertufa base to make the drainage holes for the bottom of the trough.*

4 *Put the smaller box centrally on top of the hypertufa base, making sure the vertical netting is between the two boxes. Fill the cavity with the hypertufa mix, tamping down well as you fill.*

5 *Cover the top of the hypertufa with a plastic sheet until the mix has set (which usually takes about a week). Secure the sheet in place with a weight, and protect the trough from cold.*

6 *When the hypertufa has set, remove the wooden form from the outside of the trough. If the hypertufa has stuck to the box, carefully dismantle the box with a hammer and chisel.*

7 *The surface of the hypertufa will be smooth and straight. For a more natural-looking appearance, scrub the outside of the trough with a wire brush or coarse-grained sandpaper to roughen the surface.*

8 *Remove the smaller box and the dowels, using a hammer and chisel if necessary. To encourage moss growth, paint the outside of the trough with liquid manure.*

Siting containers

An open position, with sun for at least part of the day, is ideal for most plants. Do not place containers in windy sites, unless tough plants are being grown, or on lawns, since it is difficult to maintain the surrounding grass. Avoid slopes, which cause instability, and put containers as close as possible to a tap or hose.

Raise troughs and sinks off the ground, up to a height of about 18in (45cm); the plants may then be viewed comfortably and water will drain away readily. Stone or brick pillars at the corners of a container provide sturdy, stable supports. These must bear the weight of the container without danger of tipping and should not block the holes. Tilt any sink containing just one hole so that excess water can drain.

Placing rocks and tufa

Virtually any type of rock may be used in troughs and sinks. Rocks give height and allow a greater depth of soil mix. A few large rocks are better than many small ones. Niches and crevices in the rocks can also be used to support plants, especially if hard tufa is used. Tufa's light weight and the ease with which planting holes can be excavated in it make it ideal. Roots spread into the porous rock, which is well aerated but also retains water.

Whatever type of rock is used, bury it from one-third to one-half of its depth in the soil mix to make sure that it is firmly seated.

Filling the container

Most rock garden plants thrive in standard soil mix, preferably with some additional drainage material. Add about one-third by volume of ¼–⅜in (6–9mm) stone chips, and mix in some slow-release fertilizer. Acidic-soil-loving plants need an acid-free soil mix, with added granite or sandstone chips.

Cover the drainage holes with squares of plastic-coated window screen or similar netting. Fill the bottom of the container one-quarter to one-third deep with coarse stone, gravel, or stone chips. Add a layer of fibrous peat or inverted, thinly cut sod. Fill up with slightly moist soil mix, and firm it gently.

Position pieces of rock or tufa on the soil mix, and bed them in as the container is filled. Place rocks to form crevices and niches, providing both shaded and sunny faces to suit different plants, and add randomly placed smaller pieces of stone to simulate a small-scale rock garden. Water thoroughly and allow to drain completely before planting.

Planting

Choose compact, slow-growing plants that will not swamp their neighbors and quickly exhaust the available nutrients. Do not overplant the container, and replant as soon as it becomes overcrowded (see p.265).

Position container-grown plants, still in their pots, on the soil mix or make a plan on paper of the planting design. Make planting holes, carefully slide the plants out of their pots, and loosen the root balls. Place the plants in the holes, fill in with soil mix, and firm. When complete, water thoroughly. Then add a layer of top-dressing to help ensure surface drainage, using chips or gravel that complement any rocks included.

Planting in tufa

If plants are to be grown in tufa rock, use a drill or a hammer and chisel to make holes at least 4in (10cm) apart. They should be about 1in (2.5cm) in diameter and 2–3in (5–7cm) deep, angled at 30–45° on vertical or sloping surfaces, or straight down on horizontal planes. Soak the tufa, then put a little sharp sand in each hole, and add some soil mix. Use young rooted cuttings or small plants, since they establish easily. Wash the roots before planting. Ease the plants into the holes with a small dibber or a pencil and sprinkle in soil mix until the hole is full. Be sure that the neck of the plant is not standing above the hole. Firm the soil mix and wedge small pieces of tufa around the plants to hold them in place. Water thoroughly and keep the tufa moist until the plants are established. In hot, dry weather, soak the tufa regularly.

HOW TO PLANT UP AN ALPINE TROUGH

1 *If planting in tufa, first drill holes about 1in (2.5cm) wide, 2–3in (5–7cm) deep, and no less than 4in (10cm) apart. Immerse the tufa in water overnight.*

2 *Lay fine-mesh netting over the trough base, or cover the holes with pot shards, curved side up.*

3 *Partly fill the trough with a gritty, moist soil mix, firming it in stages. Set the tufa in place so that ⅓–½ of it is buried to keep it stable.*

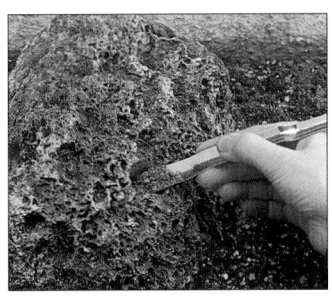

4 *Continue to fill with soil mix and firm well to allow about 2in (5cm) for top-dressing and watering. Insert a little soil mix into the tufa holes for planting.*

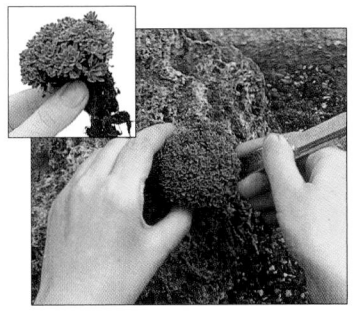

5 *Wash the roots of the plants to go in the tufa, and ease them into the planting holes. Dribble soil mix into the holes, firm, and put small rock pieces around the plants.*

6 *Set the plants, still in their pots, on the soil mix to check that the arrangement and spacing are satisfactory, then plant and firm them in.*

7 *Water the soil mix thoroughly, then top-dress the trough with a 1–2in (2.5–5cm) deep layer of coarse gravel or stone chips.*

THE FINISHED TROUGH

Helianthemum oelandicum subsp. alpestre

Saxifraga cotyledon

Oxalis 'Ione Hecker'

Saxifraga cochlearis 'Minor'

Phlox douglasii cv

Oxalis enneaphylla 'Minutifolia'

Androsace pubescens

Sisyrinchium 'E.K. Balls'

Penstemon pinifolius

Sempervivum arachnoideum

Draba aizoides

Talinum okanoganense

Saxifraga paniculata

Dianthus 'La Bourboule'

Rhodohypoxis baurii

Walls

Alpines and rock garden plants may be grown in the crevices of drystone walls, including the retaining walls of raised beds and sloping banks. Trailing plants are especially effective when grown in this way. For details on constructing a wall, see "Drystone walls," p.592.

If possible, plan for any planting in walls before construction work starts. The most practical approach is to leave planting niches at intervals in the wall and plant them up when the building work is finished.

It is also possible to position the plants as construction proceeds. This produces excellent results, since the plants may be placed at the desired level and provides good contact between the roots of the plants and any soil behind the wall. Planting during construction also makes it easier to eliminate air pockets in the soil mix and to firm around the roots.

Planting in existing walls is another option, but some of the soil will need to be removed first with a widger or teaspoon before planting. Use young plants or rooted cuttings, since these fit easily in the crevices.

HOW TO BUILD A DRYSTONE RETAINING WALL

MAKING THE FOOTINGS
Dig a trench 15in (38cm) deep; fill it with 10in (25cm) of rubble top with a large, flat stone.

PLACING THE STONES
Slope the stones backward and downward for stability so that water is carried into the soil mix.

FILLING BETWEEN STONES
As you build, fill crevices between the stones with a mix of loam, leaf mold, and sand or grit.

Planting

Use the following soil mix for filling the planting crevices in walls: 3 parts loam (or good sterilized garden soil), 2 parts coarse peat substitute or peat, and 1–2 parts sharp sand or grit. Use extra grit, sand, or stone chips for plants that are to be grown in the wall itself, since this will help to ensure good drainage. Choose plants that grow well in the exposure and conditions available in the wall. Carefully remove old soil mix from the roots and ease them into the hole, using a widger, small dibber, or pencil. Do not try to cram roots into too small a space, because this damages the plants. Holding the plant in position with one hand, trickle in fresh, moist soil mix, then firm it with the widger to remove any air pockets. It may also be helpful to wedge small stones around the collars of the plants to hold them in place and prevent the soil from becoming dislodged.

Water thoroughly from the top of the wall and spray the plants regularly until established. After several days, fill up any sunken areas with spare soil mix. Periodically check the plants, gently firming back any that have worked loose.

HOW TO PLANT IN A DRYSTONE WALL

1 *If planting in an existing wall, check that there is an adequate amount of soil mix in the crevices to support the plants.*

2 *Use seedlings or small rooted cuttings. Place them on the flat of a stone and, using a widger, ease the roots into the crevices. The plant shown here is a* Sempervivum.

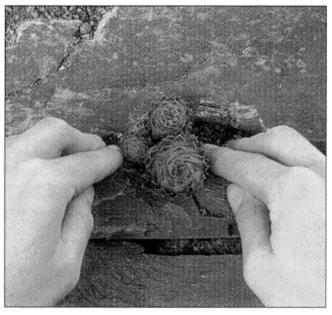

3 *Bed the plants down into soil mix, then pack more mix into the crevices to hold the plants in position. Firm the plants in with your fingers.*

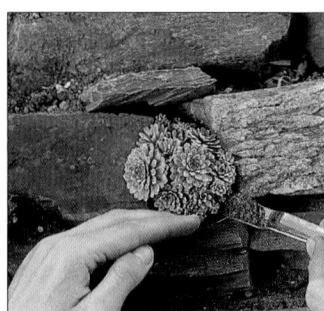

4 *For larger plants, scoop out some soil mix from the crevices. Ease the roots into the holes and add more mix while holding plants in position.*

5 *When all the plants are in position, water them from the top of the wall or with a mist spray. Keep the plants moist until established and refirm any that work loose. Planted with the* Sempervivum *are two saxifrages.*

PLANTING IN VERTICAL CREVICES

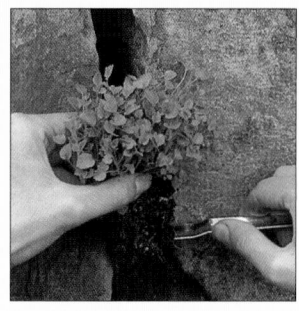

1 *Fill the crevice with a gritty soil mix. Carefully ease in the roots of the plant (here* Campanula).

2 *Cover the roots with soil mix, then wedge in a small stone, sloping it down the rock face. Firm additional mix into the crevice.*

SOFTENING
SURFACES
*Soften the edges of
steps, retaining
walls, and paving
by inserting low,
spreading plants in
gaps and crevices.
Fill in any gaps
around them with
gritty soil mix.
Take care that
growth does not
obscure steps and
make them
hazardous.*

Raised beds

A wide range of alpine plants may be
grown in raised beds, both in the
beds themselves and in crevices in
the supporting walls. The bed's
design should harmonize with the
house and yard. Depending on the
needs of the chosen plants, a raised
bed may be positioned in either sun
or shade. Fill the bed with well-
drained soil mix to suit the plants
(see "Soil for raised beds," below). If
necessary, plants may be protected in
winter with glass or plastic covers
placed over the bed.

Siting
For most alpines and rock garden
plants, raised beds should be sited in
an open, sunny position away from
the shade cast by overhanging trees
or nearby buildings and fences. Place
a raised bed in shade only if woodland or other plants requiring cooler,
shadier conditions are to be grown.

To aid mowing, a raised bed that is
positioned on a lawn should have a
surround of paving slabs or bricks set
just below the level of the grass.
Raised beds that are constructed for
elderly or disabled gardeners may
need to be built with wheelchair
access, and the beds should be of a
height and width to allow plants to be
tended easily from a seated position.
On sites where the construction of a
ground-based scree bed is not possible
because of poor drainage, a scree
may be placed on the surface of a
raised bed instead (see p.258).

Materials and design
Raised beds may be made from stone,
brick, old wooden railroad ties, or
any other suitable and attractive
material. Stone is the most costly;
new or secondhand bricks and ties
are cheaper and easier to use.

The bed may be almost any shape
but it should harmonize with the
general design of the garden. Rectangular beds are the most common.
The ideal height for a raised bed is
24–30in (60–75cm), although a
tiered bed is also attractive and may
be more appropriate where space is
limited. The width of the bed should
be no more than 5ft (1.5m) to allow
comfortable access – the center of
the bed should be within arm's reach
to allow weeding from all sides.

Large beds may need an irrigation
system; install water pipes and inlets
before filling the beds with soil mix.

Construction
Retaining brick walls for raised beds
should be vertical; the thickness of
one brick is usually adequate. They
are built in the same way as a conventional wall and may be mortared,
but small gaps should be left
between bricks at intervals for plants
to be inserted. There should also be
gaps at the base for drainage. For further information, see STRUCTURES
AND SURFACES, "Raised beds," p.593.

Raised beds may also have stone
retaining walls. If they are built without mortar they need a slight inward
slope for stability (see "Drystone
walls," p.592). Drystone walls take
time to build: each stone needs to be
chosen and positioned carefully. In
moderate climates, large crevices
may be left between the stones to be
planted with alpines. If railroad ties
are used, crevice-planting is not a
practical option.

Soil for raised beds
Use a mix of 3 parts good sterilized
garden soil), 2 parts coarse fibrous
peat substitute (such as acidic leaf
mold or compost) or peat, and 1–2
parts grit or sharp sand. For plants
that need acidic conditions, use
acidic soil and grit. To grow plants
that need different soil types in a
large bed, divide it into sections with
plastic sheeting to keep the sections
apart, and fill each with appropriate
soil mix (see p.257).

Preparing the raised bed
Fill the bottom third of the bed with
coarse gravel, stones, or rubble, then
place a layer of inverted sod or
fibrous peat substitute (or peat) over
the top to prevent the drainage material from becoming clogged. Fill the
bed with prepared soil mix, which
should be well worked into all the
corners and firmed as filling proceeds. Incorporate a slow-release
fertilizer. Some settling always
occurs, so water the bed thoroughly
and leave it for two or three weeks.
Fill any sunken areas with spare soil
mix before planting.

Adding rocks gives the effect of
a rock garden in miniature and
enhances the appearance of raised
beds. Set pieces of rock of varying
sizes into the soil mix to provide
suitable sites for a range of different
plants. Several large pieces of rock
arranged together as outcrops are
more effective than scattered rocks.

Planting and top-dressing
Make a planting plan or set out the
plants on the surface of the bed to see
how they will look. Dwarf conifers
and small shrubs, tufted and cushion-
forming alpines, trailing alpines at
the edges of the bed, and smaller
bulbs are ideal. Select plants for
year-round interest. Plant as for rock
gardens (see p.258); crevices in the
retaining walls may also be planted
up as for drystone walls (see p.262).

After planting, top-dress the bed
with stone chips or coarse grit to
match any rocks. Work a 1cm (½in)
deep layer of the top-dressing carefully around the plants and beneath
their collars. This looks attractive,
suppresses weeds, and reduces evaporation. Water the bed regularly until
the plants are established.

Winter protection
Many alpines dislike excessive
winter moisture, even in the well-
drained conditions of a raised bed.
The alpine beds can be protected
with cloches or sheets of glass or
plastic, supported with bricks or a
wire frame. Fasten down the covering so that it does not blow away.
Such protection should be put in
place in late fall and removed the
following spring. If the whole bed
needs protection, build a wooden
framework for a glass or plastic roof.
Plenty of air must circulate around
the plants to ensure that they remain
as dry as possible, so do not cover the
sides of the protective frame.

Beds for acidic soil-loving plants

Peat beds provide ideal conditions
for a wide range of acidic-soil-
loving and woodland plants.
In gardens with alkaline soils,
such beds should always be isolated from the ground with a plastic
or rubber liner so that alkalinity
cannot enter. Surround each bed
with logs, old railroad ties, or
similar nonreactive material.

Consider the needs of the plants
when deciding where to place an
peat bed, and construct the bed so
that it blends in well with the rest
of the garden. It is not necessary
to use pure peat in the bed, since
acidic peat substitutes are widely
available. A wide range of acidic-
soil-loving plants (see list, p. 254)
may be grown both in the bed and
in wall crevices to produce an
attractive display.

Siting
Choose a site that receives sun and
dappled shade, ideally facing
away from strong, hot, direct sun.
An area next to a rock garden, on
a slope, or by the side of a building
is appropriate. Peat beds on
exposed sites in full sun lose
moisture rapidly and need frequent watering. Dense shade of
trees is unsuitable, and the tree
roots nearby soon exhaust the
moisture and nutrients. Waterlogged sites and frost pockets are
not suitable, either.

A FINISHED BED
*Plant up a peat bed
bed with acidic soil-
loving rock garden
plants. Water often to
keep the soil moist,
especially in the first
year. Top-dress
the bed with bark
chips to conserve
moisture and suppress
weeds. Fertilize the
plants regularly with a
balanced fertilizer.*

Routine care

EVEN when alpines and rock plants are established in the garden, it is essential to care for them regularly. Beds, troughs, and sinks must be kept clean and free of weeds. Although the plants do not usually need nutrient-rich soil, they should be fertilized at intervals and watered whenever the soil becomes dry. Top-dressings, which improve drainage around the collars of the plants, suppress weed growth, and reduce evaporation of water from the soil, should be replenished occasionally.

Alpines and rock garden plants benefit from periodic removal of dead wood, leaves, and flowers, and should be kept trimmed. Troughs, sinks, and other containers should be replanted as soon as they become overcrowded. Check plants routinely for signs of pest infestation and disease, and treat them as necessary. In cold or wet weather, some plants may need winter protection.

Weeding

The use of clean soil mix when planting should minimize problems with weeds, at least for the first few years. Try to remove all weeds as soon as they appear, certainly before they flower and set seed. If perennial weeds do become established and are difficult to remove, paint the foliage carefully with a systemic weedkiller, which is transmitted to the roots and kills them. For further information, see PLANT PROBLEMS, "Controlling weeds," p.660.

When weeding, use a hand cultivator or weeder to loosen and aerate compacted soil around young plants, if necessary.

Fertilizing

Newly planted areas should not normally need fertilizing for some years if the original soil mix has been correctly prepared and includes slow-release fertilizer. After some time, however, the growth of the plants may begin to slow down and flowering become sparser. This can be remedied by gently scratching in around the plants a dressing of bone meal each spring, combined with a slow-release fertilizer.

Alternatively, carefully remove the top-dressing and a layer of about ½in (1cm) of soil mix from the surface of the bed and replace it with fresh soil mix and a further top-dressing of grit.

Top-dressing

The type of top-dressing used for alpines and rock garden plants depends on the plants that are grown, although it should match any of the rocks and stones that feature in beds and rock gardens as closely as possible. Any top-dressings used in troughs, sinks, or raised beds should also harmonize well with the container or retaining walls.

Coarse grit or stone chips are suitable for most situations, but limestone chips should not be used around acid-loving plants. For plants grown in peat beds, a top-dressing of bark chips will complement the plantings and conserve moisture.

Renewing top-dressings

Top-dressings may need to be renewed from time to time, since grit or stone chips gradually wash away, especially on slopes, and bark tends to decompose and mix in with the underlying soil mix. Watch for bare patches throughout the season and top up as necessary. Pay close attention to top-dressings in the fall to ensure good soil coverage in winter and to avoid compaction by heavy rain. Check again in early spring and top up as necessary. A slow-release fertilizer may be applied at the same time.

Watering

Established plants growing in rock gardens and screes root deeply into the soil and do not usually need more water than is supplied by rainfall. In droughts, however, the area should be thoroughly soaked. Do not water in very cold conditions or

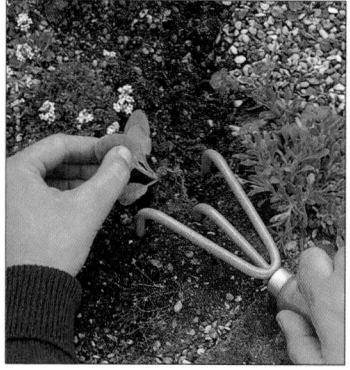

Weed around young plants with a hand fork or similar tool, which also loosens and aerates the soil. Remove any top-dressing first and replace it after weeding.

 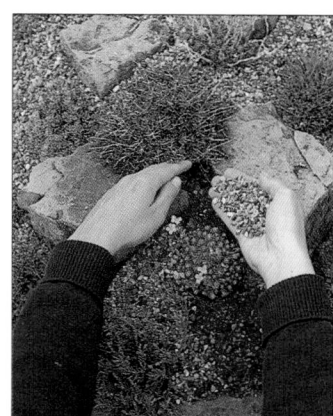

1 *Remove the old top-dressing and some soil mix (see inset). Fill in around the plants with fresh soil mix (see p.258).*

2 *Top-dress the bed with a fresh layer of coarse sand or gravel, adding some around and beneath the collars of the plants.*

during the heat of the day; early mornings or late evenings are the best times. Soak occasionally rather than giving small amounts of water frequently. If the soil mix is dry at a depth of 1¼–2in (3–5cm), water thoroughly until the water has penetrated to the full depth of the roots. During a wet summer this may be needed only two or three times, but in very dry summers it may be required more frequently.

Watering in containers, raised beds, and under cover

Alpines and rock garden plants that are grown in raised beds, sinks and troughs, under frames, and in the alpine house will need more regular watering, since the soil dries out more quickly than in rock gardens and scree beds.

It is preferable to hand-water troughs and sinks if specialized collections of plants are being grown, so that each plant may be provided with the correct amount of water. This is time-consuming, however, particularly where there are several containers to be watered.

Plants grown in pots in alpine houses and frames should be watered individually. If the pots are plunged in gravel or stone chips, water both the pots and the surrounding material. Some alpine plants have water-sensitive foliage and therefore dislike overhead watering; if this is the case, regularly soaking only the plunge material should provide sufficient moisture for these plants.

Trimming and pruning

Alpines and rock garden plants need to be cut back periodically to maintain a natural, compact shape and healthy growth, and to restrict them within their allotted space.

Pruning woody plants

To keep rock garden shrubs and woody perennials healthy, remove any dead, diseased, or damaged wood. Check the plants regularly and prune them cleanly, using pruners or sharp scissors.

Severe pruning is unnecessary because most dwarf shrubs are slow-growing and do not outgrow

In spring, after all danger of frost has passed, cut out any dieback from plants, trimming stems back carefully to healthy growth with sharp scissors or pruners.

REMOVING DEAD ROSETTES

1 *To remove dead rosettes from plants such as sax-ifrages, cut out the rosettes with a sharp knife without disturbing the rest of the plant.*

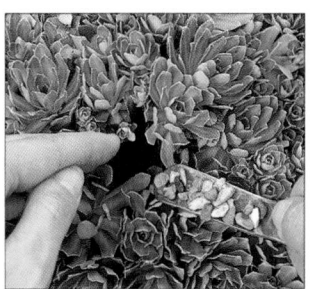

2 *Top-dress the exposed soil to prevent weeds from growing through the gaps until the plant produces fresh growth.*

CUTTING BACK AFTER FLOWERING

1 *After flowering, cut back stems (here Helianthemum) to half their length to encourage healthy, new growth.*

2 *The plants will remain compact and produce a good crop of flowers the following year.*

RENOVATING AN ALPINE BED

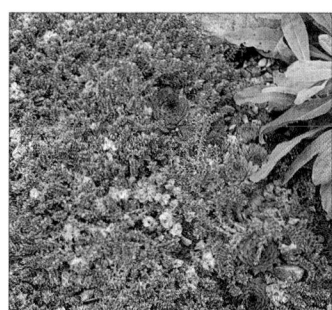

1 *Plants that spread rapidly (here* Paronychia kapela subsp. chionaea) *may eventually smother less vigorous plants nearby. Cut them back in spring.*

2 *Dig up or pull out clumps of encroaching plants. Straggly plants should be cut back severely. Make sure that plants nearby have plenty of room to grow.*

3 *Add a dressing of balanced fertilizer to the bed, before placing a fresh layer of top-dressing on the surface of the soil mix around the plants.*

their positions for many years. When pruning, aim to maintain the natural shape of the plant, especially in the case of dwarf conifers.

Removing dead flowers and foliage

Regularly remove all dead flowers and leaves, and any unwanted or unsightly seedheads, with a sharp knife, pruners, or scissors.

Pick over small alpine plants by hand, using tweezers, if necessary, to remove dead leaves and flowers. Carefully cut out dead rosettes from plants such as saxifrages; do not pull them off by hand, however, because this may loosen healthy rosettes.

Helianthemum species and cultivars, in particular, need clipping an-nually after flowering, cutting back the stems by about half their length to encourage

growth for flowering the following year. Genera such as *Arabis*, *Aubrieta*, and *Aurinia* also benefit from a hard annual pruning after flowering, which helps keep them compact and free-flowering. Some plants may produce a second flush of flowers if cut back before they set seed.

Encroaching plants

Overvigorous plants and old, straggly ones that start to encroach on their neighbors should be cut back in early spring. Mat-forming plants may simply be pulled out by hand; others may need to be lifted with a hand fork. Support nearby plants and refirm any that are accidentally lifted. Remove or cut back plants to allow a clear area of bed around all the remaining plants so that they can grow unimpeded. Hard-pruned

plants should be top-dressed with a balanced fertilizer in order to promote strong, new growth.

Winter protection

Plants in troughs, sinks, or raised beds, and some alpine bulbs, may need protection from winter moisture. Use a single, propped pane of glass, an open cloche, or, for large areas, a cold frame sash, which will give overhead protection without inhibiting air circulation. Make sure that covers are firmly secured or weighted down. Snow retention can be increased by placing a layer of evergreen branches or pine boughs loosely over the plants.

Controlling pests and diseases

Few serious problems affect alpines and rock garden plants, but some of the more common pests and diseases may need to be controlled. Regular, basic garden hygiene is often sufficient to control most problems encountered. Aphids (p.639) are likely to be troublesome if alpines are grown in too rich a soil, which induces soft, lank growth.

Coarse top-dressings around plants tend to deter slugs and snails (p.638) but some control is still necessary, particularly for choice alpines, such as *Campanula zoysii*, which are susceptible to attack from these pests. Control insects such as ants (p.656), which will excavate under cushion-forming plants. Prevent birds from disturbing newly planted specimens by covering the plants with netting.

Fungal diseases may quickly become established in alpine houses and frames (see "Hygiene," p.273).

Replanting an alpine trough

Plants in containers eventually need replanting when nutrients in the soil mix are exhausted. Water thoroughly before carefully removing the plants. Discard the soil mix and replace it with a fresh,

suitable mix (see p.196), containing a slow-release fertilizer. Trim roots and top-growth before returning plants to the container, allowing for their eventual spread. Top-dress with gravel.

Helianthemum sp.

Iris cristata

Ramonda myconi

Helianthemum sp.

Propagation

Many alpines and rock garden plants may be propagated from seed, although some plants are sterile and do not produce seeds. In addition, cultivars seldom come true from seed and must be increased in other ways. Alternative methods include cuttings and division.

Seed

Propagation from seed is the best way to produce large numbers of plants. Since many alpines flower in early spring, ripe seed is often available from midsummer and may be sown immediately. Germination will usually occur rapidly, and strong seedlings will be produced before winter. Fall-sown seeds can remain dormant until spring; if germination occurs, overwinter the seedlings in frames. It may sometimes be better to store seeds over winter and sow in early spring, although short-lived seeds should be sown as soon as they are ripe.

Seed gathering and storage
Gather seeds as the seedheads become ripe. Remove them while still attached to the stems and place them in paper (not plastic) bags to dry out. Enclose in envelopes any that might split open on drying. Store seeds in a cool, dry, well-ventilated place. Most alpines have seed capsules from which the seeds can be extracted by rubbing between the fingers. Fleshy fruits may need to be squashed and left on paper to dry.

Separate the seeds from the debris by sieving or hand-picking when dry. Put in envelopes, label, and seal, and place these in an airtight container in a cool place.

Presowing treatment
Seeds with hard coats need special treatment to allow them to absorb water. Scarify by chipping the seed coat with a sharp knife or rubbing with a file or fine abrasive paper. In some cases, soaking the seeds for 12–24 hours will accelerate the take-up of water.

Hard-cased seeds of woody rock garden plants do not respond to scarification alone; they also need exposure to cold (stratification). Store the seeds in boxes of moist sand outdoors for two or three months during winter, and sow in spring; alternatively, sow the seed in pots of seed soil mix and keep these in the freezer or refrigerator, sealed in plastic bags, for several weeks before plunging the pots in the

ground outside until the seeds germinate. Some seeds, such as *Trillium* and peonies (*Paeonia*), need alternating periods of cold and warmth to germinate successfully.

Sowing the seed
Use clean clay or plastic pots, and place a piece of screen over the drainage holes. A soil mix of equal parts sieved peat and perlite is suitable, or use soil-based sowing medium, mixed with an equal amount of perlite or sharp sand. Fill the pots and firm the medium. Tap out small seeds thinly and evenly, then space large seeds by hand, covering them to their depth with medium. Mix fine seeds with fine, dry sand before sowing, but do not cover with more medium.

After sowing, cover all but fine seeds with a ¼–½in (5–10mm) layer of ¼in (5mm) diameter grit or pea gravel, to deter mosses and liverworts and to protect the seeds from heavy rain or watering. Label the pots and stand them in water to half their depth, removing them when the surface of the medium becomes moist. Keep the medium moist.

Germination
Speed of germination depends on the type and age of the seeds, and when they are sown. Some seeds take months or years to germinate.

A cool, sheltered site outdoors is ideal for the seeds of most alpines. Plunge pots in moist sand to maintain an even temperature and reduce the need for watering. When seedlings appear, move the pots to a cold frame. Germination can be speeded up by placing the pots in gentle heat in early spring, but do not expose the seeds to high temperatures.

Pricking out and potting up
Prick out seedlings when they are ¼–½in (5–10mm) tall and when two true leaves have formed. Knock out the medium and separate the seedlings. Handle only by the leaves or cotyledons to avoid damage to stems and roots. Pot up seedlings individually in small clay pots or plastic pots, or in cell packs using low-fertility soil-based mix combined with an equal amount of grit. Fill the container, settle the soil mix, and make a hole for the roots. Put the seedling in the hole, fill with soil mix, and firm lightly.

Top-dress seedlings in individual pots with a ¼–½in (5–10mm) layer of grit. Water thoroughly with a fine spray, and place the containers

in a lightly shaded position until the seedlings are established. Water them as required. When the roots are visible through the drainage holes, pot them on.

Seeds that are slow to germinate often do so erratically, and if only a few seedlings appear, prick them out as soon as they are large enough to handle. Disturb the rest of the soil mix as little as possible, and cover it with fresh top-dressing. Put the pot back into the frame in case more seeds germinate, and pot up the seedlings as they emerge.

ROCK PLANT SEED TO BE SOWN FRESH
Anemone
Celmisia
Codonopsis
Corydalis
Cyclamen (alpine spp.)
Dodecatheon
Hepatica
Meconopsis
Primula (alpine spp.)
Pulsatilla
Ranunculus (alpine spp.)

SOWING SEED

1 *Prepare a pot by filling it with equal parts of sowing medium and horticultural sand. Firm the medium gently to level the surface and to eliminate air pockets.*

2 *Small seeds (here* Lewisia*) should be tapped out evenly over the surface of the medium. Space larger seeds by hand.*

3 *Cover the seeds with a fine layer of medium, then top-dress with grit to protect the seeds and prevent the growth of mosses. Water in and label.*

4 *Prick out seedlings when they have 2 true leaves (see inset). Lift the seedlings carefully, handling them by the leaves only.*

5 *Fill pots with equal parts of soil-based potting mix and grit. Pot up the seedlings singly, firming with a dibber.*

6 *Top-dress with grit, water, and place the seedlings in light shade. Pot on the seedlings when the roots fill the pot.*

Aubrieta deltoidea
'Argenteo-variegata'

Viola
'Jackanapes'

Helianthemum
'Fire Dragon'

(continued on next page)

Softwood and greenwood cuttings

Softwood cuttings are taken from the nonflowering, leafy shoots of a plant during periods of active growth, usually in spring.

Greenwood cuttings are taken in early summer when growth has slowed down; although slightly riper than softwood cuttings, they require the same treatment.

Taking the cuttings

Take the cuttings early in the morning, when the shoots are fully turgid. For softwood cuttings select strong, young shoots that are soft and pliable, with no trace of woodiness or hardening. In contrast, greenwood cuttings may be just beginning to harden at the base. Take cuttings about 1–3in (2.5–7cm) in length, using a sharp knife. Place them immediately in a plastic bag to conserve moisture and to prevent them from wilting.

Inserting the cuttings

Trim the base of each cutting cleanly with a sharp knife just below a node (leaf joint) and remove the lower leaves. Pinch off any shoot tips that are soft, particularly if these are showing signs of wilting.

Fill pots with standard rooting medium and make holes for the cuttings with a small dibber. Insert each cutting into the medium by up to half its length so that the lowest leaf is just above the surface.

Label the cuttings and water with a fungicide solution, then place them in a closed propagator with gentle bottom heat, or in a mist propagation unit. Alternatively, seal the pots in plastic bags. Keep the cuttings in good light but out of direct sun, because otherwise the air and soil temperature may become too hot and the cuttings will wilt.

Remove dead and diseased cuttings with tweezers, since these may infect their healthy neighbors. Watering is seldom required until after rooting. Look for signs of new growth, and check for rooting by gently pulling at the cuttings. Once they are well rooted, pot them up.

Potting up

Water the rooted cuttings well, and gently slide them out of the pot. Carefully separate them before potting them up individually, using equal parts of soil mix and grit.

Top-dress with a ½in (1cm) layer of sharp grit. Water the cuttings thoroughly and return them to the propagator, keeping them out of direct sun. Keep the cuttings well watered. Once fresh growth appears, place the cuttings in a cold frame and harden them off carefully before planting them out.

Semiripe and ripewood cuttings

Semiripe cuttings are taken in mid- to late summer from nonflowering shoots of the current season's growth. The shoots offer distinct resistance to pressure when bent gently; they should be beginning to harden at the base. Ripewood cuttings are taken from evergreen plants during late summer and fall when the wood has fully ripened.

Taking the cuttings

The cuttings will vary in length with the plant concerned from ½ to 1½in (1 to 4cm) or more. Cut them from the parent plant using a sharp knife or pruners. Make a clean cut below a node and remove soft tissue at the tips. Remove the lower leaves and dip the ends into hormone rooting powder. Alternatively, take cuttings with a heel and trim the heel with a sharp knife to remove any snags.

Potting up

The following spring, when the cuttings have rooted, repot or pot up those in frames in equal parts soil mix and grit, or plant out in a nursery bed but only after danger of frost is passed. Water well.

Keep the rooted cuttings moist and sheltered from direct sun. Apply a liquid fertilizer in the growing season. Transplant them into their permanent positions in fall.

Small cuttings root best in pots of rooting medium, topped with a ½in (1cm) layer of fine sand. Make holes in the sand and insert the cuttings by one-third to one-half of their length. Label, water with a fungicide, and place in a propagator in a cool greenhouse. Check regularly for disease. Water sparingly and, as growth begins, apply dilute liquid fertilizer.

If large numbers of cuttings are taken, they can be inserted into a cold frame with drainage at the base. Fork over the soil in the frame and then add a mixture of 1 part peat or compost and 1 part grit; top with a 1in (2.5cm) layer of sand. After inserting the cuttings, water them and close the frame. Open the frame in mild weather. If there is a danger of frost, insulate the frame.

SOFTWOOD CUTTINGS

1 *In spring, choose young, nonflowering shoots (here, from* Gypsophila repens) *and take cuttings 1–3in (2.5–7cm) long. Put the cuttings in a plastic bag.*

2 *Trim off the base of the cuttings, and the lower leaves and soft tips (see inset). Fill a pot with moist medium, inserting the cuttings by up to half their length.*

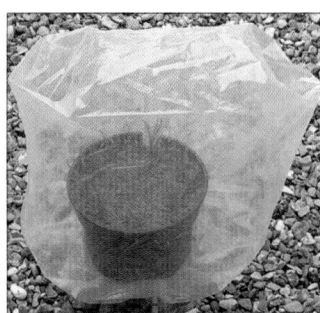

3 *Water and label the cuttings. Place the pot in a sealed plastic bag, keeping it in good light but out of direct sun.*

4 *When rooted, pot up the cuttings singly, holding them by the leaves only. Top-dress the pots, water well, and label.*

Leaf cuttings

This method is suitable for plants with fleshy leaves, such as *Haberlea*, *Ramonda*, and *Sedum*.

Using a sharp knife, cut healthy, strong, and relatively young leaves from the stem at their base. Prepare pots with a mixture of equal parts of standard rooting medium and sand. Insert each cutting at a 45° angle, so that it is just held in place by the soil mix. Enclose each pot in a plastic bag and, when the plantlets appear, pot them up individually.

Basal cuttings

Some plants, such as *Primula marginata* and its cultivars, may be propagated from basal cuttings. These are taken from young shoots at the base of the plant at, or just above, soil level. Basal cuttings are usually taken in spring but may also be taken in summer or fall.

Use a well-drained, commercial rooting medium, or a mix of equal parts of soil and peat or compost with 2 parts grit. Fill pots with medium, then firm.

Trim the base of each cutting cleanly just below a node. Make sure that the cutting is not hollow at the base. Remove the lower leaves and dip the base in hormone powder.

Insert one-third to one-half of each stem into the medium, keeping the leaves clear of the soil. Water well and place the pots in a shaded, closed propagator or cold frame. Rooting takes three to six weeks, after which the cuttings can be potted up individually or lined out in nursery beds or a cold frame to grow on.

BASAL CUTTINGS

Primula marginata

In spring, take cuttings 2–3in (5–7cm) long with new leaves and a short stem. Trim the base and remove the lower leaves, inserting the cuttings to the depth indicated.

ROCK PLANTS THAT MAY BE PROPAGATED BY CUTTINGS (CONT.)

Semiripe (cont.)
Helichrysum selago
Lepidium nanum
Lewisia
Linum arboreum

Polygala chamaebuxus

Lithodora diffusa
Origanum amanum,
  O. rotundifolium
Parahebe catarractae
Phlox 'Chatahoochee',
  P. subulata
Polygala
Rhododendron
Veronica

Dryas octopetala

Ripewood
Dryas
Eriogonum
Juniperus communis
  'Compressa'
Rosa
Salix

Rosette
Androsace
Armeria juniperifolia
Azorella trifurcata
Bolax gummifera
Draba
Helichrysum milfordiae
Jovibarba
Saxifraga
Sempervivum

Sempervivum tectorum

Leaf
Haberlea
Jancaea,
syn. *Jankaea*
Lewisia
Primula gracilipes
Ramonda
Sedum
Sempervivum

Selecting cutting material

For all types of cutting, always choose strong, healthy stems or leaves that show no sign of pests or diseases. Nonflowering shoots that are in active growth should be used. Except for basal cuttings, do not take the cuttings from the base of any plant, because this part may be weaker than elsewhere. Do not take all the cuttings from the same area on the parent plant, since this may make it look lopsided.

After taking the cuttings, immediately place them in a clean plastic bag to prevent any moisture loss. Many cuttings will root readily if they are inserted into pots of rooting medium with added grit. Alternatively, simply use washed river sand. Insert the cuttings at the depths indicated.

SEMIRIPE (Phlox)
In mid- to late summer, select shoots that are just hardening but not woody. Remove 1¼in (3cm) lengths, trimming to about ½in (1cm).

GREENWOOD (Erodium)
Take cuttings from the soft tips of new shoots in early summer. Remove 1–3in (2.5–7cm) lengths and trim them to about ½in (1cm).

ROSETTE (Saxifraga)
In early to midsummer, select new rosettes. Cut the rosettes about ½in (1cm) below the leaves. Trim each cleanly across the base.

RIPEWOOD (Dryas)
In late summer and fall, select new shoots and take cuttings that are about 1in (2.5cm) long. Trim them to about ½in (1cm) below the base of the leaves.

LEAF (Sedum)
Throughout the growing season, select mature leaves that are undamaged, cutting off selected leaves. Trim each cleanly across the base.

Division

Many alpines and rock garden plants can be successfully propagated by division. In some cases, division is the only possible method of increasing the stock if seed is rarely produced or the plant is sterile.

Plants that are particularly suitable for division include mat-forming species, which produce a mass of fibrous roots, and clump-forming plants that produce clusters of shoots that are readily separated.

ROCK PLANTS THAT MAY BE PROPAGATED BY IRISHMAN'S CUTTINGS

Achillea ageratifolia
Arenaria montana
Aurinia
Gentiana acaulis, G. verna
Phlox subulata
Primula auricula,
  P. marginata
Silene
Veronica peduncularis

ROCK PLANTS THAT MAY BE DIVIDED

Achillea ageratifolia
Alchemilla alpina,
  A. ellenbeckii
Allium sikkimense
Antennaria dioica
Arenaria montana
Artemisia schmidtiana 'Nana'
Campanula carpatica,
  C. cochleariifolia
Chiastophyllum oppositifolium
Gentiana acaulis,
  G. sino-ornata

Gentiana sino-ornata

Meconopsis
Primula allionii
Sagina subulata 'Aurea'

ROCK PLANTS THAT MAY BE PROPAGATED BY ROOT CUTTINGS

Anacyclus depressus
Carduncellus rhaponticoides
Centaurea pindicola
Gentiana lutea
Geranium
Meconopsis delavayi
Morisia monanthos
Papaver lateritium
Phlox mesoleuca
Primula denticulata
Pulsatilla
Roscoea cautleoides

A number of clump-forming plants have a tendency to die out at the center. These may be divided to rejuvenate them by replanting only the youngest, most vigorous pieces.

When to divide

Most plants are best divided in early spring, when new growth is just beginning. Do not divide plants in cold and frosty weather, or when the ground is frozen or waterlogged.

Plants can also be divided in early fall, which allows new roots to be made while the soil is still warm. Where hard winters are expected, spring division may be safer, since this allows a full growing season for establishment. Some plants, for example *Primula* and *Meconopsis*, should be divided immediately after flowering, when they enter a period of strong vegetative growth. They must be well watered after replanting until they are fully reestablished.

How to divide

Lift plants and shake off the soil. For large clumps, insert the tines of two garden forks back to back into the center of the clump; lever the plant into two halves. Tease these smaller clumps apart by hand or cut them

IRISHMAN'S CUTTINGS

1 *Lift the rooted shoots close to the base of the plant (here Veronica) and remove them with a sharp knife. Trim off sideshoots and straggly roots (see inset).*

2 *Pot up the cuttings individually. Place a little gritty soil mix in a pot, insert the cutting, then add more soil mix. Firm gently, water, and top-dress.*

with a sharp knife to produce a number of small pieces with healthy roots and growth buds. The older, woody, central part of the plant should be discarded.

If not replanting or potting up the divisions immediately, wrap them in plastic bags or moist burlap and store them out of direct sun. Divisions of most hardy plants can be replanted

HOW TO PROPAGATE BY DIVISION

1 *Plants with fibrous roots (here Gentiana acaulis) may be divided and replanted to provide new plants. Lift a clump of the parent plant and shake off the soil.*

2 *Using hand forks back to back, loosen the root mass and divide the clump into pieces. If necessary, cut away sections from the clump with a knife.*

3 *The plants should have a good root system. Replant them outdoors into their permanent positions, firming around the roots. Add top-dressing around the plants and water thoroughly with a fine spray.*

immediately into their permanent positions. If, however, plants are particularly precious, or the divisions are quite small, it may be safer to pot them up and place them in a cold frame until they are established before planting them out. Use 1 part low-fertility soil-based potting mix and 1 part grit or a lime-free mix for acidic-soil-lovers. If replanting in the open ground, make holes large enough to allow the roots to be spread out fully. Firm in and water well. Keep the soil moist until the plants are established.

Irishman's cuttings

These are essentially sideshoots that have already rooted. Thymes and other creeping rock plants produce this sort of cutting. The technique is particularly useful for plants with woody rootstocks that are not easily divided, or for those that naturally produce offsets or runners.

Before taking the cuttings, brush away surface soil from the base of the parent plant. Cut rooted pieces from the plant with a sharp knife and pot them up in equal parts of low-fertility soil-based potting mix and grit. Alternatively, plant them out in a cool, sheltered spot in the garden until well established.

Root cuttings

A limited number of alpines and rock garden plants, for example *Geranium sanguineum* and *Primula denticulata*, may be propagated from root cuttings. Take root cuttings from the healthiest-looking roots in either late fall or early winter, when the plants are dormant.

Selecting material

Choose a strong, healthy plant and lift it from the soil. Select young, vigorous roots and cut them from the parent plant. The cuttings should be about 2in (5cm) long. Cut the roots straight across at the top end (nearest the plant's stem) and use sloping cuts at the lower end (nearest the root tips). Wash the cuttings in tepid water and replant the parent stock immediately or, if old and straggly and no longer required, discard it.

Inserting the cuttings

Use pots at least 4in (10cm) deep. Put screening over the drainage holes and place over these a 1in (2.5cm) layer of low-fertility soil-based potting mix. Fill the pots with washed sand, then firm. Make several planting holes in each pot around the edges.

Insert the cuttings into the holes, with the straight ends uppermost and the tops level with the surface of the sand. Cuttings of plants with thin, wiry roots can be laid flat on the surface of the soil mix. Top-dress with fine grit. Label the pots, water thoroughly, and place them in a cold frame on a layer of grit or gravel or in a propagator. Close the frames in cold weather; otherwise, they should be ventilated freely.

Water the pots when new growth appears. When the new shoots are growing strongly, check that the cuttings have made new roots before potting them up: gently knock them out of their pots to inspect them.

Potting up rooted cuttings

Slide the cuttings out of their pots and separate them carefully. Pot them up singly, using low-fertility soil-based potting mix combined with an equal amount of sand. Instead of sand, a mix of peat or compost and sand can be used. Top-dress the pots

HOW TO PROPAGATE BY ROOT CUTTINGS

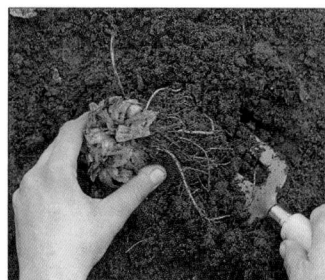

1 *In late fall or early winter, using a hand fork, carefully lift a healthy plant (*here* Primula denticulata) *with a well-developed root system.*

2 *Wash the roots clean of soil, then select thick, healthy roots for the cuttings. Using a sharp knife, cut off selected roots close to the crown of the plant.*

3 *Prepare 2in (5cm) lengths of root, cutting each one straight at the thicker end (*closest to the parent plant*) and angled at the lower end.*

4 *Place a layer of soil mix in the base of a pot, then fill almost to the brim with sharp sand. Insert the cuttings so that straight ends are just level with the sand surface.*

5 *Cover the sand with a ¹/₂in (1cm) layer of grit. Water and label the cuttings, then place the pot in a propagator or on the greenhouse bench.*

with ¹/₂in (1cm) of sharp sand or grit. Water and then place outside, out of direct sun. Leave until the new plants are established, watering as required.

Scooping rosettes

Plants that grow quickly or form rosettes, for example *Primula denticulata*, may be propagated *in situ* in early spring from root cuttings by scooping out the rosettes with a sharp knife to expose the top of the rootstock. Select strong-growing rosettes and brush the tops of the roots with fungicidal powder to prevent gray mold/*Botrytis* (see p.646); cover them with a thin layer of horticultural sharp sand.

Shoots should soon appear on each root apex. When the shoots are about 1–2in (2.5–5cm) tall, lift the clump carefully with a hand fork. Separate the clump into individual small plants that have healthy-looking, vigorous shoots and roots, pulling them apart by hand or dividing them with a sharp knife.

Pot up the young plants to grow on, using equal parts of potting mix and horticultural sand. Water thoroughly, and place outside in a shady site. Keep moist and plant out the young plants when their roots have filled the pots.

HOW TO SCOOP ROSETTES

1 *Scoop out the live crowns of rosette-forming plants (*here* Primula denticulata) *with a sharp knife, so that the tops of the roots are visible (*see inset*).*

2 *Dust the exposed roots with fungicidal powder (*see inset*) to protect them from molds and fungi. Lightly cover with sharp horticultural sand.*

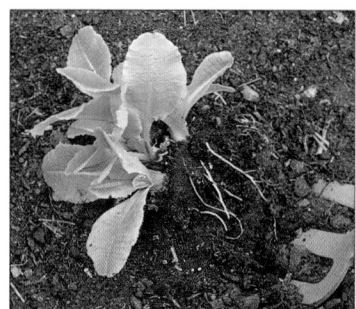

3 *When new shoots appear from the roots, lift the entire clump, using a hand fork or trowel. Take care not to damage the new roots.*

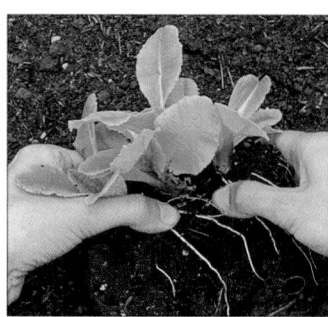

4 *Divide the clump into individual plants, each with one shoot and well-developed roots. Pot them up using equal parts of soil mix and sand.*

Alpine houses and frames

SOME high-altitude alpines grow well in the open garden in temperate climates, provided that their specific requirements of situation and soil are satisfied. Most, however, will perform considerably better if they are grown under cover. Many alpines bloom in late winter and very early spring when, if left in the open, their delicate flowers may be damaged by inclement weather, eaten by slugs or snails, or otherwise ruined in some way.

In an alpine house, plants are protected from winter moisture, cold, drying winds, and sudden, sharp cold, as well as from most pests. This enables a far wider range of alpines and rock plants to be grown, either in pots or in ground-level or raised beds, to provide an eye-catching and lasting display.

USING AN ALPINE HOUSE
Part of the house may be used to grow young plants (foreground) in beds supported by brick pillars.

Using an alpine house

An alpine house is a cold or cool/frost-free greenhouse (see p.567) designed for growing and displaying alpines and rock plants under controlled conditions. Often, half of the house is used for growing the plants, and the other half for displaying them. Alternatively, the plants can be grown in cold frames and brought temporarily into the house for display. Alpine houses are not practical in areas with very cold winters or long, very hot summers.

Displaying the plants
Alpines can be displayed in pots simply placed on the staging or, more commonly, plunged up to their rims in a layer of sand. Plunging keeps roots cool and moist and reduces temperature fluctuations, while allowing easy irrigation of plants that dislike overhead watering. Specially built display beds are an attractive option. Create miniature rock gardens in the alpine house, either waist-high where staging is strong enough to support the weight, or at ground level. These may have some permanent planting as well as areas of sand or sandy soil mix into which different plants can be plunged, according to season. Lightweight tufa rocks may be incorporated and planted up to enhance this type of display.

Siting the alpine house
Choose a firm, level site away from the shade of trees, fences, walls, and tall buildings if possible. Siting the alpine house on a north–south axis is ideal but any open, sunny position is

AN ALPINE HOUSE DISPLAY
A wide range of rock plants may be grown in pots and attractively displayed in raised sand beds in an alpine house.

acceptable. Always avoid hollows where cold air forms frost pockets, and do not site it in exposed, windy situations. Try to position the alpine house where it will harmonize with other garden features, perhaps even using it as a focal point. For further information on greenhouses, ventilation, shading, and staging, see GREENHOUSES AND FRAMES, pp.569, 570, and 573.

Using frames

Frames should be sited near the alpine house, where they may be used to protect a range of choice plants from climatic extremes, as an overflow area, or for storage when plants are not in flower. They are

very useful for bulbs that need to be kept dry when dormant, or for plants that will not tolerate the very hot conditions that may arise in summer. Frames incorporate a top sash that must be opened as required to provide good ventilation; a standard sash frame is suitable but other types are available. The sashes can be removed in summer, but they should be kept on if the frame contains dormant bulbs. Those plants that do not tolerate direct summer sun can be protected by covering the frame with mesh shading (see GREENHOUSES AND FRAMES, "Meshes and fabrics," p.570). Pots in a frame are usually plunged in a material such as washed builder's sand over a layer of stones to give them good drainage and hold them upright.

CARE OF ALPINES AND DWARF BULBS AFTER FLOWERING

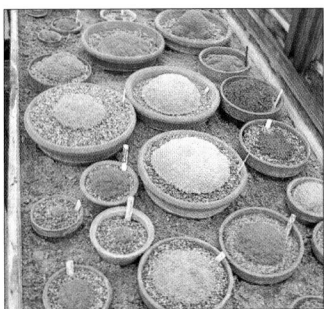

ALPINES INDOORS
After flowering, pots of alpines needing careful watering (here Dionysia spp.) should be plunged in sand under cover.

ALPINES OUTDOORS
Alpines that tolerate variable summer weather conditions, such as saxifrages, may be plunged in open cold frames after flowering.

BULBS INDOORS
Pots of dwarf bulbs that have finished flowering may be kept dry by plunging in sand or gravel under benches.

PROTECTING FLOWERING ALPINES
Alpines coming into flower may be grown in outdoor frames before bringing them into the alpine house for display.

Alpines in pots

Growing alpines in pots ensures that special watering, soil mix, or fertility requirements can be provided for individual plants.

Plastic and clay pots

Although plastic pots are suitable for growing alpines and retain moisture well, clay pots are more traditional – important if the plants are to be exhibited. The soil mix in plastic pots dries out more slowly than in clay pots, so take care not to overwater the plants. Clean and sterilize all pots before use: sterilants based on dilute solutions of household bleach are suitable, mixing 9 parts water to 1 part bleach.

Soil mixes

All alpines need a freely draining soil mix and benefit from the presence of grit, perlite, coarse vermiculite, or even styrofoam bits in the mix. Even moisture-loving plants will not tolerate stagnant conditions.

Most species grow well in soil-based potting mix combined with an equal amount of grit. Those from high alpine habitats of scree and rock-face crevices, such as some *Androsace* species and other cushion-forming plants, need a less fertile and more freely draining mix if they are to retain their neat, natural habit. In rich soil mixes, they quickly become soft and lush and are then more prone to attack by pests and diseases. For these plants use a mix of up to 3 parts grit to 1 part soil-based mix. Introduce plants to these lean mixes when they are young, since they may not adapt easily if they have been potted on from a more fertile medium.

A number of species, usually ones from woodland habitats, or those that occur in organic pockets in rocky habitats, such as *Haberlea* and *Ramonda*, require well-drained soil mixes that are rich in organic matter. For these, a mix of 1 part each of soil-based potting mix and grit, with 2 parts leaf mold, compost, or peat will be suitable. Take care to check on the individual needs of each plant in order to select an appropriate soil mix, and ensure that all ingredients for acidic-soil-loving plants are free of alkalinity.

Top-dressings

After planting up the pots (see right), top-dress them with a layer of grit or stone chips to enhance the plant's appearance, to keep the area around the neck of the plant well drained, and to prevent the growth of mosses and liverworts. Use a top-dressing that is appropriate to the pH requirements of the plant; for example, limestone chips may be used for alkalinity-loving species, or granite grit for acidic-soil-loving plants.

Some small, cushion-forming alpines are very sensitive to the presence of water around their necks so, as well as top-dressing with grit, prop small wedges of rock beneath their cushions in order to keep them clear of the surface.

Repotting

When a plant has outgrown its pot, transfer it carefully into a slightly larger pot, disturbing the root ball as little as possible. Pot on herbaceous and shrubby plants in spring and summer, when they are growing strongly; bulbs should be potted on when they are dormant. Plant to the same level as in the previous pot, firm in fresh soil mix, and then add a new layer of top-dressing.

Water well after potting by standing the pot in at least 1–2in (2.5–5cm) of water until the top of the soil mix becomes moist. Then remove the pot to avoid the risk of root rot.

Planting in beds

The beds may be at ground level or raised 3ft (1m) high. Raised beds allow plants to be tended and viewed

REPOTTING A SAXIFRAGE

1 The roots of this saxifrage can be seen growing through the drainage hole at the bottom of the pot. The plant is potbound and should be repotted.

2 Choose a pot that is one size bigger than the one that the plant is growing in. If you wish, use pot shards and gravel to take up space at the bottom of the pot.

3 Arrange the pot shards curved-side up over the drainage hole, then cover with a layer of gravel.

4 Remove the plant from its pot by tapping sharply on the base to loosen the root ball. Tease out the roots a little to encourage them to penetrate the new soil mix.

5 Add some soil mix to the correct level (so that the neck of the plant is at the same level as in the original pot), then fill in with soil mix.

6 Spread the gravel top-dressing over the surface of the soil mix, taking care to tuck it under the collar of the plant to keep it sharply drained.

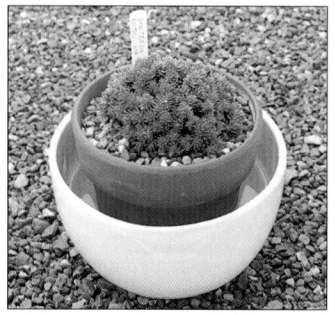

7 Place the pot in a bowl of water and leave it until the soil mix and gravel top-dressing appear damp.

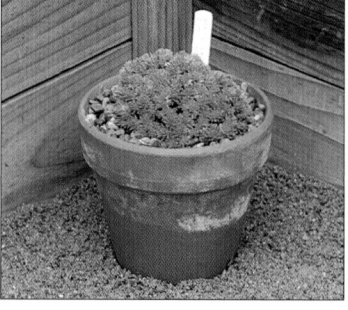

8 Remove the pot and place it on a layer of sand in a cold frame, where any excess moisture can easily drain off. This will prevent any risk of root rot.

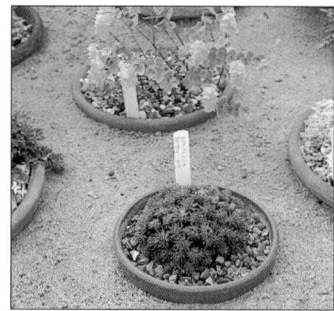

9 The repotted plant can then be plunged in sand in a cold frame or bed to grow on.

REMOVING DEAD LEAVES

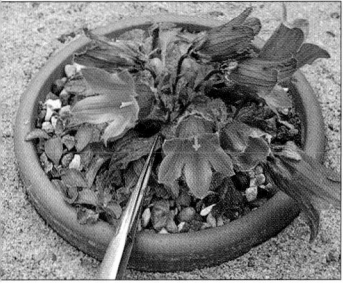

Tweezers should be used regularly to remove any brown or withered leaves from alpine plants such as this Campanula pilosa.

more easily and are especially useful for physically impaired gardeners. The staging must drain well and be solidly constructed to bear the weight of the bed (see also GREENHOUSES AND FRAMES, "Raised beds," p.572).

Use a soil mix of 3 parts good sterilized garden soil, 2 parts coarse fibrous peat or compost, and 2 parts sharp sand or grit. Add rocks to the bed to create a miniature rock garden. Tufa is particularly useful because it is lightweight and very moisture-retentive, and because plants can be grown directly in it. Plant out alpines in the bed, avoiding species that are invasive and free-seeding, but leave some gaps for plunging a succession of seasonal, potgrown specimens. Ferns and other shade-loving species may be grown under a raised bed.

Routine maintenance

Alpines have specialized growing requirements and need considerable attention throughout the growing season. Plants that are regularly repotted rarely need additional fertilizing, but when fertilizers are used, be sure that they are low in nitrogen – high nitrogen levels will lead to soft, lush growth that is uncharacteristic of alpines and more prone to pests and diseases.

Ventilation

Ventilating surfaces must occupy at least 25 percent of the glass area, since the aim is to provide the maximum possible air circulation at all times. In spring and summer, the vents and the greenhouse door can remain open permanently, unless there is strong wind or heavy rain. Use a screen of small-diameter mesh over vents and doors to keep out cats and birds. During heavy rain and windy weather, close the vents on the receiving side to avoid drip on the foliage and to reduce strong drafts

that may damage foliage and flowers. In severe winds, it is safest to close all vents and doors.

In mild winter weather, open the vents fully (unless it is windy or raining) but close them before nightfall to retain any residual warmth. In very cold weather, allow temperatures in the alpine house to rise gradually before ventilating carefully if at all; on bright, sunny days above freezing, however, open the vents as soon as possible to prevent the temperature from rising too rapidly. In damp, foggy weather, close up the house completely to keep out cold, damp air, and use a small fan to maintain air circulation.

Temperature

Shading will be necessary during sunny weather, from late spring to fall, to avoid scorching tender, new growth and to help reduce temperatures. Do not use heavy shading since this might cause etiolation or lopsided leaning of plants toward the available light source. In hot weather, frequently damp down (thoroughly wet) the house floor to reduce temperatures and maintain atmospheric humidity; plants may be lightly misted with cool water during sultry evenings.

Heating must be used to stop the pots from freezing in severe weather. A method of heating that does not produce excessive fumes or moisture is best (see GREENHOUSES AND FRAMES, "Heating," p.568).

Hygiene

Remove dead foliage and faded flowers regularly to reduce the risk of fungal attack. Check the plants for pests and diseases, and treat any outbreaks promptly (see PLANT PROBLEMS, pp.633–61). Always keep the floor of the house clean to

minimize the risk of diseases, and make sure that the glass is clean so that plants receive maximum light.

Watering

Water regularly throughout the season, especially on sunny spring and summer days, when water loss is rapid. If plants are allowed to dry out between waterings, growth may be severely checked and flower buds may shrivel. For pots standing on staging, water from above but avoid splashing the foliage. Plunged clay pots derive moisture from the surrounding material but may need additional watering in warm periods. For plants that are sensitive to moisture on their foliage, water the plunge medium around the pots.

As fall approaches, reduce watering as plants prepare for dormancy. During winter, alpines need to be kept dry but not dust dry (for plunged pots, the plunge medium should be just damp to the touch).

Winter maintenance

A spell of clear, dry weather during late summer is a good time to store the plants in a frame and clean the alpine house (see GREENHOUSES AND FRAMES, "Routine maintenance," p.577). Clean and top up the sand or grit on beds and renew labels, then transfer pots back from the frame.

Exhibiting

Alpines for showing should be in the best possible condition on exhibition day. No matter how perfect the plant, it will lose marks if poorly presented in a less than scrupulously clean pot, or if top-dressings are thin or show evidence of algal growth. Remove all evidence of weeds, pests, and diseases. Check plants for dead, discol-

TRANSPORTING PLANTS

When transporting fragile plants (here Fritillaria uva-vulpis), *make a tripod from split stakes bound at the top with twine, and tie in stems.*

ored, or misshapen leaves and faded flowers, and remove these carefully with tweezers.

Clay pots should be scrubbed clean with a wire brush or scourer. Alternatively, they may be double-potted: insert the specimen in its pot into a larger, new pot, filling any space between the pots and covering the inner rim with top-dressing. Renew all top-dressings with materials appropriate to the plant's natural habitat, then relabel. Support tall, fragile plants during travel with tripods of split stakes. Water plants thoroughly the day before the show and allow them to drain before packing them for transportation. Carry extra top-dressing to renew any lost in transit.

PREPARING PLANTS FOR EXHIBITION

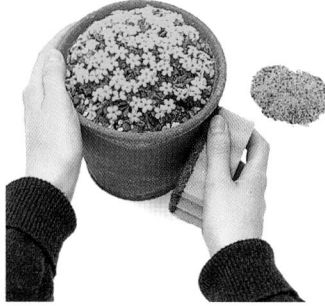

1 *Use fine sand together with a wire brush or scouring pad to clean the outside of clay pots. This will remove any algae or fertilizer salts.*

2 *Replenish the top-dressing. For this* Dionysia aretioides *the medium is coarse gravel, but stone chips, grit, or pine needles may be used, depending on the plant.*

3 *Add new, clearly written labels. Pack the pots carefully in a tray using newspaper to hold them steady, and carry extra top-dressing for last-minute renewal.*

CHAPTER

10

THE WATER GARDEN

There is a style of water feature for every garden, whether it is a formal pool graced by waterlilies and the bright gleam of goldfish, a trickling stream bordered by ferns, or a simple pond reflecting a sculptural clump of irises. Even the smallest and quietest patio garden can be brought to life by the murmur of running water and the dancing patterns of light.

A water garden provides a habitat for plants as well as wildlife, including frogs, dragonflies, and perhaps water birds. Water may be either restful or exciting: still water is valued for its reflections and tranquility, while moving water, whether in the form of a classical fountain or a rushing waterfall, adds a delightful sound and a dynamic vitality.

Designing a water garden

UNLIKE any other element in the garden, water brings an ever-changing pattern of reflections, sounds, and movement that is particularly appealing. Even when frozen, its surface creates contrasts of color and texture. A pond is a popular form of water feature but there are others: a waterfall, fountain, or watercourse, for instance.

A water feature allows you to grow plants that do not thrive in other conditions, from the floating frogbit (*Hydrocharis morsus-ranae*) and water hyacinth (*Eichhornia crassipes*) to the bog garden candelabra primroses (*Primula* spp.).

When deciding which type of water feature to create, bear in mind the size and style of the garden. If large and informal, a meandering watercourse may be suitable, while in an enclosed urban garden, a raised formal pool might be appropriate. Water may even be included in a garden for children in the form of an attractive bubble fountain, in which the water splashes over stones and is recirculated without forming an area of any great depth.

A NATURALISTIC WATER GARDEN
In an informal or semiwild garden, a gently meandering stream provides a lush, cool area by which to sit and relax. Clouds of pink rhododendrons add both height and color to the design, while marginal plantings of bright yellow Iris pseudacorus, *ferns, and rushes form a transition between the stream and the garden.*

Siting a pond

Exploit the reflective quality of water by siting a pond where it mirrors an eye-catching feature – a specimen plant or statue, perhaps. It may help to lay a reflective sheet in the proposed site to give an idea of reflections to be seen during the day and evening; check it from major viewpoints such as the house and patio.

An open, sunny position, away from buildings and overhanging trees, provides the best conditions in which to grow most water plants.

If planning to create a pond on land prone to flooding, check that there is no danger of fertilizer or pesticide residues leaching into the water from an adjacent vegetable garden or farmland. These substances invariably affect aquatic life adversely. Direct potential overflows to a suitable drainage system. Land with a high water table may cause problems because, in very wet periods, water pressure from below may push a pond liner out of shape.

Do not site a pond in a frost pocket or in a very exposed position, since this restricts the range of plants that may be grown and protection may need to be provided in winter.

Informal ponds

In an informal garden, a natural sunken pond may look most appropriate. Usually, this is in an irregular, curved shape, bordered with natural materials such as sod or stones to link it with the garden. The water surface is, however, only part of the total design; the inclusion of marginal and moisture-loving plants around the pond

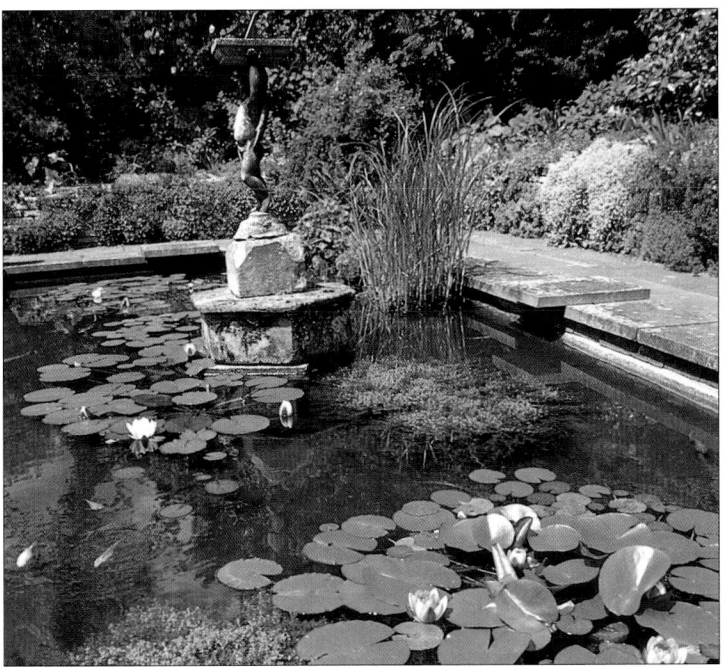

A FORMAL POOL
Waterlilies (Nymphaea) *bring elegance and color to a rectangular pool. A sundial links the informality of the plants to the pool's formal margins.*

to soften or hide its outline completely, helps create a lush and refreshing feature.

As when planting in a border or bed, consider how the plants will combine to create complementary and contrasting associations of color, texture, and form.

Formal pools

In contrast to the natural feeling of an informal pond, a formal pool makes a much bolder statement. It may be raised or sunken and is usually of a regular, geometric design. As a rule, less space is devoted to planting than in an informal pond, although plants with floating leaves and flowers (e.g., waterlilies) are often included. Sculptural plants such as certain ferns, grown next to the pool, provide attractive reflections. A fountain or waterspout to complement the style of the pool can be an ornamental addition.

Far from being disguised, the edge of the pool may form an important feature, perhaps made of attractive paving. If the pool is raised, a wide edge can form a seat that is particularly suitable for elderly or impaired people.

In many cases formal pools are sited so that they form a striking focal point in the garden: for example, at the main axis of paths, or where they may be conveniently viewed and enjoyed from the windows or terrace of the house.

Fountains

The style and size of a fountain should be considered in the context of the surrounding water and the overall design of the garden. Often used in a formal garden as a focal point, a fountain is also invaluable for adding height to a design, and for its dynamic contributions of sound, movement, and light. A fountain is particularly dramatic if lit at night.

A cobblestone or bubble fountain, in which water bubbles over stones into a small underground reservoir, looks more informal than a standard fountain and is ideal in a garden where children play.

As well as being ornamental, fountains also provide a practical function: the splashing action oxygenates the water, and this is beneficial to fish. Most water plants do not flourish in disturbed water, however, so they should not be grown close to a fountain.

Waterspouts

While a fountain or waterfall might be too large in an average garden, a waterspout can provide the pleasure of running water in the smallest garden or even in a conservatory. There are many styles, from the classical lion's head or gargoyle above a pool to a simple bamboo pipe trickling water over stones.

A waterspout is usually attached to a wall, with a pump and pipe similar to those used for a watercourse. The pump circulates water from a pool or reservoir to the rear of the spout and out through the mouth.

Streams, watercourses, and waterfalls

Few gardens have a natural stream or waterfall, but it is possible to create a circulating watercourse spilling out into a pool or underground reservoir. Making a watercourse or waterfall is an attractive way of exploiting a change of level in the garden. It may be used to link parts of the garden as well as providing points of interest between levels.

In an informal garden, a watercourse may be made to look more natural by edging it with rocks or stones and moisture-loving plants such as ferns and irises. Ornamentals that have large leaves, for example *Rheum palmatum*, are particularly valuable for watercourses made from liners or preformed units since they help disguise the edges.

Bog and wildlife areas

In an informal or naturalistic design, a bog garden makes an attractive feature. Most appropriate next to ponds, bog gardens provide a gradual and natural transition from aquatic to moisture-loving plants and ideal conditions for wildlife.

AN INFORMAL WATERCOURSE
A terrace of dams formed from thick slabs of stone creates cascades of water that spill into a shallow, cobblestone-lined pool. Overhanging plants such as ivies (Hedera)*, Japanese maple* (Acer palmatum)*, and primroses* (Primula) *help break up the rigid line of the stone. The meandering path of the watercourse also gives the design an appealing informality and charm.*

TRADITIONAL WATERSPOUT
A waterspout is attractive even in a tiny garden. Here, mellow stone complements this traditional spout.

Bog gardens
Creating a bog garden is a better way of using waterlogged land than struggling against nature by trying to drain it. While the ground next to a man-made pond is unlikely to be wet enough to provide suitable conditions for growing bog plants, using a liner under the soil will retain sufficient moisture.

Bog gardens bring freshness in late summer when many other plants are showing stress from drought. However, most bog plants die back naturally after frost, so they do not provide great interest in winter.

Wildlife ponds
A water feature increases diversity in a wildlife garden, providing a habitat for songbirds, waterfowl,

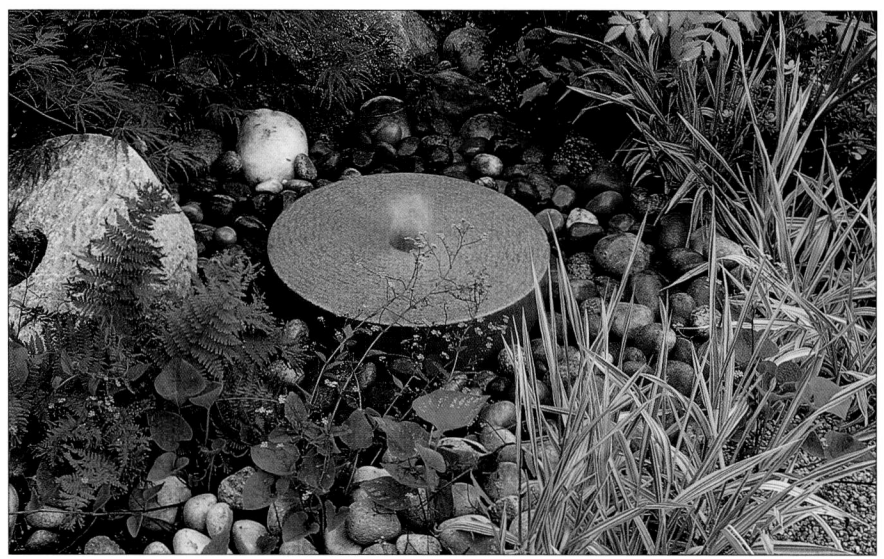

FLUID
ATTRACTION
Reservoir features such as this textured fiberglass millstone fountain create a source of movement and sound. Such simple, child-safe water features work well not only in a small garden but also as a surprise element in a much larger one.

frogs, and an enormous range of insects. Limiting the planting to only native species may attract more wildlife, although some native plants can prove invasive. The inclusion of some exotic ornamentals can make the pond a decorative feature as well. Informal ponds with muddy bottoms and shallowly sloping edges interspersed with large, flat stones are particularly suitable, providing ideal conditions for amphibians.

Container water gardens

In a small garden or patio, or where major construction work is impractical, it is still possible to have a pond by using an appropriate ornamental container, such as a sealed and lined half barrel. A container is suitable for growing only a few selected plants. Remember, however, that fish may not be able to survive in it outdoors over winter. If using a metal container, it should be sealed with a waterproof paint or liner; otherwise, it may prove to be harmful to both plants and fish.

Plants for the water garden

In any water garden, plants are vital to the design. Lush foliage and flowers enhance the pond and link it with the rest of the garden, while certain plants help maintain clear water and, in the case of oxygenators, provide good conditions for fish.

Plants suitable for a water garden range from those that thrive in deep water to those requiring moist soil only around their root tips. They are

usually grouped into six categories: oxygenators, deep-water plants, surface floaters, marginals, bog plants, and moisture-loving plants.

Oxygenators
Lagarosiphon major (syn. *Elodea crispa*) and *Myriophyllum* species are examples of oxygenators – submerged, fast-growing plants that will help clean and oxygenate the water. In sunny weather, submerged algae may turn a new pond green within a week or two of installation. Oxygenating plants, however, compete for the dissolved mineral salts on which algae thrive and starve them out so that the water eventually becomes clear once more. Such oxy-genators are essential if you are plan-ning to keep fish in the pond.

Deep-water plants
These flourish in a depth range of 12–36in (30–90cm). This category includes plants such as *Aponogeton* and *Hydrocleys*, with waterlilies (*Nymphaea*) forming the largest group (see pp.280–81). Apart from their ornamental value, their floating leaves also help reduce algae by cutting down the amount of light penetrating the water.

Surface floaters
Floating plants, such as *Trapa natans* and *Azolla caroliniana*, perform a similar function to the deep-water plants, especially during the establishment phase. It is vital not to let them cover too much of the water surface, however, since oxygenators and aquatic animals may suffer if there is not enough light.

Marginals
Marginal plants are grown at the edges of pools in shallow water usually about 3–6in (7–15cm) deep,

but occasionally up to 12in (30cm). Many of these plants are extremely attractive, such as *Iris laevigata* 'Variegata' with fans of green- and cream-striped leaves and lavender-blue flowers. They are valuable in an informal pond for breaking up the outline. In a pond installed to attract wildlife, marginals provide cover for wildfowl and various small creatures. Some species such as *Mentha aquatica* and *Veronica beccabunga* also help oxygenate the water.

Bog plants
Bog-loving plants such as *Lysichiton* or some *Caltha* species thrive in water-logged soil and can withstand occasional flooding. Under a bog-plant heading, nursery catalogs may include plants that grow in moist or even wet soil but do not tolerate a soil that is constantly waterlogged. When ordering, check with the nursery to make sure that any plants you

may have in mind for your bog garden can tolerate moderate to high water levels around their roots.

Moisture-loving plants
These thrive in soils that contain extra moisture without being water-logged. Moisture-lovers include many herbaceous perennials, such as *Astilbe*, *Ligularia*, and *Primula florindae*. They all associate well with marginal plants in the areas surrounding natural, informal ponds, where the growing conditions are ideal for them.

Planting associations
Create a varied and attractive display by mixing plants with different heights and growth habits around the pond. Similar design principles should be applied as for planting in the rest of the garden to develop a successful design with a diversity of shapes and forms (see also "Principles of planting," pp.42–5). Site *Gunnera manicata*, for example, so that its immense, platterlike leaves tower over the jutting swords of *Acorus calamus*. Use plants at the edge of the pond to act as a foil for floating plants or deep marginals –for instance, an island of waterlilies such as *Nymphaea alba* with its pure white blooms would be beautifully offset by a drift of ostrich ferns (*Matteuccia struthiopteris*).

Plants with contrasting colors and textures also provide the potential for some spectacular combinations. For example, the upright, scarlet flower spikes of *Lobelia cardinalis* would form a fine contrast with the heart-shaped, blue-gray leaves of *Hosta sieboldiana*.

Plan the planting to supply interest throughout the seasons. Including evergreen foliage plants such as

BOG GARDEN
The boggy ground next to a pond is ideal for plants such as Primula bulleyana *and* Iris laevigata. Phormium tenax *gives the design its focus.*

Bergenia at the pond edges provides continuity of form and color, while other types of plants – from the golden flowers of the marsh marigold (*Caltha palustris*) in spring to the summer-long display of the water forget-me-not (*Myosotis scorpioides*) with its delicate blue flowers – may be used for creating a changing seasonal display.

Fish

While most ornamental fish live in harmony with aquatic plant life, the inclusion of larger specimen fish necessitates certain precautions in pond design and planting. Oxygenating plants provide oxygen only in daylight, and fish may suffer from stress during warm, sultry nights unless some additional oxygen is provided – for example, from the water agitation created by the splashing of a fountain.

If planning to keep large koi, remember that they may disturb the roots of waterlilies and other deep-water plants, so anchor the soil over the roots with large stones. Pools for these fish should be at least 3ft (1m) deep and have vertical sides projecting above the surface so that the carp cannot leap out. Goldfish and orfe are easier to manage; orfe are ideal decorative fish that enjoy shallow water and feed on any insect larvae present. In the wildlife garden, native species such as sunfish may be suitable and less damaging to tadpole populations.

Planter's guide to water plants

SHALLOW MARGINALS
(6in/15cm depth of water)
Acorus gramineus,
  A. g. 'Variegatus'
Alisma parviflora

Calla palustris

Calla palustris
Caltha leptosepala,
  C. palustris, C. p. 'Alba',
  C. p. 'Flore Plena'
Carex elata 'Aurea',
  C. pendula, C. riparia
Colocasia esculenta
Cotula coronopifolia
Cyperus 'Haspan',
  C. involucratus, C. longus
Damasonium alisma
Decodon verticillatus
Eriophorum angustifolium,
  E. latifolium
Houttuynia cordata,
  H. c. 'Chamaeleon', *syn. H. c.*
  'Variegata', *H. c.* 'Plena'
Hydrocleys nymphoides

Hydrocleys nymphoides

Iris laevigata, I. versicolor
Juncus effusus, J. e. f. spiralis,
  J. e. 'Vittatus', *J. ensifolius*
Lobelia paludosa
Lysichiton americanus,
  L. camtschatcensis
Mentha aquatica
Mimulus cardinalis,
  M. cupreus, M. guttatus,
  M. ringens
Myosotis scorpioides,
  M. s. 'Mermaid'
Peltandra alba
Persicaria amphibium
Sagittaria latifolia, S. sagittifolia,
  S. s. 'Flore Pleno'
Sparganium minimum
Typha minima
Zizania aquatica

DEEP MARGINALS
(12in/30cm depth of water)
Acorus calamus,
  A. c. 'Variegatus'
Alisma lanceolatum,
  A. plantago-aquatica
Butomus umbellatus
Cyperus papyrus
Glyceria maxima 'Variegata'
Hottonia palustris
Iris pseudacorus
Nelumbo lutea, N. nucifera 'Alba
  Grandiflora', *N. n.* 'Alba
  Striata', *N. n.* 'Rosa Plena'
Phragmites australis,
  P. a. 'Variegata'
Pontederia cordata, P. lanceolata
Ranunculus lingua 'Grandiflora'
Saururus cernuus
Scirpus lacustris,
  S. l. subsp. *tabernaemontani*
  'Albescens', *S. l.* subsp. *t.* 'Zebrinus'
Sparganium erectum,
  syn. *S. ramosum*
Thalia dealbata, T. geniculata
Typha angustifolia, T. latifolia
  'Variegata', *T. stenophylla,*
  syn. *T. laxmannii*
Zantedeschia aethiopica
  'Crowborough'

DEEP-WATER PLANTS
Aponogeton distachyos
Euryale ferox
Nuphar advena, N. lutea
Nymphaea (most spp.)
Nymphoides indica, N. peltata
Orontium aquaticum
Victoria amazonica, V. regia

SUBMERGED OXYGENATORS
Callitriche hermaphroditica,
  syn. *C. autumnalis*
Ceratophyllum demersum
Ceratopteris thalictroides
Elodea canadensis
Fontinalis antipyretica
Hydrocleys parviflora
Lagarosiphon major,
  syn. *Elodea crispa*
Myriophyllum aquaticum,
  syn. *M. proserpinacoides*

Potamogeton crispus
Preslia cervina
Tillaea recurva

SURFACE FLOATERS
Azolla caroliniana, A. filiculoides
Ceratopteris pteroides
Eichhornia azurea, E. crassipes
Hydrocharis morsus-ranae
Lemna trisulca
Limnobium spongia,
  L. stoloniferum
Nymphoides aquatica
Phyllanthus fluitans
Pistia stratiotes
Riccia fluitans

Pistia
stratiotes

Salvinia auriculata,
  S. natans
Stratiotes aloides
Trapa natans
Utricularia minor, U. vulgaris
Wolffia arrhiza

BOG AND MOISTURE-LOVING PLANTS
Alnus glutinosa, A. incana
Anemone rivularis
Aruncus dioicus 'Kneiffii'
Arundo donax 'Variegata'
Astilbe x arendsii, A. chinensis,
  A. simplicifolia
Astilboides tabularis
Cardamine pratensis
Cephalanthus occidentalis
Cimicifuga americana,
  C. racemosa
Cornus alba
Eupatorium purpureum
Euphorbia palustris
Filipendula rubra, F. ulmaria
Gunnera chilensis, G. manicata
Hosta (most spp.)
Ilex verticillata
Iris ensata, I. sibirica
Leucojum aestivum
Ligularia clivorum, L. przewalskii
Lobelia cardinalis, L. fulgens

Magnolia virginiana
Osmunda regalis
Parnassia palustris
Peltiphyllum peltatum
Persicaria amplexicaule,
  P. bistorta, P. campanulata
Phalaris arundinacea
Phragmites communis
Primula alpicola, P. denticulata,
  P. florindae, P. helodoxa,
  P. japonica, P. pulverulenta,
  P. rosea, P. secundiflora,
  P. sikkimensis
Rheum alexandrae, R. palmatum,
  R. p. 'Atrosanguineum'
Rodgersia aesculifolia, R. pinnata,
  R. podophylla
Salix alba, S. babylonica,
  S. daphnoides, S. matsudana
  'Tortuosa'
Scrophularia auriculata
  'Variegata'
Senecio smithii
Taxodium distichum
Trollius x cultorum,
  T. europaeus,
  T. ledebourii

Trollius
europaeus

RECOMMENDED PLANTS FOR AQUARIUMS
Alternanthera philoxeroides
Anubias barteri
Aponogeton crispus,
  A. madagascariensis
Bacopa monnieri
Cabomba caroliniana
Cryptocoryne ciliata
Echinodorus bleheri,
  E. maior
Hygrophila polysperma
Ludwigia arcuata
Luronium natans
Myriophyllum hippuroides
Nymphoides humboldtiana
Potamogeton crispus
Salvinia natans
Utricularia exoleta,
  U. vulgaris
Vallisneria gigantea

Waterlilies

THE elegant floating cups and lush foliage of waterlilies (*Nymphaea*) are a graceful addition to any water garden, whether in an informal rural setting or a formal city courtyard. The flower forms vary from open and starlike to goblet-shaped, peonylike blooms, with colors ranging from the simple purity of white or cream to striking shades of red, yellow, or even blue. Some are offset by dark purplish green leaves, while others have foliage that is attractively mottled. Certain species have richly perfumed flowers; these are best grown in a raised pool, where their scent may be more easily enjoyed.

While most waterlilies bloom in the daytime, some tropical cultivars such as 'Missouri' and 'Red Flare' open at dusk – these are best enhanced by complementary lighting to create a bold display after dark. Native to tropical and subtropical zones, these may be grown in temperate regions in a conservatory pool or outdoors in hot weather.

For best results, waterlilies need several hours of full sun each day and should be grown in an open, sunny part of the pond; otherwise, they develop a mass of leaves but few blooms. They also prefer calm water: grow the lilies well away from a fountain or waterfall so that they are not disturbed by the movement. Tropical species usually grow more quickly than hardy ones and require high light intensity, ample fertilizer, and warm water at a minimum of 68°F (20°C).

In addition to being decorative, waterlilies help keep the water clear because their large, spreading leaves create shade, thereby helping control algal growth.

HARDY (H) AND TROPICAL (T) WATERLILIES

***Nymphaea* 'Attraction' (H)**

N. 'Pygmaea Helvola' (H)

N. 'Firecrest' (H)

N. 'Chromatella' (H)

N. 'American Star' (T)

N. 'Blue Beauty' (T)

N. 'Escarboucle' (H)

N. 'Virginalis' (H)

N. 'Marliacea Carnea' (H)

Care and cultivation

Most waterlilies have thick tubers that grow roughly vertically, with fibrous roots beneath; cultivars of *N. odorata* and *N. tuberosa* have longer, fleshy rhizomes that grow horizontally near the soil surface.

Planting

Hardy waterlilies should be planted from late spring to late summer so that they will be well established before winter; do not plant out tropicals until the risk of frost has passed.

For planting, use containers that are 12–14in (30–35cm) across and 6–7½in (15–19cm) deep, depending on the size and vigor of the cultivar. Alternatively, plant in submerged beds 12–18in (30–45cm) deep and 18–24in (45–60cm) square.

Prepare the plant by trimming back long roots and cutting off old or damaged leaves and flower buds. The older leaves make the plant too buoyant to anchor itself under water and produce little food for the plant. New leaves will quickly replace them. When planting tropical waterlilies, insert a tablet of slow-release fertilizer in the soil.

If the planted container is not too heavy, water well before placing in the pond so that any soil shrinkage can be corrected. Lower the basket into place with strings as for planting deep-water plants (see p.293).

In a new pond, the containers may be positioned on the bottom before the pond is filled. Cover them at first with only 3–6in (8–15cm) of water; raise the containers on blocks if necessary so that they have the correct depth of water above them. As the plants grow, gradually lower the containers in stages until they finally rest at the correct depth. Tropical waterlilies may be planted at their permanent depth immediately, however, since they grow quickly and prefer shallower water than most hardy cultivars.

Fertilizing

Waterlilies usually benefit from limited additional fertilizing; insert a tablet of slow-release fertilizer into the soil or soil mix approximately every six weeks during the growing season. This gradually releases small quantities of fertilizer without discoloring the water or encouraging the growth of algae.

PLANTING A TUBEROUS WATERLILY

1 *Using pruners or a sharp knife, trim back to within 2in (5cm) of the tuber any roots that are damaged or excessively long.*

2 *Cut off any dead or damaged leaves, or those with broken stalks. Retain new, young leaves and flower buds.*

3 *Line the basket and partly fill it with dampened soil. Position the tuber so that the crown is within 1½in (4cm) of the rim.*

4 *Pack soil firmly around the tuber, making sure that the crown remains 1½in (4cm) above the level of the soil.*

A FLOATING GARDEN
The strong, straight lines of a wooden deck bridge offset the platelike leaves and colorful blooms of an island of waterlilies.

Division

To maintain healthy growth, divide waterlilies when their foliage is crowding the water surface (or, ideally, before the foliage gets too lush), or when their roots have extensively outgrown the container and are spilling out of it. In spring, cut off pieces from the crown, each with a young, strong shoot and about 6in (15cm) of attached tuber, and replant in fresh soil. The old crown should be discarded.

Propagation

Most tuberous waterlilies may be propagated by means of bud cuttings; rhizomatous types may have their rootstocks divided (see p.296). Some may be raised from seed or from separated plantlets.

Bud cuttings

Some tuberous waterlilies produce sideshoots ("eyes") that may be used to propagate new plants. In spring, cut the eyes from the roots and dust them with charcoal or sulfur. Press into a prepared pot, top-dress, and immerse in water; leave the pots in a greenhouse or cold frame at 59–64°F (15–18°C). As the plants develop, pot them on and gradually increase the water depth until fall. Overwinter in a cool place and plant out the following spring.

Seed

With the exception of *N. odorata* and *N. tetragona*, hardy waterlilies do not readily set seed; however, tropical waterlilies set large quantities. Before gathering seed, enclose ripening capsules in muslin bags to prevent the seeds from floating

PROPAGATION BY BUD CUTTINGS

1 *Remove the plant from its container and wash it. Using a sharp knife, remove strongly growing buds from the root by cutting flush with the tuber.*

2 *Fill 4in (10cm) pots with soil or aquatic soil mix, firm, and press a single cutting into the surface. Top-dress with grit.*

3 *Immerse the pots in water and keep them in a greenhouse or heated frame, partially shaded; plant out the following spring.*

away. Sow hardy seed at once, before it dries out. Tropical waterlily seed should be washed and allowed to dry, then stored in bags at room temperature. Tropical waterlily seed is best sown in spring.

Sow the seeds evenly, still attached to their jellylike bladders, in pans of sowing medium. Sprinkle with medium, water, and then place the pans in a container and cover with 1–2in (2.5–5cm) of water. Hardy waterlily seed requires a minimum temperature of 55°F (13°C) to germinate, tropical seed 73–81°F (23–7°C).When the seedlings are large enough to handle, carefully lift, rinse, and plant them in pans submerged in 2–3in (5–7.5cm) of water. Pot on later into 3in (6cm) pots in 3–4in (8–10cm) of water.

After overwintering, the tubers produce young plants that may be detached and potted on.

Plantlets

Certain day-blooming tropical waterlilies produce plantlets that may form and bloom while still attached to the parent leaf. Alternatively, they may be transplanted into shallow pans in water and then grown on at a temperature of 59–64°F (15–18°C); gradually increase the water level, then pot them up into aquatic containers.

Waterlilies for barrels

Smaller waterlilies are excellent subjects for growing in a half-barrel or similar container. Make sure the container is watertight, but take care that plant-toxic materials such as tar or creosote were not used as sealants. Follow the same cultural procedures as given above. Recommended waterlilies include *Nympahea tetragona* and *N.* 'Pygmaea Helvola'.

PROPAGATION BY DIVISION

1 *In late spring, lift a mature clump when the leaves begin to appear. Dip the rhizome in water, then wash the soil from the roots.*

2 *Cut the rhizome into sections, each with 2 or 3 growth buds. Remove any damaged or overly long roots. Pot each section and keep in shallow water until it shows signs of growth.*

Constructing ponds, pools, and watercourses

FOR many years, man-made ponds were constructed mostly from heavy materials such as stone, concrete, or brick. Since the advent of plastics and fiberglass, however, it has become easier to install your own pond and also to create a more naturalistic design, if desired.

The best shape, size, and material for the pond depends to a large extent on the size and style of your garden, the preferred method of construction, and cost. Flexible liners allow you maximum freedom of shape and size. They are ideal where a natural look is required, since the edge may be easily concealed and the lining material itself is relatively unobtrusive; also, they are the best choice for large ponds. Rigid, preformed ponds are easier to install, but there is only a limited range of shapes and sizes. While they are excellent for small ponds, larger units are difficult to maneuver, and very large sizes are not available. Hard materials such as concrete make the strongest and

longest-lasting ponds, but they are the most difficult and slowest to construct.

There are several methods of constructing watercourses. Flexible liners are versatile and particularly suitable for naturalistic designs. Where strength and durability are more important, or where the design incorporates a series of shallow cascades, preformed rigid units may be more appropriate. Liners and rigid units may be used in combination.

Flexible liners

Most new garden ponds are constructed using a flexible lining sheet of synthetic rubber or plastic, which provides a waterproof barrier between the soil and the water. These liners are available in a wide range of sizes and can be cut to fit any shape. Before buying a liner, decide on the size of the pond; marking out the desired shape makes it easier to check the placement.

Butyl rubber is arguably the best pond-lining material. It is much stronger than either polyethylene or PVC, with a life expectancy of about 40–50 years, but it is also more expensive. Butyl is very pliable and is tough enough to resist tearing or deterioration caused by ultraviolet light, bacterial growth, and temperature extremes. To line an informal pond, particularly if part of the material may be exposed to sunlight, it is best to use a top-quality butyl liner that is ¼in (7mm) thick.

PVC liners are reasonably strong and tear-resistant, and some come guaranteed for ten years. They are resistant to both cold and fungal attack, but after several years of exposure to sunlight they may harden and crack. These liners are usually blue or black in color, or black on one side and beige on the other. It is usual to place them with the dark side on top since darker colors absorb light and heat and look more natural than lighter colors.

Polyethylene is the cheapest of all the lining materials; it is easily torn, and cracks after constant exposure to sunlight. Where it can be protected from light or from accidental damage, it is an economical material to use. It is particularly suitable as a lining for bog gardens, where it is covered by a layer of soil.

Measuring the liner

To calculate the size of liner required, first determine the maximum length, width, and depth of the pond. The liner should measure the maximum width of the pond plus twice its depth, by the maximum length plus twice its depth. Then add 1ft (30cm) to both width and length to allow for a 6in (15cm) flap at each edge to prevent any leakage. A pond measuring 6 x 8ft (2 x 2.5m) and 2ft (60cm) deep would require a liner 11 x 13ft (3.5 x 4m).

MAKING A POND WITH A FLEXIBLE LINER

1 Mark out the proposed shape of the pond using sand or string. Then position marker pegs at equal intervals around it, setting the first peg at the ideal level for the pond edge.

2 Use a straightedge and level to align the remaining pegs with the first one. Then excavate the hole until it is 9in (23cm) deep all around. Slope the sides slightly outward.

3 Rake the base of the hole so that it is flat. If a marginal planting shelf is desired, make a line, 9–12in (23–30cm) wide, with sand all around the hole, for the shelf.

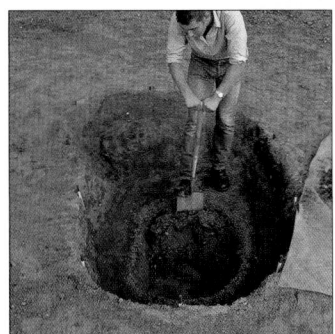

4 Dig within the marked central area to a further 20–24in (50-60cm) deep. Remove any roots and sharp stones, then rake over the base until it is level.

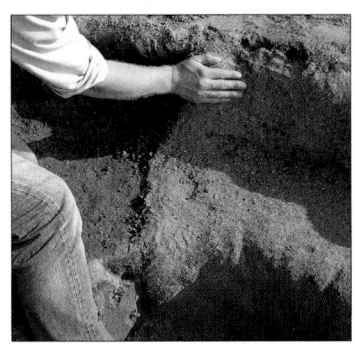

5 Press a layer of sand or sifted soil, 1in (2.5cm) deep, over the base and sides of the hole. If using underlay fabric, drape it over the hole's contours and press it down.

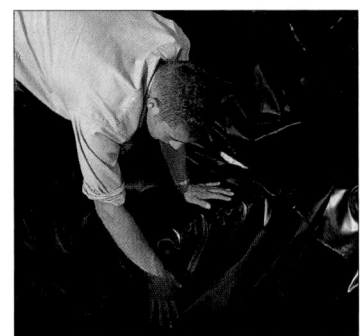

6 Carefully unroll the flexible liner over the sand or underlay until it is draped over the entire hole and there is generous overlap at the sides. Fold in the creases evenly.

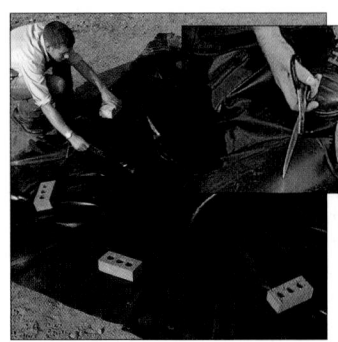

7 Fill the pond with water, using bricks to hold the liner in position. Move the bricks as the liner settles. Trim its edges, leaving a 6in (15cm) overlap.

Installation

First spread out the liner away from the site, in the sun if possible: the warmth will make it more flexible and easier to handle. Mark the required shape of the pond on the site with string and pegs, a hose, or a length of rope, then mark the soil just inside this line. Dig to a depth of approximately 9in (23cm), making the pond sides slope inward at an angle of 20° from the vertical. The slope prevents the sides from caving in, makes it easier to install the liner, and ensures that if the pond freezes in winter the ice can expand upward without causing damage.

If planning to grow marginal plants, cut a shelf about 9in (23cm) wide to provide adequate planting positions, and then continue digging at a slight angle until the desired depth (normally 20–24in/50–60cm) is reached. Check that the rim of the pond is level all around by using a straight board and level across both the length and the width of the hole. This is extremely important, since if the pond is not level water may spill over the edge. If including edging stones, remove 2in (5cm) of soil to a width of 12in (30cm) all around the pond, so that the stones can be firmly bedded in later.

Once the hole is excavated, remove any roots and sharp stones that could puncture the liner, and tamp the soil firmly. To protect and cushion the liner, spread an underlay of fiberglass insulation or heavy-duty landscape cloth, or a 1in (2.5cm) layer of damp sand in the hole. Underlays are preferable since they are both stable and durable; sand may eventually shift, leaving part of the liner exposed to damage from stones.

Drape the liner over the hole so that the center touches the base, leaving an overlap on all sides. Anchor it all the way around before starting to fill the pond. Weighed down by the water, the liner will stretch and sink to mold itself into the pond's contours. As more liner is required, remove some anchoring stones, tug the edges of the liner to make it straight, and form neat folds at the sides if it starts to crease.

When the pond is filled, remove the remaining stone weights and check again that the rim is level all around; add or take away soil if necessary until it is level. Cut off any excess liner, leaving a 6in (15cm) flap all around the edge; this surplus may be hidden beneath rocks, sod, or paving stones bedded on mortar. The stones should protrude slightly over the pond edge to hide the liner. Take care not to let any mortar slip into the water; if this happens you should empty the pond and refill it.

PREFORMED MOLDS

Preformed fiberglass or plastic ponds are available in a wide range of sizes and shapes. Most designs include planting shelves for marginal plants.

Preformed ponds

The simplest ponds to install are those preformed from fiberglass or plastic. These are available in a variety of shapes and are often contoured to provide ledges on which to grow marginal plants. Fiberglass ponds are more expensive than those made of plastic, but they are tough and weather resistant, with a life expectancy of at least ten years.

Installation

Level the site as much as possible and clear away any debris. If the mold is symmetrical in shape, invert it and mark out its outline using pegs and string. For asymmetrical shapes, stand the mold the right way up, supporting it on bricks if necessary to keep it stable and level; mark out the contours with long stakes, pushed vertically into the ground, and string or rope.

To dig a hole that matches the mold, first remove soil down to the level of the marginal shelf. The topsoil may be reserved for use in the garden, while the subsoil should be set aside for backfilling around the pond later. Place the pond in the prepared hole, and press it down firmly onto the soil to leave a clear

impression of the shape of the base. Lift out the mold, then dig out the central, deeper area that has been marked out by the pond base, allowing approximately 2in (5cm) extra depth all over the entire hole for the cushioning material.

Clear the hole of any sharp stones, tree roots, or debris; tamp the soil firmly, and line it with a 2in (5cm) layer of damp sand, heavy-duty landscape cloth, or fiberglass insulating material. Put the mold in place and check that it is level, otherwise the water will run to one end when the pond is filled.

Make sure that the pond sits firmly on the bedding layer, then add about 4in (10cm) of water. With sand or sifted soil, backfill around the sides to the same depth as the water, ramming the soil firmly under the shelf; check that there are no gaps and that the pond remains absolutely level. Continue the process of adding water, backfilling, and checking the level until the pond is full. Finally, firm the soil around the pond and mask the edges with paving stones bedded on mortar or sod.

INSTALLING A PREFORMED POND

1 *Firmly support the fiberglass or plastic mold with bricks to keep the pond level and upright, and then mark out its shape by pushing a series of stakes into the ground all around the edges. Lay a length of rope around the stakes to mark out the precise outline that will need to be excavated.*

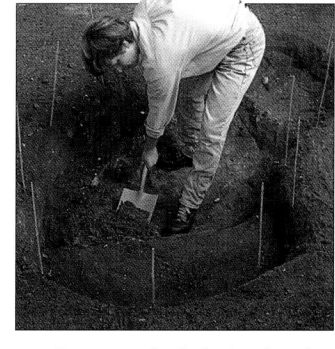

2 *Excavate the hole 2in (5cm) deeper than the mold, following its profile of shelves and base as accurately as possible.*

3 *Use a board, laid across the width of the pond, and a tape measure to check that the depth of the hole is correct, then use a level to check that the base is flat. Adjust as necessary.*

4 *Remove any tree roots and sharp stones, and then line the hole with a 2in (5cm) layer of sand. Lower the mold into place and check with a level and board that the mold is set level.*

5 *Fill with water (here pond water) to a depth of 4in (10cm). Backfill around it to the same depth with sifted soil or sand. Tamp firmly. Continue to add water, backfill, and tamp.*

MAKING A CONCRETE POND

1 *Excavate a hole to the desired size. Dig a trench, 8in (20cm) wide, around the perimeter of the base. Presoak the trench, pour in concrete, tamp, and level with the hole base. Allow to dry.*

2 *Add a layer of sand to the soil base and firm it level with the concrete foundation trench. Skim the sand with a ¹/₂in (1cm) layer of fiber-reinforced cement, overlapping the concrete by 2in (5cm).*

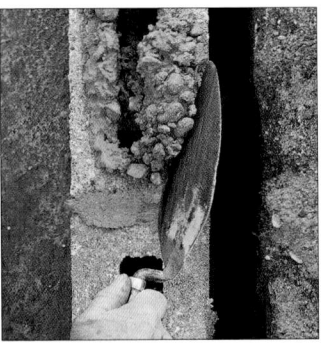

3 *After 24 hours, build walling block walls onto the foundations. Fill the voids with a fairly stiff concrete mix. Once dry, fill the gap between the block and soil walls with the same mix.*

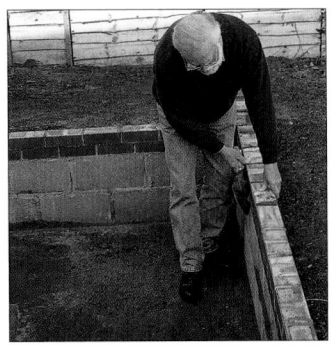

4 *To achieve a smooth, level top to the walls, mortar one or two courses of house bricks onto the walling blocks. Scoop up any excess mortar carefully, so that a smooth finish is achieved.*

5 *After 48 hours, first dampen then render the walls with a ¹/₂in (1cm) layer of fiber-reinforced cement. Build up a furrow where the base and side walls meet for additional corner strength.*

6 *Mortar coping stones (such as the concrete pavers used here) onto the wall sides so there is a 2in (5cm) overlap on the inside of the pond.*

7 *After 48 hours, brush the interior walls of the pond to remove any debris, then paint the whole inner surface with a waterproof sealant.*

Concrete pools

Often used for formal pools where its rigidity is an advantage, concrete is durable and is suitable for ponds of almost any size. Construction does, however, require more skill and expertise than is needed for installing a liner or preformed pond.

In areas prone to long periods of severe cold, concrete pools should be constructed with walls that slope outward at an angle of 30–45°; this minimizes the risk of cracking, since the ice can expand upward and outward as it freezes. Ponds of the same size that have vertical walls provide a larger area of deep water, which may be important if you plan to keep fish. Construction is more laborious than for a pool with sloping sides since the wet concrete has to be supported with a wooden form until it hardens (see below).

Construction

When digging the hole for a concrete pool, add an extra 6in (15cm) to all dimensions to allow for the volume occupied by the concrete; if there is to be a shelf for marginal plants, see "Flexible liners: Installation," p.283. Line the hole with 500-gauge plastic sheeting, then spread 2in (5cm) of concrete over the base. For added strength, place a sheet of galvanized wire reinforcing mesh over this and cover with a second 2in (5cm) layer of concrete. When the concrete has slightly hardened, roughen the surface around the edge to a width of 6in (15cm) to form a firm grip for the side walls.

After about 48 hours, or when the base is dry, install a vertical wooden form 4in (10cm) in from the sides, bracing it at the corners. Thoroughly soak the form with water, slide a piece of galvanized wire mesh between the form and the sides of the hole, then pour in the concrete. If a walled, marginal shelf is required, this form will need to be higher (see below). Leave the form for about two days to allow the concrete to set completely. For a mar-

ginal shelf, repeat the procedure with another two stages as for the main body of the pond. Remove a band of soil around the pond edge to a depth of 3in (8cm); lay crushed stone in this area as a base for the edging stones.

A few days later, apply a sealant that prevents lime in the concrete from leaching out into the water and harming the plants and fish. Finally, fill the pond and check the alkalinity of the water with a pH test kit. If close to neutral (pH7) it is safe to introduce plants, and, after two more weeks , fish. If alkaline, this may be due to hard tap water or ineffective sealant. In either case, delay planting marginals and waterlilies for a few weeks; the pH will gradually become more neutral. Oxygenators and surface-floaters generally tolerate alkaline water and may therefore be included sooner.

Raised pools

The walls of raised pools must be strong enough to resist the pressure of the water; if necessary, seek professional help. Raised pools are far more vulnerable to cold damage than sunken ponds, and a minimum depth of 24in (60cm) is needed for fish in areas where the water is likely to freeze for even a short period of time. For more advice on the depth of water needed for keeping fish in your area of the country, consult a local expert or enthusiast; there are many businesses and amateur organizations interested in keeping fish in ponds.

Construction

The best way to construct a raised pool is with double walls, built in the same way as a house cavity wall. The exterior wall can be made from walling stones or bricks. The interior wall, which will be hidden, can be constructed with a cheaper brick or walling stone. The walls need to be close enough together to be linked

RAISED POOL
Wide slabs have been used for this contemporary raised pool so that the edge also forms a seat. The adjacent patio is also made from the same slabs in order to create a harmonious design.

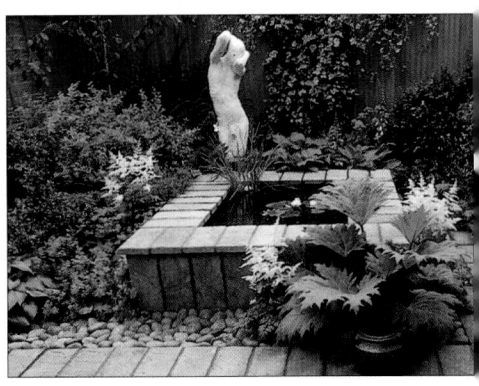

CONSTRUCTING A CONCRETE POOL WITH VERTICAL WALLS

MAKING THE POOL
Line the pool area with plastic sheeting. Build the pool in stages, allowing the concrete to set at each stage. Lay the base first, using reinforcing wire mesh between 2 layers of concrete. Once set, install a vertical form, braced at the corners, insert mesh between the pool wall and form, then pour in concrete. Repeat the process for a marginal shelf.

Galvanized wire reinforcing mesh

Concrete

Crushed stone base for edging stones

Polyethylene   Concrete   Form

MAKING A WALLED MARGINAL SHELF
A walled marginal shelf allows direct planting. Proceed as before, making the vertical form higher to retain at least 9in (23cm) of soil (left). Once set, concrete the base of the shelf as before and then the outer shelf wall. After the concrete has set, lay the edging stones so that they will overlap the water by about 2in (5cm). Apply sealant and fill the marginal shelf with soil. Plant up, and then fill with water (right).

with commercial wire wall ties. A flexible liner is used inside the interior wall.

Mark out the required shape with string and pegs, then construct concrete footings (see *How to Make a Concrete Footing*, p.590) 4–6in (10–15cm) deep and 15in (38cm) wide for the walls. Rake over the base, remove any sharp stones, and cover with a layer of fine sand or heavy-duty landscape cloth. Then construct the double side walls, incorporating the wire ties at intervals to link the two walls.

Lining a raised pool

The liner may be fitted so that an attractive stone or brick surface is exposed above the water on the inner wall: before laying the top two courses, fit the liner in the pool then over the inner wall and into the cavity of the double wall. The top two courses should then be mortared in place, securing the liner; the surplus liner is tucked underneath the coping. This prevents the appearance of conspicuous white "tide lines" on black liners when the water level drops in summer due to evaporation; it also ensures that no leakage occurs through the stone. Finally, mortar the coping stones on top of the double wall and cut off any surplus liner to create a neat edge to be covered by the coping.

Making planting beds

If including vigorous water plants in a large pond, it may be better to plant them in permanent beds or containers such as large concrete pipes or trash barrels rather than in planting baskets. These larger beds allow a greater root run, and tall plants are less likely to be displaced by wind. Beds may be sited on the marginal shelves or on the pond base for growing deep-water aquatics.

To build retaining walls on the shelves of a pond liner, first install the pond and fill it with water to stretch the liner into its ultimate shape, then lower the water level to expose the shelves. Protect the surrounding liner with a cushion of surplus liner scraps, then build the walls. The bed should be a minimum of 9in (23cm) deep and wide. Apply pond sealant to the bed (and allow it to set) before planting.

Edging a pond

While informal ponds can be edged in a naturalistic fashion with soil, grass, or rocks and pebbles, paving may be desired to enhance the clean lines of a formal pool or to create a small viewing area at one side of a pond. Safety must be the paramount consideration; slabs of any thickness should be securely mortared down on solid foundations, especially if your soil is light. If slabs are to overlap the water, they too must be mortared down; consult or hire a local contractor for information on how to do this properly and for maximum safety. Choice of materials is also important for safety around water. Traditional, natural stone surfaces (either brand-new or old reclaimed stone paving) may become extremely slippery in wet weather or if moss and algae are allowed to grow on them. By contrast, many precast concrete paving slabs have roughened surfaces, making them far less slippery.

Styles of edging

Formal pools require a crisp outline, so straight- or curved-edged, precast concrete paving is ideal. For circular pools or ponds, small units such as waterproof bricks and granite or sandstone setts are also suitable, since they will not need cutting. Irregularly shaped, random paving can be used, with the shortest edges laid along the side to create the curve. Wooden decking is appropriate to both formal and informal pools and ponds, because it can easily be cut to shape. For an informal pond, stone products such as washed cobblestones and small boulders make a gradual transition to planted surroundings and are easy to lay.

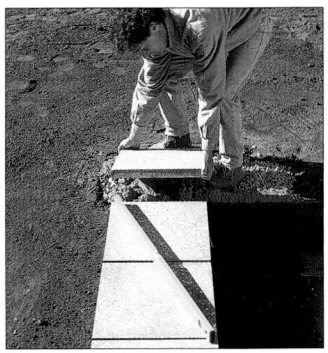

SIMPLE AND EASY EDGING
Conceal a flexible liner with rocks and stones that gradually decrease in size as they get closer to the water, creating a beachlike effect.

INFORMAL BUT MORTARED
Align irregularly shaped slabs so that one side follows around the shape of the pond's rim. Always secure them with cement for safety.

GEOMETRIC FORMALITY
Manufactured paving blocks give a uniform and clean appearance to the edge of a pool. They must be mortared into position.

Using a liner to make a watercourse

Watercourses may be constructed to meander over small changes in level, or to be faster moving over a steeper gradient with several falls and a pool at the bottom. The proposed route of the watercourse should be marked out and the position and depth of the height changes noted. Use flexible liners for a more natural appearance.

If the water movement is powered by a pump, the outlet for the proposed watercourse (usually a header pool, but this is not essential) must contain enough water not to show major variations in level when the pump is turned on and off. One unobtrusive way of creating an outlet is with an underground header pool fitted with a flexible liner. Cover the pool with a sturdy mesh and place a layer of rocks and stones on top; the water pours out between the rocks into the watercourse.

As well as the flexible liner, non-porous rock is needed to mask the watercourse edges and to create the waterfalls, while small pebbles or stones are attractive on the bottom of the watercourse.

Amount of liner required for the watercourse

The route, dimensions, and changes of level in the watercourse are the factors that determine how much lining material will be required.

If the route is fairly straight, one piece of liner may be used. This should be the maximum width plus twice the depth by the length of the watercourse, allowing for any changes in height between the top and bottom, plus about 6in (15cm) at either end of the course so that it can overlap into the header and base pools. A twisting watercourse is best made from a succession of liner pieces, each overlapping the next by 6in (15cm) to avoid unwieldy folds and excessive wastage. Allow for these overlaps when calculating the amount of liner needed.

Construction

Make a bank of soil slightly larger than the dimensions of the watercourse, with the highest point where the header pool or water source will be and the lowest point adjacent to the base pool. Then mark the outline on the soil. Starting from the lowest point, cut steps into the bank to form the falls and cascades; the flatter sections – the treads of the steps – should be made with a slight fall in the opposite direction to the water flow so that they are covered by water even when the water supply is turned off. For the header pool, dig a hole at the uppermost point at least 24in (60cm) square and 16in (40cm) deep. Rake the bottom, remove any sharp stones, then compact the soil with the back of a spade. Spread heavy-duty polyester matting or similar material over the course. The flexible liner may then be fitted into the channel, allowing approximately 12in (30cm) of liner on either side, which will later form the vertical side walls. If using more than one piece of liner to form the length of the watercourse, overlap them by 6in (15cm). Place the higher piece so that it overlaps the lower one where there is a fall or downward slope so that water flows away from the seam. Dig a channel next to the watercourse for the pipe that will circulate water from the base pool to the header pool (see *Recirculating Water in a Watercourse*, p.287).

MAKING A WATERCOURSE WITH A FLEXIBLE LINER

1 Build a soil bank to the required height and mark the shape of the watercourse. Working from the bottom, shape the steps and header pool.

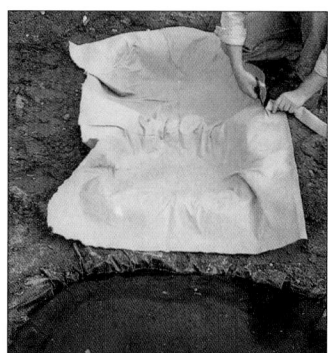

2 When complete, compact the soil with the back of a spade. Remove sharp stones and line the course with a cushioning layer of polyester matting, cutting it to fit.

3 Lay the liner in place, with the bottom edge overlapping the pool. Cut to fit, leaving 12in (30cm) on each side. Smooth the liner into the contours of the channel.

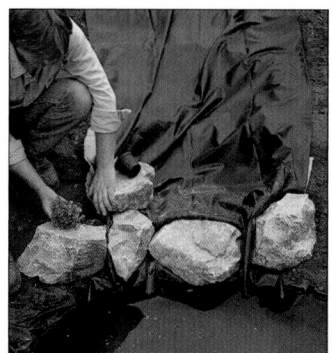

4 Starting at the base, set rocks in place to form the steps. To prevent water from escaping, tuck in the liner edges behind the rocks. Backfill firmly with soil.

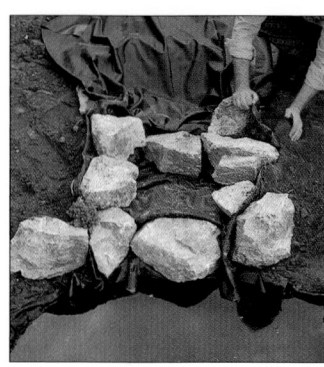

5 Continue working upward, arranging rocks and pebbles to form the falls and sides of the watercourse. Make sure the sides are steep enough to prevent water from escaping.

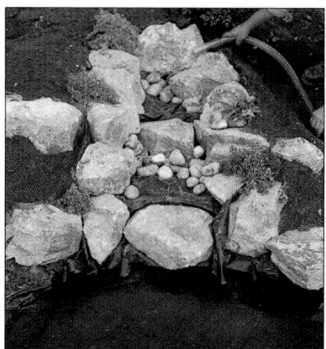

6 Position plants in the crevices between rocks to soften the edges of the watercourse. Bury the water pipe alongside so that it overhangs the header pool.

TWO KINDS OF WATERFALL

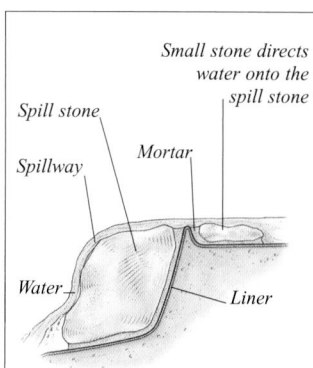

Small stone directs water onto the spill stone

Spill stone

Spillway

Mortar

Water

Liner

SPLASHING CASCADE
Positioning a single, rounded spill stone in this manner produces a more gentle-looking waterfall and creates less sound than an unbroken fall (see below).

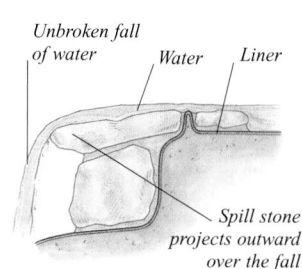

Unbroken fall of water

Water

Liner

Spill stone projects outward over the fall

UNBROKEN WATERFALL
The additional spill stone creates a taller, more active looking, louder waterfall. Be careful not to position the upper spill stone upward, which could cause water to back up before going over the fall.

RECIRCULATING WATER IN A STREAM WITH WATERFALLS

Moving from the reservoir to the header pool, each pool should be raised higher to allow water to fall naturally but must be deep enough to allow some water to be retained, should the pump be switched off.

Nonreturn valve

Water pump

Header pool

Delivery pipe concealed under soil to the side of the stream

Base or reservoir pool

Set rocks in place to form the steps and sides of the watercourse, arranging them until the grouping is satisfactory. Lift the liner at the sides behind the rocks, then pack soil in to just above the waterline. If plants at the edge are to be included, plant them at this stage in the soil behind the rocks. To provide increased stability, mortar the rocks into position using a waterproof cement.

Using rigid units to make a watercourse

Preformed modular units may be combined in various ways to incorporate falls of different heights. Strong, interlocking units are unlikely to move should any future subsidence of the underlying soil or sand occur. Installation by two people is recommended, since final adjustments in levels may require lifting one side of a unit while sand is backfilled.

Mark out the proposed area with string, then dig out the watercourse to accommodate the units. Allow extra depth for a level layer of sand beneath them. Work from the bottom up, positioning the lowest unit so that the lip overlaps the base pool and ensuring that it is level. Remove it and bolt on a vertical plate that determines the height of the waterfall. To ensure watertight seams, use a silicone sealant around each bolt. Install the linked units, making any final adjustments by backfilling or removing excess sand so that they are level. Once the first unit is level, a small amount of water may be added to increase stability.

The following units, and the final header pool, are then bolted on in the same way. Once each is attached and the levels checked, partially fill the watercourse with water, then backfill with sand around the outside edges as before. Conceal the edges with rocks and plants.

Circulating the water

To circulate water from the base pool to the header pool in a watercourse, link the two pools with a flexible pipe attached to a pump. The pipe may be pushed well down into the header pool to hide it; in this case, a one-way valve should be fitted. Alternatively, keep the end of the pipe above the water surface and disguise it at the pool edge with an overlapping stone or slab. Sink the pipe in a trench alongside the stream, then cover it with thin pieces of stone to protect it from being pierced.

Pumps and filtration

Two types of pump are available for garden use: surface-mounted and submersible models. For most small installations involving a fountain or watercourse, a submersible pump is quite adequate. Larger installations may require a surface-mounted pump that is housed in a separate, ventilated chamber.

If using a submersible pump, place it in the base pool, raised on bricks or blocks to help prevent debris from being sucked into the inlet strainer. If circulating water through a watercourse, connect a pipe to the pump to carry water up to the header pool (see diagram). Use only approved waterproof connectors with pumps and other electrical fittings. Protect outdoor wiring with armored sleeving and always include a ground fault circuit interrupter for safety.

Usually there should be no need for filtration. If there are large numbers of fish or if it is difficult to maintain submerged plants, physical or biological filtration may be needed. Filter kits that fit onto the suction inlet of submersible pumps are available, but larger installations may need a biological filter.

MAKING A WATERCOURSE WITH RIGID UNITS

1 *Mark out the watercourse. Working from the bottom up, dig a shallow trench with a slight backward slope. Bed the first unit on soft sand, its lip slightly overlapping the edge of the pond.*

2 *Repeat the process up to and including the header pool. The lip of each unit should overhang the unit below it. Hide the delivery pipe in a 15cm (6in) trench alongside the stream.*

MAKING A CANAL OR FORMAL RILL WITH CONCRETE

1 *Excavate the canal site to a depth of 8in (20cm). Cover the base and sides with soft sand, 2in (5cm) deep. Make sure the site is level, then line the canal with a heavy-duty plastic sheet.*

2 *Pour a 2in (5cm) layer of concrete onto the plastic, then tamp down and level it with a thin, straight board. Frequently check that the sides of the canal are at exactly the same height*

3 *After 48 hours, mortar a course of bricks onto the foundations to make the canal walls. Mortar decorative pavers at right angles on top of the bricks, overlapping the inside canal edge by 2in (5cm.)*

4 *After 48 hours, dampen then skim the floor and insides of the canal walls with a 1/2in (1cm) layer of fiber-reinforced cement. When dry, apply a coat of commercial water sealant.*

Small water features

To look their best, water features should be in scale with their surroundings. Fortunately, for small gardens, there are suitably diminutive features, including ones that recirculate water, that will fit into a variety of nooks and crannies. They can be used to provide an endless trickle of water over a brimming pot, a gurgling bubble fountain over pebbles, or a stylish fountain on a wall. Such moving-water features bring small spaces to life by introducing a mixture of sound and movement, adding an element of surprise, and providing a theme for interesting plant selections in the vicinity.

Small water features are much safer for small children than an open pond because there is little or no exposed water. They are also quick and easy to construct and there are no large volumes of soil to be disposed of. Those features that do not include aquatic plants, like the pebble fountain here, can also be sited in shade, whereas a planted pond could not. Maintenance is much easier, too, the main job being regular replenishment of water to compensate for losses by evaporation.

Wall fountains

Small, enclosed urban gardens, courtyards, patios, and conservatories, where there is often insufficient space for a freestanding feature, make ideal locations for a wall fountain. These range from antique stone masks (or less costly plaster or fiberglass copies) to modern metal designs. A wall trellis can be used to hide the water delivery pipe between the reservoir pool and the fountain's spout. The reservoir must have enough capacity for prolonged running of the submersible pump: a minimum of 5–6 gallons (22–27 liters) is required for even a small wall fountain. The reservoir can be open and attractively planted (see below) or concealed below ground.

Cobblestone fountains

Another successful and popular small water feature is the cobblestone fountain, which has several variations on a theme, all basically relying on water being pumped up through cobblestones or pebbles (which are supported on a piece of galvanized-steel mesh) and falling back into a reservoir pool below ground.

Cobblestone fountains are available in kit form and provide a cheap, simple, and creative opportunity to enjoy moving water within the garden. One of their greatest fascinations can be the top of the water spout, which can be adjusted either to gush or bubble gently. The source of the water spout need be no more than a rigid tube from the pump – the wider the pipe, the more restful the fountain becomes. The sound of the fountain changes as the height of the spout increases above the reservoir. A further refinement is possible by altering the water level: if the reservoir is full, splashing dominates the sound; if only half full the sound takes on an echoing dimension, emphasizing the cascading rivulets of water falling down beneath the stones.

INSTALLING A COBBLESTONE FOUNTAIN KIT

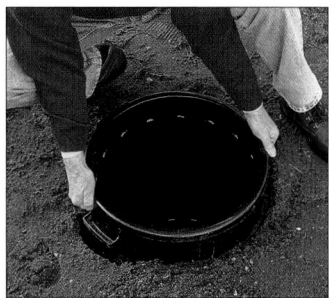

1 *Dig a hole that is wider and slightly deeper than the tub reservoir. Insert the tub, using a level to make sure it is level. Backfill around the sides, and firm the soil with a stick.*

2 *Lay a plastic sheet over the tub; cut out a circle 2in (5cm) smaller than the tub width. Connect the delivery pipe to the pump outlet. Put the pump on a brick at the bottom of the tub.*

3 *Center the galvanized-steel mesh over the hole in the plastic. Make a small hole in the mesh and feed the delivery pipe through it. Fill the bin with water to 6in (15cm) from the top.*

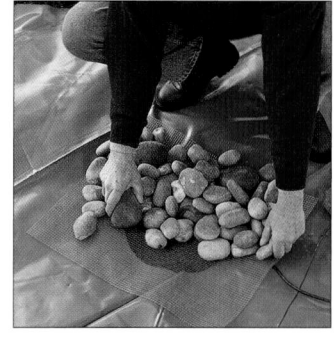

4 *Arrange a few cobblestones around the pipe and cut it to length. Then turn on the pump. Lift the mesh and experiment with the pump's flow adjuster until you achieve the desired fountain effect.*

5 *Add more cobblestones as required. Once the area onto which the water falls is established, trim the surplus plastic sheet, burying the edges, 4in (10cm) wide, under the soil. Alternatively, to allow for possible future enlargement, fold or roll up the surplus before burying it.*

MOUNTING A SIMPLE WALL FOUNTAIN

1 *Screw a trellis panel to slats on the wall. Thread the delivery pipe up behind the trellis and connect to the mask's mouth. Screw the mask in place.*

2 *Connect the delivery pipe to the pump outlet. Stand the pump on a brick in the reservoir. Fill the reservoir with water, turn on the pump, and adjust the flow.*

FINISHED FOUNTAIN
Planting in and around the reservoir conceals the pump, while climbers hide the trellis and vertical delivery pipe.

Natural and wildlife ponds

Most garden ponds attract some wildlife, but the more informal and natural they are, the more inviting they become to a wide range of creatures. You could be lucky and have a natural pond in your garden, but if not, it is possible to construct one that will have a naturalistic look and great appeal to wildlife.

A wildlife pond should be positioned where it can be seen from a house window, yet not so close that shy creatures might be deterred from visiting. Ideally some vegetation should be planted on the far side of the pond to give cover. A wildlife pond should also have a shallow beach at one edge, and a layer of soil over the bottom. The beach allows easy access for birds, amphibians, and small mammals, and the mud layer provides a home for myriad tiny creatures in summer and a hibernation spot in winter.

Lining a natural pond

Traditionally, natural ponds were lined with compacted or "puddled" clay to make them watertight, but the cost of importing clay has made this practice prohibitively expensive in all but heavy clay areas.

A more economical way to clay-line ponds is to use sodium bentonite. This powdered mineral clay swells to ten to fifteen times its volume when mixed with water, forming a waterproof gel. It is also available sandwiched in a tough, woven geotextile mat (see right), which, for ponds of more than 60 sq yd (50 sq m),

can be moved only with the use of heavy equipment.

Flexible, low-density polyethylene or PVC liners can be used, too. Since such liners will be covered by a generous layer of soil, they need not be resistant to ultraviolet deterioration.

Bog gardens make ideal companions for ponds and should be made independently with a separate lining, pierced in a number of places on the bottom to allow slow drainage.

Planting the pond

To encourage the maximum variety of wildlife, the planting in a natural pond should contain a high proportion of native species. Many of these are rampant and quickly smother smaller species, so it is a good idea to create pockets of different sizes and depths for different species (see also below).

The soil layer will encourage plants to spread. Tempting though it is to plant thickly for a natural effect, avoid really rampant growers in small ponds. Many of these have vicious root systems that can penetrate flexible liners. Eventually, even deeper zones may become choked by native marginals forming rafts with their thick, spongy roots, and periodic cutting back will be required. If not thinned, some submerged species such as water fringe (*Nymphoides peltata*) also tend to spread uncontrollably to cover the water surface, excluding sunlight. It may take some experimentation before a stable balance of planting is achieved.

QUICK TO ESTABLISH
Native plants will rapidly cover a pond surface and must be chosen carefully if a clear area of water is required. Similarly, vigorous marginals will soon surround the pond. Remember to keep open a small area for access.

Woven geotextile matting

For convenience when lining a pond, bentonite is available as an impregnated, geotextile quilt, known as Bentomat, which can be draped over the pond excavation in overlapping strips. The matting is sufficiently thick so it is not vulnerable to tunneling animals or most plant roots. The matting should be covered with a soil layer, 12in (30cm) thick, to prevent chemicals from leaching into the water.

WATERPROOFING
Line the hole with Bentomat, and then conceal it with topsoil.

CREATING A VARIETY OF HABITATS

A great advantage of using flexible liner in a water garden is the wide range of planting opportunities and levels you can provide, increasing the feature's attraction and usefulness to aquatic wildlife and other garden creatures. Varied environments maximize the variety of sheltering, feeding, and breeding sites.

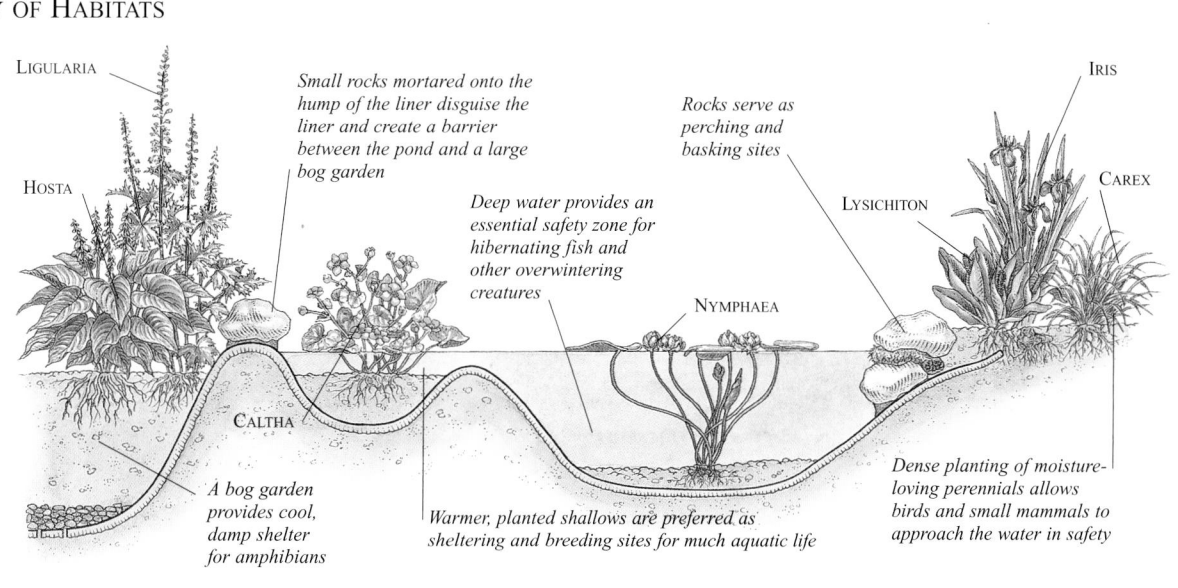

LIGULARIA

HOSTA

Small rocks mortared onto the hump of the liner disguise the liner and create a barrier between the pond and a large bog garden

Deep water provides an essential safety zone for hibernating fish and other overwintering creatures

Rocks serve as perching and basking sites

IRIS

CAREX

LYSICHITON

NYMPHAEA

CALTHA

A bog garden provides cool, damp shelter for amphibians

Warmer, planted shallows are preferred as sheltering and breeding sites for much aquatic life

Dense planting of moisture-loving perennials allows birds and small mammals to approach the water in safety

Waterside decking

WOODEN decking is an ideal material for edging water where there is also a need for an outdoor living area. It can be extended over the water, providing the illusion that water is running underneath, or more simply form a waterside seating area. Often the space underneath the deck makes an ideal place to house equipment such as clarifiers, pumps, cable switches, and transformers.

Where possible use decking squares (see also p.586) or grooved decking boards made of long-lasting hardwood; if softwood is used, be sure that it has been pressure-treated. Decking boards are usually 6–8in (15–20cm) wide, in 10–13ft (3–4m) lengths and come in various thicknesses; use a minimum of 1in (2.5cm) thickness to reduce warping.

The decking boards or squares should be secured to supporting joists, which are normally made of 3 x 2in (8 x 5cm) treated lumber and placed 30in (75cm) apart, at right angles to the line of boards. The boards or squares are then screwed onto the joists, leaving ¼in (6mm) gaps between them to allow for expansion.

The joists must be supported on perpendicular wooden beams firmly bedded on sand or crushed stone. On soft ground, trench foundations beneath the beams are advisable. Precast concrete decking pads can be used. These are 18in (45cm) square and 4in (10cm) thick and are placed 4ft (1.2m) apart. Over water, concrete footings and posts with steel supports must be used.

Wooden decking squares set with the diagonal treads at right angles to each other. This reduces the chances of slipping and gives a checkerboard effect

Bricks inserted under beams keep the decking supported and level

Beam

Joist

Last joist positioned just 16in (40cm) from the middle joist guarantees that the decking squares overhang the edge of the jetty

Beam extends under jetty joists

Decorative fascia board

Steel supports under wooden uprights prevent the wood from rotting

Brick piers to which steel supports are bolted raise a jetty area above the water

Concrete and stone footings support the decking where the ground slopes away

DIFFERENT TYPES OF FOUNDATIONS

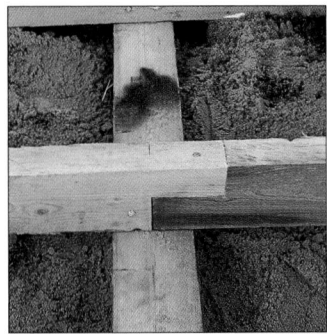

BEAMS AND JOISTS ON SAND
This simple foundation consists of a grid of wood joists laid at right angles over beams resting on 2in (5cm) of sand. This is suitable only for small decks.

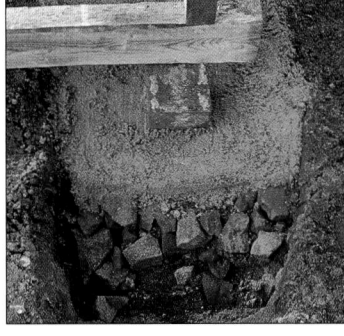

STONE OR RUBBLE FOOTINGS
For an extra-strong foundation, bed the beams in excavated trenches containing crushed stone or rubble (bricks are being used here), covered with 2in (5cm) of sand.

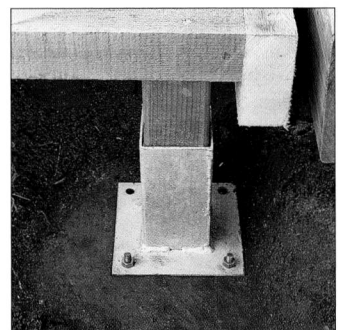

STEEL SUPPORTS
On wet ground or under water, use wood posts in steel supports bolted into concrete. These will prevent the uprights from rotting in the water.

USING A FLEXIBLE LINER

Where decking borders the water, a flexible liner should be brought up and behind the joists to prevent leaks. Where the underlay and flexible liner have to fit around a sharp corner, they should be carefully pulled and pleated before being secured with slats. Then conceal the liners from side view by nailing fascia boards to the outer edge of the liner-covered outer joists.

Beam

Joist

Fascia board

Decking square screwed onto joists

Flexible liner and underlay

Planting and stocking

WHILE most plants are grown for their ornamental features, some also help maintain the quality and appearance of water by keeping down algae (see "Plants for the water garden," p.278). There is a wide range of planting containers available, allowing flexibility when planting and making routine maintenance relatively simple.

Selecting water plants

When selecting plants, look for clean, fresh-looking, and vigorous specimens, growing in tanks that are free from algae and duckweed (*Wolffia*). Check that the undersides of the leaves are free from jellylike deposits of snail eggs, and that there are no strands of blanketweed in the foliage. Mail-order plants should appear plump and green; if they look weak and limp, they are unlikely to grow well.

If buying plants by mail order, use a specialty supplier. It is worth paying a slightly higher price since the plants are more likely to be clean and disease-free and to have been propagated in the nursery. Reputable suppliers should also pack the plants with care and ship them on the same day that they are lifted.

When buying oxygenators for a new pool, allow at least five bunches for every square yard or meter of water surface. They are often sold as bunches of unrooted cuttings about 9in (23cm) long. They should be weighted at the bottom with a stone or something similar to keep the plants anchored, in case they become loosened after planting.

Since oxygenators are extremely susceptible to drying out, they should be kept moistened in a plastic bag or submerged in water until they are ready for planting in the pond.

PLANTING BASKETS

Various planting baskets are available to meet the needs of different plants. All except those with a very closely woven mesh should be lined.

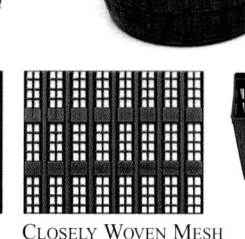

STANDARD MESH   CLOSELY WOVEN MESH

SELECTING PLANTS FOR THE WATER GARDEN

MARGINAL PLANT
GOOD EXAMPLE

Well-developed plant

Healthy leaves

POOR EXAMPLE

CALTHA PALUSTRIS

Weak growth

Weed-infested soil mix

OXYGENATOR
GOOD EXAMPLE

POTAMOGETON CRISPUS

POOR EXAMPLE

Healthy, vigorous growth

Limp, weak stems

SURFACE FLOATER
GOOD EXAMPLE

Young, fresh growth

POOR EXAMPLE

STRATIOTES ALOIDES

Damaged growth

Old, rotting foliage

Containers and planting beds

The most convenient way of growing aquatics is in specially made baskets. This makes it easy to lift and divide or replace the plants when necessary, and it is also a relatively simple matter to alter the planting arrangement when desired.

Planting baskets

Planting baskets have wide, flat bases to provide stability in the water, which is important for tall marginals on narrow shelves. They also have open lattice walls, allowing water and gases to circulate through the soil. Most should be lined with burlap or landscape fabric to prevent the soil from seeping out, although containers with a very fine mesh, which eliminates the need for a liner, are available from some suppliers.

Planting baskets range from 11in (28cm) in diameter with a 2¼ gallon (10 liter) capacity for medium-sized waterlilies, down to 1½in (4cm) in diameter with a 2fl oz (50ml) capacity, for use in aquarium planting. Larger, circular tubs without lattice walls, which are preferable for vigorous waterlilies, are also available.

Planting directly in soil beds

In wildlife ponds, aquatics may be planted directly into a layer of soil on the bottom of the pond and on marginal shelves. In most ponds, however, this is inadvisable since the vigorous species spread rapidly, swamping their slower-growing neighbors. In addition, subsequent removal or thinning out of plants can be extremely difficult.

Permanent beds

A good compromise is to build permanent planting pockets or beds on the base of the pond and around the edges during construction, which are easily planted up before the pond is filled (see also "Making planting beds," p.285). This makes it possible to maintain a natural appearance while controlling the plants' spread.

Planting

The pond should be filled with water a few days before planting to allow the water temperature to reach that of the surrounding air, and to mature. During this period, the water in the pond may become populated with

microorganisms that disperse impurities in the water and create an environment most beneficial to plants, fish, and other pond life.

Unlike the majority of terrestrial plants, aquatics should be planted while in active growth, preferably between late spring and midsummer, when water temperatures are warm and there is plenty of sunlight. If planted in late summer and early fall, the plants have little time to become established before they die down. Waterlilies must have time to build up food reserves before winter if they are to survive and grow satisfactorily the following season.

The planting medium

Aquatic plants grow quite well in good garden soil, preferably a heavy soil; if possible, use soil that has not been fertilized or manured recently. Sieve out any loose organic matter since this will rot or float when the planting basket is submerged.

Commercial soil mixes made for terrestrial plants should not be used for aquatics: besides containing peat, which tends to float, they contain added fertilizers that will encourage algal growth (see p.294). A handful of coarse bone meal mixed into the soil in a large planting basket is all the fertilizer required. If the suitability of the garden soil is in any doubt, use a prepared aquatic soil mix from a specialized supplier.

Planting depths

The ideal planting depth varies, depending on the type of plant, and can differ even within a given group of plants. Planting depths should be measured from the top of the soil in the basket or planting pocket to the water surface (see right).

It is important not to plant too deeply: without adequate sunlight for photosynthesis, plants will die. When planting young specimens, it may be necessary to stand the containers on bricks or blocks at first so that the plants are not completely submerged. As the plants grow, gradually lower the baskets until they reach the appropriate depth.

Bog and moisture-loving plants

The area bordering a natural pond is ideal for bog and moisture-loving plants, but correct growing conditions can be easily supplied next to a man-made pond by creating special planting beds.

Mark out the planting beds, then dig out at least 18in (45cm) depth of soil, removing any roots of perennial weeds such as quackgrass. Form sloping sides at the edges. Drape a flexible liner (thick-gauge plastic sheeting is suitable for this purpose) into the hole, making sure that the top edge of the liner finishes just below the existing soil level.

Although a number of vigorous, moisture-loving plants tolerate saturated soil, most will grow better if the liner is pierced to allow slow seepage of water from the bed. The slight movement of water through the soil also helps prevent stagnant conditions. Cover drainage holes with gravel so they do not become clogged up with soil.

Keep the soil moist according to the requirements of your plants. Alternatively, simplify watering by sinking a perforated, rigid pipe into the bed. Block the pipe at the far end and cover it with a layer of gravel or stones to prevent the holes from becoming blocked. Fit the pipe to a hose connector, which should remain above the soil surface.

Refill the bed with soil, and then mulch with a deep layer of coarsely sieved organic matter to help prevent moisture loss. Do not incorporate bulky additives throughout the entire bed, since sufficient moisture is retained by the liner.

Planting, which is best done in spring, is carried out in the same way as in ordinary soil, although the entire bed should be thoroughly soaked afterward. Plants that enjoy

PLANTING DEPTHS

Place plants at the appropriate depth for the species, measured from the top of the soil to the water's surface. When planting young waterlilies (Nymphaea), *raise the baskets on bricks. Lower baskets as the plants grow.*

these moist conditions will grow vigorously, so very invasive species are best confined to sunken containers to prevent them from crowding out neighboring plants.

Marginal plants

Primarily included for their ornamental flowers or foliage, marginal plants are grown at the pond edges with their roots in shallow water. Ornamental ponds usually include a shelf to accommodate marginal plants, which may be grown either in baskets or in pockets built directly onto the shelf (see also "Making planting beds," p.285).

Most marginals require approximately 3–6in (8–15cm) of water above their crowns; it may be necessary to raise the planting baskets so that the plants are at the correct depth until they are established. The more vigorous species, known as deep marginals, should be planted in 12in (30cm) or more of water, either on a deeper shelf or on the bottom.

When planting marginals, take into account their height, spread, and vigor. Plant rampant growers singly in containers to stop them from smothering slower-growing plants. If using containers, make sure there is enough room for root development; for most marginals, a container at least 9in (23cm) in diameter is necessary. Plant marginals in prepared containers or planting beds of soil and top-dress with pea gravel; if using containers, place them on the marginal shelf or the bottom of the pond, as appropriate, so that the plants are at the correct depth.

Deep-water plants

As for marginals, these plants are usually grown in aquatic containers or planting beds. Most of them are

PLANTING A BOG PLANT

1 *In the prepared bed, dig a hole sufficiently wide and deep to accommodate the root ball of the plant.*

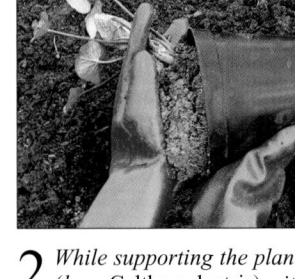

2 *While supporting the plant (here* Caltha palustris) *with one hand, gently ease the root ball out of the container, taking care not to damage the roots.*

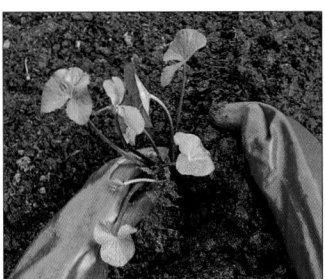

3 *Place the plant in the hole so that it is at the correct depth; the soil should always reach the same level as it did in the container.*

4 *Using your hands, thoroughly firm the soil all around the crown of the plant. Soak the entire area with water.*

Surface floaters: a caveat

When planting a pond in temperate regions, surface-floating plants can be included to discourage the growth of algae. Many plants sold for this purpose, however, are from tropical areas, and they must be used with great caution on any expanse of water other than very small ponds and aquaria These plants can gradually choke waterways, as has already occurred in some warmer regions of the world. Floating species to be wary of are water hyacinth (*Eichhornia crassipes*), water lettuce (*Pistia stratiotes*) water clover (*Marsilea quadrifolia*), butterfly fern (*Salvinia auriculata*), water chestnut (*Trapa natans*), and fairy moss (*Azolla filiculoides*). Although many of these would be killed by cold in temperate ponds and waterways, there is an increasing risk of some species surviving as global temperatures increase. Even more care should be taken when introducing alien species of aquatc weed sold as floaters. The submerged growth of many aquatic species is legendary but pales into insignificance when tropical species such as *Tillaea* and *Myriophyllum* are freely planted in large expanses of water that never freezes.

Surface-floating plants (here Stratiotes aloides) *may be placed on the water's surface. In warm weather they multiply rapidly, giving valuable surface shade.*

Planting oxygenators

Incorporating oxygenating plants is one of the first priorities when planting in a new pond. This is because their cleaning and oxygenating properties are vital to the oxygen content of the water and to the health of the fish population.

Keep the plants wet after purchasing them and until they are ready to plant. Even during the planting process, they should not be left exposed to the air longer than is absolutely necessary.

Species vary in the effectiveness with which they oxygenate the water, depending on the time of year and the pH of the water, so plant a selection of four or five species to ensure that enough plants thrive to maintain correct oxygen levels throughout the year. Keep only one species in each container to prevent stronger-growing plants from crowding out less vigorous species.

Prepare a planting basket and make planting holes in the soil, then insert a bunch of cuttings into each hole and firm them in. Cover the soil with grit or pea gravel, water thoroughly, and place the basket on the bottom of the prepared pond at a depth of 18–24in (45–60cm).

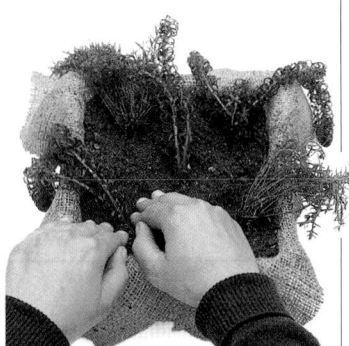

1 *Line a basket and almost fill with damp soil mix, then firm. Make planting holes and insert bunches of cuttings (here Lagarosiphon major).*

best positioned fairly shallowly at first so that their leaves are able to float on the surface of the water and photosynthesize in the sun, this providing the plants with the materials they need for growth. Lower them as their leaves grow.

Whether planting in beds or free-standing containers, settle the plants firmly in the soil, because they are very buoyant and may become dislodged. Always plant in moist soil, and soak containers well before immersing them in the pond. A top-dressing of grit, coarse sand, or pea gravel to a depth of 1in (2.5cm) prevents soil from floating out and clouding the water and discourages hungry or curious fish from disturbing the plant roots.

When submerging the containers in deep water, thread string through the sides to form handles; this makes it much easier to position the basket, which can then be gradually lowered onto the bottom.

Stocking with fish

Like water plants, fish are best introduced to the pond during the warmer months. In cooler temperatures, fish become semidormant and are more prone to stress when moved. Allow at least two weeks after planting before stocking with fish to allow plant roots to establish.

Unless there is supplementary filtration, overstocking with fish may encourage algae, which feed on excess waste. Calculate a maximum of 20in (50cm) of fish body length (when fully grown) per square yard or meter of water surface or 2in (5cm) per 1sq ft (1,000sq cm). It is advisable to stock the pond in two stages, introducing half the fish eight to ten weeks before the rest. This allows the bacteria that feed on the waste products generated by the fish to multiply to a sufficient level to deal with the waste. If too many are introduced at once, the water may become polluted and the fish starved of oxygen. Leaving a waterfall or fountain on overnight to agitate the water will provide temporary relief.

Fish are usually supplied in a large, clear, inflated plastic bag containing a small amount of water. On arrival, do not release the fish directly into the pond: they are very sensitive to sudden changes in temperature, and the water in the pond is likely to be colder than that in the bag. Float the unopened bag on the water until the water temperature in the bag is the same as in the pond. In hot, sunny weather, shade the bag with newspaper. A small amount of pond water may be gradually introduced into the bag before the fish are released. Do not lift the bag to examine the fish closely; this disturbance causes them extreme stress.

Other water creatures

As well as fish, a number of other aquatic life forms may be introduced to the pond as useful scavengers. Trapdoor snails (*Viviparus maniatus*) and related snails are often sold specifically for this purpose. Ordinary pond snails are likely to be a nuisance because they eat waterlily leaves. For larger ponds, mussels and freshwater clams are excellent scavengers, cleaning up where fish have been overfed, as well as filtering out algae. Mussels require a pan of coarse sand 2–3in (5–8cm) deep in which to burrow.

ADDING FISH TO A POND

Float the unopened bag until the water temperature in the bag matches that of the pond. Slowly introduce some pond water to the bag before gently releasing the fish.

PLANTING DEEP-WATER AND MARGINAL PLANTS

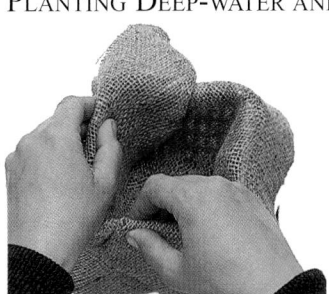

1 *Choose a planting basket to accommodate the plant roots, and line it with burlap or closely woven polypropylene.*

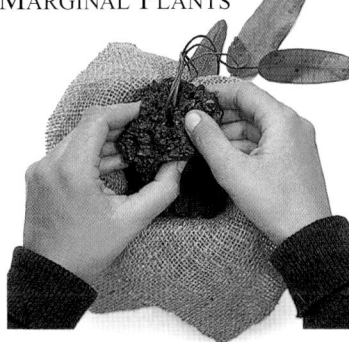

2 *Fill the basket with heavy, moist soil to a depth of at least 2in (5cm). Center the plant (here Aponogeton distachyos).*

3 *Fill with more soil to within ½in (1cm) of the rim of the basket, firming the plant in well to give it good anchorage.*

4 *Top-dress the container with washed grit or pea gravel to a depth of 1in (2.5cm).*

5 *Trim away any surplus liner with scissors. Tie string handles to the rim of the basket on opposite sides.*

6 *Hold the basket by the string handles and gently lower it onto blocks or the marginal shelf. Release the handles.*

Routine care

GOOD construction and siting, and ensuring the right balance of water, plants, and fish should help keep a pond relatively trouble-free. However, structural repairs may be occasionally necessary, for example, if the pond is damaged or leaks. Algae and weeds must also be kept in check, while many plants will benefit from periodic division.

Structural repairs

Any sudden or persistent loss of water is likely to indicate a leak. If a pond is leaking, it will be necessary to drain and inspect it. Accommodate the fish and plants in a suitable container, such as a wading pool.

Most ponds may be drained either with an electric pump or by siphoning off the water. First check visually that the pond's edges are level; water may be overflowing at the lowest point. With a watercourse, switch off the pump and check the level in the base pond: if constant, the leak is in the watercourse.

REPAIRING A FLEXIBLE POND LINER

1 *Thoroughly dry the area of damaged liner and then clean it carefully with rubbing alcohol and a soft cloth.*

2 *Apply double-sided adhesive aquatic sealing tape over the tear, then wait for it to become tacky.*

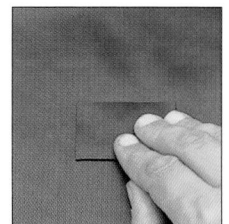

3 *Cut out a patch from spare liner and press it firmly onto the adhesive, making sure that the edges are stuck down flat.*

Flexible liners

If the water level in a lined pond drops or the flow of water in a watercourse decreases, check that no part of the edge of the liner has slipped below water level. Leaks may also be caused by punctures. The simplest way to repair a rubber liner is with double-sided adhesive tape, which is obtainable from water garden suppliers. This is used to secure a patch of rubber liner over the hole. The pond may be refilled after one hour.

Preformed ponds and units

If a pond or watercourse unit is inadequately supported or the ground underneath it is not properly compacted, it may eventually crack under the weight of the water. Repair cracks with a fiberglass repair kit. Allow the compound to harden thoroughly because it may be toxic when fluid. Before refilling the pond with water, ensure that the base is firmly bedded down and that soil is compacted around the sides to support the water pressure adequately.

With rigid, interlocking units, check the sealant around the bolts and reseal if necessary.

Concrete ponds

The most common cause of leaking is through cracks created by cold damage or subsidence. Inspect the pond carefully since water can escape through even a hairline crack. If the crack is very fine it is usually necessary to widen it slightly and brush clean any debris before sealing it with mortar. Allow the mortar to dry, then paint with sealant.

Water quality

Once a balance of plants and animal life is established, the water should remain clear without needing further attention. If there are marked changes in the numbers of fish or plants, or if there is a sudden introduction of tap or flood water, however, the water balance may be upset and a surge of harmless, but unsightly, algal growth may result.

Algae

Algae depend on sunlight, carbon dioxide, and dissolved mineral salts for their survival. Reduce the amount of light that they receive by growing sufficient plants (waterlilies, deep-water aquatics, and floaters) so that their floating leaves cover between 50 and 70 percent of the water surface. The introduction of oxygenating plants, which are efficient at absorbing minerals and carbon dioxide, helps starve out the algae. In addition, take care to keep down the amount of organic matter in the pond by regularly removing dead and decaying leaves and flowers.

Green water due to algal growth may occur in a newly planted pond, or one that has recently been cleaned out. Normally this problem clears itself within a short time.

If the water is persistently cloudy, even with adequate populations of surface and submerged leaves, it may be necessary to use an algicide or, in very acidic water, to alter the pH. Change the acidity level gradually, adding small quantities of ground limestone weekly until the water is neutral. For a small pond with a surface area of 40sq ft (4sq m) or less, introduce no more than 4oz (110g) of ground limestone at any one application.

Blanketweed

A filamentous form of algae called blanketweed (*Spirogyra*) is sometimes found in ponds with otherwise clear water; if left unchecked, it chokes the plants and restricts the free movement of fish. Remove it periodically by winding it onto a stick or lifting it out with a garden rake; in severe cases use an algicide.

REMOVING BLANKETWEED

Insert a stick into the mass of blanketweed (Spirogyra) and twist it. The weed wraps around the stick and may then be pulled free.

REPAIRING A CRACK IN A CONCRETE POND

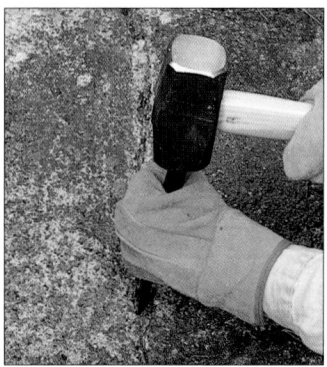

1 *If a crack is very fine, use a club hammer and chisel to widen it slightly.*

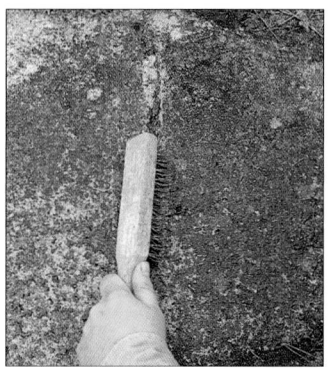

2 *Clean off any algae and debris from the surrounding area with a wire brush.*

3 *With a trowel, fill the crack with mortar or a commercial sealing compound. Allow it to dry.*

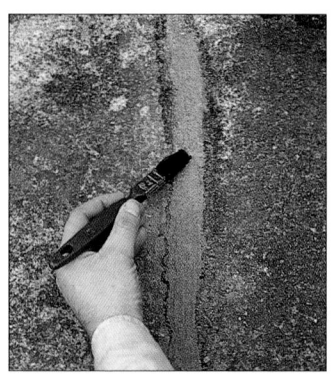

4 *Brush with a pond-sealing compound to prevent toxins from leaching out into the water.*

THINNING OUT AN OVERGROWN OXYGENATOR

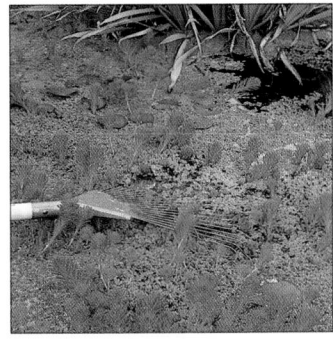

1 *In spring or fall, thin out overgrown submerged plants, either by combing them off the water's surface with a rake or by lifting out the basket and trimming back with a sharp knife.*

2 *Thinning out oxygenating plants prevents them from becoming congested. Do not remove too much growth, however, since this may leave the pond's surface area too exposed to sunlight, thus allowing algae to proliferate. Oxygenators are best thinned little and often.*

FLOATING LOG

In freezing conditions, floating a log on the water will absorb the pressure of the ice and help prevent cracks in pond walls. Break up the ice occasionally to oxygenate the water (very gently, to avoid harming fish).

In cold areas, protect tender plants by removing them from the pond and placing them in a bucket of water to overwinter in temperatures that remain above freezing. Cut off the ripe seedpods of invasive plants to prevent them from setting seed. Feed the fish before they hibernate.

If a pump is fitted, remove it from the pond and clean it thoroughly. Replace any parts that may be worn, and store it in a dry place until spring.

Clear out the dead material quickly, since decaying matter will reduce the water's oxygen content.

Pond cleaning

If the water is kept clear of fallen leaves and the plants are regularly trimmed, it should be necessary to clean the pond only every few years to remove decaying organic matter from the base. After cleaning, the water chemistry must again be carefully balanced.

Plant care and control

Water plants do not require much attention, but periodic division and repotting helps to keep them healthy and attractive. Their overall vigor normally makes it necessary for them to be kept in check rather than

encouraged, although certain water-lily cultivars will require some fertilizing (see p.280).

Thinning out and division

In late spring or early fall, thin out or divide overgrown plants or any that are crowding their neighbors. Lift container-grown plants and check whether they have become root-bound. If so, remove the plants from their containers and divide them with back-to-back forks or by hand. Tight and thick roots may need to be split with a spade or a knife. Replant the divided clumps singly.

After the first growing season, submerged oxygenating plants may become overgrown and entangled with weeds. In small ponds, the oxygenators are easily thinned by pulling out a few handfuls; in larger ponds, use a garden rake to comb out

excess growth. Alternatively, lift the container from the pond and cut back the plants by one-third to a half. Do not thin out all the plants drastically at any one time, since this causes a sudden change in the water balance and encourages algal growth.

Fall maintenance

The most important task in fall is to keep the water free from decaying vegetation. When the marginal plants begin to die down, remove dead and dying foliage regularly and prune back the excess growth of submerged plants. If there are deciduous trees and shrubs nearby, cover the surface of the pond with a fine-mesh plastic net to catch fallen leaves, and keep it in place until the trees are bare of foliage.

Winter care

In winter, ice may form, trapping methane gas released by submerged, decaying vegetation, with potentially lethal effects on the fish. Ice also exerts pressure on the sides of concrete ponds as it expands and may cause them to crack. Making sure that a small area of the pond remains ice- free prevents this and allows methane to escape into the air. Float a log on the surface or, alternatively, use a floating electric pond heater. This gives out just enough heat to maintain a small area of open water.

Pests and diseases

Pests are less of a problem in a pond stocked with fish, since the fish eat the insect larvae. Any infestations can be cleared by hand or washed off plants with a hose; insecticide sprays are unsuitable for water gardens and are highly toxic to fish. In summer, aphids (p.639) often attack the aerial parts of waterlilies and other aquatics, causing discoloration and decay. Dislodge them with a jet of water or submerge the leaves for 24 hours, weighting down infested parts with burlap.

Diseases attacking aquatic plants are relatively few, and mostly concern waterlilies. Fungal disease is indicated by the premature yellowing or spotting of the leaves. If the symptoms persist, treat the plant with copper fungicide in a separate tank.

REPOTTING A MARGINAL

1 *Plants that are growing in containers will eventually become root-bound and need thinning out. Roots protruding through the container wall indicate that a plant should be divided and repotted. The plant shown here is* Iris pseudacorus.

2 *Remove the plant from its container and divide it into smaller clumps, teasing the roots out by hand. Very tightly packed roots may be pulled apart with hand forks used back to back.*

3 *Repot each clump in a separate container filled with damp soil. Water well and top-dress with grit or pea gravel before placing in the pool. Trim off surplus burlap with scissors.*

Propagation

MOST water plants, especially marginals, may be propagated by division. Other methods are also used, depending on the type of plant: many submerged oxygenators and some creeping marginals, for example, are propagated by cuttings, while a number of floating plants naturally produce runners, plantlets, or turions, which grow into new plants. Moisture-loving species that grow around the pond edge, as well as some aquatics, may be raised from seed or increased by division.

Cuttings are best taken and plants divided in spring or early summer, when high temperatures and long daylight hours provide excellent conditions for new plant growth.

WATER PLANTS THAT MAY BE PROPAGATED BY SOFTWOOD CUTTINGS

Bacopa monnieri
Cabomba caroliniana
Callitriche hermaphroditica
Ceratophyllum demersum
Decodon verticillatus
Egeria densa
Elodea canadensis
Hydrocleys parviflora
Hygrophila polysperma
Lagarosiphon major
Limnophila heterophylla
Ludwigia arcuata
Myriophyllum
Potamogeton crispus
Tillaea recurva
Trapa natans

WATER PLANTS THAT MAY BE DIVIDED

Tubers
Aponogeton distachyos
Colocasia esculenta
Nelumbo nucifera
Zantedeschia

Rootstock
Acorus calamus
Butomus umbellatus
Calla palustris
Caltha palustris

Caltha palustris
'Flore Pleno'

Cryptocoryne ciliata
Damasonium alisma
Decodon
  verticillatus
Eriophorum angustifolium
(continued on opposite page)

Division

A large number of marginal plants may be readily propagated by division. The exact technique that should be used depends on both the plant's root system and its pattern of growth. For further information, see "Dividing perennials," p.196.

Plants with fibrous or creeping roots

Plants that have extensive fibrous or creeping roots, such as *Typha latifolia*, may be divided by levering apart the rootstocks. Simply pull the rootstocks apart with your hands; if the roots are tightly compacted, use two garden forks positioned back to back, then lever apart.

Each divided portion should include a growing point (a horizontally placed, terminal shoot). Cut off the old, brown roots and remove any dead leaves. Trim the new roots before replanting the divided portions in individual containers. Level the soil with the base of the shoots. Firm them in, then top-dress lightly with a layer of gravel. Cover the container with approximately 2–3in (5–8cm) of water.

Butomus umbellatus may be divided but may also be propagated from bulbils that form in the axils of the leaves. These are separated and then grown on individually (see LILIES, *Propagating from Stem Bulbils*, p.245).

Rhizomatous plants

For plants with strong, rhizomatous roots, such as irises, pull apart the root mass and divide it into sections with a sharp knife, each containing at least one bud and preferably some young roots. Cut off any long roots

and trim back the foliage, if needed. Do not trim the foliage back to below the water line, since the newly cut surface tissue may begin to rot.

Plant the division in a suitable container, firming the soil around the roots and just covering the rhizome. Cover the soil with a layer of gravel and immerse the basket in

the pond so that the roots are covered by about 2–3in (5–8cm) of water. Rhizomatous plants with creeping surface stems, such as *Calla palustris*, may be lifted and divided into sections, each containing a bud. The sections should be replanted individually in the same way as other rhizomatous plants.

PROPAGATING BY SOFTWOOD CUTTINGS

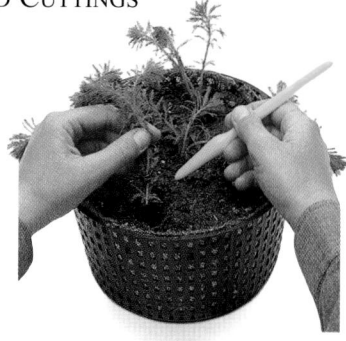

1 *In spring and summer, cut off healthy young shoots (here of* Myriophyllum). *Tie with wire into small bunches of 3 to 6 cuttings 4–6in (10–15cm) long.*

2 *Using a dibber, make holes in damp soil in a prepared planting basket lined with burlap. Insert the bunches of cuttings to a depth of about 2in (5cm).*

DIVIDING FIBROUS ROOTSTOCKS

Remove the plant from the container or lift it from the soil with a fork. Insert two forks, placed back to back, into the root mass and lever them apart, dividing the plant. Repeat to divide further, then trim and replant the divisions. The plant shown here is Acorus calamus.

DIVIDING RHIZOMATOUS PLANTS

1 *Lift the plant (here* Acorus calamus). *Split the root mass into sections with your hands. Each part should have a good root system and several healthy shoots.*

2 *Use a sharp knife to trim back long roots and foliage by approximately one-third to a half of their original length.*

3 *Line a container with burlap and partially fill with damp soil. Plant each division so that the rhizome is just covered with a thin layer of soil.*

Cuttings

Most submerged oxygenating plants may be quite easily propagated by softwood cuttings taken in spring or summer; this also helps keep plants in check. Fast-growing oxygenators, such as *Elodea canadensis* and *Potamogeton crispus*, should be regularly replaced by young stock.

Prepare the cuttings by pinching or cutting off healthy, young shoots, inserting them into pots or trays of soil, and submerging them. The cuttings may be inserted individually or tied into small bunches of six. Cuttings of some creeping marginal plants, for example *Mentha aquatica* and water forget-me-nots (*Myosotis scorpioides*), should be inserted singly rather than in bunches. The cuttings establish quickly and may be potted up and planted in position after two to three weeks.

Some tuberous waterlilies may also be propagated by cuttings, although a different method is used (see "Bud cuttings," p.281).

Runners and plantlets

Many of the floating plants that are found in tropical lakes and rivers propagate themselves by means of runners or plantlets produced on long, adventitious shoots.The water hyacinth (*Eichhornia crassipes*) and *Pistia stratiotes* can populate vast areas of warm water in this way. In shallow water, the young plantlets quickly root into the rich mud at the bottom, drawing up fresh nutrients and sending out yet more runners. The plantlets may simply be snapped off and replaced on the water surface to grow separately. In warm areas the water hyacinth can become invasive.

A dwarf form of the papyrus, *Cyperus papyrus* 'Nanus' (syn. *C. p.* var. *viviparus*), forms young plantlets in the flower head. If the head is bent over and immersed in a container of soil and water, the plantlets root and develop; these can be divided and potted up separately.

Turions

Some water plants, such as *Hydrocharis morsus-ranae*, produce swollen buds known as turions that become detached from the parent and survive the winter at the bottom of the pond. In spring these turions rise to the surface and develop into new plants.

The turions of *Hottonia palustris* develop from the mud in spring with-

PROPAGATION OF RUNNERS OR PLANTLETS

1 *Some floating plants (here water hyacinths,* Eichhornia crassipes) *form plantlets. In spring, remove a plantlet by snapping the connecting stem.*

2 *Place the plantlet directly on the water surface, supporting it gently with your hand until it floats upright.*

out floating to the surface. Since these are difficult to gather, wait for them to develop into young plants before lifting and replanting them in their new positions.

The turions may also be gathered in fall and stored in soil in a submerged seed tray covered with 6in (15cm) of water throughout the winter. In spring, when the emerging buds float to the surface, they may be gathered and potted up.

Seed

Most moisture-loving plants and some aquatics including *Aponogeton distachyos*, *Euryale ferox*, *Orontium aquaticum*, *Trapa natans*, and tropical waterlilies (see *Hardy and Tropical Waterlilies*, p.280) may be grown from ripe seed gathered in summer or fall.

Keep the seeds cool and moist until ready to sow. If using dried seeds, germination will be delayed or the seeds may have lost viability. Aquatic plant seeds should be grown in submerged or partially submerged

conditions, similar to their natural habitat. When sowing seed, first prepare containers such as seed trays or pans by filling them with an appropriate aquatic soil mix or garden soil passed through a ¼in (7mm) sieve. The growing medium should not contain any fertilizers, since they encourage algae, which could smother germinating seedlings.

Sow the seeds on the surface of the growing medium, and then cover them with a shallow layer of fine grit before placing the tray in a large watertight container, such as a plastic bowl or an aquarium. Fill the container with water until the tray is just covered, and leave it on a greenhouse bench in partial shade, or on a well-lit windowsill, at a minimum temperature of 64°F (18°C). The seeds should start to germinate the following spring.

When the first two true leaves appear, carefully prick out the seedlings into individual pots and leave them immersed in water in the greenhouse for another year. Transfer the plants to the pond when the water warms up in spring.

WATER PLANTS THAT MAY BE DIVIDED (CONT.)
Rootstock (cont.)
Lysichiton
Mentha aquatica
Menyanthes trifoliata
Myosotis scorpioides
Nuphar lutea
Peltiphyllum peltatum
Pontederia cordata
Ranunculus lingua
Sagittaria sagittifolia
Saururus cernuus
Thalia dealbata
Typha latifolia

Lysichiton camtschatcensis

Offsets
Eichhornia crassipes
Hydrocharis morsus-ranae
Limnobium stoloniferum
Marsilea quadrifolia
Nymphoides aquatica
Pistia stratiotes
Sagittaria graminea,
  S. sagittifolia 'Flore Pleno'
Salvinia auriculata,
  S.natans
Stratiotes aloides

Salvinia auriculata

Plantlets
Aponogeton undulatus
Azolla caroliniana
Baldellia ranunculoides
Ceratopteris cornuta
Eichhornia crassipes
Hottonia palustris
Nuphar advena
Nymphaea
Utricularia exoleta
Wolffia arrhiza

SOWING SEED

1 *Sow the seeds evenly by tapping them from paper onto a pan of firmed aquatic soil mix or sieved garden soil.*

2 *Cover the seeds with a shallow layer of fine grit. Then place the pan in a large plastic bowl.*

3 *Gradually add water to the bowl so that the pan is just covered. Place in a well-lit position at about 64°F (18°C) until germinated.*

CHAPTER

11

CONTAINER GARDENING

GROWING PLANTS IN containers is an exceptionally versatile way of gardening. An enormous range of plants adapt well to these essentially artificial conditions, whether they be short-lived bedding plants, which make colorful summer displays in pots, hanging baskets, or windowboxes, or relatively large shrubs and trees, which can live for many years in large containers. With such a diversity of plants to choose from, container gardens can be created almost anywhere, from spaces as confined as a patio, roof garden, balcony, or windowbox to areas in the larger garden.

Designing with containers

GROWING plants in containers is one of the most flexible of gardening techniques. For many modern gardeners, who are aiming to create a pleasing environment in a limited space, container gardening is practical and appealing. For centuries plants have been grown in containers to allow them to be placed where there is no garden soil, for example in a patio, on a balcony (see p.306), or under cover in the home (see INDOOR GARDENING, pp.346–377), greenhouse, or conservatory (see CONSERVATORY GARDENING, p.350). Plants are also potgrown to give them prominence in a display – their unique qualities being easier to appreciate when they are placed in an inconspicuous pot – or to enhance them in a container that is attractive in its own right.

Growing plants in containers also allows the cultivation of genera that may not thrive in a particular garden's soil, by using tailored formulations of soil mixes. These include acidic (ericaceous) mixes for acid-loving plants, such as rhododendrons and azaleas, or very gritty mixes for alpine plants or succulents, which need sharp drainage.

Changes in focus
In a conventional garden, plants are grown in the open ground and displays are relatively static because the components cannot easily be moved about. In such gardens, containers can play a role as focal points, for specimen planting and for filling gaps in beds and borders. In the container garden, potgrown plants are easily regrouped: with subtractions and additions, a planting design can be quickly rejuvenated or even completely transformed. Container gardening, therefore, is ideal for the experimental gardener wishing to create stimulating arrangements that can be changed when they have outlived their initial appeal.

Formal and informal styles
These two broad approaches to garden design are as relevant to container gardening as they are to gardening in the open ground. The formal style is based on geometric order, with a division of space into balanced, often symmetrical units, and the repetition of elements at regular intervals. The informal approach has little or no geometry, and the elements are arranged without obvious symmetry. At their most effective, informal arrangements take their cue from the irregularity of natural landscapes, although there is usually a carefully thought-out, underlying balance of mass, form, and space.

Many popular manufactured containers are of a regular outline that is perfectly suitable for formal arrangements. Most plants, however, naturally grow in an informal way and can be used to obscure the lines of the container. When arranging container-grown plants, it is just as easy to create an informal style – with soft, "freestyle" planting – as it is to assure formality by planting to emphasize and echo the regularity of the container's shape.

An alternative approach to the informal style is to use "found" or reclaimed containers, such as chimney pots, old sinks, or drinking troughs, whose original purpose was other than for growing plants.

300

Selecting a container

The choice of container is a matter of personal taste and aesthetics. Whether the container is manufactured or improvised, however, it must satisfy key practical requirements to make it suitable for the cultivation of plants. The most fundamental elements are that a container holds sufficient soil mix to sustain the plants and has provision for excess water to drain away.

The materials of which containers are made will also affect the final choice. These include unglazed and glazed terracotta, natural or reconstituted stone, concrete, metal, wood, fiberglass, and plastic. No material has a longer history of use than unglazed terracotta, and its warm, earthy color and matte-textured surface provide one of the most sympathetic contrasts for foliage and flowers. Terracotta lends itself to decoration with incised or relief patterns that are pleasing but not distracting. It also blends in well with most architectural features, whether they are of stone, wood, or metal.

More opulent effects can be achieved with containers of marble, or more austere ones in other types of stone. The severity of concrete containers or the strong lines of light-reflecting, galvanized zinc ones lend themselves particularly well to an ultramodern style, while wooden ones can be used to create a more rustic atmosphere. Containers in fiberglass and plastic can look inconspicuous, but both materials have practical virtues, in terms of moisture retention, for example; and

COORDINATED CONTAINER

A large earthenware pot is an ideal container for an elegant bamboo. Its subtle, earth-toned glaze echoes the bamboo fence behind, the whole lending a distinctly appropriate and stylish note to an Oriental-style garden.

the best successfully imitate much more expensive materials.

Plants and their containers should complement rather than compete with each other, and the texture, color, and surface finish of a container are considerations as important as the

material itself. To a large extent, planter selection is a matter of individual preference, but it is worth bearing in mind that containers of a strong, assertive color, a bold, high-gloss finish, or with conspicuous decoration will demand an equally strong planting design.

Size, shape, and scale

The size and shape of a container are governed by practical considerations as well those of visual appeal. The container must be large enough to accommodate the plant or plants to be grown. It is equally important to match the size of the pot to the visual mass of the planting it will hold. A small stone trough, for example, would be in scale with diminutive alpines; a tall, narrow jar would suit a vigorous trailing specimen, and a Versailles tub is ideal in both style and capacity for a topiary specimen. For a packed and colorful display of upright and trailing summer plants, a generously proportioned copper vessel (once used for boiling or washing) might be appropriate.

As a general rule, the larger the pot the better, and larger pots need less frequent watering. One advantage of smaller pots, however, is that they can be dropped into arrangements as plants reach their prime,

then removed when past their best. This technique works best in conjunction with a holding area, such as a cold frame, in which plants are brought to near perfection, and to which they are returned to recover when their display is over.

Single specimens in containers

Growing single plants in individual containers is very practical: the soil mix, watering, and feeding regime can be geared to the plant, which is also freed of competition for moisture and nutrients. It can also work well in design terms, particularly if the plant has a strong architectural shape. The spiky New Zealand cabbage palm (*Cordyline australis*) and yuccas make fine specimens, as do plants of softer, weeping form, such as cultivars of the Japanese maple (*Acer palmatum*). Arching and mound-forming grasses, such as the attractive green-and-gold variegated *Hakonechloa macra* 'Aureola', also look good alone in containers, as do species that are formally trained, such as a frame-grown common ivy (*Hedera helix*) or a clipped topiary specimen, such as boxwood (*Buxus sempervirens*). Clematis and other moderately vigorous climbers can be allowed to trail from tall containers, or be trained upward on a simple

CORRECT PROPORTIONS

This arrangement of beautifully contrasting foliage textures with hosta, fringe cups (Tellima grandiflora), and slender grasses is perfectly in scale with the broad, shallow container. The proportions of plants to pot are about two-thirds planting mass to one-third pot, an old architectural trick that gives a well-balanced and visually pleasing effect.

MIXED PLANTING
Magenta petunias form a harmonious fringe beneath rich violet heliotropes, their intensity offset by copper and soft pinks and white highlights.

obelisk. Lax shrubs, such as ground-cover roses, look perfect when trailing their stems over the container's edge, and many other quite modest plants – heathers, primroses, and violas – radiate a special charm when given the luxury of their own pot.

Mixed planting

Individual plants in their own containers can be grouped to give the impression of a mixed planting. A greater challenge is to bring together a number of plants that complement each other and give a sustained display for several weeks or even months. The keys to success are to select plants that share the same or similar cultural needs, and to create arrangements of compatible colors and contrasting forms and textures in foliage and flowers. Mixed displays are most effective with a strong structure, for example where a vertical or domed centerpiece is surrounded by lesser "uprights," with trailing plants breaking over the edge of the container to form an irregular "skirt."

A spring mixture, for example, might contrast upright dwarf irises and crocuses with a mat of small-leaved thyme (*Thymus serpyllum*); richly colored polyanthus primroses among mounds of sky-blue forget-me-nots (*Myosotis sylvatica*); or English daisies (*Bellis perennis*) with tulips as strong verticals. In summer, the choice is almost endless – by selecting long-flowering bedding and foliage plants, it is possible to assemble rich and complex arrangements to provide many months of color and fragrance.

Color themes

When packing several plants close together, color clashes become much more conspicuous than in the less condensed conditions of the open garden. In containers, it is perhaps more important to devise combinations of plants based on color harmonies or contrasts. The harmonies of closely related colors can be quiet and subtle, such as in a warm scheme based on cream, soft yellow, and pale apricot, while more heavily saturated colors – rich purples with violets and blues – create much more vibrant harmonies. Contrasts are based on complementary colors: red with green, blue with orange, or yellow with violet. The eye is comfortable with these opposites, which tone well with one another.

Alternatively, more shocking combinations can be tried, for example orange with magenta-pink. Color clashes can be stimulating, but in a small space it is often helpful to ease the tension by using pale flower colors – creams or near-whites – or foliage as a buffer. Gray-leaved plants, such as *Helichrysum petiolare*, are invaluable in this respect, as are white- or cream-variegated plants, such as small-leaved cultivars of English ivy (*Hedera helix*).

Siting containers

Planted containers can be used simply as isolated features but are often most effective in the garden when used as an integral part of a wider design. In the formal garden, for example, containers can provide accents that reinforce a sense of geometry. Similarly, looser arrangements can underline the more subtle rhythms of a more naturalistic theme.

The position of containers should be based on practical as well as aesthetic considerations. Container-grown plants may need frequent watering (sometimes twice a day) in summer, so easy access to a water supply is vital, especially in sunny sites where plants may need attention during spells of hot, dry weather.

It is worth bearing in mind, too, that thieves target gardens as well as houses, and a valuable urn or antique jar is safer placed in full view of the house, rather than in a more secluded location, and may even be best chained or bolted to the ground.

AVENUE DESIGN
A broad walk flanked by an avenue of citrus trees in terracotta pots achieves formality through repetition of simple elements. Such a design demands discipline, but the elegant effect becomes its own reward.

Defining accents

Placing containers to create a succession of accents is a useful technique for delineating areas of the garden or marking boundaries. At its simplest, a row of containers may mark a boundary, perhaps in conjunction with a wall or fence. Try lining pots along the base of a fence or along the top of a wall, provided they are secure and will not topple, or even suspend them from the wall. The effect can be achieved at little cost, perhaps with brightly painted, recycled cans planted with long-flowering and colorful geraniums. Containers can also be used to define compartments within a garden, for example when they are set singly or in clusters at the corners of a rectangular paved area.

Container accents are invaluable for enhancing other features. A squared arrangement around a circular pool, for example, forms a very effective contrast; place pots in the curved quadrants to emphasize the line of the pool's edge. Accents such as this can fulfill a dual role: they can define a shape while also softening a hard outline. This is especially useful in integrating the severe geometry of a rectangular pool into the wider garden: containers arranged around the pool echo its shape, yet, if filled with loose arrangements of plants, they soften the effect. It is best to set containers back from the water's edge so that they are not a hazard, and to reduce the risk of dead leaves and flowers falling into the water.

Containers as focal points

The main lines of a small, modern garden in a formal style rarely terminate in a natural view of a landscape

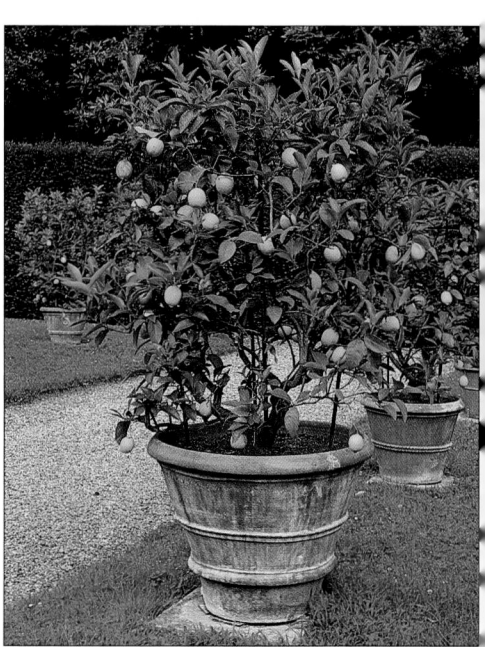

or an architectural landmark, but even on a small scale a vista that does not lead to a natural conclusion can seem unsatisfying. Features that are traditionally introduced to terminate vistas include trees and statuary, but on a smaller scale an urn, or large pot or tub, can fulfill the role equally well. Such focal points give an almost instant effect and, in comparison with statuary, are generally much less costly. Even an empty container can make an effective eye-catcher, provided that the scale is right; when planted with an upright plant or group of plants, surrounded by a fringe of trailers, the design is far more handsome.

There is no simple rule of thumb for ensuring the correct scale; it is often most satisfactory to do it "by eye." Make a preliminary test by positioning a stake where the container is to stand, and then check its position from various points along the vista. In some cases, it may be necessary to raise the container on a plinth to achieve the desired effect. This can be a ready-made, architectural plinth or can be improvised, for example, with a stack of unmortared bricks or wooden blocks, depending on the desired style.

In garden compartments, a central focal point is usually a good idea. A planted container is often a much simpler and cheaper option than a statue, sundial, or fountain. A formal herb garden divided into quarters, for example, may include a central paved or graveled area – an ideal spot for a large pot planted with an architectural specimen, such as angelica (*Angelica archangelica*). Alternatively, to maximize the growing area, the container could stand on

a plinth in the middle of the bed, but be sure that access for watering and maintenance is provided for, perhaps by means of stepping-stones.

Containers may also be used as focal points to direct the eye through the garden, for example by placing a large container at a turning point on a path, or to act as a distant feature that leads the observer on to another view or vista. In gardens where one mass of planting deliberately masks another, the unexpected has special value. A carefully placed container can introduce such an element of surprise, and an empty container of architectural quality – erect or on its side – can be just as dramatic as one full of plants.

Emphatic arrangements

Containers, especially if arranged in pairs, are an ideal way of marking a transition in the garden. This can be as simple and low-key as a one-step change of level, for example by using clipped balls of boxwood (*Buxus sempervirens*) in terracotta pots to flank the step, emphasize the change, and warn people against tripping. Longer flights of steps can be treated in a more lavish way, with paired containers at top and base and others at different landings, to create a dramatic setting. When using containers on steps, be careful to place them so they do not create a hazard.

Paired containers can also play a supporting role to another feature, such as a garden bench, that might not have sufficient impact to terminate a vista by itself. Setting matched containers on either side of a bench strengthens the central feature, which assumes greater visual weight. For strictly

TRANSITIONAL ARRANGEMENTS
Simple urns mark changes of level, while a cleverly placed Verbascum *lends emphasis with its strong vertical line. The whole design is enhanced by a marriage of complementary yellows and mauves.*

formal, long-term designs, pots could be planted with a topiary or, to mark the seasonal changes, a spring display of tulips could be followed with summer bedding plants that will bloom continuously for several months.

Paired containers can lend particular emphasis when positioned to form an "avenue." This formal pattern can work well on a relatively small scale: even in confined spaces, the effect can be monumental, for example when citrus trees in large terracotta pots or urns are placed in bays along a broad walk. On a more modest scale, pots of evergreens or seasonal flowers can be introduced to mark the main axis of a tiny garden.

Containers in beds and borders

Containerized plants, when rising above plantings in open ground, can be used to create contrast or to reinforce a color theme in beds and borders: for example, violet-purple flowers such as heliotrope (*Heliotropium arborescens*) or petunias could oppose a border theme of oranges, creams, and yellows. Subtle harmonies can be created, like the

pale pink of the double tulip 'Angélique' in pots beside beds of wallflowers, such as *Erysimum cheiri* Fair Lady Series, in shades of pink, yellow, and cream.

Container-grown plants are particularly valuable when the rest of the garden is relatively empty. Winter-flowering pansies, such as *Viola* x *wittrockiana* Universal Series, brighten dull days for many weeks in winter and early spring, and they can gradually be supplemented with a succession of bulbs, such as daffodils and tulips. In the autumn garden, container-grown shrubby plants such as *Argyranthemum*, fuchsias, and *Phygelius* will perform well until the first frosts.

Another approach is to boost beds and borders with potgrown plants plunged into the ground. This is a particularly useful way to fill gaps in a border when the foliage of summer perennials, such as Oriental poppies (*Papaver orientale* cultivars), has died back. It can also be used to supplement the display when newly planted perennials and shrubs have yet to attain their full size in a bed.

AN INFORMAL INVITATION
Planted containers here have many purposes: informality masks the severe lines of hard landscaping and draws the eye to a dramatic focal point, which, in turn, suggests an invitation to explore unseen vistas.

UNITY AND DIVERSITY
A variety of unglazed terracotta pots creates a sense of unity within a group and forms a warm but neutral foil for this colorful and attractive arrangement.

Containers in paved areas

The pleasures of gardening, and the contribution that plants make in enhancing the living environment, are being appreciated by increasingly more people. At the same time, gardens are increasingly being thought of as outdoor rooms, to be used for relaxing and entertaining, dining, and cooking. In the summer months, an outdoor room may even be much busier than living rooms indoors.

For many people, particularly in urban areas, the garden is a small paved space bounded by walls or fences: a courtyard, patio, or terrace. There are also other areas of hard landscaping in gardens, such as paths

and porches. While the range of surfaces includes a huge variety of stone, tile, gravel, or concrete, or even wooden decking, open ground is often at a premium. The only way to include plants in such sites, where soil and space are so limited, is to grow them in containers.

Plants for paved areas
A large number of plants is suitable for containers in paved areas. In enclosed gardens, especially near sunny walls, there is often a very favorable, warm, and sheltered microclimate (see p.603). Tender plants, such as the fragrant-leaved lemon verbena (*Aloysia triphylla*) or myrtle (*Myrtus communis*), often succeed here when they may not thrive in a more open garden.

In some cases, the proximity of buildings and walls means that a paved area receives little or no direct sun for all or part of the day. While painting walls white helps make such shady areas brighter, the plants that really thrive in these conditions are committed shade lovers, such as hostas and ferns. These plants grow more lush and look beautiful for much longer periods in cool shade, providing the possibilities of sumptuous arrangements of foliage color and texture.

Where direct light penetrates for several hours a day, many more plants will thrive, especially those that occur naturally in the dappled shade of a woodland setting, such as camellias and rhododendrons. When light levels are low, try moving the plants around from time to time, so that they have more exposure to sunlight; it helps promote balanced growth and encourages them to flower more freely.

Two other features of a paved environment affect the choice of plants: the weight of a pot and the watering method. Solid walls often create turbulence as they deflect wind, and unstable pots may be toppled by sudden strong gusts; the soil mix also dries more rapidly in windy conditions. Containers close to walls may also stand in a rain shadow, where natural rainfall does not penetrate (see *Rain Shadow*, p.602). Even after heavy rain, plants may not receive sufficient water, so provision must be made for adequate watering.

Choosing containers
There are no hard-and-fast aesthetic rules when choosing containers for paved areas. They can be matched closely in texture and material to architecture and hard surfaces – terracotta pots are ideal against brick, for example. An equally valid approach is to use containers that stand out in a paved setting. Glazed jars, painted wooden tubs, and galvanized metal cubes and containers are just some of the choices that can help to define a distinctive style.

Arranging containers
Any arrangement of containers must take account of practicalities. For example, it is important to leave some clear space for access and to allow enough room for the unrestricted use of furniture. However, from autumn to spring, when many paved areas are less heavily used, containers can be rearranged to provide displays that are visible from indoors. Stacked arrangements of pots loaded with bulbs, evergreens, or winter-flowering pansies (*Viola* x *wittrockiana* cultivars),

CORNERPIECE
Billowing foliage and a restricted color scheme create a beautiful cornerpiece: the red blooms pick up and echo a warm-toned brick wall.

placed in plain view of windows, allow the display to be enjoyed in warmth and comfort.

The most difficult aspect of managing changing displays is finding a place for plants before and after their most decorative season – only a limited number of those past their best can be hidden among plants in their prime. In the absence of a holding area, one solution is to rely heavily on annuals and biennials that are discarded when their season is over, leaving containers available for a succession of seasonal displays. Another option is to use containers that are ornamental in their own right; if carefully selected, they can be attractive even when empty. If more permanent plantings of bulbs, perennials, and shrubs should outlive their usefulness, they are often gratefully received by friends with more space in their gardens.

Formal arrangements
The most usual formal arrangements in paved areas are paired containers flanking doors, benches, or other furniture set against walls. Where there is room, the symmetry can be expanded to include matching clusters of containers, with additions and subtractions as the seasons advance. At times of the year when the paved area is used a lot, arrangements – formal or otherwise – are best kept to the perimeter, but this does not preclude using them as a focal point, perhaps where they can be seen from a door or window.

Although space may be limited, there is no need to restrict containers to small pots with flowers just above ground level. Such arrangements can appear humble in scale; fewer but larger plants will have much more impact. If there is no room for loose, rounded shapes, such as those of *Fatsia japonica* or the mophead *Hydrangea macrophylla* cultivars, consider naturally narrow, upright plants, such as a slow-growing conifer like *Juniperus communis* 'Sentinel', or plants such as yew (*Taxus*) and boxwood (*Buxus sempervirens*), which can be clipped to form a narrow cone or column.

To bring color to the design, use flowering plants, such as clematis and miniature climbing roses, or variegated foliage plants, such as cultivars of English ivy (*Hedera helix*), and train them onto upright obelisks or narrow, willow-wand pyramids.

Many urban gardens have a paved path between a wall or fence and the house. Without plants, these passageways can appear bleak, but there is seldom enough room at ground level for pots or tubs. One solution is to place deep, narrow troughs at the foot of the wall. They can be filled with free-standing arrangements or even with climbing plants that will cover the wall if given support. Another option is to attach containers securely to the wall top, so that plants can cascade down the wall's face. There is also a wide range of flat-backed, half-round containers available that are specifically designed to be mounted on the vertical surface of a wall or sturdy fence.

INFORMAL ENTRANCE
A plain entrance to a house is enlivened with container plants both at the door and a short distance from it to increase the feeling of depth.

Stands for containers

A plant stand with shelves at different heights provides a support for a neat and attractive display of container-grown plants; it has the advantage that a diverse display can be created within a relatively small area. The most suitable and durable ones are usually made of aluminum and are of simple design with stepped and slatted shelves. The slats allow water to drain away freely, and the setback of the shelves means that plants on the top shelf do not over-

shadow those lower down. Most stands can be attached against a wall or placed in a more open position, but some are specifically designed to fill corners, and these make good use of a potentially awkward space. An alternative to commercial stands are those made from stacked bricks, building blocks, or upturned flowerpots as uprights, and plain wooden boards as a standing surface. Such improvised structures have the advantage of being easily dismantled and reassembled as the need arises.

The position of a stand is frequently a matter of compromise, especially in the summer when the area is most heavily used. A good position for viewing from the house is against a wall opposite a door or window overlooking a courtyard or patio. In winter, when the patio is less often used, a staged display can be placed more centrally. Wherever the stand is put, the best results are usually achieved with a balanced combination of flowering and foliage plants. Even ordinary plants can make a striking display when skillfully arranged.

Informal clusters

Stray containers, unless carefully placed, can be a nuisance and a hazard in paved areas, but informal clusters can be a very effective way of displaying plants and their pots. An interesting range of plants in containers of different heights and sizes can, to some extent, mimic the layered effect of plants in the open garden. This can be enhanced by standing some containers on bricks or upturned pots to give additional prominence and by varying the height of their contents.

Any irregularly shaped cluster is a useful way of filling a corner, and informally planted containers along the borders of a patio or terrace can help soften the formal severity of paving. Very pleasing, unifying effects can be achieved by using differently shaped containers in the same material – unglazed terracotta pots, for example, are available in a wide range of shapes and sizes.

Keep it clean

The main disadvantage of clustered containers is that, inevitably, soil, dead leaves, and other detritus accumulate around their bases, which can be difficult to sweep away. A power hose is useful for keeping the surfaces clean, but it is also worth investing in wheeled bases for pots. These not only make it easier to sweep detritus away but are also an invaluable aid when moving heavy pots to re-create displays as plants fade at the end of their season.

TIERED CONTAINER DISPLAY
A banked mass of brilliant color is achieved here by using pots of various sizes, with additional height gained by means of upturned empty pots – an inexpensive alternative to staging. *The range of bronze-tinted greens found in the geranium leaves forms a linking element and is a complementary foil for the brilliant reds.*

Balconies and roof gardens

BALCONIES and areas of flat roof can be converted to architecturally pleasing spaces in which container-grown plants can be used with extraordinary effect to create gardens in the air. Large-scale roof gardens can incorporate many of the features of a garden at ground level, including seating for relaxing and entertaining, barbecues, ornamental pools, and trees and climbers on supports. Even the smallest balcony, without room for furniture, can be transformed into a green and flower-filled outdoor room – a valuable extension of the living space indoors and a beautiful frame for the world beyond.

Special challenges

Almost any balcony or flat roof area has garden potential, but such spaces present special challenges, with safety a major consideration. Plants, moist soil mix, containers, and all the other features that make up a garden constitute considerable weight, which must be within the structure's load-bearing capacity. In addition, flooring must be waterproof and adequately drained. It is always advisable to consult an architect or structural engineer before planning a roof or balcony garden, and check with local authorities about building permits. Expert advice should include suggestions for fortifying structural support, or on how to site heavy elements to use the existing load-bearing capacity of walls or crossbeams. With careful choice of materials, the accumulated weight of garden components can be minimized. For example, consider wooden decking rather than tiling as a flooring material. Select plastic or fiberglass containers rather than those made of very heavy materials, such as stone and concrete; and use soilless rather than soil-based potting mix to reduce the load even more.

Balconies and roof gardens need barriers to protect those using the space: consult relevant building regulations governing minimum standards and heights for railings and walls. Balconies and roof gardens are much more likely to be affected by turbulence and strong winds than gardens at ground level, so all containers must be firmly secured. It is important, too, that none of the contents of a balcony or roof garden falls off, putting people and property below at risk. Even within a roof garden or balcony, falling pots and large plants can cause damage to windows. Lightweight containers may need to be mounted in position or ballast added to prevent their being blown over. Bear in mind that tall, narrow-based pots are much less stable than squat, broad-based ones.

The blustery winds that are a typical feature of balconies and roof gardens may damage fragile growth and wither tender foliage on plants such as Japanese maples (*Acer palmatum* cultivars). Drying winds combined with full sun create testing growing conditions. The most successful plants are tough and drought-tolerant; however, a wide range of plants will grow well provided they receive an adequate and regular water supply. On a large roof garden, an automated irrigation system can be the most efficient way to maintain satisfactory moisture levels, provided that provision is made for dealing with excess water. It is important that the structure incorporates drainage channels so that water does not form

PARTIAL SCREENING
A see-through screen helps create an intimate, sheltered atmosphere in this roof garden. New Zealand flax (Phormium) *stands up well to windy conditions and is used here to make an impressive focal feature in a large but lightweight urn.*

SHADE IN SUMMER
This lightweight bamboo screening provides invaluable shade from strong overhead summer sun on a roof or balcony garden.

WELL-MANAGED SPACE
On this wooden deck, attractive container-grown plants are carefully grouped so that they do not impede access to the steps.

PLANTING FOR AN EXPOSED POSITION
Flowers and foliage plants, including gray-leaved Senecio maritima *and spreading* Scaevola *with fan-shaped flowers, make a wind-tolerant mixture.*

MINIMALIST FORMALITY
Strip decking, squared-up layout, and rounded topiary all contribute to the formality of a roof garden that includes both planted and empty containers.

pools, for example, after a storm. Wooden decking can be laid to disguise any drainage systems required.

Planting on balconies

Plants for balconies can be grown in pots and troughs that stand on the balcony floor, in wall-mounted containers, or in those that are securely attached to railings. When a balcony forms a garden extension to a room, the appearance of the containers and plants is most often judged from inside. Use planting to frame rather than obscure a good view, perhaps by grouping containers at either side of a clear central area. If, on the other hand, the view is dull or mediocre, use container-grown plants to block it out. In a similar way, trailing plants, spilling from pots or troughs mounted at the top of railings, can provide privacy by screening the room within from view.

Balcony plantings can be just as attractive from within as from outside a building. Balconies, like window-boxes, may be planted to complement the architecture, perhaps with designs that coordinate with plantings at ground level and on the floors above. Good trailing plants for sunny balconies include ivy-leaved geraniums; these are reasonably drought-tolerant and flower freely through summer and into autumn. Many bushy and upright plants also adapt well to life on sunny balconies, including aromatic herbs, such as hyssop (*Hyssopus officinalis*) and long-flowering annuals, such as the kingfisher daisy (*Felicia bergeriana*). While the choice for shady balconies is more limited, elegant schemes can be created using cultivars of English

ivy (*Hedera helix*) and evergreens, such as boxwood (*Buxus sempervirens*), which provide year-round interest. Add extra color with compact, shade-tolerant annuals and biennials, for example winter- and summer-flowering pansies (*Viola* x *wittrockiana*) or impatiens (*Impatiens walleriana*), which bloom for several months during summer.

Planting in roof gardens

Large balconies and roof gardens often provide viewing platforms for dramatic cityscapes. If this is the case, capitalize on the view and use planting to frame it. Whether the

CAREFULLY PLACED PLANTS
Even though plants play a subdued role on this balcony, they soften the hard lines of the essential safety barrier. While they have been chosen and placed carefully to not obscure the impressive long vista, the smaller plants do help block out the near and least attractive part of the view. Taller plants to the rear create a partial screen for shelter and privacy from neighbors.

design is formal or informal, try to group containers so that the revelation of a view is gradual. Alternatively, create frames for a series of different vistas, which will guarantee that the best view of all does not lose its novelty.

Perhaps more common than a beautiful prospect is a dreary view from a messy and overlooked space. In this case, the best option is to create a more inward-looking garden. A climbing plant, barrier, or trellis not only helps block out ugly views but also establishes an intimate atmosphere and helps reduce wind turbulence. Within the defined space, the design could be strictly formal, using a few shrubs trimmed to simple geometric shapes, or you could assemble plants to suggest the medley of a traditional cottage garden. For colorful, long-lasting displays, massed bedding plants are a good option, but there is also some opportunity to experiment with vegetables and herbs, or subtropical and tropical plants. By creating compartments with screens, or even a pergola, variety is increased and intimacy enhanced.

Whatever the chosen style, arrange containers so they do not clutter areas used for seating and entertaining. For the most wind-resistant results, choose bushy and compact plants; they are less likely to be damaged or desiccated by strong winds. Compact cultivars of most popular bedding plants are readily available, and there are many bushy shrubs to choose in preference to those that are tall and top-heavy.

Hanging containers

A variety of manufactured and improvised containers can be suspended or mounted to create a planted environment above ground level. They are particularly useful where space is limited, but even in conventional gardens there are many opportunities to use aerial displays of plants. They are invaluable for softening architectural environments; helping to lift the eye above other planting; and can be integrated into ambitious designs in which plants are arranged on several levels.

Hanging baskets

The traditional hanging basket is a simple suspended container consisting of a wire frame in which a liner holds sufficient soil mix to sustain one or, more usually, several plants. A number of other suspended containers – either ready-made or improvised – serve the same purpose and are planted and displayed in a similar way to hanging baskets.

Wire-framed baskets and other suspended containers are best planted so that the container itself is concealed by full and trailing growth. This may be achieved with a single vigorous trailer, such as *Tradescantia zebrina*, a popular house or conservatory plant that can also be moved outdoors in summer.

In general, however, it is much easier to create a floating cloud of foliage and flowers with a mixture of several different, less tender plants. The aim is to achieve a loosely rounded shape, using plants of different habit, so that growth hides the container. One approach is to use upright and rounded plants to form a crown above an irregular, hanging fringe of trailing or spreading plants. This could be achieved by including erect cultivars of geraniums and *Verbena* x *hybrida*, flanked by trailing fuchsias, lobelias, and petunias. Another option is to use containers that are in themselves ornamental, so that, even when the display is at its peak, some of the container is visible.

Hanging baskets are often hung as isolated features, perhaps to take advantage of an existing support. This might be an arch or the cross-piece of a pergola, for example. Another approach is to attach specially made supports for single or multiple hanging baskets. Brackets can be simple and inconspicuous, or ornamental and in a style that suits the surroundings. A hanging basket can make a dramatic focal point to enliven a blank wall, especially if it can be seen from a window or door. They can also be eye-catching when

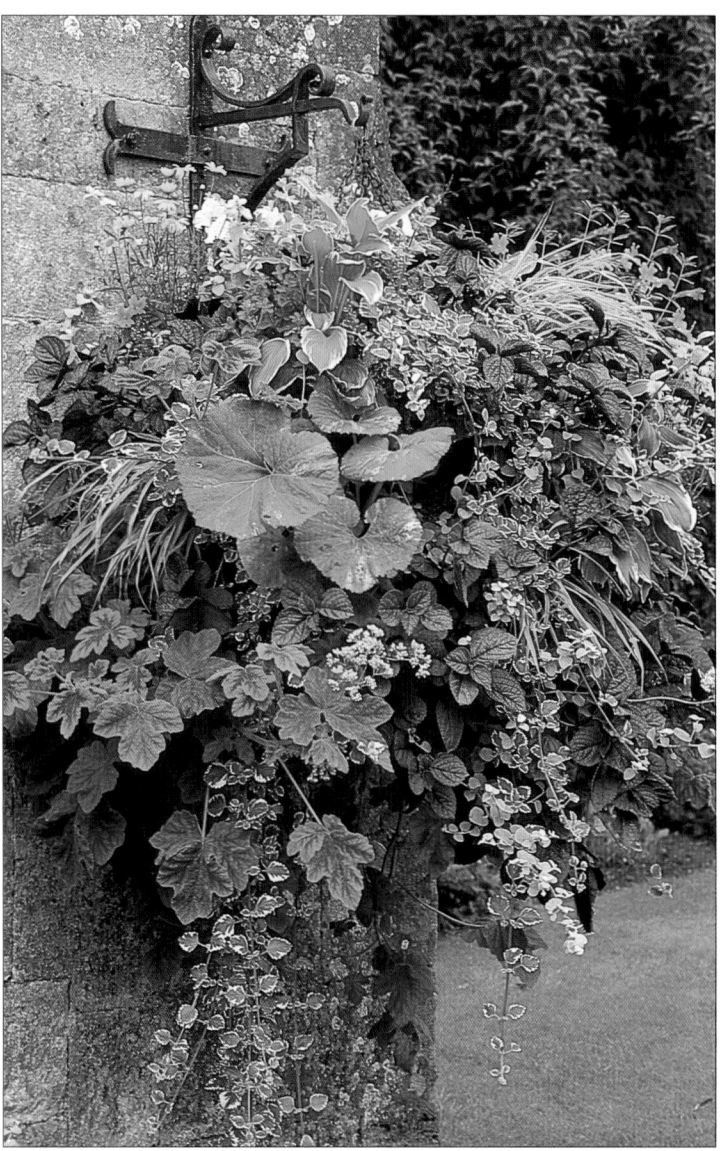

ELEVATED EYE-CATCHER
A reliance on foliage colors and textures provides a long season of interest. Here, it masks the basket, but the ornamental bracket can still be seen.

suspended from the corner of a building, but for safety they must be well above the height of passers-by.

The most obvious of the multiple arrangements are pairs of baskets, mounted, for example, on either side of a door or combined with other containers. A handsome design can be created by using a large container, such as an urn, at ground level against a wall, with hanging baskets mounted above it and on either side. The plants in the hanging baskets may match or contrast with those in the large container. For a more ambitious scheme, hanging baskets can be hung in rows, on a series of arches, or on brackets along a wall. Carefully coordinated or contrasting plantings can be dramatically staged by using several smaller baskets on either side of a large one, or by introducing variations in the height at which the

containers are suspended. Using the cross-pieces of a pergola or a trellis, a sequence of paired hanging baskets either side of a path makes an impressive avenue, although it is worth bearing in mind that such features will be time-consuming to water.

Windowboxes

These containers are available in a wide range of materials, including wood, terracotta, concrete, and plastic. They are sometimes designed to be ornamental on their own account, with painted or relief decoration. Plain wooden windowboxes can be painted to match other architectural details, but for more adventurous effects consider painting windowboxes on the front of a building in a bold color to make them stand out. The planting style and content of a windowbox depends to some extent

on the position from which it is viewed. For some apartment-dwellers, for example, their entire garden may amount to one or two windowboxes, so the view from inside matters more than that from ground level. The greatest pleasure may be had from choosing plants of refined beauty, fragrance, or aromatic foliage. If windowboxes form an integral part of the decoration of a house front, on the other hand, the view from outside is what really counts. The most valuable plants in this sort of display will be those that perform reliably over a long season, and might include an evergreen, such as boxwood (*Buxus sempervirens*).

If windowboxes are in windy, exposed positions, they may not be suitable for tall plants, which will be battered by wind; they may also block out the light. But to avoid a dull, uniformly low display, position compact but rounded plants, such as geraniums, in the center, with lower plants on either side and trailing plants cascading from the front. There are many variations to play on this theme, using a wide range of plants, including evergreens for winter or year-round effect.

Wall-mounted containers

The types of containers that can be wall-mounted include semicircular wire or strip-metal baskets, metal-frame mangers, and plastic or terracotta half-pots. Brackets can also be attached to walls to hold standard pots of small or medium size, and more solid brackets can be used to support troughs – but be sure that they are attached securely. Wall-mounted containers filled with plants are invaluable in breaking up the blankness of bare walls, whether used on their own or in conjunction with other planting. They are equally useful where windows open outward or lack a sill. The best alternative to a windowbox can be a trough mounted on brackets below the window. Wall-mounted containers are perhaps of greatest value in narrow spaces, or where a courtyard or passage is partly shaded. In a raised position, plants have greater access to light and will often thrive better when elevated than at ground level.

In general, stone or brick walls make a beautiful backdrop to plantings, but, in order to take full advantage of their possibilities, it is important to choose containers and hangers that match or contrast with the background color and texture. Full planting and generous use of trailing plants is generally the best option but, if the container itself is decorative, it should obviously be

ALL-AROUND DISPLAY
This combination of geraniums, petunias, Diascia, and Bacopa in this cascading window-box arrangement will give just as much pleasure to the occupants within as it does to the viewers in the street below.

methods, many plants are available of more compact habit, with single, semidouble, or double flowers in many colors or shades, sometimes with even more dramatic differences of flower or petal form. It is now possible to put together an extremely varied mixture, even with a limited number of plants.

Although the range is much smaller, another important group consists of annuals and biennials that flower in winter and early spring. The winter-flowering pansies (*Viola* x *wittrockiana*) create colorful displays before the main bulb season and then may continue for many weeks more. Other plants that help give continuity through spring are English daisies (*Bellis perennis*), primroses of the Polyanthus group, and wallflowers (*Erysimum cheiri*).

Most annuals and biennials are relatively easy to raise from seed; the F1 and F2 hybrids, although more expensive, provide more vigorous and uniform plants. If space does not permit raising plants from seed, there is a good selection of plants at local garden centers in late spring and early summer, and these can be a convenient way of acquiring a good range of plants in small numbers. Plant up pots just before annuals come into flower, so the container garden is almost instantaneously colorful and remains so for months.

visible. The siting of wall-mounted containers is also important. Too many, indiscriminately arranged, will create messy and rather fussy effects. A few large containers create more impact than many small ones and, in addition, will be easier to maintain, especially when watering. Nevertheless, with careful placement, either in a symmetrical or asymmetrical pattern, attractive displays can be made with individual pots of flowers. For winter and spring color, try double primroses, such as the rich violet *Primula vulgaris* 'Miss Indigo' or soft yellow 'Double Sulphur', or English daisies, such as *Bellis perennis* Pomponette Series. For summer, there is a huge range of vibrant geraniums that flower for several months, and often into autumn.

Plants for container gardening

All categories of plants – annuals, perennials, climbers, shrubs, and trees – are available for the container gardener. The traditional approach focuses on compact, long-flowering summer annuals, which are undeniably valuable for creating colorful displays; but container gardening becomes much more interesting and challenging if the repertoire of plants is extended. Using all types of plants allows for arrangements of different scale and exploits the range of habits. Foliage, for example, is often neglected in favor of flowers, yet it has special value in the container garden. Evergreens provide year-round

pleasure, and even deciduous foliage is longer lasting than most flower displays. Suitability for the available light levels is often the key issue when choosing plants for particular positions. Also be aware that the soil mix in above-ground containers freezes colder than soil in the garden, so perennial and woody plants that are normally hardy for you may not survive in a planter. As a guide, choose plants that are at least a full zone hardier or, better still, two zones, for planting in containers.

Annuals and biennials
Summer-flowering annuals, including a number of tender perennials that are usually grown as annuals, are justly popular plants for container gardening. As a result of breeding

Perennials
The perennials traditionally used in container gardening are tender ones that are raised annually from seed, or overwintered under cover. Geraniums (*Pelargonium*) are tender, shrubby perennials that make excellent container specimens. Some are F1 or

MASSED ANNUAL PLANTING
Soft mauve petunias – a plant often used in riotous combinations – can look unexpectedly eye-catching when planted alone in a large clump.

UNUSUAL ARRANGEMENT
A surprisingly successful mixture of hardy astilbes and tender begonias shows that, at times, the experimental breaking of rules is most rewarding.

309

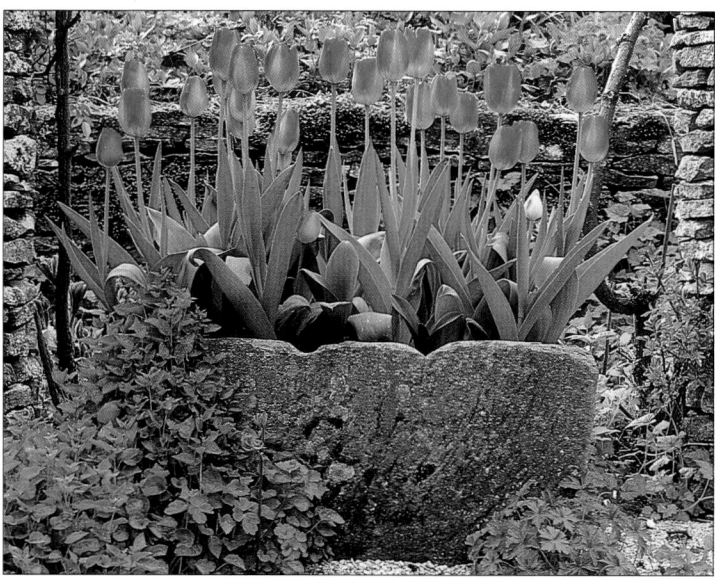

STONE TROUGH
This deep stone trough displays tulips to perfection. It is totally in scale with the planting, and the bulbs grow tall and straight in this sheltered niche.

F2 hybrids raised annually from seed, while others can be overwintered to provide material for cuttings that are brought on for the new season; the parent plant can then be discarded. The zonal and trailing ivy-leaved geraniums flower prolifically over a long season and are the most widely used in outdoor container gardening – the trailing ivy-leaved kinds are particularly useful in hanging baskets, tall containers, and windowboxes, or on balconies.

Scented-leaved geraniums are an interesting and underused group. The silver-margined, eucalyptus-scented leaves of *Pelargonium* 'Lady Plymouth', for example, are excellent for breaking up large blocks of flower color, and the leaves release their evocative fragrance when handled. The flowers tend to be small, but the spice-scented *P.* 'Copthorne' is one of several with large, attractively marked blooms.

Border perennials are not widely used in container gardening, but there is no reason not to experiment. Those with evergreen foliage help fill the gap between autumn and spring; many bergenias, for example, have large, spoon-shaped leaves that take on rich copper-red tones in fall weather, and the sprays of pink, magenta, or white flowers in spring are long-lasting. *Heuchera* is another useful genus: *Heuchera micrantha* var. *diversifolia* 'Palace Purple' has large, glossy, jagged leaves that are deep bronze-red, topped in summer by showers of tiny white flowers and pink seedheads.

The length of their flowering season makes some hardy herbaceous perennials potentially useful plants for containers. Although individual flowers are short-lived, the low-growing daylilies bloom over many weeks in mid- to late summer – those of *Hemerocallis* 'Stella de Oro' being pale orange – and most produce sheaves of attractive foliage. Other herbaceous perennials with distinguished foliage include hostas, in an enormous range of sizes, colors, and textures. A clump of the blue-gray, corrugated leaves of *Hosta sieboldiana* var. *elegans* fully justifies a container for itself.

Bulbs

In this context, the term "bulbs" also includes plants with corms, tubers, and rhizomes. It is a group that is very important in container gardening; their value lies in their remarkably reliable flowering, even though few have foliage of any great ornamental value; individual plants rarely flower for more than a few weeks. By planting a range of spring bulbs, however, a succession of colorful explosions can be enjoyed from late winter to late the following autumn.

This long season begins with snowdrops, dwarf irises, and early crocuses, and it overlaps with the earliest daffodils, which are followed by the later daffodil varieties, hyacinths, and tulips. There are many other small bulbs, such as *Scilla*, *Muscari*, and *Puschkinia*, that fit into this flowering routine. The most useful summer and autumn bulbs include lilies, dahlias, and cannas, with their huge variety in color, shape and height.

Match bulbs and containers for size and take into account the position the containers will occupy.

Tall-growing tulips, for example, are likely to suffer wind damage when planted in windowboxes. There are excellent dwarf tulips, as well as other low-growing bulbs that are better for exposed positions.

The flowers of bulbs generally last longer if the containers are in light or partial shade, but the flowers of some, including crocuses and tulips, open fully only in sun. For densely packed containers, two or even three layers of bulbs can be planted at different depths (see p.321).

With bulbs, there is inevitably a gap between planting and flowering. One way to overcome this is to keep containers in a cold frame until bulbs begin to flower. The containers can then be brought into view and then removed once flowering is over. Another option is to plant bulbs of different kinds in the same container to give a successional display, or to create mixed plantings. Many dwarf bulbs combine well with winter-flowering pansies (*Viola* x *wittrockiana*) and low evergreens, such as thymes (*Thymus*) or small-leaved cultivars of English ivy (*Hedera helix*). Bulbs can also be used as an underplanting to spring flowering shrubs such as *Skimmia*.

Although some containerized bulbs flower well for several years, the performance of most bulbs deteriorates after the first season if the soil mix is not renewed annually (if the bulbs live past the first season). For high-quality displays, it is best to plant new stock each year. Otherwise, allow bulbs to die down in their containers, then lift and store for replanting later in the growing season, or replant directly in the garden for reduced displays in subsequent years.

Trees

Many evergreen and deciduous trees can adapt to life in containers and, if well cared for, will flourish for many years, although they seldom reach the size they would attain in the open garden. Those that feature foliage, flowers, and fruits among their ornamental virtues include Amur maple, *Acer tataricum* subsp. *ginnala*, and flowering crabapples, for example *Malus* 'Red Jade'; both have spring flowers and long-lasting fruits, borne amid a blaze of autumn foliage color.

The height and architectural presence of container-grown trees, such as hornbeam (*Carpinus betulus*) or colored-bark birches, such as *Betula albosinensis* var. *septentrionalis*, lend a strong structural element to a design. They are particularly useful for screening and help create privacy and areas of cool shade.

When choosing trees for patios, courtyards, and roof gardens, scale is important. Compact conifers, such as the conical *Chamaecyparis lawsoniana* 'Ellwoodii', are among the most useful. Deciduous small trees include the Kilmarnock willow (*Salix caprea* 'Kilmarnock') with pendulous branches loaded with white then yellow catkins in spring. Trees that respond well to clipping are of particular value where space is limited. One of the most useful evergreens for container gardening is the sweet bay (*Laurus nobilis*), which can be trimmed in a variety of shapes.

Shrubs

Shrubs, which are much more widely used in container gardening than trees, span a range from large spreading specimens, which require heavy, broad-based containers, to dwarf

MONOCHROME DISPLAY
The simplicity of this arrangement of boxwood (Buxus sempervirens) and English ivy (Hedera helix) is a perfect match for its architectural setting.

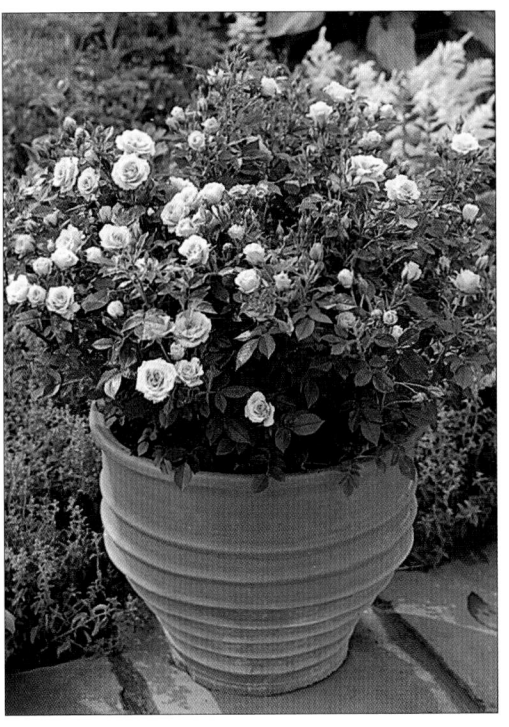

A MOVABLE FEAST
For those gardeners who feel that no garden is complete without roses, modern rose breeders have made possible their use in even the most confined of spaces. Most patio roses (the diminutive counterparts of Floribundas), such as this Rosa SURREY, bloom almost continuously throughout summer. The upright, bushy mound of growth is carefully balanced here by a wide terracotta pot.

CONTAINER SUPPORTS
Tepees and obelisks, whether bought or simply improvised, are ideal supports for climbers in pots. Here, such supports elevate a simple, cool-colored arrangement to a well-balanced focal point.

bushes, for example many dwarf conifers, which are suitable for windowboxes. When choosing a shrub, consider its scale within the setting, the plant's shape, and the qualities of foliage, flowers, and fruits that will keep the plants interesting over a long period.

Compact evergreens with good foliage and pleasing shape include a large number of dwarf conifers. Some broadleaved evergreens, such as boxwood (*Buxus sempervirens*) or *Osmanthus* x *burkwoodii*, that tolerate clipping, can be trimmed to formal or more whimsical shapes.

In some cases, it is foliage color that gives a plant a special value, as with variegated plants, such as *Euonymus fortunei* 'Emerald Gaiety'. Many low-growing cultivars of heather (*Calluna vulgaris*) provide colored winter foliage as well as flowers. With camellias, dark, glossy foliage is matched by single to fully double flowers of great beauty. Some rhododendrons also combine highly ornamental foliage and exquisite flowers; *R. yakushimanum* hybrids have a pleasingly dense habit and compact furry undersides to the new leaves that follow the flowers.

For delicate summer foliage textures and brilliant autumn colors, the Japanese maples (*Acer palmatum* cultivars) are hard to beat. Other deciduous shrubs grown mainly for their flowers include *Hydrangea macrophylla* cultivars, with flowerheads that last for months, often with pleasing color changes as they age. Fuchsias produce new flowers without interruption throughout summer

until checked by frosts. The trailing kinds are useful for spilling over the rim of hanging baskets and tall containers, while some of the erect ones, such as *F.* 'Lady Thumb', make compact bushes that are ideal centerpieces in any container.

Roses
The most suitable roses for container gardening are miniature roses, patio roses, and some of the groundcover roses. Miniatures, such as POUR TOI ('Para Ti') and LITTLE BO-PEEP ('Poullen'), are small twiggy bushes, to 1ft (30cm) high, with a myriad of tiny leaflets; they are perfect for windowboxes, needing only 8–10in (20–25cm) depth of soil. Patio roses are slightly larger bushes well covered with clustered flowers from summer to autumn; reliable performers include the brilliant orange TOP MARKS ('Fryministar'), the soft apricot-peach SWEET DREAM ('Fryminicot'), and the pale pink PRETTY POLLY ('Meitonje'). They look especially good in a stone trough or an unglazed terracotta pot.

Groundcover roses are more lax in growth and are ideal for hanging baskets and tall pots, where the sinuous stems can trail over the pot rim or basket's edge. Try PINK BELLS ('Poulbells') with its bright pink, pompon blooms, or MAGIC CARPET ('Jaclover') with its semidouble, magenta flowers.

Climbers
The versatility of climbers in containers can hardly be overstated. They can be as effective trained

upward on obelisks or other frames as they can be when used in less conventional ways. Some can simply be allowed to trail. A small-flowered clematis, such as *C. alpina* 'Frances Rivis', looks particularly elegant when spilling from tall pots or jars. Some of the more compact, large-flowered clematis, like the white-flowered *C.* 'Miss Bateman', are also successful if grown this way. Other more unusual, trailing plants include the tender perennial *Rhodochiton atrosanguineus* with its pendent, red-purple, tubular flowers.

Cultivars of English ivy (*Hedera helix*) can look just as good as trailers or climbers. The small-leaved kinds are among the best trailing evergreens for hanging baskets and for softening the hard edges of

windowboxes and other containers. These adaptable plants also lend themselves to more elaborate training. Try growing them on wire frames – they can make a very effective imitation of clipped topiary (see TOPIARY, p.118).

Strict training is usually the best way to manage vigorous climbers, including wisterias and grapes (*Vitis*). With rigorous summer and winter pruning, they can be grown as standards. But among the easiest are annuals, such as the freshly scented sweet peas (*Lathyrus odoratus*) or those like *Ipomoea tricolor* that are treated as annuals. Grow them on tepees of bamboo stakes laced together with string, on rustic pyramids made of brushwood branches, or on custom-made trellis panels.

Specialized container gardens

Container gardening is a versatile technique that, with a little imagination, can be adapted for a wide range of styles and types of gardening. Ponds and formal herb or vegetable patches, for example, usually associated with larger gardens, can be scaled down for smaller plots by using containers. It is equally possible to provide a touch of subtropical splendor in cool-temperate zones.

Fruit, vegetables, and herbs

An interesting selection of fruits and vegetables can be grown outdoors in containers such as tubs, large pots, and growing bags. Some are highly ornamental, as well as yielding reasonable crops when grown on a small scale. Crop plants grown in containers, however, generally require more attention to fertilizing and watering than they do in the open garden.

Strawberries are a good choice among fruits since they generally bear well. At the other end of the scale are tree fruits, such as apples, grown on a dwarfing rootstock; single-stemmed Ballerina apple trees are ideal but must be fertilized and watered conscientiously. Figs need root restriction to bear satisfactorily and so are suited to container cultivation. They need to be moved under cover in winter where not hardy.

Among vegetables the best choice are those that are compact, quick-growing, and highly productive. Radishes and lettuces, some of which are very ornamental, mature quickly; climbing peas and beans (on tepees) and zucchini crop well if adequately fertilized and watered. Fruiting vegetables such as tomatoes, eggplants, and peppers are particularly attractive and, since they need sun and warmth to grow well, are ideal for containers in sunny courtyards or roof gardens.

For many gardeners, the challenge is part of the pleasure of growing fruits and vegetables, but herbs are, on the whole, an easier proposition. A good range, including shrubby ones such as rosemary (*Rosmarinus officinalis*) and thyme (*Thymus vulgaris*), and annuals or biennials, such as chervil (*Anthriscus cerefolium*) and parsley (*Petroselinum crispum*), can be grown in a small space, providing leaves for culinary use from aromatic plants that are good to look at and easy to handle.

Water gardens

A pond can make an attractive water feature in a small garden. Glazed jars are among the most suitable containers for this purpose where there is no risk of freezing. If they are to be used in areas prone to severe cold, they cannot be left outdoors year-round. Other suitable containers include wooden tubs and half-barrels, glazed

VEGETABLE GARDEN
Many edible plants can be successfully cultivated in pots and other containers, provided they are watered and fertilized regularly. Here herbs such as bay, fennel, and variegated lemon balm are grown alongside a Ballerina apple tree, strawberries, and rhubarb. In temperate areas, tender plants such as citrus (in the foreground) must be moved under cover during the winter months.

TROPICAL EFFECTS
Spiky plants, such as Cordyline *and* Agave, *are strongly architectural and lend an effective suggestion of the subtropics. Their relatively somber colors are enlivened here by the hot scarlets of nasturtiums (one of the most easily grown of annuals) and* Campsis (*along the top of the wall*).

sinks, and large metal pots or cauldrons. The wood of tubs and barrels is often impregnated with chemicals that are harmful to plants and they are best lined with butyl rubber or PVC. It is also a wise precaution to seal the inside of metal containers with a rubber sealant to prevent any contamination of the water. Fish in raised containers may not survive freezing conditions and should be brought indoors in winter.

The plants that can be accommodated in a small water garden are a narrow but select group. Several waterlilies, such as the yellow, free-flowering *Nymphaea* 'Pygmaea Helvola', can be grown in water that is only 8–18in (20–45cm) deep, and shallow water is good for the mauve-flowered water hyacinth (*Eichhornia crassipes*) and the sculptural *Pistia stratiotes*. Marginal plants of suitable scale include *Juncus effusus* 'Spiralis' and *Typha minima*. Always plant an oxygenator, such as *Myriophyllum verticillatum*, to help keep the water fresh. Lift plants at the end of summer, and overwinter in frost-free conditions. See also WATER GARDENING, pp.274–297.

Subtropical container gardens

Even in cool-temperate regions, the choice of plants for containers on patios or terraces and in courtyards can help create the impression of a warmer climate. One way to achieve this is to use plants that are natives of hotter regions of the world, and give them protection from cold in a greenhouse or conservatory during the cold months, moving them outdoors for the frost-free summer months. Plants that instantly create a tropical

effect include angels' trumpets (*Brugmansia*) and *Abutilon* hybrids. The display can be enhanced – and management made easier – by adding hardy or marginally hardy plants of subtropical appearance, including the lush, large-leaved Japanese banana (*Musa basjoo*) or palms such as the Chusan palm (*Trachycarpus fortunei*). To reinforce the design, include evergreen shrubs, such as *Fatsia japonica*, with large, glossy leaves, and New Zealand flax (*Phormium*) with evergreen, sword-like leaves. Many bamboos, such as *Sasa veitchii* and *Fargesia murielae*, also have a graceful, subtropical appearance. To these can be added the frost-tender castor bean (*Ricinus communis*), which is usually raised annually from seed.

To create desert effects, cacti and other succulents are ideal. As many have low moisture and nutrient needs, they are particularly suitable for low-maintenance container gardening. Some, such as *Sempervivum*, are quite hardy, too. The tender succulent *Agave americana* and its variegated cultivars, with magnificent, swordlike leaves, are fairly tolerant of summer rainfall, as are yuccas, which make good companions.

Plants that evoke a Mediterranean climate include olive trees (*Olea europaea*), lemon trees (*Citrus limon*), bougainvilleas, and oleanders (*Nerium oleander*), all of which look beautiful in terracotta pots. They must be moved under cover in winter, but hardier plants, such as lavenders and rosemary, also fit this style. Although the last two tolerate more cold, it is best to protect them for winter where marginally hardy.

Planter's guide to container plants

TREES AND SHRUBS

See also p.59 for larger trees. For dwarf conifers, see p.62

Abutilon
Acer japonicum, A. palmatum, A. tataricum subsp. *ginnala*
Argyranthemum (subshrub)
Buxus balearica, B. microphylla, B. sempervirens
Calluna vulgaris
Camellia
Caragana arborescens 'Walker'
Codiaeum variegatum var. *pictum*
Cornus stolonifera (cvs)
Dracaena
Erica
Euonymus fortunei

Rhododendron yakushimanum

Fatsia japonica
x *Fatshedera lizei*
Fuchsia
Gardenia
Hibiscus rosa-sinensis
Hydrangea macrophylla (and cvs), *H. paniculata, H. quercifolia*
Lantana
Lavandula
Malus 'Tina'
Morus alba 'Pendula'
Nerium oleander
Physocarpus opulifolius 'Darts Gold'
Picea glauca v. *albertiana* 'Conica'
Pinus mugo v. *mugo*
Prunus laurocerasus
Rhododendron
Rosa (Groundcover, Miniature, and Patio hybrids)
Santolina
Skimmia japonica
Spiraea x *bumalda* 'Goldflame'
Viburnum davidii, V. tinus, V. trilobum 'Compactum'
Yucca

PALMS AND CYCADS

Chamaedorea
Chamaerops
Cocos
Cycas revoluta
Howea
Phoenix
Rhapis
Sabal
Trachycarpus fortunei
Washingtonia

BAMBOOS, GRASSES, AND GRASSLIKE PLANTS

Carex
Deschampsia cespitosa (cvs)
Fargesia murielae, F. nitida
Hakonechloa macra (cvs)
Himalayacalamus falconeri
Imperata cylindrica 'Rubra'
Indocalamus tessellatus
Pennisetum alopecuroides
Phalaris arundinacea 'Picta'
Phyllostachys aurea, P. flexuosa, P. nigra
Pleioblastus auricomus, P. variegatus
Shibataea kumasasa

PERENNIALS

See also Planter's guide to rock plants, Planting in troughs, p.253

Achimenes
Agapanthus
Alchemilla
Astilbe
Begonia Rex hybrids
Bergenia
Calceolaria integrifolia (cvs)
Campanula (dwarf)
Canna
Catharanthus roseus
Chrysanthemum
Dianthus

Agapanthus

Diascia
Ensete ventricosum
Fittonia
Geranium
Glechoma hederacea 'Variegata'
Hemerocallis
Heuchera
Hosta
Houttuynia cordata 'Chameleon'
Lamium maculatum
Lysimachia nummularia 'Aurea'
Musa basjoo
Nepeta
Osteospermum
Peperomia
Phlox (dwarf)
Phormium
Plectranthus
Primula Polyanthus Group
Salvia discolor, S. uliginosa
Tiarella
Tolmiea menziesii
Tradescantia fluminensis (cvs), *T. zebrina*

CLIMBERS

☆ **annual, or commonly grown as one**

Bougainvillea
Clematis, many
Clerodendrum thomsoniae
Cobaea scandens☆
Eccremocarpus scaber☆
Hedera helix
Jasminum
Lathyrus odoratus☆
Passiflora
Rhodochiton atrosanguineus☆
Stephanotis
Thunbergia alata☆
Trachelospermum

CACTI AND SUCCULENTS

See p.313

FERNS

Adiantum
Asplenium scolopendrium
Athyrium
Blechnum
Davallia
Dicksonia antarctica
Nephrolepis
Platycerium
Polypodium
Polystichum

BULBS

Amaryllis belladonna
Anemone blanda, A. coronaria (cvs), *A.* x *fulgens*
Begonia (tuberous)
Chionodoxa
Clivia
Crocus
Cyclamen
Dahlia
Freesia
Hippeastrum
Hyacinthus (cvs)
Iris (bulbous)
Ixia
Lachenalia
Lilium
Muscari
Narcissus
Nerine
Scilla (some spp.)
Tulipa

ANNUALS AND BIENNIALS

§ Perennial or subshrub commonly grown as an annual or biennial

Ageratum
Antirrhinum (dwarf cvs)
Bellis perennis (cvs)
Bidens§
Brachyscome
Brassica oleracea (ornamental cvs)
Calendula officinalis
Celosia§
Dianthus barbatus, D. chinensis§ (cvs)
Erysimum
Exacum affine§
Gazania§
Helichrysum petiolare§
Heliotropium§

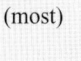

Viola x *wittrockiana*
Princess Series

Impatiens§
Iresine§
Lobelia erinus§ (cvs)
Lotus berthelotii§, *L. maculatus*§
Nicotiana§
Matthiola Brompton Series, *M.* East Lothian Series
Mimulus hybrids
Pelargonium§
Petunia§
Primula Polyanthus Group §
Ricinus communis§ (cvs)
Salvia coccinea§, *S. farinacea*§, *S. patens*§, *S. splendens*§, *S. viridis*
Scaevola§
Schizanthus pinnatus (cvs)
Solanum capsicastrum§, *S. pseudocapsicum*§
Solenostemon (syn. *Coleus*)§
Tagetes
Tropaeolum majus (cvs and hybrids)
Verbena hybrids§
Viola x *wittrockiana* §
Zinnia

FRUIT

Apples (on dwarfing rootstocks)
Blueberries
Citrus (most)

Lemon

Figs
Grapes
Peaches (dwarf)
Strawberries

HERBS

Most herbs described on pp.396–409 can be grown in containers, but pay careful attention to their annual or perennial nature and their hardiness.

Choosing containers

A SUITABLE container in which to grow plants must satisfy many criteria. It should hold sufficient soil mix to give plants adequate space for root development and to supply the moisture and nutrients necessary for growth. A container must also allow excess water to drain away, usually by means of one or more drainage holes in the base. Stability is also important; if a container is easily knocked or blown over, it may create a safety hazard and both the container and the plants in it may suffer damage.

Many commercially available containers satisfy these requirements and, being mass-produced, are relatively inexpensive. Other, more expensive ones are made individually or in small quantities, but these, along with homemade or improvised containers, often have more character and make an eye-catching statement of individual taste.

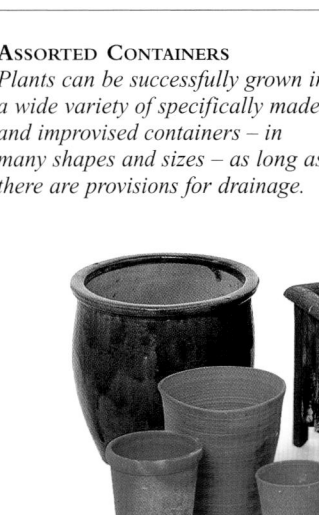

ASSORTED CONTAINERS
Plants can be successfully grown in a wide variety of specifically made and improvised containers – in many shapes and sizes – as long as there are provisions for drainage.

Materials and finishes

Containers are available in a variety of materials and finishes, each having practical and aesthetic advantages that should be taken into account before making a choice. Bear in mind where a container is to stand; its weight, for example, can be an important factor. Decide whether the style of container is to complement that of the garden or whether the container will play a functional but subordinate role to the plants it contains. Consider also matching accessories, such as trays or saucers, which are

useful for watering from below and help to keep the surfaces the pots stand on free of stains. Detached clay pot feet are particularly useful for lifting flat-bottomed containers above smooth surfaces so that excess water can drain freely.

Clay
Traditional unglazed pots of fired clay (terracotta) have been valued for centuries for their beauty as plant containers – large jars and urns can be very handsome features in a garden,

CHANGE OF USE
A galvanized tub makes an eye-catching container for a clump of mixed tulips and grape hyacinths (Muscari). With adequate capacity for soil mix, and holes drilled in the base for drainage, this old-fashioned washtub has been cleverly transformed into an unusual and attractive container for plants.

even when left unplanted. Clay is readily molded to many sizes and shapes, and can be either plain or have a molded decoration. Small to medium-sized plain pots are generally inexpensive, although costs rise as sizes increase. The most expensive are frost-resistant ones, which will not flake or crack if exposed to low temperatures during winter. Before winter cold sets in, clay containers that are not frostproof should be protected with an insulating material, such as bubble plastic, or be moved under cover. All clay pots must be handled carefully; any kind of shock is likely to cause chipping, cracking, or breakage.

Clay is a porous material, so a pot should be soaked in clean water before being filled with soil mix. Evaporation from planted clay pots helps keep plant roots cooler in summer than in nonporous ones and, while more frequent watering is necessary, there is less risk of waterlogging. This makes clay ideal for alpines and other plants that demand good drainage. The porosity also gives acceptable results with capillary watering systems (see p.571).

In most circumstances, the weight of terracotta pots filled with moist soil mix is an advantage because it produces stability. Once planted, however, they are difficult to move, and the weight can be a serious drawback

if they are placed on balconies and roof gardens (see pp.306–307).

Clay's warm, earthy color, in shades of orange- or red-brown, can at first seem rather brash but, once weathered with algae, terracotta blends unobtrusively into many settings and complements a wide range of plants. If necessary, slimy algal growth can be scrubbed off between plantings, using warm soapy water and a stiff-bristled brush.

Glazed ceramics
Whether glossy or mat, the variously colored, shaped, and textured finishes on glazed pots can make them distinctive ornamental features in the garden. In addition to brightly colored and vividly patterned glazes, those imitating the subdued green of celadon ware may also be worth considering for a more subdued design. Unless specifically labeled as frost resistant, glazed containers should not be left outdoors during winter. Since their surface is not porous, there is less water loss than from unglazed pots, and they are also easier to wipe clean.

Plastic
Plastics are versatile materials that can be molded into many different shapes, and they are now widely used in the manufacturing of inexpensive containers. The most durable pots are

CONTAINER ACCESSORIES
A saucer will protect a surface from staining, but it must not store excess water. Raise flat-bottomed pots up on pot feet so that they drain freely.

made of a polyethylene and polypropylene mix that does not become brittle in low temperatures – unlike polypropylene when used on its own.

Plastic containers are manufactured in almost any color; they can be plain, textured, or with a relief design, and the finish can be glossy or mat. Plastic is often used to simulate other materials, and perhaps this is why it is sometimes viewed as a second-rate substitute. It does, however, have many virtues. It is lightweight, for example, and therefore useful on indoor shelves, balconies, and roof gardens that are not strong enough for heavier materials. Plastic is not porous, so water is not lost through the sides of containers, and frequency of watering is less than with clay pots. Plastic pots are also more effective

with capillary watering systems than clay ones (see p.571).

Growing bags are specialized plastic containers made from flexible sheet plastic and filled with a light-weight soilless potting mix. The mix will sustain a main crop such as tomatoes and sometimes also a secondary crop, after which the mix can be spread in the garden and the container disposed of. Growing bags are functional containers that make few concessions to good looks, but they can be masked by plants in full growth if necessary.

Wood
Wood is a particularly useful material for made-to-measure containers such as windowboxes. It is also the material of first choice for a number of other traditional containers, including Versailles tubs and half-barrels, in which the staves are held together by metal bands. Hardwoods, which should come from a renewable source, last longer than softwoods, but are more expensive. Preservative treatments will extend the life of softwoods but check before using that the preservative is labeled as being harmless to plants.

Stone and concrete
Natural stone, available in many different textures and colors, is a prestige container material that is expensive and heavy. Marble, which is often used in classical urns, can be intricately carved and given a high polish, while sandstone containers

Adapting containers

Plants can be grown in almost any container that holds soil mix and permits free drainage of water. Drill drainage holes in the base of items such as galvanized metal containers, old buckets, and cans to transform them. Potential containers that are already pierced,

COLANDER BASKET
To convert a colander into a hanging container, fit chains and line it with pierced plastic.

DRILLING DRAINAGE HOLES
Masking tape placed over the position of the drainage hole gives the drill bit a secure grip.

such as colanders, or are woven, such as wicker baskets, should be lined so that the soil mix does not fall out. Use dark-colored, flexible plastic sheeting or a plastic bag of an appropriate size. Prick the bottom of the liner so that excess water can drain away freely.

are frequently left with a rough finish. Various kinds of reconstituted stone are also used in the manufacture of containers. These too are heavy and expensive, but generally cheaper than natural stone. Concrete containers may be cheaper still.

All heavy containers should be placed in their final position in the garden or conservatory before being filled with soil mix. The algal growth that develops on such materials helps to soften the initial raw appearance. Concrete and rough stone are difficult to clean.

Metal
Lead is a traditional material for cisterns, garden ornaments, and containers, and it can be introduced to reinforce a period style in a garden. Whether antique or modern, lead containers are expensive, heavy, and easily dented or distorted, because of the softness of this metal.

Cast iron was in vogue in the nineteenth century, and the numerous vase and urn shapes popular then are available again now. Cast iron, however, is expensive and will rust unless coated or painted.

Galvanized metal containers are lightweight and available in a wide range of shapes and sizes. Now often used to lend a modern flavor,

especially in urban gardens, most are sufficiently inexpensive to discard as tastes and fashions change.

Many hanging baskets and brackets are made of wire, which is usually covered with plastic to provide a suitable background color to the plants as well as to prolong the life of the container.

Fiberglass
Fiberglass is a lightweight material that is easily molded into many different shapes. It is frostproof, strong, and long-lasting; although rather brittle, it can be repaired. Because of its relative cheapness and versatility, it is often used to simulate other materials, including stone, metal, and wood.

Unusual container materials
Many domestic, agricultural, architectural, and industrial items can be transformed into highly individual containers (see "Adapting containers," above). Salvaged and recycled items, such as industrial sinks and oil drums, can also make unorthodox plant containers.

Most such containers can be decorated with paints, stains, or other materials, which are available for use on an extensive variety of surfaces and container types.

CHOOSING A SUITABLE CONTAINER

FORMAL WOODEN TUB
Matched for size and in proportion, a squared container such as a wooden Versailles tub makes a good base for this formally shaped boxwood (Buxus sempervirens).

TERRACOTTA PANS
Shallow clay pots, referred to as pans, are traditional containers for alpines and short-growing bulbs, such as Reticulata irises. They are suitable for an alpine house or for displaying plants outdoors on tiered stands.

Soil mixes for containers

THE growing medium used in containers should give plants the best chance of maximizing their ornamental or productive potential. It must be well aerated and moisture retentive, with a resilient structure that can withstand heavy watering. Ordinary garden soil should not be used; its structure, chemical balance, and nutrient levels are variable, and it will almost certainly contain weed seeds, pests, and disease organisms. The best results are achieved with precisely formulated soil mixes that are produced commercially or prepared or modified at home.

Soil mixes

There are two main types of soil mix: soil-based ones, which should contain sterilized, high-quality soil (loam) as their main ingredient; and soilless mixes, which contain no soil and are usually based on peat or a peat substitute.

Soil-based mixes

These potting mixes are free draining and have good aeration and structure,

MIXES FOR PLANTS WITH SPECIAL NEEDS

Azaleas and other rhododendrons are intolerant of alkaline soils. In a container they are best grown in an acidic mix that is soil-based but free of alkaline materials.

which encourages root development. They provide a steady supply of nutrients to sustain the long-term growth of plants and are less prone to waterlogging than soilless mixes. They also dry out more slowly, making them easier to manage in containers. Being heavier than soilless mixes, soil-based ones are especially useful in counterbalancing top-growth. Plants cultivated in a soil-based mix and then transplanted into garden soil are likely to become established quickly and develop well. The structure and nutrient content of soil-based mixes do, however, deteriorate in storage. Buy a recognized brand name from a reputable supplier, and use the mix as soon as possible.

The soil used in these mixes should have a high organic content. High-quality soil is prepared commercially by stacking sod for at least six months. It is then sterilized by heat or chemical treatment to kill pests, diseases, and weed seeds.

You might be able to find soil-based mixes based on the three standard formulations drawn up by the John Innes Horticultural Institute in England. All contain 7 parts (by volume) sterilized loam, 3 parts peat substitute or peat, and 1 part sand. To this mixture is added in specified quantities ground limestone and John Innes Base fertilizer, which consists of 2 parts hoof and horn meal, 2 parts superphosphate, and 1 part potassium sulfate.

The JI No.1 formulation has relatively little fertilizer and so is suitable mainly for growing seedlings and sowing large seed. It can also be used for slow-growing ornamentals that do not require high nutrient levels, such as alpines. To make JI No.1, mix 8 gallons (36 liters) of loam, peat substitute or peat, and sand in the proportions specified above, then add 4oz (110g) John Innes Base and ¾oz (20g) ground limestone.

JI No.2 contains double the fertilizer and limestone content of JI No.1 and is suitable for a wide range of plants needing average nutrient levels.

JI No.3, with three times the fertilizer and limestone content of JI No.1, is for vigorous plants and those such as trees and shrubs that will remain in their container for more than one growing season.

Acidic soil mixes

Although many standard formulations cover the needs of large numbers of plants, few may be suitable for rhododendrons and other plants that

COMMON INGREDIENTS FOR SOIL MIXES

LOAM
Sterilized garden soil, with good nutrient supply, drainage, aeration, and moisture retention.

GRIT
Various grades of grit are added to soil mix to improve drainage and aeration.

PEAT
Well-aerated and moisture-retentive but low in nutrients. Hard to rewet.

VERMICULITE
Expanded, air-blown mica acts like perlite but holds more water and less air.

FINE BARK
Used as a peat substitute, especially in mixes for acidic soil-loving plants.

PERLITE
Expanded volcanic rock granules retain moisture but drain freely. Aids aeration.

COIR
This peat substitute dries less rapidly than peat but needs more frequent fertilizing.

SAND
Coarse and fine sands open the texture of many soil mixes and provide extra weight.

LEAF MOLD
Used as a peat substitute and soil-mix additive, especially for woodland plants.

thrive only on neutral to acidic soils. These require special soil-based mixes that do not contain limestone. Such low-pH mixes are usually labeled "acidic" or rarely "ericaceous," referring to the acidic soil-favoring Ericaceae (heather family).

Soilless mixes

Soilless mixes are widely used in container gardening. They are usually based on 3 parts (by volume) of peat or peat substitute and 1 part sand. The content of fertilizers varies. Some also contain perlite, vermiculite, or styrofoam pellets to aid aeration and drainage.

All soilless potting mixes are relatively clean to use, lightweight, and are generally less expensive than soil-based ones. North America has huge reserves of natural peat and less than one percent has been harvested to date. Conservation practices used by the major peat companies ensure that harvested areas will regenerate. The European

practice of using other materials i unnecessary here. Occasionally pea substitutes such as fine bark, coi (coconut fiber and bark), and lea mold are used in potting mixes.

Many soil mixes based on pea need careful watering; although the surface may be dry, the layer beneath are often adequately moist Peat combines moisture retentive ness with good aeration, but it drie out rapidly and, once dry, is difficul to re-wet. Conversely, if overwatered it is prone to waterlogging. In pots soilless mixes based on peat shoul be kept evenly moist at all times.

Most soilless mixes, including peat-based ones, break down rapidly so that the mix shrinks and lose structure. In general, they do no provide such a firm roothold as soi based mixes. Also, plants move from them to the open garden fre quently adapt poorly to garden soil.

Soilless mixes are suitable for short term use, such as growing seedling and annuals and sowing large seeds

MODIFYING SOIL MIXES

Most alpines need few nutrients and free drainage, so plant them over a layer of broken pots in a 50:50 mix of standard soil mix and grit.

Although they provide a suitable medium for many plants in containers, hanging baskets, and on balconies and roof gardens, the shortcomings of soil-less mixes mean that they are not suitable for long-term plantings, such as of trees and shrubs.

Peat and peat substitutes are naturally low in nutrients, which tend to leach quickly. Regular use of soluble fertilizers can overcome this, but their effect does not last. A more efficient way of maintaining a steady nutrient supply is to incorporate slow-release inorganic fertilizers into the soil mix. These are complete formulations, some slowly degrading in the soil, others absorbing water until they burst open, spreading their fertilizer. Many discharge their nutrients over several months. The expense of slow-release fertilizers is offset by the convenience and the time saved in not needing to make frequent applications of soluble fertilizers. However, the nutrient-release pattern of slow-release fertilizers, especially long-term formulas, can be hard to predict since it is affected by the pH level, moisture content, and temperature of the soil mix.

ADDITIVES FOR SOIL MIXES

WATER-RETAINING GRANULES
When wetted, these granules expand, providing a reservoir of moisture on which plants can draw.

BALLAST AND SPACE-FILLING MATERIALS FOR CONTAINERS

BROKEN POTS
Useful to add some weight. Be sure to place the pieces curved-side up to avoid blocking the hole.

POLYSTYRENE CHUNKS
Pieces of polystyrene are ideal for filling space in a container that is initially too large for young plants

BRICKS OR OTHER RUBBLE
Heavy bricks or similar reused construction materials will increase container stability.

To maintain a reservoir of moisture in a container without waterlogging the soil mix, incorporate water-retaining granules or crystals into the growing mix. When wetted, the granules swell to make a fragmented gel. They may not be effective over very long periods, but the reduction of water loss is particularly useful in soilless mixes and in exposed containers such as hanging baskets, which dry out rapidly.

Special soil mixes

In addition to acidic mixes, there are other specialized mixes produced commercially to meet the requirements of particular groups of plants. Orchid mixes are free draining and often contain charcoal and fine bark for good aeration. Cactus mixes are even more free draining, containing a high proportion of grit, and are usually low in nutrients. Aquatic mixes, which are heavy for better anchorage, are particularly variable as the

major constituent – soil – is not of a consistent standard. Bulb fiber mix is made from undecomposed sphagnum moss, which has an open structure and is suitable for growing bulbs in containers that do not have drainage holes.

Modifying soil mixes

Commercially produced and home-made mixes can be adapted for particular plants or groups of plants. Perlite and vermiculite are commonly put in homemade mixes to improve drainage and aeration. The addition of various grades of grit and sharp sand make mixes drain more freely. Grit, for example, is often mixed in equal parts by volume to a standard soil-based mix to make a free-draining mix for alpines. Leaf mold, which is an excellent peat substitute in homemade mixes, can also be added to commercial mixes to produce a growing mix suitable for woodland plants.

Mulches

Mulches are used to cover soils or mixes to retard water loss, to even out soil temperature fluctuations, and to discourage the growth of weeds. The most useful and neatest mulch for most container plants is ground bark spread over the surface to a depth of about 1in (2.5cm). Limestone chips are suitable for plants that prefer alkaline soils, while granite chips can be used for those that need acidic conditions. Coarse gravel used as a top-dressing for trees and shrubs can also help stabilize containers. Organic mulches include leaf mold and cocoa shells; these tend to be blown about unless damp. Composted pine needles can be used for acidic soil-loving plants.

Making mixes

The main difficulty for amateur gardeners preparing their own soil-based mixes is sterilizing the soil. Special soil-sterilizing units for large-scale heat treatment are expensive, but smaller-scale units are available from specialty suppliers. To treat small quantities, put the soil through a ¼in (5mm) sieve to remove stones and lumps. Then spread it 3in (8cm) deep on a baking tray and bake for 30 minutes at 400°F (200°C) in a domestic oven. Alternatively put the soil in a roasting bag and heat in a microwave on full power for ten minutes.

Assemble the ingredients on a clean, flat surface. (For exact quantities, see "Soil-based mixes," p.316.) Mix the sterilized loam and peat or peat substitute (well moistened if it is dry). Combine the ground limestone and fertilizers with some of the sand to ensure even distribution, and incorporate this thoroughly into the remaining sand, soil, and peat or peat substitute.

MIXING INGREDIENTS

SLOW-RELEASE FERTILIZERS
These discharge nutrients over an extended period, eliminating the need for frequent liquid fertilization.

Planting large and long-term plants

A LTHOUGH many gardeners concentrate on planting annuals to create colorful container displays for late winter, spring, and summer, there are many longer-lived plants that do well in pots. They lend an appearance of maturity and provide a valuable core to a container garden, which can then be supplemented seasonally as other plants reach their peak. Large container-grown, frost-tender plants, such as brugmansias, can be placed outdoors for the summer and moved back under cover between autumn and spring.

Plants and materials

For plants to do well for several years in containers, they must have the potential for long life and be given optimum growing conditions to guarantee sustained good health.

Selecting plants

Whether buying plants or making a choice from stock raised at home, the best results are achieved by using container-grown, young but well-developed and vigorous plants that are free of pests and diseases. Look for good leaf color, and examine the undersides as well as the tops of leaves for signs of disease or pest infestation. Reject any plants with any signs of disease or damage. Slide the plant out of its container and check that the roots are well developed. If the roots are tightly congested, the plant has probably been in its container too long and may not establish quickly or well. Other signs

that indicate that a plant has been too long in its container include missing or illegible labels, containers covered with algal growth, or soil mix encrusted with liverworts or moss. If buying a bare-root tree, check that the root system is well developed and has plenty of fibrous roots. Balled-and-burlapped trees and shrubs should have a firm ball of soil and roots encased in an undamaged plastic mesh or burlap cover and should show no signs of having dried out. Before purchasing, also make a visual check from all angles to make sure that growth is evenly balanced.

Choosing containers

Containers of many different materials are suitable for growing large and long-lived plants, provided that they have adequate drainage. For plants with extensive top-growth, it is important that the container should lend weight and stability; the most suitable include broad-bottomed containers such as Versailles tubs and terracotta urns (see p.314).

Select a container that is in proportion with both the aerial parts of the plant and its root ball. It must be big enough to permit good root development and to hold sufficient soil mix to supply adequate moisture and nutrients. As a rough guide, a container should be about 2in (5cm) wider and deeper than that from which the plant is being moved. Trees, however, need more room to develop; allow a depth of at least one and a half times that of the root ball and a diameter between a sixth and a quarter of the tree's current height.

SELECTING A SHRUB

GOOD EXAMPLE
Many shrubs are sold container-grown. Choose a plant with a balanced framework of shoots and reject specimens showing signs of any pests or disease.

Healthy leaves and vigorous well-balanced growth

Label in good condition indicating that plant is fresh stock

Clean container and weed-free soil mix

Suitable soil mixes

Plants that are to remain in their containers for several years need a soil mix that will provide a steady and continuous supply of nutrients. The most suitable mixes are soil-based with slow-release fertilizer incorporated. The nutrients in mixes based on peat or peat substitute are leached relatively quickly, so plants grown in them need fertilizing at frequent intervals throughout their lives. Although potentially a disadvantage on balconies and rooftops, the weight of soil-based mixes provides stabilizing ballast and a more secure

roothold for plants than soilless mixes. Most long-term plants thrive in the standard soil-based mix Use an acidic soil mix for plants such as rhododendrons, azaleas, and camellias.

Planting a container

Before planting, assemble the container, pieces of screening, soil mix, and any supports, as well as any pot feet, bricks, or blocks on which the container is to stand. Scrub the inside and outside of containers that are being reused to remove any disease

---

PLANTING A SHRUB

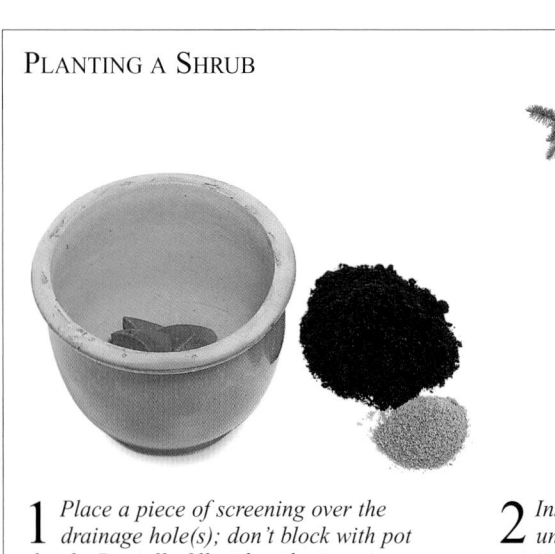

1 *Place a piece of screening over the drainage hole(s); don't block with pot shards. Partially fill with soil mix, using an acidic one with sharp sand for alkalinity-hating shrubs, such as* Picea pungens *'Glauca' here.*

2 *Insert the shrub, adjusting the soil level until the plant is at the same depth as in its original container. Fill with soil mix, firm, and water in. For a dense display, plant two specimens, adding trailing ivies underneath.*

THE FINISHED PLANTING

STAKING

Tall container-grown plants should be staked from an early age so that they develop a straight stem and even growth all around.

...causing organisms. Soak new terracotta pots in clean water. Place the container in its display position before planting; it will be heavy and difficult to move once it has been filled with soil mix.

Place a piece of screening over each of the drainage holes to prevent the soil mix from being washed out and to prevent invasion by earthworms or other creatures. Woven plastic window screening is good, as is nylon mesh, but try not to use metal screening, which decomposes quickly. Add soil mix to a depth of 2–4in (5–10cm) to start. If a support such as a stake, trellis, or tepee is required, place it in position.

Tap the container of the selected plant to loosen the root ball and carefully ease the plant out. It is important to position the plant in the new container at the same depth as it had been growing previously. This level can be detected by the soil mark, indicated by a change of color on the stem. Place the plant in the partially filled container, adjusting its height by adding soil mix if necessary. Fill with more soil mix, firming gently at intervals, until the finished surface is 2in (5cm) below the container's rim, which will leave room for water. Top-dress with an organic or grit mulch 1–1½in (2.5–4cm) deep. Water thoroughly, using rainwater for pH-sensitive plants.

Stakes and other supports

Many large container-grown plants need some form of permanent support. The most common support is a single stake that is inserted at planting, before the soil mix is added. This allows roots to spread around the stake and avoids the risk of root damage, which may occur if the stake is pushed in after planting. The stake should reach to just below the head of a standard tree or shrub. To hold the stem firmly, use an adjustable tie with a spacer to prevent bark from rubbing and adjust it regularly as the stem girth increases.

Other kinds of supports include wooden, metal, and wire frames. Metal frames are available in various shapes, including an umbrella-like support for weeping standards like wisteria. Wire frames are particularly useful for evergreen climbers, such as short-jointed cultivars of English ivy (*Hedera helix*), which can be trained to form topiary shapes (see also TOPIARY, pp.118–19).

Container-grown climbers can be trained onto trellis fans (see below). Rustic supports consisting of a tepee of bamboo stakes are effective for slender climbers such as *Rhodochiton atrosanguineus*. Wickerwork hoops – a traditional support for carnations (*Dianthus*) – can be adapted for use with shrubby perennials such as pineapple sage (*Salvia elegans* 'Scarlet Pineapple').

Planting a climber in a container

Trellis panels, often with "legs" at the base, are specially made for containers and are available in wood or plastic-covered wire. Before using, treat wooden ones with a preservative that is harmless to plants. Match the size of both the container and the trellis panel to the vigor of the selected climber. A heavy container in concrete, stone, or terracotta provides the most stable base.

Place the container in position before planting. This should be beside a wall or fence so that the trellis can be attached to it for increased stability – a planted trellis presenting a large surface area to the elements. Fill the pot with a soil-based mix. To avoid damaging the plant's roots, bed the support firmly into the soil mix along one side of the container; then plant the climber. After planting, secure the trellis top.

1 *Cover the drainage hole(s) with screening. Place the support to one side of the pot, and then work soil mix around it.*

2 *Plant the climber at the same level as in the original pot, firming the soil mix so that the surface is 2in (5cm) below the rim.*

3 *Tie the main shoots to the support, then water the plant to settle the roots. Attach the trellis to a wall or fence for stability.*

PLANTS THAT REQUIRE ACIDIC SOIL MIX

Agapetes
Andromeda
Arctostaphylos
Asteranthera ovata
Beaumontia grandiflora
Berberidopsis corallina
Billardiera
Calluna vulgaris (and cvs)
Camellia
Daboecia
Erica
Gardenia
   Rhododendron 'Vuyk's Scarlet'
Gaultheria
Hakea
Kennedia
Lapageria rosea
Lilium (some spp.)
Lithodora
Mitraria coccinea
Mutisia
Pieris
Rhododendron
Vaccinium

PLANTS THAT REQUIRE MOIST, ORGANIC SOIL MIX

Acer
Camellia
Clematis
Hibiscus
Hosta
Rhododendron
Rosa
Viola

PLANTS THAT NEED FREELY DRAINING SOIL MIX

Agave
Armeria
Artemisia
Bougainvillea
Calendula
Convolvulus

   Lavandula stoechas

Dianthus
Dorotheanthus
Erysimum
Eschscholzia
Helianthemum
Juniperus
Lavandula
Rosmarinus
Salvia
Santolina
Sempervivum
Thymus
Yucca

Pruning and training

As with the pruning of trees, shrubs, and climbers in the open garden, the aim of pruning plants in containers is to maintain good health and maximize the ornamental display. In the early stages, pruning aims to encourage the development of a well-balanced plant with evenly spaced stems. Many deciduous and evergreen plants need little pruning beyond this. To keep plants healthy, cut out out all dead, damaged, and diseased wood and, on variegated plants, remove shoots with leaves that have reverted to plain green. Such tasks can be done at almost any time of the year, although in spring you should check all plants thoroughly and deal with any problems.

Several plant groups, such as hydrangeas, roses, and clematis, however, do need annual pruning. For further information, see pruning and training ORNAMENTAL SHRUBS (pp.86–119); ROSES (pp.144–167); CLIMBING PLANTS (pp.120–143); and CLEMATIS (pp.136–138). Topiary specimens require strict formative training and subsequent regular clipping (see TOPIARY pp.118–19).

Standard specimens

Many trees, shrubs, and climbers can be grown as standards. However standards have a relatively high center of gravity, so choose a container that is heavy and broad based. Most container-grown trees are best trained as standards; the simple outline occupies little ground space and allows light to reach plants grown beneath them. Shrubs or subshrubs that respond well to this treatment include fuchsias and argyranthemums. With strict pruning, even vigorous climbers, including ornamental or fruiting vines and wisterias, can be grown as standards.

During formative training, the stem must be staked until it is sturdy enough to support the head itself, although many standards will require a permanent stake. Ties must be firm; adjust them regularly to avoid constricting the stem as it expands. With trees, retain the lower branches in the initial stages to encourage stem thickening and remove them gradually over two or three years.

With shrubs, shorten the laterals on the main stem, which should also be supported, with a stake. Retain laterals for a year to build stem strength, then remove them completely. For fuchsias, pinch out the laterals (see PINCH PRUNING, p.371). On all shrubs, allow the main stem to grow at least 8in (20cm) beyond the desired head height, then cut it back to a bud or pair of buds to encourage the growth of laterals to form the head. Subsequently, tip prune the laterals to encourage further branching and form a dense crown of foliage.

STANDARD SHRUB
When grown as a standard, shrubs such as this Syringa meyeri *var.* spontanea *'Palibin' develop a bouquetlike head that needs a heavy container to maintain stability.*

SHRUBS AND SUBSHRUBS TO GROW AS STANDARDS

Argyranthemum
Brugmansia
Buxus sempervirens
Camellia
Caragana arborescens
x *Citrofortunella microcarpa*
Ficus carica
Fuchsia
Gardenia jasminoides
Heliotropium
Hibiscus rosa-sinensis
Lagerstroemia indica
Laurus nobilis
Leptospermum scoparium
Ligustrum (some spp.)
Myrtus communis
Nerium oleander
Pelargonium
Rosa (many spp.)
Rosmarinus officinalis
Salix caprea 'Kilmarnock'
Solenostemon
Viburnum tinus

CLIMBERS TO GROW AS STANDARDS

Bougainvillea
Lonicera (some spp.)
Rosa (some spp.)
Solanum jasminoides
Wisteria
Vitis (some spp.)

TRAINING A STANDARD WOODY-STEMMED CLIMBER

STAGES OF DEVELOPMENT
In the early stages of training (here a grape), aim to develop a vigorous main vertical stem. Let sideshoots grow during the growing season so that their leaves may feed the stem, then remove them in the dormant season. Form the head by developing well-spaced laterals at an appropriate height and by pruning annually to maintain a supply of flowering spurs.

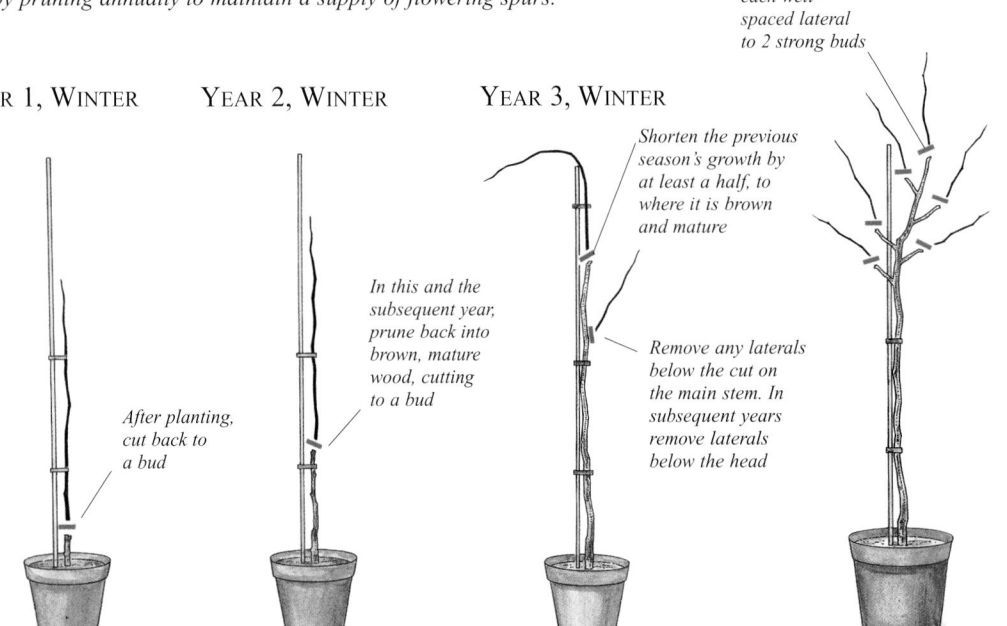

YEAR 1, WINTER

YEAR 2, WINTER

After planting, cut back to a bud

In this and the subsequent year, prune back into brown, mature wood, cutting to a bud

YEAR 3, WINTER

Shorten the previous season's growth by at least a half, to where it is brown and mature

Remove any laterals below the cut on the main stem. In subsequent years remove laterals below the head

YEAR 4, WINTER

Prune back each well-spaced lateral to 2 strong buds

YEAR 5 AND ONWARD

Shorten fruiting shoots, when they reach 12–18in (30–45cm) long, in summer

Prune flowered shoots back to two strong buds in winter

Thin spur systems as they build up and become congested

Planting seasonal displays

For many gardeners, the essential plants for container gardens are the large number of annuals that provide colorful displays all summer long. Other plants include biennials for winter, spring, and summer, and bulbs for spring, summer, and fall, all of which can be planted each year. In general, fresh bulbs planted annually give better results than those used for several years.

Annuals and biennials

A wide selection of annuals and biennials is available as young stock from garden centers even as early as midspring. Many are also easily raised from seed in a greenhouse or even an enclosed porch. If potting up early under cover, harden plants off by moving container outdoors during the day but returning them under cover at night until there is little risk of frost.

Before potting up, always water the chosen plants thoroughly. Then assemble all the essential components, such as a clean container, screening or similar mesh, soil-based or soilless mix, slow-release fertilizer, water-retaining granules, and the plants. Place the screening over the drainage hole(s) and fill the container three-quarters full with potting mix, the slow-release fertilizer, and water-retaining granules.

With the plants still in their pots, experiment with arrangements that will balance their trailing, bushy, and upright habits. In containers, it is possible to position plants closer together than in the open garden, but there must still be room for growth. Once the design is satisfactory, begin planting in a systematic way, for example, by working from the center outward or from the one side of the container to the another.

To loosen each plant, tap the container, remove the plant and place it in its new pot. Add or subtract the soil mix as necessary so that when you have finished planting, each plant is at the same depth as it was in its original container, there are no air pockets within the soilless or soil-based mix, and the final level is about 2in (5cm) below the rim. Finally, water to settle the plants in.

Annuals and biennials for winter and early spring flowering should be potted up in the fall. However, garden centers and nurseries sometimes delay making available for sale those plants that flower in late winter and early spring. These can be planted during winter provided the soil mix is not frozen.

Bulbs

Most spring-flowering bulbs such as daffodils are best planted in early autumn, as soon as they become available. Tulip bulbs, however, are best planted in late autumn or early winter, when they are less susceptible to the fungal disease tulip fire (*Botrytis tulipae*). Although bulbs can be mixed satisfactorily in a single container, it is generally better to plant different bulbs in separate containers because of the difficulties of synchronizing their flowering times.

To extend the flowering display of the same type of bulb, plant more than one layer of bulbs in the container, provided it is deep enough to take several layers as well as soil mix below and above each bulb. For most bulbs, allow a minimum planting depth equal to three times the height of the bulb. To plant two layers of daffodils or tulips, for example, place the drainage material in the base of a clean container and then cover with a layer of soil-based, soilless, or bulb potting mix not less than 2in (5cm) deep. Place in the first layer of bulbs so that they are 1–4in (2.5–10cm) apart depending on type. Cover with soil mix so that

1 Cover the drainage holes with screening, then partially fill with soil mix. Working systematically from left to right, plant some trailers, then the upright plants toward the center.

2 Continue spacing the plants evenly. Work the soil mix around the root balls and firm so that the finished surface is about 2in (5cm) below the pot rim. Water to settle the mix.

ROUTINE CARE
Throughout summer, water the plants regularly and give them a liquid fertilizer every 2 weeks. Deadhead frequently to prolong the flowering period.

CREATING A LAYERED PLANTING

1 Place a scrubbed wooden tub in its display position. Cover the drainage holes with screening, then a 2in (5cm) layer of gravel followed by a 4in (10cm) layer of fresh soil mix.

2 Plant the bedding or other plant in position, adjusting the soil mix beneath it so that it sits at the same depth as in its original container. Arrange a layer of bulbs, about 4in (10cm) apart, on the mix.

3 Cover these bulbs with soil mix and then plant a second layer, placing the bulbs in the spaces between the bulbs of the first layer. Add mix to within 3in (8cm) of the tub's rim.

4 Plant winter-flowering pansies (Viola x wittrockiana) 4–6in (10–15cm) apart. Add more soil mix, firming plants in gently, until the finished surface is 2in (5cm) below the rim. Water well.

PLANTING A WINDOWBOX

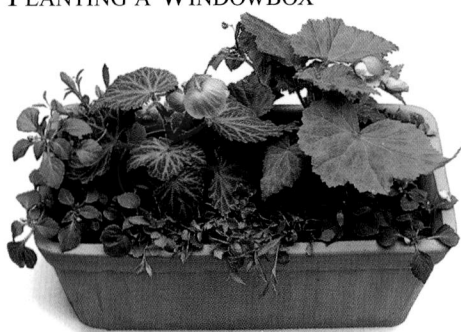

1 *While the plants are still in their pots, decide how they are to be displayed in the new container before beginning to plant up them. Begonias, lobelias, and impatiens are being used in this arrangement.*

2 *Cover the base of the windowbox with pot shards or gravel for stability, then add soil mix until the box is half to three quarters full. Slide each plant out of its pot, supporting the root ball with your fingers. Gently tease out the plant roots.*

3 *Scoop back the soil mix. Firm the plant in position so that it is at the same soil level as in its old pot and about $\frac{1}{2}$in (1cm) below the rim of the windowbox.*

4 *Pot up the remaining plants, then add more soil mix, gently pressing it in throughout the container so that there are no air pockets. Add more mix if necessary so the surface is 2in (5cm) below the rim and level. Then water thoroughly.*

just the tips are visible. Arrange a second layer of bulbs in the spaces between the first. Top up the container with soil mix until it is within 2in (5cm) of the container rim.

Lilies are among the most important bulbs for summer displays (see LILIES, p.245). They can be planted singly, or in groups of three or more in large containers. In general, lilies look better on their own or with other lilies rather than mixed with other plants in the same container. The best time to plant is in autumn, when bulbs are newly lifted. Select lily bulbs with plump, fleshy scales that are free of disease.

Lilies thrive in a well-drained growing medium, such as 4 parts soil-based mix with 1 part grit and 1 part leaf mold, to which slow-release fertilizer has been added. Stand the container on pot feet, then fill with the soil mix. Plant with the tip of the bulb 4–6in (10–15cm) below the mix surface (about two or three times the height of the bulb) and three times the bulb's diameter apart. Stem-rooting lilies, which produce roots on the stem above the bulb as well as from the bulb itself, should be planted more deeply, at about three to four times the height of the bulb.

Bulbs with bedding plants
Mixtures of spring bulbs and annuals or biennials make very effective displays in a single container. Try

planting tulips with forget-me-nots (*Myosotis*) or wallflowers (*Erysimum*), and small bulbs, such as scillas, with winter-flowering pansies (*Viola* x *wittrockiana*). Plant in autumn, with the bulbs well covered by a layer of soil-based or soilless mix and add the annuals or biennials so that when they are watered in, the surface of the mix is about 2in (5cm) below the container's rim.

Fruit, vegetables, and herbs
Although the yield is less when compared with crops grown in open ground, leafy salad crops and other vegetables such as Swiss chard, zucchini, and beans can be successfully cultivated in soilless mix if watered and fertilized regularly. Strawberries generally prefer a soil-based potting mix, but they will tolerate a soilless one. Whichever mix is used, strawberries must be kept moist at all times. Use specially made strawberry jars or adapt a wooden barrel by cutting planting holes, 2in (5cm) wide and 10in (25cm) apart at different levels in the sides. Alpine strawberries, such as *Fragaria* 'Baron Solemacher', are a good choice for a partially shaded site.

Herbs are among the most useful culinary plants for containers. Many are easily grown in pots of soil-based or soilless mix with added grit (one fifth by volume) to provide good drainage. Most need only a little extra fertilizing.

Attaching and stabilizing windowboxes

A fully planted windowbox may appear to be stable, but when placed at a height on a wall or against a building it is often subject to wind turbulence. If dislodged, such a heavy container poses a serious threat to people passing underneath and may also cause considerable structural damage. All windowboxes must be secured firmly with heavy-duty metal brackets or wedges. The wedges are ideal for sloping windowsills with a depth of at least 8in (20cm); they can be further secured in position by using mirror plates and hooks.

MIRROR PLATES
These plates are attached to the back of the windowbox then are hooked securely to the box frame.

INSERTING WEDGES ON A SLOPING SILL

1 *Place a level across a windowsill, then measure the gap between it and the sill to find the height of the wedge needed. Mark this dimension on a wood scrap that is $1\frac{1}{4}$in (30mm) shorter than the sill depth.*

2 *Mark a diagonal line to the opposite corner of the scrap. Then with another scrap, mark out an identical wedge. Cut out both wedges and treat with preservative. Nail or screw to the bottom of the windowbox.*

Planting hanging baskets

H ANGING baskets and wall-mounted containers provide great opportunities to create colorful and imaginative plant displays. Nearly all of them are of open construction and are used with a liner that holds in the soil mix and retains moisture while allowing excess water to drain away. Hanging containers must be attached to a secure overhead support or to a wall well out of the way of passersby.

A variety of styles
The standard hanging basket is of lightweight construction in wire, usually plastic coated, and is suspended by means of chains. Half-baskets of similar construction are designed to be wall-mounted. More solid baskets and containers, such as hayracks or mangers, are usually made of enameled or plastic-coated strip metal. Alternatives to openwork containers are suspended or wall-mounted pots with solid sides. Many such pots have the advantage of being self-watering, incorporating a reservoir that keeps the soil mix moist.

Types of liner
Many different liners are available, some of which are made to fit specific sizes of baskets, while others are cut to size. Most are patterned or colored so that they are camouflaged within the containers. All can be pierced to allow planting in the sides, although such holes are easier to make with some materials than others (see *Planting a hanging basket*, p.324).

Sheet plastic is among the most versatile of basket liners. It is easily

cut to size and slashed to provide drainage or planting holes. Dark-colored plastic is relatively inconspicuous, particularly as growth develops. If desired, it can, however, readily be disguised with straw or less bulky burlap, for example (see *Planting a hayrack*, below). In addition to plastic, hanging baskets can be lined with coir, foam, recycled paper, or wool (see right).

Potting mixes and additives
The most suitable mixes for most seasonal displays are soilless formulations, which are light and easy to handle. For longer-lasting displays, for example, of groundcover roses, soil-based potting mixes are preferable (see "Soil mixes for containers," p.316).

Fertilizers can be added as slow-release inorganic fertilizers or as a liquid. The addition of water-retaining granules helps reduce fluctuations in moisture levels.

Planting seasonal displays
Use trailing plants in tiers to envelop the sides of a hanging basket in flowers and foliage. Position lax plants around the rim and bushy or upright plants in the center to form a crown. If the basket can be kept frost free, plant a summer basket in midspring. Harden off gradually by moving the basket outdoors by day, and move to its final display position only when risk of frost has passed.

Use the same planting technique for spring, autumn, and winter displays. Hardy plants do not need hardening off but should be kept in a sheltered place until well established.

LINING MATERIALS FOR BASKETS

COIR *Natural look; tricky to cut for side planting.*

FOAM *Absorbent, easily cut; can be conspicuous.*

RECYCLED PAPER *Cheap, available with push-out planting holes.*

WOOL *Hard to cut, but good insulation for plant roots.*

Securing baskets
When filled, hanging baskets and other wall-mounted containers can be heavy, so they must be securely fastened to strong wall-mounted brackets or overhead supports, such as the crossbeams of a pergola. Wall-mounted containers, which must be hung plumb and level, are usually supplied with brackets; if attaching to masonry, insert wall anchors into the holes before screwing into position.

HAYRACK FIXTURES *Mark and drill holes for a hooked bracket. Use a wall anchor and galvanized screw when mounting.*

BRACKET FOR A HANGING BASKET *Holding the bracket plumb and level, mark the position of back plate holes. Insert wall anchors, then secure with galvanized screws.*

PLANTING A HAYRACK

1 *Openwork manger-style baskets must be lined. To camouflage the liner, work in straw against the inner face of the curved front of a hayrack so that, when compressed, it forms a layer 1in (2.5cm) thick.*

2 *Cut a piece of sheet plastic to make a slightly oversized liner, and fit it inside the hayrack. Fold the excess toward the straw and tuck in all around to make a neat edge. Cut slits in the liner, at the bottom for drainage and at the front, if desired, for planting holes. Fill the hayrack to one third of its depth with soil mix.*

3 *Remove plants from their pots, tease out the root balls, and insert the plants in the soil mix. Adjust the mix until the plants are at their original planting depth. Fill up and firm the mix to within 1in (2.5cm) of the rim. Mount the hayrack in position. Water well.*

Planting a Hanging Basket

1 Place the basket on a bucket or large flower pot, so that it is centered and level. Adjust the liner (here, of coir) to fit the basket snugly, making several radial cuts. (With a precut liner, simply overlap the segments.)

2 Press the liner down firmly against the bottom and sides of the basket, molding it to the basket wires. Use scissors to trim off any liner that extends above the rim of the basket, making a neat, level top edge.

3 Using sharp scissors or a craft knife, make a series of slits 2in (5cm) long in the side of the liner for planting in tiers, so that trailing plants, inserted in the slits at one or two levels below the basket rim, will fill out and mask the wire frame.

   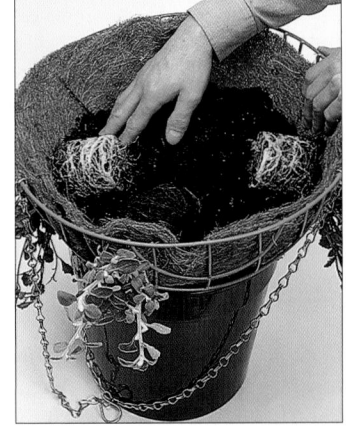

4 Add potting mix combined with slow-release fertilizer and water-retaining granules until it is level with the first tier of slits in the side of the liner. Gently firm the mix.

5 To protect the soft growth of plants that are to be inserted through the slits in the liner, wrap each plant in a piece of plastic (such as one cut from a bag) to form a cone over the stems and leaves.

6 Guide each plant cone through a slit in the liner, from the inside. When the plant is in position with the root ball on the inside and the stems outside, gently remove its plastic cover.

7 Continue planting through the sides, using the same method. Gently tease out the root balls and add mix, working it around the roots, until the basket is filled within 2in (5cm) of the rim.

8 Plant lax plants, here fuchsias, geraniums, and petunias, around the rim, spaced so that they are not immediately above the plants below.

9 Add more mix, working it in around the roots. Leave a gap for a bushy plant; Felicia amelloides 'Variegata' with blue, daisylike flowers is the centerpiece here.

10 Complete the planting and top off with mix so that the finished surface is 1in (2.5cm) below the basket rim. Water thoroughly. Allow the plants to establish in a sheltered place before hanging the basket. Meanwhile, keep the mix evenly moist, but do not overwater. In frost-prone areas, keep baskets under cover until there is no risk of frost.

Water gardens in containers

SEVERAL factors determine the success of a container water garden. The plants must be carefully selected and then placed in their appropriate light conditions if they are to achieve their potential. The pot should blend with its surroundings and provide an adequate depth and surface area of water for the chosen plants. Vigorous plants can quickly take over if the the gardener fails to exercise proper control. The surface should also be partly covered with foliage, so the water does not become fouled by algal growth.

Choosing plants
There are one or two plants, notably the deep marginal lotus (*Nelumbo*), that are very effective used on their own in a small water garden. However, the more usual approach is to scale down the planting of a conventional pond, using a mixture of marginals, deep water plants, submerged oxygenators, and floating aquatics (see WATER GARDENING, "Planting and stocking," p.291).

The number that can be accommodated depends largely on the volume and surface area of the water. In a standard half-barrel, which holds 12 gallons (50 liters), there is room for one dwarf or pygmy waterlily, three or four shallow marginals, one or two plants of a noninvasive oxygenator, and a floating aquatic.

Siting the container
Be sure the container is correctly positioned before being filled; once it holds water and plants it will be

MINIATURE POND
Floating aquatics, including the tender water lettuce (Pistia stratiotes) *and compact shallow marginals, such as variegated Japanese rush* (Acorus gramineus), *crowd the surface of this "pond" made from a half-barrel. Marginals are planted in plastic baskets and placed on bricks so that they stand just above the water surface.*

heavy and difficult to maneuver. It must be on a firm, level surface and near a water supply so that it can be filled up as necessary. The ideal site is sheltered – but well away from trees – and in sun but shaded during the hottest parts of the day.

Planting
Cover the base of the container with 2in (5cm) of washed gravel, then two-thirds fill with water. Plant aquatics individually in ordinary garden soil in plastic-mesh baskets lined with burlap to prevent the soil from

washing out. Place the plants deeply in the baskets, work the soil around the roots, and firm in gently so that the finished surface is 1in (2.5cm) below the rim. Top-dress with washed gravel. Stand containers of marginals on bricks so that the plants reach the water's surface (see *Planting depths*, p.291). Finish filling the container slowly to within 2in (5cm) of the rim to avoid disturbing the soil mix in the planting baskets. If including floating aquatics in the planting design, add them when the container has been filled.

AQUATIC PLANTS FOR CONTAINERS

Shallow marginals
(6in/15cm depth of water)
Acorus gramineus 'Ogon',
 A. gramineus 'Variegatus'
Caltha palustris
Iris laevigata, I. versicolor
Juncus effusus f. *spiralis*
Marsilea quadrifolia
Myosotis scorpioides
Typha minima

Deep marginals
(12in/30cm depth of water)
Cyperus papyrus 'Nanus'
Nelumbo 'Pygmaea Alba'

Deep water plants
Nuphar pumila
Nymphaea 'Aurora',
 N. candida, N. 'Ellisiana',
 N. 'Graziella',
 N. 'Laydekeri Purpurata',
 N. x *daubenyana* (tropical),
 N. odorata var. *minor*,
 N. 'Pygmaea Helvola',
 N. tetragona

Submerged oxygenators
Eleocharis acicularis
Fontinalis antipyretica
Myriophyllum aquaticum

Floating aquatics
Azolla caroliniana
Eichhornia crassipes
Pistia stratiotes
Wolffia arrhiza

PLANTING A CONTAINERIZED WATER GARDEN

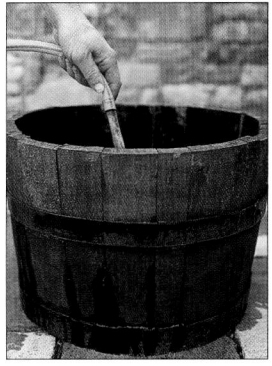
1 *Presoak the barrel to swell the wood and make it watertight and set it on a level base. Cover the bottom with gravel. Fill two thirds full with water.*

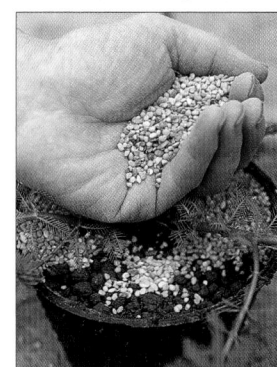
2 *Line a plastic-mesh basket with burlap, fill with garden soil, and plant up (here* Myriophyllum aquaticum). *Top-dress with gravel or coarse grit.*

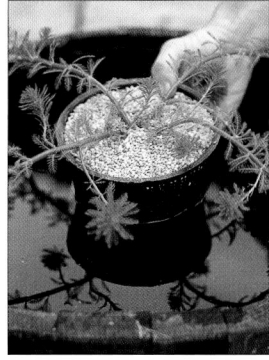
3 *Lower oxygenators, waterlilies, and other deep-water plants carefully onto the bottom of the barrel to avoid disturbing the soil in each basket.*

4 *Place bricks or half-bricks on the bottom of the barrel to raise the height of any container holding marginal plants.*

5 *Adjust the bricks until the plant is slightly exposed above the water's surface. Fill up the barrel to within 5cm (2in) of the barrel's rim, if needed.*

Routine care

THROUGHOUT the growing season, container-grown plants need regular checking. The soil mix must be kept moist, so frequent watering is essential, as is feeding during the growing season to maintain healthy growth and productivity. Dead-heading helps to prolong flowering. Plants also require protection from pests and diseases, and, if tender, from cold. Long-term plants need special attention with regard to repotting and top-dressing.

Watering

Plants in containers have access to very limited reserves of water when compared with those in open ground and so are dependent to a greater extent on the gardener for their water supply. Even after rainy weather, extra watering may be needed, as the pot plant's foliage may shed the rainwater outside the container. In addition, containers, especially windowboxes and those attached to walls, are often in a rain shadow, where the rainfall they receive is much reduced (see *Rain Shadow*, p.602). In hot, dry, or windy weather, plants may need watering two or even three times a day.

The simplest way to know when a plant should be watered is to push a finger into the soil mix to check if it is moist below the surface. Such a

WATERING HIGH-LEVEL CONTAINERS
A lance attachment with a trigger-action is a useful extension to a hose. Or, fit a stake or pole to the hose to gain the necessary rigidity and height when watering.

ADJUSTABLE CONTAINER HEIGHTS
A rise-and-fall pulley attachment allows a hanging basket to be raised, lowered, and held in a locked position. This simplifies watering and grooming of the plants in the basket.

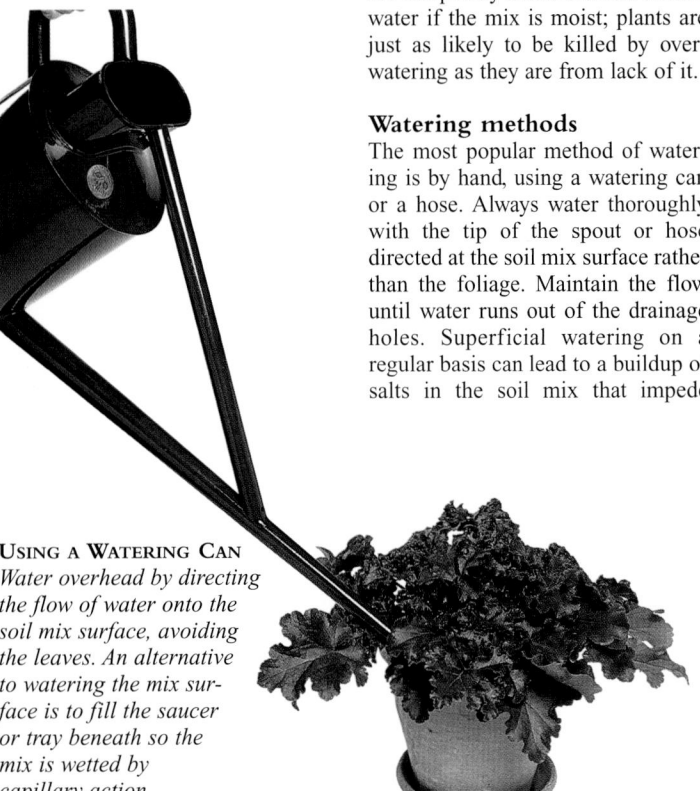

USING A WATERING CAN
Water overhead by directing the flow of water onto the soil mix surface, avoiding the leaves. An alternative to watering the mix surface is to fill the saucer or tray beneath so the mix is wetted by capillary action.

probe is especially useful for plants grown in soilless mixes based on peat substitutes; these mixes often appear dry on the surface when they are adequately moist beneath. Do not water if the mix is moist; plants are just as likely to be killed by over-watering as they are from lack of it.

Watering methods

The most popular method of watering is by hand, using a watering can or a hose. Always water thoroughly with the tip of the spout or hose directed at the soil mix surface rather than the foliage. Maintain the flow until water runs out of the drainage holes. Superficial watering on a regular basis can lead to a buildup of salts in the soil mix that impede

drainage and lead to stunted growth or rot. Tap water is usually satisfactory for most plants, but if the water is hard it will not benefit acid-loving plants such as rhododendrons. Rainwater from a water barrel can be used for these (see "Collecting water," p.606).

Automated or drip-feed irrigation systems (see TOOLS AND EQUIPMENT, "Watering aids," p.554) can be adapted for use in containers. These systems are excellent, labor-saving ways of watering containers, including windowboxes and growing bags. They do, however, need regular maintenance to make sure that lines and drip heads flow freely.

Containers above head height, such as hanging baskets and windowboxes, are difficult to reach with conventional hoses and watering cans. A rigid hose lance attachment is invaluable for this purpose and simple to use. Or, invest in a compression sprayer with a rigid extension and nozzle. Hanging baskets can also be suspended on a locking pulley system. They can be lowered for watering and raised to the required height for display.

Fertilizing

Plants growing in soil-based potting mixes containing slow-release fertilizers will receive sufficient nutrients

over a few seasons, until they are renewed when repotted or top-dressed (see p.328). Nutrient levels in soilless mixes, however, decline quickly, partly because they are easily leached out by watering. They therefore need boosting with liquid fertilizers. These are quick acting and contain a balanced supply of nitrogen, phosphorus, and potassium, the major elements needed for plant growth, along with trace elements. Apply liquid fertilizers to moist soil mix regularly during the active growing season, depending on the manufacturer's instructions regarding the strength and frequency of application.

Foliar fertilizing – the application of dilute liquid fertilizers as a foliar spray – can usefully supplement other kinds of fertilizers. Although its effect is not long lasting, it too is a fast-acting treatment for plants that are growing slowly or showing signs of stress. Apply foliar fertilizers only in dull, overcast conditions, never when plants have sunlight on them.

Grooming

The general appearance of a container garden is greatly improved by regular maintenance. By paying close attention to the plants, early infestations

TRIMMING SHOOTS

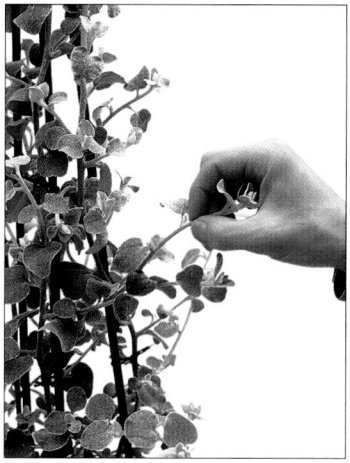

Vigorous plants, such as this trailing Helichrysum petiolare, *should be trimmed or pinched back to curb excess growth and encourage good, bushy cover.*

DEADHEADING

Pinch out dead blooms. Such deadheading encourages flowering and removes a potential source of infection by gray mold (Botrytis).

of pests and diseases are often identified. These can then be treated in their early stages before they do serious damage to the plants.

In spring, overwintered plants frequently need to be cleaned up. Prune out any frost-damaged growth and remove dead and blemished leaves; all of these are potential sources of infection by fungal diseases. Shorten any weak or straggling stems, for example those of trailing ivies, cutting back to strong buds to encourage new shoots. Pinching back overlong shoots in spring is also beneficial to most plants because it will encourage bushy new growth.

During summer, vigorous plants may need to be curbed to prevent overcrowding. Tie in climbers to their supports on a regular basis, and check that existing ties are not restricting the stems. When grown on upright supports, the stems of vigorous trailing plants, such as *Helichrysum petiolare,* should be tied in frequently, too. The stem tips and sideshoots may also need pinching back in order to provide the desired dense coverage of their upright supports.

Deadheading

The removal of dead and fading flowers prevents the formation of fruit and seed, which diverts a plant's energy from the creation of more flowers. Deadheading is a task that many gardeners find enjoyable, and this activity is the most effective way of prolonging the flowering season of a wide range of annuals that are the mainstay of the container garden in summer. Deadheading can be done by pinching the dead blooms on

many soft-stemmed annuals, or use scissors or pruners for firmer flower stems, such as those of roses.

Renewing spent plants

The usual pattern of seasonal designs is to plant for two or three main displays in a year. But sometimes, part of a display fades prematurely, leaving a conspicuous gap. Rather than starting again with a completely fresh planting, it is often possible to remove faded plants and insert replacements in the gap. This is not invariably successful, especially if pests or diseases have caused early failure of plants, and small new plants can find it difficult to compete with those that are well established.

For the best chance of success, take out as much of the old soil mix as possible, without disturbing the

roots of those that remain. Partly fill the holes with fresh, moist mix of the same type that is already in the container. Plant the replacement plants, adding more mix and working it in around the root balls. Finally, fill the soil mix to its previous level and water in thoroughly.

Pests and diseases

The pests and diseases that attack container-grown plants are much the same as those that are troublesome in the open garden (see PLANT PROBLEMS, pp.633–661). Because of the condensed nature of the container garden, however, damaged plants are more conspicuous. Even if they can be nursed back to health, diseased and damaged plants detract from the overall effect and may form a source of infection for neighboring plants. In many cases, the best policy is to discard plants that are sickly or badly damaged. If replanting entire containers, dispose of the old soil mix, clean the container thoroughly, and begin again with fresh mix.

Many problems can be avoided or contained by good hygiene and sound cultivation. Healthy plants show greater resistance to disease and recover more rapidly from pest infestations. Always use sterilized potting mix, clean all containers thoroughly before use, and check new plants to make sure that they are not carriers of pests and diseases.

Common pests

There are several particularly troublesome pests in the container garden. Aphids (see p.639) and other sap-sucking pests cause distorted and stunted growth, and unsightly

REPELLING PESTS

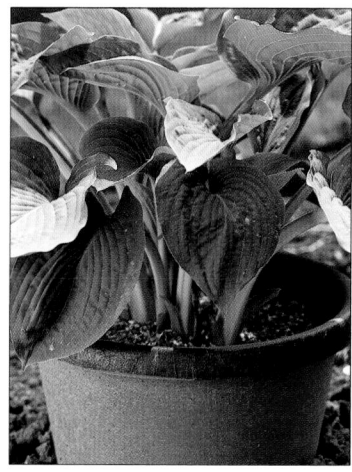

Hostas are a favorite food source for slugs and snails, so take special protective measures. A mulch of sharp sand and a copper band at the pot rim may deter them.

black sooty mold may infest the honeydew that they excrete. In addition, they often spread virus diseases.

Adult vine weevils (see p.638) cause largely cosmetic damage to leaves by cutting irregular holes in leaf margins between spring and autumn, but their curved, creamy white larvae cause far greater damage (see p.652). They feed on plant roots, frequently remaining undetected until the plant wilts. Check the roots of all new plants for signs of infestation before planting.

Slugs and snails (see p.638) eat young growth, frequently causing severe damage before their silvery slime trails are noted. They may hide under pots or their rims, so check such places regularly and dispose of the pests promptly.

Various fungal diseases, including gray mold (*Botrytis*) (see p.646), attack a wide range of plants, but by far the most serious diseases in the container garden are viral. Viruses (see p.642), which are spread by sap-sucking insects, seriously weaken plants and cause stunted, distorted, and often mottled growth. There is no effective way of treating them, and the only practical course is to destroy the affected plants.

It is largely a matter of personal choice whether or not to rely on chemical pest and disease control. Frequent checks made on the state of the plant's health allow infestations or infections to be dealt with promptly before they present serious problems (see PLANT PROBLEMS, "Integrated control," p.640). It is preferable to try an organic or biological control initially, before resorting to chemicals if these fail.

RENEWING A CONTAINER DISPLAY

1 *Deadhead flowers regularly in order to keep the display attractive. When plants have finished flowering, remove them, taking care not to damage the roots of remaining plants in the pot.*

2 *Add fresh, moist soil mix and fill the gaps with new plants or bulbs that will continue the floral display. Firm in gently and water thoroughly to help the new plants establish.*

TOP-DRESSING

1 *To top-dress a container-grown plant (here a rhododendron), remove the top 2–4in (5–10cm) of the old soil mix, taking care not to damage the plant roots.*

2 *Replace with fresh mix of a similar type and to the same level as before. Water well, and renew the mulch as is appropriate for the plant..*

Maintaining shrubs and trees in containers

Container-grown shrubs and trees require more care and attention than those in the open ground, since they have less access to moisture and nutrients. Repotting or top-dressing once a year will ensure continued growth and good health.

Repotting woody plants

If grown indefinitely in containers trees, shrubs, and many long-term shrubby perennials will become pot-bound and will exhaust the nutrients in the soil mix. A vigorous young tree or shrub is likely to outgrow its pot every one or two years. The roots of mature trees and shrubs, in which growth will naturally have slowed down, will take longer to become congested. As a general guide, mature trees and shrubs need repotting every three or four years. Check the state of the roots by laying the container on its side and easing the plant out. Often, however, the plant itself will indicate that it needs repotting by exhibiting a lack of vigor and poor color in the leaves. Growth may also appear uneven or unbalanced. If the plant is top-heavy, it will almost certainly benefit from being repotted.

Repotting is best done in early to midspring, as or just before growth begins for the new season. Mature plants can be returned to their original pots, but vigorous young plants generally need to be moved to pots that are one-and-half times the size of the old one. Expect to continue replanting them in ever larger containers until they reach maturity and growths slows.

When the tree or shrub has been eased out of its container, remove the surface mix and any weeds or moss, and discard all of this material as well as any loose soil mix. The roots are delicate and should not be handled unnecessarily, although this is a good opportunity to tease out tangled roots and shorten by up to two thirds a proportion of nonfibrous roots. If there is any delay between removal and repotting, keep the root ball covered with a sheet of plastic or damp burlap to prevent it from being desiccated by the drying effects of sun or wind.

Use an appropriate soil-based mix to which slow-release fertilizer has been added, and repot so that the surface of the plant's root ball is at the same level as before when firmed in and watered.

Top-dressing long-term plants

In years when shrubs and trees are not being repotted, their soil mix should be refreshed in spring. Having removed any mulch, the top 2–4in (5–10cm) of mix should be loosened and discarded, taking care not to damage the shallow roots of plants such as camellias and rhododendrons. The replacement soil mix must not only be fresh but also of the same type as the soil mix still in the container. It should also contain a slow-release fertilizer. Always use an acidic mix and soft water or rainwater when top-dressing acid-loving plants.

Surface-rooting plants can be top-dressed in a different way, because their fibrous feeding roots are easily damaged when the top layers of mix are removed. For surface rooters, discard the mix from the bottom of the root ball and replace it with a smaller quantity of enriched mix. The shrub will then sit lower in its pot than previously, leaving room for a smaller top-dressing.

Vacation care

The most essential requirement in the gardener's absence is regular watering. An automated irrigation system (see TOOLS AND EQUIPMENT, "Hose timers," p.555) is an ideal but expensive solution. Failing this, the best solution is arrange for a friend or neighbor to come in to water on a regular basis. To make the task easier, it is worth grouping the containers together. This massing of the plants together also has the advantage of slowing the rate of water evaporation from each; it will do so to such an extent as to be an adequate solution in itself for an absence of a few days. Place containers in a shaded and sheltered place and water thoroughly just before going away.

Evaporation can be reduced still further by packing a number of containers in a crate, tray, or similar container with drainage holes, which is filled with damp coarse sand, soil mix, or peat substitute. For short-term absences, and with relatively small plants, yet another method is to enclose small potted plants in sealed and inflated plastic bags. If the bagged plants are kept in cool shade, the rate of water loss will be negligible. This is, however, only a short-term fix; fungal diseases

REPOTTING A CONTAINER-GROWN SHRUB

1 *Carefully lay the shrub on its side. Support the main stems with one hand, then ease it out of its pot. If necessary, slide a long-bladed knife between mix and pot to loosen the root ball.*

2 *If the roots have become very congested, gently tease them out. Remove the surface mix and any moss or weeds. Prune back about a quarter of the nonfibrous roots by up to two thirds.*

3 *Place screening over the pot's drainage holes, then add the soil mix. Position the plant centrally and vertically in the pot, spreading its roots out evenly within the container.*

4 *Add more mix around the roots, gently firming it in stages, until the mix is at the same level on the plant as it was in its previous pot. Prune out any dead, twiggy, or damaged growth.*

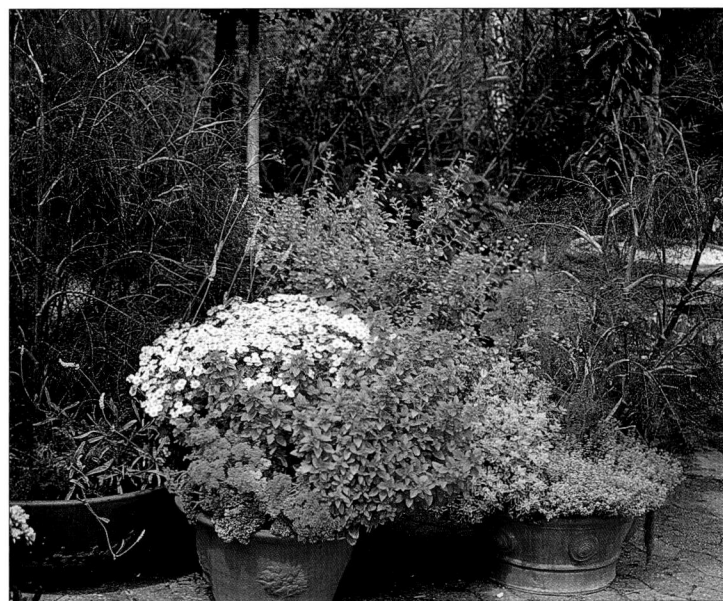

MINIMIZING MOISTURE LOSS
When containers are closely grouped, air movement between them and the plants they contain is reduced, so less water is lost to evaporation.

proliferate in such conditions, and the bags must be removed promptly when the gardener returns.

Capillary matting can be used to supply water to containers (see INDOOR GARDENING, "Care of indoor plants before going away," p.366). Another way of exploiting capillary action is to use a filled bucket as a water reservoir and strips of capillary matting as a "wick." The bucket must be raised above the container it is to serve, and the wick must be tucked into the soil mix. Commercial wicking systems are also available, which are specially designed for vacation care.

Emergency measures
If plants have wilted when you return from holiday, do not despair immediately. Even when soil mix has become so dry that it has shrunk away from the sides of the pot, plants can sometimes be salvaged by deep immersion. Partially fill a bucket with water, place it in a shady site, and plunge the plant in its container so that the top of the container is just below the surface of the water. Hold the container down until the flow of air bubbles that rises from the soil mix has ceased, then allow the plant to soak for a further 30 minutes. When the mix is thoroughly wet, remove the container from the bucket and allow to drain well. If woody plants do not revive within two or three hours, there is little point in keeping them. It is worth cutting back perennials, however; they may produce new growth from the base.

Winter protection

In frost-prone areas, container-grown plants that need protection from severe cold include all those that are known to be tender, those that are only marginally hardy, and a number of reasonably hardy plants such as rosemary (*Rosmarinus officinalis* cultivars) and lavender (*Lavandula* cultivars) that may suffer cold damage to the roots if the soil mix in the containers becomes frozen.

The most straightforward way of avoiding cold damage is to move plants under cover in autumn. Depending on the local climate, even an unheated greenhouse, conservatory, or glassed-in porch may give adequate protection to most plants, especially if they are kept almost dry during the coldest, darkest months.

In some cases, the overwintered plant can be used to provide cuttings in spring and may itself then be discarded. Where space is a problem, it can be much less space-consuming to overwinter plants as cuttings. Overwintered rooted cuttings of plants that make rapid annual growth, such as *Helichrysum petiolare*, will develop in time to use in displays for the following summer. It is always worth overwintering under cover cuttings of marginally hardy plants left outdoors, as an insurance against winter losses. *Pelargonium*, a major genus for container gardening, warrants special attention (see *Overwintering*, p.200).

If vulnerable plants are too large to be moved indoors, it may be possible to insulate them from the cold, depending on minimum temperature. Protect the plant with row cover or bubble plastic. It is important also to insulate the container. A layer of straw or burlap tied snugly around the container can provide effective insulation for the plant roots and will also help preserve the pot itself from cold damage. During winter, keep plants in a sheltered site, avoiding frost pockets. The weight of snow can break branches and stems of plants, so do not allow heavy accumulations to build up.

Spring is often a more difficult season than winter. There may be periods without frost and unseasonably warm days in which plants begin to make growth, but the risk of frost remains and its effect on unprotected, soft new growth can be devastating. The same is true of cold, dry spring winds. During a hardening-off period of a few weeks, plants that have been overwintered under cover can be gradually acclimatized to outdoor conditions. It is essential, however, to remain vigilant and provide protection at night, when there is any risk of temperatures falling below freezing. Make sure to keep a sheet of row cover handy to cover any vulnerable plant if the forecast is for a cold night.

Security

Although it is far from being a universal problem, gardens are sometimes targeted by thieves, and container-grown plants and the containers themselves are particularly vulnerable. It is difficult to take measures to put off the determined thief, without compromising the relaxed atmosphere of the garden and the quality of its display. There are, however, some sensible precautions that you can take.

Valuable containers in exposed positions close to public access arouse interest, so reposition these or chain them to a tree or other structure, although it is difficult to do this inconspicuously. The very fact that the container is chained can highlight its value. In front yards, it is generally advisable to use plain but serviceable containers. Rare or unusual plants are unlikely to be recognized as such, but they may be difficult to replace, so it is better to grow them in places away from public view.

Lights that are activated automatically by movement provide some measure of security, as do well-maintained walls, gates, and fences. Although these are not impregnable, they do provide the strongest barriers to both thieves and vandals.

PLANTS TO OVERWINTER AS ROOTED CUTTINGS

Alternanthera ficoidea
Angelonia
Anisodontea
Antirrhinum
Argyranthemum
Convolvulus sabatius
Cuphea
Diascia
Felicia amelloides
Fuchsia
Hedera helix (cvs)
Helichrysum petiolare
Heliotropium
Lantana
Lotus berthelotii,
    L. maculatus
Osteospermum
Pelargonium
Petunia (some spp.)
Plecostachys serpyllifolia
Plectranthus
Salvia
Scaevola
Senecio cineraria
Tropaeolum (some spp.)
Verbena (some spp.)

PLANTS TO OVERWINTER FOR CUTTINGS IN SPRING

Fuchsia
Impatiens (some spp.)
Ipomoea batatas
Salvia (some spp.)
Solenostemon

COLD PROTECTION

Wrap top-growth lightly but securely in row cover. A double layer of burlap tied firmly around the pot will help protect roots from cold and also help preserve the pot.

CHAPTER
12

CACTI AND OTHER SUCCULENTS

CACTI AND OTHER succulents display a unique variety of size, shape, color, and texture. Some have plump, smooth surfaces, while others have curved or straight, sometimes colorful spines or a covering of silky hair. Their forms range from symmetrical rosettes to squat globes to fluted columns and candelabra. Many bloom only briefly but bear large, brightly colored flowers. In cool-temperate climates, most cacti and other succulents are grown in the greenhouse or as houseplants, but where hardy, they can make unique garden displays of remarkable beauty. Whether grown as single specimens or grouped for contrast of form, color, and texture, the diversity of cacti and other succulents, combined with their remarkable tolerance of dry conditions, make them ideal for containers, both indoors and out.

Designing with cacti and other succulents

MANY cacti are native to the desert regions of the southern US and Mexico, where rainfall is low and intermittent and there are great extremes of temperature. In contrast, some of the most floriferous cacti originate in the warm, humid rain forests of Central and South America. These plants are usually epiphytic, which means that they grow on other plants, either weaving through host trees or lodging in niches in their branches.

Other succulent plants occur in a far greater range of habitats than cacti and, since they are found in more than 20 different plant families, show a wide diversity of characteristics. Their natural habitats include the semiarid regions of Central America, Africa, and Australasia, as well as the more temperate and cold climates of Asia and northern parts of Europe and North America.

Characteristics of succulents

Cacti and other succulents show a number of adaptations, such as reduced leaf size and loss of leaves in very dry weather, which are designed to conserve water by reducing transpiration. The distinguishing feature that is common to all, however, is the presence of water-storing, fleshy tissue in the stems, leaves, or roots. It is this tissue that allows succulent plants to withstand long periods of drought.

Cacti are easily distinguished from other succulents by structures called areoles, the cushionlike growths on their stems from which the spines, hairs, flowers, and shoots develop.

Succulent plants can be loosely divided into three groups, depending on which part of the plant contains the moisture-retaining tissue. (Some genera, for example *Euphorbia*, may be represented in more than one group.) Most cacti are stem succulents, as are some succulent plants from the Asclepiadaceae and Euphorbiaceae families. Others, including *Aloe*, *Echeveria*, *Lithops*, and *Sedum*, are leaf succulents. Plants in the third group are known as caudiciform succulents and have the water-storing tissue in a swollen rootstock (the caudex), although this often extends into the stem, such as in *Adenium obesum*. Plants that belong to this group are mostly found in the families Apocynaceae, Cucurbitaceae, and Convolvulaceae.

Form and habit

The diverse forms and growth characteristics of cacti and other succulent plants may be used to create a host of compositions. The

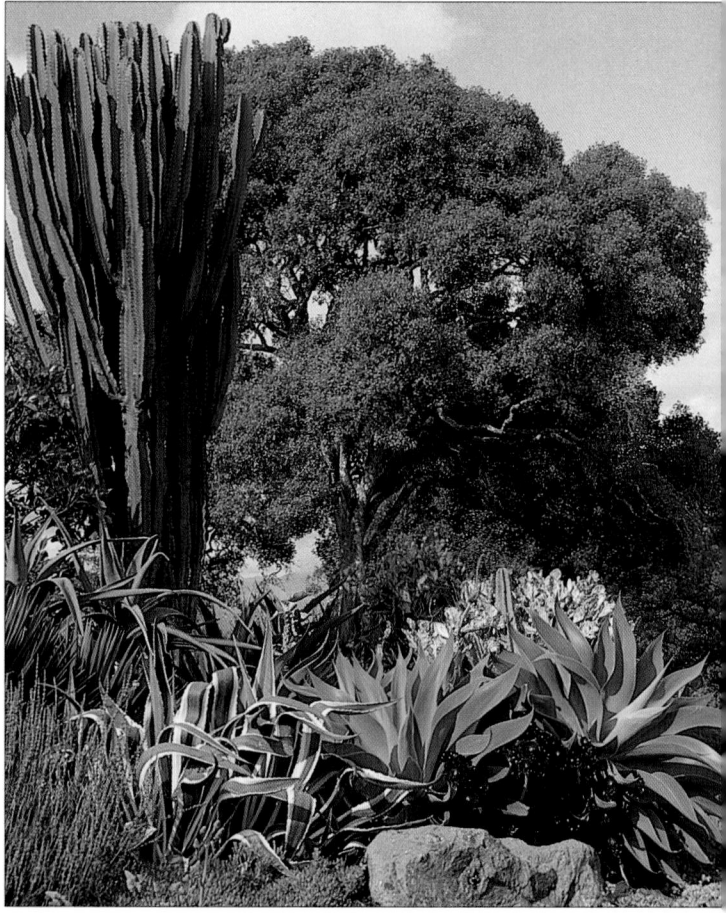

A NATURAL GROUPING
Collections of succulent plants make an impressive display. Here Euphorbia canariensis *towers above* Agave americana *'Variegata' and* A. attenuata.

FLOWERING SUCCULENTS

Thelocactus setispinus

Oroya neoperuviana

Parodia chrysacanthion

Strombocactus disciformis

Lithops pseudotruncatella **var.** *pulmonuncula*

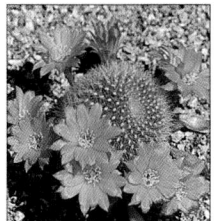
Rebutia fiebrigii

VARIETY OF FORM
The strong, architectural leaves of Agave americana (*center*) *make a sharp contrast with the orange flower spikes of the* Aloe (*left*) *and the spiky, blue-gray leaves of a* Senecio *in the foreground.*

tall columns of *Cleistocactus strausii*, for example, make strong, vertical lines that contrast well with foreground plantings of smaller, spherical forms such as *Echinocactus grusonii* and *Rebutia* species, or the characteristically flattened segments of some *Opuntia* species.

Several species have a creeping habit that adds a horizontal element to a design. *Carpobrotus edulis*, for instance, as well as *Lampranthus* and *Ruschia* species, make dense carpets of growth that provide an excellent groundcover.

Trailing succulent plants, for example *Ceropegia woodii* as well as *Schlumbergera* and *Rhipsalis* species, produce cascades of slender stems or leaves that are often displayed in hanging baskets. A number are scrambling climbers: *Aloe ciliaris* and *Selenicereus* species add height to mixed plantings if given the support of a trellis or the branch of a tree. In frost-free climates, the jointed and climbing stems of *Hylocereus* species are most attractive when sprawling over walls.

Flowering cacti and other succulents

Cacti and other succulents often produce exquisite blooms and will flower regularly once they reach maturity, although this may take between one and 40 years. Most of these plants are day-blooming, with individual blossoms sometimes lasting for several days. Some epiphytic cacti flower during the winter and have blooms that are carried in succession over long periods.

However, others bloom only briefly, the flowers sometimes appearing soon after sunset and fading as evening advances. Many of the large, columnar cacti produce buds that gradually unfold during the evening and then fade in the early morning hours.

The flowers, often of delicate appearance and silken texture, are usually exceptionally large in comparison with the size of the plant, and their color range is mainly at the warm end of the spectrum with a profusion of rich yellows, hot scarlets, and vivid carmines. A number of genera, often those of the family Mesembryanthemaceae, and some of the epiphytes, have sweetly scented blooms. Some species, especially members of the family Agavaceae, are monocarpic (they die after flowering and setting seed). A number of small, nonflowering offsets are often formed around the flowering rosette, however, and these flower in subsequent years.

Outdoor display

With careful selection and skillful arrangement, attractive collections of cacti and other succulents can be grown outdoors where winters are mild. Few succulents, however, tolerate excess moisture; even the hardy species require good drainage. These grow well in raised beds where water drains away freely. Among the hardiest are *Opuntia humifusa*, *Sedum*, hen and chickens (*Sempervivum*), *Crassula sarcocaulis*, and *Maihuenia poeppigii*.

A number of desert cacti, particularly some *Lampranthus* and *Opuntia* species, tolerate sharp drainage and high temperatures in summer and surprisingly low temperatures in winter, although not the combination of cold and wet.

In mild areas that rarely see frost, the range of plants is extended to include the spectacular rosettes of *Agave americana* and its cultivars, *A. filifera*, and *Beschorneria yuccoides*. Marginally hardy species need a freely draining site with the shelter of a warm, sunny wall for additional protection. There are hardy cacti that will survive outside over winter in all but the coldest regions given a well-drained soil. Species such as *Opuntia fragilis*, native to parts of Ontario and Alberta, will survive temperatures down to -40˚F (-40˚C) at least.

Mixed plantings
When growing nonsucculent and succulent plants together, it is important to choose plants that have similar needs for light, soil type, and watering schedules. In frost-free gardens, compatible nonsucculents include *Salvia, Nerium, Mirabilis,* and *Catharanthus* species, all of which provide additional color and variety. Bulbs and rhizomes such as

A SAMPLING OF SUCCULENTS

Beschorneria yuccoides

Maihuenia poeppigii

Sedum spectabile 'Brilliant'

Agave filifera

Opuntia compressa

Sempervivum montanum

Clivia, Cyrtanthus, and *Sprekelia* species are also good choices in mixed plantings.

In cooler regions, annual species and plants that are grown as annuals, such as *Portulaca grandiflora* and *Lampranthus* species, are suitable for planting outdoors among groups of perennial cacti and succulents.

Desert gardens
While a desert garden with a wide variety of plants is hard to achieve in most of Canada, by using hardy succulents such as sedums and hen-and-chicks (*Sempervivum*), and potted indooor cacti that are put outside for the summer, the essence of such a garden can be realized. Providing the drainage is good, the indoor plants will benefit and flower more freely.

Use smaller species at the front of the bed, so that their delicate beauty is not obscured by taller plants. Allow clump-forming plants, such as many *Echeveria, Haworthia*, and *Mammillaria* species, sufficient space to develop fully. These low-growing, cluster-forming species flower at different periods from spring to fall, to give color during the warmer months.

Tall, erect, columnar cacti and other succulents are ideal for background planting. Choose plants such as the tall, single-stemmed *Cephal-ocereus senilis*, the branching *Cleistocactus strausii*, or the towering, treelike *Euphorbia candelabrum*.

Containers outdoors

Most cacti and other succulents have shallow roots and respond well to being grown in containers. Select

A DESERT GARDEN
The branching arms of Euphorbia candelabrum *balance the surrounding globular and columnar cacti to complete this striking collection.*

containers that enhance the shape and form of the plants – a wide, shallow bowl, for example, is the natural choice for displaying low-growing and creeping species, whereas those with stronger form, such as *Agave attenuata*, are much better suited to large pots or urns.

Troughs are particularly useful for creating imaginative combinations of plants of quite different sizes and habits. Hanging baskets are suitable for displaying a variety of trailing and pendent species.

Choosing and siting the plants
In cool regions, but where temperatures seldom fall below freezing, many species will thrive outdoors in troughs and pots, provided that these are raised above the ground to allow water to drain away freely. A warm, sheltered position such as a corner of a covered patio or balcony, where the plants can more easily be protected from rain, will provide the ideal environment.

The foliage shapes of *Sedum* and neat rosettes of *Sempervivum* may be used to form a contrast with the leafy forms and brilliant blooms of *Lewisia* species and cultivars, or with the green-flowered *Echin-ocereus viridiflorus* and the scarlet, early summer blooms of *Echinopsis chamaecereus*. Other species, such as *Agave parryi*, which has symmet-

rical rosettes of plump, gray-green leaves, or *Opuntia polyacantha* with its brilliant display of yellow flowers, make striking focal points if they are planted on their own in large bowls.

In warmer climates, there is more opportunity for growing cacti and other succulents outdoors in containers. In large pots, group plants that flower at different periods and have striking forms: purple-leaved *Aeonium arboreum* 'Zwartkop' ('Schwarzkopf'); yellow-flowered *Aloe barbadensis*; and red-flowered *Crassula perfoliata* var. *minor* (*C. falcata*). These provide structural interest all year and give a succession of blooms throughout the warmer months.

Where temperatures do not consistently fall below 55°F (13°C), many dwarf cacti, such as species and cultivars of *Gymnocalycium, Mammillaria*, and *Rebutia*, survive well in outdoor bowls and troughs in the garden. These dwarf, cluster-forming species have fascinating forms and textures and put out flowers with vibrant color that can last for several weeks.

Indoor display

The protected environment of the greenhouse or conservatory, which allows practically complete control of light, temperature, humidity, and water, provides ideal conditions for an extensive range of cacti and other succulents. Most of the plants recommended for outdoor cultivation in warm climates will thrive under cover in cooler regions.

The adaptations of cacti and other succulents that help them survive in

MIXED PLANTING
The neat rosettes and delicate, nodding flower heads of Echeveria *provide a dainty contrast with the straplike leaves of* Agave filifera (*center*), *the focal point of this attractive combination.*

AN OUTDOOR CONTAINER
This varied collection of tall, spreading, and pendent cacti and other succulents creates a highly decorative and unusual feature on a balcony outdoors.

AN INDOOR BED
The bright foliage of Agave americana 'Medio-picta'*, offset by the rosettes of* Orostachys chanetii, *is a bold centerpiece in this greenhouse bed.*

harsh, arid environments in the wild also make them well suited to the warm, dry conditions of the centrally heated home, where many other plants may fail to thrive. Since different species are adapted to a variety of environmental conditions, they may be selected to suit a number of situations in the home.

The variation in their shape and habit, and their beautiful flowers, guarantee that these plants provide interest throughout the year.

Providing the right conditions

The great majority of cacti and other succulents need high light levels, warmth, and good ventilation to thrive, although some, the leafy succulents in particular, may need protection from direct sun in summer to avoid leaf scorch.

There is an important group, however, that requires shady conditions, or at least filtered light: the epiphytes that come from the humid, shaded rain forests of Central and South America. Epiphytic plants are among the most floriferous of cacti and other succulents, and they can be used to add bold splashes of color and interest to shady corners of the home or garden. The best known of this group are the Christmas cactus (*Schlumbergera bridgesii*), *Rhipsalidopsis gaertneri*, and *R. rosea*. Some of the loveliest are the magnificent hybrids created by crossing *Epiphyllum* species with those of *Echinopsis, Heliocereus, Hylocereus,* and *Nopalxochia*. The resulting hybrids produce extraordinarily beautiful and sometimes fragrant flowers in spring and summer, ranging in color from pure white through cream, yellow, and orange to red and deepest purple.

Plants for the greenhouse and conservatory

Plants in a greenhouse or conservatory can be grown in pots or open beds, either at floor level or raised on benches. Planting in open beds offers potential for growing larger species and even for creating a miniature desert garden.

When in growth, many species from warm habitats need bright light, a fairly dry atmosphere, and a temperature of 64°F (18°C) if they are to develop to their full potential and bear flowers. These conditions are more easily provided under cover than in the home, and many cacti grow and flower most successfully in the greenhouse.

Some, notably *Rhipsalis* species, require fairly high levels of humidity (80 percent) to thrive and nearly always perform best in the humid atmosphere of a conservatory. Other groups that are well suited to the conservatory and greenhouse are those that need space to grow and

GREENHOUSE DISPLAY
The rich color and diverse forms of Astrophytum, Crassula, Echeveria, Echinocactus, *and* Mammillaria, *among others, provide a sumptuous collection of plants for the greenhouse bench.*

flower well. These include the clambering *Selenicereus* (the most outstanding species is queen-of-the-night, *S. grandiflorus*) and several *Hylocereus* species, all of which do best in filtered light.

When drawing up planting plans for a greenhouse or conservatory, combine groups of cacti and other succulents that have similar cultural needs to make maintenance easier.

Container-growing indoors

Many cacti and other succulents will thrive in indoor containers if provided with warm, bright, and draft-free conditions. Use small pots for displaying individual plants, or large bowls for planting a variety of compatible species together.

Wear gloves when handling spiny plants such as *Agave, Mammillaria,* and *Opuntia,* because their sharp spines may easily become embedded in your fingers if you brush against them, causing a painful injury.

Bowl gardens

If planted with different species that have the same cultural requirements, bowl gardens are particularly suitable for growing succulent plants indoors. One or two plants with an erect habit, for example young specimens of *Cephalocereus, Cleistocactus,* or other columnar genera, could provide the focal point of the bowl. Alternatively, use a leafy succulent such as *Crassula ovata* as the main plant. Fill the rest of the bowl with smaller plants such as *Echeveria* and *Lithops.* Free-flowering cacti such as *Mammillaria, Notocactus,* and other globular cacti are also good choices for planting in a bowl garden indoors.

A HANGING BASKET
The graceful stems and flowers of Kalanchoe manginii *cascade like a waterfall against a house wall.*

Hanging baskets

Succulents in hanging baskets make colorful displays in the home or conservatory. Pendent cacti, such as *Aporocactus flagelliformis,* and trailing succulent plants such as *Kalanchoe, Rhipsalidopsis gaertneri,* and *Schlumbergera* species and cultivars, are the most suitable plants to choose, since they will trail attractively over the edge of the basket. *Sedum morganianum* and other semitrailing species are also attractive in hanging baskets.

Plant hanging baskets with just one specimen, or use several species for a harmonious but varied arrangement of shape and texture. In general, nonepiphytic plantings require bright light, but epiphytes need either partly shaded conditions or bright but filtered light, so position the baskets accordingly.

Planter's guide to cacti and other succulents

DAMP CONDITIONS

Succulents that tolerate damp conditions
Crithmum maritimum
Salicornia europaea
Suaeda fruticosa, S. maritima
Umbilicus intermedius, U. rupestris

SHADE

Succulents that tolerate shade
Lewisia Cotyledon Hybrids,
    L. leeana
Orostachys chanetii, O. spinosus
Rhodiola crassipes
Sedum dasyphyllum, S. montanum,
    S. rosulatum, S. sediforme,
    S. spectabile, S. ternatum,
    S. villosum
Sempervivum arachnoideum,
    S. ruthenicum

BOWLS AND TROUGHS

Sun
Adenium obesum
Aeonium arboreum,
    A. nobile
Agave filifera, A. stricta,
    A. victoriae-reginae
Aloe humilis, A. longistyla,
    A. rauhii
Astrophytum myriostigma,
    A. ornatum
Cephalocereus senilis
Cereus forbesii, C. peruvianus
Cleistocactus straussii
Cotyledon teretifolia,
    C. undulata
Crassula ovata,
    C. rupestris, C. socialis
Echeveria agavoides,
    E. derenbergii, E. pilosa
Echinocactus grusonii
Echinocereus blanckii,
    E. pentalophus

Echinocereus pentalophus

Echinopsis chamaecereus,
    E. eyriesii ,
    E. multiplex, E. oxygona
Espostoa lanata
Euphorbia flanaganii, E. milii,
    E. obesa
Faucaria felina
Ferocactus acanthodes,
    F. latispinus
Gasteria batesiana,
    G. liliputana
Glottiphyllum linguiforme

Gymnocalycium baldianum,
    G. gibbosum, G. mihanovichii
Haworthia cooperi,
    H. limifolia, H. reinwardtii
Jatropha podagrica
Kalanchoe blossfeldiana
Lithops bella, L. dorotheae
Lobivia densispina,
    L. jajoiana, L. pentlandii,
Mammillaria bocasana,
    M. compress, M. gracilis,
    M. hahniana, M. mystax,
    M. rhodantha,
    M. spinosissima,
    M. zeilmanniana
Opuntia microdasys
Orbea variegata
Pachypodium geayi, P. lameri
Parodia leninghausii,
    P. mutabilis
Rebutia albiflora, R. aureiflora,
    R. heliosa, R. marsoneri,
    R. minuscula, R. senilis
Sansevieria trifasciata 'Hahnii',
    S. t. 'Laurentii'
Sulcorebutia glomeriseta,
    S. steinbachii
Thelocactus bicolor,
    T. nidulans

Thelocactus bicolor

Trichocereus pachanoi,
    T. pasacana, T. spachianus

Partial shade
Epiphyllum oxypetalum
    (and hybrids)
Hoya australis, H. carnosa
Rhipsalidopsis gaertneri,
    R. rosea
Schlumbergera bridgesii,
    S. truncata (and hybrids)

HANGING BASKETS

Aporocactus flagelliformis
Ceropegia haygarthii,
    C. woodii
Epiphyllum oxypetalum
    (and hybrids)
Hatiora salicornioides
Hoya bella, H. linearis,
    H. polyneura
Kalanchoe jongsmanii,
    K. manginii, K. pumila
Rhipsalidopsis gaertneri,
    R. rosea
Rhipsalis cereuscula,
    R. mesembryanthemoides,
    R. pachyptera
Schlumbergera bridgesii,
    S. truncata (and hybrids)
Sedum morganianum

SUCCULENTS THAT TOLERATE TEMPERATURES DOWN TO 32°F (0°C)

Agave americana, A. lophantha,
    A. parryi, A. utahensis
Echinocereus viridiflorus
Echinopsis chamaecereus
Opuntia fragilis, O. humifusa,
    O. polyacantha
Sedum anglicum, S. cyaneum,
    S. dasyphyllum, S. formosanum,
    S. hispanicum, S. lanceolatum,
    S. rupestre, S. spectabile
Sempervivum (most spp.)
Umbilicus (spp. only)

SUCCULENTS THAT TOLERATE TEMPERATURES DOWN TO 45°F (7°C)

Agave attenuata, A. parviflora
Aloe arborescens, A. aristata,
    A. barbadensis, A. brevifolia,
    A. distans, A. spinosissima,
    A. variegata
Beschorneria yuccoides
Bulbine frutescens, B. latifolia,
    B. mesembryanthemoides
Caralluma europaea
Carpobrotus acinaciformis,
    C. edulis
Cereus chalybaeus,C. jamacaru
    (and other columnar spp.)
Crassula sarcocaulis,
    C. sarmentosa
Echeveria cuspidata, E. elegans,
    E. gibbiflora, E. pubescens
Echinocereus chloranthus,
    E. enneacanthus,
    E. pentalophus
Echinopsis chamaecereus
Gasteria angulata, G. distichia,
    G. verrucosa

Kalanchoe tubiflora

Kalanchoe marmorata,
    K. tubiflora
Lampranthus falcatus,
    L. multiradiatus
Lewisia Cotyledon Hybrids
Opuntia exaltata, O. rastera,
    O. robusta, O. subulata
Orostachys chanetii, O. spinosus
Oroya neoperuviana
Pelargonium acetosum,
    P. echinatum, P. tetragonum
Rosularia modesta
Senecio haworthii,
    S. macroglossus

FLOWERING CACTI

Day-flowering
Aporocactus flagelliformis
Astrophytum myriostigma

Astrophytum myriostigma

Echinocereus engelmannii,
    E. triglochidiatus, E. viereckii
Echinopsis aurea,
    E. chamaecereus,
    E. kermesina, E. multiplex
Epicactus
Gymnocalycium bruchii
Hatiora salicornioides
Heliocereus speciosus
    var. *superbus*
Lobivia famatimensis
Mammillaria blossfeldiana,
    M. bocasana, M. hahniana,
    M. microcarpa, M. nana,
    M. spinosissima,
    M. zeilmanniana
Matucana aureiflora
Nopalxochia phyllanthoides
Opuntia lanceolata,
    O. paraguayensis
Parodia brevihamata,
    P. graessneri, P. haselbergii,
    P. leninghausii,
    P. mammulosa, P. mutabilis
Rebutia aureiflora,
    R. marsoneri, R. senilis
Rhipsalidopsis gaertneri,
    R. rosea
Schlumbergera x *buckleyi,*
    S. truncata, S. t. var. *delicata*
Strombocactus disciformis
Sulcorebutia glomeriseta
Thelocactus bicolor

Night-flowering
Cephalocereus senilis
Cryptocereus anthonyanus
Echinopsis eyriesii
Epiphyllum cartagense
Eriocereus bonplandii
Espostoa lanata,
    E. melanostele
Haageocereus acranthus,
    H. setosus,
    H. versicolor
Harrisia gracilis
Hylocereus ocamponis
Pachycereus pringlei
Selenicereus grandiflorus,
    S. macdonaldiae
Setiechinopsis mirabilis
Trichocereus fulvilanus,
    T. spachianus,
    T. terscheckii

Soil preparation and planting

MANY cacti and other succulents grow naturally only in desert or rain forest conditions, but they also make striking displays out of doors in cooler climates. Whether grown indoors or outside, specially prepared, well-drained soil or soil mix is essential. A sunny site with appropriate protection from cold is also required for most species.

Buying cacti and other succulents

When buying cacti and other succulents, choose healthy, unblemished plants that show new growth or have flower buds forming. Do not buy damaged or slightly shriveled specimens, or any with dull, dry, or limp segments. Also reject plants that have outgrown their pots.

Planting in a raised bed or desert garden

Cacti and other succulents require well-drained conditions, so they benefit from being planted in a bed

RAISED BED CONSTRUCTION

Top-dressing   Soil mix   Drainage material

A raised bed has a deep gravel base and freely draining soil mix.

SELECTING CACTI AND OTHER SUCCULENTS

GOOD EXAMPLE

REBUTIA SPECIES

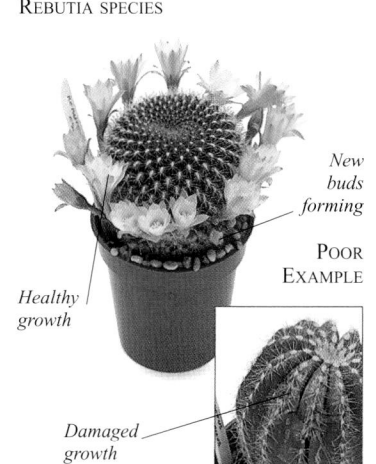

New buds forming

POOR EXAMPLE

Healthy growth

Damaged growth

GOOD EXAMPLE

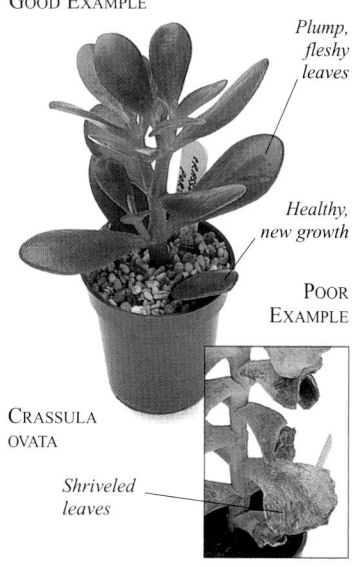

Plump, fleshy leaves

Healthy, new growth

POOR EXAMPLE

CRASSULA OVATA

Shriveled leaves

Handling cacti

Most cacti have sharp spines. When moving or planting them, either wear gloves or take other protective measures.

When handling spiny cacti, such as this Ferocactus, *wrap a loop of folded paper around the plant.*

---

that is raised at least 10in (25cm) above ground level. To provide good drainage, make the bed slightly sloping and provide a thick base of gravel or rubble that is at least one-third of the total height of the bed.

Never construct the bed on a concrete or other impermeable base, since this impedes drainage. Choose a bright, sunny site with a minimum temperature of 41°F (5°C). In cooler areas, provide adequate protection for tender species (see *COLD AND WIND PROTECTION*, pp.604–05).

Preparing the soil mix

Cacti and other succulents do not usually thrive in ordinary garden soil, because it is not sufficiently well drained. It needs to be replaced

by or supplemented with a carefully prepared growing medium. Good garden soil that has a pH level of 6–6.5 may be used as the basis of a soil mix. It must be sterilized first, however, to kill pests or weed seeds and to eliminate diseases (see "Making mixes," p.317).

To prepare the soil mix, combine 2 parts sterilized garden soil with 1 part peat or fine shredded sphagnum moss or compost, 1 part coarse sand or washed grit, and a little slow-release balanced fertilizer.

If the garden soil is alkaline, use a commercial soil-based mix combined with coarse sand or grit in a ratio of 1 part sand or grit to 3 parts soil mix. Commercial mixes may be used straight out of the bag.

Placing the plant in the bed

Water the plant, then carefully remove it from its pot. Check the root ball for disease or pest infestation (see also p.339), and treat any infections before planting.

Dig a hole of appropriate size and place the plant so that its base is at the same level in the soil as it was in its container. Fill in around the roots with soil mix, then firm, making sure that the stems and leaves are above soil level. Top-dress with grit to protect the plants from excess moisture and reduce soil water evaporation. Allow the plants to settle, then water lightly at first, gradually increasing the amount until the plants are well established and producing new growth.

PLANTING IN A BED OUTDOORS

1 *To plant a succulent (here* Espostoa lanata), *moisten the soil mix in the pot, then dig a hole large enough to accommodate the root ball in a prepared, well-drained bed. Allow space for the development of the plant and those around it.*

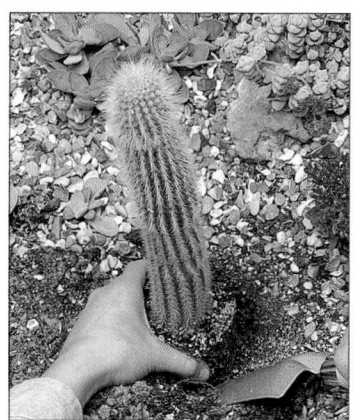

2 *Remove the cactus from the pot and place it in the hole at the same depth as it was in the pot. Firm the soil mix around the root ball.*

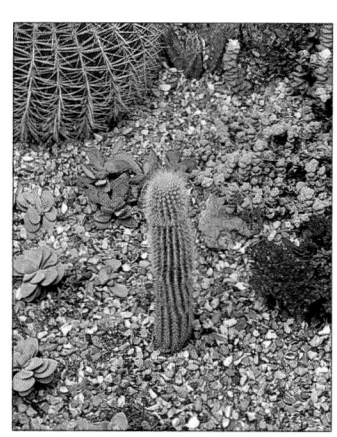

3 *Top-dress with a ¼in (5mm) layer of clean 1/8in (3mm) grit. Water after 2–3 days, when the plant has settled.*

Succulents in containers

A collection of cacti and other succulents grown in pots, bowls, or troughs provides an attractive focal point on a patio or windowsill.

Preparing the soil mix

The soil mix used should be well drained and preferably slightly acidic, with a pH of 6–6.5. Use 1 part coarse sand or grit to either 3 parts soil-based potting mix or 2 parts soilless mix. Very fast-draining mixes based on perlite and turface, and containing small amounts of organic matter, are also available. Plants intolerant of water near their roots can be grown in bricklike "stones."

A more acidic soil mix may be required if you are planting epiphytic succulents (such as certain *Hoya* species) and cacti (*Rhipsalis* and *Schlumbergera* in particular) native to forest areas. Mix 1 part organic matter (such as sphagnum moss, compost, or leaf mold) with 2 parts standard soil mix; add sand or grit to give adequate drainage.

Choosing the pot or container

Both clay and plastic containers are suitable for growing cacti and other succulents. Soil mix in plastic pots retains moisture longer than that in clay pots, which means that the plants need less frequent watering, but clay pots provide better aeration around the roots. Choose containers that have one or more drainage holes in the base to make sure that water drains away quickly. The size of pot or container should always be proportionate to the size of the plant but never less than 4in (10cm) deep; tuberous-rooted species such as *Wilcoxia* species do best in a pot with a depth of at least 6in (15cm).

Planting in containers

Always thoroughly wash all containers before use to remove possible sources of infection. Put a piece of window screening or similar mesh over the drainage hole(s). If the container is too tall for the root ball, place a layer of gravel or pot shards in the base, to approximately one-third of the depth of the container. Fill the container with soil mix to within ½in (1cm) of the rim.

Carefully remove the plant from its pot, discarding any top-dressing, and insert it into the new container so that the top of the root ball is at the same level in the soil mix as it was in the original pot. Firm the plant into the soil mix, and then top-dress with coarse gravel or grit.

When planting several cacti or other succulents in one container, space the plants so that there is room for them to develop. To create a more interesting display, decorative pieces of rock or pebbles may be added.

Allow the plants to settle for a few days before watering. Water routinely (see opposite) only when the plants are well established.

Hanging baskets

To create an attractive feature, plant trailing succulent species in a hanging basket. Make sure that the basket is completely clean. Wire baskets should be lined with a commercial liner or a layer of sphagnum moss. Do not line the basket with plastic, since this restricts drainage. If using a plastic basket that has a fixed drainage tray, place a layer of small pebbles or gravel in the base instead of sphagnum moss.

Fill the basket with an appropriate potting mix, then insert the plants in the same way as for other containers. Do not overcrowd the basket, since most suitable species have a naturally spreading or pendent habit; one to

PLANTING IN A BOWL

Crassula ovata
Cereus peruvianus
Mammillaria muehlenpfordtii
Aloe 'Black Gem'
Mammillaria polythele

1 *Select a group of plants that have similar cultivation requirements. Plan the group by positioning the pots in the container, placing the taller plants at the back. Moisten the soil mix in the pots.*

2 *Prepare the container, placing a 2in (5cm) layer of drainage material – gravel or pot shards – in the base and covering this with a layer of soil mix (such as 1 part sharp sand, 3 parts soil-based potting mix).*

3 *Remove the plants from their pots, place them in the container, and fill in with soil mix.*

4 *Top-dress the planted container with a ¼in (5mm) layer of ⅛in (3mm) gravel.*

three plants is usually sufficient to fill an average-sized basket. Top-dress with gravel or grit if extra drainage is required, then allow to settle for a few days before watering. Once the plant is established and showing new growth, routine watering can be started (see opposite).

PLANTING IN A HANGING BASKET

1 *Line a wire hanging basket with a layer of moist sphagnum moss. The layer should be 1¼in (3cm) thick when compressed.*

2 *Fill the basket almost to the brim with a mix of 1 part sharp sand to 3 parts soil-based potting mix. Prepare a hole for the plant in the center of the basket.*

3 *Insert the plant (here a Schlumbergera), spreading out the roots. Fill in with soil mix so that there are no air pockets around the roots.*

4 *Wait for 2–3 days after planting before watering the finished basket.*

Routine care

CACTI and other succulents need little maintenance in order to thrive, but they must have adequate light, warmth, and ventilation. Fertilize and water as appropriate for the particular species, and check regularly for signs of diseases or pests. Repot plants in containers as soon as they outgrow them to prevent them from becoming potbound.

The right environment

Place cacti and other succulents in a position appropriate to their individual cultural needs. Most species need full sun, although some prefer dappled or continuous shade. The ideal maximum daytime temperature in spring and summer is 86°F (30°C), and the nighttime temperature, 66°F (19°C). During the dormant season, most plants should be kept at a temperature of at least 45°F (7°C), although species that come from the tropics and equatorial regions generally require a warmer environment, with a minimum temperature of 55°F (13°C).

Ventilation
Good ventilation is essential, although cacti and other succulents should not be exposed to drafts. For plants grown in a greenhouse it may become necessary to use blinds or apply commercial shading to the outside of the glass, if ventilation is insufficient to keep the temperature below 81°F (27°C) (see "Shading," p.570). In exceptionally hot weather, watering the greenhouse floor will help to reduce the temperature. Occasionally, plants grown in the open may need some shade to protect them in extreme heat.

Watering/fertilizing

Cacti and other succulents require more water when they are growing actively (which is usually in spring and summer), and less when they are resting. Take care not to overwater them, especially during cool periods, but be sure to give them at least a trickle about once a month to prevent complete dehydration. Succulents from forested areas often bloom between late fall and early spring, so they require more water at this time.

Watering
During the growing season, moisten the soil or mix thoroughly with tepid water, allowing it to dry out almost completely before watering again. Provided that the plants are grown in freely draining soil, surplus moisture drains away quickly.

Water early in the day or in the early evening to allow any moisture on the plants to evaporate before nightfall. Alternatively, potgrown plants may be watered by placing the container in a shallow pan of water, so that the water permeates the soil mix but does not touch the stems or leaves. Remove the container from the water to drain as soon as the surface of the soil mix appears moist; the plants will quickly rot if left standing in water.

Epiphytic plants and those that need shaded conditions should be kept moist but not wet. An occasional light mist-spray maintains a reasonable level of humidity.

Fertilizing
During the growing season, fertilize cacti and other succulents to help maintain healthy, vigorous growth and to encourage flowering. Several commercial fertilizers are available but a standard, well-balanced liquid fertilizer containing all the major nutrients is satisfactory. Apply in accordance with the manufacturer's instructions at monthly intervals. Never apply fertilizer when a plant is dormant or the soil is dry, since this may damage the stems and foliage.

Hygiene

Cacti and other succulents may need occasional cleaning, since dust sometimes accumulates on the leaves or between the spines. During the growing season, houseplants may be sprayed lightly with water; succulents in the greenhouse or garden may be hosed down carefully, provided that they are not in direct sun.

Pests and diseases

Check cacti and other succulents routinely for pests and diseases. The most prevalent pests are mealybugs (p.640), scale insects (p.641), spider mites (p.640), root mealybugs (see "Mealybugs," p.640), and fungus gnats (p.656).

Diseases of cacti and other succulents are rare, although poor cultural conditions or excess nitrogen in the soil may encourage the development of black rot, which principally afflicts epiphytic cacti and *Stapelia* species. The plants become disfigured and may die. There is no treatment, so, if it appears that a plant is likely to die as a result of infection, take healthy shoots or sections as cuttings and grow them on to replace the diseased plant.

Repotting

Cacti and other succulents should be repotted as soon as the roots begin to show through the drainage holes – usually every two to three years for fast-growing species. Repot slow-growing plants every three to four years. Very lightly water a plant before repotting so the roots do not dry out while being potted.

Carefully remove the plant from its current pot. Inspect the roots, looking for signs of pests or disease, and treat if necessary. Cut out any dehydrated or dead roots, and dust the cuts with fungicide. Choose a new container one size larger than the current one and repot, making sure the planting depth is the same.

REPOTTING SUCCULENTS

1 When a succulent (here *Aloe arborescens*) has outgrown its container, repot it, selecting a container that is at least one size larger than the current one. Moisten the soil mix before sliding the plant out of its pot.

2 Gently tease out any roots that have become coiled or compressed.

3 Cover the hole(s) with a piece of screen, then put some soil mix in the pot. Position the plant at the same depth as it was before.

4 Carefully fill in around the root ball with more soil mix, firming in stages to eliminate any air pockets between the roots. Do not water until the plant is settled in the new pot, usually after several days.

Propagation

CACTI and other succulents may be propagated from seed, from leaf or stem cuttings, by division, or by grafting. Division and cuttings are the easiest methods. Raising plants from seed is slower and more difficult but provides the opportunity to obtain selected variants from within species, and to raise new hybrids by hand pollination. Grafting is useful for rare species and hybrids and for those slow-growing succulents that are difficult to propagate by other methods.

Propagating plants from seed

Seeds of cacti and other succulents vary widely in shape and size, and some of them have special requirements. Some fine seeds are slow to germinate, while some larger ones have a thick coating (such as those of several *Opuntia* species) and seldom germinate unless they have been stratified. These should be placed in a refrigerator for 48 hours.

Sowing

Sow seed under cover between late winter and late spring. Place a layer of coarse gravel, combined with a sprinkling of charcoal chips, in the base of a seed tray or pot. Fill almost to the top with sowing medium, then smooth over and firm lightly.

Sprinkle fine seeds evenly over the surface, water lightly, and barely cover with sterilized, sharp sand or a sand and grit mix. Larger seeds should be pressed into the medium, allowing ample space between them, then covered with coarse sand or grit. Stand pots or trays of larger seeds in tepid water and leave them

PROPAGATION FROM SEED

1 *Cover the base of the pot with a piece of screen, then add about ¹/₂in (1cm) of coarse gravel mixed with a little charcoal.*

2 *Fill the pot to within ¹/₂in (1cm) of the brim with moist sowing medium, and firm. Sprinkle fine seeds evenly over the surface.*

3 *Apply a fine, light mist-spray to the surface of the soil mix. Take care not to overwater.*

4 *Cover the seeds with a top-dressing of sterilized, gritty sand – only a very thin layer is required.*

5 *Label and place the pot in a pierced plastic bag. Keep in partial shade at 70°F (21°C).*

SOWING LARGE SEED

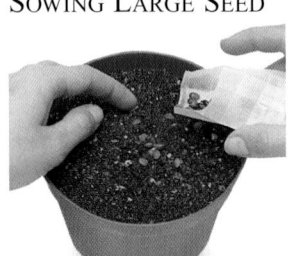

Press each seed into the medium, sowing at twice the seed's own depth. Space seeds about ¹/₂in (1cm) apart so that they have room to develop.

until the upper surface of the soil is moist, then remove the containers and let the surplus moisture drain.

Keep the containers at a temperature of 70°F (21°C). If tenting with a plastic bag, make a few small holes in the bag to admit air and reduce humidity. Keep the seeds in partial shade until they have germinated.

Care of seedlings

When the seedlings appear, remove the pots from the plastic bags or the propagator and provide additional ventilation. Spray the seedlings with fungicide to discourage damping off. Maintain a temperature of 70°F (21°C), giving further light and air as the seedlings develop.

Pricking out

After six to 12 months (depending on the species), when the seedlings are large enough to be handled without damaging them, prick them out singly into 3in (6cm) pots. Prepare the pots with screening over the hole(s) and fill almost to the brim with moist soil mix, then firm gently.

PRICKING OUT SEEDLINGS

1 *When the seedlings are large enough to handle, lift a clump from the pot, taking care not to damage the roots.*

2 *Divide the clump into individual small plants, retaining as much medium as possible around the roots (see inset).*

3 *Insert each seedling into a pot containing 3 parts cactus soil mix to 1 part gritty sand. Keep the top-growth clear of the soil mix.*

4 *Top-dress with a ¹/₄in (5mm) layer of ¹/₈in (3mm) gravel, and label. Do not water the seedlings for 3 or 4 days.*

Remove a group of seedlings and separate them out carefully. Plant out the seedlings singly, top-dress them with a thin layer of gravel, and then label each pot. Keep the young plants at a minimum temperature of 59°F (15°C). After a few days, water them sparingly, then gradually increase the amount until, usually after three or four weeks, the normal watering routine can be followed (see p.339).

Leaf cuttings

Some succulent plants, for example many species of *Crassula* and *Echeveria*, may be propagated from leaf cuttings. These should be taken from the parent plant in spring or early summer when there is plenty of new growth.

Choose firm, fleshy leaves and remove them carefully from the parent plant. Sever them with a sharp knife or pull them gently downward, making sure that a small piece of stem remains attached to the base of each. Put the severed cuttings on a clean piece of paper, and place them in partial shade at a temperature of at least 50°F (10°C); warmer is better. Leave them for a day or two until the cut end has dried.

PROPAGATION FROM LEAF CUTTINGS

1 *Remove a healthy leaf by carefully pulling it away from the parent plant. It should break off at the base with a small piece of stem attached.*

2 *Allow 24–48 hours for the wound to dry (see inset). Fill a pot with equal parts fine peat or soil mix and sand. Insert the cutting so that the base is gently but securely held in the soil mix.*

3 *Top-dress with gravel or grit, then label. After a new plantlet has formed at least a few leaves (see inset), the rooted cutting is ready to pot up into soil-based potting mix.*

Fill pots almost to the brim with equal parts of peat or screened soil mix and sharp grit or sand. Each cutting should be inserted in an upright position in a pot so that the stem of the leaf is just held in place in the top of the medium. Firm the medium around the cuttings with your fingers.

Cover the surface with a light top-dressing of gravel or grit to help keep the cuttings in position. Label the pot and place it in bright shade, making sure that you maintain a regular temperature of 70°F (21°C). Keep the young cuttings moist by watering them every day with tepid water. Use a fine mist-spray to cause least disturbance to the cuttings.

Rooting does not take long, normally occurring within a few weeks. Approximately two weeks after new growth appears, pot up the rooted cuttings into suitably sized pots of standard, soil-based potting mix. Replace the top-dressing.

SUCCULENTS THAT MAY BE PROPAGATED BY LEAF CUTTINGS

Adromischus cooperi,
  A. festivus
Aeonium arboreum
Begonia incana, B. venosa
Cotyledon ladismithiensis,
  C. undulata
Crassula ovata, C. perfoliata
Dudleya ingens, D. rigida
Echeveria agavoides,
  E. elegans
Fenestraria aurantiaca
Gasteria batesiana
Glottiphyllum linguiforme
Graptopetalum amethystinum
Haworthia attenuata,
  H. planifolia
Hoya australis, H. carnosa
Kalanchoe beharensis,
  K. tomentosa
Lenophyllum pusillum,
  L. texanum
Orostachys chanetii
Othonna dentata

Pachyphytum oviferum

Producing hybrids

When growing cacti and other succulents in a mixed collection, cross-pollination may occur (pollen from the flowers of one species or variety pollinates those of another to produce hybrid offspring). Sometimes these hybrids are improvements on other types raised and may be worth propagating. More frequently, however, they are not worth keeping.

To be sure of raising plants with the desired characteristics, it is necessary to control the pollination process. Controlled pollination can be used to produce plants of the same species (which retain the parental characteristics) or purposely to produce hybrid offspring from different species (which combine the characteristics of the parent plants).

To produce a new hybrid, choose the parent plants, usually species of the same genus, in an attempt to combine the best characteristics (such as leaf shape or flower color) of both parents. To prevent unwanted pollination by insects, just before the stigma appears receptive or the anthers are ready to dehisce, tie a small paper bag loosely over the flowers that are to be used. Transfer the pollen from the anthers of one parent flower to the stigma of the second parent by hand, using a soft, fine brush. Then recover the hand-pollinated flower with a paper bag.

Many cacti and other succulents are not self-fertile, and it is essential to cross-pollinate in order to obtain seed. If a species is self-fertile, however, cover the flowers with a bag, as above, to prevent cross-pollination by insects. A gentle tap on the bag is usually sufficient to spread pollen onto the stigmas within the flower to achieve self-pollination.

As the fruits ripen from green to red they become soft and fleshy and may release seed. If not, slice the fruits open and leave them for two or three days in a partially shaded but warm position so that the pulp dries out. Then wash the seed to remove the pulp and dry it on blotting paper before sowing.

To produce a batch of hybrid seed (here from a Schlumbergera*), dust pollen from the anthers of one of the selected parent flowers onto the stigmas of the other parent, using a fine-haired brush.*

Pachyphytum oviferum,
  P. viride
Peperomia
  dolabriformis
Sedum hintonii,
  S. sempervivoides
Senecio fulgens,
  S. jacobsenii
Streptocarpus saxorum
Thompsonella platyphylla
Umbilicus chloranthus
Xerosicyos danguyi

SUCCULENTS THAT MAY
BE PROPAGATED BY
STEM CUTTINGS OR
SECTIONS

Adromischus
Aeonium
Aporocactus
Bergerocactus
Caralluma
Cephalocereus
Cereus
Ceropegia
Cleistocactus
Cotyledon
Crassula
Echeveria
Epiphyllum
Euphorbia
Gasteria
Greenovia
Haworthia
Heliocereus
Hoya
Huernia
Kalanchoe
Nopalxochia
Opuntia
Oreocereus
Oscularia
Pachycereus
Pachyphytum
Pedilanthus
Pelargonium
Pereskia
Rhipsalis
Ruschia
Sarcocaulon
Schlumbergera
Sedum (some spp.)
Selenicereus
Senecio
Stapelia

Kalanchoe 'Wendy'

Stem cuttings and stem sections

Stem cuttings may be used to propagate many species of succulent, including *Euphorbia*, *Stapelia*, and most columnar cacti.

Take stem cuttings or sections in early to midspring. The amount and type of stem material that is removed depends on the plant. Some cacti such as *Opuntia* consist of a series of rounded pads or sections that can be severed with a sharp knife at the joint or base for propagation. For plants that have flattened, leaflike stems, for example *Epiphyllum*, make a cut across a stem to remove a short length. To avoid disfiguring the plant, remove a complete "leaf" at the point where it joins the main stem, and treat this as the cutting or cut it into several sections (see below). Most columnal cacti, and some species of *Euphorbia*, may have sections of stem removed to provide cuttings (see below).

All *Euphorbia* and some asclepiads produce a milky latex when cut. To stop the flow, dip the cutting into tepid water for a few seconds. Seal the cut on the parent plant by holding a damp cloth against the wound. Avoid getting the sap on your skin, since it can cause irritation.

Leave stem cuttings in a warm, dry place for approximately 48 hours to allow the end to dry before potting them up in suitable soil mix.

Inserting the cuttings
Insert one stem cutting centrally into a prepared pot, or place several small ones around the edge of the

STEM CUTTINGS

1 *Choose a healthy, vigorous stem (here, from* Kalanchoe *'Wendy'). Make a straight cut, severing the stem as close to the base as possible.*

2 *Trim the stem (see inset) just below a node. Remove lower leaves, if necessary, to give ½in (1cm) of clear stem.*

3 *Insert each cutting into a medium of equal parts fine peat or compost and sharp grit or sand. The leaves should be just clear of the soil mix surface.*

container. The cuttings should be inserted just deeply enough to stay upright but not too deeply; otherwise, the base of the cuttings may rot before they have rooted. Stem cuttings from succulents that bear true leaves, such as *Pereskia* species, need to have the lower leaves removed before they are inserted,

in the same way as nonsucculent plants. Apply a mist-spray of tepid water occasionally, but do not overwater, because this may cause the cuttings to rot. Rooting normally takes place after approximately a few weeks, although cuttings from some genera such as *Selenicereus* may take a month or more.

PROPAGATION FROM PAD SECTIONS

1 *Sever a pad, making a straight cut across the joint. Leave the section in a warm, dry place for about 48 hours to allow the wound to dry (see inset).*

2 *Insert the cutting into a pot containing equal parts fine peat or compost and sharp grit or sand, and label. Once rooted (approximately 3–4 weeks), pot on into standard soil mix.*

Propagation from stem sections

Many cacti and other succulents may be propagated from a small section of stem rather than from a complete one. Use lengths of about 2–4in (5–10cm), depending on the species. For columnar cacti, remove a section of stem (below), cutting it off at the appropriate point. For cacti with flattened, leaflike stems, cut the stem laterally into pieces (right). Then treat each section as a stem cutting.

LEAFLIKE STEM SECTION
Remove a stem (here Epiphyllum*) and cut it into sections.*

INSERTING A STEM SECTION

COLUMNAR STEM SECTION
Sections of stem taken from some columnar cacti may be treated as cuttings.

Cutting barely inserted into the soil mix

Drainage material

Division of offsets

A large number of clump-forming cacti and other succulents, such as *Conophytum*, *Mammillaria*, and *Sedum*, may be propagated from offsets early in the growing season.

Clump-forming offsets

Scrape away the top layer of soil from around the parent plant to reveal the base of the offsets, and carefully detach one or more from the parent plant, as required, with a sharp knife. Treat any wounds on unrooted offsets with fungicide, allowing the cut end to to dry for two to three days. Pot up rooted offsets immediately.

Rootless offsets should be inserted into soil mix made up of equal parts fine peat or compost and sand. If the offsets have already developed roots, use a standard soil mix. Use appropriately sized containers with a piece of screening over the drainage hole(s). Pot up the offsets separately and water them in lightly.

Keep the potted offsets in semi-shade for about two weeks at a minimum temperature of 59°F (15°C), and water them again after the first week. Once new growth appears, the plants should be potted on into a standard soil mix and the normal watering routine followed (see p.339).

Offset tubers

Some tuberous-rooted succulents such as *Ceropegia* produce small offset tubers around the main tuber of the parent plant. These can be treated as divisions and grown on to produce new plants. During the dormant season, remove some of the soil mix to reveal the offsets and separate them from the parent plant using a clean, sharp knife. Treat the cut surfaces of rootless offsets with

DIVISION OF CLUMP-FORMING OFFSETS

1 *Gently scrape away the top surface of the soil mix around an offset. Cut straight across the joint and allow the wound to dry (see inset).*

2 *Insert the offset just below the surface of a medium composed of equal parts coarse sand and peat or compost.*

3 *Top-dress with ¼in (5mm) of grit, label, and place in semi-shade. Water after 3–4 days.*

4 *When new growth appears, pot on into a standard soil mix, top-dressing as before.*

fungicide and allow a callus to form. Insert each offset tuber in a clean pot that contains a mix of equal parts peat or compost and coarse sand.

If the offsets have roots, place them directly into a standard soil mix. Top-dress with a thin layer of washed, sharp grit, then label. Place the pots in semishade and maintain a temperature of 64°F (18°C).

Allow the tubers to settle for three or four days, then water them regularly with a fine mist-spray. As soon as growth starts and some young shoots begin to appear, follow the normal watering routine (see p.339). Pot on into a standard soil mix as soon as the young plants have grown several shoots and they have become well established.

DIVISION OF OFFSET TUBERS

1 *Scrape away some soil mix from around the main tuber and carefully detach offset tubers. Lift them without damaging the roots, if present (see inset).*

2 *Treat wounds with fungicide, and allow to dry. If roots are present, insert into potting mix, otherwise use equal parts of fine peat or compost and sand.*

3 *Top-dress with a ¼in (5mm) layer of ⅛in (3mm) sharp grit. Label the pot but do not water for several days.*

Wigginsia vorwerkiana

SUCCULENTS THAT MAY
BE PROPAGATED BY
DIVISION OF ROOTSTOCK
Agave
Aloe
Argyroderma

Aloe variegata

Caralluma
Conophytum
Carpobrotus
Delosperma
Duvalia
Euphorbia
Faucaria
Fenestraria
Frithia
Glottiphyllum
Gymnocalycium
Haworthia
Huernia
Mammillaria
Rebutia
Ruschia
Sansevieria
Stapelia
Sulcorebutia
Titanopsis

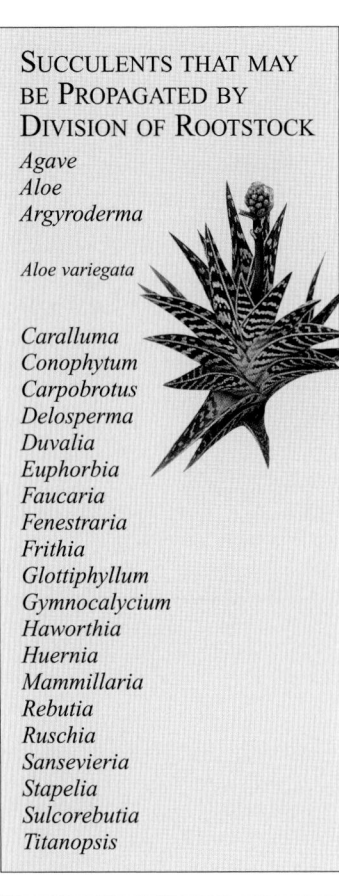

Division of rootstock

Many genera of the Aizoaceae, such as *Delosperma* and *Frithia*, some clump-forming cacti, and genera such as *Aloe*, are readily propagated by division. For some cultivars of *Sansevieria*, division is the only reliable method of retaining variegation, since leaf cuttings may produce plants that revert to plain green. Divide clump-forming cacti and other succulents early in the growing season.

Lift the entire plant from its pot, and carefully pull apart or cut the rootstock into a number of smaller pieces, each with a healthy bud or shoot and well-formed roots. Treat all cut areas with fungicide and pot up each section separately into standard soil mix. Label, water, and place in a semishaded position until well established.

Alternatively, cut away a piece of the rootstock without lifting the parent plant, and ease a section out of the soil with a hand fork. Dust the cut surfaces with fungicide and pot up as for offset tubers (see p.343). Fill any gaps that are left around the parent plant, using a standard soil mix, and water lightly.

DIVISION OF ROOTSTOCK

 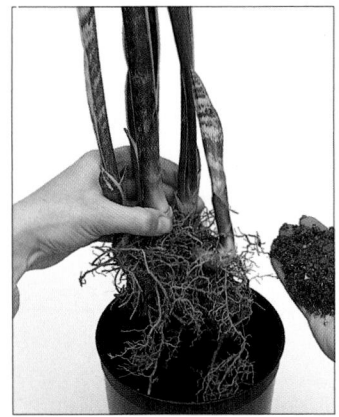

1 *Lift the plant (here Sansevieria trifasciata). Divide it into sections by cutting straight through the rootstock.*

2 *Discard old, woody material and any soft or damaged roots before replanting each new section.*

Grafting

Some cacti and other succulents, notably certain members of the Asclepiadaceae, such as *Edithcolea* and *Pseudolithos*, are slow to mature and flower when grown on their own roots. By grafting them onto established specimens of related species that are quicker to mature, they can be induced to flower in a comparatively short length of time. During the growing season the topgrowth, or scion, of the required

APICAL-WEDGE GRAFTING

1 *Prepare the rootstock by trimming off the tip, making a straight cut through the stem with a clean, sharp knife.*

2 *Make a slender V-shaped cleft (see inset) in the stock, to a depth of about ¾in (2cm).*

3 *Select the scion material and remove from the parent plant (here a Schlumbergera), cutting straight through at a node with a sharp knife.*

4 *Trim the lower end of the scion to a narrow wedge shape to match the V-shaped cleft in the stock plant.*

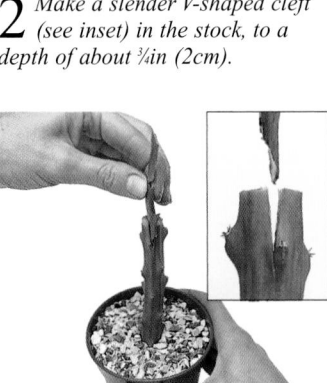

5 *Insert the scion wedge into the cleft in the stock plant (see inset), making sure that they are in close contact.*

6 *To secure the scion in place in the clefted stock, insert a cactus spine through the grafted area.*

Dab of glue on outside of graft union

ALTERNATIVE METHOD
Bind the graft firmly with a dab of superglue.

plant is grafted onto the rootstock of one of the more vigorous species. Three methods of grafting may be used: apical-wedge grafting, flat grafting, and side grafting.

Apical-wedge grafting

Epiphytic cacti are often propagated by apical-wedge grafting in order to create an erect standard or treelike plant. Use *Pereskiopsis* or *Selenicereus*, which are sturdy but of slender growth, as the rootstock.

To produce the rootstock, take a stem cutting (see p.342) of the selected plant. When this has rooted and shows evidence of new growth, it is ready to be used for grafting. Slice off the tip and then make two slanted, downward cuts into the top of the rootstock stem to produce a narrow, vertical, V-shaped slit approximately ¾in (2cm) long.

Select a healthy shoot from the scion plant and prepare it by trimming the lower end into a wedge shape to match the cleft in the stock. Insert the prepared scion wedge into the cleft so that the cut surfaces match as closely as possible. Secure the stock and scion firmly in position by either pushing a cactus spine horizontally through the graft or using a dab of superglue.

Place the grafted plant in partial shade at a temperature of 70°F (21°C). The stock and scion should unite within a few weeks. Once this has happened, remove the spine (if used), dusting with fungicide any holes made by the spine. When fresh growth appears, water and fertilize as for established plants (see p.339).

Flat grafting

This method may be used to propagate crested variants (succulents with atypical, often contorted growth), certain other succulents with tufts of hair, and *Gymnocalycium mihanovichii* and *Lobivia silvestrii*, whose seedlings may lack chlorophyll. Genera for use as rootstocks include *Echinopsis*, *Harrisia*, *Hylocereus*, and *Trichocereus*.

Make a straight, horizontal cut through the stem of the rootstock at the required height. Then remove the rib margins with a sharp knife to form a beveled edge, and trim off any spines near the cut.

Prepare the scion in a similar way, and position its base on the cut surface of the stock plant. Place rubber bands over the top of the scion and under the base of the pot to keep the scion securely in place. Make sure that the bands are not too tight.

Leave the grafted plant in a well-lit position, but not in full sun. Keep the soil mix barely moist until the scion and the stock have united (normally about a month or so), when the rubber bands can be removed. Thereafter, water and fertilize as for established plants.

When grafting asclepiads, use either the fleshy tubers of *Ceropegia* or the robust stems of *Stapelia* as rootstocks. *Ceropegia*, in particular, make excellent stock plants for some of the Madagascan and Arabian asclepiads, which may otherwise be difficult to propagate.

Side grafting

This method is useful if the scion is too slender to be grafted onto the top of the stock. It is very similar to side-veneer grafting used for woody plants. Prepare the stock by slicing off the top at an oblique angle, then trim the base of the scion to match the stock as closely as possible. Secure them together with a spine or superglue; treat as for flat grafting.

FLAT GRAFTING

1 Slice off the top of the rootstock with a sharp knife to produce a flat surface.

2 Trim the cut surface to produce a slightly beveled edge. Hold the stem without touching the wounded area.

3 Cut the scion material, slicing through at the base. Bevel the edge of the scion (inset) so that it will fit closely onto the stock.

4 Place the scion on the stock and secure firmly, but not tightly, with rubber bands. Label with the name of the scion plant.

5 Place the pot in good light at a minimum temperature of 61°F (16°C). Remove the rubber bands when new growth appears.

SIDE GRAFTING

If the scion plant is slender it can be grafted onto the side of the stock. Make a slanted cut in both stock and scion, place the cut surfaces together, and fasten with a cactus spine and raffia. Leave in good light at 61°F (16°C) until new growth appears.

SUCCULENTS THAT MAY BE GRAFTED

Flat grafting

Alluaudiopsis
Astrophytum
Austrocactus
Aztekium
Blossfeldia
Buiningia
Discocactus
Duvalia
Echinopsis chamaecereus
Edithcolea
Epithelantha
Frailea
Gymnocalycium mihanovichii (and cvs)

Gymnocalycium mihanovichii 'Red Head'

Hoodia
Lophophora
Luckhoffia
Maihuenia
Mammillaria
Mila
Nopalxochia
Notocactus
Orbea
Parodia
Pediocactus
Pelecyphora
Pseudolithos
Pygmaeocereus
Sulcorebutia
Tavaresia
Trichocaulon
Turbinicarpus
Uebelmannia

Aporocactus flagelliformis

Side grafting

Aporocactus flagelliformis
Cryptocereus
Disocactus
Lepismium (flat-stemmed spp.)
Rhipsalidopsis
Rhipsalis (spp. with rounded or angled stems)
Weberocereus (spp. with rounded stems)
Wilcoxia

Schlumbergera 'Gold Charm'

Apical-wedge grafting

Hatiora
Rhipsalidopsis
Schlumbergera
Strophocactus
Wittiocereus

CHAPTER
13

THE INDOOR GARDEN

THE GARDEN MAY be enjoyed in comfort, whatever the season, by bringing it indoors, with tender plants offering leaf and flower colors and forms as rich as those of outdoor varieties. Gardening under cover also opens up opportunities for creating different effects, from ornamental table displays of flowering pot plants to leafy terrariums or bottle gardens. In regions subject to frost, a conservatory can be transformed into a small-scale jungle with the lush foliage and exotic flowers of tropical plants, guaranteed to brighten up even the dullest of winter days. Indoor plants are also highly versatile, and some require little maintenance when bought as design accessories that are displayed, enjoyed, and then discarded. The enthusiast may also choose to grow collections of rare plants that demand more regular care and attention.

Displaying plants indoors

THE range of plants that may be grown in the home and the greenhouse offers a wealth of form, color, and texture. Plants may be chosen for their handsome foliage or the beauty of their blooms, from the exuberant hues of *Bougainvillea* to the cool elegance of calla lilies (*Zantedeschia*). Others, such as Jerusalem cherry (*Solanum pseudocapsicum*), are selected for their brightly colored fruits.

The choice depends on whether the display is to be permanent, when plants with interesting form and foliage are the best choice, or temporary, when the seasonal interest of plants such as hybrid *Cyclamen* may be used to give spots of color.

Plants can reinforce or contrast with the style of the indoor setting, whether it is a farmhouse kitchen or a formal and sophisticated urban living room. The plants may dominate the scene and give a room its essential character, create pockets of interest, or simply add to the detail. Whatever result is desired, select plants that will thrive in and enhance their intended position.

Foliage and form

Plants that have attractive foliage are invaluable for long-term indoor display. They may have huge leaves, as does Japanese aralia (*Fatsia japonica*), or a mass of dainty ones, such as those of baby's tears (*Soleirolia soleirolii*). Leaves may have subtle or striking patterns and colors, as do *Calathea* species, or interesting shapes, for example the Swiss-cheese plant (*Monstera deliciosa*).

Foliage also has different textures, ranging from the high gloss of the rubber plant (*Ficus elastica*) to the corrugated surfaces of friendship plant (*Pilea involucrata*) and the soft texture of velvet plant (*Gynura aurantiaca*). In some cases plants are chosen for their strong forms, whether they are spiky bromeliads, graceful palms and ferns, or pebble-like living stones (*Lithops*).

Grouping plants

When planning an arrangement, carefully choose plants so that those with strongly colored flowers or patterned leaves do not detract from each other. Experiment with contrasts by placing plants together before making a purchase.

Architectural plants such as palms make very fine specimen plants or striking focal points. Smaller plants have impact when arranged together on a tiered stand, but they may be used singly as a dainty finishing touch. A mass of identical plants, such as a bowl of hyacinths, makes a strong yet simple statement.

A GARDEN ROOM
Yellow Abutilon, *blue* Agapanthus, *purple and white* Streptocarpus, *and lush foliage create a gardenlike setting in which to relax.*

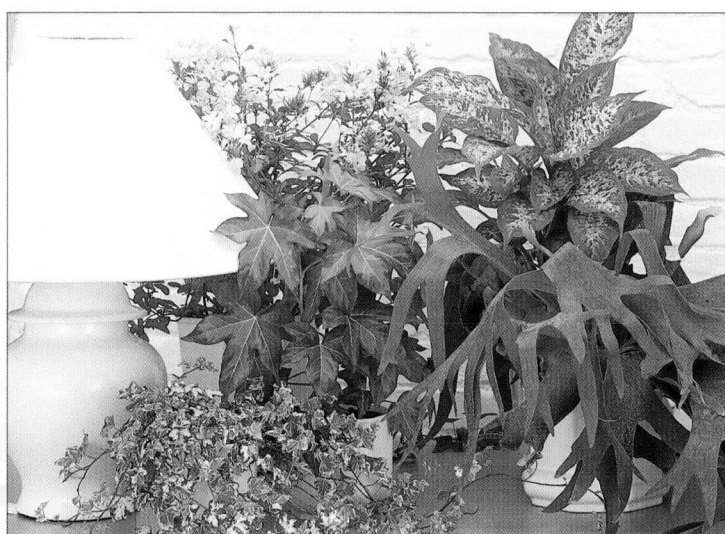

A CONTRAST OF STRONG SHAPES
Ivy (Hedera), *Dieffenbachia, Japanese aralia* (Fatsia japonica)*, and*
Platycerium bifurcatum *complement the pale blue* Plumbago.

The indoor environment

The specific temperature and light requirements of plants are the most important factors in deciding where to position them indoors (see "Planter's guide to indoor plants," p.353). If the conditions do not fulfill the plants' needs, they will soon become stressed and unhealthy. Newly purchased plants that have just come from controlled conditions are especially vulnerable.

Temperature

Although most modern houses are kept warm during the day in winter, the temperature is often allowed to drop markedly at night – a problem for many house plants of tropical origin. Place these plants where they are protected from drafts and are not subject to wide fluctuations in temperature. Do not leave tender plants on windowsills at night, especially if the drawn curtains close off residual warmth from the room, or place plants directly above radiators or heaters that are in use. To flower, indoor plants need warmth, but if the temperature is too high for the individual species, the blooms quickly fade and die.

Light

Most plants thrive in bright, filtered sunlight or in a well-lit position that is not in direct sun. Plants that have variegated leaves need more light than those with plain green leaves, but sunlight that is too strong will damage the foliage. Flowering plants such as amaryllis (*Hippeastrum*) need good light to flower well, but excessive light can shorten the life of the blooms. Indeed, few indoor plants tolerate strong, direct sunlight.

Insufficient light results in plants with pale, stunted new leaves, and drawn-out (etiolated) growth with long, thin, weak stems. Some variegated plants may begin to produce plain leaves. In time, the mature leaves will turn yellow and fall. A plant thus weakened is especially vulnerable to pests and diseases.

The amount of natural light in a room depends on the number, size, height, and orientation of the windows. Light levels fall quickly as the distance from the window increases. There is far less natural light in winter than in summer; some plants may need to be moved in response to the seasonal light variation – a plant cart is ideal for this purpose.

If plants start to grow lopsidedly toward a source of light, turn them slightly when watering them. If light levels are too low for healthy growth (most plants need 12–14 hours of daylight per day), supplementary grow lamps are effective.

Positioning the plants

With a little forethought and planning, it is possible to find a handsome houseplant that flourishes in almost every site indoors, from a brilliantly lit room to a dim passage or alcove.

The indoor setting

Consider the impact of plants in the room. Are they in proportion to the room? A tiny pot plant is lost in a large space. Is the background suitable? Plain, pale walls show flowering plants to advantage. Does the plant color blend with the decor?

Hanging baskets and shelves suit trailing plants, while positions at eye level are best for plants with delicate flowers or foliage. Train climbers, such as kangaroo vine (*Cissus antarctica*) and heartleaf philodendron (*Philodendron scandens*), on a trellis to create a screen.

Use plants to enliven empty corners or areas, such as an unused fireplace that provides an instant frame for a display. Large plants or groups may play an architectural role as room dividers or as a link between the house and the garden.

Plants for various light levels

Bright, sunny conditions suit succulent plants as well as plants with woolly, waxy, or gray leaves. Wax plant (*Hoya carnosa*), geraniums, and variegated pineapple (*Ananas comosus* 'Variegatus') also grow best in direct sunlight. Tender bonsai, kept indoors all year, may be grown under lights (see BONSAI, pp.368–69). In indirect or filtered light, grow foliage begonias such as *Begonia rex*, epiphytic orchids such as *Phalaenopsis*, and *Spathiphyllum* with their striking white spathes.

For corners that are far from a window, choose ferns and tough-leaved plants such as parlor palm (*Chamaedorea*), Japanese aralia (*Fatsia japonica*), and ivy (*Hedera*). Expose the plants to brighter light occasionally, if only for a few days.

Kitchens and bathrooms

Temperature and humidity can fluctuate in kitchens and bathrooms, especially small ones, so choose plants that can tolerate extremes. Smooth, hard surfaces contrast well with the soft, feathery forms of ferns. Bathrooms often have low levels of light, ideal for *Episcia*, Boston fern (*Nephrolepis*), or aluminum plant (*Pilea cadierei*). Trailing plants such as heartleaf philodendron make an elegant display on high bathroom shelves. In brightly lit positions, grow herbs such as chives and parsley, or dwarf tomato cultivars such as 'Patio Hybrids' or 'Pixie'.

Tolerant plants

Attractive foliage plants that are tolerant of a wide range of conditions include cast-iron plant (*Aspidistra*), spider plant (*Chlorophytum*), kangaroo vine (*Cissus*), and mother-in-law's tongue (*Sansevieria*). Flowering plants are more exacting, but potted chrysanthemums (see p.188) or forced bulbs (see p.225) may give short-term floral color.

Containers

Choose a container whose material, color, and shape blends with the decor and shows the individual plant

HAZARDS OF A WINDOWSILL

Too much sunlight, excessive heat from radiators, and drafts through the frame can seriously weaken or kill houseplants that are placed on a windowsill.

VARIATION OF LIGHT LEVELS WITHIN A ROOM

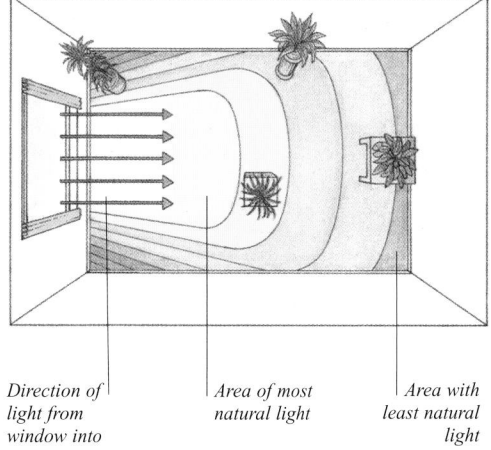

Direction of light from window into room

Area of most natural light

Area with least natural light

The farther away from a window a plant is sited, the less natural light it will receive. If the plant is 6ft (2m) away, the light level may be as little as 20 percent of that by the window. Plants that are placed close to a window but to one side of it derive little benefit from the position, especially if windowsills are very deep.

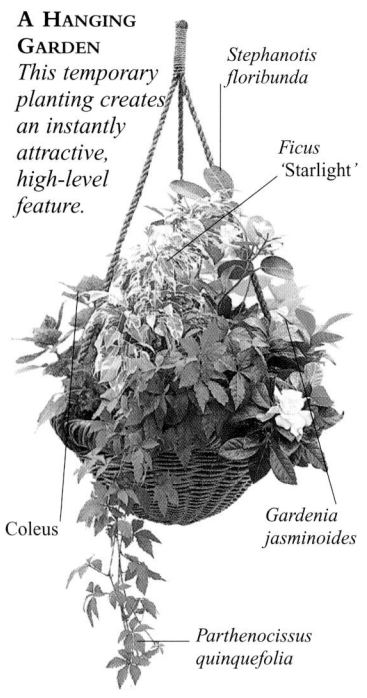

A HANGING GARDEN
This temporary planting creates an instantly attractive, high-level feature.

Stephanotis floribunda

Ficus 'Starlight'

Coleus

Gardenia jasminoides

Parthenocissus quinquefolia

or group to its best advantage. The choice is vast, both in style and ma-terials, allowing a range of effects from rustic to ultramodern. Some plastic containers are available with an integral reservoir, which reduces the need for watering. Other types are specially manufactured for hydroculture (see *Cross Section of a Hydroculture Pot*, p.367). The most unlikely household objects, such as birdcages, cooking utensils, and kettles, can make unusual and striking plant holders.

Hanging baskets

Hanging baskets are a popular feature on porches, balconies, patios, and terraces, but may also be an attractive way of growing indoor plants. Hang them in stairwells, from rafters, by windows, or from free-standing supports for an economical and colorful use of space. A group of baskets suspended at varying heights makes a fine display.

Arching fern fronds, the rosettes of epiphytes, and the cascading habit of many foliage plants lend themselves perfectly to hanging baskets. Vary the planting during the year to take advantage of seasonal displays. In a winter arrangement, Christmas cactus (*Schlumbergera bridgesii*) provides a mass of bright color, as do fuchsias in summer. Temporary arrangements may be created by planting a basket with pot plants, but they will need replanting each year. Permanently planted baskets are easier to manage, especially if devoted to a single large plant.

Choosing a hanging container
Hanging baskets are available in various materials and designs. When choosing and positioning them, take into account the fact that most plants require frequent watering. Plastic-coated wire hanging baskets are practical indoors only in rooms that have water-resistant floors; some rigid plastic baskets have drip saucers, which are a practical solution. Also available are attractive, although heavy, pottery and terracotta hanging pots, and wooden, wrought iron, or wicker baskets.

A planted basket is heavy, especially when just watered, so it must be supported by strong rope or chain from a hook or bracket attached securely to a ceiling joist or a solid wall.

Terrariums and bottle gardens

Terrariums are enclosed glass containers, often decorative in their own right, used to display small plants in the home. They were popular in the 19th century as a way of providing a suitable microclimate for ferns, but all slow-growing ornamental plants that need a humid atmosphere thrive in a terrarium. A selection of plants with contrasting leaf textures and colors is the most effective. Use flowering plants carefully because the dead blooms rot in the moist conditions. Terrariums may be built permanently into a window to house a lush arrangement of larger plants.

Bottles can also be used to create a diminutive landscape of foliage plants. As long as the neck is sufficiently wide to allow the insertion of the plants and routine aftercare, any shape or color of bottle may be used, but bear in mind that tinted glass cuts out some of the light.

Indoor lighting

A display may be enhanced by ordinary floodlights or spotlights, or given dramatic contrasts of light and shade with uplighting or downlighting. Do not place plants too close to the light source, since the heat may damage them. Ordinary incandescent bulbs do not significantly improve either food production (photosynthesis) or growth.

Plants for the office

Introducing plants into an office not only brightens it visually but may help muffle noise, refresh the air,

and create a less stressful ambience. In a modern, open-plan office that is air-conditioned and fully glazed, temperatures are constant, air pollution is minimized, and space and light are plentiful – almost ideal growing conditions. Older buildings with smaller windows and little climatic control present more challenging conditions.

Use self-watering containers, especially if the plants are sited near electrical equipment, or plunge several plants into a large container. Unless maintenance contractors are employed, be sure that responsibility for care is clearly assigned.

Suitable plants
Evergreen, shiny-leaved plants are as tough and tolerant in an office as they are in the home. The popular genus *Ficus* includes plants of every shape and size, from the lustrous, huge fiddle-leaf fig (*F. lyrata*) to the small-leaved, leathery mistletoe fig (*F. deltoidea*).

Another large and impressive genus with handsome leaves is *Philodendron*, which includes climbers and trailers. The tenacious, long-lived Swiss-cheese plant (*Monstera deliciosa*) climbs slowly but eventually reaches several feet in height and spread.

Garden rooms and conservatories

The garden may be brought indoors, either into a garden room, which is a living space furnished with container plants, or into a conservatory, which is devoted principally to planting. In temperate climates, both can be used to give winter shelter to container-grown plants that spend the summer months outdoors. A conservatory can also provide the warm, humid environment needed by tropical and subtropical plants.

The high light levels usually found in conservatories encourage colored leaves to assume intense hues and plants to flower well. Scented flowering plants, for example *Jasminum polyanthum*, are especially welcome in a confined space, where fragrance lingers in the air.

Select plants that suit the conservatory's orientation and temperature, bearing in mind that glass structures can be costly to heat in winter and very hot in summer.

Create a lush profusion of planting by taking full advantage of all the available space: grow plants at different levels in raised and ground-level soil beds, in pots on the floor, on windowsills and shelves, and in

SEASONAL COLOR
In this room, a white poinsettia (Euphorbia pulcherrima)*, carmine azalea* (Rhododendron)*, and Calamondin orange* (x Citrofortunella microcarpa) *add winter interest to a permanent framework of evergreen foliage plants.*

COOL CONSERVATORY

The foliage and flowering plants shown here are among the many that thrive in the cool, but frost-free, conditions of a lean-to conservatory to create an attractive display.

1 *Plumbago auriculata* (syn. *P. capensis*)
2 *Chlorophytum comosum*
   (syn. *C. capense* of gardens)
3 *Campanula isophylla*
4 *Saxifraga stolonifera* 'Tricolor'
   (syn. *S. sarmentosa*)
5 *Pelargonium* 'Mini Cascade'
6 *Camellia japonica*
7 *Sedum morganianum*
8 *Streptocarpus* 'Heidi'
9 *Ceropegia woodii*
10 *Callistemon citrinus* 'Splendens'
11 *Correa pulchella*
12 *Calceolaria* 'Sunshine'
13 *Nierembergia hippomanica* var.
   violacea 'Purple Robe'
14 *Prostanthera rotundifolia*
15 *Polygala myrtifolia* 'Grandiflora'
16 *Rehmannia elata*
17 x *Citrofortunella microcarpa* (syn. *Citrus mitis*)

MULTILEVEL DISPLAY
Staging, shelves, and floor space are used to maximum advantage in this cool greenhouse. Impatiens *cultivars,* Plumbago, *and* Streptocarpus *flowers are complemented by a variety of foliage plants, including ivy* (Hedera), *scented-leaved geraniums, polka-dot plant* (Hypoestes), *button fern (*Pellaea), *and piggyback plant* (Tolmiea).

hanging baskets. Large tropical or subtropical plants and climbers that are free-standing are useful for training on a trellis or wires attached to the walls; grapes will grow over and clothe the wall and roof. Use plants in the conservatory that complement those in the open garden; this will create a visual link between the two as well as a sense of space.

Indoor water features
A sunken or raised tub or a half barrel can accommodate tropical water- lilies or other tender aquatic and marginal plants. A simple and elegant waterspout will provide the restful murmur of falling water and help maintain humidity (see also THE WATER GARDEN, pp.274–97).

Growing plants in a greenhouse

The control of light, temperature, and humidity in a greenhouse will allow a much wider range of plants to be grown than in a garden that is subject to frost. It also extends the season of display and bearing from early spring until late fall, or even throughout the year if desired.

Uses of a greenhouse
A greenhouse is very useful in cool-temperate climates, where there is frost, strong wind, or excessive rain. It can be used for propagation; raising and growing tender plants or flowers for cutting; or for crops such

as salad greens, early vegetables, and even fruit. Many plants grow faster under cover and fruit or flower more profusely than they would outdoors. Marginally hardy plants can be grown in containers outdoors and transferred to temporary shelter in the greenhouse when needed.

The greenhouse may hold a specialized collection of plants such as alpines (see pp.271–73), cacti (see pp.331-345), ferns (see pp.192–93), and orchids (see pp.360–63). Alternatively, a mixed collection of foliage and flowering plants that enjoy similar conditions may provide a display throughout the year.

The greenhouse layout
The traditional, free-standing greenhouse interior consists of a central path with waist-high staging at the sides and far end. Wide greenhouses may also have staging in the center. Staging (see also p.573) is essential; even if removed in summer for border crops, it may be used at other times of the year for raising seedlings, propagating cuttings, and displaying pot plants. Slatted or meshed staging is used for pot plants to prevent water from puddling and to make sure that air circulates freely, particularly in winter.

For extra display space, use tiered staging, bench beds, or soil borders. If the glass begins at ground level, ferns and other shade-loving plants (and dormant plants) may be grown (or rested) under the staging. Raised beds are useful for displaying small

plants, such as alpines and cacti, that are planted directly in the beds or in pots plunged into gravel or sand.

The ornamental greenhouse
Although a greenhouse is often more practical in use than a conservatory, part or all of it can be devoted to ornamental displays. Groups are usually more attractive than widely spaced plants. Feature a single genus or assemble a variety of plants, displaying them in a random pattern or as a landscape in miniature. Try to include contrasts of leaf form, size, and texture; control the use of color, whether from flowers or foliage, to create a harmonious arrangement.

A lean-to greenhouse against a house wall can double as a conservatory. Make the most of the back wall by growing climbers,which need only a 12in (30cm) wide bed or pot. Paint the wall white to help to reflect light and provide a contrasting background for the plants.

The greenhouse environment

Essential requirements for success are adequate ventilation and heat, as well as shading in summer; water and electricity are also important.

The temperature range of a greenhouse depends on its purpose, but there are four basic types of greenhouse: cold (unheated), cool or frost-free, temperate, and warm. For further

AN INTERIOR GARDEN
Where space allows, a naturalistic landscape can be created within a greenhouse. Here, foliage plants including Cordyline, Eucomis, Justicia, *and* Phormium *provide a lush framework that is offset by the colorful blooms of flowering plants such as blue* Agapanthus, *pink fuchsias, and white and salmon geraniums.*

information, see GREENHOUSES AND FRAMES, "Creating the right environment," pp.567–71; see also "Planter's guide to indoor plants," opposite.

The cold greenhouse
An unheated greenhouse protects against any extremes of wind and rain and is significantly warmer, even in summer, than outdoors. It extends the growing season by providing the plants with an artificially early spring and late fall.

Depending on the severity of winter, many hardy annuals, biennials, and shrubs can be overwintered in an unheated greenhouse. Half-hardy annuals and tender bulbous plants can be started early to plant out when the garden soil has warmed up and danger of frost is past. A cold greenhouse is also useful for raising seedlings and getting an early start with vegetables. As an alpine house it may be used to provide the conditions needed for growing alpines and rock plants (see ALPINE HOUSES AND FRAMES, pp.271–73).

An unheated greenhouse does not exclude frost for more than an hour or two, so it is not suitable for overwintering plants that are not frost hardy. Sunlight, or even bright light, raises the temperature during the day, but night temperatures can drop almost as low as those in the open garden. In temperate climates, most

greenhouses built against a warm house wall give conditions similar to those in a cool greenhouse (see below), but this will not prevent tender plants from being killed by a few days (or hours) of severe cold.

The cool greenhouse
Freedom from freezing temperatures increases the range of plants that may be grown. A frost-free greenhouse is also easier to manage, since protective measures become unnecessary. Daytime temperatures of 41–50°F (5–10°C) and a minimum at night of 36°F (2°C) allow ornamentals to be enjoyed throughout the year.

In a cool greenhouse, hardy bulbous plants, particularly those with delicate blooms that are not noticed in an open garden, flower earlier, providing color in late winter and early spring. Here tender patio plants may be raised and overwintered; houseplants may be revived and propagated in warmer months; and winter-flowering plants such as fragrant Parma violets (*Viola*) may be grown in bench beds or in pots. Grown under cover, chrysanthemums and perpetual-flowering carnations (*Dianthus*) provide a good supply of cut flowers; while hardy annuals raised from seed sown in late summer give early flowers. The cool greenhouse must have a heating system capable of maintain-

ing a minimum (above-freezing) temperature in all weather conditions (see GREENHOUSES AND FRAMES, "Heating," p.568). Even if the greenhouse is not heated throughout, an electrically heated propagator, or a propagating bench, will enable the gardener to make an significantly earlier start on raising new plants in spring.

AN ORNAMENTAL COLLECTION
A warm greenhouse may be devoted to displaying a collection of plants from a particular group, such as orchids or cacti. Tropical plants such as these forest cacti thrive in the heat and high humidity provided by the greenhouse. A luxuriant show is produced by the richly hued flowers and fleshy foliage of Epiphyllum, Heliocereus, Pfeiffera, *and other forest cacti at the height of their glory.*

The temperate greenhouse
Raising the temperature to 50–55°F (10–13°C), with a nighttime minimum of 45°F (7°C), widens the scope still further. If kept in a temperate greenhouse, plants associated with the essentially frost-free climates of California, the Mediterranean, South Africa, and parts of Australia and South America may be enjoyed in harsher climates than they could normally bear. These include yesterday, today, and tomorrow (*Brunfelsia*), bird of paradise (*Strelitzia*), and *Cymbidium* orchids. If zonal geraniums are kept at 48°F (9°C) they will flower all year.

The warm greenhouse
A minimum temperature of 55°F (13°C) to 64°F (18°C) in a warm greenhouse allows cultivation of subtropical and tropical plants, as well as facilitating year-round propagation or flowering displays. Tender plants, for example a number of orchids (see pp.360–63) and many bromeliads (see pp.354–55), are at their best when grown in a warm greenhouse.

The warm greenhouse needs controllable heating throughout the year, even in summer in cooler climates. This incurs considerable heating costs in temperate zones. Equipment such as thermostats, double glazing, fans, automatic ventilation, an automated watering and damping-down system, cooling pads, and shading helps control conditions and facilitates routine care. A warm section in a cool greenhouse is a useful, cheaper option; a warm conservatory, or plant room, is another possibility.

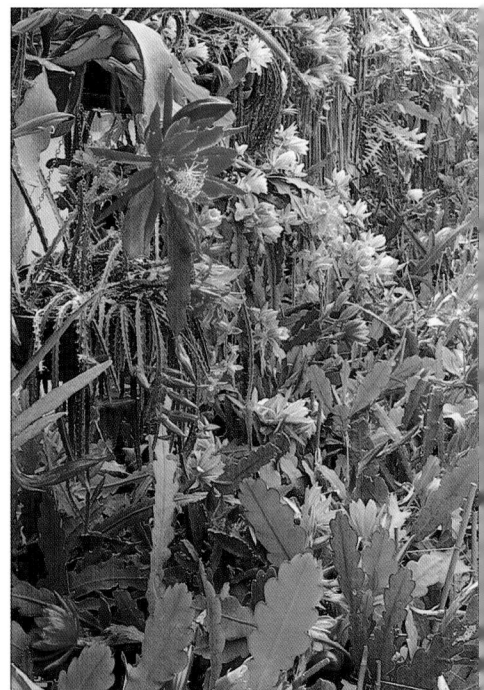

Planter's guide to indoor plants

Warm Greenhouse
(Minimum 55–64°F/13–18°C)
Flowering plants
Aeschynanthus☺
Anthurium
Aphelandra☺
Brunfelsia☺
Columnea☺
Euphorbia fulgens,
　E. pulcherrima1
Hibiscus rosa-sinensis
Hoya bella
Justicia
Kohleria☺
Medinilla☺
Pachystachys
Ruellia☺
Saintpaulia☺

Sinningia
'Red
Flicker'

Sinningia☺
Smithiantha☺
Spathiphyllum☺

Foliage plants
Aechmea☺(and most bromeliads)
Aglaonema☺
Begonia rex☺(and other spp.)
Calathea☺
Chamaedorea☺(and most palms)
Codiaeum☺
Dieffenbachia☺
Dracaena☺
Ficus
Fittonia☺
Maranta☺
Peperomia☺
Philodendron☺
Tradescantia,☺

Temperate Greenhouse
**(Daytime 50–55°F/10–13°C;
night minimum 45°F/7°C)**
Flowering plants
Achimenes
Begonia☺
Catharanthus
Cyclamen ☺
Exacum☺
Haemanthus
Impatiens☺

*Impatiens,
Novette Series
'Red Star'*

Schlumbergera☺
Strelitzia
Streptocarpus☺

Foliage plants
Asparagus
Jacaranda
Solenostemon (syn. *Coleus*)☺

Cool Greenhouse
**(Daytime 41–50°F/5–10°C;
night minimum 36°F/2°C)**
Flowering plants
Abutilon
Bougainvillea
Browallia
Calceolaria☺
Callistemon
Cestrum
Chrysanthemum ☺
x Citrofortunella
Cuphea
Datura
Freesia
Fuchsia
Gerbera
Hippeastrum
Hoya
Jasminum
Lachenalia
Lantana
Lapageria
Nerium
Passiflora
Pelargonium
Plumbago
Primula
Schizanthus
Senecio

*Senecio articulatus
'Variegatus'*

Sprekelia
Streptosolen
Tibouchina ☺
Veltheimia
Zantedeschia
Zephyranthes

Foliage plants
Aspidistra
Chlorophytum
Cissus rhombifolia
Rhoicissus
Ricinus

Cold Greenhouse
Flowering plants
Agapanthus (hardy spp.)
Anemone
Antirrhinum (hardy spp.)
Camellia (hardy spp.)
Cheiranthus (hardy spp.)
Crocus
Cyclamen (hardy miniature spp.)
Dicentra
Erica
Hyacinthus
Jasminum (hardy spp.)
Narcissus
Rhododendron (hardy azaleas in
　shady greenhouse)

Foliage plants
Adiantum (hardy spp.)
Euonymus
Fatsia
Hedera (hardy spp.)
Laurus nobilis
Phormium
Tolmiea

Plants that Prefer Direct Light Indoors
Warm room (64°F/18°C and over)
Ananas☺
Bougainvillea
Euphorbia pulcherrima
Ficus
Hibiscus rosa-sinensis
Hippeastrum
Justicia
Opuntia
Solanum pseudocapsicum☺

Cool room (40–64°F/5–18°C)
Billbergia
Browallia
Campanula isophylla☺
Capsicum☺
Chlorophytum
Clivia
Crassula
Cyclamen☺
Cyrtanthus
Echeveria
Gerbera
Hyacinthus
Jasminum
Kalanchoe
Nerine

*Pelargonium
'Caligula'*

Pelargonium
Solenostemon ☺
Streptocarpus☺
Veltheimia

Plants that Prefer Indirect Light Indoors
**Warm room – medium light
(64°F/18°C and over)**
Adiantum☺
Aechmea☺ (and all bromeliads)
Caladium
Codiaeum☺
Cryptanthus☺
Dieffenbachia☺
Howea
Hypoestes
Kohleria☺
Mandevilla☺
Maranta☺
Neoregelia☺
Peperomia☺

Pilea☺
Saintpaulia☺
Sansevieria
Schefflera
Sinningia☺
Spathiphyllum☺
Streptocarpus☺
Syngonium☺
Thunbergia
Tradescantia☺

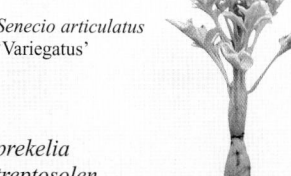

*Pilea
cadierei*

**Warm room – low light
(64°F/18°C and over)**
Asplenium
Calathea☺
Chamaedorea☺
Cissus
Dracaena☺
Episcia☺
Fittonia☺
Hedera☺
Philodendron☺

**Cool room – medium light
(40–64°F/5–18°C)**
Epiphyllum☺
Epipremnum
Fatsia
Grevillea☺
Monstera
Platycerium☺
Primula malacoides☺,
P. obconica☺
Schefflera
Sparmannia☺

**Cool room – low light
(40–64°F/5–18°C)**
Aspidistra
x Fatshederaa
Hedera☺
Pteris☺
Rhoicissus

Hydroculture
Anthurium
Chamaedorea☺
Cissus
Codiaeum☺
Dieffenbachia☺
Dracaena☺
Euphorbia milii
Ficus benjamina
Hedera☺
Monstera
Nephrolepis☺
Saintpaulia☺
Schefflera
Spathiphyllum☺
Streptocarpus☺
Yucca

Key
☺ *Requires high humidity*

Bromeliads

BROMELIADS, the 2,000 or so members of one of the most diverse and exotic families, the Bromeliaceae, are a fascinating group of plants that can make curiously beautiful specimens for the home, the warm greenhouse, or conservatory. Most are tropical epiphytes growing naturally on tree branches and rock faces, clinging by means of anchorage roots. These plants obtain moisture and nutrients via their leaves directly from the atmosphere, often from mists and low, moisture-laden clouds. Others are terrestrial, growing in the ground.

Almost all bromeliads are rosette-forming, frequently with strikingly colored or variegated foliage, and many produce flamboyant blooms. Their forms range from the long and graceful, silvery strands of Spanish moss (*Tillandsia usneoides*) to the imposing *Puya alpestris*, which holds its massive spike of tubular, metallic blue flowers above a rosette of arching, spiny foliage.

Displaying epiphytes

Most epiphytes are displayed to their best advantage if attached to a tree or branch, simulating the way that they grow in nature. This also helps the epiphytes avoid basal rot, which may occur if plants are grown in soil mix. Old, branched sections of trees cut to size are ideal.

METHODS OF DISPLAY

BINDING WITH MOSS
Wrap moistened sphagnum moss around the roots of large plants (here a cultivar of Tillandsia latifolia) *and attach to the mount by binding with wire, nylon line, or raffia. The moss must be kept moist at all times.*

USING ADHESIVE
Place adhesive onto the mount and plant base (see inset), then gently press the plants (here Tillandsia tectorum, *above, and* T. ionantha) *into position.*

Bromeliad trees
If using an upright branch, secure it firmly in a deep container with concrete or, if small, a strong adhesive. Alternatively, an artificial tree or branch may be constructed from a metal or wire framework covered in bark. There is a wide range of epiphytes suitable for displaying in this way, including many species from the genera *Aechmea*, *Catopsis*, *Guzmania*, *Neoregelia*, *Nidularium*, *Tillandsia*, and *Vriesea*. Use young plants if possible, since they are easier to mount and tend to become established more quickly.

Prepare the plants by gently removing any loose matter from around the roots, then wrap the roots in moistened sphagnum moss and bind them to the support. Soon the plants will root onto their support, and then the binding may be removed. Some smaller plants may be lodged securely in crevices without being bound, or attached with adhesive, as described for *Tillandsia*, below.

Displaying *Tillandsia*
Tillandsia species may be mounted individually or in groups on pieces of driftwood or cork bark, on rocks, or even on natural crystal. Position each plant with a small amount of adhesive. Make sure that the base of the rosette is free from adhesive so that new root growth is not inhibited. Press the plant onto the mount and secure it with a rubber band, twine, or wire until the glue has set.

Epiphytes as pot plants
A number of naturally epiphytic genera, particularly those with colored foliage, and the usually epiphytic species and cultivars of *Aechmea*, *Billbergia*, *Neoregelia*, *Nidularium*, and *Vriesea* may also be grown as po

BROMELIADS SUITABLE FOR GROWING INDOORS

Tillandsia stricta

Tillandsia caput-medusae

Neoregelia carolinae f. tricolor

Bromelia balansae

Ananas bracteatus 'Tricolor'

Aechmea fasciata

Cryptanthus bivittatus

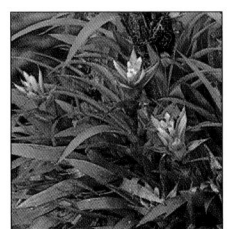

Guzmania lingulata

Guzmania lingulata var. minor

Vriesea splendens

plants, provided that an appropriate medium is used. It must be an extremely open, porous mixture high in organic matter. For this, use half coarse sand or perlite, and half peat or leaf mold. To make sure that any extra moisture drains away swiftly, add pieces of partly composted tree bark to the potting medium.

Growing terrestrials

There are several hundred terrestrial bromeliads belonging to the genera *Abromeitiella*, *Ananas*, *Dyckia*, *Hechtia*, *Portea*, and *Puya*. In regions where temperatures never fall below 45–50°F (7–10°C), a wide variety of terrestrials may be grown outdoors. *Fascicularia bicolor* may be grown without protection in temperatures as low as 32°F (0°C).

Terrestrial bromeliads often have stiff, spiny leaves and a spreading habit. While they may be grown in pots as houseplants, they perform much better if given more space in a greenhouse or conservatory border or, where conditions permit, out of doors. With their eye-catching foliage and strong outlines, they make a distinctive addition to the garden, particularly if combined in designs either with cacti and other succulents or with subtropical plants.

Routine care

Because most bromeliads originate from tropical rain forests, they need warm, humid conditions in order to thrive; most need a minimum temperature of 50°F (10°C). In the right conditions they require little maintenance but special attention is needed in order to maintain the necessary humidity if grown indoors.

Watering

Since epiphytes draw moisture from the air, they should be mist-sprayed once every day rather than watered conventionally at their roots. Use soft water or rainwater when possible, particularly for genera that do not tolerate alkalinity, such as *Aechmea*, *Neoregelia*, *Nidularium*, *Tillandsia*, and *Vriesea*. In spring and summer, add a dilute (quarter-strength) liquid orchid fertilizer to the spray every four to five weeks to keep the plants healthy and vigorous (see ORCHIDS, "Fertilizing," p.362).

Where plants are growing with sphagnum moss around their roots, keep the moss moist by regularly spraying it with tepid water, and also mist-spray the foliage occasionally. Bromeliads whose rosettes form a

DIVIDING ROOTSTOCKS

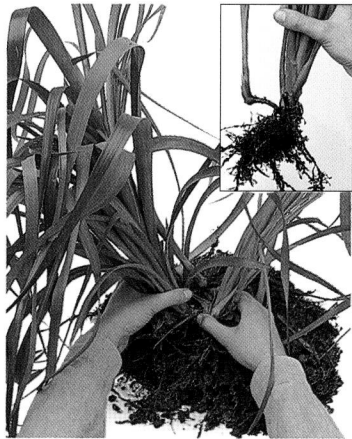

Gently tease or cut the offset away from the parent plant (here Billbergia nutans) so that the root system remains undamaged.

natural well or urn in the center should be kept filled with water, particularly in hot, dry conditions. Occasionally change the water and apply foliar fertilizer to the leaves.

Propagation

Bromeliads may be propagated by vegetative methods or by seed. Most epiphytic plants produce offsets that may be removed and grown on separately, while stoloniferous terrestrial kinds may be divided at the start of the growing season.

Offsets of epiphytes

Many epiphytic bromeliads are monocarpic, meaning that the rosettes flower only once and then die. Before they flower, however, they form offsets around the base of the mature rosette. The offsets should be left in place

until they are about one-third the size of the parent plant. In many cases, the offsets may be removed by hand, but some will need to be cut off with a sharp knife, as close to the parent plant as possible. Replant the parent plant.

Once removed, the offsets should be transferred immediately into prepared containers of free-draining medium, with their bases just held firm in the medium (see "Epiphytes as pot plants," opposite). Keep the young plants slightly shaded at about 70°F (21°C), and lightly mist-spray them with tepid water daily.

Offsets of the nonmonocarpic species may be detached from the parent plant and attached to mounts in the same way as for adult plants. The offsets may have no roots, but these will soon develop if the plants are regularly mist-sprayed and if a few strands of moist sphagnum moss are added at the base of the rosettes to retain moisture.

Offsets of terrestrials

Some terrestrial bromeliads, for example some *Ananas* and *Hechtia*, have stoloniferous rootstocks that also produce offsets. At the start of the growing season, lift the parent plant from the ground, or remove it from its container, so that the offsets may be cut off without injuring the parent plant. Then replant the parent and pot up the offsets in a mix of 1 part shredded peat, 1 part leaf mold, and 1 part coarse sand or grit.

Raising plants from seed

Most bromeliad seeds are sown like other seeds, although it is important to sow them immediately after they are fully ripe because, with only a few exceptions, they do not remain viable for very long.

A less conventional method is used for *Tillandsia* seeds. These are sown on bundles of conifer twigs, such as *Thuja*, that are packed with well-moistened sphagnum moss and then bound together. Hang the bundles in a slightly shaded position, mist-spray them regularly, and make sure that there is free air circulation but no drafts. If kept in a temperature of about 81°F (27°C), seeds will germinate in around three to four weeks. Young plants may then be transferred to branches or other types of support and grown on.

HOW TO PROPAGATE TILLANDSIA BY SEED

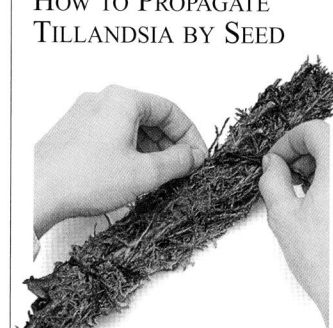

1 *Make a bundle of* Thuja *twigs interspersed with moist sphagnum moss, binding it with string, raffia, or wire.*

2 *Sprinkle the seeds evenly over the prepared bundle; they will adhere readily to the moist moss.*

3 *Water the seeds with a light mist-spray, and then hang up the bundle in position (see inset). Continue to mist-spray on a regular basis.*

HOW TO PROPAGATE BY DIVISION OF OFFSETS

1 *When the offsets are about one-third of the size of the parent (here* Aechmea*), sever them at the base with a knife. Retain any roots they may have.*

2 *Pot each offset into a mix of equal parts shredded peat, leaf mold, and sharp, gritty sand, inserting it so that the base stays on the surface.*

Soil preparation and planting

STRONG, healthy plants, suited to an indoor environment, are vital for success. Since pot plants grow in a limited amount of soil, it is important to use appropriate soil mixes and to maintain the level of nutrients in the soil mix with correct fertilizing.

Choosing plants

If possible, buy plants that have been grown locally or have been acclimated if brought in from distant growing areas. Each plant should be labeled with its full name and some cultivation details.

Look for sturdy plants with strong stems, healthy foliage, and vigorous growing points; reject any that have weak growth, dieback, or discolored, wilting, or brown-edged leaves. Choose younger plants, which should adapt more easily than larger specimens to new conditions. Do not buy potbound plants or those with dry, weedy, or moss-covered soil mix – they have been starved of nutrients and seldom recover fully. Make sure that the growing tips and leaves are free of pests and diseases.

Flowering plants should have plenty of buds that are just starting to color. Climbing plants should be correctly pruned and trained. Do not

SELECTING A HOUSE PLANT

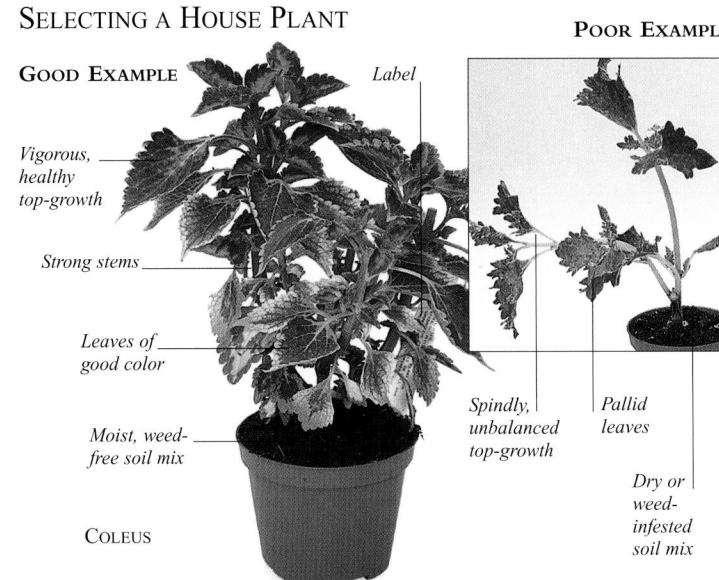

GOOD EXAMPLE — Label — POOR EXAMPLE
Vigorous, healthy top-growth
Strong stems
Leaves of good color
Moist, weed-free soil mix
COLEUS
Spindly, unbalanced top-growth — Pallid leaves
Dry or weed-infested soil mix

buy tropical plants in winter, since sudden fluctuations in temperature may have damaged them. If transporting plants in cold weather, wrap them in newspaper for insulation.

Positioning a plant

Place each plant in a room that provides the levels of temperature, humidity, and light that it requires.

Flowering houseplants that are of subtropical or tropical origin flower poorly or not at all if kept too cool or in poor light, whereas many foliage plants tolerate cool and shady areas. Cacti and other dry atmosphere plants need light, airy, and dry conditions; plants such as *Begonia rex* require more humidity. If conditions in your home are not ideal for a particular plant, a different cultivar of the same genus may be more suitable.

Soil mixes

Always use good-quality, prepared potting soil mixes for indoor plants. Soil-based mixes are generally most suitable, because they contain and retain more nutrients, dry out less quickly, and are easier to rewet than peat-based mixes. They are also heavier, providing stability for big pot plants.

Peat-based soil mixes are used for most commercially available house plants. They have little inherent fertility compared with soil-based mixes, and plants grown in them require careful, regular fertilizing. These soil mixes tend to lose their structure in time, causing poor aeration and watering difficulties.

Alkalinity-intolerant plants such as camellias need acidic soil mixes. Other groups of plants such as orchids (see pp.360–63) need specialized mixes. For further information, see SOILS AND FERTILIZERS, "Soil mixes," p.621.

Grouping plants

For ease of management, plants with similar needs for water, humidity, temperature, and light should be grouped together. If planting into

Plant supports

Various supports are available for houseplants. Choose one that is suitable for the growth habit of the plant, taking into account its speed of growth and eventual size.

Plants with aerial roots grow well up a moss pillar. Tie in the shoots until the roots penetrate it; keep the pillar damp by misting. Trailing or climbing plants with several stems may be trained onto wire hoops. Use a single hoop or several, depending on the plant's vigor. A balloon shape of up to eight wires is attractive, allowing good air circulation and access to light for plants with many stems.

Many climbers support themselves by means of twining stems, leaf stalks, or tendrils, and grow readily up bamboo tripods; they may need tying in at first. Single-stemmed plants need only a stake for support; insert the stake before planting to avoid damaging the roots. For details of support aids, see TOOLS AND EQUIPMENT, "Ties and supports," p.558.

PHILODENDRON SCANDENS
Moist moss
Natural direction of growth
Shoot pinned to moss pillar

Wire hoops tied together at the top
JASMINUM OFFICINALE

FICUS BENJAMINA 'VARIEGATA'
Stake
Plastic twist-tie

TRACHELOSPERMUM JASMINOIDES
Tripod formed by tying 3 stakes together with twine

MOSS PILLAR
Twine stems with aerial roots around a pillar, tying them in so that they are in contact with the moss.

WIRE HOOP
Train trailing plants around wire hoops inserted into the potting mix. Tie them in regularly as they grow, adding extra hoops if necessary.

STAKE
Insert a stake into the soil mix before planting. Tie in the stem of the young plant.

BAMBOO TRIPOD
Encourage stems or tendrils of climbing plants to twine around the stakes by tying them in.

the same container, make sure that the soil mix suits all the plants. In permanent arrangements, use plants with similar growth rates; otherwise, vigorous specimens may swamp their more delicate neighbors.

To increase the humidity level in a dry, centrally heated building, group individually potted plants on wet gravel in shallow bowls or trays. Alternatively, place plants on up-turned pots in a tray of water, with their roots above water level.

Plunging pot plants

Plants arranged in large containers may be plunged in their individual pots into water-retentive material, such as turface, to reduce water loss and improve the local humidity. (Turface can absorb up to 40 percent of its own weight in water, so a watertight outer container should be used.) Any plant that is past its prime or too big can then be readily removed. Alternatively, divide (see "Propagation by division," p.372) and replant it.

Bark and peat are useful as plunge materials, but plants may root into the medium, making them difficult to remove. Overwatering peat may result in waterlogging, which can rot the roots. Moisture meters are useful to help determine when the plants need water.

Planting a hanging basket

For the balcony, conservatory, or greenhouse, use slatted or plastic-coated wire baskets with a 2in (5cm) mesh. Insert plants through the sides to form a ball of flowers and foliage. Indoors, where dripping water would cause damage, use solid baskets, with attached drip trays or an outer container that has no drainage holes. Water such hanging baskets with care to avoid waterlogging.

While planting the basket, place it on a bucket or large pot to keep it stable and clear of the ground. Wire baskets tend to dry out very quickly, but a lining of plastic sheeting reduces moisture loss. The plastic-lined basket is unattractive initially but is soon obscured by the growing plants. Alternatively, line the basket with long-strand sphagnum moss; a plant saucer placed between the moss and the soil mix forms a small reservoir of moisture. Multipurpose soil mixes based on peat or soil are suitable, although soil-based mixes are easier to rewet.

Plant the basket in stages from the base. If necessary, cut the plastic to insert plants through the sides; a roll of paper around their top-growth protects them during this process.

SINKING PLANTS INTO A LARGE CONTAINER

Schefflera arboricola 'Gold Capella'

Cordyline australis 'Purpurea'

Ficus benjamina 'Reginald'

Hibiscus rosa-sinensis

Begonia rex

Fatsia japonica 'Variegata'

Fill the container to about half of its depth with turface , then position the plants in their pots on the surface. Fill in with more turface, making sure that each pot is sunk up to its rim.

HOW TO MAKE A SLATTED WOODEN BOX

1 *Measure and mark ¾ x ⅜in (20 x 20mm) lumber into 14 side pieces, each 10in (25cm) long. To get a straight edge, use a panel saw and miter box to cut the lengths. Place one of the side pieces over a scrap of wood and attach to the workbench.*

2 *Mark drilling holes on one face of the side piece, centered on the width and ½in (1.5cm) in from each end. Drill the holes using a ⅛in (3mm) wood bit. Mark and drill similarly placed holes on the other side pieces, always drilling with the scrap underneath.*

3 *Cut out a 10in (25cm) square of plywood board. Mark and drill holes ½in (1.5cm) in from each side at the corners of the square, using the ⅛in (3mm) wood bit. Mark and drill 7–9 evenly spaced holes for drainage, using a ⅜in (8mm) wood bit.*

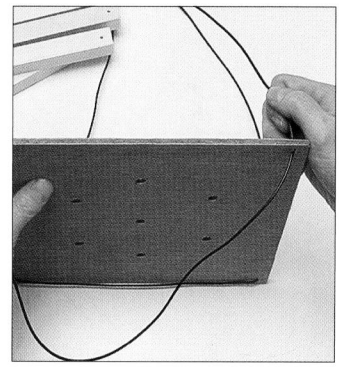

4 *Use pliers to cut 2 lengths of strong, plastic-coated wire, at least 12in (30cm) long. Working from the same side, thread each length of wire through 2 corner holes in the plywood board, then pull flush with the board.*

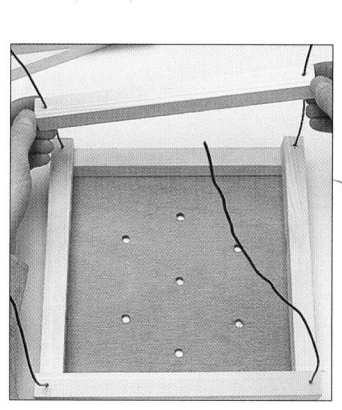

5 *Make sure that there are 4 equal lengths of wire above the board, then build up the sides of the box. After threading the final side piece, twist each wire end around a pencil to make a secure loop. Cut off excess wire. Finish with a nontoxic paint.*

Creeping fig (Ficus pumila 'Variegata')

Blechnum chilense

RECOMMENDED PLANTS FOR TERRARIUMS

Acorus gramineus 'Pusillus'
Adiantum raddianum
Asparagus densiflorus
　'Sprengeri'
Begonia prismatocarpa,
　B. prismatocarpa 'Variegata',
　B. 'Tiger Paws'
Callisia
Chamaedorea elegans
Cissus discolor
Codiaeum
Dizygotheca elegantissima
　(seedlings)
Dracaena sanderiana
Episcia
Ficus pumila
Fittonia verschaffeltii
Hedera (miniatures)
Hypoestes phyllostachya
Ludisia discolor
Maranta leuconeura
Nertera granadensis
Pellaea rotundifolia

Pellionia daveauana
Peperomia caperata
Pilea cadierei, P. spruceana
Plectranthus oertendahlii
Pteris cretica
Saintpaulia (miniatures)
Selaginella
Sinningia pusilla
Soleirolia soleirolii
Sonerila margaritacea

Fittonia
verschaffeltii

Syngonium hoffmannii
Tradescantia cerinthoides,
T. fluminensis, T. spathacea

Planted baskets are heavy, so make sure that supporting chains and hooks are sound. A universal hook allows the basket to be rotated to receive an even amount of light.

Planting in a terrarium

Before planting, clean the terrarium thoroughly to avoid contamination with algae and fungal diseases, which thrive in enclosed and humid environments. Choose a mixture of tall, upright plants and smaller, creeping ones and decide how to arrange them before starting to plant.

Since a terrarium is self-contained, it must have a layer of drainage material, such as turface, gravel, or pebbles, as well as some horticultural charcoal, which absorbs any gaseous by-products and helps keep the soil mix fresh. A lightweight, free-draining, but moisture-retentive soil mix is the most suitable planting medium for terrariums. Extra peat or perlite can be added to keep the soil loose and well aerated.

Use young plants with root systems that are sufficiently small to establish easily in shallow soil mix. Soak them thoroughly before planting, and remove dead foliage that might encourage rot. Insert the plants into the soil mix, allowing space for them to spread. If the terrarium is too small to accommodate a hand easily, attach a spoon to a stick to assist planting, and a cork or thread spool to another stick to make a firming implement. Cover bare areas with moss or pebbles to stop the soil mix from drying out, and water lightly before replacing the lid.

Once established, terrariums require very little or no watering (see "Maintaining terrariums and bottle gardens," p.365). If excess condensation appears on the glass, ventilate it a little until there is only a slight misting of the glass in the morning.

PLANTING A TERRARIUM

1 Plan the arrangement with taller plants either at the back (as here) or in the center, depending on whether the terrarium will be viewed from the front only or from all sides. The plants used here are:

Asparagus densiflorus 'Sprengeri'

Maranta leuconeura

Ficus pumila 'Variegata'

Selaginella martensii

Soleirolia soleirolii

Selaginella kraussiana 'Aurea'

2 Cover the terrarium base with a 1–2in (2.5–5cm) deep layer of pebbles and a few pieces of horticultural charcoal. Add 1in (2.5cm) of moist soil mix.

3 Remove each plant from its pot and shake off any loose soil mix. Gently tease out the roots, reducing the size of the root ball, to help the plant establish.

4 Use a widger or other small implement to make hollows for the plants, and insert them carefully, allowing space between them for further growth.

5 Fill in around the plants with more moist soil mix and firm the surface. A cork glued to the end of a thin stake provides a tamper of suitable size.

6 Using tweezers, place a layer of moss (or pebbles) over any bare areas of soil mix between the plants. This will prevent the soil mix from drying out.

7 Spray the plants and the moss lightly with a fine mist of water and replace the lid. The terrarium is now ready for display.

GROWING PLANTS IN A SOIL BENCH

Fittonia argyroneura

Streptocarpus

Zonal geranium

Ficus benjamina

Surface level with greenhouse window

Soil-based potting mix, about 12in (30cm) deep

3in (7cm) layer of coarse gravel for drainage

15in (38cm) deep bench

Drainage holes

Strengthened wooden frame

Prepare the soil bench for planting by placing a layer of drainage material in the bottom and then filling the bench with soil-based potting mix. Plant a selection of ornamentals for a fine display in the greenhouse.

Soil preparation and planting under cover

Conservatories and greenhouses allow control of the environment and extend the range of plants that can be grown in temperate or cool climates.

Soil beds and bed benches

Although conservatory and greenhouse ornamentals may be grown in pots, a large number, particularly climbers and woody shrubs, can be planted permanently in soil borders. For a new conservatory, consider at the planning stage if soil borders are needed. Raised and well-drained soil beds provide a good method of display. Prepare soil beds well, since ornamentals may be in place for some years. Make the beds four weeks before planting to allow the soil to settle, and at least 12in (30cm) deep, with 3–6in (7–15cm) of drainage material at the base.

A bench bed is useful for propagating and raising different plants, and for growing specialized plant collections. Bench beds are shallow raised beds, usually at waist height, on supporting frames or pillars. They are ideal for small plants and for use with soil-heating cables (see p.574), mist units (see p.574), and automated watering systems (see p.571). Site the bench to make maximum use of available light.

Bench beds are usually built from aluminum or wood, lined with wire mesh or perforated plastic. They should be at least 6in (15cm) deep

and no more than 3ft (1m) wide for easy access. A 3in (7cm) layer of drainage material is sufficient.

Soil mixes under cover

For soil beds, use a well-drained, soil-based mix enriched with organic matter at a rate of about 2.2 gallons/ 10sq ft (10 liters/sq m). Do not use unsterilized garden soil, since it can harbor pests, diseases, and weeds. No safe chemical soil sterilization methods are available to amateurs; heat-sterilizing units, although effective, are expensive and hard to find.

In general, use soil-based mixes under cover because they contain nutrients and trace elements that do not leach out as readily as in less rich peat-based mixes; soil-based mixes are also easier to rewet.

It is important to select the appropriate soil mix for specific purposes and for groups of plants with special needs. Most container-grown plants require a good-quality, soil-based mix that is free-draining and of approximately neutral pH. Tropical plants prefer more organic, leafy soils, so incorporate additional leaf mold in the soil mix before filling containers or soil beds. Most ferns, heathers, and many lilies (*Lilium*) need an acidic soil mix, as do hydrangeas, in order to produce blue flowers rather than pink ones.

Ornamental plants grown in borders need a dressing every year of 2–3oz/sq yd (50–85g/sq m) of a balanced fertilizer with a mulch of well-rotted compost in spring for strong growth. If the planting needs

renewal after several years, remove and dispose of the plants, having propagated them first. Then dig in some well-rotted compost or manure and add a slow-release granular fertilizer before replanting.

In beds of ornamental plants, there is seldom such a buildup of pests and diseases that it is necessary to change or sterilize the soil. With crop plants grown in borders where pests and diseases can increase rapidly, the soil usually needs to be replaced annually or sterilized if a suitable method is available. Crop plants are better cultivated in growing bags or containers, where the soil mix can be disposed of if problems occur. Always make sure the bases of containers with

drainage holes do not come into contact with the border soil. This avoids cross-contamination by pests and diseases.

Planting

Always select plants that grow well in the range of temperatures provided (see "Planter's guide to indoor plants," p.353). Make sure that ornamentals or crop plants are planted at spacings that allow free air circulation and so inhibit the spread of pests and diseases. Position the plants to receive optimum light and ventilation for their growing requirements. Make full use of temperature, light intensity, humidity, and air-circulation controls that are provided in a well-built and fitted-out greenhouse.

Planting a bottle garden

Bottle gardens provide an attractive way of growing very small, slow-growing plants in an enclosed microclimate. Many of the smaller plants grown in terrariums are suitable (see *Recommended Plants for Terrariums*, opposite).

Use any clean, plain or slightly colored glass bottle, as long as the neck is wide enough to allow plants to be inserted easily. If the neck is too narrow to take your hand, make special tools from thin stakes, loops of wire, and common household utensils, such as a dessert fork and teaspoon, to help with planting and routine care.

With the aid of a wide funnel or cardboard tube, pour turface into the bottle to provide a 1¼in (3cm) layer of drainage material and add a handful of horticultural charcoal to keep the soil mix fresh. Cover it with a 2–3in (5–7cm) layer of dampened, peat-based potting mix. If the bottle is to be viewed

from the front, use a tool to bank up the soil mix at the back. Level the soil mix if the bottle is to be viewed from all sides.

Begin planting at the sides of the bottle and work in toward the center. Remove the plants from their pots, and shake off any excess soil mix. Carefully lower each plant into a planting hole, using tweezers, tongs, or a length of wire twisted into a noose. Space the plants at least 1¼in (3cm) apart to allow room for growth. Cover the roots with soil mix, and use a cork tamper to firm it gently.

Trickle a cupful of water down the sides of the bottle to dampen the soil mix, then cover bare areas with sphagnum moss to keep it moist. Clean the inside of the glass with a sponge attached to a stake or stiff wire. If the bottle garden is not sealed after planting, water occasionally, but do not allow water to stand.

Hypoestes phyllostachya 'Purpuriana'

Asplenium nidus

Dracaena sanderiana

Hedera helix 'Eva'

Saintpaulia cv

Selaginella kraussiana

Hypoestes phyllostachya 'Splash'

Sphagnum moss

Orchids

INCLUDED in the orchid family are some 750 genera, nearly 20,000 species, and many thousands more hybrids. Their exotic blooms and intriguing habit make them very desirable ornamental plants, mostly for indoor display, although there are a significant number of beautiful terrestrial species that are quite hardy. When choosing which to grow from the vast range of types available, consider the conditions and care that you are able to provide. Some orchids have fairly rigorous demands for growing conditions, but many hybrids are specially bred for ease of cultivation and can be successfully grown and propagated in the home.

Terrestrial orchids

As the name suggests, these orchids grow in the ground in widely varying habitats. Most of those that inhabit temperate to cold regions die down after flowering and exist in a resting state as tubers or similar underground storage organs during the winter. These hardy terrestrials often have flowers that, although individually small, bloom in dense spikes. Many are attractive plants for the rock garden or alpine house (see pp.271–73).

Some terrestrials, such as the slipper orchids belonging to the genus *Paphiopedilum*, come from warmer regions, where they inhabit sheltered sites such as the forest floor. Never needing to face harsh weather conditions, these remain evergreen throughout the year, but – because they do not tolerate frost – they need to be cultivated in a greenhouse.

Epiphytic orchids

Epiphytic orchids, which form a very large proportion of those grown by enthusiasts, are fundamentally different in their structure and habit of growth. As implied by their name (derived from the Greek *epi*, upon, and *phyton*, plant), they make their homes in the branches of trees.

They are not parasites (because they do not feed off the tree) but lodgers: they take their nourishment from substances dissolved in rainwater and from debris accumulated around their roots. A few orchids known as lithophytes live in a similar manner on rocks. In temperate climates, epiphytes need to be grown under cover.

Sympodial and monopodial

Epiphytes have two methods of growth: sympodial and monopodial. Sympodial orchids, such as *Cattleya* and *Odontoglossum* species and hybrids, have creeping rhizomes. Each season new growths arise from growing points on the rhizomes and develop into swollen stem structures known as pseudobulbs. Flowers of the different sympodial species vary greatly and may appear from the top, base, or side of the pseudobulbs.

Monopodial orchids grow in what is called an indeterminate manner. The stem continues to elongate indefinitely, growing taller and taller as new leaves and stem are produced at the apex. Monopodials include many of the most spectacular orchid genera, such as *Phalaenopsis* and *Vanda*. These are native to the warmer regions of the world, climbing their way up toward the light through dense jungle foliage. Most monopodials bear their flowers in branched, often gracefully arching, flower heads from axillary points along their stems; aerial roots are also often produced from these points to give new growth.

Choosing plants

If you are a beginner, it is best to obtain plants from a specialized orchid nursery, where they will have been carefully grown an ideal environment. Specialists are also a valuable source of advice on suitable species for the conditions you have at home. Hybrid orchids are generally the easiest to grow, being themselves bred partly for vigor and ease of care. The species thrive best in environ-ments similar to those in which they grow naturally, and these conditions are not always easy to re-create.

Thanks to commercial techniques of mass production, many orchids are no longer prohibitively expensive. For a modest price, plants that are attractive but have not yet won a special award from the American Orchid Society or other national societies may be bought when you visit specialized nurseries and see them in flower. Least expensive of all are unflowered seedlings that may take several years to come into bloom; the result is uncertain, but there is always the exciting possibility that one of the seedlings may be a future major award-winner.

RECOMMENDED ORCHIDS

Dendrobium nobile

Cymbidium Strath Kanaid

***Vanda* Rothschildiana**

Paphiopedilum callosum

Cattleya bowringiana

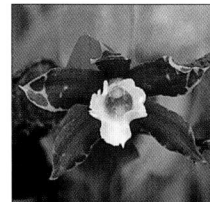

Miltonia candida var. *grandiflora*

Cultivation

The unusual structure and growth habit of epiphytic orchids gives them a reputation for being very delicate and therefore difficult to grow. With knowledge of a few guidelines and careful preparation, however, most of the difficulties can be avoided.

Potting mix

Although most epiphytes can be grown in pots, their roots are specially adapted to open conditions on trees (or rocks, in the case of lithophytes), so they cannot endure the close-textured soil mixes suitable for most other plants. Orchid potting mixes must drain very freely after watering; if they remain wet for long, the roots are likely to rot.

Chopped pine or fir bark makes an excellent potting medium, with some additions to keep the mixture open and prevent it from becoming sour. A suitable mix is as follows: 3 parts medium-grade bark (dust-free), 1 part coarse grit or perlite, 1 part charcoal pieces, and 1 part broken dry leaves or shredded coconut fiber (coir) or peat. A wide range of specialized mixes can usually be obtained from orchid nurseries.

Terrestrial orchids also require a much more free-draining potting mixture than most plants. A suitable potting mix can be made up of 3 parts fibrous peat, 3 parts coarse grit, and 1 part perlite, with the addition of 1 part charcoal.

POTTING MATERIALS FOR EPIPHYTIC ORCHIDS

The different components combine to provide the perfect growing medium: bark and peat retain moisture, grit aids drainage, and charcoal prevents the mix from becoming too acidic.

FIBROUS PEAT

CRUSHED CHARCOAL

COARSE GRIT

MEDIUM BARK

ORCHID POTTING MIX

Potting

When a plant has filled its container, it should be transferred to a new pot a size or two larger to provide space for further growth. Choose a pot that will accommodate the roots and allow for one or two years' growth but no more; a pot that is too large for the root system is likely to lead to stagnant conditions in the potting mix. To fill space, many growers fill the bottom quarter of the pot with pot shards, pieces of plastic foam, or very coarse grit. Shards and grit add extra weight to plastic pots, making them less likely to be knocked over.

Hold the plant with one hand so that the crown is just below the rim of the pot and place the potting mix around the roots, tapping the pot sharply to settle the mix. Use relatively dry mix, which should be thoroughly watered after repotting. The plant, especially the roots, should be disturbed as little as possible, and kept out of strong light.

Some epiphytes do well in containers that allow more air to reach the roots, such as hanging baskets made of wire or wooden slats. Such containers are essential for species of *Stanhopea,* because their flowers grow down through the potting mix to emerge on the underside.

When potting on sympodials, old pseudobulbs of two to three seasons' growth that have lost their leaves (usually called back bulbs) may be removed and used for propagating (see p.363). Place the rear of the plant against one side of the pot, leaving space on the opposite side for the new growth to develop.

Support

Many orchids are sturdy enough not to need support. Others, however, require careful staking to look their best, particularly those with long flowering stems that carry many heavy blooms. Use upright stakes or sturdy wires, to which the stems may be tied as unobtrusively as possible. Do this as the stems are growing and before the flower buds open. Avoid changing the position of the plants or the display will be spoiled because the flowers will face in different directions.

Growing on bark

Some orchids that do not grow successfully in containers will thrive if mounted on pieces of either bark or tree fern with moss at their roots, although they then require a constantly humid atmosphere. Initially they must be tied firmly to the slab;

nylon thread is ideal for this purpose. New roots should soon appear; these will adhere firmly to the slab and thus secure the plant.

Routine care

For successful cultivation, it is vital to provide orchids with their particular care requirements; these vary according to the species.

Temperature

While the hardy terrestrials (notably *Cypripedium* species) do well in the rock garden or alpine house, others may also be grown in unheated conditions in mild areas. They include the cool-growing genera *Pleione* and *Bletilla,* which need only enough heat to provide frost-free conditions.

A cool greenhouse, with a minimum night temperature in winter of 50°F (10°C), is suitable for a large number of different orchids, including some *Brassia, Coelogyne, Cymbidium, Dendrobium, Laelia, Odontoglossum, Oncidium,* and *Paphiopedilum* species and hybrids.

The intermediate house, with a minimum winter night temperature of 55–60°F (13–15°C) will greatly extend the range of possibilities to

include species and hybrids of *Cattleya* and its relatives, and a wider selection of the *Odontoglossum* group and of *Paphiopedilum* and *Phragmipedium* species and hybrids, as well as many other attractive and beautiful orchids.

The warm house, with a minimum night temperature of at least 65°F (18°C), provides the necessary conditions for species and hybrids of *Phalaenopsis* and *Vanda* and their many relatives, as well as the heat-loving species and hybrids of *Dendrobium,* and many orchids from the hot and humid lowlands of the tropics and subtropics.

Watering and humidity

These are perhaps the most important factors in orchid cultivation. Watering should be frequent enough to avoid drying, but not so frequent that the potting mix becomes soggy – once or twice a week for most of the year is usually sufficient. In the summer months plants may need watering every day, and during the period of shorter winter days only once every two or three weeks.

Rainwater is usually recommended, but drinkable tapwater is safe. Water plants in the early morning. Do not let water remain too long on

HOW TO DISPLAY EPIPHYTIC ORCHIDS
Most epiphytes may be grown in pots, although they may also be successfully cultivated in a hanging basket or on bark. Keep the plants in a constantly humid atmosphere until established.

GROWING ON BARK
Tie moistened moss to a piece of bark, then attach the roots of the orchid (here Dendrobium 'Happiness'*) with nylon thread.*

POT-GROWN
Choose a pot that allows for no more than 2 years' growth. Add some standard orchid potting mix, plant the orchid (here Zygopetalum mackayi)*, add more mix, then firm in.*

HANGING BASKET
Plant the orchid in standard orchid potting mix in a hanging basket lined with sphagnum moss. The flower stems of some orchids (here Stanhopea tigrina*) grow through the mix to emerge below.*

the foliage, or it may cause leaf spotting if the plants are exposed to hot sun. Overwatering must be avoided, but water thoroughly, so that the potting mix is evenly moist. Allow the mix to become nearly (but not quite) dry before watering again. If in doubt, delay watering.

During the growing season, orchids need a high level of humidity. This may be achieved by damping down the orchid house by spraying water over the paths and soil and on the staging between plants. Do this early in the morning; as the day progresses, the water will be drawn up as vapor. This daily damping down may be discontinued when the natural conditions are cold and damp. Be careful, however, because in extremely cold weather the heating system may make the air very dry, and the greenhouse may need to be damped down more often.

Orchids grown in the home as windowsill plants must be chosen from those that do not demand very high humidity. Even these may benefit from additional local humidity by standing them on a layer of moist gravel or expanded clay aggregate in a tray or deep saucer.

Fertilizing

Since modern orchid potting mixes contain little nourishment, orchids will need fertilizing during their growing period. Liquid fertilizers are the most convenient, and these can be added during watering. Any commercial, general-purpose brands sold for pot plants may be used. Orchids are not heavy feeders, so it will be necessary to dilute the fertilizer to half the strength recommended for other pot plants. Fertilize the orchids once every three weeks from spring to fall, and only every six weeks (if at all) during winter.

Ventilation

Most orchids, especially the popular cool-greenhouse kinds, require free-moving air conditions. They dislike cold drafts, however, which can cause flower buds to drop and slow down growth. Ventilators should be only partially opened in spring, when sunny days may be accompanied by chilly winds, and closed well before the temperature starts to drop in the late afternoon. As days become warm, ventilators may be opened wider and for a longer time. Remember, however, that water vapor is quickly lost through open ventilators and humidity is reduced, so that extra damping down is needed. A small electric fan, inexpensive to buy and run, will keep the air moving without letting out humidity or letting in drafts.

Shading

Although different orchids may have different light requirements, from the shade-loving *Paphiopedilum* orchids to the sun-loving *Laelia* species and hybrids, some form of shading is needed to protect new growth from being scorched by the sun and to prevent the greenhouse from overheating. The cheapest method is to use a greenhouse shading compound. White is more efficient than green in reflecting back the sun's rays, and it becomes almost transparent in rain, letting in more light on dull days. More effective, but more expensive, are manual or automatic roller blinds, made either of wood slats or plastic mesh.

Dormancy

An important and integral part of an orchid's life cycle is the dormant period, when growth slows or stops. During this time, which in the case of some orchids may last only a few weeks and in others several months, they need very little water, if any, in order to survive.

Although plants' requirements vary, the general rule is that those orchids that lose their leaves when dormant should not be watered until new growth begins. Water sparingly at first, then normally (taking care not to overwater). Plants that keep their leaves will need to be given only a little water during the dormant period to avoid dehydration.

Propagation

Vegetative propagation methods are the easiest for the amateur to learn. They also have the advantage of

HOW TO PROPAGATE BY KEIKIS

1 *When a new plantlet with aerial roots (a "keiki") has formed from a node, cut it away carefully from the parent plant with a sharp knife.*

2 *The selected cutting should have healthy leaves and an evenly developed root system.*

3 *Holding the plantlet by its stem at planting level, pot up the young plant in a 3in (6cm) pot with the roots just below the surface of the potting mix.*

HOW TO PROPAGATE BY STEM CUTTINGS

1 *Using a sharp knife, cut off a section of stem at least 10in (25cm) long, just above a leaf node or at the base of the plant.*

2 *Divide this into lengths of about 3in (7cm), cutting midway between leaf nodes. Each cutting should have at least one node.*

3 *Lay the cuttings in a tray on a layer of moist sphagnum moss and store in a humid place out of direct sunlight.*

4 *After several weeks, the dormant buds will have developed into plantlets, which will then be ready to pot up.*

producing offspring that are identical to the parent plant, so that the results are predictable.

Keikis

The simplest cuttings, which are commonly known to orchid growers as keikis, are small plantlets that appear adventitiously (that is, atypically) from the nodes on stems of monopodial orchids, such as *Dendrobium*. As soon as these plantlets have developed a few vigorous roots, they should be carefully severed from the parent plant with a sharp knife and then potted into a standard orchid potting mix. Water them sparingly at first, but remember to spray the leaves with a fine mist until the roots have become established and the plants have had a chance to become accustomed to their new environment.

Stem cuttings

Cuttings may also be made from the stems (often called canes) of many *Dendrobium* and *Epidendrum* orchids. With a sharp knife, cut off sections up to 12in (30cm) in length. Divide these into cuttings 3–4in (7.5–10cm) long, each with at least one dormant bud. Lay the cuttings on damp sphagnum moss or a similar moist material and keep them in a humid, shaded place. When the buds have produced plantlets, detach these and pot them up separately.

Division

The usual method of propagating sympodial orchids such as *Cattleya*, *Cymbidium*, and *Odontoglossum* is by division. Simply cut through the rhizome between pseudobulbs and pot up the pieces separately. Each piece should have at least three healthy pseudobulbs and a healthy dormant bud to produce new growth.

Back bulbs offer another way of propagating sympodials such as *Cymbidium*. Remove a back bulb, preferably one with roots, by cutting the rhizome just beyond it. Insert the back bulb in grit, sharp sand, or standard orchid potting mix, with the cut side of the bulb nearest the edge to allow space in the center for new growth. Place in a cool, shady place, and keep moist. Shoots should appear in two or three months. When the bulbs have developed roots, pot them on.

Commercial techniques

Growing orchids from seed is a difficult technique and requires specialized knowledge and skills. Orchids raised commercially from seed are germinated in flasks of nutrient jelly in a laboratory environment. They may also be propagated by meristem culture: microscopic pieces of plant tissue are grown on under laboratory conditions to mass-produce replicas of the original plant. As a result, first-class cultivars may now be purchased at a reasonable price. However, both techniques are highly specialized. They are seldom practiced by amateurs.

HOW TO PROPAGATE BY DIVISION

1 *When the orchid has grown too large for its pot and has several leafless bulbs, it may be divided. The plant shown here is a Cymbidium.*

2 *Remove the orchid from its pot, then divide the plant by separating or cutting it into 2 sections; each section should have at least 3 healthy pseudobulbs.*

3 *When dividing the orchid, any leafless back bulbs may be pulled away. Discard shriveled ones, and retain those that are firm for potting up separately.*

4 *Trim each section of the divided plant by removing surplus potting mix and cutting off any dead roots with pruners.*

5 *To replant each section, hold the plant, with the oldest pseudobulbs at the back of the pot and at planting level, and place the potting mix around it. New growth will develop in front of the plant.*

PROPAGATION BY BACK BULBS

1 *Plant back bulbs singly at one side of a 3in (6cm) pot. Place the cut side of the bulb nearest the edge.*

2 *Within 2 or 3 months a new shoot will grow toward the center of the pot.*

PROPAGATION IN FLASKS

Meristem culture takes place under sterile conditions. Microscopic pieces of plant tissue are placed in a flask on a special nutrient medium such as agar jelly; they then develop into young orchid plants.

Routine care

UNLIKE plants grown outdoors, indoor plants are not subject to the extremes of the seasonal cycle so they need relatively little attention. They require only watering and fertilizing, and generally an annual potting on, to perform at their best.

Watering and humidity

A common problem with indoor plants is overwatering. In general, water when the surface of the soil mix is nearly dry or the pot feels light. Some plants, such as African violets (*Saintpaulia*) and their relatives, do best in an evenly moist soil.

Water plants frequently while they are in active growth, less in winter when they are dormant – twice a month or even less may be enough. Wet the soil mix thoroughly, but do not leave the pot standing in water. Some plants, such as cyclamen, are susceptible to root rot; to water them, stand the pots in a little water until the soil mix is dark and damp. If tapwater is hard, use distilled water or rainwater for alkaline-intolerant plants.

Buildings are often poorly ventilated and the atmosphere too dry for many indoor plants. Maintain the necessary humidity by grouping pot plants on wet gravel in trays or in containers (see "Grouping plants," p.356), or on capillary matting (see "Care of indoor plants before going away," p.366).

Cool- and warm-vapor electric humidifiers are available. Bowls of water placed in a room so that the water evaporates are also effective. Plants that need high humidity benefit from being mist-sprayed with soft water. Use sprays sparingly on plants with hairy leaves, and avoid sunlight since spots of cold water on the leaves can damage them.

Cleanliness

Always remove dead leaves and flowers promptly, since they may harbor diseases or pests. Do not allow dust or grime to build up and block the light; dust the foliage with a soft brush. Thoroughly spray the plants occasionally to keep them clean and fresh, but do not spray cacti or plants with hairy leaves unless the weather is warm enough for any excess moisture to evaporate rapidly, or the leaves may rot. Use leaf shine only on glossy-leaved plants; check first that it is compatible with individual species.

Fertilizing

Pot plants grow in relatively small volumes of soil mix and soon use up the available nutrients. Frequent watering also leaches out nutrients, so the plants could starve if they do not have regular fertilizing throughout the growing season.

Balanced fertilizers are available in various forms: water-soluble or liquid (most convenient for indoor plants), granular, and solid. Always be careful to follow the manufacturers' instructions, and never apply fertilizer to dry soil mix, because it will not soak through evenly and may damage the roots.

Pinching out

The appearance of many pot plants, especially trailing plants, can be improved by pinching out growing tips on young plants to encourage more sideshoots. This keeps the foliage bushy and increases the number of flower buds. Pinch only plants that are in active growth.

MAINTAINING PLANT HYGIENE

CLEANING SMOOTH-LEAVED PLANTS
Gently wipe each leaf (here variegated Ficus elastica*) with a clean, moist, soft, and lint-free cloth.*

REMOVING DEAD LEAVES
Pinch out dead leaves and stems at the base of the plant (here Nephrolepis exaltata*), or cut them out.*

Neglected plants

With the exception of orchids and palms, most plants that have weak, leggy, or damaged growth, or sparsely spaced leaves, produce new, vigorous growth if cut back hard to a healthy bud or joint in early spring. Cut back a neglected fern to the crown; keep it moist and in medium light to induce new growth.

Plants that root readily are best renewed from cuttings, while some plants are rejuvenated by air layering (see p.377). Revive exhausted plants by repotting or with a rest in a shaded greenhouse. To rescue an overwatered plant, remove all the sodden soil mix from the root ball, trim off rotting foliage and roots, and repot it in fresh soil mix. Refresh an underwatered plant by immersing the pot in water until the bubbles stop rising, then let the pot drain.

Potting on and top-dressing

Indoor plants also need periodic potting on to accommodate their growth and to replenish the soil mix. A pot-bound plant has retarded growth, and water runs straight through the soil mix. Pot on before this so that the plant develops well. A few plants, such as amaryllis (*Hippeastrum*), enjoy confined roots, so pot them on less often and top-dress occasionally.

The best time to pot on is at the start of the growing season, although fast-growing plants may need potting on several times in one season. The process may delay flowering because the plant initially concentrates its energy on new root growth. Avoid potting on a dormant plant.

Potting on

Make sure that the root ball is completely moist so that it comes easily out of its pot without damaging the roots. Turn the pot upside down, then slide the plant out into your hand. If the pot is too big to lift easily, run a knife around the inside, then lay the pot on its side. Support the plant

HOW TO RENEW TOP-DRESSING

HIPPEASTRUM

1 *Use a widger to remove the top 1–2in (2½–5cm) of the old soil mix, taking care not to damage the plant's roots.*

2 *Replace it with fresh, moist soil mix to which a small amount of fertilizer has been added. Firm the soil mix well around the crown, then water.*

PRESERVING HUMIDITY AROUND POT PLANTS

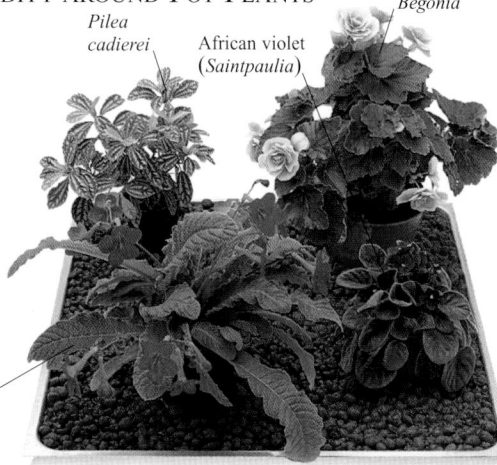

Create suitably humid conditions for indoor plants by providing them with their own microclimate. Loosely pack a shallow tray with turface or gravel and fill it with water. Group several pot plants on the tray. Keep the water filled up so that the gravel or turface remains wet.

Pilea cadierei

African violet (*Saintpaulia*)

Begonia

Streptocarpus

with one hand and roll the pot, gently tapping the sides with a wood block to loosen the soil mix fully before removing the plant.

Put fresh soil mix in the new pot until the plant is positioned at the same depth as before, with space allowed for watering. Make sure that the roots are spread out and the plant centered. Fill in with more soil mix, and firm gently. Water, but do not fertilize the plant for four to six weeks, so that it will send out new roots into the soil mix in search of food. Keep the plant out of direct sun for a few days to recover.

Repotting

If a plant is in the largest available container, has grown to its full size, or is very slow-growing, repot it into the same size pot to renew the soil mix. Take the plant out of its pot, removing as much of the old soil mix as possible. Prune out damaged or diseased roots before repotting the plant in fresh soil mix.

Top-dressing

Do not routinely repot plants that react badly to root disturbance, or enjoy confined roots. At the start of each growing season replace the old, surface soil mix with fresh soil mix enriched with balanced fertilizer. Repot only when necessary.

Hanging baskets

Hanging baskets need regular care. Never allow the soil mix in a basket to dry out. Water it thoroughly; in very warm weather, this will need to be done both morning and evening. If the plants wilt, soak the basket in a bowl filled with water.

Fertilize plants in a basket regularly with a balanced liquid fertilizer, and control any pests. Deadhead flowering plants, clip back trailing plants that are too long, and thin out any messy or tangled growth. Remove and replace any dead plants.

Maintaining terrariums and bottle gardens

A closed container rarely needs water, but if required, use a long-necked watering can to trickle water against the glass; this avoids disturbing the soil mix. Use just enough water to clean the glass and moisten the surface. If the glass is continuously obscured by mist, the soil mix is too wet – remove the cover or cork until it clears. To get rid of condensation or algae inside the glass, use a small

HOW TO POT ON AN INDOOR PLANT

1 *Before potting on a plant (here* Dracaena deremensis *'Souvenir de Schriever'), make sure that its root ball is moist by watering it thoroughly an hour beforehand. Select a pot that is one or two sizes larger than the old one. Make sure the pot is clean (whether washed, disinfected, or new) to avoid spreading diseases. The fresh soil mix should be of the same type as that in the old pot.*

2 *Remove the plant by inverting the pot and sharply tapping the rim on a hard surface to loosen the root ball. Support the plant as it slides out of the pot.*

3 *Gently tease out the root ball with your fingers or a small fork. Put some moist soil mix in the base of the new pot.*

4 *Insert the plant so that its soil mark is level with the rim base. Fill in with soil mix to within 1/2in (1.5cm) of the rim, firm, water, and place in position (right).*

Keeping plants from year to year

To renew flowering plants grown for winter color indoors, plunge them in their pots into outdoor beds when all danger of frost is past. Choose a relatively cool spot, with indirect light, and keep them watered with soft (lime-free) water. At the end of summer, repot or top-dress them, bring them back indoors, and fertilize them regularly once flower buds appear. To keep a cyclamen successfully after it has flowered, do not water it until new growth starts, then remove old roots and repot in soil-based potting mix so that the corm is level with the surface. Put it in a cool, well-lit place, and water regularly.

WINTER-FLOWERING POT PLANTS
In late spring, transfer the plants, here azaleas (Rhododendron)*, to a plunge bed in semishade outdoors. Sink each pot up to its rim in weed-free soil or another suitable plunge material, allowing space for the plants to grow. Bring them in before frost threatens, and keep them cool until the buds open.*

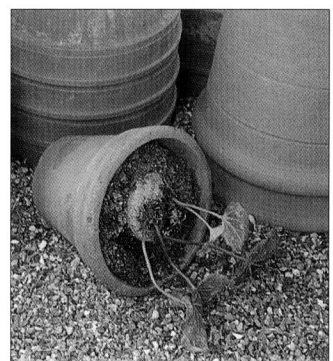

CYCLAMEN
Let the leaves die down after flowering. Place the pot on its side under a shrub or a greenhouse bench, or in a cold frame.

REPLANTING A TERRARIUM

Asparagus densiflorus 'Sprengeri'

Ficus pumila 'Variegata'

Hypoestes phyllostachya 'Splash'

Dracaena reflexa cv

Selaginella kraussiana 'Aurea'

Fittonia verschaffeltii

Selaginella martensii

1 *When a terrarium becomes overgrown, carefully remove any plants that have grown too large. Divide them or select new, small plants. Try to leave the surrounding soil mix undisturbed.*

2 *If needed, trim the remaining plants with scissors. Thin out the surface moss where necessary by removing some with tweezers, keeping adjacent plants firmly in place with a cork-and-stake tamper.*

3 *Divide low-growing plants that have outgrown their allotted space. Use a widger to replant the divisions and the new plants (see inset). Firm with a little fresh soil mix, using the tamper.*

4 *Trickle water down the inside of the glass until the soil mix is just damp, then replace the lid.*

sponge attached to a stake. Keep the container out of direct sunlight and move it occasionally, especially if it is in a shaded place in winter. Remove dead leaves, and control pests and diseases.

Trim the plants from time to time so that each has enough light and space. A razor blade inserted into the end of a stake is useful for pruning plants in small-necked bottle gardens. If any plants encroach upon others, either replace them with smaller plants, or replant the entire container (see above).

Plants in greenhouses

These need regular, sometimes daily, attention, even if the greenhouse is equipped with automatic systems. Watering, ventilation, misting, and fertilizing are especially important in summer, as is heating in winter, and proper hygiene at all times. Routine care of pot plants, including fertilizing and potting (see pp.364–65), is similar to that of indoor plants.

Watering
In the enclosed greenhouse environment, correct watering is crucial. The amount needed varies with the season and the weather. In summer, water more on sunny than on cloudy days. Use a hose in a big greenhouse, with a low water pressure to avoid washing surface soil mix away from the roots. A watering can is best in a small or mixed greenhouse, where plants have differing water needs:

some pot plants may need watering several times on a hot day. Stand the can in the greenhouse until the water temperature is the same as that of the plants. Do not overwater, especially in winter, since wet soil leads to rotting. For full instructions on watering (e.g. by capillary matting, drip feeds, or trickle systems), see p.571. Self-watering pots are also useful; an outer pot holds water that is borne by capillary action along a wick to the soil mix in an inner pot.

Humidity
Plants need moist, but not stagnant, air. In hot, sunny weather, damp down by splashing the floor, particularly hard surfaces, with water each morning and evening, or more often in very hot weather. This keeps the greenhouse humid and temporarily cools the air. (Soil floors hold the most moisture, while tiled or concrete floors dry most quickly.) If the air is too humid, plants cannot transpire water vapor from the

leaves to keep cool, and may overheat and wilt, so ventilate the greenhouse to dry out the air. In very hot climates, or for plants with particular needs, automated cooling systems and special humidifiers may be necessary (see GREENHOUSES AND FRAMES, "Humidity," p.570).

Dank, cold air encourages fungal diseases to attack plants. In winter, keep the air dry by ventilating the greenhouse when weather permits, or install a fan or a dehumidifier.

Care of indoor plants before going away

When going away, make sure that indoor plants do not dry out. To keep water loss to a minimum, move plants into the shade, and use one of the following watering methods. Group pot plants on a capillary mat on an upturned tray, draining board, or shelf. Let the mat trail into another tray, a sink, or bathtub that is filled with water to supply the plants. Holes in plastic pots allow the water through, and

clay pots are as good if saturated beforehand. Stand large or single pots on wick waterers, which draw water into the soil mix from a reservoir by means of a wick. Alternatively, water

the plant thoroughly, allow it to drain, and place it in a sealed plastic bag to avoid moisture loss. Check for and control any pests or diseases before going away.

Guzmania lingulata

Syngonium podophyllum 'Albolineatum'

Aglaonema

CAPILLARY MATTING *Adiantum capillus-veneris*
Place pot plants on one end of a piece of wet matting. Leave the other end submerged in a water reservoir. The plants must be above the water so that they can draw it up as they need it.

Ficus pumila 'Variegata'

PLASTIC BAG
Hold a clear plastic bag away from the foliage with split stakes. Seal with a plastic twist-tie or fold the neck of the bag under the pot.

Temperature regulation

Use ventilation to control temperatures in the greenhouse and avoid severe fluctuations that can harm plants. Too much ventilation slows growth; too little leads to high temperatures. On windy days, ventilate the greenhouse on the leeward side to avoid harmful drafts. For further information, see GREENHOUSES AND FRAMES, "Ventilation" (p.569) and "Shading" (p.570).

Hygiene

Keep the greenhouse clear of all debris that may harbor pests, and remove dead leaves and flowers before they rot. Wash or renew the gravel on benches if it is infested with tiny snails or clogged with soil. Each fall, take the plants outside and clean the greenhouse. Choose a still, warm day when the change in their environment is least likely to harm the plants. A thorough scrubdown is preferable; otherwise, give the greenhouse a sweeping and hosing down (see GREENHOUSES AND FRAMES, "Routine maintenance," p.577).

Cold protection

In unheated greenhouses, where winters are not harsh, prevent plant roots from freezing by keeping them nearly dry. Cover plants with a layer of plastic sheeting or newspaper, and cover beds with straw. Insulate the base of shrubs and climbers with straw or similar material, secured with netting or twine. Plunge small pots in sand.

Pests and diseases

Regularly check buds, growing points, and the backs of leaves, and take early remedial action. Destroy badly infested plants, and isolate less affected specimens until they are clear of trouble. Isolate newly purchased plants for two weeks, and control pests and diseases before placing them with other plants. Particular problems may be caused by black vine weevil larvae (p.652) and spider mites (p.640), especially in dry, centrally heated air.

In warm, moist greenhouse conditions, pests and diseases such as gray mold/*Botrytis* (p.646) and powdery mildew (p.640), aphids (p.639) and hence viruses (p.642), and whiteflies (p.639) can spread rapidly. During the annual cleanup, (see "Routine maintenance," p.577) remove plants likely to be harmed by chemicals; spray the greenhouse to control any pests or diseases before replacing the plants. See also PLANT PROBLEMS (pp.633–61).

Hydroculture

This system has developed from hydroponics, which is a technique for growing plants in water to which all necessary nutrients are added. In hydroculture, "water roots" (which are slightly different from plant roots growing in soil) are supported in an open-mesh pot of inert growing medium and nutrients are added to water in an outer, watertight container. A calibrated, floating marker in a clear plastic indicator measures "maximum," "optimum/best," or "minimum" water levels.

Hydroculture has several advantages: it is easy to provide the plants with a precise and appropriate amount of air, water, and nutrients; the growing medium is clean, well drained, odorless, free from overacidity and clogging, which discourages weeds, pests, and diseases; and growth is often faster and stronger than in soil. Bulbs, cacti, orchids, and many plants that are commonly grown in offices flourish under hydroculture; see also "Planter's guide to indoor plants," p.353.

Preparing plants

Plants are best obtained from specialty nurseries or raised from cuttings, although some will transfer from soil. Between early spring and early fall, choose a young, healthy plant and remove it carefully from its pot. Soak the root ball in water at room temperature for half an hour until the soil comes away from the roots, then gently rinse the roots clean.

Planting

If using a fertilizer cartridge, clip it firmly into the culture pot base before planting. Wash and soak some turface, then half fill a culture pot with it. Place the plant in the pot, then spread out its roots

WASHING PLANT ROOTS

Wash off soil traces under slowly running, cool water while holding the plant (here a Dieffenbachia*).*

CROSS SECTION OF A HYDROCULTURE POT

The inner culture pot holds the plant and the growing medium (here turface), which may be placed in any suitable watertight container.

Water level indicator in molded holder

TURFACE

Inner culture pot of flexible plastic

Turface

Open mesh to allow free flow of water and nutrients

Outer, watertight container

Water

Plant developing "water roots"

Recess for fertilizer cartridge

A TABLETOP DISPLAY

Chamaedorea elegans

Aucuba japonica 'Variegata'

Syngonium podophyllum

Euphorbia milii

Pilea 'Norfolk'

Group several plants in inner culture pots in a larger bowl.

and carefully fill the pot to its rim with turface. Insert the water level indicator. Place planted culture pots either singly or in groups in watertight containers; clear glass is unsuitable because it lets light reach the roots. Water to the "optimum/best" mark on the indicator. Keep the plants at 64–77°F (18–25°C). If they have previously been grown in soil, cover them with clear plastic bags to prevent them from drying out while water roots develop.

Watering

The roots, kept moist by the capillary action of the porous growing medium, dislike being in water for long periods, so let the level drop to "minimum" before watering. Occasionally keeping to "minimum" level for 2–3 days encourages new root formation. Never keep to "optimum" for more than two weeks. Before going away, fill the containers to "maximum" level or stand the

culture pots in a tray. Add water and nutrients until the level rises to about 1¼in (3cm).

Fertilizing

Various soluble fertilizers are available; follow the supplier's instructions. Minerals in the tapwater react with the fertilizers to release nutrients, which are then absorbed as needed by the plant.

Propagation from cuttings

Prepare cuttings in the normal way (see p.374), then root them in a jar of water or plant directly in small culture pots. Insert the cuttings 1–1½in (3–4cm) deep in 1/16–1/8in (2–4mm) turface. Cover them with a plastic bag or place in a propagator to reduce evaporation, and keep them in bright, indirect light for two weeks. As soon as new growth appears, remove the cover. Start normal watering and fertilizing two weeks after planting.

TYPES OF FERTILIZER

Slow-release cartridge, containing granular fertilizer, to clip into base of inner pot

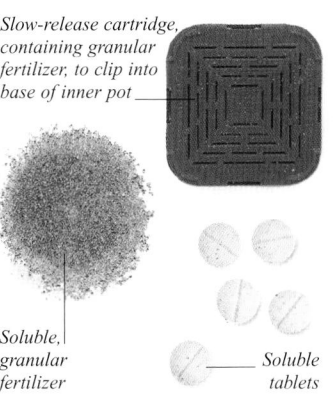

Soluble, granular fertilizer

Soluble tablets

Fertilizers for use with hydroculture pots are formulated for tapwater of various hardnesses.

Bonsai

BONSAI is the art of producing miniature trees and shrubs, mainly through specialized pruning techniques. Several styles of bonsai have been developed, all of which aim to produce a graceful plant resembling a full-sized tree or natural feature such as a waterfall or mountain. Bonsai are grown in shallow containers, indoors or outdoors, depending on the species.

Bonsai styles

There are five basic styles with many variations. All are based on the ways trees grow naturally and are defined by the angle of the trunk, so choose the right style for your plant.
Formal upright This has a tapered trunk, well-placed branches, and grows straight upward, indicative of an open growing area.
Informal upright This shape is often seen in nature, curving or bending to adapt to its growing conditions.

Slanting This bonsai has a trunk leaning by up to 45° as if to reach the light; its roots often become more substantial to anchor the tree.
Semicascade This grows up out of its pot then dips down so that the tip ends above the bottom of the pot.
Full cascade This grows at an upward slant and dips into a sinuous fall, with its tip level with or below the bottom of the pot. This form is grown in a tall container for balance.

Many other styles are recognized: over-rock or clinging-to-rock styles and group plantings (also called forests), are particularly popular.

Bonsai choices

The basic bonsai shape is created by pruning a young plant while also pruning its roots and restricting them in a container. Pruning requirements vary according to the species; the information below is intended only as a general outline.

Choosing the plant

There are two basic groups: hardy bonsai, which are summered outdoors and protected in winter, and tender bonsai, which may be kept indoors all year and even grown under lights.

Many small-leaved, woody plants are suitable for training as bonsai. Popular hardy evergreen choices include *Pinus thunbergii* and *Juniperus procumbens* 'Nana', which provide year-round foliage. Many *Pyracantha* and *Cotoneaster* have the bonus of colorful berries.

Among hardy deciduous species, honeysuckles (*Lonicera*) and hawthorns (*Crataegus*) have small leaves, whereas maple (*Acer*) species have striking foliage that changes color throughout spring, summer, and fall. Azaleas (*Rhododendron*) and *Wisteria* have spectacular blossoms, whereas *Betula pendula* and *Euonymus alatus* feature attractive bark. Easy-to-grow tender bonsai include weeping fig (*Ficus benjamina*), with interesting aerial roots, and

dwarf pomegranate (*Punica granatum* 'Nana'), which bears small leaves and fruit. *Serissa foetida* is available in single- and double-flowered forms. *Schefflera actinophylla* has large leaves that reduce over time; whereas *Cuphea hyssopifolia* has small, very narrow leaves and pinkish purple flowers.

Buy a healthy, potgrown plant with balanced branches and a sturdy trunk. Alternatively, bonsai may be raised from seed, cuttings, or seedlings, and the plants shaped from the outset. Container plants may be planted out for several years before training to thicken the trunk.

Selecting a container

In the art of creating a bonsai, it is essential to choose the right container. Choose one that is in scale with the tree and, if for a slanting tree, deep enough to balance the top-growth. Ceramics (with unglazed interiors), wood, plastic, or stone may be used. The container needs drainage holes and a base rim or small feet to elevate the pot: this increases drainage and aeration and discourages pests. Hardy bonsai need a frostproof pot.

Creating a bonsai

To create the chosen style, prune the roots and top-growth when planting the new bonsai. Then plant the tree and wire the trunk and branches to produce the desired form.

BASIC BONSAI TOOLS

Bonsai tools can be bought singly or in sets. This basic set includes trimming shears (left) for use on branches, leaves, and roots; a concave branch cutter (center) for pruning; and a wire cutter (right) for trimming and removing wire.

BONSAI STYLES

FORMAL UPRIGHT

Straight trunk tapering toward the apex

Balanced branch spread

SEQUOIADENDRON GIGANTEUM

INFORMAL UPRIGHT

PUNICA GRANATUM

Delicate branches with bushy foliage

Curving trunk

SLANTING

PINUS MUGO

Evenly spaced branches

Slanting trunk

SEMICASCADE

Plant grows upward then dips down

Tip ends above bottom of pot

Deep pot for balance

PYRACANTHA

FULL CASCADE

Downward growth is encouraged

Tip growing down to level of pot bottom

Deep pot for balance

RHODODENDRON INDICUM 'HAKUREI'

Initial root and top pruning
Remove the bonsai from its original container. Trim the roots, as sparingly as possible, to make a shallow root system that will fit the selected container. Shorten or completely remove shoots and branches to emphasize the basic framework of the chosen style and to stimulate shoots and buds to form near the branches.

Planting
Prepare the container by placing nylon mesh over the drainage holes. To secure the root ball, thread an anchorage wire through two drainage holes; pull the ends of the wire up and over the sides of the container.

Spread a soil-based mix in the base of the pot and position the bonsai so that it faces in the best direction for viewing. Pull the anchor wire across or through the root ball, twist the ends together, and bend them down. Work dry soil mix between the roots, then backfill. Top-dress with moist moss or gravel.

Wiring
Most bonsai need to be trained with wire to produce the desired shape. Wrap wire (usually copper, aluminum, or copper-coated aluminum in various gauges) evenly around trunk and branches. Between late fall and early spring is generally the best time to wire; to make the tree more flexible, stop watering three days before wiring. For deciduous trees and most tender bonsai, wiring can be left in place for three to six months; for evergreens, six months to a year. Check and renew wiring often to prevent the wire from cutting into the branches.

Routine care
Bonsai need detailed attention to maintain their shape. Protect outdoor plants from cold and wind. Treat pests and diseases as soon as they are noticed (see pp. 633–61).

Watering and fertilizing
Water regularly – a few times a day in hot or windy conditions. For moisture-loving species, insert wicking (such as nylon yarn) in the soil, and place the wick tip in water.

Give bonsai a balanced fertilizer during the growing season. In fall, apply a fertilizer high in phosphorus and potassium. Never fertilize newly root-pruned or repotted bonsai.

Pruning top-growth
Top-growth needs pruning to remove unwanted branches and leaves and encourage more, smaller branches

and leaves. Species grown as bonsai are usually pruned at the same time as full-sized plants. For bushy, short-noded growth, cut back regularly any long, straggly shoots. Different species have specific needs; seek advice from a specialist.

Root pruning and repotting
Root pruning encourages stronger, more fibrous roots. It is usually done in the spring when repotting. Root prune and repot every year for new bonsai, and every two to three years for mature plants. Trim roots by one-third, cutting them at an angle so that they heal quickly; replant with fresh soil mix in a clean pot.

HOW TO CREATE A BONSAI

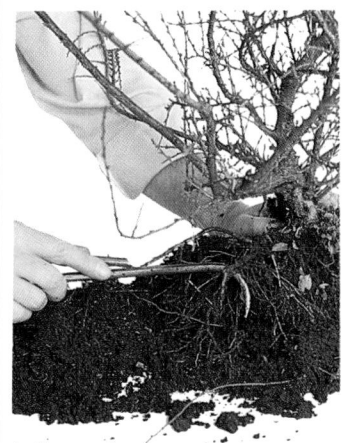

1 *Gently loosen, then remove the soil from the root ball. Comb the roots, carefully pulling them outward and downward.*

2 *Prune long and downward-growing roots. Rotate the plant (here Cotoneaster horizontalis) to determine the best angle for viewing.*

3 *Using trimming shears, remove all growth that is not appropriate to the chosen style. Shorten branches and thin them out to reveal the trunk.*

4 *Prepare the container, anchor the plant, then fill with soil mix. Here a large root remains above the surface as an extra feature. Top-dress with moss and stones, firming them into place.*

5 *New leaves will grow to fill out the bonsai, which is an informal upright shape. The alternating branches form a balanced plant, and the foliage is well distributed with the greatest mass at the base and the smallest at the apex.*

WIRING TECHNIQUES
Wire branches while they are supple when young, or in late fall or early spring. Leave room for branches to thicken. Start the wire in the soil, and wind it up the trunk and around the lowest branch. Wire together higher branches for support. Use fine-gauge wire at the apex.

Wire the apex together with an upper branch

Wire two branches with the same piece of wire

Coil wire for the lowest branch around the trunk, then along the branch

Wire starts in the soil behind the trunk

Training and pruning plants grown under cover

THE basic principles of training and pruning under cover are much the same as for outdoors, although it may be necessary to adapt them to accommodate extended flowering periods and limited space. Climbing plants that are too tender to be grown in the open may be readily cultivated under cover. If properly trained and pruned, they make efficient use of confined space and provide shade for other plants.

Plant supports

Plants that need support when grown under cover include ornamental climbers, some shrubs, annuals, fruiting vegetables, fruit trees, and grapes (*Vitis*). True climbers find their own ways up supports (see "Climbing methods and supports," p.122), while shrubs, grown as climbers against a wall, need tying in.

Some grapes require a permanent, rigid support securely attached to the framework of a wooden greenhouse or to the glazing bars of an alloy-framed one. Wires, stretched horizontally along the walls of the greenhouse, are useful for training all climbers. In lean-to greenhouses,

CLIMBING PLANTS FOR GROWING UNDER COVER

Prune after flowering
Allamanda cathartica
 'Hendersonii' ⊚
Bougainvillea
Clerodendrum thomsoniae⊚
Distictis buccinatoria
Jasminum
Kennedia rubicunda
Mandevilla splendens⊚

Mandevilla splendens

Pandorea
 jasminoides
Passiflora
Senecio
Solanum wendlandii⊚
Stephanotis floribunda⊚
Thunbergia

Prune as required
Agapetes macrantha
Asarina erubescens
Cissus
Cobaea scandens
Gynura aurantiaca⊚
Hoya
Ipomoea horsfalliae
Stigmaphyllon ciliatum

KEY
⊚ *Requires high humidity*

ESTABLISHING THE SUPPORT FRAMEWORK

Stretch wires tightly between vine eyes (see inset). Tie in the stronger shoots and prune them to downward-growing buds to encourage horizontal growth.

stretch the wires between vine eyes attached to the rear wall to avoid cutting out light. Alternatively, attach the wire to drilled and bolted vertical wall supports. Keep the wires taut by using a straining bolt at the end of each wire. Space the wires at equal intervals: grapes require a 10in (25cm) spacing; fruit trees 15–18in (38–45cm). Tie in the stems of climbers with soft string to horizontal or vertical support wires.

Netting may be attached to the framework of the greenhouse and used to support plants. Plastic netting deteriorates and needs replacing after one or two seasons, so it is not suitable for perennials. Instead, use plastic-coated wire netting.

There are some useful specially made, wire-mesh frameworks and various forms of wooden trellises available: attach them securely to supports mounted to the greenhouse wall. Train the plants gently along netting or mesh as they grow, and tie them in with soft string.

Annual ornamental climbers or fruiting vegetables such as tomatoes may be tied with soft string to bamboo stakes placed vertically at 6–12in (15–30cm) intervals. Alternatively, drop lengths of strong string from secure hooks in the roof to the base of the plants. Tie the string loosely below the plant's first true leaf, then wind it around the stems and run it back to the frame. Never let the string become too tight around the stem of the plant. For details of the treatment needed for particular plants, see the pruning and training sections in the relevant chapters.

Pruning plants grown indoors

Like plants that are grown outdoors, many indoor plants require regular pruning to maintain their vigor and encourage flowering. Others simply become too big for the space available or need cutting back in order to maintain an attractive and balanced framework. Most plants may be trained and shaped by pruning, cutting back, or pinching out. Drastic pruning is required only to remove old, weakened sections or to renovate a neglected plant.

Always use tools with well-sharpened blades to avoid damaging the remaining stems, and make a downward, sloping cut above a bud to stimulate the growth of new shoots. A sharp knife is ideal for working on soft stems; use a pair of pruners for woody ones.

When and what to prune
The best time for pruning depends on the flowering season of the plant and on the age of wood on which plants bloom. Some plants flower only on the new season's growth, and on these the old growth may be safely cut back in the spring without harming the production of the next season's flowers. Others flower on older wood so should be cut back after flowering. See guidelines given on pruning ornamental shrubs (pp.101–8), climbers (pp.132–5), and on pruning to produce fruit on grapes (pp.456–59) and tree fruits (pp.429–54).

CUTTING BACK AFTER FLOWERING

Cut back the flowered shoots to leave two or three buds. This encourages the production of next season's flowering shoots, which should be tied horizontally into the wires.

Pruning to restrict growth
Under cover, space for shrubs and climbers is always limited. Although major problems can be avoided by choosing the most suitable plant for the size of the greenhouse, it may be necessary to restrict growth to stop plants from blocking the light. Climbers that grow in the ground need to be rigorously controlled after they have filled their allotted space, since they may overwhelm other plants.

Few shrubs and ornamental climbers grown under cover flower on old wood (but do check first), so pruning back fairly hard after flowering is generally advisable and safe. The time of flowering varies not only from species to species but also according to temperature and location. Cut back overly long stems in fall; remove stray shoots whenever they appear, regardless of whether it is time to prune or not.

Some plants flower for much of the year under cover, yet they must be pruned to control them. In early spring, cut out the previous season's growth on mature *Abutilon* hybrids and cut back *Coronilla* and *Hibiscus*. *Hoya* species and cultivars continue to flower on old flowered stems, so do not remove them. *Agapetes* flowers on old wood but may need cutting back to induce bushiness.

Pinching out
To improve the shape and increase the number of flowering shoots on young, climbing, or trained shrubs, pinch out the tips of new shoots throughout the growing season.

Shrubs that respond well to this treatment include fuchsias, *Abutilon*, *Brunfelsia*, *Centradenia*, *Hibiscus*, *Reinwardtia*, and *Tibouchina*.

FALL PRUNING TO RESTRICT GROWTH

In fall, cut out the weaker shoots and reduce dense growth. This allows plenty of light to penetrate the foliage and encourages the development of strong shoots to form a sturdy framework.

Pinch pruning

Also known as "finger-and-thumb pruning," the technique of repeated pinch pruning as a plant develops can be used to produce decorative shapes in a range of tender subshrubby plants, such as coleus (*Solenostemon*), fuchsias, *Helichrysum*, and *Pelargonium*. Simple shapes such as fans and cones are well within the grasp of a novice gardener; with experience, all kinds of forms are possible – the favorites being a ball, pillar, and pinch-pruned standard. Pinching, although a fairly simple technique, must be repeated at frequent, regular intervals troughout the growing season. No tools are generally required.

Shaping the plant

Plants must be healthy in order to respond well to this technique. Site plants growing under cover in a well-lit, well-ventilated position. Always pinch prune young plants right from the start, encouraging them to form bushy mounds before beginning to form a more specific shape.

With your finger and thumb, pinch out the tip of the shoot just above an opened leaf. Remove only the very tip to stimulate the maximum number of buds into producing sideshoots. Side buds will then break and develop into shoots. When these have developed two to four leaves (or two pairs), repeat the process.

Pot young plants on regularly, while they are maturing. For some shapes, such as a fan, two or more specimens should be planted in the same pot. Do not pinch prune a week or so before or after potting to enable root systems to reestablish well. After that, start pinching the growing tips out of young plants regularly once again to encourage dense growth and a compact form.

FINISHED COLEUS FAN

Training frames and supports

Once plants are in their final pot, a supporting framework may be erected around them to assist training to the desired shape. Bamboo stakes, wire, and wire netting, both large- and small-gauge, can be used to create a variety of interesting forms, such as cones, pillars, and fans. If a large framework is needed, be sure that the pot is also sufficiently large to give the trained plant stability. The head of a pinch-pruned standard usually needs no frame but is formed entirely by bushy growth, pinch pruned regularly and carefully over time to create and maintain an even shape However, no subshrub can, in one season, produce a stem sturdy enough to support the head of a standard, so staking is required initially until the main stem thickens.

Routine care

Pick off discolored leaves as seen. Give young plants a fertilizer high in nitrogen to stimulate growth, then, when pinching stops, switch to a high-potash fertilizer to stimulate flower development or, in coleus, to allow the leaf color to develop fully.

With flowering plants, such as fuchsias, once the shape is formed to your satisfaction, stop pinching about two months before flowers are desired, to give the terminal flower buds time to develop. Flowering should be simultaneous – and dramatic. With foliage plants, where flowers are not wanted (such as coleus and *Helichrysum*), continued pinching will prevent the formation of flower buds.

In cool climates, plants can be moved out of doors after the danger of frost has passed, either onto a patio or planted out as summer bedding, then if desired brought back under cover to overwinter. In spring, trimming and pinching are resumed as new growth begins.

Do not fertilize flowering plants while they are overwintering.

PINCH PRUNING A COLEUS FAN

1 *Pinch out all shoots as they develop until the plants are 10in (25cm) tall. Then pinch only on two opposite sides, developing a flattened shape to the plants.*

SUPPORTING FRAMEWORK
When the plants are 20in (50cm) tall (see left), they will need the support of a framework, made from stakes arranged and tied as a fan.

2 *Carefully insert the stakes that form the fan's ribs into the pot, along the flattened outline of the plants, and tie in cross-bars to brace them.*

3 *Using figure-eight knots and soft twine, tie in stems to the stakes wherever possible, gently drawing some growth down to the horizontal.*

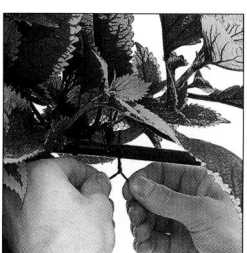

4 *Allow all shoots that extend toward the perimeter of the fan to grow on, tying them in at regular intervals to the stake framework. Continue pinching all shoots on the flat faces of the fan.*

SIDE VIEW OF FAN
Once the frame is covered, the fan shape can be maintained by pinching all growth. This will also stimulate the production of brightly colored young leaves.

371

Propagation

PROPAGATING indoor plants is an economical way to increase your stock and to replace old plants with younger, more vigorous specimens. Successful propagation requires clean conditions, warmth, light, and sufficient humidity.

The easiest method of propagation is by division, which produces only a few plants at one time. The majority of new plants for growing indoors or under cover are grown from seed or cuttings, however, since these methods usually yield a greater number of new plants. Some plants may be increased by layering.

Propagation by division

Division is a quick way to propagate plants. Many plants produce plantlets, runners, offsets, or bulbils, which root themselves and may be severed from the parent and potted up.

Dividing the rootstock

Before dividing a pot plant, water the root ball thoroughly and allow it to drain. Herbaceous and clump-forming plants may be gently pulled apart or cut into separate pieces, each with its own root system, and repotted. Use a sharp knife to separate the fleshy roots of rhizomatous plants; retain vigorous sections with young growth and fibrous, feeding roots. Prune any long, thick roots, and any that are damaged. Dust the wounds with fungicide. Replant each division in a clean pot using a similar soil mix to that used for the parent plant. Water the plants appropriately and keep them in good light, but out of direct sun, until they are established. See also "Potting on and top-dressing," p.364.

Dividing plantlets

Plantlets are small versions of the parent plant that grow on its leaves, sto-lons, stems, or inflorescences. Once they are large enough to handle, detach them with about 1¼in (3cm) of the leaf stalk or stolon, where appropriate. Insert the plantlet stalk in a pot of peat-based soil mix so that the plantlet rests on the surface. Water the pot and cover it with a clear plastic bag to preserve the humidity. Roots should form in about three weeks. After this, the plantlet may take several more weeks to resume growth, at which point it is ready to pot on.

Dividing rooting runners

Some plants, such as *Saxifraga stolonifera* (syn. *S. sarmentosa*) and *Episcia*, spread by runners. If these are rooted individually in pots of soil mix, they may then be severed from the parent to make new plants.

Dividing offsets and bulbils

Offsets are small plants that develop around the base of plants. Choose a well-developed one with some roots. Cut or break it off cleanly from the main stem and insert it in a pot of moist soil mix. Cover the pot with a

INDOOR PLANTS THAT MAY BE DIVIDED

Plantlets/runners
Chlorophytum
Episcia, some◉
Haworthia
Saxifraga stolonifera◉

Maranta leuconeura
var. *kerchoviana*

Rootstock
Adiantum◉
Anthurium
Aspidistra
Calathea◉
Cyperus
Maranta leuconeura◉
Phlebodium aureum◉
Phyllitis◉
Pteris cretica◉
Sansevieria
Stromanthe◉

KEY
◉ *Requires high humidity*

HOW TO PROPAGATE POT PLANTS BY DIVISION

1 *Thoroughly water the plant (here* Calathea) *an hour before dividing it. Support the plant, then invert the pot and tap its rim on a hard surface. Slide out the plant.*

2 *Remove surplus soil mix, either by gently shaking the plant or by teasing some of the medium away with your fingers, so that the roots are accessible.*

3 *Use hands or a hand fork to separate the root ball into sections, each with a portion of roots. Take care not to damage the stems or fibrous roots.*

4 *Using a clean, sharp knife, trim back any thick roots so that the divisions will fit into their new pots, but take care to leave the delicate fibrous roots intact.*

5 *Select sections with healthy, young shoots (see inset) for replanting. Insert each section in a pot of moist, soil-based mix. Gently firm the medium and water well to encourage the roots to establish. Label the pot.*

PROPAGATION BY ROOTING RUNNERS

1 *Peg down runners (here* Saxifraga stolonifera) *in individual 3in (6cm) pots of moist, standard rooting medium. Keep them well watered.*

2 *After a few weeks, separate each rooted plantlet, still in its pot, from the parent by cutting the runner close to the young plant. Label the pot.*

clear plastic bag until new growth is produced.

Some plants produce bulbils on the fronds or in the leaf axils. Detach these and root them in moist, soil-based medium. For further information, see LILIES, *Propagating from Stem Bulbils*, p.245.

Growing indoor plants from seed

The seed of pure species breeds true, but that of many hybrid indoor plants does not. Uniform results may be obtained, however, from selections, or first generation (F1) hybrids of biennials, annuals, and a few perennials, such as cyclamen and geraniums.

Sowing media and containers

Use a medium prepared specifically for seed (see SOILS AND FERTILIZERS, "Propagation media," p.622). It should be a free-draining and open-textured medium that holds moisture without becoming sodden or forming a hard crust on the top.

A variety of containers can be used, such as half pots, pans, and half or quarter seed trays. Always use a size of container that is appropriate to the number of plants required. Special cell packs that allow each seed to grow in its own individual plug of soil are also readily available.

When to sow

Most seeds are spring-sown, but seeds of early spring-flowering species are usually sown in fall. Annuals may be sown in several batches from spring to early summer for a succession of blooms. Seeds of many exotic species are spring-sown but often germinate freely if sown as soon as they are ripe. It may be difficult, however, to keep the young seedlings alive in winter.

Preparing the seed

Some seeds need special treatment to help them germinate. Seeds with hard coats often need presowing treatment, such as soaking in warm water. The time required varies from about ten minutes for *Cordyline australis* to 72 hours for banana seed. Other hard-coated seeds, such as *Caesalpinia pulcherrima*, will not germinate if the seed coat is not chipped with a knife or file. If the seed is too small to handle, gently abrade it between two sheets of fine sandpaper. Follow the supplier's instructions on the seed packet to ensure success.

Sowing the seed

Overfill the container with standard sowing medium and tap it on the bench; scrape off the surplus so that the medium is level with the container rim. Firm the medium to within ½in (1cm) of the rim.

Water the medium before sowing the seed, and allow the container to drain well. (Watering with a watering can after sowing may bunch the seed or wash it together, leading to problems with overcrowding and damping off later.)

Sow all seed thinly and evenly. Tiny seed is easier to sow if it is first mixed with horticultural sand. Place large seeds far enough apart to allow seedlings to grow without being thinned later on. Alternatively, sow the seeds singly into small pots, cell packs, or soil blocks.

As a general rule, cover seeds with medium to the depth of their smallest diameter. Very tiny seeds, however, or seeds that require light to germinate, should be left uncovered on the surface of the medium.

Cover the container with a sheet of glass, a plastic bag, or a propagator lid to stop the medium from drying out and maintain humidity. Place the container in the correct temperature, in bright but not direct light, and allow the seed to germinate.

Germination temperatures

Seeds usually germinate at 10°F (5°C) higher than the minimum needed by the same plant in growth. As a general rule, a temperature of 59–64°F (15–18°C) is suitable. The correct temperature varies for different seed, so follow the instructions given on the seed packets. Plants that are raised under cover for growing outside germinate at 50°F (10°C) or less. Many tropical or subtropical plants need 75–9°F (24–6°C) to germinate. If it is hard to maintain such temperatures indoors, consider using a heated propagating case. Although there are many different types and sizes, most have thermostats that allow a specific temperature to be maintained.

Aftercare of sown seed

Wipe off any condensation on covers to discourage fungal diseases. After seven to ten days, check the containers daily for signs of germination and remove the covers as soon as the seedlings appear. Germination times vary greatly, however; some larger seeds may take several months to germinate. Keep the medium moist; use either a watering can or, for very delicate seedlings, a mist-sprayer.

Fertilizing should not be necessary if seed was sown in a medium containing a small amount of nutrient. However, seedlings that are to stay in their container for some time may benefit from a liquid fertilizer as they grow. If the seedlings start to bend toward light, turn them daily and shade with cardboard or netting if there is danger of sun scorch.

Pricking out the seedlings

When the seedlings are ½in (1cm) high, they may be pricked out into larger pots or packs. Water them first, allow them to drain for an hour, then loosen them by tapping the side of the container. Lift the seedlings out of the container using a small, flat implement. If the seedlings are clumped together, use a dibber or pencil to tease them apart. Handle the seedlings carefully by the leaves since the stems are easily damaged.

Use a dibber to make holes in some fresh soil mix in a container. Lower each seedling into place so that it is at the same depth as before. Place more mix around the roots and lightly firm in each seedling. Small seedlings

---

INDOOR FLOWERING PLANTS THAT MAY BE RAISED FROM SEED

Alonsoa
Begonia☺
Browallia
Caesalpinia pulcherrima
Campanula☺
Clitoria
Cobaea
Cordyline australis
Cuphea
Cyclamen☺
Exacum affine☺
Impatiens☺
Jacaranda mimosifolia
Pelargonium (modern zonal hybrids)
Primula x *kewensis*☺,
P. malacoides☺,
P. obconica☺,
P. sinensis☺

Primula malacoides

Salpiglossis
Schizanthus
Senecio x *hybridus*
Sinningia
Streptocarpus
Thunbergia
Torenia

KEY
☺ *Requires high humidity*

RAISING INDOOR PLANTS FROM SEED

1 *Mix very fine, dustlike seed (here* Campanula) *with dry, fine sand in a bag; this makes it possible to sow the seed more evenly. Sow larger seed by hand.*

2 *Sow the mixture thinly onto a pot of moist sowing medium, using a small fold of paper held close to the surface of the medium. Label and place in a propagator.*

3 *When the seedlings are large enough to handle by their leaves, use a dibber to prick them out into a container of moist soil mix.*

4 *Once the seedlings have become established, pot them on singly into individual pots or cell packs to grow on. Water and label each pot.*

should be set about 1in (2.5cm) apart, and larger ones about 2in (5cm). Water the seedlings with a fine spray. For seedlings that are sown individually in a cell pack, lift the seedling with its plug of soil mix, and pot it up.

Potting on

Once the roots of plants have filled the containers, they need potting on (see p.364). The new pot should be large enough to allow for a 1in (2.5cm) gap all around the root ball. Insert the plant so that the base of its stem is level with the surface of the soil mix. Settle the soil mix by tapping the pot on a bench, firm it lightly, and water with a fine spray.

Once potted on in normal soil mix, the new plants can be treated as mature specimens. Be sure that the correct conditions are maintained; different indoor plants have widely varying requirements.

Propagation from cuttings

Most tender indoor plants may be readily propagated from softwood (tip) cuttings (rooted in a medium or in water), leaf-bud, or leaf cuttings. Semiripe or woody cuttings may be taken from indoor shrubs. The important factors for success with cuttings are timing, hygiene, warmth, and humidity.

Semiripe cuttings

Take cuttings of semiripe wood from the current season's growth, in summer after the main flush of fast, spring growth but before the wood is fully mature. Suitable material is firm, but flexible, and offers some resistance if bent. Plants grown under cover may reach maturity before midsummer, so check new shoots carefully from early summer onward. For details of the technique, see ORNAMENTAL SHRUBS, "Semiripe cuttings," p.110.

Leaf-bud cuttings

Genera such as *Ficus* and *Hoya* may be increased by leaf-bud cuttings, a type of semiripe cutting. Cut stems into 1–2in (2.5–5cm) lengths, each with a single leaf and leaf axil bud. Then insert them into pots of rooting medium and place the pots in a propagator at a temperature of 59–64°F (15–18°C). For further details, see ORNAMENTAL SHRUBS, "Leaf-bud cuttings," p.111.

Softwood cuttings

These are taken in early spring. Select new, short-noded sideshoots and remove them with a clean, sharp knife. When preparing the cuttings, make precise cuts so that no snags are left on the stems. Dip the base of each stem in hormone rooting powder and, using a dibber or a pencil, insert several cuttings into each pot of standard rooting medium. The cuttings may be placed close together or arranged around the edges of a pot, making sure that their their leaves do not touch.

Place the pot in a propagator or cover it with a plastic bag to reduce water loss – make sure that the bag does not touch the cuttings, however. Leave the pot in a warm, bright position but out of direct sunlight. Check the cuttings each day or two and, if necessary, clear any condensation by opening the propagator or bag for a short time.

It should take about four to six weeks for new roots to form. At this stage, when young growth can be seen, transfer the cuttings to individual pots of peat- or soil-based mix to grow on. Keep the young plants in a warm, lightly shaded place until they are well established.

INDOOR PLANTS THAT MAY BE PROPAGATED BY SOFTWOOD CUTTINGS

Abutilon
Acalypha ⊕
Aeschynanthus ⊕
Alloplectus ⊕
Bougainvillea

Brunfelsia pauciflora

Brunfelsia pauciflora ⊕
Callisia
Catharanthus
Cissus
Codiaeum ⊕
Columnea ⊕
Crassula ⊕
Crossandra ⊕
Epiphyllum ⊕
Epipremnum
Euphorbia pulcherrima
Ficus benjamina
Fittonia ⊕
Gardenia ⊕
Gynura ⊕
Hibiscus

Hibiscus rosa-sinensis 'The President'

Hoya
Impatiens ⊕
Iresine ⊕
Ixora coccinea ⊕
Jasminum mesnyi
Justicia
Kalanchoe
Mandevilla splendens ⊕
Pachystachys
Passiflora
Pelargonium
Pellionia
Pentas lanceolata
Peperomia ⊕
Pilea ⊕
Plumbago auriculata
Polyscias ⊕
Rhipsalidopsis gaertneri,
    R. rosea
Rhipsalis ⊕
Rhoicissus capensis
Ruellia ⊕
Schlumbergera ⊕
Solenostemon (coleus)
Sonerila ⊕
Sparmannia ⊕
Stephanotis ⊕
Streptosolen
Syngonium ⊕
Tibouchina ⊕
Tradescantia ⊕

KEY
⊕ *Requires high humidity*

PROPAGATING FROM SOFTWOOD CUTTINGS

1 *Fill a 5in (13cm) pot with moist rooting medium, then tamp it down until it is level.*

2 *Using pruners or a clean, sharp knife, cut off some new, short-noded shoots 4–6in (10–15cm) long, just above a node. The plant shown here is* Gynura aurantiaca.

3 *Trim each cutting just below a node, removing the lower leaves to create a length of clean stem at the base (see inset). Do not leave snags, which might rot.*

4 *Dust the cuttings with hormone rooting powder and insert them in the pot so that the leaves are just above the medium.*

5 *Water and label the cuttings. Place the pot in a propagator in a warm, light place and maintain a soil temperature of 64–70°F (18–21°C) until the cuttings are rooted and ready to pot on.*

Rooting softwood cuttings in water

The simplest method of rooting softwood cuttings is to place them in a glass or jar of water in a bright, warm position. Prepare each cutting as for a normal softwood cutting, ensuring that the lower leaves are cleanly removed. Support the cutting on netting placed over the glass so that the stem is suspended in the water. When the roots develop and there is fresh growth, pot up the cuttings. Prepare pots with drainage material and 1in (2.5cm) of soil mix. Hold each cutting in a pot with its roots spread and fill in with soil mix until the roots are covered. Firm and water the cuttings thoroughly.

Propagating from leaves

Some plants may be propagated easily from whole leaves or leaf sections. In some cases, the leaves are inserted in a medium (or water), while in others they are scored or cut up before being inserted or secured flat onto the medium. Each leaf should produce a number of small plantlets where the leaf veins have been cut.

Whole leaves

Certain plants, often those with fleshy leaves growing in rosettes such as African violets (*Saintpaulia*) and gloxinias (*Sinningia speciosa*), as well as Rex and rhizomatous begonias and some succulents (see p.341), may be increased from leaf cuttings.

For the cuttings, choose healthy, undamaged, fully grown leaves and cut them off close to the base of the leaf stalks. Trim each stalk with a straight cut 1¼in (3cm) below the leaf blade. Insert the cuttings individually into prepared pots of rooting medium (1 part sand and 1 part peat), label, and water. Place the pots in a propagator or cover each one with a clear plastic bag or improvised cloche (see below). As soon as each leaf cutting produces plantlets, remove its cover. Grow on until plantlets are large enough to be teased apart and potted on individually. Alternatively, leaves with long stalks (especially African violets) may be rooted in water, although rooting tends to take longer than in a medium.

Scored or cut leaves

The leaves of plants with prominent veins, such as Rex begonias and various members of the family

PROPAGATING SOFTWOOD CUTTINGS IN WATER

1 *Using a sharp, clean knife, remove healthy, short-noded cuttings 4–6in (10–15cm) long from a healthy, vigorous plant (here a coleus). Cut each just above a node.*

2 *Trim each cutting below a node and remove the lower leaves to create a length of clean stem at the base (see inset).*

3 *Insert the stems through a piece of chicken wire over the top of a jar of water. Be sure that the stems are in the water.*

4 *Keep the water filled up so that the lower end of each cutting is always below the surface. A network of roots should develop.*

5 *When the cuttings are well rooted, carefully plant each one into a 3in (6cm) pot of sandy soil mix.*

HALF-LEAF SECTIONS

1 *Divide the leaf (here Streptocarpus) by cutting out the midrib and exposing the veins.*

2 *Insert the sections, cut edges down, in shallow trenches. Gently firm them in.*

PROPAGATING INDOOR PLANTS FROM LEAF CUTTINGS

1 *Cut healthy leaves from the parent plant (here Saintpaulia). Insert each stalk in a small pot of rooting medium so that the leaf blade barely touches the medium.*

2 *Water, label, and cover the pots. Small covers made from the bases of plastic beverage bottles are suitable. Leave them in a warm, light place out of direct sunlight.*

3 *Each leaf should produce several plantlets. When these develop, remove the covers and grow them on until they are large enough to pot up individually.*

Gesneriaceae, for example *Strepto-carpus*, will produce small plantlets if they are scored or cut up and the cut veins are then kept in contact with a moist medium. The leaves may be divided either in half (cut lengthwise through the midrib) or into small sections, or they may be scored through.

Whichever method is used, keep the container in a propagator or in a clear plastic bag in a bright place but out of direct sunlight. Inflate the bag so that it does not touch the leaf sections, and seal it. The leaves being propagated should be kept at 64–75°F (18–24°C).

When clumps of plantlets develop from the cut veins, carefully lift and separate them, retaining a little medium around the roots of each one, and pot them up individually into 3in (6cm) pots of soil mix.

Some succulent plants, including *Sansevieria* and those that have flat-tened, leaflike stems such as *Epi-phyllum*, may also be propagated from "leaf" sections, although these are treated slightly differently. For details, see CACTI AND OTHER SUC-CULENTS, "Propagation from stem sections," p.342.

PROPAGATION FROM CUT LEAVES

1 *Select a young, healthy leaf (here* Begonia rex*) and make a ¹/₂in (1cm) long incision with a sharp knife straight across each of the strongest veins on the underside of the leaf (see inset).*

2 *Place the leaf, cut side down-ward, on a tray of rooting medium. Pin its veins to the medium. Label and place the tray in a propagator or a plastic bag.*

3 *Leave the tray in a warm place out of direct sunlight. When the plantlets have developed, carefully separate them from the leaf (see inset) and pot them on singly.*

LEAF SQUARES

1 *Cut 4 or 5 square sections the size of a postage stamp from a healthy leaf. Each piece should include a strong vein.*

2 *Place the sections, veins downward, on moist medi-um. Pin with wire hoops, then treat as other leaf sections.*

Propagation of tuberous begonias

When begonia tubers die back naturally in fall, store them in their pots at 41–50°F (5–10°C) in a dry place over winter. Alternatively, lift and clean the tubers, dust their crowns with fungicide, and store them in boxes of dry sand, vermiculite, or peat.

At the beginning of the growing season, place the tubers in a tray of moist, sandy soil mix (1 part sharp sand, 1 part peat-based soil mix). Place them in a temperature of 55–61°F (13–16°C). When new buds are clearly visible, cut the tubers into sections, making sure that each has at least one bud and some roots. Dust the sections with fungicide and allow them to dry for a few hours in a warm place. When the cut surfaces have formed calluses, pot up the sec-tions in soil-based mix. Do not firm the mix heavily or water it, since this encourages fungal attack.

Alternatively, allow new shoots to develop on the tubers, and use these as basal cuttings. Take the cuttings so that each retains an eye. Dip the base of each cutting in hormone rooting powder and insert them, ³/₄in (2cm) deep, around the edge of a pot or pan of soil-based mix.

1 *In fall, lift the dormant tubers and clean them. Dust the crowns with fungicide and overwinter them in a dry place.*

2 *In spring, place the tubers, concave side upward, 2in (5cm) apart and 1in (2.5cm) deep, in a tray of moist, sandy soil mix.*

3 *When shoots appear, cut the tubers into sections, each with a bud and some roots. Dust cut sur-faces with fungicide and allow to dry.*

4 *Pot up the sections singly in 5in (13cm) pots, with the top of each level with the soil mix surface. Water a little, and label.*

5 *Keep the pots in a propagator in a warm, frost-free place until the sections are established, then pot them on singly.*

BASAL CUTTINGS

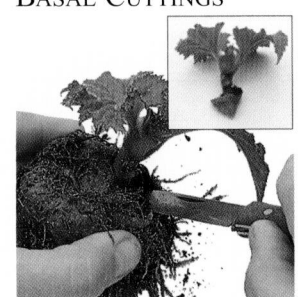

Remove 2in (5cm) shoots from the tuber, each with an eye of tuber at the base. Pot them up and treat as divided tubers.

Propagation by layering

Layering involves wounding the stem of a plant, inducing it to produce roots, and then separating the rooted stem. This method has a high success rate, since the layered stem receives nutrients from the parent plant while it is developing.

Some indoor plants may be propagated by layering – either in air or in soil mix. Air layering produces a fairly large, new plant from an older specimen but it may take some considerable time. Simple layering in soil mix provides new stock quite quickly.

Air layering

This is an excellent method for replacing old or damaged house plants, for example the rubber plant (*Ficus elastica*) and its relatives. The top of the plant, or tip of a branch, may be encouraged to form new roots, and is then severed from the parent.

Choose a section of stem of new growth that is straight, about 4in (10cm) long, and at least as thick as a pencil. Cut the bottom off a clear plastic bag to create a transparent sleeve and slip it over the stem or, if the leaves are too large to do this, fold a clear plastic sheet around the stem and tape up the seam. Secure the sleeve below the selected area of the stem.

Using a sharp knife, make a shallow, upward-slanting cut in the side of the stem, then wedge this tongue open with moist sphagnum moss. Alternatively, on woody plants, score two rings ½–¾in (1–2cm) apart below a healthy leaf joint on the selected area of the stem; the scores should be just deep enough to penetrate the bark without harming the wood. Carefully peel off the bark between the rings, leaving the cambium undisturbed.

In both cases, dust the cut area with rooting powder. Pack the sleeve with damp sphagnum moss and seal it to prevent the moss from drying out. If the stem of the plant is heavy, provide sturdy support.

It may be many months before the roots show. If the sphagnum moss begins to dry out, open up the plastic sleeve, add a little water, and reseal. When the roots begin to grow, sever the layered stem from the parent and pot it up into a soil-based mix. Water the young plant carefully until it is established.

Simple layering

Climbing or trailing shoots may be layered while they are still attached to the parent plant.

Choose a long, vigorous shoot and peg it down into a small pot of moist rooting medium or soil mix. After three to four weeks, roots should start to grow into the medium and new shoots begin to form. The rooted layer may then be detached from the parent plant. Several shoots may be layered at the same time, each in its own pot. When severing the new plants, always take care not to spoil the shape of the parent plant. For further information, see CLIMBING PLANTS, p.143.

SIMPLE LAYERING

Select a long, healthy shoot and peg down the young growth into a small pot filled with moist rooting medium. Leave it until roots have formed before detaching it from the parent plant.

Parent plant

Long, vigorous stem

Leaf node

Wire staple

Moist rooting medium

PHILODENDRON SCANDENS

HOW TO PROPAGATE BY AIR LAYERING

1 *Trim the leaves (here* Ficus elastica 'Tricolor') *from a straight length of stem (see inset). Slide a plastic sleeve over the stem and seal the lower end with tape.*

2 *Fold down the sleeve. Hold the stem firmly and cut a "tongue" in it, making a slanted, upward incision ¼in (5mm) deep and 1in (2.5cm) long.*

3 *Apply hormone rooting powder to the wound and push moist sphagnum moss into the incision, using a split stake or the back of a knife blade.*

4 *Roll the sleeve back into position around the packed incision. Fill the sleeve with more moist sphagnum moss.*

5 *When the sleeve is tightly packed with sphagnum moss, secure the upper end to the stem with tape.*

6 *When the new roots are visible through the sleeve, cut through the stem just below the root ball with pruners. Remove the plastic sleeve.*

7 *Gently loosen the moss ball and tease out the roots. Pot the rooted layer into a container that allows a 2in (5cm) space around the root ball. Fill this with soil-based mix and firm it very gently, making sure that the new roots are not damaged. Water, label, and place the pot in a shaded position until the young plant is established.*

377

CHAPTER
14

THE LAWN

FROM THE VELVETY green carpet in formal gardens to the closely mowed turf of a sports field or the rough grass under trees, there are many different types of lawn. Whether it is viewed as a showpiece in its own right, a contrast for beds and borders, a playing surface for children, or simply a relaxing haven, the lawn can be functional and attractive. For centuries, grass has been chosen to create lawns because it is visually appealing, pleasant to walk on, tolerates wear, and may be cut low without being damaged. Other species, such as chamomile and *Dichondra*, may also be used for lawns, but they are generally much less durable than grass. Frequently undervalued as merely a flat surface underfoot, the lawn may be used to complement other plantings, soften hard surfaces, separate and define features, and unify the garden as a whole.

Creating lawns

A HEALTHY, well-maintained lawn is an attractive feature that also provides an area in which to walk, play, and relax. For some, a lawn is primarily ornamental, while for others its function is paramount, and wearability is the most important consideration. Grass may be used for sports, in orchards and wild gardens, and for paths and on banks.

Some broad-leaved plants, for example chamomile (*Chamaemelum nobile*), may also be used to form lawns. They should, however, be considered primarily ornamental, to be admired rather than extensively used, because they are less tolerant of wear than grass (see "Nongrass lawns," p.383).

When deciding on the type and shape of the lawn as well as where to site it, consider how it will link to the rest of your property – to other plants, features, and the overall layout – so that it forms a compatible, unifying part of the design.

Grass

Grass is the plant most commonly chosen for a lawn because it is durable and attractive. It may also be repeatedly cut low without damage, because the growing point is at the base of the plant.

Mowed lawns

Mowed areas of grass include high-quality lawns, utility lawns, and sports fields. A primarily ornamental, high-quality lawn is suitable where a perfect, uniform appearance is paramount; it tolerates some wear but requires a considerable amount of maintenance to keep it in pristine condition. If the grass is likely to be subject to heavier wear, opt for a utility lawn; this should also be reasonably attractive, but it may contain minor imperfections and requires less maintenance.

Sports areas demand a durable surface that can be cut low. To stop unnecessary additional wear, they are best sited separately from the main lawn.

Long grass and meadows

As part of a wild garden or orchard, unmowed grass and a flower-filled meadow are very attractive but not very practical for a utility lawn, since the grass is relatively long. Meadows need very little maintenance, however, and therefore may be suitable for an area such as a slope, where mowing is difficult. Meadows often thrive on less than fertile soils.

In informal or semiwild gardens, bulbous plants such as daffodils look pretty when they are naturalized in a grassy area. The bulbs are best planted in an established area of medium or long grass that does not need frequent mowing, such as on a bank (see also BULBOUS PLANTS, "Planting in grass," p.222).

Mixing long and short grass

Using different grasses in various parts of the garden, or varying the height of cut, helps define separate

A FORMAL LAWN
Here, the close-clipped, pristine expanse of a high-quality formal lawn provides a uniform, fine-textured foil for an elegant planting of white Agapanthus, *silver-gray* Senecio, *and other complementary plants, plus it makes a platform to offset an ornamental garden seat and pots of marguerites* (Argyranthemum frutescens).

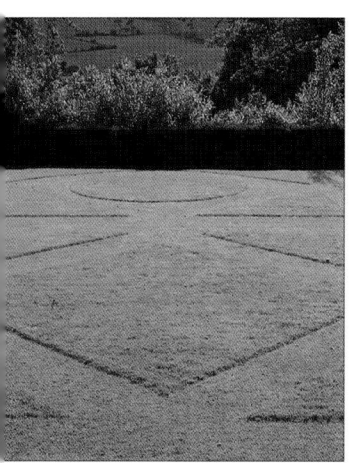

CONTRASTING TEXTURES
Altering the height of cut creates low-relief geometric patterns and provides definition or interesting textures in an area of lawn.

Form and position

The lawn may well be the largest single area in the garden, so it is important to plan its shape and position carefully within the context of the overall design. Take into account both practical and esthetic considerations so that the lawn will be pleasant to use, convenient to maintain, and an enhancing part of the overall plan.

Shape
The shape of the lawn may harmonize with the garden style or be used to dictate it. A symmetrical layout of geometrically shaped lawns bordered by paths would be elegant and appropriate in a highly stylized formal garden. In a small garden, a simple shape such as a circle could be visually striking and might be echoed imaginatively by the introduction of a circular pond or patio and containers packed with ornamental plants.

A curved, irregular design lends the garden an appealing fluidity, linking the different elements with a sweeping plane of uniform color. Broad, flowing curves can be created to set off the planting in a border and to lead the eye to a focal point, such as an architectural plant or a fountain. Steer clear of fussy scalloped edges or awkward angles, however, because they may detract from the impact of any planting and generally make mowing difficult.

Space permitting, it may be more pleasing to have more than one lawn: for example, two or more of similar or complementary shapes could be linked by paths or archways. The farther-away lawn could possibly be partially screened so that it provides an intriguing, half-glimpsed reflection of the nearer one.

INFORMAL LAWN
The bold, curving sweep of an informal lawn is echoed by a winding gravel path beyond and a ribbon of gold-leaved plants in an adjacent border.

areas and adds textural contrast. For example, a closely mowed path running through a tall, flower-rich meadow provides an eye-catching shift in height, color, and texture, and it also encourages people to walk only on the path.

On large-scale properties, consider having a small, low-cut, high-quality lawn sited near the house, where its fine appearance may be easily enjoyed; a path or steps could then lead to a larger utility lawn farther away, while an area of long grass and wildflowers could be included at the far end of the property. Mixing grasses in this way is both practical and attractive, providing contrasting but complementary ornamental, play, and wildlife-attracting areas. Mowing time is also reduced, since part of the area requires cutting only infrequently.

Design functions
As well as being attractive in its own right, the lawn may fulfill different design criteria for both plants and hard features. Uniform areas of grass create a natural bond between otherwise disparate elements, leading the eye from one part of the garden to another. A statue or specimen tree sited in a lawn has maximum impact, since the surrounding sea of plain color separates it from other more distracting elements. In a large lawn, one or two flower beds or trees may be extremely effective if they are positioned so that they break up the green expanse. Resist the temptation to dot the entire lawn surface with eye-catching features: besides making maintenance somewhat more time-consuming, the overall picture may be cluttered and disjointed.

The uniform texture and color of grass form a neutral background that enhances other planting particularly well. The level surface acts as a foil for more sculptural plants – the strong silhouette of a columnar tree or the jutting spread of a prostrate shrub – as well as for the variety of shapes, colors, and textures found in a mixed or herbaceous border.

Paths and access
Narrow areas of grass are usually subject to concentrated wear and are difficult to mow; for these reasons, paths narrower than about 3ft (1m) may be impractical. For a frequently used route across a lawn, such as from the house to the garden shed, consider laying stepping-stones or a hard path to prevent uneven wear.

If possible, leave at least one side of the lawn open for access; if there are only one or two narrow openings, the grass may become damaged at these points.

Edging
Edging the lawn with a band of paving stones or bricks helps define its shape and also that of the borders, and it has practical advantages. It makes it easier to cut the lawn right up to its edge while avoiding the risk of damaging other plants. Sprawling or trailing plants may be allowed to overhang the edge, breaking up any awkward rigidity but without depriving the grass beneath of light. In addition, ornamental containers may be set on the hard edging as focal points or to provide an interesting change of visual level. Alternatively, a narrow mowing strip of bare or mulched soil may be created at the edge of a lawn. This is particularly useful if the lawn is adjacent to a wall or fence, since the grass may be more easily mowed up to the edge.

GRASS PATHS
Including a closely mowed grass path through the garden allows a clear view of adjacent plants. Here, a broad, straight path contrasts with the informal planting of daffodils and shrubs and clearly indicates where people are expected to walk.

Climatic considerations

Turfgrasses are commonly divided into two main groups, depending on their temperature tolerance. Those that grow mainly in a temperate climate, preferring temperatures of 59–75°F (15–24°C), are known as cool-season grasses, while those that grow best in subtropical or tropical climates, thriving in temperatures of 79–95°F (26–35°C), are known as warm-season grasses. The latter are not normally used for lawns in temperate regions because they turn brown during winter as they become dormant. They will not survive the low temperatures found in much of Canada and are not covered here because their use is minimal.

Cool-season grasses

Temperate or cool-season grasses are widely used for lawns throughout North America. The grasses that are most commonly found in cool-season lawns are bents (*Agrostis*), tall and fineleaf fescues (*Festuca*), bluegrasses (also known as meadow grasses, *Poa*), and perennial ryegrass (*Lolium perenne*).

Bents are low-growing and, of all grasses, are the most tolerant of close mowing. They are widely used on high maintenance areas such as lawn bowling greens, which are mowed almost daily. In the home lawn their presence should be discouraged because, if allowed to grow to the height of an average lawn, they leave brown, dead-looking patches when mowed. They also require large amounts of fertilizer and water and are drought intolerant.

Fescues are fine leaved and may be cut low; they are quite hard wearing, and some species grow in poor soils. They also tolerate dry conditions, the competition from tree roots, and shade, making them the best choice for growing under trees. Their fertilizer requirements are moderate, but they grow poorly in high temperatures and should never be closely mowed then. Red fescue (*Festuca rubra*) is tolerant of acidic soils but does poorly in areas with hot and humid summers. Tall fescue (*F. arundinacea*) is more hardwearing than the other species and is a good choice for areas that receive heavy foot traffic. It will take more heat and sun that the other species but must not be cut too short or it will quickly begin to die out.

Bluegrasses are more resistant to wear but cannot be mowed very low, and some have quite coarse leaves. They are the grass of choice for most of Canada and are at their best in

HIGH-QUALITY OR UTILITY?

Grass varies in appearance, growth rate, and wear resistance: high-quality grass (right) has a fine texture; utility grass (far right) is better for a family lawn.

HIGH-QUALITY   UTILITY

spring, when they recover from winter and start into growth sooner than most other species. They spread by stolons (underground shoots) and can rapidly fill in any bare patches, but perform poorly unless grown in sunlight. Bluegrasses need at least six hours of full sun each day to thrive and are able to withstand high summer temperatures, although they grow best in cooler weather. Do not cut lower than 2in (5cm) during the growing season, although this height can be reduced in late fall to lessen the risk of diseases such as snow-mold during winter.

Ryegrass is extremely hard wearing and tolerates most soils, including heavy clay, but is coarse textured and does not like to be closely mowed. It is short lived but germinates rapidly and is frequently included in seed mixes to act as a nurse for other, more desirable species, giving them shelter until they become established.

Annual bluegrass (*Poa annua*) is also found in many lawns, but is often considered a weed by gardeners since it quickly runs to seed, forming coarse patches among fine-leaved grasses.

Cool-season grasses are often sown as mixtures of more than one species, although in some areas Kentucky bluegrass, which is also known as smooth-stalked meadow grass (*Poa pratensis*), and tall fescue are grown on their own. If sowing a single-species lawn, however, it is common to mix several cultivars together, because this improves the lawn's disease resistance and overall color (see "Choosing the right cultivars," opposite).

Selecting the right grass

Before selecting seed or sod, assess the relative importance of the lawn's appearance, wearability, and maintenance needs. Of the many grass mixtures available, some are best for areas of heavy use, while others give

attractive color and texture. The grass seed should also be suited to the growing conditions such as soil type, drainage, and degree of shade.

High-quality lawns

To create formal, high-quality lawns, select grass species that create an attractive, uniform texture and color.

For the highest quality lawns, a mixture of Kentucky bluegrass, perennial ryegrass, and red fescue is the best choice for most soils in eastern Canada and on the west coast. On the prairies, where additional water can be given, use a mix of equal parts Kentucky bluegrass and red fescue. A high-quality lawn can only be achieved by growing the right grasses for your region, fertilizing at the correct time, mowing frequently to the correct height, and giving supplementary water during periods of drought. For special areas, such as home putting greens, bents may be used, but they require close, frequent mowing to remain green.

Utility lawns

Lawns that are primarily functional, perhaps providing a play area for children or a space for outdoor entertaining, need to be relatively durable, but they must still provide an attractive, even surface. Grasses for this

PLAY AREAS
If the lawn is to include an area for games or play, as here, use a particularly durable grass mixture in order to prevent the lawn from becoming patchy.

purpose do not usually create the perfect texture and color of a high-quality lawn, since this is inevitably of secondary importance.

For hard-wearing lawns, the major grass is perennial ryegrass; it is usually mixed with red fescue, Kentucky bluegrass and chewings fescue (*Festuca rubra* var. *commutata*). New varieties of tall fescue are very hard wearing and hardy to at least -20°F (-30°C), but they must not be mowed lower than 2½in (6cm). On the prairies, use a 50/50 mix of Kentucky bluegrass and red fescue where additional water can be given, or one of the native grasses that can withstand drought conditions where it cannot.

The more desirable grass varieties have the smallest seeds. The price of commercial lawn seed mixes reflects this; an inexpensive grass seed mix contains a higher percentage of poor, large-seeded species and therefore far fewer seeds. Read the label carefully before buying a grass seed mixture to be sure it contains the best species for the location and purpose you have in mind.

Games and sports areas

Areas of grass used for playing ball games or sports require particularly wear-tolerant species and selected cultivars. Some sports fields must also tolerate a very low cut and have a fine finish to minimize the effect of the grass on the run of the ball.

A mixture of bluegrass, ryegrass, and fescues as for high-quality lawns (see above) tolerates some wear and is suitable for areas such as a croquet lawn. Bowling greens and putting greens need the very fine-leaved grasses such as bentgrass. These are very high maintenance species that will not stand up to heavy use and need specialized care to keep them in

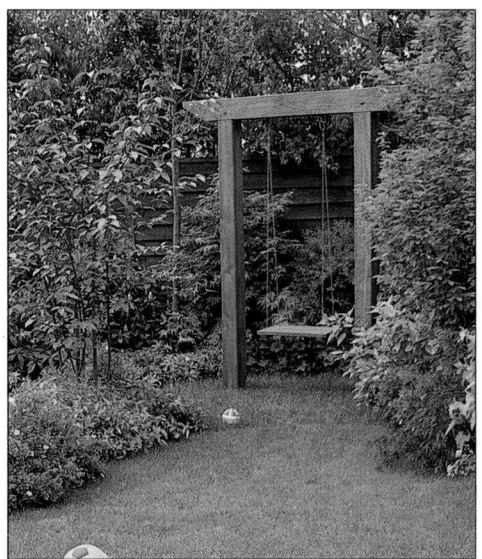

top shape. If a more hard-wearing surface is needed, such as for football or soccer, it is better to opt for a mixture containing ryegrass or tall fescue (see "Utility lawns", opposite).

Meadows

For meadows, whenever possible use grass species that are native to the area: as well as being more likely to flourish, they do not look incongruous or artificial (see also WILDFLOWER AND MEADOW GARDENING, p.395). Usually a meadow seed mixture consists of slow-growing grasses and various native, broad-leaved flowering species. In addition to climate, factors such as soil type, soil moisture, and exposure may influence the choice of species sown; some prefer extremely dry, well-drained conditions, whereas others grow well on marshy ground.

Bents and fescues are usually included, while a short-lived grass such as Italian ryegrass (*Lolium multiflorum*) may be added to provide initial, fast groundcover. If mowed, the Italian ryegrass will die out within two years, leaving behind the fine-leaved grasses and broad-leaved flowering plants. Some species need an overwintering or cold period before they will germinate and so may not appear in the first year after sowing.

Meadows should be mowed at least once each year unless you want them to revert to nature. Mowing will kill off most tree and shrub seedlings that may have germinated, although some aggressive species such as poplar (*Populus*) may survive and require removal by hand.

Problem areas

For lawns in difficult sites, such as shady, wet, or dry areas, choose a grass mixture that is specially designed for such conditions. If the problem is extreme, it may be better to grow groundcover plants instead (see GROUNDCOVERS, p.178).

Cool-season In wet, shady areas, grass does not readily grow into a dense, vigorous turf, but some species are more tolerant than others: rough-stalked bluegrass (*Poa trivialis*) with Kentucky bluegrass, and red fescue will form a lawn that will stand up to both wear and close mowing. In dry shade, use mostly red fescue, with some Kentucky bluegrass added for a better appearance. For areas where grass is desired but cannot be kept permanently (because of dense shade or excessive wear, for example), perennial ryegrass can be broadcast in spring and fall to provide an adequate groundcover throughout the growing season.

In very dry regions, use grasses native to such areas, such as western wheatgrass (*Agropyron smithii*) or buffalograss (*Buchloe dactyloides*), both of which grow naturally on the great plains of North America, or fairway crested wheatgrass (*A. cristatum*), native to the dry, cold plains of Russia and Siberia. The wheatgrasses generally produce medium- to low-quality lawns; cut to a height of 2in (5cm) or more to prevent weed encroachment.

Choosing the right cultivars

Many modern grass cultivars have been specially bred to provide qualities that are particularly valued in lawns, such as uniform color, disease resistance, tolerance of wear, and compact growth. When selecting grass seed, therefore, make sure that the mixture includes not only the correct species but also a modern cultivar of that species. New cultivars are introduced annually, so check with the retailer which cultivars are the best available for your particular lawn requirements. The grass mixture should not contain agricultural cultivars; these are bred to produce vigorous vertical leaf growth for grazing and need frequent mowing. They also tend to spread less and so do not always produce a dense, uniform cover.

Nongrass lawns

Although lawns are usually established with grasses, other evergreen species are sometimes used. These include chamomile (*Chamaemelum nobile*), *Cotula* species, *Dichondra micrantha*, and even various species of moss. Unlike many grasses, these groundcover plants do not stand up to heavy, continual wear, so they are rarely the best choice for the main lawn; they may, however, be used for primarily ornamental areas. Grow them in a patio or courtyard garden to provide a welcome patch of green; as a living edge for the base of a fountain, raised pond, pedestal urn, or statue; or next to a patio or path to creep over edges and relieve the rigidity of the hard surface.

Chamomile leaves release a sweet, applelike fragrance when crushed underfoot, but they do not tolerate heavy wear. The nonflowering clone 'Treneague' is naturally low-growing and especially suitable for lawns. *Cotula*, which has fernlike leaves, is considerably more durable because it

FLOWERS IN GRASS
*The grass in this informal orchard is dotted with bright yellow buttercups (*Ranunculus*) and the vivid red, white, and purple cups of naturalized tulips.*

forms a thick carpet of creeping stems; it also flourishes in moist conditions. *Dichondra*, a ground-hugging plant, has small, round leaves that look like waterlily pads. It grows most successfully in warm areas; it does not survive temperatures lower than 25°F (-4°C). Prepare soil as for a lawn, and plant small rooted cuttings spaced about 12in (30cm) apart. In shade, plants may grow up to 6in (15cm) tall and will need regular mowing; in sun, they remain low.

A few of the very tough perennial ground cover plants can also be used as a grass substitute and will quickly make a complete cover that will take considerable traffic. Bugleweed (*Ajuga reptans*) thrives in either sun or shade and will form a thick carpet of purple-tinged foliage that persists through the winter. If mowed immediately after flowering, it will not spread by seed into nearby flower beds, but still spreads by runners.

Bishop's weed (*Aegopodium*), also known as goutweed and ground elder, is an invasive spreader that also forms a dense mat that will withstand considerable wear, but it dies down in the fall. Either the plain green or the variegated form is suitable. They should be mowed back a couple of times each summer to keep them low, to encourage new foliage, and to prevent them from seeding.

Another option is to create a tapestry lawn with a patchwork quality by growing a number of low, mat-forming plants together. It is best to use plants that grow at a similar rate, such as the various creeping thymes, for example *Thymus praecox* var. *arcticus* 'Coccineus', *T. p.* var. *a.* 'Doone Valley', and *T. caespititius*; otherwise, one species may gradually predominate and upset the balance of the original design. As for other nongrass lawns, tapestry lawns should not be heavily used.

MOSS LAWN
Where grass may be difficult to grow, such as in the dappled shade of deciduous trees, a moss lawn provides an adaptable alternative. Unlike a grass lawn, however, it should be walked upon only in order to maintain it.

Soil and site preparation

THOROUGH site preparation is the key to establishing a successful new lawn. Although the treatment may be time-consuming and expensive, in the long run it is easier and cheaper to prepare the site properly at the outset than to try to alleviate problems at a later stage. The general principles of preparation apply to all sites, but decisions on drainage, soil improvement, and irrigation should depend on the individual site and the climate.

Clearing the site

It is important to clear the site completely, removing any large stones and rubble and all plant growth, including any tree stumps or roots. If the site is already partially grassed but in too poor a condition to be worth renovating, then remove all the turf (see also "Renovating a neglected lawn," p.393).

Eradicating weeds
Eliminate any perennial weeds with underground rhizomes or deep taproots, such as couch grass or quackgrass (*Elymus repens*), dandelion (*Taraxacum officinale*), bindweed (*Convolvulus arvensis*), and Canada thistle (*Cirsium arvense*), because they regenerate rapidly from small pieces of root or rhizome. It is very difficult to dig these out entirely, so before cultivating the soil, spray with a systemic weedkiller and then allow the weeds to die back completely before raking them away. Once the lawn grass is established, broadleaved weeds may still be controlled using selective weedkillers, but weed grasses will be more difficult to eliminate, so it is sensible to use a weedkiller to clear the ground initially.

Annual weeds such as lamb's-quarters (*Chenopodium album*) and shepherd's purse (*Capsella bursapastoris*) may be controlled by mowing after the grass has germinated. However, it is preferable to remove annual weeds before sowing.

Preparing the soil

The ideal topsoil for a lawn is a well-drained, sandy loam at least 8in (20cm) and preferably 12in (30cm) in depth, overlying a well-structured and freely draining subsoil. In these conditions the grass becomes deep-rooted and obtains ample water and nutrients from the soil.

Other soils may also be suitable, but if the soil does not drain freely and the lawn is likely to be heavily used, even in wet conditions, then the drainage should be improved. If the topsoil is very shallow or poor, it may be necessary to add new topsoil; this may be moved from other parts of the garden or bought, although for large areas the latter can be very expensive.

If the soil has a naturally high sand content, and is therefore too freely draining, incorporate some well-rotted organic matter to help retain nutrients and water (see "Soil structure and water content," p.614). Be careful, however, not to add too much; organic matter quickly rots down, and this may result in soil sinkage and an uneven lawn surface in later years.

After clearing the site, plow, rototill, or dig over the entire area, removing any large stones that are brought to the surface, then rake the ground to produce a fine tilth. Breaking up the soil in this way makes subsequent leveling easier, as well as relieving compaction and improving the soil structure. On heavy clay soils, however, rototilling or plowing may create a compacted layer (hardpan) below the soil surface, which could impede drainage: if necessary, break it up using a subsoiling machine or by double digging. For further information, see "Soil cultivation," pp.612–14.

Drainage
Lawns on free-draining soils, and those in regions with low rainfall, are unlikely to require draining. In heavy clay soils, drainage may be improved by digging washed and sieved river sand into the soil. Up to 6in (15cm) can be added, but this is expensive and laborious. In any soil that is not freely draining, installing a drainage system during the preparation stage will avoid continual and expensive attempts to alleviate the problem after the lawn is established.

The best type of drain for lawns consists of a row of pipes laid in a trench that is backfilled with gravel. The ideal depth of the drain and the distance between drains will vary from site to site depending on the type of soil and the rainfall. For most loamy soils receiving moderate rainfall, one drain every 15–25ft (5–8m) is needed. Heavier clay soils or sites in areas with a high rainfall will need drains laid at closer intervals (see also SOILS AND FERTILIZERS, "Improving drainage," p.617).

Adjusting the soil pH
For new lawns, the pH is unlikely to need adjusting, unless previous use has left the site in poor condition. Most grasses grow well at pH levels of 5.5–7. Fineleaf and tall fescues and bents grow best at pH 5.5–6.5, while perennial ryegrass (*Lolium perenne*), Kentucky bluegrass (*Poa pratensis*), and many warm-season grasses grow better at pH 6–7. Soil-testing kits for measuring pH are available from garden centers.

If the soil is very acidic (below pH 5), dig or rototill lime into the soil; the exact amount depends on the degree of acidity (see "Liming," p.619). Then leave the site for about a week before applying fertilizer. Lime may be added once the lawn is established, but since large amounts spread on grass may encourage certain diseases, use only a small quantity, and repeat the following year if necessary. If uncertain about what to do, seek advice from an agricultural or horticultural college, or your provincial Ministry of Agriculture.

Leveling the site

In gardens that have only minor undulations and deep topsoil, the site may be roughly leveled by raking soil from the high spots to fill the hollows, firming at intervals to settle the soil. Although it is not essential for the ground to be precisely level, awkward bumps and hollows may

---

HOW TO LEVEL THE GROUND

1 Firm the site well, especially at the edges, by tamping with the back of a rake or by treading. Mark some pegs at the same point on each peg. Insert a row of pegs at the site edge. If next to paving, the marks should be level with its surface.

2 Add a second, parallel row of pegs about 3ft (1m) from the first row. Place a level on top of these to check that they are level with the previous row. Adjust the pegs as necessary.

3 Repeat the process to create a grid of pegs all at the same level. Rake up the soil to the top of the marks on the pegs, adding topsoil to fill any hollows. Once the ground is level, the pegs may be removed.

ACCURATE LEVELING

To level the ground, first create a grid of premarked pegs and knock them into the soil at the same depth. Add or remove soil until it is level with the marks on the pegs.

cause problems when mowing. In some instances – for example, for an orchard or an area of rough sports grass – leveling by eye should be sufficient. But if a perfectly level surface is required, such as for a formal lawn, a more accurate method should be used.

Achieving an accurate level

After leveling the ground roughly, an exact level may be achieved by knocking pegs into the ground all at the same depth to form a grid.

Start from a straight edge such as a path or patio, or create a taut line with string. Then take a number of identical pegs and make a mark on each one at the same distance from the top. Starting from the straight edge, knock the pegs into the ground at equal intervals so that the marks are at the required level of the lawn, or approximately ¾in (2cm) below this if sodding. Add a second row of pegs and then additional rows until the site is covered by a grid of pegs.

Use a level – placed on a straight wooden board if necessary to span across the rows – to check that the

pegs within the rows are all at the same height. Then adjust the level of the soil so that it is aligned with the mark on each peg.

Substantial leveling

If the site needs more substantial leveling or the topsoil is very shallow, the subsoil must be leveled first. To do this, remove the topsoil, rototill or dig over the subsoil, then rake, level, and firm it roughly before replacing the topsoil in an even layer at least 8–12in (20–30cm) deep. To prevent the filled areas from sinking later, firm them thoroughly at intervals, adding more topsoil if necessary, and allow the site to settle before preparing the surface.

Creating a slope

Making the lawn slope gently away from the house or patio improves drainage and guarantees that water does not drain into the foundation. A method similar to leveling is used, but each successive row of pegs is marked farther up or down to form a sloping grid. For example, to create a gradient of 1:100, make the marks on

each row of pegs successively lower by ¹⁄₁₀₀ of the distance between the rows. If sloping the lawn down toward the house, install a drain or soakaway (see "Drainage systems and soakaways," p.617) to prevent water from reaching the house.

Final site preparations

Once the soil has been drained and leveled, the final surface may be prepared so that the site is ready for establishing a lawn.

Firming and raking

Using a lawn roller or by treading, firm the soil evenly to be sure there are no soft spots that might later sink, making the lawn vulnerable to scalping during mowing. One rolling should be sufficient; however, it may be necessary to tread the area about three times before the soil is settled enough, but take care not to compress the soil too much, and do not firm wet soil because it will become compacted. Even so, the soil may settle even more over the course of the next year or two, leaving small hollows. These can be leveled when they occur by applying a sieved sandy top-dressing (see p.392).

After firming, thoroughly rake the surface to produce a fine tilth. The soil should be level, without humps or hollows, and with a fine crumb texture. If sowing seed, remove any stones larger than about ½in (1cm) across during raking; if sodding, it is necessary to remove only those stones over 1in (2.5cm).

Leave the prepared site for about three to four weeks to allow any weed seeds to germinate; any weeds should then be either hoed off or treated with a contact weedkiller. Gently rake them off several days later, once they have died, taking care not to disrupt the leveled soil.

Fertilizing

A few days before establishing the lawn, and once the surface has been prepared, apply fertilizer to the site. This should contain the three major nutrients to ensure good growth: nitrogen (N), phosphorus (P), and potassium (K). Sites that have not been fertilized for many years may be deficient in all three. Phosphorus is especially important during the early stages of growth. Use either a simple fertilizer such as superphosphate or, preferably, a balanced granular fertilizer that contains all three nutrients, such as 7–21–7; apply all fertilizers according to the manufacturer's instructions. Organic lawn fertilizers are also available.

CREATING A SLOPE

Decide how many rows of pegs will be used, and then mark the pegs for each row at different heights in order to achieve the desired gradient (see left). Using a level, create a grid of pegs as for leveling, then rake soil up to the marks.

INSTALLING A DRAIN

Position the drain at the lowest point, sloping the ground away from the house. Dig a trench, lay pipes at the base, and cover with crushed stone. Add topsoil, then sod or seed.

Slope away from house / Topsoil / Drain at lowest level / Drain at lowest level / Crushed stone / Gravel / Pipe

PREPARING THE SOIL SURFACE

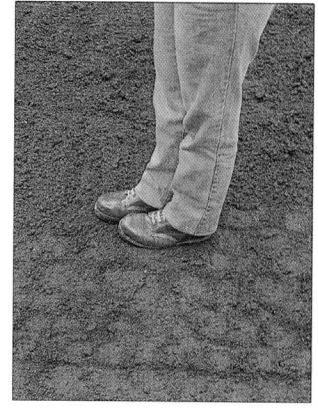

1 *Firm the surface by walking on it evenly, or by tamping it with the back of a rake. Repeat, if necessary, until the entire site is well firmed.*

2 *Rake the soil to a fine tilth, then leave it to allow weeds to germinate. Apply a glyphosate-based weedkiller, then, after the weeds look unhealthy, rake them off, including their roots.*

3 *Apply a base dressing of a balanced granular fertilizer, then lightly rake it into the surface of the soil.*

Establishing a lawn

THERE are various methods of establishing a lawn. For cool-season grasses in temperate areas, the gardener may choose between seeding and sodding; for warm-season grasses in subtropical and tropical regions, vegetative propagation methods may also be used.

Seeding a lawn is usually the cheapest method, but it takes up to a year before the lawn can be subjected to heavy wear. Establishing a lawn by vegetative may take longer and is more costly than seeding. Sodding, although more expensive, gives an immediate visual effect, and the lawn may be used within four to six months; it is advisable to use sod if you have pets that may disturb grass seedlings before they are established.

Sodding

There is a wide range of sod types available, including specially and commercially grown sod, meadow and treated meadow sod, and fine-grass sod; the type chosen depends on considerations of site and expense. Always buy sod from a reputable garden center or sod farm.

If possible, inspect the sod before buying it to make sure that it is in good condition, of the right quality (see "Selecting the right grass," p.382), and that the soil is a free-draining loam rather than a heavy clay. Check that there are no weeds, pests, or diseases, nor an excessive amount of thatch (the organic matter consisting of decaying grass, stolons, and rhizomes that accumulates on the soil surface); there should, however, be enough organic matter to hold the sod together. If possible, purchase only sod that is certified free of weeds and other crop grasses.

Commercially grown sod
Commercially grown sod is widely available and contains different grasses for various uses. It is raised from the newest grass cultivars and treated to make it free from weeds and disease. Sod that is certified free of troublesome weeds is also available from better producers at a slightly higher price. If you need a very large quantity of special sod and are prepared to wait 18 months for it to be grown and harvested, it may also be grown to order, but this is costly.

Meadow sod
This is usually grown for agricultural purposes and therefore is less fine in texture; it may have been either sown recently or grown in a long-established field. It is usually the least expensive sod, since it may contain coarse, vigorous agricultural grasses and broad-leaved weeds. The quality varies greatly, however, so it is especially important to buy meadow sod from a reputable supplier to make sure that it is of reasonable quality. If the weeds are eliminated by the use of selective weed-killers, the improved sod is described as treated meadow sod. Lawns established with meadow sod may be coarse and need more frequent mowing. Meadow sod is appropriate for use only where low quality is acceptable and minimal traffic is expected.

Fine-grass sod
Considered by many to be the best sod available, fine-grass sod contains fine fescues (*Festuca*) and bents (*Agrostis*). It is used mainly for croquet lawns and golf putting greens and requires high maintenance. In the home garden, it should be mowed at least every second day, or the lawn will turn brown upon mowing. Commercially grown sod, with new cultivars, is sold at larger sod farms.

Sizes of sod
Sod is available in a wide range of sizes and shapes. High-quality sod is often sold in 1ft (30cm) squares and lower quality sod in lengths of 3 x 1ft (90 x 30cm). Major producers usually supply sod of all qualities in units of 1sq yd (1sq m).

Storing sod
Sod is best lifted and relaid in its new position within the same day. If there is an unavoidable delay, lay the sod flat on paving or plastic sheeting, preferably in a slightly shaded area, and keep it watered; in hot weather, it may dry out very quickly, so check it regularly. If the sod is left rolled up, it will not receive enough light, so the grass will turn yellow and eventually die.

Laying sod

Sod may be laid at almost any time of the year except during prolonged spells of extreme temperatures. If possible, choose a time when rain is expected in the next day or two. Sod should be laid on moist, but not wet, soil to encourage rapid rooting.

Starting at the edge of the site, lay the first row of sod in a straight line. Standing on boards placed on the sod, rake over the soil on which the

1 *Lay the first row of sod alongside a straight edge such as a patio or path. Place each new piece exactly flush with its neighbor.*

2 *While kneeling on a board placed on the first row of sod, lay the next row with the sod joints staggered. Proceed in the same way for the rest of the lawn.*

3 *Tamp down each piece with the back of a rake to make sure that there are no air pockets. Alternatively, roll the lawn with a light roller.*

4 *If no rain is forecast, water the sod well. Keep the pieces moist until they have rooted into the topsoil, or they may shrink and gaps will appear.*

next row is to be laid. Lay this next row so that the pieces form an alternate bond, like bricks in a wall.

Do not finish a row with a small segment of sod beside the edge, because it will be vulnerable to damage (such as being kicked out) and drying out. If necessary, lay the last complete piece of sod at the edge, and fill the gap behind with the trimmed segment. Lay additional rows until the site is covered.

STORING SOD

Lay the sod as soon as possible; if it is essential to store it, spread the pieces out flat – green side up – so that they receive enough light, and keep them watered.

Shaping the edge
When all the sod has been laid, cut the edges to fit the final shape of the lawn. For a curved edge, lay a hose or rope along the curve, then cut just inside it. For a straight edge, use a string between pegs to mark the lawn edge. Align a board with this guide line and cut along it using a half moon or power edger. Repeat the procedure until the entire edge has been cut.

Aftercare

Either tamp down the sod with the back of a rake or roll the lawn with a light roller to make sure that there are no air pockets between the sod and the soil. In wet conditions do not roll until the sod has rooted and knitted together. Brushing a light top-dressing (see p.392) between the pieces of sod to encourage the roots to spread may be helpful.

Do not allow the sod to dry out before the grass has rooted through. It is essential to water the sod thoroughly so that it reaches the soil below; otherwise, the pieces of sod may shrink in dry or hot weather, leaving large gaps between them.

Moving sod

Sometimes it may be necessary to lift and re-lay sod. Cut and lift it in uniformly sized pieces so that they fit together when they are re-laid.

Cutting

First, divide the sod to be lifted into lengths 12in (30cm) wide by cutting along the edge of a board with a

TRIMMING THE LAWN EDGE

CURVED EDGE
Lay a hose or rope to the required shape and secure with wire hoops. Standing on a board, cut just inside the hose.

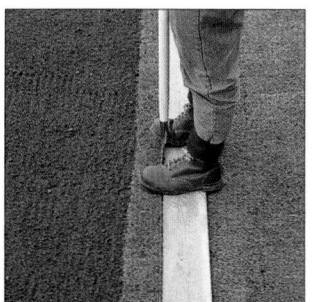

STRAIGHT EDGE
Stretch a taut string along the required line and align a board with this. Then, standing on the board, cut along its edge.

LIFTING SOD FOR RE-LAYING

1 *Cut into strips the sod to be lifted: insert 2 short stakes a little way apart, 12in (30cm) in from the sod edge, and lay a board flush against them. Stand on the board and cut along its edge.*

2 *Cut each strip into pieces about 18in (45cm) long, then undercut the sod to a depth of at least 1in (2.5cm). To stack them, lay grass to grass, soil to soil, on a path or piece of plastic sheeting.*

half-moon edger. Move the board 12in (30cm) in from the previous cut to form each new length. Then cut each length at right angles to form pieces about 18in (45cm) long. Alternatively, a mechanical sod lifter may be rented; this cuts the sod to the size and depth required and also lifts the newly cut pieces.

Lifting

Once cut, lift the pieces of sod with a flat spade, carefully severing each piece from the underlying soil and roots. As work begins, remove a wedge of sod next to the first piece to be lifted, then insert the spade under the sod without damaging the edge of the piece. Undercut each piece of sod to a uniform depth of at least 1–1¼in (2.5–3cm). Stack the lifted pieces of sod grass to grass, soil to soil, on a hard surface such as paving. (For further information, see "Storing sod," opposite.)

Trimming

After the sod has been lifted, trim it all to the same depth using a specially constructed shallow box the same size as the cut sod. Leave one of the shorter sides open and, if possible, cover the remaining top edges with a smooth metal strip. Place each piece of sod upside down in the box and, using a sharp blade, remove the excess soil by slicing along the top of the box.

Seeding

Grass seed is best sown in warm, moist conditions so that it will germinate and establish quickly: early fall is usually best. Spring-sown grass is also successful, but the soil is colder than in fall and there is

more competition from weeds. Seed may be sown in summer if irrigation is available, but in hot conditions young grass seedlings suffer heat stress and may wilt or even die.

Sowing rates

Grass sowing rates vary, depending on the mixture or species (see *Sowing Rates*, p.388). Although there is some leeway to allow for factors such as depletion caused by birds eating the seeds, it is important not to sow seed in much greater or smaller quantities than the recommended rate. Sowing too little seed may allow weed seedlings space to compete with the grass, and the lawn will take slightly longer to establish. Sowing too much seed may cause other problems by producing humid conditions among the seedlings. This encourages damping off (p.655), which can damage the young lawn in a very short time, particularly in warm, humid weather (see also "Lawn problems," pp.657).

Sowing seed

Seed may be sown either by hand or, faster and more evenly, by a machine. First calculate the amount of seed needed by multiplying the size of the area to be sown (in square yards or meters) by the recommended sowing rate (the amount of seed per square yard or meter). Before sowing the seed, shake the container to mix the seeds thoroughly and make sure that small seeds do not settle to the bottom, thus giving an uneven distribution of grass types.

Sowing by machine

This is the best way to sow seed over a large area. Measure out the correct

amount of seed for the lawn and divide it in half. For even coverage, sow half of the seed in one direction and half at right angles to this. A well-defined lawn edge may be achieved by laying plastic sheeting or burlap at the site edge and running the machine just over it; this also prevents the uneven distribution that may occur when stopping the machine at the end of a strip. Excess seed may be gathered and resown.

Sowing by hand

If sowing by hand, first divide the area into small, equal-sized sections; this makes it easier to sow the seed evenly. Then measure out the correct amount of seed for one section and accurately divide the batch of seed in half. Transfer one half-batch into a measure, such as a small cup, to make it easier and faster to measure out each subsequent amount. Work on one section at a time, scattering half the seed of a batch in one direction, then sow the other half at right angles to this before moving on.

Aftercare

After sowing, lightly rake over the surface. Rolling after seeding is recommended to assure good seed-to-soil contact. In addition, use of a natural product (such as grain straw) or a lightweight synthetic seeding cloth helps prevent soil erosion and also helps keep seed from drying out. Weeds that may appear from using straw will disappear with repeated mowing. If using cloth, remove it after the grass is growing well (about 1in/2.5cm tall). Seeding cloth will also protect the seed and seedlings from bird damage.

The young grass is certain to need watering before it is properly established. To avoid having to walk on the newly germinated seedlings and damaging them, set out sufficient sprinklers and hoses to cover the area immediately after sowing. They can be connected to the tap in turn if several are needed. Remove them when the lawn is ready for its first cut, and the marks of the sprinklers and hoses will soon disappear.

Germination will occur in one to two weeks, depending on grass species, soil and air temperature, and moisture. Water the site regularly in dry weather, since young grasses are very susceptible to drought.

Cutting

When the grass has reached approximately 2in (5cm), cut it to a height of 1in (2.5cm). For the first two or three cuts use a rotary mower, as a reel mower with a roller may tear up young plants, but make sure the mower blade is freshly sharpened to avoid uprooting the seedlings. Then rake and remove all excess clippings if the mower has no grass catcher.

If the lawn was sown in late summer or early fall, mow when necessary through late fall in order to maintain the grass at about 2in (5cm) high. During the following spring, gradually adjust the height of the cut until the desired height is reached, depending on the type of grass used (see also "Frequency and height of cut," p.389). Young grasses are vulnerable to damage by wear, so try to use the lawn as little as possible during its first growing season.

Hydromulching

Hydromulching may be considered as a method for establishing very large utility lawns. Grass seed is mixed with water, fertilizer, and fiber mulch, and then sprayed directly onto the seedbed. The mixture holds the seeds in place and helps retain moisture while protecting the seed from birds and other pests.

Hydromulching generally costs more than seeding, but less than sodding. Unlike seeding, however, the procedure can be used successfully during the summer. Apply hydromulch only on dry days and do not let the slurry come into contact with lawn furniture, bicycles, grills, and other objects that may be harmed by the chemicals it contains.

Because of the equipment involved, hydromulching is usually done by lawn care companies who will need easy access for machinery to the area involved. Kentucky bluegrass and perennial ryegrass are most frequently used but other species could be applied equally easily.

Establishing a non-grass lawn

Lawns can easily be established from various evergreen non-grass species, including chamomile and moss.

Chamomile
To create a new lawn from chamomile, (*Chamaemelum nobile*), prepare the site as for a regular lawn, including a dressing of fertilizer on the soil. Plant pot-grown specimens, rooted cuttings, divisions, or seedlings at 6–12in (15–30cm) intervals, depending on the size of the plants and the speed at which you need them to fill in.

If possible, use the non-flowering variety 'Treneague', which is very low growing but can be difficult to find commercially. Flowering forms may be raised from seed, but these are taller and will require more frequent trimming to remove the dead flowerheads.

Keep the site well watered until the plants are established and show signs of new growth. Once the plants have covered the soil, trim the lawn with a rotary mower, nylon-line trimmer, or hand shears, as needed.

Moss
Although it is generally regarded as a lawn problem, moss can be used to create entire lawns. Usually associated with dampness and shade, mosses grow either in sun or shade in a variety of soils, from moist to dry, acidic to alkaline, light to heavy. Drier conditions favor gray mosses, while green mosses thrive on wet soils.

Moss lawns may be introduced in any season. Work compost into the soil, water, then lay down cushions or mats of moss, including some of the

ESTABLISHING A LAWN BY SOWING SEED

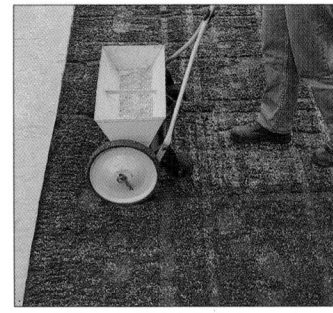

1 *If using a machine, sow half the seed in one direction and half at right angles to this. For a defined edge, lay down plastic sheeting and push the machine just over it at the end of each row.*

ALTERNATIVE STEP
If sowing by hand, mark the site into equal areas. Weigh enough seed for a single area, then scatter it evenly, half in one direction and half at right angles to this.

2 *After sowing, lightly rake over the surface. In dry conditions, water the site regularly to encourage the seeds to germinate.*

3 *The grass seedlings should take 7–14 days to emerge. Once the grass is about 2in (5cm) high, cut it to a height of 1in (2.5cm) with a rotary mower.*

organic matter in which it was growing – pine needles, forest litter, rotting wood – and press firmly. Obtain (always with permission) moss from woods, farms, or neighbors. It transplants well.

Mist the transplanted material and new growth daily; do not walk on the moss until established. Use a broom to sweep leaves and debris away. Moss lawns need periodic weeding and no mowing. They can be walked on occasionally to perform maintenance tasks, but they are never suitable for hard wear.

Thyme
This makes a very good, fragrant, lawn that will withstand a reasonable amount of foot traffic. Space plants about 12in (30cm) apart for a fairly fast cover, wider than this if you are patient; each plant will cover about 4 square feet (370 sq. cm) in time. This is very low growing and only needs trimming once a year to remove the flower stalks after they fade.

Different varieties have different colored foliage, flowers, and fragrance, so you can create a chequerboard effect or design patterns.

However, the hardiness varies slightly between the named forms, and some of the colored-leaved varieties in particular are slightly more tender than the plain green ones. Do not use the culinary thyme (*Thymus vulgaris*) for this purpose, as it grows much taller than the creeping wild thyme (*T. serpyllum*).

Bugleweed
Bugleweed (*Ajuga reptans*) will make a hard wearing lawn, although the purple color may seem a bit strange at first. It grows rapidly, and plants spaced 12in (30cm) apart will soon cover the soil, making a dense carpet that smothers weeds.

It is useful in areas that are bounded by a barrier, such as between the house wall and a front walk where mowing can sometimes be difficult. The barriers help to contain the plant and prevent its runners spreading into other areas. Mow once each year, immediately after flowering, to prevent seeding. Variegated varieties such as *A.r.* 'Gaiety' and 'Silver Beauty' are visually more pleasing but tend to revert to the plain form unless carefully watched.

SOWING RATES

MIXTURES	oz/sq yd	g/sq m
Fineleaf fescues and bents	5/16 – 1/2	10 – 15
Perennial ryegrass and other species	5/8 – 3/4	20 – 25
Tall fescue and Kentucky bluegrass	3/4 – 7/8	25 – 30
SINGLE SPECIES		
Bents *(Agrostis)*	1/16 – 1/8	3 – 5
Carpetgrass *(Axonopus)*	1/4 – 3/8	8 – 12
Bermudagrass *(Cynodon dactylon)*	1/8 – 1/4	5 – 8
Centipedegrass *(Eremochloa ophiuroides)*	1/2 – 3/4	15 – 25
Fineleaf fescues *(Festuca spp.)*	1/2 – 5/8	15 – 20
Perennial ryegrass *(Lolium perenne)*	3/4 – 1	25 – 35
Bahiagrass *(Paspalum notatum)*	7/8 – 1 1/8	30 – 40
Kentucky bluegrass *(Poa pratensis)*	1/4 – 1/2	8 – 15
Tall fescue *(Festuca arundinacea)*	3/4 – 1	25 – 35
Buffalograss *(Buchloe dactyloides)* burrs	1/4 – 3/8	8 – 12
Zoysiagrass *(Zoysia)*	1/8 – 5/16	5 – 10

Routine care

O NCE the lawn is well established, regular maintenance is needed to ensure its health and attractive appearance. The amount required depends on the lawn's size and type as well as the site and climate. In general, the most frequent tasks are mowing and watering, but annual maintenance may also include such things as fertilizing, top-dressing, aerating, and, where necessary, controlling moss, weeds, pests, and diseases. For large lawns, using mechanical or power tools, which may be rented, often makes maintenance tasks faster and easier (see "Lawn-care tools," pp.552–3).

Mowing

In addition to making the lawn a pleasure to walk on, regularly cutting the grass helps create a dense, healthy turf with an even, attractive finish. Mowing is needed most frequently in mid- to late spring and early fall for cool-season grasses, and late spring and summer for warm-season grasses. However, during drought conditions, it is best either not to mow at all or to set the mower to a higher cut. Delay mowing during very wet or cold weather: wet grass can clog the mower or the mower may slip, and mowing in frost damages the grass. When using a power mower, always wear sturdy or steel-toe shoes with nonslip soles and heels, especially if mowing on a slope. Wear goggles if mowing in stony ground or near graveled areas.

Mowers

For most lawns, either a reel or a rotary mower will provide a suitable finish. A reel mower that incorporates a roller provides the finest finish for a high-quality lawn, but a rotary mower gives a perfectly acceptable surface for a utility lawn.

For most lawns, rotary mowers are the best all-around choice; they are widely available, fast, and efficient, and they provide good results. For large properties, riding mowers let the operator cut the grass with a commanding view of the lawn and comparatively little physical effort. Riding mowers are obviously inappropriate for small lawns as well as greatly uneven or stony lawns.

However, nonmotorized reel mowers are becoming an increasingly popular choice, especially among the ecologically aware. Reel mowers, also called push mowers, do not use gasoline, so they do not put out harmful fumes, and they are far less poten-

tially hazardous to use than rotary mowers. Also, the user of a reel mower is likely to get some good exercise, since the energy needed to get a smooth cut comes from the operator rather than from electricity or a gasoline engine. For more information, see "Lawn mowers," p.551.

Frequency and height of cut

The frequency of mowing and the height of cut depend on a number of factors, including the type of grasses grown, how the lawn is used, and the time of year, but little and often is a good general rule to follow. Try to remove no more than one-third the leaf growth at any one time. If the grass is cut sporadically and drastically, it will struggle to recover after each mowing, which will result in a noticeable decline in the lawn's quality. Frequent mowing is necessary during the spring flush of growth. The need for mowing tapers off with the arrival of summer, and it may not be necessary to mow at all during the warmest part of the summer. Growth begins again with cooler weather. In mild areas, an occasional mowing may be required in winter.

High-quality lawns may be cut as low as ½in (1.25cm), but they need to be mowed frequently – every two or three days in active growth – to maintain their appearance. Utility lawns should be left to grow longer than this, because the grasses do not tolerate such a low cut; this also helps protect the surface against drying out.

It is not necessary to mow all areas to the same height. Try two or three heights of cut for different grass areas to add texture and interest to the garden. For practical reasons, cut the main area to be used for walking or playing to a height of about 2–3in (5–8cm). Keeping the grass at this length protects the surface against drying. Areas under trees may require less frequent mowing – every two to three weeks during summer, especially fineleaf fescues.

MOWING STRIPS

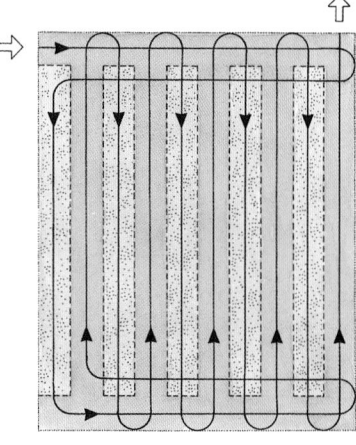

REGULAR SHAPE
First mow a wide strip at each end of the lawn for turning space, then mow up and down the lawn in slightly overlapping runs.

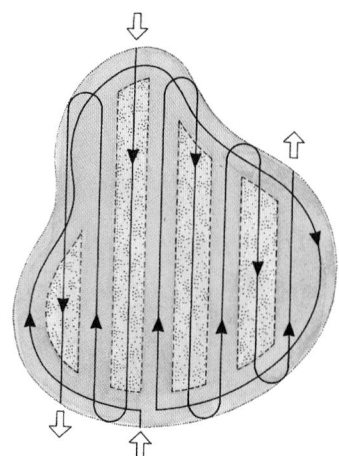

IRREGULAR SHAPE
Mow a strip around the lawn edge, then mow a straight strip up the center. Mow up and down one-half of the lawn, then the other half.

Grasses in shade should be mowed slightly higher, so as much leaf area as possible is available to absorb the available light. Leave any areas of meadow at 6in (15cm) or more; they will need no more than three cuts per year and should not be cut until the flowering species have shed their seed in midsummer (see WILD-FLOWER AND MEADOW GARDENING, p.395). Since they are mowed infrequently, these areas produce much more growth and debris, which should be raked up and removed after each mowing.

Mowing efficiently

Efficient mowing, especially with a riding mower, can save a great deal of time. If the lawn is square or rectangular, first mow a wide strip at either end of the lawn to provide turning space. Then mow up and down in straight strips, slightly overlapping the previous run to make sure that all the grass is mowed.

If the lawn is of an irregular shape, first mow all around its edge. Then, starting at the center of one end, mow a straight line down the middle by

picking out an object or tree beyond the end of the lawn and then pointing the mower directly toward it. Mow straight strips up and down one-half of the lawn, then return to the center and mow the other half in a similar fashion.

Mowing sports fields

On areas to be used for ball games such as croquet or putting, vary the direction each time you mow to prevent a grain from developing. Grain is produced by grass growing in one direction, and it will influence the run of a ball.

Grass clippings

On fine lawns where a high-quality finish is required, use a mower that gathers grass clippings as it cuts or rake them up afterward, then add them in layers (alternating with other material) to the compost pile. On most utility lawns, using a modern mulching mower, which cuts the clippings into small pieces and drops them in the wake of the mower, will actually require less mowing time overall and will benefit the lawn.

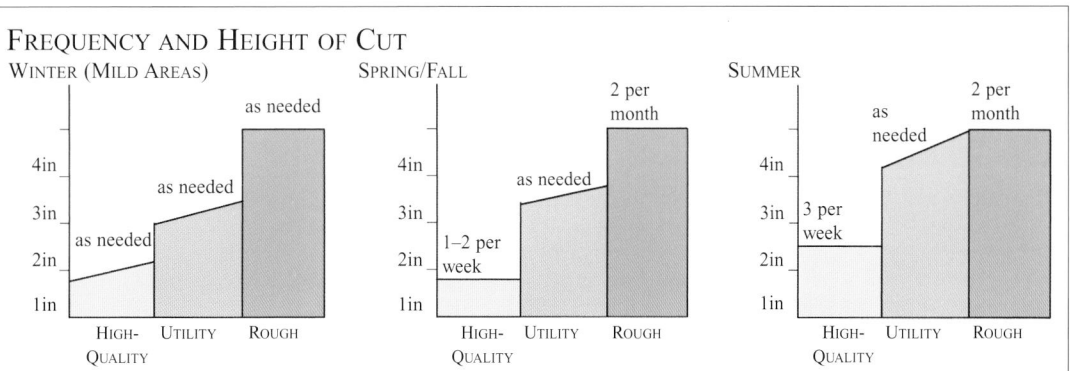

FREQUENCY AND HEIGHT OF CUT

WINTER (MILD AREAS)

SPRING/FALL

SUMMER

Utility lawns containing earthworms will benefit from clippings left on the lawn; the clippings will be recycled by the earthworms and the plant nutrients returned to the soil. Another related way to recycle nutrients is by composting. Even leaving fine clippings on the lawn to break down slowly is preferable to relegating them to landfills, where their components will be unavailable to the ecosystem for years to come.

Removing fallen leaves
In fall and winter, clear away any fallen leaves from the lawn by brushing or raking them up and removing them; a layer of leaves left on the lawn reduces evaporation, and the resulting humidity can encourage lawn diseases.

Trimming edges
After mowing, create a neat finish by trimming the lawn edges with long-handled edging shears, a mechanical edging machine, or a nylon-line trimmer with an adjustable head for edging (see "Lawn-care tools," pp.552–3). If the lawn edges become irregular, recut them once or twice a year with a half-moon edger, cutting against a board for a straight line; for very large lawns, it is faster and less laborious to use a power edger for this task.

CLEARING LEAVES

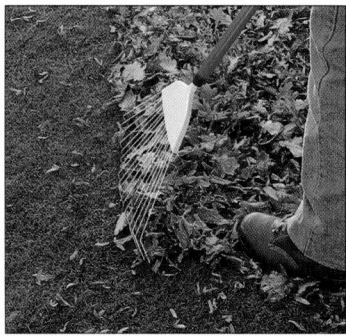

Remove any fallen leaves and debris by brushing the lawn briskly with a spring-tined rake. For large lawns, use a leaf sweeper or blower to speed up the task.

Watering

Grass generally resists drought well once established, but growth slows down and the lawn turns brown in prolonged dry spells. To maintain growth and color, it is essential to water the lawn thoroughly in very dry periods. Water in the early morning to minimize evaporation, and avoid watering in early evening or at night, since this may increase damage from fungal diseases.

Start to water as soon as you notice that the grass does not spring back up after the lawn has been walked on (called "footprinting"). In most areas, 1in (2.5cm) of water per week will keep a lawn green throughout summer. However, it hotter, more arid areas, daily evapotranspiration (ET) rates are published in local newspapers and should be monitored. In those areas, watering should be conducted to replace 80–100% of ET. After watering, the soil should be moist to a depth of 4–6in (10–15cm). Shallow watering encourages roots to remain near the surface, making the lawn more susceptible to drought. Dig a small hole to check that the soil is damp to the required depth, then make a note of the time that it took to water the lawn sufficiently. An electric moisture meter may also be used for evaluation.

On heavy soils, where the drainage is restricted, it is important not to apply too much water, since this restricts oxygen and mineral intake by the roots. If water remains on the lawn for some time after heavy rain or watering, the lawn may need additional drainage (see "Improving drainage," p.617).

Grass that needs regular watering is best served by a built-in, pop-up underground sprinkler system. Such systems may also be set to operate automatically as well as manually but are much more expensive than a sprinkler or hose. For information, see "Watering aids," pp. 554–55.

Fertilizing

As with all plants, grasses require nutrients to grow, and regular applications of fertilizer help produce a vigorous, healthy lawn. Most of the nutrients essential for growth are plentiful within the soil, but three – nitrogen (N), phosphorus (P), and potassium (K) – are often applied as a supplement. Nitrogen is the most commonly added nutrient: it is removed in grass clippings and is essential for the production of new growth. Nitrogen-deficient grass is generally yellow-green and lacking in resilience and vigor. Fertilizers are the easiest and most usual way to

apply nutrients to lawns; both organic and inorganic products are available (see also "Soil nutrients and fertilizers," pp.618–19). The exact amount of fertilizer that is required depends on how quickly water drains from the soil, how much rainfall or irrigation is received, whether or not grass clippings are removed, and on the type of grasses grown. On heavy clay soils that are rich in nutrients, and where rainfall or irrigation rates are low, only light fertilizing is necessary. However, light, sandy soils that are well watered and that lose nutrients quickly by leaching need greater amounts.

Types and constituents of fertilizer
For most lawns in cool areas, three applications of fertilizer a year are sufficient (see chart, opposite). Local recommendations should be considered first, but, in general, apply a spring fertilizer as soon as the grass begins to green up, then in late summer/early fall, then in late fall. Select a fertilizer that contains a mixture of both slow- and fast-release nitrogen; this helps the lawn green up within two to three days and stay green for several weeks. Potassium should be applied in amounts equal to 50–100% of the nitrogen applied.

In most of Canada, the late fall fertilizer should be one of the new winterizing types. These are available in two forms. One is low in nitrogen but high in phosphorus and potassium. This is applied in late fall and helps the grass withstand the harsh winter. The other is high in nitrogen and is applied just before freeze-up. The nitrogen is absorbed by the plant, which goes dormant shortly after, ready to burst into growth with the warm days of spring.

Weed-and-feed compounds help control moss and broad-leaved weeds and fertilize the lawn all in one operation. Do not assume, however, that a weed-and-feed fertilizer will eliminate all of your lawn weeds. As with pesticides, the herbicide's effectiveness depends on applying it properly to the weeds it can control at the correct time. Always read the package carefully.

CUTTING THE EDGE OF THE LAWN

EDGING BY MACHINE *Periodically recut the lawn edge to retain the lawn's shape and create a well-defined finish. For large lawns, use a power edger: align the cutting blade along the required new edge, then guide the machine forward.*

TRIMMING THE EDGE *After mowing, trim the grass overhanging the lawn edge with long-handled edging shears, or use a nylon-line trimmer adapted to work vertically.*

EDGING BY HAND *If recutting the edge manually, use a sharp half-moon edger, cutting along the line of a board for a straight edge.*

WATER PENETRATION

Shallow watering may make the lawn vulnerable to drought (right); apply enough water to moisten the soil to a depth of about 4–6in (10–15cm) (far right).

 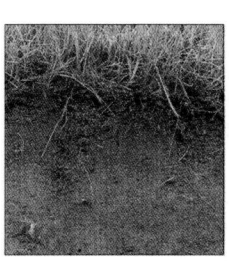

HOW TO APPLY FERTILIZER

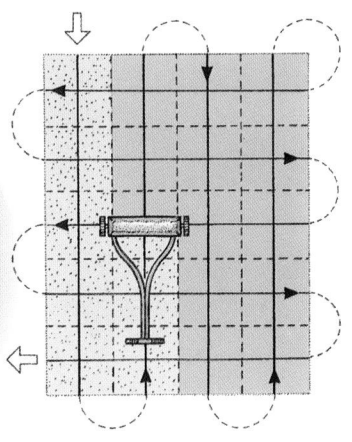

Measure the correct amount of fertilizer for the area, then divide it in half. Apply the first half in one direction, working up and down the lawn in adjoining but not overlapping runs. Apply the second half at right angles to this. Close off the supply when you turn the machine at the end of each run.

How to apply fertilizer

It is essential to apply fertilizer evenly to avoid variations in growth and the risk of damaging or even killing the grass. Any variation in the rate of application will generally be more than obvious within a week, and excessive doses may create a dead patch. Although fertilizer may be spread manually, it is both easier and more accurate to machine-apply it. Probably the simplest method is to use a drop-type spreader. This is pushed up and down the lawn so that each pass abuts the previous one without overlapping it. To provide even coverage over the lawn, it is best to divide the fertilizer into two batches and apply half in one direction and the rest at right angles to it.

Alternatively, a cyclone or broadcast spreader may be used to apply the fertilizer over a larger area. To reduce the risk of fertilizer being distributed unevenly, set the machine to half the application rate, and make adjacent runs at half the distance apart of the machine's spread. For example, if the extent of the spread is 6ft (2m), make the runs as close to 3ft (1m) apart as you can.

Before applying fertilizer, calibrate the spreader to obtain the correct distribution rate. To calibrate a spreader,

UNEVEN DISTRIBUTION

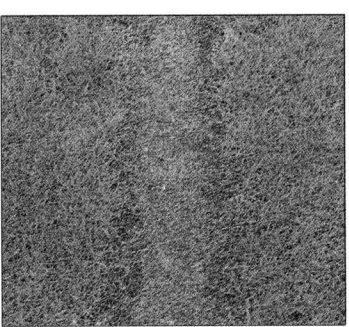

Take care to apply fertilizer evenly, because uneven distribution may make the lawn patchy, and it could damage or kill areas of grass.

first find a dry, flat area of concrete or asphalt, and mark out a measured area of 4sq yd (4sq m), for example. Set the spreader to medium and fill it a quarter full. Using the machine, spread the fertilizer as evenly as possible over the marked area, then sweep up all the fertilizer within the area and weigh it. Divide this weight by the area, in this case 4sq yd (4sq m), to give the application rate in ounces per square yard (grams per square meter). Adjust the machine setting accordingly, then check the application rate again over the same measured area. Continue until the rate is correct. In addition, many fertilizer bags contain settings for many manufacturers' brands of spreader. These settings do not replace calibration but are a good guide.

Annual maintenance

In addition to routine tasks such as mowing and watering, regular maintenance is required to keep a lawn healthy and to reduce the risk of serious pest or disease problems (see chart, below). A maintenance program should involve aeration (including thatch removal or scarifying), fertilizing, and the control of weeds, moss, pests, and diseases (see "Lawn weeds," p.394, and "Pests and diseases," p.394).

It is also important for the continued good health of the lawn to top-dress the grass as well as to rake or brush it regularly to clear away leaves and other debris (see "Removing fallen leaves," opposite).

Tasks that may be necessary at least once a year include recutting any edges that have become uneven or jagged, and repairing any damaged or worn patches of grass by resodding or reseeding (see "Repairing lawn damage," p.393). Winter is the most convenient time to check all equipment carefully, since the lawn does not need regular attention. Sharpen all cutting edges, oil tools where necessary, and send the mower for servicing so that it will be in peak condition for the first cut of the new season.

Dethatching

It is important to reduce excessive thatch, the organic matter consisting of decaying blades of grass, rhizomes, and stolons that accumulate on the soil surface. A certain amount of thatch – up to about $\frac{1}{2}$in (1cm) deep – is beneficial, since it reduces evaporation and helps protect the lawn from wear. In excess, however, it prevents water from reaching the soil beneath and may itself become saturated, interfering with drainage. The removal of thatch also encourages new grass growth.

Aerating the lawn

Aeration is vital, since it allows deep root growth and so helps the lawn become established, as well as reducing soil compaction.

There are several ways of aerating the soil. These include scarifying, slicing (also called slitting), hollow tining (also known as coring), and spiking. It is preferable not to undertake these tasks in dry conditions, however, since they make the lawn more vulnerable to drought. Early spring is the best time, since the grass is growing rapidly and will recover

ANNUAL MAINTENANCE PROGRAM

MAINTENANCE PROCEDURE	EARLY/MID SPRING	MID/LATE SPRING	EARLY/MID SUMMER	MID/LATE SUMMER	EARLY/MID FALL	MID/LATE FALL	WINTER
Mowing	Roll before mowing if sod is lifted by frost	Mow weekly. Adjust mower to summer cut height	Mow 1–3 times a week as required	Mow 1–3 times a week (set mower higher in dry periods)	Adjust height of cut as growth rate slows	Set mower to winter cut height	Lightly mow if there is new growth
Watering		May be needed in dry regions	Water as necessary	Water well in dry periods	Occasionally water if dry		
Fertilizing		Apply spring fertilizer	Apply summer fertilizer		Apply fall/winter fertilizer or apply late-fall fertilizer		
Aerating and scarifying	Dethatch if necessary when dry enough	Lightly scarify			Spike or slice areas subject to heavy wear	Aerate lawn if not done in early fall	
Weed and moss control	Apply annual-grass weedkiller	Apply weed-killer if needed			Apply contact weedkiller if needed		
Insect and disease control	Check for snow mold. Rake lawn if present		Look for chinch bug and treat if found	Look for white grubs and treat if necessary			
Other procedures	Rake off winter debris. Recut edges if required	Reseed or re-sod if necessary			Reseed or renovate if necessary	Remove fallen leaves	Remove leaves. Service mower

SCARIFYING

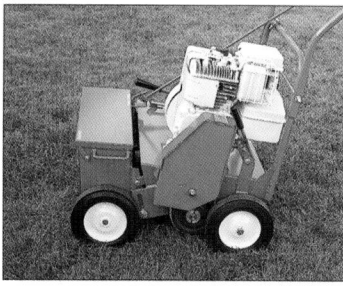

BY MACHINE
For large areas of lawn, use a mechanical or power scarifier. Work the machine back and forth across the lawn as if mowing.

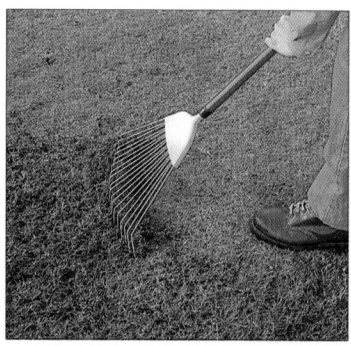

BY HAND
Pull a spring-tined rake vigorously across the lawn to remove thatch and dead moss. Make sure that the tines of the rake reach well down into the soil surface.

quickly from these renovation procedures. First mow the lawn to its normal height. After maintenance work, apply a low-nitrogen fertilizer, and avoid using the lawn for one to two weeks to encourage recovery.

Scarifying
This technique helps remove thatch and permits air to enter the surface of the lawn. These processes are important, since the soil organisms that nat-

urally break down thatch require air to live. For small areas, scarifying may be done manually by vigorously raking the lawn with a spring-tined rake. This is hard work, however, so it may be worth renting a mechanical or power scarifier instead. To remove the maximum amount of thatch, scarify the lawn in two directions, one at 90° to the other. Any moss should be killed prior to scarifying so that it will not spread to other parts of the lawn (see "Moss," p.394).

Slicing
For slicing (sometimes referred to as "slitting"), a machine penetrates the soil with a flat, sharp blade to 3–4in (8–10cm) deep. The blades cut through the thatch, allowing air into the soil and thereby encouraging a dense, healthy turf.

Hollow tining, or coring
This removes some thatch, aerates the soil, and relieves soil compaction, all in one operation. A mechanical or hand tiner removes a core of grass, thatch, and soil, making a series of holes across the lawn, about 4in (10cm) apart. Allow the cores to remain on the lawn surface. Once they have dried, they can be crushed by being raked or by walking on them, becoming a top-dressing. Hollow tining may take longer to do than spiking and slitting, because soil is removed rather than simply being pushed sideways.

Spiking
This allows air into the soil, thereby encouraging root growth; it can also relieve soil compaction. Use a mechanical or hand spiker or, for small areas, a garden fork. Angle the spikes back slightly to raise the turf gently without breaking it up. This encourages deep root growth by creating fissures in the soil.

AERATING

AERATING BY MACHINE
For large lawns, use a mechanical or power aerator. Work the machine in slightly overlapping runs.

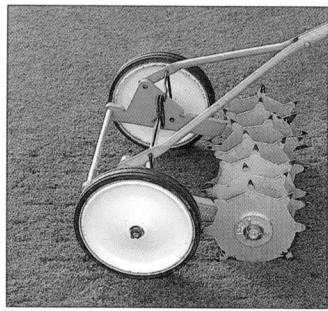

SLICING
Slicing, which must be done with a specialized machine, allows air into the soil. Push the machine back and forth across the lawn.

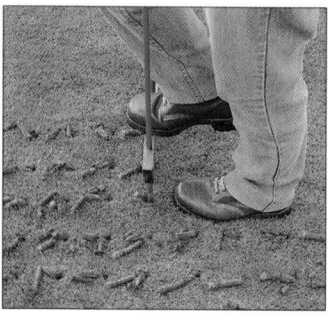

HOLLOW TINING
Use a specifically designed tool, working methodically across the lawn to lift out cores of grass and soil ¼–¾in (0.5–2cm) wide.

SPIKING
For small lawns, spiking using a garden fork is adequate. Insert the fork straight in, then lean it back slightly to create a larger hole.

Top-dressing
Where soils are shallow and the lawn is poor, it will be beneficial to top-dress the lawn. Top-dressing also helps break down thatch by keeping the lawn open and aerated, fills core holes, and helps to level the surface. For most lawns, a sandy mixture of 6 parts medium-fine sand, 3 parts sieved soil, and 1 part peat, compost, or leaf mold is suitable;

alternatively, a sandy topsoil may be used. Apply the top-dressing with a drop-type fertilizer spreader or a shovel; do not apply a layer any deeper than ¼in (6mm) at any one time. Spread the selected top-dressing across the lawn with a rake or flat board to achieve uniform distribution. Using a flat board also helps level any slight irregularities in the surface of the lawn.

TOP-DRESSING

Medium-fine sand

Sieved soil

Peat

1 *Prepare the top-dressing by mixing medium-fine sand with topsoil and peat or leaf mold. Pass the mixture through a ¼in (5mm) mesh sieve.*

2 *Weigh out the correct amount of top-dressing for the lawn area, then apply it on a dry day. For a large lawn, it is best to use a spreader.*

ALTERNATIVE STEP
For small areas, the top-dressing may be applied by hand. Spread it evenly over the lawn with a shovel or spade.

3 *Use the back of a rake to work in the dressing, keeping a steady pressure to distribute the dressing evenly. Then water the lawn thoroughly.*

Rolling

Rolling is not essential, but if done in spring it may help resettle the surface after any maintenance work carried out the previous fall or after any upheaval caused by frost action. A roller should not be filled more than about a quarter full with water and should not be used at all on clay soils. The traditional practice of rolling lawns frequently is unnecessary and could cause the problems associated with compaction.

Renovating a neglected lawn

In some cases, a neglected, patchy lawn may be improved by renovation; however, if the lawn is infested with weeds or moss, it may be preferable to remove the old turf and establish a new lawn. The best time to start renovation work is in either early spring or late summer. Avoid midsummer, when the lawn is under heat stress.

A renovation program involves a series of procedures that restore the lawn to a good condition. First, in early spring, cut the grass to about 2in (5cm) using a rotary mower, and remove any clippings. Apply a high-nitrogen fertilizer such as 10–6–4 at about a quarter of the recommended rate. Repeat the fertilizer application every three to four weeks, except when the lawn is experiencing heat stress. Water thoroughly during drought. Once the daytime temperature is above 70°F (21°C) but below 86°F (30°C), apply a selective weed-killer. Reseed any remaining bare patches at least eight weeks before freeze-up to give the new grass time to become established before winter arrives. At the beginning of fall, aerate the lawn (except any newly seeded areas) and apply a fall/winter fertilizer. A regular maintenance program should then be followed so that the lawn is kept in optimum condition. See *Annual Maintenance Program*, p.391.

Repairing lawn damage

If an area of the lawn becomes damaged or patchy, it may usually be repaired by removing the unwanted part, then sodding or seeding. Using sod or seed that is the same type as the rest of the lawn is important; if the lawn type is unknown, use a piece of sod from a less prominent part of the lawn to replace the damaged area. If the problem of lawn damage occurs repeatedly, it may be necessary to consider introducing a completely different and more durable surface, such as gravel or paving (see STRUCTURES AND SURFACES, pp.578–99).

Repairing a damaged edge

Edges that have been damaged in only one or two small areas may be repaired quite simply. Using a half-moon edger and a straightedge, such as a short wooden board, mark out a small section of sod containing the damaged part. Slice under the section of sod with a spade, and push it toward the lawn edge until the poor area is outside the lawn. Then trim off the damaged part to align the sod with the existing lawn edge. This leaves a gap within the lawn, which should be gently forked over and a granular or liquid fertilizer added. Then resod or add a little soil and reseed the newly exposed area with an appropriate grass mixture. Be sure that the repair will grow to be flush with the rest of the lawn. Alternatively, lift the sod, then turn it around and replace it so that the damaged area is within the lawn. Repair the damage by sodding or seeding, making sure that any new sod is laid lmore or less evel with the surrounding lawn.

Repairing a damaged patch

If there is a damaged patch within the lawn, first cut out and lift a piece of sod containing the damaged area. Fork over the soil, then fertilize it, if required, and lightly firm the soil.

HOW TO REPAIR A DAMAGED EDGE

1 *Using stakes and string, mark out a small, straight-sided section of sod containing the damaged part. Cut out the area with a half-moon edger.*

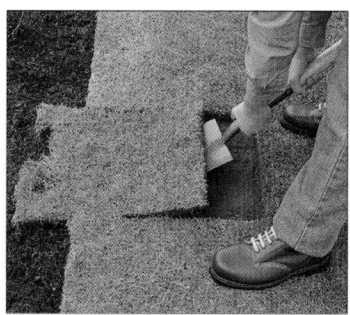

2 *Carefully undercut the sod with a spade, then slide it forward until the damaged part is beyond the lawn edge.*

3 *Align a board with the lawn edge, then cut along it to trim off the damaged section so that the sod is level with the rest of the lawn edge.*

4 *Cut a new piece of sod to fit the resulting gap, then ease it into the hole. If it is too large, trim it so that it forms an exact fit.*

5 *Adjust the soil level beneath the new sod, if necessary, by adding or removing soil until the new piece sits level with the rest of the lawn.*

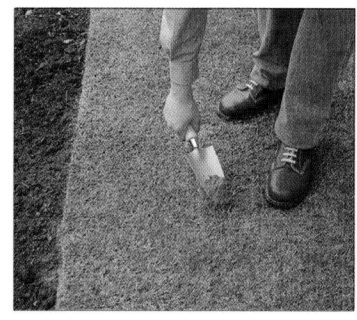

6 *Once the level is correct, tamp the new piece firmly into place by standing on a board and shifting your weight.*

7 *Sprinkle some sandy top-dressing over the repaired area, particularly into the seams, and water thoroughly.*

ALTERNATIVE METHOD

1 *Cut out a section containing the damaged part. Turn it so that the damaged piece faces the lawn, and firm it into place.*

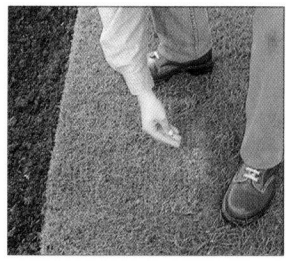

2 *Add a little sandy soil, if necessary, so that the damaged part is level with the rest of the lawn, then sow grass seed over the damaged section, and water well.*

HOW TO REPAIR A DAMAGED PATCH

1 *Using a half-moon edger and the edge of a board, cut around the damaged area, then undercut the sod with a spade and remove it.*

2 *Lightly fork or rake over the area of exposed soil to loosen it, then apply a liquid or granular fertilizer if required.*

3 *Carefully tread over the soil to settle it and firm the surface before resodding.*

Lay a new piece of sod to fit the exposed space, raising or lowering the soil level beneath, if necessary, so that the new sod is level with the rest of the lawn, then tamp it down in position with the back of a rake or your hands. Top-dress and water the repaired surface well.

Leveling a hump or hollow

Small humps or hollows within the lawn may be leveled easily. First cut a cross through the sod on the problem area and peel back the cut sod. To level a hollow, fork over the soil beneath and fill in with topsoil, then lightly firm the ground. For a hump, remove the excess soil until the ground is level, and firm. Fold back the cut sod, then tamp it down with the back of a rake before top-dressing and watering.

On larger areas, it may be necessary to remove complete sections of sod entirely, level the soil beneath (see "Leveling the site," p.384), and then carefully re-lay the sod over the original area.

4 *Place a new piece of sod in the hole, cutting it to fit with a half-moon edger.*

5 *Check that the new sod is level with the rest of the lawn; if necessary, adjust the soil level beneath the sod. Then firm in the sod and water well.*

Lawn weeds

Although some weeds such as slender speedwell (*Veronica filiformis*) and white clover (*Trifolium repens*) may look attractive in utility lawns, they are considered undesirable in high-quality, closely mowed lawns. Many broad-leaved weeds can survive in grass that is mowed, but excessive numbers may make the grass suffer, so, even in a utility lawn, control may be needed. Unless lawn clippings are gathered, mowing may spread weeds that can root from small pieces of stem. On small lawns, dandelions (*Taraxacum officinale*) and plantains (*Plantago*) may be cut out by hand, but for a large lawn, it is easiest to use a selective weedkiller when the weeds are growing actively. This may be in granular or liquid form and can be part of the lawn fertilizing program.

Moss

Almost always undesirable, moss may be found in lawns for many reasons, including soil compaction, poor drainage, low fertility, insufficient light, mowing too closely, and extremes of soil pH; it can be a problem even in the best-kept lawns. Treat moss with a chemical moss killer, then remove it by scarifying (see p.392). If the problem continually recurs, identify and correct the possible causes; these may involve improving soil aeration, drainage, and fertility and, on light soils, top-dressing to assist water retention. Adopting an annual maintenance program should help control the problem. For further details see PLANT PROBLEMS, "Lawn weeds," p.661

Pests and diseases

There are several species of insect that live in the soil and feed on grass roots. These include white grubs, the larvae of June bugs and Japanese beetles, chinch bugs, and sod webworms. Moles and ants can also cause problems by excavating soil and forming hills.

Several lawn diseases, including brown patch (see "Drought," p.655), dollar spot, fairy rings, snow mold, and red thread, attack lawns, particularly in hot, humid areas; snow mold is a problem in cold regions, too, and may occur under snow. Preventive sprays may be necessary, but in cooler temperate and maritime climates it is usual to spray only in serious cases. For treatment of pests and diseases, see "Lawn problems," p.657.

LEVELING A HOLLOW OR HUMP

1 *Cut a cross right through the hump or hollow in the sod, using a half-moon edger. The cross should reach just beyond the problem area.*

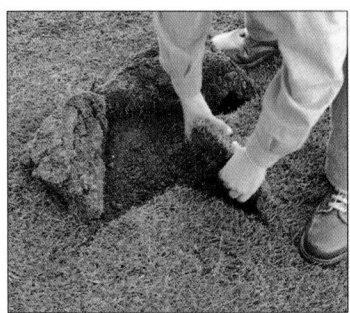

2 *Fold back the cut sections of sod, taking care not to pull them too roughly to avoid cracking.*

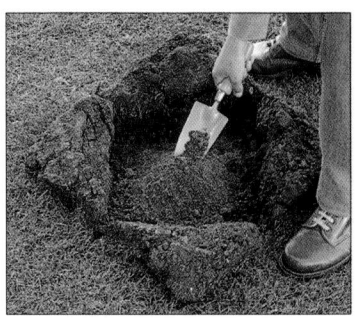

3 *For a hollow, fill in the ground beneath with a good sandy topsoil; for a hump, remove some of the soil until the entire surface is level.*

4 *Replace the folded-back sod and lightly firm to check that the level is correct. Adjust the soil level beneath (if necessary), firm, top-dress, and water well.*

Wildflower and meadow gardening

Wildflower gardening stems in part from a wish to conserve native species that are threatened by the erosion of their natural habitats. While it is not possible to re-create such habitats exactly, growing even a small area of wildflowers contributes to their conservation and attracts a variety of insects (often beneficial) and other wildlife into the garden.

Creating a wildflower area is often the best way of using part of the garden that does not lend itself to more conventional cultivation, perhaps because it is too exposed, sloping, or dry, or has poor soil.

Wildflower gardens

Wildflower habitats are extremely diverse and include meadows or flower-rich grasslands (see p.383), prairies, alpine meadows, wetlands, and woodlands (see p.20).

When planning a wildflower area, assess the site, taking into account climate, soil type, and drainage, and the degree of sun, shade, and shelter. The growing conditions will determine the plants that will thrive and look natural in the setting.

An open, sunny site with well-drained soil is ideal for a meadow with purple coneflower (*Echinacea purpurea*), Indian blanket (*Gaillardia aristata*), and butterfly weed (*Asclepias tuberosa*). A more exposed site may suit an alpine meadow with short grass and low-growing plants, such as

little red elephant (*Pedicularis groenlandica*) and blue-eyed grass (*Sisyrinchium bellum*) that will not be damaged by wind. Damp or waterlogged ground may be used for a bog garden (see p.277) with plants such as turtlehead (*Chelone glabra*).

Observe the local wild flora, since this will indicate which species to grow, but never take plants from the wild without gaining permission from the landowner. You can also include some non-native plants that require the same conditions and are in keeping with the planting style.

Seasonal variation
Depending on the site and the selected plants, the main display may be planned for a particular season or to extend over a longer period. A woodland habitat favors spring-flowering plants, for example, because the tree canopy lets through more light than it does later on. Meadows are at their peak in summer but have a long span of interest, from the spring-flowering bluets (*Houstonia caerulea*) through fall-flowering New England asters (*Aster novae-angliae*).

Establishing a meadow garden

A meadow garden should preferably be established on soil that is low in fertility, using a mixture of fine grasses such as bents (*Agrostis*)

THE WILDFLOWER MEADOW
Many wild species bloom more profusely under cultivation than in the wild, providing a rich food source for bees, butterflies, and their larvae.

and fescues (*Festuca*) that will not outgrow and suppress the flowering plants. Typical meadow flowers include perennials such as bottle gentian (*Gentiana andrewsii*) and annuals such as California poppy (*Eschscholzia californica*).

Sowing and planting
Eliminate vigorous, perennial weeds such as docks (*Rumex*) and dandelions (*Taraxacum officinale*) with a systemic weedkiller. Then strip off any sod, and remove the upper layer of fertile topsoil for use elsewhere. Cultivate the soil to a fine tilth, firm by treading or rolling, and rake lightly. The stale seedbed technique may be used (see SOILS AND FERTILIZERS, p.614) to reduce weed competition. In early fall or spring, sow the wildflower seed mixture (with fine sand for even distribution) at a rate of ⅛oz/sq yd (4g/sq m) or as advised by the supplier.

If establishing wildflowers in existing grassland or in an orchard, reduce the soil fertility over one or two years by mowing regularly and removing the clippings. Then introduce potgrown plants, using a small bulb planter to remove cores of sod.

Maintenance
During the first summer after seeding, spot-treat any invasive weeds, such as thistles or plantains, as they appear. If annuals were included in

the seed mix, they will bloom the first year, but the perennials will not bloom until the second summer. Mow the meadow in the fall, after plants have seeded, cutting to 3–4in (7–10cm). Rake up and remove the clippings so that soil fertility remains low. In areas where open fires are permitted, you may adopt a burnoff program to remove plant debris, but do this with great care.

AIDING NATURAL DISTRIBUTION
After cutting, allow clippings to dry, and then shake out the seeds. It is worth gathering some to sow for plug or potted plants for next year.

FLOWERING PLANTS FOR DIFFERENT HABITATS

Rudbeckia hirta
(meadow)

Monarda fistulosa
(meadow)

Caltha palustris
(bog)

Sanguinaria canadensis
(woodland)

Arisaema triphyllum
(woodland)

Erythronium americanum
(woodland)

395

CHAPTER

15

THE HERB GARDEN

WHETHER GROWN ON their own as an ornamental feature, with other plants in a border, or among the ordered ranks of a vegetable patch, herbs are an invaluable addition to any garden. They have long been prized for their culinary, cosmetic, or curative uses, but they also make highly decorative garden plants. Although few have showy flowers, many are graced by attractive foliage, and almost all are worth growing for their scent alone, ranging from the tang of lemon balm to the aniseed aroma of fennel and the sweet apple perfume of chamomile. Their fragrances are hard to resist, and their nectar-filled flowers tempt bees and butterflies, adding the animated hum of insects to the herb garden.

Designing with herbs

HERB growing combines the delights of the flower garden with the productivity of the vegetable plot. The results are decorative, excellent in aroma and flavor, and inexpensive to produce. By definition, an herb is any plant that has culinary or curative uses, so the range is surprisingly wide. Herbs include trees and shrubs, not just herbaceous perennials and annuals.

Historically, herbs have been used for flavoring and preserving food, and, in addition, for making medicines and toiletries. Their aesthetic appeal has always been important too, and their ornamental qualities, as well as their practical uses, are of equal value today.

STRUCTURED INFORMALITY
Growing a rich profusion of herbs brings a wealth of fine scents and contrasting textures to the garden. In this herb garden, clipped dwarf hedges add structure, while bold blocks of herbs such as golden marjoram contrast with casual plantings of feathery fennel and low alpine strawberries.

Herbs in the home

Although fresh and dried herbs are widely available, they rarely have as fine an aroma or flavor as those harvested from your own garden. Enjoy their scents indoors as well as outside by using them fresh in flower arrangements or dried to make potpourri or to fill herb pillows.

For the adventurous, herbs may also be used to make richly colored dyes: tansy flowers (*Tanacetum vulgare*) produce yellow dye, and sorrel roots (*Rumex acetosa*) yield a soft pink color. Exotic paper may be embedded with herb flowers and leaves. Furniture wax can be made with marjoram (*Origanum vulgare*).

Culinary uses
Freshly harvested herbs are an important ingredient in many classic combinations, such as tomato and basil salad, potato salad with chives, and May wine with sweet woodruff. Some flowers can be used as an edible decoration: borage, chives, elder, and pot marigold are all simple to grow and produce attractive flowers. Stalks, such as angelica for crystallizing or branches of rosemary for barbecues, are also easily grown but are rarely available otherwise. Aromatic seeds and spices are easier to obtain but again are simple, and mostly cheap, to produce.

Certain herbs, such as lemon balm and peppermint, may be infused in boiling water to make herb teas. They are a good alternative to ordinary tea and coffee, because they do not contain tannin or caffeine. Most are made from dried leaves, flowers, or seeds, although they may also be made from fresh herbs.

Medicinal herbs
In many parts of the world, herbal medicine is commonplace, and the herb garden is a source of home-grown treatments for all sorts of ailment. Mint, for example, is a mild local anesthetic, a powerful antiseptic, and a remedy for digestive problems. Herbs are also grown for processing into drugs by the pharmaceutical industry. In general, it is inadvisable to use herbs for medicinal purposes without expert knowledge or advice.

Cosmetic and scented preparations
A number of herbs have beneficial effects on the condition of skin or hair and are included in beauty products. Rosemary, chamomile, and mint are used in shampoos and conditioners; thyme as an antiseptic for mouthwashes; and pot marigold and elderflower in skin lotions.

Aromatic herbs may be enjoyed all year if they are made into scented household articles such as linen sachets and pomanders. Commercially, they are also used in perfumery. Extracting oils and essences is, however, usually too complex to undertake at home.

Herbs in the garden
A surprising number of herbs grown today are still the wild species, but many cultivars are also now available, differing in habit or in the color of their foliage or flowers. This diversity makes them even more valuable as decorative garden plants,

while their scent and other properties are usually similar, if not identical, to the species.

The appeal of herbs lies largely in their fragrance, which, in contrast to that of other plants, usually derives from the foliage rather than the flowers. Essential oils are released when the leaves are warmed or crushed; on a sunny day, the scent from an herb garden fills the air.

A few herbs have brightly colored flowers, which may be used to great advantage: the orange of pot marigolds (*Calendula officinalis*) offset by bronze fennel (*Foeniculum vulgare* 'Purpureum'), or the blue of borage (*Borago officinalis*) with silver-gray wormwood (*Artemisia absinthium*), for example.

Certain herbs are reputed to benefit other plants: some pungent plants such as southernwood (*Artemisia abrotanum*) are said to repel insects if crushed or infused. Growing chamomile (*Chamaemelum nobile*) in the garden is supposed to increase the health and vigor of nearby plants.

Where to grow herbs

Herbs, like other plants, should be grown in conditions that are similar to their natural habitat to be sure that they are healthy and vigorous. Many herbs are Mediterranean in origin, and these usually prefer plenty of sunshine and a freely draining soil.

Several herbs tolerate a damp, partially shaded site, provided that they are not waterlogged or in dense or permanent shade. Most variegated and golden cultivars thrive in light shade. As a rule, gray-foliaged

HERBS THAT TOLERATE MOIST SHADE

Angelica (*Angelica archangelica*)
Chervil (*Anthriscus cerefolium*)
Chives (*Allium schoenoprasum*)
Elder (*Sambucus nigra, S. n.* 'Aurea', *S. n.* 'Marginata')
Feverfew (*Tanacetum parthenium, T. p.* 'Aureum')
Lemon balm (*Melissa officinalis, M. o.* 'All Gold', *M. o.*'Aurea', *M. o.* 'Variegata')
Lovage (*Levisticum officinale*)
Mints (*Mentha*)
Parsley (*Petroselinum crispum*)
Sorrel (*Rumex acetosa*)
Sweet cicely (*Myrrhis odorata*)
Tansy (*Tanacetum vulgare*)
Woodruff (*Asperula odorata*)

herbs do not tolerate high humidity. Pineapple mint (*Mentha suaveolens* 'Variegata') and golden forms of lemon balm (*Melissa officinalis*) and feverfew (*Tanacetum parthenium*, syn. *Chrysanthemum parthenium*) retain their color best when lit by either morning or evening sun but shaded at midday.

Herbs may be grown in a variety of situations. A separate herb garden in an attractive design provides an appealing feature and need not take up much space. It may be preferable to have a culinary herb patch, or herbs in containers, within easy reach of the kitchen. Some herbs are decorative enough to be grown with other plants in a bed or border, while others may be better sited in the vegetable garden. Culinary herbs should always be sited away from possible contamination by pets or roadside pollution.

Herb gardens
If there is space, it is worth creating a separate herb garden to grow many different herbs together for a strong impact and to reap the benefit of their combined scents in one place. Making a special feature of the plants allows plenty of opportunity to create an interesting pattern or design using blocks of complementary or contrasting colors. As well as being a highly ornamental way of displaying the herbs, it makes harvesting easier. Herb gardens are traditionally bordered by low, clipped hedges of boxwood (*Buxus sempervirens*), but a less formal edging of hyssop (*Hyssopus officinalis*) or lavender (*Lavandula*) would also be suitable.

Beds and borders
Herbs may also be grown with other ornamental garden plants. This is useful where there is no space for a separate herb garden, or for herbs that are border plants in their own right, such as bee balm (*Monarda didyma*) and rue (*Ruta graveolens*). Gray-leaved species are especially fine in a silver border or as a contrast to plants with blue, pink, or purple coloring such as purple sage (*Salvia officinalis* 'Purpurascens').

Stately architectural plants are valuable as focal points on their own or at the back of a border. Fill gaps in borders with colorful annuals such as poppies (*Papaver*), blue borage (*Borago officinalis*), and dark-leaved basil (*Ocimum basilicum* 'Purpurascens').

Planting aromatic herbs next to doorways, paths, and seats makes it easy to enjoy their scents to the fullest. Low, spreading herbs, such

as wild thyme (*Thymus serpyllum*), lawn chamomile (*Chamaemelum nobile* 'Treneague'), and creeping savory (*Satureja spicigera*), are suitable for rock gardens or en masse to form a fragrant carpet. These and other, more upright, herbs such as chives (*Allium schoenoprasum*) make an unusual and attractive edging to a border or path.

Herbs in the vegetable garden
For culinary herbs that are used in large quantities, such as parsley (*Petroselinum crispum*), the vegetable patch may be the best site. This may also be the most convenient place for fast-growing herbs such as chervil (*Anthriscus cerefolium*) and dill (Anethum graveolens) that are sown in succession and do not transplant successfully. The herbs may be grown in straight rows among the vegetables or as an ornamental border around the edge of the vegetable garden.

Growing herbs in containers
Many herbs grow well in containers. From a hanging basket to a plastic pail, almost any container is suitable, provided that it has drainage holes (if not, add a layer of drainage material before planting in it).

In small gardens or on balconies, the entire herb garden may consist of containers, imaginatively positioned on walls, steps, shelves, and windowsills, as well as at ground level. If space is at a premium, using a strawberry jar (a pot with planting pockets) offers an attractive and functional way of growing a number of different plants together. Even if you have a separate area for herbs or grow them with other ornamentals or vegetables, it is often convenient to have one or two pots of commonly used herbs near the door.

Some of the best herbs for containers are chervil, parsley, chives, compact marjoram (*Origanum vul-*

CARTWHEEL BED
A cartwheel design provides a decorative and practical way of growing a small selection of herbs.

CONTAINER GARDENING
Even in the smallest garden, there is room to grow a variety of aromatic herbs in a group of pots.

gare 'Compactum'), rock hyssop (*Hyssopus officinalis* subsp. *aristatus*), and thymes (*Thymus*). Large plants such as rosemary (*Rosmarinus officinalis*) and bay (*Laurus nobilis*) often look good grown as single specimens in pots or tubs. Growing slightly tender herbs such as myrtle (*Myrtus communis*), lemon verbena (*Aloysia triphylla*), and rose-scented geranium (*Pelargonium graveolens*) in containers is convenient because they may be brought inside during winter. They also make good conservatory plants.

Paving and patios
Planting herbs in the gaps between paving stones is an attractive option for herbs that prefer well-drained conditions, such as thymes and creeping savory. Allow the plants to spread so that an occasional light tread releases their fragrance.

Patios are often ideal for displaying a variety of tender or Mediterranean herbs that enjoy warmth and shelter, while an exotic touch may be added by including plants such as lemon trees (*Citrus limon*), cardamom (*Elettaria cardamomum*), or ginger (*Zingiber officinale*) grown in ornamental containers.

Raised beds
Growing herbs in raised beds makes it easier to enjoy their fragrance at close quarters as well as being practical for the physically impaired, providing good access for planting, maintenance, and harvesting. Raised beds must have strong retaining walls and should be no more than approximately 30in (75cm) wide and at a comfortable height for working (see also STRUCTURES AND SURFACES, "Raised beds," p.593).

Raised beds are also a good option on paved areas against a wall (but not above the level of the basement walls) and in any site where the soil is not free-draining. Choose small, compact herbs for raised beds, and control their spread by regular pruning and dividing.

Designing an herb garden

Whether informal or formal, an herb garden should be designed so that it is compatible with the style of the rest of the garden and the house. Take into account maintenance resources when planning: in general, informal herb gardens need less initial structural work than formal ones, and routine care may be less time-consuming, depending on the plants used and the size and complexity of the design. It is also possible to combine elements of both formal and informal designs; for example, a well-defined, symmetrical pattern of paths could form a framework for a free planting of herbs of different heights, habits, and colors.

Informal designs

An informal design largely depends for its success upon the complementary habits and colors of the herbs. Many variegated and colored-leaved forms such as golden marjoram (*Origanum vulgare* 'Aureum') and purple sage are especially dramatic in such a design. Try green- and gold-leaved plants together, for example, or those with purple and silver foliage.

There is greater freedom to use plants of different heights and habits than in a formal design: tall ones may be used strikingly without upsetting the balance and impact of the

FORMAL HERB GARDEN
This well-planned layout is divided by brick paths, which provide a formal framework for a number of geometric herb beds.

design, and the overall impression of colorful harmony and rich abundance allows greater flexibility for experimenting with bold, innovative, or even daring combinations. Consider including a few simple pots or rustic containers as well.

Formal designs

These designs are usually based on geometric patterns and framed by low hedges or paths. Each small bed created by the pattern is then planted with one kind of herb, giving bold blocks of color and texture. At its simplest, the design may take the form of a cartwheel bedded into the soil with a different herb planted in each segment. These designs often look particularly impressive when viewed from above, so consider siting the herb garden where it may be viewed from an upper win-

dow (such as from a bedroom) or a slope. When choosing plants, do not include tall, invasive, or sprawling herbs that may spoil the rest of the design when fully grown.

A formal garden with paths is labor intensive initially but soon looks mature and needs little structural maintenance. One that includes a framework of dwarf hedges that require regular clipping may be considerably more demanding. The

hedging may outline the design or take on the complex shapes of a knot garden. Suitable plants for dwarf hedges include boxwood, hyssop, lavenders, shrubby germander (*Teucrium fruticans*), and winter savory (*Satureja montana*) planted about 9–12in (22–30cm) apart.

Making a plan

To draw up a plan, first measure the site and surrounding features accurately, taking account of any changes in grade. Also note where shadows fall at different seasons as well as at different times of day.

Whether the garden is to be formal or informal in style, remember that herbs should be within arm's reach for convenient routine care and harvesting. For beds or borders in open ground, access by paths or stepping-stones will greatly help reduce harmful soil compaction.

Transfer the measurements to graph paper, working to scale. In order to compare a number of different designs, draw each design on a sheet of tracing paper laid over the master plan.

Finally, decide on which herbs to grow and mark them on the plan. Take into account their cultivation requirements, habit, color, eventual height and spread, and the amounts that will be required for harvesting. Herbs in containers may also be included in the garden design to provide focal points.

HERBS IN A PATIO GARDEN
Enliven a patio or courtyard, and soften the effect of the hard elements, by planting herbs directly into the gaps between paving or in gravel.

PLANNING A FORMAL HERB GARDEN

There are many possible formal designs, although imagination should be restrained by considerations of balance and proportion. Cartwheel and chessboard layouts are popular, but unusual geometric patterns also provide plenty of opportunity to create an eye-catching feature.

Directory of common herbs

Chives
(*Allium schoenoprasum*)

Herbaceous, clump-forming perennial with hollow, grasslike leaves and mauve flowers. Good as a low edging for borders. May be forced for winter use (see p.405). Use the leaves, which have a mild onion flavor, as a garnish and flavoring in salads, dips, soft cheeses, and soups; the edible flowers make a decorative addition to salads.
Harvesting and storing Cut leaves and flowers as available to use fresh. For freezing and drying, cut leaves before flowering and chop finely.
Propagation By seed sown in spring (see p.194) or by division in fall (p.196).
Related species and variants Variations in height, flower color, and flavor are available. Chinese, or garlic, chives (*A. tuberosum*) have a mild garlic flavor and white flowers.

Lemon verbena
(*Aloysia triphylla*)

Upright, deciduous shrub with pointed, oval leaves. Plants will be cut back by frost but grow again from the base outdoors in mild areas. The leaves have a strong lemon scent and are used in herb teas, desserts, potpourri, and teas.
Harvesting and storing Pick leaves during the growing season for using fresh or for drying.
Propagation By softwood cuttings (see p.109).

Dill
(*Anethum graveolens*)

Upright annual with flat heads of greenish yellow flowers and feathery, blue-green leaves. Do not plant dill near fennel, since this may result in cross-pollination and the loss of its distinctive flavor. Runs to seed quickly. Use the leaves or, for a stronger flavor, the aromatic seeds in soups, sauces, potato salad, pickles, and fish dishes.
Harvesting and storing Pick leaves in spring and summer before flowering. Cut seedheads as they ripen in summer.
Propagation By seed sown in spring and early summer (see p.210); may not transplant well.

Angelica
(*Angelica archangelica*)

Biennial with large, divided leaves and large flower heads. A bold, architectural plant. Unless seeds are required, remove seedheads before ripening to prevent unwanted seedlings. The young stalks may be candied; the leaves are used in cooking, especially in fruit desserts and fish dishes.
Harvesting and storing Gather fresh leaves in spring and summer. Cut the young stalks for crystallizing in spring or early summer. Cut seedheads as they ripen in summer.
Propagation By seed sown in fall (see p.210); seeds lose viability within three months of ripening.

Chervil
(*Anthriscus cerefolium*)

Annual with bright green, fernlike leaves. Runs to seed quickly in hot, dry conditions. The leaves have a fine, subtle flavor reminiscent of parsley and anise. Use the leaves in egg dishes, salads, soups, and sauces.
Harvesting and storing Gather leaves before flowering. Freeze or dry them gently to preserve their delicate flavor.
Propagation By seed sown at monthly intervals from spring to early fall (see p.210); do not transplant. May also be sown in trays under cover in early fall for winter use.

Horseradish
(*Armoracia rusticana*)

Perennial with large, coarse leaves. Plants are persistent and difficult to eradicate. The thick, white-fleshed roots have a pungent flavor and are grated into coleslaw, dips, and sauces, especially horseradish sauce. Young leaves are used in salads or sandwiches.
Harvesting and storing Pick the young leaves in spring. Harvest the roots in fall when the flavor is at its peak, or as required.
Propagation By division (see p.196), 6in (15cm) root cuttings (p.199), or by seed (p.194).

Southernwood
(*Artemisia abrotanum*)

Semievergreen subshrub with finely divided, gray-green foliage. May be used to form a low hedge, trimmed in summer; it is also attractive in mixed borders. Flowers are rarely produced in colder climates. Use the aromatic leaves in potpourri and as an insect repellant.
Harvesting and storing In summer, pick leaves as required for using fresh or for drying.
Propagation By softwood cuttings in summer, semiripe heel cuttings in late summer, or hardwood cuttings in fall (see pp.109–112).

Wormwood
(*Artemisia absinthium*)

Deciduous subshrub with deeply divided, grayish green leaves. Good as a border plant or informal hedge. Prune to within 6in (15cm) of the ground in spring. The aromatic leaves are intensely bitter; they were formerly used to flavor alcoholic drinks (such as absinthe) but are now regarded as toxic. The foliage is attractive in herbal decorations.
Harvesting and storing Pick foliage in summer for use fresh or dried in arrangements.
Propagation By softwood cuttings in summer (see p.109) or by semiripe heel cuttings in late summer (p.111).
Variants 'Lambrook Silver' is a cultivar with silver-gray foliage.

French tarragon
(*Artemisia dracunculus*)

Perennial with upright stems and glossy, narrow leaves. In colder areas it may need winter protection, but it can be forced for winter use. The leaves are commonly used in béarnaise sauce, fines herbes, tartar sauce, and egg and chicken dishes, as well as to flavor vinegar.
Harvesting and storing Cut sprigs of foliage throughout the growing season, leaving two-thirds of the stem to regrow. The leaves are best frozen but may also be dried.
Propagation By division of rhizomes in spring (see p.197) or by stem tip cuttings in summer (p.198). Seed is not available: that sold as tarragon is the Russian species.
Related species Russian tarragon (*A. dracunculoides*) is a hardier species, but it unfortunately has an inferior flavor.

Borage
(*Borago officinalis*)

Upright annual with hairy foliage and intense blue flowers. Add the cucumber-flavored leaves and the flowers to cold drinks and salads. Crystallize the flowers for use in cake decoration or as a garnish.
Harvesting and storing Pick young leaves and use fresh. Gather the flowers (without calyces) in summer to use fresh, freeze in ice cubes, or crystallize.
Propagation Sow seed from spring to early fall (see p.210). Self-sows in light soils.
Variants There is also a form with white flowers, *B. o. f. alba*.

Pot marigold
(*Calendula officinalis*)

Bushy, hardy annual with bright orange flowers. A colorful plant for borders and containers. Deadhead to prolong flowering. Use the petals to flavor and color rice, cream cheese, and soups, and to garnish salads. Chop the young leaves into salads. Dried petals may be used to add color to potpourri.
Harvesting and storing Pick open flowers in summer and remove petals for drying. Gather leaves when young.
Propagation By seed sown in fall or spring (see p.210). Self-sows freely.
Variants Double-flowered forms in shades of cream, orange, and bronze are widely available.

Caraway
(*Carum carvi*)

Biennial with feathery leaves and, in the second year, flat heads of tiny white flowers. Aromatic seeds are used in baking, confectionery, cheeses, and meat stews such as goulash. Add the leaves to soups and salads.
Harvesting and storing Gather leaves when young. Gather the ripe seedheads in summer.
Propagation By seed in fall (see p.210).

Chamomile
(*Chamaemelum nobile*)

Creeping, vigorous perennial, forming a dense mat of finely cut, feathery leaves. Good at the edge of paths and borders, or between paving stones. May be planted as an ornamental lawn (see p.383). Use the apple-scented leaves in potpourri; the aromatic flowers are used in potpourri and herb teas.
Harvesting and storing Pick leaves at any time as required. Gather flowers when fully open in summer, and dry whole.
Propagation By division in spring or fall (see p.196), or by stem tip cuttings of sideshoots in summer (p.198).
Variants 'Treneague' is a dwarf, nonflowering form that is particularly suitable for lawns and gaps in paving. *C. n.* var. *flore-pleno* has attractive double flowers.

Cilantro/Coriander
(*Coriandrum sativum*)

Annual with divided foliage and small white or pale mauve flowers. The plants have a distinctive odor and are not commonly grown indoors. The lobed lower leaves (known as cilantro) are used in curries, chutneys, sauces, and salads. The seeds (coriander), which have a sweet, spicy flavor, are used in baking, chutneys, and sausages.
Harvesting and storing Pick young leaves for using fresh or for freezing. Gather seedheads as they ripen.
Propagation By seed in fall or spring (see p.210).

Cumin
(*Cuminum cyminum*)

Annual with delicate leaves and white or pale pink flowers. Requires heat for the seeds to ripen. The aromatic seeds are used in curries, pickles, yogurt, and Middle Eastern dishes.
Harvesting and storing Gather seedheads as they ripen.
Propagation By seed sown in late spring in a warm site or under cover (see p.211).

Fennel
(*Foeniculum vulgare*)

Perennial with fine filigree leaves and clusters of yellow flowers. A tall, graceful plant for borders. Use the leaves and leaf sheaths for their anise flavor in salads and meat and fish dishes. Seeds are used in baking, fish dishes, and herb teas.
Harvesting and storing Cut leaves and leaf sheaths when still young. Gather seedheads as they ripen.
Propagation By seed sown in spring (see p.194) or by division in fall (p.196).
Variants 'Purpureum' is an attractive bronze cultivar; Florence fennel (*F. v.* var. *dulce*) is grown as an annual for use as a vegetable (see p.534).

Woodruff
(*Galium odoratum,* syn. *Asperula odorata*)

Creeping perennial with star-shaped white flowers that appear above the whorls of narrow leaves in spring and early summer. An excellent groundcover in damp shade. The dried leaves are used in potpourri and herb tea.
Harvesting and storing Gather the leaves for drying just before the flowers open in spring.
Propagation By division in fall or spring (see p.196) or by seed sown in early fall (p.194), but germination may be slow.

Hyssop
(*Hyssopus officinalis*)

Semievergreen subshrub with spikes of small, dark purple-blue flowers. Suitable for growing as a low hedge. The aromatic leaves are used sparingly in soups, bean dishes, stews, game, and pâté.
Harvesting and storing Gather leaves any time for fresh use; pick young leaves in early summer to dry.
Propagation By seed (see p.113), division (p.116), or by softwood cuttings in spring (p.109).

Orris
(*Iris 'Florentina',* syn. *I. florentina*)

Perennial with off-white flowers and sword-shaped leaves. The thick rhizome is bitter when fresh but develops a violet scent after drying and prolonged storage. It is ground for using as a fixative in potpourri and linen sachets.
Harvesting and storing In fall, dig up rhizomes at least three years old. Peel, split, and dry, leaving them for up to two years before grinding.
Propagation By division of rhizomes in late spring or early fall (see p.197).

Bay
(*Laurus nobilis*)

Small evergreen tree or large shrub with dark, leathery, pointed leaves. Makes an excellent topiary or container plant. Use the leaves in *bouquet garni* and for flavoring stock, marinades, sauces, custards, and meat and fish dishes.
Harvesting and storing Pick leaves any time for using fresh. Dry mature leaves in summer.
Propagation By semiripe heel cuttings of side shoots in late summer (see p.77) or by layering in summer (p.79).
Variants 'Aurea' has yellow-flushed leaves.

Lavender
(*Lavandula angustifolia*)

Evergreen, bushy shrub with narrow, gray-green leaves and upright, mauve flower spikes. The flowers are used in potpourri, linen sachets, herb pillows, and tea. They may also be crystallized or used to flavor oil or vinegar.
Harvesting and storing Gather flowering stems in summer, and air-dry.
Propagation By cuttings of semiripe, nonflowering shoots in summer (see p.110).
Variants and related species 'Hidcote' is more compact, and 'Nana Alba' has white flowers French lavender (*L. stoechas*) has purple flowers crowned by purple bracts and is less hardy.

Lovage
(*Levisticum officinale*, syn. *Ligusticum levisticum*)

Perennial with divided leaves and clusters of pale green flowers; a tall plant, suitable for the back of a border. The leaves have a strong flavor, resembling celery and yeast, and are used in soups, stocks, and stews; add the raw young leaves to salads. The aromatic seeds are used in baking and vegetable dishes, and the young stalks may be crystallized. Blanch plants under pots in spring for use as a vegetable.
Harvesting and storing Pick young leaves in spring and freeze or dry. Gather young spring stalks for crystallizing. After they have been under pots for two to three weeks, cut blanched stalks in spring, , leaving central shoots to grow.
Propagation By seed sown when ripe in late summer (see p.194), or division in spring or fall (p.196).

Lemon balm
(*Melissa officinalis*)

Clump-forming perennial with oval, toothed leaves. Add the lemon-scented leaves to cold drinks and to sweet and savory dishes, or infuse them to make herb tea.
Harvesting and storing Pick leaves before flowering for using fresh or for drying.
Propagation By seed sown in spring (see p.194) or division in spring or fall (p.196).
Variants Yellow-variegated cultivars, such as 'Aurea', are available; grow them in partial shade to avoid leaf scorch.

Mint
(*Mentha spicata*)

Herbaceous perennial with tiny mauve flowers in summer. May be invasive (see p.405). Use the leaves to make mint sauce, in salads and drinks, and with potatoes or peas.
Harvesting and storing Pick leaves before flowering and dry or freeze, or chop and infuse in vinegar.
Propagation By stem tip cuttings rooted in spring or summer (see p.198), or by division in spring or fall (p.196).
Related species The numerous species and cultivars have slightly differing foliage and scents. Some, such as pineapple mint (*M. suaveolens* 'Variegata'), have variegated leaves. Peppermint (*M.* x *piperita*) has purplish green leaves used in peppermint tea and in syrups, candy, and desserts, while eau-de-cologne mint (*M.* x *piperita* 'Citrata') has purple-flushed foliage and a perfume. Bowles' mint (*M.* x *villosa* 'Alopecuroides') has rounded leaves with a fresh spearmint aroma and purplish pink flowers.

Bee balm
(*Monarda didyma*)

Herbaceous perennial with heads of red claw-shaped flowers in summer. An excellent border plant for moist soil. Infuse the aromatic leaves in tea for an "Earl Grey" flavor, and add them to summer drinks, salads, pork dishes, or potpourri. Use the flowers to add color to salads and potpourri.
Harvesting and storing Pick leaves in spring or just before flowering in summer for using fresh or for drying. Gather flowers in summer.
Propagation By seed in spring (see p.194), stem cuttings in summer (p.198), or division in early spring (p.196).
Related species and variants Cultivars with red, pink, white, or purple flowers are available. *M. fistulosa* has lavender flowers.

Sweet cicely
(*Myrrhis odorata*)

Herbaceous perennial with flat heads of tiny white flowers in summer. The fernlike leaves, which have an anise flavor, are used mainly in fruit dishes to reduce acidity but may also be added to salads. The thick taproot can be eaten raw or cooked as a vegetable. The large seeds are added to fruit dishes.
Harvesting and storing Pick leaves in spring and early summer for drying. Gather unripe seeds in summer and dry or pickle them. Dig up roots in fall for using fresh.
Propagation By seed sown outdoors in fall (see p.195). Self-sows readily.

Basil
(*Ocimum basilicum*)

Annual with toothed, pointed-oval leaves. In colder regions, basil must be grown under cover or in a warm position. Grows well in pots on a sunny windowsill. The highly aromatic leaves are used in salads, vinegars, pesto, and pasta dishes.
Harvesting and storing Pick leaves when young in summer and freeze, dry, or use to flavor herb oil or vinegar. Pack leaves in jars of oil to preserve them.
Propagation By seed sown in warmth in late spring (see p.211).
Related species and variants 'Purpurascens' is an attractive, purple-leaved cultivar with pink flowers. The compact bush basil (*O. b.* var. *minimum*) is hardier but has less flavor.

Marjoram
(*Origanum vulgare*)

Herbaceous perennial with tiny white or mauve flowers in summer. Needs warmth and full sun for its flavor to develop. The aromatic leaves are used widely in cooking, especially in pizzas and pasta sauces.
Harvesting and storing Pick leaves for immediate use or for drying or freezing, just before flowers open.
Propagation By seed sown in spring (see p.194), division in spring or fall (p.196), or by basal stem or root cuttings of nonflowering shoots in summer (pp.198–99).
Variants The various species and hybrids differ in hardiness, flavor, and flower and foliage color. Golden marjoram (*O. v.* 'Aureum') is one well-known cultivar. The low-growing 'Compactum' is ideal for containers and edging.

Parsley
(*Petroselinum crispum*)

Biennial with bright green, crinkled leaves and, in its second summer, flat heads of tiny, greenish yellow flowers. Good for growing in pots. Use the leaves whole or chopped as a garnish and in *bouquet garni*, sauces, and egg and fish dishes.
Harvesting and storing Pick leaves of plants in their first year and use fresh or freeze.
Propagation By seed sown at intervals from early spring to late summer (see p.210).
Variants *P. c.* 'Neapolitanum' is a flat-leaved parsley with a stronger flavor.

Anise
(*Pimpinella anisum*)

Annual with deeply divided leaves and, in late summer, heads of tiny white flowers. In colder regions, it must have a sunny, sheltered position for the seed to ripen. Add the leaves to fruit salads. The aromatic seeds are used in baking, confectionery, and sweet and savory dishes.
Harvesting and storing Pick lower leaves in spring for immediate use. Gather seedheads as they ripen in fall.
Propagation By seed sown in late spring in its final position, because it is difficult to transplant successfully (see p.211).

Rosemary
(*Rosmarinus officinalis*)

Evergreen shrub with dense, needlelike leaves and pale blue flowers in spring and summer or all year in milder regions. May be grown as an informal hedge. The leaves, which have a strong, resinous aroma, are used in meat dishes, such as

lamb, and to make potpourri and hair rinses. The flowers may be added to salads.
Harvesting and storing Pick leaves and flowers as required for immediate use. Gather sprigs during the growing season for drying.
Propagation By seed sown in warmth in spring (see p.112), semiripe cuttings in late summer (p.110), or layering in fall (p.114).
Variants Cultivars with flowers in shades of blue, pink, and white are available. The erect cultivar 'Miss Jessopp's Upright' is suitable for hedging. 'Severn Sea' has bright blue flowers and a dwarf, arching habit ideal for containers. 'Arp' is hardiest and has paler leaves.

Sorrel
(Rumex acetosa)

Upright perennial with dock-like leaves. Remove the flower spikes to prolong leaf production. Protect with covers for a winter supply. The young, tender leaves, which have a sour taste, are used in salads, soups, and sauces.
Harvesting and storing Pick young leaves before flowering for using fresh or freezing. Frozen leaves can be used in cooked dishes.
Propagation By division in either spring or fall (see p.196), or by seed sown in spring (p.194).
Related species The low-growing species, known as French, shield, or buckler-leaf sorrel (*R. scutatus*), has small, fine-flavored leaves.

Rue
(Ruta graveolens)

Evergreen subshrub with divided, gray-green foliage and greenish yellow flowers in summer. Handling rue on sunny days may cause a severe skin rash. Use the pungent leaves very sparingly in salads and sauces, and to flavor cream cheese.
Harvesting and storing Pick leaves as required for immediate use, protecting hands with rubber gloves on sunny days.
Propagation By seed sown in spring (see p.112), or cuttings of semiripe side shoots in late summer (p.110).
Variants 'Variegata' leaves irregularly variegated with cream; 'Jackman's Blue' more compact .

Sage
(Salvia officinalis)

Evergreen subshrub with gray-green foliage and purplish blue flowers. An excellent plant for shrub borders and rose gardens. The aromatic leaves are used in poultry stuffings, rich meat dishes, and herb teas, and to flavor cheese.

Harvesting and storing Pick leaves as needed to use fresh. Gather leaves before the flowers open for drying.
Propagation By seed sown in spring (see p.112), softwood cuttings in summer (p.109), or semiripe heel cuttings in early fall (p.111).
Variants Cultivars include purple sage (*S. o.* 'Purpurascens') with purple leaves, 'Tricolor' with white-streaked, pink-flushed leaves, and 'Albiflora' with white flowers.

Lavender cotton
(Santolina chamaecyparissus)

Evergreen subshrub with narrow, divided, silver-gray leaves on upright stems. In summer, it bears masses of yellow button flower-heads. It is good as a low hedge, especially to provide a contrasting color in knot gardens.
Add the aromatic leaves to potpourri, and dry the flowers for decorative use.
Harvesting and storing Pick leaves for drying in spring and summer. In summer, gather flowers as they open for drying.
Propagation By cuttings of semiripe sideshoots in late summer (see p.110).
Variants 'Lemon Queen' has bright green foliage and cream flowers; 'Nana' is a dwarf form, only 6in (15cm) tall; *S. virens* has green leaves.

Winter savory
(Satureja montana)

Evergreen subshrub with tiny, white to pink flowers in summer, and small, narrow, aromatic leaves. Use the leaves in bean and cheese dishes.
Harvesting and storing Pick any time for using fresh. When flower buds appear, gather leaves to dry or freeze.
Propagation By seed sown in spring (see p.112), division in spring or fall (p.116), or by softwood cuttings taken between late spring and early summer (p.109).
Related species Creeping savory (*S. spicigera*) is a low species ideal for containers, edging, and rock gardens. Summer savory (*S. hortensis*) has lilac flowers and a fine flavor.

Bible leaf
(Tanacetum balsamita)

Rather coarse perennial with small, daisylike flowers in late summer and oval gray-green leaves. The leaves have a citrus-mint fragrance; use them sparingly in cooking and also in potpourri.
Harvesting and storing Gather leaves in spring and summer for using fresh or for drying.
Propagation By division (see p.196).

Feverfew
(Tanacetum parthenium, syn. *Chrysanthemum parthenium)*

Perennial or annual with light green, chrysanthemum-like leaves; in summer and fall it is covered with long-lasting, daisylike flowers. An easy-to-grow, attractive plant for borders and containers. Use the pungent leaves in sachets to deter clothes moths. The aromatic flowers are added to potpourri.
Harvesting and storing Pick leaves and flowers in summer for drying.
Propagation By seed sown in spring or fall (see p.194), division in fall (p.196), or basal stem cuttings in summer (p.198). Self-sows freely.
Variants Cultivars vary in height and foliage, with single or double flowers. The golden-leaved 'Aureum' is highly recommended.

Thyme
(Thymus vulgaris)

Evergreen, low-growing subshrub with tiny leaves and, in summer, pale lilac flowers. May be grown as an edging for borders, between paving stones, and in containers. Add the aromatic leaves to *bouquet garni*, stuffings, sauces, soups, stocks, and meat dishes.
Harvesting and storing Pick leaves at any time to use fresh. Gather flowering tops for drying, stripping leaves and flowers from the stalks when quite dry. Fresh sprigs may also be infused in oil or vinegar.
Propagation By seed (see p.112) or division in spring (p.116), layering in spring or fall (p.114), or by semiripe heel cuttings in late spring or early summer (p.111).
Related species and variants The many species and cultivars vary in height, foliage, and flower color. Wild thyme (*T. serpyllum*) is a low, mat-forming plant with mauve flowers. *T. praecox* var. *arcticus* 'Coccineus' and 'Snowdrift' have, respectively, magenta and white flowers, and 'Doone Valley' has scented foliage with gold markings. *T. x citriodorus* has lemon-scented leaves and lilac flowers. *T. vulgaris* 'Silver Posie' has silver-margined leaves.

Ginger
(Zingiber officinale)

Tender, deciduous perennial with tall, canelike stems and lance-shaped leaves. The thick, tuberous rhizome is highly aromatic and is used in baking, preserves, confectionery, chutneys, sauces, and many Oriental dishes, including sushi.
Harvesting and storing Dig up young rhizomes and peel them for using fresh or preserving in syrup. For drying, dig up the rhizomes as the leaves turn yellow.
Propagation By division of rhizomes as they start to sprout (see p.197).

Soil preparation and planting

THE ideal site for an herb garden is sunny and open but sheltered, with neutral to alkaline soil, and good drainage. These growing conditions suit the majority of common herbs such as lavender (*Lavandula angustifolia*), winter savory (*Satureja montana*), sage (*Salvia officinalis*), marjoram (*Origanum vulgare*), rosemary (*Rosmarinus officinalis*), and thyme (*Thymus vulgaris*), most of which are Mediterranean in origin.

Preparing the site

If possible, prepare the ground well in advance, preferably in fall. First, remove all weeds, taking care to eliminate any persistent perennial weeds such as quackgrass (*Elymus repens*), using a weedkiller if necessary. Then dig over the soil, leaving it in a rough state over the winter to be broken down by frost.

In early spring, remove any weeds that have appeared, fork in well-rotted organic matter (such as compost or mushroom compost), and rake the soil to a fine, level tilth. The objective is to provide a free-draining and reasonably fertile soil. Fertilizing with manure or inorganic fertilizers is not recommended, especially for Mediterranean herbs, since it produces soft growth that has little aroma or resistance to cold.

On heavy clay soil, it may be necessary to improve the drainage (see SOILS AND FERTILIZERS, "Improving drainage," p.617); alternatively, the herbs may be grown in raised beds or containers. Most herbs tolerate a slightly acidic soil; if the pH is below 6.5, however, add a dressing of lime when preparing the soil (see SOILS AND FERTILIZERS, "Liming," p.619).

Planting invasive herbs

If planting invasive herbs such as mints (*Mentha*), tansy (*Tanacetum vulgare*), or woodruff (*Galium odoratum*, syn. *Asperula odorata*) in open ground, restrict their spread by growing them in sunken containers. Old buckets, large pots, or even heavy-duty plastic bags are suitable, although it is usually necessary to make drainage holes. For best results, lift and divide the plants each spring and replant young, vigorous pieces in the containers using fresh soil mix; if not replenished, nutrients are quickly depleted and the herbs may deteriorate and become more prone to disease, such as rusts (see p.641).

1 *Dig a hole large enough to accommodate a large pot or old bucket. Make drainage holes in the pot, then place it in the hole and fill with a soil and compost mixture.*

2 *Plant the herb (here mint), firming in well; add enough soil mix to conceal the pot's rim, and water thoroughly. Each spring, replant and replace the soil mix in the pot.*

Herbs in winter

Although herbs are harvested mainly in spring and summer, the availability of many can be extended almost all year.

Sown in late summer or early fall, a number of herbs such as chervil (*Anthriscus cerefolium*), cilantro (*Coriandrum sativum*), and parsley (*Petroselinum crispum*) continue to grow throughout the winter if they are protected from severe cold by cloches or a cold frame. They also grow well in pots placed on a sunny windowsill.

Herbaceous perennials that die down in winter, such as chives (*Allium schoenoprasum*), French tarragon (*Artemisia dracunculus*), and mints (*Mentha*), may be forced for winter use. In early fall, dig up mature plants, divide them, and replant in containers of soil-based potting mix. If kept in a bright place that is free from frost and drafts, they produce fresh shoots throughout the winter that may be harvested regularly. Discard forced plants in spring or plant them out; if planted out, do not pick their leaves for at least a season to allow them time to recover.

Evergreen herbs, such as winter savory, thyme, and rosemary, may be gathered throughout the year, but limit winter harvesting to reduce stress to the plants.

Planting container-grown herbs

Container-grown herbs may be planted throughout the year, but the best time is in spring when they establish rapidly. If they have been kept in a heated greenhouse during the winter, gradually harden them off in a cold frame before planting them out.

Water well before planting, because dry root balls are difficult to wet once below ground. To avoid trampling and compacting the soil in a bed, it is best to stand on a board in order to reach the planting positions. Set out the herbs (still in their pots) according to your planting plan and check that each has sufficient room to develop, depending on its growth rate and spread.

Whatever the weather, water thoroughly after planting in order to settle the soil around the plants and provide even moisture for new root growth. After planting, pinch out the tips of clump-forming herbs and trim back shrubby herbs to encourage new sideshoots and to develop a bushy habit.

HOW TO GROW HERBS FOR FRESH WINTER USE

1 *Choose a dry, preferably overcast, day in early fall to lift a clump of herbs (here chives) from the garden using a fork.*

2 *Divide the clump into smaller pieces with your hands or a hand fork. Shake loose as much of the soil as possible from the roots.*

3 *Plant up the divided pieces into pots or trays of soil mix. Water well and cut back the top-growth.*

4 *Place the plants in a bright, frost-free place. Once they are about 4in (10cm) high, harvest the leaves regularly to maintain a supply of new growth.*

Planting an herb garden to a design

Whether creating an intricate, formal design or a simple, informal one, plan carefully, both on paper and on site, to ensure success. Make plans well in advance: start in the winter for planting in the spring, or as early as the preceding summer if you are raising the plants yourself.

As for all planting, thoroughly prepare the ground, clearing any weeds and raking the surface of the soil to a fine tilth (see "Preparing the site," opposite).

Once you have determined the design and the planting plan on paper, mark the basic outline of the herb garden, including any paths, on the prepared site. Make any adjustments to the layout at this stage if required. Container-grown herbs are convenient because they can easily be set out according to the plan and the arrangement checked before the actual planting begins.

If using sod or heavy materials such as paving, bricks, or stone, lay them before planting. Paths made of lighter, loose materials, such as grit, gravel, or shredded bark, may be laid before or after planting. When making paths of grit or gravel, provide retaining boards or edging tiles to prevent the paving material from spreading onto the plants in the beds.

1 *On ground prepared for planting, mark out the herb garden according to the planned design, including any paths or paved areas. Use stakes and string, or grit. Remove the string after planting.*

2 *Lay out the plants, still in their pots, to check the overall look and spacing. If using grit or gravel for the paths, sink boards at the edges to keep the material in place.*

3 *Once the design is completed, plant and water the herbs. Planting them densely achieves the desired result more quickly.*

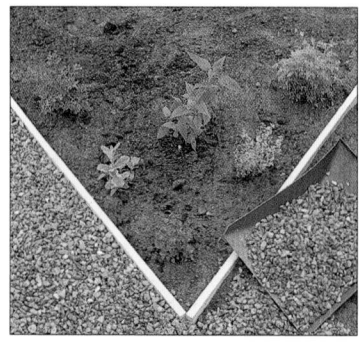

4 *Lay the paths, adding grit or gravel evenly in between the boards; level the surface.*

5 *Keep the herb garden watered and weeded. Pinch out growing tips to promote bushy growth, and prune as necessary.*

DESIGN FOR AN HERB GARDEN

1 Chives (*Allium schoenoprasum*)
2 Compact marjoram (*Origanum vulgare* 'Compactum')
3 Bee balm (*Monarda didyma*)
4 Wormwood (*Artemisia absinthium*)
5 Hyssop (*Hyssopus officinalis*)
6 Wild thyme (*Thymus serpyllum*)
7 Silver-variegated thyme (*Thymus vulgaris* 'Silver Posie')
8 Marjoram (*Origanum vulgare*)
9 Pineapple mint (*Mentha suaveolens* 'Variegata')
10 Chamomile (*Chamaemelum nobile*)
11 French sorrel (*Rumex scutatus*)
12 French tarragon (*Artemisia dracunculus*)
13 Yellow-variegated sage (*Salvia officinalis* 'Icterina')
14 Parsley (*Petroselinum crispum*)
15 Sweet cicely (*Myrrhis odorata*)

16 Lavender cotton (*Santolina chamaecyparissus*)
17 Creeping savory (*Satureja spicigera*)
18 Golden lemon balm (*Melissa officinalis* 'Aurea')
19 Chinese chives (*Allium tuberosum*)
20 Orris (*Iris* 'Florentina')
21 Borage (*Borago officinalis*)
22 Pink hyssop (*Hyssopus officinalis* 'Rosea')
23 Purple sage (*Salvia officinalis* 'Purpurascens')
24 Pink lavender (*Lavandula angustifolia* 'Rosea')
25 Thyme (*Thymus vulgaris*)
26 Dark-leaved basil (*Ocimum basilicum* 'Purpurascens')
27 Rosemary (*Rosmarinus officinalis*)
28 Summer savory (*Satureja hortensis*)
29 Southernwood (*Artemisia abrotanum*)
30 Sweet marjoram (*Origanum majorana*)
31 Bible leaf (*Tanacetum balsamita*)
32 Golden feverfew (*Tanacetum parthenium* 'Aureum')
33 Chervil (*Anthriscus cerefolium*)
34 Pot marigold (*Calendula officinalis*)
35 Bronze fennel (*Foeniculum vulgare* 'Purpureum')
36 Woodruff (*Asperula odorata*)
37 Lavender cotton (*Santolina chamaecyparissus* 'Lemon Queen')
38 Sorrel (*Rumex acetosa*)
39 Lemon thyme (*Thymus* x *citriodorus*)

This small garden includes a wide range of aromatic and culinary herbs. They have been grouped in beds of restricted color and divided by symmetrical paths for a traditional, formal design, softened by the informal plant groupings within the beds.

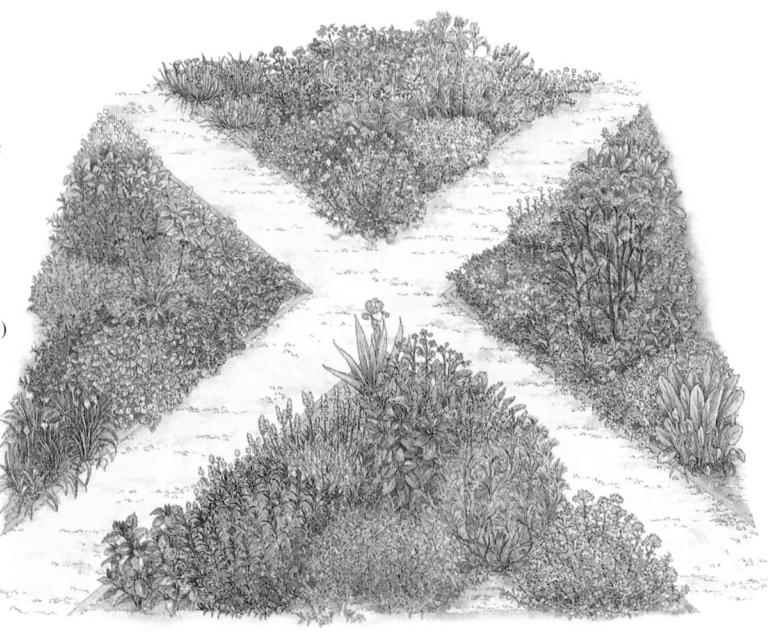

Routine care

Most herbs flourish and require little attention once established. Maintenance largely consists of cutting back plants in spring and summer to encourage healthy growth, and neatening dormant plants in winter. Herbs in containers usually need routine watering and fertilizing during the growing season, while periodic repotting or top-dressing is also necessary. Growing herbs in the right conditions should minimize any pest or disease problems; take action as necessary (see PLANT PROBLEMS, pp. 633–61) but then wait one or two weeks after treatment before using the herbs.

Cutting back

Herbs that are valued for their fresh, young foliage may be cut back to produce a regular supply of leaves. Remove flowering stems of sorrel (*Rumex acetosa*) as they appear. Chives (*Allium schoenoprasum*) and marjoram (*Origanum vulgare*) may be left until after flowering because the flowers are attractive and useful

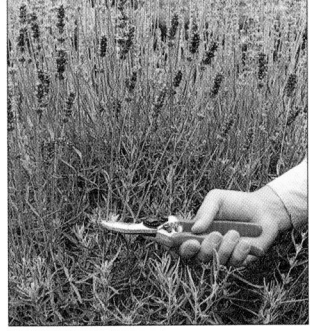

1 *In late summer or early fall, cut off all the dry flower stalks with pruning shears and lightly clip the shrubs to maintain a neat, tighter finish.*

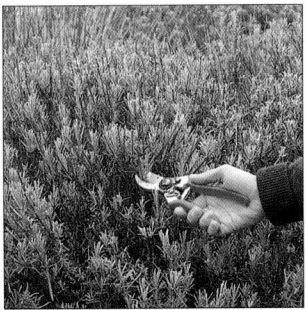

2 *Early the following spring, cut back shoots by 1in (2.5cm) or more of the previous year's growth, making sure that some green growth remains.*

as flavorings. Variegated forms of marjoram, mint (*Mentha*), and lemon balm (*Melissa officinalis*) fade, but they produce bright new foliage if the plant is cut back hard shortly before flowering.

The growth of invasive herbs should be checked regularly. Even when planted in sunken containers, they produce surface runners which must be removed before they spread too far. Remove any reverted, plain shoots from variegated herbs as soon as they appear.

Deadheading and pruning

Unless planning to save the seed, remove the dead flower heads from most herbs so that energy is channeled into growth. Deadheading annuals such as borage (*Borago officinalis*) lengthens the flowering season. Certain herbs such as angelica (*Angelica archangelica*) self-sow prolifically; these may become a nuisance if they are left to set seed.

Deadhead and prune shrubby herbs such as lavender (*Lavandula*) and thyme (*Thymus*) by trimming lightly with shears after flowering. Hard pruning in spring encourages sideshoots and new growth from the base; thyme, however, is best pruned lightly but often during the growing season.

Mulching

Mulch only established herbs that thrive in moist soil, such as mint and bee balm (*Monarda didyma*). In summer, mulch after rain to retain moisture and to enrich the soil as older mulch breaks down. Use an inorganic mulch such as grit around Mediterranean or gray-leaved plants in heavy soil to reduce the risk of rot.

Fall cleanup

The extent to which herbs are cut back in fall partly depends on personal preference. In cold areas, leaving the dead foliage of herbaceous perennials until spring helps protect them against cold and wind. Remove any dead leaves that have fallen on thyme and other low-growing, evergreen herbs because they may encourage fungal attack.

Winter protection

In cold weather, tender herbs should either be brought under cover or otherwise protected (see COLD AND WIND PROTECTION, pp.604–05). In spring, cut them back and plant them out again, or propagate new plants from cuttings. The hardiness of a number of herbs such as sage,

1 *Each spring, replace or divide and replant the herbs in a strawberry jar if they have outgrown the pot or need rejuvenating.*

2 *First lift the plants from the top, then dig out the soil mix, carefully removing the plants from the pockets. Tip out any remaining soil mix.*

3 *Add fresh soil mix up to the level of the lowest pockets. Divide or replace the old plants. Place each plant at the inside of a pocket, then gently pull the foliage through the hole.*

4 *Pack soil mix around the roots and up to the next level, firming well after each addition. Water thoroughly.*

rosemary, and lavender varies according to the species or cultivar; check this when buying.

Herbs in containers

Most herbs are easy to grow in containers and require little maintenance. They are, however, more prone to drying out than plants in the open ground, so in hot weather, check soil moisture daily and water thoroughly when dry. During the growing season, liquid-fertilize the herbs every two weeks.

During cold periods, bring herbs in containers under cover in good light. Frostproof pots may be left outdoors, but insulate them by burying them to their rims in the ground.

Repotting

Inspect herbs periodically to check that they are not becoming potbound. Watch for such signs as roots protruding through the base of the pot and rapid drying out. Repot during the growing season to encourage new root growth.

If repotting is impractical, renew the top 1–2in (2.5–5cm) of soil mix, incorporating well-rotted organic matter or a slow-release fertilizer. It will then be unnecessary to fertilize the herbs for about a month.

Propagation

Hᴇʀʙs may be propagated by a wide variety of methods, depending on the type of plant and the quantity of new plants required. Sowing seed is a simple, inexpensive way to raise a large number of plants and is necessary for annuals and biennials, although it may also be used for other plant groups. Cuttings are used to propagate various perennials as well as shrubs and trees, while division is suitable for a number of perennials, and layering is a good method for some shrubby herbs. For further information on propagating individual species and cultivars, see "Directory of common herbs," pp.401–04.

Raising new plants from seed

Most herbs are easy to grow from seed; they may be sown in containers or, where large quantities are required, in drills in the open ground. Seed may also be sown directly into the cracks between paving stones, where it would be difficult to insert plants. Prepare a finely raked seedbed for any seedlings that you intend to transplant outside from containers.

Spring is generally the best time for sowing seed, although some annual herbs may also be sown in early fall.

Annuals and biennials
Hardier annuals, such as pot marigolds (*Calendula officinalis*) and borage (*Borago officinalis*), may be sown in the spring or – to provide flowers late in the next spring – in fall. Sow biennials such as caraway (*Carum carvi*) and angelica (*Angelica archangelica*) outdoors in late summer or early fall for flowering the following summer. Thin out the seedlings twice: once after germination so that two or three remain at each position, and again after a few weeks so that only the strongest is left in place.

Short-lived herbs that are used regularly in large quantities, such as parsley (*Petroselinum crispum*), cilantro (*Coriandrum sativum*), and chervil (*Anthriscus cerefolium*), may be sown at intervals of three to four weeks from early spring to early fall. This provides a succession of foliage for harvesting throughout the year, although in some areas it may be necessary to provide protection from cold with cloches or similar covers. Annual herbs of the carrot family (Umbelliferae) – chervil (*Anthriscus*

cerefolium) and dill (*Anethum graveolens*), for example – are quite difficult to transplant successfully and are best sown directly into their final positions.

Basil (*Ocimum basilicum*) is one of the more difficult herbs to grow from seed unless kept warm and moist. In colder areas, sow basil seed very thinly indoors in pots or trays in late spring, and keep it at a minimum temperature of 70°F (21°C). Prick out the seedlings once they are large enough to handle, and keep them in a sunny, well-ventilated place. In cold, damp conditions, basil seedlings are prone to damping off (p.655) and gray mold/*Botrytis* (p.650). Plant them out once all danger of frost is past or grow them in containers under cover. In warm climates, basil may be sown directly outdoors (see ANNUALS AND BIENNIALS, "Sowing in open ground," p.211).

Perennials
If raising perennial herbs from seed, sow the seed in warmth in spring and grow on the seedlings in pots until they are large enough to be hardened off and planted out. Plant and care for them as for container-grown herbs (see p.405).

Most cultivars of perennial herbs do not come true from seed, however, and must be propagated by either cuttings or layering. An exception to this is variegated rue (*Ruta graveolens* 'Variegata'). Nonflowering forms, such as lawn chamomile (*Chamaemelum nobile* 'Treneague'), cannot be raised from seed; new plants should be propagated by cuttings or division.

Mound layering

This method is particularly suitable for propagating shrubs such as sage (*Salvia officinalis*), rosemary (*Rosmarinus officinalis*), lavender (*Lavandula*), and thyme (*Thymus*) that tend to become woody at the base or center with little or no new growth. In spring, mound freely draining soil over the base of the plant, leaving just the top exposed. This stimulates new shoots to develop roots in a manner similar to stooling (see ORNAMENTAL SHRUBS, p.115). Leave the soil in place, replenishing it if it is washed away by heavy rain, until new roots have been established in late summer or fall. Cut off the shoots from the parent plant, then pot them up or plant them out.

SOWING BASIL SEED IN CONTAINERS

1 *Tap seeds from a fold of paper onto firmed medium. Lightly cover with some sieved medium, and keep moist at a minimum temperature of 70°F (21°C).*

2 *Once the seedlings are large enough to handle, carefully lift them with a widger, holding them by the leaves, not by the stems, to prevent damage.*

3 *Prick out seedlings singly into cell packs of firmed soil mix, then keep moist in a sunny, well-ventilated place. Plant them out after frost danger, or grow them in containers under cover.*

MOUND LAYERING SHRUBBY HERBS

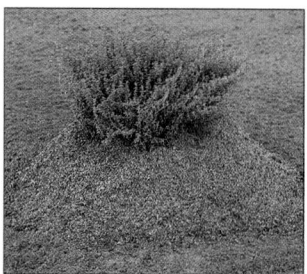

1 *To stimulate rooting, mound 3–5in (7–12cm) of sandy soil over the crown of the plant (here thyme) so that just the tips of the shoots are visible.*

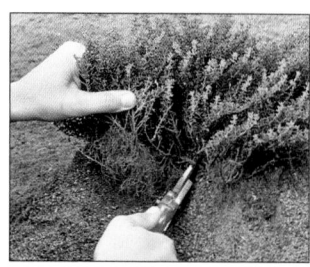

2 *Once the layered stems have established new roots, remove them with a knife or pruning shears. Pot up the rooted layers individually, or plant them out.*

HERBS TO PROPAGATE BY MOUND LAYERING

Hyssop (*Hyssopus officinalis*)
Lavender (*Lavandula angustifolia, L. stoechas*)
Lavender cotton (*Santolina chamaecyparissus, S.virens, S.rosmarinifolia*)
Rosemary (*Rosmarinus officinalis*)
Sage (*Salvia lavandulifolia, S. officinalis*)

Salvia officinalis

Southernwood (*Artemisia abrotanum*)
Thyme (*Thymus cilicicus, T. x citriodorus* and cvs, *T. vulgaris* and woody cvs)
Winter savory (*Satureja montana*)
Wormwood (*Artemisia absinthium*)

Harvesting and preserving

THE flavor of herbs varies according to the growing conditions, the season, and the time of day. Because the level of essential oils fluctuates with light and temperature, it is important to harvest herbs at the right time to ensure that they are at their peak. There are various methods of preserving herbs so that their scents and flavors may be enjoyed all year. For advice on specific herbs, see the "Directory of common herbs," pp.401–04.

Harvesting

Herbs should be harvested on a warm, dry day after the dew has dried but before the plants are exposed to hot sunshine, which evaporates the essential oils. Always try to harvest herbs in a way that helps to maintain the plant's shape and vigor. Choose straggly or invasive

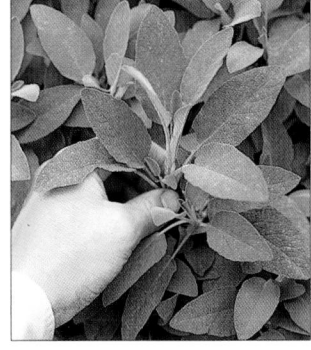

1 *Pick healthy, unblemished shoots or leaves (here sage) on a dry morning, before the heat of the day releases the herb's essential oils.*

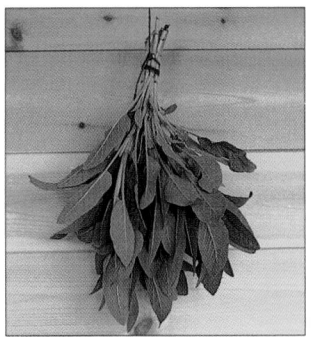

2 *Tie the shoots into bundles, then hang them upside down in a warm place. Once dry, strip the leaves from the stalks and store them in dark glass jars.*

shoots, and with clump-forming herbs such as chives (*Allium schoenoprasum*) and parsley (*Petroselinum crispum*) pick the outer leaves to encourage new growth in the center. Use only foliage free from damage and insects.

Leaves and shoots may be picked at any time during the growing season but are at their best before flowering. Evergreen herbs may be harvested in winter but this should be limited. Handle aromatic leaves gently: bruising releases the essential oils. Use or preserve herbs as soon as possible after harvesting.

Gathering flowers, seed, and roots

When harvesting flowers, pick them on a warm, dry day, when they are fully opened. Gather seed in summer or early fall by cutting off whole seedheads as they turn brown but before they are completely ripe and starting to shed. Roots may be lifted at any time of year, but the flavor is best in fall.

Preserving

The main methods of preserving herbs are drying and freezing. In addition, a number of herbs are suitable for flavoring vinegars, oils, or jellies, and a few may be crystallized (candied) for decorating cakes and desserts. Store dried herbs in dark glass or ceramic containers, because exposure to light speeds the deterioration of their aromas.

Air-drying

Do not wash herbs, because this may encourage molds to develop. Dry herbs by hanging them upside down in a warm, dry place away from direct light. Alternatively, place leaves, flower heads, or petals in a single layer on a rack covered with muslin, netting, or paper towels. Leave them in a warm, dark, well-ventilated place until crisp.

Microwave drying

For microwave drying, wash the herbs, pat them dry, then place in a single layer on paper towels. Microwave them for two to three minutes, checking every 30 seconds and rearranging if necessary to provide even drying. Cool, then crumble and store as for air-dried herbs.

Drying seedheads

Cut seedheads in summer or early fall as they turn brown, then place

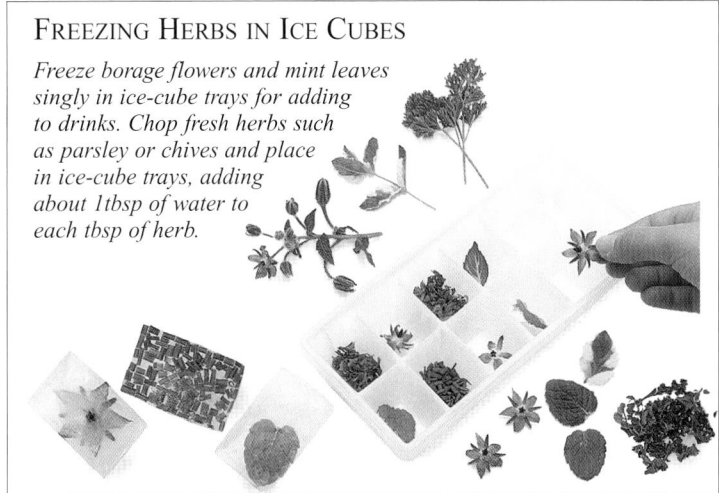

Freeze borage flowers and mint leaves singly in ice-cube trays for adding to drinks. Chop fresh herbs such as parsley or chives and place in ice-cube trays, adding about 1tbsp of water to each tbsp of herb.

them in a paper bag or hang them upside down and cover them with muslin to hold the seeds as they fall. Keep them in a warm, dry place to ripen; remove the seeds when dry and store them in jars or bags. Seed to be used for sowing should be kept in a cool, dry, frost-free place.

Drying roots

Most roots are best used fresh, but some may be dried and ground. First wash the roots thoroughly, then peel, chop, or slice them, before spreading them out on absorbent paper. Dry them in either a cool oven or at 122–40°F (50–60°C) in a dehydrator until brittle, then crush or grind them before storing.

Freezing

Many soft-leaved herbs such as parsley and basil retain their color and flavor better when frozen than when

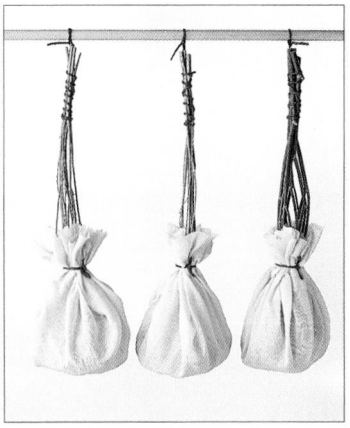

Cover the seedheads with muslin or a paper bag, secured in place with string or a rubber band, then hang them upside down in a warm place until dry.

dried. Pack whole sprigs into labeled plastic bags and freeze them; they crumble easily for use once frozen. For long-term storage, blanch them before freezing by dipping them first in boiling water, then in ice water. Pat dry and freeze.

Freezing in ice

Herbs may be frozen in water to form ice cubes. This is a good way of preserving borage flowers and mint leaves to use as a decorative addition to drinks, and the ice also protects the herbs from damage during storage. Herbs for cooking should be chopped before freezing, because this is difficult to do once they have thawed. Place the ice cubes in a sieve and drain the water before use.

Making herb oils and vinegars

Many herbs, such as French tarragon, thyme, oregano, and lavender, may have their flavors preserved by being steeped in oil or vinegar.

To make flavored oil, loosely fill a clear glass jar with the fresh herb, add a flavorless oil such as safflower, then seal. For a sweet oil such as lavender, use almond oil as the base instead. Leave the jar in a sunny spot for two weeks, shaking or stirring daily. (For a stronger flavor, replace the herbs and repeat the process.) Strain and bottle, adding a fresh sprig of the herb for identification. Basil leaves may be preserved by being packed in oil; the leaves themselves may be used in pasta sauces and other cooked dishes and the oil in salad dressings.

Herb vinegars are made in a similar way, using wine or cider vinegar, but the herbs should be lightly crushed before steeping. Warm the vinegar, pour it over the herbs, and proceed as above.

CHAPTER

16

THE FRUIT GARDEN

THE SATISFACTION OF growing, harvesting, and tasting your own fresh fruits is one of the great pleasures of gardening. A fruit garden may be highly decorative as well as productive: some plants have attractive, fragrant blossoms or fine foliage while, in many cases, the fruits themselves are as ornamental as they are edible. A wide range of fruits can be grown in most areas; in cooler regions, growing under cover makes it possible to cultivate an extensive variety. In a large garden, there may be room to devote an area exclusively to fruit, whether in a formal layout with neat rows of trees, bushes, and canes, bordered by trained fans or cordons, or in an informal orchard. If space is limited, incorporate fruits into the rest of the garden by edging a bed with alpine strawberries or by growing a grapevine over a pergola; even in a small patio garden, there should be space for one or two citrus trees in pots or wall-trained apples or pears.

Planning the fruit garden

Fruits have traditionally held a prominent place in the garden, and today, with a wide range of cultivars and many dwarf fruit trees available ideal for the average garden, fruit growing is increasing in popularity. There are always some fruits that will thrive in the given climatic and growing conditions, although the majority prefer a good soil and a sunny situation. In warm climates, a wide range of fruits may be cultivated outdoors; however, some fruits that require periods of cold dormancy before flowering will not usually be successful.

Where only a few fruit plants are required, the gardener may prefer to grow them within the ornamental garden rather than in a specialized fruit garden; many fruit trees are suitable for growing as specimens in a lawn. Alternatively, if space is very limited, most fruits may be cultivated in containers, either free-standing or trained against a support.

If planning to grow plants in large numbers, however, it is best to create a separate fruit area within the garden; this makes it possible to grow fruits with similar requirements together and to protect them against pests and cold damage. This is possible even in a small garden, as long as suitable rootstocks are chosen and trees are carefully trained. If grown as espaliers, fans, or cordons around the borders of a garden, fruit trees may be both ornamental and a source of fresh crops.

Another consideration may well be the type of blossom you wish your trees to bear: some cultivars of many different types of fruit produce flowers in particularly attractive colors and/or larger than usual sizes. However, do not plant a cultivar (especially of a tree fruit) selected for its fruit strictly for the beauty of its flowers: the plant will still need the care required for producing sound fruit, and you may find yourself spending more time maintaining the tree and its unwanted fruit than enjoying its beautiful flowers.

Thoughtful planning as well as careful selection of cultivars and methods of training make it possible to provide fresh fruit supplies over several months, and if there is some storage and freezing space available (and you are willing to spend the time in the kitchen), the produce from a fruit garden may be enjoyed all year.

In cool areas, the range of fruits that may be grown is even wider if some protection under cover is available. Reliable crops of peaches, nectarines, figs, grapes, or more tender fruits may be obtained by growing plants in a greenhouse, although ample room is needed for even a single tree. Protection and shelter are required by many of these fruits if they are grown outdoors.

FAN-TRAINED PEACH TREE
A fan-trained peach tree grown against a wall provides a dramatic accent as well as a high yield of fruit from a limited space. Growing fruit in this way also provides some protection in cooler areas.

TREE FORMS

When selecting a tree form, there are three main factors to consider: growth habit, space, and maintenance. An espalier, for example, is ideal for growing against a wall, particularly for apples, which develop naturally on short spur shoots. Several cordons will occupy the same space as a fan and so might be better in a small garden. Multiple cordons may be grafted with more than one cultivar, which provides an opportunity to have one "arm" as a pollinator for the main cultivar. Free-growing forms, such as bush or spindle, need pruning only once a year, while more elaborate shapes, such as cordons and espaliers, require training and pruning more often.

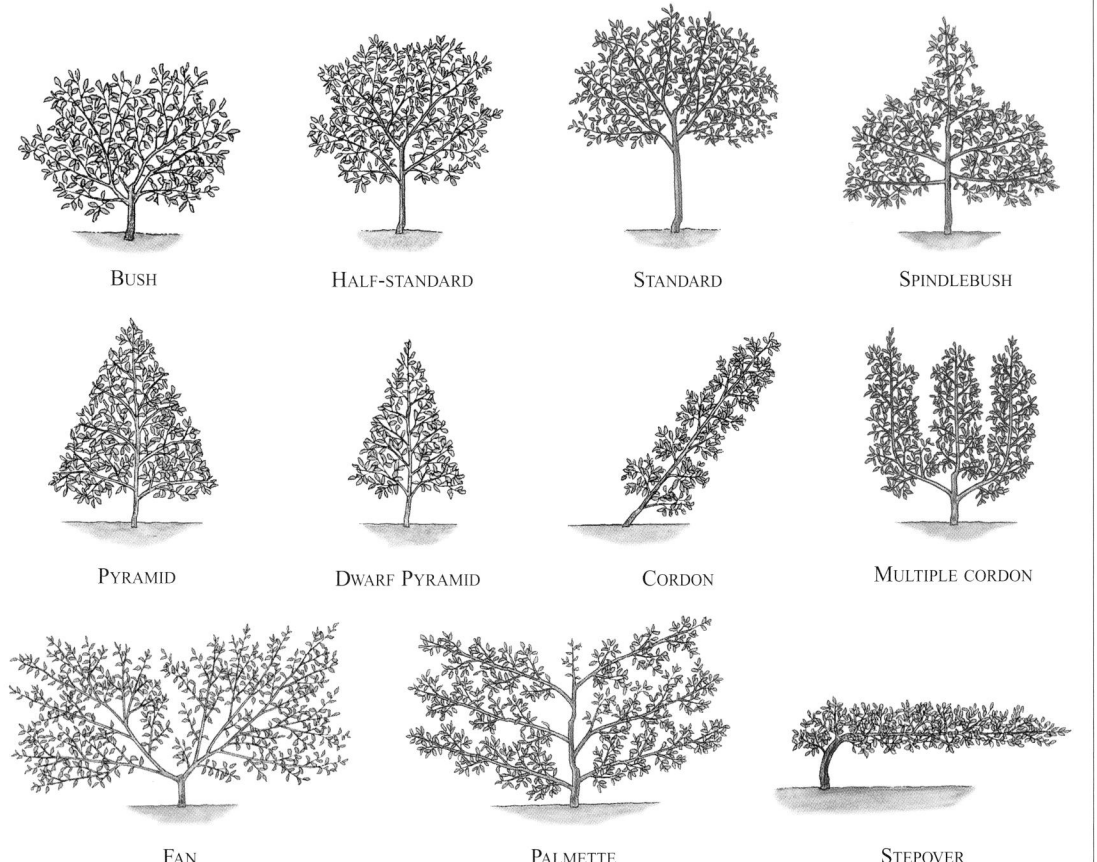

BUSH HALF-STANDARD STANDARD SPINDLEBUSH

PYRAMID DWARF PYRAMID CORDON MULTIPLE CORDON

ESPALIER FAN PALMETTE STEPOVER

The range of fruits

The different groups of fruit plants may be categorized according to their stature, their growth and fruiting habit, and their hardiness.

Tree fruits include apples, peaches, and figs. The term embraces both pome fruits (those having a core with small seeds, such as apples and pears) and stone fruits (those containing stones, such as cherries, peaches, and plums), as well as a few other fruits, including mulberries and persimmons.

The word "vine" is used to describe woody, fruiting climbers such as kiwi fruits and grapes; in some countries, the term is applied only to *Vitis vinifera*, the grape.

The category soft fruits includes bush fruits, cane fruits, and strawberries, which are herbaceous. Bush fruits are naturally shrubby, forming a compact, bush shape, although they may also be trained into other forms. Blackcurrants, redcurrants, whitecurrants, and gooseberries are the most commonly grown bush fruits. Plants described as cane fruits produce canelike shoots that bear the fruits; raspberries, blackberries, and hybrid berries, such as loganberries, are in this group. Most develop

their canes in one season and bear fruit on these the next, while producing new canes that will fruit the following year.

Certain fruit-bearing plants cannot withstand frost and need warm, subtropical temperatures to develop and ripen fully; these may be categorized as tender fruits. Tender fruits include citrus, pomegranates, pineapples, tree tomatoes, and prickly pears. Some are also tree fruits but have been grouped here with tender fruits because of their need for consistently warm temperatures.

Nuts include all plants that produce fruits with a hard outer shell around an edible kernel, for example hazelnuts, almonds, and pecans.

Unrestricted and trained forms

Many fruits, particularly tree fruits, and to a lesser extent vines and some soft fruits, may be trained into a variety of forms. When deciding which forms to grow, bear in mind the space available, the relative ease of harvesting, and the degree of pruning and training needed to produce a plant that crops well. The choice of

rootstock for fruit trees also determines their ultimate size (see "Rootstocks and tree size," p.417).

With the correct technique, tree and bush fruits may be trained almost as desired. The principle is to train young shoots into the required shape while they are still pliable; the branches then retain this form with regular, basic pruning.

Unrestricted tree forms

These forms develop, with limited pruning, in much the same way as a natural tree; they include the bush tree, standard, half-standard, and spindlebush. The bush and spindlebush are more compact than the standard and half-standard and are suitable for small gardens.

A bush tree has a trunk up to 3ft (90cm) tall, with branches radiating out from the top third. It has an open center, thus allowing the branches maximum light and space. Bush trees are small to medium sized; that is, 5–12ft (1.5–4m).

The half-standard is similar to the bush, but the trunk measures 3–5ft (1–1.5m) with an overall height of 12–15ft (4–5m). The standard is similar in form but with a trunk measuring 5–7ft (1.5–2.2m) and an overall height of 15ft (5m) or more.

The spindlebush is a small tree growing up to 7ft (2.2m) tall with branches that radiate out from the leader at a wide angle. It has fewer branches than other lightly pruned forms, but each branch is pruned to be as productive as possible. The lowest branch is usually about 18in (45cm) from ground level.

Trained forms

Some fruit trees and bushes are suitable for growing in trained (or restricted) forms. These forms include cordons, fans, and espaliers. They need careful training initially and are then maintained by regular summer pruning to restrict vegetative growth, with a minimum of winter pruning. Most require support wires, secured either to free-standing posts or against a wall or fence. Wall-trained forms are often favored in cool climates for fruits such as peaches because the fruits receive maximum sun and also benefit from the reflected heat of the wall. All the trained tree forms are ideal for small gardens, since they make it possible to cultivate a variety of fruits in a restricted space. Maiden plants that have been grafted onto dwarfing rootstocks are usually used for training restricted forms.

FAMILY TREES
In a small garden, a convenient way to grow a variety of fruits is to plant a family tree, in which two or more cultivars are grafted onto the same rootstock so the tree bears different fruits on different branches.

FRUIT FOR FROST-FREE AREAS
Oranges grow well outdoors only in warm, virtually frost-free regions such as Florida, California, Mediterranean countries, and South Africa. They often produce 2 crops a year and may bear flowers at the same time as an earlier crop is maturing. In colder climates, citrus can be grown in a greenhouse, provided that it is warm and large enough.

A cordon is restricted to a single stem 5–6ft (1.5–2m) long, clothed with fruiting spurs to produce a high yield in a small area. It is usually planted at an angle of about 45° but may also be grown vertically or horizontally. Most commonly used for apples and pears, it is also useful with red- and whitecurrants and gooseberries. Double (sometimes known as U), triple, or multiple cordons may be formed by pruning a maiden plant so that it forms two or more parallel stems. Cordons that have more than a single stem are usually trained vertically.

A fan is trained with the main branches radiating in a fan shape from a short, 10in (25cm) trunk and is suitable for tree fruits that are grown against walls and fences, especially peaches and cherries.

An espalier is trained with matching pairs of horizontal branches extending at regular intervals from a central stem. Each branch is clothed in short, fruiting spurs. The number of pairs of branches is variable, depending on space and tree vigor.

This method is particularly suitable for apples and pears grown against walls or fences.

Unlike the other trained forms, the pyramid is free-standing; its branches radiate from a central trunk, with an overall pyramidal form that is maintained by regular summer pruning to produce trees of small to medium size. Dwarf pyramids are grown on a more dwarfing rootstock.

Family trees

Family trees carry several cultivars – usually three – of the same fruit on a single tree. Such trees provide for a succession of fruit and are a very useful space-saving measure. Used originally by the Greeks and Romans, they were reintroduced during the 1950s and have become an increasingly popular way to grow apples and pears.

When young, a tree is grafted with two other cultivars suitable for cross-pollination and of similar vigor. Good apple combinations include:

'Egremont Russet' with 'James Grieve' and 'Sunset'; 'Bramley's Seedling' with 'Red Pippin (Fiesta)' and 'Falstaff'; and 'Charles Ross' with 'Discovery' and 'James Grieve'. Successful family pear trees include 'Beth' with 'Conference' and 'Concorde'; and 'Williams' Bon Chrétien' with 'Conference' and 'Doyenne du Comice'.

All such trees are available on a variety of rootstocks, and it is important to select one that will suit your soil and grow to the tree size required. 'MM106' is used for medium-sized apple trees, and 'Quince A' for pears. Apple 'M9' and pear 'Quince A' are for smaller family trees. Smallest of all is 'M27', which is best for pot-grown family apple trees. 'Quince C' rootstock is generally reserved for a few of the most vigorous cultivars such as 'Doyenné du Comice'.

Trees grown on 'M9', 'M27', and 'Quince A' must be permanently staked because of their small, brittle root system.

Be aware that there are some family trees grafted with as many as five different cultivars onto the rootstock. You must pay close attention to the condition of all of the cultivars to make sure one does not overgrow and outcompete any others.

Integrating fruits into the garden plan

Fruits may be grown either in a separate area on their own or intermingled with other plants. The choice depends on space, personal prefer-

ence, and the range of fruits to be included. In either case, assess the impact that the fully grown fruit plants will have on the adjacent or surrounding plants. Planning and siting are particularly important, because most fruits are long-term plants that require consistently good conditions to flourish and crop well over many years. In addition, with the exception of a few fruits such as strawberries, it is seldom practical or worthwhile to transplant them to other positions as they grow larger.

The planned fruit garden
Where a range of different fruits is desired, it is well worth growing the plants together in a single area.

TRAINED CORDONS
Apple cordons make good use of a fence, with alpine strawberries providing an edge for the border.

When planning a fruit garden, take into account the preferred growing conditions of each type of plant and recommended planting distances; for example, site tall fruit trees where they will cast the least shade on smaller bushes nearby. Also make sure that the space allocated for each plant is sufficient for it to develop naturally to its mature size.

Plants that have similar cultivation requirements may be grouped together to simplify practical operations such as applying fertilizer: for example, redcurrants and gooseberries need more potassium than other fruits. Grouping plants also makes it easier to protect them from birds (with a fruit cage) or wind damage (with a windbreak).

For an ornamental border, edge the fruit garden with a row of trained trees; cordons or dwarf pyramids are especially suitable because they need a minimum of support and occupy comparatively little space.

In planning the position of fruit trees (particularly apples, pears, sweet cherries, and some plums), remember that a self-sterile cultivar should be sited near a cultivar with which it will cross-pollinate (see

"Pollination requirements," p.418), or it will produce few if any fruits.

For many fruits, there is a wide choice of cultivars that ripen at different times; this makes it possible to plan for a succession of fruits that may be regularly harvested, rather than dealing with a single glut. Some fruits, late-ripening apples and pears for example, may be stored for long periods, so if a steady supply is required, more space should be devoted to these than to earlier-ripening cultivars.

Fruit in the small garden

There are various ways to make the most of a limited area for fruit growing so that it provides a high yield and is an attractive feature. Whenever possible, choose trees grafted on dwarfing rootstocks (see "Rootstocks and tree size," opposite), and use training methods that make the best use of the available space. Train trees and soft fruits such as redcurrants and gooseberries into cordons against the house or garden wall, rather than as bushes, since cordons need less room for a comparable fruit yield than fans or espaliers. Grow grapes over a sturdy pergola or

ornamental arch. Cane fruits may also be trained in a variety of ways, depending on space. Strawberries may be grown in vertical grow bags attached to a stake, fence, or other structure, or in a classic strawberry jar on the patio.

If there is room for only a single tree, then it is essential to choose a self-fertile cultivar (see "Pollination requirements," p.418). It is also worth selecting plants with a prolonged cropping season, unless there is ample storage and freezer space.

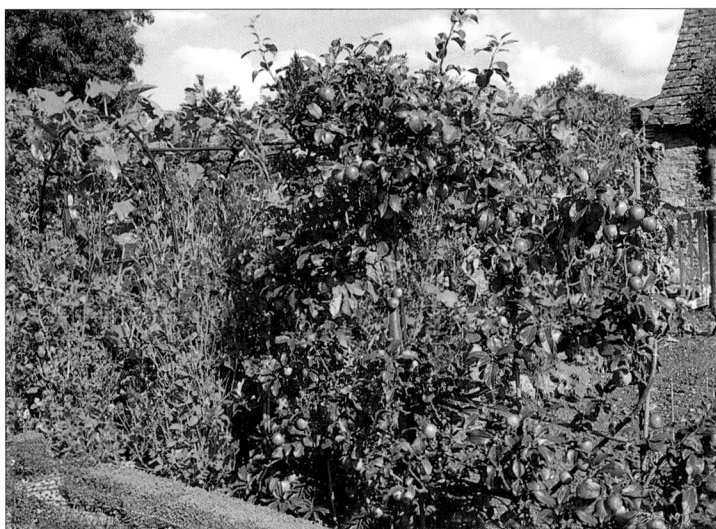

ORNAMENTAL DIVIDER
Apple espaliers form an attractive screen providing a fine display of spring blossoms that are followed by handsome fruits in fall.

PLAN FOR A LARGE FRUIT GARDEN

A large plot, 35 x 54ft (11 x 17m), provides space for a wide range of fruit. Here, the apple and pear cultivars will bear over a long period, and the soft fruit has been grouped for easier maintenance. The more tender peaches and grapes thrive in a lean-to greenhouse.

1 Apple 'Discovery' (on 'M26'/'Ottawa 3')
2 Apple 'Lodi' (on 'M26'/'Ottawa 3')
3 Apple 'Red Delicious' (on 'M26'/'Ottawa 3')
4 Apple 'Sunset' (on 'M26'/'Ottawa 3')
5 Apple 'Cox's Orange Pippin' (on 'M26'/'Ottawa 3')
6 Apple 'Golden Delicious' (on 'M26'/'Ottawa 3')
7 Plum 'Redcoat' (on 'Pixy')

8 Plum 'Victoria' (on 'Pixy')
9 Damson 'Prune' (on 'Pixy')
10 Pear 'Rescue' (on 'Quince A')
11 Pear 'Bartlett' (on 'Quince A')
12 Pear 'Doyenné du Comice' (on 'Quince A')
13 Pear 'Golden Spice' (on 'Quince A')
14 Blackcurrant 'Boskoop Giant'
15 Blackcurrant 'Ben Lomond'
16 Blackcurrant 'Ben Sarek'
17 Redcurrant 'Red Lake'
18 Gooseberry 'Careless'

19 Gooseberry 'Leveller'
20 Raspberry 'Autumn Bliss'
21 Sour cherry 'Meteor'
22 Raspberry 'Royalty'
23 Loganberry (thornless)
24 Tayberry
25 Blackberry 'Lucretia'
26 Grape 'Black Hamburgh'
27 Peach 'Harbrite'(on 'St. Julien A')
28 Strawberry 'Kent'
29 Sweet cherry 'Stella' (on 'Colt')
30 Fig 'Brown Turkey'

Mixed planting

In a primarily ornamental garden or one where there is insufficient space for a dedicated fruit garden, fruits may be planted among other plants. One or more fruit trees may make attractive specimens in the lawn or grown in containers on a sunny terrace or patio. Fruit cordons or dwarf pyramids can be framed as an ornamental divider, providing an unusual and productive screen, with attractive blossoms in spring and ripening fruits in late summer to fall. Trained forms of bushes or trees may be grown on almost any type of garden structure, such as a pergola, fence, or shed, provided that the exposure is suitable.

When fruits are planted with ornamentals, make sure that all the plants' needs are compatible. For example, if the fruits need nets for protection from squirrels, this may impede the growth of surrounding plants and look out of place. Particular care is also needed to ensure that pesticide sprays do not adversely affect any nearby ornamental plants.

Strawberries are often grown among other plants either in a vegetable garden or along the edge of a border or raised bed (a popular use of alpine strawberries).

Choosing a site

A sunny, sheltered position, where the plants will produce fruits of good quality and flavor, is ideal. Sites with some light shade are also acceptable but provide fewer ripening hours so are best used for soft fruits or early-ripening cultivars of apples, pears, and plums. Plants on a south-facing slope may produce crops earlier than elsewhere, but since they also flower earlier, they are more likely to suffer frost damage.

FRUIT IN A BORDER
The compact, rounded shape of a lemon tree laden with fruit punctuates an informal planting, providing a charming contrast to the colorful display of roses and herbaceous plants. Gardeners in warmer climates may enjoy this sort of planting.

SMALL FRUIT GARDEN

This small fenced area supports no fewer than 17 fruit cultivars, providing abundant crops from early summer to fall. The plot measures only 12 x 28ft (4 x 9m), with a 6ft (2m) fence surrounding it. Careful choice of cultivars and rootstocks coupled with correct training of the trees allows a wide range of fruits to be accommodated. The apple and pear cordons provide especially good yields from a limited space.

1 Sweet cherry 'Stella' (on 'Colt')
2 Pear 'Earlibrite' (on 'Quince C')
3 Pear 'Bartlett' (on 'Quince C')
4 Pear 'Doyenné du Comice' (on 'Quince C')
5 Raspberry 'Marcy' (summer-fruiting)
6 Plum 'Victoria' (on 'Pixy')
7 Raspberry 'Autumn Bliss' (fall-fruiting)
8 Peach 'Redhaven' (on 'St. Julien A')
9 Gooseberry 'Careless'
10 Gooseberry 'Leveller'
11 Whitecurrant 'White Grape'
12 Redcurrant 'Red Lake'
13 Apple 'Lodi' (on 'M9')
14 Apple 'McIntosh' (on 'M9')
15 Apple 'Sunset' (on 'M9')
16 Blackcurrant 'Ben Sarek'
17 Sour cherry 'Meteor' (on 'Colt')

Growing against supports

Walls, fences, pergolas, and arches all provide an ideal site for growing trained trees, especially if they are exposed to maximum sun. These structures make good use of space and allow the fruits to develop and ripen well; fruits trained on supports are also easier to protect from pests and frost than fruits in the open garden. The wall or fence must be high enough to accommodate the chosen fruits: 4ft (1.2m) would be enough for soft fruits, or for apples or pears trained as cordons or espaliers, but a height and spread of 6ft (2m) or more are required for a fan-trained apple, pear, cherry, plum, or peach. Pergolas and arches are likely to provide sufficient height, but make sure there is space for the plants to grow as they mature. The structure must be able to support normally or abnormally heavy crops, even in strong winds.

Frost and wind

Avoid planting in frost-prone sites, because flowers, unopened buds, and fruitlets are all susceptible to damage. The coldest air accumulates where the ground is lowest, and a frost pocket will form in a valley floor or at the foot of a sloping garden. Also remember that totally open, exposed areas (such as an open field or area away from buildings and trees) may experience frost, whereas a more protected area will escape it or have less frost. Shaded areas remain frost-covered longer than sunny ones – the duration of the frost is often as critical as its severity.

Exposure to wind discourages pollinating insects and therefore greatly reduces the regularity of cropping. Strong winds also cause considerable crop damage. Drafty sites, such as between two buildings, should be avoided, but a well-placed windbreak may be very effective in diverting or filtering wind to improve the conditions. Trees or large shrubs are preferable to solid barriers because they filter wind that would otherwise swirl over the barrier and damage plants on the other side (see CLIMATE AND THE GARDEN, "How a windbreak works," p.603).

Growing fruits under cover

Crops native to warm climates, such as peaches, nectarines, and grapes, are ideal for greenhouse cultivation in cooler climates, but skill and attention to detail are required to maintain them in good condition and obtain satisfactory crops. If fruits are to be grown with other plants in the same greenhouse, ensure that their temperature, humidity, and ventilation requirements are compatible. It is important that the greenhouse have the maximum possible number of side and top vents to provide a free flow of air. As for planting in open ground, the soil needs to be fertile and well drained for the plants to thrive.

A number of tender fruits such as tree tomatoes and pomegranates may be grown successfully under cover. In milder climates they are often grown as ornamental plants, since they seldom crop heavily, even under glass.

Trained fruits

Tree and soft fruits that are suitable for training may also be treated in this way when grown in a greenhouse. Check that there is enough space for the chosen cultivar to develop and grow to its mature size, and ensure that suitable hardware for training the plant in the chosen form is in place before planting.

A CORDON ARCH
Fruit trees trained as vertical cordons over a series of arches provide an attractive architectural feature as well as abundant crops of fruit. The structure must be sufficiently strong to support the weight of trees heavily laden with fruit.

Fruits in pots

Strawberry plants that are grown in individual pots in a greenhouse or under a cover will produce ripe fruits earlier than those in the open, thereby prolonging the fruiting season if both cultivation methods are used. Tender fruit trees such as citrus may be grown in pots that are placed outdoors during summer and returned under cover for winter.

Growing fruits in containers

Container growing is useful for cultivating fruits where space is limited. The pots should be placed in sunny, sheltered sites and may be used on paved areas such as patios to provide ornamental features as well as crops of fruits. It is also a way of controlling the root growth, and therefore the vigor, of plants such as figs that (particularly in temperate climates) may make excessive vegetative growth at the expense of the crop.

Container-grown fruit trees can also be moved in and out of cover to avoid frost or to give the plant a higher or lower temperature, according to its seasonal needs. Early-flowering trees such as peaches and nectarines in particular benefit from doing this,

and many people in northern gardens enjoy their own citrus by growing the trees in sufficiently large pots outdoors in summer and then bringing them under cover for winter. Most citrus can be kept at temperatures just a few degrees above freezing without harm, but they will not grow, bloom, or produce fruits at those low temperatures.

Most fruits may be grown successfully in a large pot, half barrel, or similar container with a diameter of at least 12in (30cm). Some tree fruits, especially apples and peaches, now have cultivars that grow no more than a few feet tall and wide and can be grown in a 12in (30cm) pot. Strawberries may be grown either singly in 4in (10cm) pots or in strawberry jars (containers with side planting pockets). Fruits need more regular care in containers than when in the open ground, particularly with watering and fertilizing, because the root systems are confined and easily dry out.

Deciding which plants to grow

Whether planning an entire fruit garden or choosing just two or three trees, it is vital to select plants that

will thrive in the given soil and climatic conditions without growing too large for their allotted space.

It also makes sense to choose exceptionally well-flavored, less commercial cultivars that are seldom available in stores. Nurseries and organizations that specialize in heirloom cultivars can be very helpful in this respect; consult them or their printed material, and don't overlook information available online. More unusual fruits, such as currants or hybrid berries, are also worth considering, because they are often expensive to but (if they can be found). If freezing soft fruits such as raspberries or strawberries is a priority, seek out and plant cultivars that are suitable for that purpose.

Check the compatibility of different cultivars for pollination purposes before deciding which to grow (see "Pollination requirements," p.418). The final choice should also depend on the size of the crop required and the harvesting time.

Rootstocks and tree size

Tree size is determined largely by the rootstock onto which the tree has been grafted. Choose rootstocks that are of appropriate vigor for the planting area or training space available. Apple trees grown on dwarfing rootstocks such as 'M26' or 'M9', for example, are likely to suit most gardens; their relatively small size makes picking, pruning, and spraying easier. If a large tree is required, select one that is grown on a more vigorous rootstock. For further details, see pp.418 and 429.

Pollination compatibility

Most cultivars of apples, pears, sweet cherries, and some plums are not satisfactorily self-fertile. They therefore need to be planted close to one or more suitable cultivars of the same fruit that are in flower at about the

same time so that insects are able to cross-pollinate all the trees. For example, the apple cultivars 'State Fair', 'Delicious', and 'Wolf River' need to be planted together for all to be cross-pollinated successfully. When planning a fruit garden, take into account the minimum number of trees required for pollination to occur, and position compatible cultivars adjacent to each other to help ensure satisfactory fertilization and bearing.

Crop size and timing

Within the limits of space available, the amount of fruits that are required will determine the number of plants that should be obtained, bearing in mind that crop levels inevitably vary from year to year. The amount of storage or freezer space available may govern the size of crop that can be handled. Try to balance the numbers of early-, mid-, and late-ripening cultivars of each fruit grown in order to provide a consistent supply over a long period rather than producing a brief glut.

Early-ripening apples and pears do not keep well for more than a day or two, so do not grow more than can be consumed quickly: one or two cordons yielding 5–11lb (2–5kg) per tree should suffice. If you have plenty of storage space, plant a high proportion of late-ripening cultivars, the fruits of which can be stored for several months. Plums are also liable to produce gluts, and the fruits must be used quickly unless they are frozen or otherwise preserved.

When deciding whether to plant early- or late-ripening cultivars, remember to take climatic factors into account. For example, late-ripening apples or pears are not a good choice for a region with a short summer or if the proposed site is shady, because there will not be enough time or sun for the fruit to ripen fully.

GRAPE CANOPY
A grapevine thrives in the warm but well-ventilated atmosphere of a conservatory or greenhouse. Care must be taken to prevent the ripening bunches from becoming scorched by the sun.

Site, soil preparation, and planting

FRUIT-BEARING plants require soil that is well structured, adequately drained, and fertile. Before planting fruits, therefore, choose and prepare a suitable site so that it provides the necessary conditions.

Preparing the site

Prepare the site at least two months before planting. Remove all weeds, especially perennial ones, before preparing the soil (see PLANT PROBLEMS, "Weeds," pp.658–61).

Soil types
A loam is ideal and produces high yields of good-quality fruits. Clay soils may produce very good crops if drainage is good, but they are slow to warm up in spring; growth and therefore cropping may be later. On sandy soils, plants come into growth earlier, since the soil warms up quickly in spring. Heat is lost equally rapidly, however, which creates a greater risk from frost and cold; sandy soil is also prone to drought. Sandy soils are usually less fertile than others, so the quality and flavor of fruits grown on these may be inferior to those of fruits that are produced on more fertile soil.

On alkaline soils, lime-induced chlorosis caused by manganese and iron deficiencies (see p.643) may be severe, causing leaves to turn yellow and adversely affecting the quality and yield of fruit. In extreme cases, it will prove impossible to grow certain fruits satisfactorily; pears and raspberries, in particular, suffer badly. The use of chelated iron alleviates the problem, but regular treatment may be necessary and is expensive. Annual mulches of farmyard manure and compost help by providing some of the trace elements required.

Improving the soil
For soft fruits, dig in generous amounts of well-rotted manure or garden compost and fertilizer to improve water retention and fertility. In preparation for planting tree fruits, fertilizers should not be used unless the soil is very poor, since this may encourage excessive soft growth rather than fruiting wood.

Drainage problems
Although poor drainage is more likely on heavy clay soils, it may occur in many types of soil. Improve the soil structure where possible (see "Soil structure and water content," p.614), and install a drainage system if necessary (see SOILS AND FERTILIZERS, "Installing drains," p.617). Where drains cannot be installed, plant fruits in raised beds (see STRUCTURES AND SURFACES, "Raised beds," p.593).

Adjusting the pH level
Soil with a pH level of 6–6.5 is ideal for all fruits except blueberries, which need an acidic soil of pH 4–5.5. Soils below about pH 5.8 will need liming (see p.619). If planting in soil with a pH level over 7, topdress regularly with ammonium sulfate and mulch with acidic compost to lower the pH in the short term.

Preparing the support for a trained fruit tree or bush
If a fruit tree or bush is to be trained against a solid support such as a wall or fence, attach horizontal parallel wires to the support with vine eyes and a straining bolt to keep the wires taut as the fruits develop. The eyes should hold the wires 4–6in (10–15cm) from the support to allow air to circulate around the branches and leaves of the plant. The spacing of the wires will vary, depending on the type of fruits grown. If using a free-standing post-and-wire support, secure the wires firmly to the posts. Just before planting, attach bamboo stakes to the wires at the appropriate angles, and tie in the young plants to begin the training process.

Buying plants

Always choose fruits that will thrive in the conditions in your garden. Check that the ultimate size of the plant or tree will fit the available space and that there is room to train it into the desired form. Pollination needs also must be considered before deciding which cultivars to buy.

Specialty fruit nurseries are often the best and most reliable source of supply. They offer a wide range of old and new cultivars and will also advise about suitable rootstocks. Wherever possible, buy plants that are certified free from disease.

It is best to buy young plants, since these become established quickly and may be shaped and trained to your own requirements. Plants are available bare-root or in containers. Container-grown plants are available throughout the year, but bare-root plants only in late fall and in spring when the plants are dormant and may safely be lifted. Reject plants with a potbound root

BARE-ROOT TREE

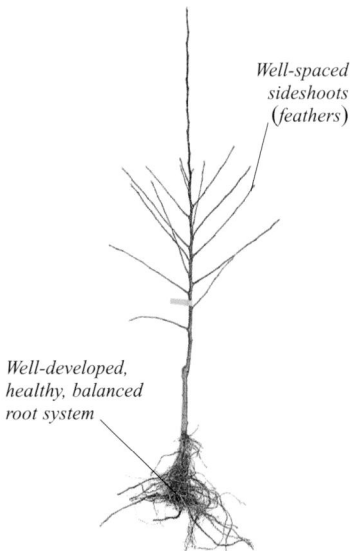

Well-spaced sideshoots (feathers)

Well-developed, healthy, balanced root system

CONTAINER-GROWN TREE

Moist, weed-free soil mix

Vigorous, healthy roots that have not become congested and potbound

system, since these seldom develop well. When buying bare-root plants, make sure that the roots have not dried out, and select plants with balanced main and fibrous roots.

Choose fruit trees that are healthy, with sturdy growth and, if two or three years old, with well-spaced laterals. Inspect plants carefully, and do not buy any with signs of pest infestation, damage, or disease, or those that are lacking in vigor.

Pollination requirements
Most soft fruits and some tree fruits are self-fertile: they produce a crop without needing a pollinating cultivar nearby, and may therefore be grown singly. Apples, pears, nearly all sweet cherries, and some plums are not reliably self-fertile, however. To produce a successful crop, self-sterile cultivars need to be cross-pollinated by another cultivar of the same fruit. Usually, one polli-

ROOTSTOCK

A graft union between rootstock and scion is identifiable by a noticeable kink in the stem 4–12in (10–30cm) above the soil mark, especially on young fruit trees that have only recently been propagated. When planting, make sure that the graft union is not below soil level.

nating cultivar is sufficient, but some apples and pears must be grown close to two other cultivars for all trees to produce good crops.

For cross-pollination to occur, the flowering periods must overlap. This is not a problem in most of North America, where blooming seasons are so short that all flowering periods overlap. In areas with longer seasons, cultivars are sometimes divided into several flowering groups, from early to late. Cultivars for cross-pollination should be in the same, preceding, or following group. Nurseries and catalogs generally provide this information.

Certain cultivars of some fruits, however, will not cross-pollinate. For sweet cherries and pears, these are classified in incompatibility groups, which are indicated in the plant lists. Seek advice if in doubt. A few sweet cherry cultivars will pollinate all other cultivars in flower at the same time; these are known as universal pollinators.

Selecting rootstocks
Many tree fruit cultivars offered for sale will have been grafted onto a compatible rootstock, since cultivars do not breed true from seed and cannot be raised consistently from cuttings. The rootstock controls the growth rate and size of the mature tree, while the scion determines the cultivar of fruits produced. Some rootstocks have a dwarfing effect (useful for a small garden) and induce early fruiting. A few rootstocks are resistant to certain diseases.

Selecting fruit trees

Young fruit trees may be purchased at several stages of growth – choose the one most appropriate for the form that the tree is to take. Maiden whip trees (with side shoots) take at least one year longer than other forms to train and fruit. One-year-old feathered maidens are popular with experienced growers because their sideshoots enable the earliest possible training. Two-year-old trees fruit more quickly, and good specimens are easily trained. Three-year-old, trained trees are more expensive and can be harder to reestablish.

Planting in open ground

Container-grown plants may be planted at any time of year except when the ground is frozen or waterlogged, or during drought. Plant bare-root plants in late fall or early spring while they are dormant; soak the roots well before planting. In frosty periods, heel them in temporarily in moist, frost-free soil until conditions are suitable for planting.

Planting fruit trees

If planting a number of trees, measure the site and mark out the planting positions with stakes. Dig a hole at least one-third wider than the tree's root system; firm the base of the hole and slightly mound it.

Insert a stake into the hole 3in (8cm) away from the center to allow for the tree's growth in girth as it matures. The stake height depends on the form into which the tree is to be trained (for details, see under individual fruits). Trees on dwarfing rootstocks need permanent staking; remove the stake of those on other rootstocks after three years.

Place the tree in the hole, making sure that the soil mark on the stem is at ground level, and spread out the roots. Do not cover the union between rootstock and scion; otherwise, the scion may root and the rootstock's influence would be lost.

Backfill in stages with soil, while another person holds the tree upright, shaking it gently from time to time so that the soil settles in between the roots. Firm the soil; when the hole is nearly full, break up the soil around the edges to obtain a uniform soil firmness over a greater area. Firm and level the area, and attach the tree to the stake using a soft, pliable tie with a firm cushion between tree and stake to prevent chafing. Protect the tree from rabbits and other animals with chicken wire.

Fruit trees to be planted against a wall or fence should be positioned 6–9in (15–22cm) away from the support, with the branches sloping gently inward. This ensures that the roots are in good soil and allows for future expansion of the trunk.

Planting soft fruits and climbers

Bush and cane fruits are planted as for fruit trees, but no staking is needed. Plant only up to the soil mark: planting too deeply inhibits a plant's growth. For climbers, make the planting holes or trench wide enough for the roots to be fully extended, and train the shoots against a support.

Planting in containers

Water the young plant thoroughly before planting. Use a moist, soil-based potting mix, leaving 1in (2.5cm) between the soil mix surface and the rim of the pot for watering. Water again after planting, and keep the soil mix moist until growth begins, then water regularly.

PLANTING CORDONS

IN THE OPEN GROUND
Space trees 2¹/₂ft (75cm) apart (top). Attach a stake at an angle of 45° to horizontal wires (bottom left) stretched between sturdy posts. Tie each tree securely to a stake (bottom right).

AGAINST A FENCE *Attach wires 4–6in (10–15cm) away from the fence to allow for the growth of the trees and give good air circulation. Plant the trees 6–9in (15–22cm) from the fence.*

PLANTING A FRUIT BUSH

1 *Dig a hole large enough to accommodate the roots of the bush when spread out. Place a stake across the hole to check that the level of the surrounding soil is the same as the soil mark on the main stem.*

2 *Backfill the hole with soil; pushing on the soil gently to ensure that no air pockets remain between the roots. Rake over the soil lightly to level the surface.*

PLANTING A FRUIT TREE

1 *Dig a hole one-third wider than the tree's root system. Drive in a stake to a depth of 18in (45cm) about 3in (8cm) from the center of the hole.*

2 *Slightly mound the soil at the base of the hole and place the tree in the center. Use a stake to check that the soil mark on the stem is level with the soil surface.*

3 *Spread out the tree's roots, then gradually fill the hole with soil. Firm to make sure that the tree is well anchored and that there are no air pockets between the roots.*

4 *Attach a buckle-and-spacer to the top of the stake and then to the tree so that the cushion is between the stem and the stake (see inset). Adjust as necessary.*

Routine care

$\mathbf{M}$OST fruit plants need regular maintenance to make sure that they are healthy and produce high-quality crops. Routine operations vary, depending on the type of fruit, growing conditions, and season.

Fruit thinning

Fruit thinning is necessary for a number of tree fruits, particularly apples, pears, and plums, to provide good-sized, high-quality fruits. It also prevents branch breakages by ensuring balanced crop distribution. In addition, thinning helps to prevent biennial bearing (to which some fruit cultivars are prone), that is, bearing heavy crops one year and little or no fruit the next.

Thin initially by hand or with scissors to remove disfigured fruits; later, thin again to leave the fruits room to develop fully and to receive enough sun and air to ripen. Details of how and when to thin are given under each fruit.

Fertilizing, mulching, and watering

Apply manures and fertilizers when needed, observing crop performance and checking for any leaf discoloration that may denote nutrient deficiencies. In hot, dry summers, watering will usually be necessary; a trickle watering system (see p.555) uses water most efficiently.

Care of tree fruits
In early spring, mulch newly planted trees and any that are not thriving with manure or compost. First check

HOW TO THIN FRUIT

1 *Thinning of some fruits is required to obtain fruit of a good size and quality. If it is left unthinned, the fruit is usually small and of poor flavor.*

2 *Remove unhealthy or disfigured fruits first, then reduce the remainder to at least 2–3in (5–8cm) apart, depending on the type of fruit.*

that any problem is not caused by a pest or disease; if it is, treat as recommended in PLANT PROBLEMS, pp.633–61. Once the trees reach flowering size, apply a balanced fertilizer at a rate of 3–4oz/sq yd (105–40g/sq m) in early spring. Do not overfertilize, particularly with nitrogen, since this may produce soft, disease-prone growth.

If a particular nutrient is needed, use specific fertilizers: potassium sulfate to correct potassium deficiency; ammonium nitrate to supply nitrogen; superphosphate to provide

phosphorus. Apply these in spring at a rate of 1oz/sq yd (35g/sq m), except superphosphate, which is normally applied at three times this rate every three or four years. Correct magnesium deficiency (p.643) by spraying the foliage, after flowering, with a solution of Epsom salts. In severe cases, repeat the treatment after three weeks. Other deficiencies, especially of manganese and iron (p.643), may also arise. If, more rarely, deficiencies of zinc, copper, or other elements are suspected, seek the advice of an expert.

Apply fertilizers evenly over the entire branch spread (see below). Where trees are grown in grass, mow regularly and leave the clippings *in situ*; they rot down and return nutrients to the soil, helping particularly to avert potassium deficiency.

Care of soft fruits
Mulch soft fruits regularly in spring with rotted farmyard manure. Use fertilizers as indicated for tree fruits; nitrogen and potassium are the most essential nutrients. Apply fertilizer over the whole area; in the case of raspberries, spread the dressing at least 2ft (60cm) on either side of the row. With strawberries, dig in manure before planting.

Fruit in containers

Although soil-based potting mixes contain nutrients, plants should be fertilized in the growing season in order to replace the nutrients as they are used; nitrogen and potassium in particular are often needed. Fruit plants in containers require watering

more frequently than those planted in open ground. Check the soil mix regularly – at least once a day in hot, dry weather – and keep it moist.

Each winter, fruit trees and bushes in pots should be top-dressed or repotted. To top-dress, remove the top 1in (2.5cm) of soil mix with a hand fork and replace with fresh soil mix. In alternate winters, where possible, repot the plant. Remove the plant from its container, and gently comb away some of the old soil mix from the root ball, using a hand fork or wooden stick. Cut out any coarse roots, taking care not to damage the fibrous roots, and repot into a larger, clean container (see also "Planting in containers," p.419).

Stakes and ties

The stakes and ties of all fruit trees should be checked regularly. When the cushioning or ties are weak or worn out, the tree may rub against the stake, and *Nectria* canker (p.655) on apples or bacterial canker on apples and stone fruits may develop. Check the base of the stake: this may rot and then the tree may topple in high winds, particularly just before a heavy crop is to be gathered. On trained trees, be sure that branches are not tied too tightly to stakes or wires, since this will restrict growth and damage the tree. Loosen any ties if necessary.

Supporting branches
Tree fruits grown in unrestricted forms may need to have their branches supported when the tree is heavily laden with fruit, even if the

FERTILIZING FRUIT TREES

Using string and a peg, mark a circular area around the tree, slightly beyond the spread of the branches. This indicates where fertilizer should be applied: over the entire span of the tree's root system.

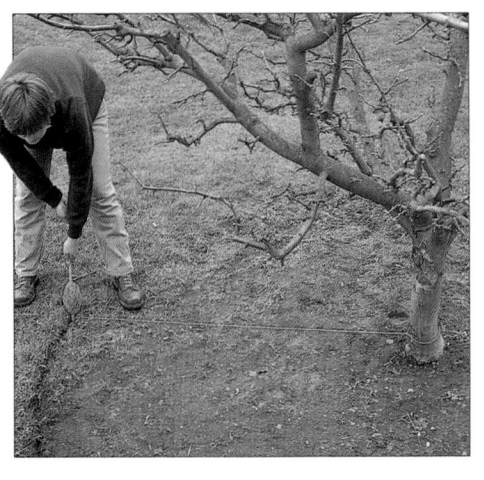

SUPPORTING LADEN BRANCHES

Tie several pieces of nylon string to a centrally placed pole attached to the main trunk. Use a nail to stop the string from slipping down the pole. Tie at least one string to each heavily laden branch (away from the fruits) to support it.

fruits have been correctly thinned. If only one or two branches are affected, support them on forked stakes or rope them in to stronger branches. If several branches are overloaded, secure a sturdy stake either to the trunk or to the main stake and tie a rope to each branch and to the top of the stake; this technique is known as "maypoling."

Protecting plants

Fruit trees and bushes may need to be protected from bad weather or cold with windbreaks or insulation. Protection against birds and animals may also be necessary.

Wind protection
Maintain windbreaks (see p.603) properly so that they remain effective, and prune natural barriers such as trees or shrubs if they become thin to encourage bushier growth. Check that posts supporting windbreak netting or fences are secure and repair them as necessary.

Cold protection
Most cold damage is caused by spring frosts that kill or injure buds, flowers, or fruitlets overnight. Severe winter cold may cause bark splitting and dieback, so in areas where low temperatures are common, select cultivars that are bred to withstand the conditions. In warmer regions, there should be few problems; if necessary, cover small trees and bushes with polyester fabric or spun polypropylene sheets.

Very slight cold seldom causes any serious damage: 28°F (-2°C) is frequently the danger point. The duration of the cold is usually more important than the temperature alone: 27°F (-3°C) for a quarter of an hour would cause little or no damage, whereas sustained over three hours, it could cause substantial losses.

If frost is forecast, protect strawberries, bushes, and even small trees by using old curtains, burlap, or layers of newspaper to cover the plants completely and trap warm air around them. Remove the covers each day once the temperature has risen above the freezing point. For further information, see COLD AND WIND PROTECTION, pp.604–05.

Protection from animals
In winter, squirrels often damage fruit buds by feeding on the nutritious center of the buds and discarding the outer bud scales. This damage is much more serious than the loss of ripe fruit, because it denudes whole branches permanently, making

it necessary to prune them back to obtain new young shoots, which will not fruit for two or more seasons. The best protection is to place nets over the trees or bushes. If snow is forecast, support the net or remove it temporarily, since the weight of the snow on the net may damage branches underneath.

Ripening fruit should also be protected against birds. Small areas may be temporarily covered with netting, but for large areas it is preferable to erect a fruit cage instead. It is impractical to protect large fruit trees, although those trained against

supports may be enclosed by attaching netting to the support. The mesh of any net used must be small enough to exclude tiny birds. Protect strawberries in a patch with a low, temporary cage.

Pest, disease, and weed control

It is advisable to check plants once a week for signs of pest and disease problems; they may then be treated at an early stage before extensive

damage has been caused (see PLANT PROBLEMS, pp.633–61). If viral diseases (p.642) are suspected, seek professional advice to confirm that this is the problem; strawberries, raspberries, loganberries, blackberries, and blackcurrants are especially vulnerable. The only practical solution is to dig up infected specimens with their roots and discard them; otherwise, the virus may spread to adjacent plants.

Weed control is also essential. Remove seedling weeds and mulch to inhibit germination of weed seeds. Perennial weeds should be dug out or spot-treated as soon as they are noticed. For further details, see "Weeds," pp.658–61.

Plants under cover

In much of Canada, some fruits may need to be grown under cover. These include all the tender fruits, as well as a number of other fruits that either have flowers that are vulnerable to damage by spring frosts or require a longer ripening period, for example peaches and many late-ripening varieties of grape.

In subtropical climates, fruit trees are rarely grown under cover, since the only climatic problems encountered are exceptionally cool periods and heavy rainfall, which most are able to tolerate.

Plants that need to be under cover all year are best grown in greenhouses; walk-in polytunnels are of limited use because temperature levels and adequate ventilation are hard to maintain (see also GREENHOUSES AND FRAMES, "Choosing a greenhouse," pp.562–65).

Particular care is needed to maintain free air circulation around plants grown in greenhouses to discourage diseases that may be caused by the increased heat and humidity. Support wires for trained fruits should be secured at least 12in (30cm) away from the glass or plastic of the greenhouse. Control any pests and diseases and apply fertilizer as recommended under individual tree fruit entries. For details of pruning fruits grown in a greenhouse, see "Pruning under cover," p.424.

Growing tender fruits (for example citrus, guava, pomegranate, and olive) in containers makes it possible to bring them under cover when necessary. In cool areas, place tender plants grown in pots outside in a sunny position in spring and bring them under cover again in fall. Overwinter the plants in the greenhouse at a temperature of at least 50°F (10°C).

PROTECTING AGAINST BIRD AND ANIMAL DAMAGE

BUD STRIPPING
Animals stripping buds from branches over winter cause permanent damage, leading to unproductive, bare wood.

NETTING STRAWBERRIES
Protect fruit by erecting a frame 4ft (1.2m) high and draping and tying ³/₄in (2cm) mesh netting over it. Secure the base so that birds and squirrels cannot get underneath.

FRUIT CAGE
Fruit bushes or small fruit trees may be protected by a fruit cage constructed from metal supports covered with wire or plastic netting.

PROTECTING TRAINED TREES
Fruit trees trained against supporting wires may be protected with a ³/₄in (2cm) mesh net attached at the top and secured firmly to the support.

Pruning and training

FRUIT trees and bushes need correct, regular pruning and (in many cases) training to yield a good crop. The degree and method required depend on the desired shape and the fruiting time and habit as well as on the individual type of fruit. Relatively limited pruning is needed to produce an open-center bush tree, for example, whereas extensive formative pruning and training are required for a fan or espalier to produce a symmetrical network of well-trained branches.

Aims of pruning and training

Initially, young trees and bushes should receive formative pruning and training to produce the desired shape (such as a cordon) and to develop a strong, balanced framework. With established plants, the aim of subsequent pruning is to maintain the health and shape of the plant and ensure a good yield of fruit.

Pruning
This is the cutting out of unwanted shoots and branches, either because they spoil the plant's framework or because they are unproductive. Correct pruning maintains an open, uncrowded structure to allow the maximum amount of sun to reach the ripening fruits and to simplify spraying and harvesting. It also includes the removal of dead, diseased, damaged, or old, unfruitful wood.

On young plants, pruning may be combined with training to form a particular shape. Unwanted shoots are removed completely; those retained may be cut back to stimulate the growth of sideshoots. The established, cropping tree, bush, or plant is pruned to encourage optimum growth and fruit production.

Training
The selection and, in many cases, the tying in of shoots to create a specific shape is known as training. Forms close to the natural shape, such as the bush, require much less training than, for example, a fan, which is produced by precise selection, spacing, and tying in of individual shoots onto a supporting framework of stakes and wires.

Over- and underpruning
Take care not to over- or underprune, because both of these restrict fruitfulness and may encourage disease. Repeated severe pruning results in increased, vigorous, vegetative growth and little or no fruit, since few fruit buds are able to develop. This is especially damaging on a plant that is already vigorous. Underpruning leads to overcrowded branches that will receive less sun, which is essential to ripen the fruit; the branches may also rub together, exposing the tree to the risk of diseases such as *Nectria* canker (p.655). Pruning a young tree too lightly may also cause early overcropping that could stunt the tree and even break branches by overloading them.

When to prune

The time of pruning depends both on the specific treatment and on the kind of fruit. In the pruning procedures described here and under the individual fruits, "year one" refers to the first 12 months after planting, "year two" to the following 12 months, and so on.

Winter pruning is standard practice on untrained apple, pear, and quince trees; on grapes; and on black-, red-, and whitecurrants, gooseberries, and blueberries. Water shoots, which take much energy from the tree and spoil its shape, should be cut flush to the branch from which they arise. Any diseased wood and borer-infested branches (see "Stem borers," p.646) should also be removed. Summer pruning is essential on trained forms of tree fruits, grapevines, currants, and gooseberries. This reduces their vigor and contains them within the limited space they occupy; it also concentrates the plants' energies on fruit production. Many tender fruits are pruned directly after fruiting.

How to prune

When deciding on the extent of pruning, always take into account the vigor both of the individual shoot and of the whole tree. Vigorous growth should be pruned lightly; this usually involves thinning out a percentage of shoots completely and leaving the remainder unpruned. Prune weak growth more severely, but check first that no disease, such as canker, is causing the weakness.

Where to cut
It is important always to prune to just above a healthy bud and to make a clean cut; cutting midway between buds or leaving a ragged end may cause dieback and increase the shoot's vulnerability to disease. If removing a shoot or branch completely, cut it back to the point of origin but leave the bark ridge and branch collar intact rather than cutting flush with the parent stem.

INCORRECT PRUNING

UNDERPRUNING
A tree that is pruned very lightly or irregularly will develop overcrowded shoots that will not receive sufficient light to ripen the fruits. The branches may also rub together, increasing the risk of certain diseases.

OVERPRUNING
If a fruit tree is pruned excessively, this will stimulate a mass of vigorous vegetative shoots. These shoots will produce few, if any, fruit buds, so the crop will be poor.

WHERE TO MAKE A PRUNING CUT

CUTTING TO A BUD
Cut just above a bud at a 45° angle, sloping the cut away from the bud. Do not cut too close (you might damage the bud), nor too far away (the stem may die back).

CUTTING TO A REPLACEMENT SHOOT
As when cutting to a bud, make an angled cut sloping away from the replacement shoot.

CUTTING BACK TO A MAIN BRANCH
Make a clean cut, leaving the branch collar intact (inset, top). The tree is then less susceptible to disease, and the wound heals faster (inset, bottom).

REMOVING A BRANCH

1 *Using a pruning saw, make the first cut approximately 12in (30cm) away from the trunk. Saw at right angles to the branch from underneath, to about a quarter of the way through.*

2 *Start the second cut at the top of the branch, slightly farther out than the first cut. Saw right through the branch; if it breaks away, the bark will tear only as far as the first cut.*

3 *When making the final cut, take care not to damage the bark ridge at the top of the branch or the collar at the base. If necessary, start the cut from below and cut down from above to meet it.*

4 *Pare away rough edges with a sharp knife. The exposed area will seal itself more quickly with the bark ridge and collar left intact. This also reduces the risk of disease entering the wound. Do not apply wound paint: it might seal in an existing infection.*

To prevent the branch or bark from tearing before cutting is completed, undercut first before finishing the cut from above. Cut back to the point of origin or to a well-placed, healthy branch as a suitable replacement. Do not leave a stub, or the cut end will die instead of healing. Pare away any rough edges with a sharp knife.

Fruiting habits

How a plant is pruned depends on its fruiting habit. For example, sweet cherries form fruit mainly on spurs on two-year and older wood, so many of the older shoots must be retained. Sour cherries, however, fruit on one-year-old shoots; when pruning, leave most of the young shoots but remove some of the old, unproductive wood.

Training for shape

A young tree is usually bought as a "feathered maiden" (a one-year-old tree with sideshoots). Initial pruning consists of selecting shoots to be retained, shortening them as required, and removing unwanted shoots. If a young tree is bought as a maiden whip (a one-year-old tree without sideshoots), it should be cut down to a bud after planting, the height depending on how the tree is to be trained. This encourages the growth of sideshoots. When these develop, the tree, now two years old, is equivalent to a feathered maiden. Formative pruning continues for the first two or three years until the desired shape has been obtained.

Training for fruitfulness

The vigor and fruitfulness of shoots may be adjusted by raising or lowering selected laterals or, with oblique cordons, the whole tree. Horizontal growths are more fruitful than vertical ones, so tying a lateral closer to the horizontal makes it produce more fruit. If one lateral is less vigorous than another and more sideshoots are needed, raising it will stimulate vegetative growth. For an established, cropping tree or bush, pruning is more important than training; even on an untrained tree, less fruitful or unbalanced shoots may be tied down in summer to increase their yield.

PRUNING A MAIDEN WHIP TO FORM A FEATHERED TREE

WINTER, YEAR 1
To produce vigorous "feathers" (sideshoots) on a maiden whip tree, cut it back with an angled cut just above a bud at the required height.

WINTER, YEAR 2
By the following winter, a number of new sideshoots should have been produced below the pruning cut.

TRAINING ON STAKES

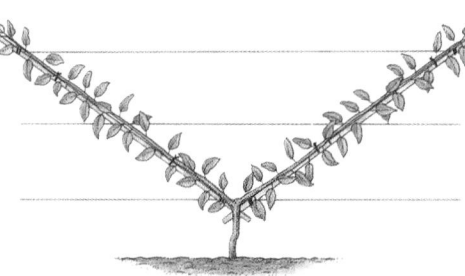

1 *The vigor of laterals of trained trees may be altered by adjusting the angle at which they are trained. This technique corrects uneven growth on either side of the same tree.*

2 *Lower a young, strong-growing lateral, with its stake, at the start of or during the summer to reduce its vigor; raise a lateral to encourage it to grow more quickly. Retie the stakes to the wires.*

3 *By the end of summer, the branches may be returned to their original positions; they should be more even in length.*

Curbing excessive vigor

Extremely vigorous trees that produce rapid vegetative growth at the expense of cropping may benefit from root pruning. On apples and pears only, bark-ringing (see p.431) may also be used as a last resort to curb vigor; it should not be used on stone fruits because it may kill them. Both methods will induce the formation of fruit buds, so the beneficial effects will be seen in increased blossoms and fruiting one or possibly two years later.

Root pruning

Trees may be root pruned at any age, but only when they are dormant. When pruning the roots of a young tree, first lift it by digging around it, then remove soil carefully from around the fibrous roots, taking care not to damage them. Cut back a few of the thick roots in the process. Then replant the tree firmly and stake it.

Larger trees need to be root pruned *in situ*, with the root system on one side of the tree pruned one winter, and the other side a year or two later. To do this effectively, make a trench 18in–4ft (45cm–1.2m) wide, depending on the size of the tree, to expose the main roots. These should be severed and a section of each root removed. Then fill in the trench, firm, and mulch; in some cases, staking may be required to provide support until the tree is fully stable.

Pruning under cover

Prune back branches and shoots of plants grown in a greenhouse so that they do not touch the glass or plastic surfaces, because otherwise they may suffer sun scorch and growth will be constricted or damaged. Regular pruning also allows more light to reach the developing fruits and helps them to ripen.

Renovation

If a tree is too old to bear well, and it has split, rotten, or severely diseased branches or trunk, it should be removed. If the trunk and the main branches are sound, however, and the tree is merely overcrowded, it can be rejuvenated by means of renovative pruning, followed by correct and diligent routine care.

Renovative work should be carried out in spring or summer on stone fruits and in winter on apples, pears, and other pome fruits. Cut out any

branches that are dead, damaged, or diseased, or so low that they may trail on the ground when laden with fruit. Also remove crowded or crossing branches, because these will shade the developing fruits, and, if they rub together, may become prone to diseases such as canker. On a vigorous tree, it is advisable to stagger this pruning over more than one year; pruning too severely on a single occasion may only induce more vigorous, vegetative growth.

Once this initial thinning has been achieved, more precise pruning, such as spur thinning, may be carried out (as described for routine pruning under individual fruit entries). Chemical inhibitors are available to curb the regrowth of water shoots around the cuts, but wound paints are not recommended because they may seal in any infection.

ROOT PRUNING TO IMPROVE FRUITING

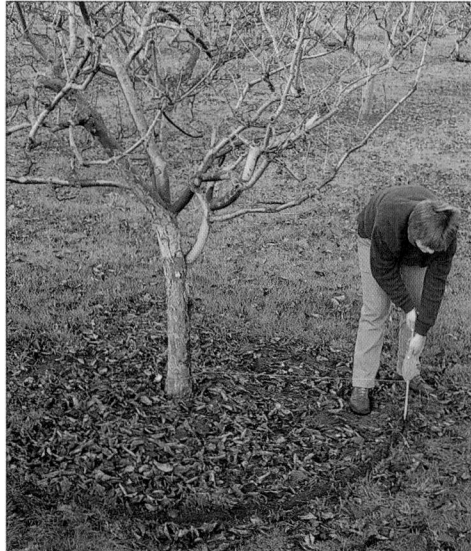

1 *Mark out the position for a trench around the tree using string and a peg. The trench should form an even semicircle just below the outermost spread of the branches. Prune the root system on only one side of the tree one winter; prune the other side a year later.*

2 *Dig out a trench around the tree at the marked line; it should be at least 18in (45cm) wide and approximately 24in (60cm) deep.*

3 *At the base of the trench, use a fork to remove soil from around the thick roots without damaging the fibrous roots.*

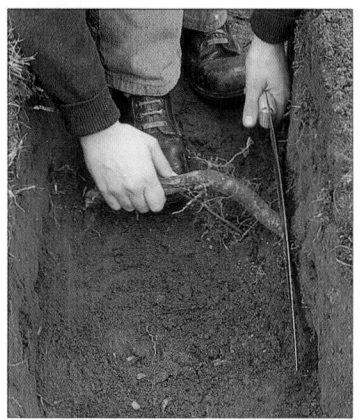

4 *Sever every thick, woody root on either side of the trench with a pruning saw, discarding the central section. Leave the smaller, more fibrous roots unpruned.*

5 *Backfill the trench with soil, firm well, then cover the area with an organic mulch to retain moisture and help the tree reestablish. Stake if necessary.*

RENOVATING A NEGLECTED TREE

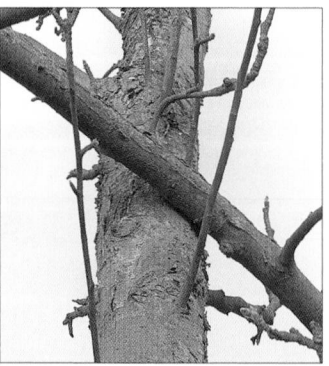

1 *Remove overcrowded, rubbing, or crossing branches to let in light and air by cutting them back to their point of origin, or to a vigorous sublateral facing in the required direction.*

2 *Any branches that are physically damaged or clearly affected by a disease such as canker (shown above) should be removed completely or cut back to a healthy shoot.*

Harvesting and storing

MANY home-grown fruits may be enjoyed long after their normal harvesting time if correctly harvested and stored. While most are at their best eaten fresh, a number keep their flavor well even after prolonged storage. For details on harvesting and storing specific fruits, see the individual fruit entries.

Harvesting

Most fruits are best picked when fully ripe for using fresh. Fruits for storing are usually harvested slightly earlier, however, when they are mature but not yet completely ripe and still firm. Since not all the fruits on a single plant ripen at the same time, it is usually necessary to harvest over a period; this provides a succession of fresh supplies.

For tree fruits such as apples and pears, test for ripeness by holding a fruit in the palm of your hand, then gently lift and twist. If ripe, the fruit will come away easily complete with its stalk; if unripe, it should be left for a day or two.

When harvesting, use any damaged, diseased, or bruised fruits immediately, since they will rot quickly; rot then spreads rapidly to adjacent fruits in storage.

Soft fruits must be picked completely dry; otherwise, many may be affected by rot unless the fruits are used immediately. Regular picking, at least every other day, is advisable for strawberries, raspberries, blackberries, and hybrid berries.

Always take care not to damage the plant when harvesting – by pulling fruit off sharply, for example. Some types of fruit, such as cherries, grapes, and mangos, should be cut off the plant to avoid the risk of accidental damage.

Storing

There are various ways of keeping fruits for later use, including cool storage, freezing, and preserving; the most suitable method depends on the type of fruit. Some fruits, especially those that have a high acid and sugar content, such as apples, apricots, and figs, may also be oven-dried at 120–140°F (49–60°C). Drying ovens for home use are available.

FREEZING SOFT FRUITS

Spread out soft fruits, such as raspberries, on trays so that they are not in contact with each other, then freeze them. Once they are frozen, they may be packed into suitable containers and kept in the freezer until they are needed.

When preparing fruits for storage, handle them carefully to avoid bruising. Always store different cultivars in separate containers that are free from any residues or aromas that may taint the fruits.

Cool storage

Apples and pears in particular may be kept for several weeks, or even months, in the right conditions – consistently cool, dark, and slightly damp. Various other tree fruits, such as lemons, may also be stored this way, although they do not usually keep for such a long period. Most nuts keep well for up to a few months. Soft fruits cannot be stored in this way. The required temperature and degree of humidity vary for different fruits, but most should be stored in slatted trays and boxes to allow free air circulation. Some apple and pear cultivars, however, tend to shrivel and are better kept in clear plastic bags. Check unwrapped fruits regularly and remove any that show signs of disease or rotting.

Freezing

This is ideal for most soft fruits, except strawberries, and for a number of tree fruits. Small fruits such as raspberries are usually frozen whole, while large fruits such as apples are best chopped or sliced to ensure even and thorough freezing. Remove any stalks (and fruit stems of currants), then open-freeze whole fruits spread out on trays. Once they are frozen – after two to four hours – transfer the fruits to plastic boxes or bags, excluding as much air as possible, and keep them frozen until needed. Strawberries and some soft-fleshed tree fruits such as plums are often puréed before being frozen.

Preserving and canning

All soft fruits, and a number of tree fruits such as apricots and plums, may be made into preserves. In most cases, the entire fruit is used, while some such as grapes and blackberries are better strained, with only the juice used to make jelly.

Citrus fruits, pineapples, and most stone fruits, such as cherries, may be canned in sugar syrup – with alcohol (such as rum, brandy, or cognac), if desired – to preserve them. Citrus peel may also be candied or dried for use in baking.

STORING APPLES

1 *Wrap each fruit individually in tissue paper to prevent rot and keep it in good condition.*

2 *Carefully fold the tissue paper around the fruit, holding the fruit lightly to avoid bruising it.*

3 *Place each wrapped fruit on its folded end in a wooden slatted box or other well-ventilated container, and store in a cool place.*

ALTERNATIVE METHOD

Store fruits of cultivars that tend to shrivel quickly in a plastic bag. Make several holes in the bag before filling it with no more than 6lb 8oz (3kg) of fruit. Seal the bag loosely.

FRUITS THAT FREEZE WELL

Apples **Sl**
Apricots **Sl**
Blackberries and all hybrid berries **Sk**
Blackcurrants **Sk**
Blueberries **Sk**
Cherries (sour) **Sk**
Cherries (sweet) **Sk**
Damsons **Sk** (with or without stones)
Gages **Sk**
Gooseberries **Sk**
Grapes **Sk**
Nectarines **Sl**
Peaches **Sl**
Plums **Sk, Sl**
Raspberries **Sk**
Redcurrants **Sk**
Whitecurrants **Sk**

KEY

Sk *Remove stalks (and stones where applicable)*
Sl *Remove cores or stones and slice and peel if required*

Propagation

TREE fruits (except figs) are usually propagated by grafting; figs, grapes, and many soft fruits by cuttings, although if *Phylloxera* (see p.455) is a problem, grapevines should be grafted. Some fruits produce runners, layers, or suckers; all produce new plants. Several tender fruits and some nuts may be grown from seed, but hardy fruits seldom grow true to type from seed.

Bud-grafting

Both chip-budding and T-budding are used to increase the stock of fruit trees. They are economical methods of propagation, since a new tree is produced from a single bud. Grafting should be carried out in mid-summer, using as the rootstock an established plant with a stem that is at least 1/2in (1cm) thick. A bud from the scion plant is cut from a ripe shoot (the budstick) of the current season's growth and grafted onto an incision in the rootstock.

Propagating by chip-budding
Select a healthy budstick and carefully remove a bud (the budchip), taking care not to damage the cambium layer. Remove a sliver of rind from the rootstock and place the budchip onto the exposed wood of the rootstock so that the cambium layers are in close contact. Bind the budchip tightly onto the rootstock to hold it in place. When the bud and rootstock have united, the bud will start to swell and the binding may be removed. The following winter, trim the rootstock just above the grafted bud to encourage a strong shoot to develop from the graft in spring.

CHIP-BUDDING

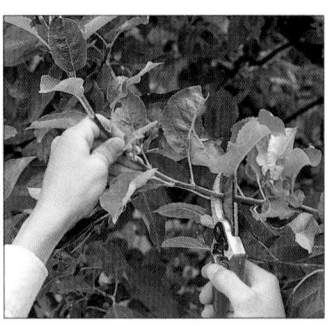

1 *Choose a vigorous shoot of the current season's ripened wood as the budstick. The shoot should be approximately pencil thick and have well-developed buds.*

2 *Hold the budstick firmly and, using a clean, sharp knife, slice off the soft tip and remove all the leaves to produce a clear length of stem.*

3 *To remove a budchip, first slice into the budstick about 3/4in (2cm) below a bud. Cut down to a depth of about 1/4in (5mm), slanting the blade at an angle of 45°.*

4 *Make another incision about 1 1/2in (4cm) above the first. Slice downward behind the bud toward the first incision, taking care not to damage the bud.*

5 *Remove the budchip, holding it by the bud to keep the cambium layer clean. Place the budchip in a plastic bag to prevent it from drying out.*

6 *To prepare the rootstock, stand astride the plant and, using a sharp knife, remove all the shoots and leaves from the bottom 12in (30cm) of stem.*

7 *Make a shallow cut in the stock. Remove a sliver of rind to reveal the cambium layer (see inset), leaving a "lip" at the base. Do not touch the exposed wood.*

Budchip in position on rootstock

8 *Place the budchip onto the prepared lip of rind, offset if necessary, so that the exposed cambium layers of budchip and rootstock match and touch.*

9 *Bind the budchip to the rootstock with plastic tape. Carefully remove the tape after a few weeks when the budchip has united with the rootstock.*

10 *Late the following winter, remove the top of the rootstock. Cut cleanly with pruners just above the grafted bud, using an angled cut.*

11 *During the summer, a shoot from the grafted bud will develop. The new tree is then at the maiden whip stage (see "Selecting fruit trees," p.419).*

Propagating by T-budding

In this technique, the preparation of the rootstock and scion bud is similar to chip-budding, except that two slits are made in the rootstock, to form the shape of a T. This allows the bark of the rootstock to be lifted slightly so that the scion bud may be tucked behind it. Removing the scion bud with a leaf stalk attached makes it easier to handle; the stalk is removed before the bud is bound to the rootstock. The rootstock should be cut back the next winter.

For this technique to be successful, the bark of the rootstock must lift smoothly: in dry weather, rootstocks need to be watered for up to two weeks before T-budding takes place.

Whip-and-tongue grafting

This is a common method of grafting for tree fruits. It may be used as an alternative to budding, but it is usually more successful with pome than with stone fruits. Use well-established rootstocks that have been planted either the previous winter or, preferably, two winters before grafting takes place.

The scion material should have at least three buds and should be taken in midwinter from a healthy shoot of the previous season's growth. Heel it in until ready for grafting. In late winter or early spring, prepare the stock by cutting off the top of the stem and removing any sideshoots.

Using a sloping cut, slice off a small piece of bark from the top of the remaining stem; make a shallow incision in the exposed cambium layer, to create a tongue.

Trim the scion to a length of three or four buds, then, using a sloping cut, slice off a small piece of bark close to a bud but on the opposite side to it. Make another shallow incision, to match that in the stock, and hook the resulting tongue onto the one on the rootstock. Make sure that the two cambium layers are in close

---

T-BUDDING

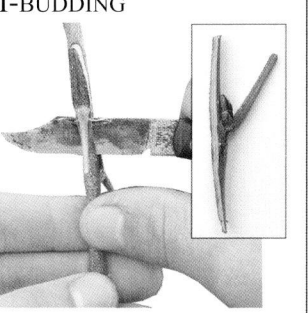

1 *From the current season's growth, select a ripened shoot as the scion, and remove the leaves. Remove a bud by slicing underneath it (see inset).*

2 *Make a T-shaped cut in the stock about 9in (22cm) above ground level, and open the flaps of bark.*

3 *Place the bud behind the flaps of bark, trimming the top level with the horizontal cut on the stock. Bind the bud as for chip-budding.*

WHIP-AND-TONGUE GRAFTING

1 *In midwinter, remove healthy, vigorous hardwood shoots from the scion tree. Cut lengths of about 9in (22cm), cutting obliquely just above a bud.*

2 *Make bundles of 5 or 6 scions. Choose a well-drained, sheltered site and heel them in to keep them moist but dormant, leaving 2–3in (5–8cm) above the soil surface.*

3 *In late winter or early spring, prepare the rootstocks just before bud break. Cut off the top of each rootstock about 8–10in (20–25cm) from ground level.*

4 *Trim off any shoots from the rootstock with a sharp knife, then make a 1¹/₂in (3.5cm) upward-sloping cut on one side to receive the scion.*

5 *Make a slit ¹/₂in (1cm) deep about one-third of the way down the exposed cambium layer, to form a tongue into which the scion may be inserted (see inset).*

6 *Lift the scions, cut off any soft growth at the tips, and trim to 3 or 4 buds. For each, cut off a piece of bark behind a bud that is about 2in (5cm) from the base.*

7 *Without touching the cut surface with your hand, cut the cambium layer (see inset) to match the tongue in the rootstock.*

8 *Place the scion into the tongue on the stock (inset, top). Use the arches of the cambium layers as a guide (inset, bottom) to ensure the exposed surfaces fit together well.*

9 *Bind together stock and scion with clear plastic tape. When the cut surfaces start to callus, remove the tape by carefully scoring it downward.*

contact, then bind the graft firmly. Remove the binding carefully when a callus has formed around the graft union. By spring, buds on the scion will have started to grow. Select the best shoot that develops (keeping others pinched back) to form a maiden whip tree (see "Selecting fruit trees," p.419).

Cuttings

Hardwood, softwood, and leaf-bud cuttings may be used to propagate certain fruits. Always select cutting material from a healthy parent plant that crops regularly.

Hardwood cuttings

Figs, grapes, currants (white, red, and black), and gooseberries may be propagated from hardwood cuttings, usually taken in fall.

Select a well-ripened shoot of the current season's growth and trim off the leaves and soft tip. Remove some or most of the buds, depending on the fruit being propagated, and trim off the top and base. The exact preparation and length of the cuttings vary slightly; details are given under individual fruit entries.

If the soil is well cultivated, the cuttings may be inserted into a narrow trench in the open ground. If the soil is heavy, sprinkle sand into the bottom of the trench to improve drainage, or place the cuttings in a pot of moist, sandy soil mix. Transplant the cuttings one or two years later.

Softwood cuttings

Guavas, pomegranates, tree tomatoes, and blueberries are propagated from softwood cuttings (where the climate is warm enough for the wood to ripen sufficiently, blueberries may also be propagated from hardwood cuttings). Take the cuttings in midsummer and place them in pots of rooting medium (see p.622). Harden off the young plants before transplanting to their permanent positions.

Leaf-bud cuttings

Stocks of blackberries and hybrid berries may be increased quickly by leaf-bud cuttings (see p.466). Take the cuttings in late summer: remove short lengths of stem, each with a bud and leaf attached; insert them in medium with the buds just above the surface. Once rooted, the cuttings may be potted up or planted out.

Runners, layers, and suckers

Some fruits send out runners, layers, or suckers, which root naturally at stem nodes while still attached to the parent plant. This process may be exploited to increase fruit stocks.

Runners

Strawberries (but not all alpine strawberries) produce creeping horizontal stems, or runners, which root where they come into contact with the ground and may be used for propagation. As the runners are produced, spread them out evenly. Allow them to root, and then lift and sever them (see p.464).

Layers

Blackberries and hybrid berries may be propagated by layering, although some hybrids are slow to root. The tip of a shoot is induced to root by carefully pegging it down in the soil or in a pot of moist soil mix (see *Tip Layering*, p.465). A year later, when the tip has rooted and produced new growth, it may be severed from the parent plant and transplanted to its permanent position.

Suckers

Established cane fruits such as raspberries naturally produce suckers that are usually hoed off. If retained, rooted suckers may be lifted and severed in fall, when the plants are dormant but the soil is still warm. Transplant the rooted suckers directly to their permanent positions (see *Propagating by Suckers*, p.468). Figs, hazelnuts, and filberts also produce suckers: if the suckers have good root systems, sever them with a spade and replant in the same way.

Seed

Propagation from seed is the usual method of increasing stock of many tender fruits, including avocado (see p.479), guava, and papaya.

The alpine strawberry is one of the few hardy fruits that can be raised successfully from seed (see p.464). Hazelnuts, walnuts, and chestnuts may also be raised from seed with a reasonable chance of success, although cultivars selected for the quality of their fruit need to be propagated vegetatively. For details, see ORNAMENTAL TREES, "Raising trees from seed," p.78.

HARDWOOD CUTTINGS

1 Dig a narrow trench 6in (15cm) deep. If the soil has a high clay content, sprinkle a little sand into the bottom of the trench to improve drainage.

2 Choose a mature stem from the current season's growth (here, from a fig tree). Remove lengths of at least 12in (30cm), cutting flush with the main stem.

3 Cut off all the leaves and the soft growth at the tip of each cutting, then trim to about 9in (22cm). Make an angled cut above the top bud and a straight cut at the base.

4 Place the cuttings in the prepared trench, spacing them 4–6in (10–15cm) apart and burying two-thirds of the stems. Firm the soil, and label.

5 The cuttings will take several months to root. Toward the end of the following growing season, they should have developed sturdy new growth.

6 After leaf drop in fall, carefully lift the rooted cuttings, wrapping the roots in plastic to keep them from drying out. Transplant the cuttings to their permanent positions to grow on.

Tree fruits

Pears

Apples

Apples

Quinces

Apples

Medlars

THE fruits in this group are the largest-growing forms in the nontropical fruit garden. They may be divided into two main categories: pome fruits, such as apples and pears, have a seed-containing core, while the stone fruits, such as cherries, peaches, and apricots, have a hard central stone, or pit. There are also certain other fruits within this group that fit into neither of the above categories, such as figs, mulberries, and persimmons.

Cultivating tree fruits is a long-term undertaking that requires careful planning. The size and shape or form of the trees are important considerations. Left to grow naturally, many tree fruits would become much too large for the average-sized garden. However, smaller forms grown on dwarfing rootstocks have been developed. Fruit trees may also be trained and pruned as fans,

espaliers, or cordons, and grown flat against walls or fences, making it feasible to grow them in even the smallest of spaces.

Another factor to consider is the number of trees required. Many fruit trees are self-sterile and, to produce fruit, need at least one other tree of the same type to act as a pollinator. Even self-fertile trees bear more heavily if pollinators are present.

Some tree fruits, such as figs, prefer a long, hot growing season and are difficult to cultivate in cooler climates. Growing them under cover provides protection and improves fruit and crop size, as well as flavor.

Once a tree fruit has been selected and planted, it is important to follow the correct pruning methods. Good pruning not only builds a strong framework of branches but also encourages and maintains maximum bearing for many years.

Apples (*Malus sylvestris var. domestica*)

Apples are one of the most widely grown hardy fruits, and both dessert and culinary cultivars offer a great variety of flavors and textures.

Tree size may be considerably reduced now that dwarfing rootstocks are more widely available. This allows a number of different apples to be grown in small gardens where only one large tree could have been accommodated before. Apple trees may readily be trained into almost any shape. Cordon-, espalier-, and fan-shaped forms are particularly useful for growing trees against walls and fences.

The extensive choice of cultivars covers a period of ripening from mid-summer to late winter, and fruit may be stored until midspring, given suitable conditions. There are cultivars and rootstocks suitable for most climates, including those with severe winters. For flowering to occur, the trees must be subjected to at least 900 hours below 45°F (7°C) to meet the chilling requirement. Apples are not grown successfully in tropical or subtropical regions, since they do not receive adequate chilling.

Site and planting

When planting, make sure that each tree has sufficient space to develop to its full size. Select the most appropriate size of tree (determined by the rootstock) for your garden. In most

cases, more than one apple tree will be required for pollination.

Site

A sunny, sheltered site is essential for consistently good crops. Walls for trained fruit should not be shaded and should preferably be in full sun. For shaded gardens or those in a region with short summers and cool temperatures, choose cultivars that ripen early. Where late frosts occur, select late-flowering cultivars so that the blossoms will not be damaged.

Apples will grow in most well-drained soils (see "Preparing the site," p.418). The more dwarfing the rootstock, however, the more fertile the soil should be.

Rootstocks

Choice of rootstock depends on the tree size required and the soil type. Many apple rootstocks are prefixed by M or MM, which stand for Malling and Malling Merton respectively, the research stations in the UK where the rootstocks were developed. The 'Ottawa' range of rootstocks was developed at the Central Experimental Farm, Ottawa, Ontario. A wide range

of rootstocks is available, from 'M27', which is very dwarfing, to the vigorous 'M25'. For normal garden purposes, 'M9' is recommended for dwarf trees, 'M26' for larger ones, and 'Ottawa 3' for medium-sized trees (see *Planting Distances*, p.430). Cultivars on 'M27' bear fruit within three years of being grafted but require good growing conditions. Where the soil is poor, use a more vigorous rootstock: for example, where a dwarf tree is required use 'Ottawa 3'. The vigor of the cultivar also determines the size of the mature tree. Triploid cultivars grow larger than diploids (see below); use a more dwarfing rootstock for a triploid than for a diploid to attain a tree of similar size.

Pollination

No apples are reliably and consistently self-fertile: diploids must be planted near a second, compatible cultivar; triploid apples, which will not pollinate other cultivars, require two compatible cultivars nearby to pollinate them. Cultivars are divided into groups according to their time of flowering; a cultivar from one

group may be cross-pollinated by another from the same group or one in the group before or after it if flowering times overlap. However, short North American blooming seasons make flowering group designations less meaningful. Some cultivars are incompatible: of those listed on pp.430 and 431, 'Cox's Orange Pippin' will not pollinate 'Kidd's Orange Red' or 'Suntan' and vice versa. If in doubt about compatibility, ask a fruit nursery for advice.

Planting

Bare-root trees are best planted when dormant, preferably in fall because the soil is still warm; they may be planted until late winter (except when it is frosty), but keep them moist in spring so that they establish well. Container-grown trees may be planted at any time, unless the ground is frozen or very wet; water before planting so that the roots are moist. Using the soil mark as a guide, plant each tree at its original planting depth (see *Planting a Fruit Tree*, p.419).

If the tree is to be trained, fit the supports and wires securely in place before planting (see under individual tree forms for details). For all untrained trees, staking when planting is essential and should be permanent for those on dwarfing rootstocks.

Planting distances (see p.430) depend on how the trees are to be trained, as well as on the vigor of the chosen rootstocks and cultivars.

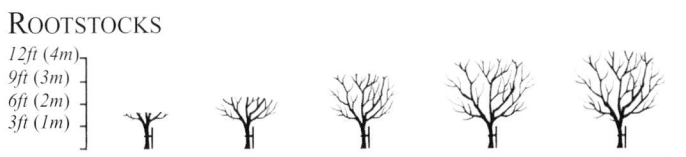

ROOTSTOCKS

12ft (4m)
9ft (3m)
6ft (2m)
3ft (1m)

'M27'   'M9'   'M26'   'Ottawa 3'   'MM111'

RECOMMENDED DESSERT
APPLES

Early
'Akane'
'Discovery'
'Empress'
'George Cave'
'Ginger Gold'
'Gravenstein' **P**
'Jerseymac'
'Pristine' **D**
'Red Astrachan'
'Transparent'
'William's Pride' **D**
'Zestar!'

'George Cave'

Midseason
'Arlet'
'Blushing Golden'
'Corail'
'Cox's Orange Pippin'
'Delicious'
'Empire'
'Fameuse'
'Freedom' **D**
'Gala'
'Golden Delicious'
'Golden Supreme'
'Honeycrisp'
'Jonafree' **D**
'Jonagold' **P**
'Idared'   'Worcester
'Liberty' **D**   Pearmain'
'Macoun'
'McIntosh'
'Ribston Pippin'
'SirPrize' **D**
'Spartan'
'Spitzenburg'
'Wealthy'
'Winter Banana'
'Worcester Pearmain'

Late
'Ashmead's Kernel'
'Calville Blanche d'Hiver'
'Cameo'
'Enterprise' **D**
'Fuji'
'Golden Russet' **D**
'Goldrush' **D**
'Granny Smith'
'Idared'
'Keepsake'
'Lady'
'Mutsu' **P**
'Northern Spy'
'Orleans Reinette'
'Pink Lady'
'Ruxbury Russet'
'Stayman'
'Winesap' **P**
'Winter Banana'
'Wolf River'

KEY
D *Disease resistant*
P *Poor pollen source*

Routine care

Establish a regular maintenance program to make sure that trees stay healthy and bear well. Fertilize and mulch periodically as required. Blossom and fruit thinning are annual tasks required to ensure satisfactory bearing. Check trees regularly for signs of pests and diseases, and damage from rubbing stakes and ties.

Blossom thinning and biennial bearing

Certain cultivars, such as 'Northern Spy', tend to produce heavy crops in alternate years, with little or no blossoms or fruit in intervening years. This is known as biennial bearing.

Blossom thinning can largely correct this; it involves removing nine of every ten blossom clusters by pinching them out, leaving the rosette of young leaves around each intact. The tree then produces a moderate, rather than heavy, crop, and its resources are channeled into producing fruit buds for the following year, which would otherwise have been fruitless. On large trees, where it would be impractical to thin blossoms over the entire tree, biennial bearing can be corrected by blossom thinning a few branches.

If trees that normally bear regularly start to bear biennially, this may be due to the loss of blossoms from frost and the resulting loss of crop; this may then induce a tree to overbear the following year. The tree may not have sufficient resources to develop adequate fruit buds for the third year, so a biennial tendency is set in motion. Disease or pest infestation causing a setback in one year may have a similar effect.

Fruit thinning

Thinning is essential where heavy crops have set, to improve fruit size, quality, and flavor and to help prevent branches from breaking. On young trees, overheavy bearing strains the tree's resources and slows the growth of new buds. Some thinning is possible on the young fruitlets, but it is simpler to carry out the whole task in early summer, after the "June drop," when the tree naturally sheds imperfect and infertile fruits.

Use pruners to remove the center (or "king") fruit of each cluster, which is sometimes abnormally shaped; then cut out any fruits that are damaged. In about midsummer, thin the clusters again so that there is one good fruit per cluster. Fruit of dessert cultivars should be spaced 4–6in (10–15cm) apart, and that of culinary cultivars 6–9in (15–22cm) apart. These distances may vary

according to the individual cultivar and the size of fruit required.

Fertilizing, watering, and mulching

Water trees in spells of hot, dry weather, apply fertilizer annually, and mulch as necessary (see "Care of tree fruits," p.420). If growth is poor, apply ammonium sulfate in spring at a rate of 1oz/sq yd (35g/sq m) of area under the canopy.

Stakes and ties

Inspect stakes and ties regularly to check that they are not rubbing against the bark of trees and that ties

are not too loose; adjust them as necessary. Trees grown on dwarfing rootstocks such as 'M9' and 'M26' produce few taproots and need permanent staking to provide support.

Pests and diseases

Common pests that may be troublesome include tent caterpillars (p.640), wasps (p.651), codling moths (p.651), European apple sawflies, apple maggots (p.651), apple psyllids, and spider mites (p.640). Diseases include scab (p.650), brown rot (p.650), powdery mildew (p.650), bitter pit (see "Calcium deficiency," p.650), and *Nectria* canker (p.655).

PLANTING DISTANCES

TREE FORM	ROOTSTOCK	DISTANCE BETWEEN TREES	DISTANCE BETWEEN ROWS
Bush	'M27'	4–6ft (1.2–2m)	6ft (2m)
	'M9'	8–10ft (2.5–3m)	10ft (3m)
	'M26'	10–14ft (3–4.75m)	15ft (5m)
	'Ottawa 3'	11–18ft (3.5–5.5m)	18ft (5.5m)
Half-standard	'MM111'	24–8ft (7.5–9m)	24–8ft (7.5–9m)
Standard	'MM111', 'M25' (or Seedling crab)	24–32ft (7.5–10.5m)	24–32ft (7.5–10.5m)
Spindlebush	'M9' or 'M26' (and triploids on 'M27')	6–7ft (2–2.2m)	8–10ft (2.5–3m)
	'Ottawa 3'	6–7ft (2–2.2m)	11ft (3.5m)
Cordon	As bush	30in (75cm)	6ft (2m)
Fan/espalier	'M9'	10ft (3m)	
	'Ottawa 3'	14ft (4.75m)	
	'MM111'	18ft (5.5m)	
Dwarf pyramid	'M27'	4ft (1.2m)	6ft (2m)
	'M9' or 'M26'	5ft (1.5m)	6–7ft (2–2.2m)
	'Ottawa 3'	6ft (2m)	7ft (2.2m)

APPLE THINNING

 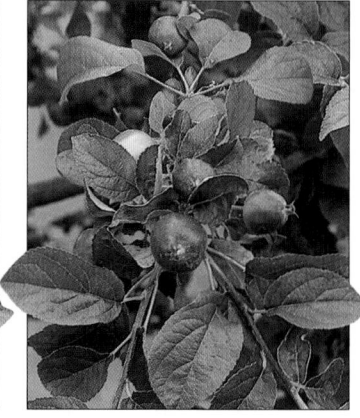

1 *Thinning is essential if the apple tree is carrying a heavy crop. After the "June drop," which is a normal occurrence, the remaining fruits will require further thinning if the crop is still heavy.*

2 *Remove enough fruitlets (especially any that are malformed) to leave about 4–6in (10–15cm) between dessert apples and 6–9in (15–22cm) between culinary apples and only 1 fruitlet per cluster.*

Pruning and training techniques

Apple trees produce flowers and fruit mainly on two-year-old and older shoots and on short spurs produced on the older wood. Two-year-old shoots carry both large fruit buds and smaller, pointed growth buds. Fruit buds produce flower clusters and then fruit, while growth buds form into fruit buds for the following year or into sideshoots or fruiting spurs. One-year-old shoots may also carry fruit buds, but these flower later than those on older wood. Tip-bearing cultivars produce markedly fewer spurs (see right).

Once their branch framework is established, trained trees need to be pruned (mainly in summer) to maintain shape, curb vegetative growth, and stimulate the production of fruit buds. Untrained trees require moderate pruning in winter to stimulate growth for the next season's fruit and to maintain an open, well-balanced structure so that they bear well and the fruit is of good quality.

FRUIT BUDS AND GROWTH BUDS

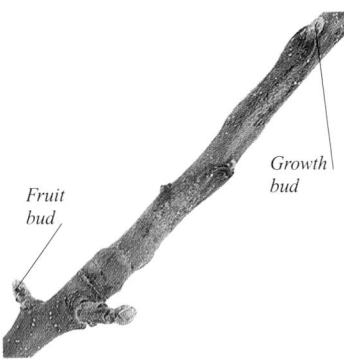

Large fruit buds develop on 2-year-old and older wood. The smaller buds are growth buds and are found mainly on 1-year-old wood.

Fruit bud

Growth bud

NICKING AND NOTCHING

NICKING
To weaken bud growth, make a nick in the bark just below the bud and into the cambium layer.

NOTCHING
To stimulate bud growth, make a notch through the bark into the cambium layer just above the bud.

Tip bearers and spur bearers
Cultivars differ in the way they bear their fruit. Tip bearers carry much of the crop at, or near, the shoot tips; spur bearers carry it along the whole shoot on short-jointed spurs.

Some well-known cultivar names such as 'Delicious' encompass many different varieties. When buying new trees, determine whether they are spur or tip bearers. Spur bearers, easily trained as cordons, espaliers, and fans, are preferable for small gardens. Tip bearers are best grown as standard, half-standard, or bush forms; once established, they need renewal pruning only (see p.433).

Nicking and notching
Sometimes it may be necessary to correct the balance of the branch framework of a trained tree. This may be achieved by nicking, which weakens the growth of a particular bud, or notching, which strengthens it. Notching may also be used to stimulate the production of sideshoots on bare lengths of stem.

Nicking and notching are most effective in spring when the sap is rising. Make a nick or a small incision with a sharp knife just below a growth bud to inhibit it; make a notch just above it to increase its vigor and stimulate new growth.

Bark-ringing
On excessively vigorous apple and pear trees (but not on stone fruits) that produce unsatisfactory crops, bark-ringing may be used as a last resort to curb vegetative growth and induce a greater fruit set. In late spring, remove a narrow band of bark from around the trunk through to the cambium layer at a height of about 3ft (1m). This reduces the flow of nutrients and hormones back to the roots, so that they are concentrated in the upper part of the tree.

Bark-ringing must be carried out carefully, or the tree may die. First measure out the width of the band, which must be only ⅛in (3mm) on a small tree, graduating to no more than ½in (1cm) on a very large tree, then score the band with a knife. Cut through the bark and the cambium layer and remove the bark within the band down to the hardwood all the way around. Seal the wound at once with several layers of waterproof adhesive tape – it must cover the wound without touching the cambium layer.

RECOMMENDED CULINARY APPLES

Early
'Chenango Strawberry' **De**
'Earligold'
'Jerseymac'
'Melba' **De**
'Parkland'
'Red Astrachan'
'Redfree' **D**
'Twenty Ounce'
'William's Pride'
'Yellow Transparent'

Midseason
'Blenheim Orange' **P**
'Collet' **De**
'Cortland' **De**
'Cox's Orange Pippin'
'Elstar'
'Empire'
'Enterprise' **D**
'Freedom' **D**

'Mutsu'

'Golden Delicious' **De**
'Golden Nobel'
'Gravenstein' **P, B**
'Jonagold'
'Liberty'
'McIntosh' **De**
'Macoun' **De**
'Sweet Sixteen'

Late
'Braeburn'
'Calville Blanche d'Hiver'
'Edward VII'
'Idared'
'Golden Russet' **De**
'Granny Smith' **De**
'Haralson'

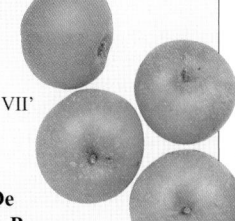

'Edward VII'

'Melrose' **De**
'Mutsu' **De, P**
'Newton Pippin' **De**
'Northern Spy' **B**
'Novaspy' **De**
'Rhode Island Greening' **B, P**
'Rome'
'Stayman'
'Winesap' **De**
'York Imperial'

KEY
B *Biennial bearing*
D *Disease resistant*
De *Dessert use also*
P *Poor pollen source*

BARK-RINGING

1 *Stick tape around the trunk as a guide for 2 parallel cuts. The ring may be ⅛–½in (3mm–1cm) wide, depending on the age and size of the tree.*

2 *The parallel cuts should be made through both the bark and the cambium layer. Carefully remove the ring of bark with the blunt side of the knife blade.*

3 *Wind waterproof tape around the ring so that it covers the wound without touching the cambium layer. Remove the tape when the wound has healed.*

The wound should heal over by the fall, when the waterproof tape may be removed. The following year, the tree should produce many more blossoms and, if conditions favor it, a much heavier crop of fruit because the reaction of any wounded plant is to reproduce.

Winter pruning

There are three main techniques for winter pruning, all of which stimulate new growth. Spur pruning and thinning should be done only on cultivars that produce plenty of spurs, not on tip bearers. Renewal pruning is appropriate for spindlebushes and all tip bearers, as well as for vigorous cultivars that would be overstimulated by hard pruning. Regulated pruning is suited to cultivars that are naturally very vigorous, particularly triploids such as 'Gravenstein', 'Mutsu', 'Spigold', 'Winesap', and 'Jonagold'.

It may be necessary to vary the degree and type of pruning from year to year depending on the extent of growth, the quantity of fruit produced, and the age of the tree.
Spur pruning involves cutting back branch leaders and young laterals to stimulate the growth of sublaterals and fruiting spurs. The extent of pruning required depends on the tree's vigor – the greater the vigor, the lighter the pruning, since pruning stimulates growth.

Shorten branch leaders on vigorous trees by only a few buds (but on weaker ones by up to one-third) to stimulate new sublaterals to form. Shorten young laterals to three to six buds where growth is good but to three or four buds on weaker trees so that spurs form. On a stronger tree, shoots up to 6in (15cm) long may be left unpruned.
Spur thinning is necessary as a tree ages to prevent fruits from becoming overcrowded. If left unthinned, the spurs become entangled and carry inferior fruit. When spur systems become congested, remove the older wood in favor of the younger. In time, it may be necessary to saw off whole spur systems to allow room for new ones to develop.
Renewal pruning involves the annual cutting back of a proportion of older, fruited shoots to their base to stimulate the growth of new, young wood. Keep the center of a bush tree open by pruning out any vigorous growth that is crossing or shading other laterals so that all the branches are well spaced. Remove only a little of the tip from branch leaders and none at all on vigorous trees.
Regulated pruning consists of removing shoots and sometimes long

sections of large branches that are crowded or crossing, particularly in the center of the tree, to keep the branch framework open. Remove old wood to make room for new shoots. Do not tip prune the branch leaders.

Summer pruning

This is carried out to keep trained trees within their allotted space. It involves removing a large proportion of the new growth each summer to slow down vegetative growth.
The Modified Lorette System is the standard method of summer pruning in temperate climates with cool, unpredictable summers. It is carried out once the young shoots have become woody at the base. Maiden (new) laterals more than 9in (22cm) long that grow directly from the main stem or a main branch should be reduced to three leaves above the basal cluster. Prune back sideshoots arising from spurs and existing laterals to one leaf above the basal cluster. Continue to prune in this way as shoots mature.

WINTER PRUNING
SPUR PRUNING

1 *Cut back young laterals to between 3 and 6 buds of the current growth, depending on the vigor of the shoot.*

2 *Prune back the current season's growth on branch leaders by a quarter to one-third.*

SPUR THINNING

On older trees, spur systems may become too dense. Thin these out by removing weak spurs and any on the undersides of the branches.

RENEWAL PRUNING

Prune out a good proportion of the older shoots that have already borne fruit (left). This will encourage new shoots to develop (right).

REGULATED PRUNING

On this tree there is congested growth. Correct this by removing any branches that are crossing or touching each other, and thin out any sublaterals or laterals that are overcrowded.

SUMMER PRUNING (MODIFIED LORETTE SYSTEM)

Prune trees when the lowest third of all new growth has become woody.

Cut back laterals on the main stems to 3 leaves above the basal cluster.

Basal cluster

Trim any sideshoots to 1 leaf.

BEFORE PRUNING

AFTER PRUNING

To help prevent sideshoots, or secondary growths, from developing behind the pruning cut, leave a small number of the longer shoots unpruned; tie these shoots securely to other branches so that they are roughly horizontal and draw the sap down. Do not shorten any of them until after fruiting. Then, in midfall, cut back any secondary growth shoots to one bud.

The Full Lorette System should be used in warmer climates. Prune back new laterals to about 2in (5cm), repeating at intervals through the summer. Shorten the laterals to ³⁄₄in (2cm) once they are woody at the base. Prune any secondary growths in late summer in the same way.

APPLE BUSH
YEAR 1, WINTER PRUNING

Prune back the leader to a selected lateral, leaving 2 or 3 strong laterals below it.

Cut back each of these laterals by two-thirds to an upward-facing bud. Remove all other laterals.

YEAR 2, WINTER PRUNING
Sublaterals that are not needed for secondary branches should be pruned back to 4 or 5 buds.

Prune back branch leaders and well-placed sublaterals by half to outward-facing buds.

Bush

The open-center or goblet-shaped bush is comparatively simple to maintain; it is ideal for larger gardens where there is plenty of space.

Formative pruning
Start with a well-feathered maiden tree; the laterals will form the first branches. After planting, while the tree is dormant, cut back the leader to a strong lateral 24–30in (60–75cm) above ground level, leaving at least two or three well-spaced laterals below it radiating out like the spokes of a wheel. These form the basis of the branch system; shorten them by two-thirds, cutting to an upward-pointing bud. Remove all other laterals.

If a maiden whip is used, or a feathered maiden tree that has few or no suitable laterals, cut back the leader in winter to a strong bud 24–30in (60–75cm) from the base, then make a small nick under the top two buds; this depresses their growth and encourages shoots from the lower buds to grow. Remove any unwanted laterals completely.

By the end of the following summer, three or four strong, healthy laterals should have developed to produce a plant equivalent to a pruned, feathered maiden.

Strong growth should develop the following summer. If one lateral grows faster than the others, tie it down nearly horizontally to slow its growth. Remove any inward- or downward-growing and weak shoots.

In the second winter, select several well-spaced shoots arising from the original laterals to build up the branch framework, and shorten them by half, cutting to outward-facing buds. If any are not needed for the framework, shorten them to four or five buds, and remove completely any shoots crossing the open center. As

ESTABLISHED BUSH, SPUR PRUNING IN WINTER

Prune vigorous branch leaders, leaving two-thirds of the previous season's growth. Weaker branch leaders should be cut back by two-thirds.

Cut back to 5 or 6 buds any young sideshoots growing from permanent branches to form spurs.

growth continues in the second summer, remove any vigorous, upright shoots that unbalance the shape of the tree. By the third winter, the final branch formation should be established, with eight to ten main branches as well as several subsidiary ones.

Routine pruning
Only winter pruning (see opposite) is necessary for bushes once the framework is established; the pruning required will depend on the amount of growth made by the tree and on whether it is a tip or spur bearer. A tip bearer requires renewal pruning. Spur bearers require spur pruning and thinning.

Standard and half-standard

Few gardens are large enough to accommodate a standard or half-standard tree, but these make fine specimen trees where there is space.

Two or three years' training and pruning is needed to produce a clear stem of 4–4¹⁄₂ft (1.2–1.35m) for a

ESTABLISHED BUSH, RENEWAL PRUNING IN WINTER

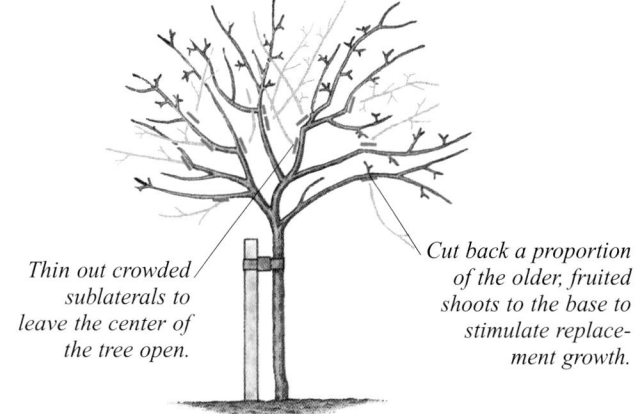

Thin out crowded sublaterals to leave the center of the tree open.

Cut back a proportion of the older, fruited shoots to the base to stimulate replacement growth.

half-standard, or 6–6¹⁄₂ft (2–2.1m) for a standard. After planting a feathered maiden or maiden whip, tie in the leading shoot to a stake and cut any laterals back hard to 1in (2.5cm) in winter. In spring and summer, periodically pinch or cut back any feathers to a few leaves; this helps thicken the main stem. Repeat this procedure in the second year.

In the following winter, remove most of the laterals and cut back the leader to the desired height for either a half-standard or a standard; if the tree is not of the required height, grow it on for a third year. Several laterals should then develop below the cut; select and retain three or four well-spaced laterals to form the basic branch framework. Then train as for an open-center bush (above).

Subsequent pruning of the tree is also as for a bush, but growth will be much stronger because the tree is grafted on a vigorous or a very vigorous rootstock. Carry out regulated pruning on the established tree; it is necessary to prune hard only if the tree is not growing satisfactorily.

Spindlebush

A spindlebush is trained into the shape of a pyramid or cone, to a height of 7ft (2.2m); once established, only renewal pruning and pruning to keep the shape are required.

Numerous variations of the spindlebush have been developed, but the basic aim is to keep the three or four lowest branches dominant by removing shoots that would otherwise develop in the center of the tree. Any shoots that do develop higher in the tree are allowed to fruit and are then pruned back hard, to be replaced by fresh growth.

Formative pruning
Plant a strong feathered maiden, supporting it with a 6ft (2m) stake. Cut back the leader in the winter to about 3ft (1m), or to just above the topmost lateral if this is higher. Select three or four vigorous and evenly spaced laterals that are about 2–3ft (60–90cm) from the base. Prune back each lateral by half to a downward-pointing, healthy bud and remove all other laterals.

If growth is strong, tie down any upright laterals toward the end of the first summer, in order to suppress growth and encourage the tree to fruit. If growth is weak, the upright laterals do not need to be tied down until the next summer.

Tie down the laterals with strong string secured to wooden or hooked metal pegs driven into the ground at an angle around the tree. If using wooden pegs, hammer a large U staple into the top of each one so that a string may be secured to it. Tie each string loosely to the branch so that it pulls down the branch to a 30° angle. Long branches may need to be tied in two places.

Remove any excessively vigorous shoots growing upward from the main stem or laterals; do not attempt to tie them down, since they may break. Train the central stem vertically by tying it to the stake.

The second winter after planting, shorten the central leader by one-third of the new growth, cutting to a bud on the opposite side of the pruning cut made the previous winter. This helps maintain a straight stem. Make sure that the strings are not constricting the tied-down shoots; once the growths have hardened and will remain in a more

or less horizontal position, remove the strings. The following summer, tie down some of the vertical shoots and remove completely any that are exceptionally vigorous or too close to the main stem, or that unbalance the branch framework.

By the third winter, laterals higher in the tree should have developed and been tied down to form further tiers of branches. They should be nearly horizontal, since this encourages early fruiting, and should not overshadow the lower framework branches if this can be avoided.

In the third summer, when the tree should produce fruit for the first time, tie down selected new sideshoots in late summer and remove any excessively strong shoots.

Routine pruning
From the fourth or fifth year onward, renewal pruning (see p.432) is necessary in winter: shorten some of the old, fruited wood. Some of the shoots, particularly those that are higher in the tree, should be pruned back hard close to the trunk to encourage the development of replacement growths.

If the central leader is too vigorous, it may be cut back a little to a weaker lateral that will replace it. This concentrates vigor in the lower branches and helps retain the pyramid shape, allowing maximum light to reach the fruits. In summer, continue cutting out completely any excessively vigorous and strongly upright-growing shoots.

Cordon

A feathered maiden may be trained as an oblique cordon on wires secured to posts or to a wall. Space three horizontal wires 24in (60cm) apart; the lowest should be 30in (75cm) from the ground. Attach the wires 4–6in (10–15cm) clear of the support to allow free air circulation. Attach a stake to the wires at an angle of 45°, then plant a feathered maiden by it (see "Training for shape," p.423) and tie in the main stem to the stake.

Formative pruning
In the winter immediately after planting, shorten all lateral shoots that are over 4in (10cm) in length to

APPLE SPINDLEBUSH
YEAR 1, WINTER PRUNING

Prune the leader by making an angled cut just above a suitable bud about 3ft (1m) from the ground.

Cut back 3 or 4 strong laterals by half to downward-facing buds. Remove other laterals.

YEAR 1, SUMMER PRUNING

Tie down each of the 3 or 4 main laterals to pegs in the ground so that the branches are at a 30° angle.

Cut to the base any vigorous upward-pointing laterals or sublaterals.

YEAR 2, SUMMER PRUNING

Repeat summer pruning as for Year 1, concentrating on removing any upright growths.

ESTABLISHED SPINDLEBUSH, WINTER PRUNING

Cut back to 1 bud any large, old, upper branches with loppers or pruners.

Cut out any weak unproductive spurs completely

Prune sublaterals on the lower 4 permanent branches if they are unproductive, crossing, or inward-growing three or four buds. For tip-bearing cultivars, shorten the leader by about one-third; do not attempt to prune the cordon further.

From the first summer onward, prune the new shoots in mid- to late summer, once they have become woody at the base. Not all shoots mature together, so pruning should continue over several weeks. Use the Modified or Full Lorette System (see "Summer pruning," p.432). The time of pruning depends on climate and on which system is used.

Routine pruning

Winter pruning is essential to prevent congestion: reduce overgrown spur systems and completely remove those that are overcrowded. If the cordon is not producing enough well-spaced laterals, shorten the leader by about a quarter of its length to encourage strong growth.

Once a cordon has extended beyond the top wire, lower its angle of growth slightly to provide space for the leader to extend. When it reaches the top wire, trim it back to one leaf of new growth in late spring. Alternatively, if the leader is vigorous, cut it back in late spring to a sideshoot near the top wire to curb its growth.

Continue on the Modified or Full Lorette System; on an established cordon, this largely involves cutting sideshoots to one leaf.

Double cordon

A double cordon is usually grown vertically but may be grown at an angle if desired. Feathered maidens and maiden whips may be trained as double cordons. The process is similar in each case, except that maiden whips must form sideshoots before training can begin (see "Forming a double cordon," right).

If using a feathered maiden, prune the leader to two sideshoots of equal vigor, one on either side, about 10in (25cm) above soil level. Do this during the winter immediately after planting. Tie the sideshoots to stakes at an angle of 35°. Train the new growth upward in summer while it is still supple, with at least 18in (45cm) between the vertical arms of the U; each arm is subsequently treated as a single cordon.

Fan

A wall or fence is an ideal support against which to grow a fan-trained apple tree; select a cultivar on a dwarfing rootstock so that it may be comfortably accommodated in the available space. Attach horizontal support wires about 6in (15cm)

APPLE CORDON
YEAR 1, WINTER PRUNING

Cut back laterals that are over 4in (10cm) to 3 or 4 buds. Do not prune laterals that are shorter than this.

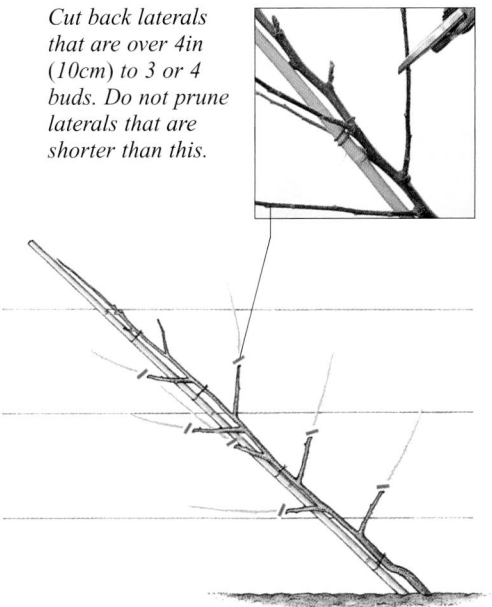

YEAR 1, SUMMER PRUNING

Once the bases of the shoots have become woody, prune all new growth to 3 leaves.

Trim back any sideshoots to 1 leaf.

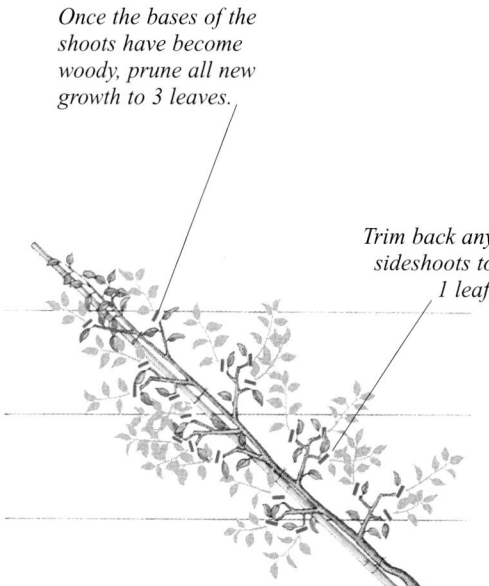

ESTABLISHED CORDON, WINTER PRUNING

Thin spurs as they become congested on older cordons.

ESTABLISHED CORDON, SUMMER PRUNING

When the bases of the laterals have become woody, cut back the new growth to 1 leaf.

Trim any maiden laterals to 3 leaves.

Forming a double cordon

To train a maiden whip as a double cordon, cut back the newly planted tree to about 10in (25cm) from soil level during its first winter, leaving a strong bud on either side below the cut. The following summer, when new shoots have been produced, tie the two uppermost shoots to stakes at an angle of 45°, lowering them to 30° later in the season. When the shoot tips are more than 18in (45cm) apart, train them upward by tying them to vertical stakes.

Once the basic U shape of the double cordon has been formed, the two vertical arms should each be pruned in the same way as a single cordon.

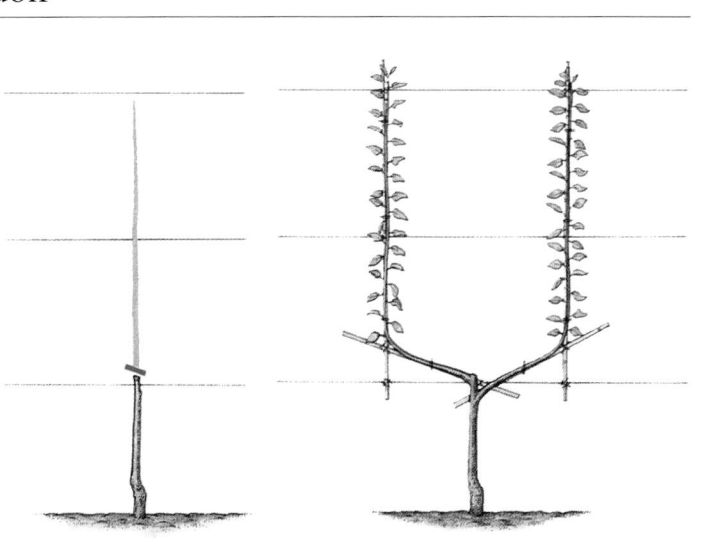

apart, starting at 15in (38cm) from soil level. The initial development of the framework is as for peaches (see p.447); once established, it should be pruned on the Modified Lorette System (see p.432), with each arm being treated like a single cordon. This encourages fruiting spurs to develop along the arms.

Espalier

For this tree form, one or more pairs of opposite shoots are trained at right angles to the main stem onto support wires 15in (38cm) apart. An espalier usually has two or three tiers, but more are possible with trees of sufficient vigor and where there is room to accommodate them. If a maiden whip is used, the first tier of branches may then be trained more readily at the required height.

Formative pruning

After planting a maiden whip, prune back the leader to a bud just above the lowest wire. The following summer, train the uppermost shoot vertically to form a new leader; as the two strongest laterals below this develop, tie each to a stake at an angle of 45° to form the first branch tier. Cut or pinch back all other, lower shoots to two or three leaves.

Tie down the laterals of the first tier into their horizontal position toward the end of the first growing season. If the two main arms develop unevenly, lower the more vigorous shoot to check growth and raise the weaker shoot to induce vigor. Once the two are balanced, tie them into their horizontal positions (see also *Training on Stakes*, p.423).

The following winter, remove completely any laterals that have developed other than the main arms. To create the second tier, first look for two strong buds about 15in (38cm) above the first tier, then cut back the central leader to the bud above these. Shorten each first-tier

arm by one-third to a downward-facing bud; where growth is very vigorous, leave the arm unpruned.

The bud to which each arm is cut back will produce a shoot that should be trained horizontally during the second summer after planting. Cut back other sublaterals according to the Modified Lorette System (see p.432). The second pair of arms will form, and these should be trained in the same way as the first pair. Repeat this process as necessary to obtain the required number of tiers.

Routine pruning

Once the arms of the topmost tier are well established, prune back the

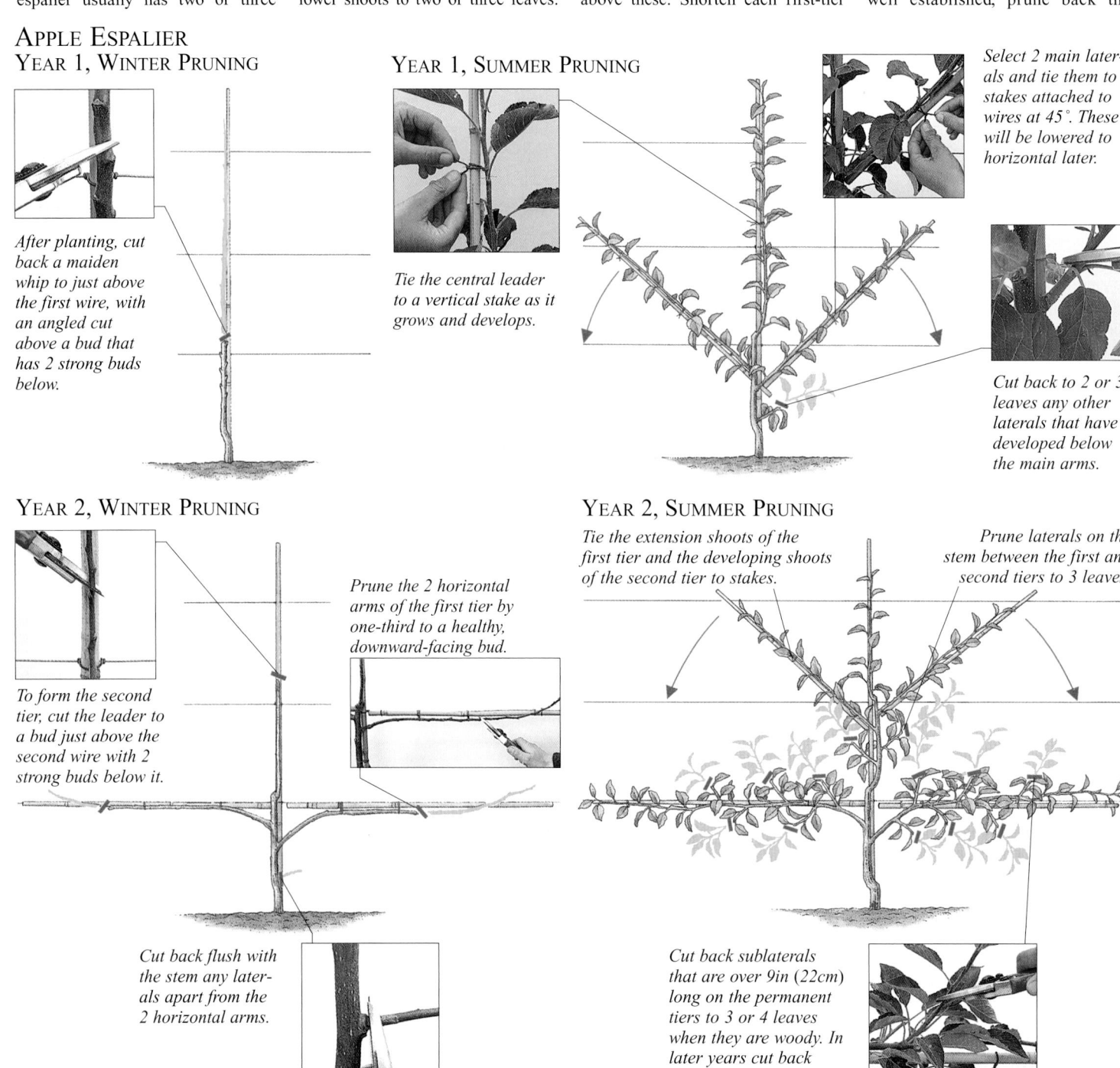

APPLE ESPALIER
YEAR 1, WINTER PRUNING

After planting, cut back a maiden whip to just above the first wire, with an angled cut above a bud that has 2 strong buds below.

YEAR 1, SUMMER PRUNING

Tie the central leader to a vertical stake as it grows and develops.

Select 2 main laterals and tie them to stakes attached to wires at 45°. These will be lowered to horizontal later.

Cut back to 2 or 3 leaves any other laterals that have developed below the main arms.

YEAR 2, WINTER PRUNING

To form the second tier, cut the leader to a bud just above the second wire with 2 strong buds below it.

Prune the 2 horizontal arms of the first tier by one-third to a healthy, downward-facing bud.

Cut back flush with the stem any laterals apart from the 2 horizontal arms.

YEAR 2, SUMMER PRUNING

Tie the extension shoots of the first tier and the developing shoots of the second tier to stakes.

Prune laterals on the stem between the first and second tiers to 3 leaves.

Cut back sublaterals that are over 9in (22cm) long on the permanent tiers to 3 or 4 leaves when they are woody. In later years cut back sublaterals to 1 leaf.

PICKING

Support an apple in the palm of your hand and twist it slightly. If the apple comes away easily, it and others on the tree are ready for picking.

central leader in winter to just above this tier. The espalier should thereafter be pruned in summer following the Full or Modified Lorette System (see p.432).

Dwarf pyramid

The dwarf pyramid is a compact tree form suitable for a small garden or for a container. It needs permanent staking if grown on an 'M27' or 'M9' rootstock; cultivars on other rootstocks need staking for four to five years. For pruning details, see "Pears: Dwarf pyramid," p.439.

Secondary growth often develops after summer pruning. These unwanted shoots inhibit the formation of fruit buds, so prune two to three weeks later than usual to help retard their growth if this is a problem. If secondary growth continues to appear, leave one or two shoots unpruned to act as sap-drawers (see "Summer pruning," p.432).

Harvesting and storing

Early-ripening apples should be gathered just before they are fully ripe or they soon become mealy. Late-maturing cultivars must not be picked too soon, however, or the fruits will shrivel in storage.

Wrap sound, undamaged fruits individually in tissue paper and, keeping different cultivars separate, store them in slatted boxes or crates in a cool place (see p.425). Fruits from young or overvigorous trees store less well than those from more mature trees and should therefore be used first. For further information on harvesting and storing, see p.425.

Propagation

Apple trees may be propagated by chip-budding or T-budding in summer (see pp.426 and 427) or by whip-and-tongue grafting in early spring (see p.427). If possible, use certified scions and rootstocks.

Grafting over

Grafting over is a technique used to grow a selected cultivar on an established apple or pear tree to replace part of the original cultivar. This is done to introduce a new pollinator for adjacent trees or to try a new cultivar; because the roots and main branch system are already established, the new cultivar bears fruit quickly. There are two methods: top-working and frame-working.

Top-working

Initially, this entails heading (cutting) back most of the main branches to within 24–30in (60–75cm)

of the main branch fork in spring. Leave one or two smaller branches unpruned to act as sap-drawers to reduce the number of new shoots that form around pruning cuts. Trim the cuts where branches have been sawn off. Two or three scions are used per branch, but only the most vigorous one is grown on; the presence of the others may initially help keep canker from developing in the cut surface. Scions may be either rind- or cleft-grafted (the latter is rarely used by amateurs and is not described here).

For rind grafting, take dormant scions from the previous season's growth of the desired cultivar and prepare them with angled top cuts and tapering basal cuts. Cut away a sliver of bark on the other side of the tapering cut to prevent the bark from being damaged when inserted into the branch. When rind grafting branches of about 1in (2.5cm) in diameter, place two scions opposite each other. Larger branches can accommodate three evenly spaced scions. Make a vertical cut for each

scion in the bark of the prepared branch. Carefully lift the bark and slide the scion into position underneath. Bind the graft firmly into position and seal the cut surfaces with grafting wax. Scion growth is rapid and ties must be released.

Retain the most vigorous scion and remove the others. Frequently, more than one shoot will develop from the selected scion; allow the best one to grow unchecked as the basis for the new branch. Shorten any others if they are less vigorous than the retained shoot, but remove them completely if they are of equal vigor. After three or four years the new cultivar should start to bear regularly. Subsequently, prune the new branch according to the individual tree form.

Frame-working

In this method, most of the branch framework is retained and many scions are grafted onto different parts of the tree. Frame-working is preferred by commercial growers since trees bear more quickly than if top-worked.

HOW TO RIND GRAFT

1 *In early spring, cut off most of the main branches to within 24–30in (60–75cm) of the trunk. Leave 1 or 2 branches uncut to draw the sap.*

2 *Make a vertical cut 1in (2.5cm) long through the bark of 1 of the trimmed branches. If it is 1in (2.5cm) in diameter, make 2 evenly spaced cuts; if larger, make 3 cuts.*

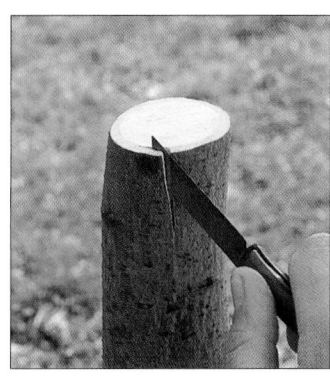

3 *Use the blunt side of the knife blade to ease the bark away from the cambium layer.*

4 *Prepare scions 3 buds long, each with an angled cut at the top and a 1in (2.5cm) tapering cut at the base. Insert them with the tapering cut facing inward.*

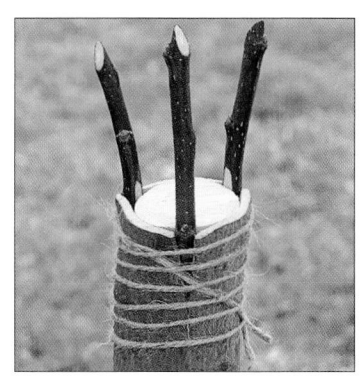

5 *When 2 or 3 scions have been inserted into the branch, bind the grafts tightly with strong string, winding it around the whole branch to hold the scions in place.*

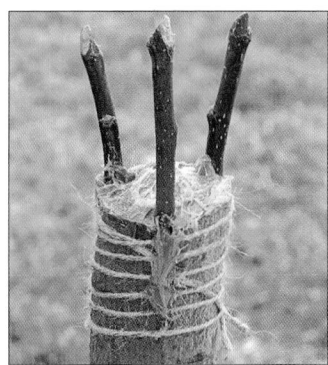

6 *Apply grafting wax to the exposed areas. When the scions have united with the branch, retain only the most vigorous one and remove the others.*

Pears (*Pyrus communis var. sativa*)

Pears need more consistently warm conditions than apples to bear reliably. Late-ripening cultivars require dry and warm conditions throughout late summer and early fall. They have a winter chilling requirement of 600–900 hours below 45°F (7°C).

Pears may be trained much like apples; bush, dwarf pyramid, cordon, and espalier forms are the most suitable for small gardens. Pears are usually grown on quince, rather than pear, rootstocks because this produces smaller trees. Some new rootstocks are in development.

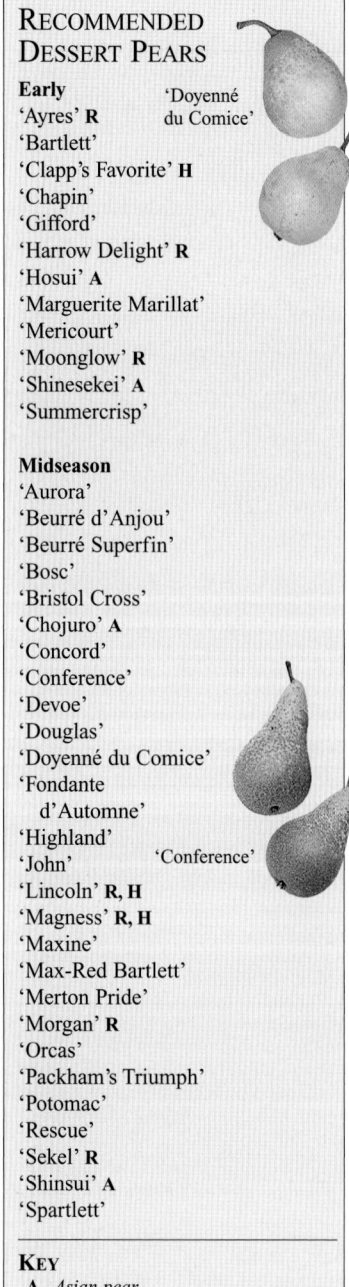

RECOMMENDED DESSERT PEARS

Early
'Ayres' R
'Bartlett'
'Clapp's Favorite' H
'Chapin'
'Gifford'
'Harrow Delight' R
'Hosui' A
'Marguerite Marillat'
'Mericourt'
'Moonglow' R
'Shinesekei' A
'Summercrisp'
'Doyenné du Comice'

Midseason
'Aurora'
'Beurré d'Anjou'
'Beurré Superfin'
'Bosc'
'Bristol Cross'
'Chojuro' A
'Concord'
'Conference'
'Devoe'
'Douglas'
'Doyenné du Comice'
'Fondante
    d'Automne'
'Highland'
'John'
'Lincoln' R, H
'Magness' R, H
'Maxine'
'Max-Red Bartlett'
'Merton Pride'
'Morgan' R
'Orcas'
'Packham's Triumph'
'Potomac'
'Rescue'
'Sekel' R
'Shinsui' A
'Spartlett'
'Conference'

KEY
A *Asian pear*
H *Notably hardy*
R *Resistant to fireblight*

Site and planting

Pears flower earlier than apples, in mid- to late spring, and may be damaged by frosts. Pears are not fully self-fertile; cross-pollination is needed for a good crop.

Site
Pears require a warm, sheltered, and sunny site. The soil should retain moisture but must be well drained, particularly for trees on quince rootstocks (see below). Pears tolerate wetter conditions than apples. Trees on poor or sandy soils produce fruits of inferior flavor, while those on shallow alkaline soils may suffer from lime-induced chlorosis, a nutritional problem caused by deficiencies of manganese and iron (see p.643). Such sites may be improved by mulching regularly with large amounts of organic matter and occasionally applying chelated iron and manganese.

Rootstocks
As well as producing relatively small trees, growing pears on quince rootstocks induces early fruiting. 'Quince A' is moderately dwarfing (similar to 'M26' in apple); 'Quince C' is more dwarfing (similar to 'M9' in apple). A few cultivars, however, do not make a good union with quince rootstocks and may need double-working (see p.440).

Pollination
Provision for cross-pollination should always be made by planting two compatible cultivars. Some cultivars are triploid, and a very few are male sterile: these require two pollinators near them. Incompatible cultivars are indicated in *Recommended Dessert Pears*, left and opposite, and *Recommended Culinary Pears*, opposite.

Planting
Plant pears in fall when the soil is still warm or by early winter at the latest. This allows trees to establish before

ROOTSTOCKS

12ft (4m)
9ft (3m)
6ft (2m)
3ft (1m)

'Quince C'   'Quince A'

coming into growth, which may occur very early in a mild spring. Planting distances (see below) depend on the choice of rootstock and the form in which the trees are grown (see "Pruning and training," right).

Routine care

Regular maintenance, including fruit thinning, fertilizing, and watering, and checking for pest and disease problems, is similar to that required for apples (see p.430). For general information, see pp.420–21.

Fruit thinning
After the natural shedding of fruitlets at or soon after midsummer, thin out to leave one fruit per cluster if the crop is heavy, but two per cluster if bearing is lighter.

Fertilizing, watering, and mulching
Water and fertilize trees as needed (see p.420). It is particularly important to give pears adequate nitrogen: in spring, apply light dressings of up to 1oz/sq yd (35g/sq m) of ammonium sulfate to maintain levels during the growing season. Mulch around newly planted trees in spring.

Pests and diseases
Pears may be affected by rabbits (see "Small animals," p.656), wasps (p.651), aphids (p.639), caterpillars (p.639), fire blight (p.642), pear thrips, scab (p.642), and brown rot (p.650). Pear leaf blister mites produce pustules in the leaves. Destroy affected leaves in summer. Some pear cultivars, especially

'Conference', may develop parthenocarpic fruits. These are cylindrical and may be produced when partial fertilization has occurred; the fruit continues to grow misshapen. Provide a suitable pollinator and give shelter to encourage more pollinating insects.

Pruning and training

Pruning requirements and techniques are similar to those for apples, but pears tolerate harder pruning once they have started to bear. Fruiting occurs predominantly on two-year-old and older wood. On pears, spur production is usually more prolific than on apples, and spurs should be thinned regularly on established trees. Very few pear cultivars are tip bearers.

Training and pruning to develop a cordon or an espalier are as for apples. Both are pruned by the Modified Lorette System in temperate areas or, in warmer climates, by the Full Lorette System (see "Apples: Summer pruning," p.432). A fan is formed in the same way as for peaches (see p.447), but, once established, prune as for an apple fan (see p.435). Pears are normally pruned two or three weeks earlier than apples, soon after midsummer.

Where excessive vigor occurs at the expense of bearing, root pruning (see p.424) where possible or, as a last resort, bark-ringing (see p.431) may be carried out.

Bush
Initial training and pruning of a bush are as for apples (see p.433). Several pear cultivars (for example 'Doyenné du Comice') have an upright growth habit; when pruning branch leaders of these cultivars, cut to an outward-pointing bud. Shoots that are upright should be tied down at the base before they ripen fully, as part of the initial training process, to encourage a wider angle of growth. Pruning on very vigorous bushes is normally much lighter after the second year. Where vigor is lacking, shorten new laterals to five or six buds or fewer, adjusting this recommendation if the tree's vigor improves.

The few tip-bearers (for example 'Merton Pride') need to be renewal pruned as described for tip-bearing apples (see p.432). Established spur-bearing trees need considerable spur shortening and thinning, and occasional branch thinning, in winter.

PLANTING DISTANCES

TREE FORM	ROOTSTOCK	DISTANCE BETWEEN TREES	DISTANCE BETWEEN ROWS
Bush	'Quince C'	11ft (3.5m)	18ft (5.5m)
	'Quince A'	14ft (4.75m)	18ft (5.5m)
Cordon	'Quince A' or 'C'	30in (75cm)	6ft (2m)
Espalier	'Quince C'	11ft (3.5m)	
	'Quince A'	14ft (4.75m)	
Fan	As espalier	As espalier	
Dwarf pyramid	'Quince C'	4ft (1.2m)	6ft (2m)
	'Quince A'	5ft (1.5m)	6ft (2m)

Dwarf pyramid

Prune back the leading shoot of a feathered maiden after planting to 20–30in (50–75cm) from the ground, and reduce any laterals to 6in (15cm); remove weak or low laterals. In the first summer, prune extension growth on the laterals, and any new laterals, to five or six leaves to downward-facing buds. This encourages horizontal growth and induces early fruiting. Cut back sub-laterals to three leaves. The following winter, prune the leading shoot to leave 10in (25cm) of the new growth, cutting to a bud on the opposite side to that of the previous year's pruning. In each subsequent year, prune the leader to buds on alternate sides. When the leader reaches the required height, prune back in late spring to leave one bud of the new growth.

Once the initial framework has been formed, nearly all pruning is carried out in mid- to late summer, depending on season and location. It is important that shoots have become

PEAR, DWARF PYRAMID

YEAR 1, WINTER PRUNING

Cut back the leader with an angled cut just above a bud, 20–30in (50–75cm) from the ground.

Prune back each lateral to a downward-facing bud about 6in (15cm) from the main stem.

Cut back entirely any low laterals on the main stem.

YEAR 1, SUMMER PRUNING

Prune new laterals growing directly from the main stem to 5 or 6 leaves.

Cut back new growth at the tips of the main laterals to 5 or 6 leaves on the extension growth.

Cut back any sub-laterals growing from the main laterals to 3 leaves. These will start to form spurs for the following summer.

YEAR 2, WINTER PRUNING

Prune the previous season's growth on the leader to about 10in (25cm).

YEAR 2 AND ROUTINE SUMMER PRUNING

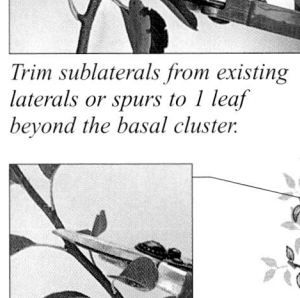

Trim sublaterals from existing laterals or spurs to 1 leaf beyond the basal cluster.

Cut back new growth at the ends of the permanent branches to 5 or 6 leaves.

When the leader reaches the required height, prune it to 1 bud of the previous season's growth.

Cut back laterals growing from the main branches to 3 leaves.

ESTABLISHED DWARF PYRAMID, WINTER PRUNING

BEFORE
The spurs on the darker wood at the base of this shoot are congested and require thinning.

AFTER
Thin by removing any unproductive or overlapping spurs. Trim out excess fruit buds to leave 2 or 3 evenly spaced buds per spur.

RECOMMENDED DESSERT PEARS (CONT.)

Midseason (cont.)
'Starkcrimson'
'Twentieth Century' **A**

Late
'Atago'
'Beurré Bosc'
'Comice'
'Duchess' **R**
'Dumont'
'Golden Russet Bosc'
'Golden Spice' **R**
'Gorham'
'Highland'
'Joséphine de Malines'
'Kieffer' **R**
'Luscious'
'Niitaka' **A**
'Olympic'
'Shinko' **A**
'Thomas' **H**
'Warren' **R**
'Winter Nelis'
'Ya Li' **A**
'Yoinashi' **A**

'Joséphine de Malines'

RECOMMENDED CULINARY PEARS

Midseason
'Bartlett'
'Catillac'

Late
'Seckel'
'Vicar of Winkfield' **T**

'Catillac'

KEY
A *Asian pear*
H *Notably hardy*
R *Resistant to fireblight*

woody at their base before they are pruned; the operation is therefore spread over three or four weeks, and a few shoots may not be ready to prune until early fall. Do not shorten shoots that are 6in (15cm) or less in length. Cut back branch leaders to six leaves of new growth and prune any sublaterals to one leaf above the basal cluster. Any shoots arising directly from the main branches should be shortened to three leaves. If any secondary growth develops, leave a few of the shoots unpruned as for apples (see "Summer pruning," p.432) to draw the sap.

The only major operation for winter pruning is the shortening of the central leader already described plus, in later years, some spur thinning and shortening. If the spur systems are allowed to become congested, the tree loses vigor and small, overcrowded fruits are produced.

Harvesting and storing

Time of picking is most important, especially for cultivars that ripen in late summer and early fall. If left on the tree too long, the fruits will have turned "sleepy" and brown at the center. Gather them at the first sign of a change of ground color on the skin from dark to slightly lighter green. If in doubt, gently lift and twist a fruit:

if it comes away easily, it is almost ripe and will be at peak flavor in a few days. If the stalk breaks, wait for a few days longer to harvest any more fruit. Several harvests need to be made because all fruits do not ripen simultaneously. Fruits of late-ripening cultivars and those grown in cool climates must be left on the tree until mature to develop their full flavor.

Store pears in cool conditions, laying them in slatted boxes. Do not wrap them, since this makes the flesh discolor. The fruits of later-ripening cultivars should be conditioned before eating: keep them at room temperature for a day or two and eat when the flesh gives under gentle pressure by the thumb near the stalk. The flavor is then at its fullest.

Propagation

For most pear cultivars, chip- or T-budding or whip-and-tongue grafting (see "Propagation," p.426) onto a 'Quince A' or 'Quince C' rootstock is usually successful. Grafting over may also be used to change the cultivar of an existing tree to another, preferable cultivar (see p.437).

Double-working pear cultivars

The few pear cultivars that are incompatible with quince rootstocks need to be double-worked: a cultivar that is compatible with both the quince rootstock and the selected scion cultivar is used as an interstock between the two. The cultivar 'Beurré Hardy' is the most widely used interstock; 'Vicar of Winkfield' may also be used for all pear cultivars that require double-working. These include 'Dr. Jules Guyot', 'Marguerite Marillat', and 'Packham's Triumph'. Two methods of double-working may be used: double chip-budding and double grafting.

Double chip-budding entails carrying out chip-budding for two years in succession: in the first year, a scion of the interstock is budded onto a suitable quince rootstock; in the second year, a scion of the selected cultivar is

DOUBLE BUDDING
Insert the budchip 2in (5cm) above the first graft and on the opposite side, so that the resulting stem will grow out straighter when the bud develops. Cut off the interstock above the new bud once the scion shoot has developed. Remove any shoots on the interstock.

budded onto the interstock on the opposite side. The method is as for chip-budding (see p.426).

For double grafting the same principle should be followed. Graft the interstock onto the quince rootstock in early spring using the whip-and-tongue method (see p.427). In late winter or early spring, cut back the grafted interstock and graft the

DOUBLE GRAFTING
This follows the same principle as double budding: cut back the interstock a year after it is grafted, once the sap starts to rise, and graft on the required scion. Leave 2in (5cm) between grafts; position the scion graft on the opposite side from the previous one.

incompatible cultivar scion onto the interstock. Alternatively, the incompatible cultivar scion may be budded onto the interstock in summer, following the grafting of the interstock in spring. Remove all shoots from the interstock as they arise, but retain those from the cultivar scion for strong growth in future seasons.

Quinces *(Cydonia oblonga)*

Quinces are fruits grown mainly in temperate regions. As bushes, they reach 10–15ft (3.4–5m); they may also be trained as fans. The fruits are apple- or pear-shaped and are covered with grayish white down. The most widely grown cultivars are 'Champion', 'Orange', 'Portugal', and 'Smyrna'. Quince trees have a chilling requirement of 100–450 hours below 45°F (7°C) to flower.

Site and planting

Quinces require a reasonably sunny site. The protection provided by a nearby wall may be beneficial in cold areas (hardy to zone 5b). Moisture-retentive, slightly acidic soils are preferred; marked alkalinity usually causes lime-induced chlorosis.

'Quince A' is normally used as a rootstock. Where trees are grown on their own roots, suckering may be difficult to control. Quinces are generally self-fertile, but the provision of pollinators is claimed to improve bearing levels. Plant quinces in

spring if bare-root, or throughout the year if container-grown, spacing them at approximately 12–15ft (4–5m) apart.

Routine care

Cultivation requirements are as described under "Care of tree fruits," p.420. Once established, quinces need little attention. Occasional fertilizing at the standard rate may be necessary, particularly on poor soils, while watering and mulching may also be required. Quinces are comparatively easy to grow, but fungal leaf spots (p.641) may be troublesome.

Pruning and training

Quinces fruit on spurs and on the tips of the previous summer's growth. Bushes may be left into multistemmed trees or pruned in the early stages as for apples (see p.433), with an open-centered, well-spaced branch framework.

Pruning of established trees is minimal, with occasional thinning in

winter of old, overcrowded growth. Not every lateral should be pruned, however, since this removes too many fruit buds.

Harvesting and storing

Pick the fruits when the skins have turned from green to gold, usually in late fall. Store fruits in boxes in a cool, well-ventilated, dark place. Do not wrap the fruits: quinces stored in plastic bags will discolor internally.

QUINCE TREE
Leave a generous grass-free area around young quinces, so that all the nutrients are absorbed by the trees and not shared with the grass.

Because quinces have a strong aroma, they should be stored separately, so that they do not contaminate the flavor of other fruits. Quinces are often used in preserves.

Propagation

Quince trees may be propagated either by chip-budding onto 'Quince A' rootstocks in summer (see p.426) or by taking hardwood cuttings in fall (see p.428).

Medlars (*Mespilus germanica*)

Medlars are decorative, spreading trees with golden fall color and large white or pinkish white flowers in mid- to late spring. Medlar trees are most commonly grown as bushes, or as half-standards where larger specimens are required. They are self-fertile and have a chilling requirement of 100–450 hours below 45°F (7°C). The fruits are apple-shaped and somewhat flattened with prominent, horny calyces. Their flavor is an acquired taste; the fruits are used to make preserves.

RIPENING MEDLARS
The small, brown fruits ripen in fall and measure 1–2in (2.5–5cm) across.

Site and planting
A sunny, sheltered site is preferable, although medlars tolerate partial shade (hardy to zone 7). They may be grown in a wide range of soils, with the exception of those that are highly alkaline or poorly drained. Adequate moisture is essential to obtain strong growth and a good crop of fruits.

Trees grown for the quality of their fruits are usually grafted on 'Quince A' rootstocks, although half-standards are sometimes available on seedling pear rootstocks.

Medlar trees are best planted in late fall to winter. Half-standards should be spaced at a distance of 25ft (8m), and bushes at 14ft (4.75m).

Routine care
Cultivation requirements are generally as for apples (see p.430). Medlars may sometimes be affected by leaf-eating caterpillars (p.639) and fungal leaf spots (p.641).

Pruning and training
Train a bush tree as for apples (see p.433). For half-standards, pruning is initially as for apples. Once the main framework is established, occasionally thin branches in winter to maintain an open framework, removing overcrowded, diseased, or dead growth.

Harvesting and storing
Leave fruits on the tree for as long as possible so that they develop their full flavor. Pick them in late fall

MEDLARS

when the stalk parts easily from the tree, preferably in dry weather. The fruits are unpalatable immediately after picking and must be stored before use. Dip the stalks in a strong salt solution to prevent rot, then store the fruits, calyces downward, on slatted trays, so that the fruits do not touch. Use when the flesh has become soft and brown.

Propagation
Propagate by chip- or T-budding (see pp.426 and 427) or whip-and-tongue grafting (see p.427).

Plums, gages, damsons, and bullaces (*Prunus spp.*)

Among the many kinds of plum are European plums (selections of *Prunus domestica*); gages (*P. domestica* and *P. insititia*); damsons, Mirabelles, and bullaces (*P. insititia*); cherry plums (*P. besseyi* hybrids); and the Japanese plums (*P. salicina*, syn. *P. triflora*). Crosses of Japanese plums with native American plums (such as *P. americana*) have produced hybrids that combine the size and sweetness of the Japanese plums with the hardiness of American plums.

Regions with cool-temperate climates are ideal for European plums, damsons, and bullaces; in warmer areas with earlier springs, Japanese plums and Mirabelles are more widely grown. All types of plum prefer areas that have plenty of sun and relatively low rainfall. Myrobalan plums are rarely grown for their fruit but are often used as vigorous rootstocks.

There is a wide range of cultivars adapted to different climates, and with more dwarfing rootstocks now available, plums are ideal for even small gardens. Damsons usually make smaller trees than plums. The compact pyramid tree and dwarf bush forms are particularly suitable for small gardens. For the choicest fruit in cool climates, grow fan-trained trees on warm, sunny walls. European plums and damsons have

a chilling requirement of 700–1,000 hours below 45°F (7°C), and the Japanese plum one of 500–900 hours.

Site and planting

Plums need a warm, sheltered site to ensure that the flowers are pollinated successfully. Pollination requirements are complex – some cultivars are self-fertile, whereas others require suitable pollinators nearby.

Site
All plums flower early in spring, Japanese plums markedly so and cherry plums earlier still, so that spring frosts are always a hazard. They are, therefore, best planted in a relatively frost-free site. Plums need to be sheltered from wind to avoid damage to the trees and also to encourage pollinating insects.

Most soils are suitable, but avoid those that are highly alkaline or poorly drained. Plums on poor, sandy soils need extra fertilizing and watering (see "Fertilizing, watering, and mulching," p.442).

Rootstocks
'Pixy' (dwarfing) and 'St. Julien A' (moderately vigorous) are best for small to medium-sized trees, 7–12ft (2.2–4m). For trees up to 13ft (4.5m), choose 'Myrobalan B'

ROOTSTOCKS

12ft (4m)
9ft (3m)
6ft (2m)
3ft (1m)

 'Pixy'   'St. Julien A'   'Brompton'   'Myrobalan B'

(incompatible with some cultivars) or 'Brompton' (universally compatible). 'Marianna' is excellent for Japanese plums but is incompatible with some European plums. Plum trees tend to produce suckers, but this is less common with modern rootstocks.

Pollination
European plums and damsons may be self-fertile, partially self-fertile, or self-sterile. Fortunately, some very popular cultivars, such as 'Stanley', are self-fertile, but planting suitable pollinators nearby will ensure more consistent bearing. Cultivars that are not self-fertile must always be plant-

ed with compatible pollinators nearby. Some Japanese plums are self-fertile, but most give better results when planted near a suitable pollinator. Plum cultivars that will not pollinate certain others are indicated in the lists of recommended cultivars on pp.442 and 443, which also give details of flowering times. Seek advice about pollination of individual trees when buying.

Planting
This should be completed as early as possible in late fall or early winter because growth starts early in spring. In cold areas, plant in spring only.

PLANTING DISTANCES

TREE FORM	ROOTSTOCK	DISTANCE BETWEEN TREES	DISTANCE BETWEEN ROWS
Bush	'St. Julien A'	12–15ft (4–5m)	18ft (5.5m)
Half-standard	'Brompton' or 'Myrobalan B'	18–22ft (5.5–7m)	22ft (7m) minimum
Fan	'St. Julien A'	15–18ft (5–5.5m)	
Pyramid	'St. Julien A' or 'Pixy'	8–12ft (2.5–4m)	12–20ft (4–6m)

RECOMMENDED PLUMS
AND RELATED FRUITS

European plums
'Angelina Burdett'
'Belle de Louvain' **Psf**
'Bluebell' **Ss**
'Bluefre' **Psf**
'Earliblue'
'Empress'

'Opal'

'Iroquois' **Sf**
'Imperial Epineuse'
'Italian Prune',
   syn. 'Fellenberg'
'Kirkes' **Ss**
'Lombard'
'Longjohn' **Sf**
'Mirabelle' **Sf**
'Mount Royal'
'Opal' **Sf**
'Polly' **Sf**
'President'
'Seneca'
'Stanley' **Sf**
'Sugar' **Sf**
'Valor'
'Veeblue' **Ss**
'Verity'
'Vision' **Ss**
'Victoria' **Sf**
'Yellow Egg'

'Cambridge Gage'

Japanese plums
'Abundance'
'Burbank' **Ss**
'Duarte'
'Early Golden' **Ss**
'Formosa'
'Fortune'
'Methley' **Sf**
'Ozark Premier' **Ss**
'Santa Rosa' **Psf**
'Shiro' **Ss**
'Starking Delicious'
'Vanier' **Ss**

'Victoria'

Gages
'Cambridge Gage'
'Coe's Golden Drop'
'Count Althanns' **Sf**
'Golden Transparent Gage' **Sf**
'Green Gage', syn.
  'Reine Claude' **Sf**
'Jefferson' **Ss, H**
'Oullins Golden Gage' **Sf**

'Coe's Golden Drop'

'Reine Claude de Bavay' **Sf**
'Washington'

KEY
Sf *Self-fertile*
Psf *Partly self-fertile*
Ss *Self-sterile*
H *Notably hardy*

All trees are best staked for two years; stake those on 'Pixy' rootstocks permanently. Planting distances (see p.441) are determined by the chosen tree form and by the vigor of the rootstock.

Routine care

Fertilize and water trees regularly, and check for pests and diseases. Fruit thinning should be carried out as necessary. If spring frosts are likely, protect wall-trained trees in bloom with a burlap cover (see COLD AND WIND PROTECTION, pp.604–05).

Fruit thinning
This is an important procedure both to give larger, better-flavored fruits and to reduce the risk of branches breaking from the heavy weight of too many fruits. Fruitlets may be thinned early if the set is heavy. After the stones have formed and natural fruit drop has occurred, thin the remaining fruit to about 2–3in (5–8cm) apart for small fruits and 3–4in (8–10cm) for larger cultivars (such as 'Victoria'). Scissors are best for this job since they are quicker to use than pruners.

Fertilizing, watering, and mulching
Plums require plenty of nitrogen; apply a spring dressing at the rate recommended under "Care of tree fruits," p.420. Mulch annually with well-rotted manure or compost, and water as required, particularly in prolonged spells of hot weather. Plums planted against fences or walls will need more regular watering than those grown in the open.

Pests and diseases
Plums may be attacked by rabbits (see "Small animals," p.656), wasps (p.651), aphids (p.639), and plum curculio (p.650). Diseases that may

affect plums include black knot gall (p.647), bacterial canker, and brown rot (p.650). Any trees that are badly infected with black knot, bacterial canker, or (less commonly) viruses (p.642) should be dug up and discarded without delay.

All stone fruit trees may be affected by the physiological disorder known as gummosis. Trees that have this problem exude a translucent, amber-colored, gumlike substance from the trunk and branches, while plums may also form gum around the stone within the fruit. The gum is produced by the trees as a result of stress caused by disease, adverse soil conditions, or physical damage caused by, for example, strong winds or a heavy crop. If gummosis is noticed, try to identify the cause and alleviate the problem if possible.

Birds may also be troublesome; if they attack the fruit buds, it may be necessary to place fine mesh nets over the trees during the winter to prevent damage (see also p.651).

PLUM BUSH
YEAR 1, EARLY SPRING PRUNING

Prune back 3 or 4 laterals by about two-thirds to a half, cutting to outward-facing buds.

Cut off any laterals below those selected flush with the main stem.

Prune out the leader above the topmost selected lateral, using an angled cut.

Pruning and training

Plum trees produce fruit at the base of one-year-old shoots, as well as on two-year-old wood and spurs. Once trained, they require less pruning on unrestricted forms than apples or pears. In cool-temperate climates it is essential to prune in summer (after training) to minimize the risk of black knot (p.647). Trained trees require routine summer pruning to maintain their restricted shape. Remove any damaged or diseased branches immediately, cutting back to healthy wood.

Bush
In early spring when the buds are breaking, start training a newly planted feathered maiden. Select three or four strong, evenly spaced laterals, the highest at about 3ft (90cm) from ground level, and prune them by about two-thirds or a half to healthy, outward-facing buds. These laterals will form the

YEAR 2, EARLY SPRING PRUNING

Prune back 3 or 4 of the strongest sublaterals that develop from each of the framework laterals by about half.

Remove other weak, badly placed, or narrow-angled laterals completely.

THE REWARDS OF PROPER CARE

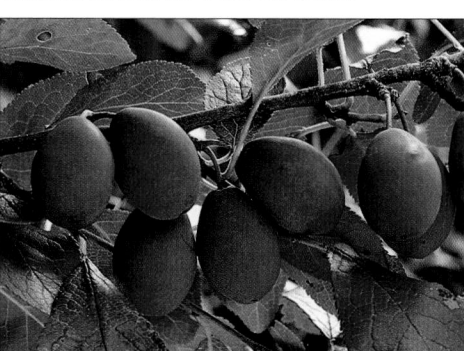

Plum trees develop fruit at the base of one-year-old shoots and then along the stems on two-year-old wood and spurs.

basic framework of branches. Then prune out the leader, making an angled cut above the highest of the selected laterals. Cut back to the main stem unwanted laterals below those selected.

The following early spring, choose three or four of the strongest sublaterals that have developed on each of the pruned laterals and shorten them by half. To achieve a balanced framework, trim off weak or badly placed laterals and pinch out any shoots growing from the main stem. Subsequently, restrict pruning of young trees to the removal in summer of excessively vigorous or awkwardly placed growths. With older trees, thin some branches in summer to avoid overcrowding.

If using a maiden whip, prune it to about 3ft (90cm). The following spring, laterals should have developed, and it may then be trained as a feathered maiden.

Half-standard
Choose three or four well-spaced laterals on a feathered maiden; cut back the leader just above the uppermost lateral at 4½ft (1.35m), then prune each of the chosen laterals by one-third to a half. Remove any lower laterals. Subsequent pruning of the sublaterals and training to form an open-center head is the same as for a bush. Half-standard trees are less easy to manage than pyramid or bush plums when mature because of their greater size.

Spindlebush
Similar in shape to a plum pyramid (see p.444), the spindlebush requires a little more space but does not need the same annual summer pruning. Pruning and training are as for apple spindlebushes (see p.434), but prune in early spring when the buds break.

Tie down upright shoots and keep the top of the tree in check by removing the more vigorous shoots and retaining the less vigorous ones to produce fruit. In this way the conical shape is maintained.

Fan
Train a plum fan initially as for a peach fan (see p.447) to produce main branches or ribs to train against horizontal support wires. When

(see p.444)
(see p.434)
(see p.447)

RECOMMENDED JAPANESE–AMERICAN HYBRID PLUMS
'Alderman'
'AU Producer'
'AU Roadside'
'Elite' **H**
'Ember'
'Kahinta'
'La Crescent'
'Pembina'
'Perfection'
'Pipestone'   'Waneta'
'Redcoat'
'South Dakota'
'Superior'
'Toka'
'Underwood' **H**
'Waneta'

RECOMMENDED CHERRY PLUMS
'Beta'
'Compass'
'Deep Purple'

'Prune'

RECOMMENDED DAMSONS
'Blue Damson'
'Farleigh' **Psf**
'French Damson'
'Prune', syn. 'Shropshire' **Sf**

KEY
H *Notably hardy*
Sf *Self-fertile*
Psf *Partly self-fertile*

ESTABLISHED PLUM FAN
SPRING PRUNING

Thin new sideshoots to about 4in (10cm) apart.

Cut out any sideshoots that are growing toward the center of the fan or are badly placed.

SUMMER PRUNING

Tie in any laterals needed to extend the framework or to replace older wood.

Cut back sideshoots that are not needed for the permanent branch framework to 5 or 6 leaves.

Cut back wrong-pointing or awkward shoots to those facing in the required direction or flush with the stem.

AFTER FRUITING

In fall, after the fruit has been harvested, prune back to 3 leaves all the sideshoots that were shortened to 5 or 6 leaves earlier in the summer.

training the young fan, retain some sideshoots to fill in gaps and pinch back others to one bud. Remove any very vigorous sideshoots or those growing at an awkward angle.

On an established fan, remove sideshoots growing inward toward the wall, fence, or center of the fan in spring or as soon as they appear. Thin the remainder to 4in (10cm) apart and pinch or cut them back to six leaves during the summer unless they are required to fill spaces in the fan framework. After the crop has been picked, shorten these shoots to three leaves.

Pyramid

Plant a feathered maiden against a strong stake and, in early spring, cut back the central leader to a healthy bud at a height of about 5ft (1.5m). Remove any laterals growing below 18in (45cm) from the ground. Shorten the remaining laterals over 9in (22cm) long by half their length. When the bases of the young shoots are turning woody later in the summer, cut back extension growth on the main branches and new (maiden) laterals to about 8in (20cm); at the same time, reduce sublaterals to about 6in (15cm). To start forming the pyramid shape, cut main branches and sublaterals back to downward-facing buds so that growth is more or less horizontal. Remove any laterals that are very vigorous or upward-pointing. Tie in the central leader to the stake, but do not prune it until the following spring, then shorten it by two-thirds of its new growth. Once the tree has reached a height of about 6ft (2m) on 'Pixy' or 8ft (2.5m) on 'St. Julien A', cut back the central leader. This should be delayed until late spring, however, because this reduces its subsequent growth; cut it back to a bud about 1in (2.5cm) from the old wood. Continue annual summer pruning as previously described, cutting branch leaders to downward-pointing buds and removing any excessively vigorous, upright shoots, especially those growing in the upper parts of the tree, to maintain the pyramid shape.

On mature pyramids, overcrowding will develop; in summer, trim off any badly placed, old wood as necessary. Maintain the pyramid shape by keeping any vigorous or dominant upper branches in check.

Harvesting and storing

For the best flavor, allow fruits to ripen fully; for freezing or preserving, pick them when ripe but still firm. In wet weather, gather the ripening crop before brown rot or wasps spoil it. Split skins may occur with some cultivars in moist conditions. Keep the fresh fruits in a cool, dark place and use within a few days.

Propagation

Chip- or T-budding is most usual (see pp.426 and 427); whip-and-tongue grafting (see p.427) is less reliable for plums than for apples and pears.

PLUM PYRAMID

YEAR 1, EARLY SPRING PRUNING

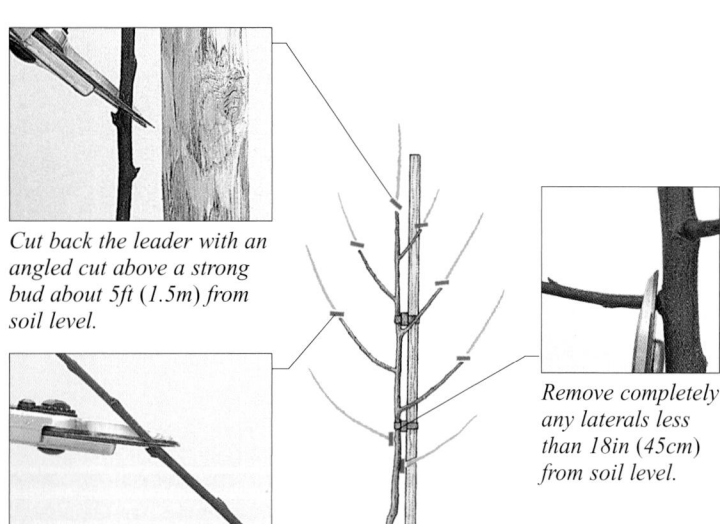

Cut back the leader with an angled cut above a strong bud about 5ft (1.5m) from soil level.

Prune the remaining laterals by half to a downward-facing bud.

Remove completely any laterals less than 18in (45cm) from soil level.

YEAR 1, SUMMER PRUNING

Any new laterals forming too narrow an angle with the main stem should be removed. Do not prune the central leader.

Cut back any sublaterals to 6in (15cm) with an angled cut just above a leaf.

Cut back new growth at the tips of the main branches to about 8in (20cm).

YEAR 2, EARLY SPRING PRUNING

Just before bud break, shorten the central leader by two-thirds of its new growth.

ESTABLISHED PYRAMID, SUMMER PRUNING

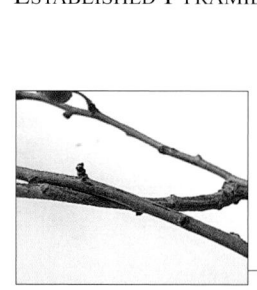

Remove any laterals that are crossing or overcrowded.

Repeat the routine summer pruning of main branches and sublaterals.

Cut back any dead or unproductive wood to a healthy shoot or to the point of origin.

Peaches and nectarines (*Prunus persica* and *P. p. var. nectarina*)

Peaches and nectarines are grown in many temperate regions. They have a chilling requirement of 600–900 hours below 45°F (7°C). Sunny, reasonably dry summers are essential to produce good crops; in cooler climates, peaches may be grown under cover. A range of cultivars is available for different climates (see *Recommended Peaches*, right, and *Recommended Nectarines*, p.446); they are yellow-, pink-, or white-fleshed. On cling peaches the flesh tends to cling to the stone; other peaches are known as freestone. The nectarine is a smooth-skinned form of the peach and requires very similar treatment, although it prefers warmer growing conditions.

Peaches and nectarines are usually grown in bush form, but fans are popular in temperate climates since they allow the fruits to receive maximum sunlight for ripening. Some naturally compact (genetic dwarf) cultivars are ideal for growing in pots.

Site and planting

Peaches flower early in the year and so should be protected from frost; a south-facing wall is an ideal site.

Site

Maximum sun is necessary, in a sheltered site that is not susceptible to spring frosts. In cooler climates, a sunny wall or a greenhouse is needed. Peach trees in areas with high rainfall may be badly affected by peach leaf curl (p.644) unless given some protection (see "Routine care," right).

Deep, fertile, slightly acidic soils (pH 6.5–7) are ideal for growing peaches. If grown on sandy soils they need extra fertilizing and watering; shallow, alkaline soils often give rise to lime-induced chlorosis.

Rootstocks

The plum rootstock 'St. Julien A' is used to provide a moderately vigorous tree; 'Brompton' is used if more vigor is required. In some areas, seedling peach rootstocks are preferred, using vigorous selections resistant to root-knot nematodes.

HAND-POLLINATION

Peaches may be hand-pollinated once the blossoms are fully out. On a warm, dry day, use a small, soft brush to transfer the pollen from the anthers of one flower to the stigmas of another.

Pollination

Nearly all cultivars are self-fertile. An exception is 'J. H. Hale', which requires a nearby pollinator that flowers at the same time (seek advice when buying). In areas with wet or uncertain weather, pollination may be erratic or poor, but this can be improved by hand-pollination.

Planting

Plant peach trees by midwinter if possible, because growth starts very early. Stake bush trees for the first two years. Planting distances vary depending on the tree form and rootstock (see chart, below).

Routine care

For details of maintenance and cultivation requirements, see "Care of tree fruits," p.420. Lime-induced chlorosis may lead to manganese-/iron deficiency (p.643), which must be treated as soon as possible. Protect

PROTECTING PEACH FANS

In fall, at leaf drop, cover the tree with a plastic shelter open at both ends for ventilation. This keeps the leaf buds dry and inhibits spores of peach leaf curl from germinating.

the developing foliage of fan-trained peaches against peach leaf curl, and frost to some extent, with a plastic lean-to in winter and early spring.

Fruit thinning

To produce large fruits, thinning will be needed. When the fruitlets are about the size of hazelnuts, thin them to one fruit per cluster. Later, when they are walnut-sized and some fruitlets have been shed naturally, thin the peaches to a spacing of 6–9in (15–22cm); in warm climates closer spacing may be used.

Fertilizing, watering, and mulching

In dry areas, watering is necessary to support both growth and fruiting.

RECOMMENDED PEACHES

Early
'Candor' **W, S, Y**
'Dixired' **Y**
'Earliglo' **Y**
'Early Redhaven' **Y**
'Erly-Red-Fre' **Wh**
'Garnet Beauty'
'Harbelle' **S, Y**
'Harbinger' **S, Y**
'J.H. Hale' **Y, Wh, H**
'Raritan Rose' **H, Wh**
'Redhaven' **Y**
'RisingStar' **Y**
'Sweet Scarlet' **S, Y**
'Tejon' **Y, Lc**

'Earliglo'

Midseason
'Bonanza' **Gd, Y**
'Bonita' **Lc**
'Belle of Georgia' **Wh, H**
'Fairhaven' **Y**
'Harken' **Y**
'Harrow Diamond' **Y, H**
'Loring' **Y**
'Madison' **Y, H**
'Peregrine' **Wh**
'Reliance' **Y, H**

'Peregrine'

Late
'Babygold No. 5' **Gd, Y, C**
'Canadian Harmony' **Y**
'Cresthaven' **W, Y**
'Fayette' **W, Y**
'Redskin' **Y**
'Zachary Taylor' **C, Y**

KEY
W *Warm climate needed*
Gd *Genetic dwarf (good for pot culture)*
C *Cling*
S *Semifreestone*
Y *Yellow flesh*
Wh *White flesh*
Lc *Low chilling requirement*
H *Notably hardy*

ROOTSTOCKS

12ft (4m)
9ft (3m)
6ft (2m)
3ft (1m)

'St. Julien A'   'Brompton'

PLANTING DISTANCES

TREE FORM	ROOTSTOCK	DISTANCE BETWEEN TREES	DISTANCE BETWEEN ROWS
Bush	'St. Julien A'	15–18ft (5–5.5m)	18ft (5.5m)
	'Brompton' or seedling peach	18–24ft (5.5–7.5m)	24ft (7.5m)
Fan	'St. Julien A'	11–15ft (3.5–5m)	

THINNING

1 *As they form, thin peaches to 1 fruit per cluster, removing first any fruits growing toward the wall or fence.*

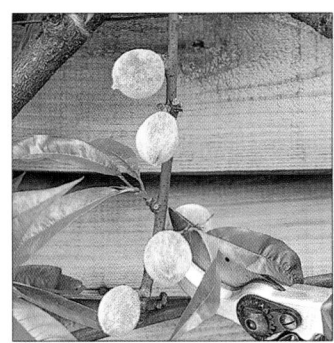

2 *These remaining fruits will need thinning again later, in order to leave 1 fruit every 6–9in (15–22cm).*

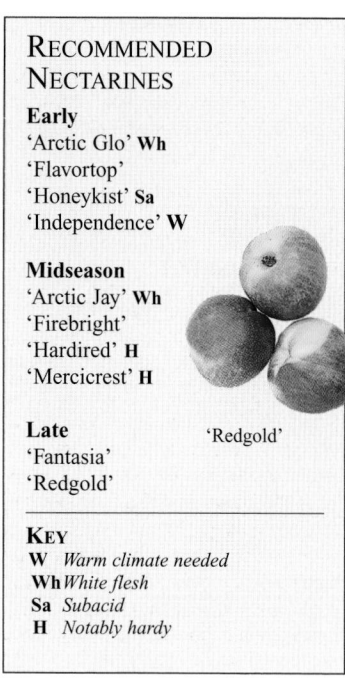

RECOMMENDED
NECTARINES
Early
'Arctic Glo' **Wh**
'Flavortop'
'Honeykist' **Sa**
'Independence' **W**

Midseason
'Arctic Jay' **Wh**
'Firebright'
'Hardired' **H**
'Mercicrest' **H**

Late   'Redgold'
'Fantasia'
'Redgold'

KEY
W *Warm climate needed*
Wh *White flesh*
Sa *Subacid*
H *Notably hardy*

Mulching in spring once the soil has warmed up helps the soil retain its moisture. An adequate nitrogen level is essential to promote new growth for bearing, and potassium is needed to enhance hardiness and fruit quality.

Pests and diseases
Peaches may be attacked by aphids (p.639), spider mites (p.640), earwigs (p.638), and root-knot nematodes (p.652); diseases include peach leaf curl (p.644), bacterial canker, gray mold/*Botrytis* (p.646), and gummosis (see "Plums: Pests and diseases," p.442).

Growing under cover

Peach trees under cover are best fan-trained so that the fruits receive maximum sun. The greenhouse must be able to accommodate a minimum span of about 9ft (2.75m). Fertile, moisture-retentive soil is essential. A trained tree should be grown against suitable support wires spaced at 6in (15cm) intervals, starting at 15in (38cm) from the ground. Secure the wires so that they are held about 9in (22cm) away from the glass. Full ventilation is essential in winter to allow adequate chilling.

In early spring, but not too early if no heat is available, reduce ventilation to start the tree into growth. Keep the temperature at 40–50°F (8–10°C) for up to two weeks and then raise it to 68°F (20°C).

Trees under cover grow rapidly; always fertilize and water them well. Occasional copious watering is preferable to frequent light applications. Spray the foliage with a mist of tepid water, and damp down the greenhouse floor on hot days.

Pollinate the trees by hand when in bloom (see *Hand-pollination*, p.445). Do not spray or damp down during the flowering season, since this may prevent pollination. Start again once the flowers have dropped, to help control spider mites; stop spraying and damping down when the fruits begin to ripen.

Fruit thinning is essential to make sure that the fruits develop to their full size (see p.445).

Pruning and training

Peach and nectarine trees bear fruit only on shoots produced the previous year. The first fruits usually develop the third year after planting. Pruning is aimed at encouraging new growth and replacement shoots to maintain a well-balanced, open branch framework. There are three different kinds of bud: plump fruit buds; small, pointed growth buds; and triple buds that have a plump, central fruit bud with growth buds

PEACH BUSH

YEAR 1, EARLY SPRING PRUNING

Select 3 or 4 strong laterals. Cut back each by two-thirds to an outward-facing bud.

Trim back to the stem any unwanted laterals.

Prune back the leader to the topmost lateral.

Cut back flush with the stem any side-shoots below the main laterals.

YEAR 1, SUMMER PRUNING

Remove any shoots that are growing inward or downward.

YEAR 2, EARLY SPRING PRUNING

Prune weak sublaterals to about 4in (10cm).

Before bud break, cut back the strongest laterals and sublaterals by a half to form the main branches.

ESTABLISHED BUSH, EARLY SUMMER PRUNING

Cut back to a replacement bud or shoot up to a quarter of shoots that have fruited.

Remove old, unproductive wood, as well as any crowded or crossing branches.

on either side. On branches where extension growth is required, prune back to a growth bud, or, if there is no growth bud, to a triple bud.

Bush

Plant a feathered maiden between late fall and late winter. In early spring select three or four strong, well-spaced laterals with the topmost one about 2½–3ft (75–90cm) from the ground; prune back the leader to just above the top lateral. Prune back each of the selected laterals by two-thirds and remove all other unwanted laterals. During summer, remove any badly placed or low shoots that have developed.

The following early spring, before bud break, select strong laterals and sublaterals to form the basic framework. Cut these back by about half to a bud; prune any other sublaterals to about 4in (10cm).

Once the tree is well established, keep the center open by removing some of the older, fruited shoots each summer; occasionally, unproductive branches may need to be cut out.

Fan

Partially trained fans are sometimes available; if buying one of these, make sure that it has been correctly trained (as shown below). A fan should be developed from two branches trained out approximately 12in (30cm) above the ground at 40°. The central leader immediately above them should have been removed to channel vigor equally to both sides of the tree. A fan that retains its long, central leader and has side branches radiating out at an angle along its length will produce excessive growth at the top of the fan, leaving the base bare.

Formative pruning
Set up support wires as for an apple fan (see p.435). After planting a feathered maiden, choose two laterals about 12in (30cm) above the ground and remove the leader above them. Prune the selected laterals to about 15in (38cm) to form the first two "arms" and tie them to stakes at 40°. Prune back all other laterals to one bud as a reserve until the two main shoots have developed.

In summer, tie in the leader and selected sideshoots to stakes as they develop, to start forming the framework "ribs." Select and train in two equally spaced shoots on the upper side of each branch and one underneath. Pinch back any other shoots on the stem to one leaf, and remove any shoots on the ribs that are badly placed. Before bud break in the second spring, cut back the extension growth on the two main arms by one-third to a strong bud to promote growth and the fan's development.

In early summer, continue tying in the selected developing shoots. Pinch back weak shoots and remove any that are very vigorous or pointing in the wrong direction.

The following early spring, shorten these new ribs by a quarter. During the third summer, select further shoots to complete the main ribs or branches of the fan. Any space in the center of the tree will soon be filled in by sideshoots. Thin sideshoots produced from the main branches early in the season to 4–6in (10–15cm) apart. Retain those lying naturally along the plane of the fan, but remove any that are awkwardly placed or growing straight outward or inward toward the wall or fence. Tie in the retained shoots; they should produce fruit the following year. Pinch back overlapping shoots to four to six leaves.

Routine pruning
The aim of pruning in spring is to ensure a constant supply of well-placed young shoots each year. At the base of each flowered shoot that will carry fruit in the forthcoming summer, there are usually two buds or young shoots; pinch out (disbud) one of these to prevent growth from becoming congested. The remaining one will carry fruit the following year. A second bud about halfway up the shoot may also be retained as a reserve in case the other one becomes damaged. After harvesting, remove the fruited wood, and tie in a replacement shoot at the base of each shoot that is cut out.

Continue this process annually; retain two replacement shoots if there is space in the framework. Without rigorous pruning, a peach tree soon becomes congested with old wood that bears no fruit.

PEACH FAN
YEAR 1, EARLY SPRING PRUNING

Choose 2 laterals, 1 on either side, 12in (30cm) from the ground, to form the main arms. Cut out the leader just above the higher lateral.

Prune back each arm to about 15in (38cm) to a strong bud to encourage sideshoots or "ribs" to form.

Tie each main arm to a bamboo stake attached to the wires at 40°.

Cut back lower laterals to 1 bud.

YEAR 1, SUMMER PRUNING
Choose 2 sideshoots on the top of each arm and 1 underneath and tie them to well-spaced stakes attached to the wires. Pinch back other shoots to 1 leaf.

YEAR 2, EARLY SPRING PRUNING

In early spring, cut back the extension growth on the 2 main arms by one-third to strong buds facing in the required direction.

YEAR 2, EARLY SUMMER PRUNING

Train in developing sideshoots by tying them to stakes to extend the permanent framework.

Cut back any wrong-pointing sideshoots to the point of origin, and remove any shoots emerging below the 2 main arms.

YEAR 3, EARLY SPRING PRUNING

Cut back each of the main ribs by a quarter to stimulate further growth and extend the framework.

YEAR 3, SUMMER PRUNING

Pinch back any shoots that overlap the ribs to 4–6 leaves as they develop.

As the remaining sideshoots develop, tie them to stakes to fill in the framework. These shoots should fruit the following year.

YEAR 3, EARLY SUMMER PRUNING

Thin young sideshoots to 4–6in (10–15cm) apart by pinching out unwanted shoots. Pinch out any shoots that are growing toward the wall or fence or in the wrong direction.

ESTABLISHED FAN, PRUNING AFTER FRUITING

Cut back each fruited shoot to a suitable replacement near its base.

Tie in the replacement shoot to fill the gap. These shoots should be evenly distributed over the entire fan.

Harvesting and storing

Harvest the fruits when they are fully ripe. Rest them in the palm of your hand and apply gentle pressure with your thumb on the part of the fruit nearest the stalk. If the flesh gives slightly, the fruit is ready for picking. For the finest flavor, peaches and nectarines are best eaten as soon as possible after picking. If necessary, they can be stored for a few days by placing the fruits in a container lined with soft material and keeping it in a cool place.

Propagation

Peaches and nectarines are usually propagated by chip- or T-budding (see pp.426 and 427) in summer. Seedling peaches are variable in quality but are often vigorous and may produce excellent crops.

Apricots (*Prunus armeniaca*)

Apricots are more difficult to grow than many other fruits. Not all cultivars thrive in certain areas, so always seek advice when selecting trees. The chilling requirement for apricots is 350–900 hours below 45°F (7°C), most cultivars being at the lower end of this range. They flower extremely early in the year.

Although dry, sunny summers are needed for successful bearing, drought conditions may cause serious bud drop late in the season. In cool climates, apricots may be grown under cover or fan-trained against a warm wall. In warm areas, the bush form is popular.

Site and planting

Apricot trees should be planted in a sunny, sheltered, and frost-free site in order to produce good crops of fruit. In cool areas, it is essential to grow them against a sunny wall or in a greenhouse to protect the flowers from low temperatures and frost in late winter and early spring.

A deep, slightly alkaline loam is the most suitable soil. Apricots are least likely to thrive on sandy and alkaline soils. It is also best to avoid planting them on heavy soils, particularly in areas that have cool, wet winters, since this may make them prone to dieback.

For rootstocks, both seedling apricots and peaches are widely used. A seedling peach rootstock tolerates wetter conditions than a seedling apricot rootstock and produces a smaller tree. The plum rootstock 'St. Julien A' is also often used; this is moderately vigorous.

Apricots are self-fertile; in cool areas, however, flowers should be pollinated by hand.

Plant in late fall or very early winter (see *Planting Distances*, opposite) before bud break. Stake bush trees securely for the first two years.

PLANTING DISTANCES

TREE FORM	ROOTSTOCK	DISTANCE BETWEEN TREES	DISTANCE BETWEEN ROWS
Bush	'St. Julien A'	15–18ft (4.5–5.5m)	18ft (5.5m)
	Seedling peach or apricot	18–22ft (5.5–7m)	22ft (7m)
Fan	'St. Julien A'	15–18ft (4.5–5.5m)	

Routine care

In general, maintenance and cultivation requirements are as for other tree fruits (see "Care of tree fruits," p.420).

In warm regions where heavy bearing is common, blossoms may need thinning to counteract biennial bearing (see p.430). Remove badly placed fruitlets, and carry out the main thinning after any fruits have dropped naturally and the stones have started forming. Thin so that there is a single fruit on each truss; leave about 3in (7cm) between fruits.

In cool areas, branch dieback occurs frequently; cut back affected branches to clean wood as soon as possible. Earwigs (p.638), bacterial canker, brown rot (p.650), and gummosis (see "Plums: Pests and diseases," p.442) cause problems. Use peach rootstocks where nematodes are prevalent.

Pruning and training

Fruits are borne both on one-year-old shoots and on older spurs. Pruning is aimed at maintaining the shape of the tree and removing any old, unproductive wood. If young trees are too vigorous, they may be root pruned (see p.424). Prune and train an apricot bush as for plums (see p.442).

Initial fan training of apricots is as for peaches (see p.447). On an established fan, thin young shoots to 4–6in (10–15cm) apart as they develop in the spring, and remove any shoots that are pointing downward, toward the center of the fan, or inward to the wall. Pinch back the sublaterals to six leaves if they are not required to fill gaps, and reduce any sideshoots to one leaf later in the season. After fruiting, prune sublaterals to three leaves.

Harvesting

Pick the fruit when it is fully ripe and comes away easily from its stalk. Use immediately, because fresh apricots do not store well; alternatively, they may be frozen, used in preserves, or dried (see "Storing," p.425).

Propagation

Apricots may be propagated by chip- or T-budding (see pp.426 and 427), using seedling peach roostocks or 'St. Julien A' rootstocks.

RECOMMENDED APRICOTS

Early
'Goldbar'
'Goldrich'
'Goldstrike'
'Harcot'
'Hemskerk'
'Shaha' W
'Sunrise' H
'Tomcot'
'Veecot'

Midseason
'Alfred' H
'Farmingdale' H
'Goldcot' W
'Harglow'
'Hargrand' W
'Perfection'
'Puget Gold' W
'Rival'
'Sun-Glo'
'Westcot' H

Late
'Blenheim'
'Farmingdale' H
'Harlayne' W
'Harogem' W
'Moorpark'
'Vivagold'

KEY
W   *Warm climate needed*
H   *Notably hardy*

'Hemskerk'

ESTABLISHED APRICOT FAN, EARLY SUMMER PRUNING

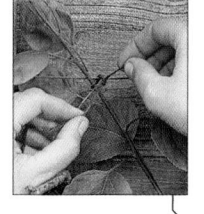
To fill gaps in the framework, tie in young sideshoots once they have hardened at the base.

Cut or pinch out altogether any shoots pointing downward or toward the wall or fence.

Cut or pinch back to 5 or 6 leaves any sublaterals not needed as replacement shoots.

THINNING

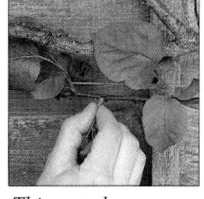
Thin out the young shoots to leave them 4–6in (10–15cm) apart. Tie them in to the wires as they develop.

AFTER FRUITING

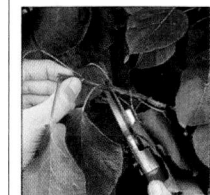
Using pruners, cut back to 3 leaves the shoots that were reduced to 6 leaves earlier in the summer.

Sweet cherries *(Prunus avium)*

Sweet cherry trees may grow to a height and spread of 25ft (7.5m) or more and, since most cultivars are self-sterile, two trees are often necessary to produce a crop. There are as yet no reliable dwarfing rootstocks (see p.450), so sweet cherries are best suited to an orchard or large garden. For an average garden, choose a self-fertile cultivar. Ideally, the tree should be fan-trained on a wall or fence: this restricts growth and makes it easier to protect the tree from birds and from rain just before picking, which may cause the fruits to split. Sweet cherries have a chilling requirement of 800–1,200 hours below 45°F (7°C).

Duke cherries are thought to be hybrids between the sweet cherry and the sour cherry. They are not very widely grown but, where chosen, require treatment and spacing similar to sweet cherries. Some Duke cherry cultivars are self-fertile, and combinations of sour cherries and Duke cherries are compatible.

Site and planting

Sweet cherries need a warm, sheltered site to produce a good crop. It is important to choose cultivars carefully to make sure that they will pollinate each other; this should be checked before buying trees (see "Pollination requirements," p.418).

ROOTSTOCKS

15ft (5m)
12ft (4m)
9ft (3m)
6ft (2m)
3ft (1m)

'Colt'   'Malling F12/1'

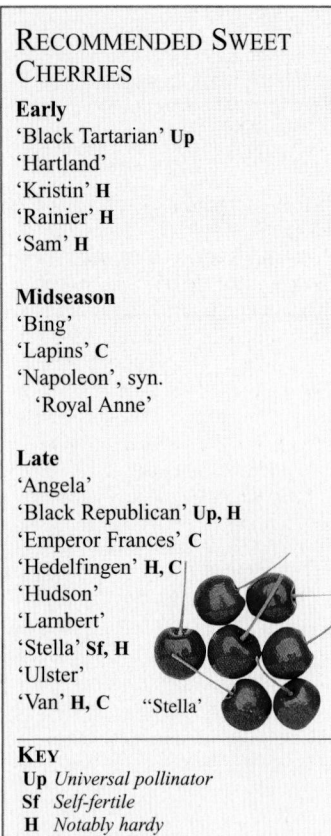

RECOMMENDED SWEET
CHERRIES

Early
'Black Tartarian' **Up**
'Hartland'
'Kristin' **H**
'Rainier' **H**
'Sam' **H**

Midseason
'Bing'
'Lapins' **C**
'Napoleon', syn.
  'Royal Anne'

Late
'Angela'
'Black Republican' **Up, H**
'Emperor Frances' **C**
'Hedelfingen' **H, C**
'Hudson'
'Lambert'
'Stella' **Sf, H**
'Ulster'
'Van' **H, C**

"Stella"

KEY
Up *Universal pollinator*
Sf *Self-fertile*
H *Notably hardy*
C *Resists cracking*

Site

Choose an open, sunny, and sheltered site. If the cherry is to be grown as a fan, the support must be at least 8ft (2.5m) high and 15ft (5m) wide, with a reasonably sunny exposure; a tree grown on a cold wall will produce fruit of poor quality and flavor. A good, deep, well-drained soil is essential, because trees grown on shallow, poor soils produce small fruits and are less long-lived.

Rootstocks

'Colt', a semidwarfing rootstock, is suitable for bush or fan-trained trees in small gardens. 'Malling F12/1', which is very vigorous, is used where there is space. Two new dwarfing rootstocks, 'Inmil' and 'Camil', are under trial; their longevity and bearing potential are as yet unproven.

Pollination

The pollination requirements of sweet cherries are complex. The majority are self-sterile, and they fall into distinct groups within which any combination is incompatible. Unless a self-fertile cultivar is obtained, it is important to choose a pair of trees that are from different groups and that flower at the same time. A few sweet cherries are universal pollinators; that is, they will pollinate any cherries that flower at about the same time (see *Recommended Sweet Cherries*, left).

Planting

Sweet cherries should be planted in late fall or winter if bare-root, or at any time if container-grown. Construct the necessary supports and wires before planting fan-trained plants. Allow 15–18ft (5–5.5m) between trees that are to be fan-trained and between half-standards.

Routine care

Fruit thinning is unnecessary. Little or no fertilizing should be needed, apart from mulching (see "Care of tree fruits," p.420.) If growth is poor, apply ammonium sulfate at the rate of 1oz/sq yd (35g/sq m) of canopy area. Sweet cherries need thorough watering when dry, but sudden watering may cause the fruits to split.

As the fruits begin to color, protect them from birds by draping netting over fan-trained trees. Bush and half-standard trees are difficult to net, however, so pick fruits as soon as they ripen.

The most likely pests and diseases to afflict sweet cherries are cherry aphids (see "Aphids," p.639), tent caterpillars (p.640), brown rot (p.650), black knot (p.647), and bacterial canker; cut out any branches with signs of black knot or bacterial canker as soon as they are noticed.

Pruning and training

Sweet cherries fruit on spurs on two-year-old and older wood. Mature trees should be pruned in summer to restrict vegetative growth and induce the formation of fruit buds. Train and prune half-standards and bushes as for plums (see p.442).

Fan

Sweet cherry fans are established as for peaches (see p.447). If there are conveniently placed laterals on a feathered maiden, however, it may be possible to select four rather than two laterals to speed up the development of the fan. Tie these laterals to stakes (attached to wires), which radiate out at 35–45° from the stem. In the spring following planting, prune back the selected shoots to 18–24in (45–60cm) and remove all other laterals that have developed.

During the summer, select two or three well-placed shoots from each branch and tie them in to fill the available space; remove the remainder. All branches or ribs on the young tree may be tip pruned at bud break (but never earlier) to reduce the risk of black knot and bacterial canker.

On older fans, spurs may be thinned or shortened in spring (see "Apples: Winter pruning," p.432) and branch leaders pruned to shorten replacement laterals to reduce height. In summer, pinch back all shoots not needed for the framework to six leaves, then to three after fruiting. Upright or very vigorous growths should be removed or tied horizontally to prevent the fan from becoming unbalanced.

Harvesting and storing

Pick fruits when fully ripe, complete with stalks, and eat or cook them immediately. If the fruits are to be frozen (see p.425), pick when firm.

Propagation

Chip- and T-budding are the usual ways to propagate (see pp.426 and 427). 'Colt' rootstocks are compatible with all cultivars, as is the more vigorous 'Malling F12/1' rootstock.

ESTABLISHED SWEET CHERRY FAN, SUMMER PRUNING

Tie in sideshoots that are needed to replace old wood or to fill bare spaces.

Cut back to 5 or 6 leaves any new growth not needed to extend the fan framework.

AFTER FRUITING

After the crop has been harvested, cut back all the laterals that were pruned to 6 leaves in early summer to 3 leaves.

Sour cherries (*Prunus cerasus*)

Sour or acid cherry trees are much smaller than sweet cherries, and all cultivars are self-fertile, so they are more suitable for the average garden. The fruiting habit also differs in that the crop is borne mostly on one-year-old shoots produced the previous summer. The fruit is not usually eaten raw but is prized for preserves and other culinary uses. Sour cherries have a chilling requirement of 800–1,200 hours below 45°F (7°C).

Site and planting

Site and soil requirements are generally as for sweet cherries (see p.450), but sour cherries are hardier and may also be grown against a north- or east-facing wall or fence.

The recommended rootstock, as for sweet and Duke cherries, is 'Colt'. It is best to obtain cultivars such as 'Meteor' (the most popular) from a specialized fruit supplier since inferior, less fertile selections exist. Plant trees to be trained as bushes and fans 12–15ft (4–5m) apart, and for fans provide a minimum support height of 7ft (2.2m).

Routine care

Sour cherries have the same cultivation requirements as sweet cherries (see p.450). Greater attention to fertilizing, particularly with nitrogen, may be necessary to encourage young replacement shoots, but do not overdo. Irrigation is important in dry areas. Netting is essential to protect the fruits from birds (see p.421). Since sour cherries may be trained into small tree forms, such as the bush or dwarf pyramid, they may be grown in a fruit cage. Sour cherries are affected by the same pests and diseases as sweet cherries (see "Routine care," opposite).

Pruning and training

Sour cherries are pruned on a renewal system to produce a constant supply of one-year-old wood on which fruit is produced. A proportion of the older wood should be removed each year. Prune trees in spring and summer, since this reduces the risk of leaf diseases.

Fan
This is trained as for a peach fan (see p.447). Renewal pruning to encourage young growth once bearing starts is important because of the restricted space. In spring, on an established fan, pinch out badly placed or overcrowded new shoots and thin the rest to leave them 4in (10cm) apart. Tie these into support wires as they develop. Retain one or, where space permits, two developing shoots low down on each fruiting shoot. Tie in one of these to replace each fruiting shoot that is cut out after harvesting. The second shoot may be used as a reserve in case the first is damaged, or to fill a gap in the fan. To rejuvenate older fans, prune them back to young shoots on older wood in spring and fall.

ROOTSTOCK

12ft (4m)
9ft (3m)
6ft (2m)
3ft (1m)

'Colt'

RECOMMENDED SOUR CHERRIES

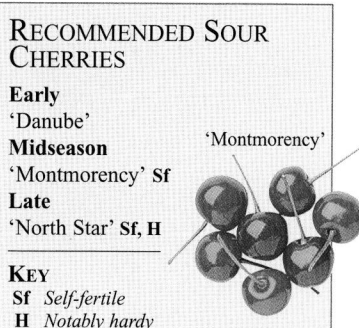

Early
'Danube'
Midseason
'Montmorency' **Sf**
Late
'North Star' **Sf, H**

'Montmorency'

KEY
Sf *Self-fertile*
H *Notably hardy*

ESTABLISHED SOUR CHERRY FAN

SPRING PRUNING

Remove any wrong-pointing young shoots, cutting them back flush with the stem.

Thin the young, developing shoots to about 4in (10cm) apart, if necessary.

SUMMER PRUNING, AFTER FRUITING

Cut back each fruited shoot to a suitable replacement near its base.

Tie in the replacement shoots to maintain even spacing. These should fruit the following year.

Remove any wrong-pointing shoots that have developed and were not removed in the spring, cutting them back flush with the stem.

ESTABLISHED SOUR CHERRY BUSH, PRUNING AFTER FRUITING

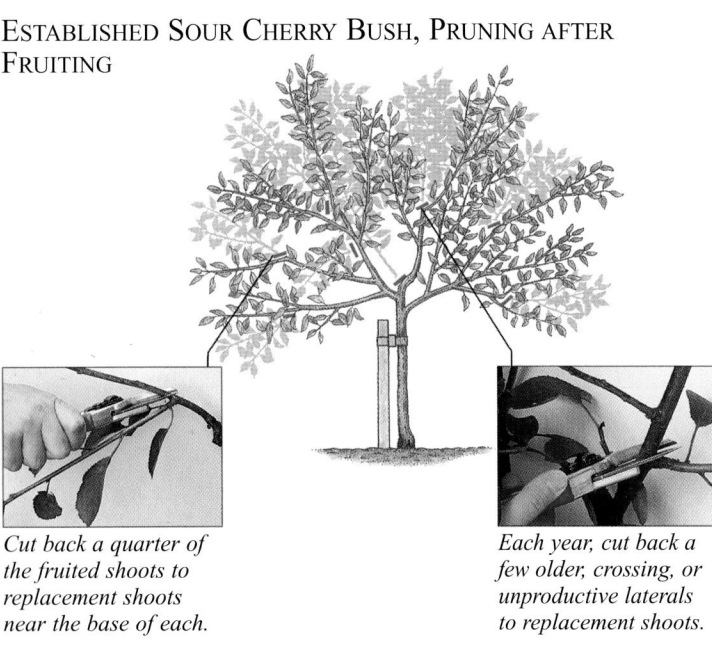

Cut back a quarter of the fruited shoots to replacement shoots near the base of each.

Each year, cut back a few older, crossing, or unproductive laterals to replacement shoots.

Bush
The bush is built up as for a peach bush (see p.447). After the third or fourth year, once the bush is established, renewal pruning is essential. In early fall, after fruiting, cut back a quarter of the fruited shoots, preferably to replacement shoots, to maintain even spacing and leave room for the young growth that will carry the next year's crop. Remove old wood at the same time. If pruning is neglected, fruiting will decrease and be restricted to the tree's outer edge.

Harvesting
Hand-picking may injure the shoots and encourage infection, so cut stalks with scissors. Cook, freeze, or preserve soon after picking (see "Harvesting and storing," p.425).

Propagation
The usual methods are chip- and T-budding (see pp.426 and 427). All cultivars are compatible with 'Colt' and 'Malling F12/1' rootstocks.

HARVESTING SOUR CHERRIES

Harvest by cutting each stalk close to the lateral, not by pulling, which may damage the bark and increase the risk of bacterial canker.

Persimmons (*Diospyros kaki* and *D. virginiana*)

Asian persimmons (*Diospyros kaki*) are deciduous, slow-growing trees that will eventually reach a height of 30–50ft (10–15m) and a spread of about 30ft (10m). The fruits are globular, and they may be yellow, orange, or red when ripe. The hardier American persimmon (*D. virginiana*) attains similar dimensions; the fruits are typically smaller than those of Asians.

Outdoor cultivation of Asian persimmons in areas with a minimum temperature of 50°F (10°C) is possible, but a range of 61–72°F (16–22°C) during fall is preferable. Most Asian cultivars have a low chilling requirement of 100–200 hours below 45°F (7°C). During the growing season they need at least 1,400 hours of sunshine to fruit. American persimmons are hardier, with a greater chilling requirement.

Site and planting
A sheltered and sunny site is preferable. A well-drained and fertile soil is essential, with a pH of 6–7.

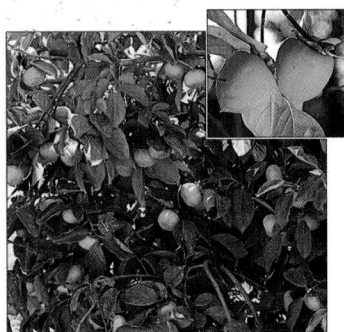

ASIAN PERSIMMON

Mature trees are relatively drought-resistant, but they require irrigation if there is inadequate rain in the growing season.

Vigorous seedlings of *Diospyros kaki* are suitable as rootstocks, but *D. virginiana* is most frequently used for this purpose.

Although some persimmon cultivars have both male and female flowers on the same tree, a number have only one or the other. The most widely grown cultivars have only female flowers; these will produce fruit without pollination, but the fruits are small and astringent. A pollinator cultivar, with male flowers, must therefore be grown nearby. A ratio of one pollinator plant to eight or ten female-flowering plants is usually adequate. Trees should be spaced at about 15ft (5m).

Prepare planting holes in well-manured ground; add organic material and general-purpose fertilizer.

Routine care
Apply fertilizer around the trees every three to four months, using a general-purpose mixture with medium nitrogen levels. Conserve moisture in the soil by mulching with organic matter, and water regularly in the dry season. Keep the ground around the trees weed-free.

The major pests that affect persimmons grown in the open are thrips (p.640), mealybugs (p.640), scale insects (p.641), and fruit flies. Common diseases that may cause problems include crown gall (p.647) and anthracnose and other fungal leaf spots (p.641).

Growing under cover
If growing persimmons in a greenhouse, plant them in prepared beds or in large containers with a minimum diameter of 14in (35cm); use a very fertile soil mix incorporating a general-purpose fertilizer with medium nitrogen levels. Maintain a temperature of at least 61°F (16°C) and a humidity of 60–70 percent. Water regularly during the growing season and apply a general-purpose fertilizer every three to four weeks.

It is necessary to pollinate the flowers by hand for a successful fruit set (see *Hand-pollination*, p.445). During the summer, move plants in containers into the open; leave them outside in the fall until their chilling requirement has been met.

Pruning and training
Cultivars vary greatly in vigor. Dwarf and semidwarf cultivars are trained in a similar way to an apple spindlebush (see p.434). Prune young trees for the first three years during the dormant season to form a framework. Restrict all subsequent pruning to the removal of crowded or unproductive branches, and to cutting back branch leaders annually by about one-third of their new growth.

Harvesting and storing
Pick fruits when they are fully ripe. Cut fruits from the tree, leaving the calyx and a short fruit stalk attached. Seal the fruits in clear plastic bags and store them at 32°F (0°C); they should remain in good condition for up to two months.

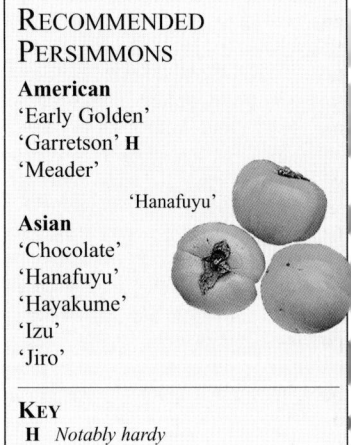

RECOMMENDED PERSIMMONS

American
'Early Golden'
'Garretson' H
'Meader'

'Hanafuyu'

Asian
'Chocolate'
'Hanafuyu'
'Hayakume'
'Izu'
'Jiro'

KEY
H *Notably hardy*

Propagation
Persimmon trees may be propagated by seed, by grafting, from cuttings, or from rooted suckers.

Sow seed taken from mature fruits immediately in containers; kept at 82°F (28°C), it usually germinates in two to three weeks. In 12 months, the seedlings provide stocks suitable for grafting. Handle seedlings carefully when transplanting.

Cultivars may be propagated by chip- or T-budding (see pp.426 and 427) or by whip-and-tongue grafting (see p.427). Softwood cuttings (see p.77) taken in summer and treated with hormone rooting powder should root in a mist unit with basal heat.

Rooted suckers may be detached from the base of the parent tree (provided that it has not been budded or grafted). Establish them in containers before planting them out in their final positions.

Figs (*Ficus carica*)

Figs are among the oldest fruits in cultivation and belong to the family Moraceae. They have a low chilling requirement of 100–300 hours below 45°F (7°C) and thrive in regions with a long, hot growing season.

Site and planting

Figs require a sunny position and in cool areas need a wall for more warmth and protection from severe cold; this should be at least 10–11ft (3–3.5m) wide by 7ft (2.2m) high.

Figs prefer slightly alkaline, deep, rich, moisture-retentive soils and a warm, dry climate. Cooler, wetter conditions induce too much growth, with poorer crops. When the pH is less than 6, lime the soil (see p.619).

Where space is limited, a concrete or brick pit, or box, may be built below soil level to restrict the root system and produce a smaller tree. The pit should be 2ft (60cm) square and have a base that is not solid but filled with broken bricks or stones to a depth of 10–12in (25–30cm); this will assist drainage and restrict root growth downward.

In cool climates, figs may also be grown in pots placed in a sunny, sheltered site and transferred to cold but frost-free conditions in winter. Use a container 12–15in (30–38cm) in diameter, with several large drainage holes and filled with a soil-based potting mix.

No specific rootstocks have yet been introduced, and trees are grown on their own roots. Modern cultivars are self-fertile.

Select two-year-old, potgrown specimens and plant these in spring, teasing the roots gently loose from the soil ball before planting. Space unrestricted trees 20–26ft (6–8m) apart; those planted in a pit need only half this spacing.

Routine care

To overwinter branches carrying the embryo figs, tie a dense layer of straw around them (see also COLD

FRUIT PLACEMENT

Ripening fruits

Embryo fruits

AND WIND PROTECTION, *Burlap and Straw Cover*, p.604). At the same time, remove any unripe figs from the previous summer. It may be necessary to protect the ripening fruits against birds and wasps.

Fertilizing, watering, and mulching

A spring mulch of well-rotted manure is all that is normally required, but trees with restricted roots need extra nutrients. This may be in the form of a balanced fertilizer applied at a rate of 2oz/sq yd (70g/sq m) of root area, and supplemented during the summer with occasional liquid fertilizer. Avoid overfertilizing.

Watering is essential in hot, dry weather, especially where the roots are restricted. Potgrown figs need regular watering throughout the growing season. Repot them and prune the roots every two years.

Pests and diseases

Figs in the open are usually problem-free, but wasps (p.651) and birds (p.651) may attack fruits. When growing fig trees under cover, spider mites (p.640), mealybugs (p.640), whiteflies (p.639), wasps (p.651), mice (p.653), and *Nectria* canker (p.655) may be troublesome.

Growing under cover

In cool areas, fan-trained figs may be grown under cover and will bear more regularly than in the open. The roots must be contained to restrict growth. Once growth starts, water regularly, but reduce watering as the fruits ripen, to prevent the skins from splitting. Prune as for figs grown outdoors, but leave a more open tree to allow as much light as possible to reach the leaves and fruit.

Pruning and training

In warm climates, figs need only light pruning and are usually grown in bush form. Two crops per season are normally produced, an early one from embryo figs (about the size of small peas) formed late in the previous season, followed by the main crop, which is both formed and ripened during the same summer. Meanwhile, further embryo fruits develop to repeat the process.

In cool climates, figs are trained either as open bushes or as fans. Only the first crop from embryo figs will have time to ripen. Remove

ESTABLISHED FIG BUSH
SPRING PRUNING

Cut back cold-damaged shoots to healthy wood, and thin out wrong-pointing shoots and any that are overcrowded.

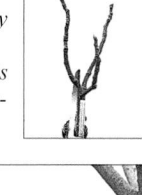

Cut out a proportion of the remaining shoots or, on older trees, branches to 1 bud to promote new growth.

SUMMER PRUNING

Pinch out the tip of each new shoot when it has developed 5 or 6 leaves.

those that do not ripen to concentrate the tree's energies into producing new embryo fruits.

Bush

Purchase a tree with three or four branches rising about 2ft (60cm) above ground. Prune these back by half their length in the first winter to encourage further branches to form and establish a basic framework. Potgrown trees should branch at 15in (38cm) from the base so that they are compact and not top-heavy.

Pruning of established trees differs with the climate. In warm climates in spring, shorten spreading branches to more vertical shoots and leave some growth in the tree's center to protect the bark from sun scorch. In cooler climates, remove all crowded, crossing, or frost-damaged branches; keep the center open by taking out all upright shoots and pruning to buds on the lower sides of branches.

Lengths of bare wood should be cut back to one bud to promote new growth. In the summer, pinch out new shoots or sideshoots to five or six leaves to encourage fruit to form.

Fan

Plant a two-year-old tree with two or three strong shoots. Tie down the two best-placed as for peach fans

RECOMMENDED FIGS

Early
'Calimyrna'
'Celeste'
'Osborne Prolific'
'White Marseilles'

Midseason
'Alma'
'Black Mission'
'Brown Turkey'
'Kadota'
'King'

'Brown Turkey'

Late
'Conadria'

(see p.447) and tip prune lightly. Prune back trees without suitable sideshoots to about 15in (38cm) to encourage lateral growth. The fan is then developed as for peaches but with greater space between branches to allow for the fig's larger foliage.

Prune the established fan in early spring to remove old, fruited wood and any that is cold-damaged or badly placed; leave the younger wood. Also prune back a proportion of younger shoots to one bud to induce fresh growths close to the main branches. Wherever possible, tie in the unpruned shoots to fill any spaces and remove all others. Pinch out the tips of new growths to five leaves in midsummer. The resulting new shoots should then develop embryo fruits for overwintering.

Harvesting and storing

Pick the fruits when fully ripe. Ripe fruits tend to hang down, are very soft to the touch, and may have slight splits in the skin. Figs are best eaten fresh but may also be dried.

Propagation

Seed-raised plants vary in fruit quality. Hardwood cuttings of one-year-old wood from selected cultivars should be used. Take cuttings (see p.428) 12in (30cm) long and insert them in well-prepared, well-drained ground. Protect them with covers. Figs may also be propagated by rooted suckers severed from the parent tree and transplanted.

ESTABLISHED FIG FAN
SPRING PRUNING

Once all risk of frost has passed, cut all cold-damaged shoots back to their point of origin.

Cut back a proportion of young shoots to 1 bud to encourage replacement growth that will produce embryo fruits.

Tie in the shoots so that they are evenly spaced over the fan.

Cut off wrong-pointing shoots to the point of origin or to a well-placed sublateral.

Cut back a proportion of old, bare wood to 1 bud or node to promote new growth.

SUMMER PRUNING

Pinch back new shoots to 5 leaves to encourage embryo fruits to form in the leaf axils.

Mulberries (*Morus nigra*)

Mulberries belong to the Moraceae family. Black mulberries reach a height of 20–30ft (6–10m) and are grown for their fruit. White mulberries (*M. alba*) are not usually grown for their fruit.They grow up to 10ft (3m) tall. The chilling requirement is high, and the trees begin growth late in the season.

Site and planting
Moist, slightly acidic soils are preferable. Mulberries are usually grown on their own roots and are self-fertile. Plant in late fall, spacing trees 25–30ft (8–10m) apart; in cold areas, plant in spring.

Routine care
Cultivation is similar to that of apples (see p.430). Mulch and water in dry weather. Mulberries are generally pest- and disease-free.

Pruning and training
Mulberries are grown as either half-standards or standards. Prune only to establish a strong framework of four to five branches, and thereafter remove branches only if they are badly placed or crowded. The trees should be pruned when fully dormant in winter since shoots and roots bleed profusely if cut or damaged between early spring and fall. If

bleeding does occur, cauterize the wounds as quickly as possible with a hot poker or other iron implement.

Harvesting and storing
Pick the fruit when fully ripe in late summer, or allow it to drop onto a suitable temporary surface (such as a sheet of plastic) to keep it clean. Eat mulberries fresh, or freeze them.

Propagation
Mulberries may be propagated by simple or air layering (see p.114) or by hardwood cuttings about 7in (18cm) long, taken with a heel (see p.111), known as "truncheons."

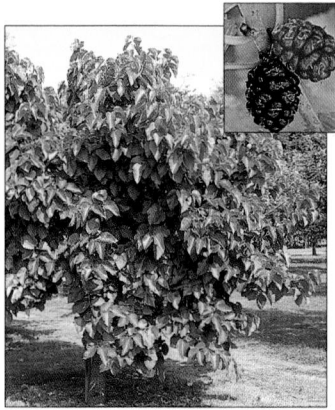

BLACK MULBERRY

Vines

VINES require warm, sheltered positions for successful fertilization and to ripen their fruits. Grapes, kiwi fruits, and passionfruits all belong to this group. In cool areas, they should be given a sheltered environment, or they may be grown under cover. These vines bear on long, flexible stems of one-year-old wood and need to be pruned after fruiting each year to encourage them to produce a supply of new shoots; these grow rapidly and need to be carefully trained into their supports so that they receive the maximum amount of light and air.

Red table grapes

White table grapes

Kiwi fruits

Grapes (*Vitis vinifera*)

Through the ages, grapes have traditionally been one of the choicest fruits for eating or for making wine. The European grape (*Vitis vinifera*) and its cultivars are generally considered to be of the highest quality. American grapes (*V. labrusca, V. riparia, V. rupestris*) have been hybridized with *V. vinifera* to widen the choice of cultivars for table and wine grapes in cooler climates and to improve disease resistance. In the warm, humid Gulf Coast region of the US, *Muscadina rotundifolia* (formerly *Vitis rotundifolia*) is grown.

The fruits need a hot, dry summer to ripen. Warm-temperate regions suit a wide range of cultivars; many cultivars may be grown successfully in cooler climates, however, in protected sites or in greenhouses. Decorative pergolas, arches, or other structures may support them. Pruning methods vary: cultivars grown for table grapes are pruned to produce fewer, higher-quality fruits; those grown for wine grapes are pruned to obtain the greatest quantity of fruits. Grapes are usually self-fertile and wind-pollinated.

Table grapes

It is comparatively easy to produce high-quality table grapes in warm areas. In cooler climates, they may be grown against a sunny, warm wall or, preferably, in a greenhouse. For details of greenhouse cultivation of table grapes, see "Growing under cover," right.

Site

A warm, sheltered, sunny site free from frost at flowering time is ideal. Grapes need a reasonably fertile, well-drained soil, with a pH around 6–7.5. Avoid planting them on very rich soil, since this encourages excess growth at the expense of fruits. Sharp drainage is essential for success because grapes will not tolerate wet soils; improve the soil or install a drainage system if necessary

(for details, see SOILS AND FERTILIZERS, "Improving drainage," p.617).

In cool climates, grapes grown on a warm, sunny wall give reasonably good results but will not match the quality of grapes grown under cover. Early-ripening cultivars should be used for wall cultivation to obtain table fruits by late summer. Support vines with horizontal wires, held in place by vine eyes, 1–2in (2.5–5cm) from the wall.

Grapes are usually grown on their own roots, except in areas where *Phylloxera* is a hazard (see "Pests and diseases," right); in this case, seek local advice on which rootstock to use. The use of a rootstock may have other advantages, too, such as greater tolerance of a high pH or wet soil conditions, and control of overly vigorous growth.

Planting

Cultivate the soil thoroughly before planting. In poor or sandy soils, add well-rotted manure or compost, then firm the area and water well. The soil by a wall is often dry, so thorough preparation, with the addition of ample organic matter, is usually required to improve water retention. Plant bare-root vines in early spring; specimens in containers may be planted at any season. Space single cordons at least 4ft (1.2m) apart, double or U cordons at twice that spacing; the arms of multiple cordons should be 24in (60cm) apart.

Routine care

Water thoroughly during the growing season whenever conditions are dry, reducing watering gradually as the fruit ripens. Particular care is needed with grapes grown on a wall, since they may be in a rain shadow. Mulch to retain moisture. Once vigorous young shoots develop, apply a high-potassium fertilizer every two to three weeks; if growth is poor, give high levels of nitrogen instead. Stop fertilizing as soon as the fruits start to ripen.

If using the cordon system, retain no more than one bunch per 12in (30cm) of vertical stem, or rod, for best-quality grapes; remove intermediate bunches at an early stage. Thin the fruits to obtain both well-shaped bunches and large, evenly sized grapes (and to discourage mildew). Use grape-thinning scissors and a small forked stick to expose portions of the bunch so that small fruits in the center may be removed. Some cultivars need a second thinning as the fruits develop.

Pests and diseases

Grapes are affected by many problems, including scale insects (p.641), black vine weevils (p.638), spider mites (p.640), whiteflies (p.639), wasps (p.651), downy mildew, gray mold/*Botrytis* (p.650), shanking of grapes (p.650), and root-knot nematodes (p.652). Under cover, mealybugs (p.640) and powdery mildew (p.650) may also be troublesome.

Grape *Phylloxera* is a serious pest in warmer climates, where this aphidlike insect attacks the roots of European grapes; galls may also form on the leaves. The attack causes severe stunting and is often fatal. However, the use of resistant rootstocks and resistant hybrids of American cultivars has greatly reduced its incidence. In the Gulf Coast region, Muscadine cultivars and related hybrids resistant to Pierce's disease (PD) must be planted.

Growing under cover

In cool climates, grow grapes in a greenhouse, preferably with heating. Other crops with compatible temperature and humidity requirements may also be grown in the greenhouse. In a lean-to greenhouse, the warmth from the back wall is particularly beneficial, especially if there is little or no direct heating. Greenhouses with both top and side ventilation give the best results.

The soil must be fairly fertile, weed-free, and well drained, with a pH of 6–7.5. Drainage must be 2½ft

(75cm) deep: grapes are deep-rooted. Plant as for grapes grown outdoors. Hand-pollinate by gently but firmly tapping the stems or supports around midday or by drawing your hand gently down the flower cluster. This will release pollen onto the flowers below.

Either train vines directly onto the back wall or plant them at the foot of the glass wall, training them on support wires that are 9in (22cm) or more from the glass. Plant vines at

THINNING GRAPES

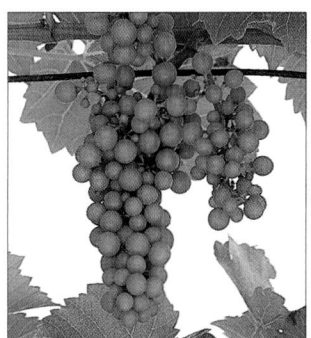

1 *Once the bunches have been thinned to 12in (30cm) apart, the fruits will need thinning as they swell to increase the size of the grapes and to allow air circulation between them.*

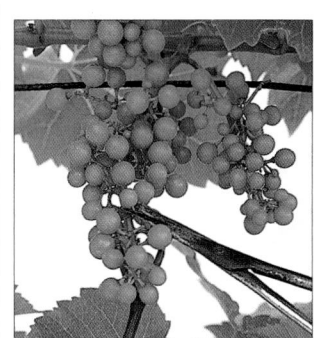

2 *With a forked stick and grape scissors, expose portions of the bunch and snip off unwanted grapes. The bunch should then be wide at the top, tapering toward the base.*

one end of free-standing houses, then train up and along the roof on wires. For details of cultivation, see "Routine care," p.455. A soil auger may be used to gauge levels of moisture in the soil; use tepid water for the first waterings of the season.

Control the ventilation; carefully keep it at a maximum in winter to ensure adequate winter chilling of the vines. Reduce it to a minimum in late winter to induce growth and vary it according to the weather to maintain even temperatures. Slight ventilation is advisable, and adequate warmth is needed at flowering to aid pollination. After fruit set, good air circulation is needed to control gray mold/*Botrytis* and mildew.

Damping down and mist-spraying help control spider mites. Do not damp down on dull days, or during flowering or ripening periods.

Fork over the bed carefully in late winter, avoiding the root area; remove ½in (1cm) of soil from the surface and replace it with soil-based mix. After the first watering, mulch with well-rotted manure or compost around the base of the vines.

Once the fruits ripen, they need a "finishing period" during which they remain on the vine to attain maximum color and flavor: allow two to three weeks for early cultivars, and longer for late-ripening ones. Provide good ventilation, netting ventilators to exclude birds if these are a problem.

Pruning and training

The usual method for table grapes is to develop single or double (U) cordons or rods on which permanent fruiting spurs are formed. These produce high-quality fruits.

Grapes fruit on the current season's growth. Spring and summer pruning, therefore, is aimed at restricting new growth from the rods so that one bunch of grapes develops from each spur. It also restricts the growth of foliage sufficiently to expose the developing fruit to sun, particularly in cool climates. In hot climates, take care that sun scorch does not occur. Carry out winter pruning before midwinter in order to restrict bleeding.

Single cordon After planting, while the vine is dormant, shorten the stem to a strong bud a few inches above the ground. In summer, train one leading shoot onto a vertical bamboo stake, and pinch or cut back any laterals to five or six leaves. Shorten all the sublaterals (shoots that are growing from the laterals) to one leaf. Remove any shoots that develop

GRAPE, SINGLE CORDON
YEAR 1, WINTER PRUNING

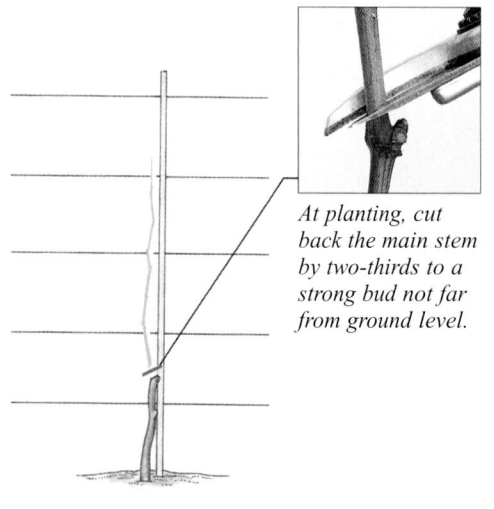

At planting, cut back the main stem by two-thirds to a strong bud not far from ground level.

YEAR 1, SUMMER PRUNING

Pinch back to 1 leaf any sublaterals that form from the laterals.

As the main leader develops, tie it in to the vertical stake.

Cut back each of the main laterals to 5 or 6 leaves.

YEAR 2, WINTER PRUNING

Cut back the leader by about two-thirds of the new growth.

Prune back the laterals that have formed to 1 strong bud.

YEAR 2, SUMMER PRUNING

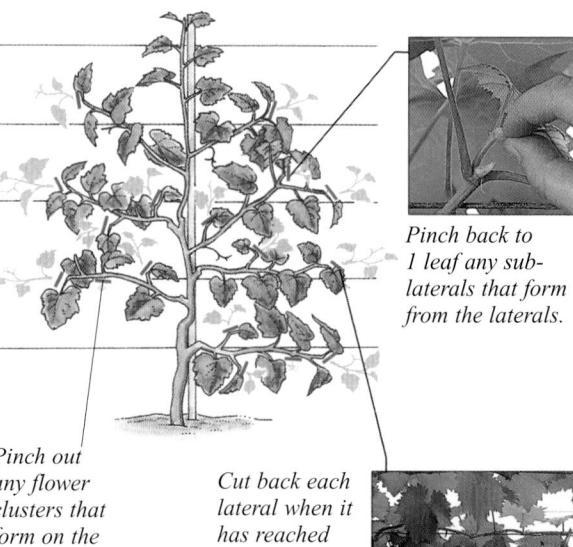

Pinch out any flower clusters that form on the laterals.

Cut back each lateral when it has reached 5 or 6 leaves.

Pinch back to 1 leaf any sublaterals that form from the laterals.

from the base.

During the second winter, reduce the leader by two-thirds of the new growth to well-ripened wood and laterals back to one bud. In the second summer, tie in the leading shoot as it extends. Pinch or cut the sideshoots to five or six leaves and sublaterals to one leaf. Remove any flower clusters; do not allow the vine to fruit until the third year.

In the third winter, shorten the leading shoot by two-thirds of its new growth, and cut back all the laterals to one strong bud to create spurs that will bear fruiting shoots.

Routine pruning Carry out routine pruning from the third year onward. In spring, let two shoots grow at each spur and pinch out others. Retain the stronger of the two for fruiting, and pinch back the weaker to two leaves,

keeping it as a replacement in case the fruiting shoot breaks. In summer, as flower clusters develop, retain the best, pruning out the others to leave one per lateral. Stop laterals at two leaves beyond the chosen flower clusters. Pinch out laterals not carrying flowers at about five leaves and any sublaterals at one leaf.

Each winter continue to remove two-thirds of the new growth from the leader, but when it has reached the top of its support, cut it back annually to two buds. Cut laterals to one strong bud. If spur systems become congested in later years, either remove part of the system with a pruning saw or, if there are too many spurs on the rod, remove some of them completely. The spurs should be 9–12in (22–30cm) apart. The rod should be untied from its wires to

about halfway down its length and bent over until nearly horizontal for a few weeks during winter to encourage the even development of shoots the following spring; afterward, retie the rod vertically.

Double cordon This may be formed by training in two shoots horizontally in the first summer. Prune each back to 2ft (60cm) the following winter. The next year, train the extension growths vertically. These form two vertical arms; prune each arm as a single cordon.

Multiple cordon Train in two shoots in the first summer and in winter prune each back to 2ft (60cm). Train the extension growths horizontally, and choose a strong shoot every 2ft (60cm) to train vertically in order to form the number of arms required. Once established, prune each arm as

HARVESTING TABLE GRAPES

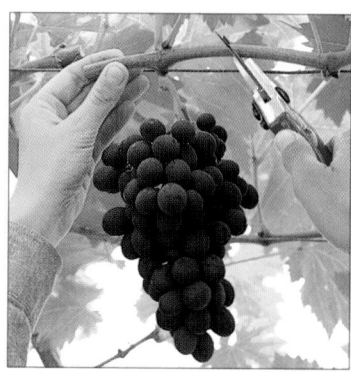

Avoid touching the fruits, which could spoil any powdery bloom. Cut each bunch complete with a handle consisting of 2in (5cm) of woody stem from either side of the bunch.

YEAR 3, WINTER PRUNING

Cut back the leader, removing about two-thirds of the new growth.

Cut back laterals to 1 strong bud.

SPRING PRUNING

When shoots form at each spur, thin to 2 shoots, one to form the main lateral, the other as a backup shoot.

ESTABLISHED SINGLE CORDON, SUMMER PRUNING

If any lateral is not fruiting, cut back the tip to 5 or 6 leaves.

Cut all fruiting laterals back to 2 leaves beyond the flower cluster.

Pinch back any sublaterals that form on the laterals to 1 leaf.

Pinch out any weak flower clusters to leave no more than 1 per lateral.

ESTABLISHED SINGLE CORDON, WINTER PRUNING

When the leader reaches the top of the support, cut the new growth back to 2 buds.

Cut the vine loose, and tie the upper half in a near-horizontal position.

Cut back all lateral shoots to the first strong bud.

If spurs become congested, saw off any surplus wood with a pruning saw.

MULTIPLE CORDON

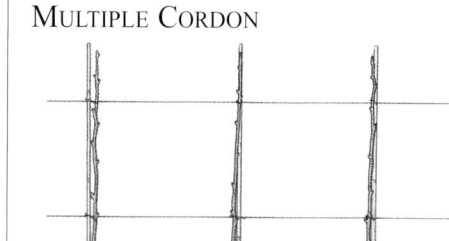

A multiple cordon may be trained with as many vertical rods as space allows. Once established, each arm is pruned in the same way as a single cordon.

a single cordon.

Alternative pruning methods Some cultivars will not produce adequate fruit-bearing shoots from the basal buds left by spur pruning. In such cases, longer lengths of mature wood, or canes, are retained when winter pruning the buds from which fruit-bearing shoots will be produced. Other canes are cut back to three or four buds to produce strong new growths to replace the old fruiting canes the following winter. This process is repeated annually. Many other renewal systems may also be used to train table grapes (for details on the double Guyot system, see "Pruning and training: Guyot system," opposite).

Harvesting and storing

Tie back or remove some of the foliage to allow more sun to reach the ripening fruits. Cut ripe bunches from the vine with a short piece of woody stem – the handle – and place in a container with soft lining so that the fruits are not damaged and their bloom (coating) is not spoiled.

Bunches may be stored for a week or two at room temperature by cutting a longer handle and placing this in a narrow-necked container of water, with the fruit hanging down on the outside of the container.

Propagation

Grapes may be propagated by hardwood cuttings or grafting (for details, see "Wine grapes: Propagation," p.460, and "Bud-grafting," p.426).

Wine grapes

Grapes may be grown for wine in areas with long, dry, sunny summers and adequate soil moisture. In cooler climates, early and midseason cultivars grown on warm walls or under cover give good results.

Site and planting

Most well-drained soils with a pH of 6–7.5 are suitable. Clear weeds before planting. Rootstocks are as for table grapes (see "Table grapes: Site," p.455). The flowers are usually self-fertile, and are pollinated by the wind. Before planting, erect a row of support posts. Attach a single wire 15in (38cm) above the ground and double wires at 30in and 4ft (75cm and 1.2m). Loop both double

GRAPE, DOUBLE GUYOT
YEAR 1, WINTER PRUNING

After planting in winter, cut back the plant to about 6in (15cm) from the soil level, leaving at least 2 strong buds.

YEAR 1, SUMMER PRUNING

Prune any laterals that develop back to 5 leaves.

As it develops, tie in the leader to a vertical stake with twine in a loose figure-eight knot.

Remove any competing shoots developing below the main leader.

YEAR 2, WINTER PRUNING

Prune the leader back to about 15in (38cm) from soil level, just below the bottom wire, to leave 3 good buds.

YEAR 2, SUMMER PRUNING

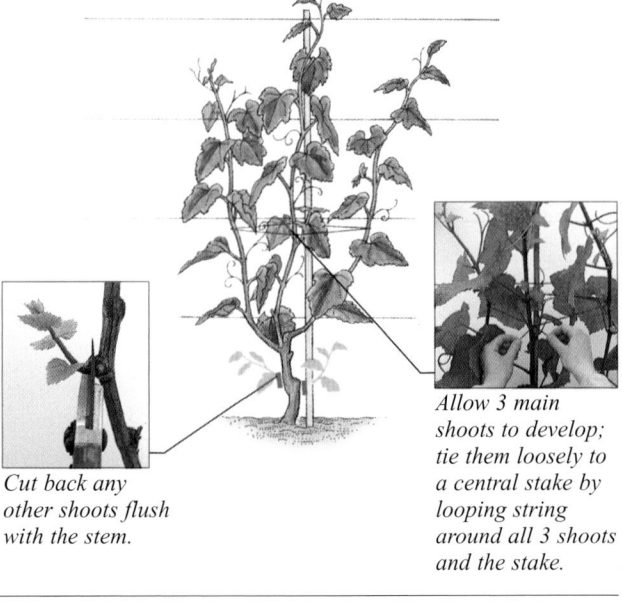

Cut back any other shoots flush with the stem.

Allow 3 main shoots to develop; tie them loosely to a central stake by looping string around all 3 shoots and the stake.

wires around the posts to form a figure eight. Plant one- or two-year-old vines in winter, 5–6ft (1.5–2m) apart, in rows 6ft (2m) apart.

Routine care

Remove any weeds, and water to establish young vines in dry conditions; water bearing vines only in drought conditions, since too much water reduces grape quality. Give a light, annual, early spring application of a balanced fertilizer, and apply potassium sulfate in alternate years. Use a foliar spray of magnesium sulfate to correct magnesium deficiencies (see p.643). Mulch every other year with plenty of well-rotted compost, or annually if the soil quality is poor. Fruit size is not important for wine quality, so thinning is necessary only in cold areas to improve sugar levels.

Pruning and training

Some cultivars need spur pruning (see "Table grapes: Pruning and training," p.456); many, however, require annual replacement of old canes to fruit regularly.

Guyot system This is widely used for wine grapes, since it produces a prolific crop in a limited space. It involves annual training of horizontal rods, from which fruiting shoots are trained vertically. In the double

YEAR 3, WINTER PRUNING

Gently bend down the 2 strongest sideshoots and tie them to the bottom wire, 1 on either side. As shoots develop from these, train them vertically.

Prune these shoots back to 8–12 buds, to leave 2ft (60cm) of strong growth.

Prune the third central shoot back, leaving at least 3 or 4 good buds to encourage the formation of new shoots during the following season.

YEAR 3, SUMMER PRUNING

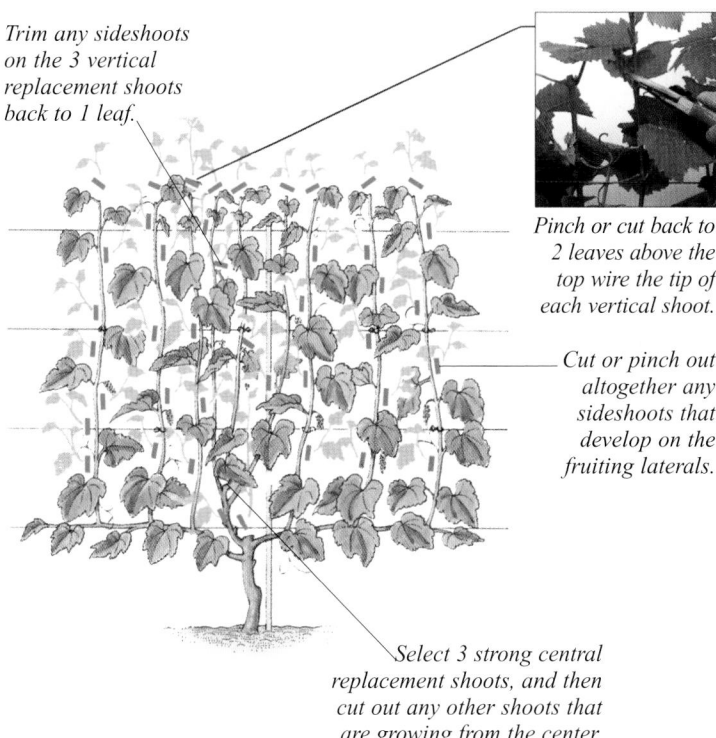

Trim any sideshoots on the 3 vertical replacement shoots back to 1 leaf.

Pinch or cut back to 2 leaves above the top wire the tip of each vertical shoot.

Cut or pinch out altogether any sideshoots that develop on the fruiting laterals.

Select 3 strong central replacement shoots, and then cut out any other shoots that are growing from the center.

ESTABLISHED DOUBLE GUYOT, WINTER PRUNING

Cut the central shoot back to 3 buds. These buds will then develop into new shoots for training in the following winter.

Remove all the fruited wood by cutting the basal horizontal laterals flush with the main stem, leaving the 3 replacement shoots.

Carefully bend down the 2 remaining shoots to the left and right and tie them to the first or second wires. Tip prune to 8–12 buds.

ESTABLISHED DOUBLE GUYOT, SUMMER PRUNING

Pinch out the tips of the fruiting shoots, keeping 2 leaves above the top wire.

Pinch or cut back to 1 leaf any sideshoots that have been produced on the 3 vertical replacement shoots.

Cut out overcrowded shoots that are either likely to obscure the developing fruits or are surplus to your requirements.

Pinch out completely any sideshoots on fruiting shoots.

Guyot, two rods on each plant are trained in this way; in the single Guyot system, only one.

To train a vine by the double Guyot system, cut it back during the first winter to two strong buds above ground level. In the first summer, let one shoot develop and tie it to a vertical stake or wires. Remove other

REMOVING FOLIAGE

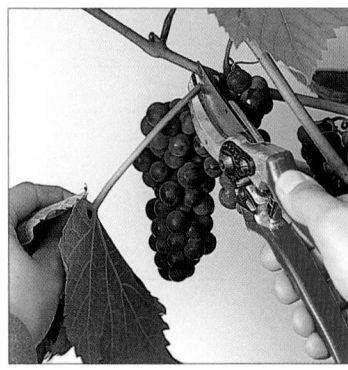

When the grapes are developing, cut off any leaves that shade the ripening fruit directly. Do not remove too many, because this may cause scorch from excess sunlight.

HARVESTING WINE GRAPES

Bunches of wine grapes may be harvested simply by cutting the stalk with pruners.

low shoots and cut any laterals to five leaves. In the second winter, cut back to just under the lowest wire, making sure that there are at least three strong buds remaining.

The next summer, let three strong shoots develop and tie them in vertically. Remove low shoots. In the third winter, tie down two of the shoots to the bottom wire, one on either side. Tip prune these to eight to 12 buds; they will produce fruiting shoots the following summer. Cut the third shoot back to three or four buds to produce replacement shoots, so that the entire process may be repeated. (For the single Guyot system, allow two shoots to develop; tie down one and cut back the other.)

During the third summer, select three of the best central shoots growing from the rod and tie loosely to a central post or stake; cut out other, weaker, central shoots. Pinch back to one leaf any sideshoots that form on the three replacements. Train the shoots from the two arms vertically through the parallel wires. If growth is strong, allow a few bunches of grapes to develop on them. Pinch or cut out shoot tips at two leaves above the top wire; remove any sideshoots on the fruiting shoots.

Routine pruning For winter pruning, cut out all old, fruited wood, leaving three replacement shoots. Tie two of these down, one on either side, and tip prune as for the third winter. Prune the third shoot to three strong buds. Routine summer pruning and training of replacement shoots is as for the third summer. Cut out any overcrowded shoots obscuring the fruits. Remove any leaves shading the grapes six weeks before they are expected to ripen.

Harvesting
Cut the bunches from the vines with pruners; the grapes should be fully ripe and completely dry.

Propagation
Propagate from hardwood cuttings prepared in winter when pruning, using wood from the hardened base of one-year-old shoots. To plant in the open, take sections about 8in (20cm) long, trimming above and below a bud, and insert the cuttings 6in (15cm) deep in sandy soil.

Under cover it is possible to use shorter one- or two-bud cuttings. Grow these singly in 3½in (9cm) pots or insert five cuttings in an 8in (21cm) pot. Place the pots in a cold frame. Pot on each young rooted plant the following summer.

HARDWOOD CUTTINGS

Trim the stems into lengths of about 8in (20cm), making an angled cut above a bud at the top and a flat cut below a bud at the base. Insert each cutting to two-thirds its length into a trench in sandy soil.

TWO-BUD CUTTINGS

1 *While pruning at leaf drop, trim off a long section of mature wood from the current season's growth. Then remove any remaining leaves or tendrils.*

2 *Divide the stem into cuttings with 2 buds, with an angled cut above the top bud and a horizontal cut between 2 nodes below the lower bud. Remove a ½in (1cm) length of rind above the lower cut.*

3 *Insert cuttings in a medium of 2 parts peat, 1 part soil, and 1 part sand, the lower bud just below the surface. Label, water, and place in a protected spot.*

4 *When the cuttings have rooted, they should be potted on individually into 4in (10cm) pots to grow on.*

Kiwi fruits (*Actinidia deliciosa*)

Deciduous trailing climbers, kiwi fruits were originally known as Chinese gooseberries. The vines will grow up to 28ft (9m) in length. The berries have hairy brown skin and green pulp, with small black seeds.

Warm, moist conditions are preferable during the growing season, with the optimum temperature range being 41–78°F (5–25°C). Dormant plants will, however, tolerate several degrees below freezing and require chilling for a period of at least 400 hours below 42°F (7°C) to encourage good flower production.

Site and planting
Kiwi fruits can be grown only in the open in sunny, sheltered areas, since plants in growth are sensitive to adverse weather conditions. The soil should be well aerated, deep, and rich in organic matter, with a pH of 6–7. Incorporate a general-purpose fertilizer into the site at a rate of 2–4oz (50–110g) per plant.

Kiwi fruits are dioecious, with plants bearing either male or female flowers. One male is needed for every eight or nine female plants to ensure adequate fertilization.

Erect a post and wire support, with wires at 12in (30cm) intervals. Plant either rooted cuttings or grafted plants 12–15ft (4–5m) apart in rows 12–18ft (4–6m) apart, staking the vines until they are tall enough to reach the supporting wires.

Routine care
Mulch the plants heavily and apply a general-purpose fertilizer rich in phosphorus and potassium. Water regularly, particularly in prolonged dry periods. Keep rows weed-free. Fruit thinning is rarely necessary.

RECOMMENDED KIWI FRUITS
'Abbot' **F**
'Blake' **F**
'Chico No. 3' **M**
'Hayward' **F**
'Matua' **M**
'Monty' **F**
'Saanichton' **F**
'Top Star' **F**

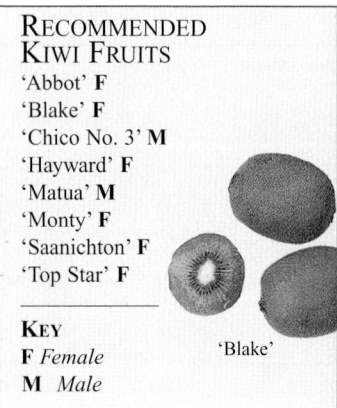

KEY
F *Female*
M *Male*

'Blake'

HOW TO SUPPORT KIWI FRUIT

A common method is to train the plants as espaliers on horizontal wires with 2 main laterals per plant arising from the main stem, with fruiting laterals (see inset) at intervals of about 20in (50cm).

Plants grown in the open may be liable to root rot (see *Phytophthora* root rots, p.652). Under cover they may be infested with thrips (p.640), scale insects (p.641), and root-knot nematodes (p.652). Fruit rot may also occur as a result of infection of the petals. Infection spreads to the fruits, which then drop early. The spread of the disease is promoted by high humidity. Spraying flowers at petal fall with a fungicide will give reasonable control.

Growing under cover
This is rarely practical due to the long, trailing growth of the plants; in exposed conditions, however, plants grown in the open may be protected from excessive wind and hail by a light plastic screening material.

Kiwi fruits may be grown in walk-in polytunnels if the appropriate environmental conditions can be provided. Soil preparation and cultivation details are the same as for plants grown in the open.

Pruning and training
Commercial crops are often grown on a T bar or overhead pergola structure. Another commonly used system is to train plants as espaliers on horizontal wires: each plant then has two main laterals arising from the main stem, and fruiting branches at intervals of 20in (50cm). For details, see "Apple: Espalier," p.436.

The fruits are produced on one-year-old wood, so all fruited side-shoots should be cut back to two to four buds in the dormant season.

Harvesting and storing
Kiwi fruits start to bear fruit three to four years after planting. Harvest them as they soften. Snap or cut them from the branch, with the calyx attached; keep them cool. If wrapped in plastic film, fruits store for several months at 32°F (0°C).

Propagation
Both soft- and hardwood cuttings may be rooted successfully. Softwood cuttings should be taken in spring; trim to 4–6in (10–15cm) and insert in rooting medium (see p.370). Hardwood cuttings are taken in late summer; these should be 8–12in (20–30cm) long and inserted in sandy soil mix (see p.428).

Selected cultivars may also be grafted onto vigorous seedling stocks; the most common methods are T-budding and whip-and-tongue grafting (see p.427).

Passionfruits (*Passiflora spp.*)

Passionfruits are climbing plants, with individual stems reaching many feet in length. The globular fruits are either yellow or purple when ripe, and may be up to 3in (7cm) in diameter. Two recommended selections are the yellow-fruited *P. edulis* f. *flavicarpa* 'Brazilian Golden' and the purple *P. edulis* 'Black Knight'.

The optimum temperature range for the purple passionfruit is about 68–82°F (20–28°C). The yellow passionfruit prefers temperatures over 75°F (24°C) and does not tolerate frost; purple types may withstand frost for short periods. Moderate to high humidity is required for satisfactory growth.

Site and planting
Select a sunny site, protected by windbreaks if necessary. Soils may vary in type but must be well drained, with a pH of about 6.

Cross-pollination by insects, normally bees, is usual, but hand-pollination may be necessary in wet weather; hand-pollination has been found to increase the yield of plants that are grown in the open.

Passionfruits require support, in the form of a wire trellis. Before planting, insert sturdy uprights, 10ft (3m) long, at intervals of 12ft (4m) each way. Link adjoining uprights in rows by tying with one or two strands of wire.

Take care to prepare the planting holes thoroughly, adding both organic material and a general-purpose fertilizer with medium to high levels of nitrogen. Establish the plants at about 10–12ft (3–4m) apart each way, or less if only a few plants are grown. The yellow form is usually planted 3m (10ft) apart each way.

Routine care
Apply a general-purpose fertilizer that has a medium to high nitrogen content at a rate of 1–2lb (0.5–1kg) per plant per year, preferably in equal dressings at intervals of three to four months. Apply an organic mulch in spring, and weed and water regularly during the dry season.

Pests affecting plants in the open as well as under cover include fruit flies, aphids (p.639), spider mites (p.640), and various scale insects (p.641). Root-knot nematodes (p.652) and *Fusarium* wilt (p.646) may also be serious in some subtropical areas. "Woodiness" is caused by cucumber mosaic virus (see "Viruses," p.642), which is transmitted by aphids. Because passionfruit vines are susceptible to nematodes and various wilt diseases, replace the plants every five or six years with healthy seedlings, rooted cuttings, or grafted plants.

Growing under cover
This is possible in temperate areas, but fruits may not be produced unless the optimum temperatures and conditions are provided; hand-pollination is generally necessary. Provide wire supports as for outdoor plants. Grow plants either in prepared beds or in large containers at least 14in (35cm) in diameter. Use a well-drained, fertile soil mix with

PASSIONFRUITS

a high organic content, and incorporate a general-purpose fertilizer into the soil mix before planting. Maintain a minimum temperature of 68°F (20°C) and humidity of 60–70 percent. Apply a liquid or general-purpose fertilizer once a month, and water regularly.

Pruning and training
Train two main growing stems along the wires to form a permanent framework. If these have not produced laterals by the time they are 2–3ft (60–90cm) long, pinch out their tips. Allow the lateral shoots, on which the fruits will be produced, to hang down as they develop each spring. Prune these laterals so that they are never less than 6in (15cm) from the soil. Once the plant is established, each winter cut back the current season's fruited shoots, since these will not bear fruit again.

Harvesting and storing
Pick fruits when they begin to change color, from green to either purple or yellow. The fruits should be ripe eight to 12 weeks after fruit set, depending on the cultivar. Fruits may be stored for up to 21 days if maintained at an even temperature of at least 43°F (6°C) and at a constant humidity level of 85–90 percent.

Propagation
This is usually by sowing seed or raising cuttings; passionfruits may also be propagated by bud-grafting.

Seed may be extracted from the fully ripe fruits, and should be fermented for three to four days, then washed and dried. Sow the seed under cover in trays or 3–3½in (6–9cm) pots of sowing medium, and keep at a temperature of at least 68°F (20°C). When the germinated seedlings are 8–14in (20–35cm) tall, transplant them to open ground, after hardening off, or grow them on under cover.

Cuttings 6–8in (15–20cm) long should be prepared and inserted in-to a tray or pot filled with rooting medium. Apply bottom heat and mist-spray to encourage rooting.

For details of bud-grafting, see p.426. Healthy bud-grafted plants should be transplanted into their permanent positions to grow on when approximately 6in (15cm) tall.

If nematodes or wilt diseases are a serious problem, the purple cultivars may be grafted onto resistant rootstocks. Vigorous seedlings of the yellow-fruited type are normally used for this purpose.

Soft fruits

Aᴸᴸ the usually cultivated soft fruits are bush or cane fruits, except for strawberries, which are herbaceous perennials. Bush fruits include blueberries, gooseberries, and black-, red-, and whitecurrants. Cane fruits include blackberries, hybrid berries, and raspberries. All produce succulent fruits that are eaten fresh, or preserved, canned, or frozen. Most soft fruits grow best in temperate climates. They prefer a well-drained, moisture-retentive, and fertile soil. A sunny site is best and gives fine-quality fruit, but in most cases a little shade is tolerated. Almost all cultivars are self-fertile. Pruning methods depend on whether fruit is produced on one-year-old wood, on older wood and spurs, or on both.

Blackberries

Yellow raspberries

Blueberries

Strawberries

Boysenberries

Redcurrants

Raspberries

Strawberries (*Fragaria* x *ananassa*)

Strawberries are low-growing, herbaceous plants that may be grown in most gardens, either in the open ground or in containers. There are three distinct types of strawberry plant: summer-fruiting, everbearing, and alpine.

Summer-fruiting strawberries produce nearly all their fruit in an intensive two- to three-week period in midsummer. Some cultivars also give a smaller fall crop.

Everbearing (perpetual-fruiting) strawberries bear briefly in summer, cease for about two months, and then produce a succession of fruits in fall. They grow best in regions that have mild, frost-free fall weather.

Alpine strawberries produce small, delicately flavored fruits from midsummer to fall.

Variations in daylength (see THE VEGETABLE GARDEN, p.489) affect the formation of flowers in some cultivars. It is therefore important to choose those appropriate for the latitude of the particular garden: nearer the tropics, for example, the cooler temperatures that are essential for growth and bearing may be found only at high altitudes.

Site and planting

Strawberries are best grown where new plantings may be made regularly on fresh ground, since bearing, fruit size, and plant health deteriorate if the same ground and plants are used after the third year. If you have room, grow one-, two-, and three-year-old plants in succession, discarding the oldest plants and planting new runners in fresh ground each year.

Site

Sunny, warm sites give the best-flavored fruit. Sandy soils produce the earliest crops, loams and well-drained clays the heaviest and most flavorful; alkaline soils do not produce good results. Slightly acidic conditions with a pH of 6–6.5 are ideal. Good drainage is vital to avoid soilborne diseases. Planting strawberries after potatoes can be risky, since the ground may be infected with *Verticillium* wilt (p.645).

To prolong the fruiting season, plantings may be split. Choose a warm, sheltered position for the earliest crops; sunny, open ground for the main crop; and a less sunny site for late-ripening fruits.

Pollination

Most strawberry cultivars are self-fertile. Some cultivars, however, fruit only if several plants of a different cultivar that flowers at the same time grow nearby.

Planting

The planting time for strawberries depends on geographical location. Seek expert advice if in doubt. In cool-temperate regions, late summer to early fall planting is best and ensures the heaviest crops the following summer. For later plantings, remove flowers in spring to allow plants to become well established before they begin to bear fruit.

Use plants of certified stock, if possible, and plant in fresh ground, where strawberries have not been grown for at least three years. Replace plants every two or three years, and grub out and discard any old plants nearby to prevent the spread of viral diseases. Clear all weeds and apply generous amounts of well-rotted farmyard manure, unless plenty remains in the soil from the preceding crop. On hungrier sandy or gravelly soils, rake in a dressing of a balanced fertilizer as well, at a

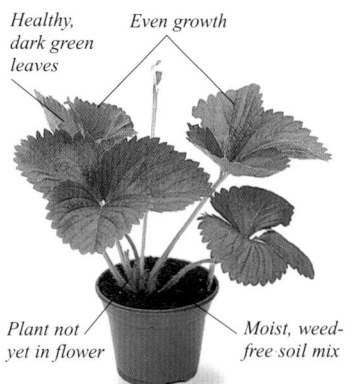

Healthy, dark green leaves

Even growth

Plant not yet in flower

Moist, weed-free soil mix

rate of 3oz/sq yd (105g/sq m), just before planting. Space strawberries at 18in (45cm) intervals in slightly raised rows, 2½ft (75cm) apart, so that rainwater runs off. Plant with the base of the central crown at soil level, firm in the plants, and water well. On wet sites, plant in raised beds (see STRUCTURES AND SURFACES, "Raised beds," p.593).

Strawberries may also be planted through sheets of black plastic, which smother weeds, retain soil moisture, and encourage early bearing by

PLANTING STRAWBERRIES UNDER BLACK PLASTIC

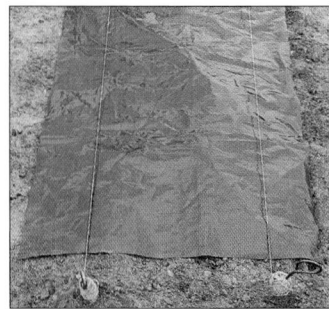

1 In moist soil, mark out a 3ft (90cm) wide bed with string. Mound the soil in the center, and cover the bed with a length of black plastic 4ft (1.2m) wide.

2 Dig a narrow trench on either side of the bed and, using a spade, anchor the edges of the plastic sheet firmly in the trenches to keep it from blowing away.

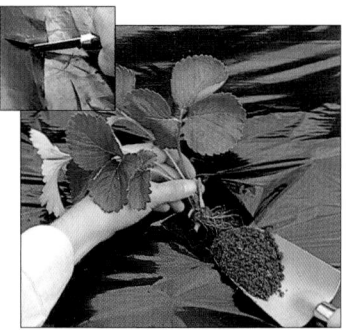

3 Make cross-shaped cuts in the plastic (see inset) at 18in (45cm) intervals. Plant the strawberries through the slits and firm the soil around their crowns.

4 Tuck in the cut plastic around the crowns of the plants. The finished row of strawberries should be slightly raised so that rain drains away from the plants.

warming the soil. Anchor the plastic firmly, then make planting slits at the required intervals.

Routine care

Strawberries need regular watering. Ripening fruits should be netted against pests, and kept off the soil to keep them clean. Remove surplus runners, weed, and regularly check for pests and diseases. Flowers may need protection from cold in spring: double-thickness sheets of newspaper are very effective.

Protecting the fruits

Before the fruit clusters develop fully, lay clean, dry straw or commercial mats beneath them to prevent soil splash on the fruits; this is unnecessary for plants grown through plastic. Protect the fruits from birds before they redden, using posts to support fruit nets (see p.421). Nets also help discourage raccoons.

HOW TO KEEP STRAWBERRIES CLEAN

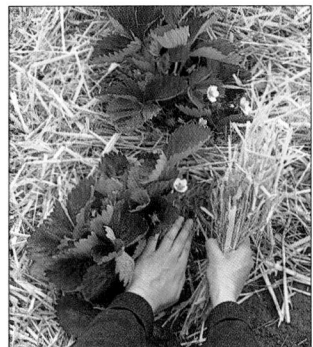

When the strawberries are in flower or the fruits are forming, put a thick layer of straw underneath and between the plants to prevent the ripening fruits from touching the soil.

ALTERNATIVE METHOD

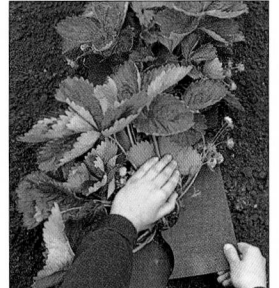

Alternatively, strawberry mats may be laid carefully around the crowns to protect the developing fruits.

REMOVING RUNNERS

Remove excess runners as they develop. Pinch them out close to the parent plant, taking care not to damage any other foliage.

Controlling runners

Pinch out runners as they appear, unless they are needed to help form matted rows (see "Growing under cover," below).

Watering and weeding

Water strawberries when newly planted, then regularly during the growing season, especially after flowering to promote the development of quality fruits. Water plants under plastic only in very dry weather, watering through the planting slits. Keep beds free of weeds.

Pests and diseases

Strawberries may be eaten by small animals (see p.656), squirrels (p.651), millipedes (p.638), and slugs (p.638), and are vulnerable to aphids (p.639), viruses (p.642), gray mold/*Botrytis* (p.646), fungal leaf spots (p.641), and spider mites (p.640). Discard diseased or stunted plants. Red core and strawberry beetles are not widespread but are serious where they occur. Red core is a soilborne disease, more prevalent in heavy soils, causing the foliage to collapse and die. The only remedy is to change the site. Strawberry beetles take seeds from the outside of the fruits, encouraging rotting. They feed on weed seeds, so weed beds well; control the beetles with slug pellets.

Growing under cover

Strawberries grown in a heated greenhouse fruit up to one month earlier than those grown outdoors, but have less flavor. Establish runners in 3in (6cm) pots of seed soil mix as early as possible (see p.464). Before the roots fill the pots, transplant into 6in (15cm) pots of potting mix. Keep the plants outside until midwinter, protected from heavy rain, then move them into the

PICKING FRUITS

Pick dessert strawberries by the stalk to avoid bruising the fruit. Strawberries for jam may be picked without the stalk.

greenhouse in a position of maximum light. When new leaves form, maintain minimum temperatures of 45°F (7°C) at night and 50°F (10°C) during the day.

Adjust the ventilation to maintain these temperatures. Water and damp down frequently to keep a moist atmosphere and reduce the risk of spider mite infestation. Increase the temperature by about 5°F (3°C) when flower clusters start to develop; during flowering, raise the temperature again by the same amount and stop damping down. Pollinate flowers by hand with a soft brush; do this around midday on a bright day. Remove late-forming flowers to improve the size of the ripening fruits. To enhance flavor, lower the temperature as fruits begin to ripen.

For plants grown in the open, cloches placed over plants in late winter advance ripening by about three weeks, and polytunnels by one to two weeks (see p.576). Both should be well ventilated on warm days. Under covers or plastic tunnels, strawberries may be grown in matted rows, in which the planting distance is halved to give maximum yield. Runners may be retained to increase the density of the planting. Revert to the usual spacing after the first year by removing every other plant; otherwise, fruit quality deteriorates and routine care becomes increasingly difficult.

Harvesting and storing

Harvest dessert strawberries when fully ripe, complete with stalks, and use them at once for the best flavor. Pick strawberries for jam when ripe but still firm. Pick the fruit every other day and remove diseased or damaged fruit. Strawberries may also

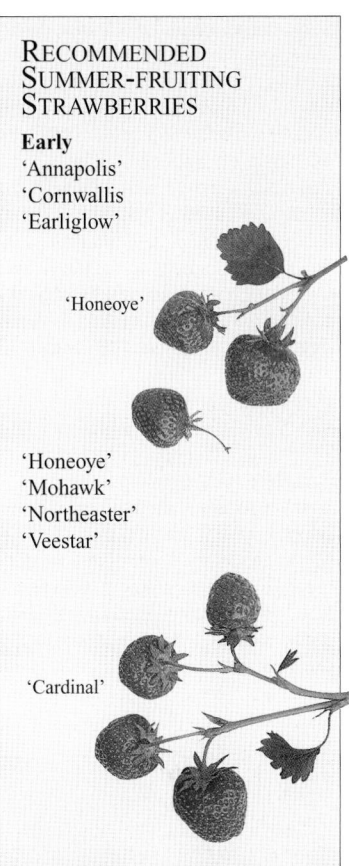

RECOMMENDED SUMMER-FRUITING STRAWBERRIES

Early
'Annapolis'
'Cornwallis'
'Earliglow'

'Honeoye'
'Mohawk'
'Northeaster'
'Veestar'

Midseason
'Cardinal'
'Catskills'
'Cavendish'
'Guardian'
'Jewel'
'Kent'
'Lester'
'Raritan'
'Redchief'
'Scott'
'Secord'
'Tennessee Beauty'

Late
'Allstar'
'Bounty'
'Sparkle'

RECOMMENDED EVERBEARING STRAWBERRIES

'Autumn Beauty'
'Fort Laramie'
'Ogallala'
'Ozark Beauty', syn.
    'Cross's Beauty'
'Puget Beauty'
'Rockhill'
'Tribute'
'Tristar'

RECOMMENDED ALPINE STRAWBERRIES

'Alexandria'
'Baron Solemacher'
'Mignonette'
'Pineapple Crush'

be canned or preserved. If frozen, the fruits, except those of the cultivar 'Veestar', lose their firmness.

After harvesting, clear surplus runners, weeds, and straw from the site. Cut off the old foliage from plants, taking care not to damage the young leaves. Apply a balanced fertilizer and water it in if the soil is dry. Where plants are growing through a plastic mulch, make a fresh planting unless they are thriving.

Propagation

Each year, plant one or two certified virus-free young plants well away from established fruiting beds. Control aphids and remove all flowers. The plants will produce a healthy supply of runners for up to two years; then start afresh with new, certified stock. Some everbearing cultivars produce few runners.

CLEARING THE FOLIAGE AFTER HARVESTING

As soon as the crop has been picked, remove the old foliage to leave 4in (10cm) of stem above the young leaves and crown. Discard straw, foliage, and other debris from around the plants to minimize the risk of pests and diseases.

HOW TO PROPAGATE BY RUNNERS

1 *Plant certified virus-free plants especially to produce runners. As runners form, spread them out evenly around the parent plant.*

2 *Once a runner has rooted and is making vigorous new growth, lift it carefully, using a hand fork, without damaging the roots.*

3 *Sever the rooted runner from the parent plant. Transplant it to well-prepared soil or pot it up singly for planting out later.*

Alpine strawberries

Alpine strawberries (*Fragaria vesca* Semperflorens Group) have small, fragrant, sweetly flavored fruits and make a neat and attractive edging for flower borders or vegetable plots. They tolerate cooler conditions than most other strawberries and prefer partial shade in the summer in warm areas. Their fruiting season lasts from midsummer to late fall.

Plants deteriorate after about two years, so should be propagated regularly from either runners or seed.

To separate seed from the fruits, leave the strawberries to dry, then squash them between finger and thumb. Sow the seed in pots of standard sowing medium and maintain them at 64–75°F (18–24°C). Prick out seedlings when they have two true leaves. Plant out young strawberries in early summer.

HOW TO PROPAGATE FROM SEED

ALPINE STRAWBERRY

1 *Use dried fruits, squashing them gently between finger and thumb so that the seeds fall off. Hold the fruits over a clean container to gather the seeds.*

2 *Fill a 3in (6cm) pot with sowing medium. Sprinkle the seeds thinly on the surface, then cover them with a thin layer of medium and a layer of fine grit.*

Blackberries and hybrid berries (*Rubus fruticosus* and *Rubus* hybrids)

The fruits of cultivated blackberries and hybrid berries such as loganberries and boysenberries are borne on canes in late summer. The hybrids have arisen from crosses between different *Rubus* species or cultivars.

Site
Before planting, the ground should be well prepared and fertilized, as for raspberries (see p.466). Buy blackberries and hybrid berries from specialty nurseries and, if possible, choose plants that are included in a certification program to ensure healthy, virus-free stock. Thornless cultivars are usually less vigorous than prickly ones. Blackberries and

hybrid berries are all self-fertile and consequently may be grown singly.

Blackberries and hybrid berries need a sunny or partially shaded position. Do not plant them in exposed sites.

Provide support for the canes: walls and fences, with horizontal wires set up at 12in (30cm) intervals, are ideal.

A post 10ft (3m) long sunk 2ft (60cm) into the ground may also be used as a basic support, but for vigorous cultivars erect a post-and-wire fence. Position the posts at 12–15ft (4–5m) intervals with four horizontal wires running between them, the lowest at 3ft (90cm) from the ground, the highest at 6ft (2m). On light,

sandy soils, provide extra support for the end posts by bracing them with diagonal wooden props. This will help prevent the wires from sagging under the weight of the canes.

Planting
Plant during late fall; if the weather is severe, delay until late winter or early spring. Some hybrids may be killed in very cold areas, so seek local advice. Plant shallowly, spreading out the roots well and firming the soil at the base of the plants. Space vigorous cultivars 12–15ft (4–5m) apart, less vigorous ones 8–10ft (2.5–3m) apart. After planting, shorten the canes to 9in (22cm).

BUYING HEALTHY BLACKBERRY PLANTS

Strong, healthy cane

Well-developed, fibrous roots

METHODS OF TRAINING

ALTERNATE BAY
*Train new canes to one side of the plant,
while the older ones fruit on the other side.*

FAN
*Fan-train fruiting canes individually to the left
and right, and train new canes centrally.*

ROPE
*Train fruiting canes in groups along wires,
leaving new canes to grow centrally.*

WEAVING
*Weave fruiting canes through the lower wires.
Train new canes centrally and along the top wire.*

RECOMMENDED BLACKBERRIES

Early
'Brazos'
'Cherokee'
'Cheyenne'
'Comanche'

'Comanche'

Late
'Chester'
'Darrow'
'Dirksen'
'Hull'
'Olallie'

RECOMMENDED HYBRID BERRIES

Tayberry

Boysenberry
Jostaberry
Loganberry
Marionberry
Sunberry
Sylvanberry
Tayberry
Youngberry

PRUNING ESTABLISHED BLACKBERRIES
AFTER FRUITING

*Cut down all the fruited
canes to ground level
near the base of the stem.*

*Cut down all the
fruited canes to
ground level near
the base of the
stem.*

TIP PRUNING COLD-DAMAGED STEMS

*Inspect the canes for
signs of cold damage in
early spring and, if
necessary, cut back the
tips of affected canes to
healthy wood.*

Routine care
Maintenance requirements are as for raspberries (see p.466).

Pests and diseases
Problems may be caused by raspberry borers, fruit worms, gray mold/*Botrytis* (p.650), and viruses (p.651), although resistance varies between hybrids.

Pruning and training
The plants fruit on one-year-old wood, so training needs to separate fruiting canes from newly developing ones. For small gardens, the rope and fan methods (see above) are best. The alternate bay and weaving systems use much more space, but weaving is the best method for vigorous plants.

After bearing, cut out the fruiting canes at ground level. Retain and tie in those canes that have grown during the current season, but remove any that are weak or damaged. In early spring, cut back the tip of each cane if it shows any signs of die-back resulting from cold.

Harvesting and storing
Pick the fruits regularly; unlike raspberries, the central plug stays within the picked fruit. For exhibiting, pick fruits complete with their stalks. Blackberries may be stored by canning, preserving, or freezing.

Propagation
To provide a few new plants, use tip layering (see below). In summer,

TIP LAYERING

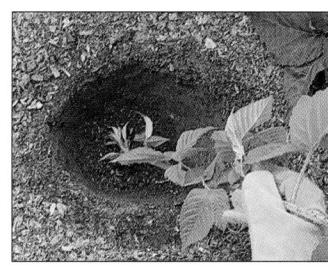

1 *Bend over the tip of a healthy, vigorous shoot and place it in a hole 4in (10cm) deep. Fill the hole with soil and firm down well.*

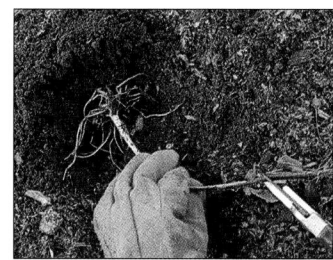

2 *Once the tip has rooted in late fall, cut the old stem close to the young, rooted plant to sever it from the parent. Pot up the new plant, if required, or transplant in spring.*

bend a shoot to ground level and place the tip in a hole dug in the soil. Cover it with soil and firm. Once the tip has rooted in late fall, sever it from the parent plant. Transfer the young plant to its final growing position in spring.

To produce a larger number of young plants, remove shoots, 12in (30cm) long, of the current season's growth in late summer; take leaf-bud cuttings from them, with a leaf and a piece of stem. Place several cuttings in one 5½in (14cm) pot in a moist atmosphere or cold frame; they should root in six to eight weeks. Harden them off and plant them out in late fall or, where winters are harsh, in early spring. Transplant the young canes to their final positions a year later.

HOW TO PROPAGATE BY LEAF-BUD CUTTINGS

1 *Select a strong, healthy shoot from the current season's growth, taking at least 12in (30cm) of stem with plenty of well-developed leaf buds.*

2 *Make a cut ½in (1cm) above a bud: slice downward to remove the bud and a portion of stem about 1in (2.5cm) long, with a leaf attached.*

3 *Place 3 cuttings in a 5½in (14cm) pot, with the stem portions at an angle and growth buds just above the soil. Water, label, and place in a cold frame.*

Raspberries (*Rubus idaeus*)

A number of raspberry cultivars have been produced by crossing the European wild red raspberry (*Rubus idaeus*) with the American raspberry (*R. idaeus* var. *strigosus*) and the North American black raspberry (*R. occidentalis*).

Raspberries are a cool-season crop, growing best where there is plenty of moisture. Fruits vary in color from dark red to yellow. There are two main types of raspberry: summer-fruiting, which has a short season of heavy bearing in midsummer, and fall-fruiting, which has an extended bearing period beginning in late summer and continuing until the start of severe frost.

Site and planting

The site needs thorough preparation before planting, since raspberries do not bear well on poor soils, particularly if in competition with weeds. Raspberries are self-fertile.

Site

Raspberries should be planted in a sheltered, sunny position. They tolerate partial shade, and in hotter regions some shade may be a positive advantage.

The soil should be rich in organic matter and moisture-retentive but also well drained, because raspberries do not tolerate poor drainage. Sandy, alkaline, and poor, stony soils need an annual, heavy dressing with organic material, and regular watering. In addition, if raspberries are grown on alkaline soil, they may suffer from chlorosis (see "Manganese/iron deficiency," p.643).

Preparation

Clear all perennial weeds before planting, since they are extremely difficult to deal with later. Prepare an area at least 3ft (90cm) wide, and dig in plenty of well-rotted manure.

Construct permanent supports. For a post-and-wire support, set a single row of sturdy posts 10ft (3m) apart. Run three lengths of wire or nylon string between the posts, setting them at heights of 30in (75cm), 3½ft (1.1m), and 5ft (1.5m). Keep the wires or strings taut and tie in the canes with twine by continuous lacing (weaving between the canes and wires) to prevent the canes from being blown along the row.

The parallel wires method requires two rows of posts, with posts at the above spacing and rows 30in (75cm) apart. Run two pairs of parallel wires along the posts, one pair at 30in (75cm), the other at 5ft (1.5m), then crisscross between them with wire or strong string. The canes are supported by the crosswires and do not need to be tied in.

For the Scandinavian system, erect two rows of posts, as above, but with 3ft (90cm) between rows, then run a single wire along each row at a height of 3ft (90cm). Twist fruiting canes along the wires, allowing new canes to grow in the open, central space.

Obtain certified virus-free canes; otherwise, use suckers taken from established plants of known good health and bearing performance.

Planting

Plant dormant canes in well-manured ground at 15–18in (38–45cm) intervals, in rows 6ft (2m) apart. Plant in fall or early winter, since this

SUPPORTING AND TRAINING METHODS

The post-and-wire method is useful if space is limited. The parallel wires method gives the canes more room but is not suitable in windy conditions. The Scandinavian system bends young canes around each other and the wire; the canes are not tied in or tip pruned. This method needs more space than the others.

SCANDINAVIAN SYSTEM

POST AND WIRES

PARALLEL WIRES

HOW TO PLANT RASPBERRIES

1 *Prepare a trench 2–3in (5–8cm) deep in well-manured ground. Plant the canes 15–18in (38–45cm) apart. Spread out the roots carefully, then backfill the trench with soil.*

2 *Firm the soil around the bases of the canes, making sure that they remain vertical. Prune canes back to a bud about 10in (25cm) from the ground. Rake the soil lightly.*

encourages the canes to establish quickly. Spread out the roots evenly at a depth of 2–3in (5–8cm), and gently firm them in. Prune the canes to 10in (25cm) from the ground.

Routine care

In spring, mulch with well-rotted manure. Apply this on either side of the row, taking care not to bury the canes. If manure is unavailable, apply regular dressings of a balanced fertilizer (see "Care of soft fruits," p.420) and mulch with compost or leaf mold to conserve moisture.

Flowers usually appear too late to be damaged by cold and so do not need protection. Remove weeds, and water the plants regularly and thoroughly. Remove any suckers more than 9in (22cm) from the main row.

Pests and diseases
Raspberry fruit worms and borers (p.646) are the main pests. Gray mold/*Botrytis* (p.650), spur blight/cane blight, and viruses (p.651) may also be a problem.

Pruning and training

As soon as new canes are established, by about midsummer, cut out the canes that were shortened at planting time.

Summer-fruiting raspberries should have all fruited canes removed at ground level after bearing. Tie in the new canes (see *Supporting and Training Methods*, opposite), spacing them 3–4in (8–10cm) apart. Cut out damaged and weak canes so that those remaining receive as much

light and air as possible. Loop over and tie in tall canes to prevent wind damage.

Fall-fruiting raspberries (see p.466) should have all canes cut to ground level in late winter. The new canes grow, then fruit in the fall.

The following spring, trim canes to 6in (15cm) above the topmost wire, cutting back any tips with cold damage. Remove dead, diseased, or crowded canes or any growing more than 9in (22cm) from the row.

Harvesting and storing

Pick the fruit when it is firm to ripe for preserves and freezing, and when it is fully ripe for eating fresh, harvesting every other day if possible.

HOW TO REMOVE UNWANTED SUCKERS

If suckers become overcrowded or are growing too far outside the row, as here, lift them and sever from the parent plant.

PRUNING AT THE END OF THE FIRST SEASON

1 *By about midsummer, cut down to ground level the old canes that were shortened when planting was carried out.*

2 *Tie the current season's strongest canes to the support wires (see inset) when they reach about 3ft (90cm). Remove weak shoots and those growing more than 9in (22cm) from the row.*

RECOMMENDED RASPBERRIES: SUMMER-FRUITING

Early
'Boyne' **R, H**
'Canby' **R**
'Madawaska' **R**
'Reveille' **R**
'Southland' **R**
'Trent' **H**

'Southland'

Midseason
'Dundee' **Bf**
'Festival' **R, H**
'Hilton' **R**
'Royalty' **Pu**
'Sentry' **R**

Late
'Brandywine' **Pu**
'Cumberland' **Bf**
'Newburgh' **R**

FALL-FRUITING
'Autumn Bliss' **R**
'Fall Gold' **Y**
'Golden Harvest' **Y, H**
'Heritage' **R**

'Autumn Bliss'

KEY
Bf *Black fruit*
R *Red fruit*
Pu *Purple fruit*
Y *Yellow fruit*
H *Notably hardy*

ESTABLISHED RASPBERRIES, PRUNING AFTER FRUITING

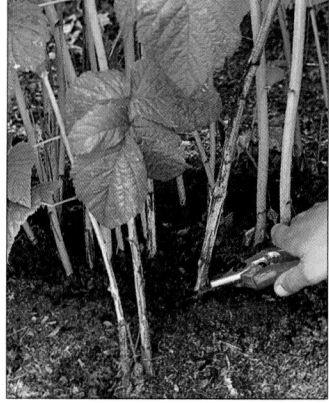

1 *When all the fruit has been picked, cut back all the fruited canes to ground level.*

2 *Tie the current season's strongest canes to the support wires when about 3ft (90cm) tall, spacing them 4in (10cm) apart. Here the continuous lacing method is used.*

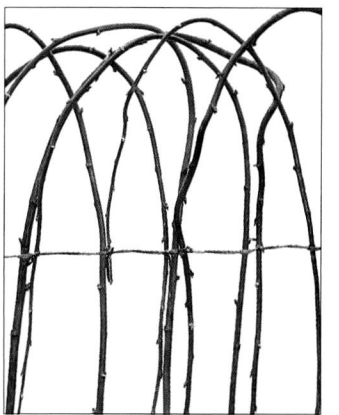

3 *At the end of the growing season, loop any tall canes over the top wire and tie them in.*

SPRING PRUNING

Before the growing season begins, tip prune all the canes to a healthy bud. Wherever possible, the cut should be made about 6in (15cm) above the top supporting wire.

Detach the fruit from the central plug and the stalk; fruits for exhibiting should be picked complete with stalk, however. Remove and discard diseased or damaged fruits promptly to prevent the spread of infection to healthy fruits.

Propagation

In late fall, select and mark strong suckers that are growing away from the main fruiting row, then lift and replant them while they are dormant. Make sure they are from plants that are known to be healthy and free-bearing; where doubt exists, use certified virus-free canes from fruit nurseries instead.

PROPAGATING BY SUCKERS

Lift suckers carefully in fall and sever them from the parent plant. Remove any remaining foliage. Make sure the suckers are healthy, and replant where new stock is required. Water in thoroughly.

Fall-fruiting raspberries

These should be sited in a sunny, sheltered position where the plants will quickly become established and the fruits should ripen in as short a time as possible. The fruits are borne freely on the upper part of the current season's canes. Planting and cultivation requirements are as for summer-fruiting raspberries.

Pruning of fall-fruiting raspberries is carried out in late winter before growth starts; the fruited canes are all cut down to the ground to stimulate new canes, which will fruit in the fall.

LATE-WINTER PRUNING
Before new growth starts, cut down all the canes to ground level. Fruit will be produced in fall on the new season's canes.

Blackcurrants (*Ribes nigrum*)

Blackcurrants thrive only in cool-temperate regions. The bushes flower early and so are prone to cold damage on exposed sites. They fruit in mid-summer. (In parts of the US their cultivation is prohibited because they are hosts for a rust disease on white pine.) Jostaberries, a hybrid between blackcurrants and gooseberries, are cultivated in the same way.

Site and planting

The ground should be well prepared before planting to provide the best conditions for the continual production of new fruiting shoots. Remove all weeds from the site before planting, and dig in plenty of manure or garden compost.

Site
Choose a sunny site, sheltered from cold winds; some shade is tolerated. Protect blackcurrants from spring frosts if necessary (see COLD AND WIND PROTECTION, pp.604–05). Blackcurrants grow in a range of soils, but deep, moisture-retentive soil is most suitable. Avoid wet, poorly drained ground. A pH of 6.5–7 is preferable; lime very acidic soils (see p.619). Blackcurrants are self-fertile.

Planting
Plant disease-free bushes from certified stock. Bushes sold under certification programs are normally two years old, but one-year-old plants from disease-free stock are also ideal. Planting in late fall is preferable; blackcurrants may be planted throughout the winter in mild areas. Always handle plants

carefully to avoid damaging the basal buds. Space the bushes 4–5ft (1.2–1.5m) apart, with the same distance between rows. After planting, cut down all the shoots to one bud to encourage strong, new growth.

Routine care

In spring, apply a mulch of well-rotted manure as well as nitrogen and potassium fertilizers at a rate of 1oz/sq yd (35g/sq m). If manure is not available, increase the amount of fertilizer (see "Care of soft fruits," p.420) and mulch around the base of bushes with compost or leaf mold to conserve soil moisture.

Water in dry weather, but not as the fruits ripen, since this may cause the skins to split. Net bushes to protect ripening fruits from birds.

Pests and diseases
Sawfly larvae (p.639), aphids (p.639), and gall mites (p.644) may affect blackcurrants. Gray mold/

Botrytis (p.650), powdery mildew (p.650), and fungal leaf spots (p.641) may also be troublesome.

Pruning and training

Regular pruning is essential to maintain high yields. Most of the fruits are borne on shoots produced the previous season. Pruning, together with adequate feeding, encourages strong, new shoots to develop.

Cut all stems to one bud above ground level after planting. The following year, remove downward-pointing or weak shoots. Thereafter, prune established bushes before late winter by cutting to the base a quarter to one-third of two-year-old wood, and any older, weak wood. No tip pruning is required. New shoots are pale tan, two-year-old wood is gray, and older wood black.

If a bush needs rejuvenating, cut out a greater proportion of the old wood, retaining only those branches from which strong, young shoots

NEW AND FRUITED SHOOTS

Pale new shoot

Dark fruited wood

have developed. If few shoots develop yet the bush is healthy, cut down the entire plant to just above ground level in winter. Most bushes then rejuvenate well if fed and mulched, but one year's crop is sacrificed. The new shoots may need thinning, with the strongest retained. After ten years or so it is better to replace a bush than to try to rejuvenate it.

BLACKCURRANT BUSH
YEAR 1, WINTER PRUNING

Immediately after planting, cut back all stems to 1 bud above soil level.

YEAR 2, WINTER PRUNING

The bush should develop 7 or 8 strong, new-shoots. Cut back any weak or low-growing shoots to about 1in (2.5cm) above soil level to encourage new growth from the base.

ESTABLISHED BUSH, PRUNING AFTER FRUITING

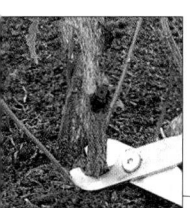

Cut out the old wood and a quarter to one-third of 2-year-old stems to stimulate new growth.

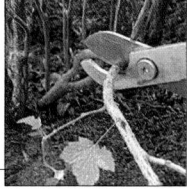

Remove any weak, damaged, or low-growing shoots, cutting close to the main stem.

RECOMMENDED BLACKCURRANTS

Early
'Amos Black'
'Boskoop Giant'

'Ben Lomond'

Midseason
'Ben Lomond'
'Ben More'
'Climax'
'Crandall'
'Wellington XXX'

Late
'Consort'
'Raven'
'Tinker'   'Ben More'

Very late
'Champion'

Harvesting and storing

Blackcurrants are borne on fruit stems in bunches. Harvest the fruits when dry and ripe but still firm. Remove the whole bunch, not the individual fruits, which may otherwise be damaged. Early-ripening cultivars soon shed their fruits, but late-ripening cultivars retain their fruits much longer. Fruits may be either eaten fresh or stored by canning, preserving, or freezing.

Propagation

Blackcurrants are propagated from hardwood cuttings (see p.428) taken from healthy bushes in fall. Retain all buds on the cuttings to encourage basal shoots to grow.

HARDWOOD CUTTINGS

Insert 8–10in (20–25cm) cuttings in a trench, leaving 2 buds exposed.

Redcurrants and whitecurrants (*Ribes sativum*)

These fruits require a cool climate. Whitecurrants are a color variant of redcurrants. As with blackcurrants (opposite), cultivation is prohibited in parts of the US.

Site and planting

Redcurrants and whitecurrants need a sunny site but tolerate some shade; in hot climates, some shade may be necessary. Protect plants from winds to prevent stems from breaking, and in high temperatures to prevent scorch (see p.643).

Prepare the soil well before planting, as for blackcurrants (opposite). Heavier, moisture-retentive, but well-drained soils are preferable. Potassium deficiency may occur on very sandy soil. All cultivars are self-fertile.

When buying young bushes, make sure that the plants are from healthy stock that bears well. Plant in fall or winter: space bushes 4–5ft (1.2–1.5m) apart, cordons at 12in (30cm), and fans at 6ft (2m).

Routine care

For details of care, see blackcurrants (opposite). Maintain high potassium levels by applying potassium sulfate if necessary (muriate of potash may scorch the foliage).

Pests and diseases
Net the plants throughout the winter to prevent birds from damaging the buds. If the buds are damaged, delay winter pruning until just before bud break, and then prune to healthy buds. Aphids (p.639), sawfly larvae (p.639), gray mold/*Botrytis* (p.650), and spider mites (p.640) may affect plants.

Pruning and training

Redcurrants and whitecurrants are normally grown as open-center bushes but may be trained on wires as cordons, double cordons, or fans. Fruits develop on spurs produced by pruning back the sideshoots.

Bush
A one-year-old bush should have two or three strong, young shoots; shorten these by half in late winter. Remove any that are less than 4in (10cm) from the ground to produce a short leg.

The following winter, shorten new growth by half to form the main branches, pruning to an outward-pointing bud. Prune any sideshoots

REDCURRANT BUSH
YEAR 1, WINTER PRUNING

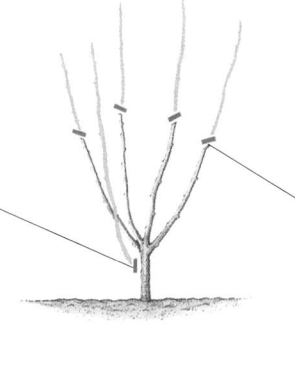

Remove any sideshoots growing within 4in (10cm) of soil level by cutting flush with the stem. This will form a short leg at the base.

Prune each stem to an outward-facing bud (or to an upright shoot) about halfway along its length.

YEAR 2, WINTER PRUNING

To form the permanent branches, shorten leaders and sideshoots by half of the new growth, cutting to outward-facing buds.

Cut back to 1 bud any sideshoots crowding the center or growing downward.

ESTABLISHED BUSH, WINTER PRUNING

Prune sideshoots to 1 bud.

Cut 2–3in (5–7cm) from the tips of the leaders to stimulate new growth the following season.

growing inward or downward to one bud. Prune established bushes by cutting back sideshoots to one bud and tip pruning main branches.

Cordon

Single cordons are usually trained vertically. Set up wires at 24in (60cm) and 4ft (1.2m) from the ground. Select a main shoot on a one-year-old plant and train it against a stake;

prune back the shoot by half, then cut back all other shoots to one bud.

In summer, prune sideshoots to five leaves of new growth. Shorten these sideshoots to one or two buds in winter, and prune the leader by a quarter of the new growth. When the leader reaches the top of its support, trim it to one bud. A double cordon is developed by training two shoots at about 30° to the ground as for

apples (see "Forming a double cordon," p.435); they are subsequently trained vertically when 12in (30cm) apart. Each branch is then pruned as for a single cordon.

Fan

Fan-trained redcurrants and whitecurrants are established as for a peach fan (see p.447). Each branch should then be pruned as for a cordon.

Harvesting and storing

Harvest redcurrants and whitecurrants as for blackcurrants. The plants tend to retain ripe fruits a little longer than most blackcurrants. Fruits may be canned, preserved, or frozen.

Propagation

Take hardwood cuttings in early fall. Use young shoots 12–15in (30–38cm) long, and remove all but the top three or four buds, to produce a plant with a short stem.

Insert the cuttings in moist, fertile soil, burying them by about half their length, and firm well. Once rooted, transplant the young plants to their final positions.

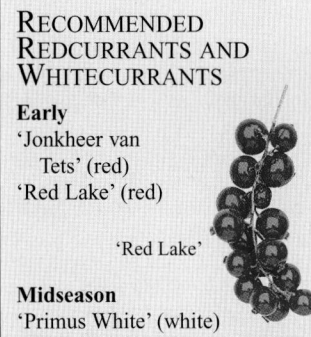

RECOMMENDED REDCURRANTS AND WHITECURRANTS

Early
'Jonkheer van Tets' (red)
'Red Lake' (red)

'Red Lake'

Midseason
'Primus White' (white)
'White Imperial' (white)
'Wilder' (red)

'White Imperial'

Late
'Cherry' (red)

HARDWOOD CUTTINGS

Cuttings should be 12in (30cm) long. Retain only the top few buds.

REDCURRANT CORDON
YEAR 1, WINTER PRUNING

Cut back the leader by half of its new growth to stimulate new sideshoots.

If there are any sideshoots at planting, cut them back to 1 bud.

YEAR 1, SUMMER PRUNING

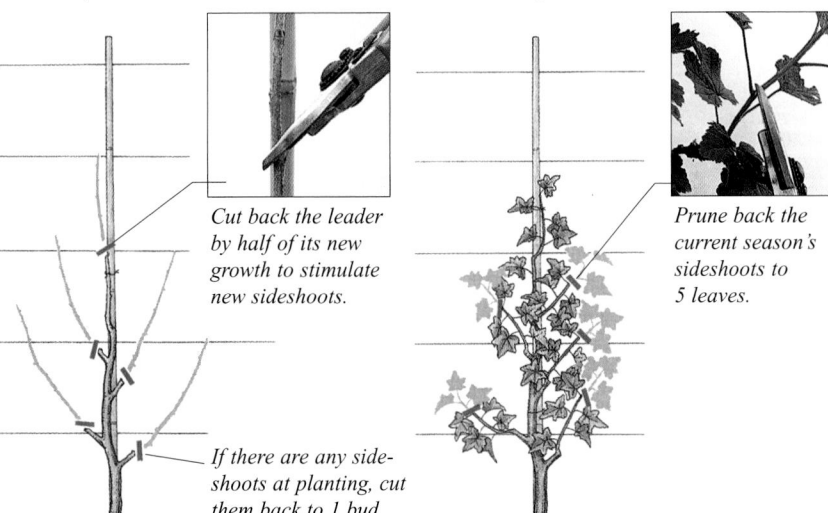

Prune back the current season's sideshoots to 5 leaves.

ESTABLISHED CORDON, WINTER PRUNING

If the leader has reached the top wire, prune to 1 bud; otherwise. prune it back by a quarter of the summer's growth.

Trim back to the point of origin any shoots growing less than 4in (10cm) from the ground.

Cut back all the sideshoots to 1 or 2 buds to encourage the development of new spurs near the main stem.

Gooseberries (*Ribes uva-crispa*)

Gooseberries are easy to grow but, like currants (also *Ribes*), need cool conditions and, if summer temperatures are high, adequate shade. Fruits ripen yellow, red, white, or green, depending on the cultivar. Methods of cultivation, pruning, and training are similar to those used for redcurrants.

Site and planting
Growing conditions and planting distances are as for redcurrants (see p.469). All cultivars are self-fertile. As with blackcurrants (p.468), cultivation is restricted in parts of the US, since the plants host a rust disease that affects white pine.

Routine care
General maintenance is largely as for blackcurrants (see p.468). Gooseberries require high potassium levels and regular mulching, ideally with well-rotted manure. New shoots on young bushes are vulnerable to breakage and need protection from

strong winds. If the crop is heavy, thin the fruits in late spring.

Pests and diseases
Deer (p.656) may cause severe bud loss, so protect plants where feasible. If the buds have been attacked, delay winter pruning until bud break.

then prune to live buds. Plants may be affected by powdery mildew (p.650), which attacks the tips of shoots; sawfly larvae (p.639); and bacterial or fungal leaf spots (p.641).

Pruning and training

Young plants may be trained as bushes, cordons, or fans as for redcurrants. A number of gooseberry cultivars, such as 'Leveller', have a natural drooping habit, however. To prevent stems from trailing to the ground, prune to upward-pointing buds, particularly when training young bushes.

GOOSEBERRY BUSH
YEAR 1, WINTER PRUNING

Prune back all the shoots by a half to three-quarters to an outward-facing bud.

ESTABLISHED BUSH, REGULATED PRUNING, WINTER

Cut out older branches to prevent overcrowding and to maintain an open center.

The bush should have mainly young shoots, evenly spaced, pointing up- or outward.

ESTABLISHED BUSH, SPUR PRUNING, WINTER

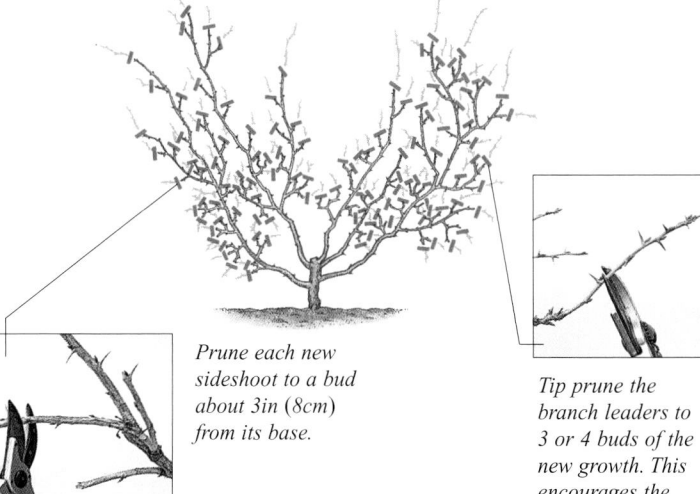

Prune each new sideshoot to a bud about 3in (8cm) from its base.

Tip prune the branch leaders to 3 or 4 buds of the new growth. This encourages the formation of spurs.

Bush For initial pruning, see redcurrants (p.469); aim to create an open-center bush on a stem 4–6in (10–15cm) long. Established bushes may be pruned by regulated or spur pruning in winter.

Regulated pruning is the simpler method: remove low, crowded, and crossing shoots to maintain well-spaced growth at the center of the bush. Also remove any old, unproductive branches and select new, young shoots to replace them.

Spur pruning is more labor intensive: all the sideshoots are shortened to a suitable bud 3in (8cm)

GOOSEBERRY STANDARD

from the main branches. The branch leaders also need to be tip pruned.

Standard Cultivars to be trained as standards are grafted onto *Ribes odoratum* or *R. divaricatum* stock. Select one shoot of the rootstock and train it vertically, keeping any sideshoots short. It will take about three years to grow to a suitable height. When the stem has thickened and reached about 3¹/₂–4ft (1.1–1.2m), trim off the sideshoots and graft on the selected cultivar using whip-and-tongue grafting (see p.427). Use a strong stake to support the stem. The scion will develop and branch naturally the following summer. The next winter, establish the framework as for a bush, and then prune and train in the same way.

Cordon and fan These are trained as for redcurrants (see opposite). Once established, prune in summer, reducing new sideshoots to five leaves. In winter, shorten shoots to 3in (8cm) and tip prune leaders.

Harvesting and storing

Fruits should ripen by midsummer. Gooseberries for cooking may be picked green as part of thinning, but allow dessert-quality cultivars to ripen fully for the best flavor, ensuring that they are protected from

RECOMMENDED GOOSEBERRIES

Early
'Abundance' (red) **A**
'Catherine' (yellow) **A**
'Early Sulphur' (yellow) **A**

'Downing'

Midseason
'Clark' (red) **Rm, E**
'Colossal' (green) **E**
'Downing' (green) **A**
'Hinnomaeki' (red) **A**
'Leveller' (yellow) **E**
'Pixwell' (red-purple) **Th, A**
'Poorman' (red) **Rm, A**
'Welcome' (red) **A**
'Whinham's Industry' (red) **E**

'Whinham's Industry'

Late
'Captivator' (red) **Th, A**
'Fredonia' (red) **A**
'Lancashire Lad' (red) **Rm, E**
'Ross' (red) **A**
'White Lion' (white) **E**

KEY
Rm *Some resistance to mildew*
Th *Nearly thornless*
A *American cultivar*
E *European cultivar*

birds. Yellow-, white-, and red-berried cultivars should be left to ripen to their full color before they are picked. All freeze well.

Propagation

Layering is the easiest method. American gooseberries are easy to root from hardwood cuttings; the European varieties may take two years. When the rooted cutting is lifted, rub off all low buds and sideshoots; otherwise, troublesome suckers will develop.

HARDWOOD CUTTINGS

1 *In early fall, take cuttings of well-ripened young shoots. Trim to 12–15in (30–38cm) with an angled cut above a bud at the top and a straight cut at the base. Insert in a trench to half their length.*

2 *The following fall, carefully lift the rooted cuttings. Remove basal buds or shoots less than 4in (10cm) from the base (see inset) before transplanting the young plants.*

Blueberries (*Vaccinium corymbosum* and *V. ashei*)

Highbush blueberries (*Vaccinium corymbosum*) are derived from the American wild blueberry. They produce clusters of dark purplish blue fruit with a gray bloom. Blueberries require a cool, moist climate and 700–1,200 hours below 45°F (7°C), except for cultivars adapted to very warm areas (for example, 'O'Neal'). All need very acidic soil. Highbush blueberries grow to a height of 4¹/₂–6ft (1.3–2m) and are deciduous, with striking fall color.

Rabbit-eye blueberries (*Vaccinium ashei*) are grown in the same way as the highbush group but tolerate less acidic soils and drier conditions. They are cultivated mainly in the US and Australia. The fruits are smaller and grittier than highbush blueberries.

Bearing, in mid- to late summer, is light at first, but yields of 5lb (2.25kg) of fruit per bush may be obtained after five or six years, and considerably more on older bushes. Although blueberries are self-fertile, the plants produce larger crops when two or more cultivars are planted close together.

Site and planting
Blueberries need a sunny location, although they tolerate some shade. The soil must be well drained. Clear all perennial weeds from the site before planting, and if the soil is alkaline, correct this by mixing a 6in (15cm) layer of acidic compost with the existing soil to a depth of at least 2ft (60cm). Alternatively, apply flowers of sulfur at a rate of 2–4oz/sq yd (50–120g/sq m).

Blueberries may also be grown in large pots or tubs with a diameter of 12–15in (30–38cm), filled with acidic soil mix.

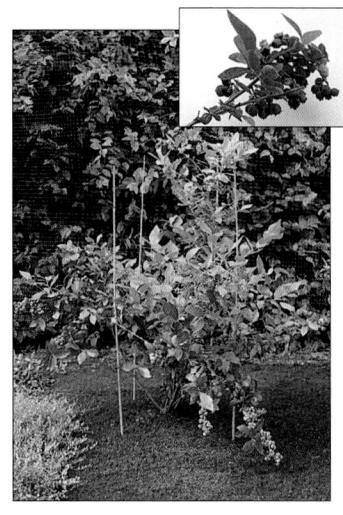

HIGHBUSH BLUEBERRY BUSH

Plant in late fall or early spring, spacing bushes 5ft (1.5m) apart. Cover the roots with 1–2in (2.5–5cm) of soil, and mulch with acidic compost or leaf mold. Growing a mixture of cultivars results in better fertilization and heavier crops.

Routine care
To promote growth and bearing and to maintain acidity, apply a dressing each spring of ammonium sulfate at 1oz/sq yd (35g/sq m), potassium sulfate at 1oz/sq yd (35g/sq m), and bone meal at 3oz/sq yd (105g/sq m). Keep plants mulched with acidic compost, and water with rainwater. Avoid root disturbance when weeding.

Pests and diseases
The fruits may be eaten by birds, so provide protection by netting the bushes (see "Protection from animals," p.421). Other pests and diseases rarely cause trouble.

ESTABLISHED BLUEBERRY BUSH, WINTER PRUNING

Cut weak or unproductive shoots back to where a strong new shoot can take over.

Cut older, nonfruiting branches to ground level to stimulate new basal shoots.

Cut back any low or downward-pointing branches to their point of origin or to a branch growing in the required direction.

Pruning and training
Blueberries fruit on two- or three-year-old wood. New bushes need little pruning for two or three years, but cut out weak shoots to provide a strong basic framework.

Thereafter, prune to ensure regular production of new shoots from the base, as for blackcurrants (see p.468), by cutting out some of the oldest wood each year.

Harvesting and storing
The fruits ripen over a period of several weeks. Pick over the bushes carefully, harvesting only the ripe fruits, which part easily from the cluster. Blueberries may be successfully stored for later use by preserving, canning, or freezing.

Propagation
Take 4–6in (10–15cm) softwood cuttings in midsummer, dip them in hormone rooting powder, and then insert them in an acidic, peat/sand rooting medium. Place the cuttings in a propagator until rooted, then transplant to a larger pot. Harden off before planting out.

RECOMMENDED HIGHBUSH BLUEBERRIES

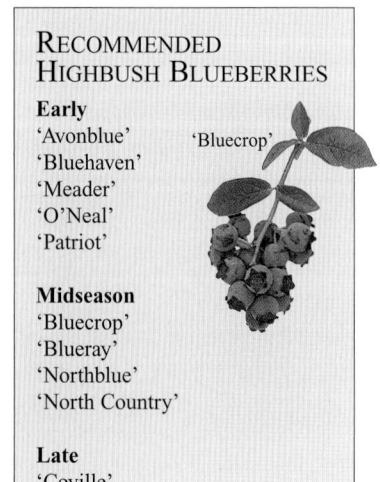

'Bluecrop'

Early
'Avonblue'
'Bluehaven'
'Meader'
'O'Neal'
'Patriot'

Midseason
'Bluecrop'
'Blueray'
'Northblue'
'North Country'

Late
'Coville'
'Elizabeth'

BLUEBERRY SOFTWOOD CUTTINGS

1 *Select suitable softwood material and take cuttings at least 4in (10cm) long. Cut just above a leaf joint.*

2 *Trim the base of each cutting just below a node with a sharp knife, and remove the leaves from the lower third of the cuttings. Dip the ends of the cuttings in hormone rooting powder.*

3 *Prepare a pot of acidic rooting medium. Make holes with a dibber, then insert each cutting so that the basal leaves are just above the medium. Water, label, and place the pot in a propagator.*

Tender fruits

Most tender fruits originate from tropical and subtropical regions, where they thrive in the warm, dry conditions. Apart from olives, which need to be treated to remove their bitterness, many may be eaten straight from the tree, or stored for a short period of time in suitable conditions. Members of the citrus family that are too acidic for eating, such as lemons and limes, are grown either for their juice or for use in preserves and marmalades. Since tender fruits are generally grown in hot climates, where the soil may be lacking in nutrients, it is important to prepare the site adequately when planting: an extra 4–6oz (110–80g) of slow-release fertilizer forked into the bottom of the planting hole will help the plants establish quickly.

In cool-temperate climates, some tender fruits may still be grown, in containers or under cover, as long as the correct temperature and humidity levels are provided. Although many do not consistently ripen their fruits under cover, they nevertheless make attractive ornamentals.

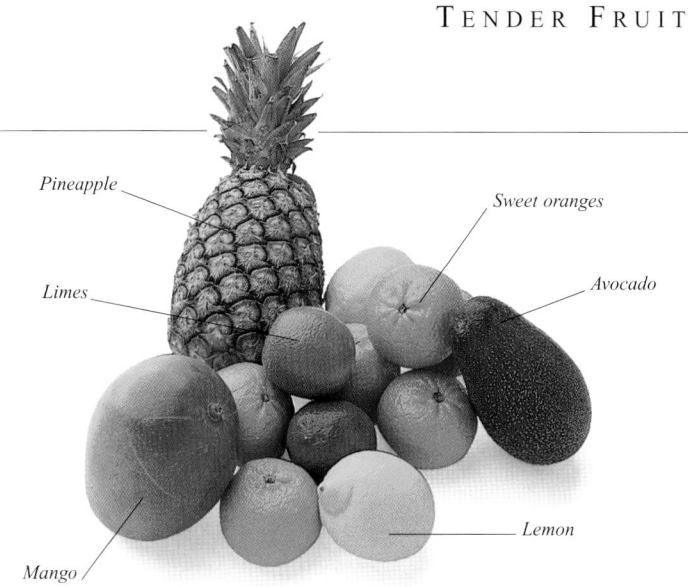

Pineapple

Sweet oranges

Limes

Avocado

Mango

Lemon

Pineapples (*Ananas comosus*)

Pineapples are tropical perennials that produce terminal fruits, each composed of up to 200 seedless fruitlets. For best results they need full sun and temperatures of 64–80°F (18–30°C) with humidity of 70–80 percent. Cultivar groups include the Cayenne Group, the Queen Group, and the Spanish Group; the Spanish has the sweetest flavor.

Site and planting
Select a sunny site that is sheltered from strong winds. Pineapples tolerate a wide range of soils but prefer a sandy, medium loam with a pH of 5–6.5. Plant suckers about 12in (30cm) apart, with 24in (60cm) between rows, or at a spacing of 20in (50cm) each way.

Routine care
Use a general-purpose fertilizer with medium potassium and high nitrogen levels at intervals of two to three months, at a rate of 2oz (50g) per plant. Correct any iron and zinc deficiencies by spraying with a 2 percent solution of ferrous or zinc sulfate. Water pineapples regularly in dry weather, and apply an organic mulch to conserve soil moisture.

Pests and diseases
Pests that may affect pineapples include mealybugs (p.640), root-knot nematodes (p.652), scale insects (p.641), spider mites (p.640), and thrips (p.640).

The most serious disease affecting pineapple plants in the open is heart-rot, caused by *Phytophthora cinnamoni* and *P. parasitica*, fungi that often affect pineapples grown in wet conditions. Since this is difficult to treat, it is advisable to guard against infection by planting resistant cultivars where these are available. All suckers that are required for propagation should be dipped in a fungicide, since the fungus enters through wounds.

Growing under cover
Plant rooted pineapple cuttings in well-prepared beds with good drainage, or use pots at least 12in (30cm) in diameter. Use a soil mix with a high organic content, and apply a liquid fertilizer every three to four weeks. Maintain a temperature of at least 68°F (20°C) and humidity of about 70 percent. Water regularly and thoroughly, particularly while young plants are establishing.

Harvesting and storing
Harvest the fruits when they begin to turn yellow by cutting the stem 1–2in (2.5–5cm) below each fruit. Pineapples may be stored for up to three weeks at 46°F (8°C) and at 90 percent humidity.

Propagation
The terminal crown shoot may be used as a cutting; remove it with about 1/2in (1cm) of the fruit attached. Pineapples may also be

PROPAGATING PINEAPPLES FROM SUCKERS

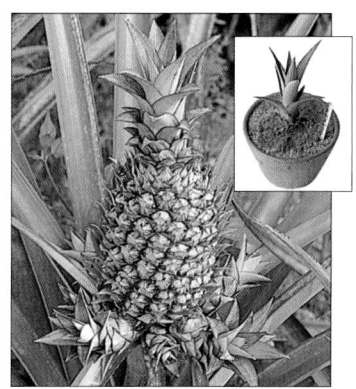

Sever basal shoots or suckers and allow to dry before inserting in a sandy rooting medium (see inset).

propagated by suckers that arise from the leaf axils, the base of the stem, or below the fruit; these may be detached with a sharp knife. Dip the cut surfaces of shoots in a fungicide, then allow them to dry for several days. Remove the lower leaves and insert the cuttings in pots of sandy rooting medium. Pot them on into 6in (15cm) pots when rooted.

PINEAPPLE

PROPAGATING PINEAPPLES FROM THE CROWN SHOOT

1 *Scoop out the crown shoot of a ripe pineapple with a sharp knife, making sure you do not cut through the base of the shoot. Dip the wound in fungicide, then allow to dry for several days.*

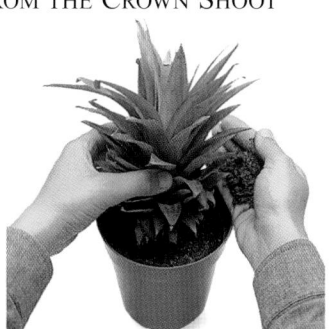

2 *Insert the prepared cutting into a pot of sandy rooting medium and maintain at a temperature of at least 64°F (18°C). The cutting should be rooted and ready to pot on within a few weeks.*

RECOMMENDED PINEAPPLES

Cayenne Group
'Hilo'
'Smooth Cayenne'
'Sugar Baby'

Queen Group
'Natal Queen'
'Ripley Queen'

Spanish Group
'Red Spanish'
'Singapore Spanish'

473

Papayas (*Carica papaya*)

Papayas are slender, generally single-stemmed, tropical trees growing up to 12–15ft (4–5m), with a spread of 3–6ft (1–2m) at the crown. The fruits may be up to 8in (20cm) long when mature. Temperatures of 72–82°F (22–8°C) with humidity of 60–70 percent are normally required for fruiting; some cultivars will withstand temperatures as low as 59°F (15°C), although flowering and fruiting may then be poor.

Site and planting
Choose a warm, sunny site with protection from strong winds. Papayas require fertile, well-drained

RECOMMENDED PAPAYAS
'Fairchild' **D**
'Higgins' **Mo**
'Kapoho' **Mo**
'Solo' **Mo**
'Sunrise' **Mo**

'Higgins'

'Sunset' **Mo**
'Waimanalo' **Mo**
'X-77' **Mo**

KEY
D *Dioecious*
Mo *Monoecious*

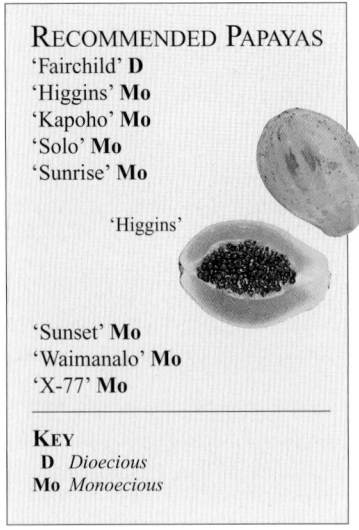

soil with a pH of 6–7; good drainage is essential, since the trees are sensitive to waterlogging.

Many cultivars of papaya are dioecious, with male and female flowers produced on separate plants, but monoecious cultivars are sometimes available. One male tree is usually sufficient to pollinate five or six female trees. Pollination is normally by insects and wind. Plant at a spacing of 8–10ft (2.5–3m).

Routine care
Apply a general-purpose, balanced fertilizer, 2lb 3oz–3lb 6oz (1–1.5kg) per tree per year, in two or three separate dressings during the growing season. Water regularly in dry conditions, and conserve moisture with an organic mulch. Papayas may be affected by viruses and nematodes after three or four years; if this happens, replace diseased papayas with seedlings or young plants of named cultivars.

Pests and diseases
Common pests in the open are root-knot nematodes (p.652); papaya diseases include anthracnose (see "Fungal leaf spots," p.641), bunchy top virus (see "Viruses," p.642), and damping off of seedlings (p.651). Papaya trees grown under cover may also be attacked by aphids (p.639), thrips (p.640), whiteflies (p.639), and mealybugs (p.640).

Growing under cover
In temperate areas, papayas may be grown successfully under cover if adequate light and temperature levels are provided. Raise seedlings or cuttings as described under "Propagation," below. Transplant them when they are 8–10in (20–25cm) tall into prepared beds, or pots with a minimum diameter of 14in (35cm). Use a fertile soil mix, to which a slow-release fertilizer has been added. Maintain a temperature of at least 72°F (22°C) and humidity of 60–70 percent. Apply a liquid fertilizer or light dressings of fertilizer with medium to high nitrogen content every three to four weeks. The plants should be watered regularly.

Pruning and training
Remove any lateral branches, since these are unproductive. After fruiting, prune to 12in (30cm) from the ground; of the new shoots that arise, select the strongest as the new leader and cut back the others.

Harvesting and storing
Harvest the fruits when they are orange to red. They may be stored at 50–55°F (10–13°C) with 70 percent humidity for up to 14 days.

Propagation
Seed is the usual method of propagation. Sow the seed under cover in trays or, preferably, in bottomless

PAPAYA TREE

pots 2½–3½in (6–9cm) in diameter. Handle the seedlings carefully, since papayas are sensitive to root disturbance. Harden them off, then plant them out when they are 12–18in (30–45cm) tall. To obtain adequate numbers of female plants when dioecious cultivars are used, plant seedlings in clumps of three or four, thinning to one female plant after flowering begins. Monoecious seedlings may be planted singly.

Cuttings are usually obtained by pruning mature trees to 12–16in (30–40cm) from the ground and using the new shoots as cuttings. Dip their bases in hormone rooting powder, and grow on under cover.

Citrus (*Citrus* spp.), including kumquats (*Fortunella* spp.)

The genus *Citrus* includes oranges, lemons, and a number of other edible species (see opposite). Citrus form small, widely branching trees on trunks of 20–24in (50–60cm) in circumference. The trees will reach a height of 10–30ft (3–10m) and a spread of 15–25ft (5–8m). Limes are the most compact; grapefruits are among the largest and most vigorous. Lemon trees have a more upright habit than the other species. Also discussed here is the kumquat, formerly included within the genus *Citrus* but now classified as *Fortunella*. Its cultivation requirements are similar to those of *Citrus*.

Citrus is a subtropical genus. All species and hybrids are evergreen and have aromatic leaves. For optimum growth, they require a temperature of 58–86°F (15–30°C), although most species will survive short periods at 32°F (0°C). They thrive at altitudes of 320ft (100m)

or above, with humidity levels of 60–70 percent, unless otherwise stated. Flowering is not seasonal but occurs during warm periods with regular rainfall; flowers and fruits may coincide. Many species of citrus make excellent plants for growing in containers under cover in temperate areas.

Site and planting

Citrus prefer a sunny exposure and should be protected by windbreaks in exposed areas. They tolerate a wide range of soils but do best in fertile, well-drained, slightly acidic soils (pH 6–6.5). Young citrus respond well to highly fertile soil.

Rootstocks
Sweet orange may be used, since it is compatible with all widely grown citrus species and cultivars. Rough

lemon rootstocks produce early-bearing, vigorous trees resistant to tristeza (quick decline) viruses, but their fruits may have thick rinds and a low acid and sugar content. Sour orange is also a good universal rootstock, but it is susceptible to tristeza viruses.

Trifoliate orange (*Poncirus trifoliata*) is a dwarfing rootstock that is suitable for cooler areas. It has some resistance to nematodes but is not compatible with certain cultivars of lemon. Cleopatra mandarin and Rangpur lime are also used as rootstocks. Seedling rootstocks may also be raised – for those details, see "Propagation," opposite.

Pollination
Most citrus, including sweet orange, are self-fertile, so a pollinator is not normally required; many, for instance the 'Washington' sweet orange, also produce seedless fruits.

Planting
Planting distances vary between 15ft (5m) and 30ft (10m) each way, depending on the vigor of the species or cultivar chosen, so seek advice from the nursery when purchasing a tree.

SWEET ORANGE TREE

Citrus are sensitive to waterlogging, so on a site where the soil is not sufficiently well drained, plant each tree on a slight mound, 2–3in (5–7cm) high, to allow any excess water to run off.

Routine care

During the first few years, give citrus trees a balanced fertilizer that has a high nitrogen and medium potassium level at a rate of 2lb 3oz (1kg) per tree per year. The fertilizer should be given in two or three doses, applied at regular intervals around the base of each tree, when the trees are in active growth. Double the quantity of fertilizer after five years. A mulch helps retain moisture.

Remove all weeds around the bases of the trees, and water thoroughly in dry weather, particularly when the flowers or fruits are developing. The nonseasonal habit of fruiting makes fruit thinning unnecessary. Remove any suckers.

Pests and diseases

Various mealybugs (p.640), scale insects (p.641), thrips (p.640), spider mites (p.640), aphids (p.639), root and crown rots (see "*Phytophthora* root rots," p.646), fungal leaf spots (p.641), and scab (p.650) may affect citrus grown in the open and under cover. Root-knot nematodes (p.652) may be serious pests on some soils. In the tropics and subtropics, fruit flies may be a problem.

Many citrus species and cultivars may be infected with tristeza virus, which is spread by aphids and causes stem pitting on grapefruits, limes, and citrons. Infected trees will lose vigor and produce small fruits. The virus is most likely to affect cultivars that are budded onto sour orange rootstocks. Spray for aphids, or use alternative rootstocks.

Growing under cover

In temperate areas, several cultivars of sweet orange, tangerine, lemon, and lime, as well as the Seville orange and kumquat, may be grown as ornamentals under cover, although they may not be relied on to bear fruit. Before planting, prepare the beds well, or use large containers, at least 2ft (60cm) in diameter, filled with a nutrient-rich soil mix. Maintain a minimum temperature of 68°F (20°C) with at least 75 percent humidity, and water the citrus plants regularly. Apply a liquid fertilizer each month once the young trees are well established.

Pruning and training

Shorten the main branches of newly planted trees by one-third in the first year. This encourages lateral growth and produces a rounded shape. After fruiting, prune only to remove dead, diseased, or crossing branches and any that touch the soil. Citrus may also be trained as standards or half-standards (see p.433), particularly if grown as ornamentals.

Harvesting and storing

Citrus fruits may take from six to eight months, or even longer, from fruit set to ripen, depending on the climate (the lower the temperature, the longer the period required). In areas of low sunshine, mature citrus fruits may remain green.

Harvest the fruits when they have ripened by cutting them at the fruit stalk with pruners or a sharp knife, or by pulling the fruit stalk from the tree with a slight twist. Undamaged fruits may be stored for several weeks at 38–42°F (4–6°C).

Propagation

Some citrus may be raised from seed. Most citrus seeds are polyembryonic and therefore clonal, reproducing characteristics of the parent tree. The quality of fruits from non-polyembryonic cultivars is variable. For named cultivars the usual means of propagation is by budding.

To raise citrus trees from seed, use fresh seed, sowing it in trays or pots of sowing medium at a depth of 1¼–2in (3–5cm). Water the seeds frequently and maintain a temperature of 77–90°F (25–32°C). When the seedlings are large enough to handle, prick them out into 4 or 4½in (10 or 12cm) pots. When they are 8–12in (20–30cm) high, transplant them into 8–12in (20–30cm) pots, or plant them out, after hardening them off. Alternatively, repot seedlings into 10–15in (25–38cm) pots and plant in the open when they are 2–3ft (60–90cm) tall.

T-budding (see p.427) is the usual method of propagating citrus vegetatively. Use seedling citrus stocks with stems ½in (1cm) in diameter. After three to four weeks, remove the budding tape and cut the stock growth above the budded area halfway across. When the bud shoot is 1in (2.5cm) long, the stock growth above the budded shoot may be removed entirely.

RIPE SWEET ORANGES

Species of citrus

Limes (*Citrus aurantiifolia*)

Limes fall into three groups. Key limes, also known as West Indian or Mexican limes, have small, thin-skinned fruits with seeds; fruits are used when the skin is yellow. 'Tahiti'-type limes (actually *C. latifolia*) are larger and seedless. The third group includes 'Bearss' and other tart limes.

Most limes are grown as seedlings but may also be reproduced by budgrafting onto lemon rootstock.

Sour, Seville, or bitter oranges (*Citrus aurantium*)

The sour, or bitter, orange is used mainly as a rootstock. The fruits, which are used for making marmalade, are about 3in (7cm) in diameter, rounded, with thick peel. They are fairly acidic, but some forms of the species bear fruits of lower citric acid content.

Lemons (*Citrus limon*)

Most lemon cultivars produce seeded fruits that may remain green, rather than turning yellow, even when fully mature. To grow successfully in the open, they require an altitude of 960–1,600ft (300–500m), with little variation in temperature, and need a minimum temperature of 68°F (20°C).

An interesting hybrid between lemon and lime is the "lemonime"; this may be grown in the open in subtropical areas or as an ornamental under cover in temperate areas.

Citrons (*Citrus medica*)

The fruits of the citron are ovoid and yellow, with a thick rind and a rough surface, and may be up to 6in (15cm) long; the pulp is acidic with little juice.

No specific citron cultivars have been recorded. Citrons are grown mainly for their peel, which is usually candied for use in confections.

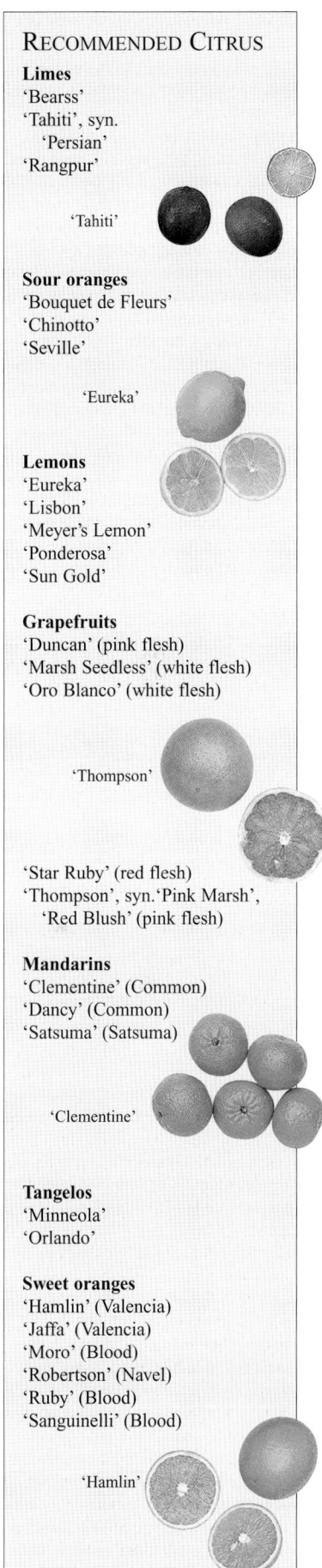

RECOMMENDED CITRUS

Limes
'Bearss'
'Tahiti', syn.
   'Persian'
'Rangpur'

'Tahiti'

Sour oranges
'Bouquet de Fleurs'
'Chinotto'
'Seville'

'Eureka'

Lemons
'Eureka'
'Lisbon'
'Meyer's Lemon'
'Ponderosa'
'Sun Gold'

Grapefruits
'Duncan' (pink flesh)
'Marsh Seedless' (white flesh)
'Oro Blanco' (white flesh)

'Thompson'

'Star Ruby' (red flesh)
'Thompson', syn. 'Pink Marsh',
   'Red Blush' (pink flesh)

Mandarins
'Clementine' (Common)
'Dancy' (Common)
'Satsuma' (Satsuma)

'Clementine'

Tangelos
'Minneola'
'Orlando'

Sweet oranges
'Hamlin' (Valencia)
'Jaffa' (Valencia)
'Moro' (Blood)
'Robertson' (Navel)
'Ruby' (Blood)
'Sanguinelli' (Blood)

'Hamlin'

'Valencia' (Valencia)
'Washington' (Navel)

Citrons make attractive garden plants; however, in areas where they are not hardy, they may be grown under cover (see p.475).

Grapefruits (*Citrus paradisi*)
The fruits of the grapefruit are large, rounded, up to 4–6in (10–15cm) in diameter, and yellow. Most cultivars are well adapted to growing at or just above sea level, provided the temperature exceeds 77°F (25°C). There are two principal groups of grapefruit in cultivation, one with white pulp, the other with pink flesh, ranging in color to deep red. Seeded and seedless cultivars are available in both grapefruit groups.

Mandarins or tangerines
(*Citrus reticulata*)
Mandarins, or tangerines, generally require temperatures above 64°F (18°C), but very high temperatures may result in loss of fruit quality.

Cross-pollination between trees frequently occurs; this gives rise to fruits with many seeds. Some varieties have a particularly loose skin that makes the fruits easy to peel.

The Satsuma Group is the one most frequently cultivated. The fruits of cultivars in this group are mainly slightly flattened and seedless, with a well-developed orange color and sweet flavor. Some cultivars have a "navel," a miniature fruit that develops at the end of the fruit. The other three groups are the Cleopatra Group, which is widely used as a rootstock but has unpalatable fruits itself; the King Group; and the Common Mandarin Group (which includes the cultivar 'Clementine').

Tangelos and ugli fruits
(*Citrus reticulata* x *C. paradisi*)
These hybrids between the grapefruit and the mandarin inherit characteristics from their parents: the

fruits are larger than those of the mandarin but have easily peeled skin. They may be grown under cover in temperate areas, where they occasionally bear fruit.

Sweet oranges (*Citrus sinensis*)
Most sweet oranges, including the widely grown 'Jaffa' orange, belong to the Valencia (or Common) Group. The fruits are medium to large and spherical to ovoid, with few or no seeds. Oranges in this group may be slightly acidic, but they have an excellent flavor.

Sweet oranges are usually grown from seed, but a few cultivars are propagated vegetatively by budding. Seedlings are also used as rootstocks for grafting with other species. Sweet orange cultivars are classified into three groups: Navel oranges, Blood oranges, and Valencia oranges.

Navel oranges have a small secondary fruit at the main fruit apex

and are usually seedless. They have an excellent flavor and grow well in slightly cooler climates; California is noted for its Navels. Blood oranges are similar, but their pulp, flesh, and juice are red (except when grown at high temperatures).

Two sweet orange crops at different stages of development may be borne on a tree at the same time.

Kumquats (*Fortunella japonica*, *F. margarita*)
Originating in China, kumquats are fairly hardy: they can withstand temperatures down to 23°F (-5°C) for short periods. The fruits, which are eaten unpeeled, are small and yellow. Those of *Fortunella japonica* are rounded in shape, while those of *F. margarita* are ovoid.

The Calamondin (x *Citrofortunella microcarpa*) is a mandarin-kumquat hybrid; it is grown as an ornamental in temperate regions.

Tree tomatoes (*Cyphomandra betacea*)

Also known as tamarillos, tree tomatoes are subtropical trees growing to 10–15ft (3–5m), with a spread of 5–8ft (1.5–2.5m). They are most productive at 68–82°F (20–28°C) with 70 percent humidity. The red, orange, or yellow fruits are ovoid and may be 3in (7.5cm) long.

RIPE TREE TOMATOES

Site and planting
Tree tomatoes require a sunny situation and need protection from the wind in exposed sites. Fertile loam soils produce the best results. Allow a planting distance of about 10ft (3m) each way.

Routine care
A general-purpose fertilizer with medium to high nitrogen should be applied every two to three months at a rate of 4oz (110g) for each tree. Water well during dry periods, and use an organic mulch around the base of the plants to prevent loss of moisture from the soil.

Pests and diseases
Tree tomatoes in the open may be affected by aphids (p.639). They are susceptible to cucumber mosaic virus and potato virus Y (see "Viruses," pp.642 and 651); *Phytophthora palmivora* and *P. infestans* (see "Tomato/potato late blight," p.642) may also cause problems. Under

cover, plants may be attacked by thrips (p.640), whiteflies (p.639), and spider mites (p.640).

Growing under cover
Tree tomatoes may be grown in containers with a diameter of at least 14in (35cm) or in well-prepared beds. Use fertile soil mix, to which a general-purpose fertilizer has been added. Maintain the correct temperatures and humidity, water regularly, and apply a liquid fertilizer every three to four weeks.

Pruning and training
When plants reach a height of 3ft (1m), remove the growing point to encourage branching. Little pruning is needed apart from removing crowded and crossing branches and diseased or dead wood.

Harvesting and storing
Tree tomatoes usually fruit one to two years after planting. Detach the fruits using a sharp knife when they

TREE TOMATOES

start to change color. They may be stored for up to two weeks at a temperature of 39–43°F (4–6°C).

Propagation
Sow seed under cover; pot the seedlings individually into 4in (10cm) pots when they are 1¼–2in (3–5cm) tall. When they reach 6–10in (15–25cm), harden off and plant out in the open. Propagation is also easy from softwood cuttings: select shoots 4–6in (10–15cm) long and use a sandy (but not acidic) medium. Follow the procedure as for blueberries (see p.472).

Loquats (*Eriobotrya japonica*)

A member of the family Rosaceae, the loquat is an attractive evergreen tree growing to 22ft (7m) or more tall, with a spread of about 15ft (5m). Loquats are best suited to a subtropical environment and need a minimum temperature of 59°F (15°C) to flower and fruit regularly. They are grown commercially in both

California and Florida. In cooler climates loquats may be successfully grown under cover, since they are able to withstand relatively low temperatures for short periods. Some cultivars have a low chilling requirement.

Loquats bear clusters of fragrant cream-colored flowers, followed by

bunches of round yellow fruits 1¼–3in (3–8cm) long with tough skins. The pulp is soft and sweet.

Rootstocks for loquats include quince (*Cydonia oblonga*), hawthorns (*Crataegus* spp.), and vigorous seedlings. Most loquat cultivars are self-pollinated, but cross-pollination by insects may occur.

Site and planting
Select a warm, sunny situation. Windbreaks should be erected to reduce wind damage and moisture evaporation. Loquats tolerate a wide range of soils, but a well-drained, fertile loam is most suitable. The trees should be planted at a distance of 12–15ft (4–5m) each way.

Routine care

Apply a top-dressing of general-purpose fertilizer at a rate of about 16oz (450g) per tree every three to four months. Loquats must be regularly watered to keep the roots moist during dry periods; regular applications of organic mulch help to reduce water loss. Keep the surrounding area free of weeds.

To ensure the production of large fruits, thin the bunches at an early stage of their development. Remove any that are weak or damaged, leaving healthy, evenly spaced fruitlets.

Pests and diseases

Plants in the open have few problems. Under cover, however, loquats may be attacked by thrips (p.640), mealybugs (p.640), spider mites (p.640), and whiteflies (p.639).

Growing under cover

Young seed-raised plants may be grown in containers or planted out in well-prepared beds when they are about 18in (45cm) tall. Use a soil-based mix, with a slow-release fertilizer incorporated, and maintain a temperature of at least 64°F (18°C) during the summer. Water them regularly, and apply a liquid fertilizer every month.

Pruning and training

Minimal pruning is required for loquats, other than tip pruning all overvigorous shoots and removing wayward branches; any crossing, damaged, dead, or diseased branches should also be removed.

Harvesting and storing

Harvest when the fruits soften and begin to turn rich yellow or orange. Short-term storage is possible at temperatures of 41–50°F (5–10°C).

Propagation

Loquats may be propagated by seed, sown ¾–1¼in (2–3cm) deep in containers filled with a sandy sowing medium, and maintained at not less than 64°F (18°C). Transplant the seedlings to their final positions when they are 3–4in (7–10cm) high. Other techniques that may be used for propagating loquat cultivars include T-budding (see p.427), side-veneer grafting (see *Propagating Trees by Side-veneer Grafting*, p.80), and air layering (see THE INDOOR GARDEN, p.377).

RIPE LOQUATS

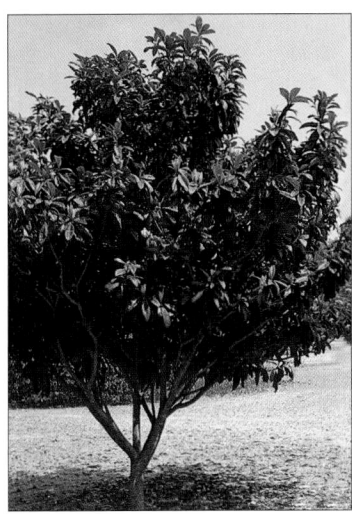

LOQUAT TREE

Mangos *(Mangifera indica)*

Mangos are tropical evergreen trees that often reach 100ft (30m) when grown from vigorous seedlings. If dwarfing rootstocks and compact-growing clones are used, the trees' height may be restricted to 22–30ft (7–10m). The spread is about 25ft (8m) for dwarf types.

Mango fruits vary from 2 to 12in (5 to 30cm) in length and may weigh from 3½oz (100g) up to about 4lb 6oz (2kg). They have a leathery skin and may be orange, yellow, green, or red, depending on the cultivar. The single seed may constitute 25 percent of the total volume of the fruit. Cultivars are available that are adapted to growing in subtropical areas with a temperature range of 70–77°F (21–5°C) and humidity above 60 percent; the higher temperature is regarded as the optimum for most cultivars. For successful flowering and good fruit set, mangos require a high light intensity and a dry period.

Site and planting

Select a warm, sunny exposure. If necessary, provide protection from strong winds, since high moisture loss may seriously affect the growth of the trees; very low humidity may worsen the situation and lead to leaf scorch, seed abortion, and fruit drop.

Soil type is less important for mangos than it is for most other tree crops, and both sandy loams and medium clays are suitable, provided they are well drained. Mangos need a pH of between 5.5 and 7.5.

Dwarfing rootstocks are rapidly becoming available; these are often more suitable, particularly for small gardens, than nonselected local cultivars. If dwarfing rootstocks are not available, polyembryonic seedlings produced from parent trees selected for their high quality of fruit and yield are to be preferred.

Pollination is successful only in relatively dry weather, since high humidity and heavy rainfall limit fertilization (flowering usually begins after a period of cool or dry weather). A solution of potassium nitrate, applied as a spray, may promote flowering. Pollination is mainly by insects, although some mango cultivars are self-fertile.

Space compact and dwarf cultivars 25ft (8m) apart each way; more vigorous cultivars require a spacing of 30–40ft (10–12m).

Routine care

Apply a general-purpose fertilizer, with medium potassium and high nitrogen levels, at a rate of 2lb 3oz–3lb 5oz (1–1.5kg) per tree per year. This should be applied in three or four doses during the growing season; after the fourth year of growth, double the amount.

Water mangos well during dry periods, particularly in the first three years of growth, since plenty of moisture is essential for root development. An organic mulch retains moisture and suppresses weeds. Fruit thinning is rarely necessary.

Pests and diseases

In the tropics, mangos are liable to attack by fruit flies and mealybugs (p.640); various types of scale insect (p.641) may also be a problem. Diseases that may affect trees in the open include fungal leaf spots (p.641) and powdery mildew (p.640).

Mangos grown under cover may also be subject to damage by aphids (p.639), whiteflies (p.639), thrips (p.640), spider mites (p.640), and certain forms of powdery and downy mildews (p.640).

MANGOS

Growing under cover

Mangos grown from seed are likely to be too vigorous for growing under cover unless they have been grafted onto a dwarfing rootstock, when they will form attractive, ornamental trees. They may be grown in large containers or well-prepared beds. In temperate regions, flowering will generally occur under cover only toward the end of the growing season, and only if the optimum growing conditions have been provided. Fruiting cannot be guaranteed, however, and is dependent on successful pollination.

Transplant young plants when they are about 3ft (1m) tall. They will require a soil mix containing a slow-release fertilizer with a medium potassium and high nitrogen content. Ensure that a minimum temperature of 70°F (21°C) and humidity of about 75 percent are maintained. Mangos grown under

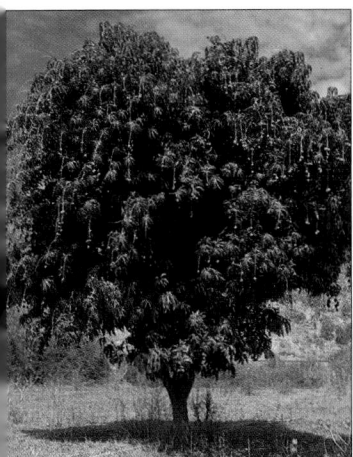

MANGO TREE

RECOMMENDED MANGOS

'Aloha'
'Cooper'   'Tommy
'Edgehill'   Atkins'
'Haden'
'Kent'
'Tommy Atkins'
'Villasenor'

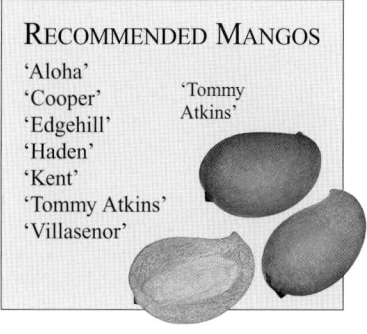

cover should be watered regularly and given liquid fertilizer monthly. Supplement this with sprays of a nitrogenous fertilizer if the leaves turn yellow due to lack of nitrogen.

Pruning and training

Restrict pruning to tip pruning the leading shoot when it is about 3ft (1m) long to encourage lateral branching. Remove overcrowded or very vigorous growth during the early years to ensure an evenly spaced, rounded tree canopy. Once the tree is established, pruning is limited to the removal of diseased, dead, or crossing branches, or those that are congested.

Harvesting and storing

Mangos fruit three to four years after planting. The fruits should be picked when they begin to change color. Handle them carefully to avoid any damage by bruising.

Any mangos that are slightly immature may be stored at 48°F (10°C) for two to four weeks, maintaining humidity of 90–95 percent; they should ripen during this time.

Propagation

Propagation from seed is possible for polyembryonic cultivars, or various methods of grafting may be used instead. For seed propagation, remove the pulp of ripe fruits. To hasten germination, soak the seed in water for 48 hours and carefully remove the seed coat. Sow immediately in beds or containers, using well-prepared sowing medium, and with the convex side of the seeds uppermost. Lightly cover them with medium, and water them.

The resulting seedlings may be polyembryonic and similar to the parent tree, but they are also likely to be very vigorous and take five to eight years to bear fruits that may prove variable in quality. A mango seed usually produces at least one such vigorous seedling resulting from self- or cross-pollination; any such seedlings should be discarded. The remaining seedlings are ready for transplanting to containers at least 6in (15cm) in diameter within six to eight weeks and may be used for rootstocks. Alternatively, they may be grown on as fruiting trees.

Mangos may also be propagated vegetatively, although stem cuttings often fail to root successfully. Approach-grafting is a good alternative. Take a container-grown rootstock that is about one year old. Place the container near the scion branch still growing on the parent tree. Using a sharp knife, take a shallow, vertical slice 2–2½in (5–6cm) long from the side of the rootstock and scion, thus exposing the cambium layers. Place the matching cut surfaces together and bind them firmly. After two to three months the two should have united. Cut the top off the rootstock and sever the scion from the parent plant.

Other successful methods of propagating mangos are by T-budding (see p.427) and air layering (see THE INDOOR GARDEN, p.377).

Olives (*Olea europaea*)

Olives are evergreen trees, growing 28–40ft (9–12m) tall, with a spread of 22–8ft (7–9m). The fruits may be gathered while they are still green, or when they are fully ripe and have turned black. They may measure up to 1½in (4cm) long.

Olives grow well in subtropical areas with an optimum temperature range of 41–77°F (5–25°C). They need long, hot summers for the fruits to ripen fully, followed by winter temperatures that are low enough to meet the chilling requirement of the specific cultivar. Seek advice on which cultivars grow best in your area. Winter temperatures below the optimum will result in cold damage. Hot, dry winds and cool, wet weather during the flowering period reduce fruit set. In temperate areas olives are occasionally grown as ornamental trees in warm gardens, but they seldom flower or fruit. Given suitable growing conditions, an olive tree may attain a great age.

RECOMMENDED OLIVES

European cultivars
'Ascolano'
'Barouni'
'Leccino'
'Manzanillo'
'Mission'
'Picual'   Black table
'Salonenque'   olives
'San Fernando'
'Santa Caterina'
'Sevillano'

Site and planting

A wide range of soils is suitable, although low to medium fertility is preferable, since soils that are very fertile are likely to result in excessive vegetative growth. The site must be well drained. Olives grow well on alkaline soils, including those with a high level of salts, provided that the pH level does not exceed 8.5. Windbreaks should be used in exposed areas.

Most cultivars are self-fertile, but pollinators may be necessary to increase fruit yield in cooler climates. Olives are pollinated by insects and also by wind; high humidity levels inhibit pollination.

The usual planting distance varies from 22ft (7m) to 40ft (12m) each way, depending on the habit of the cultivar. All olives should be staked to avoid wind damage. Closely planted trees may be thinned by removing alternate trees when the canopies begin to overlap.

Routine care

Top-dress with a general-purpose fertilizer with medium to high levels of nitrogen at a yearly rate of about 1–2lb (0.5–1kg) per tree, applied in two or three doses when the trees are in active growth. Applications of potassium and, possibly, boron supplements may be necessary on some soils. Water olives regularly during dry periods, particularly for the first two to three years after planting. Mulching with organic material is also beneficial. Keep the planting area free of weeds.

OLIVE TREE

OLIVES

Fruit thinning may be necessary if the trees show signs of biennial bearing (see "Apples: Blossom thinning and biennial bearing," p.430). Thinning is generally done by hand, but applications of a spray containing alpha naphthalene acetic acid four to 18 days after flowering may also be effective.

Pests and diseases

Olives grown in the open may be affected by various types of scale insect (p.641) and root-knot nematodes (p.652). Olive diseases include *Verticillium* wilt (p.645). Trees grown under cover may be affected by whiteflies (p.639), thrips (p.640), and spider mites (p.640).

Growing under cover

Rooted cuttings or budded plants should be grown either in prepared beds, or in containers no smaller than 12–14in (30–35cm) in diameter; use a fertile soil mix that incorporates a slow-release fertilizer with medium levels of potassium and nitrogen. Apply a liquid fertilizer every three to four weeks, and water the trees regularly.

Maintain a high temperature – above 70°F (21°C) – in summer and as low a temperature as possible in winter. Olives grown in containers may be placed in the open during the summer months.

Pruning and training

Prune newly planted olives by removing the leading shoot when it is about 5ft (1.5m) tall; select three or four strong laterals to provide the basic framework. Subsequent pruning consists of removing older branches to encourage the growth of new shoots, since fruits are produced on one-year-old wood mostly at the edges of the tree canopy.

Harvesting and storing

Olive trees grown in the open are likely to flower and fruit in three to four years from planting; yields tart here.

generally increase until the tree is 15 years old, after which they remain fairly constant.

Olives are processed to remove their bitterness. Fruits used for fermenting should be harvested when they are fully ripe but still green. Olives for eating without being processed may be harvested when black and firm, then packed in dry salt. When thoroughly dehydrated, the olives are stored in oil.

Fruits that are required for oil production should be left on the tree until they are fully ripe. They are harvested by shaking the tree so that the olives fall onto a cloth or fine netting placed on the ground below the tree canopy.

Propagation
Olives are usually propagated by stem cuttings, but selected cultivars may also be increased by bud-grafting. Cuttings may be either hardwood (from one- or two-year-old wood) or leafy, semiripe cuttings from the current season's growth.

Hardwood cuttings, which are taken during the winter, should be about 12in (30cm) in length. Remove the leaves from the lower half of each cutting, and soak its base for 24 hours in hormone rooting solution. Insert the cuttings to half their length in rooting medium, leaving them

for about 30 days to root while maintaining a temperature of 55–70°F (13–21°C). Transplant the cuttings singly into pots, and raise them in greenhouse conditions.

Alternatively, take semiripe cuttings 4–6in (10–15cm) long (see ORNAMENTAL TREES, p.77). Named olive cultivars may be propagated by T-budding (see p.427), always budding onto vigorous, olive seedling rootstocks.

Prickly pears (*Opuntia ficus-indica*)

This member of the cactus family is grown mainly in the subtropics. Although many of its forms are relatively low-growing and spreading in habit, some may eventually attain a height of 6ft (2m).

Most prickly pears will tolerate semiarid conditions, with an optimum temperature range of 64–77°F (18–25°C); they will survive at lower temperatures, with a minimum of 50°F (10°C). Full sunlight is essential for satisfactory growth.

The stems of prickly pears consist of flattened, elliptic sections, 12–20in (30–50cm) long, which

PRICKLY PEAR

are almost spineless in many of the cultivated forms but very spiny on wild and naturalized plants.

Prickly pear fruits, which are produced from the upper part of the sections, are purple or red when ripe, and about 2–4in (5–10cm) long. They contain a soft, juicy pulp with many seeds. Prickly pears are pollinated by insects.

Site and planting
Prickly pears thrive in subtropical regions, where they are able to tolerate lengthy periods of drought. They are sensitive to poor drainage and saline conditions, however, and prefer sandy, well-aerated soils, with an ideal pH of 5.5–7.

Rooted sections are usually established 6–7½ft (2–2.4m) apart, with a spacing of 6–10ft (2–3m) between each row.

Routine care
Fertilizers are not normally required, unless the soil is particularly poor. Keep the planting site weed-free. Pests are rarely a problem. Some species of *Pythium* (see "Damping off," p.655), however, may affect prickly pears in humid conditions.

Growing under cover
Use a sandy soil mix to which a slow-release fertilizer has been added. Maintain the temperature at

PROPAGATING PRICKLY PEARS FROM STEM SECTIONS

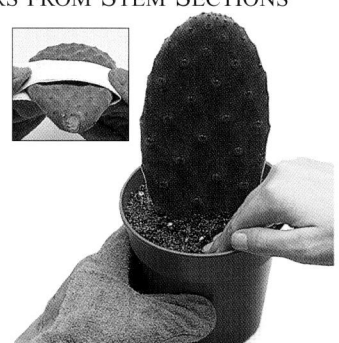

1 *Using a sharp knife, cut a "pad" (single section) away from the parent plant. Wear gloves, since the spines irritate the skin.*

2 *After allowing the section to dry out for a few days, place it in a sandy soil mix and firm it in. The section should be well rooted in 2–3 months.*

64–77°F (18–25°C), with humidity of 60 percent or below. Little watering is required once the plants have become established.

Harvesting and storing
Prickly pears produce fruits three to four years after planting. Detach the fruits carefully from the stem sections using a sharp knife. They are best eaten within a few days after they have been harvested but may be stored for short periods in cool conditions if necessary.

Propagation
Detach whole stem sections from the parent plant; if these are very large, cut them horizontally into two or three pieces. Allow them to callus in a sunny, sheltered place for several days before inserting them into a sandy soil mix. The sections should take two to three months to root; they may then be potted on into 6–8in (15–21cm) pots, or transplanted to their final positions. Water the new plants regularly until they are established.

Avocados (*Persea americana*)

The avocado is a subtropical evergreen tree that may grow to a height of 30–45ft (10–15m), with a similar spread. Its fruits are pear-shaped, with a large, central, rounded seed. Fruit size and skin texture vary with the cultivar, and colors range from green to russet. The main types of avocado are Guatemalan, Mexican, and hybrids of the two.

The optimum temperature range for growth and fruit development is

68–82°F (20–28°C), with humidity of over 60 percent; some Mexican and Guatemalan cultivars are able to withstand temperatures as low as 48–58°F (10–15°C), but they do not usually produce flowers at such low temperatures.

Site and planting
Avocado trees may be grown in the open in subtropical areas, provided the temperature is within the range

given above. Their branches are brittle, so it is necessary to provide windbreaks in exposed areas to prevent them from being seriously damaged by the wind.

Select a site with maximum exposure to sun if possible. Avocados need a well-drained soil, since their roots are extremely sensitive to waterlogging. Medium loam soils with a pH of 5.5–6.5 are preferable, but a sandy or clay loam may be

RECOMMENDED AVOCADOS

'Bacon' (Mexican)
'Duke' (Mexican)
'Fuerte' (Mexican x Guat.)
'Green Gold' (Mexican x Guat.)
'Hass' (Guat.)
'Reed' (Guat.)
'Rincon' (Guat.)
'Zutano' (Mexican)

'Rincon'

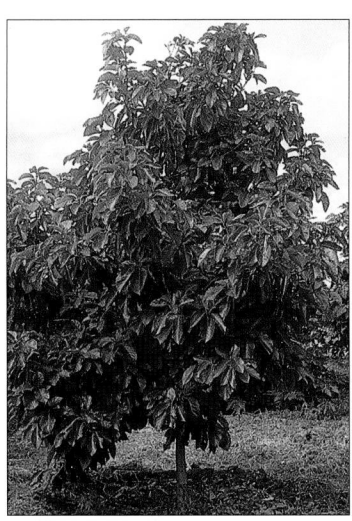

AVOCADO TREE

suitable, provided it has been improved and the drainage is good (see also "Preparing the site," p.418).

If grafted plants are to be used, those on rootstocks that are known to be both vigorous and resistant to avocado root rot (*Phytophthora cinnamoni*) are preferable. Avocados may be self-pollinated, but the best crops are produced if at least two cultivars are planted near each other. Choose cultivars whose flowering periods coincide or overlap. When planting, allow 20ft (6m) each way between the trees.

Routine care
Apply a general-purpose fertilizer with a medium potassium and nitrogen content when the trees are in active growth. The recommended rate is 3lb 4oz–4lb 6oz (1.5–2kg) per tree every year, preferably in two or three doses. Use an organic mulch around the base of each tree, leaving 10in (25cm) clear around the stems.

Water avocado trees during dry periods, particularly during the first three years when they are becoming established. Keep the area around the base of the trees free from all weeds.

It is not normally necessary to thin the fruits on avocado trees.

Pests and diseases
Avocados may be affected by avocado root rot (see "*Phytophthora* root rots," p.646) and *Cercospora* spot or blotch (see "Fungal leaf spots," p.641). They may be attacked by such pests as whiteflies (p.639), thrips (p.640), spider mites (p.640), and mealybugs (p.640).

Growing under cover
Establish young plants either in well-prepared beds or in containers with a minimum diameter of 8in (21cm). Maintain temperatures of 68–82°F (20–28°C) and humidity of 70 percent. For container-grown plants, pot on into containers at least 12in (30cm) in diameter, taking care not to disturb the plants' root systems.

Water containerized avocados regularly, and apply either a general-purpose fertilizer with a medium level of both potassium and nitrogen at intervals of two to three weeks, or a liquid fertilizer. In temperate climates, flowering and fruiting are rare under cover, due to the trees' daylength and light intensity demands.

Pruning and training
Avocado trees need little pruning beyond shaping the tree during its early growth to ensure that an evenly spaced, rounded canopy develops. Once the tree is established, remove any diseased, damaged, or crossing branches after fruiting.

Harvesting and storing
Seed-raised trees start to bear fruit when they are between five and seven years old; budded or grafted plants are productive at three to five years after planting. The fruits may remain on the tree for up to 18 months without maturing, but they usually ripen rapidly after harvesting.

Cut the fruits from the tree using pruners. Handle them carefully to avoid bruising. Store them at temperatures above 48°F (10°C) and at 60 percent humidity. Any damaged fruits should be discarded.

Propagation
Avocado trees are easily grown from seed and reproduce virtually true to type. Select healthy, undamaged seeds and soak them in hot water at 106–30°F (40–52°C) for 30 minutes to inhibit infection from avocado root

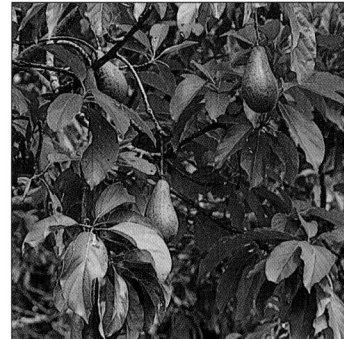

RIPE AVOCADOS

rot. Cut a thin slice from the pointed end, then dip the wound in a fungicide. Sow the seed in sandy sowing medium with the cut end slightly above the soil surface; germination takes about four weeks. The seedlings may be grown on in containers until they are about 12–16in (30–40cm) tall. They should then be ready for transferring to their final positions.

To propagate named cultivars onto disease-resistant rootstocks, side-wedge grafting (see PRINCIPLES OF PROPAGATION, p.630) or saddle grafting (see ORNAMENTAL SHRUBS, p.116) may be used.

GROWING AVOCADOS FROM SEED

1 Soak the seed in hot water, and then prepare it by cutting about ¹/₂in (1cm) off the pointed end with a sharp knife. Dip the wound in fungicide.

2 Place the seed in a 6in (15cm) pot of moist sandy sowing medium so that the cut top of the seed is just above the soil surface.

3 Several weeks later the seed will germinate to produce a shoot and roots.

Guavas (*Psidium guajava*)

Guava trees grow to a height of up to about 25ft (8m) and have a spread of 22ft (7m). They are widely grown in both tropical and subtropical regions and thrive in temperatures ranging from 72–82°F (22–8°C). The preferred humidity level is 70 percent or less: a higher level may reduce the quality of the fruits produced.

Guava fruits are 2–4in (5–10cm) in diameter, with either white or pink flesh. The flowers are normally pollinated by insects.

Site and planting
A sheltered site is preferable, protected by windbreaks if necessary. Guavas tolerate a wide range of soils, but a well-drained loam is ideal. The pH may range from 4.8 to 8, but a pH of approximately 6 is most desirable.

When planting, allow a spacing of 15ft (5m) in each direction between the trees. The young trees should be securely staked in areas that are exposed to strong winds.

Routine care
Guavas respond well to applications of a general-purpose fertilizer with a medium potassium and nitrogen content. Use this at a rate of 2lb 3oz–4lb 6oz (1–2kg) of fertilizer for each tree per year, divided into two or three top-dressings during the growing season. Weed the area around the bases of the trees, keep them well watered, and apply a mulch of organic matter, which helps to retain soil moisture.

GUAVAS

GUAVA TREE

Pests and diseases

Pests are rarely a serious problem, but in the open, aphids (p.639), fruit flies, and scale insects (p.641) may require control. Plants under cover may also be infested by whiteflies (p.639) and thrips (p.640). Guava seedlings are sensitive to damping off (p.655).

Growing under cover

Guavas may be grown in either well-prepared beds or large containers at least 12–14in (30–35cm) in diameter, using a fairly rich, commercial soil mix to which a slow-release fertilizer has been added. Maintain a minimum temperature of 72°F (22°C), with humidity of 70 percent. Water plants regularly, and apply liquid fertilizer every three to four weeks. To improve the chances of fruiting, cross-pollination by hand may be necessary. A relatively dry atmosphere should be maintained during the flowering period.

Pruning and training

When the young trees are about 3ft (1m) tall, cut back the leading shoot by about two-thirds to encourage branching. Subsequent pruning can be limited to the removal of any dead, crossing, or diseased branches, and any low branches that droop down and touch the soil.

Harvesting and storing

Guavas cultivated in the open generally fruit after one to three years, depending on cultivar and environmental conditions. The fruits ripen about five months after fertilization and may be picked when they begin to turn yellow. Handle them carefully, since they bruise easily.

They may be stored for up to three to four weeks at a temperature of 45–50°F (7–10°C), with relative humidity of 75 percent.

Propagation

Guavas are usually propagated from seed. For the increase of specific cultivars, air layering, cuttings, or bud-grafting may be used.

Sow seed in a fertile, sterile sowing medium in trays or 3in (6cm) containers; germination normally occurs in two to three weeks. The seedlings may vary in quality: pot the strongest ones on into 6in (15cm) pots when they are 8in (20cm) tall. Harden the young plants off and transplant them when they are 12in (30cm) tall.

Selected guava cultivars may be chip-budded (see p.426) onto vigorous seedling guava rootstocks, the stems of which should have a diameter of at least ¼in (5mm). No specific rootstocks are recommended; select only strong, healthy plants, preferably self-pollinated, as parents for rootstock seeds.

Guavas may also be increased by softwood cuttings 5–6in (12–16cm) long (see p.626). Plants produced by

RECOMMENDED GUAVAS

'Beaumont' (pink flesh)
'Malherbe' (pink flesh)
'Mexican Cream' (white flesh)
'Miami White' (white flesh)

'Parker's White'

'Parker's White'
 (white flesh)
'Patillo' (pink flesh)
'Patnagola' (white flesh)
'Red Indian' (pink flesh)
'Ruby' (pink flesh)
'Supreme' (white flesh)

these buddings or cuttings may be planted out when they are about 12in (30cm) tall. In the open, guavas may be increased by simple layering (see ORNAMENTAL TREES, p.79) or by air layering (see THE INDOOR GARDEN, p.377). With the latter, hormone rooting powder applied to the girdled sections increases the success rate.

Pomegranates (*Punica granatum*)

Pomegranates form small ornamental trees or bushes 6–10ft (2–3m) tall with a spread of 3–5ft (1–1.5m). They are evergreen in the subtropics but deciduous in cooler climates. The globular fruits are up to 4in (10cm) in diameter, with leathery yellow or red skins. The optimum temperature range is 64–77°F (18–25°C), but temperatures just below freezing are tolerated for short periods. Dry weather and a high temperature, ideally 96°F (35°C), are required for fruiting. In temperate climates, therefore, pomegranates are usually grown for their orange-red summer flowers and fall color; a dwarf cultivar of the species, *Punica granatum* 'Nana', fruits freely under cover in temperate areas.

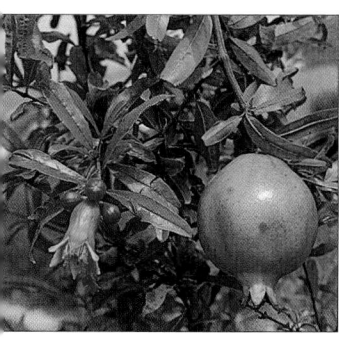

POMEGRANATE FLOWER AND FRUIT

Site and planting

Select a sunny exposure, sheltered by windbreaks in exposed conditions. Heavy loam soils with a pH level of about 7 are generally suitable, if they are well drained. Most cultivars are self-fertile. Plant seedlings, rooted cuttings, or suckers 12–20ft (4–6m) apart each way.

Routine care

Once plants are established, apply a general-purpose fertilizer every two to three months at a rate of 4oz (110g) for each tree per year. Mulch the site and keep it free of weeds; water the trees regularly during dry weather. Cut out all suckers.

Pests and diseases

Pomegranates grown in the open are generally trouble free; under cover, they may be affected by whiteflies (p.639), aphids (p.639), spider mites (p.640), and thrips (p.640).

Growing under cover

Plant pomegranates in well-prepared beds or containers with a minimum diameter of 14in (35cm), using a fertile soil mix with slow-release fertilizer added. Maintain a temperature range of 64–77°F (18–25°C) and humidity of 60–70 percent. Apply a liquid fertilizer every three to four weeks, and water the plants regularly. Plants in containers may be moved into the open in summer.

Pruning and training

Select three or four main branches to form a framework, and remove any crowded, crossing, or diseased branches. Cut out any suckers not required for propagation.

Harvesting and storing

Fruiting should start about two to three years after planting. Harvest the pomegranates when they turn yellow or red; they may then be stored for several weeks at 39–43°F (4–6°C).

Propagation

Pomegranates are usually propagated from cuttings or root suckers. Insert hardwood cuttings (see p.428) in sandy soil mix, and give bottom heat until they have rooted. Softwood cuttings (see *Blueberry Softwood Cuttings*, p.472) require bottom heat and mist (use a medium with a neutral pH). Pot on both types into 4–6in (10–15cm) pots when they have rooted. Root suckers may be carefully separated from the parent plant and replanted. Alternatively, dry off the seed; sow it in pots or trays of seed soil mix, maintaining a temperature of 72°F (22°C).

POMEGRANATE TREE

RECOMMENDED POMEGRANATES

'Papershell'
'Ruby'
'Spanish'
'Wonderful'

'Wonderful'

Nuts

Pecans

Walnuts

Hazelnut

Chestnuts

Almonds

SEVERAL nut-bearing trees and bushes are suitable for gardens; they prefer a sunny, open situation. Some, such as sweet chestnuts, walnuts, and pecans, eventually form large trees and make handsome specimens. In small gardens, an almond tree may make a fine feature, although it may produce nuts only in warm climates. Hazelnuts and filberts may be pruned as compact bushes in a fruit garden or planted in informal groups in a wild garden. Most nuts (but not almonds) are monoecious, having separate male and female flowers on the same plant.

Pecans (*Carya illinoensis*)

Pecans are deciduous trees that may grow to 100ft (30m) high with a spread of 50–70ft (15–20m), so they are suitable only for large gardens. They grow best in warm-temperate climates: temperatures over 100°F (38°C) may lead to bark damage and the production of low-quality nuts; flowers may be damaged if the temperature drops below 34°F (1°C). Pecans have a chilling requirement of 150–250 hours below 45°F (7°C) in order for flowering to occur. The nuts are ovoid, ¾–1in (2–2.5cm) long, and most cultivars have a relatively thin shell.

Pecans are monoecious, but the male flowers are often open before the females on the same tree, so it is best to grow two or more cultivars near each other to be sure that fertilization takes place. Since pecans are wind-pollinated, heavy rainfall when the trees are flowering adversely affects pollination; after such conditions, crops may be poor.

Site and planting
Choose selected cultivars that have been grafted onto pecan seedling stock, since trees raised from seed may not produce fruit of good quality. Pecans quickly develop a long taproot, so plant young trees: older, potgrown plants with congested roots are seldom successful. Pecans need a site that is sheltered from strong winds and thrive on deep, fertile soils with a pH of 6–6.5.

Plant the trees when they are dormant (see *Planting a Fruit Tree*, p.419), spacing them 25ft (8m) apart.

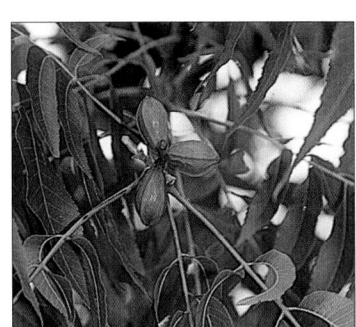

PECANS

Routine care
Apply a top-dressing of a balanced fertilizer at a rate of 2–4oz/sq yd (70–140g/sq m) under the canopy annually. Keep the planting site free of weeds, and water the trees during dry periods until they are established. Pecans are moderately resistant to drought but require plenty of water during the summer months.

Pecan trees are seldom affected by pests and diseases; *Phytophthora* root rots (p.646) and aphids (p.639) may sometimes be a problem.

Pruning and training
Train pecans with a central leader initially (see "Central-leader standard trees," p.72). Once the trees are established, pruning is restricted to removing crossing and congested branches and any dead wood.

Harvesting and storing
The first crop may be produced after five years; full production is reached after 15–20 years. The nuts are usually harvested by hand. They may be stored in cool, dry, airy conditions for several months.

Propagation
Whip-and-tongue grafting of selected cultivars onto vigorous pecan seedling rootstocks is the most usual method of propagation (see p.427). The seedlings to be used as stock plants should be raised in deep pots or plastic sleeves, since their long taproots are sensitive to damage during transplanting.

RECOMMENDED PECANS
'Chariton'
'Desirable'
'Early Best'
'Hastings'
'Gloria Grande'
'Lucas'
'Mohawk'
'NC-4'
'Snags'

Chestnuts (*Castanea* spp.)

A fungal disease has made the native American chestnut (*Castanea dentata*) all but extinct. Better results come from the Chinese chestnut (*C. molissima*) and Spanish chestnut (*C. sativa*). These trees produce excellent fruit, but their malodorous flowers are definitely a liability. Choose modern Chinese–American hybrids or hybrids of Chinese, Japanese, and European chestnuts, such as 'Colossal'. Chestnuts are monoecious and wind-pollinated.

CHESTNUTS

Site, planting, and routine care
A fertile, moisture-retentive soil with a pH of 6 is preferred; allow 30–40ft (10–12m) between trees (see *Planting a Fruit Tree*, p.419). Water young trees. Fertilizing is unnecessary on prepared sites. Trees may be affected by *Armillaria* root rots (p.653).

Pruning and training
Train as central-leader standards (see p.72). On established trees, remove congested, crossing, or dead branches.

Harvesting and storing
Nuts are borne after about four years. Harvest in fall. Cook nuts fresh, or hull the nuts, soak them for 48 hours, discarding any that darken, then dry and store in a cool, airy place.

Propagation
Propagate from selected cultivar by bud-grafting or whip-and-tongue grafting onto seedling stock of chestnut (see pp.426 and 427).

Hazelnuts and filberts (*Corylus avellana* and *C. maxima*)

Hazelnuts and filberts are valued for their nuts and their winter catkins. Unpruned, they reach a height and spread of 12–15ft (4–5m). They are deciduous and monoecious, bearing best in cool, moist summers. The chilling requirement is 800–1,200 hours below 45°F (7°C). Winter temperatures below 13°F (-10°C) may damage the male flowers (catkins), although the female flowers are usually less vulnerable. The outer husk or calyx of the hazelnut does not completely envelop the nut. The filbert has a husk that is longer than the nut and often completely encloses it; a subgroup of filberts has frilled husks and is known as frizzled filberts. Hazelnuts and filberts are wind-pollinated; many are self fertile. Recommended cultivars include 'Barcelona', 'Daviana',

HAZELNUTS

FILBERTS

'Du Chilly', 'Ennis', 'Royale', 'Rush', and 'Winkler'; 'Rush' and 'Winkler' are the hardiest. The nuts of hazelnuts and filberts are brown and irregularly egg-shaped.

Site and planting
A partially shaded, sheltered position is preferable. A soil pH of 6 is best; very rich soil may cause excessive soft growth at the expense of bearing. Adequate moisture with good drainage is important. Plant in fall or early winter, 15ft (5m) apart (see *Planting a Fruit Tree*, p.419).

Routine care
Weed and mulch regularly; water in dry spells. On poor soils apply a balanced fertilizer in spring at a rate of 3oz/sq yd (105g/sq m) under the canopy. Trees are usually trouble-free, but they may be attacked by nut weevils unless sprayed in late spring and again in early summer.

Pruning and training
Hazelnuts and filberts are usually grown as open-center bushes, each with an 18in (45cm) stem and eight to 12 main branches. On young plants, prune the leaders in winter to 22in (55cm); good laterals should then develop. Remove any shoots growing down low on the main stem and all but the best-placed, strongest shoots needed to develop the framework. Shorten these by a third in winter. The following winter remove any excessively strong, upright growth and, if necessary, tip prune sideshoots to form a framework.

Established bushes bear heavier crops if pruned in late summer using

BRUTTING HAZELNUTS

In late summer, strong shoots of the current season's growth that are about 12in (30cm) long are broken and left hanging. This helps with the formation of new flower buds.

a technique known as "brutting." Break the longer sideshoots halfway along their length, and let them hang. This opens up the bush and encourages more female flowers to form. In winter, when the catkins release pollen, shorten the brutted shoots to three or four buds; remove old or overcrowded shoots.

Harvesting and storing
Nuts are borne after three to four years. Gather them when the husks begin to yellow. Dry, then store.

Propagation
Suckers produced from roots may be used for propagation. In winter, remove them, each with a root ball, and grow on in a nursery bed or plant directly in their final positions. Trees may also be propagated by simple layering (see p.114) in fall.

Walnuts (*Juglans regia*)

English walnuts (strictly speaking, Persian) are deciduous trees that may reach a height of 60ft (18m) with a similar spread; they are suitable only for large gardens. Named cultivars should always be planted for nuts, since seedlings may produce poor-quality nuts. Walnuts are monoecious and wind-pollinated. Most are self-fertile, but some cultivars produce male catkins and pollen before the female flowers are receptive. To overcome this problem, plant nearby a reliable pollinator such as the old French cultivar 'Franquette'. Walnuts have a chilling requirement of 500–1,000 hours below 45°F (7°C). The gnarled nuts develop within a pitted shell.

Site, planting, and routine care
A well-drained, moisture-retentive soil is best. Walnuts prefer a pH of

RECOMMENDED WALNUTS
All cultivars listed are self-fertile.
'Broadview'
'Colby'
'Hansen'
'Lake'
'Metcalfe'
'Somers'
'Young's B1'

6.5–7 but tolerate some alkalinity. Since flowers and young shoots are susceptible to frost damage, avoid cold sites. Walnuts have a long tap-root, so select young plants rather than older, potgrown ones whose roots may be congested. Plant in late fall or winter (see *Planting a Fruit Tree*, p.419), with 40–60ft (12–18m) between trees.

Walnuts may be slow to establish, but after two to three years, once the root system is well developed, stronger growth occurs. Bacterial leaf blotch and blight may be a problem (see "Bacterial leaf spots and blotches," p.641).

Pruning and training
Walnuts should be trained as central-leader standards (see p.48). Prune in midwinter since the trees do not bleed when they are dormant. Remove any strong shoots that make a narrow angle with the stem, to leave a well-balanced framework of evenly spaced branches. Thereafter, little pruning is required apart from cutting out overcrowded, crossing, or congested branches in winter and removing dead wood as required.

Harvesting and storing
Walnut trees may need many years before they start bearing. Walnuts for pickling should be picked in summer before the hulls and shells harden. In early fall, the hull or casing cracks to release the nut, still in its shell.

Almonds (*Prunus dulcis*)

Left unpruned, almonds grow about 15–20ft (5–6m) tall, with a similar spread. They bear regularly only in areas with warm, dry summers and frost-free winters. The chilling requirement is 300–500 hours below 45°F (7°C). In cooler areas they are often grown as flowering ornamentals. Almonds are insect-pollinated. Most cultivars are partly self-fertile, but crops will be better if a pollinator is planted nearby. The nuts are flattened and pointed, with a pitted shell resembling that of a peach.

Site, planting, and routine care
Almonds require a sheltered, frost-free site and a well-drained soil, preferably with a pH of 6.5. Plant them 20–22ft (6–7m) apart (see *Planting a Fruit Tree*, p.419).

Cultivation of almonds is as for peaches (see p.445). Peach leaf curl (p.644) and bacterial canker may affect almond trees.

Pruning and training
Almonds are usually pruned and trained as bushes, as for peaches (see p.446). Nuts are borne on one-year-old wood. In summer, on established trees, remove a quarter of the old shoots that have borne in previous seasons to encourage fresh growth.

Harvesting and storing
The nuts are borne after three to four years. Gather them as their hulls start

WALNUTS

Harvest the crop before the shells become discolored. Clean then gently dry the nuts. Store them in cool, airy, slightly humid conditions.

Propagation
The usual methods are whip-and-tongue grafting (see p.427) or chip-budding (see p.426) cultivars onto seedlings of the American black walnut (*Juglans nigra*). In cool climates, keep a grafted tree under cover until the graft has taken, then move the container to a protected site in the open. Plant young trees in their final positions in fall or winter.

ALMONDS

to crack. Clean and dry the almonds before storing them.

Propagation
Almonds are usually propagated by chip-budding (see p.426). Root-stocks vary according to soil type: almond seedlings are often used for dry regions, while peach seedlings are more suitable for heavier soils.

RECOMMENDED ALMONDS
'Ayles' **Sf**
'Ferraduel' **Psf**
'Ferragnes' **Psf**
'Guara' **Sf**
'Steliette' **Sf**

KEY
Sf *Self-fertile*
Psf *Partly self-fertile*

CHAPTER

17

THE VEGETABLE GARDEN

MORE AND MORE people are discovering the satisfaction of growing their own vegetables. They do so for many reasons: for some it is the freshness and flavor rarely to be found in store-bought produce, while for others it is a chance to grow unusual varieties they cannot otherwise obtain. Another motive, for those who favor organic methods, is the knowledge that their produce is not tainted with harmful chemicals. Then again, there are gardeners who find a well-tended vegetable patch just as beautiful as a perennial border. Modern science and methods of cultivation, coupled with the vigor and disease resistance of many of today's cultivars, enable even newcomers to experience the considerable pleasure and satisfaction of bringing to the table fine vegetables that they have sown, tended, and harvested in their own gardens.

Designing a vegetable garden

A HEALTHY, productive area for growing vegetables may be created in a garden of any size, from a large, sunny patch to the smallest townhouse garden. The vegetables may be grown in a separate plot or integrated with flower beds.

Good growing conditions are essential if vegetables of quality are to be produced. Virtually any site can, however, be made suitable, perhaps by erecting windbreaks if it is exposed, or taking the necessary steps to improve soil fertility and drainage. This cannot be done overnight, but within a year or two very satisfactory results may be obtained.

Choosing the site

Most vegetables lead short but pampered lives, so the ideal situation for a vegetable garden provides warmth, sunlight, shelter, and fertile, well-drained, loamy soil with an adequate water supply. The chosen site should be open but not exposed, and not overshadowed: trees cast shade, drip on plants, and remove nutrients and moisture from the soil, and buildings may create shade and tunnel damaging winds across the plot.

Shelter from wind
Providing shelter from wind is one of the most important factors in vegetable growing. Wherever possible,

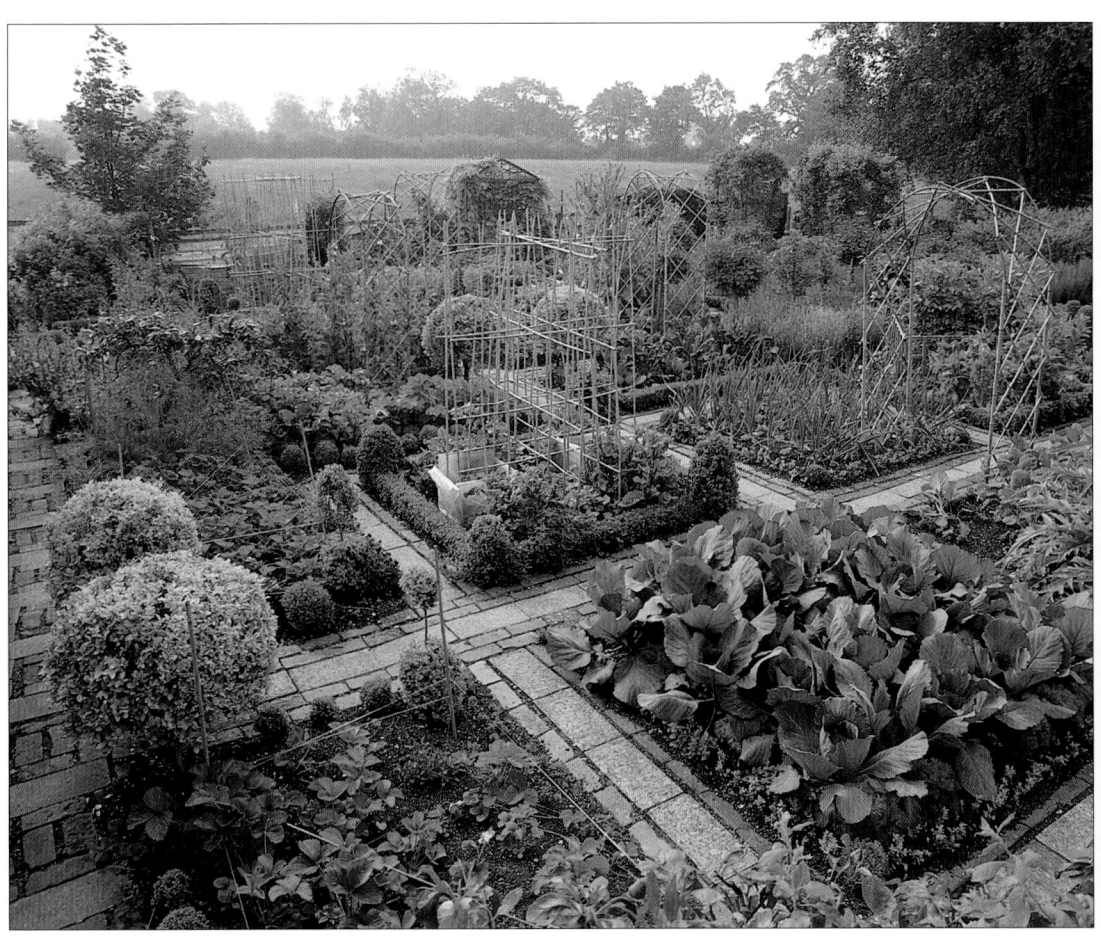

A WELL-DESIGNED GARDEN
This thriving vegetable garden is both well designed and properly maintained, with an open, but not exposed, site.

The beds all contain different crops, and a network of paths allows easy access to each bed.

avoid windy sites: even light winds may decrease vegetable yields by 20–30 percent, and strong winds are often devastating. Vegetables in coastal gardens may be damaged by desiccating, windborne salt spray.

Windbreaks
In gardens exposed to wind, windbreaks should be erected. They should be about 50 percent permeable, allowing the wind to filter through, rather than being solid structures that force the wind over them and create an area of turbulence on the other side (see also COLD AND WIND PROTECTION, pp.604–05, and CLIMATE AND THE GARDEN, "Wind," p.602).

Effective windbreaks may be either a living barrier, such as a hedge, or a structure, such as a fence or a screen of windbreak netting. Hedges are attractive but take time to become established, require maintenance, take up considerable space, and compete for soil, water, and plant nutrients; they are therefore only appropriate in large gardens. For further information, see HEDGES AND SCREENS, pp.82–84. A windbreak of trees should be considered only in a very large garden. In smaller gardens, fences, lattice, or windbreak netting fastened to posts or stakes is more practical.

A windbreak gives shelter for a distance roughly five times its height. An exposed garden may need a windbreak approximately 6ft (2m) high. In this case, nets and posts must be strong, because they will be subjected to great strain in high winds. Lower, short-term windbreaks can be erected between rows

of plants or beds; netting windbreaks no more than 18in (45cm) high and 10–13ft (3–4m) apart, attached to stakes, are very useful.

If gaps in buildings or trees create a wind tunnel across the garden, erect a barrier extending 3ft (1m) beyond the gap in each direction. Deciduous shrubs or a hedge may be planted in the gap, with an artificial windbreak to shelter the plants until they are established.

Slopes
A sloping site is harder to work than a flat one. Soil erosion after heavy rain may be a problem on steep slopes; setting the beds across the slope may help. A site on a south-facing slope is an advantage in cool-temperate climates because it warms up rapidly in spring. In hot climates, site beds on a north-facing slope because here they will have relief from intense sun.

Positioning
The orientation of vegetable beds often makes little difference to open-ground crops, although greenhouses and frames must be oriented correctly to maximize their efficiency. Position tall crops, such as pole beans, carefully: in temperate climates, place them where they will not shield dwarf-sized plants from the sun, and in hotter climates use them to provide some shade.

Sites below garden walls
In temperate and northern climates, the ground at the foot of a south-facing garden wall is a warm, sheltered place that is useful for growing early spring and late fall crops and,

ALLOCATING SPACE
Each element in this garden has been sited to produce optimum growing conditions for the crops. The greenhouse and frame are positioned to receive maximum light, the hedge filters the prevailing wind, and tall plants, such as the scarlet runner beans, do not overshadow the smaller vegetables.

in summer, tender, sun-loving crops such as tomatoes and eggplants. Keep these beds fertile and well watered so that the soil does not dry out. North-facing walls may be used to provide some shade for plants such as lettuces and peas that suffer in high temperatures.

Maintaining soil fertility
A friable loam (the "ideal" soil, made up of a balance of sand, silt, and clay particles) is ideal for growing vegetables: it is rich in plant nutrients (and can hold onto nutrients added to it) and supports a pop-

ulation of earthworms and microorganisms that break down organic matter into nutrient-retaining humus. It has a good structure and remains workable even in adverse conditions: it does not become sticky during wet weather or dusty in dry periods, but always retains a crumbly texture, so that the soil is well aerated. This is important for both the organisms living in the soil and the roots of the vegetables themselves. An ideal soil is both well drained and moisture-retentive and for most vegetables should be slightly acidic (pH 6–6.5). In such a soil, most vegetables grow quite well.

Soil types
Vegetables may be grown successfully on a range of different soil types. At one extreme are the porous, sandy soils, which warm up quickly in spring and are ideal for early crops. Nutrients are washed out rapidly from these soils, however, and crops that are planted in them often need extra fertilizing.

At the other extreme are heavy clays. Naturally sticky and cold (and sometimes waterlogged), clay soils warm up slowly in spring but are rich in nutrients, and, once their structure has been improved by incorporating organic matter (and if necessary, drainage), they are fertile and retain moisture well. Heavy feeders such as the cabbage family grow well on clay soils. For further information, see "Soil and its structure," pp.610–11.

In practice, most soils are a mixture of different types, and although few of us start with perfect soil, it can usually be improved by working in organic matter regularly.

SURPRISING BEAUTY
A vegetable garden, or individual plants or groupings, can provide considerable visual as well as eating pleasure. This simple composition of lettuce and weathered wooden edging could lend its beauty to a humble vegetable patch or to a magnificent mixed border.

Using organic matter

Crops continuously remove nutrients from the soil and from naturally decomposing organic matter. In almost all soils, fertility must be maintained by replenishing the supplies of both fertilizers and organic matter. The main organic materials available to gardeners are animal manures (preferably with a high straw content but little sawdust or wood shavings), spent mushroom compost, seaweed, or compost.

A layer of organic matter 3–4in (8–10cm) deep, applied over most of the ground each year, should maintain structure, fertility, and nutrient-holding capacity. It may be spread on the surface or dug into the soil. If organic matter is spread on the soil surface in fall in milder areas, it may be left for the worms to work in, at least partially. This is particularly beneficial on light soils, where heavy winter rainfall can cause nutrients to be washed out. Any organic matter remaining on the surface in spring should be forked in as soon as the soil can be worked. Well-rotted organic matter is a useful mulch and can be used at any point in the growing season.

In fall, dig organic matter into heavy soils and into light soils that freeze solid in the winter, spreading it evenly throughout the soil as deeply as possible (see also "Mulching," p.496).

INTERCROPPING
Lettuces and sweet corn planted together mature at varying rates. The fast-growing lettuces are ready to harvest before the corn is fully grown. This also works well with onion sets and radishes, as well as spinach and beans.

Green manuring

This is the practice of growing crops (particularly grasses and legumes, such as rye and vetch, respectively) specifically to dig into the soil to improve its fertility. In the vegetable garden, a green manure may be grown and dug in between crops or over the winter to augment plant nutrients and avoid leaving the soil bare (see SOILS AND FERTILIZERS, "Green manures," p.619).

Drainage

Good drainage is essential; where there is a serious problem, it may be necessary to lay tile drains (see SOILS AND FERTILIZERS, "Improving drainage," p.617). In most cases, working in organic matter improves drainage markedly, this will encourage earthworms, which improve the soil structure by forming a network of drainage channels.

Preserving soil structure

Good soil structure is easily destroyed by physically damaging the soil, for example by walking on it or cultivating it when it is either very wet or very dry, or from heavy rain beating down on the surface, or from rototilling it excessively, thus producing a hardpan layer. Laying out the garden in narrow beds (see "The bed system," right) to minimize the need to walk on the soil, and keeping the surface continuously mulched (see "Mulching," p.496) will help preserve the soil structure.

Planning the vegetable garden

The layout of a vegetable garden is determined by the size, shape, and nature of the garden and the demands of the household. The quantity and choice of vegetables to be cultivated depends on the aims of the gardener. These may be to attain self-sufficiency; to produce gourmet vegetables and well-flavored, unusual cultivars that are unavailable locally; to grow produce for the freezer; or to save money.

The following are a few guidelines that give an indication of the main factors to be considered.

A place for perennials

Most vegetables are grown as annuals on a different piece of ground each year. The few perennial vegetables, such as rhubarb, asparagus, and globe artichokes, should be grouped in a permanent bed at one side or end of the garden, separated from the annual vegetables. If there is space, they may be intercropped with fast-growing vegetables.

Vegetables in containers

Gardeners who are limited to terraces, concrete yards, patios, roofs, or balconies often grow vegetables in containers to provide an attractive and productive display. Although vegetables are more difficult than flowers to grow successfully in containers, they are still worth the effort involved. Place containers on paths and low walls to make the best use of the space available, and plant them up with dwarf and decorative cultivars. Suitable containers include terracotta pots and wooden barrels, as well as commercial brands of growing bags filled with soil mix.

Growing vegetables in rows

A traditional vegetable garden consists of one to a number of rectangular plots each several yards (meters) wide, in which vegetables are grown in widely spaced rows. This method allows easy access between individual rows.

The bed system

Although the traditional layout of vegetable plots is still used, the modern trend is to grow vegetables in smaller, narrower beds, with the plants evenly spaced in all directions. This is known as the bed system. In practice, the beds may be of any shape or size: square, round, or even crescent-shaped, as long as the center of the bed is reached easily from the path, so that all sowing, planting, routine care, and harvesting can be done without walking on the soil. The paths between the beds may be of soil, grass, concrete, bark, stones, brick, sawdust, or any other suitable material.

The main benefit of growing vegetables in narrow beds is that the soil structure is preserved by using the access paths between the beds rather than walking on them. Also, organic matter and manure are concentrated on areas where the crops grow, rather than being wasted on pathways and working areas where they are not used by the plants.

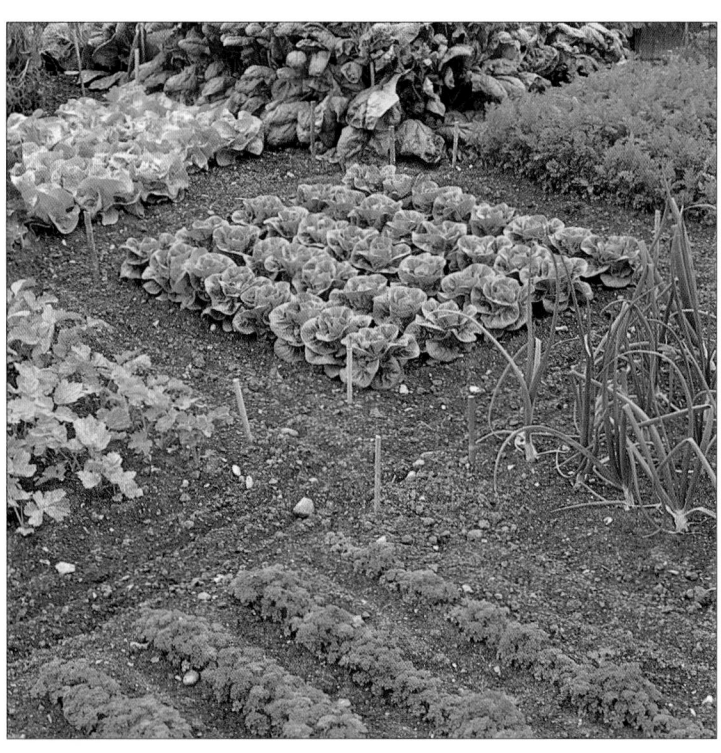

A PATCHWORK OF CROPS
Square beds with soil paths between them provide a neat framework for manageable rows of vegetables. A plot laid out like this allows a variety of crops to be grown and is designed for a simple method of crop rotation.

High yields may be obtained from narrow beds by growing plants in patches at equidistant spacing, which makes the best use of available space and minimizes competition between plants. Uniform spacing also helps to suppress weed germination by allowing fully grown broadleaved vegetables to make a canopy over the soil.

A place for herbs

For practical purposes, it is best to grow herbs as near the kitchen as possible and within easy access of paths. Compact herbs such as chives, marjoram, thyme, cilantro, and parsley make neat, attractive edgings to vegetable beds; the larger perennials such as mint, sage, and rosemary are often best grown in a separate bed. For further information, see THE HERB GARDEN, "Where to grow herbs," p.399.

Vegetables in flower beds

Because many properties are no longer spacious enough to allow a complete area to be dedicated exclusively to vegetables, there has been a move toward integrating vegetables into flower beds or, alternatively, planting them in groups of beds designed in an attractive pattern. Wherever possible, vegetable cultivars are selected for their decorative qualities, and then grouped to display them attractively.

This approach is known as "edible landscaping" in North America and "potager gardening" in Europe. There is great opportunity for gardeners to develop their own ideas. The only requirement for growing vegetables in flower beds is making sure that the soil fertility is maintained at the level necessary for the chosen vegetables.

Climatic factors

Most vegetables grow only when the average daytime temperature rises above about 43°F (6°C) between spring and fall. The number of growing days with suitable daytime temperatures that occur between these seasons is governed by factors such as latitude, altitude, and degree of exposure, and largely determines what may be grown outdoors in any locality.

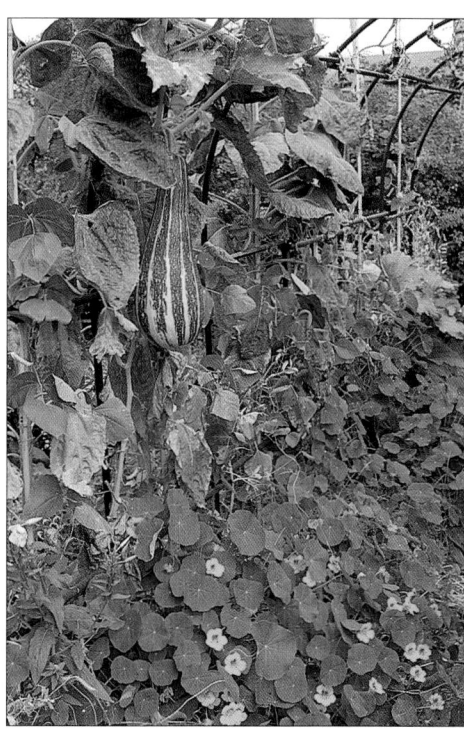

A PRODUCTIVE DISPLAY
This example of edible landscaping groups a squash climbing a supporting arch with a profusion of yellow and red nasturtiums beneath. All thrive in warm, sunny conditions.

Temperature requirements

Vegetables are sometimes classified as warm- or cool-season crops, depending on their physiological needs, particularly those relating to temperature. Most brassicas and several bulb and stem vegetables cannot withstand the intense heat of summer, whereas more tender vegetables such as tomatoes are damaged or killed by freezing or near-freezing temperatures. Cultivars of some vegetables have been bred to resist cold, and the growing season of many vegetables may be extended by growing them under cover (see p.499). See individual vegetables for specific requirements.

Daylength

The number of daylight hours, or daylength, differs according to the latitude and season, and vegetable cultivars have a varying response to daylength at different stages of growth. Short-day plants grow and seed only if the daylength is less than 12 hours; long-day plants only if it is more than 12 hours.

This affects the sowing time, particularly of crops that are grown for their seeds, such as beans; others must be harvested before flowering. Onions, for example, are naturally long-day plants: when the daylength is 16 hours or more, onions stop making leafy growth and start to develop a bulb. The more leafy growth that has been made up to this point, the larger the bulb that forms. Onion seeds should therefore be sown early in the year so that the plant will develop as much leafy growth as possible before the daylength increases.

Cultivars are available that have been adapted to long or short days or that are daylength neutral. Examples are mentioned under individual vegetables later in the chapter; the safest course is to choose cultivars recommended for your area.

COMBINING VEGETABLES AND HERBS
This informal garden has vegetables intermingled with herbs. Scarlet runner beans climb up an arch, parsley and chives surround red and green lettuces in the center bed, and sweet corn develops among feathery dill.

VEGETABLES IN A WINDOWBOX
Vegetables can thrive in small containers such as this windowbox. Here shallow-rooted lettuces, young cabbages, tomatoes, and strawberries have been chosen not only for their culinary uses but also for their decorative qualities.

The bed system

FRUIT and vegetables are best grown in open ground, either on the flat or in raised beds. In these situations the soil benefits from rainfall and weathering, and the plants have a free root run. In the traditional garden, it is usual to set aside a particular garden area specifically for fruit and vegetables. This area can be a wide, open plot, but an excellent, more modern alternative is to set out the vegetable garden as a series of narrow beds divided by pathways.

The traditional vegetable patch

In the traditional kitchen garden, long rows of vegetables usually run across the plot. This is a perfectly good way to grow produce; it allows large areas of ground to be cultivated and used with maximum flexibility.

Growing crops, however, requires constant access for sowing, thinning, planting out, watering, top-dressing, pest and disease control, weeding, harvesting, and clearing. Each task involves walking on the ground, which compresses the soil. This reduces the air in the soil, impedes drainage, and results in poor growth. Compaction can be reduced by taking care not to walk on wet soil and by walking on boards to spread the weight, but narrow beds totally avoid the need to walk on cropped areas.

Using beds

In a bed system, the cropping area is divided into semipermanent or fixed beds. The beds should be narrow enough to bring their central areas within arm's reach, so that all cultivation tasks can be carried out from the dividing pathways without stepping onto the soil. This avoids soil compaction and has the additional advantage that harvesting and other tasks can be done soon after rain without the usual risk of damaging soil structure. There is also less need to dig beds once they are established and fertile, and what cultivation is necessary is greatly reduced because of the smaller cropped area. Since the regular addition of bulky organic manures is concentrated on a smaller area, it is easier to build up high levels of fertility, and to improve soil aeration and drainage, which in turn leads to stronger root growth.

The concentration of cropping areas into relatively confined spaces makes the bed system an ideal solution for worthwhile vegetable production in small gardens. The increase in soil fertility and lack of need for access along crop rows allows plants to be grown at closer spacings. Lettuces, for example, may be grown 8in (20cm) apart each way in staggered rows, as opposed to rows 12in (30cm) apart in more traditional layouts. Each plant gains the maximum root space in the smallest possible area, making the best use of the soil available and increasing the total yield.

The close spacing of plants has additional indirect benefits. Irrigation using low-level distribution systems such as seep hoses (see p.555) becomes more manageable, since smaller areas are served; water can also be saved by using more conventional watering techniques. Close

CLOSE CROPPING
The high soil fertility in this raised bed permits close and equidistant plant spacing in staggered rows. Narrow beds like these are also particularly convenient when using a standard width of horticultural row cover to protect crops.

MAKING A RAISED BED

1 *Measure and mark out beds. Edge with 6 x 1in (15 x 2.5cm) boards, sunk into a 2in (5cm) slit trench and supported by wooden pegs driven into the ground every 3–4ft (1–1.2m).*

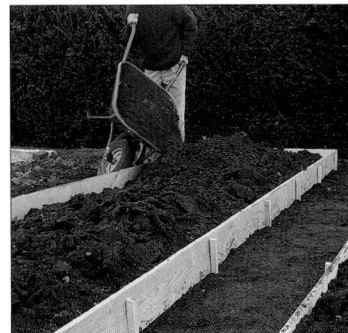

2 *Fill the bed with good-quality topsoil that has been enriched with organic matter, such as well-rotted manure or compost. Take care to avoid creating air pockets at the edges and corners.*

3 *Spread out the soil evenly using a rake. Break up any lumps, aiming to achieve an even, firm texture. Make the finished soil surface roughly level with the top of the boards, filling up as necessary.*

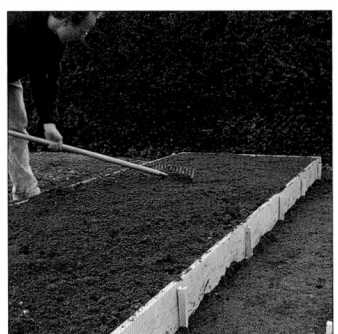

4 *Level the soil with the back of the rake to leave a smooth finish. Fill up with more soil as necessary in later weeks as the filled bed settles and the level of the soil falls.*

PLANTING IN A BED

The bed should be no more than 5ft (1.5m) wide, so that the center is within easy arm's reach from either side. All work can then be carried out from the surrounding paths without any need to walk on the soil, thus avoiding damage to the soil structure.

spacing results in more effective smothering of annual weed growth, so weeding is also reduced.

Using a bed system can make crop rotation (see p.492) much easier, because each crop group can be allocated to a bed and moved on to a different one the following year according to the rotation requirements.

Planning bed layouts

Beds may be rectangular, square, or even curved; the prime consideration is that they must allow the whole bed to be cultivated from the paths.

The ideal width is 4ft (1.2m); this can be increased to 5ft (1.5m) if this makes better use of available space, or reduced to 3ft (1m) for areas that are to be protected with glass or plastic cloches. Narrow strips are particularly suitable for strawberries, for ease of mulching and harvesting.

The bed length can be adjusted to suit the site and, while their orientation is not of vital importance, running them from north to south generally ensures the most even distribution of sunlight.

The width of the paths between beds needs to be at least 18in (45cm) wide to allow for easy access, both on foot and with wheelbarrows.

Types of beds

Many terms are used to describe beds: they include flat or semiflat beds, deep beds, and raised beds. A flat or semiflat bed is simply marked out from the surrounding garden and cultivated. With repeated annual addition of bulky organic dressings, soil depth is increased as the bed surface is gradually raised above path level.

Deep beds

Organic growers often aim to minimize soil cultivation to preserve its natural structure and fertility and reduce the growth of weeds. Deep beds are an ideal way of achieving this. In deep beds, soil is improved to the required depth with one thorough cultivation that incorporates large amounts of organic matter (see *Double digging*, p.614). After this, further digging is avoided so that a natural soil structure develops, encouraged by the organic matter and a high worm population. Further organic matter is added only as mulches and top-dressings. The only disturbance to the soil surface occurs when planting, so weed seeds below germination level remain dormant, and only weed seedlings from wind-blown seeds need to be removed.

Raised beds

Raised beds are constructed by marking out beds and building the sides up to 12in (30cm) high, using wood (such as railroad ties) bricks, or cement blocks. Walls can be dispensed with, but in that case, the base of the bed should be about 12in (30cm) wider than the finished top to ensure stability.

Raised beds bring all the advantages of flat beds but have improved drainage and warm up faster in spring. Making a raised bed higher along one side than the other, so that the sloping surface faces the sun, warms the bed even more effectively and promotes early plant growth.

Raised beds provide a means of gardening successfully on the most unpromising ground, such as where a site is naturally very badly drained or perhaps even concreted over.

Higher beds can also extend the pleasure of gardening to people of limited mobility. Walls can be built up to 24–36in (60–90cm) and the base filled with rubble (for good drainage). The bed is then topped with 12–18in (30–45cm) of fertile soil.

Making paths

Paths between beds can be maintained as soil areas from which weed growth is regularly skimmed off. A mulched path requires more initial effort but reduces longer-term maintenance, especially if it is laid over a weed-suppressing landscape fabric. When topped with bark or gravel, this creates a firm, hard-wearing surface.

Grass pathways are most successful when a durable edging (for example rigid plastic or concrete blocks) is laid around the beds; the grass surface must stand above the edging to allow for unobstructed mowing.

The "no-dig" system

Cultivating the soil creates conditions in which weeds flourish; it exposes weed seeds to the light needed for germination. It may also cause a natural soil structure to deteriorate as air incorporated by digging causes more rapid breakdown of organic matter. The "no-dig" system is a method of cultivation used by organic gardeners to preserve soil structure and reduce loss of nutrients. It relies on minimal soil disturbance and regular surface applications of organic matter (applied well in advance of cropping so earthworms can incorporate it) to help suppress weeds, conserve moisture, and maintain soil fertility and structure. The success of the technique demands thorough initial weed clearance, especially of perennial weeds, by means of sheet mulches (or herbicides, for those gardeners who choose to use them). The no-dig technique is well suited to bed systems and can be very useful in reducing the labor of trenching and hilling up potatoes.

NO-DIG POTATOES

1 *To grow potatoes, lay the tubers on the soil surface, then cover with a 6–8in (15–20cm) layer of mulch.*

2 *Cover the mounded mulch with black plastic, attaching it securely. Make slits for potato shoots to grow through.*

MAKING A PATH BETWEEN BEDS

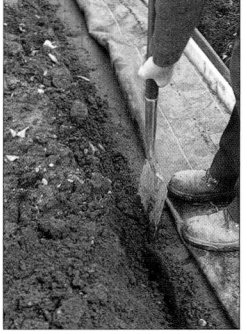

1 *Mark out, level, and firm the path. Cut a 1in (2.5cm) slit along each edge. Cut fabric to length and 8in (20cm) wider than the path.*

2 *Fold the fabric edge into the slit on one side. Secure with 4 x 1in (10 x 2.5cm) wood edging and hammer level. Pull fabric taut, and repeat on opposite side.*

3 *Cut crosses in opposite pairs in the fabric close to each board, 6ft (2m) apart. Knock a wooden peg through each cross, to 1in (2.5cm) below the board top.*

4 *Apply the mulch (here of bark chips). Rake and tamp down, so that the mulch is level with the board tops and the support pegs are concealed.*

Rotation

Rotation is a system by which vegetable crops are grown on different areas of the plot in succession in consecutive years.

Advantages of rotation

The principal reason for rotating crops is to prevent a buildup of soil-borne pests and diseases specific to one group of crops. If the same type of host crop is grown every year in the same soil, its pests and diseases increase rapidly in number and often become a serious problem, whereas in the absence of their host they gradually die out. Various types of nematode, clubroot (which attacks almost all brassicas) and onion white rot are some of the problems that may be alleviated by rotating crops.

Other benefits stem from rotating vegetables. Some crops, for example potatoes, blanket the soil so well that they smother most weeds, so it is useful to follow them with crops that are difficult to weed, such as onions. Most vegetables in the legume family, including peas and beans, fix nitrogen in the soil by means of nodules on their roots and make it available for the next crop. Therefore nitrogen-hungry crops such as leafy brassicas, potatoes, or spinach should follow legumes.

Several vegetables, including perennial types and many salad plants, do not fall into a principal rotation group. Salad plants stay in the ground for a short time and are therefore useful for intercropping. As with other vegetables, they should not be grown in the same patch of ground year after year. Perennial vegetables are best grown in a permanent bed of their own and so are not rotated.

Drawbacks of rotation

A weak point in the rotation theory is that rotation should take place over more than three or four years: clubroot and white rot infections can persist for up to 20 years. Rotations on that scale are out of the question in most gardens. Another shortcoming is that, in practice, the distance between beds is often so small that soilborne pests and diseases can easily spread from one to the next.

Planning for rotation

Despite the disadvantages, rotation is a sensible practice, and gardeners should try to build it into their plans.

Draw up a list of the main vegetables that you want to grow, with a rough indication of quantities. Growing vegetables that are climatically unsuited to the area is usually unsatisfactory, particularly in small gardens. List the various beds in the vegetable garden. Group the selected vegetables in their rotation groups, with a miscellaneous category for vegetables not in the main groups (see right).

Month-by-month planning

Make a chart with a column for each month of the year, and for every vegetable on your list fill in the months during which it will be in the ground. Remember that this period may be shortened by raising plants in containers (see "Sowing indoors," p.495) for transplanting later, and lengthened by the use of some form of cover early and late in the season (see "Growing under cover," p.499). Some crops, such as parsnips and cabbages, are sown once a year; but with others, such as lettuces and radishes, repeat sowings may provide a continuous supply throughout the growing season.

Planning a layout

Allocate each bed (or several beds if needed) to a different rotation group of vegetables, and write in the most important crop that each bed will grow. Refer to your month-by-month chart, and indicate a suitable crop to precede or follow it. For example, if Brussels sprouts are cleared in mid-spring, they may be followed by carrots, lettuces, or peas. Except where winters are very harsh, assume that most pieces of ground can bear two crops a year. Use this basic plan to rotate crops in subsequent years.

Consider the overall plan as a rough guide only. Many factors, in particular the weather, have a direct bearing on the success and failure of crops. The key to success lies as much in flexibility as in strict adherence to the plan. Keeping detailed records of your planting is an invaluable guide to improving performance in future seasons.

Intercropping

For maximum yield over a given area, crops of vegetables may be combined in a single bed. A fast-growing crop, such as radishes, is planted at the same time as a slow-growing crop, such as parsnips. A checkerboard pattern gives maximum efficiency, but alternate rows also work well. Fast growers make almost immediate use of the available space, but they reach maturity before the slow-growing crops need the room. Make sure that the short-term crop is not shaded by more slowly maturing vegetables.

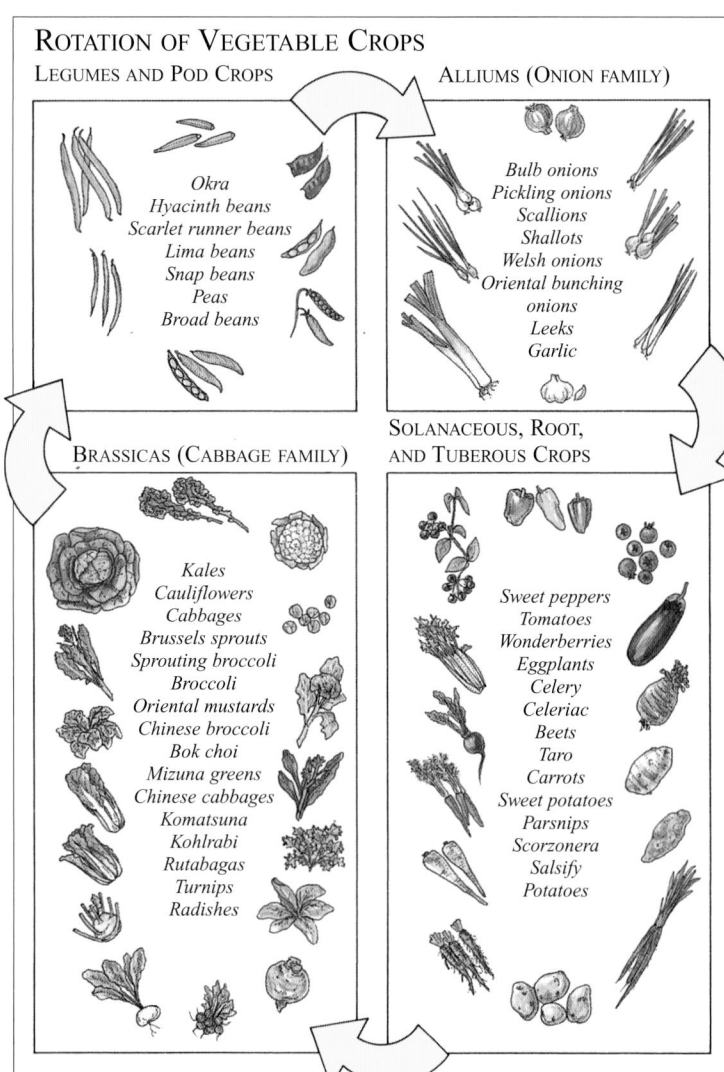

ROTATION OF VEGETABLE CROPS

LEGUMES AND POD CROPS

Okra
Hyacinth beans
Scarlet runner beans
Lima beans
Snap beans
Peas
Broad beans

ALLIUMS (ONION FAMILY)

Bulb onions
Pickling onions
Scallions
Shallots
Welsh onions
Oriental bunching
onions
Leeks
Garlic

BRASSICAS (CABBAGE FAMILY)

Kales
Cauliflowers
Cabbages
Brussels sprouts
Sprouting broccoli
Broccoli
Oriental mustards
Chinese broccoli
Bok choi
Mizuna greens
Chinese cabbages
Komatsuna
Kohlrabi
Rutabagas
Turnips
Radishes

SOLANACEOUS, ROOT, AND TUBEROUS CROPS

Sweet peppers
Tomatoes
Wonderberries
Eggplants
Celery
Celeriac
Beets
Taro
Carrots
Sweet potatoes
Parsnips
Scorzonera
Salsify
Potatoes

INTERCROPPING
Vegetables may be arranged to maximize yields by alternating rows of fast- and slow-growing crops (here, lettuces and brassicas). The fast-growing lettuces will have been harvested by the time the brassicas have reached maturity.

Sowing and planting

THE most common method of raising vegetables is from seed. There are several methods for sowing outdoors or under cover; use the most suitable for the chosen cultivar and the space available. Care in the early stages gives healthier, more productive crops. Thin or transplant seedlings to their final position in the garden, greenhouse, or container before they become overcrowded.

Choosing seed

In the past, seed was sold only as ordinary, "naked" seed, but it is now also available prepared in a variety of ways to make sowing and germination easier.

Purchasing seed

Always buy good-quality seed, preferably vacuum-packed to preserve viability. Many of the best cultivars are F1 hybrids, bred by crossing two selected parents. Although expensive, they are very vigorous and productive. Vegetable seeds differ widely in their viability: to be safe, buy seed dated for the current year, or test a sample before sowing (see "Pregerminating seed," below).

Prepared seed

Pelleted seeds are individually coated with clay to form tiny balls that are easier to sow evenly than naked seed. This is useful for handling particularly fine seeds such as those of carrots. Pelleted seeds should be carefully placed in a drill one by one, which saves transplanting later. They are sown in the normal way, but the clay coating must be kept moist until after germination.

Seed is also available embedded, evenly spaced, in paper sheets or tapes, which disintegrate in the soil after sowing. The tapes are laid in a drill and covered with soil as for ordinary seed. The backing gives protection in the early stages of germination and reduces thinning.

Pregerminating seed

To start ordinary seed early, it may be pregerminated indoors. This is useful for seed that germinates slowly in cold soil and may rot before germination. Space seeds on damp paper towels and put them in a warm place. Keep them moist until germination, then sow them carefully in containers or in open ground. This method may also be used to test a sample of old seed for viability before sowing.

Storing seed

Packets often contain more seed than is required for the current season. If stored incorrectly, seed will lose its viability quite quickly. To save seed with the least loss of viability, fold over the packet and seal it with tape. Put all the packets in a food-storage container with a tight-fitting lid. Before sealing the container, add a stay-dry package (such as those that come with electronic equipment) to absorb moisture. Store the container in the coldest part of the refrigerator. Most vegetable seeds can be frozen without any harm.

Sowing outdoors

Vegetables are sown either *in situ*, where they grow to maturity, or in a seedbed from which they are transplanted to their permanent position. *In situ* sowing is used for crops that are harvested young, such as scallions and radishes, or vegetables that do not transplant well, such as carrots and parsnips. Most other vegetables may be sown in a seedbed, in rows up to 6in (15cm) apart.

Successful sowing outdoors requires warm, well-prepared soil. Germination occurs for most vegetables once temperatures are over 45°F (7°C), so do not sow seed in cold soil. In several cases, lettuces for example, germination is poor at high temperatures. Particular temperature requirements for germination are given under individual vegetables. Soil temperature may be measured with a soil thermometer, but most gardeners use their knowledge of the soil to assess if it is warm enough for germination to occur.

Preparing the ground

Before sowing, dig the soil, then rake the surface until it has a fine texture or tilth, removing stones and large clods. Rake when it is neither very wet and heavy nor very dry. If soil sticks to your shoes, delay until it has dried out a little, but not so much that it is dusty.

If sowing in wet soil, standing on a board prevents damaging the structure of adjacent soil. This is not necessary with the bed system (see p.490–91) since the seed may be sown from the surrounding path.

Guidelines for sowing

Seeds are sown at different depths according to their size. Unless otherwise directed, sow small seed such as onions about 1/2in (1cm) deep,

SOWING IN A DRILL

1 *Mark out the drill using pegs and string. Use the corner of a hoe or a trowel to make the drill, ensuring that it is the depth required for the seed.*

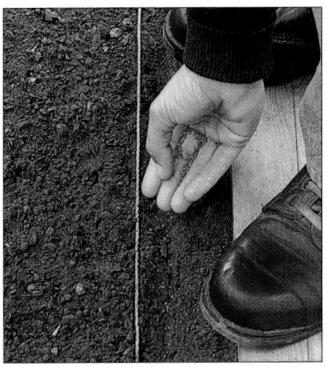

2 *Sprinkle the seeds thinly and evenly along the drill. Stand on a board placed parallel to the drill to prevent compaction of adjacent soil. Cover the seeds without dislodging them.*

ALTERNATIVE METHODS

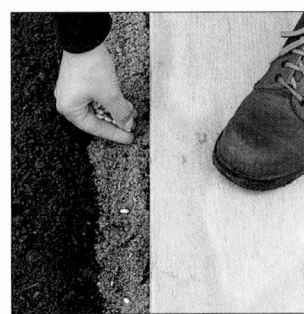

WET CONDITIONS
If the soil drains slowly or is very heavy, sprinkle a layer of sand at the base of the drill, sow the seed, then cover it.

DRY CONDITIONS
When the soil is very dry, water the base of the drill, then sow the seeds and lightly press them in before covering with dry soil.

brassicas 3/4in (2cm) deep, peas and corn about 1in (2.5cm) deep, and beans up to 2in (5cm) deep. The most important requirement is to sow thinly so that seedlings are not crowded in the early stages. Various methods of sowing are described below; whichever method is used, it is vital to preserve surface moisture. In dry weather, cover the soil after sowing with plastic sheeting or newspaper. Remove any covering when the first seedlings appear.

Sowing in a drill

This is the most common method of sowing vegetables. Mark a row with a string line and make a small, even channel (a drill) in the soil to the required depth. Take pinches of seed to scatter along the drill. Either space the seeds evenly, or station sow at intervals in groups of three or four

seeds to be thinned later to one seedling per station. If the seed is sown *in situ*, space the stations half the required distance between the mature plants to allow for losses; stations may be closer if seedlings are to be transplanted. Consider station sowing fast-growing crops such as radishes between slow-growing crops such as parsnips: the radishes are pulled up before the intervening space is needed by the parsnips. After sowing, cover the seed with soil, drawing it back lightly with a hoe or rake, firm the area gently, and water with a fine spray from a hose or watering can.

If sowing in unavoidably wet conditions, line the drill before sowing with dry, light material such as sand or vermiculite. If conditions are very dry, water the drill before sowing, lightly press each seed into the soil,

SOWING IN A WIDE DRILL

1 Use a draw hoe to mark out parallel drills 6–9in (15–23 cm) wide and flat at the base.

2 Sow seeds the required distance apart in the drill.

3 Cover the seeds with soil, using the hoe. Take care not to dislodge them.

4 Protect seeds from birds or animals by pegging wire netting over the drill.

then cover them with dry soil. This slows down the rate of evaporation and helps the seeds stay moist until they germinate.

Wide drills

Use wide, flat drills for plants that are grown closely together, such as peas, early carrots, and seedling crops. Make each drill up to 9in (23cm) wide and to the required depth. Space the seeds evenly in the drill, and cover carefully.

Large seed

The seed of beans and squash may be sown individually by placing a seed in a hole made by a small dibber or a finger. Make sure that each seed is at the base of the hole and in contact with the soil. Sowings of tender plants such as melons may be covered with glass jars or cut-off plastic bottles, which are removed once the seedlings emerge.

Broadcasting seed

In this method, the soil is first raked to produce a fine tilth; the seed is then scattered as evenly as possible, either by hand or from a packet. Rake the soil lightly again afterward to cover the seed.

Cut-and-come-again seedling crops

Many leafy or salad vegetables may be sown for harvesting at the seedling stage when they are at their most nutritious. Once cut, they often resprout to produce a second and third crop. This method is a very productive way to make use of a small area, and such crops are ideal for sowing under or between slower-maturing vegetables.

To obtain seedling crops, sow seed either broadcast or in wide drills or rows about 3in (8cm) apart; seedlings do not need thinning and are often ready for their first cut in a few weeks.

Successional crops

Vegetables that grow fast but rapidly pass their prime or run to seed (lettuces, for example) should be sown little and often. To avoid both gluts or gaps in cropping, wait until one sowing has emerged before making the next.

Thinning

Young seedlings need to be thinned to prevent overcrowding. Thin to the final spacing in stages, rather than immediately, to allow for any loss from pests and diseases; at each stage, aim to leave a seedling just clear of its neighbors. If the seeds have been sown *in situ*, continue to thin until they are at the spacing required for mature plants. Very small seedlings should be thinned by nipping them off just above ground level to avoid disturbing the roots of adjacent plants. Clear thinnings away since their scent may attract pests. Seedlings of plants such as lettuces, cabbages, and onions may be lifted for transplanting, and the soil gently refirmed around the remaining seedlings.

Planting

Plant or transplant vegetables when they are as young as possible so that they can grow without further check. Exceptions to this are plants raised in cell packs or containers (see opposite). Do not transplant root vegetables once the taproot has started to form, since this may distort it.

BROADCASTING

1 Prepare the area to be sown by raking carefully in one direction to produce a fine tilth. Sprinkle the seed thinly and evenly over the surface.

2 Rake lightly at right angles to the original direction to cover the seed, then water thoroughly with a fine spray from a hose or can.

THINNING SEEDLINGS

To thin small seedlings, nip them out at ground level so that the roots of the remaining seedlings are not disturbed.

Before taking plants from a seedbed, water around their roots; if the ground into which they are being planted is dry, water it lightly. Pick up a plant by a leaf rather than the stem or roots, which are easily damaged. Make a hole slightly bigger than the roots and position the plant in the hole, replacing the soil so that the lower leaves are just above soil level. Firm around the stem to anchor the plant. In hot weather, water seedlings,

TRANSPLANTING SEEDLINGS

Lift seedlings gently, keeping as much soil around the roots as possible. While moving them, place the seedlings in a clear plastic bag to retain moisture.

PLANTING DEPTH

Plant vegetable seedlings so that their lowest leaves are just above soil level. Planting too high exposes the stalk, which may not support the weight of the mature vegetable.

and then shade them with fine-mesh netting or newspaper cones until they are established. Keep the soil moist for a few days after planting (see "Critical watering periods," p.496).

Spacing
Different vegetables have individual spacing requirements, which sometimes determine their final size. Traditionally, vegetables are grown in rows with a recommended spacing between the plants, as well as between the rows.

They may alternatively be grown with equidistant spacing between the plants – the average of the recommended spacing between plants and rows; so plants 6in (15cm) apart, in rows 12in (30cm) apart, may alternatively be grown 9in (23cm) apart each way. This method probably gives the best results: plants have an equal share of light, air, moisture, and soil nutrients, and as they mature they form a canopy over the soil, which suppresses weeds (see also "The bed system," p.490). Vegetables may also be grown close together within widely spaced rows.

Sowing indoors
Vegetable seed may be sown indoors, in a cool greenhouse, or on a windowsill. This is helpful in climates with cool or short summers, for tender vegetables, and for those that need a long growing season. It is also a way of producing healthy seedlings and overcoming problems with germination, since the temperature is more easily controlled.

After germination, keep most seedlings at a lower temperature in a spacious, light, protected environment until they are planted out. Where this is not possible, it may be practical to buy more mature plants.

Seed trays
Sow seed in a small pan or seed tray, in standard sowing medium (for details see ANNUALS AND BIENNIALS, "Sowing in pots or trays," p.212). When the seedlings have two or three small leaves, prick them out into a seed tray of soil mix, spaced 1–2in (2.5–5cm) apart. Seedlings usually need to be kept slightly warm. Put them in a well-lit, draft-free place to grow quickly and evenly. Transfer larger plants to individual pots before planting them out.

Cell packs and small containers
Cell packs are individual units in which seeds are sown and plants grown for planting out directly. This

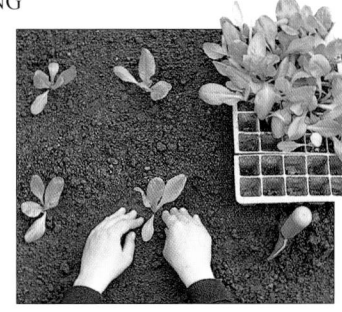

1 Fill the cell pack with sowing medium, and make a hole ¹/₄in (5mm) deep in each section. Sow 1 or 2 seeds per section. Cover with medium, then water.

2 Remove each plant from the cell pack. Make a hole to take its root ball. Place the plant in the hole with its lower leaves just above the surface; firm and water.

produces plants of high quality that grow on well: seedlings have no competition and so develop a healthy root ball, which is hardly disturbed when planted out in their final position. They do, however, need more space and medium in the early stages than those that are planted in trays.

Many sizes of cell are available, all designed to fit into a standard tray. Small containers include clay or plastic pots, degradable pots, and soil blocks made of compressed medium. The medium may be enclosed in netting, because roots can easily penetrate it as they grow.

Sow two or three seeds per unit; then thin the seedlings to leave the strongest. In some cases, such as onions and leeks, several seeds are sown and grown together, planted out as a unit at a wider spacing than usual, and grown on to maturity.

Hardening off
Plants raised indoors must be acclimatized to lower temperatures and wind before being planted in the open. Harden off by placing seedlings outdoors for increasing lengths of time. Eventually leave them out overnight against a wall, and then plant out.

Vegetative propagation
A few vegetables are usually raised vegetatively from offsets, tubers, corms, bulbs, or cuttings. This may be because they rarely set seed or, if raised from seed, are variable, or because vegetative propagation is faster. Details are given under individual vegetables (pp.501–542).

Growing vegetables in containers
Containers are useful for growing vegetables where space is limited, or to extend the vegetable garden into a paved area. They are used in the greenhouse, especially if the soil is infected with soilborne diseases, and it is impractical to sterilize or replace it. Vegetables need richer growing medium and more consistent and thorough watering than flowers and so are hard to grow well in containers unless they are carefully maintained.

Choosing the vegetables
The best vegetables for containers are compact, quick-maturing plants, such as lettuces, radishes, and beets, or robust, undemanding, leafy vegetables, such as Swiss chard. Fruiting vegetables, such as peppers, eggplants, and tomatoes, also flourish. Fast-maturing seedling crops also grow well. Dwarf cultivars are excellent since they do not need support. Do not use vegetables that are deep-rooting, slow to mature, or very tall or large, such as brassicas, parsnips, or celery. Raise plants for containers in cell packs; sow cut-and-come-again seedling crops in the container.

Preparing the container
The larger the container, and the greater its volume of soil or soilless mix, the better. Large vegetables

that are gross feeders, such as potatoes and tomatoes, generally need a container at least 10in (25cm) deep and wide. For large or top-heavy vegetables, the container must be strong and stable.

Good drainage is essential. If there are no drainage holes, make several of at least ¹/₂in (1cm) diameter in the base; cover them with screening to prevent blockage. For growing bags, follow the maker's instructions; drainage holes are not usually made, since they would allow infection to enter when laid on diseased soil.

The soil or soilless mix must be light and well aerated, since frequent watering will compact it. Lighten garden soil with well-rotted compost mixed with coarse sand and sphagnum moss.

In hot and windy weather, containers dry out rapidly by evaporation through the top and, if not made of plastic, the sides. To minimize this, do not put them in exposed sites or at the foot of a hot wall. Line nonplastic containers with plastic sheeting perforated with drainage holes.

Fast-maturing, compact lettuces

Dwarf broad beans

Stable plastic container to retain moisture

Peas supported by peasticks (bushy twigs)

Routine cultivation

THE best vegetables are produced when the plants are maintained in the optimum conditions for growth. Keep them free from weeds, and water them thoroughly as required. Mulches may be used to retain moisture and to suppress weeds. The level of nutrients needs to be maintained as the crop grows.

Watering

Most vegetables need reasonably moist soil; they vary, however, in the amount of water they require as well as when they most need it (see "Critical watering periods," below). Overwatering may lead to loss of flavor in tomatoes and carrots, and, in root crops, to the development of leaves at the expense of root.

How to water
It is more efficient to water heavily and occasionally rather than frequently and lightly; very young plants, however, should be watered lightly and frequently so that they never dry out. Light watering evaporates rapidly without reaching the plants' roots, and encourages shallow surface rooting rather than the deep rooting that enables plants to withstand drought. Direct the water at the base of each plant. Water in the evening when less moisture will evaporate, and allow time for the plants to dry before nightfall.

Watering equipment
Water young plants with a fine spray from a can. For general watering in small gardens, a can may be adequate; in larger gardens, use a handheld hose, regulating the flow with a nozzle attached to the end.

A practical choice in vegetable gardens is either a soaker hose or a porous hose laid among the plants (see also TOOLS AND EQUIPMENT, "Soaker hoses," p.555). These allow water to flow through fine holes, usually watering a strip about 12in (30cm) wide. The tubing can be easily moved from crop to crop, and some types of porous hose may be buried shallowly in the soil.

Critical watering periods
There are periods in the growing cycle of vegetables when water is particularly beneficial; these vary according to the individual vegetable. In prolonged dry weather, confine watering to these periods.

Germinating seeds, seedlings, and newly transplanted plants should never be allowed to dry out, so water frequently and lightly.

Leafy and salad vegetables, such as spinach, chard, most brassicas, and lettuces, require frequent watering to help them crop heavily. The most critical period is between ten days and three weeks before maturity; during this period, but only in very dry conditions, apply a single heavy watering of 5 gallons/sq yd (23 liters/sq m). Outside this period, give half this amount weekly during dry weather.

The critical point for fruiting crops such as tomatoes, peppers, beans, zucchini, cucumbers, and peas is when the flowers are forming and fruits or pods are developing. If conditions are dry during this time, water weekly at the rate for leafy crops (above). Do not water heavily before the critical period, since this produces leafy growth at the expense of fruit.

Root crops, such as carrots, radishes, and beets, need moderate watering during the growing period. In the early stages, water at a rate of 1 gallon/sq yd (5 liters/sq m) if the soil is dry. Increase this rate four-fold when the roots start to swell, watering every two weeks if dry conditions persist.

Minimizing the need to water
To conserve soil moisture, particularly in dry areas, dig the soil deeply, working in plenty of organic matter to improve soil structure and moisture retention and to encourage deep rooting. Keep the soil surface mulched (see "Mulching," right) and keep down weeds, which compete for moisture. Do not hoe in dry weather, since this encourages moisture to evaporate from the soil. Erect windbreaks to protect from desiccating winds (see "Shelter from wind," p.486). In areas prone to drought, adopt slightly wider spacing so that the roots can spread farther to take moisture from a larger area.

Controlling weeds

A vegetable garden should be free of weeds. They compete for water, nutrients, and light, may physically suffocate plants, and may harbor pests and diseases (see PLANT PROBLEMS, "Weeds," pp.658–61).

Perennial weeds
Wherever possible, clear a vegetable garden of perennial weeds before starting to grow crops. Dig out

A soaker hose laid between rows of vegetables ensures that the water will reach the roots of the plants and penetrate deeply into the soil.

deeply rooted and spreading perennials, taking care not to leave in the soil small pieces of root that will sprout again. Where a weed problem is very serious, either use appropriate weedkillers or smother the weeds with a lightproof mulch, such as old carpet or heavy black plastic. Most weeds (except very persistent ones) will die if covered for six to 12 months. While crops are growing, take care to prevent or control perennial weeds.

Annual weeds
These germinate and grow very rapidly and become a nuisance if they are allowed to seed freely in the vegetable garden. Pay particular attention to weeding in the first three weeks after crops germinate, when

they are most affected by competition. Pull up weeds by hand or hoe shallowly to avoid bringing deeper weed seeds to the surface. Remove the weeds to prevent rerooting.

Minimizing weed growth
During the growing season, weed growth may be greatly reduced by mulching crops (see below) and also by growing vegetables at equidistant spacing (see "Spacing," p.495). Once they have reached a reasonable size, most form a canopy over the ground, which suppresses weeds.

Stale seedbeds
Spring sowings or plantings are the most vulnerable to annual weeds. Where the soil has not been cultivated recently and may be full of weed seeds, prepare the soil in advance; allow the first flush of weeds to germinate, and hoe them off before sowing or planting (see also SOILS AND FERTILIZERS, "The stale seedbed technique," p.614).

Mulching

A mulch is a layer of organic or inorganic material laid on the soil around plants. Where the surface is kept mulched, the need to cultivate is lessened or even eliminated.

Organic mulches
Bulky organic mulches add nutrients to the soil and improve the soil structure. They may be in the form of compost, spent mushroom compost, dried lawn clippings, seaweed or well-rotted, straw-rich, animal manures. Do not use any materials derived from wood, such as sawdust and pulverized or shredded bark,

Many vegetables such as beans drop their flowers if the soil around their roots dries out. Water the crops well, then apply a mulch by carefully forking it onto the border. A mulch prevents soil-moisture evaporation and also insulates the soil, suppresses weeds, and protects the surface from heavy rain and erosion.

unless they are at least two years old, because their decomposition uses up soil nitrogen.

Organic mulches are best applied to growing crops in spring and early summer when the soil is moist. They maintain the temperature and moisture levels of the soil once they are applied so, if possible, mulch after the soil has warmed up in spring but before it starts to dry out. Never mulch cold, wet, or very dry soil. In areas with high rainfall and on heavy soil, however, an organic mulch is best spread on the ground in fall to allow the worms to work it in.

In practice, it is often easiest to apply organic mulches when planting, watering plants first if necessary. Alternatively, mulch young seedlings that are already planted and growing strongly and are at least 2in (5cm) high. A mulch may be 1–3in (2.5–7cm) deep or more; aim for a deep mulch if the purpose is to keep down weeds.

Plastic film mulches
These are sheets of plastic that may be black, white, transparent, or colored. Depending on which kind is used, they raise soil temperatures to bring on crops early, suppress weeds, reflect heat up to ripening fruit, and keep fruiting vegetables clean and free from soil splash. Shiny film mulches help deter flying pests.

Black films are mainly used to suppress weeds, although they also raise the soil temperature. Early potatoes may be grown under black films instead of being hilled up (see "Potatoes," p.541).

White films are used mainly to reflect light and warmth onto ripening fruit such as tomatoes and melons. Some films are made with the lower side black to suppress weeds, and the upper side white to reflect light. These films raise soil temperatures about 12°F (7°C) more than black films. Transparent films are used mainly to warm up the soil in spring, or to prevent soil splash.

It is simpler to lay films before planting or sowing crops. If desired, lay soaker or porous hoses in position first, then lay the film on the ground or over the bed to be covered. Make slits 3–4in (7–10cm) deep in the soil around the bed, and anchor mulch by tucking the edges into the soil, carefully using a spade or a shovel. This is simpler on slightly mounded beds. To plant, cut cross-shaped slits in the film with a knife, make a hole in the soil beneath, then carefully ease the plants through into the soil and firm. Sow large seeds, such as corn, by making holes in the plastic and pushing the seeds

PLANTING THROUGH A BLACK-AND-WHITE PLASTIC MULCH

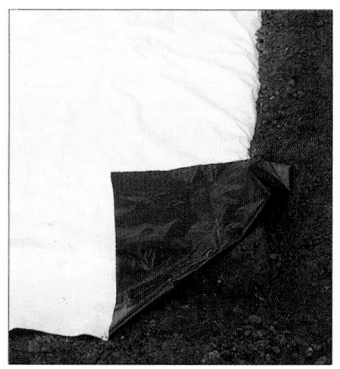

1 *Dig a trench around the area to be planted, lay down the mulch with the white side upward, and secure its edges firmly into the soil.*

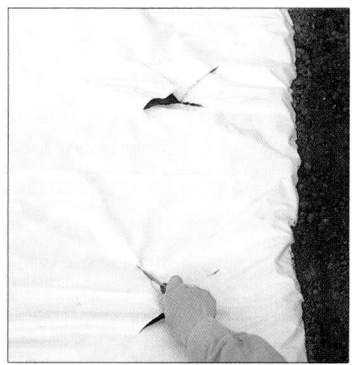

2 *Make cross-shaped slits in the plastic the required distance apart, then dig a hole in the soil large enough to take the plant's root ball.*

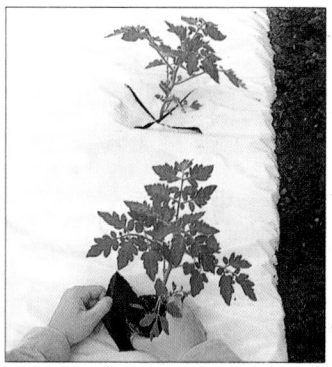

3 *Remove the plant (here a tomato) from its pot, and place it in the hole. Firm the soil around the root ball and water. Stake if necessary.*

through. When seedlings appear, guide them through the holes so that they are not trapped.

When necessary, water carefully through the planting holes. Slugs may be attracted to films: lift the film edges carefully and remove them or use a commercial slug killer.

Fertilizing

In fertile garden soils, into which plenty of organic matter is regularly worked, most vegetables will grow satisfactorily without the use of additional fertilizers. However, because it takes a few years to build up soil fertility, supplementary fertilizing will be necessary on poor soils or to correct deficiencies and, in some cases, to obtain higher yields.

Soil nutrients
Plants need a range of nutrients; the three most important for vegetables, and those most commonly in short supply, are nitrogen (N), phosphorus (P), and potassium or potash (K). For further information, see "Soil nutrients and fertilizers," pp.618–19.

Maintain adequate levels of phosphorus and potassium with an annual application of compost at 5–11lb/sq yd (2–5kg/sq m) or manure at 12lb/sq yd (5.5kg/sq m). You can also use inorganic fertilizers such as superphosphate (for P) and potassium sulfate (for K) at levels that are recommended by the manufacturer, or apply them in complete fertilizers that contain N, P, and K.

Potassium is washed out of soil slowly, so reserves last into the following season. Phosphorus is not lost through leaching but may be "locked up" in insoluble forms and not available to plants; reserves may need replenishing if soil analysis indicates that they are low. Nitrogen is constantly leached out, and reserves need to be replenished continually by adding either organic matter (which releases nitrogen as it breaks down) or inorganic fertilizers.

Vegetables vary in their need for nitrogen. For further information, see *Nitrogen Requirements*, p.498, which indicates the broad requirements of different groups using a fertilizer with 21 percent N content. Rates therefore vary according to which fertilizer is used; nitrogenous fertilizers include ammonium nitrate and potassium nitrate.

Applying fertilizers
Fertilizers are sold in dry forms (dusts, granules, and pellets) and as concentrated liquids (see "Types of fertilizer," p.618). They can be applied either as a base-dressing before sowing or planting, or as a top-dressing to give a boost during growth (see "Applying fertilizers," p.619).

Apply nitrogenous fertilizers in spring, a month before sowing or planting; additional applications may be made later in the growing season. Never apply nitrogen in fall, because most of the nutrient will be washed out of the soil before most vegetables are planted. Phosphorus and potassium fertilizers are applied at any time, often in fall or, where complete fertilizers are used, at the same time as nitrogen, in spring.

Fertilizing in organic systems
If extra fertilizing is necessary, use slower-acting organic fertilizers. Manure "tea" is useful in many cases.

Soak a burlap bag of dried manure, preferably from sheep, in a barrel of water until the resulting liquid is the color of weak tea. Use this for little risk of overfertilizing.

Various commercial and general-purpose liquid fertilizers are available, some based on animal manures and others on seaweed extracts. The latter appear to be particularly beneficial to growth, even though their nutrient levels are not very high. They are either watered in or applied as a foliar fertilizer.

Container-grown vegetables

The soil mix in containers can dry out very rapidly in hot weather. To conserve moisture, keep the upper surface mulched with up to 2in (5cm) of organic material, stones, or a sheet mulch. Be prepared to water thoroughly twice a day.

Occasional fertilizing may be necessary; use an organic or inorganic fertilizer at diluted strengths, according to the manufacturer's instructions. Top-dress the soil mix in the container in spring, and change the soil mix completely every two or three years when it becomes compacted and less productive.

Pests and diseases

Healthy plants can resist most pest and disease attacks. Therefore good care of plants will keep problems caused by pests and diseases to a minimum. Learn to recognize the most common pests and diseases in your garden, and take the appropriate preventive measures wherever feasible. Avoid using chemicals in the vegetable garden as far as possible. Apart from inherent dangers and the risk of residues in the soil as well as on the plants, they may kill the natural enemies of many pests and diseases. If using chemical controls seems unavoidable, try to use organically approved products at least. In a few cases, biological control – the introduction of a pest's natural enemy – may be used. For general information and details about specific pests and diseases, see PLANT PROBLEMS, pp.633–61.

Healthy practices

To reduce problems with pests and diseases, keep the soil fertile and well drained, work in plenty of organic matter, and rotate crops regularly (see p.492). Grow suitable crops for the climate, choosing (wherever possible) cultivars with pest and disease resistance or tolerance (see the lists of recommended cultivars for individual vegetables, pp.501–42). Always purchase disease-free plants. Raise plants in cell packs wherever feasible and harden off plants raised indoors. If growing plants under cover, always use clean seed trays and pots and sterilized soil mix.

Common pests

Animals that may attack vegetables include deer, rabbits, groundhogs, mice, moles, and birds. In cases of persistent attack, erect wire fences or nets around the garden or over crops, use humane animal traps, and deter large birds with humming wire and small ones with strands of black

thread. In damp climates slugs and snails may be the most serious of all pests. They are primarily night-feeders – gather them after dark by flashlight and discard them. Where chemical controls are used, they must be handled carefully.

Soil pests, such as slugs and cutworms, commonly attack young plants, sometimes biting through the stems of plants at ground level. They tend to be worse in newly cultivated ground. Thorough digging exposes them to the birds. Many soil pests are night-feeders and may be easily caught by flashlight .

Microscopic soil pests known as nematodes or eelworms attack certain groups of plants, including potatoes. Rotate crops to prevent the pests from becoming established, and grow resistant cultivars where they are available.

Sucking insects, including many species of aphid, as well as carrot rust flies, cabbage root maggots, and thrips, damage a range of plants by sucking the sap; they may spread virus diseases in the process. Knowledge of the pests' habits may help to prevent attacks – by making earlier or later sowings, for example. Use sticky yellow traps to catch aphids, collars (see *Collaring Seedlings*, p.501) to deter pests such as cutworms, and netting barriers against carrot rust flies (see p.538). Chemical or organic sprays may control outbreaks.

Various caterpillars attack a wide range of plants. Newly planted brassicas, in particular, are prone to attack by cutworms. A collar of aluminum foil will protect young plants. Pick caterpillars off by hand or use the biological control *Bacillus*

thuringiensis, or organic or chemical sprays. Fine nets placed over vegetables prevent butterflies or moths from laying eggs on the plants. Small beetles such as flea beetles nibble leaves of brassica sand eggplants; control them with sprays, and protect plants with row covers. Large beetles such as Colorado potato beetles pose serious problems.

Pests may multiply very rapidly in high temperatures. The most serious are whiteflies and spider mites, both of which attack a wide range of crops. They have become very resistant to most standard chemical sprays. As soon as these pests are noticed, introduce some form of biological control to restrict their numbers (see p.634).

CREATING HEALTHY GROWING CONDITIONS

Keep vegetable beds (here of ornamental cabbages and carrots) and paths free of weeds and debris; remove diseased plant material. Water and fertilize carefully – excess can be as damaging as too little. Thin seedlings early to avoid stunting, and remove the thinnings. Encourage rapid germination of homegrown plants by sowing indoors if conditions are adverse outside.

Common diseases

Diseases are caused mainly by fungi, bacteria, and viruses. Infected plants develop a range of symptoms that in some cases merely disfigure plants, but in others will kill them. Damping-off diseases, for example, infect and usually kill young seedlings; dig up and put affected plants in the garbage.

Diseases spread very rapidly in conditions that are favorable to their development, and once established are difficult to control. Preventive measures and good garden hygiene are vitally important to prevent diseases from spreading and becoming established. A few sprays may be used in anticipation of an attack. Choose disease-resistant cultivars.

Clubroot, a soil infection, is one of the most serious problems affecting members of the cabbage family. Raising the soil pH by applying lime (see "Liming," p.619), and raising plants in sterile soil in packs so that they are vigorous, may help to control this infection.

Physiological disorders

Some problems experienced with growing vegetables are due to incorrect cultural conditions. The most common problem is premature bolting (flowering and setting seed) caused by sudden low or high temperatures, drought, or sowing at the wrong time. Fruits may fail to set due to lack of pollination, erratic watering, or drought. If there are mineral deficiencies in the soil, cauliflower curds may fail to grow. Further details are given under individual vegetables (see pp.501–42), with advice on how to create healthy growing conditions.

NITROGEN REQUIREMENTS (USING FERTILIZER WITH 21 PERCENT N CONTENT)				
VERY LOW 1/2OZ/SQ YD (12G/SQ M)	LOW 1–1 1/3OZ/SQ YD (25–35G/SQ M)	MEDIUM 1 1/2–2OZ/SQ YD (45–55G/SQ M)	HIGH 2 1/2–3 1/2OZ/SQ YD (70–100G/SQ M)	VERY HIGH 4OZ/SQ YD (110G/SQ M)
Carrots Garlic Radishes (Peas do not require any extra nitrogen)	Asparagus Beans (all) Celeriac Chicory (all) Cucumbers Endive Florence fennel Gherkins Globe artichokes Kohlrabi New Zealand spinach Okra Onions (all) Parsnips Peanuts Rutabagas Salsify Scorzonera Summer squash Tomatoes Turnips (and turnip tops) Zucchini	Amaranths Broccoli Broccoli raab Cabbages (for storage) Cauliflowers Eggplants Hot peppers Jerusalem artichokes Kales Lettuces Potatoes (early) Rhubarb (young) Spinach Sprouting broccoli Sweet corn Sweet/chili peppers Sweet potatoes Taro Watermelons Winter squash Wonderberries	Beets Brussels sprouts Celery Leeks Malabar spinach Melons Potatoes (maincrop) Spinach beet Swiss chard	Bok choi Cabbages (spring, summer, winter) Chinese broccoli Chinese cabbages Komatsuna Mizuna greens Oriental mustards Rhubarb (cutting years)

Growing under cover

THE productivity of a vegetable garden may be increased greatly in climates with a short growing season by growing plants under cover in a protected environment for some or all of their life cycle. The shorter the growing season, the more useful cover will be.

Under cover, air and soil temperatures are increased, and crops are sheltered from chilly winds. This lengthens the growing season by up to two months. The quality and yields of many crops are improved by higher temperatures and shelter.

Cover may be used to start crops early in spring for planting outside when temperatures rise. Some summer vegetables that would not mature outdoors during the growing season may ripen under cover; in cool climates, okra and eggplants, for example, ripen fully only under cover. The winter cropping period of many vegetables may be extended; lettuces, peas, oriental brassicas (see p.507) and spinach, for example, all stop growing in the open but continue under cover.

Make the most of cover by making sure that the soil underneath is fertile and weed-free. Vegetables require extra watering under cover – mulch them where practical to cut down on watering. Plants started under cover may be set back if abruptly exposed to the elements. Harden them off gradually where appropriate.

Greenhouses and frames

Cover may be provided by anything from a greenhouse to a cold frame or a plastic polytunnel. For full details, see GREENHOUSES AND FRAMES, pp.560–77.

Greenhouses
A permanent, glazed greenhouse provides an excellent growing environment. It is easily ventilated and retains heat at night better than plastic film. Diseases may build up in soil if crops such as tomatoes are grown for several consecutive years. The soil must then be changed or sterilized, or crops grown in containers. Supports may be required for tender climbing vegetables.

Walk-in polytunnels
These are made of heavy-duty, clear plastic sheeting on metal supports. They are cheaper and easier to erect than greenhouses, and they may be

LOW POLYTUNNEL

Use wire hoops pushed into the ground 3ft (90cm) apart to support plastic film, which is tied at each end to a stake. Tie strings over the plastic and secure them at the base of each hoop.

moved to a different site if required. Ventilation is hard to control, however, increasing the risk of pests and diseases if temperatures rise rapidly; holes may be cut in the film in summer and taped over in winter. The film needs to be replaced every two or three years.

Low polytunnels
These are cheap, mobile, and flexible; the lightweight plastic film may be rolled back for ventilation and watering. They provide shelter from wind and are useful in most gardens, especially for the final stages of hardening off seedlings and protecting vegetables in unsettled spring and fall weather. Low polytunnels are limited by their height and flimsiness, however, and give little protection from low temperatures. They also need to be well anchored in windy situations.

Garden frames
Being relatively small, frames are most beneficial in gardens lacking space for a greenhouse or polytunnel. Some types are portable. They are easily ventilated, and may be heated by electric soil-heating cables. They are useful for raising and hardening off seedlings. Their low height limits the range of crops that may be grown, although the lids may be removed to allow semihardy crops to mature. Garden frames may be blacked out for forcing crops such as Belgian endive and endive.

Covers
Although individual covers protect only a small area, when placed end to end they can be used to cover an entire row. To make maximum use of covers, move them from one crop to another during a season; for example, protect overwintering salad greens, then start early potatoes or dwarf beans in spring, then ripen early melons in midsummer.

Sheet covers

These are various types of sheet covers, including perforated plastic film, netting films, nonwoven row covers, and improvised materials such as old bedsheets. All may be laid over low polytunnel hoops or directly over crops after sowing or planting, and anchored shallowly in the soil or weighted down. The covers are lifted by the crops as they grow.

Sheet covers promote earlier crops and higher yields by raising air and soil temperatures and by protecting plants from wind and (in some cases) insect pests. All give better ventilation than unperforated plastic films.

Weed beds carefully before laying sheet covers, since they are awkward to lift for weeding later.

Perforated plastic films
These are perforated with tiny slits or holes. They are generally used in the early stages of growth. Disadvantages include overheating in hot weather, minimal frost protection, and the risk of plants being chafed. To harden plants, slit plastic films down the center a few days before removing them completely.

Netting films
Fine netting films are strong and last for several seasons. They are well ventilated so may usually be kept on until plants mature. They have little effect on temperature but do protect against wind. Provided that they are well anchored at the edges, they also protect against many insect pests.

Nonwoven row covers
These light, soft, nonwoven films usually last one season. Depending on the films' weight, they may protect against frost and flying insect pests; the films are more permeable to light and air than plastics. Many vegetables may be grown under fleecy film until they are nearly mature.

USING SHEET COVERS

PERFORATED PLASTIC FILM
These are spread over a bed of seedlings and hilled up at the edges so that they are loose enough to allow for growth. Perforated plastic film protects the seedlings but allows ventilation.

NETTING FILM
This protects plants against insect pests and wind damage.

NONWOVEN ROW COVER
This is effective against light frost and deters insect pests.

Harvesting and storing

How and when vegetables are harvested, and whether they are used fresh, stored, or both, depends on the nature of the vegetable and the climate. The shorter the growing season and the more severe the winter, the greater the incentive to store vegetables, either naturally or by freezing. For details, see individual vegetables (pp.501–42) and *Vegetables that Freeze Well*, below.

Harvesting

Follow the guidelines under individual vegetables for how to harvest. Most vegetables are harvested at maturity, but some, notably leafy plants and brassicas, may be cut at various stages and will often resprout for a second and third crop.

Cut-and-come-again harvesting
This method of harvesting is suited to vegetables that resprout after an initial cut has been made, enabling them to be used fresh over a fairly long period. Crops may be harvested at the seedling stage, or later when they are semimature or mature.

Harvest seedling crops when they are 2–4in (5–10cm) high, cutting about ³⁄₄in (2cm) above soil level. Some, for example arugula and cress, may be cut and left to resprout several times in succession. See also "Cut-and-come-again seedling crops," p.494.

Some semimature or mature crops, if harvested by cutting 1–2in (2.5–5cm) above soil level, will resprout, producing more leaves and, in some cases, edible flowering shoots (see "Harvesting and storing oriental brassicas," p.507).

The technique is suited to certain types of lettuce, endive, sugar loaf chicory, Oriental greens, and Swiss chard. It is useful in cool climates in fall and early winter because plants treated this way survive lower temperatures than they would otherwise and may be very productive, especially under cover.

Storing

The length of time that vegetables may be stored depends on the storage conditions and on the vegetable or cultivar. For details, see individual vegetables. The main cause of deterioration after harvesting is water loss, so aim to keep this to a minimum. Do not store damaged or diseased specimens: they may rot.

Vegetables often freeze well; almost all need to be blanched either in steam or boiling water and cooled quickly before freezing. The only exception to this is sweet peppers, which may be frozen without any initial preparation.

Leafy vegetables and brassicas
Leafy vegetables and various types of brassica, such as broccoli and cauliflowers, have such a high water content that few of them store well. An exception is the winter-storage cabbage, which may be stored either hanging in nets or on a bed of straw, in a frost-free shed or cold frame. Several brassicas freeze well; some

VEGETABLES THAT FREEZE WELL

Asparagus 1
Beets 1 3
Broad beans 1
Broccoli 1
Broccoli raab 1
Brussels sprouts 1
Carrots 1 3
Cauliflowers 1 2
Celery 2
Chinese broccoli 1
Chinese cabbages 1 2
Eggplants 1 2
Hot peppers 1 2
Hyacinth beans 1
Kales 1
Kohlrabi 1 2
Lima beans 1
New Zealand spinach 1
Okra 1
Parsnips 1 3
Peas 1
Pole beans 1
Potatoes (small and new potatoes only) 1
Rhubarb 2
Rutabagas 1 2
Scallions 2
Scarlet runner beans 1
Snap beans 1
Spinach 1
Spinach beet 1
Sprouting broccoli 1
Summer squash 1 2
Sweet corn 1
Sweet peppers 1
Swiss chard 1
Tomatoes 1
Turnips 1 2 3
Winter squash 2
Wonderberries 1
Zucchini 1

KEY
1 Blanch
2 Dice, slice, purée, or shred
3 Freeze only when young

STORING STRINGS OF ONIONS
Braid together the dried onion leaves to form strings of bulbs. These may be hung outside in warm weather to dry even more, and then brought indoors to be stored in frost-free conditions.

cultivars are bred for the purpose. Freeze only top-quality produce.

Fruiting vegetables
Vegetables such as tomatoes, eggplants, and cucumbers usually have an optimum time for harvesting, although fruits may also be harvested immature. If they are to be stored for winter use, they are best made into preserves or deep frozen.

Sweet peppers keep in good condition for many months if whole plants are pulled up and hung in a dry, frost-free place. Certain cultivars of winter squash may be stored for several months. Leave the fruit on the plant until it is mature, then pick and cure it in the sun to harden the skin so that it forms an effective barrier to water loss, and store it in a dry, frost-free environment (see also "Winter squash," p.519).

Bulbs
Certain cultivars of onion, shallot, and garlic will keep for many months. Lift the crop when mature or nearing maturity, and dry it in the sun (or under cover in wet climates), until the outer skins are papery. Handle the bulbs carefully to avoid bruising. Hang them as braided strings, in nets, or spaced out on trays, in well-ventilated, frost-free conditions (see also *Storing Onions in a Box*, p.529).

Root vegetables
Some root vegetables, such as carrots and potatoes, may be either harvested young and eaten immature or left to mature and lifted and stored at the end of the season. A few, such as parsnips, are extremely hardy and may be harvested at any time the soil is not frozen solid.

Prepare vegetables carefully for storing, removing any foliage, since this will rot. Store only healthy, unbruised specimens. Potatoes are susceptible to freezing; store them packed in lightproof sacks in a frost-free place.

Root vegetables such as beets and carrots easily lose moisture, so store them in layers in boxes of moist sand or peat in a cool shed or cellar (see *Storing Carrots*, p.538). They may also be stored in outdoor piles: stack them on straw and cover with more straw, and, in colder areas, a layer of soil to give protection against freezing (see *Making a Rutabaga Pile*, p.537).

STORING RED CABBAGES

Lay the cabbages on slats covered with straw in a cool, well-ventilated, frost-free place. Leave gaps between them to allow free air circulation and discourage rot.

Western brassicas

WESTERN brassicas include kales, cauliflowers, cabbages, Brussels sprouts, sprouting broccoli, broccoli, turnip tops, broccoli raab, kohlrabi, rutabagas, and turnips. They are usually cooked, but some are used raw. For kohlrabi, rutabagas, and turnips, see pp.534, 536, and 537 respectively.

COLLARING SEEDLINGS

Newly planted brassicas are especially prone to attack by cutworms. Protect the plant by pushing a collar of aluminum foil or half a frozen-juice can into the soil around the plant.

Western brassicas are naturally biennial but are cultivated as annuals for their leaves and roots, and as biennials for flower heads and shoots. Each type displays considerable variation, and there is often a range of cultivars for different seasons. Western brassicas are cool-season crops with varying degrees of frost tolerance; most perform poorly at high temperatures, so in warm climates grow them in winter. In temperate climates, they may provide crops for much of the year.

Siting Western brassicas
An open situation with fertile, well-drained, moisture-retentive soil is required. Rotate brassicas (see p.492) to avoid a buildup of clubroot. If this is a problem, lime the soil (see p.619) to bring the pH to 6.5–7. Most Western brassicas need medium levels of nitrogen (see p.498), but they should not be planted on freshly manured ground since this causes overlush growth that is prone to pests. A base-dressing may be applied to the area before planting (see "Applying fertilizers," p.497).

Sowing and planting Western brassicas
Western brassicas prefer firm soil; they may be planted after a previous vegetable crop without forking the

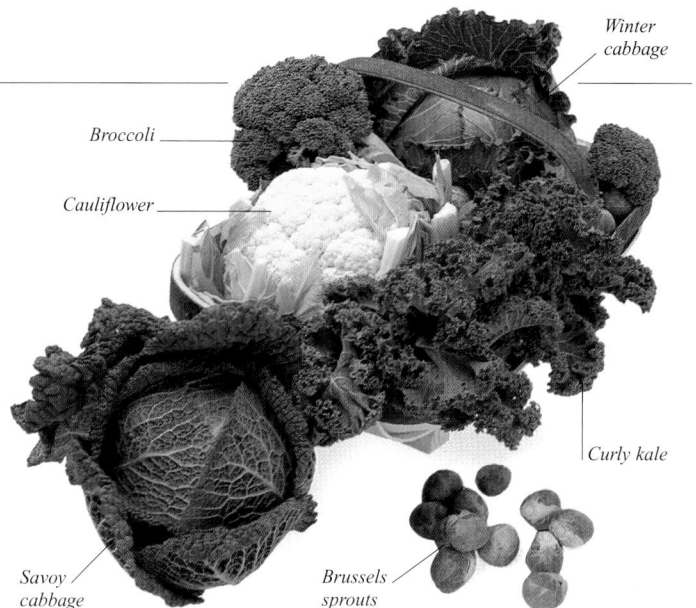

Broccoli
Cauliflower
Winter cabbage
Curly kale
Savoy cabbage
Brussels sprouts

soil. Sow *in situ*, in a seedbed, or indoors in trays or cell packs for transplanting. If the soil is infected with clubroot, sow in cell packs, transferring to pots before planting out. Tall, top-heavy brassicas such as Brussels sprouts should be planted 4in (10cm) deep. Hill up the stem as it grows by building a small mound of soil around it to a depth of about 4in (10cm); in windy sites, support the stem with a stake 3ft (1m) high. Plant brassicas firmly, with the lower leaves just above soil level. In some cases, spacing may be varied to determine the size of the brassica.

Cultivating Western brassicas
Mulch Western brassicas after planting to suppress weeds. In dry weather, water as for leafy vegetables (see "Critical watering periods," p.496). Apply a nitrogenous fertilizer during growth.

Flea beetles (p.638), slugs and snails (p.638), damping off (p.655), cabbage root maggots (p.652), whiptail, and cutworms (p.652) all affect young plants. Caterpillars (p.639), whiteflies (p.639), mealy aphids (see "Aphids," p.639), and clubroot (p.642) attack plants at all stages of growth.

Kales (*Brassica oleracea* Acephala Group)

Grown as annuals or biennials depending on the type, dwarf kales are 12–16in (30–40cm) tall, with a 12in (30cm) spread; tall types grow to 3ft (90cm) and spread up to 24in (60cm). Some American kales are known as collards. Plain (such as the tall 'Champion') and curly-leaved types (such as the medium-sized 'Blue Surf') and curly-broad hybrids (such as the tall 'Westland Winter') usually produce leaves from a central stem. The leaves of all kales, and the spring-flowering shoots and young leaves of broad-leaved types, are used cooked or raw. Kales are the hardiest brassicas, some surviving at 5°F (-15°C); many also tolerate heat. All prefer fertile, well-drained soils and need medium nitrogen levels (see p.498).

Sowing, planting, and routine cultivation
Sow seed in early spring for summer crops, and in late spring for fall and winter crops. Sow *in situ* or in seedbeds, cell packs, or seed trays for transplanting; dwarf forms should be spaced 12–18in (30–45cm) apart, tall forms 30in (75cm) apart.

Give overwintering types a nitrogenous top-dressing in spring to encourage growth. In severe winters, grow dwarf cultivars under cloches or low polytunnels. Kales are usually unaffected by pests and diseases.

Growing under cover
For very early, tender kales, sow seed in early spring in rows 6in (15cm) apart, or in wide drills. Either harvest them as large seedlings, or thin the seedlings to 3in (7cm) apart and cut when they form plants 6in (15cm) tall, leaving the stumps to resprout for a second harvest.

Harvesting and storing
Some cultivars mature seven weeks after sowing, but plants can stand a long time in the ground. Snap off the leaves as required in fall and winter to encourage new growth. Pick the shoots in spring when they are about 4in (10cm) long, before the flowers open. Kales freeze well.

CURLY KALE

ORNAMENTAL KALES
Ornamental kales are grown mainly for winter decoration in the garden or for garnishing salads. Leaves are variegated green, red, white, and/or purple.

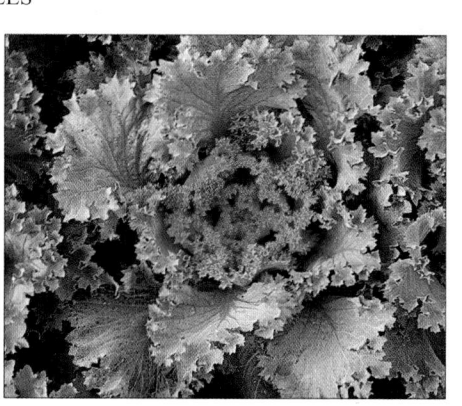

Cauliflowers (*Brassica oleracea* Botrytis Group)

Grown as annuals or biennials, cauliflowers form an average head (or curd) of about 8in (20cm) in diameter; the plants are 18–24in (45–60cm) tall, with a spread of up to 3ft (90cm). They are classified by the main season of use, usually winter (with a distinction between those for frost-prone and frost-free areas), early summer, and summer/fall, although these groups overlap (see *Cauliflower Types*, below). Most types of cauliflower have creamy or white curds, but there are attractive, distinctively flavored types with green or purple curds. The curds, and in some cases the young leaves surrounding them, are cooked or used raw in salads. Smaller curds, or mini-cauliflowers, about 2in (5cm) in diameter, may be specially grown from early summer cultivars.

Cauliflowers are a cool-season crop and do not usually grow well in areas with high summer temperatures. Several cultivars are frost hardy, but cauliflowers may only be harvested all year in areas with frost-free winters. For soil and site, see "Siting Western brassicas," p.501; overwintering cauliflowers need a sheltered situation outside,

and are not usually grown to maturity under cover. All cauliflowers need a moisture-retentive soil, with medium nitrogen levels (see p.498) and a pH of 6.5–7.5.

Sowing and planting
Success with cauliflowers depends on sowing the correct cultivar at the appropriate time, and allowing plants to develop with as few checks to growth (from transplanting or dry soil, for example) as possible. Where drought is likely in summer, grow fast-maturing mini-cauliflowers or spring-heading types, which will benefit from fall rains.

The main sowing times and spacings are given in the chart below. Cauliflowers are usually sown in seed trays, cell packs, or a seedbed for transplanting, but may be sown *in situ* and thinned to the correct spacing. Generally, the later the planting, the larger the cauliflower will grow and the wider the spacing required. Seed germinates best at a temperature of about 70°F (21°C).

For a very early summer supply, sow seed in fall, in seed trays or cell packs, then pot up seedlings in small pots. Put the pots into a well-ventilated frame or under cloches for the winter. Alternatively, sow *in situ* in frames or under cloches, thinning to 2in (5cm) apart. Harden off seedlings before planting them out in spring. For a later crop, sow indoors in gentle heat in early spring, and prick out into small pots.

For summer/fall and winter groups, sow the first batch indoors in seed trays or cell packs, or *in situ* in frames or under cloches. Successive sowings may be made either in a seedbed outdoors, or in cell packs for transplanting later on.

To obtain mini-cauliflowers, select an early summer cultivar to be sown in spring or early summer; sow several seeds per station, 6in (15cm) apart, thinning to one seedling after germination. Alternatively, raise plants in packs and plant them out 6in (15cm) apart. For a continuous supply, make successive sowings.

Routine cultivation
Cauliflowers need regular water throughout the growing period. In dry conditions, water at a rate of 5 gallons/sq yd (23 liters/sq m) every two weeks. Overwintering cauliflowers require low nitrogen levels when planted or they will be too soft to survive the colder conditions. A nitrogenous fertilizer or organic liquid fertilizer may be applied in spring.

To prevent white curds from discoloring in sunny weather, tie the leaves over the curds. This may also be done in winter and spring to protect curds of overwintering types from the elements; most modern cultivars, however, have leaves that naturally tend to cover the curds.

PROTECTING CAULIFLOWER CURDS

 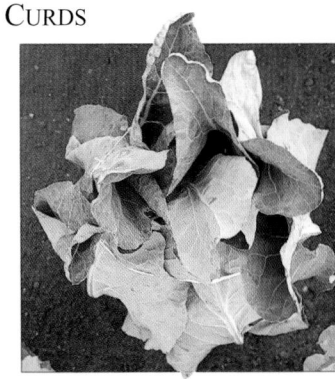

1 *In winter and early spring, mature curds of overwintering types may need protection from severe cold and hard frost.*

2 *Wrap the leaves up around the central curd, securing them with soft string, to prevent cold damage.*

Pests and diseases
For cauliflower pests and diseases, see "Cultivating Western brassicas," p.501. Cauliflowers are also attacked by pollen beetles (p.649).

Harvesting and storing
The time from sowing to maturity varies from approximately 16 weeks for summer/fall cauliflowers to about 40 weeks for winter ones. Cut the curds while they are still firm and tight. Mini-cauliflowers mature about 15 weeks after sowing and should be picked immediately since they deteriorate quickly. All cauliflowers, and in particular the mini-cauliflowers, freeze well.

RECOMMENDED CAULIFLOWERS

Winter
'Glacier'

Early summer
'Early Dawn'
'Early Snow Ball'
'Milkyway'
'Minuteman'
'Pathfinder'
'Quasar'
'Snow Crown'

Summer/fall
'Amazing'
'Cumberland'
'Fremont'
'Serrano'
'White Rock'
'White Sails'

'White Sails'

Green cultivars
'Chartreuse'

Purple cultivars
'Burgundy Queen'
'Graffiti'
'Violet Queen'

MINI-CAULIFLOWERS

PURPLE-HEADED CAULIFLOWER

CAULIFLOWER TYPES

GROUP	WHEN TO SOW	WHEN TO PLANT	SPACING	WHEN TO HARVEST
Winter (frost-free areas)	Late spring	Summer	28in (70cm)	Winter/very early spring
Winter	Late spring	Summer	25in (63cm)	Early spring
Early summer	Fall/early spring (sow under glass)	Spring	21in (52cm)	Early to midsummer
Summer/fall	Mid- to late spring	Early summer	22–5in (55–63cm)	Late summer to late fall

Cabbages (*Brassica oleracea* Capitata Group)

Most cabbages are grown as annuals. Plants are generally 8–10in (20–25cm) tall, with a spread of up to 28in (70cm). The average head is about 6in (15cm) in diameter.

They are grouped according to their season of maturity, although there is some overlap between the groups. Leaves are dark or light green, blue-green, white, or red, and smooth or crinkled (savoy). Cabbage heads are pointed or round, and vary in their density. Spring greens are either loose-leaved cultivars or standard spring cabbages harvested before the head forms. Cabbage leaves are eaten either cooked or raw and sliced in salads. They may also be pickled. Stems and stalks may be sliced finely and cooked if they are tender enough. Some types of winter cabbage may be stored.

Cabbages grow best at 59–68°F (15–20°C). Do not plant in temperatures over 77°F (25°C). The hardiest cultivars may survive temperatures as low as 14°F (-10°C) for short periods. Cabbages are not usually grown under cover.

To grow well, cabbages need soil that is fertile, moisture-retentive, and organic with a pH level above 6. Spring, summer, and fresh winter cabbages require very high nitrogen levels, and winter-storage cabbages medium nitrogen (see p.498). Do

MATURE SPRING CABBAGES

not give spring cabbages a nitrogenous base-dressing at planting, since the nitrogen will probably be washed from the soil over winter; top-dress in spring instead.

Sowing and planting

Sow the chosen cultivars at the correct time for their group (see *Cabbage Types*, below). Sow seeds in seedbeds or cell packs and transplant seedlings to their final position on average five weeks later. Appropriate spacing varies according to type (see chart below) and it may be

modified to vary the size of the head; adopt closer spacing for smaller heads, and wide spacing to produce larger heads. A collar may be placed around each seedling stem when transplanting to protect against cutworms (see *Collaring Seedlings*, p.501). Ensure that young seedlings have sufficient moisture until they are well established.

For spring greens either grow a greens cultivar, spacing the plants about 10in (25cm) apart, or use a heading spring cultivar and space plants 4–6in (10–15cm) apart. Cut

FALL CABBAGE

RED SUMMER CABBAGE

SAVOY CABBAGE

RECOMMENDED CABBAGES

Spring
'Earliana'
'Early Marvel'
'Emerald Acre'
'Golden Cross'
'Greensleeves' (greens only)
'Primax'
'Savoy Express'
'Stonehead'

'Golden Cross'

Early summer
'Cheers'
'Dynamo' F1
'Golden Acre'
'Gonzales' F1
'Primero' F1 (red)
'Spivoy' F1
'Tastie' F1

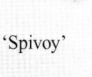

'Spivoy'

Summer
'Blue Vantage'
'Cheers'
'Gourmet'
'Red Dynasty'
'Savoy Ace'
'Savoy Queen'
'Super Red'
'Taler' (savoy)

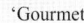

'Gourmet'

Fall
'Emblem'
'Grand Prize'
'Megaton' F1
'Primavoy' (savoy)
'Vantage Point'

Winter (for storage)
'Danish Ballhead'
'Hilton'
'Multikeeper'
'Ruby Perfection' (red)
'Sanibel'

Winter (to use fresh)
'Aquarius'
'Celtic' F1
'Ice Queen' F1
 (savoy)

'January King 327'

'January King 327'
'Julius' F1 (savoy)

CABBAGE TYPES

Group (Time of Maturity)	Description	Main Sowing Period	Average Spacing
Spring	Small, pointed or round heads	End of summer	12in (30cm)
	Loose-leaf greens	End of summer	10in (25cm)
Early summer	Large, mainly round heads	Very early spring (sow under cover)	14in (35cm)
Summer	Large, round heads	Early spring	14in (35cm)
Fall	Large, round heads	Late spring	20in (50cm)
Winter (for storage)	Smooth, white-leaved, winter white types	Spring	20in (50cm)
Winter (to use fresh)	Blue, green, and savoy leaf types	Late spring	20in (50cm)

HARVESTING SPRING GREENS

Plant spring cabbages 6in (15cm) apart. When they have grown on, but before they start to form a compact heart, harvest alternate plants, cutting them at the base. Use these as spring greens.

HOW TO OBTAIN A SECOND CROP

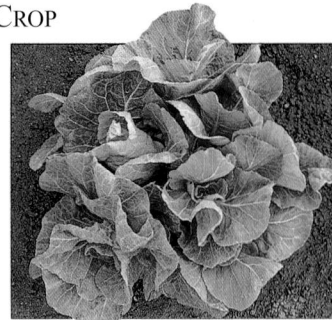

1 *To produce a second crop of greens, make a cross-shaped cut in the stalk after harvesting the cabbage head.*

2 *A few weeks later, several miniature heads should have sprouted, ready for a second harvest.*

them young as loose greens; every second or third plant may be left to heart up if a heading cultivar is used.

Routine cultivation

To increase their stability, hill up winter cabbages as they grow. Protect spring cabbages under cloches or floating row covers, and apply a liquid fertilizer or a nitrogenous top-dressing in spring; fertilize others in the growing season. Keep moist throughout growth (see "Critical watering periods," p.496).

Pests and diseases

For pests and diseases that may affect cabbages, see "Cultivating Western brassicas," p.501. Southern blight (p.647) may also occur.

Harvesting and storing

Spring and summer cultivars vary in their ability to stand in good condition once the head has matured; modern cultivars often stand longer than traditional ones. Normally the plant is dug up once the head has been cut, but spring and early summer cultivars may produce a second crop if the head is cut to leave a 4in (10cm) stalk in the ground. Using a sharp knife, make a shallow cross in the top of the stem to encourage new growth. Provided that the soil is kept fertile and moist, three or four more small heads may develop together on the stalk.

Storage cabbages (winter white cultivars and appropriate red cabbages) should be lifted before heavy

PREPARING CABBAGES FOR STORING

Before storing cabbages, carefully remove any loose or discolored outer leaves without damaging the head (see inset). Inspect the cabbages regularly while they are in storage, and remove leaves that are rotting.

frost. Dig them up and carefully remove any loose outer leaves. Place them on slatted supports or straw on the floor of a shed, or suspend them in nets. Store the heads at just above freezing point, with relatively high humidity. They may also be stored in a cold frame, provided that it is ventilated on warm days to discourage rotting (see also *Storing Red Cabbages*, p.500). Cabbages may keep for four or five months.

Brussels sprouts (*Brassica oleracea* Gemmifera Group)

These are biennials grown as annuals, varying in height from about 14in (35cm) for the dwarf forms to 30in (75cm) for the tall forms, with a spread of up to 20in (50cm) in both cases. Brussels sprouts are loose-ly divided by their time of maturity into early, midseason, and late groups. The earlier types tend to be dwarfer and less hardy. The mod-

ern F1 cultivars are an improvement over the older, open-pollinated ones; they perform better on fertile soils, are less prone to lean (since they have a stronger root system), and have more compact, even sprouts. The tight sprouts that develop on the stem are cooked or shredded raw into salads. The mature leaves at the top of the plants may also be eaten. There is a well-flavored, but less productive, red cultivar, 'Rubine'.

Brussels sprouts are typical cool-season brassicas; the hardiest cultivars survive temperatures of 14°F (-10°C). If sown in succession where winters are mild, Brussels sprouts provide a constant crop from early fall to late spring. Apply a high-nitrogen fertilizer shortly before planting (see p.498). Avoid using freshly manured ground since this encourages blown and loose, rather than firm, sprouts. For soil and site requirements, see "Siting Western brassicas," p.501.

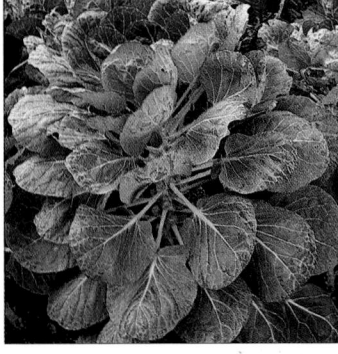

DWARF BRUSSELS SPROUTS PLANT

HILLING UP BRUSSELS SPROUTS

About a month after planting out, hill up Brussels sprouts by drawing the soil around the base of the stem to increase stability. At this stage they may also be staked if they are in an exposed site.

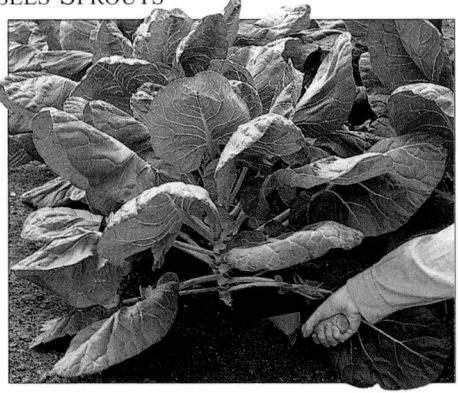

Sowing and planting

Starting with the early-maturing cultivars, sow in succession from mid- to late spring as the soil begins to warm up. For a very early crop, sow in gentle heat under cover in early spring. Sow in seed trays or in

a seedbed for transplanting, or *in situ* in firm ground; most Brussels sprouts do not grow well in cell packs.

Thin out or transplant to the required spacing in early summer, generally four to five weeks after sowing. Plant dwarf cultivars about

18in (45cm) apart, and tall cultivars about 2ft (60cm) apart. Use closer spacing to produce smaller sprouts of a more uniform size, and wider spacing for large sprouts that mature in succession and so may be picked over a longer period. Wide spacing also encourages good air circulation, which keeps plants healthy and disease-free. Plant tall cultivars deeply and hill up the stems as they grow to provide extra stability. Keep young plants moist until they are well established.

REMOVING LEAVES

Snap off any yellowing or diseased leaves that develop, because these may carry fungal diseases that could spread to the whole crop. This also improves air circulation.

Brussels sprouts, with their slow rate of growth, may be intercropped in the first few months with fast-maturing vegetables.

Routine cultivation
Keep beds weed-free. Since plants are widely spaced, extra watering is required only in very dry conditions, when they should be watered at the rate for leafy crops (see "Critical watering periods," p.496). A top-dressing of a nitrogenous fertilizer or an organic liquid fertilizer may be applied in late summer if the plants are not growing vigorously. Remove any withered or diseased leaves from the stems as they appear.

If sprouts are wanted for freezing, grow an early cultivar that matures in fall, and nip off the sprout top or growing point in late summer, when the lower sprouts are roughly ½in (1cm) in diameter. All the sprouts will then mature for picking together, rather than in succession.

Pests and diseases
The most common problems are mealybugs (p.640), which can colonize the individual sprouts, and downy mildew. For other diseases likely to affect Brussels sprouts, see "Cultivating Western brassicas," p.501.

Harvesting and storing
Brussels sprouts are ready to harvest about 20 weeks after sowing. Their flavor is improved after they have

been exposed to some frost. Pick the lowest sprouts first by snapping them off at the base; the upper sprouts will continue to develop. If the sprouts are intended for freezing, pick them before the outer leaves become damaged by winter weather; freeze only top-quality sprouts. Sprout tops may be harvested by cutting them off at the end of the season.

After harvesting, dig up the plants and break up the stems with a hammer. This deters the buildup and spread of brassica diseases and enables the stems to rot down more quickly when composted.

Where winters are very severe, uproot the whole plants before the ground freezes and hang them in a cool, frost-free place; the sprouts will remain fresh for several weeks.

F1 AND OPEN-POLLINATED SPROUTS

Modern F1 hybrids produce sprouts that are compact, evenly spaced, and of uniform size. Traditional open-pollinated cultivars are more likely to produce blown sprouts widely varying in size.

F1 HYBRID

TRADITIONAL CULTIVAR

RECOMMENDED BRUSSELS SPROUTS
Early
'Jade Cross E'
'Oliver' F1

'Jade Cross E'

Midseason
'Bubbles'
'Prince Marvel'
'Vancouver'

Late
'Harley'
'Red Rubine'
'Trafalgar' F1

Sprouting broccoli (*Brassica oleracea* Italica Group)

These large, biennial plants may reach a height of 2–3ft (60–90cm) and a spread of 2ft (60cm). There are purple and white forms; the purple is more prolific and hardier. The flowering shoots that develop in spring are eaten cooked.

Sprouting broccoli is considered one of the hardiest winter vegetables, surviving temperatures of about 10°F (-12°C). Because it is a slow-maturing vegetable that occupies the ground for up to a year, it requires a fertile soil and medium nitrogen

levels (see p.498). Avoid shallow and sandy soils and sites exposed to strong winter winds.

Sowing, planting, and routine cultivation
Sow in spring, either in a seedbed or in cell packs. Transplant from early to midsummer, spacing plants at least 2ft (60cm) apart, and planting them deeply for stability.

Plants may need staking in the fall in areas where they will overwinter. If birds peck at the leaves, cover the plants with netting to protect them for the winter. For further cultivation requirements, see "Cultivating Western brassicas," p.501.

Pests and diseases
Sprouting broccoli is, in theory, affected by common brassica pests, but in practice is fairly trouble-free. Pollen beetles (p.649) attacking the flowering shoots are an increasing problem in some areas.

RECOMMENDED SPROUTING BROCCOLI
'De Ciccio'
'Italian Sprouting'
'Purple Sprouting'

'Purple Sprouting'

'San Marzano'

Harvesting and storing
Pick shoots as they mature. Snap them off when they are about 6in (15cm) long, while the flowers are in bud. Pick regularly to encourage the production of more shoots; plants may crop for up to two months. Sprouting broccoli freezes well.

PURPLE SPROUTING BROCCOLI

Broccoli (*Brassica oleracea* Italica Group)

Regular (nonsprouting) broccoli is grown as an annual or biennial, and produces compact plants about 18in (45cm) tall, with a spread rarely over 15in (38cm). Cultivars are classified as early, midseason, and late, with the earliest maturing the fastest. F1 hybrids are more productive than the original cultivars. The compact terminal head and the young side shoots are best eaten lightly cooked; they are also eaten raw.

Broccoli is a cool-season crop and should not be grown in areas where the average mean temperature is above 59°F (15°C). Young plants tolerate some frost, but it may damage embryonic and young heads once they start to develop. Broccoli needs an open site in moisture-retentive, fairly fertile soil with medium nitrogen levels (see p.498).

Sowing and planting

Sow in succession from spring to early summer for a crop during summer and fall. Broccoli seedlings do not transplant well, so either sow two or three seeds per station *in situ*, or sow in cell packs and transplant seedlings to moist ground, disturbing the roots as little as possible. For an early crop, make the first sowings indoors; these plants are, however, especially prone to bolting when transplanted.

HARVESTING BROCCOLI

1 *Just before the flower buds open, harvest the first central head by cutting through the stalk.*

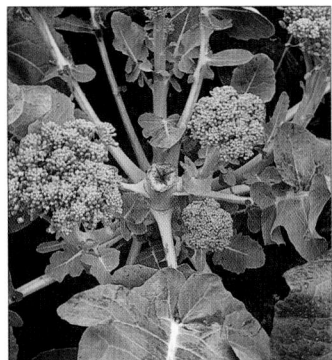

2 *This encourages sideshoots to develop; these can also be harvested, and more sideshoots will be produced.*

Broccoli plants grow well at various spacings. For the highest overall yield, space plants 9in (22cm) apart each way, or 6in (15cm) apart in rows spaced at 12in (30cm). Closer spacing produces smaller terminal shoots, which mature together and are suitable for freezing.

Routine cultivation

Keep the bed weed-free. Broccoli plants need plenty of water to crop well – 2 gallons/sq yd (11 liters/sq m)

every two weeks. In very dry conditions, water as for leafy crops (see "Critical watering periods," p.496). A nitrogenous top-dressing or an organic liquid fertilizer may be applied once the terminal heads have been cut in order to encourage additional side shoots to develop.

Pests and diseases

For pests and diseases that may affect broccoli, see "Cultivating Western brassicas," p.501. Problems

may also be caused by pollen beetles (p.649) and downy mildew.

Harvesting and storing

Broccoli is a fast-maturing brassica, ready 11–14 weeks after sowing. The main head should be cut when it is 3–4in (7–10cm) in diameter, while still firm and before the flower buds open. Sideshoots will subsequently develop; cut these when they are about 4in (10cm) long. Broccoli freezes well.

RECOMMENDED BROCCOLI

Early
'Dividend' F1

'Dividend' F1

'Packman' F1
'Regal'
'Southern Comet' F1

Midseason
'Everest'
'Premium Crop' F1

Late
'Barbados' F1
'Windsor'

Turnip greens and broccoli raab (*Brassica rapa*)

Over the centuries different brassicas have been grown for cutting in the immature stages for use as quick-maturing greens. The two types commonly used for this purpose today are turnip greens (*Brassica rapa* Rapifera Group) and broccoli raab (*Brassica rapa* Utilis Group), which

is also known as turnip rape and by a number of Italian names such as *cime di rapa*, rapini, and *broccoletti*.

They are grown as annuals or biennials, generally with single stems that reach a maximum height of about 12in (30cm). The leaves, young stems, and sweetly flavored

young flower heads are eaten cooked as spring greens, or raw in salads.

Turnip greens and broccoli raab are cool-season brassicas. Grow them in spring and fall in hot climates, or all year where summers are cool. All turnip cultivars are suitable; broccoli raab has no named cultivars. Both grow best in fertile, moisture-retentive soil and require low to medium nitrogen levels (see p.498).

Sowing, planting, and routine cultivation

Sow thinly broadcast or in rows 4in (10cm) apart. For larger plants, thin to 6in (15cm). For an early crop in cold areas, make the first sowing indoors in early spring. Plants need little attention subsequently.

Harvesting and storing

Harvest plants within seven to eight weeks of sowing. Make the first cut when they are leafy and 4in (10cm) tall, or wait until the immature flowering shoots appear and the plant is

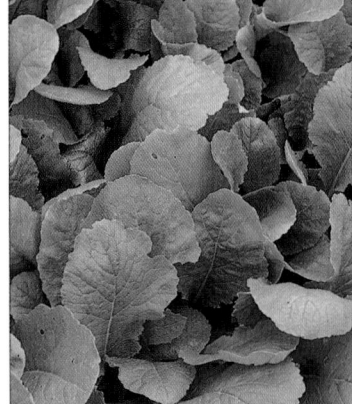

TURNIP GREENS

8–10in (20–25cm) tall. Cut about 1in (2.5cm) above ground level. In cool weather, the plants resprout to give two or three further cuttings over a period of four or five weeks. Cut as long as the stems are tender. Use turnip greens and broccoli raab fresh, since they do not store well.

BROCCOLI RAAB

Oriental brassicas

Loose-leaved Chinese cabbage

Tight-headed Chinese cabbage

Bok choi

Bok choi

SEVERAL Oriental brassicas are now becoming popular in the West. They have many features in common with Western brassicas but tend to be faster growing and have a wider range of uses than Western brassicas. If they are given the right conditions they are highly productive. They are grown as annuals or biennials.

Oriental brassicas are cultivated mainly for their leaves and leafy stems, but also for their young, sweetly flavored flowering shoots. Leaf shape and color vary from the glossy, white-ribbed leaves of some bok choi cultivars, and the feathery green leaves of mizuna greens, to the purplish green of Oriental mustards. Oriental brassicas are nutritious, succulent, and crisp, and are mild to peppery in flavor. Cook them, preferably by stir-frying or steaming, or use young leaves and shoots raw in salads.

Oriental brassicas are best suited to climates with cool summers and mild winters, although many cultivars are available that are adapted for hotter climates. Most will withstand light frost, especially if harvested when they are semimature as a cut-and-come-again crop (see p.494). A few Oriental brassicas, such as komatsuna and some of the mustards, are extremely hardy.

In temperate climates, Oriental brassicas grow best in late summer and fall. Where winter temperatures fall only a few degrees below freezing, they may be grown as a winter crop under cover in unheated structures; if planted late in the summer they may crop from fall to spring, although they will stop growing at low temperatures.

Oriental brassicas require similar conditions to Western brassicas (see "Siting Western brassicas," p.501) but, being fast-growing, hungry, and thirsty plants, the soil must be rich in organic matter, moisture-retentive, and fertile. They never develop well in poor, dry soil. Most of them have very high nitrogen requirements (see p.498).

Sowing and planting Oriental brassicas

All standard methods of sowing may be used; where there is a risk of plants going to seed prematurely (bolting), sow seed in cell packs or *in situ*. Many have a tendency to bolt when days are lengthening, particularly when this is combined with low spring temperatures. In these cases, in northern latitudes, delay sowing until midsummer, unless plants are started off in heat or cultivars with bolting resistance are used. If bolting continues to be a problem, grow Oriental brassicas as seedling crops, and harvest the leaves before the plants start to bolt.

Their rapid rate of growth makes Oriental brassicas ideal for intercropping among slower-maturing vegetables, especially for cutting as a cut-and-come-again seedling crop, when their flavor is superb.

Cultivating Oriental brassicas

Oriental brassicas are generally shallow-rooting and so need regular watering. In very dry conditions, water at the rate for leafy crops (see "Critical watering periods," p.496). They should also be kept mulched.

Oriental brassicas and Western brassicas are susceptible to the same pests and diseases (see "Cultivating Western brassicas," p.501). Those with tender leaves are very prone to slugs and snails (p.638), caterpillars (p.639), and flea beetles (p.638). They may be grown under fine nets to provide some protection.

Harvesting and storing Oriental brassicas

Most Oriental brassicas mature within two to three months after being sown. They may be harvested at four different stages from seedling to mature plant.

They may be harvested at the seedling stage using cut-and-come-again techniques (see "Cut-and-come-again harvesting," p.494), or left a few weeks longer and cut as semimature plants. When the plants are fully mature they may be either harvested all at once or alternatively cut about 1in (2.5cm) above ground level so that they sprout again for a second crop. The flowering shoots that develop naturally from mature plants may also be harvested before the flowers open.

In the West, Oriental brassicas are mainly used fresh, although most will keep for a few days if refrigerated. In the Orient, leaves are pickled or dried, and Chinese cabbages are stored for off-season supplies.

Oriental mustards (*Brassica juncea*)

The mustards are a varied group of annuals and biennials, forming large, often coarse-leaved plants. Leaf texture may be smooth, blistered, or deeply curled; some cultivars have purple leaves. The mustards are naturally very robust and less prone to pests and diseases than most oriental brassicas. Several, including the purplish green 'Miike Giant', 'Osaka Purple', and 'Xue Li Hong' survive at least 14°F (-10°C). The distinctive flavor may be piquant, becoming stronger as they run to seed. The leaves are used cooked but may also be eaten raw in salads when young or if sliced.

Sow from mid- to late summer in temperate climates for harvesting from fall to spring, and in late spring in cold regions for harvesting in summer. The seed is small and is sown in shallow soil *in situ* or in cell packs. Thin or plant out seedlings 6in (15cm) apart for harvesting young, and 14in (35cm) apart for growing to larger plants. If they are planted under cover in fall, plants are more tender, but will run to seed earlier the following spring.

Oriental mustards mature in six to 13 weeks, depending on the cultivar. Cut single leaves as required.

PURPLE-LEAVED ORIENTAL MUSTARD

Chinese broccoli
(*Brassica rapa* var. *alboglabra*)

These annuals, also known as Chinese kale, form stout plants with thick, blue-green leaves, growing up to 18in (45cm) tall. The succulent, flavorful, chunky flower stems, which may be ¾in (2cm) thick, are generally cooked.

Chinese broccoli tolerates higher summer temperatures than many other brassicas, and it withstands light frost. In warm and temperate climates, sow from late spring to late summer. For a very early crop, make a first sowing under cover in spring to transplant outside. For a protected early winter crop, plant under cover in fall. In cool climates, delay sowing until midsummer since sowings made earlier than this may bolt.

Sow seed *in situ* or in cell packs. For small plants, to be harvested whole as soon as the flowering shoots appear, grow plants 5in

CHINESE BROCCOLI

(12cm) apart with 4in (10cm) between rows. For large plants, to be cropped over a longer period, space plants 12in (30cm) apart each way. Cut the main shoot first, as for broccoli (see opposite); further side-shoots will continue to develop for harvesting later. Large plants take nine to ten weeks to mature.

Bok choi
(*Brassica rapa* var. *chinensis*)

Bok choi is a biennial usually grown as an annual, forming a loose head of fairly stiff leaves with wide midribs that broaden out markedly and overlap at the base. There are many types, the most common being white-ribbed and green-ribbed, available as F1 cultivars 'Joi Choi' (white) and 'Mei Qing Choi' (green). They vary in size from squat forms about 4in (10cm) tall to large plants 18in (45cm) tall. Bok choi is succulent and mild in flavor, and may be eaten either cooked or raw.

Bok choi grows best at cool temperatures of 59–68°F (15–20°C). Most cultivars will tolerate some frost in the open but survive lower temperatures under cover grown as winter cut-and-come-again crops. A few are suited to hotter climates.

In temperate climates, sow seed throughout the growing season. There is some risk of premature bolting with spring sowings, so confine these to cut-and-come-again seedling crops. Sow seed *in situ* or in cell packs. Spacing depends on cultivar and size of plant required, ranging from 4in (10cm) apart for small cultivars to about 18in (45cm) apart for the largest cultivars. In late summer, transplant bok choi under cover for a fall crop.

Bok choi may be harvested at any stage from seedlings to the young flower shoots of mature plants.

BOK CHOI

HARVESTING SEEDLINGS

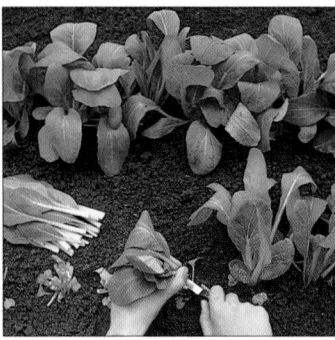

Bok choi may be harvested at the seedling stage. If they are cut about 1in (2.5cm) from the ground, new leaves will sprout.

Seedling leaves will be ready for harvesting in three weeks. They may be cut 1in (2.5cm) above ground level and will resprout. Mature plants may be cut higher and will also resprout for a second harvest.

Mizuna greens (*Brassica rapa* var. *nipposinica*)

Mizuna greens are annuals or biennials, depending on climatic conditions. They have dark green, glossy, deeply serrated, almost feathery leaves and slender, white, juicy stems forming a rosette up to 18in (45cm) in diameter and about 9in (23cm) tall. They are highly decorative, especially when grown as an edging or in blocks. Mizuna greens are eaten cooked, or raw when leaves are harvested young and tender.

They are very adaptable, capable of tolerating both high summer temperatures (provided that they are in moisture-retentive soil) and winter temperatures down to 14°F (-10°C).

They may be sown throughout the growing season. Resistance to bolting is good and seed may therefore be sown in seed trays or cell packs, in a seedbed for transplanting, or *in situ*. For a tender winter crop, sow in late summer to transplant under cover. Space plants 4in (10cm) apart for small plants harvested young, and up to 18in (45cm) apart to obtain large plants. Mizuna greens are useful for intercropping if cut at the seedling stage.

Mizuna greens mature eight to ten weeks after sowing and may be harvested at all stages; seedling leaves may be ready within two or three weeks (see "Harvesting and storing Oriental brassicas," p.507). The plants are vigorous, and are capable of resprouting several times after they have been cut initially.

MIZUNA GREENS

Chinese cabbages (*Brassica rapa* var. *pekinensis*)

These are annuals or biennials usually grown as annuals. Chinese cabbages have dense, upright heads. The leaves are marked by prominent white veins, the broadened midribs overlapping at the base rather like bok choi. The barrel type forms a stout head about 10in (25cm) high, the cylindrical type a longer, less compact head up to 18in (45cm) high. Leaf color ranges from dark green to almost creamy white, especially in the center. There are also some very attractive loose-headed types. Mild-flavored with a crisp texture, Chinese cabbages are excellent in salads and lightly cooked.

For preferred climatic conditions see "Bok choi" (left). Most headed types are likely to bolt if they are sown in spring, unless a temperature of 68–77°F (20–25°C) is maintained during the first three weeks of growth. It is best to delay sowing until early summer. Some loose-headed types may be sown in spring. If they start to bolt, treat them as cut-and-come-again crops, although the leaves of some cultivars may be rough-textured and hairy when young. Sow seed in cell packs or *in situ*; thin or transplant seedlings to 12in (30cm) apart. Plenty of moisture throughout growth is vital. Chinese cabbages have soft leaves that are susceptible to pests (see "Cultivating Oriental brassicas," p.507).

Chinese cabbages mature eight to ten weeks after sowing. They can be harvested at any stage, since they respond well to cut-and-come-again treatment both after the main heads have been cut, and during growth, as semimature plants.

RECOMMENDED CHINESE CABBAGES

'China Pride' (barrel)
'Jade Pagoda' F1 (cylindrical)
'Kasumi' (barrel)

'Jade Pagoda'

HARVESTING CHINESE CABBAGES

1 *Harvest Chinese cabbage (here a loose-leaved cultivar) by cutting about 1in (2.5cm) above soil level.*

2 *After a few weeks, new leaves will have formed and may be cut. Stumps may resprout several times.*

Komatsuna (*Brassica rapa* var. *perviridis*)

The komatsuna group, also known as mustard spinach, is extremely diverse; its members form large, productive, robust, healthy plants, often with glossy leaves that may be up to 12in (30cm) long and 7in (18cm) wide. The flavor of the leaves resembles cabbage, with a touch of spinach, and they are eaten cooked, or raw, finely sliced in salads.

Komatsuna plants tolerate a wide range of temperatures and will survive 10°F (-12°C). Some cultivars are suitable for tropical climates.

Plants are less likely to bolt from early spring sowings than most Oriental brassicas, and they are more drought-tolerant. For sowing and spacing, see "Mizuna greens" (left). Komatsuna makes a satisfactory winter crop under cover.

KOMATSUNA

Leaves may be harvested at all stages (see "Harvesting and storing Oriental brassicas," p.507). Mature plants are usually ready to be harvested eight weeks after sowing.

Leafy and salad vegetables

THIS group of vegetables is grown for the great variety of leaves that it produces, which may be eaten raw in salads, or cooked. The freshly picked leaves are both delicious and highly nutritious. The range of leaf color also gives them decorative value. Careful choice of cultivar and the right growing conditions ensure a year-round supply. If seeds are sown in succession, gluts of crops maturing together may be avoided. Due to the high moisture content of the leaves, many store for only two or three days; however, a few are suitable for freezing.

Butterhead lettuce

Loose-leaf lettuce

Spinach

Romaine lettuce

Belgian endive

Amaranths (*Amaranthus* spp.)

These rapidly growing annuals reach a height of about 24in (60cm) and a spread of 12–15in (30–38cm). *Amaranthus cruentus*, the most commonly grown as an edible crop, has oval, light green leaves; amaranth cultivars are mostly local – they include 'Fotete', 'Green Spinach', and 'Stubby'. *A. tricolor*, or Chinese spinach, has red, yellow, or green leaves and greenish white flowers; cultivars include 'Lal Sag Rouge', 'Tampala', 'Banerjee's Giant', and 'Crystal'. *A. caudatus* has pale green leaves and is often grown as an ornamental plant for its vivid red, tassellike flowers. Amaranth species are also known as African or Indian spinach. The leaves of the plants and immature flower buds are cooked and eaten in the same way as spinach.

Amaranths are tropical and subtropical plants that require temperatures of 72–86°F (22–30°C) with a humidity of above 70 percent to crop well. They may also be grown in temperate climates in greenhouses or outdoors in a sunny, sheltered site. Moderately deep, well-drained, fertile soil with a pH of 5.5–7 and medium to high nitrogen levels are required (see p.498).

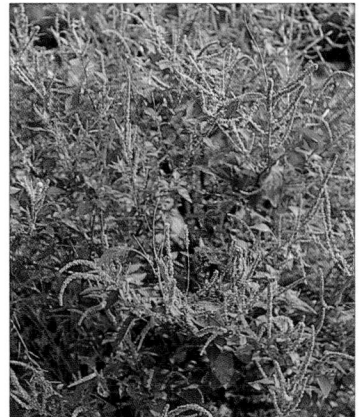

AMARANTHUS CRUENTUS

Sowing and planting
Sow outdoors in spring, once the temperature is high enough, in rows 8–12in (20–30cm) apart. Thin seedlings to 4–6in (10–15cm) apart when they are about 2–3in (5–7cm) high. Protect with plastic covers or under cloches until the young plants have become established.

In cool areas, or for an earlier crop, seed may be sown in trays in a greenhouse; prick out seedlings into 3 or 3½in (7 or 9cm) pots when they are large enough to handle. Transplant them outdoors when they are 3–3½in (7–9cm) tall, spacing them 4–6in (10–15cm) apart.

Routine cultivation
Keep amaranth beds weed-free, and water regularly. Apply a balanced fertilizer or organic liquid fertilizer every 2–3 weeks. Give additional dressings of nitrogen and potassium every three weeks on less fertile soils. Apply an organic mulch around the base of the plants to retain moisture and warmth. When the plants are 8in (20cm) tall, pinch out the growing point to encourage lateral shoots and to produce a heavier crop.

Pests and diseases
Downy mildew, powdery mildew (p.640), caterpillars (p.639), and aphids (p.639) may affect amaranths outside, and thrips (p.640) and damping off (p.655) under cover.

Growing under cover
When seedlings are 3in (7cm) tall, transplant them to 8in (21cm) pots, grow bags, or beds, spacing them 15–20in (38–50cm) apart each way. Keep them at a minimum temperature of 72°F (22°C). Water, and maintain 70 percent humidity by damping down in hot weather.

Harvesting and storing
Amaranths are ready to harvest eight to ten weeks after sowing. Using a sharp knife, cut young shoots up to 4in (10cm) long when the plants are about 10in (25cm) tall; they will produce further shoots over several months. Continue picking them as required. Amaranths are best eaten fresh; alternatively, they may be stored for up to one week at 32°F (0°C) and 95 percent humidity.

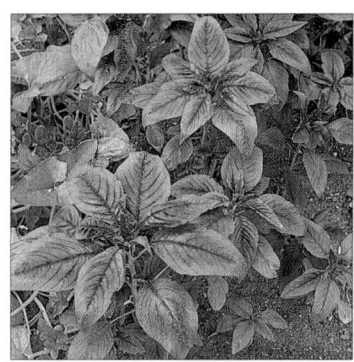

AMARANTHUS TRICOLOR

Malabar spinach (*Basella alba*)

Also known as Ceylon, Indian, or vine spinach, these short-lived, twining perennials may grow to 12ft (4m) tall if supported. Var. *alba* has dark green leaves; var. *rubra* has red stems and leaves. The oval or round leaves are eaten cooked; the purple berries are not normally eaten.

Malabar spinach is a tropical and subtropical plant that requires a temperature of 77–86°F (25–30°C). Lower temperatures reduce the growth rate, resulting in smaller leaves. Larger leaves are, however, produced in light shade. Well drained and highly fertile soil with a pH of 6–7.5 and high nitrogen levels (see p.498) are required for good growth.

Sowing and planting
Sow in seed trays or 3 or 3½in (7 or 9cm) pots, maintaining the required temperature range. When the seedlings are 4–6in (10–15cm) tall, transplant them to well-prepared beds, spacing the plants 16–20in (40–50cm) apart each way.

Routine cultivation
Support plants by staking or by tying in the stems to a vertical or horizontal trellis. Keep plants weed-free and water as necessary. Mulch with organic material. Apply a balanced granular or liquid fertilizer every two to three weeks during the growing period. When the seedlings reach a

SUPPORTING MALABAR SPINACH

Malabar spinach may be supported on a trellis parallel to the ground, raised about 12in (30cm) above soil level. The stems should be evenly spaced on the trellis so that they do not become overcrowded.

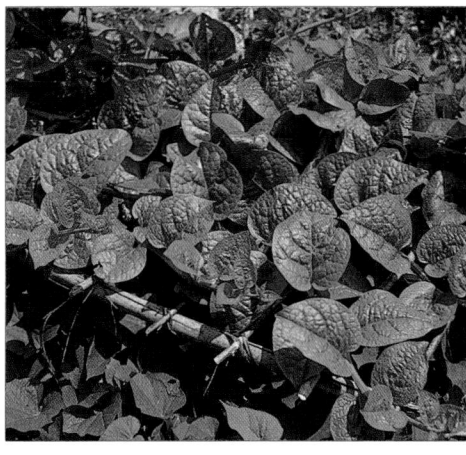

height of about 18in (45cm), remove the growing point to encourage branching. Remove flowering shoots to encourage leaf production.

Propagate plants by taking cuttings 4–6in (10–15cm) long; insert them in small pots until rooted and then transplant as described for seedlings.

Pests and diseases
Malabar spinach is generally free of pests and diseases. Root-knot nematodes (p.652) may, however, affect plants, and aphids (p.639), leafhoppers (p.640), whiteflies (p.639), and spider mites (p.640) may also be troublesome.

Growing under cover
Transplant seedlings to growing bags or to 8–10in (21–25cm) pots. Remove the growing tips when the seedlings are about 12in (30cm) tall to encourage branching, and damp down regularly to maintain high humidity. Tie in developing shoots.

Harvesting and storing
Harvest ten to 12 weeks after transplanting by cutting young terminal shoots about 6–8in (15–20cm) long; this encourages further shoots to develop over several months. Eat leaves within two days of picking, or refrigerate them for a few days.

Swiss chard and spinach beet (*Beta vulgaris* Cicla Group)

These spinachlike biennials belong to the beet family. Swiss chard, also known as seakale beet, forms large, glossy-leaved plants. The individual leaves may be up to 18in (45cm) long and 6in (15cm) wide. The midribs widen into broad leaf stalks up to 2in (5cm) in diameter that may be white, red, creamy yellow, or pink. Leaf color varies according to cultivar, from deep green ('Fordhook Giant') to greenish yellow ('Lucullus') and reddish green ('Rhubarb Chard'). 'Bright Lights' has multicolored stems and bright green leaves. Leaves and

WHITE-STEMMED SWISS CHARD

midribs are usually cooked. Spinach beet, or perpetual spinach, forms smaller-leaved plants, with narrow green leaf stalks. It is eaten lightly cooked or raw.

Although chard and spinach beet are essentially cool-season crops, growing best at 61–64°F (16–18°C), they tolerate higher summer temperatures than spinach (see p.513) without bolting, and survive winter temperatures of 7°F (-14°C). They may be grown in a wide range of soils other than acidic ones, provided the soil is moisture-retentive and fertile, containing plenty of organic matter. Plants may remain in the ground for up to 12 months, requiring high nitrogen levels (see p.498).

Sowing and planting
For a continuous supply, sow seed in spring (plants may crop until late spring the following year), and again in mid- to late summer (for plants cropping until the following summer). Sow *in situ* in rows 15in (38cm) apart for spinach beet or, for Swiss chard, 18in (45cm) apart; thin seedlings early to 12in (30cm) apart. Plants may be grown closer together

RED-STEMMED SWISS CHARD

in more widely spaced rows, but avoid overcrowding, since this may encourage downy mildew.

Alternatively, seed may be sown in seed trays or cell packs for transplanting. Germination is usually rapid. Spinach beet may be sown closely for use as a cut-and-come-again seedling crop (see p.494).

Routine cultivation
Chard and spinach beet are naturally healthy and vigorous and usually require little attention. Give an organic mulch to keep down weeds and preserve moisture; apply a

nitrogenous fertilizer or organic liquid fertilizer during the growing season if plants are developing slowly.

Pests and diseases
Earwigs (p.638) may attack seedlings. Bacterial or fungal leaf spots (p.641) and downy mildew may also be problems.

Growing under cover
In mild climates, chard and spinach beet are excellent winter crops under cover. Sow in cell packs in late summer and transplant under cover in early fall, or broadcast spinach beet for cut-and-come-again seedling crops (see p.494). They often crop through winter and spring.

Harvesting and storing
Leaves are ready to be harvested eight to 12 weeks after sowing. Cut the outer leaves first and continue picking as required; alternatively, harvest the whole plant by cutting the leaves about 1in (2.5cm) above ground level. Further leaves are then produced from the base over many months. Both Swiss chard and spinach beet may be frozen.

Endive (*Cichorium endivia*)

RECOMMENDED ENDIVE

Curled (early and summer)
'Frisan'

Green curled
'Tosca'

Escarole (all sowings)
'Full Heart Batavian' **Ow**
'Galia'

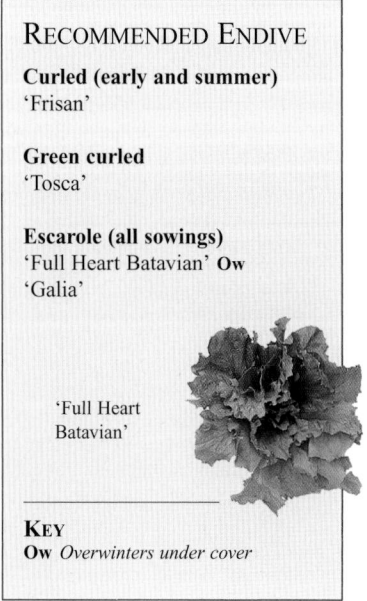

'Full Heart Batavian'

KEY
Ow *Overwinters under cover*

Endive is an annual or biennial plant that forms a flat or semiupright leaf rosette 8–15in (20–38cm) in diameter. The most distinct types of endive are serrated- or curled-leaved endive, green curled endive, and broad-leaved escarole; there are also intermediate types. Outer leaves are dark to light green and the more tender, inner leaves creamy yellow. Endive is slightly bitter and is blanched to make it sweeter. Used mainly in salads, it is shredded to reduce bitterness or may be cooked.

Endive is a cool-season crop that grows best at 50–68°F (10–20°C), but withstands light frost in the open; the hardier cultivars survive 15°F (-9°C). Bitterness generally increases at high temperatures. Some curled types are quite heat-tolerant, while escarole types tend to

withstand greater cold. There is a risk of premature bolting from spring sowings if temperatures fall below 41°F (5°C) for an extended period. Endive performs much better than lettuce in the low light levels of northern winters and therefore makes a useful winter greenhouse crop.

For soil and site requirements, see "Lettuces," p.512. Summer crops may be grown in light shade; always grow fall crops on well-drained soil to avoid the risk of rotting. Endive has a low nitrogen requirement (see p.498).

Sowing and planting
Choose appropriate cultivars for each season. Sow in late spring for a summer crop or in summer for a fall crop, either *in situ* or in cell packs or seed trays. Thin or plant out the

seedlings 10–15in (25–38cm) apart, using the widest spacing for spreading cultivars. Curled types may be sown as cut-and-come-again seedling crops (see p.494), most usefully in late spring and late summer.

Routine cultivation
To blanch leaves, choose nearly mature plants with dry leaves and blanch a few at a time since they deteriorate rapidly after blanching.

For complete blanching *in situ*, cover each plant with a bucket. For partial blanching, lay a large plate or piece of cardboard over the center. With escarole types, bunch up the leaves and tie them together. Protect the plants against slugs until they are ready for harvesting, which is after about ten days. In fall, plants for blanching should be lifted before

BLANCHING ENDIVE

1 *Make sure the endive is dry, then lay a plate over the center to blanch the leaves partially.*

2 *The center should have turned white and be ready for harvesting after about 10 days.*

severe weather disfigures them; transplant them into a darkened frame or dark area under greenhouse staging, then blanch as for Belgian endive (see below).

Pests and diseases
Slugs (p.638) and aphids (p.639) are the most common problems. For other pests and diseases that affect endive, see "Lettuces," p.512.

Growing under cover
Protecting plants under cover provides a year-round supply. For use in winter and early spring, transplant seedlings in early fall from seed trays or cell packs under cover. Sow as a cut-and-come-again seedling crop (see p.494) under cover in spring for harvesting early, and in early fall for a late crop.

Harvesting and storing
Harvest endive between seven and 13 weeks after sowing, depending on the cultivar and season. Pick leaves as needed, or cut across the crown, allowing the plant to resprout. Mature plants respond well to cut-and-come-again treatment (see "Cut-and-come-again harvesting," p.500). Endive leaves do not store well so should be eaten fresh.

Chicory (*Cichorium intybus*)

There are many types of chicory, all with a distinctive, slightly bitter taste. Nearly all are very hardy and are useful crops for growing in cooler months. Their diverse colors make them attractive in salads, and some types may also be cooked. All types have low nitrogen requirements (see p.498).

Belgian endive

Similar in appearance to dandelion (*Taraxacum officinale*), this biennial has pointed leaves about 8in (20cm) long, with a spread of about 6in (15cm). Its chicons (the whitened, compact, leafy shoots obtained from lifting the roots and forcing and blanching them to make them sweeter) may be eaten raw or cooked. The green leaves may also be used, but taste more bitter.

Belgian endive grows best at 59–66°F (15–19°C). It is generally forced for winter use. Grow the plants in an open site in reasonably fertile – but not freshly manured – soil.

The plants require a fairly long growing season. Sow seed outdoors *in situ* in spring or early summer, in rows 12in (30cm) apart. Thin the seedlings to about 8in (20cm) apart. Keep plants weed-free. Water them to prevent the soil from drying out.

Belgian endive may be forced *in situ* in light soils and areas with mild winters. In early winter, cut the green leaves about 1in (2.5cm) above ground level. Cover the stumps with soil, making a ridge about 6in (15cm) high; the chicons will grow and force their way through.

Force indoors if the garden soil is heavy or winters are severe, or if an earlier crop is required. Dig up the plants in late fall or early winter. Cut the leaves to 1in (2.5cm) and trim roots to about 8in (20cm); reject any that are very thin. The roots may be forced immediately or stored for forcing a few at a time in succession during the winter and early spring. To store the roots, lay them flat in boxes with moist sand between each of the layers and keep them in a frost-free shed or cellar until they are required.

To force indoors, plant several of the prepared roots in a large pot or box filled with soil mix or garden soil, and cover with an inverted pot or box of the same size. Block any drainage holes to keep out light. Keep the soil moist, and maintain a temperature of 50–64°F (10–18°C). Roots may also be planted under greenhouse staging or in a garden frame. Make a lightproof area by stretching black plastic over wire hoops or attaching it to a wooden support. Do not use plastic in spring

if temperatures soar, since aphid damage and rotting may occur. Belgian endive is normally free of pests and diseases.

Harvest chicons forced outside after eight to 12 weeks when about 4in (10cm) high by moving the soil and cutting the heads 1in (2.5cm)

above the neck. Plants forced indoors should be ready after three to four weeks. Stumps may resprout to give a second crop of smaller chicons. Keep chicons wrapped or refrigerated after cutting since they become green and bitter on exposure to light.

FORCING AND BLANCHING BELGIAN ENDIVE

1 *In late fall or early winter, lift the mature plant carefully. The central leaves may be tender enough to eat.*

2 *Using a sharp knife, trim the leaves to 1in (2.5cm) from the crown, then slice off the base of the root and any side roots, leaving the root 8–9in (20–22cm) long.*

3 *Put a layer of moist soil mix or garden soil into a 9in (24cm) pot. Place 3 trimmed roots in the mixture and firm so that they stand upright, then fill the pot to within 1in (2.5cm) of the rim and firm, leaving the crowns exposed.*

4 *Line another pot with aluminum foil or black plastic to cover the drainage holes, and place it over the roots to block the light. Keep at 50–64°F (10–18°C). Harvest the chicons 3–4 weeks later by cutting just above soil level.*

Radicchio

This is a varied group of perennials usually grown as annuals. The typical radicchio, also known as red chicory, is a low-growing plant with bitter, reddish green outer leaves and a compact heart. It is eaten raw in salads, shredded to reduce bitterness, or may be cooked.

Radicchio tolerates a wide range of temperatures and soil conditions, but is mainly grown for use in the cooler months. Cultivars vary in their frost tolerance. 'Red Treviso' is quite hardy; it may be forced in the same way as Belgian endive (see p.511). The new F1 hybrids produce more solid heads than traditional cultivars. Sow in early and midsummer, *in situ* or in seed trays for transplanting. Plant 10–14in (25–35cm) apart, depending on the cultivar. Transplant summer-sown crops under cover in fall.

Eight to ten weeks after sowing, pick single leaves or harvest the whole head. Radicchio stands a long time after maturing; in temperate climates, protect with low tunnels in late fall so that the plants develop more solid heads.

Sugar loaf chicory

Sugar loaf chicory is green-leaved, forming a conical head not unlike Romaine lettuce in both shape and size. Its inner leaves are naturally blanched and slightly sweet. For use, and for climate, soil, and cultivation requirements, see "Radicchio" (left).

Sugar loaf chicory may be sown in spring as a cut-and-come-again seedling crop (see p.494); harvest the seedlings before temperatures rise, causing leaves to coarsen. For mature plants, thin seedlings to 10in (25cm) apart, and harvest in late summer to fall. The plants tolerate some cold and provide winter crops if grown under cover.

Harvest leaves as needed, or cut the mature heads. The heads keep for a few weeks in cool, dry, frost-free conditions. They may also be piled up, turned inward, and covered with straw to form clamps (see *Making a Rutabaga Pile*, p.537).

SUGAR LOAF CHICORY

Lettuces (*Lactuca sativa*)

Lettuces are annual, low-growing plants; they usually have green leaves, although some cultivars have red or reddish green leaves.

There are several distinct types. Romaine (cos) lettuces have long, substantial, well-flavored leaves with loose hearts; semicos types are shorter with very sweet, crunchy leaves. Butterhead, or Boston, lettuces have smooth, soft leaves, which form a rounded, compact heart; crispheads (known as icebergs when marketed with the outer leaves removed) have crispy leaves forming a heart. Loose-leaf lettuces, typified by the Salad Bowl types, do not form hearts so are slow to bolt and may be cut over a long period; their leaves are often indented and are very decorative. They are the most nutritious form of lettuce and may also be used for cut-and-come-again seedling crops (see p.494).

Lettuces vary from 4in (10cm) to over 12in (30cm) in spread. The Romaine types are about 10in (25cm) tall, others about 6in (15cm) high. Lettuces are primarily used as salad vegetables, but outer and older leaves may also be cooked or used in soups.

Lettuces are cool-season crops, growing best at 50–68°F (10–20°C). Cool nights are essential for good results. Some cultivars are tolerant of heat or cold. Germination is poor above 77°F (25°C); at these temperatures, plants tend to bolt rapidly and may become bitter, although loose-leaf lettuces are slower to bolt than other types.

Grow in an open site, or in light shade in very hot weather. Lettuces need fertile, moisture-retentive soil and, although they fall into none of the rotation groups, should not be

LOOSE-LEAF LETTUCES ('LOLLO ROSSA')

grown in one patch of soil for two years in a row to prevent the build-up of fungus disease. They require medium nitrogen levels (see p.498).

Sowing and planting
Cultivars appropriate for the season must be sown. For a year-round supply in cool climates, sow from early spring to late summer at two- to three-week intervals. At the end of summer or in early fall, sow hardy cultivars that overwinter outdoors or under cover to produce a spring crop. In warm climates, only heat-tolerant cultivars should be sown during the summer.

In cool climates, sow seed *in situ*, in a seedbed, or in trays or cell packs for transplanting. Sowings in summer are best made *in situ*, since seedlings may wilt when transplanted unless they have been raised in cell packs. Seed may become dormant in high temperatures; this is most likely to occur several hours after sowing and may be overcome by watering after sowing to cool the soil, by putting seed trays or cell packs in a cool place to germinate, or by sowing seed in the afternoon so that the critical period occurs at night when temperatures are lower.

HARVESTING LOOSE-LEAF LETTUCES

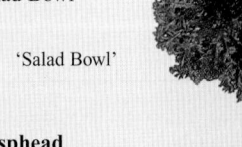

Loose-leaf lettuces may be harvested by cutting across the leaves 1in (2.5cm) above ground level. Leave the stump to resprout.

RECOMMENDED LETTUCES

Romaine
'Freckles' (bicolor)
'Paris Island Cos'
'Rosalita'

'Paris Island Cos'

Semicos
'Winter Density' **Ow**

Butterhead
'Burpee Bibb'
'Buttercrunch'
'Pirat'
'Sangria' (bicolor)
'Tom Thumb'

Loose-leaf
'Black-seeded Simpson'
'Grand Rapids'
'Green Ice'
'Lollo Rossa'
'Oakleaf'
'Salad Bowl'

'Salad Bowl'

Crisphead
'Great Lakes'
'Iceberg'
'Ithaca'
'Minetto'
'Summertime'

'Great Lakes'

KEY
Ow *Overwinters under cover*

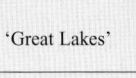

Transplant lettuces in moist conditions when they have five or six leaves, with the base of the leaves positioned just above soil level. In hot weather, shade young plants until they are established. Space small cultivars 6in (15cm) apart, and larger ones about 12in (30cm) apart.

Sow hardy cultivars for over-wintering outdoors *in situ* or under cloches or in frames; thin to about 3in (7cm) apart in fall and to the full distance apart in spring. Floating row covers or cloches, over the plants, improve their quality and help them to mature earlier.

Most types of lettuce may be grown as cut-and-come-again seedling crops, especially loose-leaf types, including the traditional European "cutting" cultivars, and some Romaine types (see "Cut-and-come-again seedling crops," p.494).

Routine cultivation
Keep lettuce beds weed-free. Apply a nitrogenous fertilizer or organic liquid fertilizer if growth is slow. In dry conditions, water the plants at a rate of 5 gallons/sq yd (23 liters/sq m) per week. The most critical watering period is about seven to ten days before maturity (see also p.496). In late fall or early winter, protect lettuces with covers to improve the quality of the crop.

Pests and diseases
Problems include aphids and root aphids (see "Aphids," p.639), cutworms (p.647), slugs (p.638), mosaic virus (see "Viruses," p.642), downy mildew, boron deficiency (p.647), and gray mold/*Botrytis* (p.646); in addition, birds may attack seedlings. Some cultivars show aphid resistance and others have some

PROTECTING SEEDLINGS

Protecting seedlings with perforated film helps them mature more quickly early in the season.

tolerance to mosaic virus and downy mildew.

Growing under cover
In cool climates, earlier lettuce crops may be obtained by sowing or planting in early spring in an unheated greenhouse, beneath cloches or floating row covers, or in cold frames. Some cultivars may also be grown under cover in winter for early spring cropping; for midwinter crops, gentle heat is usually required.

Harvesting and storing
Loose-leaf lettuces should be ready about seven weeks after sowing, butterheads after ten or 11 weeks, and Romaine and crispheads after 11 or 12 weeks. Cut Romaine, butterhead, and crisphead types soon after maturing to prevent bolting. They may be stored for a few days in a refrigerator. Pick the leaves of loose-leaf types a few at a time, as required, since they do not store well, or cut across the plants 1in (2.5cm) above soil level, leaving the stumps to resprout.

Spinach (*Spinacia oleracea*)

This fast-growing annual reaches a height of 6–8in (15–20cm), with a spread of about 6in (15cm). The highly nutritious leaves are smooth or crinkled, and round or pointed, depending on the cultivar. They are eaten lightly cooked or, when young, raw in salads.

Spinach is a cool-season crop, growing best at 61–64°F (16–18°C), although it will grow well at lower temperatures. Small plants and seedlings may survive 15°F (-9°C). Grow cultivars recommended for the area; many are prone to bolt in long days (see "Daylength," p.489), especially after a cold period or in hot, dry conditions. Recommended cultivars that may be used as seedling crops or mature plants include 'Melody', 'Space', and 'Tyee'.

Spinach tolerates light shade in summer, and needs a soil with medium nitrogen levels (see p.498). For other soil requirements, see "Swiss chard and spinach beet," p.510.

Sowing and planting
Sow in cool seasons as spinach will not germinate in temperatures above 86°F (30°C). Sow *in situ*, placing individual seeds about 1in (2.5cm) apart in rows spaced about 12in (30cm) apart. For a continuous crop, sow in succession, after seedlings of the previous sowings have appeared. Thin early as for Swiss chard (see p.510), to about 3in (7cm) for young plants, or to 6in (15cm) apart for large plants.

Spinach may also be grown as a cut-and-come-again seedling crop

(see p.494) for use in salads. For this, sow in early spring and early fall under cover, and also in late summer to overwinter where winters are not too harsh. For routine cultivation, pests and diseases, and growing under cover, see "Swiss chard and spinach beet," p.510.

Harvesting and storing
Cut leaves between five and ten weeks after sowing at any stage once the plants are about 2in (5cm) tall. Either cut individual leaves, or cut the heads about 1in (2.5cm) above the ground and leave them to resprout; alternatively, pull up whole plants. In warm areas, harvest plants young, before they start to run to seed. Use the leaves fresh soon after picking, or store by freezing.

SPINACH

New Zealand spinach (*Tetragonia tetragonioides*, syn. T. expansa)

A creeping perennial, New Zealand spinach is also grown as an annual. The plants have thick, triangular leaves about 2in (5cm) long with a spread of 3–4ft (90–120cm). The leaves are used in the same way as spinach (see above).

New Zealand spinach tolerates drought and high, even tropical, temperatures, but cannot withstand frost. It grows best in an open site on reasonably fertile and moisture-retentive soil, and needs low nitrogen (see p.498). It is generally less prone to bolting than spinach.

Seeds may be slow to germinate, so to aid germination soak them in

water for 24 hours before sowing. In cool climates, sow seed indoors and plant out at 18in (45cm) each way after all risk of frost has passed. Otherwise sow seed *in situ* outdoors after the last frost, thinning in stages to the final spacing. Keep the seedlings weed-free (mature plants cover the soil, suppressing weeds). Pest or disease problems are rare.

Start picking the young leaves and the tips of the stems six or seven weeks after sowing. Pick frequently to encourage further young growth for three or four months. New Zealand spinach should be used fresh immediately after picking, or frozen.

PICKING NEW ZEALAND SPINACH

Pick the young leaves and tips of stems of New Zealand spinach before seedheads start to form. Plants will continue to make new growth that may be harvested until the first frosts.

Minor salad vegetables

THERE are many lesser-known vegetables worth cultivating to use raw in salads, either on their own or mixed with other vegetables. They are suitable for growing in small gardens and containers. The leaves are distinctly flavored and nutritious, especially if used young. Apart from summer purslane and iceplants, all tolerate a few degrees below freezing, or even lower temperatures on well-drained soil with wind protection. In cool climates, most may be grown under cover in winter for higher yields. Most are fast-maturing but make lusher growth in nitrogen-rich soil. Many are best sown as cut-and-come-again seedling crops (see p.494). They are usually free of pests and diseases.

Upland cress (*Barbarea verna*)

This biennial, low-growing plant has a spread of 6–8in (15–20cm); upland cress is also known as American land cress. The glossy, deep green leaves have a strong flavor similar to watercress, and are used as a watercress substitute, either raw or cooked. Upland cress is very hardy, often remaining green in winter. It grows best in the shade; it runs to seed rapidly in heat, becoming coarse and very hot-tasting. It may be intercropped between taller vegetables or used as a bed edging.

Grow upland cress in fertile and moisture-retentive soils. Sow seed in spring for an early summer crop, or in late summer for a fall and over-wintering crop. It may be grown in unheated greenhouses in winter. Sow *in situ*, thinning to 6in (15cm) apart, or in seed trays to transplant. Pick leaves seven weeks after sowing when they are 3–4in (7–10cm) long.

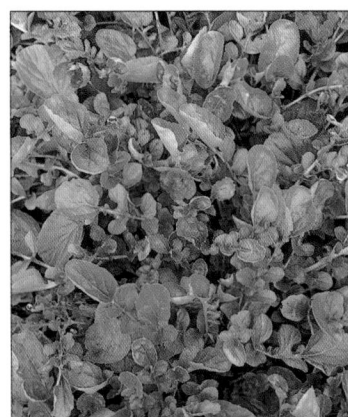

UPLAND CRESS

If a few plants are left to run to seed in spring they seed freely, and the seedlings may be transplanted where they are needed. Flea beetles (p.638) may attack young plants.

Mustard (*Brassica hirta*)

Mustard is similar to cress in its habit and is often partnered with it. It is grown for the sharply flavored seedling leaves which may be used raw in salads. It is a cool-season crop that runs to seed very rapidly in hot weather. Its leaves tend to become coarse if it is grown in areas with heavy rainfall.

In temperate climates, outdoor sowings are most successful in spring and fall *in situ*, using any of the methods suggested for cut-and-come-again seedlings (see p.494).

Mustard, like cress, is a useful crop for growing under cover from fall to spring. It may be sown without soil either on moist paper towels in a saucer placed on a windowsill, or in a sprouter; alternatively, it may be sown in a seed tray of soil mix or soil. These methods may be used all year. Mustard germinates faster than cress, so if the two are required together, the mustard should be sown two or three days later than the

MUSTARD

cress. A sowing every seven to ten days ensures a continuous supply of this vegetable.

Harvest mustard by cutting as required when the seedlings are about 1½–2in (3.5–5cm) tall. It runs to seed much more rapidly than cress and will normally provide no more than two or three cuts.

Salad rapini (*Brassica napus*)

This annual plant has light green, mild-flavored leaves and is often used as a substitute for mustard in salads. It is fast-growing but slower to run to seed than either mustard or cress. The leaves are used raw as seedlings, while larger leaves may be cooked as greens.

Salad rapini survives temperatures of 14°F (-10°C), and tolerates moderate heat. The plants grow in a wide range of soils. In temperate climates, sow under cover in early spring and late fall; sow in succession outdoors until early fall. Indoors, grow on a windowsill as for mustard (left). Outdoors, sow broadcast, or in rows or wide drills. Make the first cut after ten days; when plants reach 24in (60cm), harvest small leaves over several months.

Arugula (*Eruca vesicaria*)

This spicy Mediterranean plant is used in salads; older plants may be cooked. Arugula is also known as rucola, salad rocket, Mediterranean rocket, or roquette. It grows best in moisture-retentive soil in cool weather; in cool climates, it is good under cover in winter, and as a cut-and-come-again seedling crop. Sow broadcast or in rows to cut as seedlings, or thin to 6in (15cm) to cut when larger. Seedlings are ready in three weeks. Flea beetles (p.638) may attack arugula.

Cress (*Lepidium sativum*)

This fast-growing plant is grown for its seedling leaves, which are used raw. Cress is also known as garden cress, curly cress, or peppercress. There is a fine-leaved and a broad-leaved form. It is a moderately hardy, cool-season crop, running to seed rapidly in hot weather unless sown in light shade. In cool climates, cress grows well under cover in the winter months. It may stop growing at very low temperatures, but starts again when temperatures rise. It is useful for inter- and undercropping.

Except in very cool areas, cress is best sown in spring and late summer or early fall; avoid sowing in hot weather. Either sow on moist paper towels in a saucer and place on a windowsill or sow in a sprouter; this will give one cut. To obtain several consecutive cuts, sow in a seed tray of light soil, or broadcast in the

Cut leaves of salad rapini at any stage from seedling to 3in (7cm) long. In good conditions, three cuts of seedling leaves may be possible.

ARUGULA

BROAD-LEAVED CRESS

ground in single rows, or in wide drills. Cut ten days after sowing when seedlings are up to 2in (5cm) high. If sown in the ground, up to four successive cuts may be made.

Iceplants (*Mesembryanthemum crystallinum*)

Grown as perennials in warm climates and as tender annuals elsewhere, iceplants have a sprawling habit, succulent stems, and thick, fleshy leaves, covered with sparkling bladders. The leaves and young stems taste refreshing and slightly salty. They are used raw in salads or cooked like spinach.

Iceplants need a sunny position in light, well-drained soil. In warm climates, sow *in situ* outdoors; in cool climates, sow indoors in the spring, transplanting to 12in (30cm) apart after all risk of frost has passed. Slugs (p.638) may attack seedlings. Plants may be propagated by means of cuttings (see PERENNIALS, "Stem tip cuttings," p.198). The first picking of the young leaves and tender pieces of stem may be made about

ICEPLANTS

four weeks after planting. Harvest plants regularly to encourage further growth, and remove any flowers that appear. Leaves and stems keep fresh for several days.

Miner's lettuce (*Montia perfoliata*)

This is an annual with heart-shaped leaves and dainty flowering shoots. The mildly flavored, slightly succulent leaves, stems, and flowering shoots are used raw in salads. Also called winter purslane or claytonia, it thrives in cool weather. It prefers well-drained conditions but grows well even in poor, light soil. Once established, it self-seeds rapidly; the shallow-rooted, invasive seedlings are easily pulled up.

Make the main sowing in late summer for a fall and early winter crop outdoors. Sow in spring for a summer crop. Grow either broadcast as a cut-and-come-again seedling crop (see p.494), or in rows, or 4in (10cm) wide drills; seed may be

MINER'S LETTUCE

sown *in situ* or in seed trays. Thin seedlings to 6–9in (15–23cm) apart. Start cutting 12 weeks after sowing, allowing plants to resprout.

Summer purslane (*Portulaca oleracea*)

This low-growing plant has slightly succulent leaves and stems that are used raw or cooked. There are green- and yellow-leaved forms; the green type has thinner leaves, is more vigorous. and is possibly better flavored, but the yellow or golden form is attractive in salads. The plants need a warm, sheltered site with light, well-drained soil.

Grow summer purslane either as a cut-and-come-again seedling crop (see p.494) or as single plants. In cool climates, sow in a seed tray in late spring, planting out 6in (15cm) apart, after all risk of frost. Make early and late summer sowings under cover as a cut-and-come-again seedling crop. In warm climates, sow *in situ* throughout summer. Cut the seedlings, or young shoots of

GOLDEN SUMMER PURSLANE

single plants, from four to eight weeks after sowing. Cut regularly, always leaving two basal leaves, and remove any flowers that develop. Slugs (p.638) may attack plants.

Watercress (*Rorippa nasturtium-aquaticum*)

An aquatic perennial, watercress (also known as *Nasturtium officinale*) has nutritious, sharply flavored leaves that are used in salads and soups. Its natural habitat is fresh running streams, with slightly alkaline water at about 50°F (10°C).

Root cuttings by placing stems in fresh water; they will soon root and may be planted at the edge of a stream in spring, spaced 6in (15cm) apart. Watercress may be grown in moist garden soil, but it is easier to grow in 6–8in (15–20cm) pots. Put a layer of gravel or moss in each pot, fill with rich soil, and stand it in a dish of cool, clean water. Plant three or four rooted cuttings per pot,

WATERCRESS GROWN IN A POT

and stand it in a sheltered position in good light. Change the water at least daily in hot weather. Cut leaves as needed.

Dandelions (*Taraxacum officinale*)

Vigorous perennial weeds, dandelions spread up to 12in (30cm). Wild and cultivated forms are grown for the young leaves, which are used raw. The cultivated forms are larger and slower to run to seed. Dandelion leaves are slightly bitter, but blanching sweetens them. The flowers and roots are also edible. Dandelions tolerate a range of well-drained soils.

Sow in spring in seed trays for transplanting, or *in situ*, spacing 14in (35cm) apart. Blanch in succession from late summer, covering dry plants with a large, lightproof bucket. Harvest the leaves when they are elongated and creamy yellow. Dandelions die back in winter but reappear in spring; the plants will continue to grow for several years.

BLANCHING DANDELION

When the plant has several leaves, cover it with a bucket 12in (30cm) tall. Harvest the creamy yellow, elongated leaves after a few weeks.

Corn salad (*Valerianella locusta*)

Grown for fall and winter salads in cool climates, this annual forms small, mild-flavored plants. Corn salad is also known as lamb's lettuce or mache. There are two types: the floppy, large-leaved type, and the smaller, upright type with darker green leaves, which is reputedly hardier. It tolerates a wide range of soils. In cold climates, grow it under cover in winter to obtain more prolific and tender-leaved plants. Corn salad is a useful crop for inter- or undercropping vegetables such as winter brassicas.

Corn salad may be grown as a cut-and-come-again seedling crop (see p.494) or as individual plants. Sow from midsummer onward *in situ*, broadcast, in rows, or in wide drills. Keep the seeds moist until germination. Thin seedlings to 4in (10cm) apart. Corn salad is slow-growing

LARGE-LEAVED CORN SALAD

and may take 12 weeks to mature. Harvest leaves individually or cut across the plants, leaving them to resprout for a second cut.

Fruiting and flowering vegetables

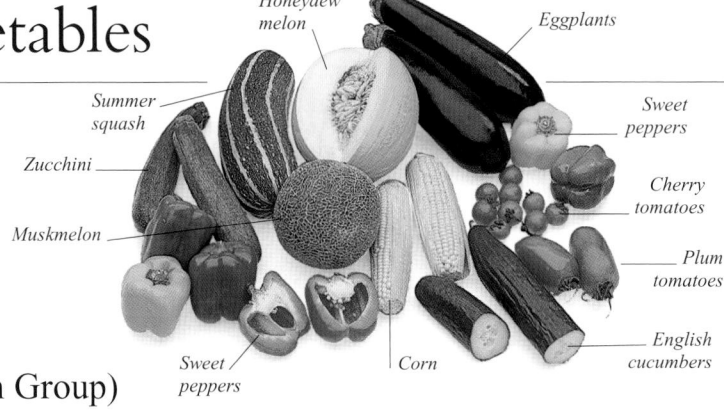

Honeydew melon
Eggplants
Summer squash
Sweet peppers
Zucchini
Cherry tomatoes
Muskmelon
Plum tomatoes
Sweet peppers
Corn
English cucumbers

SOME of the most exotic and succulent vegetables fall into the fruiting and flowering group of vegetables. Many – tomatoes, peppers, eggplants, and melons, for example – are tropical or subtropical in origin; in cooler areas these may need to be grown under cover or in a warm situation. In cool climates, other vegetables such as squash, corn, and pumpkins need to be germinated indoors, but they may be planted outdoors to grow to maturity. All need a warm, sheltered situation to ripen their fruits and for pollination to be successful.

Sweet peppers (*Capsicum annuum* Grossum Group)

Also called bell peppers, these annuals have a bushy habit and may grow up to 30in (75cm) tall with a spread of 18–24in (45–60cm). The fruits are usually oblong, range in size from 1¼–6in (3–15cm) long and 1¼–3in (3–7cm) in diameter, and may be green, cream, yellow, orange, red, or dark purple. The mature fruits are eaten cooked or raw, whole and stuffed, or sliced.

Sweet peppers are tropical and subtropical plants needing a minimum temperature of 70°F (21°C) with a humidity of 70–75 percent. Temperatures over 86°F (30°C) may reduce fruit set and cause buds and flowers to drop. In temperate climates, plants may be grown under cover or outside in a sunny, sheltered site. Moderately deep, fertile, well-drained soil with medium nitrogen levels (see p.498) is required.

Sowing and planting
Sow seed in spring indoors in trays of soil mix with a pH of 5.5–7. Prick out the seedlings into 3–3½in

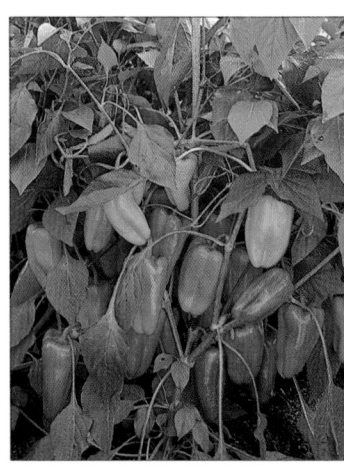

SWEET PEPPERS

(7–9cm) pots and plant out ten to 12 weeks after sowing, spacing them 18–20in (45–50cm) apart each way. In cooler regions, pot on seedlings and do not plant out until all risk of frost has passed and nights are warm, or flowers will drop.

Routine cultivation
Pinch out the terminal growing point of established plants to encourage a bushy habit, and stake cultivars over 24in (60cm) tall. Water regularly to prevent leaf and bud drop, and mulch with organic material. Apply a balanced fertilizer every two weeks. Protect plants outdoors with plastic covers, if necessary.

Pests and diseases
Plants may be attacked by aphids (p.639); they may also be affected by spider mites (p.640), whiteflies (p.639), caterpillars (p.639), blossom end rot (see "Calcium deficiency," p.650), and thrips (p.640).

Growing under cover
Sow as above in early spring. When the seedlings are 3–4in (7–10cm) tall, pot them into 8in (21cm) pots or transplant into grow bags or well-prepared greenhouse beds. Space plants at least 20in (50cm) apart and stake taller cultivars. Maintain the

RECOMMENDED SWEET PEPPERS

'Ace' F1
'Bell Boy' F1
'Big Bertha'
'Blushing Beauty' F1

'Red Knight'

'Californian Wonder'
'Cherry Sweet'

'Valencia'

'Giant Marconi'
'Gypsy' F1
'Lipstick'
'Red Knight' F1
'Tequila' F1
'Valencia' F1

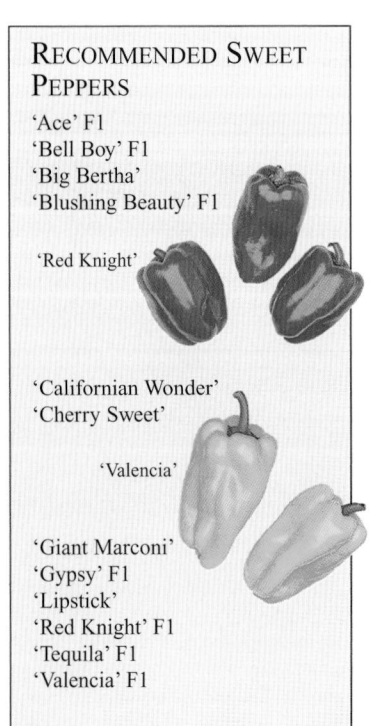

RIPENING SWEET PEPPERS
As they ripen, the fruits change from green to red, yellow, orange, or dark purple, and the flavor becomes sweeter.

recommended temperature and a humidity of 70–75 percent by regularly damping down.

Harvesting and storing
Harvest the peppers 12–14 weeks after transplanting and before the first frost if the plants are growing outside. Some cultivars are best used when the fruits are green, but others may be left on the plants for two to three weeks until they change color to red or creamy yellow. Cut off individual peppers; they may be stored in cool, humid conditions for up to 14 days at 54–59°F (12–15°C). Entire plants may also be stored if pulled before first frost (see "Fruiting vegetables," p.500).

HARVESTING SWEET PEPPERS

Some peppers are best harvested when green; others may be left to turn red or yellow. Cut the stalk about 1in (2.5cm) from the fruit.

Chili peppers (*Capsicum annuum* Longum Group)

This form of *Capsicum annuum* has pointed fruits up to 3½in (9cm) long. Popular cultivars include 'Jalapeño', 'Anaheim Chili', 'Fooled You', and 'Serrano'.

The plants are cultivated in the same way as sweet peppers (see left); chili peppers are slightly more tolerant of high temperature levels, however. They may be picked for use at any stage when the color is green to red. If they are growing outside, they should be harvested before the first frost is expected.

The hot flavor, which increases with the maturity of the chili fruit, comes from the white pith and seeds inside. If the flavor is too hot, the pith and seeds may be removed and discarded.

RIPENING CHILI PEPPERS

RED CHILI PEPPERS

Hot peppers (*Capsicum frutescens*)

These plants, also known as cayenne peppers, are branching perennials that grow to 5ft (1.5m) tall and bear small, narrow, orange, yellow, or red fruits that may hang from the branches or be carried upright, depending on the cultivar. They are highly pungent and are used in sauces and as a general flavoring.

Hot peppers are tropical and subtropical plants and therefore cannot tolerate frost. Space plants 24in (60cm) apart in each direction, and cultivate in the same way as sweet peppers (see opposite), although they generally require more water. Staking is not normally necessary.

Hot peppers need a long growing period, and the first fruits are usually produced about 15–18 weeks after planting. They should be allowed to ripen fully before being picked. They may be frozen or dried and stored for several months.

HOT PEPPERS

RECOMMENDED HOT PEPPERS

'Cayenne Long Slim'
'Cherry Bomb'
'Early Jalapeno'
'Hungarian Yellow Wax Hot'
'Super Cayenne' F1

'Super Cayenne'

Watermelons (*Citrullus lanatus*)

Watermelons are annual, tropical or subtropical plants with spreading stems that grow to 10–12ft (3–4m). Their fruits are rounded or oblong, green or cream, striped or mottled, and may grow to 24in (60cm) in length; they are eaten raw. Plants need a temperature of 77–86°F (25–30°C) and are grown outdoors where the growing season is long; they need at least 70 frost-free days. Well-drained, sandy soils with medium nitrogen levels (see p.498) and a pH of 5.5–7 are needed. Incorporate a general-purpose fertilizer and well-rotted manure into the soil before planting.

WATERMELON

Sowing and planting
Sow in early spring under cover, in trays or 3–3½in (7–9cm) pots, at a temperature of 72–77°F (22–25°C). When the seedlings are 4–6in (10–15cm) tall, harden them off. Plant them out after all risk of frost has passed, spaced at least 3ft (1m) apart. Protect from wind and cold weather with plastic screens.

Routine cultivation
Mulch to retain moisture, and apply a balanced granular or liquid fertilizer every two weeks until fruits begin to develop. Pinch out the growing points of the main shoots when they are 6ft (2m) long and train side-shoots between other plants in the row. To assist formation of fruits, hand-pollinate the flowers (see "Summer squash and zucchini," p.520). Reduce sublateral growths from the sideshoots to two or three leaves after fruits start to develop, and place a pad of dried grass or a block of wood beneath each fruit to protect it from soilborne pests and diseases.

Pests and diseases
Humidity levels over 75 percent encourage leaf diseases, particularly powdery mildew (p.640) and mosaic virus (see "Viruses," p.642). Likely pests include aphids (p.639), root-knot nematodes (p.652), and fruit flies.

Growing under cover
Watermelons are extremely vigorous and are not normally grown in a greenhouse. They may be grown under plastic covers, spaced 3ft (1m) apart; remove covers at flowering time to reduce humidity and encourage insect-pollination.

Harvesting and storing
Harvest ten to 14 weeks after sowing; mature fruits give a hollow sound when tapped. They may be stored 14–20 days at 50–54°F (10–12°C).

RECOMMENDED WATERMELONS

'New Queen' F1

'New Queen'

'Nova' F1
'Sugar Baby'
'Sunshine' F1
'Sweet Favorite ' F1
'Tiger Baby'
'Yellow Doll'

Melons (*Cucumis melo*)

These annuals grow on long, spreading vines or as compact bushes. The three major types are cantaloupe, winter or casaba, and muskmelons (including honeydew), while some do not classify easily. Cantaloupes have gray-green, thick, rough skins with deep grooves and orange flesh. Winter melons have smooth yellow or yellow and green striped skin, and yellow or green flesh. Muskmelons are usually smaller than cantaloupes and often have fine reticulated markings on smooth skins; they have orange flesh. Honeydews have smooth skins and green flesh. Winter melons and some cantaloupes are suitable for greenhouse culture.

Melons are tropical plants requiring a minimum temperature of 64°F (18°C) for germination, rising to 77°F (25°C) during the growing period. In very sunny, sheltered sites, growing in the open is possible but in temperate climates plants are grown in cold frames or in a greenhouse. They need a well-drained, fertile soil with a pH of 6.5–7, a high organic content, and high nitrogen levels (see p.498). Add a general-purpose fertilizer and well-rotted compost or manure.

Sowing and planting
Sow seed under cover in early spring in trays or in 3–3½in (6–9cm) pots (two seeds per pot), removing the weaker seedling if both germinate. After about six weeks, and when all risk of frost is past, the seedlings should be hardened off and planted out, spaced 3ft (1m) apart with 3–5ft (1–1.5m) between rows. Plant each seedling on a slight mound, and protect young plants until they are established from wind and cold weather with individual covers or plastic tunnels.

MUSKMELON

RECOMMENDED MELONS

Cantaloupes
'Ambrosia' F1
'Earlisweet' F1

'Ambrosia'

Muskmelons
'Athena' F1
'Earlidew' (honeydew)
'Fast Break' F1

'Athena'

Winter melon
'Crenshaw'

Other
'Angel'
'Honey-I-Dew'
'Gallicum'

PINCHING MELONS

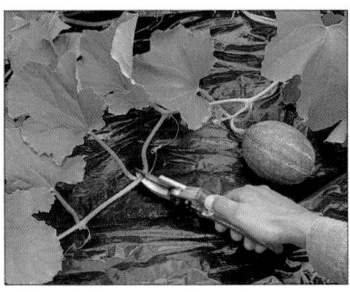

Allow 1 flower per lateral to set, and then pinch or cut out the growing tip of each lateral at 2–3 leaves beyond the developing fruit.

Routine cultivation

After five leaves have developed, pinch out each growing point to encourage further shoots. When these are well developed, reduce them to about four of the most vigorous shoots. Train two shoots on either side, between adjacent plants in the row. Remove any protective covering when the plants begin to flower to encourage insect-pollination. Hand-pollinate them if required (see "Summer squash and zucchini," p.520).

Thin to one fruit per shoot when the fruits are 2.5cm (1in) in diameter, and pinch all sublaterals at two to three leaves beyond the developing fruits. Pinch out the main shoots when they are 3–4ft (1–1.2m) long and remove any further sublaterals that form. Place a pad of dried grass, a tile, or a piece of wood beneath each developing fruit to protect it from soilborne diseases.

Water regularly and apply a liquid fertilizer every ten to 14 days as the fruits begin to develop; reduce watering and fertilizing as fruits ripen.

Pests and diseases

Aphids (p.639), powdery mildew (p.640), spider mites (p.640), whiteflies (p.639), *Verticillium* wilt (p.645), spotted cucumber beetles (p.649), and striped cucumber beetles (p.655) may cause problems.

Growing under cover

To raise melons in a cold frame, plant seedlings singly in the center. After pinching, train four laterals to grow toward the corners. As the plants develop, increase ventilation and gradually reduce humidity. Once the fruits start forming, remove the sashes, replacing them at night in cold weather. In hot weather, shade lightly.

Melons may be grown in a greenhouse if the distance from the base of the side walls to the ridge is at least 6ft (2m). Plant seedlings onto well-prepared mounds (see "Cucumbers and gherkins," below). Grow as single or double cordons, training on stakes tied to horizontal wires up to the ridge. Space plants 15in (38cm) apart for single cordons, 2ft (60cm) for double cordons. They may also be grown in growing bags or 24–25cm (9–10in) pots placed on greenhouse staging.

For a single cordon, pinch out the growing point when the main shoot is 6ft (2m) long to encourage lateral growth. Pinch laterals at five leaves and sublaterals at two leaves beyond the flowers. For a double cordon, pinch out the main shoot and let two shoots develop vertically; train as above. Support developing fruits in 2in (5cm) mesh slings attached to the ridge. To aid pollination do not damp down during flowering. Maintain a temperature of 75°F (24°C) at night and 86°F (30°C) in the day.

Harvesting and storing

Harvest 12–20 weeks after sowing. Cantaloupe and muskmelons are sweet-smelling when mature, and the fruit stalks crack. Separate the fruits gently from the stalks. Store for 14–50 days at 50–59°F (10–15°C), depending on the cultivar.

Cucumbers and gherkins (*Cucumis sativus*)

Most are annual trailing vines that grow to 3–10ft (1–3m); there are a few compact bush cultivars. The immature fruits are eaten raw, pickled, or served in soup.

Cucumbers are characteristically rough-skinned, spiny, and 4–6in (10–15cm) long. Modern cultivars, many of Japanese origin, are smoother and up to 12in (30cm) long, with improved cold tolerance and disease resistance. They are mainly grown outdoors and are insect-pollinated. Gherkins are cucumbers with short, often stumpy fruits up to 3in (7cm) long, harvested young, and used mainly for pickling. Apple and lemon cucumbers are round, yellow-skinned ridged cucumbers that grow up to 2½in (6cm) in diameter. English and greenhouse fruits are smooth and over 12in (30cm) long. They do not require pollination to set fruit and, if pollinated, may produce bitter, swollen fruits; use the modern all-female cultivars to remove the risk of accidental pollination.

Cucumbers are warm-season vegetables, growing best between temperatures of 64–86°F (18–30°C). They have no frost tolerance, and most are damaged at temperatures below 50°F (10°C). In northern latitudes, outdoor types may produce male flowers alone early in the season; female flowers, then fruits, occur later. Grow cucumbers in a sheltered site in fertile, organic soil that is well drained but moisture-retentive: the roots must not dry out. Lime very acidic soils. The plants need low nitrogen levels (see p.498).

Greenhouse types must be grown with minimum night temperatures of 68°F (20°C) and in high humidity. Never grow outdoor types in the same greenhouse with all-female cultivars, since undesirable cross-pollination will occur.

Sowing and planting

Cucumbers transplant badly, so seed for outdoor varieties should be sown *in situ* after all risk of frost has passed or alternatively in small pots or cell packs. If sowing outside, prepare holes at least 12in (30cm) wide and deep, working in plenty of well-rotted compost or manure as you backfill. Cover with about 6in (15cm) of manured soil made into a small mound to ensure sharp drainage. Place seeds on their side about ¾in (2cm) deep, sowing two to three per pot or site.

Seed germinates at a minimum soil temperature of 68°F (20°C). Thin to one seedling after germination. Seed sown in pots needs a minimum temperature at night of

GHERKIN

60°F (16°C) until the seedlings are planted out, about four weeks after sowing. Space climbing types 18in (45cm) apart; bush types, and climbing types if trailing over the ground, should be spaced about 30in (75cm) apart. In cool climates, protect plants from strong winds after planting.

Routine cultivation

Grow trailing types up supporting fences, nets, or stakes, or allow them to twine up strings. Nip out the growing point after five or six leaves have appeared, and train the resulting stronger growths up the support, tying them in if necessary. When these shoots reach the top of the support, nip them out two leaves beyond a flower; laterals will develop on which more fruits will form. As fruiting continues, fertilize plants

SOWING AND PLANTING OUT

1 *Fill a small pot with sowing medium to within 1in (2.5cm) of the rim. Place 2 or 3 seeds on their sides in the medium, then cover them to a depth of about ¾ in (2cm). Water well and label. Save the strongest plant.*

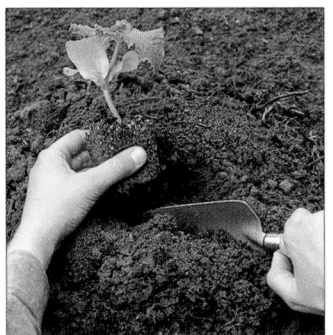

2 *Prepare a hole 12in (30cm) wide and 12in (30cm) deep, and fill with well-rotted compost. Pile the soil on top to make a mound about 6in (15cm) high. Plant the cucumber on top of this mound. Firm in and water.*

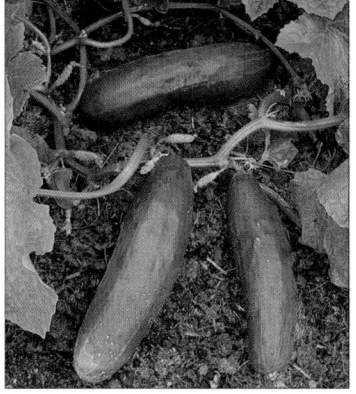

BUSH CUCUMBERS

every two weeks with a high-potassium fertilizer or equivalent organic liquid fertilizer. Regular watering is essential during the growing period, particularly after transplanting, so that plants establish quickly, and during flowering and fruiting to ensure healthy fruit formation (see "Critical watering periods," p.496).

Pests and diseases
Snails (p.638), aphids (p.639), powdery mildew (p.640), cutworms (p.647), spider mites (p.640), whiteflies (p.639), squash vine borers (p.641), cucumber mosaic virus (see "Viruses," p.642), spotted cucumber beetles (p.649), and striped cucumber beetles (p.655) may cause problems.

Growing under cover
Grow as in the open using appropriate cultivars – the all-female selections are recommended. Pinch the main shoot of each plant at the top of the supports and nip off sideshoots beyond the first leaf. Damp down greenhouses to control pests.

Harvesting and storing
Harvest cucumbers regularly from about 12 weeks after sowing, when the sides of the fruits are parallel and they are about 6–8in (15–20cm) long. Harvest gherkins when they are 1–3in (2.5–7cm) long.

CLIMBING CUCUMBERS

RECOMMENDED CUCUMBERS AND GHERKINS

Ridged cucumbers
'Burpless Tasty Green' F1
'Bush Champion' F1

'Bush Champion'

Smooth cucumbers
'Fanfare'
'Marketmore TG'
'Sweet Slice'

Japanese cucumbers
'Suyo Long'
'Tasty Jade'

Gherkins
'Calypso'
'Cross Country'
'Patio Pickles'

'Cross Country'

Winter squash (*Cucurbita maxima, C. moschata, C. pepo*)

This is a very diverse group of annuals, with fruits ranging from 1lb (450g) to well over 66lb (30kg). They include pumpkins and the inedible ornamental gourds. The skin may be smooth, warted, or ridged, and green, cream, blue-green, yellow, orange, red, or striped, the color often changing with maturity. Their shapes range from round, long, squat, or onion-shaped to a two-layered turban shape. Most form very large trailing plants with huge leaves; some are compact and bushy. Both young and mature fruits may be eaten cooked, either fresh or after storage. Shoots and young leaves may be cooked and flowers eaten raw or cooked. Some cultivars have edible seeds.

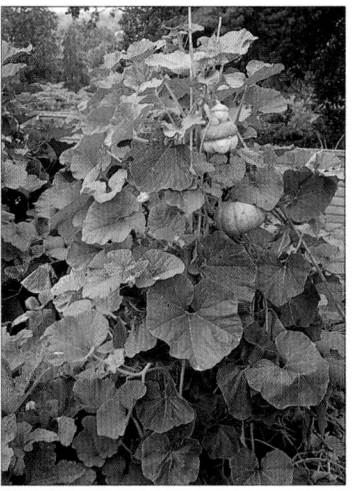

WINTER SQUASH ON A TRIPOD

For climate, site, and soil preparation requirements, see "Cucumbers and gherkins," opposite. Winter squash require medium to high nitrogen levels (see p.498).

Sowing and planting
Seed may be soaked overnight before sowing to hasten germination. Sow as for cucumbers (see opposite). Space plants 6–10ft (2–3m) apart, depending on the cultivar. For large cultivars, prepare holes up to 18in (45cm) deep and 24in (60cm) wide. Insert a marker stake when planting so that the center of the plant can be found if watering is necessary. Protect and mulch after planting.

Routine cultivation
A top-dressing of a general fertilizer may be applied soon after planting. Shoots may be trained in circles on the ground using bent wire to hold down the stems, or grown on supports, such as tripods. Where only a few large fruits are needed, remove all but two or three of the other fruits while still young.
   Winter squash are deep-rooting, so watering should be needed only in very dry weather.

Pests and diseases
Slugs (p.638) may attack in early stages; later, squash vine borers (p.641), cucumber mosaic virus (p.642), spotted cucumber beetles (p.649), and striped cucumber beetles (p.655) may cause problems.

Harvesting and storing
Cut away any foliage shading the fruits to encourage them to ripen. Harvest winter squash 12–20 weeks after planting. Leave fruits for storing on the plant to mature as long as possible: the stem starts to crack and the skin hardens when the fruit is ripe. Pick before the first frost, cutting each fruit with a long stalk.
   After harvesting, most storage types must be exposed to the sun for ten days to cure (further harden) the skin so that it forms a barrier, slowing the rate of water loss. Cover the fruits at night if frost threatens, or cure indoors at 81–90°F (27–32°C) for four days. Acorn types may be stored without first being cured. Store winter squash at about 50°F (10°C) in a well-ventilated place. They may be kept from four to six months, and, in some cases, even longer, depending on the conditions and the cultivar grown.

CURING WINTER SQUASH

When it is ripe, cut the squash off the plant with as long a stalk as possible. Leave the squash in the sun for about 10 days so that the skin hardens.

RECOMMENDED WINTER SQUASH

'Ambercup'
'Blue Hubbard'
'Buttercup'
'Cornell's Bush Delicata'
'Early Butternut' F1
'Golden Hubbard'

'Buttercup'
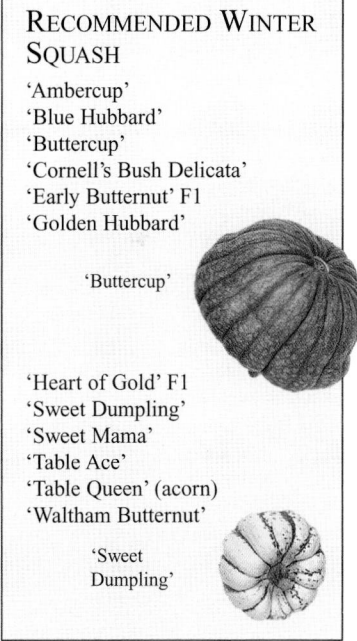

'Heart of Gold' F1
'Sweet Dumpling'
'Sweet Mama'
'Table Ace'
'Table Queen' (acorn)
'Waltham Butternut'

'Sweet Dumpling'

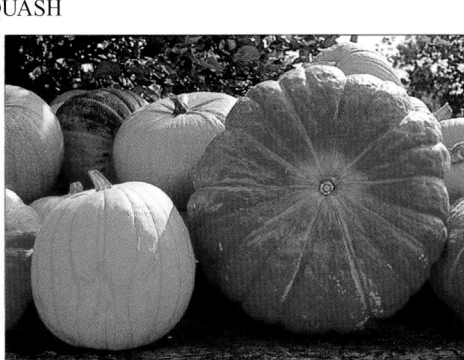

Summer squash and zucchini (*Cucurbita pepo*)

Summer squash and zucchini are annual plants that trail for several feet or form compact plants of 3ft (90cm) spread. They most commonly have cylindrical fruits about 12in (30cm) long and 5in (13cm) in diameter. Zucchini are normally harvested young, as are other squash whose fruits are tender-skinned when young. Summer squash may be trailing or bushy with green, yellow, white, or striped skin. Custard squash have flattish, fluted-edged fruits; crookneck squash have swollen fruits with a bent neck. There are also round-fruited cultivars. Spaghetti squash are squashlike in shape but with hard skins; cooked, the flesh resembles spaghetti. All the fruits are generally cooked. Young leaves and shoot tips may also be cooked, and flowers eaten raw or cooked.

Summer squash are warm-season crops, needing temperatures of 64–81°F (18–27°C). Frost intolerance, soil, and soil preparation are as for cucumbers (see p.518). They need low nitrogen levels (see p.498).

Sowing and planting
Sow as for cucumbers (see p.518) when the soil temperature is at least 59°F (15°C). Place each seed about

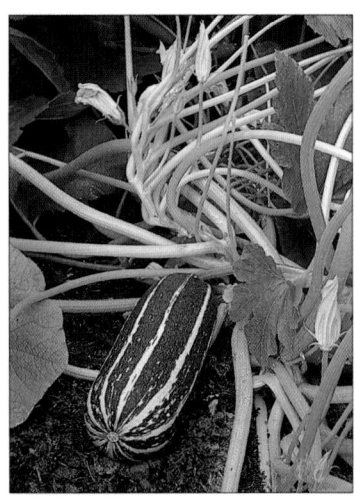

BUSH SQUASH

Hand-pollinating

Summer squash and zucchini are generally insect-pollinated, but, in cool periods, if fruits are not setting, it may be necessary to hand-pollinate. The female flower has a tiny bump (the embryonic fruit) behind the petals, which the male flower lacks (see below); this makes it easy to distinguish between them.

MALE FLOWER

FEMALE FLOWER

Embryonic fruit

To hand-pollinate, take a male flower, remove all the petals, and press it against the female flower. Alternatively, use a fine paintbrush to transfer the pollen from the stamens of the male flower to the stigma of the female.

1in (2.5cm) deep. Sow *in situ* after all risk of frost has passed, or germinate indoors. Space bush types 3ft (90cm) apart, and trailing types 4–6ft (1.2–2m) apart. In cool areas, protect young plants with cloches or floating row covers. In hot areas, floating row covers will protect young plants against insects. Mulch after planting.

Routine cultivation
Trailing types may be grown up strong supports. The shoots may also be trained in circles, using bent wire to peg down the stems. Toward the end of the season, nip off the ends of the shoots. Fertilize and water as for cucumbers (see p.518).

Pests and diseases
Slugs (p.638) may attack in early stages; squash vine borers (p.641), cucumber mosaic virus (see "Viruses," p.642), spotted cucumber beetles (p.649), and striped cucumber beetles (p.655) may cause problems.

Growing under cover
This is appropriate only in cool climates when a very early crop is required. Use bush cultivars.

Harvesting and storing
Harvest squash seven to eight weeks after planting. Some types may be stored for a few weeks if they are kept well ventilated at about 50°F (10°C) with high humidity. Spaghetti squash may be stored for several months. Pick zucchini when they are about 4in (10cm) long, preferably with the flower attached, since this indicates freshness. Harvest shoots from the top 6in (15cm) of stem; new growth is soon made. If harvesting flowers, pick male ones after the females have set.

HARVESTING ZUCCHINI

Cut zucchini when they are 4in (10cm) long, with a short stalk. Handle the fruits carefully to avoid bruising them. Regular harvesting will encourage more fruits.

RECOMMENDED SUMMER SQUASH

'Butterstick'
'Clarimore' F1
'Golden Crookneck'
'Magda'
'Papaya Pear' F1
'Peter Pan'
'Scallopini' F1

'Early White Bush'

'Seneca Prolific'
'Starship'
'Sunburst'
'Sundance'

'Vegetable Spaghetti'

Spaghetti squash
'Orangetti' F1
'Pasta' F1
'Vegetable Spaghetti'

Zucchini
'Ambassador' F1
'Black Beauty'
'Black Jack'
'Elite' F1
'Gold Rush' F1
'Jaguar' F1
'Raven' F1
'Spineless Beauty'

Globe artichokes (*Cynara scolymus*)

These perennial plants have blue-gray leaves and thistlelike flowers. Globe artichokes may grow up to 4–5ft (1.2–1.5m) tall with a 3ft (90cm) spread. They are grown for the green and purple flower buds, which have edible, fleshy pads (the hearts) at the base of the outer scales

and the top of the flower stem; the hearts are cooked or pickled. A reliable cultivar is 'Green Globe'.

Globe artichokes grow best in cool climates at 55–64°F (13–18°C) and tolerate light to medium frosts. They need an open but not exposed site, with fertile, well-drained soil into

which plenty of compost or well-rotted manure has been dug, and low levels of nitrogen (see p.498).

Sowing and planting
Globe artichokes are normally increased by division. Using a sharp knife, two hand forks, or a spade,

divide healthy, established plants in the spring; each division should have at least two shoots with a tuft of leaves and a good root system. Plant these divisions 24–30in (60–75cm) apart and trim the tips of the leaves to 5in (13cm). Globe artichokes may be raised from seed either indoors or

DIVIDING GLOBE ARTICHOKES

In spring, lift an established plant and divide it using two hand forks, a spade, or a knife. Each division should have at least two shoots and strong roots.

outdoors in spring, but the results are variable; thin or plant out seedlings at the correct spacing. Replace plants every three years or so to maintain good yields. The cultivar 'Imperial Star' will produce flower heads the first year. Sow early or plant out hardened-off young plants. It needs spring frosts to produce well.

Routine cultivation

Keep the planting area free of weeds and well mulched to conserve soil moisture. Do not allow the roots of globe artichokes to dry out in summer or become waterlogged in winter. If severe cold is expected,

hill up the base of each plant, covering with a thick layer of straw; remove the covering in spring.

Pests and diseases

Lettuce root aphids (see "Aphids," p.639) may cause problems.

Harvesting and storing

In favorable conditions, some heads may be cut in the late summer of the first season. More flowering stems will be produced in the second season. Pick before the scales open, when the buds feel plump. Remove the hairy choke and stalk before freezing; the hearts may be pickled.

GLOBE ARTICHOKE

Tomatoes (*Lycopersicon esculentum*)

These are annual plants in temperate areas and short-lived perennials in the tropics. The main trailing stem of the staking (indeterminate) types grows to over 8ft (2.5m) long in warm climates, with vigorous sideshoots. The shorter semideterminate types and the bush (determinate) types stop growing earlier than the staking types, and the stems end in a fruit cluster. Compact dwarf types may grow up to 9in (23cm) across and as tall.

Ripe tomato fruits are red, yellow, orange, pink, or white, and round, flat, plum- or pear-shaped. The tiny currant tomatoes (*Lycopersicon pimpinellifolium*) are ½in (1cm) in diameter; cherry types, 1in (2.5cm); and giant beefsteak types, up to 4in (10cm). All are eaten raw or cooked.

Tomatoes grow best at 70–75°F (21–24°C) or higher temperatures, but do not grow well below 61°F (16°C) and do not tolerate frost. They need high light intensity. In cool climates, grow them in a sheltered site outdoors or under cover; they are often grown in containers. Tomatoes tolerate a wide range of fertile and well-drained soils, with a pH of 5.5–7; lime very acidic soils (see "Liming," p.619). Crops need to be rotated (see p.492).

Prepare the ground by working in plenty of well-rotted manure or compost at least 12in (30cm) deep, since tomatoes are deep-rooted gross feeders. Apply a general fertilizer before planting; tomatoes need high levels of phosphorus (see "Soil nutrients," p.497) but low levels of nitrogen (see p.498).

Sowing and planting

In warm climates, sow seed *in situ* in spring and thin seedlings to the correct spacing. In cool climates, six to eight weeks before the last frost is expected, sow seed ¼in (6mm) deep,

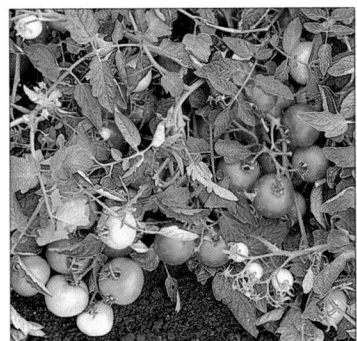

BUSH TOMATOES

at about 80°F (27°C), in seed trays or cell packs. Transplant into 2–3in (5–7cm) pots at the two- or three-leaf stage; give the seedlings ample ventilation, space, and light. They can stand short periods of low temperatures if day temperatures rise to compensate. Harden off before planting out when night temperatures are over 45°F (7°C) or soil temperatures at least 50°F (10°C) and the risk of frost is over. Plant out when all danger of frost is past.

For extra-early crops, warm the soil by putting water-filled crop protectors into position about eight weeks before the last frost date. Tomato transplants can be put out two to four weeks later. In windy locations, shield new transplants with plastic or paper sleeves held away from the plants.

Staking types Plant indeterminate and semideterminate types on stakes with 15–18in (38–45cm) between plants in single rows 18in (45cm) apart, or in double rows with 3ft (90cm) between the pairs of rows.

Alternatively, plant in homemade or commercial tomato cages, which provide support without the need to tie in. Make sure that the mesh is large enough to get your hand through for picking.

Indeterminate cherry tomatoes such as 'Sweet 100' can grow 12ft (4m) tall or more. The plants may be trained up heavy strings.

Bush and dwarf types Bush types sprawl on the ground; space them 12–36in (30–90cm) apart, depending on the cultivar. Dwarf types may be more closely spaced than this. Cover with cloches or floating row covers in the early stages. Bush types grow well when mulched with black plastic (see "Mulching," p.496).

Routine cultivation

All types of tomato should be watered and mulched heavily once the soil is warm. In dry conditions, water tomatoes weekly at a rate of 2 gallons (9 liters) per plant. Plants

GROWING IN A WIRE CAGE

Tomatoes may be grown in wire cages as an alternative to staking. Firmly push the cages into the soil around newly set plants.

in containers need more frequent watering and supplementary feeding with a tomato fertilizer. Take care not to overwater or overfeed.

Staking types Tie in plants to the support stakes or wires as they grow, and remove all suckers (side shoots) when they are about 1in (2.5cm) long. In late summer, remove the terminal shoot two leaves above a flower cluster to allow the remaining fruits to develop and ripen before the first frost. In cool climates, remove supports at the end of the season, bend the plants over *in situ* on straw, then cover them to encourage the crop to ripen.

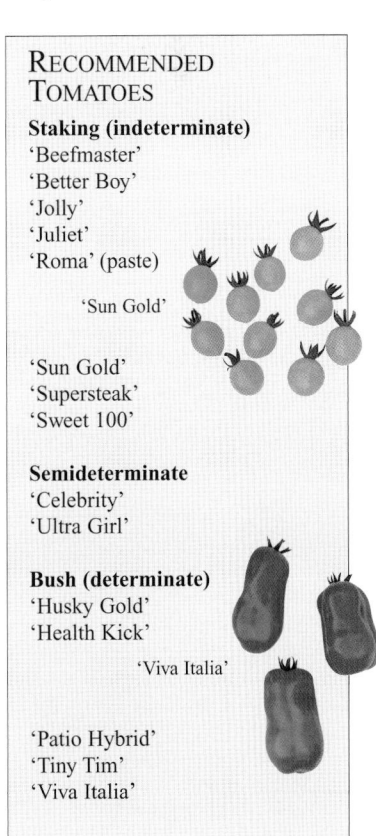

RECOMMENDED TOMATOES

Staking (indeterminate)
'Beefmaster'
'Better Boy'
'Jolly'
'Juliet'
'Roma' (paste)

'Sun Gold'

'Sun Gold'
'Supersteak'
'Sweet 100'

Semideterminate
'Celebrity'
'Ultra Girl'

Bush (determinate)
'Husky Gold'
'Health Kick'

'Viva Italia'

'Patio Hybrid'
'Tiny Tim'
'Viva Italia'

TRAINING STAKING TOMATOES

1 *On staking tomatoes, regularly pinch out suckers (sideshoots) as they develop.*

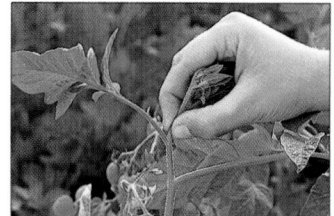

2 *In late summer, nip out the tip of the main shoot 2 leaves above the top flower cluster.*

Pests and diseases
Tomato plants are affected by damping off in seedlings (p.655), leafhoppers (p.640), potato cyst nematodes, and tomato late blight (p.650). They are also affected by whiteflies (p.639), several mosaic viruses (see "Viruses," p.642), gray mold/*Botrytis* (p.646), magnesium deficiency (p.643), boron deficiency (p.647), Southern blight (p.647), foot and root rots (p.653), and blossom end rot (see "Calcium deficiency," p.650). Use disease- and nematode-resistant cultivars, indicated in catalogs by V, F, and N after the cultivar name. Interplanting with French marigolds may deter whiteflies.

Growing under cover
In cool climates, tomatoes may be grown in greenhouses or polytunnels. Polytunnels, which can be moved to a fresh site, are better than greenhouses, where soilborne diseases may develop unless the soil is replaced every three years. Alternatively, crops may be grown in containers or by ring culture (plants are grown in "rings" or bottomless pots filled with soil mix, resting on pea gravel). Cultivars may also be grafted onto disease-resistant rootstocks. After the first cluster has set, apply a high-potassium fertilizer or an organic liquid fertilizer weekly.

Harvesting and storing
Pick fruits as they ripen. Harvest the earliest bush types seven to eight weeks after planting. Before frost, pull the plants up by the roots and hang them upside down indoors to ripen. Harvest staking types after ten to 12 weeks. Tomatoes freeze well.

GROWING BAGS

Tomatoes may be planted in growing bags outdoors or in greenhouses. Growing in bags prevents the plants from being infected by soilborne diseases.

Wonderberries (*Solanum* x *burbankii*)

These annual plants grow to about 30in–3ft (75cm–1m) tall with a spread of 24in (60cm). Several cultivated forms of the wonderberry, or sunberry, are grown; all have oval, light green leaves as well as round, purple berries up to ½in (1cm) in diameter. The leaves and young shoots are used like spinach. The unripe fruits contain a poisonous alkaloid, so pick only ripe berries, and cook them thoroughly.

Wonderberries are tropical and subtropical plants requiring temperatures of 64–77°F (18–25°C) with a humidity of at least 70 percent. They may be grown in the open in sunny, sheltered sites, but in temperate areas, greenhouse cultivation is recommended. A fertile, well-drained soil with a pH of 5.5–7 is preferable; medium nitrogen levels are required (see p.498).

Sowing and planting
Sow seed in spring in trays in the greenhouse. Prick out the seedlings when they are large enough to handle, into 3–3½in (7–9cm) pots. When they are 3–4in (7–10cm) tall, harden them off and transplant them; space plants 16–20in (40–50cm) apart, leaving about 24in (60cm) between rows.

Routine cultivation
Wonderberries need high levels of soil moisture; mulch well and water regularly. Apply a general-purpose fertilizer or an organic liquid fertilizer every 10–14 days. Pinch out the growing point when plants are 12in (30cm) tall to encourage lateral branching, and stake plants that grow higher than 24in (60cm). Keep the ground around the plants free from weeds.

Pests and diseases
Aphids (p.639) are the major pest. Under cover, red spider mite (p.640) and thrips (p.640) may also attack plants.

Growing under cover
When seedlings are about 4–6in (10–15cm) tall, transplant into 8in (21cm) pots or growing bags, leaving at least 20in (50cm) between plants, or transplant into well-prepared greenhouse beds, spacing plants 20–24in (50–60cm) apart each way. Reduce the level of humidity during flowering to promote pollination.

Harvesting and storing
Harvest shoots 9–11 weeks after transplanting; continue removing shoots 4–6in (10–15cm) long to encourage lateral growths. To produce berries, do not remove shoots

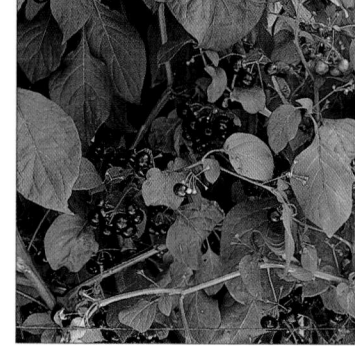

WONDERBERRIES

but allow the plants to become bushy and to flower. Harvest the fruit about 14–17 weeks after sowing, removing bunches with a sharp knife. Ripe berries may be stored for 10–14 days at 50–59°F (10–15°C).

Eggplants (*Solanum melongena*)

Short-lived perennials normally cultivated as annuals, eggplants form small bushes about 24–8in (60–70cm) tall with a spread of about 24in (60cm). Also known as aubergines, cultivars differ mainly in the shape, size, and color of the fruits, which may be oval, pear-shaped, or round, dark purple, yellowish green, or white, and weigh 7–18oz (200–500g). The fruits are generally sliced and cooked.

Eggplants are tropical and subtropical plants requiring temperatures of 77–86°F (25–30°C), with a minimum humidity of 75 percent. Below 68°F (20°C), growth may be checked. Grow in full sun and protect newly planted plants from cold winds and low temperatures, which may stunt growth and cause bud drop.

Eggplants require a deep, fertile, well-drained soil and medium nitrogen levels (see p.498).

Sowing and planting
In spring, sow seed under cover in trays using a light, slightly acidic (pH 6–6.5) soil mix: soak the seed in warm water for 24 hours first to encourage germination. Prick out into 3–3½in (7–9cm) pots. In warm climates, plant out the seedlings into well-prepared beds when they are 3–4in (7–10cm) tall, spacing them about 24–30in (60–75cm) apart each way. Pinch out the terminal

RECOMMENDED EGGPLANTS

'Black Beauty'
'Burpee Hybrid'
'Easter Egg'
'Ichiban'
'Little Fingers'

'Easter Egg'

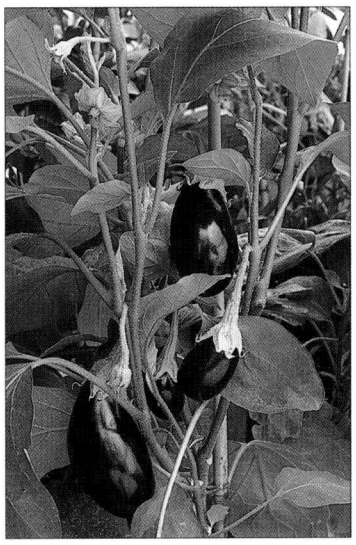

EGGPLANTS

growing points of the plants to promote a bushy habit. In temperate climates, pot them up singly into 6in (15cm) pots; plant out after all danger of frost has passed.

Routine cultivation
Stake cultivars over 24in (60cm) tall. Keep plants well watered, otherwise leaves and buds are liable to drop, and mulch to preserve moisture. Apply a balanced granular or liquid fertilizer every two weeks during the growing season. Prune back mature plants to stimulate growth. To produce large fruits, restrict the number per plant to five or six.

Pests and diseases
Eggplants may be attacked by aphids (p.639). Spider mites (p.640), mealybugs (p.640), caterpillars (p.639), thrips (p.640), and powdery and downy mildew (p.640) may also be troublesome.

Growing under cover
Sow seed in early spring at 68–86°F (20–30°C). When the seedlings are 3–4in (7–10cm) tall, transfer them to 8in (21cm) pots or growing bags, and pinch out the tips. Maintain the temperature above the minimum required during the growing period. Damp down greenhouses to help discourage spider mites.

Harvesting and storing
Harvest 16–24 weeks after sowing, when fruits reach full color and are unwrinkled. Cut the fruit stalks close to the stem. Eggplants may be stored for up to two weeks in humid conditions at 54–59°F (12–15°C).

HARVESTING EGGPLANTS

Cut eggplants while the skin is still shiny; once it loses its shine, the flesh will taste bitter. Cut the stalk at least 1in (2.5cm) from the fruit.

Sweet corn (*Zea mays*)

Sweet corn is an annual that grows to at least 30in–5½ft (75cm–1.7m) and has an average spread of 18in (45cm). Male tassels and female ears (cobs) are borne on the same plant. The ears are golden, white, or bicolored white and yellow, and cooked or eaten raw when young. New "supersweet" (sugar-enhanced) cultivars are available.

Sweet corn needs a long growing season of 70–110 frost-free days after planting. It requires temperatures of 61–95°F (16–35°C), but pollination is poor in hot, dry conditions; in warm climates, grow in an open site. In cool climates, grow early-maturing cultivars in a frost-free, sheltered site. Sweet corn is shallow-rooting and grows on a wide range of fertile, well-drained soils with medium nitrogen (see p.498).

Sowing and planting
Seed does not germinate at soil temperatures below 50°F (10°C). In warm climates, sow seed in spring *in situ*, 1in (2.5cm) deep and 3in (7cm) apart, thinning to the correct spacing after germination. Seed may be sown through plastic mulches. In cool climates, sow indoors in cell packs and plant out seedlings when the soil temperature reaches 55°F (13°C), or sow *in situ* after all risk of frost has passed. In wet soils, use treated seed, which will not rot.

To ensure good pollination and full ears, plant corn in blocks of at least four plants each way. The average spacing is 12in (30cm) apart; short cultivars may be closer, tall ones farther apart. In cool climates, cover with floating row covers or

SWEET CORN PLANTED IN A BLOCK

Male and female flowers are carried on the same plant. The male flowers (inset, top), which release pollen, are produced in tassels up to 16in (40cm) in length at the tip of the plant. The female flowers (inset, bottom) are silky strands, under which each ear forms. The strands are sticky to collect pollen. The female flowers are wind-pollinated, so plant in a block rather than a row to ensure good pollination.

cloches after sowing or planting, removing them at the five-leaf stage. The supersweet types need higher temperatures to germinate and grow and should not be planted with other types, because the sweetness will be lost if they are cross-pollinated. Baby corn is obtained by planting early cultivars about 6in (15cm) apart and harvesting ears when they are about 3in (7cm) long.

Routine cultivation
Hoe shallowly when weeding to avoid damaging the roots. In exposed areas, hill up the stems to 5in (13cm) to increase stability. Watering is not necessary, except in very dry conditions, until flowering starts and when the kernels are swelling.

Water at a rate of 5 gallons/sq yd (23 liters/sq m). Mulching with several thin layers of grass clippings helps reduce evaporation.

Pests and diseases
Spotted cucumber beetle larvae, asparagus beetles (p.638), cutworms (p.647), smuts (p.651), corn rootworms (p.652), armyworms (p.656), and raccoons (see "Small animals," p.656) may attack.

Harvesting and storing
Pick just before required, since the sweetness deteriorates within hours; supersweet types retain their sweetness for two or three days. Sweet corn freezes well, especially if removed from ears before freezing.

RECOMMENDED SWEET CORN

Early
'Early Sunglow'
'July Gold'
'Kandy Kwik' F1

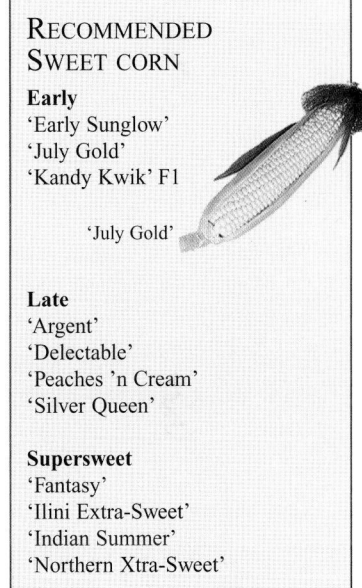

'July Gold'

Late
'Argent'
'Delectable'
'Peaches 'n Cream'
'Silver Queen'

Supersweet
'Fantasy'
'Ilini Extra-Sweet'
'Indian Summer'
'Northern Xtra-Sweet'

TESTING SWEET CORN FOR RIPENESS

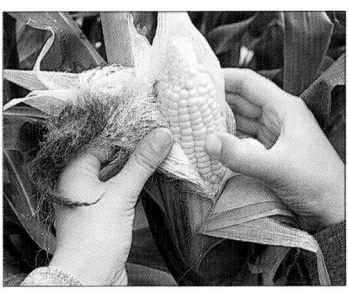

Once the silks have turned brown, peel back the husks and press into a kernel with a fingernail. If the liquid that appears is milky, the ear is ripe; if watery, it is underripe; and if doughy, overripe.

Podded vegetables

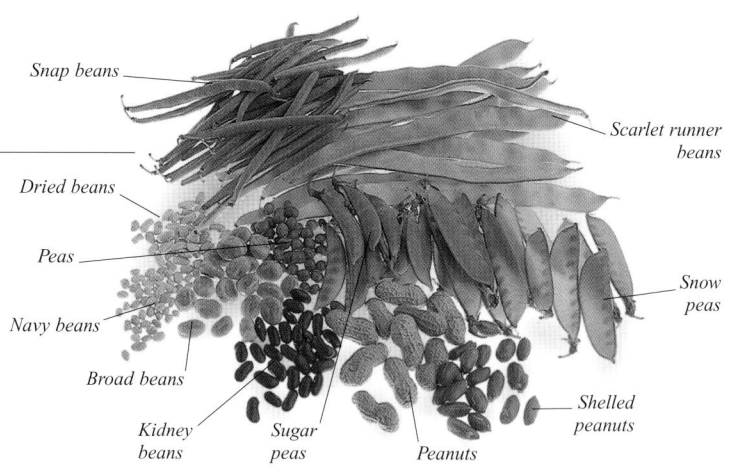

Snap beans

Scarlet runner beans

Dried beans

Peas

Snow peas

Navy beans

Broad beans

Kidney beans

Sugar peas

Peanuts

Shelled peanuts

VEGETABLES in this group all produce seedpods. Some are grown for these pods, which may be cooked and eaten whole, while others are grown for the seeds, which are extracted and cooked or eaten raw. The seeds of some may be dried; most may be frozen. Several of the plants are decorative as well as functional and may be used for screening or trained over arches. Podded vegetables often need sheltered conditions at specific temperatures for pollination; they usually require a rich soil to which organic matter has been added before planting.

Okra (*Abelmoschus esculentus*)

These tender annual plants are also known as lady's fingers. The fast-maturing cultivars may grow to 3ft (1m) with a spread of 12–16in (30–40cm); the slow-maturing ones (mainly grown in the South) are up to 6ft (2m) tall. The pods are 4–10in (10–25cm) long and white, green, or red. Recommended cultivars include 'Clemson Spineless', 'Green Velvet', and 'Burgundy'. Immature pods are eaten as a cooked vegetable; mature pods may also be dried and powdered for use as a thickener.

In warm-temperate and subtropical areas, plants may be grown in the open in favorable, sunny conditions. Seeds germinate only at soil temperatures of at least 61°F (16°C); after germination a stable temperature in the range 68–86°F (20–30°C) is needed for optimum growth. Most modern cultivars are daylength neutral (see "Daylength," p.489). Plant in well-drained soil, adding plenty of organic material during preparation. Okra plants need low to medium nitrogen levels (see p.498).

Sowing and planting
Soak seed for 24 hours before sowing to aid germination. When soil temperatures reach 61–64°F (16–18°C), sow seed *in situ* in rows 24–28in (60–70cm) apart, leaving 8–12in (20–30cm) between plants. In warm-temperate areas, sow in spring under cover at 68°F (20°C) or above, in trays or 3–3½in (7–9cm) pots. When seedlings are 4–6in (10–15cm) tall, harden off and transplant to well-prepared beds, spacing as above.

Routine cultivation
Stake tall plants and protect from strong winds with screens or plastic covers, if necessary. Remove all weeds, water regularly, and apply an organic mulch to retain soil moisture. Pinch out the growing points when seedlings are about 24in (60cm) tall to promote branching. Apply a general-purpose granular or liquid fertilizer at two-week intervals to encourage rapid growth. Do not overfertilize with nitrogen, since this delays flowering.

Pests and diseases
Plants are most likely to be damaged by aphids (p.639), caterpillars (p.639), and powdery mildew (p.640). Whiteflies (p.639), spider mites (p.640), thrips (p.640), and fungal leaf spots (p.641) may also be troublesome.

Growing under cover
Seedlings may be transplanted into well-prepared beds in the greenhouse or in growing bags, spacing the young plants at least 16in (40cm) apart. Maintain a temperature above 68°F (20°C) and a humidity of over 70 percent. Spray the plants as necessary to control pests and diseases, and apply an organic liquid or general-purpose fertilizer.

Harvesting and storing
Each plant may produce up to a few dozen pods. The pods may be harvested approximately eight to 11 weeks after sowing, depending on the cultivar. Sever the pods from the plant with a sharp knife when they are still small and tender; overmature pods will be fibrous. Pods may be stored in perforated bags at 45–50°F (7–10°C) for up to ten days.

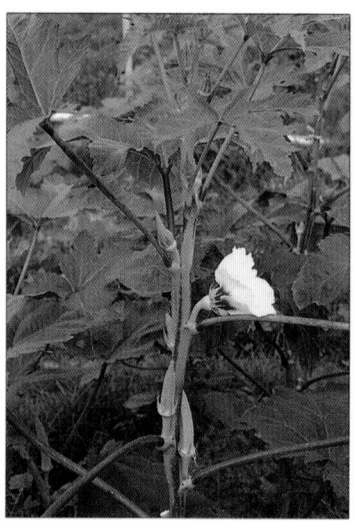

OKRA

Peanuts (*Arachis hypogaea*)

These tender annual plants, also known as groundnuts and monkeynuts, originated in South America. Plants grow to a height of 24in (60cm) with a spread of 12in (30cm) for the more upright Spanish-Valencia types, or up to 3ft (1m) for the less common, prostrate, Virginia types. The Spanish-Valencia types are often divided into Spanish, with two seeds per pod and light brown seed coats, and Valencia, with up to four seeds per pod and dark red seed coats. The stems of the Valencia types are usually thicker than those of the Spanish. The Virginia forms have two seeds per pod, with dark brown seed coats.

The fertilized flowers produce shootlike structures that penetrate the soil where the immature fruits develop into peanuts. Removed from their pods, the nuts are eaten fresh or roasted, or used in cooking.

Peanuts are tropical plants that need average temperatures of about 68–86°F (20–30°C) and a relative humidity of 80 percent, although some forms grow well in the warmer subtropics. A frost-free site is essential. Rainfall at flowering time may adversely affect pollination.

Peanut cultivars are generally daylength-neutral (see "Daylength," p.489). Sandy, well-drained loams with a pH of 5.5–6.5 containing extra calcium, potassium, and phosphorus are preferable. The plants also need low nitrogen levels (see p.498).

Sowing and planting
Sow seeds *in situ*, removed from their shells, in spring or when soil temperatures exceed 61°F (16°C). In cooler climates, sow under cover in trays or 3½in (9cm) pots, keeping temperatures over 68°F (20°C).

When the seedlings are 4–6in (10–15cm) tall, harden them off and transplant them to well-prepared beds. Whether directly sown or transplanted, the plants should be spaced 6–12in (15–30cm) apart with about 24–28in (60–70cm) between rows. Protect them with individual covers or polytunnels where necessary.

Routine cultivation
Hill up around the roots when the plants are 6in (15cm) tall, and hoe regularly to encourage the fertilized flowers to penetrate the soil. Remove all weeds, and water well in dry periods. Do not water plants during the flowering period, since this may lead to poor pollination.

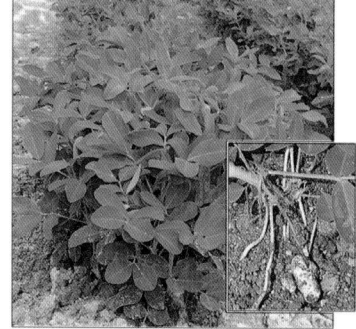

SPANISH-VALENCIA PEANUT PLANT

Pests and diseases
Plants may be affected by aphids (p.639), thrips (p.640), and caterpillars (p.639); spider mites (p.640), and whiteflies (p.639) may also cause problems. Fungal leaf spots

(p.641), root and stem rot (see "Southern blight," p.647), and rosette virus (see "Viruses," p.642) may also be troublesome.

Growing under cover
Sow seed as described above. Transplant the seedlings when they are 4–6in (10–15cm) tall into growing bags, or well-prepared greenhouse beds. Maintain a temperature over 68°F (20°C), reducing humidity at flowering time to aid pollination.

Harvesting and storing
Harvest the pods 16–20 weeks after sowing for the upright types, and three to four weeks after this for the prostrate types. Virginia types, which produce two seeds per pod, may require up to 25 weeks from sowing to harvesting. Assess the stage of maturity by uprooting one or two pods. Dry the pods in the sun, then remove the peanuts for storing in cool, dry conditions. They keep for several months.

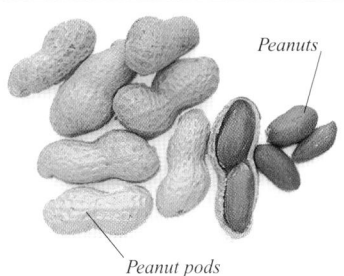

Peanuts

Peanut pods

Hyacinth beans (*Lablab purpureus*)

These dwarf or climbing, short-lived tender perennials are also known as dolichos beans and lablab beans. Both long- and short-podded cultivars occur. Climbing forms may grow to 12–20ft (4–6m), while dwarf forms reach 3ft (1m) with a spread of about 2ft (60cm). The pods range in color from green to purple. Young pods and mature seeds are eaten cooked; the latter should be cooked thoroughly. Young seedlings, raised in the dark, may be used as bean sprouts, either raw or cooked.

Hyacinth beans may be grown in subtropical and warm-temperate regions in sunny sites. The plants require a temperature of 64–86°F (18–30°C) with a minimum humidity of 70 percent; cool weather may adversely affect pollination since it discourages pollinating insects. Daylength-neutral cultivars are available (see "Daylength," p.489).

Most soils are suitable for hyacinth beans, particularly those high in organic matter; good drainage is essential. Some cultivars respond well to applications of superphosphate. Hyacinth beans need low nitrogen levels (see p.498).

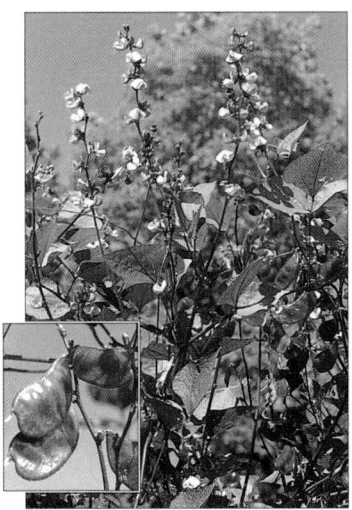

HYACINTH BEANS

Sowing and planting
Sow *in situ*, in spring or at other times of the year if temperatures are high enough. In temperate areas, sow seeds under cover, in trays, or in 3–3½in (7–9cm) pots at a depth of 1in (2.5cm). When the seedlings are 4–6in (10–15cm) tall, harden them off and transplant into well-prepared beds. Space climbing cultivars 12–18in (30–45cm) apart, allowing 30–36in (75–100cm) between rows; space the dwarf cultivars 12–16in (30–40cm) apart with a distance of 18–24in (45–60cm) between rows.

Routine cultivation
Climbing cultivars should be supported by individual stakes at least 6ft (2m) high or as for scarlet runner beans (see below). Water the plants regularly, and mulch to conserve moisture. Protect young plants as necessary and remove all weeds. Apply a general-purpose granular or liquid fertilizer every ten to 14 days until flowering. Pinch out the growing points of dwarf cultivars to encourage a bushy habit; the shoots of climbing cultivars should be trained or tied in to the stakes.

Pests and diseases
Aphids (p.639), thrips (p.640), caterpillars (p.639), root-knot nematodes (p.652), powdery mildew (p.640), fungal leaf spots (p.641), and some viruses (p.642) may be troublesome; whiteflies (p.639) and spider mites (p.640) may also affect plants.

Growing under cover
Transplant seedlings to growing bags or well-prepared beds in the greenhouse, spacing the plants at least 20–24in (50–60cm) apart. Alternatively, seedlings may be grown on in 8–10in (21–5cm) pots (two plants may be grown in the larger pots). Maintain a temperature of at least 68°F (20°C), and reduce humidity by providing adequate ventilation at flowering time to improve pollination. Hyacinth beans may also be propagated from softwood cuttings (see PRINCIPLES OF PROPAGATION, "Stem cuttings," p.626), taken early in the growing season, which root readily in high humidity.

Harvesting and storing
Harvest the young pods six to nine weeks after sowing, when they are fully grown but before the seeds develop; the mature pods containing seeds may be harvested after ten to 14 weeks, before they become fibrous. If the plants remain healthy after the first crop, cut back the main stems to about half their length to encourage a second crop. Hyacinth beans freeze well.

Scarlet runner beans (*Phaseolus coccineus*)

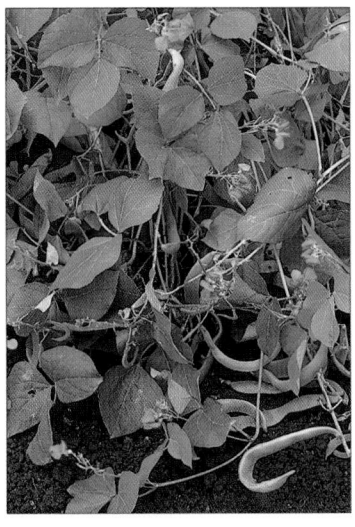

SCARLET RUNNER BEANS

These perennial climbers are grown as annuals in temperate and cool climates. Plants grow to over 10ft (3m) tall, with a spread of about 12in (30cm); some naturally dwarf cultivars form bushes about 15in (38cm) tall. They have pink, red, white, or bicolored flowers.

The flat pods, over 10in (25cm) long and up to ¾in (2cm) wide, are eaten cooked; immature seeds and dried mature seeds may also be cooked. With some cultivars, it may be necessary to remove the strings along the pods.

Scarlet runner beans are a temperate or cool-season crop that does not withstand frost. Plants need a growing season of about 100 frost-free days, and they grow best at 57–84°F (14–29°C). At higher temperatures, especially if combined with high humidity, the pods may not set unless the plants are in light shade. In cool climates, choose a sheltered situation to encourage pollinating insects. Plants are deep-rooting and need fertile, moisture-retentive soil. Prepare the soil by digging a trench one spade deep and 60cm (24in) wide, working in well-rotted straw or compost. Runner bean crops should be rotated (see p.492) and need low nitrogen levels (see p.498).

Sowing and planting
Before planting climbing types, erect a strong support system of poles or stakes over 8ft (2.5m) long, tied to a horizontal pole or to each other to form a tepee. Commercial supports or towers are available. Plants may

RECOMMENDED SCARLET RUNNER BEANS

Standard
'Apricot Runner'
'Emperor'
'Painted Lady'
'Prize Winner'

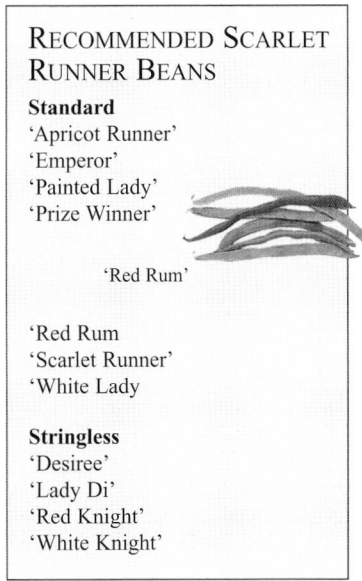

'Red Rum'

'Red Rum'
'Scarlet Runner'
'White Lady'

Stringless
'Desiree'
'Lady Di'
'Red Knight'
'White Knight'

also be twisted up nylon netting, strings, or wires pegged to the ground; do not use plastic-coated netting, since the plants do not cling to it. Sow seed *in situ* 2in (5cm) deep, after all risk of frost has passed, bearing in mind that a minimum soil temperature of 59°F (15°C) is needed for germination. In cool areas, sow seed indoors in seed trays and harden off seedlings before transplanting outside. Grow climbers in double rows 2ft (60cm) apart or in circular tepees, spacing the plants 6in (15cm) apart. Bush forms may be grown in groups at the same spacing. Mulch well to retain moisture after germination or planting out.

BEAN SUPPORTS

There are various ways to support climbing beans, depending on the space available. Mature plants will obscure the support structure beneath.

CROSSED STAKE ROW

Two rows of 8ft (2.5m) stakes, crossed and secured to a horizontal bar

WIGWAM

8ft (2.5m) stakes tied near the top

NETTING SUPPORT

4in (10cm) square nylon net mounted on a pole frame

TRAINED ON A TEPEE

Routine cultivation
Protect seedlings with covers or floating row covers. To convert climbing forms into bushes, nip out the growing shoots when plants are 9in (23cm) high. Such plants crop earlier but have lower yields.

Watering is especially important when the flower buds appear and pods are setting (see "Critical watering periods," p.496). At these times water at a rate of 1–2 gallons/sq yd (5–11 liters/sq m) twice a week.

Pests and diseases
Slugs (p.638) in the early stages, pollen beetles (p.649), fungal leaf spots (p.641), foot and root rots (p.646), halo blight (see "Bacterial leaf spots and blotches," p.641), Southern blight (p.647), and viruses (p.642) may be troublesome in scarlet runner beans.

Harvesting and storing
Harvest after 13–17 weeks. Pick pods when they are at least 7in (17cm) long and tender; picking prolongs the cropping period. Scarlet runner beans freeze well.

Lima beans (*Phaseolus lunatus*)

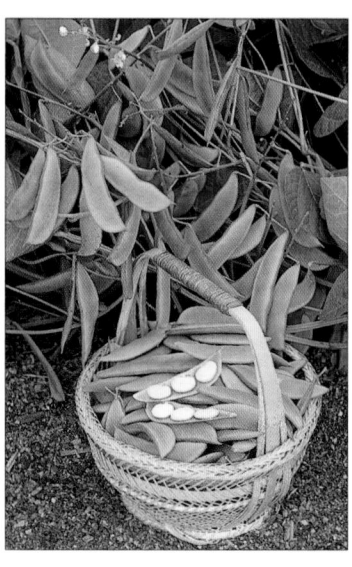

DWARF LIMA BEANS

Also known as butter beans, lima beans are tender annuals and short-lived perennials. Some forms of lima bean climb, while others are dwarf and branching. Climbing cultivars may grow to a height of 9–12ft (3–4m), dwarf cultivars to 3ft (90cm), spreading to 16–18in (40–45cm). The young pods and mature seeds are eaten cooked; the seeds may also be dried or germinated in the dark for use as bean sprouts.

The lima bean is a tropical plant requiring a minimum temperature of 64°F (18°C) for germination. Temperatures above 86°F (30°C) may adversely affect pollen formation. In subtropical and warm-temperate areas, growing in the open is possible only in full sun, using plastic screens or covers for protection until the plants are fully established.

Small-seeded cultivars flower only in short daylengths of about 12 hours, but the large-seeded cultivars are normally daylength neutral (see "Daylength," p.489).

Most cultivars thrive in a wide range of soil types, but a sandy, well-drained loam with a pH of 6–7 is preferable. Lima beans require low to medium nitrogen levels (see p.498). The procedures for sowing, planting, routine cultivation, and growing under cover are as described for hyacinth beans (see p.525).

Pests and diseases
Aphids (p.639), thrips (p.640), caterpillars (p.639), whiteflies (p.639) and spider mites (p.640) may cause problems. Diseases include powdery mildew (p.640), fungal leaf spots (p.640), and viruses (p.642).

RECOMMENDED LIMA BEANS

Climbing
'Florida Butter'
'King of the Garden'

Dwarf
'Dixie Butterpea'
'Eastland'
'Fordhook 242'

'Fordhook 242'

Harvesting and storing
Harvest whole pods young; mature seeds about 12–16 weeks after sowing. Store both above 39°F (4°C) at 90 percent humidity for up to two weeks. Lima beans may be frozen.

Snap beans (*Phaseolus vulgaris*)

These tender annuals have pole (climbing), bush, and intermediate forms. They are also known as French, green, or string beans. Height and spread are as for scarlet runner beans (see p.525). The pods are 3–8in (7–20cm) long. They may be round, flat, or curved in shape; diameter ranges from pencil thickness (for the filet types) to about ¾in (2cm); they may be green, yellow, purple, red, or green flecked with purple. The yellow waxpod types have a waxy texture and excellent flavor. Types vary in the stringiness of the pods; stringless cultivars are widely available. Snap beans may be eaten raw in salads or lightly steamed.

Some related beans are grown specifically for drying the seeds. These include kidney, pinto, navy, and white beans; all are grown as for snap beans. Dried seeds are used in stews.

Snap beans grow in similar conditions to scarlet runner beans (see p.525) but the seeds need a minimum temperature of 54°F (12°C) to germinate. The optimum growing temperature is 61–86°F (16–30°C); seedlings do not tolerate temperatures below 50°F (10°C). The plants are self-pollinated and grow best in rich, light soil. Good drainage is essential to prevent root rot. Work plenty of well-rotted compost or manure into the soil before planting, and always rotate crops (see p.492). Seed may be dressed with the appropriate bacterial inoculant, or Rhizobium granules may be applied to the soil at planting; this treatment increases current and subsequent yields by encouraging the formation of nitrogen-fixing root nodules. Snap beans usually need low nitrogen levels (see p.498).

PREGERMINATING SNAP BEANS

1 *Spread the beans out on moist tissue paper in a tray without drainage holes. Keep damp, at a minimum of 54°F (12°C).*

2 *When the delicate shoots begin to appear and before they turn green, carefully pot up the beans or sow them directly in their final position outside.*

Sowing and planting
Seed may be pregerminated before sowing. Sow seed or pregerminated seed 1½in (4cm) deep *in situ* or indoors as for scarlet runner beans (see p.525), and make successive sowings throughout the summer. If necessary, warm the soil beforehand with cloches. Space pole forms as for scarlet runner beans. Bush types may be grown at an equidistant spacing of 9in (22cm) in staggered rows for the highest yields. In cold climates, protect after planting with covers or floating row covers.

Routine cultivation
Support pole types as for scarlet runner beans; use twigs to support intermediate types. Stems may also be hilled up to keep plants upright. Mulch and do not allow plants to dry out completely; extra watering at a rate of 5 gallons/sq yd (23 liters/sq m) may be necessary in dry conditions at flowering time.

Pests and diseases
Slugs (p.638), root aphids and black bean aphids (see "Aphids," p.639), fungal leaf spots (p.641), foot and root rots (p.646), halo blight (see "Bacterial leaf spots and blotches," p.641), and viruses (p.642) may affect snap beans. Under cover, spider mites (p.640) may be a problem.

Growing under cover
In cool climates, bush snap beans may be grown in a greenhouse or polytunnel, or under individual cloches. Space plants as in the open.

HILLING UP
Plant out the beans 6in (15cm) apart, and once they have formed several pairs of leaves, hill them up to support them.

Harvesting and storing
Harvest after seven to 13 weeks. Pick young beans regularly to use fresh or freeze. For shelled beans, see below; store in an airtight jar.

DRYING BEANS

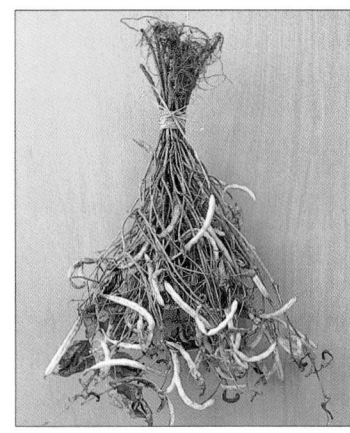

In damp climates, pull up plants and hang them by the roots in a dry, frost-free place. Once dried, remove the pods and extract the beans.

RECOMMENDED BEANS
Pole
'Blue Lake'
'Kentucky Blue'
'Kentucky Wonder'

Bush
'Bush Blue Lake'
'Dorabel' (wax)
'Goldcrop' (wax)
'Provider'
'Rocdor' (wax)
'Roma II'
'Royal Burgundy' (purple podded)
'Tenderlake'

'Royal Burgundy'

Beans for drying
'Jacob's Cattle'
'Maine Yellow Eye'
'Vermont Cranberry'

Peas (*Pisum sativum*)

Peas are annuals that grow from 18in (45cm) to over 6ft (2m) tall and have an average spread of 9in (23cm). Plants cling to supports with tendrils; modern semileafless types are almost self-supporting. Peas are grouped according to the time taken to mature. The early groups are dwarfer and lower yielding. Pods are usually green, but there are purple-podded cultivars.

Shelling-pea types are grown for the fresh peas in the pods; some may be dried. Petits pois are small, fine-flavored peas. Wrinkle-seeded cultivars are usually sweeter but less hardy than smooth-seeded types. Edible-podded types (snow peas and sugar peas) may be eaten before the peas mature. Snow peas have flat pods and are eaten young; round-podded sugar types are used when semimature. Peas and pods are often cooked but may be eaten raw.

SEMILEAFLESS PEAS

Peas are a cool-season crop, growing best at 55–64°F (13–18°C). The flowers and pods cannot withstand frost. Grow peas in an open site in reasonably fertile, moisture-retentive, well-drained soil; they will not tolerate cold, wet soil, or drought. Work

plenty of well-rotted compost or manure into the soil before planting. Peas should be rotated (see p.492). The plants have nitrogen-fixing nodules on their roots so do not require any extra nitrogen during growth.

Sowing and planting
Make the first outdoor sowings as soon as the soil is about 50°F (10°C). Germination is much slower at lower temperatures. The first sowings may be made under covers or floating row covers using dwarf cultivars. For successive crops, either sow seeds at 14-day intervals, or sow cultivars from different groups at the same time so that they mature in succession. Avoid midsummer sowings in warm areas, since high temperatures also impede germination. If sowing an early type late, allow about ten weeks before frost is expected for the pods to ripen. Where

winters are mild, sow hardy, early-maturing cultivars in late fall to overwinter.

Sow the seed 1¼in (3cm) deep in patches so that plants can support each other, spacing individual seeds 2–3in (5–7cm) apart. Alternatively, make a flat-bottomed drill up to 9in (23cm) wide, spacing seeds 2in (5cm) apart each way (see "Wide drills," p.494). The drills should be 24–36in (60–90cm) apart, the wider spacing for tall cultivars. Seed may also be sown in double rows 9in (23cm) apart, spacing seeds ½in (1cm) apart.

Routine cultivation
Protect seedlings against birds with horizontal netting as pea guards. Once the tendrils have developed, remove the guards and erect supports: use wire netting, pea nets, or brushwood on either side of a drill.

Semileafless and dwarf types need less support. When the peas have several leaves, mulch them to keep the roots cool.

Once plants are flowering and forming pods, water every week (unless rainfall is high) at a rate of 5 gallons/sq yd (23 liters/sq m).

Pests and diseases

Aphids (p.639) and pea moths are the most common pests; mice (p.653) may also be troublesome since they eat seeds. Damping off (p.655), foot and root rots (p.646), Southern blight (p.647), and *Fusarium* wilt (p.646) are occasional problems.

Growing under cover

Early spring and late fall sowings may be made under cover; grow dwarf peas to maturity under cloches for early or overwintering crops.

Harvesting and storing

Harvest early types 11–12 weeks after sowing, and maincrop peas after 13–14 weeks. Pick snow pea

SUPPORTING PEAS

When seedlings have developed tendrils, push peasticks into the ground, as upright as possible, all around the outside of the patch (above). As the peas grow, the tendrils wrap around the peasticks and the peas grow up them (right).

types when the immature peas are just forming inside the pods, or leave them to mature and then shell them normally. Pick shelling peas and

sugar types when the pods have swollen. All may be frozen. For how to store pods on plants, see *Drying Beans*, p.527.

RECOMMENDED PEAS

Early
'Knight'
'Laxton's Progress'
'Little Marvel'
'Maestro'

Maincrop
'Green Arrow'
'Lincoln'
'Mr. Big'
'Olympia'

Sugar peas
'Cascadia'
'Oregon Sugar Pod'
'Sugar Anne'
'Sugar Bon'

'Sugar Bon'

'Sugar Daddy'
'Sugar Snap'
'Sugar Sprint'

Broad beans (*Vicia faba*)

These annual plants are also known as fava beans. They range in height from 12in (30cm) for dwarf cultivars to about 5ft (1.5m), with an average spread of 18in (45cm). Broad beans are grouped according to the time they take to mature. The broad pods are up to 1in (2.5cm) wide and 3–6in (7–15cm) long, with green, white, or pinkish red seeds 3/4–1in (2–2.5cm) long. The immature bean seeds, as well as the young pods and leafy shoot tips, may be cooked. The shelled beans freeze well.

Broad beans are a cool-season crop, growing satisfactorily only at temperatures below about 59°F (15°C). Some cultivars are very hardy, the immature plants surviving 14°F (-10°C) on well-drained soil. Some that are adapted to higher temperatures have recently been bred. Grow spring and early summer sowings in an open site, and fall sowings for overwintering in a sheltered site in reasonably fertile, well-manured soil. Rotate broad bean crops (see p.492). The plants need low nitrogen levels (see p.498) because their root nodules fix atmospheric nitrogen.

Sowing and planting

Sow seed *in situ* in spring and early summer as soon as the ground is workable. Seed germinates at fairly low temperatures. For an early crop, sow seed in late fall to

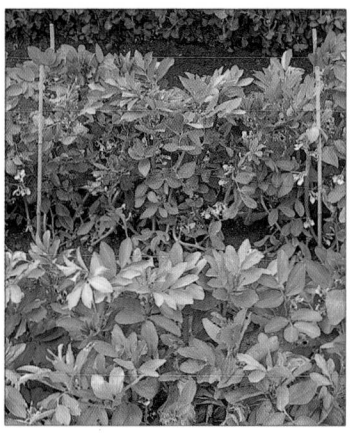

DWARF BROAD BEANS

early winter of the previous year – the plants need only be 1in (2.5cm) high before winter. In very cold areas, seed may be sown indoors in winter and transplanted outside in spring after the risk of frost has passed.

Sow seed about 1½in (4cm) deep, spaced about 9in (23cm) apart each way. Grow either in double rows, with 3ft (90cm) between the pairs of rows, or evenly spaced in blocks across a bed. The taller cultivars may be supported with strands of wire attached to strong stakes or poles placed around the rows or blocks of plants. If necessary, dwarf cultivars may be supported with twigs to keep their pods clear of the ground. Overwintering crops and those sown in early spring may

be protected with covers or floating row covers in the early stages of growth.

Routine cultivation

Do not allow the plants to dry out; water as for snap beans (see p.526). Once flowering starts, pinch out the growing tips to encourage pods to form and to combat aphids. Hill up overwintering plants to protect them against the elements.

Pests and diseases

Tropical root rots, aphids (p.639), chocolate spot, and foot and

PINCHING OUT

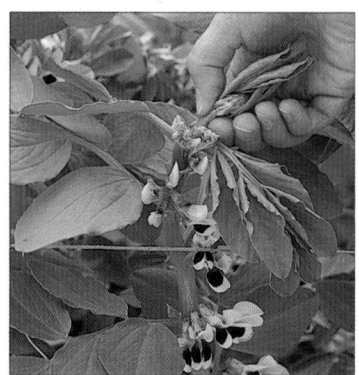

When the beans are in full flower, pinch out the growing tip of each plant. This will remove any black aphids and concentrate the plant's energy into producing beans.

root rots (p.646) may affect broad beans, causing problems at all stages of growth.

Harvesting and storing

Harvest broad beans that were sown in spring after 12–16 weeks, and those sown in fall after 28–35 weeks. Pick them while the pods are fresh and plump with the swelling beans and before they become old and leathery.

The beans may be frozen, or dried at the end of the growing season for use during the winter months as for snap beans (see p.526).

RECOMMENDED BROAD BEANS

Dwarf
'Sutton'   'Imperial Green
                         Longpod'
Tall
'Aquadulce
  Claudia' (fall sowing)
'Aquadulce Loreta' (fall or
  early spring sowing)
'Broad Windsor Long Pod'
'Express'
'Imperial Green Longpod'
'Jubilee Hysor'

'Witkiem Major'

'Jumbo'
'Medes'
'Witkiem Major'

Bulb and stem vegetables

Leeks

Garlic

Scallions

Bulb onions

Celery

Florence fennel

Red bulb onions

Asparagus

Shallots

VEGETABLES grown for their bulbs or stems include members of the onion family as well as a varied group of other plants that, with the exception of Florence fennel, are mostly quite hardy and slow-maturing. Celeriac, kohlrabi, and Florence fennel form swollen stems just above ground level, rather than true bulbs. The onion family should be rotated as one group; for rotation groups for the other vegetables, see p.492. Both asparagus and rhubarb are perennial vegetables that should be planted in permanent beds that have been specially prepared for them.

Bulb onions (*Allium cepa*)

These are grown as annuals. The bulbs may be rounded or flattened or have a long torpedo shape. They normally have brown or yellow skins with white flesh, although some have red skin and pinkish white flesh; the leaves grow 6–18in (15–45cm) long. Immature and mature bulbs are eaten either raw or cooked. Some cultivars are suitable for storage. The green-leaved thinnings may be used as scallions (see p.530).

Bulb onions are a cool-season, cold-tolerant crop, growing best at 55–75°F (13–24°C). Cool temperatures are required in the early stages of growth. Cultivars need different daylengths in order for the bulbs to swell; long-day types should be chosen for northerly latitudes, and short-day types for southerly latitudes (see also "Daylength," p.489).

Grow them in an open site, on fertile, medium to light soil that is well drained. Prepare the soil by digging in a good deal of well-rotted manure, preferably the fall before planting. Do not plant on newly manured ground. An all-purpose fertilizer may be worked into the seedbed before sowing. They have low nitrogen requirements (see p.498).

Sowing and planting
Onions may be raised from seed or sets (small bulbs specially grown and harvested immature the year before). Seed is cheaper but slower to develop; sets are easier to grow but usually available for only a few cultivars. Bulb onions require a long growing season, particularly if large bulbs are required or if they are to be stored.

Sow in spring when the soil is workable, on a firm seedbed, sowing seed very thinly ½in (1cm) deep, in rows 9–12in (23–30cm) apart. Thin out the seedlings in stages. For the highest yield of medium-sized onions, space 1½in (4cm) apart; for larger onions, thin seedlings to 2–4in (5–10cm) apart.

To extend the growing season in northern latitudes, start under cover in seed trays or cell packs at 50–59°F (10–15°C) from late winter to early spring. Harden off seedlings at the two-leaf stage and plant out at the appropriate spacing. Cell packs may also be multisown with five seeds per section and each section planted out as a unit, with 10in (25cm) between units (see also *Transplanting Leeks*, p.531).

Certain cultivars may be sown in summer or fall to overwinter for earlier crops the following year. This is inadvisable where winters are very severe or very wet, since seeds may rot before germination. Traditional summer-sown cultivars are reasonably hardy and may be sown *in situ* in late summer, thinning to 1in (2.5cm) apart in fall and in stages to the final spacing in spring. Japanese overwintering onions are also suitable for sowing at this time; they are hardier than other bulb onions, but are unsuitable for storage. The precise sowing date for these is critical. Sow during the summer at the recommended date for the area, spacing and thinning as above.

Most sets are planted in the early spring. If using heat-treated sets, consult the suppliers for planting times. Plant at the above spacing in shallow furrows so that the tips protrude just above the soil. Recently introduced sets for planting during fall may be available.

Routine cultivation
Keep the site weed-free, especially when the onions are young and susceptible to competition from weeds. Onions are fairly shallow-rooted and need little water once established, except in very dry conditions. Overwintering onions may be given either a nitrogenous fertilizer or an organic liquid fertilizer if necessary in spring.

Pests and diseases
Onion maggots (p.654), onion white rot (p.654), downy mildew, and, in storage, onion neck rot are common problems that affect onions.

Harvesting and storing
Spring-sown bulb onions will take 12–18 weeks to mature, summer-sown onions up to 42 weeks. Pull or lift them as needed to use fresh.

For storage, wait until the leaves have died back naturally (do not bend them over by hand), and then carefully uproot all the onions. In

> ### RECOMMENDED BULB ONIONS
>
> **Onions for fall harvesting**
> 'Albion' F1
> 'Carmen' F1 (pink)
> 'Norstar'
> 'Super Star' F1
> 'Yellow Granex' F1
>
> **Red onions (use fresh or store)**
> 'Florence Red'
> 'Mars'
>
> 'Florence Red'
>
> 'Red Burgermaster'
> 'Redwing'
>
> **Traditional and Japanese overwintering onions**
> 'Beltsville Bunching'
> 'Frontier'
> 'Hardy White Bunching'
> 'Ishikuro'
> 'Kincho'
> 'Stuttgarter'
> 'Walla Walla Sweet'

STORING ONIONS IN A BOX

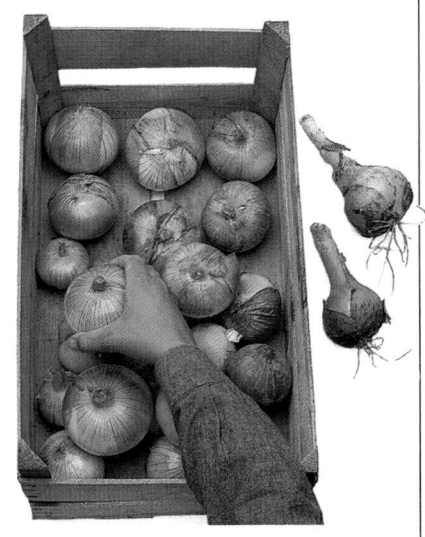

Prepare onions carefully for storing. Bull-necked onions (those with thick necks above the bulbs, see far right) should be rejected. Be careful not to damage any onions for storing, since this encourages rot. Place them in layers in a box and store them in a place that is well ventilated and frost-free.

sunny conditions, leave them in the sun to dry for about ten days, either hung in nets or supported off the ground on an upturned seed tray to allow maximum ventilation. In wet conditions, hang them indoors in a cool place. The outer skins and leaves must all be thoroughly dry before the bulbs are put into storage.

Handle the bulbs gently, since any bruises will encourage storage rots. Do not store onions that are bull-necked; these should always be used first. Store onions either hanging in nets or braids (see *Storing Strings of Onions*, p.500) or packed carefully in layers in boxes. They must be kept at 32–45°F (0–7°C) and in low humidity (i.e. below 40 percent). Average storage life is three to six months, depending on the cultivar.

Scallions

Traditional European scallions, or bunching onions, are cultivars of bulb onions suitable for using young. Pull them when the green leaves are 6in (15cm) tall, with a whitened shank and tiny bulb. A widely grown cultivar is 'White Lisbon'. For climate, soil requirements, and pests and diseases see "Bulb onions," p.529. Lime acid soil (see p.619).

In spring, sow thinly *in situ*, in rows 4in (10cm) apart, or bands 3in (7cm) wide and 6in (15cm) apart. For continuous crops, sow every three weeks in summer. Overwintering cultivars (e.g. 'White Lisbon Winter Hardy') may be sown in late summer for an early spring crop; protect them in winter with covers. Water the onions in dry conditions. Scallions are ready for pulling after two months.

THINNING SCALLIONS

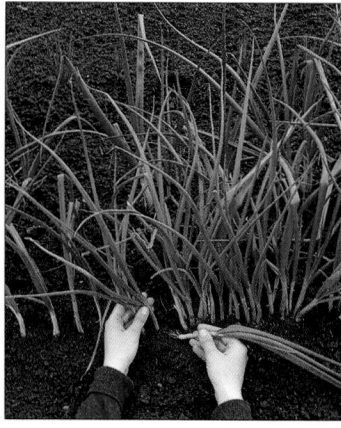

If densely sown, harvest seedling scallions to leave the others spaced 1in (2.5cm) apart. Those remaining will continue to grow and may be harvested when required.

Pickling onions

These bulb onion cultivars produce small white bulbs (also known as cocktail onions) in northerly latitudes, and larger bulbs in southerly latitudes. They may be used when they reach about thumbnail size, either fresh or for pickling. Cultivars include 'Silver Queen' and 'Snow Baby'. They prefer fertile soil but tolerate fairly poor soil. For climate, cultivation, and pests and diseases, see "Bulb onions," p.529.

In spring sow seed *in situ*, either broadcast or in bands about 4in (10cm) wide, spacing seeds ½in (1cm) apart. Thin only if larger onions are required. Harvest onions after about eight weeks when the foliage has died back; use fresh, or dry and store as for bulb onions (see p.529) until required for pickling.

PICKLING ONIONS

Shallots (*Allium cepa* Aggregatum Group)

These distinctively flavored, onion-shaped bulbs form clumps of about a dozen bulbs. There are yellow- and red-skinned forms; all may be used fresh or after storing, and are eaten raw or cooked. The green leaves of young shallots may be used fresh as scallions.

Climate and soil requirements, routine cultivation, and pests and diseases are as for bulb onions (see p.529). Shallots are very hardy. Buy virus-free sets that are ideally about ¾in (2cm) in diameter. Plant in early spring, or during winter in mild areas. Plant as for bulb onion sets (see p.529), spacing the sets about 7in (18cm) apart each way. Each set will develop into a clump, maturing in early summer. For an early crop of green leaves, plant small sets in fall, spacing them in the ground, or in seed trays under cover, about 1in (2.5cm) apart.

Harvest green leaves as needed. For good-sized bulbs, do not pick the leaves; lift the bulbs once the foliage has died down. To store, dry as for bulb onions (see p.529); good stocks store for up to a year.

PLANTING SHALLOTS

Make a drill ½in (1cm) deep. Push the sets into the drill about 7in (18cm) apart so that the tips show above the soil.

SHALLOTS

Welsh onions (*Allium fistulosum*)

These onions are very hardy perennials. They have hollow leaves up to 18in (45cm) tall and ½in (1cm) in diameter, growing in clumps of 9in (23cm) diameter on average; the bases of the leaves are thickened at and below ground level. The leaves remain green all year, even at temperatures as low as 14°F (-10°C), so they are a useful winter vegetable. The leaves and tiny bulbs may be eaten either raw or cooked.

Climate and soil requirements, cultivation, and pests and diseases are as for bulb onions (see p.529). Sow seed *in situ* in spring or summer in rows about 12in (30cm) apart. Thin the seedlings in stages until they are about 9in (23cm) apart, or propagate by dividing established clumps and carefully replanting the younger outer sections of the clumps to the above spacing. Leaves may be

WELSH ONIONS

harvested from 24 weeks after sowing; cut individual leaves as required, or pull up part or all of the clump. Established clumps can become very thick and should be divided every two or three years. Welsh onions do not store well.

Oriental bunching onions

These have been developed from Welsh onions. They are perennials usually grown as annuals or biennials for harvesting at any stage from seedlings to large plants. Mature plants have thickened white shafts 1in (2.5cm) in diameter and 6in (15cm) high. All parts are edible. There are cultivars for planting and harvesting year-round, and for a wide range of climatic conditions.

For soil requirements, see "Bulb onions" (p.529). Sow seed *in situ* in spring and summer, in rows 12in (30cm) apart. Thin out in stages up to 6in (15cm) apart, depending on the size required. Seed may also be sown in trays and planted out. Sow the hardiest cultivars, such as 'White Evergreen' or 'Ishikuro', in fall and overwinter to use in early spring. Some cultivars, such as 'Ishikuro' may be hilled up several times during growth to obtain long, white shafts. Young leaves may be picked four weeks after sowing.

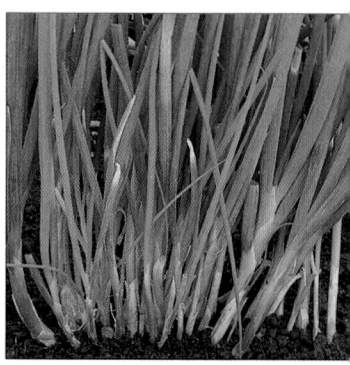

ORIENTAL BUNCHING ONIONS

Leeks (*Allium porrum*)

These are biennials grown as annuals, reaching 18in (45cm) tall and 6in (15cm) across. The edible part is the sweetly flavored, thick white shank that forms below long blue-green leaves. This may be blanched by hilling it up or by deep planting. Leeks with short, thick shanks are called pot leeks. All types are used cooked, as a vegetable or in soups.

Leeks are a cool-season crop and grow best below 75°F (24°C), but will tolerate higher temperatures if kept moist. Cultivars range from early and moderately hardy to late and very hardy. Grow in open sites on fertile, moisture-retentive soil, working in plenty of manure or compost and a nitrogenous fertilizer if the soil is low in nitrogen (high levels are needed; see p.498). Do not plant on compacted soils. Leeks must be rotated (see p.492).

Sowing and planting
Leeks need a long growing season; start them as early in the year as possible, sowing in succession. Sow ½in (1cm) deep in an outdoor seedbed for transplanting when 8in (20cm) tall. Alternatively, sow *in situ* in rows 12in (30cm) apart. Thin or transplant

LEEK PLANTS

SOWING IN A CELL PACK

Fill a cell pack with sowing medium to within ½in (1cm) of the top. Sow 4 leek seeds in each cell pack on the surface of the medium. Cover with a thin layer of soil mix, and water.

the seedlings at the three-leaf stage to 6in (15cm) apart. Use closer spacing if smaller leeks are preferred. For well-blanched stems, make holes 6–8in (15–20cm) deep with a dibber and drop a seedling in each; make sure that the roots reach the soil at the base. Water gently, then allow soil to fall in around the plants as they grow. Leeks may also be planted on the flat and blanched by hoeing up soil around the stems, 2in (5cm) at a time, as they grow.

To extend the growing season, sow under cover as for bulb onions (see p.529). Leeks respond well to being multisown in cell packs with up to four seeds per cell. Plant out the groups of seedlings at an even spacing of 9in (23cm).

Routine cultivation
Water thoroughly until the leeks are well established, and thereafter only in exceptionally dry conditions. Keep beds weed-free. Mulch to retain soil moisture if necessary.

Pests and diseases
Stem and bulb nematodes, onion maggots (p.654), rusts (p.641), and onion white rot (p.654) may all be troublesome.

TRANSPLANTING LEEKS

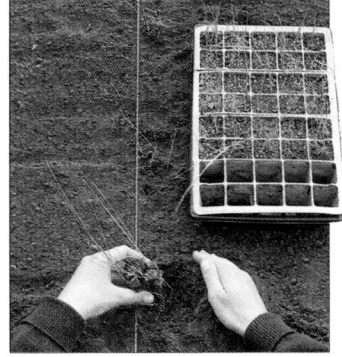

Each section of a cell pack may be planted out as a whole; plant the clumps 9in (23cm) apart.

SINGLE SEEDLINGS

Leeks sown outdoors may be transplanted to their final position in holes 6–8in (15–20cm) deep and 4–6in (10–15cm) apart.

Harvesting and storing
Leeks may be harvested 16–20 weeks after sowing but can stand for many months. Lift them as required from summer onward; the hardy cultivars may be lifted throughout

HEELING IN LEEKS

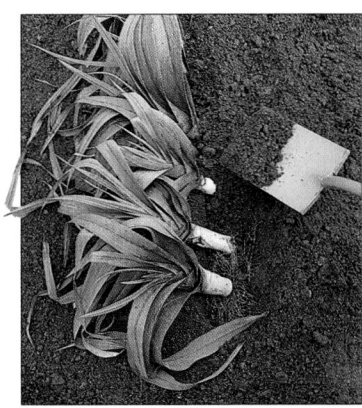

To store outdoors, lift the leeks and lean them against one side of a V-shaped trench. Cover the roots and white stems with soil and firm lightly. Lift and use as required.

winter into spring, except in very severe climates. Leeks do not store well out of the ground. If the site they occupy is required for another crop, dig up the plants and heel them in elsewhere.

RECOMMENDED LEEKS
'Arkansas' l
'Autumn Giant' m
'Dawn Giant' m
'Giant Musselburgh' e
'Jersey' m, l
'Jolant' e
'King Richard' e
'Large American Flag' l
'Leefall' l
'Lincoln' (all season)
'Tadorna' l
'Titan' e

KEY
e *early*
m *midseason*
l *late*

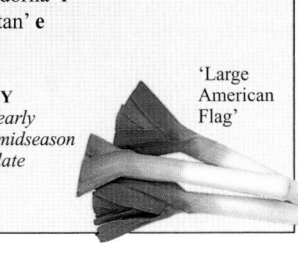
'Large American Flag'

Garlic (*Allium sativum*)

Biennials grown as annuals, garlic plants grow up to 2ft (60cm) tall with a spread of about 6in (15cm). Each produces an underground bulb up to 2in (5cm) in diameter. There are pink- and white-skinned forms, and many selections are available that are adapted to different climatic zones. Garlic is grown mainly for the strong-flavored cloves that form the bulb and may be stored for a year-round supply. The cloves are

used either fresh or after storing for seasoning and may be eaten both cooked and raw.

Garlic tolerates a wide range of climates but needs a period of one to two months at about 32–50°F (0–10°C) in winter. Some variants are extremely hardy; use those recommended for your area. Garlic grows best in an open, sunny position on light soil that does not have to be very fertile, so do not grow it

on freshly manured ground. Good drainage is vital. Garlic needs very low levels of nitrogen (see p.498).

Sowing and planting
For planting, split off individual cloves at least ½in (1cm) in diameter from a mature bulb. Always use healthy, virus-free stock. To produce large bulbs, garlic needs a long growing season, so wherever possible plant cloves in the fall. In

very cold areas and on heavy soils, delay planting until the early spring, or plant the cloves in cell packs in winter, one per section. Then place the cell packs in a sheltered position outdoors to provide them with the necessary cold period. Plant them out in the ground after they have started to sprout in spring.

Plant the cloves upright with the flat base plates downward, at about twice their own depth. Space them

PLANTING GARLIC CLOVES IN CELL PACKS

Plant one clove 1in (2.5cm) deep in each section of a cell pack. Cover the cloves with more soil mix.

about 7in (18cm) apart each way or 4in (10cm) apart in rows 12in (30cm) apart. The bulbs tend to push themselves upward as they grow.

Routine cultivation
Little attention is required during growth other than keeping the beds free of weeds. For pests and diseases that may affect garlic, see "Bulb onions," p.529.

Harvesting and storing
Garlic takes between 16 and 36 weeks to mature, depending on the variant and time of planting. Uproot the plants as soon as the leaves have started to die back so that the bulbs do not resprout; if they are allowed to resprout, they are more likely to rot when stored.

Dry them thoroughly after lifting as for bulb onions (see p.529). Handle the bulbs very carefully when preparing them for storage to avoid bruising. Store the bulbs hanging in bunches or braids made with the dry leaves, or place them loose on trays kept in dry conditions at 41–50°F (5–10°C). Garlic may be stored for up to ten months, depending on the variant and storage conditions.

STORING GARLIC

After harvesting garlic, tie the leaves loosely together with raffia or braid them. Then hang each bunch in a cool, dry place.

Celery (*Apium graveolens*)

A biennial plant, celery grows to 12–24in (30–60cm) tall, with a spread of 12in (30cm). Traditional trench celery has white, pink, or red stems that are blanched before use. Self-blanching types have creamy yellow stems that may be partially blanched. American green types have green stems. Intermediates are also available. Celery stalks are eaten raw or cooked and the leaves used as a seasoning or garnish.

As a temperate-climate crop, celery grows best at 59–70°F (15–21°C). Depending on the cultivar and conditions, it tolerates light or moderate frost; trench cultivars with red stems are hardiest. Some have improved resistance to bolting. Grow celery in an open site in fertile, moisture-retentive, but well-drained soil; lime acidic soil (see p.619). Rotate celery (see p.492), but do not plant it near parsnips since both are susceptible to celery flies. Dig plenty of well-rotted organic matter

CELERY SEEDLINGS IN A BLOCK

into the soil before planting. For trench celery, prepare a trench 15in (38cm) wide and 12in (30cm) deep in fall before planting; work in manure or soil mix, and replace the soil to ground level. Celery needs a high level of nitrogen (see p.498).

Sowing and planting
Sow in spring *in situ* after all risk of frost is past, or indoors in seed trays or cell packs at 59°F (15°C) no more than ten weeks before the last expected frost. Use seed treated with a fungicide to avoid celery leaf spot. Sprinkle seed onto the soil mix or cover it shallowly: light is needed for germination. Do not sow too early; plants may bolt if the temperature falls below 50°F (10°C).

Thin out seedlings with four to six true leaves; plant out indoor-sown seedlings after all risk of frost is past. Reject any with blistered leaves. Plant self-blanching types 9in (23cm) apart in blocks to increase natural blanching. Young plants may be covered with cloches or floating row covers that should be removed after a month. Plant trench celery seedlings 15in (38cm) apart in single rows. They may be planted in trenches, or on the flat.

Routine cultivation
Celery requires steady growth, with no checks from water shortage or sudden drops in temperature. Apply a nitrogenous fertilizer or organic liquid fertilizer about a month after planting. Once the plants are established, water them weekly at a rate of 5 gallons/sq yd (23 liters/sq m).

To sweeten self-blanching types, tuck a thick layer of loose straw around the plants when they are 8in (20cm) tall. To blanch celery in a trench, tie stems loosely together with soft string and fill in the trench gradually, hilling up the stems as they grow. If planted on the flat, wrap specially made collars or 9in (23cm) strips of heavy, lightproof paper around the stems when the plants are 12in (30cm) tall. To extend the blanched area, add a second collar three weeks later. In winter, cover trench celery with straw to protect against cold.

Pests and diseases
Slugs (p.638), celery flies (see "Leaf miners," p.641), cabbage root maggots (p.652), boron deficiency

RECOMMENDED CELERY

Self-blanching
'Galaxy'
'Golden Self Blanching'

Trench
'Matador'
'Picador'
'Ventura'
'Victoria'

American green
'Tango'
'Utah 52–70'

'Utah 52–70'

LIFTING CELERY

Lift self-blanching celery plants before the first frosts. Clear the straw from around the stem, and use a fork to uproot the whole plant.

(p.647), and fungal leaf spots (p.641) are the most common pests and diseases of celery.

Harvesting and storing
Harvest self-blanching and green celery 11–16 weeks after planting and trench celery in late fall. Cut the stalks before they become pithy. Before frost threatens, lift and store the remaining plants in high humidity in a cool, frost-free place. They will keep for several weeks.

BLANCHING CELERY

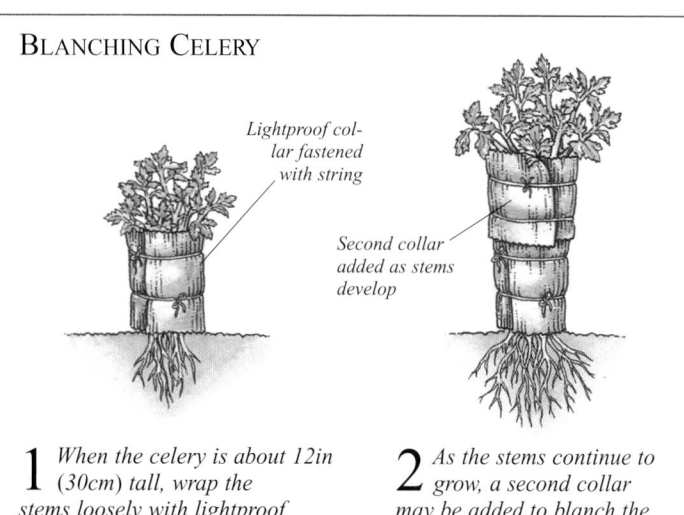

Lightproof collar fastened with string

Second collar added as stems develop

1 *When the celery is about 12in (30cm) tall, wrap the stems loosely with lightproof paper so that the leaves are still exposed to the light.*

2 *As the stems continue to grow, a second collar may be added to blanch the new growth.*

Celeriac (*Apium graveolens* var. *rapaceum*)

This is a biennial plant that grows 12in (30cm) high with a spread of 15in (38cm). The swollen "bulb" at the stem base is cooked and also grated raw in salads. The leaves are used for seasoning and garnishing.

Celeriac is a cool-temperate crop, withstanding 14°F (-10°C) if the crowns are protected with straw. Plants tolerate light shade if the soil is moist. For soil requirements, see "Celery," opposite; celeriac needs low nitrogen levels (see p.498).

Sowing and planting

Celeriac needs a six-month growing season for the bulb to develop. Germination may be erratic. Sow seed indoors in early spring, preferably in cell packs. If using trays, prick out seedlings to 2–3in (5–7cm) apart or pot them singly into small pots or cell packs. Harden off the young plants before planting out when they are about 3in (7cm) tall. Space them 12–15in (30–38cm) apart with their crowns at soil level, not buried.

Routine cultivation

Mulch after planting and water well, especially in dry conditions. Plants may be fertilized (see "Celery," opposite). Toward the end of the summer, remove some of the coarse outer leaves to expose the crowns, encouraging the bulbs to develop. To protect from frost, tuck a loose layer of straw 4–6in (10–15cm) thick around the crowns.

Pests and diseases

Celeriac may be affected by the same pests and diseases as celery (see opposite), but is normally healthy.

PLANTING OUT CELERIAC FROM A CELL PACK

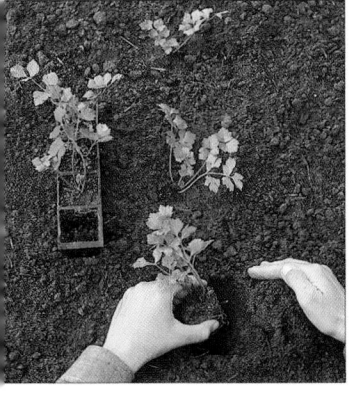

Plant out celeriac from a cell pack when it is 3–4in (8–10cm) high with 6 or 7 leaves. Space the young plants 12–15in (30–38cm) apart; take care not to bury the crowns.

CULTIVATING AND PROTECTING CELERIAC

1 *Toward the end of the summer, as the swollen stem bases develop, remove a few of the outer leaves to expose the crowns.*

2 *Before the first frosts, mulch around the base of the plants with a 6in (15cm) layer of straw to protect the crowns.*

Harvesting and storing

Celeriac may be harvested from late summer until the following spring. The bulbs are ready for use when they are 3–5in (7–13cm) in diameter.

The flavor is best and the bulbs will keep longer if the roots are left in the ground over winter. Where winters are very severe, dig up the plants in early winter without damaging the bulbs; trim off the outer leaves, leaving a central tuft, and store the plants in boxes of damp soil in a cool, frost-free place.

RECOMMENDED CELERIAC

'Brilliant'
'Diamant'
'Monarch'
'President'
'Prague'

'Brilliant'

Asparagus (*Asparagus officinalis*)

Asparagus is perennial and may be productive for up to 20 years. Its light, fernlike foliage grows over 3ft (90cm) tall, with a spread of about 18in (45cm). It is cultivated for the delicious young shoots or spears that push through the ground in spring. Male and female plants are available; the females produce berries. Male plants are higher yielding; very productive, all-male, F1 hybrid cultivars are now also available. Asparagus is normally eaten cooked.

Asparagus is a cool-season crop, growing best at 61–75°F (16–24°C) in regions with cool winters that provide the necessary dormant period. Choose an open site, avoiding exposed situations and frost pockets. Asparagus tolerates a very wide range of moderately fertile soils, although acidic soils should be limed (see p.619). Good drainage is essential. Do not make a new asparagus bed where asparagus has been grown before, since soilborne diseases may persist. Remove all perennial weeds from the site and prepare the ground by digging it over and working in manure or soil mix. Asparagus may also be grown in raised beds to improve drainage. It has low nitrogen requirements (see p.498).

Sowing and planting

Asparagus is traditionally grown by planting one-year-old purchased plants, or crowns, in spring. The crowns are fleshy and must never be allowed to dry out before planting.

Grow them about 15in (38cm) apart, either in single or double rows, with the rows spaced 12in (30cm) apart. Plant the crowns about 4in (10cm) deep by first making a small trench with a central, mounded ridge along the flat base. Spread out the roots evenly over the ridge and cover them with soil to the level of the crowns. Fill in the rest of the trench with soil gradually as the stems grow, leaving 3–4in (7–10cm) of the stems exposed.

Raising asparagus from seed is cheaper, but the results are more variable. Sow seed 1in (2.5cm) deep *in situ* in spring, and thin out to about 3in (7cm) apart. Plant out the largest the following spring, or, if preferred, sow

PLANTING ASPARAGUS CROWNS

Dig a trench about 12in (30cm) wide and 8in (20cm) deep with a central, mounded ridge that is 4in (10cm) high. Place the asparagus crowns on the ridge about 15in (38cm) apart. Spread the roots out evenly and cover them with about 2in (5cm) of soil to the level of the crowns.

RECOMMENDED ASPARAGUS

Traditional
'Larac' (white)
'Martha Washington'
'Mary Washington'
'Purple Passion'
'Viking'

All-male cultivars
'Guelph Millennium'
'Jersey Giant'
'Jersey King'
'Jersey Knight'

'Jersey Giant'

CUTTING BACK ASPARAGUS STEMS

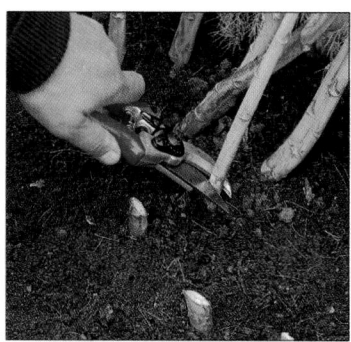

Using pruners, cut back the stems in fall to within about 1in (2.5cm) of ground level.

seed indoors in cell packs in early spring at 55–61°F (13–16°C). The seedlings grow rapidly and may be planted out in permanent positions in early summer.

Routine cultivation
Asparagus requires little attention other than keeping the beds weed-free. Hoe shallowly in order to avoid damaging the roots. When the foliage turns yellow in fall, cut the stems back to approximately 1in (2.5cm) above the soil.

Pests and diseases
Slugs (p.638) at an early stage and asparagus beetles (p.638) on more mature plants are the most serious

pests. The soilborne fungal disease crown rot may destroy plants in long-established beds.

Harvesting and storing
Asparagus must be allowed to build into a strong plant before it is harvested in midspring. Good modern cultivars may be cut lightly in the second season. The following year, limit cutting to a six-week period; subsequently, cutting may continue over eight weeks if the plants are growing well. Harvest the spears when they are about 6in (15cm) high and fairly thick. Cut at an angle, taking care not to damage nearby spears. Remaining spears will continue to grow. Asparagus freezes well.

HARVESTING ASPARAGUS

When the spears are 5–6in (12–15cm) high, cut each stalk 1–2in (2.5–5cm) below soil level.

Kohlrabi (*Brassica oleracea* Gongylodes Group)

These annual plants from the brassica family are grown for the white-fleshed, turniplike, swollen stem or "bulb" that forms just above ground. Kohlrabi reaches 12in (30cm) high and has an average spread of 12in (30cm). The outer skin is pale green (sometimes described as white) or purple. The bulbs are nutritious, flavorful, and used cooked or raw.

Kohlrabi is a cool-season crop, growing best at 64–77°F (18–25°C). Young plants tend to bolt prematurely in temperatures below about 50°F (10°C). For soil requirements, see "Siting Western brassicas," p.501. Kohlrabi grows well in light soils and withstands drought better than most brassicas. It has low nitrogen requirements (see p.498).

Sowing and planting
In mild climates, sow seed outdoors in succession from spring through to late summer, using the hardier

purple forms for late sowings. In hot climates, sow in spring and fall. Sow *in situ* either in rows about 12in (30cm) apart, thinning seedlings to about 7in (18cm) apart, or space the seeds about 10in (25cm) apart in

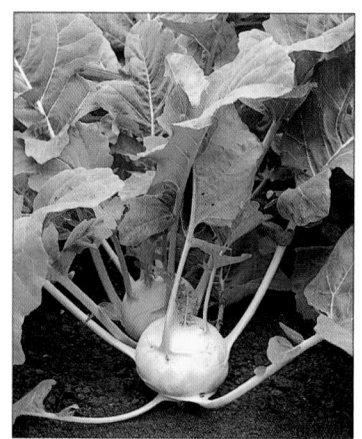

GREEN KOHLRABI

each direction. Under cover, sow earlier in gentle heat in trays or cell packs. Plant out seedlings when they are no more than 2in (5cm) high. Protect early outdoor crops with covers or floating row covers.

Routine cultivation
Kohlrabi is fast-maturing; little attention is required during growth other than keeping beds weed-free.

Pests and diseases
Clubroot (p.652), cabbage root maggots (p.652), and flea beetles (p.638) may affect plants. See also "Cultivating Western brassicas," p.501.

Harvesting and storing
Depending on the cultivar and season, kohlrabi may be ready for cutting between five and nine weeks after sowing. Traditional cultivars should be eaten when they are no larger than tennis balls or they will

RECOMMENDED KOHLRABI

Traditional
'Purple Vienna'
'White Vienna'

'Purple Vienna'

Modern
'Grand Duke'
'Kolibri' F1 (purple)
'Winner' F1

become woody; improved modern cultivars are still tender at a diameter of about 4in (10cm).

Leave later crops in the soil until heavy frost threatens, since the flavor deteriorates once lifted. In cold areas, lift in fall. Leave a central tuft of leaves on each bulb to help keep them fresh; store them for up to two months in boxes of moist sand.

Florence fennel (*Foeniculum vulgare* var. *dulce*)

Grown as an annual, Florence, or sweet, fennel is distinct from the perennial herb fennel. The plants grow up to about 2ft (60cm) high and have a spread of about 18in (45cm). The anise-flavored, flattened "bulb" of overlapping scales that develops at the base of the leaf stalks is eaten cooked or raw. The decorative fern-like foliage may be used as a flavoring or garnish.

Florence fennel tolerates a wide range of climates, from temperate to subtropical. It thrives at a warm, even temperature, but mature plants can withstand a light frost. Grow it in an open situation, in very fertile,

moisture-retentive, but well-drained soil into which plenty of organic matter has been worked. It grows well in light soils, but it must not be allowed to dry out. It has low nitrogen requirements (see p.498).

Sowing and planting
In cool northern latitudes, sow seed from early to midsummer; traditional cultivars are likely to bolt if sown in spring, so use modern, bolt-resistant cultivars for earlier sowings. In warmer climates, sow in spring for a summer crop and again in late summer for a fall crop. Florence fennel does not transplant well and may

bolt prematurely if checked, so sow seed either *in situ* or in cell packs for transplanting when the seedlings have no more than four leaves. Space the young seedlings about 12in (30cm) apart each way. Both early and late crops may be protected from frost by covering with covers or floating row covers.

Routine cultivation
Little attention is required; keep beds weed-free. Florence fennel needs to be kept moist, so water thoroughly and mulch. When bulbs start to swell, hill them up to half their height to make them whiter and sweeter.

FLORENCE FENNEL

HARVESTING FLORENCE FENNEL

1 Cut the fennel bulb about 1in (2.5cm) above soil level. Leave the base in position.

2 Feathery leaves will usually sprout from the base of the stem within a few weeks.

Pests and diseases
Florence fennel rarely suffers from any pests or diseases. Most problems stem from lack of water, fluctuating temperatures, or transplanting, all of which may cause bolting.

Harvesting and storing
Harvest the bulbs when they are well rounded, about 15 weeks after sowing or from two to three weeks after hilling up. Pull them up whole, or cut across the bulbs about 1in (2.5cm) above ground level. The stump will usually resprout to produce small sprigs of ferny foliage that may be used for flavoring or as a garnish. Florence fennel does not store well; eat it as fresh as possible.

RECOMMENDED FLORENCE FENNEL

'Fennel Fino'
'Neopolitan'
'Romy'
'Supewadremen'
'Sweet Florence'
'Zefa Fino' **Br**

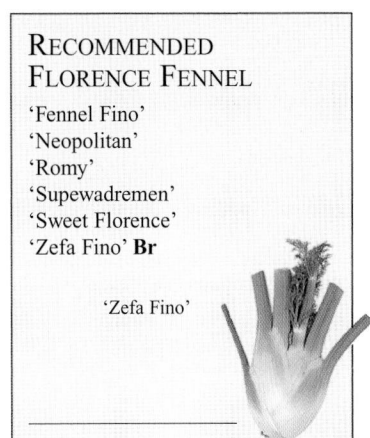

'Zefa Fino'

KEY
Br Bolt resistant

Rhubarb (Rheum x cultorum)

This perennial lasts over 20 years in good conditions. Rhubarb grows about 24in (60cm) or more high and up to 6ft (2m) across. The leaves may be 18in (45cm) wide. The pale green or pinkish red leaf stalks, which may be 2ft (60cm) long, are harvested young and used cooked.

Rhubarb is a temperate-climate crop and does not thrive at high temperatures; the roots survive lows down to -20 °F (-30°C). Recommended rhubarb cultivars include 'Valentine', 'Cherry Red', and 'Victoria'. It grows on a wide range of soils, as long as they are rich and well drained. Before planting, dig in plenty of manure or compost. Rhubarb needs medium nitrogen levels when young and very high nitrogen once it is mature (see p.498).

Sowing and planting
Rhubarb is normally propagated by planting "sets," each consisting of a fleshy rootstock with at least one bud. Sets are about 4in (10cm) in diameter. Plant them in the dormant season from fall to spring, preferably in fall. Either buy virus-free sets, or separate a set from a healthy two- or three-year-old plant, once its leaves have died back, by lifting the plant and slicing through the crown; replant the parent. On light soils, plant the set so that 1in (2.5cm) of soil covers the buds; on heavy or wet soils, plant with the buds just above ground level. Space the plants 3ft (90cm) apart.

Rhubarb may also be raised from seed, although the results are variable. Sow seed in spring, 1in (2.5cm) deep in rows 12in (30cm) apart, in a seedbed outdoors. Thin the seedlings to 6in (15cm) apart, and plant out the strongest-looking ones in their permanent positions in fall, or in spring the following year.

Routine cultivation
Mulch the plants heavily, and water them in dry weather. Apply a heavy dressing of manure or compost every

DIVIDING RHUBARB

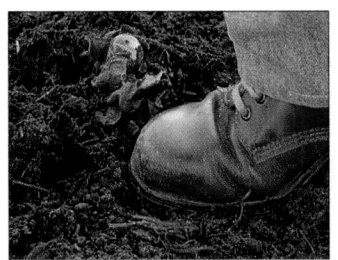

1 Lift or expose the crown. Cut through it carefully using a spade, ensuring there is at least 1 main bud on each section. Prepare the soil by digging in manure.

2 Replant the sections (sets) 2½–3ft (75–90cm) apart. Fill in around each root so that the bud is just above the surface. Firm the soil gently, then water

fall or spring and a nitrogenous dressing or organic liquid fertilizer in spring. Remove flowering stems.

Rhubarb may be forced in the dark to obtain very tender stems. Cover the dormant crowns in late winter with a 4in (10cm) layer of straw or leaves, then a forcing pot, or a large bucket, at least 18in (45cm) high; leave this on for about four weeks until stems are large enough.

Pests and diseases
Crown rot and viruses (p.642) may attack established plants.

Harvesting and storing
Harvest in spring and early summer. With plants raised from sets, start pulling lightly the first year after planting; with plants grown from seed, wait until the second year. In subsequent years, pull heavily until the quality starts to deteriorate in summer. Forced stems are ready to harvest about three weeks earlier than unforced ones.

FORCING RHUBARB

For an earlier, tender crop, cover the dormant buds (see upper inset) in winter with straw or leaves inside a forcing pot or any large container that excludes light. The plant will produce tender pink stems a few weeks later (see lower inset).

HARVESTING RHUBARB

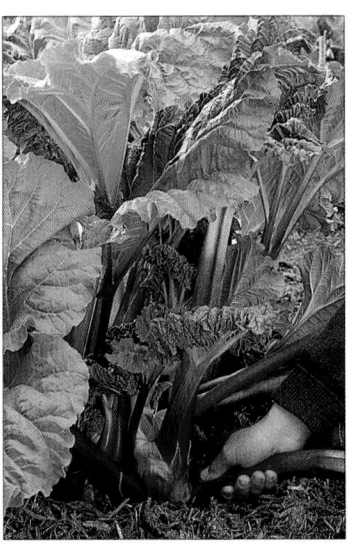

When the rhubarb stems are ready, they may be harvested by gripping each stem at the base and twisting it while pulling it upward and outward.

Root and tuberous vegetables

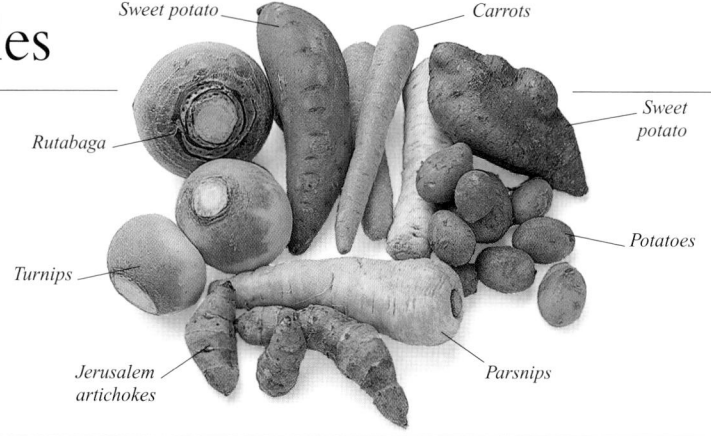

Sweet potato
Carrots
Rutabaga
Sweet potato
Potatoes
Turnips
Parsnips
Jerusalem artichokes

Root vegetables are the mainstay of the kitchen garden. As the name suggests, most are grown for their swollen roots or tubers. A few, such as turnips, beets, and taro, are also used for their young leaves; some radish cultivars also produce edible seedpods. A variety of root vegetables may be grown and harvested in succession for a steady supply; many store quite easily, sometimes still in the ground, for use throughout winter. Salsify and scorzonera may be overwintered in milder areas for their flowering shoots produced in spring.

Beets (*Beta vulgaris* subsp. *vulgaris*)

Beets are biennial plants grown as annuals. They grow to about 12in (30cm) tall and about 10in (24cm) across. The swollen root forms at ground level and may be round, flat, or cylindrical. It is on average 4in (10cm) in diameter, and about 8in (20cm) or more deep in the long forms. The flesh is normally red but may be yellow, white, or even have concentric pink and white rings. The skin is similarly red, yellow, or off-white. The sweetly flavored roots are mainly used cooked, either fresh or stored, but may also be pickled. The fresh young leaves (tops) may be used as greens.

Beets grow best and develop the deepest colors in cool, even temperatures, ideally of 61°F (16°C). Grow in an open site on rich, light soil with high nitrogen levels (see p.498). Apply half the nitrogen before sowing. Lime very acidic soils.

THINNING SEEDLINGS

When the beet seedlings have produced 3 or 4 leaves, thin clumps growing close together to the required spacing by nipping off the top green leaves at soil level without disturbing the remaining seedlings.

Sowing and planting
Beet "seeds" each contain a cluster of two or three seeds, the seedlings of which must be thinned out early. Some cultivars, such as 'Mobile' and 'Monopoly', have been bred to produce single, or mono-germ, seed, which needs little or no thinning.

To overcome slow germination, soak seed in warm water for 30 minutes before sowing. Some cultivars may bolt if sown early or in unfavorable conditions, so choose bolt-resistant cultivars for sowings early in the season.

In spring, sow seed *in situ* outdoors when the soil is workable and has warmed up to at least 45°F (7°C). Sow seed ½–¾in (1–2cm) deep, with the spacing determined by the type of beet and the size required. Grow maincrop beets in rows 12in (30cm) apart, thinning to 3–4in (7–10cm) apart. For pickling beets about 1in (2.5cm) in diameter, space rows 3in (7cm) apart, thinning seedlings to 2½in (6cm).

For earlier crops, sow in early spring under covers, in frames, or indoors in seed trays or cell packs, transplanting outside when the seedlings are 2in (5cm) tall. Sow three mono-germ or ordinary seeds per cell pack (see "Cell packs and small containers," p.495); thin as necessary. Early beets need plenty of space, so plant indoor-sown seedlings in rows 9in (23cm) apart, then thin them to 3½in (9cm) apart. For continuous supplies of young beets and beet tops, sow seed at intervals of two to three weeks until hot summer weather arrives. Sow cultivars for storage in late summer, a minimum of ten weeks before the first heavy frost is expected.

HARVESTING BEETS

Carefully grip the leaf stems and pull the beet from the soil; it should lift easily, since it is shallow-rooted. Avoid damaging the roots as much as possible, since they will bleed if they are cut.

Routine cultivation
Water only to prevent the soil from drying out, at a rate of 2 gallons/sq yd (11 liters/sq m) every two weeks. Apply the remaining nitrogenous fertilizer during active growth.

Pests and diseases
Beets may be affected by cutworms (p.647), aphids (p.639), damping off (p.651), fungal leaf spots (p.641), and boron deficiency (p.653).

RECOMMENDED BEETS
'Bull's Blood'
'Burpee's Golden' (stores well) **Br**

'Burpee's Golden'

'Chioggia Striped' **Br**
'Cylindra'
'Detroit Dark Red'
'Early Wonder'
'Formanova'
'Lutz Green Leaf'
'Red Ace' F1 **Br**
'Scarlet Supreme' F1 **Br**

KEY
Br Bolt resistant

Harvesting and storing
Harvest beets at any stage from small, immature roots 1in (2.5cm) in diameter to fully mature roots; this will be from seven to 13 weeks after sowing, depending on the cultivar, the season, and the size required. In mild areas, beets may be left in well-drained soil in winter, protected with a layer of straw up to 6in (15cm) deep, but they eventually become rather woody. Otherwise, lift them before severe frost. Twist off the leaves (cutting causes bleeding) and store the roots in moist sand in a frost-free place. Beets normally keep until midspring.

Rutabagas (*Brassica napus* Napobrassica Group)

Biennials from the brassica family, rutabagas are grown as annuals and reach a height of 15in (38cm) with a spread of 15in (38cm). The root flesh is usually yellow, but sometimes white, and the skin is generally purple, buff, or a combination of both. The large, often irregularly shaped, underground roots, which may be 8in (20cm) in diameter and as long, are sweetly flavored and used cooked. This hardy, cool-season crop grows best on light, fertile soil with low nitrogen levels (see p.498). For climate and soil requirements, see "Siting Western brassicas," p.501.

Sowing and planting
Rutabagas need a growing season of up to 26 weeks to mature fully. Sow seed from early to late spring *in situ*, ¾in (2cm) deep in rows 15in (38cm) apart, thinning early and in stages until the seedlings are about 9in (23cm) apart.

RECOMMENDED RUTABAGAS
'Laurentian'
'Purple Top Yellow'
'Virtue'

'Virtue'

Routine cultivation
Keep beds weed-free, and if conditions are very dry, water at a rate of 2 gallons/sq yd (9 liters/sq m).

Pests and diseases
Downy mildew, powdery mildew (p.640), boron deficiency (p.653), and flea beetles (p.638) may affect rutabagas. Some cultivars are resistant to mildew. For other pests and diseases, see "Cultivating Western brassicas," p.501.

Harvesting and storing
Rutabagas generally mature in fall and, being hardy, may be left in the soil until the end of the season, when they should be lifted carefully to prevent them from becoming woody. Except in very cold climates, covering with a thick layer of straw provides sufficient protection until the rutabagas are lifted. Store rutabagas in piles outdoors (see right) or in crates under cover (see *Storing Carrots*, p.538) for up to 4 months.

MAKING A RUTABAGA PILE
Choose a sheltered, well-drained site and stack the roots on an 8in (20cm) layer of straw in a pyramid, with their necks facing outward. Cover with a layer of more straw. In very cold climates, protect further with a 12in (10cm) layer of soil.

Turnips (*Brassica rapa* Rapifera Group)

These are biennials from the brassica family grown as annuals. The plants are about 9in (23cm) high with a spread of about 10in (25cm). The underground roots swell to 1–3in (2.5–7cm) in diameter and are round, fairly flat, or long. The flesh may be either white or yellow and the skin white, pink, red, or yellow. The young leaves, known as turnip greens, may also be eaten (see "Turnip greens and broccoli raab," p.506). Turnip roots are used either fresh or stored, usually cooked.

Turnips are a temperate-climate crop, growing best at about 68°F (20°C). They are reasonably hardy, tolerating light frost. For general climate and soil requirements, see "Siting Western brassicas," p.501. Grow turnips in moist soil, since they bolt prematurely in dry conditions. Early types, many small and white, grow fast and are excellent for early spring and summer crops; the hardier types are used fresh during summer and winter and for storage. They require low to medium nitrogen levels (see p.498).

Sowing and planting
Start sowing seed of early turnips in spring as soon as the ground is workable, or sow under cover. Make

HARVESTING TURNIPS

Harvest turnips by pulling them from the soil by their leaves. Do not leave them in the ground too long, or they may become woody.

successive sowings at three-week intervals until early summer. Sow maincrop types in late summer *in situ*, ¾ in (2cm) deep. Space early types in rows that are 9in (23cm) apart, thinning seedlings to 4in (10cm); space maincrop types in rows 12in (30cm) apart, thinning to 6in (15cm).

Routine cultivation
Keep beds weed-free. In dry weather water at a rate of 2 gallons/sq yd (9 liters/sq m).

Pests and diseases
Flea beetles (p.638) may affect seedlings; other problems include boron deficiency (p.653), powdery mildew (p.640), and downy mildew. Turnip gall weevils cause hollow swellings on the roots that may be mistaken for clubroot but are rarely serious; discard affected plants. For other pests and diseases, see "Cultivating Western brassicas," p.501.

Harvesting and storing
Harvest early turnips after about five weeks, maincrop types after six to ten weeks. Pull them before they become woody. Lift turnips for storage before the first frost, then store for up to three or four months in outdoor piles covered with straw.

RECOMMENDED TURNIPS
'Golden Ball'
'Hakurei' F1
'Just Right'
'Purple Top White Globe'
'Royal Crown' F1
'Tokyo Cross' F1
'White Lady' F1

'Golden Ball'

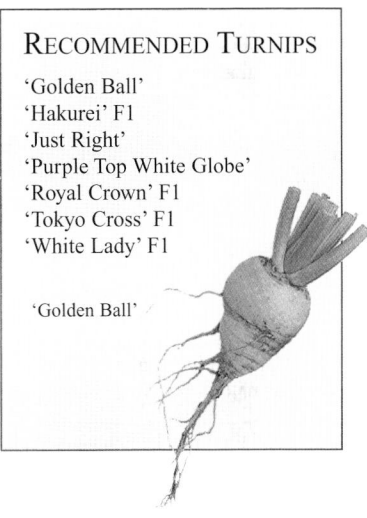

Taro (*Colocasia esculenta*)

This herbaceous, frost-tender perennial grows to about 3ft (1m) tall, with a spread of 24–8in (60–70cm). The plants have large, long-stalked leaves, which may be green or greenish purple. Taro, sometimes known as cocoyam, is grown for its large, swollen tuber, which is eaten

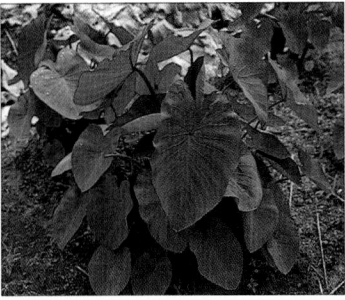

TARO PLANT

cooked. The young leaves and shoots are also edible, and may be cooked and used as greens.

Taro is a tropical and subtropical plant that requires temperatures of 70–81°F (21–27°C), with humidity levels over 75 percent. In temperate areas it needs a very sheltered, sunny site, or it may be grown under cover. Taro is adapted to short daylengths of about 12 hours (see "Daylength," p.489); it rarely produces flowers. Some forms are tolerant of light shade. Moisture-retentive soil is essential for success because many forms of taro are sensitive to dry soil conditions. Fertile soil that has a high organic content and a slightly acidic pH level of 5.5–6.5 is recommended; prepare soil before planting. Taro requires medium to high levels of nitrogen (see p.498).

Sowing and planting
Seeds are rarely available, so propagation is usually from existing tubers. Plant mature tubers or portions of tubers with dormant buds *in situ* in well-prepared beds. Space the tubers about 18in (45cm) apart with 3ft (90cm) between rows.

Taro may also be propagated by cuttings. Sever the tops of tubers with a horizontal cut; each cutting should consist of several leaves 4–5in (10–12cm) long, a central growing point, and a small portion of the tuber. Plant the cuttings in their final positions at the above spacing; if the temperature is below the optimum 70°F (21°C), plant them in 8–10in (20–25cm) pots of standard soil mix to grow on under cover until the temperature is high enough for transplanting outside.

Routine cultivation
Taro needs a constant supply of water for the highest yields, so water regularly. Apply an organic mulch to conserve moisture, and apply a general-purpose fertilizer at two- to three-week intervals. Keep beds free of weeds. The plants should be hilled up around the stems once they are established to encourage the tubers to develop.

Pests and diseases
These are rarely serious for taro grown in the open, but aphids (p.639), thrips (p.640), spider mites (p.640), and fungal leaf spots (p.641) may reduce tuber yields. Under cover, taro is vulnerable to the same pests and diseases as for those grown outside; whiteflies (p.639) may also be troublesome.

Growing under cover

Propagate from tubers (see p.537). When these have rooted, transfer them to well-prepared greenhouse beds, 8–12in (20–30cm) pots, or growing bags, ensuring that the roots are disturbed as little as possible.

Water and fertilize the plants regularly, maintaining a temperature of 70–81°F (21–27°C) and humidity of more than 75 percent by damping down. Tubers that are cultivated under cover tend to be smaller than those grown outdoors.

Harvesting and storing

Taro is slow to develop and reach maturity. Harvest the tubers 16–24 weeks after planting, when the leaves start to turn yellow and plants die down. Lift taro grown in the open carefully using a fork; plants under cover may be lifted gently out of their pots or grow bags. Try not to damage the tubers, since this encourages rot.

Healthy tubers may be stored for about eight to 12 weeks at a temperature of 52–55°F (11–13°C), with humidity of 85–90 percent.

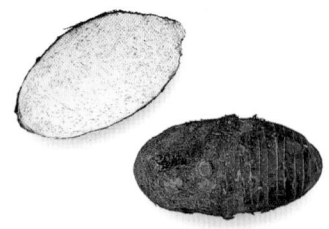

TARO TUBER

Carrots (*Daucus carota*)

These are biennials grown as annuals. Their swollen orange taproots may be up to 3in (7cm) in diameter at the neck and up to about 12in (30cm) in length. The feathery green foliage grows to about 24in (60cm), with a 12in (30cm) spread. Carrots are normally long and tapered but may be rounded. There are many types: early ones are usually small and slender and used young; maincrop types are larger and are used fresh or stored. Carrots are eaten either cooked or raw.

Carrots are a cool-season crop, tolerating the same temperatures as beets (see p.536). Grow in an open site on light and fertile soil. Deep-rooted types require reasonably deep, stone-free soil. Work in plenty of organic matter, preferably in the fall before sowing. The fertile, loose soil of established raised beds is particularly suitable for growing carrots. Rake the soil into a fine tilth before sowing. Carrots should be rotated (see p.492). They need very low nitrogen levels (see p.498).

Sowing and planting

Sow early types in spring *in situ* as soon as the soil is workable and has warmed up to 45°F (7°C). Earlier sowings may be made under covers, in frames, or under floating row covers; remove these after a few weeks. Sow maincrop types from late spring until early summer. A second sowing of early types may be made in late summer and protected with covers.

Sow seed sparingly about ½–¾in (1–2cm) deep, either broadcast or in rows 6in (15cm) apart. Thin early carrots to 3in (7cm) apart; main-crop carrots should be thinned to 1½in (4cm) to obtain medium-sized carrots or farther apart if large carrots are needed. Carrots do not transplant well unless sown in cell packs: sow seed of deep-rooted cultivars singly, those of round-rooted ones, several together. The latter, if sown in cell packs, do not need thinning and should be planted out as a group at slightly wider spacing than for maincrop carrots.

Routine cultivation

Remove weeds regularly once the carrots have germinated and until the foliage hinders further weed growth. Water at a rate of 3–5 gallons/sq yd (16–23 liters/sqm) every two or three weeks.

Pests and diseases

Carrot rust flies (p.652) may be a serious problem. The egg-laying adult flies are attracted by the smell of carrot foliage; thin in the evening, nipping off the seedlings at ground level and removing the tops from the site. Root and leaf aphids (see "Aphids," p.639), carrot motley dwarf virus (see "Viruses," p.642), and boron deficiency (p.653) may be troublesome.

Harvesting and storing

Harvest early cultivars about seven to nine weeks after sowing, main-crop cultivars after ten to 11 weeks. Pull them by hand or fork them out. On well-drained soils in areas with mild winters, carrots may be left in the soil in winter (see *Protecting Parsnips*, p.540). Otherwise lift them before heavy frost, cut or twist off foliage, and store in boxes in a cool, dry place for up to five months.

PROTECTION AGAINST CARROT RUST FLY

Surround the patch of young carrots with a protective barrier 2–3ft (60–90cm) high. The barrier may be made either of fine mesh netting or stiff, clear plastic, both of which also help warm the soil inside.

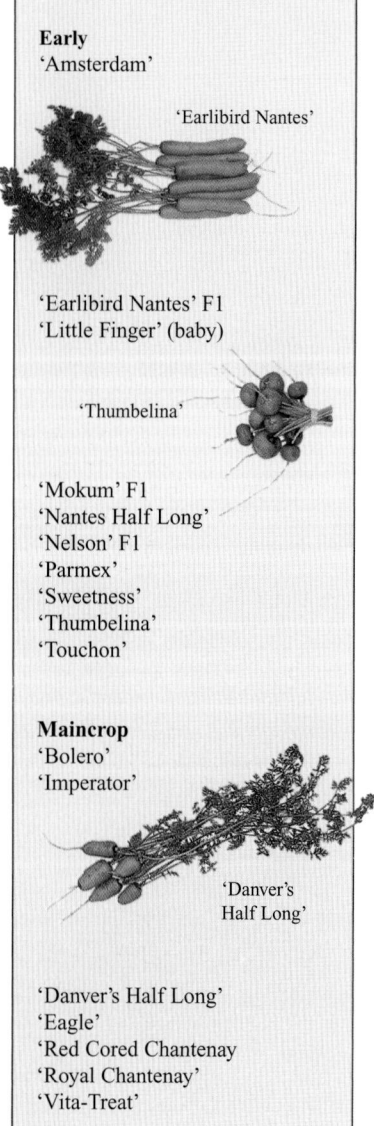

RECOMMENDED CARROTS

Early
'Amsterdam'

'Earlibird Nantes'

'Earlibird Nantes' F1
'Little Finger' (baby)

'Thumbelina'

'Mokum' F1
'Nantes Half Long'
'Nelson' F1
'Parmex'
'Sweetness'
'Thumbelina'
'Touchon'

Maincrop
'Bolero'
'Imperator'

'Danver's Half Long'

'Danver's Half Long'
'Eagle'
'Red Cored Chantenay'
'Royal Chantenay'
'Vita-Treat'

THIN SOWING

Sow carrot seeds about 1in (2.5cm) apart so that the seedlings will need little thinning later. The seed should be ½–¾in (1–2cm) deep.

HARVESTING YOUNG

Early cultivars may be harvested when they are very young. Pull them up in a bunch when they are 3–4in (8–10cm) long.

STORING CARROTS

Twist the foliage off the carrots; place roots on a layer of sand in a box. Cover them with more sand and continue in layers.

Jerusalem artichokes (*Helianthus tuberosus*)

These are perennial plants, also known as sunchokes or girasoles. The distinctively flavored tubers are 2–4in (5–10cm) long, about 1½in (4cm) in diameter and, in most cultivars, very bumpy. 'Fuseau', however, produces smooth tubers. The plants may grow up to 10ft (3m) tall. The tubers are normally cooked but may be eaten raw. Jerusalem artichokes grow best in temperate climates and are very hardy. They

tolerate a wide range of soils and require medium nitrogen levels (see p.498). They may be planted as a windbreak screen.

Sowing and planting
Plant tubers as soon as the ground is workable in spring. Those the size of a hen's egg may be planted whole; cut large ones into pieces, each with several buds. Make a drill, planting about 5in (12.5cm) deep and 12in (30cm) apart. Cover with soil.

Routine cultivation
When the plants are about 12in (30cm) tall, hill up the stems to half their height for stability. In late summer, cut the stems back to 5ft (1.5m), removing any flower heads at the same time. In very exposed sites, stake or support the stems. Water in very dry conditions. When the leaves start to yellow, cut the stems back to just above ground level.

Smooth 'Fuseau' tubers

Bumpy Jerusalem artichoke tubers

PLANTING

Make a drill 4–6in (10–15cm) deep. Place the tubers in the drill 12in (30cm) apart with the main bud facing upward. Cover carefully so the tubers are not dislodged.

Harvesting and storing
Harvest the tubers 16–20 weeks after planting. Lift them only when required, since they keep best in the ground, and take care not to damage the roots. Save a few tubers to replant or leave some in the soil for the

CUTTING DOWN

Toward the end of the summer, cut down the stems to about 5ft (1.5m), so that the plants will not suffer wind damage. The tubers will continue to develop unchecked.

following year. Otherwise, remove even small tubers, since they rapidly become invasive. In severe climates or on heavy ground, lift in early winter and store in a cellar or in piles outdoors (see Making a Rutabaga Pile, p.537) for up to five months.

Sweet potatoes (*Ipomoea batatas*)

These tender perennials are grown as annuals. They have trailing stems that grow to 10ft (3m) or more if unpruned. Cultivars vary considerably in leaf shape and tuber size, shape, and color. Tubers are eaten cooked; the leaves may be used in the same way as spinach (see p.513).

Sweet potatoes are tropical and subtropical, requiring a temperature of 75–79°F (24–26°C). In warm climates, they need a sunny site; in temperate climates, they should be grown under cover, but tuber yields are smaller. Most cultivars are short-day plants (see "Daylength," p.489).

Highly fertile, well-drained, sandy loams with a pH of 5.5–6.5 and medium to high nitrogen levels (see p.498) are required.

Sowing and planting
In the tropics and subtropics, plant sweet potatoes at the start of the rainy season. In warm and temperate climates, plant in spring. Make raised ridges about 30in (75cm) apart, then plant the tubers 2–3in (5–7cm) deep in the ridge, spacing them 10–12in (25–30cm) apart. Alternatively, take 8–10in (20–25cm) stem cuttings from mature plants and insert them to half their length just below the apex of the ridge.

Cultivars raised from seed will provide reasonable crops. Sow indoors in trays or 8–10in (20–25cm) pots at a temperature of at least 75°F

(24°C). When seedlings are 4–6in (10–15cm) high, harden them off and transplant outside.

Routine cultivation
Water and weed regularly, and mulch to conserve moisture. Train shoots to spread around the plant. Apply a general-purpose fertilizer at two- to three-week intervals until the tubers have formed. Protect from winds.

Pests and diseases
Aphids (p.639), caterpillars (p.639), root-knot nematodes (p.652), fungal leaf spots (p.641), *Fusarium* wilt (p.653), Southern blight (p.647), and various viruses (p.642) affect sweet potatoes growing outdoors. Under cover, whiteflies (p.639), thrips (p.640), and spider mites (p.640) may be troublesome.

Growing under cover
Sow seed, as described above, transplanting seedlings to grow bags or prepared beds. Alternatively, take cuttings and insert three or four into 6in (15cm) pots. Maintain a minimum temperature of 77°F (25°C) and a humidity of over 70 percent by damping down regularly. When roots develop, transfer plants to greenhouse beds or growing bags. Water regularly and remove the growing points of shoots longer than 2ft (60cm) to encourage development of lateral shoots. Keep the temperature below 82°F (28°C), and the growing area well ventilated.

Harvesting and storing
Harvest 12–16 weeks after planting, when the stems and leaves turn yellow. Crops from seed are ready three

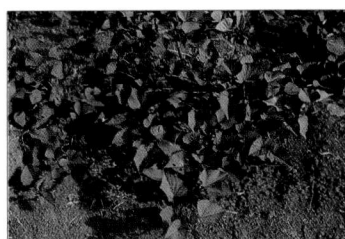

SWEET POTATO PLANT

or four weeks later. Lift the tubers, using a fork, without damaging them. In order to store sweet potatoes they must first be cured for four to seven days at temperatures of 82–86°F (28–30°C) and humidity of 85–90 percent (see "Winter squash," p.519). They may be stored in shallow trays for several months at 50–59°F (10–15°C).

STEM CUTTINGS FOR GROWING UNDER COVER

1 *Select healthy, vigorous shoots and cut them off the parent plant with pruners.*

2 *Remove the lower leaves and trim each shoot below a node to 8–10in (20–25cm). Insert in pots and grow on under cover.*

RECOMMENDED SWEET POTATOES

'Beauregard' (orange-fleshed)
'Centennial' (orange-fleshed)
'Georgia Jet' (orange-fleshed)
'Jewel' (white-fleshed)
'Vardaman' (orange-fleshed)
'White Yam' (white-fleshed)

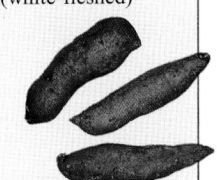

Parsnips (*Pastinaca sativa*)

Parsnips are biennials grown as annuals. The taproot grows to 2in (5cm) across at the neck and about 4in (10cm) long in short forms and up to 9in (23cm) in long types. The leaves are about 15in (38cm) long and 12in (30cm) wide. The roots are eaten cooked.

Parsnips are a hardy, cool-season crop and prefer light, deeply cultivated, stone-free soils. On shallow soils, grow the shorter forms. Lime very acidic soils, and rotate crops (see p.492). Parsnips have low nitrogen requirements (see p.498).

RECOMMENDED PARSNIPS

'Andover' (long)
'Avonresister' (short)
'Gladiator' F1 (long)
'Harris Model' (long)
'Hollow Crown' (long)
'Lancer' (long)

'Gladiator'

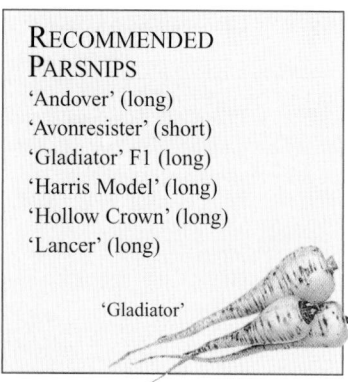

Sowing and planting

Always sow fresh seed. Parsnips need a long growing season and so should be sown as soon as the soil is workable in spring, but not in cold or wet soil. Sow seed *in situ* ³⁄₄in (2cm) deep in rows 12in (30cm) apart. Thin the seedlings to 4in (10cm) apart to produce large roots, or 3in (7cm) for smaller roots. A faster-germinating crop such as radishes may be intersown; to allow for this, station sow several parsnip seeds at intervals of 4in (10cm), and thin to one seedling per station. To start parsnips earlier, sow seed in cell packs with gentle heat under cover, then transplant seedlings before taproots develop.

Routine cultivation

Always keep beds free of weeds. In very dry conditions, water the plants as for carrots (see p.538).

Pests and diseases

Parsnips may be attacked by celery flies (see "Leaf miners," p.641), lettuce root aphids (see "Aphids," p.639), and carrot rust flies (p.652). Use cultivars resistant to parsnip

canker where possible; of those recommended, all but 'Tender and True' are resistant. Boron deficiency (p.653) may occasionally be troublesome.

Harvesting and storing

Parsnips mature in about 16 weeks. Their flavor is improved by frost and, except where the soil freezes,

INTERSOWING

In a prepared drill, sow 3 parsnip seeds every 4in (10cm), and then sow radish seeds between them, about 1in (2.5cm) apart.

they may be left in the soil during winter and lifted as required. The leaves die back in winter, so mark the ends of the rows with stakes so that the plants are easily found to harvest. Where winters are severe, cover the rows with 6in (15cm) of straw to keep the soil from freezing and to make lifting easier. Young parsnips may be lifted and frozen.

PROTECTING PARSNIPS

In severe climates, cover the plants with layers of straw to a depth of 6in (15cm). Hold in place with wire hoops and mark each row.

Radishes (*Raphanus sativus* and *Raphanus sativus* Longipinnatus Group)

There are several types of radish, some biennial and others annual; all are grown for the swollen roots. Small, round types have roots up to 1in (2.5cm) in diameter; small, long types up to 3in (7cm) long. The leaves of both may grow to about 5in (13cm) high. Large forms include oriental radishes (Longipinnatus Group), known as daikon or mooli, and the large, overwintering, winter radishes. The roots of large, round cultivars may be over 9in (23cm) in diameter, those of large, long cultivars up to 24in (60cm) long, while the plants grow 24in (60cm) tall with a spread of 18in (45cm).

Radish skin color is red, pink, white, purple, black, yellow, or green; the flesh is normally white. Small roots are used raw when fresh, and large roots are used raw or cooked, fresh or stored. Immature seedpods from cultivars such as 'Münchner Bier', and young seedling leaves from most cultivars, are edible raw.

Radishes are mainly a cool-season crop, but there are cultivars suited to a wide range of growing conditions. Some daikon and all overwintering types are frost-tolerant. Grow radishes in an open site, although midsummer crops tolerate light shade.

Radishes prefer light, rich, well-drained soil, preferably manured for the previous crop, and very low nitrogen levels (see p.498). Radishes should be rotated (see p.492).

Sowing and planting

Sow standard, small types outdoors throughout the growing season, starting when the soil is workable. Sow at 15-day intervals for a continuous crop. Very early and late sowings may be made under cover, using small-leaved cultivars bred for growing under cover. Delay sowing most oriental daikon until summer to prevent bolting. Some bolt-resistant cultivars may be sown earlier. Sow overwintering radishes in summer.

Radishes are normally sown *in situ*. Small types grow very fast and may be used for intercropping (see "Parsnips," above). Broadcast seed very thinly, or sow ¹⁄₂in (1cm) deep in drills 6in (15cm) apart. Thin the seedlings to at least 1in (2.5cm) apart, never allowing them to become overcrowded. Alternatively, seeds may be spaced 1in (2.5cm) apart so that no thinning is needed. Sow large types about ³⁄₄in (2cm) deep, in rows about 9in (23cm) apart, thinning to 6–9in (15–23cm), depending on the

cultivar. Small types may be used for cut-and-come-again seedling radish leaves (see "Cut-and-come-again seedling crops," p.494).

Routine cultivation

Radishes should never be allowed to dry out. In periods of dry weather, water the crop every week at a rate

HARVESTING

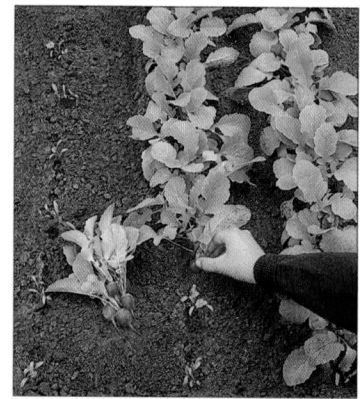

Radishes are ready to harvest 3–4 weeks after sowing. If the radishes are being used for intercropping, pull them up carefully without disturbing the roots of the other seedlings in the row.

RECOMMENDED RADISHES

Small
'Champion'
'Cherriette'

'French Breakfast'

'Cherry Belle'
'D'Avignon'
'Easter Egg'
'French Breakfast'
'Long White Icicle'
'Snow Belle'
'Sparkler'
'Valentine'

Daikon
'April Cross' F1
(slow bolting)
'Miyashige'
'Summer Cross' F1

Overwintering
'Black Spanish Round'
'China Rose'
'China White'

'Black Spanish Round'

of 2 gallons/sq yd (9 liters/sq m). Overwatering, however, encourages leaf rather than root development.

Pests and diseases
Radishes may be attacked by flea beetles (p.638), cabbage root maggots (p.652), and slugs (p.638).

Harvesting and storing
Small radishes mature three to four weeks after sowing, most large types after eight to ten weeks. Pull small types soon after they mature, since most will become woody if they remain in the ground for long. Large types, however, may be left in the ground for several weeks with no risk of deterioration. Overwintering radishes may be left in the soil for lifting when required, except where the soil freezes or if they have been grown in heavy soil. In these cases, lift the roots and store them in boxes of moist sand in a frost-free place, or outside in piles for three or four months (see *Making a Rutabaga Pile*, p.537). Where radish seed is required for propagation, leave a few plants to produce some seed. Harvest the pods while they are still young and green, then dry them and gather the seeds.

Scorzonera (*Scorzonera hispanica*)

This hardy perennial is normally grown as an annual. Plants grow to about 3ft (90cm) tall and have yellow flower heads. The black-skinned, white-fleshed roots are 8in (20cm) or more long, and about 1½in (4cm) across at the neck. They have an unusual flavor and are eaten cooked. Both the young leaves and shoots (chards) of overwintered plants are edible, and the young flower buds and their flower stalks are also eaten cooked. For soil, climate, and manuring requirements, see "Carrots," p.538. A fertile, deep, light soil is essential for good roots to develop. Scorzonera has low nitrogen requirements (see p.498).

Sowing and planting
Sow fresh seed *in situ* in spring about ½in (1cm) deep, in rows about 8in (20cm) apart, thinning out seedlings to 4in (10cm). Water at a rate of 3–5 gallons/sq yd (16–23 liters/sq m) in dry spells. For routine cultivation, see "Carrots," p.538. Pests and diseases rarely affect scorzonera.

Harvesting and storing
The roots need at least four months to develop. They may be left in the soil throughout the winter (see *Protecting Parsnips*, opposite), or lifted and stored in boxes in cool conditions. Start lifting the roots for use in the fall and continue into spring. If they are only pencil-thin, leave the remaining plant roots to thicken for harvesting the following fall.
For chards, cover the plants with about 5in (13cm) of straw or leaves in early spring. The young, blanched leaves will push through this layer. Cut them when about 4in (10cm) tall.

For flower buds, leave a few roots in the soil during winter with no covering; these will flower the following spring or early summer. Pick the unopened buds with about 3in (7cm) of stem.

SCORZONERA ROOTS

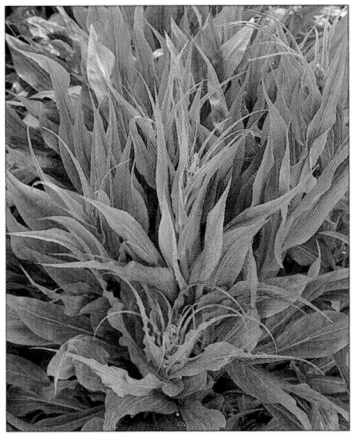

SCORZONERA PLANTS

Salsify (*Tragopogon porrifolius*)

A biennial with purple flowers, salsify is known as vegetable oyster or oyster plant, due to its taste. It is similar to scorzonera in appearance and use and has the same climate, soil, cultivation, harvesting, and storage requirements. Salsify roots need to be eaten in their first winter.

SALSIFY ROOTS

If the roots are overwintered, the flower buds may be eaten the following spring. Pick the buds with short stalks, preferably in the morning before they open.

Potatoes (*Solanum tuberosum*)

Potatoes are tender perennials that grow to an average height of 2ft (60cm), with a similar spread. There are numerous potato cultivars, displaying enormous variation in their underground tubers.
A typical mature tuber is about 3in (7cm) long and 1½in (4cm) wide with white or pinkish red skin and white flesh, but there are yellow- and blue-fleshed cultivars, often used in salads. Potatoes are eaten cooked, fresh or after storing.
Potatoes are a cool-season crop, growing best at 61–64°F (16–18°C). Neither plants nor tubers tolerate frost. Depending on the cultivar, they require a growing season of 90–140 frost-free days. They are divided into early, second early, and maincrop groups, depending on the number of days required to mature. The earlies grow fastest but are generally lower yielding. Potatoes need at least 20in (500mm) of rainfall or irrigation during the season.
Grow potatoes in an open, frost-free site; they need well-drained, fertile soil at least 2ft (60cm) deep that is rich in organic matter. Although tolerant of a wide range of soils, acid soils (pH 5–6) are preferred.
Potatoes are subject to several soilborne pests and diseases, and so crops must always be rotated (see p.492). Prepare the ground well by digging in plenty of organic matter. A complete fertilizer may be worked in just before planting. Early potatoes need medium nitrogen; high nitrogen is required for maincrop potatoes (see p.498).

Planting
Grow cultivars recommended for the area. Plant small tubers (known as seed potatoes) that have been specially raised and are certified disease-free. In northern latitudes with a short growing season, potatoes (especially the earlies) are sprouted indoors to start them into growth about six weeks before planting. Place the tubers in a shallow tray, with the eyes or buds uppermost, in even light in a cool but frost-free room. Planting is easiest when the sprouts are about ¾in (2cm) long, but they may be planted with sprouts of any length. For large early potatoes, leave only three sprouts per plant, rubbing off the others. Otherwise, the more sprouts per tuber, the higher the yield.

SPROUTING SEED POTATOES FOR PLANTING

To sprout seed potatoes, place them in a box or tray in a single layer with the end of the potato containing the most "eyes" uppermost. Store in a light, frost-free, but well-ventilated place until the sprouts have grown to about 2cm (¾in) in length.

Plant outside when there is no longer risk of heavy frost and once the soil temperature has reached 45°F (7°C). Make drills 3–6in (7–15cm) deep or make individual holes, and place tubers upright with the eyes or sprouts at the top, covering them with at least a 1in (2.5cm) layer of soil. Plant early potatoes 14in (35cm) apart in rows 17in (43cm) apart, second early and maincrop potatoes 15in (38cm) apart in rows 27in (68cm) and 30in (75cm) apart respectively.

In cool areas, cover early potatoes with clear plastic sheeting or nonwoven row covers (see p.499). When shoots emerge, cut holes in the covers and ease the foliage through. Remove floating covers about a month later, cutting them down the center first to acclimatize the potatoes to cooler conditions for a few days. Early potatoes may also be planted under black plastic, which excludes light and makes hilling up unnecessary; this is not recommended for maincrop potatoes, since watering is difficult. Lay the plastic on the ground, anchor the edges in the soil, and plant the potatoes through cross-shaped slits in the plastic. Alternatively, plant the potatoes, cover them with plastic, make slits, and pull the stems through when the plants start to push up the plastic.

Potatoes are sometimes grown from seedlings, plantlets, or eyes. These are planted in seed trays and transferred outside, after hardening off, once all risk of frost has passed.

Routine cultivation

If frost threatens after the leaves have appeared, cover them at night with a light layer of straw or newspaper. Plants normally recover from light frost damage. Unless grown under black plastic, potatoes need to be hilled up to prevent tubers near the surface from becoming green and unpalatable and sometimes toxic. When the plants are about 9in (23cm) tall, hoe up soil around the stems to a depth of about 5in (13cm). This may be done in stages.

In dry conditions, water early potatoes every 12 days at a rate of 3 gallons/sq yd (16 liters/sq m). Delay watering maincrop potatoes until the young potatoes are the size of marbles – check the size of the tubers by scraping back the soil beneath one plant – then give one watering of at least 5 gallons/sq yd (23 liters/sq m). Potatoes may be given an organic liquid fertilizer or a nitrogenous topdressing during growth.

Pests and diseases

Cutworms (p.652), snails (p.638), Colorado potato beetles (p.639), potato cyst nematodes, millipedes (p.638), and blackleg on potatoes may be troublesome. For details of potato late blight (including resistant cultivars) and other problems affecting potatoes, see "Potato tuber problems," p.653.

Harvesting and storing

Harvest early potatoes when, or just before, the flowers open. Potatoes under black plastic may be harvested by lifting the sheeting – they should be on the surface. Leave healthy maincrop potatoes in the soil for as long as possible; in fall, cut the haulm (the stems) of each plant to about 2in (5cm) above ground level, and leave the potatoes for another two weeks to harden the skins, before lifting. In areas with warm, wet summers where potato blight is prevalent, cut the haulm in late summer and discard the foliage; lift the potatoes two weeks later.

Lift potatoes for storage on a dry, sunny day and leave them in the sun for two hours, then store them in the dark in paper sacks in a cool, frost-proof place. Give extra protection if frost threatens. Potatoes may also be stored for up to six months outdoors in well-insulated piles (see p.537) or in a cellar. Young, or new, potatoes may be frozen. For new potatoes to be eaten during winter, plant a few tubers in the middle of summer and then cover them in fall.

RECOMMENDED POTATOES

Early
'Caribe'
'Eramosa'
'Norland'
'Superior'
'Warba'
'Yukon Gold'

'Warba'

Second early
'Acacia Russet'
'All Blue'
'All Red'
'Red Cloud'
'Ruby Gold'
'Viking'

Maincrop
'Butte'
'Cherokee'
'Chieftain'
'Desiree'
'Green Mountain'
'Kennebec'
'Pink Pearl'
'Russet Burbank'
'Shepody'

'Rose Finn Apple'

For salads
'Asparagus'
'German Yellow'
'Lady Fingers'
'Rose Finn Apple'
'Ruby Crescent'
'Russian Banana'

PLANTING POTATOES

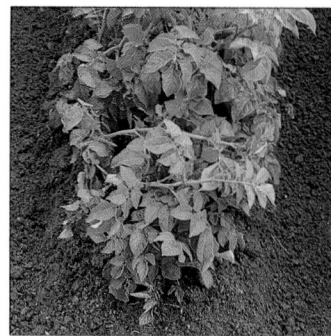

1 *When planting maincrop potatoes, make a drill 3–6in (7–15cm) deep, using a draw hoe. Place them in the drill 15in (38cm) apart with the sprouts upward. Cover carefully once planted.*

2 *Draw up the soil around the stems when the foliage is about 9in (23cm) high. Hilling up prevents tubers that form near the surface from turning green and being unfit to eat.*

ALTERNATIVE METHOD

1 *To plant under black plastic, unroll the plastic and anchor it by burying the edges. Make a cross-shaped cut where each potato is to be planted. Place each potato 4–5in (10–12cm) deep in the soil under each cut.*

2 *Once the haulm has been cut, the plastic can be pulled back and the crop of potatoes will be lying on the soil surface, ready to harvest. Yields may be lower than when growing by hilling up.*

HARVESTING POTATOES

In fall, cut the haulm (stems) cleanly with a knife to about 2in (5cm) above ground level. Leave the potatoes in the ground for another 2 weeks before lifting.

Salsify (*Tragopogon porrifolius*), see Scorzonera, p.541

MAINTAINING THE GARDEN

PRACTICAL ADVICE ON TOOLS AND EQUIPMENT, GREENHOUSES, AND BUILDING MATERIALS AND TECHNIQUES; UNDERSTANDING SOIL TYPE AND CLIMATE, HOW PLANTS GROW AND REPRODUCE, AND HOW BEST TO DEAL WITH PROBLEMS

1
TOOLS AND EQUIPMENT

KEEPING A GARDEN looking its best year-round involves a certain amount of maintenance, from mowing the lawn to hedge trimming to seed sowing. While it is unnecessary and expensive to invest in an entire catalog's worth of garden equipment, having the correct tool for the job makes work easier and faster and produces a better result. Besides basic tools that will be in almost constant use, there will be other items that you cannot do without; these might include a sprinkler for watering, a wheelbarrow for moving garden materials and refuse, or a supply of seed trays. Assessing the type and amount of work you do in the garden makes it easier to decide which tools and equipment you need; choosing them with care ensures that they will be durable and comfortable to use as well as practical and economical.

Buying and using tools

Most modern gardening tools are based on traditional designs, although some may be improvements or variations on old concepts. A few completely new tools, however, have been successfully introduced. For example, until the 1980s, shredders and nylon-line trimmers were hardly known; yet they are now firmly established because they fulfill a demand not met by traditional tools.

Before buying a tool, the most important point to bear in mind is its function – it must perform correctly the task it is meant to do. Consider exactly what you need a particular tool for and how frequently you will use it. A simple, inexpensive pair of pruners, for example, will be adequate if wanted only for pruning a few rosebushes once a year. However, if they are needed for intensive use, it is better to invest in a high-quality, more heavy-duty pair. Before purchasing a tool, wherever possible always try to check that it is:
• the best type of tool for the task;
• the right size and model to suit your needs;
• comfortable to use.
In large gardens, or for laborious or time-consuming tasks, consider using power tools; however, because they are expensive and need careful handling, be sure that they are really needed before going ahead.

To ensure that tools perform well and last a long time, it is important that they are properly maintained. Immediately after use, clean off any soil, grass clippings, or other plant material and wipe metal parts with an oily rag; all pruning and cutting tools will also need regular sharpening. Tools that are not needed over the winter months should be especially well oiled and then stored in a dry place.

In addition, factors such as expense and storage space must be taken into account: if a tool is needed only infrequently, renting may be a more sensible option, especially for relatively expensive, bulky tools.

Renting tools

If you decide to rent, reserve equipment in advance, especially tools likely to be in seasonal demand, such as power aerators and cultivators. Check whether the rental firm will deliver and pick up.

The condition of rented tools varies considerably. Some, especially power tools, may even be potentially dangerous to operate. Always:
• Check for missing or loose parts. These may not be obvious, but if in doubt, do not accept the tool.
• Look for loose bolts and other hardware on tools such as power cultivators that are subject to vibration.
• Ask for power tools to be started, and check carefully for excessive vibration and noise.
• On electrical tools, look for frayed, cut, or exposed wires. Do not assume that the wiring is satisfactory just because the tool works adequately.
• For two-cycle engines, determine the gas/oil ratio and keep an adequate supply on hand. Check and refill periodically.
• On four-cycle engines, check the oil in the engine and transmission.
• Ask for a demonstration or instructions if you have never operated the tool before. This is particularly important with tools such as chain saws, which can be dangerous to use.
• Buy or rent any recommended protective clothing such as goggles, gloves, and ear protectors.
• Before signing the delivery note, comment on the contract or delivery note if you have noticed any faults.

Safe use of tools

If you are not sure how to use a tool, ask for advice when buying or renting, or contact the manufacturer. Correct use gives good results and helps prevent accidents. Make sure that the weight and length are suitable: a tool that is too heavy will be difficult to handle; one that is too short may cause back strain. Keep power tools in good repair and follow safety recommendations. Avoid the risk of shock: plug electrical tools only into receptacles protected with ground fault circuit interrupters (GFCIs). The GFCI cuts the power in microseconds when a shock-producing ground fault occurs (see also "Electrical safety," p.550).

DIGGING CORRECTLY
Keeping your back straight, not curved, when digging, hoeing, or raking helps prevent backache.

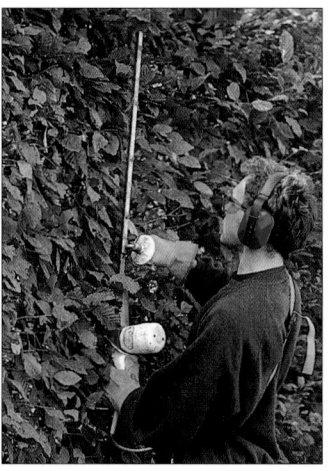

USING POWER TOOLS
Take particular care when using power tools, and always wear appropriate protective clothing.

Cultivation tools

The type of cultivation tools required depends on the nature of your garden. If you grow mainly vegetables or are cultivating a new garden, tools for digging will be a priority. If, however, the garden is well established with lawns and perennial borders, surface cultivation tools such as hoes will be more important.

Spades

A spade is an essential tool, excellent for general cultivation, lifting soil, and digging holes for planting. There are two major types: standard digging spades, and the smaller and lighter border (also called ladies') spades. Some manufacturers also produce an intermediate-sized or medium spade that is suitable for general digging but is lighter than a standard spade.

Some spades have a tread, which makes it easier to push the blade into the soil and less likely to damage footwear; these spades are, however, heavier and more expensive. For extensive digging, a larger spade (known as a "heavy"), which has a 8 x 12in (20 x 30cm) blade, may prove quicker to use.

If you find digging difficult or if the soil is very heavy, it may be worth buying an automatic spade to make the task less of a strain.

Forks

Garden forks are used for general cultivation, lifting root crops (which are more likely to be damaged with a spade), and shifting bulky material such as manure, mulch, and compost. Most garden forks have four heavy metal prongs, and are generally available in two sizes: standard and border (or ladies'). Less common are medium, or youth, forks, an intermediate size between standard and border forks.

Other variations are also sometimes found. For example, a potato fork has broad, flat prongs and, generally, a larger head than a standard fork; it may be easier to use than a spade when digging heavy ground.

The head and neck of a fork should be forged in a single piece, with no welds or rough surfaces; the shaft should fit into a long socket in the neck. Some forks have shorter necks, the head held in place by two long metal plates riveted to the front and back of the wooden shaft. These are usually weaker and are uncommon.

STANDARD DIGGING SPADE
This is useful for shifting large amounts of soil, but it is heavy and therefore may be unsuitable or uncomfortable for some gardeners. It has a rectangular blade of about 7 x 11in (19 x 28cm).

D-type molded hilt gives a good grip

Plastic hilt is comfortable, even in cold weather

Tread makes digging easier

Coated blade may be easily cleaned

STAINLESS STEEL BLADE
This is useful for a spade, since it makes lighter work of digging and never rusts.

AUTOMATIC SPADE
Operating on a spring-and-lever system, the spade throws the soil forward without the need to bend. It is expensive but may be worthwhile for those with back trouble.

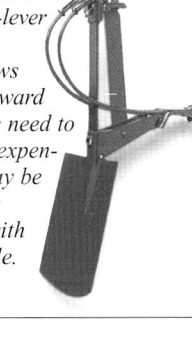

BORDER SPADE
With a blade only 5 x 9in (13 x 3cm), this is designed for digging in confined spaces, for example a planting hole in a border, but it is also good for any general light work.

STANDARD FORK
This fork is useful for cultivating heavy soil, lifting vegetables, and shifting large loads, but some people may find it heavy to maneuver. Its head is about 8 x 12in (20 x 30cm).

Neck and head formed from one piece of metal for strength

Head

POTATO FORK
Primarily for lifting potatoes, this flat-tined fork may also be used for digging or moving compost and garden waste.

Wooden shaft fitting into long socket in neck

BORDER FORK
This is best for light work in borders and similar restricted areas. The size of the head – 5½ x 9in (14 x 23cm) – makes it suitable for anyone needing a small, lightweight fork.

Which metal?

Carbon steel is used for most garden tools. If it is routinely cleaned and oiled after use, this metal should not rust. Although stainless steel is more expensive, it does make digging easier because soil falls away from the blade more readily, and it has the additional advantage of being rustproof. Tools that have a nonstick coating may make clearing and working the soil easier, but the coating may wear off after long use.

Handles and hilts

A spade or fork shaft should be the correct length for the user's height to minimize back strain. The standard shaft length is 28–29in (70–73cm); a longer shaft, available up to 39in (98cm) long, will almost certainly be more comfortable for people over 5ft 6in (1.7m) tall.

Shafts are made from wood or metal, the latter sometimes covered with plastic or nylon. Both are generally strong, but even metal shafts may break if put under too much stress and, unlike wooden ones, they cannot be replaced. Metal shafts, even plastic-coated, are colder than wood to hold in winter. Try out the tool, as if using it, to assess which type feels best.

D-TYPE HILTS
These are the most common type, but they may be uncomfortable for those with large hands, particularly when wearing gloves.

Y-TYPE HILTS
Similar to D-type hilts, but they may be weaker, since they are formed by splitting the shaft wood.

T-TYPE HILTS
These have a crosspiece joined to the shaft end. Some gardeners find them comfortable, but they are not commonly available and may need to be ordered.

545

Hoes

Hoes are excellent for weeding and aerating soil; some types may be used to form seed drills. The Dutch hoe is probably the most versatile and is ideal for weeding between rows of plants and for creating drills. Apart from draw, digging, and onion hoes, there are other hoes available for specific uses.

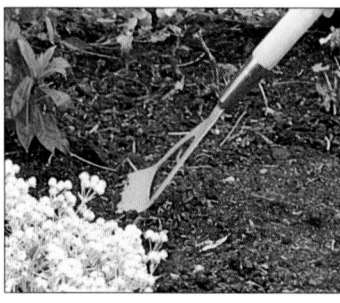

USING A DUTCH HOE
Hold the hoe so that the blade is parallel to the soil surface.

DUTCH HOE
This traditional hoe, also called a scuffle hoe, is good for weeding around plants. It removes surface weeds without damaging plant roots.

COMBINATION HOE
This is suitable for chopping off weeds, drawing drills, and hilling up. Use the prongs to break up soil and draw seed drills.

TRIANGULAR HOE
Use the point for drawing a V-shaped drill; the flat side is for weeding narrow spaces in between plants.

DIGGING HOE
This has one or two chisel-like blades. It is used with a swinging motion to break up small areas of hard ground.

Short-handled hoe for use in confined areas

ONION HOE
This small hoe (above), also called a hand, or rock garden, hoe, is for weeding between onions and other closely grown plants where a standard hoe might cause damage. It is like a short-handled version of a draw hoe and is used while squatting or kneeling.

Molded handle ensures a secure grip

DRAW HOE
This hoe (right) is good for chopping weeds, drawing up soil around plants, making flat-bottomed drills, and, with the blade corner, making V-shaped drills.

Curved neck makes the hoe easier to use in between plants without damaging them

Rakes

Rakes are excellent for leveling and breaking up the soil surface before planting and for gathering garden debris. There are two main types: general garden rakes and lawn rakes (see "Rakes and aerators," p.553).

A flathead rake is stronger than a bowhead rake. The more teeth a rake has, the faster an area is covered: 12 teeth are adequate, but 16 or more are preferable for large areas. A 3ft (1m) wide wooden rake is useful in a large garden.

Heads and shafts

Most rake and hoe heads are made from solid carbon steel; stainless steel ones are more expensive and do not work any better, although they are easier to clean and do not rust. Some rakes have a nonstick coating.

Shafts may be made from wood, aluminum, or plastic-covered metal. Shaft length is important: you should be able to stand upright while hoeing or raking to reduce strain on the back. Most people find a 5ft (1.5m) shaft comfortable, but a longer handle may be preferred.

FLATHEAD RAKE
This has short, wide, rounded teeth and is valuable for leveling soil, clearing the ground, and general garden cleanup.

BOWHEAD RAKE
This lighter rake may be preferred by some gardeners.

Trowels and hand forks

A trowel is useful for digging holes for small plants and bulbs and for working in containers and raised beds. A hand, or weed, fork may be used for weeding, lifting small plants, and planting.

Most trowel blades and hand fork prongs are made from stainless steel, coated steel (e.g. chrome-plated), or ordinary carbon steel. Unlike carbon steel, stainless steel does not rust and is easy to keep clean, but it is expensive. Coatings gradually tend to wear off in time. Some trowels have extra-long handles – up to 12in (30cm) – for more leverage. Hand forks with handles 4ft (1.2m) long reduce the need to bend when weeding the back of a border. Wooden, plastic, and plastic-coated handles are all generally comfortable to hold; metal ones tend to be cold.

HAND FORK
Often used for lifting small plants or loosening the soil when weeding. Unlike a trowel, it does not compact the soil, so it may be preferable to use when planting in heavy soil.

WIDE-BLADED TROWEL
This is useful for planting bulbs and bedding or other small plants, especially in confined areas such as containers and windowboxes.

NARROW-BLADED TROWEL
Sometimes known as a rock garden or transplanting trowel, this is ideal for working in very confined areas, such as rock gardens, as well as for general transplanting tasks.

Hand-weeding tools

For weeding between paving, bricks, or rocks, a Cape Cod weeder with its narrow, hooked blade, is ideal. An asparagus knife has a pronged blade suitable for levering up lawn weeds.

SPECIALIZED WEEDERS
A Cape Cod weeder (right) can be used in narrow crevices. An asparagus knife (far right) may be used to lift lawn weeds without damaging the sod.

Manual cultivators

A hand, or pronged, cultivator is used to break up the surface of compacted soil or to loosen weeds. It has a three- or five-pronged metal head on a long shaft and is pulled through the soil, generally from a standing position. Some adjustable models have removable, central prongs.

Specialized hand cultivators may be useful for certain tasks. A star-wheeled cultivator, or miller, for example, forms a fine tilth when pushed back and forth through the soil and is good when preparing a seedbed or surface from sod.

ADJUSTABLE MODELS
Cultivators with removable central prongs are suitable for tasks such as cultivating each side of a row of seedlings. Some models have a detachable handle, which may be fitted onto other types of compatible tool head, for example a rake or hoe.

A single detachable handle may be combined with a variety of tool heads

STAR-WHEELED CULTIVATOR
This creates a fine tilth for a seedbed.

REMOVABLE PRONGS
When working in very confined areas, it may be useful to remove some prongs to make the head smaller.

Rototillers

A rototiller, or power cultivator, is used for tackling laborious tasks like turning over the soil in neglected ground. It breaks up compacted soil and reduces it to a tilth fine enough for planting. It is impractical for use in densely planted areas, however, and does not eliminate the need for hand digging. Gas-powered cultivators are powerful and generally have a wide range of attachments but need more routine maintenance than electric ones. Electric cultivators are excellent for small jobs, being easier to maneuver, less noisy, and cheaper than gas-powered types. Trailing cords may be a problem, however.

On most cultivators the handle height is adjustable. Some also have handles that pivot and lock sideways; this allows you to walk alongside the machine rather than behind it, preventing you from trampling the ground already cultivated.

Cultivators come in three main types: front-, mid-, and rear-engined. **Front-engined cultivators** have tines behind the driving wheels. They are easy to steer but, because of the way the weight is distributed, are suitable only for shallow cultivation. **Mid-engined cultivators** are propelled by tines rather than wheels. This may make control difficult, but the engine weight over the rotors makes deep cultivation easier than with a front-engined type. **Rear-engined cultivators** are best for maneuvering in difficult places and for forming deep holes. The tines, on a boom at the front, are swept from side to side as the cultivator is propelled along. These machines may be hard to control.

MINI-ROTOTILLER
Useful in small or confined areas, a mini-rototiller is much easier to maneuver than a standard rototiller. A special attachment allows rear wheels to be fitted for easier transporting to and from the work site.

ROTOTILLER
This front-engined gas model is stable and easy to control. It is expensive but does an excellent job of straightforward cultivation over a large area.

Throttle control (accelerator)
Dead-man's handle cuts the power if the grip is relaxed
Forward/reverse lever
PTO engagement lever
Bumper bar
Engine
Battery
High/low gear lever
Lever adjusts depth of cultivation
Overlapping tines leave no areas of unturned soil
Rear tines produce a fine finish for a seedbed

HILLING ATTACHMENT
Used in place of the tines, this tool throws soil on either side of the row so is useful for hilling up row crops.

Pruning and cutting tools

When pruning, it is important to use the appropriate tool for the task and to make sure that it is sharp so that it cuts cleanly, easily, and safely. Using a blunt blade can leave a plant with a ragged wound that is prone to infection or that can cause dieback. Take particular care when working with power tools such as hedge trimmers or brushwood cutters (see "Electrical safety," p.550).

Pruners

Pruners are used for pruning woody stems up to about ½in (1cm) thick and soft shoots of any thickness; they may also be used for taking cuttings for propagation. They can be used single-handed and are more controllable and easier to handle safely than a knife, particularly by inexperienced gardeners.

There are three main types of pruner: bypass, curved, or side anvil; parrot-beak; and anvil. Bypass and parrot-beak pruners have a scissorlike action; anvil pruners have a sharp, straight-edged upper blade that cuts against a square-edged lower anvil. In some designs (swing-anvils), the blade is pivoted in such a way that it remains parallel to the anvil as it cuts, preventing the stem from sliding out.

For cutting soft-stemmed plants, a light, comparatively cheap pair is adequate. For pruning fruit trees and shrubs with woody shoots up to ½in (1cm) thick, a pair of heavy-duty pruners is preferable.

If possible, try out the pruners to check that they are comfortable and easy to operate. The handle material and shape, how wide they open, and the pressure of the spring keeping them open all vary considerably.

BYPASS PRUNERS
These use a scissorlike action. They have a sharp, convex, steel upper blade that cuts against a concave or square steel lower blade to make a clean cut.

Brightly colored handles are easy to spot

Molded grip is comfortable to use

Sharp steel blade makes a clean, precise cut

Safety catch may be moved with your thumb

FLOWER GATHERERS
These are designed to grip the stem after cutting.

SAFETY CATCH
This catch clips the handles together.

RATCHET SYSTEM
This makes cutting tough stems easier.

ANVIL PRUNERS
These must always be sharp; otherwise, the blade crushes the stem against the anvil instead of cutting it.

PARROT-BEAK PRUNERS
These give a clean cut but may be damaged if used to cut wood more than ½in (1cm) thick.

Metal handles may be very cold to hold, but most handles are now plastic or plastic-covered metal. All pruners should be fitted with a safety catch that locks the blades in the shut position. Check that it is easy to operate with one hand and that it cannot be flicked off accidentally.

Pruner blades may be made from stainless steel, carbon steel, or coated steel. Coated blades are easy to wipe clean, but are unlikely to last as long as high-quality stainless or carbon steel blades, which keep their sharpness and cut cleanly and easily.

When buying high-quality pruners, ensure that they can be dismantled for sharpening without special tools and that new blades are available.

Some models have a ratchet system for cutting through a shoot in stages. These require less effort and so are suitable for those who find conventional models a strain, but they are slower to use.

Flower gatherers, or flower pickers, hold the flower stem after cutting. They are invaluable if cutting flowers often; otherwise, pruners or scissors will suffice.

Maintenance

Clean the blades of cutting tools after each use with an oily rag or steel wool to remove any sap that has dried on, then lightly oil them. Periodically tighten the blade tension of garden shears; this makes them cut more efficiently and produces a better finish.

Most pruning tools are easy to sharpen. Remove blades that are badly blunted or damaged, and regrind or replace them.

Long-handled pruners or loppers

A pair of long-handled pruners, or loppers, is useful for removing woody stems ½–1in (1–2.5cm) thick, where pruners might be damaged, and for thinner branches that are difficult to reach.

The long handles give additional leverage, making it easier to cut through thick stems. They are usually wood or plastic-covered tubular steel or aluminum. Blades are made of stainless steel, carbon steel, or coated steel, as for pruners.

The weight and balance of long-handled pruners are important, because you may need to hold them

at full stretch or above your head. Make sure that you will be able to operate them easily and without strain.

Most long-handled pruners have a bypass blade motion, others an anvil action. Both are satisfactory designs, and the choice is a matter of personal preference. Designs with a ratchet are sometimes available and are particularly useful for cutting through thick or tough branches and to reduce the strength needed for cutting.

All long-handled pruners require regular maintenance to keep them in peak working condition.

LONG-HANDLED BYPASS PRUNERS
Using long-handled pruners makes it possible to prune stems that are high up or that are too tough or thick for pruners.

Buffers prevent jarring when operating pruners

ANVIL PRUNERS
The blades open wide for cutting thick stems.

Tree pruners

A tree pruner is suitable for cutting branches up to 1in (2.5cm) thick that would otherwise be out of reach. The cutting device is positioned at the end of a pole that is usually 6–10ft (2–3m) long, although some extend to 15ft (5m). The carbon steel blade is operated by a lever system or a cord; both are efficient, although the lever system is more popular. Some cord models have telescopic poles so that the length may be adjusted; they are also more convenient to store. Tree pruners may have saw or fruit-picker attachments.

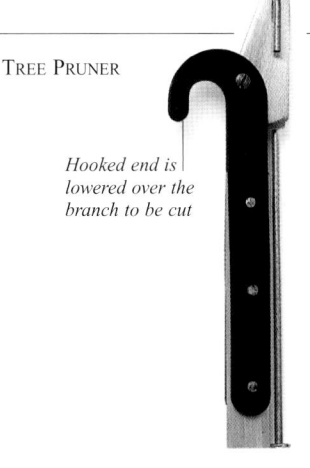

TREE PRUNER

Hooked end is lowered over the branch to be cut

Pruning saws

Use a pruning saw for severing branches more than about 1in (2.5cm) thick. Because sawing in a confined space between other branches (often at an awkward angle) may be difficult, various types of pruning saw have been developed. Those that are most commonly available are general-purpose pruning, Curved or rigid-handle curved, double-edged or two-edged, folding, and bow saws. If pruning is a major task in the garden, it may be necessary to have more than one saw for different types of work. A curved saw is one of the most useful pruning saws for an amateur.

All pruning saws should have hardpoint, heat-treated teeth, which are harder and stay sharper longer than ordinary teeth. They must be professionally sharpened. Saw handles are plastic or wood; choose whichever feels more comfortable and has a secure grip. Be sure to score a groove in the branch, and then insert the saw blade to reduce the risk of its slipping during use.

GENERAL-PURPOSE PRUNING SAW
Invaluable for most pruning jobs, this saw has a small blade, generally not more than 18in (45cm) long, so that it can be easily used in confined areas and at awkward angles.

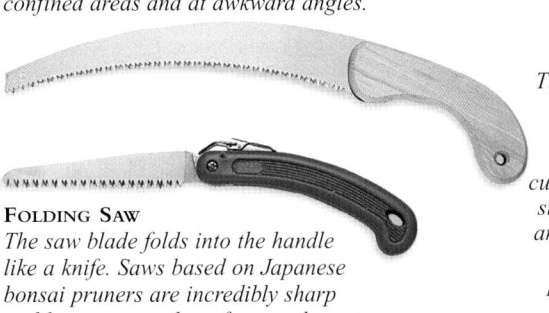

FOLDING SAW
The saw blade folds into the handle like a knife. Saws based on Japanese bonsai pruners are incredibly sharp and leave a smooth surface on the cut.

CURVED SAW
This is excellent for confined spaces because it has a curved blade and cuts only on the pull stroke. In restricted areas, it is easier to use pressure on a pull, rather than a push, stroke.

DOUBLE-EDGED PRUNING SAW
This is very versatile, since it has both coarse and fine teeth, but it may be difficult to operate in confined spaces without the top teeth damaging a nearby branch.

BOW SAW
This is used to cut through thick branches quickly, but is too large to operate in a confined area.

Garden knives

A garden knife may be used for light pruning tasks instead of pruners, and it is more versatile. It is also convenient for taking cuttings, preparing material for grafting, harvesting certain vegetables, and cutting string.

There are various types of garden knife available, including general-purpose, grafting, budding, and pruning or peach pruners. Most knives have a carbon steel blade that is either fixed or folds into the handle. If choosing the folding type, check that it is easy to open, and that the spring holding the blade in position is neither too strong nor too slack. Always dry knife blades after use, and wipe them with an oily rag. Sharpen knives regularly to the same angle as when new.

Most gardeners prefer a knife with a plastic or wooden handle rather than a metal one, which may feel cold and uncomfortable.

GENERAL-PURPOSE GARDEN KNIFE
This is useful for all cutting tasks except heavy pruning.

MULTIPURPOSE KNIFE
There are various models available. This one has a large blade for general use and pruning, a small one for grafting, and an attachment for budding.

GRAFTING
This straight-bladed knife is suitable for general tasks and for making accurate cuts when grafting.

BUDDING
The blade projection is used for pushing open the rootstock incision when propagating by bud-grafting.

PRUNING
The large blade curves downward for a controlled cut when pruning.

Garden shears

Shears are used mainly for trimming hedges but are also invaluable for cutting small or awkward areas of long grass (see also "Lawn-care tools," pp.552–3), clipping topiary, and cutting back herbaceous plants.

For soft-stemmed hedges, a light pair is adequate. For large hedges with tough, woody stems, a heavy-duty pair will be needed.

Weight and balance are important; before buying, check that the shears are centrally balanced and the blades are not too heavy, or they will then be tiring to operate.

Most shears have straight blades although a few have wavy-edged blades: these cut through mature wood easily and help trap the shoots so that they are not pushed out with the scissor action of the blades. They are difficult to sharpen (see also "Maintenance," opposite).

STANDARD SHEARS
Shears usually have one notched blade to hold a thick shoot during cutting.

SINGLE-HANDED SHEARS
These have a spring mechanism similar to pruners that allows them to be operated with one hand. Some types have blades that swivel – useful for cutting at an angle or vertically (as for edging a lawn). They are suitable only for cutting grass or very soft stems.

Hedge trimmers

For gardeners with large hedges to cut, a power hedge trimmer may be worthwhile, because it takes much less time and effort to use than ordinary, manually operated shears.

The longer the blade, the faster the hedge can be cut and the easier it is to reach a tall hedge or across the top of a wide one. Hedge trimmers with very long blades are heavy and often poorly balanced, however. A 16in (40cm) blade is adequate for normal garden use, but if cutting extensive hedges a 24in (60cm) blade saves considerable time. Blades may be either single- or double-sided; the latter speed up the cutting time but are not as easy to control as single-sided blades, so hedge shaping may be more difficult.

The ease of handling is also influenced by the blade action. Models with reciprocating- or double-action blades, which move against each other, are generally preferred by most gardeners. Single-action models, in which one moving blade cuts against a second, stationary blade, cause vibration and can therefore be tiring to operate.

The finish of the cut is largely controlled by the spacing of the teeth along the blade. Teeth that are narrowly spaced produce a smooth, even

PROTECTIVE CLOTHING
When operating power tools, wear protective clothing such as goggles, ear protectors, and thick gardening gloves (see also p.557).

POWER HEDGE TRIMMER
This makes hedge trimming faster and easier than using garden shears. Electric models are light and easy to maneuver, while gas versions are powerful and unhampered by trailing cords.

finish on a hedge that is regularly trimmed, while more widely spaced teeth usually cope better with thicker twigs but leave a rougher cut.

Gas or electricity?
Hedge trimmers may be powered by gas, batteries, or electricity. Gas hedge trimmers may be operated anywhere and are generally powerful and relatively free from vibration. They are, however, noisier, heavier, and more expensive than electric or battery-powered ones and usually require more maintenance.

Electric hedge trimmers are more commonly used by amateurs and are better for small jobs. Being lighter, they are easier to handle than gas trimmers; they are also cleaner to use and cheaper to buy.

Electric hedge trimmers are the most convenient for hedges within 100ft (30m) of a power supply. As with other electric tools, the trailing cord can be inconvenient and even hazardous; the machine must not be used in wet conditions. Safety features are very important when handling such a potentially dangerous

tool: for example, they should always be operated with a residual current device, commonly called a ground fault circuit interrupter (see also "Electrical safety," below).

Battery-powered hedge trimmers are good for hedges in a distant part of a large garden or where there is no convenient power supply. They are usually run from a spare car battery. When fully charged, they are reasonably powerful, but maintaining a charged battery and moving it around can be time-consuming and laborious. They are more expensive than electric models.

Rechargeable hedge trimmers

Hedge trimmers powered by a rechargeable battery are cordless, easy to maneuver, and comparatively cheap. They are excellent for small, regularly trimmed hedges, but they lack the power to cut thick shoots and long hedges satisfactorily. Since there are no trailing cords, rechargeable machines present fewer safety hazards than other types of electric trimmer. They can be recharged using the unit provided with the tool.

Brushwood cutters

A rotating metal blade is useful for heavy-duty tasks

A brushwood cutter is excellent for slashing through tough weeds, undergrowth, and very long grass. The rotating head has a metal fine-toothed blade or slasher. This makes it suitable for far heavier tasks than those that can be tackled with a nylon-line trimmer (see "Lawn-care tools," p.552), but it is more tiring to operate. Some models take plastic

blades, but these are not as tough or durable. In addition to their cutting blade, some may be fitted with a nylon line for trimming grass.

Since they need powerful engines to work effectively, most brushwood cutters are gas-driven. Electric models are usually lighter, less noisy, and require less maintenance, but they are less efficient for heavy work.

Electrical safety

• Keep cords only just as long as is necessary. Trailing cords are inconvenient and potentially hazardous, because they may be cut by moving blades.
• Have outside sockets installed by a qualified electrician at suitable points in the garden to keep cords short and safe.
• If extension cords are needed, make sure they have the same number of wires as the tool: if the tool is grounded, the extension cord should be, too.
• Double-insulated tools do not require a grounded (3-prong) socket or extension. All other electric tools do.
• Do not use an electric tool during or just after rain, since this may cause electrical shorts.
• Always disconnect the power supply before adjusting, inspecting, or cleaning a tool.
• Never touch a severed or damaged cord before disconnecting it from the socket.
• Sockets should be fitted with a ground fault circuit interrupter.

Chain saws

Chain saws are suitable for sawing logs or large branches and for extensive tree surgery and felling. Because they cut with a powered, toothed chain revolving at high speed, they can be dangerous and should be handled with great care; it is advisable to be trained in their safe use.

Electric chain saws are useful for small jobs and are cheaper than gas types, but strict safety precautions are essential (see right).

Gas-driven chain saws are more powerful and therefore suitable for very large gardens or woodlands, but they are noisy, heavy, often difficult to start, and create fumes.

ELECTRIC CHAIN SAW
An electric chain saw is suitable for most sawing tasks. It is lighter and easier to handle than a gas-powered version and generally requires less maintenance.

Side handle to help balance saw

On-off switch

Chain brake

Revolving, toothed chain cuts through the wood

Reservoir containing oil, to lubricate the chain

Cord and plug

Lawn mowers

When choosing a lawn mower, take into account the size of your lawn and the type of cut required. If only a small area needs mowing, a manual lawn mower should suffice, but for a larger lawn buy a power mower. There are reel and rotary mowers available: reel models usually provide the finest cut, while rotary types are better for longer, tougher, or overgrown grass.

Grass should be mowed more closely during periods of rapid growth and left longer when less growth occurs, such as late fall, or when hot and dry in summer, so check that the height of cut is easily adjustable (see also THE LAWN, "Frequency and height of cut," p.389). For a fine finish without loose grass, choose a mulching mower or a model with a grass catcher (see also "Grass clippings," p.389).

Manual lawn mowers

Manual mowers are relatively cheap, quiet, have no awkward cords, and require very little maintenance.

There are two types of manual lawn mower: those driven by wheels at the side, and those operated by a chain drive from a heavy rear roller. A side-wheel mower is easy to push but may be difficult to use at the edge of a lawn – if its side wheels are not in contact with the grass, they do not turn the reel blades. Since there is no rear roller, it does not produce a strip pattern on the turf. Mowers with a rear roller make it easy to mow over an edge.

Power lawn mowers

There are two basic types of power lawn mower: reel and rotary. They run on gas or electricity. Power mowers are potentially dangerous on steep slopes, because they are designed for flat surfaces.

Reel mowers

These mowers either are entirely self-propelled or have a power blade; the latter type may be heavy and tiring to operate. Most reel mowers have a rear roller, which is essential if you want a lawn with a strip pattern; the heavier the roller, the more pronounced the strip.

Gas-driven reel mowers often have broader cutting widths than electric ones. This reduces the cutting time but makes them more difficult to maneuver.

PUSH REEL MOWER
The scissor-cut action of this mower cuts grass very cleanly, and it adds no pollutants to the environment. However, reel mowers can be tiring to use, since the energy needed to cut the grass comes from the operator.

REEL MOWER BLADES
The blades are set along a reel that rotates forward and cuts against a fixed blade.

MULCHING MECHANISM
The arrows show the flow of cut grass within the blade housing before the particles drop onto the lawn.

MULCHING ROTARY MOWER
The mulching action returns the nutrients in the cut grass back into the lawn.

ROTARY MOWER
The replaceable metal blade cuts horizontally, so it is unlikely to scalp uneven turf. The action of the blade (see inset) pushes leaves or cut grass into the bag attachment.

RIDING MOWER
Preferable for any large lawn, this may also be used as a mulching mower or to gather leaves in the fall.

Large-volume grass collector reduces the frequency of emptying

Rotary mowers

These have replaceable metal or plastic blades that cut grass with a scythelike motion as they rotate horizontally. Rotary mowers have wheels; only a few rotary mowers are fitted with rollers. They work better than reel mowers for sites that are slightly uneven or have long grass, but most models cannot cut very low. Riding mowers, convenient for large lawns, are almost always rotary models.

Which power source?

Electricity is more convenient and cleaner than gas but is not suitable for powerful engines. If used for very long grass or extensive areas, an electric mower may overheat. Convenience and safety should also be considered. Access to a power supply is essential, although the trailing cord may be a hazard. Do not use electric mowers on wet grass.

Gas lawn mowers are not hampered by cords but are more expensive to purchase and maintain. They may not start readily unless they are fitted with an electric ignition.

Safety

- Blades must be well protected so that they do not come into contact with the operator's feet. However safe the mower appears, the operator should always wear strong, protective shoes.
- The blade brake must stop the blades from rotating within five seconds of being turned off.
- The mower should have a lock-off switch, which requires two operations to turn on an engine. This reduces the risk of a child accidentally switching it on.
- A dead-man's handle should be fitted. Held in when mowing, this turns off the engine when released.

Maintenance

A few simple precautions keep a mower working efficiently.
- After use, disconnect power, then clean engine and blades.
- Replace blunt blades promptly.
- Oil and lubricate regularly.
- Service the mower yearly.
- Periodically check that spark plugs are clean and adjusted.
- Clean filters and air intakes of gas mowers regularly.
- Periodically check the oil level on four-cycle engines.
- Drain the tank before you store a gas-powered model.

551

Lawn–care tools

In addition to lawn mowers, a number of other tools are useful for maintaining a healthy and attractive lawn. Manual tools are usually adequate for smaller lawns, but, for large areas, power tools are faster and less tiring to operate.

Edging tools

A neat, well-defined edge provides the perfect finishing touch to a well-mowed lawn and emphasizes the lawn's shape and outline (see also *Cutting the Edge of the Lawn*, p.390). There are two main lawn edging tools: half-moon edgers and long-handled shears, although power edging machines and certain nylon-line trimmers may be used.

Shafts for long-handled shears are wood, steel, or plastic-coated steel; all are strong, and the choice is really a matter of personal preference.

LONG-HANDLED EDGING SHEARS
These are useful for trimming overhanging grass around a lawn edge. The handles should be sufficiently long so that there is no need to stoop. If either too short or too heavy, the shears may be tiring to operate.

HALF-MOON EDGER
Also known as an edging iron or lawn edger, this is used with a rocking motion to cut away worn or uneven lawn edges and to remove small pieces of sod for repair. It has a sharp, curved metal blade attached to a long wooden or metal handle.

Tang of blade is well secured to shaft neck

Lawn edging materials

To prevent a lawn from gradually decreasing in size when turf is removed with tools such as a half-moon edger, outline the lawn with bricks, paving slabs, terracotta edging tiles, or metal or plastic edging strips. This helps ensure an even edge and inhibits grass from spreading onto paths and borders. A brick or paving-slab edge also enables side-wheel mowers to be driven right to the lawn edge. Plastic strips, which are usually green, are less likely than metal edging strips to damage mower blades and are much cheaper. However, plastic strips may deteriorate quickly.

Nylon–line trimmers

A nylon-line trimmer is useful for trimming grass in awkward areas that cannot easily be reached by a mower. It may also be used for soft-stemmed weeds, although a more powerful brushwood cutter may be needed for tough undergrowth (see p.550). The cutting line is flexible and easily replaced, so it is possible to work right up to a wall or paving without damaging the tool. (Do not trim up to trees as it can kill them.) It is also safer than a fixed blade or cutter if there is an accident. Always wear goggles, since flying stones are hazardous.

As for most other power tools, nylon-line trimmers may be driven by electricity or gas, and similar considerations of safety, convenience, and weight apply. Electric models are more common and are suitable for gardens where they are needed for small areas only.

They are light and easy to operate, but their area of use is restricted by the cord length. For safety, they should have a dead-man's handle and be plugged into a receptacle with a ground fault circuit interrupter. Never use them on wet grass (see also "Electrical safety," p.550).

A gas-driven nylon-line trimmer is ideal for larger gardens and for areas where there is no power supply. It is more expensive and needs more maintenance than an electric trimmer. It is also heavier and therefore may be more tiring to operate. For safety, it should have a quick, easy way to stop the engine.

Garden rollers

A garden roller, which may be made of metal or water-filled hollow plastic, is used to level the surface during initial ground preparation before sowing grass seed or laying sod. It also settles the soil around young grass seedlings. Rolling established lawns regularly is no longer recommended, however; on heavy soils particularly, it tends to compact the turf and therefore impede drainage, which may lead to problems such as moss and poor grass growth.

TRIMMER
This has a flexible nylon cutting line that rotates at high speed to cut through grass and other soft-stemmed plants or weeds. Some models have an adjustable head that may be tilted vertically for trimming lawn edges.

A shaft handle makes the tool easy to operate

Shield protects user from whirling cutting line

CUTTING GUIDE
This keeps the nylon line just off the ground to stop it from cutting too low and to trim evenly.

Long-handled lawn shears

Long-handled lawn shears are helpful for trimming grass in awkward places, such as beneath overhanging plants or around trees, paving, or walls, and for cleaning up any stalks missed during mowing. The blades, set at right angles to the handles, are positioned parallel to the ground, not vertically as in edging shears.

While lawn shears are useful for very small areas, they have largely been superseded by power nylon-line trimmers, which are faster and more versatile. However, trimmers are heavier to hold and maneuver than shears and are more expensive, since they are power tools.

LONG-HANDLED LAWN SHEARS
These may be useful for cutting grass in small areas that would be difficult to cut with a mower.

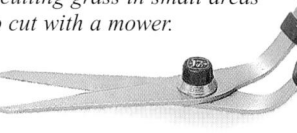

Rakes and aerators

Tools for clearing up fallen leaves and garden debris, and for reducing thatch (a layer of decaying organic matter) and soil compaction, help keep a lawn in good condition.

Lawn rakes are primarily used to gather up fallen leaves. Some types may be helpful in removing thatch and dead moss. There are three types of lawn rake: spring-tined, flat-tined, and scarifying, or aerator, rakes (see also "Rakes," p.546). In addition, power lawn rakes, which are suitable for large lawns, are available.

Aerating, whether by spiking, scarifying, slitting, or hollow-tining, helps reduce thatch – which should not exceed a layer ½in (1cm) in depth – and lets air into the soil. The result of proper dethatching and aerating is to encourage healthy, vigorous turf with deep root growth (see also THE LAWN, "Annual maintenance," p.391).

On small areas, aerating may be done by spiking the turf with a garden fork, but for most lawns a more powerful tool, for example a hollow-tined aerator also known as a plugger, or star-wheeled slitter attachment (see right), will be needed. Although a slitter aerates the soil faster than a hollow-tined aerator, its tines may not penetrate the turf deeply enough to be effective.

SPRING-TINED LAWN RAKE
This is used for clearing out dead grass and moss, removing small stones and debris, and lightly aerating a lawn. Its light head has long, flexible, rounded wire tines.

FLAT-TINED LAWN RAKE
Excellent for gathering up leaves and loose material, this has long, flexible, flat tines of plastic or metal, and a light head to minimize damage to new growth.

SCARIFYING RAKE
This cuts deeply into thatch and even into the sod itself. Its rigid metal tines are usually flat, with sharp points. Because it may be heavy and tiring to use, a model with wheels either side of the rake head may be preferable.

HOLLOW-TINED AERATOR (PLUGGER)
This hollow-tined power aerator penetrates deeply through the sod into the soil. The tines remove cores of sod and soil, opening up compacted sod.

STAR-WHEELED SLITTER ATTACHMENT
This attachment for riding mowers (see p.465) aerates the soil faster than a hollow-tined aerator.

Sweepers and blowers

At its simplest, a leaf sweeper may be an ordinary stiff broom or brush used to sweep away small debris; this kind of basic sweeper is ideal for clearing pathways and small areas of the garden.

For large lawns, however, using a power leaf blower saves both labor and time. The leaves are quickly and easily blown into rows or piles, which may then be raked up and discarded or added to a compost pile.

Some power models have flexible attachments designed for use in flower beds, borders, and other areas of the garden that are particularly hard to reach. Larger models of power blower, especially push models, may prove worthwhile in large gardens, but they are expensive to buy and they may be noisy to operate. Smaller models may be cheaper and quieter in addition to being lighter.

Fertilizer spreaders

A fertilizer spreader is suitable for the accurate distribution of fertilizer, grass seed, and granular weedkillers. It consists of a hopper on wheels with a long handle. Check that the application rate is adjustable and that the flow may be switched off when turning at the lawn edge. After setting the application rate, always check that it is correct by fertilizing a test area first (see "Applying fertilizers," p.619). A hose attachment for applying a fertilizer with water is useful for treating a lawn (see *Hose-end Attachments*, p.554).

BACKPACK BLOWER
This blower is carried on the operator's back and is very useful for small, tight, and irregularly shaped areas.

FERTILIZER SPREADER
A spreader applies fertilizer evenly, thus avoiding scorching the grass.

PUSH LEAF BLOWER
This cleans up garden leaves by blowing (rather than sweeping) them into a pile for collection. It is very useful for large, paved surfaces.

HANDHELD BLOWER
This is useful for smaller jobs.

Watering aids

Irrigation makes it possible to grow plants that require more water than is provided by rainfall, and to grow plants both indoors and in the greenhouse. Equipment such as hoses and sprinklers helps make routine watering easier and faster.

Watering cans

A watering can is practical in the house, greenhouse, or for small areas outside. Choose a lightweight can that will not be too heavy to carry when full. The opening of the watering can should be wide enough to make filling easy, and the can itself should feel comfortable and well balanced. A can that has a strainer at the base of the spout helps prevent the nozzle from becoming clogged by debris in the water.

Water barrels

A water barrel gathers and stores rainwater from the house or greenhouse roof, invaluable during dry periods and for acid-loving plants. The barrel should have a tap, plus a lid to keep out insects and debris, which pollute the water and might block the tap. If necessary, raise the barrel on blocks to allow room for a watering can beneath the tap. Some water barrels divert water back to a drain when the barrel is full.

GARDEN WATERING CANS
These should have a generous capacity to reduce the need for repeated refilling. For general-purpose use, a 2 gallon (9 liter) can, which holds 18lb (8kg) of water, is a convenient size.

PLASTIC OR METAL?
Most watering cans are now made from plastic, but traditional galvanized metal ones, which are heavier and more expensive, are still available; both types are sturdy and durable.

GREENHOUSE WATERING CAN
This has a long spout, so that it is easy to reach plants at the back of a bench, and an interchangeable nozzle for fine and coarse sprays for watering seedlings and mature plants.

INDOOR WATERING CAN
This should have a long spout to reach into plant pots and window-boxes, and to help control the flow.

Caution with weedkiller

Do not use the same watering can for watering the garden and for dispensing liquid weedkillers. Keep a special can with a dribble bar, clearly marked, for applying chemicals.

Which nozzle?

Coarse-spray nozzle

Fine-spray brass nozzle

Fine-spray, brass-faced, plastic nozzle

A fine nozzle is best for seeds and seedlings, because the resulting spray does not damage them or wash the soil mix or soil away from them. For more established plants, a coarse-spray nozzle, which delivers the water faster, is preferable.

Nozzles are manufactured in a choice of materials: brass, brass-faced plastic, and all-plastic. Plastic is less durable and cheaper than brass but is still satisfactory for most uses. In general, metal nozzles give a finer spray.

Using a dribble bar, which is attached to a watering can, makes it more accurate than a nozzle for applying weedkiller. It also reduces spray drift, which can be a problem with a nozzle.

Hoses

A hose is invaluable for irrigating distant parts of the garden and for areas that require copious watering. Most hoses are made from PVC; they vary in the way they are finished or reinforced, which affects their flexibility and their resistance to kinking. Any kinks interrupt water flow and eventually weaken the hose wall. Double-walled and reinforced hoses are resistant to kinking but relatively expensive.

Some hoses are available in a wall-mounted, retractable reel, in order to facilitate storage, while others are mounted on wheels. These allow water to flow through the hose even when partially wound, so the hose can be stored neatly yet always ready for immediate use. Whichever type of hose you choose, you should make certain that it is long enough that it can reach all parts of the garden; some types may be lengthened with an extension.

A flat hose is mounted on its own reel and cannot be used unless the entire hose is unreeled. Flat hoses are made in fixed lengths with connectors and nozzles prefitted. Some flat hoses kink readily unless they are laid in a straight line; they may also be difficult to wind up because all of the water must be drained out first.

HOSE REEL
A reel with a handle or wheels is easy to move around the garden. Some reels allow water to flow through the hose, even when partially wound.

Sprayers

Use sprayers, either portable devices or attachments fitted to the end of a hose, to apply pesticides, weedkillers, and fertilizers, and to water or mist-spray plants. Compression types, pumped up before use, are most suitable for general use; small trigger-pump sprayers are for misting house plants or applying pesticides to a few plants. For a large area, use a knapsack sprayer.

TRIGGER-ACTION HOSE ATTACHMENT
Nozzle allows spray to be adjusted to jet or mist
Trigger

FERTILIZER PULSE HOSE ATTACHMENT
Central chamber for fertilizer

COMPRESSION SPRAYER
The sprayer is pumped up with the handle and is suitable for treating large areas.

HOSE-END ATTACHMENTS
Most attachments simply allow the intensity and range of the water spray to be adjusted. Some have trigger action.

Garden sprinklers

A garden sprinkler automatically delivers a fine spray of water over a specific area. Because it works while unattended, it saves time and effort. It also distributes the water economically, since the spray, when applied over a long period, penetrates the soil better than water delivered from a watering can or hand-held hose. A sprinkler is generally attached to a garden hose.

There are various types of sprinkler to suit a variety of needs: some are best for a lawn, for example, while others are preferable for irrigating a flower bed or vegetable patch. The simplest is a standing sprinkler, which usually waters a limited, circular area. It is suitable for lawns but is liable to form puddles, so it must be moved around to achieve an even distribution. In a flower bed the spray is often obstructed by foliage, giving unsatisfactory results, although some models have a long spike to raise the head above the surrounding plants.

Other forms of sprinkler in which water pressure is used to rotate the sprinkler heads give better, more even coverage. Rotating sprinklers and pulse-jet sprinklers swing around to deliver water in a wide circle. Oscillating sprinklers deliver water over a rectangular area through a series of holes in a bar that rocks back and forth.

A traveling sprinkler (also called a walking sprinkler) is useful for large, level areas such as a big lawn; it is convenient but expensive. The sprinkler delivers spray over a rectangular area while being propelled along a straight track (usually a hose) by the force of the water. The rate of travel and size of area covered on either side of the track depend on the water pressure.

TYPES OF SPRINKLER

STANDING SPRINKLER
Standing sprinklers are intended primarily for use on lawns, most being mounted on a spike to push into the ground. They usually deliver water in a circle, but a few water in a semicircular, rectangular, or fan shape.

ROTATING SPRINKLER
Good for lawns, beds, and borders, this type of sprinkler covers a large circular area and applies the water evenly. The spray is delivered through nozzles on the arms, which are attached to a spinning pivot, driven by the force of the water. Those that are fitted with long stems are the best type for watering beds and borders.

PULSE-JET SPRINKLER
This type of sprinkler is invaluable for covering large, circular areas of lawn, beds, or borders. It has a single jet on a central pivot, which rotates in a series of pulses, ejecting spurts of water. Except on lawns, the delivery head is generally set on a tall stem for increased coverage.

OSCILLATING SPRINKLER
This is best used at ground level; it is not suitable for positions where surrounding foliage will interfere with the range of the spray. Water is sprayed through the brass jets in the oscillating arm. This sprinkler delivers water fairly evenly over a rectangular area, the size of which may be easily adjusted.

Underground sprinkler systems

These are permanent systems, ideal for irrigating lawns and rock gardens. They are unobtrusive and simple to operate and are best installed when the area needing irrigation is first constructed, preferably by a professional. PVC pipes and connecting joints are laid in the form of a grid so that they supply various watering heads, to which hoses or sprinklers are attached. The sprinkler from each head delivers an even supply of water to a given area.

Always continue watering until the ground is thoroughly wet, because this helps even out the distribution to any overlapping areas. This type of watering system is usually the most expensive: it requires anti-siphon valves to meet water authority standards, and possibly a water meter and other fittings.

Soaker hoses

Soaker (or seep) hoses are useful for irrigating lawns or rows of plants. They are hoses with small perforations along their length. With the holes facing upward, a soaker hose produces a fine spray over a rectangular area and can be used to water lawns. With the holes placed toward the ground, water is directed to the base of plants – an excellent way to irrigate vegetables and other plants grown in rows. Choose a soaker hose carefully, because some cannot be used as sprinklers, since their holes are so small that the water just trickles out even when the holes are facing upward.

Porous hoses are a variation on soaker hoses. A network of porous hoses enables water to seep slowly into the soil. They are particularly suitable for newly planted beds and borders. The connections may be varied and the system moved around as required on the soil surface, or the hoses may be buried 4–6in (10–15cm) below the surface as a permanent irrigation system.

Hose timers

Hose timers may be used with ordinary garden sprinklers or more elaborate watering systems. They fit between a tap and the hose or irrigation pipe. Most hose timers turn off the water after a predetermined time. The more sophisticated ones also turn on the water. Some may be linked to a soil-moisture detector that overrides the program if the ground is already sufficiently wet.

COMPUTERIZED TIMER
This allows you to irrigate plants while you are busy or away by programming watering times and duration in advance.

WATER TIMER
This can be set to turn off the water after a preset period, from about 5 minutes to 2 hours.

Trickle, or drip-feed, systems

These are used for plants that benefit from individual watering. The water drips gently beside the plant, minimizing soil disturbance around the roots. A trickle system works well in a shrub border, along a hedge, or for vegetables. It can also be used for plants in containers, growing bags, and windowboxes. Ideal in arid regions where water is scarce or very costly, a trickle system does not give plants more water than they need. However, unless fitted with a hose timer it can waste water. Also, it needs regular cleaning to prevent the tubes and drip heads from becoming blocked with algae and debris.

TRICKLE WATERING SYSTEM
The delivery hose is connected to a unit that filters the water and reduces the pressure. The water then flows along a network of tubes supported by spikes stuck into the ground. Systems of this kind can be extended by buying additional drip heads and lengths of tube.

Filter removable for cleaning
Connector for tube
Hose connection
Central unit reduces water pressure
Drip head
Spike
Cleaning tool

General garden equipment

In addition to tools for cultivating and maintaining the garden, a wide range of other accessories such as carrying equipment and planting aids may be useful, depending on your own individual requirements.

Wheelbarrows

Wheelbarrows are useful for transporting plants, soil, and materials such as compost and garden debris. They may be made of metal or plastic, the former being more durable. Painted metal soon rusts if the paint is chipped; even galvanized metal trays rust eventually. Plastic trays, although lighter, may split.

Most traditional wheelbarrows have an inflatable tire to cushion the load. Check regularly and inflate the tire as needed; an underinflated tire makes pushing the wheelbarrow very difficult, especially if the tray is heavily loaded. Garden carts, as barrows with two wheels and a single handle are usually called, are stable and easy to load and unload, but are less maneuverable than standard barrows on uneven ground.

Sheets and bags

A carrying sheet or bag is suitable for transporting light but bulky garden waste such as hedge clippings. When not in use, it takes up very little space. It should be lightweight,

CARRYING BAG

CARRYING SHEET

TRUG

with strong handles, and made of a tough, tearproof material, such as woven plastic. Carrying bags have a larger capacity than sheets. Trugs and baskets are good for light tasks, such as carrying flowers or fruit.

TYPES OF WHEELBARROW

TRADITIONAL WHEELBARROW
Most barrows have a single tire and a shallow tray, although some models may be fitted with an extension to increase their capacity.

GARDEN CART
For transporting large or heavy loads, this is generally preferable to a traditional wheelbarrow.

Plastic bags

Clear plastic bags are excellent for a number of purposes: preventing cuttings material from drying out after raking them, for example, and for covering cuttings in pots to raise humidity around them. Most food and freezer bags are suitable provided that they are not too thin, since they are then less effective at retaining moisture.

Kneelers and knee pads

A kneeler or knee pads, cushioned and covered with a waterproof material, make kneeling more comfortable, particularly when weeding or planting. Knee pads are simply strapped to the knees; they are often sold in only one size, so check that

Compost bins

A compost bin should have a lid to keep warmth in, easy access to the compost by slats or panels, and a capacity of at least 10cu ft (0.28cu m) to generate sufficient heat to accelerate the rotting process. Avoid wire mesh bins or those with large gaps between the slats, because they allow the heat generated to escape.

Traditional, wooden compost bins are available precut for easy

they fit before buying. Kneeling stools support the knees on a slightly raised platform and have hand rests to give support when kneeling down and standing up. They may also be turned upside down for use as a small stool for working at raised beds or greenhouse benches.

KNEELERS
A kneeling stool (top) can be inverted for use as a stool and is light to carry. A cushioned pad (bottom) keeps knees clear of damp, hard ground.

self-assembly. Plastic compost bins are generally more efficient than metal or wooden ones, because they conserve moisture and reduce the need to water. There are plastic bins available that may be rotated to turn the compost, but this does not necessarily make good compost more quickly than a well-designed, traditional bin (see SOILS AND FERTILIZERS, *Making a Compost Bin*, p.621).

Incinerators

Open-mesh incinerators, some of which may be folded up after use, are good for burning dry material such as twigs and leaves. Galvanized steel, drum-type incinerators are suitable for slowly burning damp, woody material. However, open burning, once a standard gardening practice, is now illegal in many areas; seek advice before you buy. Many gardeners prefer to recycle garden waste by shredding and composting it.

Shredders

A compost shredder chops woody or tough garden waste, such as old corn stems, hedge trimmings, and prunings, until it is fine enough to break down quickly on a compost pile. Shredders are usually electrically powered and should not be left outdoors when not in use. They are heavy to move around, so choose one with wheels, unless there is space to use and store it in one place.

For safety, make sure that the power is automatically disconnected when the hopper is removed (see "Electrical safety," p.550). The funnel should be easy to use, but you must not be able to touch the blades.

Power should cut out if inlet funnel is removed

Three sturdy legs provide stability for shredder

USING A SHREDDER
The inlet funnel should not allow direct access to the blades. Wear goggles and gloves to shield against flying debris and thorny stems.

Planting and sowing aids

General garden tools or household items are often used for planting and sowing; for example a stick or pencil, instead of a dibber, will make a planting hole. Specialized tools, however, do make some tedious and repetitive jobs simpler and quicker.

Seed sowers and planters
These facilitate accurate and even sowing of seed. There are four main types: shakers, plungers, wheeled sowers, and seed-tray sowers.
Shakers are hand-held devices that may be used for sowing seed in prepared drills. Skill is required to ensure even seed distribution.
Plungers insert each seed individually to a predetermined depth.
Wheeled seed sowers are good for distributing seeds evenly in an outdoor drill. With a long handle, they can be worked from a standing position, making sowing less tiring.
Seed-tray sowers are thin, plastic or wooden boards with molded protrusions on one side. When pressed onto the sowing medium they firm the surface and make evenly spaced holes for sowing seed.

Bulb planters
A bulb planter is useful if planting a number of bulbs individually; for planting groups of small bulbs, a trowel or hand fork is better. A bulb planter removes a plug of soil or sod, which is then replaced on top of the bulb after planting; models with a clawlike action release the plug by pressure on the handle.

Gardening gloves

There is a wide range of gardening gloves for various purposes: some keep hands clean when working with soil or other media; others also provide protection against thorns.

Leather and fabric gloves are useful for tasks such as pruning roses to guard against thorns. When buying leather ones, check that the leather extends far enough to protect all of your palm. All-leather or suede gloves give very good protection but may be uncomfortably hot in warm weather. Gauntlet types cover the wrists and lower forearms.

Many gloves are made of fabric and vinyl. Some are impregnated with vinyl, others just have a vinyl grip on the palms. They are good for most jobs and keep hands cleaner than fabric alone. Vinyl-coated gloves are useful for messy jobs, such as mixing concrete, but are too thick for jobs needing a sensitive touch.

FABRIC WITH VINYL GRIP

SUEDE GAUNTLETS

SUEDE AND FABRIC

COTTON FABRIC

Dibbers and widgers

A dibber is a pencil-shaped tool used for making planting holes. Use a small dibber to transplant seedlings or insert cuttings, and a large one for transplanting vegetables such as leeks that require a wide hole to allow space for growth, and for planting through a sheet mulch. A widger, which is like a narrow spatula, is good for lifting seedlings and rooted cuttings with the minimum of root disturbance.

Garden lines

A garden line is used mainly in vegetable plots as a guide for forming straight rows, but it is also invaluable for other tasks, such as marking out areas when planning or designing, or forming a straight edge when planting a hedge or constructing a wall or patio.

GARDEN LINE
Most garden lines have a pointed stake at either end for inserting into the ground. Grooves allow you to stretch a level line between the stakes.

Sieves

Garden sieves generally have a mesh of ⅛–½in (3–12mm) and are used to separate out coarse material from soil or other medium. Choose a sieve with a large mesh to remove twigs and stones from soil before sowing, potting up, or planting; use one with a smaller mesh when covering fine seeds after sowing. Those with a wire mesh tend to be more effective and durable than plastic ones.

Thermometers

A greenhouse thermometer measures the current air temperature. A minimum-maximum thermometer records both the lowest and highest temperatures; it is the best type for both garden and greenhouse use, since it also helps determine the warmest and coldest parts of the garden. A soil thermometer registers soil temperature and is helpful in deciding when to sow seed.

MINIMUM-MAXIMUM THERMOMETER

GREENHOUSE THERMOMETER

Rain gauges

A rain gauge is used for measuring amounts of rainfall or irrigation; it is helpful for identifying areas of the garden that are affected by rain shadow. It should have clear markings and a smooth inside surface for easy cleaning. Many gauges have a short spike for inserting into the ground.

Measurements are clear so that water level is easy to read

Spike for stability

PLASTIC RAIN GAUGE

PLANTING AND SOWING TOOLS

SMALL DIBBER

WOODEN GARDEN DIBBER FOR OUTDOOR USE

BULB PLANTER

WIDGER

WHEELED SEED SOWER

METAL GARDEN DIBBER

WIRE-MESH SIEVE

SIEVE WITH FINE PLASTIC MESH

Ties and supports

Ties are used for various purposes in the garden, but in particular to secure a climbing, scrambling, or fragile plant. Ties must be secure without constricting the stem. Use a light material such as twine or raffia on soft-stemmed plants, which are damaged easily. Supports are needed to protect some plants from wind or rain.

General ties

Garden string or twine in 3-ply is adequate for most tying jobs. Raffia, which is good for binding joins after grafting and as a lightweight tie, and soft strings, such as green twine, may disintegrate after a year or so. Clear plastic tape and special rubber ties are excellent for use in grafting. Tar-impregnated string or polypropylene twine is a reliable, weather-resistant tie but, if used to secure plants to a support, may need to be loosened and retied annually.

Plastic-coated tying wire is strong and, since it lasts for several years, needs adjusting as the plant grows. It is good for attaching labels to training wires or as a trellis and joining stakes. It may come on a reel with a convenient built-in cutter.

Plant rings

These are split rings of wire; plastic-covered rings are also available. Plant rings are designed to be opened and closed easily around a

plant stem and its support. They are suitable for light jobs, such as attaching a house plant to a stake.

Tree ties

Rubber tree ties are strong, durable, and useful for securing a young tree to a stake. They should be easily adjustable so that an expanding stem is not constricted. Select one with a buffer so that the stake does not chafe the stem, or use a padded tie in a figure-eight form (see also "Tree ties," p.65). Nail ties to the stakes.

Wall hardware

Specially designed plant stickers may be used for tasks such as securing the stem of a climber directly to a

wall or any other support. Lead-headed nails are stronger, and they have the additional advantage of a soft spur that may be bent over to attach stems and small branches to a wall.

Vine eyes hold stretched wires to which wall plants are then secured. On wall masonry, use flat vine eyes; for lumber and wall anchors, screw in eyelet vine eyes.

Stakes

Bamboo stakes are excellent for supporting single-stemmed plants, but they eventually split and rot. More permanent and expensive are PVC stakes and plastic-covered steel rods. Support clumps of border plants with metal link or ring stakes (see PERENNIALS, "Staking," p.190). Trees and standard roses should be supported with sturdy wooden stakes.

Labels and markers

Labels for garden use should be durable, weather resistant, and large enough to contain all the information you want to note. Plastic labels are cheap and may be reused; if written on with pencil, they should remain legible for a season. Most plastic labels discolor gradually with age and become brittle, but they are ideal for labeling trays of seeds and cuttings. Looped labels and those with ties may be secured around the stem of a plant and are useful if labels at eye level are required.

For more permanent, water-resistant markers, use those coated with a black material; these are written on by scratching through to the white plastic beneath, but they cannot be marked with a new name. Aluminum labels, which are more expensive, will last almost indefinitely, but the lettering may need to be renewed every few years.

Netting

Netting is available in various materials and mesh sizes for a range of uses, such as supporting plants, protecting fruit from birds, and shading greenhouse plants (see "Shading," p.570). For plant support, choose a mesh of 2in (5cm) or more; it may be hard to disentangle plants from a smaller mesh. For many annual climbers and some clematis, thin, flexible plastic netting is adequate; heavier plants need semirigid plastic nets. For fruit protection, use commercial plastic netting with a mesh of 1/2–3/4in (1–2cm). Protect seedlings and winter vegetables from birds with 1in (2.5cm) mesh

netting. Wire netting may be placed around plants to provide protection from animals such as rabbits. It is also useful for reinforcing concrete when constructing a pond or trough.

Use a plastic snow fence to protect plants in exposed sites (see Windbreaks, p.605). Knitted plastic netting may deteriorate in about four years, whereas molded plastic should last at least twice as long. Windbreak webbing is even more long-lasting but very obtrusive. Durability is less important if a temporary windbreak is needed.

NETTING

PLASTIC NETTING
Shade netting

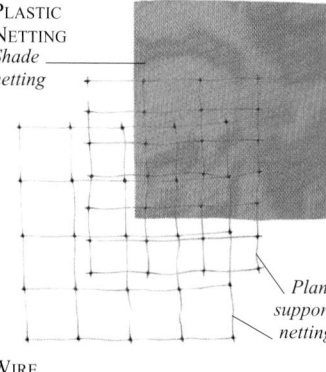

Plant support netting

WIRE NETTING

Chicken wire

Pig wire

WALL HARDWARE

FLAT VINE EYE

EYELET VINE EYE

LEAD-HEADED NAIL WITH SPUR

PLANT SUPPORTS AND TIES

STAKES AND SUPPORTS
Tree stake
Bamboo stake
Rose stake
Green bamboo stake
Moss totem
Split stake

TREE TIE

GARDEN TWINE

ROSE TIE

PLASTIC TIES

PLANT RINGS

TWIST TIES

RING STAKE

LINK STAKES

Pots and trays

Pots are available in a wide range of sizes, but there are two basic shapes: round and square. Although round pots are more traditional, square pots hold more medium for the same width and pack neatly together, thereby saving space. Round pots are classified by the inside diameter at the rim; square ones by the length of the rim along one side. Most pots have slightly sloping sides so that a plant and its root ball may be easily removed intact for repotting or planting out.

Most pots are made of clay (terracotta) or plastic. Clay is traditional, heavier, and more expensive; plastic, however, is more common, lighter, and cheaper. Most plastic pots are manufactured from polypropylene, which deteriorates in cold weather. Pots made of a polypropylene/polyethylene mix do not become brittle in cold weather and are preferable for using outdoors. Pots made of polyethylene only are cheapest and least durable.

Standard pots are at least as deep as they are wide; they are the most common type of pot. Bulb or seed pans are one-half as tall as they are wide at the top; they are useful for germinating seeds. Azalea pots are three-fourths as tall as they are wide at the top; they are often used commercially for plants with relatively small rootballs, such as evergreen azaleas. Use sweet pea tubes for very deep-rooted seedlings. For plants that will remain in the pot for some time, long Toms are preferred.

TRAYS AND CELL PACKS
These are used for sowing seeds, inserting cuttings, or growing on young plants. Use a rigid, outer tray to hold flimsy, single-use inserts containing plastic cells. Cell packs are useful for pricking out seedlings and sowing seeds singly.

POTS AND PANS
Pots as well as other containers, such as troughs and urns, are used for cultivating and displaying plants both indoors and outside. The smaller pots, pans, and azalea pots are suitable for propagating and growing on young plants.

Ornamental terracotta pots

Standard pots

Large standard pot

Azalea pot

Seed pan

Pans

Seed, seedling, and cutting pots

Other special-use pots include lattice pots (which have mesh sides), hydroculture pots (a form of double pot), and forcing pots, which are placed over plants to exclude light. Tarpaper ring pots, sometimes used for greenhouse tomato culture, are bottomless and hold medium on top of a growing aggregate.

Degradable pots and pellets
These are good for plants that resent root disturbance, since they can be planted out into the bed. A plant's roots grow through the sides and base of the pots into the surrounding ground. They are generally made from compressed peat and various other fibers (often sphagnum moss and wood fiber, sometimes impregnated with fertilizer).

Peat pellets are good for seeds and rooting cuttings and must be expanded with water before being used. Many gardeners create their own degradable pots from cones made from double-thickness newspaper.

Pot saucers
These are particularly useful for indoor use, when watering plants from beneath and to catch surplus water, which should then always be emptied to prevent waterlogging the growing medium. Saucers are available to match clay or plastic pots.

Seed trays
Traditional wooden seed trays have largely been replaced by plastic ones, which are easier to clean but often more fragile. Very thin plastic trays are cheap and flexible but are unlikely to last more than a year or two. Strong plastics are more rigid and expensive; they may become brittle and split with age but, if stored away from sunlight and extreme cold when not in use, they should last for several years.

Which material?

Plastic pots are:
- lightweight and ideal where less weight is important (on indoor shelves or balconies);
- inexpensive;
- easy to clean;
- durable, although they may eventually split or crack;
- more or less impermeable, so medium dries out more slowly than in clay pots;
- good for use with capillary watering systems (see p.571);
- available in various colors.

Clay pots are:
- heavy and stable, so are good for large plants that might be top-heavy in a plastic pot;
- expensive but attractive, so they are often preferable for displaying plants;
- difficult to clean;
- breakable and, unless frostproof, may crack or flake;
- porous, so the medium is less likely to become waterlogged, although plants may need more frequent watering;
- excellent for alpines, because they provide extra drainage;
- fair for capillary watering systems (see p.571).

Cell packs
With cell packs or modular systems, plant roots are not damaged when separating each unit, whereas seedlings grown in seed trays suffer some initial root damage when transplanted. Expanded plastic foam trays with individual planting cells insulate the medium, encouraging growth. They are useful for seeds or pricked-out seedling. They are as expensive as good-quality polypropylene seed trays but do not last as long.

LONG TOM
This pot suits deep-rooted plants that would be restricted by a standard pot.

TARPAPER RING POT
This specialized bottomless pot holds medium over a growing aggregate.

SWEET PEA TUBES
These are for growing seedlings that develop long or brittle taproot systems.

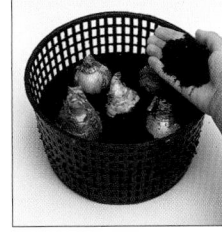

BULB BASKET
This basket protects bulbs from animals and is also easy to lift after flowering.

BIODEGRADABLE POTS
Use for propagating plants that resent root disturbance when transplanted.

LATTICE POT
This pot for aquatics lets in water, but it should be lined with burlap to retain soil.

2
GREENHOUSES
AND FRAMES

MANY PEOPLE RESIST the idea of installing a greenhouse in the mistaken belief that it is always expensive or that it requires extensive specialized gardening knowledge to maintain and use it properly. Not so. As well as being the perfect all-weather gardening space, a greenhouse can be an extremely cost-effective investment, allowing you to propagate and grow plants that can later be transferred outside to the garden itself at relatively little cost. Cold frames, like greenhouses, are a boon to gardening and can easily be integrated into the smallest of spaces. Gardening under cover more than compensates for the initial cost and effort, and it opens up an entire world of gardening pleasures.

Gardening under cover

Greenhouses, cold frames, and cloches (covers) are useful additions to any style of garden and are available in a range of sizes to fit whatever space is available. Each type of structure has a distinctive function, but they are usually used in conjunction with each other. The most productive gardens use all three.

Unheated structures

Unheated greenhouses are used primarily to advance or extend the growing season of hardy and half-hardy plants. Cold frames fulfill a similar function, although they are also often used for hardening off plants that have been propagated in the greenhouse and for storing dormant plants. Cloches are used *in situ* over plants in the garden itself.

Heated structures

A heated greenhouse is far more versatile than either an unheated greenhouse or a cold frame, and it allows a much wider variety of plants to be grown. These include many frost-tender species that do not grow satisfactorily in temperate or cold climates without protection. In addition, a heated greenhouse provides a suitable environment in which to propagate plants.

GREENHOUSE STYLE
This traditional-style greenhouse is an integral part of the garden, which extends right up to the sides of the greenhouse. The hedges and trees provide shelter, but they are not close enough to reduce light penetration significantly. The wooden framework will need to be treated every year or so with wood preservative to give weather resistance, but otherwise only minimal maintenance is required.

ELEGANT DESIGN
Greenhouses with plastic-covered frames can be extremely attractive as well as functional. This one is a decorative garden feature in its own right.

Siting the greenhouse

A greenhouse is best positioned so that it blends in with the overall garden design. It should be positioned in a sheltered site where enough light is available for the plants to grow and thrive. Too much shade will limit the range of plants that may otherwise be grown easily, whereas an exposed site will make the greenhouse expensive to heat or may mean that the plants are not adequately protected on cold nights.

Early planning

It is always worth spending the time to make sure you have chosen the right spot before buying a greenhouse. If possible, make detailed notes in winter or spring of where shadows are cast in the garden by houses and any neighboring garages, trees, or other large, nearby features. Do not site a greenhouse where it will be in shade for more than a few hours each day. Orienting the greenhouse north–south by its longest axis makes the best use of light in summer. For raising annuals and vegetables in spring, or overwintering tender specimens, an east–west orientation provides good light for much of the day.

If there is a possibility that you will want to extend the greenhouse in the future, or build a second smaller one, allow enough space on the site to meet your current and future needs.

Free-standing greenhouse

The best place to site a free-standing greenhouse is in a sheltered, light area away from buildings and large trees. If the site is high or exposed, choose a position that is sheltered by a hedge that acts as a windbreak, or build a fence or other screen. Windbreaks should not cast too much shade onto the greenhouse itself, however. They need not be tall; an 8ft (2.5m) hedge provides shelter for a distance of 40ft (12m) or more.

Do not position a free-standing greenhouse near or between buildings, since this could create a wind tunnel that may damage the greenhouse and the plants inside. Locations at the bottom of a slope or near walls, hedges, or fences on the side of a slope should not be used to site a greenhouse, because cold air may become trapped there (see CLIMATE AND THE GARDEN, "Frost pockets and frost damage," p.601).

Lean-to greenhouse

Place a lean-to greenhouse against a wall that receives both sun and shade. Do not site it where there is sun for most of the day; otherwise, the greenhouse may overheat in summer, even with shading and a good ventilation system.

Access

Bear in mind the need for easy access. A site reasonably close to the house is preferable to one at a distance. Also make sure that there is a clear area in front of the greenhouse door for loading and unloading. Any paths leading to the greenhouse should be level. They should preferably have a hard, resilient surface and be wide enough to accommodate a wheelbarrow.

Utilities

Choose a greenhouse site that will be accessible to water and electricity connections, if these services are needed. Consider including both hot and cold water for convenience, especially in winter. Although electricity is not essential for heating, it is necessary for lighting as well as for some thermostatic controls, timing switches, heating cables and mats, and other items.

POSITIONING THE GREENHOUSE

If the greenhouse is used mostly in the summer, its longer axis should run north to south. If good light in spring is a priority, however – when the sun is lower in the sky – orient the greenhouse east to west to make the best use of available light.

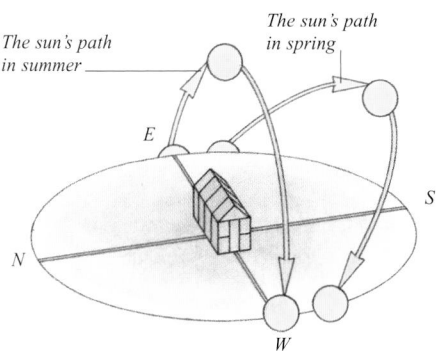

The sun's path in summer
The sun's path in spring

CHOOSING THE SITE

An open but sheltered site is best for a greenhouse – it should not be positioned in the path of a wind tunnel. If there is no natural protection from the wind, construct a windbreak.

This greenhouse is in an open position, away from the shade cast by buildings and trees.

A line of trees provides shelter from the prevailing wind.

GOOD POSITION

POOR POSITIONS

This greenhouse lies in the shade cast by the nearby tree. Leaf drop may cause problems if the tree is deciduous.

This greenhouse lies directly in the path of a possible wind tunnel. It is also too close to the hedge, which may make maintenance difficult.

A wind tunnel may be created between 2 adjacent buildings.

Shade cast in summer

Shade cast in winter

Choosing a greenhouse

Before buying a greenhouse, carefully consider how it will be used in order to select the most suitable style, size, and materials. For example, a greenhouse that is used as a garden room will differ significantly from one that is used to propagate plants. If growing tropical and subtropical plants, an attractively shaped greenhouse, perhaps with room for staging in the center, might enhance the floral display.

Many different styles of greenhouse are available. Some make best use of space or provide optimum ventilation; others conserve heat well or allow better light penetration. When priorities have been decided, the final choice of style will depend on personal preference.

Conventional greenhouses

The more conventional types of greenhouse are suitable for a very wide range of plants. They include traditional span, Dutch light, three-quarter span, lean-to, and Mansard (or curvilinear) greenhouses. All of

TRADITIONAL SPAN

DUTCH LIGHT

these may have an aluminum or wooden framework, and either all-glass or part-solid walls (except Dutch light greenhouses). Conventional greenhouses also have a wide range of compatible accessories, including staging and shelves.

Traditional span
The vertical sides and even-span roof of a traditional span greenhouse are extremely practical in terms of

growing space and headroom. For raising seedlings and growing border crops, a traditional span greenhouse is likely to provide the best use of space for the least cost.

Dutch light
The sloping sides of Dutch light greenhouses are designed to allow in maximum light, so these greenhouses are suitable for border crops, especially low-growing ones such

as lettuce. The large panes of glass (lights) are expensive to replace because of the size – the traditional dimensions are 30¾ x 59in (77 x 145cm). The glass panes slide into the frame and are secured using cleats attached with galvanized nails.

The panes of glass on the roof overlap slightly to keep out rain and increase rigidity of the panes. This may cause loss of heat, if the panes overlap too loosely.

THREE-QUARTER SPAN

LEAN-TO

MANSARD

Three-quarter span
A three-quarter span greenhouse is positioned with one of its sides against a wall. Light is a little more restricted than in a free-standing model, so this type of greenhouse is best positioned beside a sunny wall, although this may mean that additional shading is required in summer. The wall provides extra warmth and insulation in the greenhouse, especially if it is a house wall (see also "Lean-to," right).

Lean-to
Where there is insufficient space for a free-standing structure, a lean-to greenhouse is an invaluable choice, particularly if a mainly decorative showhouse is favored.

Many are similar in appearance to conservatories and may be used as garden rooms. Installing electricity, natural gas, or a water supply in a lean-to that is adjacent to a house wall is cheaper and generally involves less work than laying wires

or pipes to a greenhouse that is some distance from the house. In addition, the warmth of the house wall may reduce the level of heating required. The wall stores heat, from both the sun (especially if the wall is south-facing) and the home heating system, which is then released into the greenhouse.

The wall also provides good insulation, so that less heat escapes from a lean-to than from many other types of greenhouse.

Mansard
The Mansard (curvilinear) greenhouse has slanting sides and roof panels that are designed to allow maximum entry of available light. The full benefit is gained only in an open position with no shade from surrounding buildings or trees. A Mansard greenhouse is suitable for plants that need maximum light during the winter, when daylight hours are short and light levels are also correspondingly low.

DOME-SHAPED

POLYGONAL

ALPINE HOUSE

Specialized greenhouses

There are many specialized types of greenhouse, including dome-shaped, polygonal, alpine house, conservation, mini, and polytunnel, all of which differ markedly in appearance from the more conventional types. Some are designed as highly decorative garden features in their own right, while others may offer particularly good value or be suited to specific types of plant.

Dome-shaped

This is an elegant design that is particularly useful in exposed positions, since it is stable and offers less wind resistance than traditional greenhouses. Light transmission is excellent, because the multiangled glass panes and aluminum frame allow in maximum light. Dome-shaped structures may have limited headroom around the edge, and plants may also be difficult to reach. Extensions are not generally available, and fixtures may be limited to those produced by the manufacturer.

Polygonal

Octagonal and other polygonal greenhouses are frequently chosen where appearance is important, and they may provide a focal point within the garden. They are generally more expensive than traditional greenhouses of similar size and, because they are not very common, there may be a limited choice of accessories. The irregular shape may also restrict growing space. Fitting replacement panes of glass in a polygonal greenhouse is more difficult than in a conventional structure.

Alpine house

This type of greenhouse is traditionally wooden-framed with louver vents extending all along the sides for the most effective ventilation. Usually, alpine houses are barely heated even in winter, so less insulation is required than for a warmer house. Unsuitable for tender plants, they are used for plants that thrive in bright, well-ventilated conditions, yet which require some overhead protection from dampness and rain. Their shape is similar to that of a traditional span greenhouse.

CONSERVATION

MINI

POLYTUNNEL

Conservation greenhouse

This type of greenhouse has many special features that are designed to save as much energy as possible. The roof panels are angled to allow optimum light penetration in winter yet reduce hot summer sun, and mirrored surfaces are also used to reflect light within the greenhouse itself. Solar collectors may be used to store heat in winter. Double glazing and insulation are included as standard features.

Mini-greenhouse

This provides a useful, low-cost introduction to greenhouse gardening. Mini-greenhouses are usually aluminum and placed against a wall or fence. They should preferably face southeast or southwest so that maximum light penetrates. It is the best choice if only a small number of plants is to be grown, since space is limited. However, there is often useful space beneath the staging for overwintering plants or for storage.

Access may be a problem – all work needs to be done from the outside. Ventilation may be inadequate, and rapid temperature changes often occur. This type of house is normally used only during the spring peak growing season.

Plastic polytunnel greenhouse

Where visual appearance is not important and low-cost protection is required – such as in the vegetable garden – a polytunnel greenhouse has many benefits. It consists of a large, tunnel-shaped frame covered with heavy-duty transparent plastic sheets. It is widely used for crops that require some protection but not the warm conditions of a traditional greenhouse. Polytunnels keep out some of the winter cold and provide useful wind protection throughout the year. Since they are light and relatively easy to move, they are often used in plots where crop rotation is carried out.

For a large growing area, commercial polytunnels are a cost-effective investment, but for a small garden, a more traditional shape may be a better choice. Some polytunnels include staging, although most are intended primarily for growing crops at ground level, directly in the soil, in pots, or in growing bags.

Ventilation may be a problem. The door offers a reasonably efficient method of ventilation, especially in large tunnels with openings at each end. Some have sides that roll up. The plastic sheeting should be routinely checked and replaced every year or two, since it gradually becomes brittle and likely to rip, as well as opaque, thereby restricting light penetration.

Choosing the size

You home greenhouse will almost inevitably seem too small once it is filled with plants so, if possible, buy one that can be extended. Although a large greenhouse costs more to heat than a small one, it is possible to partition off a section in winter, and leave the remainder unheated (see "Thermal screens," p.568).

Space considerations

A greenhouse that is used primarily for ornamentals should have plenty of room inside for staging, which may be tiered, and possibly a central or end display. To provide space for propagation and growing on, it may be necessary to divide up the space with a partition. Alternatively, use a cold frame for propagation.

Length, width, and height

A length of 8ft (2.5m) and a width of 6ft (2m) are the minimum, practical dimensions for a general-purpose, traditional greenhouse. A smaller greenhouse than this limits the range of plants that may be grown and may make it difficult to control the environment. Drafts and rapid heat buildup in summer tend to be more of a problem in small greenhouses and may lead to sudden fluctuations in temperature. In greenhouses that are more than 6ft (2m) wide, it may also be difficult to reach pots and ventilation toward the back of the staging. Erecting staging or platforms to a width of 2ft (60cm) on either side allows a path of the same width to run down the middle.

If border crops are to be grown, choose a greenhouse that is 8ft (2.5m) wide with borders to a width of 3ft (1m). A width of 8ft (2.5m) is also suitable if a wider path is required for a wheelchair or to enable a wheelbarrow to be used easily.

Many small greenhouses have low eaves and comparatively low ridges, which make it tiring to work over the border or staging for long periods. To gain more height, build the greenhouse on a brick base, or dig out a sunken path.

Choosing the materials

Greenhouses are made in a variety of materials. The most important considerations when choosing both the framework and glazing for the greenhouse are practicality, expense, and the amount of maintenance required. The appearance of the materials may also be important.

BUYING A GREENHOUSE

Before buying a greenhouse, use the following as a checklist. It may prevent disappointment later.

Ridge height should be at least 5¹/₂ft (1.7m). Remember to allow for protruding roof-ventilator openings.

Roof ventilators are usually inadequate as supplied. The total ventilation area should equal one-sixth of the floor area. Extra ventilators may be needed.

Glass should be easy to replace; use panes of a standard size – 24in (60cm) square or 18 x 24in (45 x 60cm). The large panes of Dutch light greenhouses are expensive to replace. Consider double glazing if winter temperatures fall below 10˚F (-12˚C), although this adds considerably to the cost.

Crossbracing on aluminum alloy greenhouses must be strong enough to make the structure rigid.

Doors may be hinged or sliding. They must be wide enough: 24in (60cm) is the minimum practical width. For wheelchair or wheelbarrow access, they should be wider and without a lip. Sliding doors are easily adjusted for ventilation and are less likely to slam in wind than hinged doors. Check that doors are a good fit when closed; otherwise, they may let in drafts.

Eave height determines the headroom. It should be at least 4¹/₂ft (1.35m) for ease of working.

Use ground anchors if the structure is not secured to a brick base.

A kick panel at the foot of the door minimizes the risk of breaking the glass panel.

Gutters and downspouts reduce the risk of water cascading from the roof and damaging the plants nearby.

A base may be an optional extra. Bear this in mind when comparing prices, since most wooden-framed greenhouses need one. Some have a step that makes wheelchair access and use of a wheelbarrow difficult.

Side ventilators allow free circulation of air. Louver windows must close tightly to minimize heat loss in cold weather.

Use base insulation to reduce heat loss in the winter, unless border crops are to be grown.

The framework

Wooden frameworks have been the traditional choice and are generally considered to be the most attractive. They may be expensive, however, and are also heavy to construct. If possible, choose a durable hardwood. Cedar, cypress, and redwood are excellent choices. They are rot-resistant, do not warp easily, and, if treated every year or two with a quality wood preservative, retain their color well.

Some woods are regionally abundant or are the traditional choice. Check with a local contractor or building supply store to determine which wood is best for your needs and budget (see also "Wooden framework," p.577).

Greenhouses with aluminum alloy frames are almost completely maintenance-free. They do not retain heat quite as well as wooden

CONSTRUCTION MATERIALS

WOOD
A wooden frame is the traditional choice for garden greenhouses. Hardwoods are low maintenance.

ALUMINUM
Aluminum alloy frames are light but extremely sturdy and need only minimum maintenance.

STEEL
Plastic-coated steel frames are very strong but must be treated regularly to prevent rust.

frames, but the difference is minimal and should not be considered a serious disadvantage.

Galvanized steel is also often used for greenhouse frames. Steel frames are light and easy to construct but extremely strong. They are cheaper than wooden or aluminum frames but must be painted regularly (see "Metal framework," p.577). Aluminum and steel frames are narrower than wooden ones and allow larger panes of glass to be used, resulting in better light penetration.

Glass panes

Regular glass is the most satisfactory glazing material for a greenhouse. It allows excellent light penetration, far better than modern high-tech substitutes. It is easy to clean, does not discolor, and retains

considerably more heat than plastic glazing materials. Glass is not as durable as plastic glazing, however, so breakages and cracks may be a problem, since damaged panes must be replaced quickly.

Plastic glazing

Plastics are generally more expensive and less durable than glass. They discolor more readily and also tend to become scratched over time, which is both unsightly and, more important, may cut down on the amount of light that is transmitted if the discoloring is severe.

Acrylic sheets are used to glaze the curved eaves of many greenhouses because the acrylic may be shaped easily to give an elegant outline to the structure. Condensation occurs more readily on its surface than on a

conventional glass pane. Rigid polycarbonate sheets are also often used to glaze greenhouses. They are easy to handle, lightweight, virtually unbreakable, and have good insulating properties. They are relatively easily scratched, however, and tend to discolor.

Twin-walled polycarbonate has particularly good insulating qualities, but its opacity may be a major problem in the greenhouse.

Sizing

Most local glass merchants will cut glass panes to size for little cost. However, it is important to make sure that any measurements you give are accurate. Calculate them carefully, making sure that there will be sufficient clearance for the glass to engage with the mounting system

GLAZING MATERIAL

Rigid plastic glazing material is light and easy to install. This is twin-walled polycarbonate, which provides good insulation.

that is to be used. If plastic glazing material is used, it will be supplied in sheets; it is not usually difficult to cut to size at home using a sharp craft knife and straightedge.

Erecting the greenhouse

A greenhouse requires far less maintenance and lasts much longer if it is properly erected in the first place. The information listed below is necessarily of a general nature because it applies to many different greenhouse types and designs. Always follow the manufacturer's instructions for particular advice. If in doubt on any point, check with either the supplier or the greenhouse manufacturer.

Before beginning to construct a greenhouse, look into the applicable local building codes. Greenhouses often require a building permit, and building inspectors may well be involved throughout the process.

Preparing the site

Always erect a greenhouse on firm, level ground; otherwise, the frame may warp and become twisted and cause the glass to crack. The site must first be cleared of weeds, since persistent weeds are very difficult to eradicate when the greenhouse is erected in position. If the site selected for the greenhouse has been recently dug over, allow the soil to settle for a few weeks, and then compact it with a heavy roller.

Foundations

Aluminum greenhouses that are smaller than 6ft wide and 8ft long (2 x 2.5m) do not usually require a thick concrete base. Simply dig a hole at each corner approximately 10–18in (25–45cm) deep, then wedge in the ground anchors (see p.566) with stone chips and pour in a concrete mix to secure them.

If a more substantial foundation is required, dig a trench approximately 10in (25cm) deep, filling it with 6in (15cm) of compacted stone chips. Mount the anchoring bolts in place and finish off with poured concrete or paving slabs, making sure that the ground is level.

Brick bases

A brick base must be constructed to the precise measurements provided by the manufacturer, on solid concrete footings deep enough to withstand your winter conditions. Check with local contractors for the footing depths recommended for your area. For further instructions, see *How to Make a Concrete Footing*, p.590.

Wooden greenhouses

The sections of a wooden greenhouse are usually supplied complete and only need to be bolted together and then attached to the base.

Base

Either use interlocking concrete blocks for the base, or build a solid concrete foundation or brick base (see "Foundations" and "Brick bases," left and above).

Sides, gable ends, and roof

Before the greenhouse is delivered, check what kind of bolts or hardware are required and whether they will be supplied. First bolt the sides and gable ends together to form the main framework. Follow the supplier's advice for the exact method of attaching this to the base or founda-

tions, since designs vary. The foot of the frame may contain integral anchorage points for securely bolting it down. Bolt any internal partitions to the frame, then add the roof sections and bolt them in place.

Some wooden greenhouses are supplied as sections with unglazed frames, with the glass or plastic glazing supplied separately. Other wooden structures have preglazed frames, but these are heavy to move – two or more people may be needed to support them.

If the wood has not been treated and is not rot-resistant, it is important to paint all the woodwork with a preservative at this stage, before the greenhouse is glazed.

Glazing

If putty is to be used for glazing, it is usually supplied with the greenhouse. Apply it to the glazing bars, and seat the glass carefully. The glass panes are usually secured in place with galvanized steel or brass sprigs. If these are not supplied by the manufacturer, they may be purchased from a hardware store.

If a dry glazing system (that is, one that does not require putty) is to be used, simply follow the supplier's instructions.

Whichever method is used, glaze the sides and gable ends first, overlapping the panes by ½in (1cm). Use soft metal overlap clips to hold the glass panes firmly together.

BUILDING A BRICK BASE

If using a brick base for the greenhouse, lay proper foundations first. Check with the greenhouse manufacturer before building the base to make sure that the dimensions are correct. Also check your winter soil-freezing depth.

CONCRETE FOUNDATIONS

For solid greenhouse foundations, dig a trench to match the dimensions of the greenhouse, filling it with stone chips and a layer of concrete.

GLAZING BARS AND CLIPS FOR METAL GREENHOUSES

GLAZING BARS
These form the framework of the greenhouse.

W-SHAPED WIRE CLIP
Use this type of clip to hold glass and plastic panes firmly in place.

SPRUNG BAND CLIPS
An alternative to wire clips, these attach onto the frame.

Ventilators and door
Ventilators are supplied as an integral part of the preassembled sections, so the number you ordered should be in place. Screw on hinged doors and simply insert sliding doors into the runners.

Metal greenhouses

Greenhouses with metal frames are delivered in home-assembly kit form, and the frame is supplied in sections – the base, sides, gable ends, and roof. The sections are in turn divided into separate component pieces that need to be bolted together.

Base
Assemble the base first, making sure it is perfectly level and square to prevent any warping and twisting of the frame. Measure from each corner to the one diagonally opposite – the measurements must be the same. The base must be securely anchored; this is particularly important in windy or exposed areas.

If attaching ground anchors to a concrete foundation, use the anchor-

A GROUND ANCHOR

Rubble and concrete

Ground anchor

Small greenhouses may be secured using ground anchors. Wedge them in place with stone chips before pouring in a concrete mix.

ing bolts provided; otherwise, simply set the ground anchors in rubble and concrete at each corner of the base.

Sides, gable ends, and roof
Assemble the sides, gable ends, and roof sections in the sequence recommended by the manufacturer in the instruction sheet. The sides are usually put together first.

First make sure that everything has been included. Then, before assembling, lay out on the ground all the pieces for each section, in their correct relative positions. Bolt the pieces for each section (sides and gable ends) together. Decide at this point where the vents are to be positioned and leave suitable gaps for them, as necessary. Do not tighten the nuts until all the sections are fully assembled and have been loosely put together.

Bolt the sections together one to another, and then to the base, then bolt on the roof bars and ridge bar.

Ventilators
Ventilator frames are assembled separately, then bolted onto the roof and sides as required, before glazing. This gives greater flexibility than with wooden greenhouses when choosing both the number and position of ventilators. The hinges of roof ventilators usually slide in a groove in the molding.

Glazing
Glazing strips are usually used for metal greenhouses. Cut the strips to the appropriate length, and then press them into the grooves in the glazing bars – shaped pieces of metal that form the framework to hold the glass securely in position.

Glaze the sides of the greenhouse first, placing the glass squarely between the glazing bars, leaving about ⅛in (3mm) clearance on each side of the glass panes for the glazing clips to be attached. The upper panes of glass should overlap the lower ones by about ½in (1cm). Secure them with overlap glazing clips – pieces of metal bent into S shapes that hook over the lower pane and hold the upper one firmly in place.

Once each pane is in position, use glazing clips, pressing them into place between the glazing bars and panes to hold the glass. A little pressure will be required to overcome the natural spring in the metal.

Glaze the gable ends of the greenhouse and then the roof, using the same technique.

Hanging the door
Metal greenhouses usually have sliding doors. These should be bolted together and slid into the runners

Installing electricity, natural gas, and water

Installing an outdoor power supply is not a job for the amateur. The installation of electricity in a greenhouse must be properly carried out by a qualified electrician, although considerable savings may be made by excavating the trench for the cord yourself and then refilling it later when the job is completed. Alternatively, the cord may be run overhead if your greenhouse is close to the house and it will not be unsightly. Your electrician will be able to advise you whether or not this is a practical option. Armored, insulated cords and waterproof hardware should always be used for safety.

Electricity has many practical uses in the greenhouse: it provides power for heating, lighting, propagators, timers, heating cables, and electrically powered garden tools of various types.

Natural gas is useful for heating the greenhouse. If the greenhouse is sited close to the house, it may be possible to extend the system; otherwise, use an outside tank. Consult your local utility to discuss the feasibility and cost of installing lines for natural gas. You might save money by offering to do the digging yourself.

If you already have an outdoor faucet, you may be able to add a branch to its pipe and run it to the greenhouse. In regions with cold winters, either the system must be buried below the frost line or, if the greenhouse will not be used during the winter, provisions must be made to drain all the lines before the onset of severe cold.

provided in the end frame. A stop is supplied for bolting on afterward to prevent the door from coming off the runners if it is opened too quickly. The door should be glazed when it has been placed in position.

Installing the staging

The staging supplied by the manufacturer is designed to be bolted or screwed to the framework. This is best done at the same time as the greenhouse is erected, especially for octagonal and dome-shaped greenhouses, which have staging specially designed to fit. If solid staging is used, leave a gap of several inches between the inside of the greenhouse and the staging to allow free air circulation.

FITTING A PANE IN A METAL GREENHOUSE

Attach overlap glazing clips to the base of the pane. Wearing gloves, lift the pane into place, gently pressing the top edge into position before hooking the bottom edge onto the lower pane. Secure the pane with glazing clips (see inset), pressing them gently until they slot into position.

Creating the right environment

Creating the right balance of conditions in a greenhouse to suit the plants grown in it is the essence of successful greenhouse gardening.

For tender plants, the temperature maintained is vital. In a heated greenhouse, choose an efficient, reliable, and economical heater. In any greenhouse, good insulation to retain heat and keep out drafts must be balanced with the need for thorough ventilation. Shading is essential in most greenhouses during warm and hot months to help prevent the plants from overheating; see PRINCIPLES OF PROPAGATION, *Shading Greenhouses (Temperate climates)*, p.630.

Atmospheric humidity should be kept at a level that suits the plants being grown. Automatic methods of watering tend to increase humidity so, for most plants, special humidifiers may not be essential. Special lighting is often useful to increase the growth potential of plants.

Greenhouse temperature

The choice of plants to be grown in a greenhouse is determined largely by the temperature at which it is maintained (see "The greenhouse environment," p.351). There are four categories of greenhouse: cold, cool, temperate, and warm. The environment is controlled slightly differently in each type.

Cold

A cold greenhouse is not heated at all. Insulation (see p.568) is needed to keep out the worst of the winter cold, and some form of shading (see p.570) is needed in summer. Thorough ventilation (see p.569) is important throughout the year.

A cold greenhouse can be used to grow summer crops, to overwinter slightly tender plants where winters are mild, or to propagate cuttings (although a propagator will increase the success rate; see p.574). An unheated greenhouse may also permit an early display of spring bulbs.

An unheated greenhouse is suitable for alpines – some types are specifically designed to provide maximum ventilation for these plants (see "Alpine house," p.563), although any greenhouse with louver ventilators along the sides is adequate.

Cool/frost-free

A cool greenhouse is one that is heated just enough to keep out frost. This means that a minimum daytime temperature range between 41°F (5°C) and 50°F (10°C), and a nighttime temperature of no less than 35°F (2°C), is needed.

To be sure that these temperatures are maintained, a heater capable of a large temperature lift is a necessity in winter, in case the outside temperature falls many degrees below freezing. A gas heater with a thermostat (see p.568) is most likely to do this efficiently.

Insulation, thorough ventilation, and shading control are necessary, as with cold greenhouses.

A frost-free greenhouse may be used to grow all the types of plant mentioned for cold greenhouses. In addition, frost-tender plants can be overwintered, and summer crops or flowering pot plants grown. A propagator will be needed for germinating seeds. Young seedlings will benefit from the extra light provided by a grow lamp (see p.571).

Temperate

A slightly warmer greenhouse with a minimum daytime temperature range between 50°F (10°C) and 55°F (13°C), and with a minimum nighttime temperature of 45°F (7°C), is suitable for growing a good selection of hardy, half-hardy, and tender pot plants, as well as vegetables.

Additional warmth is necessary in spring for propagation, supplied by a propagator or by boosting the ordinary heating for the required period. Supplementary lighting from a grow lamp is useful. Shading and good ventilation are required, especially in warm and hot months.

Warm

A warm greenhouse has a daytime temperature range between 55°F (13°C) and 64°F (18°C) or higher, with a minimum nighttime temperature of 55°F (13°C). Such high temperatures allow the amateur gardener to grow a large range of plants,

THE GREENHOUSE EFFECT

Light passes through glass as short-wave radiation, warming everything inside, including floor, platforms, soil, and plants. Heat then reradiates from the warmed objects as long waves, which cannot pass through the glass, and so increases heat inside the greenhouse.

including tropical and subtropical ornamentals, fruits, and vegetables. Use a warm greenhouse for propagating plants and raising seedlings without propagation equipment, although a grow lamp will be useful.

Very good ventilation (preferably automatic), cooling pads, an efficient method of shading, and high humidity (see p.570) in hot weather are essential.

HOW TO BALANCE THE ENVIRONMENT OF A GREENHOUSE

	HEATING (see p.568)	INSULATION (see p.568)	VENTILATION (see p.569)	SHADING (see p.570)	HUMIDITY (see p.570)	WATERING (see p.571)	LIGHTING (see p.571)
COLD No minimum temperature	None.	Insulate against severely cold drafts and damp, foggy weather in winter.	Thorough ventilation is essential to prevent damp, stagnant conditions in winter.	Shade vulnerable plants in summer with a shading wash, blinds, meshes or fabric, or rigid sheets.	Unlikely to be a problem in summer. Maintain a "dry" atmosphere in winter by ventilating.	Water by hand in winter. Use a capillary system, soaker hose, or trickle system in summer.	Grow lamps are unlikely to be needed for the type of plants grown.
COOL Minimum temperature 35°F (2°C)	A thermostatically controlled electric heater is preferable, but gas or kerosene heaters may also be used. A cold alarm is useful if tender plants are grown.	In winter, as for a cold greenhouse. In spring, good insulation is extremely important if frost-tender plants are grown.	Ventilate freely, especially if a gas or kerosene heater is used, to disperse water vapor and toxic fumes.	Shade to control the temperature in summer – shading washes or blinds do this most efficiently. Install automatic blinds, if possible.	Damping down is beneficial to increase humidity in summer.	As for a cold greenhouse, except that an overhead system may also be used in summer.	Grow lamps may be useful, especially in spring when natural light is poor, for plants at an early stage of development.
TEMPERATE Minimum temperature 45°F (7°C)	A heater (preferably electric) with a thermostat is required. A cold alarm is also essential.	As for cold and cool greenhouses. Thermal screens are useful in spring for propagation.	As for a cool greenhouse. Automatic vent openers are extremely useful in summer.	As for a cool greenhouse.	Maintain high humidity in spring and summer, especially around cuttings and seedlings.	An automatic watering system is useful throughout the year.	Grow lamps are useful in winter and spring for extending daylength.
WARM Minimum temperature 55°F (13°C)	As for a temperate greenhouse.	Good insulation is essential throughout the year to minimize heating costs.	Automatic vent openers on several vents simplify temperature control enormously.	Automatic blinds are desirable in summer.	High humidity is required throughout the year.	As for a temperate greenhouse.	As for a temperate greenhouse.

Heating

It is important to maintain the correct temperature in the greenhouse for the range of plants you have chosen to grow. Select a heater that is powerful enough to maintain the required minimum temperature efficiently. Other factors to consider when choosing a greenhouse heater include convenience, the cost of installation, and running costs.

Electric heaters

These are generally the most reliable, efficient, and convenient to use in the cool or temperate greenhouse, although an electricity supply will be needed to run them (see "Installing electricity, natural gas, and water," p.566). They are usually thermostatically controlled, which means that no heat is wasted, and they do not require regular refueling or maintenance. In addition, electric heaters do not produce fumes or water vapor.

A number of different types of electric heater is available. These include fan heaters and waterproof tubular heaters, both of which heat the greenhouse effectively. Convector heaters are also used but these do not distribute heat as efficiently. Tubular heaters need to be fitted to the sides of the greenhouse, just above floor level. Other heaters may be moved around as desired.

Electric fan heaters are particularly useful because they promote good air circulation, which helps maintain an even temperature and minimizes the spread of disease. They may also be used to cool the greenhouse in warm weather if the heating element is switched off.

Natural gas or propane heaters

Gas heating systems can be run off your house lines (see "Installing electricity, natural gas, and water," p.566) or from an outside tank. They are not as convenient to use as electric heaters: although they may have thermostats, they may not be calibrated in degrees, so you will need to experiment.

If an outside tank is used, most suppliers will routinely check it to keep it filled, depending on the temperature. Consider having two bottles connected by an automatic switchover valve in case one runs out. Propane gas releases fumes and water vapor as it burns, so ventilation is important.

Kerosene heaters

These are not as efficient as electric or gas heaters in their use of fuel, because they are not controlled by a thermostat. Kerosene heaters may therefore be expensive to run if a high temperature needs to be maintained, since some energy may be wasted. However, they are inexpensive to buy in the first place, and there is no installation cost.

When using kerosene heaters, thorough ventilation is required, because some plant-toxic fumes and water vapor are produced as a byproduct of combustion; a humid, stagnant atmosphere may encourage disease if ventilation is poor. Other drawbacks include the need to transport and store fuel, and to check the fuel level and wick every day (to make sure it is burning cleanly).

Circulated hot water

Solid fuel (that is, coal, coke, and wood) hot water systems are now rarely used in greenhouses. Oil- and gas-fired circulated hot water systems are sometimes used, but seldom in small greenhouses.

Although the distribution of heat through hot water pipes provides good heat transfer, often only about 50 percent of the energy released is used. Greenhouses attached to a house may be heated by connecting them to the home heating system. Check with local contractors and utilities for details.

Thermometer and cold alarm

If the heater in a greenhouse is not thermostatically controlled, use a maximum/minimum thermometer to check that the correct overnight temperatures are being maintained for the plants being grown.

In regions where the temperature can be severe, a cold alarm is a useful safeguard if the greenhouse contains tender plants. If the air temperature unexpectedly drops to near freezing, for example through a power failure or heater breakdown, an alarm bell will sound remotely (this will usually be somewhere in your home), allowing you time to protect the plants.

A COLD ALARM

Install a cold alarm if growing tender plants that may be damaged or killed if the temperature falls.

INSULATION MATERIAL

Bubble plastic is useful for insulating a greenhouse and reduces heat loss considerably. Cut it to size, then attach it securely to the framework.

Insulation

Insulation in the greenhouse may reduce heating costs considerably. If a minimum temperature of 45°F (7°C) is required, for example, the cost of insulation may be recovered within just a few seasons – in a single winter in particularly cold areas. The higher the temperature to be maintained, and the colder the region, the more cost-effective insulation is likely to be. Care in choosing the right material is required, however, since some insulation materials may reduce the amount of light reaching the plants.

Double glazing

The most efficient method of insulating the entire greenhouse is to fit double glazing. This is best done at the time of construction, if possible. Double glazing is expensive, but the long-term money and energy savings can be great.

Flexible plastic insulation

Bubble plastic, which consists of double or triple skins of transparent plastic with air cells in between, is a very efficient method of insulation. A single layer of plastic sheeting is not as efficient as bubble plastic at reducing heat loss, but it is less expensive and does not cut out so much light. Plastic sheets can be used in winter as a form of double glazing. To attach the insulation material, use suction-pad fasteners or clips that fit into the greenhouse frame.

Thermal screens

These consist of sheets of clear plastic or translucent material, such as a cross-laminated fabric, that are attached to wires between the eaves and drawn horizontally across the greenhouse in the evening. They are useful for conserving heat at night, because they restrict the amount of heat that rises above the eaves, trapping the warmth lower down around the plants.

Vertical screens may also be used to partition off a heated section at one end of the greenhouse with plastic sheeting, leaving the remainder of the area unheated. Plants can be overwintered and early seedlings raised in the heated section.

Special kits for making thermal screens are available, or plastic sheeting and the necessary hardware may be obtained separately.

Base insulation

Base insulation on the floor of glass-to-ground greenhouses reduces heat loss significantly. In winter, place plastic foam panels along the foot of the glass panes to provide extra insulation, removing them before summer border crops are planted.

THERMAL SCREENS

Horizontal screen between the eaves

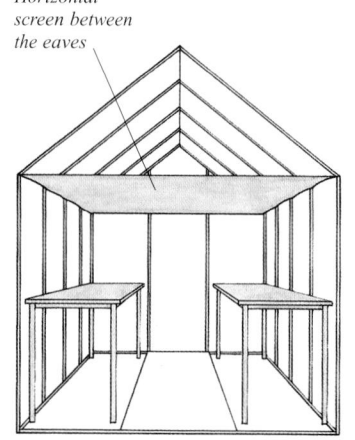

Vertical screen that acts as a partition

Thermal screens can be drawn horizontally between the eaves. They can also be drawn vertically to partition off a section of the greenhouse that needs to be heated to a higher temperature.

Ventilation

Good ventilation is essential in a greenhouse, even in winter, to avoid a buildup of stuffy or damp, stale air, and to control temperature. In warm areas, air circulation is very important in summer to prevent serious disease problems. It is important that the area covered by ventilators should be equal to at least one-sixth of the floor area.

Extra ventilation

Few greenhouses are supplied with enough ventilators as standard, so order additional air vents or extractor fans when buying a greenhouse. This is an especially important consideration with wooden greenhouses, since it is usually difficult to add them later.

To prevent water vapor and fumes from building up to an unacceptable level, extra ventilation is particularly important if kerosene or natural gas heating systems are used.

Wind ventilation system

Air exchange in a greenhouse occurs when external air movements, caused by gusts of wind, replace interior warm, humid air with fresh air. If ventilators are placed on the sides and roof of the greenhouse, and are also staggered, this will ensure that air circulates throughout the entire area – if vents are placed directly opposite one another, air will simply blow straight through the greenhouse.

Doors may also be kept open in summer to increase ventilation. Consider adding a screen door to keep out birds and pets.

Chimney ventilation system

Chimney-effect ventilation depends on warm, humid air rising out of roof vents and being replaced by fresh air that is drawn in as a result through lower ventilators. For greatest efficiency, position them along the lower sides of the greenhouse, either above or below the staging.

Fan ventilation system

Fan ventilation is a mechanically driven system that works by extracting air from the greenhouse at head height, or slightly higher, and drawing in fresh air through vents lower down and usually at the opposite end of the greenhouse.

Hinged ventilators

These may be mounted to the sides or roof of the greenhouse and should open wide, to an angle of about 45°. This will allow maximum airflow, while at the same time preventing direct gusts of wind from entering the greenhouse and possibly causing damage to the plants or even to the structure itself.

Louver ventilators

Usually positioned below the height of the staging, louver window ventilators are particularly useful for controlling the flow of air throughout the greenhouse in winter, when roof ventilators may allow too much heat to escape. The louver vents must close tightly, however, so that they exclude all drafts.

Automatic vent openers

Autovent openers simplify temperature control significantly, since they are designed to open automatically whenever the temperature rises above a predetermined level. These devices are essential if a heating system that has no thermostat has been installed in the greenhouse.

With any type of greenhouse, automatic vent openers should be mounted to at least some of the hinged or louver ventilators. This is easily done by closely following the manufacturer's instructions.

They may be set to open at a range of temperatures, but make sure that the automatic system you choose will function within the temperature range required. Set this to operate at a temperature that is just below the optimum for the plants in order for the vents to open before the temperature inside rises to an unsuitable level.

Many autovent designs are available. Some work by the expansion and contraction of a wax plug contained in a metal or plastic cylinder; the movement of the wax works a piston that opens and closes the ventilator. Other models make use of metal rods that alter their shape as the temperature rises and falls.

Evaporative coolers

In hot, dry climates, evaporative coolers are useful. They are relatively inexpensive to buy and run.

Extractor fans

The type of extractor fan that is designed primarily for use in kitchens and bathrooms is also ideally suited for use in the greenhouse. An additional bonus with using these extractor fans is that most come with a thermostatic control, an essential requirement for greenhouses.

Choose a fan that is powerful enough for the size of your greenhouse. The extraction rate is usually quoted in cubic feet or cubic meters per hour. As a general guide, a 6 x 8ft (2 x 2.5m) greenhouse requires a fan capacity of 10,000cu ft (300cu m) per hour, but a smaller one may be perfectly adequate if other types of ventilation are also used.

A louver window – positioned at the opposite end of the greenhouse from the extractor fan and set lower down – is essential to provide a flow of fresh air to replace the stale air that is drawn out by the fan.

Buy a fan that comes with louver flaps that close when the fan is not actually working so that drafts are excluded. To extend the working life of the fan, the motor should not be set to run constantly at maximum capacity. It is much better to choose a model that is slightly more powerful than is strictly necessary for the greenhouse.

THE PRINCIPLES OF GREENHOUSE VENTILATION

WIND EFFECT *Fresh air blows into the greenhouse, circulates, and then escapes through an open vent on the opposite side.*

CHIMNEY EFFECT *Warm air rises and escapes through open vents in the roof, drawing fresh, cooler air in lower down.*

FAN VENTILATION *Air is drawn out by a fan at the top of the greenhouse and drawn in through open vents lower down.*

LOUVER VENTS

These are mounted on the side of the greenhouse above ground level to improve the flow of air through the interior. The opening mechanism has a lever and is simple to operate (see insets).

HINGED VENTS

Vents that open by a hinge mechanism are normally installed on the roof of the greenhouse. Make sure that they open wide and that they are securely in place when open.

AUTOVENT OPENER

This autovent works by the expansion and contraction of wax in a cylinder as the greenhouse temperature rises and falls.

Shading

This will help control the temperature of the greenhouse if the ventilation system is insufficient. It also protects vulnerable plants from too much direct sunlight, reducing the risk of leaf scorch and preventing flower colors from fading in strong sunlight. Shading applied primarily to control heat should be on the outside of the greenhouse; internal shading is unlikely to reduce the temperature significantly.

The amount of shade required in a greenhouse depends on the season and the plants being grown. In the months of strongest sunlight, shading that reduces the light by 40–50 percent is suitable for a typical mixed greenhouse. Ferns generally prefer approximately 75 percent filtered light, while most cacti and other succulents require very little or no shading at all.

Shading washes
These are often the most efficient method of reducing heat from the sun, while still allowing enough light to penetrate for good plant growth. Paint or spray the wash onto the outside of the glass at the beginning of the sunny season. Reapply if heavy rains prematurely remove the shading before late summer.

Shading washes are inexpensive, but they may be messy to apply, and their appearance is sometimes unattractive in a small garden where the greenhouse is a major feature. Some washes become more transparent when wet, so that on rainy days or in dull weather they allow more light to penetrate.

Blinds
These are used mainly on the outside of the greenhouse to control temperature. They are more versatile than shading washes, since they may be rolled up or down, depending on the intensity of light required. They can also be used where only a section of the greenhouse needs to be shaded. However, manually operated blinds need constant attention. Automatic blinds, which come into operation as soon as the temperature rises to a predetermined level, are more convenient to use but are relatively expensive.

Meshes and fabrics
Flexible mesh shading materials are suitable for either interior or exterior use. They are less adaptable than blinds because they usually remain in position for the entire season. They are used more commonly to provide shading for plants that do not require high light levels than to reduce temperatures.

Woven and knitted fabrics are also suitable for both interior and exterior greenhouse use. The amount of light reduction varies considerably, depending on the type of fabric fitted. The quality of light allowed through to the plants is usually perfectly adequate for good growth, although the temperature is not significantly reduced.

FLEXIBLE MESH

Plastic mesh netting can be cut to length and used either internally or externally for shading plants in a greenhouse.

SHADING THE GREENHOUSE

Shading washes are applied to the outside of a greenhouse to prevent the temperature inside from rising too high, without greatly reducing light. The washes may be left on throughout the season.

ROLLER BLINDS

Blinds are a versatile method of shading the greenhouse. They should be durable, since they will be in place for long periods.

Cross-laminated fabric and some plastic meshes are recommended for internal shading only.

Tinted bubble plastic can also be used for shading. It cuts down the light by almost 50 percent, but it reduces temperature only slightly.

Rigid sheets
Rigid polycarbonate sheets (usually tinted) are sometimes used for shading in greenhouses. The sheets may be mounted either inside or outside, as recommended by the greenhouse manufacturer. They cut down the light considerably and, unless they are clear or white, the quality of light transmitted may not be sufficient for good plant growth.

Humidity

Humidity is a measure of the quantity of water vapor in the air. The humidity of the air influences the rate at which plants transpire; this is their mechanism for drawing water (along with nutrients) from roots to leaves, where the water then evaporates from leaf pores. As water evaporates, the plant is cooled down.

Establish the preferred humidity levels of the plants in your greenhouse, then control the amount of moisture in the atmosphere to suit them. Humidity can be increased using various techniques (see "Increasing humidity," right) and reduced by ventilation (see p.569).

Plant requirements
Many tropical plants from humid climates require high levels of humidity for healthy growth and will not survive in a very dry atmosphere.

However, a very humid atmosphere reduces the rate of transpiration and evaporation to a level that may be harmful to some plants. They may suffer damage from overheating unless cooler, drier air is brought in by ventilation.

If the air is dry and the humidity level low, plants transpire more rapidly, often losing a great deal of moisture. Plants that are not adapted to cope with low humidity will wilt as a result, unless additional water is supplied at the roots. Dry-climate plants often have specific anatomical features that reduce the rate of transpiration in drought conditions (see CLIMATE AND THE GARDEN, "Drought," p.602). However, it is very expensive to reduce humidity below the ambient level, which in summer can be 95 percent.

Measuring humidity
The level of humidity in a greenhouse depends to an extent on the temperature of the air. Warm air is capable of holding more moisture than cold air before it becomes saturated. Relative humidity is a measure of the amount of water vapor in the air expressed as a percentage of saturation point at the same temperature. A humid atmosphere is defined as having a relative humidity of about 75 percent; a dry atmosphere has a relative humidity of about 35 percent.

Wet and dry bulb thermometers, used in conjunction with hygrometric tables, may be used to measure the relative humidity of the atmosphere. Hygrometers, which have a dial that gives readings for both the temperature and the humidity, are also available. As a general guide, a relative humidity below 75 percent, but above 40 percent, is beneficial for most greenhouse plants during the growing season. At levels above 80 percent, diseases such as gray mold/*Botrytis* and mildew may become a problem.

In winter, humidity should be maintained at a lower level, but the exact level required will depend on the types of plant grown and the temperature of the greenhouse.

Increasing humidity
Greenhouses can be damped down during warm and hot months by splashing water – predominantly on the floor and on any staging – from a watering can or hose. This has the result of increasing the level of atmospheric humidity. An automatic spray system simplifies humidity control, especially for plants that require very high humidity. In a small greenhouse, mist-spraying by

hand or providing a tray filled with water that slowly evaporates into the air is usually adequate.

Watering

A traditional watering can is still the most efficient, if perhaps the most time-consuming, method of watering a mixed collection of plants in a small greenhouse. Since you can easily monitor the flow, all of the plants are watered according to their individual requirements.

An automatic watering system is a useful addition to the greenhouse in summer. If the greenhouse is left unattended on a regular basis, however, an automatic system becomes essential, since some pot plants may need to be watered several times a day if the weather is very hot.

Capillary systems
Watering systems that rely on capillary action to draw up water are often used in a greenhouse.

Plant pots may be placed on a ¾–2in (2–5cm) layer of clean sand (which retains moisture well) that is spread on the greenhouse staging and kept permanently wet. Moist sand adds considerable weight to the staging, however, so make sure that it is sturdy enough to take the extra load. In addition, protect wooden staging from the wet sand by lining it with sheets of plastic or aluminum foil; otherwise, it will rot. Alternatively, place the sand in aluminum trays.

Add a length of plastic gutter to the edge of the bench and keep it filled with water. This can be done by hand or automatically from an overhead tank connected to the water supply, in which case the system should be controlled by a float valve.

Capillary matting, which is widely available in rolls and is simply cut to the required size, is far lighter, easier to keep clean, and just as acceptable as sand. To keep the capillary matting continuously moist, trail the edge into a water trough or other reservoir of water. The water may be filled up by hand or supplied automatically, as above.

For a capillary system to be effective, there must be sufficient contact between the medium in the pots and the source of moisture so that water is continuously supplied to the plants' root systems. Plastic plant pots usually allow good contact between the medium and the moist sand or matting. Clay pots, however, may each require a wick. This is cut out of a piece of spare capillary matting or nylon yarn and placed in the drainage hole to bridge any gaps between the medium and the mat.

During the winter months, do not use capillary watering systems in the greenhouse, since most plants are dormant, or are growing only slowly, and therefore require a reduced intake of water. The perpetually damp mat or sand may also increase humidity in the greenhouse to unsatisfactory levels for the plants (see "Humidity," opposite).

Overhead systems
A system of overhead pipes, with nozzles from which water is sprayed onto the plants below, is widely used in commercial greenhouses. This is an ideal system for watering a large number of plants that are all at a similar stage of growth. However, it is not suitable for the small amateur greenhouse that contains a wide variety of plants. Overhead watering systems are also expensive to install and create too humid an atmosphere if used in the winter.

Soaker hoses
These are widely used in the garden and can also be used inside the greenhouse to water border crops or to keep capillary matting moist. In very hot weather, however, soaker hoses may not supply a sufficient flow of water to the plants.

Trickle irrigation systems
This type of irrigation system consists of a series of small-bore tubes, each with an adjustable nozzle. The tubes are placed in the individual pots or growing bags, or near plants growing in the greenhouse border.

Most trickle irrigation systems are fed with water from a reservoir that is filled in turn from a hose connected to the water supply. It is possible, however, to use water directly from the supply.

The rate of water delivery must always be monitored very carefully and adjusted according to the needs of the plants. These needs vary depending on the time of year and the vagaries of the weather.

Lighting

If a power supply is already installed in the greenhouse (see "Installing electricity, natural gas, and water," p.566), lighting units are not expensive to add at any time, and running costs are also low. In addition, the lights produce a little extra heat for the plants. Ordinary fluorescent lamps provide enough illumination to work by comfortably.

WATERING SYSTEMS

Overhead reservoir

Tubes supply each plant with water

Gutter filled with water

Capillary matting

CAPILLARY WATERING
An overhead reservoir feeds water to a gutter attached to the staging. The matting soaks up water, which is absorbed by soil mix in the trays.

TRICKLE IRRIGATION
Trickle systems supply water directly to each pot by means of tubes, which could be from an overhead reservoir.

Grow lamps
The special quality of lighting produced by grow lamps is required to increase daylength (see THE VEGETABLE GARDEN, "Daylength," p.489) for specific purposes during the fall and winter months, when light levels are consistently low.

Fluorescent tubes that produce good light to improve plant growth can be obtained from specialty suppliers and garden centers. They do not produce much heat and so can be placed close to the plants. The lights come with reflectors that cast the light downward, where it will do the most good. For best effect, the tubes should be mounted 10–12in (25–30cm) above the foliage. Mercury fluorescent lamps and mercury vapor lamps also provide a suitable quality of light to encourage good plant growth.

Metal halide lamps are the best, if most expensive, form of grow lamp, emitting light that is close to the spectrum of natural light. They illuminate a large area but cast their light in a circular pattern, which may be inconvenient in a small greenhouse, since the corners may not be adequately lit.

Most grow lamps suitable for use in the greenhouse need special hardware because of the moist, humid atmosphere. If in doubt, ask the advice of a qualified electrician.

Light meters
Where lighting is important, light meters are useful, since they measure light levels much more accurately than can be judged by eye. Some meters are supplied with information about the light levels preferred by a wide range of commonly cultivated plants.

A GROW LAMP

This provides additional light to improve plant growth. Secure it directly above the plants, if possible.

Using the space

To make the best use of the limited space in a greenhouse, plan the layout carefully. Cultivation in raised beds, borders, growing bags, or containers placed on the ground, staging, or shelves are all suitable methods; often, a combination is best.

Raised beds

These are used mainly in alpine houses, where sharp drainage is required. Raised beds may be expensive to construct using new bricks, but old bricks are satisfactory. Leave a large gap between a raised bed and the wall of a greenhouse so that air can circulate and moisture from the soil mix does not penetrate the wall. For details see STRUCTURES AND SURFACES, "Raised beds," p.593.

Beds that are raised to normal bench height are suitable only for lean-to greenhouses or for those with a tall brick base. For small plants that do not require a great depth of soil, a stone trough placed on brick pillars or legs may be used. Alternatively, construct a raised container by placing rigid metal sheets or paving slabs on top of brick pillars, making the walls by laying several brick courses around the top. Line the bed with a sheet of heavy plastic, pierced frequently to make sure the bed will be adequately drained. A layer of coarse gravel at the bottom also improves drainage.

Raised beds for taller plants need not be so high and so do not need to stand on brick pillars. They are usually built up from ground level with basal seep holes for drainage and simply filled with soil mix.

Borders and growing bags

A glass-to-ground greenhouse is required to grow plants directly in a border, to ensure that plants receive enough light. Borders with a width of 3ft (1m) are acceptable in a greenhouse that is 8ft (2.5m) wide. Make the beds wider if staging is placed over the borders, so that the staging does not interfere with the in-ground plants. Plants in containers may also be placed on top of the border.

The soil mix in greenhouse borders may become infected with disease if the same plants are grown repeatedly over many years. If this is the case, or if the greenhouse floor is concreted over, growing bags may be used. Growing bags provide a convenient method of cultivation, since they retain moisture well and remove the need to dig and fertilize the soil.

INSIDE THE GREENHOUSE

Organize the elements within the greenhouse sensibly to make the best possible use of the limited space. Here is a well-planned layout for a lean-to greenhouse.

Vent

Automatic vent opener

External shading blinds

Water reservoir irrigating the plants in the tray beneath

Thermometer

Display shelf for plants

Louver vents

Seedlings and cuttings growing in trays

Fan heater

Pots sunk into sand underneath the bench

Paved area

Shelf mounted on the wall

Electric sockets

Heated propagator

Water supply

Slatted bench staging

Shade-loving plant beneath staging

Growing bag

DISPLAYING THE PLANTS

Plants in the greenhouse should be arranged to make attractive displays. If the greenhouse is heated, a wide variety of plants may be grown throughout the year to maintain the display of flowers and foliage. Place dormant plants beneath the staging to make more room for other plants in season.

before planting. Most of the nutrients in the soil mix contained in the growing bags are used up during the season, so fresh bags should be used each year.

Staging

Staging is important for any ornamental or mixed greenhouse, since bringing plants closer to the light encourages healthier growth. Even if removed for summer border crops, staging is necessary for propagating and growing on young plants.

Positioning the staging
The most satisfactory arrangement for a small or mixed greenhouse is to have a central path with staging along the sides, and possibly across one end. Remove half of it for border crops when necessary, and retain the permanent staging to display ornamentals. The permanent staging should be positioned on the side where it will cast the least shade on the border crops.

Central staging
Larger ornamental greenhouses that are designed primarily as show-houses may have staging placed in the center, with a path around the edge. Two staging benches can be placed back to back, preferably with tiered staging in the center to enhance the display of plants.

The right size and height
For convenience, make the benches 18–24in (45–60cm) wide. Wider benches are useful in a large greenhouse but they may be difficult to reach across. All staging needs to be of sturdy construction to support the weight of plants, containers, and soil mix. Always leave a generous gap between the back of any staging and the sides of the greenhouse to allow air to circulate.

Most amateur greenhouses also have to serve as a potting shed. A convenient height for staging that is also used as a work surface is approximately 30–36in (75–90cm); it should be lower if a seated working position is required.

Free-standing staging
It is sometimes useful to have staging that can be dismantled and stored away, bringing it into the greenhouse for short periods, for instance when raising seedlings in spring. Free-standing staging may not fit the greenhouse quite as well as

FREE-STANDING STAGING

Movable benches allow great flexibility, since they can be moved around to accommodate the plants or removed altogether.

FIXED STAGING

Most greenhouse manufacturers supply permanent staging that is made from the same materials as the greenhouse. It is best installed at the same time as the greenhouse is constructed.

staging that is built in, and may not look as attractive, but is more flexible in use. It must be easy to assemble and sturdy since it will be in use for many years. If border crops are grown for most of the year, open-mesh staging, which folds back neatly against the side of the greenhouse when it is not needed, is convenient for short periods.

Free-standing modular staging systems can be built up into tiers and provide an attractive way of displaying plants. Slatted, mesh, or solid modular systems are available.

Permanent staging
Built-in staging and shelves may put a strain on the framework of a greenhouse, especially light aluminum alloy structures. Gravel or sand, if used, adds extra weight to the staging, particularly when it is wet. Buy staging that is specially built, if possible. If in doubt, check with the greenhouse manufacturer before installing any permanent staging.

Slatted and mesh staging
If you are growing alpines or cacti and succulents in pots, it is preferable to use slatted or mesh benches, which allow a freer flow of air than solid staging. However, slatted and mesh staging are not suitable for use with capillary watering systems.

SLATTED STAGING

Wooden-slatted staging is an attractive choice. The slats allow better air circulation around the plants than solid-surface staging does, but slats are not suitable for a capillary watering system unless pots are placed in trays on the bench.

For a wooden greenhouse, use wooden-slatted benches; for an aluminum alloy or galvanized steel greenhouse, metal or plastic-mesh benches are more appropriate.

Solid-surface staging
Solid staging allows more pots to be accommodated than slatted staging (it is difficult to keep pots upright between the slats), but it may require more ventilation.

If using a capillary watering system, choose solid aluminum staging that has a level surface for the matting or sand. Some types of staging have reversible sections that produce raised flat surfaces for mats if placed one way, and dishlike sections for sand or gravel if reversed.

Shelves

Shelves in the greenhouse can be used for both storage and display. Permanent shelves often cast shade on the plants below, so it is preferable to install fold-away shelves, which may be used in spring when space is short and then put away for the rest of the year.

In a small greenhouse, where there is not enough headroom for hanging baskets, shelves can be used to display trailing plants.

Propagation aids

The propagation of many plants requires higher temperatures than can realistically be maintained in the greenhouse. Therefore, to save on utility bills, propagation aids are often used to provide the extra heat required. They may also increase the success rate when sowing seed or rooting cuttings. For the greenhouse, choose a propagator that is large enough to hold at least three standard seed trays.

An electric power supply in the greenhouse is essential if heated propagators, mist units, or heating cables are to be used. Mist units also require a constant water supply as well as a power supply.

Unheated propagators are of limited use in the greenhouse, but they usually provide sufficient humidity for rooting cuttings in summer.

Heated propagators

A heated propagator should have a heating element that is capable of providing a minimum soil mix temperature of 59°F (15°C) in winter and early spring, when temperatures outside may fall below freezing.

If tropical plants are to be propagated, the unit must have a more powerful heating element that can maintain a temperature of 75°F (24°C). The propagator should preferably come with an adjustable thermostat, which allows greater flexibility of temperature.

Use rigid plastic lids, since these are more likely to retain the heat than thin plastic covers. Adjustable ventilators are useful, because they allow moisture to escape and prevent the atmosphere inside the propagator from becoming too humid.

Domestic propagators

Some small heated propagators are designed for windowsill use. Usually holding just two seed trays, they are generally too small to be of practical use in the greenhouse, and they often do not have a thermostat. They may not generate enough heat in a cold or cool greenhouse, since the heating element is intended to operate in a room indoors.

A WINDOWSILL PROPAGATOR

Propagators designed for windowsills are best used in a greenhouse only during summer, when temperatures are high.

Heating mats

These are designed to be used with unheated propagators or ordinary seed trays, either of which may be placed on the heating mats. A plastic hood must be placed over seed trays to maintain warmth and humidity. Heating mats do not raise the temperature as efficiently as heated tray propagators (see below) and are suitable for only one or two trays.

Heated tray propagators

These have a self-contained heating element in the base, and are more useful than heating mats (see above), especially if they come with an adjustable thermostat.

Mist units

Cuttings may often be rooted more rapidly and in greater numbers in a mist unit than by using other more traditional means. Mist units are convenient, since they remove the need to water cuttings frequently.

The easiest and most convenient mist units to use are self-contained, enclosed units that include a heating element, thermostat, transparent cover, and a misting head. The constantly humid atmosphere created by the misting head provides a suitable environment in which to root cuttings quickly, by maintaining a constant film of water on the propagating material. Heat loss by evaporation is also reduced. There is also less risk of the cuttings being affected by fungal diseases because, when the misting head is in operation, most disease spores are washed out of the air and from the leaves before they can infect plant tissues. On a small scale, a similar environment is created by enclosing a pot of cuttings in a clear plastic bag.

For large numbers of plants, a mist propagation unit is more practical. Some units are designed for use without a cover on an open greenhouse propagating bench. They are used in conjunction with heating cables and require a specially constructed greenhouse bench. If sited in a greenhouse where a mixed collection of plants is grown, however, the

A MIST PROPAGATION UNIT

A soil thermostat controls the temperature of the soil mix, which is heated by cables. The misting head is controlled by a sensor (connected to a solenoid) located near the cuttings. When the atmosphere becomes too dry, the misting head is activated.

high humidity created by an open mist unit may prove unsuitable for some types of plant. In this situation, it would be preferable to install a closed mist unit.

Heating cables

Intended primarily for heating the soil mix in a conventional propagator or on a mist bench in the greenhouse, heating cables may also be used to heat the air in an enclosed space, such as a cold frame or homemade propagator. The safest system to use is a cable with a wired-in thermostat that is connected to an insulated, fused socket.

Cover any heating cable with wire mesh to protect it from being accidentally cut.

Heating cables are sold in lengths that are designed to heat a given area. A 75-watt cable, for example, measures 20ft (6m) and provides enough heat for a bench area of 7sq ft (0.7sq m) in a greenhouse that has some form of heating. A cable with a higher wattage would of course be needed for practical use in a similar area in an unheated greenhouse or in a cold frame that is outside the greenhouse.

The cable should be laid at a depth of 2–3in (5–7cm) in a series of S bends (making sure the loops do not touch) in a bed of moist sand.

USING HEATING CABLES

In this propagating case, cables are used to heat both soil and air. Each set of cables has a thermostat, which ensures that the temperature never falls below a preset level.

Cold frames and covers

Cold frames and other covers relieve pressure on greenhouse space, but they are also extremely useful in their own right. They are likely to be used most intensively in spring to harden off plants raised in a greenhouse, but they may also be used throughout the year to grow a wide range of crops. They are most useful where winters are mild because they are unheated, but even in areas with severe winters they can be used to add several weeks at either end of the season.

Cold frames

The most popular type of cold frame has glass (or clear plastic) sides as well as glass sashes (frame tops that contain the panes of glass), although sometimes wood and bricks are used for the construction. Glass-to-ground models usually have a metal framework for extra strength.

Frame sashes

Choose a frame that has removable or sliding sashes for easy access. Some also have sliding front panels, which may be useful to supply extra ventilation. Hinged sashes that are wedged open still provide protection from heavy rain, but sliding sashes

are often removed entirely during the day, leaving the plants very vulnerable to heavy rain. Lightweight aluminum frames with their sashes wedged open may be at risk in strong winds, however, so choose a model that has a hinged top and adjustable casement stays to secure the sashes safely.

Wooden frames

Traditional wooden frames are now difficult to obtain and are usually expensive, but they can be made cheaply at home from secondhand timber. The wooden sides retain heat well. It is not very difficult to attach heating cables (see opposite) to the inside of the frame to provide extra warmth. Paint or stain the wood to preserve it.

Aluminum alloy frames

These are available from horticultural specialists and are relatively inexpensive. They vary considerably, usually sold packed flat for easy transportation and assembled on site. Aluminum alloy frames let in more light than either wooden or brick frames, but they do not have such good insulating qualities and may not be as strong. It may be necessary to use ground anchors for lightweight frames.

HOW TO USE COLD FRAMES

PLANTING IN THE FRAME

Plants may be grown directly in the cold frame, if required. Always prepare the base with a thick layer of drainage material, such as rubble or coarse gravel, before adding a 6in (15cm) layer of good garden soil or a suitable soil mix.

PROTECTING CROPS

Here, the cold frame has been placed directly onto the soil in the vegetable plot. Vegetables are growing through slits in a plastic sheet laid on the surface of the soil.

VENTILATION METHODS OF COLD FRAMES

HINGED SASHES
Hinged tops can be wedged open on warm days to prevent the plants from overheating.

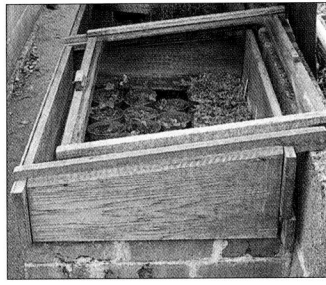

SLIDING SASHES
Sliding tops are less vulnerable to gusts of wind, but they do not protect plants from heavy rain.

Brick frames

These are rarely used nowadays, but they may still be built at home if a cheap supply of old bricks is available and if the sashes can be made. Brick frames are generally warm and draftproof.

Suitable sizes

The minimum practical size for a cold frame is 2 x 4ft (60cm x 1.2m). Often, however, the frame has to fit into whatever space is available (as near the greenhouse as possible), so choose the largest affordable frame that fits the space.

Height is important if the frame is to be used for plants in pots or for tall vegetable crops. In order to increase the height of a frame temporarily, raise it on loose bricks.

Insulation

The variety of plants that can be successfully overwintered in a frame is increased if the frame is well insulated. The frame needs to be draftproof; there should be no gaps around the glass or framework, and the top and any sliding front panels must fit well.

Glass-to-ground and plastic-sided frames may need insulating in cold weather with sheets of plastic foam. Cut the sheets to size, then place them against the inside of the frame to reduce drafts and heat loss.

On cold nights, particularly when a deep freeze is predicted, frames may require additional outer protection: use layers of burlap or old carpet to cover the tops, tied down firmly or held in position with pieces of heavy wood. This protective covering should always be removed during the day; otherwise, plants may suffer from lack of light. Another way is to use several layers

of thick, clear plastic sheeting for extra protection. This can be left in place during the day, since it does not reduce the light to the same degree.

Ventilation

Good ventilation is essential in warm weather. Most frames have sashes that can be wedged open to allow fresh air inside. Often, the sashes also slide along to allow more ventilation and are eventually removed completely when young plants need to be hardened off.

Light

Aluminum frames (but not brick or wooden frames) may be moved around the garden to take advantage of the best light at various times of the year. If a frame is permanently sited, it should be positioned where it will receive the maximum amount of light in winter and spring, provided that the site is not too exposed.

Frames need shading in summer, but one that lets in as much light as possible is best for year-round use.

Glazing materials

Glass is the best glazing material for cold frames; it transmits light well, allows the frame to warm up quickly, and retains heat better than most plastic materials. Broken or cracked panes should be replaced as soon as possible, so a frame that allows the individual panes to be replaced easily should be chosen. Some are glazed using glazing clips or glass panels that slide into the framework, making glass replacement relatively quick and simple.

Where glass may be a potential danger for children or animals, or where the cost of the frame is the main consideration, use plastic glazing material.

Covers

A range of cover designs and materials is available, so choose a cover that suits the types of plant to be grown. Covers tend to be used mainly in the vegetable garden, but they are equally useful for protecting ornamental plants and seedlings that benefit from a little extra warmth early in the season.

Materials

Glass is the best choice if covers are to be used extensively for most of the year and moved from crop to crop. It has good light transmission and allows the frame to warm up quickly in sunlight. Clear plastic material (of various thicknesses) is an alternative. Plastic covers are generally less expensive than those made of glass but do not allow such good light penetration, nor do they retain as much heat.

Single-thickness plastic is the least satisfactory material for retaining heat, but it is cheap and useful where high temperatures are not necessary. Plastic covers last longer if they have been treated with an ultraviolet inhibitor and are stored out of direct sunlight when not in use.

The minimum thickness that is suitable for covers is 150 gauge, but 300, 600, or 800 gauge provides much greater protection. PVC is thicker and more rigid, and has similar qualities to polypropylene (see below). Molded PVC and PVC sheeting should last for at least five years or more if treated with an ultraviolet inhibitor.

Covers made from twin-walled polycarbonate offer good insulation and should last for ten years or more. Polypropylene is used in some injection-molded covers and in corrugated sheets; it retains heat better than plastic, but not as well as glass or twin-walled polycarbonate. It lasts for five years or more if treated with an ultraviolet inhibitor.

BARN COVER

End pieces

These are an important part of most covers – without them, a cover may become a wind tunnel, damaging the plants inside. The end pieces should fit well to preclude drafts, but they should be easy to remove to provide additional ventilation when required.

Tent cover

A tent cover is inexpensive and simple to construct from two sheets of glass to form a tent shape. It is suitable for germinating seeds, protecting young seedlings in spring, and covering low-growing plants.

Tunnel cover

A tunnel cover may be made from either rigid or flexible plastic. Generally, flexible-plastic, continuous-tunnel covers are used for crops such as strawberries and early carrots. The plastic must be supported by wire hoops (positioned over the row of plants) and tensioned with wires. Heavy-duty plastic that has been treated with an ultraviolet inhibitor should be used.

Rigid models are generally more attractive but more expensive than tunnel covers that are made of flexible plastic. They are also easier to move around, since they do not need to be dismantled first.

Some tunnel covers have self-watering features (see right).

TENT COVER

TUNNEL COVER

Barn cover

This has almost vertical sides supporting a sloping, tent-shaped top. Its extra height makes it useful for relatively tall plants, but extra materials and complicated hardware make it more expensive than a tent cover.

Some glass and rigid plastic barn covers have lifting or removable tops to provide ventilation in warm weather while still offering wind protection. This makes weeding, watering, and harvesting easier.

Flexible PVC is sometimes used for barn covers, but these tend to be lower and therefore less versatile than those using other types of material, unless the top is removable or can be wedged open.

Dome-shaped cover

Made from rigid plastic, dome-shaped covers are easy to move around but are more expensive than tent or tunnel covers. They have more space at the edges than tent and tunnel covers, although the overall height may be no greater.

Self-watering cover

Watering plants beneath covers is difficult and time-consuming if the covers need to be lifted or moved. A self-watering cover is designed to allow rainwater to trickle through gradually to the plants below. Alternatively, it may have a tubular system that is connected to a hose.

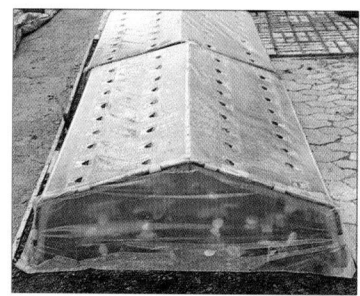

SELF-WATERING COVER

Floating row cover

A floating row cover (also known as a floating mulch) consists of a sheet of perforated plastic sheeting or a light garden blanket, which is placed over the ground where crops have been recently sown.

Floating row covers are permeable, allowing rainwater to penetrate to the soil below. This is a great advantage, since it reduces the need to water. The perforations in plastic floating row covers enable the sheet to stretch a little as the crop grows beneath it. Garden blankets are sufficiently lightweight to rise with the growing crop. Both perforated plastic and blanket floating row covers allow air to pass freely through the material and also have useful insulating properties. Garden blankets also protect plants from light frosts. For further information, see THE VEGETABLE GARDEN, p.499.

The sheets or blankets should be anchored firmly into the soil at the edges of the beds with soil, stones, or pegs. Entire beds may be covered with a floating row cover, if desired, or pieces can be cut to fit smaller areas or even individual plants.

Individual cover

These are usually used to protect individual plants in the early stages of growth. They may also be placed over any small, vulnerable plants during severe winter weather, such as hard frost, deep snow, heavy rain, and high winds.

Homemade individual covers such as waxed paper protectors and cut-off plastic bottles, are easy to make and are much less expensive than store-bought models but may not be as attractive.

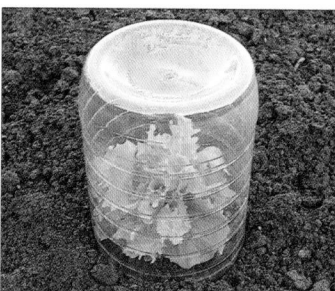

INDIVIDUAL COVER

Wall-of-water cover

This unusual design is useful for single plants and consists of a circle of hollow, clear plastic tubes, into which water is poured. The tubes form the wall of the cover, which alters in shape depending on the water level. If the tubes are half filled, they cave in at the top, protecting the plant from above as well as from the sides.

WALL-OF-WATER COVER

Routine maintenance

Regular maintenance is necessary to preserve greenhouses and to keep frames and covers clean. Fall is usually a convenient time to attend to the maintenance work: cleaning and disinfecting the greenhouse structure and equipment at this time of year minimizes problems from overwintering pests and diseases.

It is important to do this work on a mild day before the very cold weather begins. Tender plants can then be put outside while the preparations for winter are carried out.

CLEANING BETWEEN PANES

To remove dirt from between overlapping panes in the greenhouse, use a thin, rigid strip of plastic to loosen any deposits before spraying or hosing down with water.

Exterior maintenance

Choose a dry, still day for routine work on the outside of the greenhouse. Before making a start, gather together all necessary materials for cleaning, repairing, and repainting.

Cleaning glass and plastic glazing

Glass should be cleaned with water only, using a hose and long-handled brush, but if it has become very dirty, better results are achieved by brushing with a solution of lime remover. Protect your skin and eyes by wearing gloves and goggles, and rinse off the solution thoroughly with running water.

A commercial window cleaning solution may also be used but it will not remove ingrained dirt. Dirt also tends to become trapped between overlapping panes. Push a thin plastic label between panes to loosen dirt and algae, then use the water jet from a hose to remove it. Shading washes are best removed by rubbing them off with a cloth.

Repairing glass

Panes of glass and plastic panes that are slightly cracked may be temporarily repaired with transparent glazing tape. Broken and badly cracked panes, however, should be replaced completely and as soon as possible after the damage is noticed, to prevent harm to plants.

To replace a pane in an aluminum alloy greenhouse, remove the spring glazing clips and the adjoining pane, if necessary, and reglaze using the old clips (see p.566).

If the panes are bedded on linseed putty (as in many older wooden greenhouses), remove the glazing tacks and the panes of glass carefully. Chip away the putty with a small chisel to leave a smooth surface. Clean the glazing bars with sandpaper before reglazing.

Apply a priming paint to any unpainted or untreated wood on the glazing bars. Pay particular attention to knots in the wood, which may be potential entry points for moisture. When the paint is fully dry, replace the panes by setting them on a bed of putty or glazing mastic, using glazing tacks to hold them.

Gutters and downspouts

Check that gutters and downspouts are in good repair. Use a hose to clear any blockages. Small leaks in gutters can be sealed with mastic or other sealant, but badly leaking sections of gutter will need to be replaced completely.

Metal framework

Aluminum greenhouses require only minimal structural attention. Although they lose their bright color, the grayish patina that forms protects the metal from the weather.

Steel frames and hardware should be checked for rust and, if necessary, treated with rust remover. Repaint every few years.

Wooden framework

Cut out any rotting wood and replace it, applying wood preservative and replacing rusty hinges as necessary. Softwood greenhouses need regular painting: strip off flaking paint, wash down, then apply primer and good-quality exterior paint. Hardwood greenhouses are more rot-resistant, requiring only a coat of wood stain every year or two, which also restores the color.

Ventilators

Windows and ventilator fans should be checked for ease of operation, working parts oiled if necessary, and glass or plastic cleaned. Also ensur-make that any fan-blade guards are securely in place.

Inside the greenhouse

Before cleaning and disinfecting the inside of a greenhouse or frame, turn off any electric power supply at the source, cover electric sockets and hardware with plastic, and remove all plants to a safe place.

Cleaning and disinfecting

Glass and plastic glazing materials should be cleaned as described under "Exterior maintenance," above. Clean the glazing bars by scrubbing with a disinfectant solution. Fine steel wool can be used, but not on anodized (colored) aluminum.

Scrub brickwork and paths with a garden disinfectant, then rinse with clean water. The disinfectant can be used, diluted according to the manufacturer's instructions, to sterilize the staging and other surfaces. Apply it with a paintbrush or as a coarse spray, wearing protective gloves, a face mask, and goggles.

Sanitation

Before returning plants to the greenhouse, check them for pests and diseases and treat as required. For details on which pests and diseases are likely to affect the plants you grow, consult the "Routine care" sections of the appropriate chapters.

MAINTAINING THE GREENHOUSE

An annual check in fall should be enough to keep your greenhouse in good working order.

Check all ventilators, making sure that they are watertight.

Check for rusty hinges, then treat with rust remover or replace.

Give panes a thorough cleaning, inside and out.

Replace cracked panes.

Repair broken ventilator hardware.

Clear leaves and trash from gutters.

Cover electric sockets with plastic before cleaning inside the greenhouse.

Remove weeds from inside the greenhouse.

Check for dirt between overlapping panes. Clean as necessary.

Strip areas of flaky paint, then repaint or treat with preservative.

Remove rotten wood and replace it.

Clean and disinfect all inside surfaces.

3
STRUCTURES
AND SURFACES

THE STRUCTURES AND hard surfaces of a garden act as the framework around which plants can grow and mature over the seasons. If thoughtfully designed, built features can add welcome height to any planting design as well as providing privacy and shelter. Paths can lead visitors along planned routes; a deck attached to the house makes a perfect setting for a meal.

As well as being practical, structures and surfaces are often attractive features in their own right. They may be designed so that they contrast or blend with the planting: the bold shape of a circular patio would make a striking contrast with the gentler lines of sprawling plants, whereas a rustic pergola is an attractive support for climbers such as roses and clematis.

Designing with structures and surfaces

Hard landscape elements are vital in helping to form the framework of a garden design and may be as ornamental as they are functional. In a new garden, features such as a patio or a pergola are valuable for providing interest while the plants are growing and becoming established. In a more mature garden, sympathetically designed structures complement softer elements such as a lawn or the planting in a border, and give the garden solidity and substance all year round.

When planning and designing structures, consider them in the context of their setting and in relation to each other. Materials, style, size, and shape should all be compatible, both with the house and the overall design of the garden. A terrace or wall adjacent to the house often looks most attractive if built of the same materials, forming a cohesive link between house and garden. Local materials are often preferable, because they tend to look appropriate in the setting. The degree of formality is another important consideration; in a formal garden, for example, a mellow brick wall boundary would be ideal, while in an informal cottage garden a picket fence or wooden pole fence would be more suitable.

Structures may be used to link, define, or separate different elements or parts of the garden. A gently

DESIGNING WITH HARD LANDSCAPE
Hard materials have been used here to form the main framework of the design, creating interest while the planting is becoming established and providing a contrast for the softer shapes of the plants. The curving path adds a sense of movement, while the innovative use of mixed materials provides satisfying textural contrasts.

curving path leads the eye along the garden, providing a unifying line, while a wide, straight path separates the features on either side. Steps create an interesting change of level and demarcate separate areas as well as joining them visually and providing access from one part to another. If the steps adjoin a patio, they may look best if constructed from the same materials and in a similar style – curved steps appropriately linked to a circular patio, for example.

The order in which you undertake construction work largely depends on your individual priorities and the requirements of the site. It might be necessary to erect a flanking wall first, because it will help retain the soil of a raised bed. In another garden, laying a path might be the first priority to allow easy access with wheelbarrows to the rear of a site where work is in progress.

This chapter covers most straightforward structural projects that may

be undertaken by an amateur, from hard surfaces such as patios, terraces, and paths, to boundaries and divisions (for example walls or fences) as well as other structures, such as raised beds and pergolas. In addition, certain hard elements are covered fully in other chapters: see THE WATER GARDEN, pp.275–97, for details on constructing ponds and watercourses; see THE ROCK GARDEN, pp.248–73, for rock gardens, alpine troughs, and peat beds.

Patios and terraces

A patio is an ornamental feature as well as a functional one, providing an area for meals and relaxation, with plants in beds or containers, and perhaps a raised pool. A raised paved area, with a balustrade or low wall, is more accurately described as a terrace. Patios and terraces are usually paved, although wooden decking (see pp.585–6) is popular as an alternative in some areas.

Choosing a site

Patios and terraces are usually sited close to the house, often with glass doors allowing direct access. This is convenient for providing power sources for lights and other equipment, but if the site is not warm and sheltered, it may be better to choose an alternative position. Designing the patio at an angle of 45° to the house, perhaps at a corner, may ensure that it receives sun for most of the day. A patio may also be built away from the house to make use of an attractive view across the property.

Two or more small patios may be more useful than one large one. One may be sited in an open, sunny spot, and the other in a cooler position to provide a welcome, shady retreat on a summer's day.

Shelter and privacy

A warm, sheltered patio can be enjoyed both earlier and later in the season than one that is subject to strong winds. If the site is exposed to winds, provide both shelter and seclusion with screens, such as a trellis, covered with climbing plants. A pergola (see pp.597–8) roofed with lattice will screen the patio from above and provide shade. Think twice before siting a patio under large trees, however: these will cast too much shade, they drip long after rain has stopped, their roots may dislodge and heave the paving, insects could be troublesome, and falling leaves may become a nuisance.

PREPARING THE SUBBASE FOR PATIOS AND PATHS

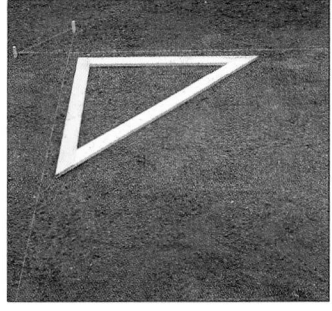

1 *Mark out the area with pegs and string, setting the string at the ultimate level of the path or patio. Use a builder's square to check that the corners are set at right angles.*

2 *Dig down to firm subsoil and tamp down with a plate compactor. Allow for a 4in (10cm) depth of crushed stone, a 2in (5cm) layer of sand, if needed, plus the thickness of the surface layer.*

3 *Drive in a grid of leveling pegs every 6ft (2m). For a patio, incorporate a slight slope so surface water drains away. Use a level and board to ensure that pegs are level with strings.*

4 *Spread a 4in (10cm) layer of crushed stone over the entire site, and then compact it so that it is level, using the pegs as a guide. Add sand, if necessary, and compact the area again.*

DRAINAGE SLOPE

Mark pegs at the same distance from the top of each, then pound them in, in rows 6ft (2m) apart – the first at the top of the slope. Put a 1in (2.5cm) scrap of wood on a peg in the second row. Make the two rows level, remove the scrap, and repeat.

1in (2.5cm) scrap of wood

Leveling pegs

Slope of patio

A suitable size

Size is less important for a terrace that is simply a link between house and garden than for a patio that is to serve as an outdoor room. It should be in proportion to the garden: if too small it may look trivial, if too large it may overpower a small garden. Allow about 4sq yd (3.3sq m) for each person likely to use it. For a family of four, a patio about 16sq yd (13sq m) is a practical size.

Choosing a surface

Simplicity is the key to good design. If the patio is to accommodate furniture, climbers, and container plants, paving should be unobtrusive. Bear in mind that colored paving may look fussy and often weathers to dreary shades. Variety is best achieved by mixing textures: small areas of brick or gravel among paving slabs, railroad ties intersecting bricks or clay pavers, or cobblestones with stone slabs.

Also decide if, for example, a hard-wearing surface is needed, or one that is not slippery when wet: choose from such materials as concrete (p.580), paving slabs (p.581), natural stone (p.582), tiles (p.582), bricks and pavers (p.583), or granite setts and cobblestones (p.585).

Foundations

Patios, paths, and driveways (see p.587) need firm foundations to ensure that the paved surface remains stable once in use. The load-bearing requirements must also be taken into account: few patios will be required to support very heavy loads, but driveways need more substantial foundations because they may be used by heavy vehicles as well as cars. Climate is another factor: in areas with long cold and dry periods, for example, concrete foundations may crack if not sufficiently deep; seek local advice as necessary.

Before undertaking any excavation work, check the location of all the utility pipes and cables on your property with the local utility company to avoid damaging them.

Water runoff

To drain off water, the surface of a patio should slope slightly; a fall of about 1in/6ft (2.5cm/2m) is usually sufficient. Calculate the combined depth of the subbase and surface material and mark this as a line at the same distance from the top of each of a number of leveling pegs. Insert one row at the top of the slope so that the mark is at soil level, the top of the peg indicating the desired level of the finished paving. Insert a second row of pegs 6ft (2m) down the slope. On each peg in this row in turn, place a small, 1in (2.5cm) thick scrap of wood (a shim) and lay a level on a board between this peg and one in the first row. Adjust the height of the lower peg until the top of the shim and the upper peg are level. Remove the shim and repeat the process, working down the slope. Then rake the soil so that it is level with the mark on each of the pegs. The tops of the subbase and the surface material of the finished construction should be level.

Basic procedure

Remove any plant growth from the area, including tree roots, then dig out loose topsoil to reach firm subsoil. Consolidate this using a plate compactor. For most patios and paths, but not those that might bear heavy loads (see "Load-bearing surfaces," p.580), firm subsoil and, if needed, a 4in (10cm) layer of crushed stone covered with 2in (5cm) sand, is a serviceable foundation. Use more crushed stone if necessary to bring the surface of the subbase up to the required level.

On unstable soils, such as muck or heavy clay, or where frost penetrates deeply into the soil, footings should run deeper than normal, as far down as 10in (25cm). Check the footing depths specified by your local building codes before proceeding with any further construction.

HOW TO LAY CONCRETE

1 *After marking out the site, dig it out to a depth of 8in (20cm). Drive leveling pegs into the ground 3ft (1m) apart along the string lines. Set them horizontal using a board and a level.*

2 *Remove the string lines and nail wooden boards to the inner faces of the pegs, butted end to face at the corners. This form holds the concrete in place until it sets hard.*

3 *Divide large sites into sections no more than 12ft (4m) long using forms. Spread crushed stone 4in (10cm) deep and firm it down with a roller.*

4 *Starting with the first section, tip in the concrete and spread it level so that it is slightly higher than the form. Work the concrete well into the edges.*

5 *Using a wooden beam that spans the width of the form, compact the concrete with a downward chopping motion. Then slide the beam from side to side to level the surface.*

6 *Fill any hollows that appear after leveling using fresh concrete, then level it again.*

7 *Lay a protective waterproof covering such as a plastic tarp over the concrete until it dries. Remove the form when the concrete has set hard.*

Load-bearing surfaces

For areas such as driveways that need to support heavy weight, lay a sub-base of at least 4in (10cm) of compacted crushed stone or rubble, with a further 4in (10cm) of concrete on top. This concrete may be used as the top surface or as a base for another material such as asphalt or pavers bedded in mortar. On clay or unstable soils, or if the surface is to be used by heavy vehicles, lay 6in (15cm) of concrete on top of the base. If mixing your own concrete for the foundations, see below. In large areas of concrete, it is essential to leave expansion gaps (see "Expansion joints," p.588).

Concrete

Concrete is relatively quick and easy to lay and makes a hard-wearing and long-lasting surface. It may be made more attractive by adding a textured finish (see p.588).

Ordering concrete

If you intend to lay a large area of concrete and there is access for large vehicles, having premixed concrete delivered will make the job easier and quicker. Give the supplier the site measurements and information about the intended use of the surface to make sure the correct amount and mix is delivered, or use a supplier who will mix it for you on site. This saves time and effort but requires advance preparation and usually some helpers, since you need to tackle the job immediately.

Concrete and mortar mixes

The following proportions for concrete and mortar mixes are suitable for most projects. For an explanation of terms, see p.585.

Wall footings, drive foundations, and bases for precast paving
1 part cement
2½ parts sharp sand
3½ parts ¾in (20mm) aggregate
(or 5 parts combined aggregate to 1 part cement, omitting the sand)

***In situ* (poured) concrete paving**
1 part cement
1½ parts sharp sand
2½ parts ¾in (20mm) aggregate
(or 3½ parts combined aggregate to 1 part cement, omitting the sand)

Bedding mortar (for bedding paving, and jointing paving bricks)
1 part cement
5 parts sharp sand

Masonry mortar (for garden brickwork)
1 part masonry cement
3 parts fine sand

All these proportions are measured by volume and not by weight. The consistency of the mix required for different jobs varies considerably. When mixing either concrete or mortar, start by adding only about half a part of water to one part of cement. This will provide a very stiff mix. Continue to add water gradually until you reach the consistency you need.

In hot climates, setting retardants may sometimes be necessary in mortar and concrete mixes, while in cold climates, antifreeze products may need to be incorporated. Seek local advice, if uncertain. It is best to avoid laying concrete and mortar when the weather is close to freezing or above 90°F (32°C).

Laying concrete

First mark out with string the area to be concreted, and excavate as deeply as needed for local conditions. Drive a number of wooden leveling pegs into the ground at intervals of 3ft (1m) around the edge, using the string as a guide. Nail boards to the inside faces of the leveling pegs to make a form at least 8in (20cm) deep, which confines the concrete until it sets.

Divide up large sites into small sections no more than 12ft (4m) long using more boards. On top of the subsoil, spread at least 4in (10cm) of compacted crushed stone. Taking one section at a time, pour the freshly mixed concrete inside the form to a depth of 4in (10cm) and work it well into the edges. Use a wooden beam spanning the width of the form to compact the mix, then level the concrete by drawing the beam back and forth in long, smooth strokes. Use a trowel or wood float in corners.

Utility meters

Utility meters must always be unobstructed to allow easy access for readers. Most meters may be hidden behind a fence or surrounded by shrubs (which should not be thorny, however).

When constructing or planting nearby, be aware that the utility company may at some time need to destroy plantings or structures in order to service or replace the meter.

Call the utility company before digging. Pay particular attention to meters when using heavy equipment, since even an accidental hit from a shovel may do serious damage.

Paving slabs

Concrete paving slabs are popular for patios, paths, driveways, and other structures (for example, to create a solid walkway under a pergola). They are available from many garden centers and building supply stores in a range of sizes, textures, and colors, and they are easy to lay once the base has been prepared appropriately and properly (for instance, to meet local ordinances or to provide a deep enough base to prevent winter damage). Some designs may be available only in limited areas. Large suppliers usually produce catalogs and may deliver directly to the consumer.

Sizes and shapes

Most slabs are sold either 24 x 24in (600 x 600mm) or 24 x 36in (600 x 900mm), with smaller slabs made to integrate with them. Not all slabs have a shaped edge designed to butt join; a half slab may be slightly less than half the size of a full one, to allow for mortar between the joints.

Circular slabs are suitable only for stepping-stones and small areas of paving with an infill of a loose material, such as gravel. Hexagonal slabs are useful if you prefer a pattern without regular, parallel lines; half slabs are available for a straight edge. Some slabs are available with a "bite" out of one corner, so that when four slabs are laid together a planting hole is created at the center.

Quantities

If laying a pattern with slabs of different sizes or colors, draw a plan on graph paper to calculate the number of each required, and allow up to 5 percent extra for breakages (especially if many have to be cut; see "Cutting paving slabs," p.582). Try to work to dimensions that minimize the need to cut slabs.

Laying paving slabs

If laying a patio, establish a line to use as a straight edge, and make sure there is a slight slope for drainage; the patio should always slope away from a building. A house wall is a practical base line to work from, but you may want to leave a small gap between the wall and paving for planting. In that case, start from a level line that is parallel to the house wall. With pegs and string, mark out the area to be paved, making it a size and shape that requires the fewest slabs to be cut. If the slabs are not to be butted, allow about ¼–½in (0.5–1cm) for the mortar joints. Seek advice from your supplier if you are in any doubt

Preparing the site

Clear the site and prepare a subbase with crushed stone (see p.579). If you intend to cement the stones in place, you will need wooden spacers about ½in (1cm) thick to place between the paving slabs to allow room for filling with mortar.

Positioning the slabs

Work from one corner, placing a row of slabs in each direction with spacers between to make sure that the dimensions are correct. Adjustments are easy to make at this stage. Using a bricklayer's trowel, lay a strip of bedding mortar along each edge where the slab is to be laid, to form an area slightly smaller than the slab. If the slab is 18in (45cm) across or more, lay a cross of mortar within the box. The mortar ridges should be about 1¼–2in (3–5cm) high. This "box and cross" method combines strength with easy adjustment. Lay the slab in position, then tamp it down with the handle of a club hammer or mallet. Use a level to check that it is firm and straight.

PAVING SLAB STYLES

TEXTURE
Surface textures range from smooth to stippled, scored, or roughly pebbled.

HEXAGONAL PAVERS
These are an attractive alternative to rectangles or squares. Half blocks are used for straight edges.

WEATHERED PAVERS
If a more natural look is desired, a variety of weathered stone pavers is available.

POINTED SLABS
Some slabs are pointed to give special patterns or effects. Those with a "bite" taken out may be fitted together for a planting hole.

PAVING PATTERNS
A variety of pleasing patterns may be created with different shapes and sizes of paver.

CAST AND PRESSED SLABS
Cast slabs (sloping edges) are for light/medium use. Pressed slabs (straight) are lighter but stronger.

HOW TO LAY PAVING SLABS

1 *Mark out the area and prepare the subbase (see p.579). Lay strips of mortar to form a square just smaller than the slab. Include a cross strip for large slabs.*

2 *Position the slab and tamp down. Use a level to check that it is even. Repeat, using spacers for ½in (1cm) mortar gaps between the slabs.*

3 *Remove the spacers before the mortar sets. Fill the joints with a stiff mortar. Tamp down. Joints should be recessed about 1/16in (2mm). Brush mortar from the slabs.*

USING A JIGGER
This device has a central slit. After aligning the slit and joint, the gap can be filled without spilling mortar on the slabs.

Repeat with successive slabs, using spacers between each one. Check the levels in each direction after every three or four slabs. Remove the spacers while you can still reach them without walking on the paving, nd before the mortar sets. If you need to walk on the paving before the mortar has dried, stand on boards to distribute your weight more evenly over the entire area.

HOW TO CUT SLABS

1 *Place the slab on a firm, flat surface and, using the corner of a chisel and a straightedge, score a groove on both faces and edges to mark the cutting line.*

2 *Using a chisel and club hammer, carefully work along the scored line to deepen the groove on the faces and edges of the paving slab.*

3 *Raise the slab onto a length of wood. Align the groove with the edge of the wood, then tap the slab sharply with a hammer handle until it splits.*

Finishing

After a couple of days, fill the joints with a very stiff mortar mix (it should almost be crumbly to avoid staining the surface of the paving). Rub a dowel or a rounded piece of wood over the pointing for a crisp finish, leaving it about $1/16$in (2mm) below the paving surface. Alternatively, brush a dry mortar consisting of 1 part cement to 3 parts sand into the joints.

Brush surplus mortar off the surface. Spray the joints with a fine mist from a hose-end sprayer or a watering can fitted with a fine nozzle. Sponge mortar from the surface immediately, before it stains the slabs.

Cutting paving slabs

If you have many slabs to cut, it is best to rent a power masonry saw. For only a few, use a broad-edged cold chisel and club hammer. Always wear goggles when cutting paving blocks. With a corner of the chisel, score the line where you need to cut all around the slab, then create a groove about $1/8$in (3mm) deep along this line; you may have to work around the slab several times, using the chisel to define and deepen the groove. If the slab has to fit into a tight space, cut it about $1/4$in (6mm) smaller than needed to allow room for any rough edges that may be left when the slab splits.

Place the slab on a firm surface and raise the smaller part of the slab to be cut on a length of wood. Tap it sharply with the handle of a club hammer until a split forms along the line of the groove. Trim any protrusions carefully with the chisel to make a smooth edge.

Random paving

Random paving has an informal appearance. It can be laid on sand, which will allow plants to be grown between the joints, or on mortar for a firmer finish; if using the latter, fill in the joints with bedding mortar.

Defining the edges

Use string lines to mark out the area to be paved and prepare a subbase for the paving (see p.579). Allow a slight slope for drainage (see "Water runoff," p.579) if necessary. Define the edges by laying a few yards (meters) of edging material first, working from one corner if laying a patio, or the two edges if laying a path. This may simply be large pieces of random paving, with at least one straight edge, which can be laid to form the sides of the patio or path, or it could be wood, brick, or concrete. If using paving slabs, mortar these into position, even if bedding the remaining slabs on sand.

Laying the random paving

Rough-lay an area about 3ft (1m) square without mortar, fitting the pieces together like a jigsaw puzzle. Keep the gaps small. It may be necessary to trim some pieces to size. Introduce a large piece occasionally, and fill in with smaller ones.

Bed the pieces on sand or mortar, using a level on a straight edge to ensure that they are even. Use a mallet or block of wood and a hammer to bed each piece firmly in position. Lift pieces and add or remove sand or mortar as necessary until all paving stones are level.

Filling the joints

If bedding random paving on sand, finish off by brushing dry sand into the joints. If using mortar, mix a stiff, crumbly, almost-dry mortar, and use a pointing trowel to fill the joints (see "Finishing off," left). If using a dark-colored stone, such as slate, use a concrete dye (a powder that you mix with the sand and cement) to make the joints less conspicuous. The color will look different when dry, so test the dye on a small area and allow it to dry before deciding on the amount of color to add.

Natural stone

Natural stone looks good, but is expensive and difficult to lay. Some types, such as sandstone, may be available cut into regular sizes and with an even edge. "Dressed" stone looks more natural; it is trimmed to a regular shape and has an attractive, uneven finish. Lay sawed or dressed stone in the same way as paving slabs, adding or removing mortar to produce a level surface.

Fieldstone is irregular and has no straight edges. This stone is suitable for laying as random paving, and it looks much more appealing than broken concrete slabs, but it can form an uneven walkway. Upper and lower faces may differ; try to match them.

Tile surfaces

Quarry tiles, which are made of clay fired to a very high temperature, are useful for linking outdoor and indoor areas – perhaps where the paving inside a conservatory links with that outside. Glazed ceramic tiles may be more ornamental, giving an enclosed patio the impression of a

HOW TO LAY RANDOM PAVING

1 *Using string lines and pegs to mark the height of the edges, prepare a subbase (see p.579). Lay the edging pieces first, placing their straight edges facing outward.*

2 *Lay large slabs in the center, filling in with smaller ones. Check that central slabs are level with the edging pieces and bed them on sand or mortar. Use a piece of wood and a club hammer.*

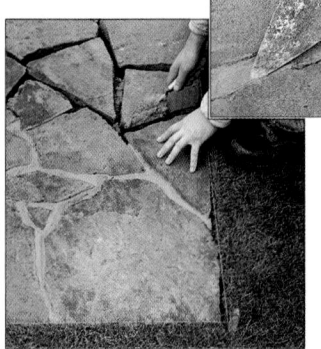

3 *Fill the joints with almost-dry mortar, or brush in sand. With a mortar finish, use a trowel to bevel the mortar so that any surface water will always drain away from the slabs.*

Mediterranean courtyard for example, but many are not frostproof. When selecting tiles, always check that they are suitable for using outdoors in your area. Tiles are difficult to cut, especially if they are not rectangular, so where possible design the area to make use of full tiles.

Laying tiles

Since tiles are thin and sometimes brittle, they need to be laid on a concrete subbase (see "Load-bearing surfaces," p.580). Quarry tiles may be laid on bedding mortar (see p.580). Soak the tiles in water for a couple of hours before use so that they do not absorb too much moisture from the mortar.

Glazed ceramic tiles are best glued to a level concrete base using outdoor tile adhesive (obtainable from a building supply store). Spread this on the back of the tiles, following the manufacturer's instructions, then press the tiles into position on the prepared concrete base.

Finish off an area of glazed tiles with a grout (available from building supply stores) to fill the gaps, perhaps colored to match or contrast with the tiles.

Bricks and pavers

Bricks and clay or concrete pavers (also called interlock) are most effective when laid in small areas. A large expanse may be divided up with other materials, such as gravel or railroad ties. Alternatively, lay bricks in two or more complementary patterns or colors.

For a patio situated next to a house built of brick, using bricks or pavers is an excellent way of visually linking the house and garden.

Choosing bricks

The range of bricks available is quite wide; it is possible to find a type that suits virtually any patio or terrace.

For a large volume of bricks, contact a brick company to see if they will deliver. Building supply stores sell bricks in any quantities. Be sure to choose bricks that are appropriate for outdoor paving and resistant to wetting and freezing.

Choosing pavers

Clay pavers are as attractive as bricks and are usually produced in shades of red. They have a thinner profile than concrete pavers or bricks. Concrete pavers may lack the warm colors of bricks, but they will make a practical surface. They are generally found in gray, blue-gray, or buff shades and are produced in a range of shapes.

Laying bricks

First make a suitable subbase (see p.579). Bricks should ideally be bedded on mortar. First lay the edging strips (or edging bricks), bedded on concrete footing and then fixed with mortar between the joints. Prepare the bedding mortar (see p.580) and lay it to a depth of 1in (2.5cm). Bed the bricks onto this, spacing them evenly to leave joints for mortar; use thin strips of hardboard or wood as spacers between bricks if desired. Once an area is complete, brush a dry mortar over the bricks. To remove air pockets, press this into the gaps with a narrow piece of wood. In damp weather, moisture from the ground and air will set the pointing; in dry weather, speed up setting by spraying with water.

HOW TO LAY BRICK PAVING

1 *First, prepare the subbase (see p.579), allowing space for the edging bricks. Use string lines and pegs to set the edging bricks at the desired height.*

2 *Mortar in the edging bricks, and bed the others in the required pattern, tamping them level. At intervals, check levels in all directions.*

3 *Spread a thin layer of dry mortar over the surface, and brush it between the joints. Sprinkle with water to set the mortar, then clean the surface.*

Patterns in brick

Bricks can be laid in several different ways to create attractive patterns. Three examples are shown below.

BASKET WEAVE

INTERLOCKING BOXES

HERRINGBONE

Types of brick

Bricks are available in a wide variety of styles, textures, and colors, providing an attractive and practical building material. Take care to choose the most appropriate type. They should be suitable for the proposed purpose and coordinate well with the house, patio, or other hard landscape features.

ENGINEERING BRICKS
Engineering bricks are very durable. If used for paving, make sure they have good wet-weather grip. They may cost more than ordinary bricks.

CORED BRICKS
Cored bricks have holes. They may be used on edge for paving with a narrower profile but are not economical for large areas.

FACING OR STOCK BRICKS
These are used to face buildings, providing an attractive finish. They are available in a variety of colors and may be rough or smooth in texture. They may be unsuitable for paving, since they may not be able to withstand severe weather conditions.

BRICKS WITH "FROGS"
A frog is an indentation in one face of a brick. Frogged bricks may be used for paving if they are laid on edge or the frogs face downward.

Cutting bricks and pavers

Bricks and thick pavers may be difficult to cut. If cutting is necessary, it can be done by the company that supplied the material or by using a rented masonry saw. Using these options, it is possible to cut bricks accurately, neatly, and quickly. Alternatively, they may be cut to the desired shape with a chisel and club hammer (see "Cutting paving slabs," p.582), although the cuts made by these tools may not be as clean.

Laying pavers

Pavers are bedded onto sand using a plate compactor; they nest together with small gaps between. Since the pavers can be lifted and relaid, this type of paving is sometimes called flexible paving. Blocks 2½–2¾in (6–6.5cm) thick are adequate for garden projects.

Preparing the site and laying edge restraints

First, prepare a subbase suitable for local conditions (see "Foundations," p.579). Where there are no existing firm edges (such as walls), lay permanent edging strips. The simplest way to do this is to use specially made edge restraints or edging pieces, which are available from paving manufacturers. These must be set into position in concrete. Alternatively, 1½ x 4in (3.8 x 10cm) pressure-treated lumber held in place with strong pegs at least 2in (5cm) square may be used.

Large areas should be broken up into manageable sizes, such as 3ft (1m) squares, using temporary wooden rails. Spread a layer of sharp sand evenly to a depth of about 2in

Pavers, tiles, setts, and cobblestones

Pavers (also called interlock) vary greatly in size, color, and thickness. They are also finished in many different ways, so that their texture and final shape (either formal and geometric or more informal and natural) contribute greatly to the style of the garden. Considerably more distinctive results may be achieved using terracotta tiles, granite setts, Belgian blocks, or cobblestones.

CLAY PAVERS
These red pavers may be laid either as stretchers, that is longitudinally, or as headers, placed end on.

WIRE-CUT CLAY PAVERS

Wire-cut clay pavers have a dragged finish and a roughened surface on all sides, which serves to provide extra grip in the finished paving.

INTERLOCKING PAVERS
These clay or concrete pavers can be used to create unusual patterns. Pressed pavers in blocks (far right) are produced in a range of colors.

TERRACOTTA TILES
Like bricks, terracotta tiles are made of clay but allowed to dry in the sun. They are porous and may crack if used in areas prone to frost.

GRANITE SETTS
Cut from hard granite, this form of paving is extremely durable. Like cobblestones, their roughened surface creates a natural look.

IMITATION GRANITE SETTS
These reconstituted stone pavers are lighter and cheaper than granite. Belgian blocks have a more weathered look.

BELGIAN BLOCKS

COBBLESTONES
Cobblestones (below) are large, rounded stones formed by the action of the ocean or glaciers. They can be set in mortar to form an interestingly textured finish, but they are uncomfortable to walk on and should be used only in small areas or in combination with other paving materials. When laying cobblestones, form firm edges with bricks or lengths of concrete edging, set in concrete.

HOW TO LAY FLEXIBLE PAVING

1 *After preparing the subbase (see p.580), set edging strips of concrete or wood in position around the edges of the site. Use a level and a club hammer to tap the edges level.*

2 *Divide large areas into bays 3ft (1m) square with boards. Add 2in (5cm) of sand. Level the sand to the tops of the boards with a length of wood. Remove the boards and fill the vacated spaces with sand.*

3 *Lay the pavers to the required pattern, working from one corner of the site. Lay only whole blocks at this stage, leaving until last any cut ones required to fill the gaps in the design.*

4 *Vibrate the pavers into the sand or tamp down with a club hammer and length of wood. Brush dry sand over the surface and make 2 or 3 passes with a plate compactor.*

(5cm). The top surface of the sand should be just high enough that about one-third of the paving block will protrude above the surrounding wooden rails. Adjust the amount of sand as work proceeds.

Positioning and bedding the pavers

Do not walk on the sand while laying the pavers, and keep it dry. Work from one corner of the site to lay the pavers. When some are laid, place a kneeling board over the pavers to continue working. Lay as many whole blocks as possible, then fill in with cut pavers around any obstacles as necessary (see "Cutting paving slabs," p.582).

When about 6sq yd (5sq m) of paving has been laid, bed the pavers into the sand. The easiest way to do this is with a plate compactor, but do not go too near the incompleted edge. If laying only a small area of paving, the blocks can be tamped down with a heavy club hammer over a block of wood that is large enough to span several pavers at once. Continue to lay pavers and bed or tamp them down.

When the whole area is finished, brush dry sand into the joints and settle in position with the plate compactor. Create a mowing edge of bricks, pavers, or concrete slabs where it is difficult to mow right up to the lawn edge, such as along a flower bed. Bed the paving material on mortar, with the top just below the grass level, so that the mower is not damaged.

A COMBINATION OF PAVING EFFECTS
A mixture of different paving materials, including square stone slabs, random paving, and brick edging, blends well with informal planting.

Setts and cobblestones

Bed granite or imitation setts on 2in (5cm) of bedding mortar (see p.580) and brush stiff mortar into the joints (see "Finishing," p.582). Spray the surface with water to clean it and set the mortar mix.

Cobblestones may also be set in mortar. They are uncomfortable to walk on, so use for small areas or with other materials. When laying, form firm edges with bricks or lengths of concrete edging. Lay 1½in (3.5cm) of bedding mortar on 3in (7.5cm) of compacted crushed stone.

Terms explained

Aggregate is crushed stone or gravel used to make concrete. Fine aggregate contains particles up to ¼in (½cm), coarse aggregate from ¼in to 3in (½cm to 7cm). Combined aggregate contains sand and stone.
Bedding mortar is used for laying paving stones. It is made with sharp sand instead of soft (builder's) sand.
Cement is a gray powder containing limestone, the setting agent of concrete and mortar.
Concrete is a hard-setting building material made of a mixture of cement, aggregate, sand, and water.
Crushed stone has angular particles that are graded by size, the finest grade being stone dust.
Dry mortar is a stiff mix often used to fill the joints in paving.
Masonry cement has additives that make it unsuitable for concrete. Use only for mortars.
Mortar is a mixture of cement, sand, and water used principally for bricklaying.
Portland cement is a type of cement. Use ordinary Portland cement for most concreting jobs. It can also be used for mortars.
Sand is graded by particle size. Sharp sand is gritty, clean, and contains no salt. Avoid or wash ocean-beach sand, since salt stops cement from hardening.

Decks

Wooden decking is popular as a hard surface in warm, dry climates. Decks may be used anywhere, however, provided that pressure-treated lumber is used.

It is best to build the deck on a level or gently sloping site. For a raised deck on a steeply sloping site, it is advisable to seek specialized assistance, since it would need to be well designed and constructed.

In some areas there are building regulations that state that all exterior areas of decking must be able to support a stipulated minimum weight. It may also be necessary to obtain a building permit in some areas and have the work inspected. If in any doubt concerning the regulations, check your local building ordinances. Simple parquet decking (see p.586), which is laid on gravel and sand, should not require a building permit.

WOODEN DECKING
A wooden patio or veranda overlooking the garden makes a very imposing feature, especially when crowned with a pergola to provide summer shade. However, wooden decking needs to be very well constructed, and it is usually best to have the job done by experts. Features such as rails, steps, and wooden supports require regular maintenance (see p.586).

Wood for decking

Western red cedar is a good choice because of its natural rot resistance, although regularly treating it with a preservative ensures a longer life. Other wood is suitable but must be pressure-treated with a preservative. When using pressure-treated lumber, always paint cut ends with a wood preservative. Short lengths of lumber can be made up into decking panels to produce a wide variety of practical, attractive patterns.

CHECKERBOARD   HERRINGBONE   PARALLEL SLATS   ANGLED CHECKERBOARD   PARALLEL JOINTED

Slatted decking

This type of decking is suitable for level or gently sloping ground. It is simple to construct and requires little specialized hardware.

For an area beside a house, construct a concrete foundation (see *How to Lay Concrete*, p.580) with a gentle fall away from the house for water drainage. Onto the concrete base, mortar a row of bricks spaced about one brick apart at right angles to the intended direction of the decking. Add more rows of bricks at intervals of 16in (40cm). Check constantly that all the bricks are level, because they will support the joists.

Lay joists 2 x 3in (5 x 7cm) over the bricks, inserting a sheet of plastic between the bricks and the joists. If joining lengths of wood, make sure there is a brick beneath the point where the joists abut, and screw a plain bracket across the join. Always check that joists are even, using a level and a straightedge to ensure accuracy.

DECKING STEPPING-STONES
Decking can be used to create an unusual "stepping-stone" path across a pond. When positioned and angled for aesthetic impact, the squares add a stylish, geometric element to informal planting and the soft play of light on the pond surface. Here, parallel slats are laid in alternate directions to add a dynamic sense of movement to the overall design.

Lay 1 x 10in (2.5 x 25cm) boards at right angles to the joists. Allow 1/2in (1cm) gaps for free drainage and a little movement in the wood. Make sure that joins in the decking are staggered from row to row and that the boards are butt-joined over a supporting joist. Secure the boards with brass or other rustproof screws, countersunk beneath the surface. Fill the holes with a wood filler that matches the color of the wood.

Finish the deck neatly with a low brick or block edging, cutting the decking so that it overlaps the edging by 2in (5cm). Alternatively, a length of facing wood can be screwed or nailed along the cut edges.

Parquet decking

It is possible to buy parquetlike wooden squares intended primarily for paths, which can also be used for decking. Alternatively they can be easily made. About 3ft (1m) square is a practical size. Buy 2 x 4in

(5 x 10cm) treated wood, cut into 3ft (80cm) lengths, and sand the ends smooth. Two lengths form the supports at opposite sides of the square, while the others are laid across them as slats. Use spacers to make sure that these slats fill the area evenly, and fix with two nails at either end. Prepare a base on firmed ground or subsoil with 3in (7cm) of compacted gravel topped with 3in (7cm) of sand. Level and tamp before laying the squares in alternate directions. Nail them together if necessary to ensure their stability, driving the nails in at an angle.

Applying stains

Western red cedar turns a very obvious red color when wet. It may, however, be stained any color to suit the surroundings. It is best to use stains that allow any moisture in the wood to escape; if trapped beneath an impermeable layer, it would eventually cause the surface color to lift. Wooden surfaces to be stained should be dry and free from dirt. Follow instructions regarding stirring or thinning, and apply the

stain with a good-quality paint brush, brushing in the direction of the grain. Do not overload the brush, which leads to uneven coverage, but work the stain well into the wood. Several applications will be needed, waiting until each coat is completely dry before applying more.

Maintenance

All wooden surfaces need regular maintenance. Once a year, check for splits or cracks. Damaged boards will need to be replaced. Check that no bolts, screws, brackets, or nails have rusted. If galvanized hardware is scratched, the protective coating may be damaged and rust will appear. Brass hardware, which does not rust, is preferable in wooden decking. If the stain wears thin in areas of heavy foot traffic, clean the surface and reapply the stain (see above). Fungal growths may appear at some stage. Fungicides are available, but it is better to remove growths by brushing with a stiff broom. In some regions, termites can cause problems in decking; if in doubt, consult a pest control firm.

SUPPORT FOR WOODEN DECKING

Boards butt-joined over a joist

Joists butt-joined over a supporting brick

Moisture-proof membrane

When joining two lengths of wood to form a joist, make sure that the join lies over one of the supporting bricks. Lay the boards at right angles to the joists, positioning all butt joins directly over a supporting joist.

Paths and steps

Paths and steps play a major role in good garden design. They help form the framework of the garden, link its various elements, and may lead the eye to a focal point. Consider setting a path at an angle, off center, or following an indirect route. Steps provide interesting changes of level and create very different effects, depending on whether they are straight or curved, wide or narrow, and shallow or steep.

Practical considerations
Paths to the garden shed or the greenhouse need to be wide enough to take a wheelbarrow and should also provide a dry and solid surface. Paths to the front door or for strolling through the garden should be sufficiently wide for two to walk abreast: about 3–4ft (1–1.2m).

Materials and design
The choice of materials and the laying pattern may be used to set or enhance the garden style. Combining materials, such as paving stones with cobblestones, bricks with gravel, or concrete paving slabs with bricks or clay pavers, often makes an appealing design for a path.

Stepping-stone paths may be laid in many parts of the garden. They are a good choice, for example, when you do not want to spoil the line of a lawn, but they can become muddy in wet weather. Before you start, place the paving stones on the surface to check the spacing; they should be spaced at a natural pace. On lawns, set them into the grass so that their surface is safely below mowing level.

Where winters are relatively dry, paths may be made of wood, either in the form of log sections used as stepping-stones or to make a series of square, slatted units as described in "Parquet decking," opposite.

On sloping sites, steps may be an essential part of a path. They may also be valuable as a design feature even on a relatively flat site. Steps should harmonize with their setting: in a woodland garden, for example, shallow log risers and gravel treads would be suitable while brick risers and concrete slab treads might be more appropriate in a modern setting.

Driveways
A driveway can have a considerable impact on a design, especially in a small garden. There may be little choice in where to position a driveway, unless a new garage is to be built at the same time. It is possible to make a driveway look attractive by choosing a suitable surface and positioning ornamental plants nearby.

Asphalt

Asphalt is best used for driveways and paths that need not be attractive – the path to the shed, for example. It can also be used to cover a damaged concrete path. Add texture by rolling stone chips into the surface. If asphalt is not locally available in small quantities, use cold patch. Asphalt is best laid in warm weather. Unless it is well laid, asphalt may break up after a few years; for heavily used areas such as a main driveway, hire a qualified contractor to lay the asphalt.

Preparations
Asphalt can be laid on any firm surface such as concrete or gravel. Never lay it on bare earth or crushed

BRICK PATHWAYS
A brick path can become a design feature in its own right, adding texture and color to a garden entrance. Here, the soft pink of the brick harmonizes with the surrounding plants and leads the eye to the rose-covered arch and the less formal grass area beyond.

stone, since it will be difficult to obtain a firm and level surface that will last. If necessary, make a stable base by spreading a mixture of gravel and sand 2–3in (5–7cm) thick over firm ground or compacted crushed stone. If an old path or driveway is the base, first paint inside any holes or cracks with driveway sealer and leave for about 20 minutes before filling them with asphalt. To ensure good water drainage, lay a driveway on a slight slope.

The edges of an asphalt path often weaken and crumble, so use concrete edging blocks (obtained from building supply stores), bricks, or lengths of pressure-treated lumber to provide a firm edging.

Application
Apply a layer of driveway sealer to bind the surface. Stir it first, then pour it from the container and spread with a stiff brush. Apply the asphalt and rake to an even depth of about ¾in (2cm).

Firm the surface by tamping it with the back of a rake to remove large air pockets, then make several passes with a heavy garden roller. Keep the surface of the roller damp to prevent the asphalt from sticking to it. Fill up any visible depressions, then roll the surface again. If using stone chips, sprinkle evenly and roll again to bed them in.

Bricks and pavers

The sympathetic coloring of bricks and clay pavers makes them excellent materials for paths within the garden. Because the individual units are small, it is relatively easy to adjust to changes of level and even to

lay a path to a curve. A variety of effects can be created, depending on the laying pattern used (see "Patterns in brick," p.583).

Construction
Mark out the proposed line of the path with pegs and string, calculating where cut bricks or pavers may be needed to create a sharp curve. If the path will be subjected to heavy wear, prepare a deep foundation (see "Load-bearing surfaces," p.580). For one that will receive lighter use, a 3in (8cm) subbase of crushed stone firmed and leveled with stone dust should be sufficient.

First lay a suitable edging (see "Edging paths," p.588) along one side of the path, then lay the path itself in sections about 3ft (1m) long. Pavers should be bedded in a 2in (5cm) layer of dry sand (see "Laying pavers," p.584), while bricks require a 1in (2.5cm) bed of mortar (see "Laying bricks," p.583). As you complete each section, tamp the bricks or pavers into place, checking that they are level with a straightedge and level. Then lay the edging on the other side of the path to complete this section. Repeat the process for each section until the path has been laid.

To finish off a path made of pavers, brush dry sand into the joints. For a brick path, brush a dry mortar mix in between the joints (see "Finishing," p.582), making sure that there are no large air pockets. If necessary, compact the mortar using a piece of wood slightly thinner than the width of the joints. Finally, sprinkle with a fine spray of water from a watering can or wash down gently with a hose-end sprayer to moisten the mortar and clean the bricks.

SUBTLETY WITH STONE
Here, the mottled texture of the embedded stones is complemented by Alchemilla mollis and defined by seams of moss.

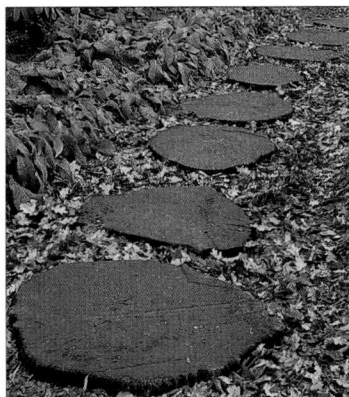

LOG SECTIONS
Logs sawed into sections make a harmonious series of stepping-stones through an area of woodland, blending perfectly with the setting.

Concrete

Concrete poured *in situ* is a practical and durable surface material that is especially useful for wide paths and driveways. Its appearance can be made more attractive by adding texture (see below). Concrete can also be colored using special dyes added to the mix. Since the color often looks different once the concrete has dried, use dyes with caution. Color a small test piece first, then let it dry, rather than judge the final appearance by the wet mix.

Divide a wide concrete path with rows of bricks or lengths of broad wood that will become part of the finished design. These will avoid the need for laying expansion joints during construction.

Preparing a base

Prepare a suitable foundation (see "Basic procedure," p.579). Next, make the form to hold the concrete in place until it sets. Use lengths of wood 1in (2.5cm) thick, and at least the depth of the concrete. Use 2 x 2in (5 x 5cm) pegs, not more than 3ft (1m) apart to hold the form in place. Lengths of wood may be joined

by nailing a block of wood to the outside of the two pieces to bridge them together.

Making curves

To make gentle curves, mark out the shape that you want to create, and hammer pegs into the ground set closely together. Soak lengths of softwood in water to make them pliable, and then bend and nail them to the pegs. Sharp curves can be made in a similar way, with the addition of a series of saw cuts on the inside of the curve. The saw cuts should reach about halfway through the wood to increase its flexibility. Alternatively, use several thicknesses of thin hardboard, which is easy to bend and shape.

Expansion joints

Concrete will crack if not laid with breaks to allow for expansion and a degree of movement. Divide the area into sections no more than 12ft (4m) long, using fixed pieces of wood as temporary divisions. If using pre-mixed concrete, where the load has to be used all at once, use hardboard cut into sections, and leave these in position until the concrete has set.

Adding texture

A concrete path poured *in situ* can be made more attractive by adding texture. Use these techniques on a few sections only, or alternate patterns between sections, to create an interesting overall result.

Exposed aggregate gives a pleasant, nonslip finish. Spread gravel or crushed stone evenly over the concrete before it sets, then tamp it gently into the surface. When the concrete is nearly hard, brush the surface to expose more of the aggregate, then spray it with water to wash away fine particles. Different textures and colors can be created by using aggregates with particles of various sizes and colors.

Brushed finishes are easy to create. After tamping the concrete gently, push the bristles of a soft broom over the surface to produce a fairly smooth finish; for a ridged effect, use a stiff broom once the concrete has begun to set. You can also brush in a series of swirls, or straight or wavy lines.

Stamped patterns can be made with special tools or with inventive objects such as pastry cutters and seashells. This technique is best kept to very small areas. To create leaf impressions, use large leaves, such as sycamore, pressing them into the surface with a trowel, and then brushing them out once the concrete has hardened.

Coarse texture

Medium-coarse texture

Fine texture

1 *Dig out the base of the path to a depth of 7in (18cm) and set the edges. Compact the base. Drive in pegs at 3ft (1m) intervals to anchor the edge restraints.*

2 *If the path borders a lawn, excavate an extra 1in (2.5cm) so that the path is below grass level (inset). Put down layers of crushed stone, sand and coarse gravel, and pea gravel. Rake level.*

Laying concrete

Mix the concrete (see p.580) and pour it into the form. If mixing in small batches, fill alternate bays, then remove the dividers once the concrete has set and pour concrete into the remaining bays. Use a length of wood to tamp the concrete level, working from the center toward the joints. If the path or driveway is wide, using a tamping board with another person will make the job easier. Tamping leaves a slightly ridged surface. If a smooth finish is required, use a wood float in gentle, sweeping motions. A steel float will produce an even smoother surface.

Concrete paving slabs

Paving slabs are available in a wide range of colors, shapes, and finishes. They are easier to lay than concrete poured *in situ* but are more difficult to lay to a curve than bricks or pavers. They combine well with other materials, for instance with cobblestones set along the edge or with small strips of gravel between each slab. This is a useful technique for creating curved paths, since it makes the uneven joints less obtrusive. For details on laying paving slabs, see p.581.

Grass

Grass paths are useful for linking a series of lawns, or for broad walks between beds. They should be as wide as possible: this helps them stand up to concentrated wear. They also need less water than narrow sod. Put down sod for a grass path in the same way as for a lawn (see THE LAWN, "Laying sod," p.386).

Gravel

Gravel is easy to lay, presents no problems when creating curves, and is not expensive. There are drawbacks, however: unless well bedded and used with retaining edges, loose gravel can get onto adjoining surfaces, it can be uncomfortable and noisy to walk on, and it is not an easy surface on which to push a wheelbarrow or a stroller.

Construct a firm base by excavating the ground to take about 4in (10cm) of compacted crushed stone, 2in (5cm) of a sand and coarse gravel mix, and 1in (2.5cm) of gravel. For a fine finish, use pea gravel.

In a formal setting with mainly straight edges, concrete edging strips can be used; in other settings, bricks or treated lumber may be more appropriate. If using wood, anchor it with pegs about 3ft (1m) apart. Apply the gravel in several stages, raking and rolling it to produce a slight camber for drainage. To help compaction and create a solid path, water the gravel occasionally with a fine spray while rolling.

Edging paths

Plastic edge restraints sold as lawn edging are easily cut to size and hold a path of bricks or pavers in place invisibly. Lengths of treated lumber may also be used, held in place with wooden pegs. It is possible to use boards temporarily while building the path, then remove them and fill in the gaps with concrete. For a brick edging, lay matching or contrasting bricks on edge. Secure them with mortar; this also helps stop weeds from growing.

Building steps

To calculate the number of steps you need to build, divide the height of the slope by the height of one riser (including the depth of the paving slab and mortar). It may be necessary to adjust the height of the steps to fit the slope. Mark the position of the risers with wooden pegs, and then excavate the soil to form a series of soil steps.

Make a concrete footing (see p.590) for the base riser, and allow it to set. Then construct the riser using bricks or blocks set in masonry mortar (see p.580). Check that they are even using a straightedge and level, and backfill behind the riser with compacted crushed stone or sand and gravel.

Prepare a bed of mortar on top of the riser and lay the first tread; it should slope forward slightly to shed water, and overlap the riser at the front by 1–2in (2.5–5cm). Mark the position of the next riser on the tread, and mortar it into position.

Tread-to-riser ratio

For ease of use, it is important that the width of the tread and the height of the riser are in the correct proportion to each other. As a general rule, the width of the tread and double the height of the riser should total about 26in (65cm). First, choose the height of the riser, double it and deduct it from 26in (65cm) to give the width of the tread. You may wish to add 1–2in (2.5–5cm) for an overhang.

For the steps to be safe, the treads should measure at least 12in (30cm) from front to back. The height of the risers is normally between 4in (10cm) and 7in (18cm).

Paving-stone treads

Brick risers

Gravel

WOOD AND GRAVEL STEPS
Railroad ties are filled in with gravel to create a curving flight of gently rising steps, with flanking plants softening the edges.

HOW TO BUILD STEPS INTO A BANK

1 *Measure the height of the bank to work out how many steps are needed (see left). To do this, drive a peg into the top of the slope and a post at the bottom. Tie string horizontally between the two, then measure the distance between ground level and the string.*

2 *Use string and pegs to mark the sides, then run strings to mark the fronts of the treads. Dig out the steps and compact the earth at each tread position.*

3 *Construct a footing for the riser, 6in (15cm) deep and twice the width of the bricks. Fill with concrete over a 3in (7cm) crushed-stone base.*

4 *When the concrete has set, lay the first riser on the footing. Use a string line stretched between pegs to be sure the bricks are straight and level.*

5 *Backfill with crushed stone to the height of the bricks and tamp down. Set the paving slabs on ½in (1cm) of mortar, with a small gap between them.*

6 *The slabs should have an overhang of 1–2in (2.5–5cm) at the front and a slight forward slope for drainage. Mark the position of the second riser on the slabs, then mortar the bricks in place. Fill in and set the treads as before. Continue for the remaining steps. Finally, mortar the joints between the slabs.*

Walls

Boundary walls have been a feature of gardens since the early days of enclosures, and in the 19th century, walled gardens were a common feature on large estates. Now, however, large boundary walls are uncommon, having given way to less expensive fences or hedges.

Garden walls are often decorative as well as practical. If they have a planting cavity, low walls can be particularly attractive and, because they require less substantial foundations and supporting piers, they are also easy and inexpensive to build.

Materials

Boundary walls may be constructed from various materials, including brick, and for low walls precast concrete walling blocks. Screen block walls (opposite) are a practical and decorative alternative to solid walls and are also suitable for dividing off parts of the garden. These blocks are made specifically for outdoor use. When buying bricks, however, always check with the supplier that they are suitable for garden walls: bricks should be frostproof and able to withstand moisture penetration from both sides.

Walls may also be constructed from a combination of materials, for example brick with facing panels of local stone such as schist. Large, plain walls may be painted with a masonry paint (usually white or a pale color) on the garden side. This reflects the light and contrasts well with wall shrubs or other plants.

How high to build?

There may be restrictions placed on the height of walls in local building codes, so check this before building. A low block wall is a straightforward job that anyone handy with materials and tools should be able to tackle. Brick and concrete block walls higher than about 3ft (1m) require advice from an expert and should have a strengthening pier every 8ft (2.5m).

COMBINED MATERIALS
Brick and flint are juxtaposed here to create a striking garden divider. The mixture of straight and curved lines reinforces the blend of styles. When combined in this way, diverse materials enhance each other.

Concrete footings for walls

The width of the footing for all walls should be two to three times the width of the wall. For walls lower than 3ft (1m), deep and substantial foundations are not necessary.

For a half-brick wall (i.e. the width of a single brick), dig a trench the length of the wall and 15in (38cm) deep. Place 5in (13cm) of crushed stone in the bottom and tamp it down. Then pour in 4in (10cm) of concrete, allowing it to harden completely for a few days before laying the bricks or concrete blocks. For a

---

Walling materials

Bricks are the most popular choice of walling material, although concrete blocks manufactured to imitate natural clay bricks may also be used. If you want to build a wall to match the brickwork of existing buildings, used bricks are available in many colors and styles.

SMOOTH-TEXTURED BRICKS
These are most suitable for facing the front of a wall. They come in a variety of colors.

MOTTLED ENGINEERING BRICKS
These contribute a rough-hewn appearance; they are also the hardest of all the bricks.

PRECAST CONCRETE BLOCKS
These contain medium-textured gravel.

ROCK-FACED CONCRETE BLOCKS
The brick red color imitates the look of clay bricks. They are also available colored to look like sandstone.

SMOOTH BLOCKS
These concrete blocks suit a modern design.

HOW TO MAKE A CONCRETE FOOTING

1 *Mark out the site of the foundations with string lines stretched between wooden pegs. Dig a trench to the required depth (see text).*

2 *Check that the base is level and the sides vertical. Drive in pegs to the level for the concrete. Align with a level and a length of wood spanning the pegs.*

3 *Soak the trench with water and allow it to drain. Then add 5in (13cm) of crushed stone and tamp it down. Pour in concrete, slicing into the mix with a spade to dispel air bubbles.*

4 *Compact the concrete by tamping it down firmly with a length of wood. Level it to the tops of the pegs. Leave the surface rough as a key for the mortar for the first course of bricks.*

How to Build a Screen Wall

1 *Once the concrete footing has dried fully – at least two days – set out the position of the wall with two string guides, 2 bricks' width plus ½in (10mm) apart. Dry-position the lowest course, ½in (10mm) between bricks.*

2 *Chalk the brick positions on the footing. Throw a mortar bed ½in (10mm) thick along all the entire first course. As you set each brick on it, check that it is level from end to end and front to back.*

3 *Before laying, butter an end face of each brick with ½in (10mm) of mortar. Fill the gap.*

4 *Throw a mortar bed on top of the first course of length-wise bricks (the stretcher) and lay the next course (the header) at right angles to the first. Check constantly and adjust all levels.*

5 *Raise up both ends of the wall by 4 courses, alternating stretchers and headers. Scrape off excess mortar as you bed each brick. Neaten joints with a pointing tool. Then complete each course.*

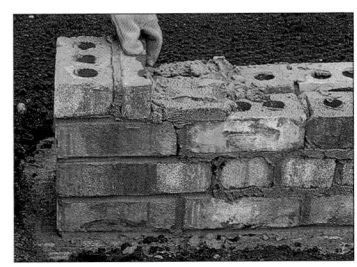

6 *On the fourth row, insert a half brick after the first header to maintain staggered joints and avoid having a weak joint running down the wall. As you build, regularly check all levels as before.*

7 *Complete the wall with a header course, laying the bricks on edge. To help deflect rainwater, point the mortar joints by running a pointing tool against the vertical then horizontal joints.*

---

full-brick wall, which is two bricks wide, or for a double wall with a space for planting cavities, dig the trench 2in (5cm) deeper and add 2in (5cm) extra concrete. For a brick or concrete block wall, the top of the footing need only be 6in (15cm) below ground level. For a concrete screen, the top of the footing may be just below ground level, provided reinforcing rebars are used. On heavy clay or in cold areas, increase the depth of the footing so that it is below the frost line. For higher walls, seek the advice of a specialist.

Combination bricks

"Combination blocks" that give the appearance of being several individual bricks may look crude close up, but once in a garden setting, and especially when weathered, they are far less noticeable. They make simple garden wall construction very much quicker and easier. Some are regularly shaped, while others interlock like a jig-saw puzzle for greater stability.

COMBINATION COPING BLOCK

Bricklaying

To ensure that the first course is straight, stretch two parallel strings along the footing, the space between them equal to the width of the wall. Lay a ⅜in (1cm) bed of masonry mortar (p.580) along the footing. The first brick of a course is laid un-mortared, then the second is "buttered" on one end and laid up against it. As you lay, check frequently with a level that the bricks are even and horizontal. If too high, tap them down gently with the trowel handle. Insert more mortar under any that are too low. Check also that the mortar joints are all ⅜in (1cm) thick.

Repeat the process for subsequent courses. For walls with planting cavities, leave weep holes (unmortared gaps between bricks) for drainage in the first course that is completely above ground level.

Before the mortar dries, use a pointing trowel to give the joints a neat, beveled finish. Vertical joints should all be beveled in the same direction; horizontal ones should slope slightly downward to aid water runoff.

Brick bonding
There are many brick bonding patterns. If you are a beginner at brick-laying, keep to one that is easy to lay and does not require many cut bricks. The simplest of all is a running, or stretcher, bond, in which all the bricks are laid lengthwise.

Screen walling

In parts of the garden where a brick wall would form too solid a barrier, a screen wall of specifically made, pierced concrete blocks (see left and above) may be more appropriate. Walls of this kind are supported at each end and at 8–10ft (2.5–3m) intervals by piers built of hollow pilaster blocks. These are normally reinforced with rebars set in the footing and filled with mortar or concrete. Even so, screen walls are not strong, so for walls higher than 6ft (2m) seek professional advice.

Some popular bonds

Running bond is used for walls one brick thick. Flemish and English bonds use both stretchers and headers (bricks laid respectively lengthwise and widthwise) in a full-brick wall.

RUNNING BOND

FLEMISH BOND

ENGLISH BOND

TYPES OF COPING

A DECORATIVE FINISH
Upright stones have been set in mortar as a coping for a dry limestone wall.

A FULL-BRICK WALL
This Flemish-bonded wall is topped by a course of headers – bricks laid across the full width of the wall.

STONE COPING
Large stone slabs form a solid coping that complements a wall of flints mortared in courses.

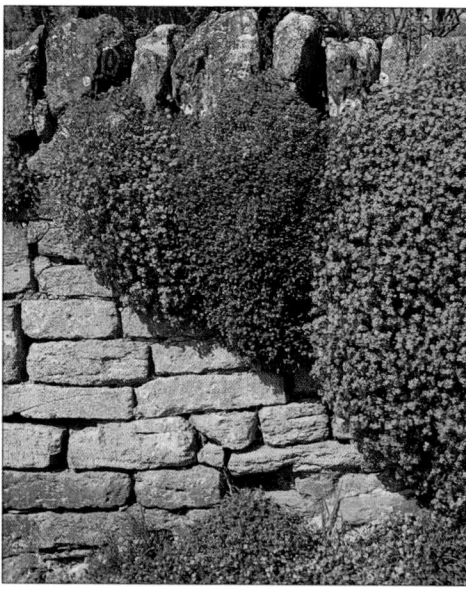

SOFTENING THE WALL
The hard line of the wall's edge is softened by a display of trailing flowering plants to create a colorful curtain. The crevices between the dry-laid stones provide ideal spaces for many rock garden plants.

Coping

Coping, which forms the top course of a wall, prevents frost damage by shedding rainwater so that it does not seep into the joints. It also gives the wall a finished appearance.

Specially made, curved coping bricks are available, but these are often only the width of the wall and are strictly cappings, since they do not throw the drips clear of the wall. Wider concrete slabs are used for copings on brick as well as concrete block walls. Coping is especially important for precast concrete block walls, because it helps bond the blocks. Suppliers often call coping for concrete blocks "cap blocks."

Drystone walls

Drystone walls may be laid on concrete footings (see p.590) or a foundation of crushed stone. They may be planted with alpines (see p.262), and look attractive if a cavity is left in the top for trailing plants.

Dig a trench and make a firm base of compacted crushed stone or gravel. The base of the wall should be one or two courses below ground level. Use a taut line to maintain a level construction, and build up the wall with broad tie-stones and smaller random stones to bond the wall together. The wall should be wider at the bottom than at the top. To achieve a consistent slope, or "batter," make a batter board, a wooden frame in the shape of the desired cross section of the wall. An inward slope of about 1in for every 24in (2.5cm for every 60cm) is usually sufficient. Use a level to keep the batter board perpendicular. Finish with large, flat stones or a row

of vertical stones laid on edge (and mortared if desired) as a decorative coping.

Retaining walls

Retaining walls may be used to terrace a garden or contain the soil in a raised bed (see opposite). Dry stones, special concrete blocks, or bricks may be used. Seek professional advice for any retaining wall more than 2½ft (75cm) high or one on a steep slope, because it may be necessary to reinforce it to withstand the pressure of soil and water. Rather than building one large retaining

wall, terracing the garden in a series of shallow steps may be better. In some regions, permission is required to build a high retaining wall, and regulations may demand that contractors be hired to construct it from poured concrete.

Insert a drain (see "Installing drains," p.617) running horizontally along the back of the wall, and backfill the lower half of the wall with crushed stone. If using concrete blocks or bricks, build the wall on a concrete footing (see p.590) set below the lower soil level, and leave weep holes for drainage between every second or third brick in the lower courses of the wall.

Drystone walling is a good choice for a low retaining wall, since alpines can be grown in the exposed face. Place large stones on a firm foundation of concrete or compacted crushed stone, and lay subsequent courses of stone with an inward slope (a batter) of 1–2in for every 12in (2.5–5cm for every 30cm) of height. The wall should be perpendicular on the retaining side (see THE ROCK GARDEN, *How to Build a Drystone Retaining Wall*, p.262). If it is not to be planted with crevice plants, the wall may be mortared to make it stronger (see "Bricklaying," p.591); otherwise, pack garden soil between the stones for additional stability.

Constructing retaining walls

Coping

Weep hole

Gravel backfill

Mowing edge

Any retaining wall used to hold back soil on a slope must be extremely strong. Bear in mind that the higher the wall, the stronger it will need to be. Remember, too, that wet soil is heavier than dry soil, and water must be allowed to drain out through weep holes left at the base of the wall. If the units of construction are large, the retaining wall will be even stronger than if small bricks or blocks are used.

CONSTRUCTION
On the left is a section of a brick wall with a vertical, unmortared joint acting as a weep hole. On the right is a wall built of hollow concrete blocks. Hollows may be filled with wet concrete, or with soil for plants.

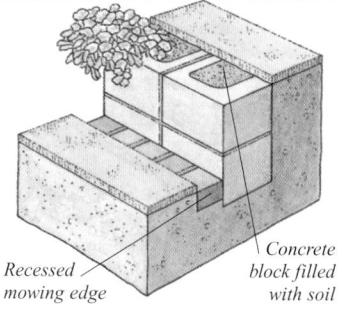

Recessed mowing edge

Concrete block filled with soil

PREFORMED BLOCKS
There are several shapes of commercial preformed concrete blocks especially made for retaining walls. They can be laid with butt or open joins and can be positioned to form shallow curves without being cut.

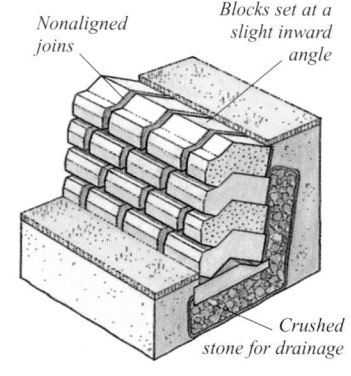

Nonaligned joins

Blocks set at a slight inward angle

Crushed stone for drainage

Raised beds

Raised beds provide a strong design element in a garden, perhaps surrounding a sunken garden or providing changes of level. Small groups of raised beds, or a series of linked beds, are ideal for an area that is mainly paved, while a single, distinctive raised bed makes a good contrast for an attractive specimen plant.

Where the soil in a garden is poor, or unsuitable for growing certain plants, raised beds can be extremely useful: they enable acidic conditions to be created in a garden with alkaline soil, for instance. Moreover, plants in raised beds have more room to develop and need less attention than those in tubs or other containers, in which the soil dries out fast.

Raised beds have the great advantage that they can be reached from a sitting position. A well-planned series of raised beds makes gardening possible for physically impaired gardeners. The height of the beds will need to be tailored to the requirements of the individual gardener, and the width must be narrow enough for the whole bed to be within easy reach. The beds should be linked by easily negotiated, wide garden paths (see pp.587–8). In areas with cold winters, raised beds will freeze more deeply than the open ground. This may limit to some extent the range of plants that can be grown.

Materials

Raised beds may be built from a wide range of materials: mortared bricks (see "Types of brick," p.583), concrete walling blocks (see "Walling materials," p.590), unmortared natural stone (see "Drystone walls," opposite), railroad ties, or sawed logs. Brick or concrete block walls may be topped with a coping (see opposite) wide enough to sit on.

Brick beds

A large rectangular brick bed is easy to construct but may appear rather unimaginative. A number of smaller linked beds at different heights will create a more visually stimulating feature, as will a circular raised bed. Always choose frostproof bricks; ordinary house bricks may be unsuitable – check with the supplier. A half-brick wall is usually strong enough for this purpose.

Rectangular beds

Prepare a footing (see *How to Make a Concrete Footing*, p.590) at a depth that allows the first course of bricks

to lie below ground level. When the footing has set, use a masonry mortar mix (see p.580) to lay the courses of bricks (see "Bricklaying," p.591). Lay whole bricks at right angles to form the corners.

Circular beds

For a circular bed, the bricks should ideally be cut to give a smooth curve, but full bricks may be used. First lay the bricks loosely to a radius of about the right size that does not create wide gaps at the edge. Prepare the footing and, when this has set, lay the bricks so that they almost touch on the inside edge of the wall. Use wedges of mortar to fill the gaps on the outer face. Stagger the courses as with a conventional bond, and use half bricks all the way around the final course to give it a smooth curve.

Acidic soil-loving plants

If plants that require acidic soil are to be grown in the raised bed, line the inside of the walls, when completed, with a butyl rubber liner or several coats of a waterproof paint. This stops lime in the mortar from leaching into the bed.

Concrete block beds

Concrete walling blocks are a good choice for raised beds if matching materials have been used for other garden structures and surfaces. The blocks may be too large for circular beds but are ideal for rectangular ones. The beds are constructed in a similar way to brick beds.

Natural stone

Raised beds may be built using natural stone laid dry. Use the technique for drystone retaining walls (see "Drystone walls" and "Retaining walls," opposite), but keep the beds low and small.

For a bed higher than about 24in (60cm), it is best to mortar the stones securely in place. Even with a low bed, it may be necessary to use a certain amount of mortar at the corners for stability.

Railroad ties

Railroad ties, which blend unobtrusively with most plants and garden surfaces, are ideal for large, low, raised beds, but they are heavy and difficult to handle: do not make the

MATERIALS FOR RAISED BEDS

Half-brick wall using a running bond

Soil level

Crushed stone base

1in (2.5cm) concrete footing

BRICK BED
Ideally, brick beds should be built with frostproof bricks. After preparing the concrete footing (see p.504), lay the first course of bricks below soil level. Stagger the courses to strengthen the walls.

Railroad ties laid like bricks in a running bond

Rammed gravel base

TIES
Railroad ties are particularly good for low raised beds. No footing is needed, because the ties are themselves very stable. Make sure they have not been treated with a preservative that is toxic to plants.

walls more than three ties high. They may be purchased in full or half lengths; try to build walls in multiples of these to eliminate the need for sawing. If it is necessary to cut special lengths, you will need to use a chain saw.

It is not necessary to provide a footing, since the length and weight of the ties make them inherently stable. Create a level surface to lay them on, using rammed gravel, then bond the ties like bricks. If more than two courses high, drill vertical holes in the ends of each tie, then insert rods or pipes long enough to sink 1ft (30cm) into the soil.

Sawed logs

Logs make attractive edgings for woodland-style beds, and for very low informal beds in a natural setting. For higher raised beds, logs of a uniform size and thickness should be used. Ideal logs may not be readily available, however, and the corner

joints are difficult to construct. If this type of raised bed is to be built, it may be better to buy the sawed logs in easily assembled kit form, available from home centers and garden-supply stores.

Watering

The growing medium in a raised bed will drain more rapidly than the soil of in-ground garden borders, so it is important to water plants more frequently. In particular, the soil in immediate contact with the retaining walls tends to dry out and shrink. In extreme conditions, this could expose the fibrous feeding roots of plants growing around the edges. The frequency with which this happens is in direct proportion to the amount of clay that was used in the fill soil: the more clay in the mix, the more shrinkage takes place; the more organic matter, the less it happens (see SOILS AND FERTILIZERS, "Using soil additives," p.615).

Fences

Fences are commonly used as property boundary markers, but they may also act as windbreaks or as decorative features within the garden. They may be erected more quickly and cheaply than brick- or block-built walls, and many have the additional advantage of affording almost instant privacy. In general they do, however, require more maintenance than a wall. To make a fence into a decorative element, it may be clothed with climbers or have trellis paneling attached to the top.

The first step before erecting any fence is to mark out the line of fencing with a string line. If it is to be on a boundary between two properties, all the fencing and fence posts must be on your side of the boundary. For other legal requirements regarding fences, see "Laws on fences," p.596.

Basic elements

Fences are made from three basic elements: posts, rails, and siding.

Posts are the heavy vertical members that have one end inserted into the ground. They are usually made of lumber but can be made of manufactured metal (see also *Erecting a Fence using Metal Post Supports*, opposite).

Rails are medium-weight horizontal members attached between the posts; they often act as support for the siding (see right). On wooden fences, these rails are usually made of 2 x 4in (5 x 10cm) lumber. The number of rails on a wooden fence depends on the height of the fence: usually two for fences up to 5ft (1.5m) tall, and three on taller fences.

Bottom and center rails can be inset into posts for a smooth finish. (Top rails are usually positioned across the top of the fence.) The inset cuts made in the posts, into which the rails are fitted, are called dado cuts. To avoid weakening posts, do not cut dados into opposite sides of the post at the same level.

Horizontal board fences, which are made up of boards nailed directly to the posts, do not need rails, although a top rail is often used.

Siding is a collective term, often used to describe the thinner dimension lumber that runs vertically from the top to the bottom rails or horizontally across the rails.

Siding comes in many forms, from the pickets on a picket fence to the alternate overlapping boards on a wavy-edged fence that gives complete privacy. Many fence designs call for vertical siding boards to be nailed to the rails at different spacings, depending on the privacy, sunlight, and air circulation desired. The panels of a panel fence (see p.595) are another form of siding. Used loosely, "siding" includes chain link mesh and other nonwood materials.

Fence types

Basketweave fencing is usually sold as prefabricated panels, generally in a range of heights. Thin interwoven slats of pine or fir are attached to a light softwood frame. It provides good privacy but is not very strong.

Closeboard fencing consists of overlapping vertical feather-edged boards, usually of softwood, as siding nailed to a pair of horizontal rails. The thick edges of the boards are nailed over the thin edges. It may be constructed *in situ*, but is also available (as shown here) in the form of panels. Closeboard is one of the strongest forms of fencing, and it also offers good security and privacy.

Wavy-edged fencing has siding of overlapping, irregularly edged board; it is a locally common form of panel fencing (see also p.595). It provides an adequate level of security.

Shingle fences consist of overlapping cedar shingles (wooden "tiles") that are nailed to a wooden framework to produce a strong, solid fence. They offer good security and privacy, depending on their height.

Wattle hurdles are flimsy panels of interwoven woody stems. Two examples are shown here. They may be made *in situ* or bought as ready-made panels. They are held in place by sturdy stakes and are particularly useful when a new hedge is becoming established in a garden, offering interim privacy as well as good protection against both small and large animals. Within a relatively short period of time, however, they can begin to look ragged and unattractive, and they are also troublesome to maintain and repair.

Lattice fences are made from sawed lumber or rustic wood. They resemble large partitions of a diamond-shaped trellis. They are useful for an informal boundary marker, but they offer little privacy.

Picket fences have vertical wooden "pales" spaced about 2in (5cm) apart, affixed to horizontal rails, and are more decorative than functional. Plastic picket fences are available that require far less maintenance than traditional wooden ones. Neither kind offers much security or privacy.

Ranch-style fencing uses as siding thin planed boards attached horizontally to sturdy posts. The wood is either painted or simply treated with preservative. There are plastic versions of this style of fencing available, which need less maintenance, but neither is secure.

Splitwood fencing consists of split vertical stakes about 3in (7.5cm) apart, linked by strands of galvanized wire. It is suitable only as a temporary fence.

Post-and-rail fences have two or more horizontal poles or rough-sawed wooden rails set between adjacent posts. They form an inexpensive boundary marker.

Interference fencing has horizontal boards attached on both sides of the posts, the boards on one side facing the gaps on the other. It makes a better windbreak than a solid fence, and it provides acceptable if not total privacy.

Chain link consists of a wire mesh, which is usually attached to concrete, wooden, or iron posts. Galvanized wire mesh lasts for about ten years, plastic-coated wire mesh longer. It is a good choice where an animal-proof boundary is required. It is also the first choice where maximum security is needed, because it can be topped with barbed wire, and you can see through it. Since chain link fences are generally less expensive than fences with wood siding, they are often used where a large barrier of 6ft (2m) or higher is needed.

Welded wire consists of an open wire mesh stapled to wooden posts and rails. It is used primarily to fence off larger animals where appearance is unimportant.

Post-and-chain fences may have chains of metal or plastic, attached to wooden, concrete, or plastic posts. They are used to mark boundaries where more substantial fences are not required.

Posthole diggers

If a number of holes are needed for fence posts, buy, rent, or borrow a manual posthole digger or a posthole digger attachment for a garden tractor outfitted with a hydraulic system. (There are several types of manual digger; each has its merits, so consult a specialist before buying.) Using a manually operated posthole digger may be strenuous, depending on the site, type of soil, and amount of moisture in the soil. Power diggers are much easier to use and save time and effort.

HOW TO ERECT A PANEL FENCE

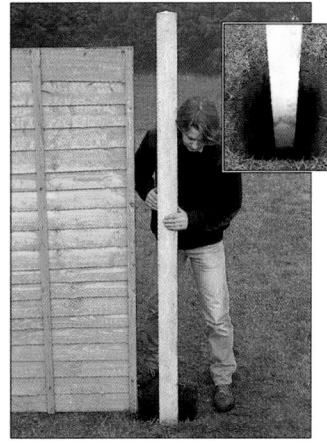

1 *Dig a hole 30in (75cm) deep and pack a 6in (15cm) layer of crushed stone in the base. Insert the first post and check the above-ground height of the post against the fence panel.*

2 *Pack crushed stone around the post and pour in concrete. Tamp it down. Add more concrete and tamp again. Keep checking with a level to make sure the post is vertical.*

3 *Lay a fence panel on the ground to position the next hole accurately. Use a string line as a guide, then dig the next hole.*

4 *Fit a gravel board between the post holes. Level the ground until the board lies horizontally. Check with a level.*

CONCRETE SPURS

Wooden post
Bolts
Gravel board
Concrete foundation
Concrete spur

To avoid damage through contact with damp soil, bolt wooden fence posts to a concrete spur set in a concrete foundation.

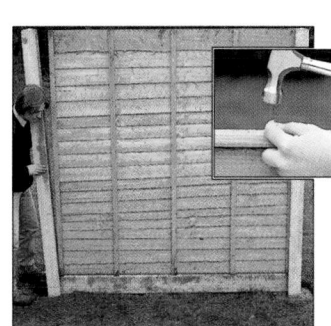

5 *Slot the panel into the groove in the first post. Insert the next post and pack into position with crushed stone. Secure molded wooden coping to the panel top.*

Panel fences

One of the simplest forms of fencing is a panel fence. It may be constructed using wooden or concrete posts. With concrete posts, the panels are simply slotted into grooves on either side of the post. For details, see *How to Erect a Panel Fence*, left. Another advantage of concrete is that it does not rot.

If you prefer wooden posts, the panels have to be screwed or nailed into position. Protect the bases of wooden fence posts by using either metal post supports or concrete spurs (see below). The latter are short posts that are embedded in a firm concrete foundation. They are bought ready-made with two holes through which the wooden posts are bolted to the spur just above ground level.

To build a fence with wooden posts, dig a hole for the first post, then stretch a line along the run of the fence to be sure that it is straight. For a panel 6ft (2m) high, you will need 8½ft (2.75m) lengths of wood for the posts and the post holes should be 30in (75cm) deep. Fill the bottom with a 6in (15cm) base of crushed stone, then stand the post in the hole and pack it with more crushed stone to hold it in position. Check that it is upright with a level. Using the panel as a width guide, dig a hole for the second post, making sure that it is aligned with the string line. Level the ground between the post and the hole and lay a gravel board – a length of wood (or concrete) fixed between fence posts at ground level to prevent panels from coming into contact with the soil and rotting. A wooden gravel board should be secured to the first post with galvanized nails. Attach a fence panel to the post using 3in (7cm) galvanized nails driven through predrilled holes, or screw them together with metal fixing brackets. Place the second post into its hole, making sure that it is vertical and fits closely against the fence panel; attach the gravel board and panel. Repeat with the remaining posts, gravel boards, and panels.

ERECTING A FENCE USING METAL POST SUPPORTS

1 *Place a scrap of wood and the fixing accessory in the socket of the post support. Use a sledgehammer to drive the support directly into the ground.*

2 *Keep checking that the support is being driven in vertically. Hold the level against all 4 sides in turn.*

3 *Insert the fence post into the socket at the top of the support and secure it by nailing through the slatted holes. Some sockets are fitted with clamping bolts.*

4 *Using a string guide, hammer in more post supports. Nail the fencing (here a panel of picket fence supported on bricks to keep the rails horizontal) to the posts.*

INSET RAILS

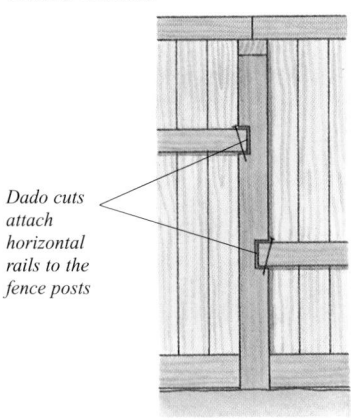

Dado cuts attach horizontal rails to the fence posts

For a smooth finish, set rails into posts using dado cuts. Alternate the cuts to avoid weakening the post.

Saw the tops of the posts to an equal height above the panels if necessary. Treat any sawed surfaces with wood preservative, and finish each post with an overhanging wooden cap that deflects rainwater.

Lodge the posts firmly in position with wedges of scrap lumber and crushed stone, and use a level to check that they are vertical. Pack a stiff concrete mix (see p.580) around the base of each post, and use a trowel to create a slope away from each side as a runoff for water.

Metal post supports

Metal post supports may be sunk into the ground and wooden posts inserted into them (see *Erecting a Fence using Metal Post Supports*, p.595). This technique reduces the length of the boards needed for fence posts and keeps them out of the soil, which prolongs the life of the wood. Use 24in (60cm) metal post supports for fences that are up to 4ft (1.2m) high and 30in (75cm) supports for fences up to 6ft (2m).

Before driving the support into the ground, fit a scrap of wood from a post into the socket. This protects the support. Most manufacturers provide an attachment that fits over the scrap while the support is hammered into place.

Make sure that the spike is entering the ground at an exact right angle. To do this, hold a level against each of the four sides of the socket in turn. Secure the post by tightening the clamping bolts in the socket, or if these are not provided, attach the post with screws or nails through the slatted holes. For added strength and durability, metal post supports may also be set in a foundation of crushed stone and concrete.

Sloping ground

There are two ways to erect a fence on sloping ground: the fence may be constructed as a series of stepped horizontal sections, or it may slope with the ground. The method you should use is largely dictated by the type of fencing you want to use.

A stepped fence

Panel fences, which cannot be satisfactorily cut, should be stepped. The upright posts need to be longer than they would be on level ground, the extra height depending on the width of the fence panels and the gradient. The triangular gap beneath each panel may be filled by building a low brick wall, stepped so that the panels sit on it. You can also cut angled boards and attach them in the gaps.

A sloped fence

To build a fence that slopes with the ground, set a temporary post at the top of the slope and stretch a line

SLOPING GROUND

STEPPED FENCE
Horizontal fence panels are erected as they would be on level ground and stepped down a brick wall built onto the slope.

SLOPED FENCE
The line of the fence runs parallel to the slope; the posts and the boards are set at the same height as they would be on level ground.

between this and the bottom post. Use a fencing system that consists of individual boards nailed to rails (such as a picket fence). Instead of running horizontally between the posts, the rails should run parallel to the slope. Cut the base of each board at an angle to match the slope. Attach the boards to the rails vertically, resting them on another board.

Wood and wood preservatives

Native conifer lumber (arborvitae in the East, red cedar and redwood in the West) is an excellent fencing material. The lumber is easy to work with and is exceptionally resistant to the elements. It also weathers attractively. Other durable hardwoods, including cedar, may also be suitable, but tend to be more expensive.

If possible, buy lumber that has been pressure-treated, and be sure to treat any surfaces that you cut. Unless fences are made of naturally rot-resisting wood such as redwood or cypress, treat them regularly with a wood preservative. Reapply creosote or water-based preservatives every four years, the solvent-based products every two or three years.

Creosote is a widely used treatment for preserving fencing. It has a very powerful smell, however. Wear protective clothing when applying this substance, since it is poisonous if swallowed, inhaled, or absorbed through the skin. Creosote is not recommended for fences used to support plants. Solvent-based preservatives may also be effective. These come in a range of colors.

Water-based preservatives are less unpleasant to use and less toxic to plants. They prevent the growth of surface molds and improve the appearance of the wood (they may alter the wood's color slightly). However, they are generally less effective at controlling rot.

Preservative should be applied to dry wood only. When erecting a

fence, any cut ends should be soaked in preservative for 24 hours before use. Keep all preservatives away from plants, and always wear gloves.

Maintenance

Broken wooden support posts are one of the most common maintenance problems. If the damage to the support post is at soil level, the most effective method of repair is to use a concrete spur (see p.595). This is a short post sunk into the ground alongside the existing wooden one and bolted to it to give extra support.

Dig a hole 18–24in (45–60cm) deep around the damaged post and saw off the rotten part. Paint the cut end of the wooden post with a wood preservative. Place the concrete spur in the hole, resting it against the post, and pack crushed stone around the base to support it. Push bolts through the holes in the spur, then tap them with a hammer hard enough to leave an impression on the wooden post. Remove the bolts and spur, then drill holes through the post for the bolts. Bolt the concrete spur onto the post, tightening the nuts from the spur side so that the wooden post is not damaged.

Make sure that the post and spur are vertical, if necessary bracing them in position temporarily with stakes driven into the ground. Then fill the hole with a fairly stiff concrete mix (see "Concrete and mortar mixes," p.580), ramming it down firmly as you work to remove any air pockets. After about a week, once the concrete has set, remove the supporting stakes and saw off any surplus length from the protruding bolts, taking care not to leave rough ends, which could cause injuries.

Broken rails are easily repaired with special metal brackets. Some of these brackets are designed to brace a broken rail in the middle, while others will support a rail that has rotted where the end fits into the post. Both types are simply screwed into place.

Laws on fences

As soon as you decide to put up a fence, check your local ordinances to determine which laws relate to fences in your area. They may govern such things as height, materials, and location. Unless you are certain of where your boundaries lie, have your property surveyed. If you build a fence on your neighbor's land, it becomes the property of your neighbor. You may be able to build on the property line with your neighbor's agreement; otherwise, the fence will need to be on your own land.

It is advisable to obtain a neighbor's agreement on property line, fence design, materials, height, and perhaps on working out a cost-sharing agreement. Your neighbor may also be prepared to share the cost of repairing the fence.

Trellises

Trellises, which are usually made of wood, are both a practical and a decorative feature in a garden. They may be secured to the tops of fences or walls or attached against them. Alternatively, they may be used on their own as partitions or screens. Curved and more intricately designed trellis panels are available for creating garden arbors. Panels come in a range of shapes and patterns, most consisting of standard diamonds or squares; herringbone trellises are particularly suitable for screening.

Trellises are most frequently used to support climbing plants. For a free-standing screen, a heavy duty trellis is essential, particularly if it is to support vigorous climbers; the wooden frame should be at least 1in (2.5cm) in depth. If the trellis is to be used to extend the height of a wall or a fence, a lighter weight may be acceptable. When buying a trellis, make sure it has been pressure-treated, and treat any sawed ends with a wood preservative (see opposite). Trellises primarily intended for supporting climbers are also available in wire and plastic.

Erecting a trellis

For a free-standing trellis, panels may be attached to fence posts in the same way as ordinary fence panels (see "Panel fences," p.595). To attach panels to a fence with wooden posts, use metal post extenders. Remove the post cap and slide the metal extender over the top of the post. Insert the required length of extension post and replace the original cap on top of the extension. To include a lightweight trellis above a masonry wall, attach lumber pieces 3/4 x 2in (2 x 5cm) to the sides of the trellis and screw them to the wall. If the trellis is to be mounted against a wall, allow at least 4in (10cm) between the wall and the trellis for good air circulation. Hinged hardware allows access for maintenance (see CLIMBING PLANTS, "Attaching a trellis panel to a wall," p.128)

TRELLISES

Trellises can complement the architectural detailing of the structure to which they are attached as well as provide support for climbing plants. They are available in a wide variety of shapes and woods. A jointed trellis is much sturdier than a concertina-style trellis held together by small staples.

LATTICE PANEL

DIAMOND-SHAPED LATTICE PANEL

LARGE-SQUARED TRELLIS

Pergolas and rustic work

The word "pergola" originally meant a covered walkway formed by plants grown up a trellis. Today the term describes any structure consisting of uprights supporting horizontal beams, over which plants are grown.

Traditionally, pergolas were made of rustic poles, but sawed lumber is often a better choice, especially where the pergola is combined with wooden decking or where the house forms one of the supports. Sawed lumber may be used in combination with brick columns or with painted scaffold poles serving as uprights. Hardwoods such as oak are often used for sawed lumber pergolas, but softwoods are perfectly adequate, provided they have been pressure-treated with a preservative.

Pergola construction

Draw your design on graph paper to work out the quantities of materials required, but buy a little more than you think you will need, because you may wish to modify the design slightly during construction. The height of the pergola should be at least 8ft (2.5m) if plants are to be grown over it, to allow room to walk beneath. If the pergola spans a path, the uprights should be positioned far enough apart to allow for the growth of plants on either side.

Supports

Set wooden support posts in gravel and concrete in holes at least 2ft (60cm) deep (see "Panel fences," p.595), or use metal post supports (see p.595). If you are building a pergola over a patio, special metal shoes designed to be set in a concrete base are available. To avoid breaking up an existing concrete or paved surface, build a brick shoe and set the post into it (see *Joints and Supports*, p.598).

Sawed lumber support posts should be 4 x 4in (10 x 10cm) in cross section. Scaffold poles may be used instead of wooden uprights but must be set in concrete because of their greater weight. Alternatively, if the weight that is to be carried is substantial, build brick or concrete block columns on substantial footings (see "Bricklaying," p.591).

Crossbeams

For crossbeams (roof beams), use either the same lumber as for the uprights or boards 2 x 6in (5 x 15cm) in section. These are sometimes sold preshaped and notched to fit

WOODEN PERGOLA ON A BRICK PATIO
The materials used to construct this pergola are few and simple, yet the design is most effective. A large square trellis has been mounted behind the square brick pillars that support the crossbeams.

JOINTS AND SUPPORTS

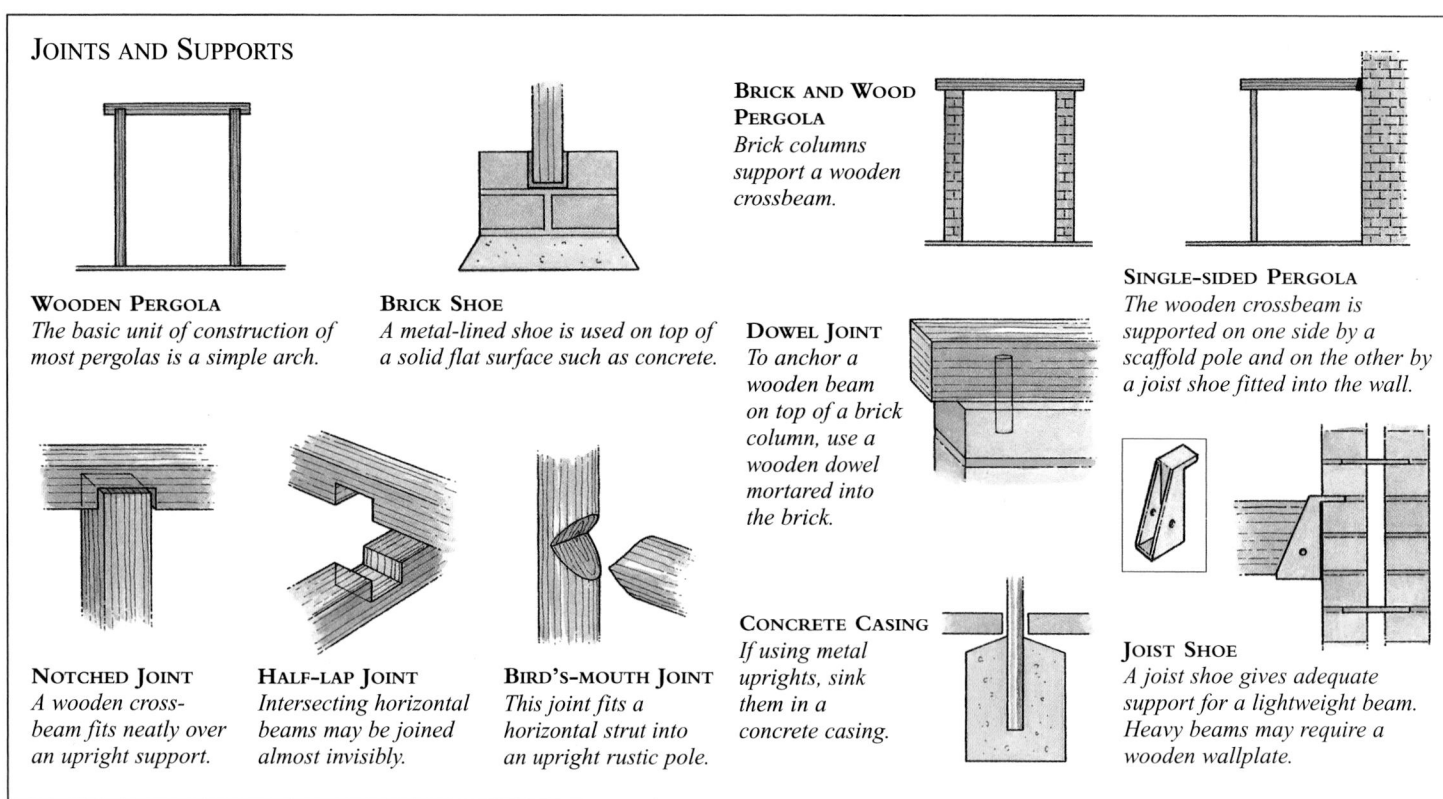

WOODEN PERGOLA
The basic unit of construction of most pergolas is a simple arch.

BRICK SHOE
A metal-lined shoe is used on top of a solid flat surface such as concrete.

BRICK AND WOOD PERGOLA
Brick columns support a wooden crossbeam.

DOWEL JOINT
To anchor a wooden beam on top of a brick column, use a wooden dowel mortared into the brick.

SINGLE-SIDED PERGOLA
The wooden crossbeam is supported on one side by a scaffold pole and on the other by a joist shoe fitted into the wall.

NOTCHED JOINT
A wooden cross-beam fits neatly over an upright support.

HALF-LAP JOINT
Intersecting horizontal beams may be joined almost invisibly.

BIRD'S-MOUTH JOINT
This joint fits a horizontal strut into an upright rustic pole.

CONCRETE CASING
If using metal uprights, sink them in a concrete casing.

JOIST SHOE
A joist shoe gives adequate support for a lightweight beam. Heavy beams may require a wooden wallplate.

over the tops of the uprights. Lighter lumber may be used for decorative rafters laid between the crossbeams.

Joints for beams and uprights
It is possible to assemble all the overhead woodwork by means of galvanized brackets and screws, but the structure will be stronger, and more attractive, if you use carpentry joints (see above). To attach an overhead beam to an upright, use a simple notched joint. This kind of joint is especially useful if the crossbeams are to project beyond the uprights – to serve as supports for hanging containers, for example.

Treat the cut surfaces of the joint with wood preservative (see p.596) before nailing them together. Avoid driving the nails in at right angles; skew-nailed joints hold together better when the structure flexes in the wind. If extra strength is needed, screw a T-bracket where the upright meets the horizontal.

If you are using scaffold poles to support wooden crossbeams, effective joints may be created by drilling circular holes of the same diameter as the scaffold into the beams. The depth of the holes should be half the thickness of the wood.

Wooden pergolas are often supported by a wall of the house. To attach a wooden crossbeam to the wall, you will need to use a metal joist shoe mortared into the brickwork. When the supports are brick columns, the wooden horizontals

are held with dowels, which are mortared into the brick (see above).

You may wish to roof over the pergola with a network of intersecting rafters. Where two beams of equal thickness meet, a half-lap joint gives a strong, neat finish.

Many designs also incorporate corner braces between the uprights and the crossbeams to give the pergola greater rigidity. The wood for the braces should measure about 2 x 2in (5 x 5cm) and should fit as closely as possible into notches cut in the beams.

Cut the braces to the required length, then hold them up to the framework to mark the position and shape of the notches. Use a drill and chisel to cut the notches. When all the necessary adjustments have been made, treat all the cut surfaces with preservative before nailing the braces into the notches.

Rustic work

Rustic work consists of all kinds of garden structures made from poles (usually of cedar or fir), rather than sawed lumber. A popular material for arches and screens as well as pergolas, the poles may either be dressed (with the bark stripped off) or be left with the bark on as an attractive finish. If you use poles with bark, bear in mind that the bark is likely to become a refuge for various garden pests.

The vertical poles that support the structure should be about 4in (10cm) in diameter. They may be bedded in concrete (see "Panel fences," p.595) or set in the open ground. In the latter case, sink them to 18–24in (45–60cm) of their length to ensure stability. If the bark is to be left on, strip it from the bases of the poles up to a point that extends 1in (2.5cm) above soil level when they are in position. Whether the bark is left on the poles or stripped off, soak the ends in wood preservative overnight. Set the uprights in their positions. The crossbeams and corner braces needed to complete the structure may be attached later, once the concrete around the vertical members (if concrete is used) has set.

The poles used for the main crossbeams and corner braces should have a diameter of about 3in (7cm), but thinner poles may be used for decorative latticework.

It is possible to preassemble some sections of the structure by laying them out on the ground according to the design, then cutting some poles to length and making the necessary joints. Saw all the crosspieces only as you need them to be sure that they fit exactly.

There are many joints that may be used in the construction of a rustic pergola or arch. Half-lap joints (see above), similar to those used for sawed lumber, are useful where the poles intersect. To attach a horizontal crossbeam to an upright, use a bird's-

mouth joint (see above). All cut ends should be painted with a wood preservative before you assemble the structure.

As with sawed lumber, it is always best to nail the joints together at an angle to give them extra rigidity.

Other plant supports

It is possible to provide permanent support for climbing plants without erecting a trellis or a pergola. Striking results can be achieved with relatively simple structures.

Tripods
Rustic tripods are an excellent way of integrating climbers into a mixed or herbaceous border. Dressed rustic poles are better than those with bark for this purpose, since they are less likely to attract potential pests. For large plants, use poles with a diameter of about 6in (15cm). If the tripod is in a bed, sink the poles in holes filled with gravel.

Pillars
For a more formal look along the back of a border or to flank a path, erect a row of single pillars made of brick or reconstituted stone. The bases of the pillars should be set firmly in concrete. To help climbers grow up the pillars, use plastic-covered large-mesh netting. Secure the net around the pillars by tying it together with plastic-covered wire.

Garden sheds

Sheds are valuable outbuildings for storing garden tools and equipment. A simple toolshed will keep hand tools dry and clean, but a larger shed with space to set up a workbench along one wall is a better investment.

Designs

A variety of different shed designs is available. There are three basic roof styles to select from: gable (an inverted V shape), gambrel (the shape commonly associated with barn roofs), and lean-to (a sloping half-roof – one side of the shed may be against a wall). Medium to large walk-in sheds usually have gable or gambrel roofs. Lean-to roofs are normally used only on small sheds, sometimes called garden lockers.

Prefabricated garden sheds are packaged as kits, complete with assembly instructions. Putting the directions on a videotape or CD/DVD is a new and helpful innovation.

Typically, medium to large sheds have sliding windows on one or more walls to admit light and air. Many sheds also offer an anchor kit to protect the building from strong winds, or a just-add-concrete foundation kit, which must be assembled before erecting the structure.

Materials

Garden sheds may be constructed from a variety of materials – wood, steel, aluminum, or vinyl. The choice of material depends on the intended uses of the shed as well as on expense and maintenance needs.

Wood
The single best material for a garden shed is wood; it blends in sympathetically with plants, especially after the new wood has weathered with age. Durable woods such as cedar are preferable, since they are naturally resistant to rot.

Most sheds, however, are made of softwood, which is much cheaper than cedar. Try to find a shed made of pressure-treated lumber rather than of wood that has simply been dipped or painted. Treat with a preservative when new, and maintain regularly. Wooden sheds should be lined with waterproof building paper (which can be obtained from a building supply store) to reduce the risk of moisture penetration and to protect tools from rusting.

When shopping for wooden sheds, in addition to the ten points shown and described below, check how the joints are held together. In terms of strength and longevity, bolts and wooden screws are best, followed by galvanized nails, with staples being the poorest choice.

Metal
Garden sheds made of steel cost less per square foot than wooden ones. The price varies according to the quality of galvanized steel used and how thoroughly it is coated with plastic. The higher the cost of a metal shed, the longer it should resist rust. The plastic-coated-steel sheds come in a range of colors; many of the sheds have small windows.

Sheds made of interlocking sheets of aluminum are readily available. Most have a sliding door, and some an acrylic sheet window. Often small, these sheds are intended primarily for tool storage and are virtually maintenance-free.

Vinyl
Sheds made of vinyl resin panels are easy to assemble, and require no elaborate maintenance. When necessary, simply wash them off with a garden hose and allow to air-dry.

CHOOSING A WOODEN SHED

The life of a wooden shed depends on the quality of the construction and of the wood. Whenever possible, compare erected sheds – most major suppliers will have a good selection to choose from. Pay close attention to the features indicated below.

ROOFING MATERIAL
Choose roofing felt or shingles with a stone-chip finish. Poor quality will let in moisture that will damage the wood after 3 or 4 years.

EAVES
These should overhang the sides and ends by at least 2in (5cm).

HEADROOM
Make sure that you can stand comfortably. Bear in mind that cross-braces are found in some designs.

DOOR
This should be solid with good crossbracing. Check for strong hinges and a good lock. Hardware should be rust-resistant – galvanized steel or aluminum.

ROOF
It must be strong, and it should not sag or flex if you push the center of one of the roof panels.

FLOOR
It should be firm – test it by jumping up and down on it.

EAVES TROUGHS
They can help extend the life of the shed by keeping the siding dry. If not supplied as standard, they are easy to add yourself.

WINDOWS
These must fit well and should have rustproof hardware. If hinged from the top, water is less likely to enter if they are left open in the rain. Check that there is a sloping sill and a drip groove underneath to prevent water from damaging the siding.

SIDING
Inspect the shed from the inside to make sure that no daylight is visible through the boards. See right for different types of siding.

BEARERS
If the shed is not erected on a concrete base, pressure-treated bearers help to keep the wood dry. If not using bearers, lay the shed on a moistureproof material.

TYPES OF SIDING

TONGUE-AND-GROOVE
This type usually offers good weather protection.

FEATHER-EDGED, OVERLAPPING WEATHERBOARD
This may warp or buckle unless it is thick.

REBATED WEATHERBOARD
This gives a closer fit than feather-edged weatherboard.

REBATE SHIPLAP
As well as being durable, this has an attractive finish.

WAVY-EDGED WEATHERBOARD
This rough-edged board, which is also called rustic siding, may not be weatherproof.

599

4
CLIMATE AND THE GARDEN

CLIMATE HAS A considerable influence on plant growth and, perhaps more importantly, on garden practices. Choosing plants that thrive in the prevailing climate is fundamental to success, but, although some plants will perform well only in their natural habitat, many are more adaptable and may be grown elsewhere, as long as suitable conditions are provided.

The effects of climate on plants are complex, made more so because weather is constantly changing. A plant's responses to weather are also shaped by its location, maturity, and the length and intensity of the plant's exposure to weather conditions. Through an understanding of the weather, a gardener will be better able to grow healthy plants.

Climate zones

World climate may be divided into four broad but clearly defined zones: these are tropical, desert, temperate, and polar.

Tropical climates are characterized by high temperatures and heavy, sometimes seasonal, rainfall, which support luxuriant evergreen vegetation. Deserts have average daytime temperatures in excess of 100°F (38°C) but very cold nights, and annual rainfall of less than 10in (25cm); only adapted plants, such as cacti, survive in these conditions. Temperate regions have changeable daily patterns, but rainfall is evenly spread throughout the year, and temperatures are less extreme than in the tropics or deserts; deciduous plants are more common here than evergreens, since they are better adapted to these conditions. Polar regions experience extreme cold, strong winds, and low rainfall, so little plant growth is possible.

In addition to these four broad zones, intermediate zones such as subtropical and Mediterranean are also recognized.

Regional climate

Conditions within climate zones are determined by geographical factors such as latitude, altitude, and proximity to the ocean, which increases rainfall and moderates temperature.

The North American climate
North America has a great deal of regional variation. The continent can be roughly divided into several areas based on climate, but topographical variation and proximity to large bodies of water create significant differences within regions. In both the US and Canada, coastal climates are influenced by warm air and water currents, and by rain from the surrounding oceans.

For general purposes, areas are defined (see "Gardening in different regions," pp.608–9) with respect to temperature range, number of frost-free days, precipitation, humidity, sun, wind, and the plants that may be grown in each region.

The great extremes of summer and winter temperatures in central parts of Canada are influenced by both latitude and the continental land mass. The Atlantic and Pacific oceans and the Gulf of Mexico are too far away to have any moderating effect on temperatures. During winter, the cold northern land mass has more impact.

Within Canada, growing seasons range from the very short Arctic season, with high light intensity, to longer, milder seasons in British Columbia, with lower light intensity. Areas with deep, reliable snow cover can grow a wider range of perennial plants than warmer parts with mid-winter thaws.

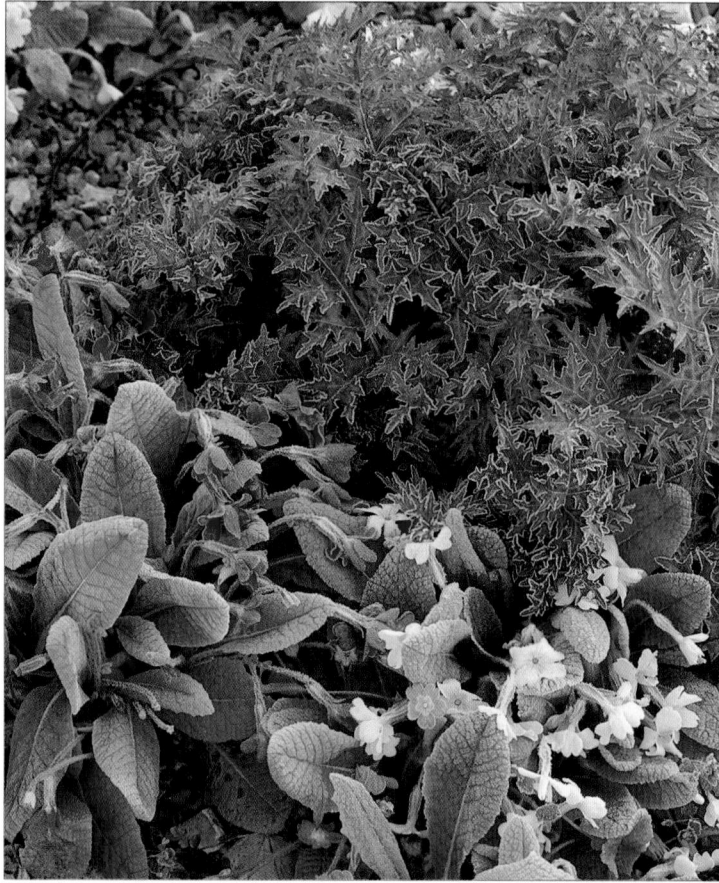

SPRING FROST
The play of light on the frost-tinged foliage and flowers of hardy plants brings an ethereal quality to the garden. Working with the weather rather than against it will give satisfying results throughout the year.

Elements of climate

The elements of climate that directly affect plants and the techniques used to grow them are temperature, frost, snow, rain, humidity, sun, and wind. Of these, temperature is usually regarded by gardeners as the most important: it determines the choice of plants to be grown as well as the length of the growing season.

Temperature

Plant processes such as photosynthesis, transpiration, respiration, and growth are vitally dependent on temperature. Each plant species has a minimum and a maximum temperature, beyond which these vital processes fail to take place. The maximum temperature is around 96°F (35°C) for most plants, while the minimum is highly variable. Where very low temperatures occur, plant tissue may be destroyed (see "Freezing and thawing," right).

Air and soil temperatures are the most important climatic factors influencing the onset and breaking of dormancy in plants. Dormancy, in turn, chiefly determines the length of a plant's growing season.

Air temperature
Sunshine produces radiant energy that raises the ambient or air temperature significantly. In temperate and cooler climates, a sheltered site that benefits from the warming effect of full sun may be used to grow plants from warmer regions that might not otherwise thrive.

An important relationship exists between altitude and air temperature: given the same latitude, highland sites are cooler than lowland ones – for every 1,000ft (300m) increase in altitude, the temperature drops by 1°F (0.5°C). High-altitude sites thus have a shorter growing season, which together with the cooler temperatures dictates the range of plants that may be grown.

Soil temperature
The temperature of the soil is important for good, healthy root growth and directly relates to the rate at which plants are able to absorb water and nutrients from the soil. The successful germination of seeds and development of shoots also depend on suitable soil temperatures (see PRINCIPLES OF PROPAGATION, "Requirements for germination," p.624).

The speed at which soil warms up and the temperature maintained during the year depend on soil type and the orientation of the site. Sandy soils warm up more quickly than clay, and well-drained, fertile soils stay warm longer than those that are compacted or infertile (see also "Soil types," p.610).

Sites with a natural, gentle incline toward the south warm up quickly in spring, because they gain more benefit from the sun than level or north-facing ground. They are therefore ideal for early vegetable crops. North-facing slopes, on the other hand, stay relatively cool and may be used to grow plants that thrive in cooler conditions.

Dormancy
Plants become dormant to limit their exposure to adverse weather; most have at least a short period of full dormancy. Many woody plants shed their leaves in fall to avoid excessive transpiration, while most herbaceous and bulbous plants die down completely in winter and remain dormant below the ground.

The temperature of the soil and air are the most important factors involved in the onset and breaking of dormancy. It is possible to exploit this knowledge by, for example, keeping plants in a dormant state through cold storage. Dormant scions for grafting may be stored until sap begins to rise in the rootstock, and shrubs may be stored in the same way, if necessary, until the soil is warm enough for planting.

On the other hand, bulbs grown in pots and winter-flowering azaleas, for example, may be awakened from dormancy and brought into early flowering by bringing them into a bright, warm place.

Frost

Frost is a great hazard in gardening and is considered to be more crucial than the average minimum temperature for the area. Otherwise hardy plants may be vulnerable to unusually low temperatures, particularly after they have produced new growth in spring, and an unexpected severe frost has serious implications.

Frost (frozen atmospheric moisture) forms on objects when their surface temperature drops below 32°F (0°C). It takes several forms: in a hoarfrost, crystals of ice are formed from water that has condensed from a humid atmosphere; black frost is more likely in a drier atmosphere and blackens the leaves and stems of plants. Ground frost results when the

FROST POCKETS

Since cold air sinks, it will always collect at the lowest point it can reach, forming a frost pocket. Valleys and ground hollows are therefore most susceptible to frost pockets, and any plants in the vicinity will suffer as a result. Cold air also collects above closely planted hedges and other solid obstructions such as walls and fences, with the same effect.

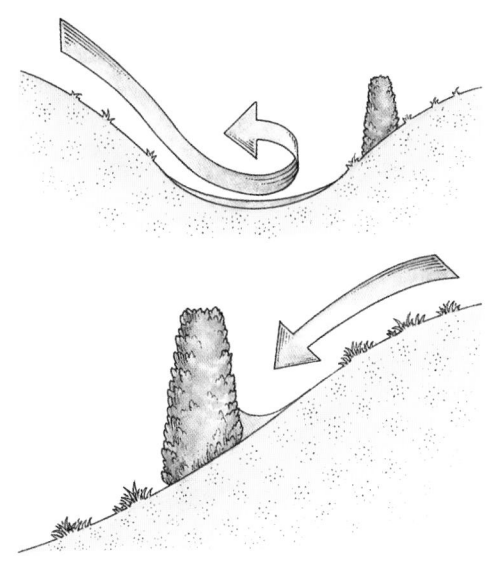

temperature of the soil falls below freezing; the depth of penetration of the ground frost depends on its intensity and duration.

Frost is most likely to occur on cold, still nights when the cold air gathers at a level just above the ground. Most at risk are woody plants whose tissue has not ripened (matured) well, usually due to a lack of sun and warmth during fall.

The risk of spring frost in any area determines the date after which it is safe to sow or plant out tender plants such as tomatoes, dahlias, and many bedding plants. The onset of the fall frost determines the end of their growing season. If tender plants are kept from year to year, they should be taken indoors or given adequate protection (see COLD AND WIND PROTECTION, pp.604–5).

Frost pockets and frost damage
Dense, cold air flowing down a slope eventually becomes trapped; any valley or hollow is therefore a potential frost pocket. The cold air accumulates in the depression and backs up the sloping sides of the valley, increasing the area of any potential damage.

Thick barriers formed by established trees or hedges along hillsides may obstruct the passage of cold air down a slope, and frost pockets will form in front of them. The problem may be avoided by thinning or removing the trees or hedges to allow cold air to flow through.

When the ground is frozen, water is no longer available to plant roots. Deep-rooted deciduous trees and shrubs are not affected even by deep frost, because many of their roots penetrate well below the frost line, but plants with shallower roots, such as small evergreen shrubs, may not be able to replace the moisture lost by continued transpiration. Severe ground frost can also cause newly planted, young, or shallowly rooted plants to heave, or rise, out of the soil; they should be carefully refirmed as soon as the thaw begins.

The risk of frost damage to plants kept outside permanently can be reduced by various protective measures (see COLD AND WIND PROTECTION, pp.604–5).

Freezing and thawing
Frost itself does not always cause great damage to plants, but alternate freezing and thawing does. Frozen cell sap expands on thawing, which destroys plant cell walls, often killing tender plants. The thaw may damage the flowers, shoots, buds, and leaves of hardier plants and sometimes even the roots. In extreme cold, the bark of some woody plants may split.

Repeated hard freezes followed by rapid thaws and subsequent waterlogging of the soil causes the greatest damage to roots. Late frosts in spring are particularly damaging to new top-growth, causing blackening of the leaves and injury to new buds and flowers.

Duration of frosts
The duration of the frost is also relevant to the amount of damage caused to the plant. For example, a temperature that drops to 27°F (-3°C) for a quarter of an hour may cause no damage, whereas the same temperature sustained over three hours could result in substantial losses.

RAIN SHADOW

Ground in the lee of a wall or solid fence (see shaded area above) receives less rainfall than ground on the windward side, since the wall or fence creates an area of rain shadow.

Snow

When atmospheric temperature falls close to (but not below) freezing, water droplets freeze in clouds or rain and may fall as snow. Snowfall produces a useful supply of water upon thawing and often provides valuable insulation for plants, particularly those recently planted and/or in heavy soil. Snow insulates the soil; it also helps reduce frost heaving. Heavy snow, however, may damage branches and twigs. Whenever practical to do so, carefully remove heavy snow from vulnerable plants (such as boxwood and many conifers) by sweeping upward with a broom

Rainfall

Water is the main constituent of cell sap and is essential for photosynthesis. Water is also essential to transpiration, whereby a plant is kept from wilting and nutrients are transported through it. Most other metabolic processes are also dependent upon water supplies.

SUNSHINE AND SHADE

Shade cast in summer

The shade cast on a garden by buildings and fences, as well as trees and large shrubs, changes according to the angles of sunlight, which differ according to season.

Shade cast in winter

Much rainfall is lost through evaporation and runoff, but most of the moisture that remains in the soil is held as a thin film around soil particles. Water and nutrients are then extracted from the soil by root hairs.

For optimum growth, plants need a steady supply of water. In reality, however, rainfall is variable in both frequency and quantity.

Waterlogging

This is a problem in badly drained soil. Most plants are well equipped to survive an occasional heavy downpour, but where waterlogging is prolonged, roots may die through lack of oxygen, except in the case of specially adapted plants. Most plants fail to establish on permanently waterlogged sites; in such locations, drainage must be improved (see p.617).

Drought

Plant development is more often restricted by too little available water rather than by too much. Drought during summer, when temperature and sunlight are at their maximum levels, is a common problem. Wilting is the first outward sign of drought; plant functions are slowed down until more water is available, and water loss through transpiration is reduced by partial closure of the stomata, the "breathing pores" found mostly on the undersides of leaves.

Humidity

Humidity levels are determined by the quantity or proportion of water vapor in the atmosphere and the moisture content of the soil.

The point at which the air becomes saturated varies according to sunlight, temperature, and wind. Atmospheric humidity is usually referred to as relative humidity, which is the amount of water vapor present in the air expressed as a percentage of saturation point.

WIND TURBULENCE

Exposed areas on rising ground may suffer severe wind damage. Gusts of air meeting resistance from the land are diverted around the sides and over the tops of hills, gathering intensity at the same time.

WIND TUNNELING

A wind tunnel created between buildings and trees may cause a great deal of damage to plants in its path, since air is forced through the narrow channel at great speed. If gardening in such an area is unavoidable, construct a windbreak to protect your plants.

The effects of humidity

In areas of heavy rainfall, atmospheric humidity is high. If necessary, humidity may be increased by damping down the areas around plants (see GREENHOUSES AND FRAMES, "Increasing humidity," p.570). This is also of great value when propagating plants to reduce loss of water by transpiration.

High relative humidity may have unfavorable effects, however. Fungal diseases, for example gray mold/ *Botrytis*, flourish in the moist conditions created by high humidity and can damage plants rapidly.

Sunlight

Sunlight provides radiant energy to raise the temperature and humidity of soil and air, and it plays a major role in stimulating plant growth.

Daylength

The duration of daylight in a given 24-hour period (daylength) is determined by latitude and season, and it affects flowering and fruiting in some plants, such as strawberries and chrysanthemums. "Short" days have less than 12 hours of daylight, while "long" days have more than 12 hours. By using artificial lighting or blacking out the natural light, the flowering times of daylength-sensitive plants may be manipulated. Germination of seeds and seedling development may also be advanced (see GREENHOUSES AND FRAMES, "Grow lamps," p.571).

Sun or shade

Some garden plants thrive in direct, strong sunshine, while others will not tolerate it. Many annuals, most fruits and vegetables, roses, and plants of Mediterranean origin all thrive best in full sun. On the other hand, many rhododendrons prefer to have some shade, whereas ivies (*Hedera*) and periwinkles (*Vinca*) tend to do best in heavily shaded areas.

Excessive sunshine

Strong sunlight may scorch the flowers and leaves of plants, especially those of house plants when they are first put out for the summer. It may also split fruits or the bark of shrubs and trees. To prevent these problems, always choose an appropriate site when planting, and for vulnerable plants provide shade in summer, particularly in greenhouses and frames (see GREENHOUSES AND FRAMES, "Shading," p.570).

Wind

Wind often damages plants and their environment, but it also has some benefits: it plays an important part in pollen and seed dispersal, and it may also be useful in cooling plants down, provided that they have enough water to prevent desiccation. In addition, gentle winds prevent the development of a stagnant atmosphere and deter plant diseases that might otherwise thrive. On the other hand, wind may discourage beneficial insects.

Wind damage

If woody plants are exposed to strong winds continually, their top-growth becomes unbalanced, giving the plants a one-sided appearance. The exposed shoot tips are also likely to be damaged or scorched. Trees that grow on hilltops and on exposed coastal sites are examples.

Strong winds and storms

The greater the velocity of wind, the more damage it causes. In high winds, shoots and stems of plants may be broken and, in gale force conditions, trees may be uprooted or their root systems seriously weakened. Strong winds may also cause damage to fences, greenhouses, and other structures in the garden. On sandy or peaty soil, the wind may cause soil erosion.

Scorching and cold damage

Strong winds in high temperatures increase the rate at which water is lost from plants, leading to desiccation of leaves and shoots. Where temperatures are low and there is continual wind, plants will suffer cold damage (see "Frost," p.601).

Effects of topography

The severity of the wind depends to a large extent on topography. Coastal sites often have no natural protection from strong, persistent, and/or salt-laden wind coming in off the water. Hilltop sites may be equally exposed, because the wind gusts around and over the hill.

Wind tunnels are created by the channeling of air between, for example, hillsides and along valleys, through tree corridors, or between adjacent buildings. This has the result of considerably intensifying wind speed and strength, so avoid planting in these areas. Windbreaks are a very useful means of providing shelter. They may be either constructed, such as fences or screens, or natural, for example tree or shrub hedges.

How a windbreak works

Whichever type of windbreak is used, it should be approximately 50 percent permeable. Solid barriers deflect the wind upward, producing an area of low pressure directly behind them, causing turbulence.

Fences or screens need to be up to

break will be different: the ground close to a hedge or fence on the leeward side will rarely receive rain and may also be sheltered from the warming effect of the sun.

WINDBREAKS

Place windbreaks at a distance of 10 times their height.

A SERIES OF WINDBREAKS
Across a large area of flat ground, construct several semipermeable fences or screens to break the force of the wind.

REDUCING WIND SPEED
A windbreak should be semi-permeable. Gusts of air still pass through but at reduced speed.

NONPERMEABLE WINDBREAK
A solid windbreak is ineffective. Air is forced upward then pulled down, creating a downdraft.

12ft (4m) high for maximum protection as a garden boundary but may be as low as 18in (45cm). To achieve the greatest benefit across a large area, windbreaks should be placed at regular intervals roughly equal to ten times their height.

Microclimate

Differences in topography frequently mean that local microclimates show variations from the more generalized pattern within a specific climatic region. A site in a natural dip or hollow may be relatively warm if it is protected from the wind; on the other hand, if the hollow is shaded from sunshine it will be relatively cool and may form a frost pocket in winter. Rainfall may be significantly less in the lee of high ground than in others in the same locality but on the windward side.

The garden and its plants further adapt the local climate and introduce features that give rise to a microclimate specific to the garden; this may differ markedly from that of the surrounding area. To alter the microclimate of a garden, the gardener can easily adapt certain features to provide specific conditions.

Orientation

The soil in raised or sloping beds that face the sun will warm up quickly in spring, producing ideal conditions for early crops or flowers. If the soil drains freely, the same area may be used for plants that prefer dry conditions.

South-facing fences and walls are excellent places to grow marginally hardy plants (including climbers, wall shrubs, and herbaceous plants)

as well as trained fruit trees, since they are in sun for much of the day. Walls and fences also absorb a great deal of heat that is then released to the plants overnight, which improves flowering and fruiting.

Wind shelter

A row of trees, a wall, or a fence provides a sheltered area for plants that might otherwise suffer wind damage, such as in an open, windswept area or along the ocean. The growing conditions on each side of such a wind-

Shaded areas

Areas of shade in the garden beneath tree canopies, hedges, or large shrubs receive the same sort of light as in natural woodland. If a greater degree of shade is required, plants may be grown against north-facing walls, although these sites may be colder.

A bog garden

The edges of a pond or stream, or a low-lying part of the garden, may be used to create the boglike conditions in which moisture-loving plants thrive.

Greenhouses and frames

Using greenhouses, frames, and other covers gives greater control over the elements, enabling the gardener to create a variety of microclimates (see GREENHOUSES AND FRAMES, pp.560–77).

THE MICROCLIMATE OF A GARDEN

The potential for several different growing environments exists in even the smallest gardens. Naturally occurring features create their own areas of microclimate. Garden features may be either exploited or manipulated to provide the conditions that plants from many different regions require.

Avoid planting in areas of wind turbulence.

Raised beds provide well-drained conditions.

Trees provide a natural windbreak.

A sunny terrace is suitable for tender and sun-loving plants.

The edges of a pond may be planted with bog plants.

A greenhouse provides a suitable environment for tender plants.

Water plants thrive in a pond.

Cold and wind protection

SELECT plants that will thrive in a given climate zone rather than attempting to alter the growing conditions. Trying to grow very tender plants in a cold climate will almost certainly end in disappointment. For species that normally do well in a site but may suffer in harsh winters, providing protection against cold and wind is a sensible precaution. Efficient wind protection enables the gardener to grow a wide range of plants and is particularly useful for large plants, for those in open ground that cannot easily be brought under cover, and for early-flowering shrubs and trees that are more susceptible to cold than later-flowering species. Protection is also needed from strong winds, which can break the stems of woody plants and damage fragile ones; winds may also carry salt spray from nearby roads or the ocean, causing browning of the foliage.

Preventive measures

Gardeners can take precautions to avoid cold damage: for susceptible plants, choose sheltered sites (such as in front of a warm wall or on a sunny bank) and do not plant in frost pockets. Tender climbers, for example, may be

PROTECTING SMALL TREES AND SHRUBS

STRAW INSULATION
Tie in the branches, then surround the tree with wire netting secured to 3 stakes in a partial circle 12in (30cm) from the tree. Pack straw into the gap, then secure the netting to a fourth stake. Cover the top with more straw. Attach a sheet of plastic to the netting.

STRAW BARRIER
Pack a thick layer of straw between 2 layers of wire netting. Surround the plant, filling any gaps with extra straw, and tie in place.

BURLAP STRIPS
Tie in the branches or leaves, then wrap the tree (here a palm) in strips of burlap, winding it around and tying it in place at intervals with string or twine Protect the base of the trunk with straw.

BURLAP AND STRAW COVER
Pack straw around the shrub's branches, working from the bottom up. Loosely wrap burlap around it, and tie with string.

NETTING OVER A FRAMEWORK
When wall-trained fruit trees blossom, protect them from frost at night with woven nylon netting, rolled down to cover the tree but held away from the blossoms by stakes.

STRAW AND NETTING FOR WALL-TRAINED PLANTS
Protect a tree or shrub against a fence or wall by packing straw behind the branches. Attach netting at the top and bottom of the fence. Pack more straw between the netting and plant until it is covered.

TRENCHING (TIPPING) ROSES

MOUNDING UP SOIL
Protect the graft union of bush roses from extreme cold by mounding up soil around the crown to a depth of 5in (12cm).

1 *Loosen the root ball, then dig a trench long enough to take the height of the bush when laid on its side and about 12in (30cm) deeper than the width of the bush.*

2 *Line the trench with a 4in (10cm) layer of straw, then lay the bush down. Pack straw around and above the shoots.*

3 *Insert stakes and tie strings between them to hold the bush down. Fill in with soil, mounding it up to cover the bush to a depth of 12in (30cm).*

grown against a house wall (which will be warmer than a garden wall) or in containers that can easily be moved to a sheltered position. Seedlings, summer bulbs, and tubers should be planted out only when all danger of spring frost has passed, and roses and other shrubs should not be fertilized late in the season, since this encourages soft growth that may then be damaged by fall frost. Allowing healthy, deadheaded herbaceous plants to die down naturally means that the foliage and stems will protect the crowns in winter, while a deep mulch of slowly decomposing organic matter provides protection for the roots of all plants. Check plants regularly in winter, firming any that have been heaved out of the ground.

Cold protection

The aim of cold protection is to insulate the plants from the extremes of freeze-and-thaw conditions by maintaining a constant temperature.

Insulation
In milder regions, wrapping plants in burlap, carpet, or several thicknesses of newspaper is effective in protecting the top-growth from damage. These materials also help moderate soil temperature fluctuations in colder areas, lessening damage to roots. Burlap helps slow the warming process caused by a thaw and keeps plants dormant through any midwinter mild spells. Straw packed around the plant beneath the burlap provides additional insulation and is suitable for wall-trained trees and shrubs, climbers, root crops, strawberries, and small fruit trees and bushes. Once temperatures rise above freezing, this cover can be removed. Wall-trained

plants need to be detached from their support, if possible, and the stems gathered together before wrapping.

Small shrubs and trees growing in areas colder than their usual winter hardiness zone can be protected by building a loose wire-netting cage around them and then packing this with dry leaves or straw. Plastic sheeting tied or stapled over the top of the cage will keep the insulating layer dry. You can also pack straw in between and behind the stems before covering over.

Mounding with mulches or soil
For perennial plants that die down to a dormant crown, place a mulch or a few forkfuls of leaves over the crown, and keep it in place with straw or prunings from evergreens. Roses and other woody plants can be protected by mounding soil around the base or laying them in a trench. In very cold regions, the soil mound should be covered with a layer of straw. Root vegetables can be protected from cold damage in the same way and can then be harvested, even during rather severe cold spells.

Covers
If only a few individual plants need protection, the best solution is to use a cover, which acts like a miniature greenhouse, warming the soil and maintaining an even temperature. Emerging shoots of frost-sensitive plants, such as asparagus, can be protected with almost any household container: an old bucket, a large plant pot, or a sturdy cardboard box will all do the job quite adequately. Specially designed plastic foam and clear plastic covers are available. More permanent cover protection

WINDBREAKS

DOUBLE NETTING
Protect fragile-stemmed plants from wind using flexible double netting.

SNOW FENCE
Lengths of plastic snow fence, attached to stakes, protect plants from drifting snow and prevailing winds.

WOVEN SCREENS
Place woven screens at intervals between the plants, setting them at an angle into the prevailing wind to deflect any strong gusts.

can be provided by glass covers, polytunnels, or cold frames. For further information, see GREENHOUSES AND FRAMES, pp.560–77.

Wind protection

Wind protection aims to reduce the wind speed before it reaches any plants, thereby reducing physical damage to branches and stems and preventing further water loss. Many tender plants have greatly improved chances of survival if they are planted in the lee of a good hedge. A 5ft (1.5m) hedge will reduce the wind speed by 50 percent for plants within 23ft (7.5m) of the hedge (see *Hedges and Screens*, pp.82–84).

Tree and shrub species vary widely in their ability to withstand wind. The most tolerant species are those with small, thick, spiny, or waxy leaves, such as x *Cupressocyparis leylandii*, arborvitae (*Thuja*), and hollies (*Ilex*). Of deciduous trees, alders (*Alnus*), alpine currant (*Ribes alpinum*), willows (*Salix*), and hawthorn (*Crataegus*) are particularly wind hardy. Windbreaks made from stakes and netting, or commercial windbreaks, can be used while the hedge grows.

COVERS FOR FROST AND SNOW PROTECTION

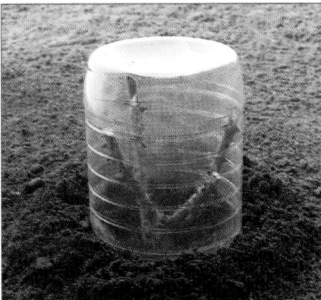

INDIVIDUAL COVER
Use to protect roses and other young shrubs, seedlings, and tender herbaceous plants. An empty water bottle makes an excellent, low-cost cover.

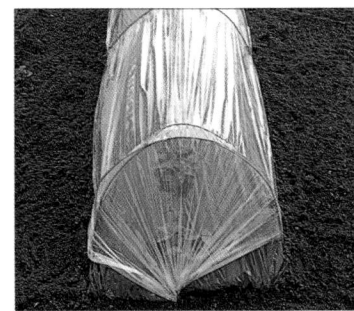

LOW POLYTUNNEL
Protect low-growing plants such as strawberries with a polytunnel stretched over wire hoops. The plastic may be raised at either side for ventilation during the day.

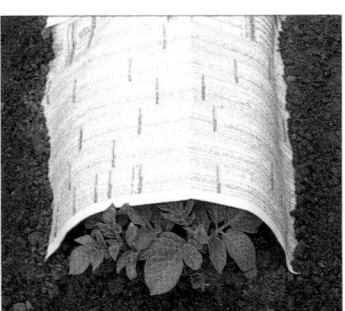

NEWSPAPER
Protect the new growth of potatoes and other tender crops against frost at night by covering them with sheets of newspaper, mounded up on either side to keep them in place.

SNOW FRAME
Use plywood panels, cross-braced with a wooden strut, to protect delicate, highly prized shrubs from heavy snowfall.

Water conservation and recycling

WATER conservation in the garden begins with choosing the right plants for the soil and climatic conditions. In dry areas, where the need for water conservation is at its greatest, select species that have fleshy or waxy-surfaced leaves, and grasses, which are well adapted to withstand drought, as are a great many plants native to Mediterranean climates. The appropriate plants must then be planted in well-prepared soil (see SOILS AND FERTILIZERS, "Soil cultivation," p.612). Improving the soil by incorporating organic matter (see "Soil structure and water content," p.614) and the use of mulches (see "Top-dressings and mulches," p.621) can largely eliminate the need for supplementary watering. It will, however, be necessary to water plants in containers, which are unable to develop extensive root systems and receive little benefit from natural rainfall. They are also much more susceptible to drying out in windy situations. Where extra watering is needed (see "Reducing high water dependency," right), apply it as efficiently as possible, using the following guidelines.

To reduce evaporation, water plants early in the morning or in the evening, but water before nightfall to allow leaf surfaces to dry. Water thoroughly when required, making sure the moisture reaches the plant roots. Refrain from simply wetting the soil surface by indiscriminate hosing or by giving a little water at frequent intervals (see SOILS AND FERTILIZERS, "Watering techniques", p.616). Inadequate amounts of water simply encourage surface rooting, which in the long term makes the plant more vulnerable.

PLANTING THROUGH SHEET MULCH
Cut a slit in a sheet mulch such as geotextile fabric, then plant through the hole. The mulch will reduce evaporation and suppress weeds.

 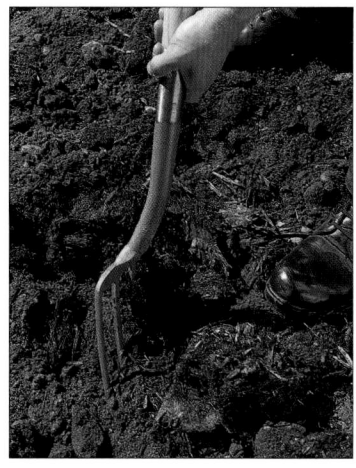

ENHANCING WATER RETENTION IN SOIL
Water absorption can be a problem on poorly structured light or neglected soil (left). Such soils should be improved by the addition of bulky organic matter, such as well-rotted farmyard manure or compost (right).

When symptoms of water stress first occur, apply no more than 5 gallons per sq yd (23 liters of water per sq m); give this every 7–10 days to maintain plant growth if necessary. Avoid the use of a sprinkler, which indiscriminately and wastefully discharges high volumes of water over a wide area.

Collecting water

In many temperate areas, the water collected from rain falling on the roof of an average house could and should be used to supplement water from the house supply, which should be used as efficiently as possible. As a rough guide to the amount of water that could be saved from a roof, multiply its surface area by the annual rainfall in the vicinity. For example, with an annual rainfall of 2ft (0.6m), runoff from a garden shed roof measuring 8 x 11ft (2.5 x 3.5m) would be more than 1,100 gallons (5,000 liters). A house roof measuring 56 x 22ft (17 x 7m) could produce nearly 16,000 gallons (72,000 liters) of water for use in your garden.

Rainwater is readily stored by connecting a water barrel or similar tank to a downspout. If the barrel or tank has a lid and is free from algae, the water will remain oxygenated for about 6 months. (Anaerobic water should not be used on plants.) Such water reservoirs should stand on a firm base; to facilitate filling a watering can from the bottom tap, they should be raised on a plinth of bricks or walling blocks.

Since rainfall occurs at irregular intervals, often in heavy bursts, a rainwater barrel will frequently overflow. The amount stored can easily be increased by using several barrels joined to one another by short pipes inserted into the overflow valves.

Reducing high water dependency

Although some garden features and crops will usually require supplementary watering, their needs can be reduced in the following ways.

New plantings
• Create a saucer-shaped depression around each plant stem to hold water and avoid runoff.
• Lay trickle, or drip-feed, irrigation, which targets water to the roots of each plant (see p.555).
• Make sure the growing medium of container-grown plants is saturated by immersing the plants in a bucket before planting; this ensures that the air is completely expelled. Water again thoroughly immediately after planting.
• Destroy competitive weeds by hoeing the soil shallowly.

Containers and hanging baskets
• Incorporate water-retaining granules in the medium.
• Level the medium to within 1–2in (2.5–5cm) of the container rim so there is space for sufficient water to soak the medium thoroughly at each watering.

• Place plants in a sheltered spot that is shaded for part of the day. Keep away from drying winds.
• Group containers together rather than placing them individually.

Food crops
• Select crops carefully, especially in dry areas. Several vegetables will fail to develop adequately if short of water at critical periods in their development. Examples are potatoes, which need plenty of water as their tubers are ripening, and tomatoes, zucchini, melons, and some beans when flowering and fruit is swelling.
• Irrigate with seep or trickle hoses so that supplementary watering is targeted where it is most needed.

Lawns
• Reduce the size of the lawn, and create gravel beds or surfaces.
• Select a mixture of lawn grass species that are relatively resistant to drought conditions.
• Raise the mower blade height at which the grass is cut, say from ½in (1cm) to 1in (2.5cm).
• Apply an appropriate fertilizer

during the fall to encourage drought resistance.

Patios
• Create partial shade with wooden structures to reduce the considerable glare from the sun on some patio surfaces. The reflection may affect adjacent plants, increasing their moisture loss. Although trees will provide shade, dry zones occur around the roots, and these can nullify the advantage of shade.
• Angle any slope on a patio so water runs off onto the garden and is not lost in adjacent drains.
• Use decking, which allows water to percolate through the gaps, rather than concrete or stone slabs.

Water features
• Convert moving water to still water features. The former inevitably has a higher evaporation rate, particularly when placed in a sunny, exposed position.
• Plant waterlilies to minimize evaporation from ponds and similar uncovered surfaces.
• Replace water loss with stored rainwater rather than house water.

RECYCLING GRAY WATER
Water from showers or baths can be diverted from dedicated downpipes to an adjacent water barrel for immediate distribution and reuse around garden plants. The water barrel must be covered with a lid not only for safety but also to prevent the accumulation of debris and algae.

SEEP HOSES
Hoses with small perforations along their entire length are an excellent way to irrigate strawberries (here) and other plants grown in a row.

TARGETED WATER OUTLETS
Trickle, or drip-feed, systems deliver water through individual drippers that are placed permanently near the roots of each plant.

Larger water tanks are also available; any recycled ones must be thoroughly cleaned of residues from previously stored fluids.

By adjusting the downspouts from rainwater gutters, water barrels can be placed against a wall, which should not be in full sun. If the barrel or a series of barrels are obtrusive, the rainwater downspout can be fitted with a small device that diverts the rainwater through a pipe to a more distant receptacle – for example, one sited behind a garden shed or trellis.

Where there is an insufficient slope for the water to run naturally into these storage tanks, a sump pump should be installed in a small barrel or receptacle at the base of the downspout. Very large storage tanks,

RAINWATER BARREL
Collect rainwater off greenhouse, shed, and house roofs by attaching pipes between each gutter and water barrel. Always buy as large a barrel as you can afford, and position it sufficiently high for a watering can to fit conveniently under its tap.

even if they are placed low enough to be gravity fed from the house, will need a pump to redistribute the water around the garden. Sump pumps that have an on/off, cut-out float on the intake are ideal, because they prevent damage to the pump if the tank runs dry and the pump has been left on accidentally. The system can be constructed so the pump drives water through a series of small diameter pipes to the areas of the garden requiring irrigation.

Rainwater diverters fitted on the downpipe or the overflow socket on a rainwater barrel can also channel the excess water to a garden pond. Ponds used for this purpose should be free of blanketweed and should preferably contain oxygenating plants. In a

large informal garden, a saucer-shaped, heavily planted pond can be created with a pebbled edging for a beachlike effect (see WATER GARDENING, "Styles of pond edging", p.285). This will conceal any large variance in water level from summer to winter. As with other water reservoirs, any pond is likely to require an electric submersible pump to redistribute the water to the rest of the garden.

Gray water
Gray water is the term used for domestic waste water other than sewage (which is referred to as black water). Since large volumes of water are available from this source – the average bathtub using 26 gallons (120 liters) – in extreme drought conditions it can be a valuable source of water, provided it is not heavily contaminated with soaps, detergents, fats, or grease. Buckets of gray water can be taken directly from a bathtub (or sink) to the garden, or the water could be siphoned to the garden using a garden hose. Siphoning aids are available from hardware stores. Pipe diverters used in the same way as rainwater diverters can be fitted to the waste-water drain from the bathroom and fed into a dedicated gray-water barrel or reservoir, for use after it has cooled.

Some types of domestic waste water are better than others. In order of preference they are shower, bathtub, bathroom sink, and utility sink, provided bleaches or strong detergents have not been used. Water from dishwashers and washing machines is unsuitable for garden use: it contains too much detergent.

Gray water should never be used on newly propagated or container-grown plants or those grown in a conservatory or greenhouse.

How to use gray water

• Store in a dedicated container, and don't mix with other water.
• Use gray water as soon as it has cooled, and never keep longer than a few hours. Storing it on summer days can quickly produce a bacterial soup, which can smell unpleasant and breed disease pathogens.
• Apply gray water on soil or soil mix adjacent to a plant; never water directly on foliage.
• Never use gray water on fruit, vegetables, herbs, or on acidic soil-loving plants: detergents are alkaline.
• Never apply gray water with a sprinkler to the lawn or to any area where the water might form puddles, since such water is unhygienic. Children may be attracted to play in the puddles, and animals may drink from them. Insects (such as mosquitoes) may breed in the water.
• Avoid using gray water with "dripper" or fine nozzle irrigation systems, because these will quickly clog up.
• Try to rotate the types of water applied to the garden, and avoid the persistent use of gray water in one particular area. Harmful sodium levels may build up if gray water is overused. This can be detected by a soil test. If the pH level is over 7.5, plant growth may be adversely affected. Overly high levels can be remedied with gypsum; apply at a rate of 1lb per 50 sq ft (1kg per 10 sq m). until the pH level reaches 7 or below.

Gardening in different regions

WITHIN a country as vast as Canada, there is wide variation in climate, soil, and planting traditions. Differences are significant even within the generally accepted regions: Maritimes, Central Canada, Prairies, and West Coast. The following accounts of these regions describe their climate and soil type and provide general gardening recommendations. The climate zone in which you live is one of the most important factors in determining what will grow well in your garden. The plant hardiness zone map printed on the endpapers is based on data prepared by Natural Resources Canada and Agriculture and Agri-Food Canada. It shows the zones of hardiness for the plants listed on pages 673–680. The US Department of Agriculture publishes a similar map, which also appears in some nursery and seed catalogs. The zone numbering, however, is different for each map, so it is essential to know which map is being used. Many other factors also influence gardening in Canada. Coastal regions and those bordering large lakes, for example, have stronger winds and more rain and snowfall than inland areas. The situation of your garden is important, too; an exposed site is several degrees colder, and accumulates less snow, than a sheltered one. The length of the growing season may be crucial for vegetables and annuals that are started outdoors. Also, gardening traditions differ in the range of ornamental plants cultivated and in the amount of ground devoted to fruit, vegetables, and lawn.

Maritime region

This region of Canada consists of the provinces of Newfoundland, New Brunswick, Nova Scotia, and Prince Edward Island, and the eastern seaboard of Quebec.

Environmental diversity in these maritime provinces, caused by size and topographical differences in the area, creates a challenge for the gardener. Soils are generally very acidic. The sea, too, inevitably has considerable influence on what can be grown, allowing greater scope in coastal areas than in the interior.

Climate
Temperatures range from -30°F (-35°C) to 95°F (35°C) and the growing season ranges from about 130 frost-free days in Kentville, Nova Scotia, down to 95 frost-free days in southern Labrador.

Some areas, such as Fredericton, New Brunswick, experience hot and often dry summers, and soil moisture conservation must be practiced. In coastal areas, rain can be heavy, particularly in spring and fall. The Avalon Peninsula of Newfoundland receives 60in (150cm) of precipitation a year, roughly one-quarter

as snow. Only one-third of the annual precipitation evaporates, leaving a moisture surplus of 40in (100cm) each year. Good drainage is therefore essential when gardening. Inclement winter rains and wet snow in coastal areas can damage woolly-leaved perennials by rotting their leaves and crown.

Humidity is higher on south-facing coastal areas than elsewhere, with daytime relative humidity from midspring to midfall of 75–90 percent; inland levels are 50–80 percent. The average annual hours of sunshine vary from 1,465 in St. John's, Newfoundland, to 1,870 in Fredericton, New Brunswick.

Incessant wind, particularly around coastal areas, can severely hinder plant growth. Winds blowing off a sea studded with icebergs and pack ice are often responsible for a late spring. In such situations, windbreaks are essential.

Soils
Much of this region has shallow, acidic (pH of 5 or lower), and nutrient-poor soils, which need additional organic matter. Most garden soils, except those

designated for acid-loving plants, will benefit from an annual application of lime and general-purpose fertilizer. Good soils are often localized and are found in such areas as Prince Edward Island and the Annapolis valley, Nova Scotia.

Soils are usually wet at the start of winter and therefore freeze quickly. Freezing, alternating with frequent midwinter thaws, may heave the plants out of the ground. This problem is particularly prevalent where soils are shallow and plants do not make deep root systems.

Planting traditions
Trees such as linden (*Tilia*), birch (*Betula*), poplar (*Populus*), oak (*Quercus*), pine (*Pinus*), and spruce (*Picea*) are popular, along with some of the smaller ornamentals such as flowering crabapple (*Malus*) and lilac (*Syringa*). *Magnolia* x *soulangiana*, *M. stellata*, and *Cercis canadensis* grow in the warmer areas of mainland Maritimes, while St. John's, Newfoundland, is noted for its Scotch laburnums (*Laburnum alpinum*). In the Avalon Peninsula and coastal Nova Scotia a wide range of rhododendrons,

azaleas, and heaths flourish, due, in part, to the naturally acidic soil. Primroses such as *Primula juliae*, *P. sieboldii*, and *P. vialii* also grow well. Many herbaceous perennials are hardy, and bulbs such as crocuses, snowdrops, daffodils, and flowering onions thrive.

Basic, short-season vegetables are successful, especially cool-season kinds such as lettuce and spinach, but those requiring warm summers – zucchini, sweet peppers, and tomatoes – do well only in the more southerly parts of the region. A wide variety of strawberries, apples, and pears are cultivated, while even grapes, such as 'Valiant' and 'Beta', and the hardiest edible kiwi grow in those areas of New Brunswick and Nova Scotia that have warm springs and summers.

Lawns are popular but need continuous care. Snow mold and chinch bug can be a problem (see p.657). Grass mixtures containing Kentucky bluegrass (*Poa pratensis*), perennial ryegrass (*Lolium perenne*), and creeping red fescue (*Festuca rubra* var. *rubra*) are favored, while wild white clover is often added to poor sites.

Central Canada region

This region consists of the provinces of Quebec (except the eastern seaboard) and Ontario. It is bounded by permafrost on the north, Prairies on the west, and the United States on the south.

Gardening is widely practiced, but usually on a limited scale – a lawn, one shade tree, and a few flowers. Most gardens have some display of flowers, but the heat of summer does not encourage the majority of people to work out in the sun; escaping to a cottage on a lake has more appeal. Soils are generally alkaline.

Climate
There is a wide temperature range between seasons, with those in winter dropping to -l0°F (-22°C) even in milder areas. Summer temperatures can reach 95°F (35°C) with high relative humidity (95 percent) in midsummer. Winter has a humidity reading down to 15 percent in cold snaps, when the wind-chill temperature can reach -58°F (-50°C).

Spring is fleeting and is condensed into a few weeks with snowdrops and single

late tulips often in flower together. The number of frost-free days ranges from about 110 in the north to 165 in the Niagara peninsula.

Rainfall is generally spread evenly throughout the year, although there is often a summer drought. Annual rainfall is around 26in (60cm) in the populated southern part of this region. Snow may be deep but comparatively short-lived in the south, while it can be very deep and persistent in the north. While this region is out of the hurricane belt, occasional tornadoes do occur and cause considerable local damage.

Soils
During the Ice Age, glaciers pushed much soil southward through Central Canada so that northern areas have mostly shallow, rocky soils, while in the south soils are deeper and richer. Since the growing season in much of the region is short, the soil has been very slow to build up again.

Much of the region has alkaline soil, the underlying rock being granite or lime-

stone. There are also areas of acidic, peat-based soils, generally the sites of silted-up lakes. These are warm soils, which are used for market gardening and early spring crops. Sphagnum moss is common in Quebec province, on the sites of ancient, large lakes, and harvesting peat moss is a major industry.

Planting traditions
Trees and shrubs are widely available in an increasing range of species and varieties. As winters become colder toward the north of the region, the selection that can be grown gradually narrows. Maple (*Acer*), linden (*Tilia*), and ash (*Fraxinus*), which were extensively planted in the past, are falling out of favor because the mature trees are too large for modern properties. Smaller trees such as crabapples (*Malus*), Japanese tree lilac (*Syringa reticulata*), and honey locust (*Gleditsia*) are becoming very popular. Spiraea, Potentilla, and French hybrid lilacs (*Syringa vulgaris*) are the most widely sold shrubs, whereas arborvitae (*Thuja*) –

often known as cedar – and alpine currant (*Ribes alpinum*) are the most favored evergreen and deciduous hedges.

Roses – particularly Hybrid Tea and Floribunda types – are found almost everywhere in the region in spite of the amount of work needed to overwinter them in most parts. Hardy shrub roses, too, are gaining in popularity, especially some new climbing types that do not require winter protection. Tree roses, however, grow successfully only in the Niagara area.

Flower gardening is also becoming more common, with a trend toward perennials, especially peonies (*Paeonia*), irises, and day lilies (*Hemerocallis*). Bulbs are widely planted, although some, especially tulips, divide up in warm soils and become too small to flower after a few years. Annuals give the main color focus for most gardens.

Vegetable production is possible over most of the region, provided that short-season varieties are used. Cool-climate crops such as lettuce and spinach do not produce over a long period because the soil warms up so quickly in spring. If started indoors and planted out early, however, they can be successfully grown.

Warm-climate crops such as tomatoes and sweet peppers produce well, providing they are not planted out until the soil is warm. In northern Central Canada, choose cold-tolerant, quick-maturing tomato varieties such as 'Sub-arctic Maxi' to improve the chances of a good crop. All but the long-season, over-wintering varieties of cabbage and their relatives can be grown successfully, especially in the north, where they benefit from the extended daylength.

In the Niagara area, tree fruits such as peaches, nectarines, apricots, sweet cherries, and grapes are widely cultivated. Elsewhere the choice is restricted to pears, plums, sour cherries, and apples. Bush fruits are not common, and the range of cultivars available to the gardener is quite limited.

Lawns are almost all of Kentucky bluegrass (*Poa pratensis*), although tall fescue (*Festuca arundinacea*) is becoming popular because it is hard-wearing. Fine lawns of bentgrass (*Agrostis*) are rarely found in amateur gardens: they require expert care in the humid summers and suffer from many diseases.

Prairie region

The prairies are bounded by permafrost on the north, Ontario on the east, the United States on the south, and the Rocky Mountains on the west.

Gardeners in this extensive territory face the very unusual challenge of choosing plants that will survive a dormant season of six months or more. Perhaps the considerable satisfaction gained from overcoming the elements is responsible for the historic enthusiasm for gardening within this region. Most of the populated parts of this region enjoy good soils with little acidity.

Climate
Because this inland region is generally at high altitude, it suffers growing seasons that are hot and dry with temperatures up to 110°F (43°C), followed by very cold winters, with temperatures falling as low as -78°F (-61°C).

The short growing season of 60–155 frost-free days (generally 90–120 days in the more populated areas) may be interrupted by frost or snow in early or late summer. Some 54in (135cm) of snow may fall during the year, and total annual precipitation is 18in (45cm). The most humid season is midwinter, with 78 percent relative humidity in the Edmonton

area; the lowest (47 percent) is late spring. The average annual hours of sunshine amount to some 2,315.

During the dormant season, areas near the mountains and foothills often experience chinooks – sudden incursions of brisk, warm air from the west. Such warm winds encourage plants to start active growth; trees and shrubs may develop leaves and then later suffer die back from cold, desiccating, winter winds through their leaves.

Although the severe winters limit the range of plants that may be grown, many borderline plants should survive if protected by windbreaks to create micro-climates around them.

Soils
Heavy clay soils (pH 6.3–7.3) are found in much of the prairie region. In grassland or grassland-forest communities these are known as chernozemic soils. In most well-populated areas, heavy "gumbo" soils are very fertile, although they severely reduce the time that a garden is workable because the gumbo is sticky in spring and bakes hard in summer. If enough organic material and coarse sand can be added, such soil can become very productive.

Elsewhere in the region, particularly in the south, soil salinity and alkalinity reduce the number of plant species that may be grown.

Planting traditions
Ornamental trees that are suited to the growing conditions are limited to only some 20 genera, imparting a distinctive continuity to the prairie landscape. *Picea pungens* 'Glauca', white birch (*Betula papyrifera*), and mountain ash (*Sorbus aucuparia*) are among the more popular ones. Trees in this region experience few attacks from insects and disease.

White-flowered *Spiraea*, which unfailingly heralds spring, is everywhere in prairie gardens. Other widely grown shrubs include yellowtwig dogwood (*Cornus stolonifera* 'Flaviramea'), redtwig dogwood (*C. alba* 'Sibirica'), lilacs such as French lilac (*Syringa vulgaris*), hardy roses, and *Viburnum*. Popular hedging plants are *Cotoneaster lucidus*, the native, red-fruited *Crataegus chrysocarpa*, and the black-fruited *C. douglasii*. Owing to their lack of hardiness, broadleaved evergreen shrubs are virtually absent from the prairie landscape, but evergreen shrubs such as *Juniperus horizontalis* are successful.

Most herbaceous perennials do very well in the region, and annuals remain popular as bedding plants. The small, spring-flowering bulbs thrive, but many of the larger bulbs, especially daffodils, tend to be short-lived.

In most areas, growing vegetables such as beans, peas, and especially root crops is extremely satisfactory because the long, sunny days bring rapid maturity. Hot spring and early summer conditions, however, do not favor cool-climate crops such as lettuce and spinach. Warm-climate crops, for example tomatoes, sweet peppers, and squash, are best planted only after the soil warms up. Shelter warm-climate crops to make them even more productive.

Tree fruit production is limited to apples, crabapples, a few pears, and plums (mostly Japanese-American hybrids).

Lawns are normally grown using Kentucky bluegrass (*Poa pratensis*) and creeping red fescue (*Festuca rubra* var. *rubra*), but environmentally aware gardeners are beginning to question the heavy applications of water needed to maintain such quality lawns. Some gardeners are therefore experimenting with "wild meadow" alternatives but as yet few have proved satisfactory.

West Coast region

This region is bounded by Alaska to the north, the Rocky Mountains on the east, the United States on the south, and the Pacific Ocean on the west.

Proximity to the Pacific Ocean is the most important factor affecting gardens on the West Coast. Air streams from the Pacific, warmed by the Japanese ocean current, cause mild, moist weather, so that the range of plants grown here is different from elsewhere in Canada. Some plants that are common elsewhere, for example hawthorns (*Crataegus*) and crabapples (*Malus*), fail to thrive on the coast, because high rainfall in late winter brings an increase in fungal diseases. Soils throughout the region are acidic due to the high rainfall and geology.

Climate
The influence of the sea results in milder winters and cooler summers than are experienced in the rest of Canada. On the coast, summer temperatures as high as 91°F (33°C) are common, whereas those in winter may drop to 0°F (-18°C). Winter temperatures are colder in the mainland mountains, and snow is common. The Rocky Mountains greatly affect the local climate; even places only a short distance

apart can have widely differing temperatures and rainfall. Occasionally, winters are extremely cold, and commonly grown shrubs may perish in an arctic high sweeping down from the north, or they can be very mild, when there may be virtually no frost all winter and pelargoniums and fuchsias survive. Vancouver averages 216 frost-free days a year; Victoria 280.

The region's closeness to the sea also affects the distribution of rainfall. Where the Pacific meets the mountains, rainfall reaches l28in (320cm), whereas the lee of the mountains receives only 25in (63cm). Relative humidity, which is high in the mornings (84–92 percent), drops in the afternoons. During summer, coastal regions experience long spells of dry weather, sometimes even drought. Vancouver, for example, averages 1,920 hours of sunshine per year while Victoria experiences 2,059 hours. The prevailing winds are easterly.

Soils
Coastal soils are acidic, while those in the mountains are often shallow and lacking in nutrients. Both soil types require the addition of copious amounts of organic

matter. Peaty soils, which produce bountiful gardens and excellent commercial crops of highbush blueberry (*Vaccinium corymbosum*), are common on the Fraser delta. Clay soils occur in the Fraser valley.

Planting traditions
The backdrop to many gardens on the West Coast is huge native trees and lush native vegetation that will quickly invade if neglected.

Conifers such as *Pseudotsuga menziesii*, *Tsuga heterophylla*, and *Thuja plicata* are established in many gardens. Gardening under these giants poses a problem in itself and frequently leads to disputes over the merits of removing these trees altogether.

An outstanding range of plants can be cultivated along the coast. Mild winters and acid soils enable azaleas, rhododendrons, camellias, *Pieris*, Japanese maples (*Acer spp.*), ferns, and heathers to thrive. Such acidic soil also benefits mophead and lacecap hydrangeas (*Hydrangea macrophylla*), which develop blue flowers rather than the usual pink ones associated with alkaline soils. Roses survive most winters but, since springs are damp, are prone to blackspot

(see "Fungal leaf spots," p.641) and powdery mildew (see p.640). Adventurous gardeners try tender plants such as *Phormium tenax*, eucalyptus, *Trachycarpus fortunei*, and *Hebe*.

Tall, late spring-flowering perennials such as delphiniums, peonies (*Paeonia*), and oriental poppy (*Papaver orientale*) need careful staking to prevent damage in spring downpours. Some annuals may even rot in a wet spring.

While lack of extreme summer heat allows many perennials and bedding plants to flower for extended periods, it does make growing warm-climate crops such as tomatoes, cucumbers, and melons, all of which prefer a hot summer, that much more haphazard. Conversely, cool-weather crops such as lettuce thrive and can be produced all summer long, especially in the foothills.

On the coast, fruits such as apples, cherries, pears, kiwis, strawberries, raspberries, and blueberries grow well. Diseases flourish on fruit trees, however, in a wet spring.

Lawns are mostly of Kentucky bluegrass (*Poa pratensis*), but fine lawn grasses such as the fescues (*Festuca*) thrive and can make excellent lawns.

5
SOILS AND FERTILIZERS

SOILS ARE HIGHLY complex and dynamic materials that are made up of minute particles of weathered rock of different types, organic matter, and plant and animal life down to the microscopic level. Healthy soil is essential to successful plant growth: it physically supports plants and supplies them with water, air, and mineral nutrients. If your soil does not at first appear to be ideal, there are a number of possible solutions; virtually any soil may be improved with a little time and effort.

It is possible, for example, to drain the soil if it is waterlogged or to improve its structure and water-holding capacity by the addition of organic matter. Nutrients are easily added to the soil with fertilizers, and lime may be added to make acidic soils more alkaline. Mulches improve plant growth because they prevent weed seeds from germinating and reduce water loss from the soil; some are ornamental. For container-grown plants, a wide range of soil mixes is available for every purpose.

Soil and its structure

Most soil is classified according to its clay, silt, and sand content. The size and proportion of these mineral particles help determine the chemical and physical behavior of the soil. Clay particles are less than $\frac{1}{16,000}$in (0.0016mm) in diameter; silt particles are up to 25 times larger than the largest clay particles; and sand particles may be 1,000 times larger – up to $\frac{1}{16}$in (1.6mm) in diameter.

Soil types

Loam soils have the ideal balance of mineral particle sizes, with between 8 and 25 percent clay, which results in good drainage and water retention, combined with high fertility.

Clay soils are heavy, slow draining, and slow to warm up in spring, but they are often highly fertile. They are easily compacted, however, and may bake hard in summer.

Both sandy and silt soils have a low proportion of clay particles, making them much less water-retentive than clay. Sandy soils are particularly light and drain freely; they need frequent irrigation and fertilizing. However, they warm up quickly in spring and are easily improved with organic matter. Silts are more retentive and fertile than sandy soils but tend to compact more easily.

Soil characteristics

Clay soils have more than 25 percent clay particles and are characteristically wet and sticky. Soils containing less than 8 percent clay are classified as either silt or sandy soil, depending on whether silt or sand particles predominate. Muck is formed where wet, acidic conditions prevent full decomposition of organic matter, which therefore remains on or near the soil surface. Alkaline soil, however, normally drains freely, and organic matter incorporated into it decomposes rapidly.

SANDY SOIL
A dry, light, freely draining soil, easy to work but relatively infertile.

MUCK
Rich in organic matter, muck is dark and moisture-retentive.

CLAY
A heavy, slowly draining soil, usually with a high nutrient value.

ALKALINE SOIL
Pale, shallow, and stony, this drains freely and is moderately fertile.

SILT
Silt is reasonably moisture-retentive and fertile but compacts easily.

Organic or muck soils are generally wet and acidic; however, they support excellent plant growth if drained, fertilized, and limed, if required. Alkaline soils are shallow and moderately fertile, and they drain freely.

The profile of the soil

Soils may be divided into three layers, or horizons: topsoil, subsoil, and a layer derived from the parent rock. Topsoil contains most soil organisms and many of the nutrients. It is generally dark: it contains organic matter that is added artificially or naturally by leaf drop. Subsoil is usually lighter in color; if it is white, the parent rock is probably limestone. If there is little or no color change between topsoil and subsoil, the topsoil may be deficient in organic matter.

Weeds and wild plants help indicate the type of soil in a garden and any characteristics it may have, although their presence is only a guide. Birch (*Betula*), blueberries (*Vaccinium*), bluebells (*Mertensia*), and hemlock (*Tsuga*) are all signs of acidic soil, as are many garden plants such as rhododendrons. Beech (*Fagus*) and ash (*Fraxinus*) indicate

A SOIL PROFILE

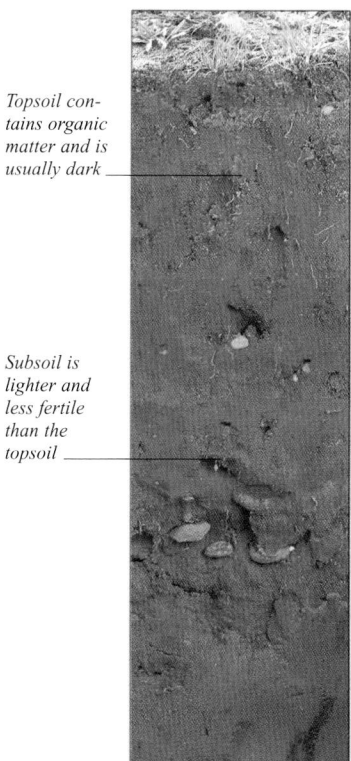

Topsoil contains organic matter and is usually dark

Subsoil is lighter and less fertile than the topsoil

Soil is usually made up of layers of topsoil and subsoil, plus a lower layer derived from underlying rock. The depth of each layer will vary.

Identifying your soil

Rub a small amount of moist soil between your fingers. A sandy soil feels quite gritty and will not stick together or form a ball, although a sandy loam is slightly more cohesive. A silty soil feels silky or soapy to the touch. A silty loam may show imprints when pressed with a finger. A loamy clay soil holds together well and may be rolled into a cylindrical shape. Heavy clay soil may be rolled even more thinly, and it develops a shiny streak when smoothed. All clay soils feel sticky and slightly heavy.

SANDY SOIL
Sandy soil feels gritty when rubbed between finger and thumb. The grains do not stick together.

CLAY SOIL
Clay soil feels sticky when wet and may be rolled into a ball that changes shape when pressed.

---

that the soil is likely to be alkaline. Wild plants may also indicate the chemical profile of the soil: nettle and dock, for example, suggest a rich, fertile soil that is high in phosphorus, while clover indicates a soil that is low in nitrogen.

Acidity and alkalinity

Soil pH is a measurement of acidity or alkalinity – the scale ranges from 1–14. A pH below 7 indicates an acidic soil, while a pH higher than 7 indicates an alkaline soil. Neutral soil has a pH of 7.

The pH of soil is usually controlled by its calcium level. Calcium is an alkaline element that almost all soils tend to lose through leaching (meaning that it is washed through the soil by water). Soils over limestone, which are rich in calcium, are more or less unaffected; other soils, especially sands and sandy loams, gradually turn more acidic.

Alkalinity may be increased, if necessary, by liming (see p.619) or introducing lime-rich material such as mushroom compost.

TESTING PH LEVEL

Soil test kits use a chemical solution that changes color when mixed with soil in a small test tube. The color is then matched against a chart that indicates the pH level of the soil sample.

A yellow or orange color indicates acidic soil

Bright green indicates neutral soil

Dark green indicates alkaline soil

Electronic pH meters and soil test kits may be used to measure pH. Make several tests across the garden, since pH may vary; readings are very unreliable after liming.

The effect of pH

Above all, pH affects the solubility of soil minerals and hence their availability to plants. Acidic soils tend to be deficient in phosphorus and sometimes contain excess manganese and aluminum. Alkaline soils tend to lack manganese, boron, and phosphorus.

Soil pH also affects the number and type of beneficial soil organisms, as well as pests and diseases. For example, earthworms dislike acidic soils, but clubroot and wireworms are common in acidic conditions. On alkaline soils, potato scab occurs more frequently.

Optimum pH

The pH range for good plant growth is between 5.5 and 7.5. A pH of 6.5 usually is optimum, depending on the plants to be grown. Muck soils have an optimum pH of 5.8, however. The highest vegetable yields

---

are generally obtained from neutral soils, but most ornamentals tolerate a wide pH range. Some are more sensitive: calcicoles (lime lovers) and calcifuges (lime haters) are adapted to extreme pH ranges and their growth suffers if they are planted in soil with the wrong pH level.

Soil organisms

Certain soil organisms are essential to maintain soil fertility. Beneficial bacteria and fungi prefer well-aerated soil and generally tolerate a wide pH, although most fungi prefer acidic conditions. One group of fungi (mycorrhizae) live in association with plant roots and improve the take-up of nutrients from the soil.

Small soil animals, such as mites, play a vital part in the breakdown of organic matter. Microscopic worms and nematodes (eelworms) help control pests, although some are themselves pests.

Larger soil animals, particularly earthworms, improve soil structure when feeding and burrowing; the passage of soil through an earthworm's body binds soil particles into crumbs, increasing aeration and improving drainage.

BENEFICIAL ORGANISMS

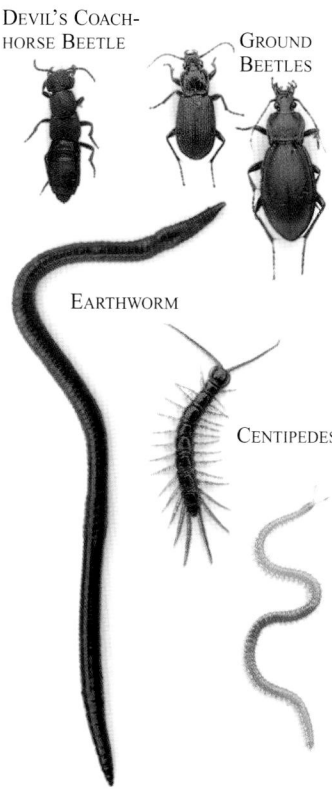

DEVIL'S COACH-HORSE BEETLE

GROUND BEETLES

EARTHWORM

CENTIPEDES

Healthy soil contains a teeming community of earthworms and other organisms that help aerate the soil and break down organic matter.

Soil cultivation

Correct methods of soil cultivation, including weeding, digging, and adding soil improvers, are vital to successful long-term plant growth.

Weeds compete with cultivated plants for space, light, nutrients, and water – in fact, all the essentials. They may also harbor diseases of many types, which makes their eradication or control vital.

Several digging techniques are used to cultivate the soil in different ways, depending on the condition of the soil and the plants that are to be grown. If the condition of the soil is poor, it may be improved by the addition of organic material, usually at the same time as digging.

Clearing an overgrown garden

Badly neglected, overgrown areas may be cleared using either tools or chemicals, so use whichever method is appropriate for the site (see also PLANT PROBLEMS, "Controlling weeds," p.660).

Mechanical clearance
Slash as much top-growth as possible using a nylon-line trimmer, brushwood cutter, or scythe, and clear it away from the area. Then, with a rotary mower, cut any remaining growth as low as possible before digging out and removing all the vegetation that is left on the site.

Alternatively, use a rototiller to churn up the soil and chop up the weeds. Make several passes with the rototiller to break up the matted vegetation, then rake it up and remove it from the surface. The chopping action of the tines, however, will cut the roots or rhizomes of perennial weeds into pieces that regenerate rapidly. After rototilling, therefore, it is essential to rake over the plot and remove by hand all remaining weeds.

Chemical clearance
Following the manufacturer's instructions carefully, spray with a systemic weedkiller, allow it to be absorbed, and then clear away the dead top-growth. If necessary, respray any vegetation that escaped the first application of weedkiller.

Remove the dead vegetation or incorporate it into the soil. Most gardeners prefer to prepare the whole site for planting, but trees, shrubs, and other vigorous ornamentals may be planted directly into holes prepared in the dead vegetation.

On sandy soil, many weedkillers are rapidly leached out, so use only contact weedkillers, which break down when in contact with soil. In organic gardens, where it is not desirable to use chemicals, or if the layout of a garden makes it difficult to apply weedkiller evenly, use mechanical or other methods of weed control, for example mulches (see p.620) and organic practices such as the deep-bed system.

Weed control

In practically all gardens the soil is full of weed seeds and fragments of perennial weed roots. Weed seeds are brought into the garden from neighboring land by the wind and in the soil or soil mix around bought plants. Cultivation, by its very nature disturbs the soil and often brings weed seeds to the surface, where they

CLEARING A SITE OF WEEDS

USING WEEDKILLER
A neglected or weed-infested site must be thoroughly cleared before planting takes place. Treat tough weeds with a chemical weedkiller.

FORKING OUT WEEDS
Fork up the roots of large weeds and pull them out, holding the main stem close to the soil so that the entire root system is removed.

are able to germinate (see "The stale seedbed technique," p.614). Soil cultivation also allows small pieces of perennial weed roots to regenerate and start a new growth cycle all over again.

It is virtually impossible to clean a soil completely of weeds, but regular weeding, rather than sporadic attempts that are then followed by periods of neglect, is the best method of control. Although tedious, hand-weeding with a hand fork is one of the most efficient methods of controlling weeds, since you can be sure that the entire plant is removed from the bed. It also causes the least disturbance to existing plants.

Hoeing
Hoes are used to remove annual weeds and also help aerate the soil (see also p.546). Unless used carefully, however, they may damage the surface roots and top-growth of nearby cultivated plants. Hoeing mainly works only in the surface soil and seldom goes deep enough to destroy the roots of perennial weeds; pull these out by hand or destroy them with a systemic weedkiller (see PLANT PROBLEMS, "Foliage-acting weedkillers," p.660).

Sterilizing the soil

Some soil pests and diseases, such as bacterial soft rot of irises and nematodes, are so aggressive and persistent that soil sterilization may be the only effective treatment to eliminate them.

Soil sterilants should be used only as a last resort, since they are indiscriminate and kill all organisms, beneficial as well as harmful. This may lead to long-term problems in the garden, because harmful pests

ROTOTILLING THE SOIL

1 *For cultivating large areas of soil, it is worth renting or buying a roto-tiller. Adjust the handlebars to a comfortable position, then press down on the handlebars so that the tiller blades penetrate the soil to their full depth.*

2 *After rototilling, rake up and remove any pieces of perennial weeds from the surface of the soil; otherwise, they will reestablish and grow again.*

SOIL STERILIZATION

Soil sterilization may be the only method of eradicating some pests or diseases. Cover the sterilized soil with weighted-down plastic (any soil used for this should be discarded).

are likely to reinvade and thrive unhindered, since there will be no natural predators to control them.

Chemical soil sterilants are highly poisonous and can be applied only by a licensed operator. The sterilant is applied as a drench that percolates and vaporizes through the pores of the soil. The soil surface is then covered with plastic to prevent the gases from escaping. After a soil sterilant has been applied, it will be several weeks before it is safe to plant in the treated soil.

Digging and forking

Cultivating the soil by digging and forking helps provide suitable conditions for good plant growth by aerating the soil and breaking up any surface crust (cap). Organic matter and fertilizers may be incorporated at the same time, if required. On heavily compacted ground, thorough digging helps improve both soil structure and drainage.

The most common method of cultivation is digging with a spade; single and double digging are in general the most effective and labor-efficient digging methods. Some garden beds, however, may not be suited to such a methodical approach to soil cultivation, especially where there are already many established plants. In these circumstances, forking and simple digging may be useful alternatives.

Disadvantages of digging

There are some disadvantages associated with digging. It increases the rate of breakdown of organic matter, particularly in sandy soils, which in the long term reduces soil fertility. In addition, while soil structure is temporarily improved by cultivation, after a while the soil settles down and may become compacted, resulting in poor aeration and drainage unless the soil is dug again.

When to dig

It is preferable to dig in fall, if possible. The soil is then exposed to winter cold and snow, which help break down large clods of soil and improve soil structure.

From midwinter until early spring, the ground is frequently wet or frozen and impossible to work. Heavy soil must never be dug when it is wet, since this may cause severe and permanent structural damage.

Using a fork

Much digging work involves lifting and turning the soil. Forks, which are shaped to penetrate the soil easily, are excellent for opening up and loosening soil – but not for lifting it. Forking is less harmful to the soil structure than using a spade, because it tends to break the clods along existing, natural fracture lines rather than along artificially sliced ones.

Forking is suitable for rough digging and for turning the soil but not for creating fine tilths (see "Forming a tilth," p.614). It is also useful for clearing weeds from the soil, particularly perennial weeds such as quackgrass (*Elymus*), but take care not to leave behind small pieces of plant that will regenerate.

Simple digging

When digging, some gardeners prefer simply to lift out a spadeful of soil, invert it, drop it back in its original position, and chop it up. This method is known as simple digging. It is a quick and relatively easy form of cultivation and is suitable for cleaning the soil surface of any debris and nonpersistent weeds, incorporating small amounts of manure and fertilizers, or creating a surface tilth. Simple digging is often the best option when working in irregularly shaped beds or around existing plants.

Single digging

Single digging is the term applied to a methodical and labor-efficient approach to cultivation that ensures an area has been completely dug to a uniform standard, and to the depth of a spade (known as a spit).

Mark out with lines the area to be cultivated. Then, beginning at one end of the plot, dig out trenches to a spade's depth and about 12in (30cm) wide. Place the soil from the first trench in a pile on the ground in front. Work backward along the plot, turning the soil from each subsequent trench into the one in front.

FORKING

Fork over the soil when it is moist but not waterlogged. Work methodically, inserting the fork then turning it over (see inset) to break up the soil and aerate it.

SIMPLE DIGGING

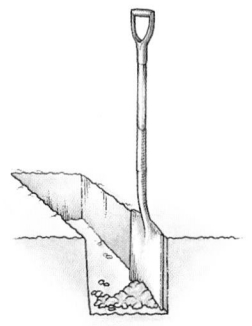

Most spades have a blade 10in (25cm) long. This is the depth of trench required when digging 1 spit deep.

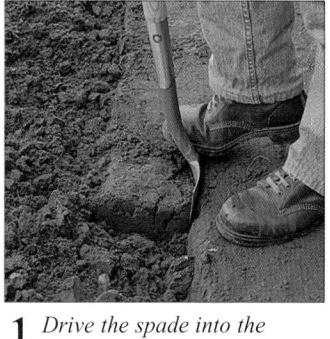

1 *Drive the spade into the soil to its full depth, keeping the blade upright. Press down firmly on the blade with the ball of your foot.*

2 *Pull back on the handle and lever soil onto the blade. Bend knees and elbows to lift the spade; do not try to lift too much, especially where the soil is heavy.*

3 *Twist the spade to turn the soil over. This introduces air into the soil and encourages the breakdown of organic matter.*

SINGLE DIGGING

Mark out the bed, then dig a series of trenches, working backward so that you do not compact the soil. Turn the soil from each trench into the one in front, using soil from the first trench to fill the last.

1 *Dig out a trench 1 spit deep and about 12in (30cm) wide. Insert the spade vertically, then lift the soil onto the ground in front.*

2 *Dig a second trench, turning the soil into the trench in front. Invert the soil to bury annual weeds and weed seeds.*

Adopt this method on regularly shaped plots and where soil uniformity is important – in vegetable gardens and formal beds, for example. Single digging is also useful where large quantities of organic matter need to be dug in, or where double digging is impractical.

Take the opportunity to incorporate lime (if needed) and fertilizers, such as bone meal, into the bottom of each trench before replacing the soil. Weeds, especially deep-rooting perennial ones, should be removed as a matter of course.

Double digging

Double or trench digging, in which the soil is worked to a depth of two spits rather than one, should be carried out if the ground has not been previously cultivated or if drainage needs to be improved.

In grassed areas, the sod may be stripped off the top, thrown into the trench bottom, and chopped up with a spade before backfilling the soil. Lime and fertilizers should also be incorporated, if required, and perennial weeds removed, as in single digging.

When double digging, it is essential that subsoil is not mixed with topsoil. On sites where the topsoil is less than two spits deep, standard double digging should be used, since this method ensures that the soil from the upper and lower spits are kept separate. The lower spit does not need to be brought to the surface – it may be forked or dug over *in situ*, although if more thorough cultivation is required it is also turned.

Mark out the area with lines, as for single digging, then remove the soil from the upper and lower spits of the first trench and from the upper spit of the second, laying it aside on the ground in three separate, clearly

SURFACE TILTH

A crumbly, even-textured soil with fine particles provides a good tilth for seed germination. It is air- and water-retentive, yet it also provides free drainage.

DOUBLE DIGGING

STANDARD DOUBLE DIGGING

Dig out trenches 2 spits deep and turn soil from each trench into the ones in front; do not mix soil from the upper and lower spits.

DOUBLE DIGGING FOR DEEP TOPSOILS

Where the topsoil is at least 2 spits deep, soil from the upper and lower spits may be mixed or transferred. Dig out 2 spits from the first trench, setting the soil aside to fill the final trench, then transfer soil from the upper spit of the second trench to the bottom of the first. Soil from the lower spit of the second trench should be transferred to the top of the first, and so on.

marked, piles. Soil may then be transferred from the lower spit of the second trench to the base of the first trench, and from the upper spit of the third trench to the top of the first. In this way, topsoil and subsoil remain completely separate. Continue digging additional trenches in the same way and, at the end of the bed, use soil that was saved from the first two trenches to fill the appropriate spits of the final two.

If the topsoil is more than two spits deep, there is no need to keep soil from the upper and lower spits separate, and all the soil from one trench may simply be transferred to the trench in front (see above).

Forming a tilth

A tilth is a fine surface soil that is suitable for seed germination. It consists mostly of small soil particles and is moisture-retentive and level. A fine surface tilth ensures good contact between seed and soil, so

---

IMPROVING STRUCTURE

To improve soil structure, dig in organic material such as well-rotted manure or compost, according to the needs of the soil.

that moisture is absorbed easily. If possible, prepare seedbeds a month before sowing by digging the soil and allowing it to weather. Just before sowing, break up clods with a rake, level the ground by treading gently, and then rake to provide the fine tilth required for seeds.

Soil structure and water content

For plants to grow and flourish over a period of many years, the soil needs to have a good inherent structure. On medium and heavy soils, in particular, plant growth depends on good soil structure.

In a well-structured soil, the particles form crumbs that exist as part of an interconnecting network of pores, through which water, nutrients, and air circulate. The structure of the soil therefore determines its ability to hold water, the rate at which it drains, and its fertility. A poorly structured soil may become too freely drained or waterlogged, and nutrients will be lost by leaching.

The stale seedbed technique

This method of cultivation involves disturbing the soil by shallow digging to bring weed seeds to the surface. Existing weeds are also removed at the same time. The weed seeds are then allowed to germinate and grow and the seedlings killed with a contact weedkiller or by shallow hoeing – this time disturbing the soil as little as possible. Seed may then be safely sown in the weed-free ground, as required. More weed seeds inevitably germinate during the season, but since the main weed flush has been destroyed, subsequent weed control will be relatively simple.

1 *As an experiment, the soil on the right of this plot has been dug over, while the soil on the left has been left undisturbed.*

2 *After a few weeks, weed seeds have germinated on the cultivated ground. The undisturbed soil has relatively few weeds.*

Poorly structured soil

A poorly structured soil tends to be too wet in winter and too dry in summer. Water frequently runs off the surface rather than percolating deep down, yet once the soil is wet it drains slowly. A soil such as this is difficult to work, and in summer it may become hard and concretelike. As a result, plant roots have great difficulty penetrating the soil, and plant growth is impeded.

Cultivating heavy soil during wet weather may make it compacted. When soil particles are compressed, the amount of air in the soil is reduced and drainage is hindered.

Walking on the soil in wet conditions damages the structure of the surface layer – the soil crumbs break down and fine particles at the surface form a crust, which then prevents air and oxygen from reaching the plants' roots and also prevents seeds from germinating. This is known as capping and may occur on some soils (particularly silts) following heavy rain or if the soil is watered too heavily.

Improving soil structure

To improve poor structure, cultivate the soil to as great a depth as possible by double digging (without mixing subsoil with topsoil), incorporating organic or inorganic additives to help bind the soil particles into crumbs. This will do much to improve both aeration and water retention. On severely waterlogged sites, a suitable drainage system may need to be installed (see p.617).

Using soil additives

The choice of additives to use is dependent on the type of soil. Most may be either applied to the surface or incorporated into the soil. Organic material such as animal manure and compost improves the structure of any type of soil and also provides valuable nutrients. In addition, animal manure encourages earthworms, which will further benefit soil content and structure (see "Soil organisms," p.611).

A light, sandy soil may be improved by forking in a top-dressing of a heavy, clay-rich topsoil. The addition of grit or sharp sand will lighten clay soils.

On compacted soil and clay soil, add manure, compost, and/or lime (but not for acidic soil-loving plants) to improve its structure by encouraging crumb formation.

On silt, add small amounts of clay to improve soil structure, and incorporate manure, compost, peat, and other organic materials to encourage crumb formation.

The amount of additive required depends on the condition of the soil, but a good rule of thumb is to apply about a 2–4in (5–10cm) layer of bulky additives. Some materials, particularly inorganic compounds and water-retaining gels, should be added in much smaller quantities, so it is important to follow the manufacturer's instructions.

Subsidiary benefits of soil additives

Additives also maintain a good balance of air and water in soil. Sand, gravel, and coarse organic matter may be used to improve drainage in silty, compacted, and heavy clay soils. Sand or gravel is often used along channels in the soil, keeping a path open for water, rather than being worked in. Some additives, such as compost, peat, well-rotted

SOIL ADDITIVES

Adding compost, well-rotted manure, or peat improves the soil structure and helps hold moisture in the soil. Mushroom compost is alkaline by reaction and therefore should not be used with plants requiring acidic conditions. Lime binds clay soil particles together into crumbs by a process known as flocculation.

MUSHROOM COMPOST   MANURE

LIME   PEAT

manure, and water-holding gels (which hold many times their weight in water) act as sponges and may be used to improve water retention in free-draining, sandy soil. On compacted soil, water-holding gels are useful for improving water retention without reducing aeration.

Additions of clay will improve the fertility of impoverished soil. Clay, peat, compost, and to some extent bark and leaves help retain nutrients that might otherwise be lost by leaching.

Problems with additives

Some additives should not be used in certain soil conditions. Fine sand, for example, added in small amounts to heavy soil may make poor drainage worse by blocking the soil pores. Use a more open material, such as gravel or coarse sand, instead.

Fresh manure gives off ammonia and sometimes other substances that may be toxic to plants. If it is not possible to compost the manure or to mature it until it is well rotted, apply it to the soil surface in the fall and leave the soil uncultivated over winter. The manure will gradually rot down and be incorporated into the soil by earthworms.

Fresh straw, leaves, and bark use up nitrogen during their decomposition process, contributing to a possible nitrogen deficiency in the soil unless additional nitrogen fertilizer is applied to the soil at the same time.

When making compost (see p.621), never use plant remains that are infected with viruses or any material that contains perennial weeds – both are difficult to control. This material should be discarded.

COMPARING SOILS

GOOD SOIL
A well-structured soil has a crumbly, moist texture, with a network of pores that holds both air and water. The soil crumbs bind together but do not form a hard cap.

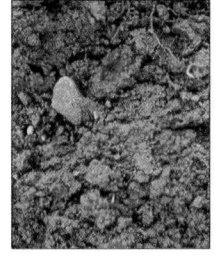

POOR SOIL
This topsoil is hard and compacted, making it almost impossible to cultivate. Drainage will be poor. Cracks appear where the soil has dried out.

SOIL PROBLEMS

COMPACTION
In compacted soil, the pores between the soil particles have been badly compressed. This results in slow drainage and poor aeration.

BLUE MOTTLING
Blue mottling on the soil surface indicates stagnant, waterlogged soil that needs to be drained. The soil may also have an unpleasant smell.

HARDPAN
This is an almost impermeable layer of severely compacted soil. Water will not drain through until the hardpan is broken up. Drains may need to be installed.

CAPPING
A crust or cap forms on the soil when soil crumbs on the surface are damaged by heavy rain or watering, or by walking on the soil when it is wet.

Water

Adequate water is crucial for good plant growth; the amount available depends to some extent on the plant itself but also on soil type and structure, and the method of watering. Water is often in short supply and should not be wasted, so it is important to use good watering and water-conserving techniques. It is also useful to know which plants are susceptible to drought (and when) and which are drought-resistant.

An excess of water in the soil (waterlogging) can be as damaging to plants as a lack of soil water. Cultivating the soil and adding organic matter and grit will do much to improve drainage in saturated soil, but on severely waterlogged sites an appropriate drainage system should be installed.

Soil water

In a well-structured soil, water is held in fine capillary pores, which are usually less than $1/160$ in (0.16mm) in diameter, with air in the larger pores; it is therefore possible for soil to be described as both moist and well drained.

Water is most readily available to plants from pores of the largest diameter. As the pores become smaller, it becomes increasingly difficult for the plants to extract moisture, which means that some soil water always remains unavailable.

Clay soils
Clay soils hold the greatest amount of water but they have a high percentage of fine capillary pores, so plants are not always able to extract enough water for their needs.

HOW NOT TO WATER

Do not water plants at a rate that causes puddling on the soil surface, since this leads to runoff and can erode the soil very quickly.

METHODS OF WATERING

BASIN-WATERING
Scoop out soil from around the base of the plant, then fill the resulting basin with water.

POT-WATERING
Bury a large pot that has a drainage hole close to the plant, then fill the pot slowly with water.

Sandy soils
Sandy soils contain coarse pores, so the water held within them is more readily available than in clay. Sandy soils, however, have a high drainage rate, and there is relatively little capillary movement of water sideways and upward.

Loams
Loams usually contain a balanced mix of coarse and relatively fine pores – the coarse pores allow rapid drainage while the finer ones retain water, much of which may be extracted by plants in dry conditions.

The water table
Moisture rises to the soil surface by capillary action from the water table below. Heavy clay soils may be saturated to 6ft (2m) above the water table, with some moisture available to plant roots as much as 11ft (3.5m) above it. Silty and most clay soils are saturated to 5ft (1.5m), with moisture available to roots 8ft (2.5m) above the water table. The figures for fine sand are 5ft (1.5m) and 7½ft (2.4m) respectively, and for coarser sand 1ft (30cm) and 3ft (1m). On gravel, there is no water rise at all.

Watering techniques

The aim of watering is to recharge the soil so that reserves will be sufficient to last until the next watering or rainfall.

Always water thoroughly so that water is available deep in the soil. Frequently applying a little water is of limited value, because much of it simply evaporates off the soil surface before it has a chance to penetrate down to the roots of plants.

Moisture takeup
The water supply to a plant is limited by the size of its root system. By improving drainage (see p.617) and rectifying compaction by double digging (see p.614), if necessary, plants are able to develop deeper root systems, with a comparative increase in growth.

The main limitation when watering, however, is the rate at which the soil takes up the moisture. On average, soil absorbs only about $3/8$in (8mm) depth of water per hour. Water applied to the soil faster than it is absorbed (for example, by a hand-held hose or watering can with a nozzle) collects in a pool on the surface until the area covered is capable of taking it all in. After watering in dry conditions, it is worth examining the soil with an auger – it may be surprising just how little the water has penetrated. If the soil around the roots of the plants is still dry, give the area several further, longer applications once the first application has soaked in.

To reduce water runoff, the ground may be modified by terracing or dishing to create a hollow basin around each plant (see above), which ensures that water reaches the roots. Pot-watering (see above), garden sprinklers (see p.555), and trickle or drip-feed systems (see p.555) are efficient methods of watering, since water is supplied to the roots over several hours.

Water-conserving techniques
Mulching the surface of the soil (see p.620) improves rain penetration and minimizes evaporation. By controlling weeds effectively (see p.660), you will ensure that no soil water is wasted on unwanted plants.

Water deficiency

Once a plant begins to wilt, its growth rate has already begun to slow down. In many areas, water use will exceed water supply during summer, so the soil suffers a net loss of moisture. Digging additives such as manure into the soil improves structure (see "Using soil additives," p.615) and water retention, which helps prevent a water deficit from occurring, but unless an existing deficit is made up by irrigation, the soil becomes progressively drier. Regular watering is therefore essential.

The local meteorological office will have figures for the typical monthly water loss from the soil and through leaves by transpiration (known as potential evapotranspiration), and also for the average monthly rainfall. These figures are useful when calculating how often to water but, for greater accuracy, it is better to take your own rainfall measurements each month.

Seasonal needs
The point at which a water deficit begins to hinder plant growth depends on the plants themselves. High-yield plants usually need plenty of water, so the soil should be kept moist. Some plants have critical periods of growth, during which time water supplies are vital: the first half of summer, for example, is much more important than the second for young ornamental trees. Fruit trees need ample water as the fruits swell, as do potato tubers. Newly planted trees are likely to require watering throughout their first season, since their top-growth is frequently out of proportion to their root system.

Watering is especially important for newly planted or transplanted plants, and those in shallow soils and in containers. Seedlings, too, have low drought resistance, and a reliable water supply is essential.

Xeriscaping
In areas of normally low rainfall, interest is increasing in xeriscaping, which promotes growing naturally drought-adapted plants under a program of water-saving methods.

Purists use only native North American plants, limiting their selections to species growing within a given radius of their gardens, or they may include any suitable North American species or cultivar. Other gardeners combine native and non-native plants.

Drip emitters and other irrigation techniques may supplement natural rainfall. Organic mulches may be used to conserve moisture; in very arid regions, however, where organic mulches may be difficult to obtain, rocks and gravel are much cheaper and are ecologically correct.

Waterlogged soil

Waterlogging occurs when the amount of water entering the soil exceeds the amount that drains out. Particularly vulnerable are those areas where the water table is high (see opposite) or where the soil is compacted and thus poorly structured.

Roots (except those of bog plants) are unable to function properly in waterlogged soil and may eventually die if drainage is not improved. Wet soil is often low in certain nutrients (notably nitrogen) and, as a result, mineral deficiencies may prove a problem. Since wet soil tends to be cold, plant growth may be slow in spring. Diseases such as clubroot also flourish in waterlogged soil.

Rushes, sedges, and mosses growing on the ground suggest that the soil may be waterlogged. A sharp dividing line between peaty topsoil and subsoil also indicates poor drainage. On waterlogged clay, the soil may have a stagnant smell and a yellow or blue-gray color.

Poor drainage may be confirmed by pouring water into a hole that is 12–24in (30–60cm) deep. If the water remains for hours or even days, the soil needs draining. If digging deeper or trying to push a sturdy metal rod into the soil meets with resistance, this indicates a layer of hardpan (see *Soil Problems*, p.615).

Improving drainage

Where waterlogging is not severe and there is excess surface water only, this may be diverted from the site by shaping garden surfaces so that the water flows into drainage ditches. To improve drainage on sites where there is a high water table, install an underground drainage system, preferably using a specialized contractor to carry out the work. If drains already exist on the site, check for blockages in the drainage ditches, or for damaged drainage pipes.

Drainage ditches and French drains

A system of open ditches is the best method of carrying away any excess water. These should be 3–4ft (1–1.2m) deep, with sloping sides. Just as efficient but less obtrusive are French drains, which are gravel-filled drainage ditches topped with upturned sod and topsoil.

Drainage systems and soakaways

A soakaway is a gravel-filled pit into which excess water runs via underground drains or drainage ditches (see below). This method of drainage is recommended for sites where there is surface compaction, since it breaks through any hardpan layer. To construct a soakaway, dig a trench approximately 5ft (1.5m) wide and up to 6ft (2m) deep. Fill it with crushed stone, topped with a layer of coarse sand or gravel, and lay sod or a grate over the top. Install drains about 24in (60cm) below ground level to lead from the surrounding land to the soakaway.

Water storage areas

Alternatively, create a water storage area where water can gather in a pond or large container, or can gradually soak away. A pond is beneficial to wildlife, but its success depends on the degree of sediment in the drainage water – too much will make a pond rich in nutrients, therefore becoming prone to silting up and excessive algal growth.

Water that is collected in containers may be recycled for use in the garden. Collecting water that is allowed gradually to soak away helps replenish groundwater reserves and reduces silt pollution of rivers.

HOW TO LAY DRAINAGE PIPES ON A FLAT SITE

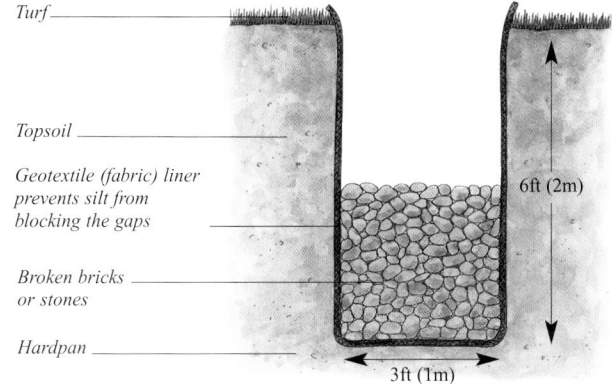

Turf

Topsoil

Geotextile (fabric) liner prevents silt from blocking the gaps

Broken bricks or stones

Hardpan

6ft (2m)

3ft (1m)

1 *In a waterlogged part of the garden, dig a hole 6ft (2m) deep with 3 x 3ft (1 x 1m) sides. Line the sides and bottom with a geotextile. Then fill the lined soakaway hole with rubble, such as broken bricks or stones, to a depth of 3ft (1m).*

Topsoil

Flexible, corrugated plastic drainage pipe slopes toward soakaway

Geotextile fabric liner ensures free flow of water

Soakaway filled with broken bricks or stones

minimum 2ft (60cm) below ground level

2 *Fold the liner over the rubble. Then place the end of a perforated plastic pipe on top of the liner, so that it is ideally 2ft (60cm) below ground level. Fill in the hole with topsoil, and put sod over the top.*

Installing drains

A system of perforated plastic pipes or tile drains laid in a herringbone pattern underground provides an efficient method of drainage. Lay the pipes or tile drains in trenches on a bed of gravel, then cover them with further layers of gravel and sand, before refilling the trench with topsoil. Water from the surrounding site can seep through the gravel and into the pipes, which then carry it to a drainage ditch or soakaway. On level ground, slope the pipes to encourage water to drain away quickly. Where the ground slopes, simply lay pipes parallel to the ground. Install drains before plants are in place, if possible, since the work causes considerable upheaval.

A DRAINAGE SYSTEM ON A SLOPING SITE

High ground

On sloping ground, lay the pipes or tile drains to run parallel to the ground. Simply butt them together in a gravel-filled trench.

Arrows show the direction of water flow

Gravel in trench surrounding pipes or tile drains

Trenches for pipes or tile drains, about 24in (60cm) deep

Gravel-filled drainage ditch or soakaway

Lowest level

Soil nutrients and fertilizers

The nutrients needed by plants are composed of mineral ions, which are absorbed in solution from the soil through the roots and used with carbon dioxide and water to make more complex compounds. Macronutrients include nitrogen (N), phosphorus (P), potassium (K), magnesium (Mg), calcium (Ca), and sulfur (S); these are required in relatively large amounts by plants.

Micronutrients, or trace elements, are equally important but required only in small amounts; they include iron (Fe), manganese (Mn), copper (Cu), zinc (Zn), boron (B), molybdenum (Mb), and chlorine (Cl).

To ensure healthy plant growth, fertilizers containing nutrients may be added to the soil, but this is necessary only when the soil is unable to provide adequate amounts of the nutrients required. On the majority of soils, only nitrogen, which promotes vigorous growth, phosphorus, which improves flowering and fruiting, and potassium, for assisting strong root growth, need to be added regularly. This is because the most common nutrient deficiency problems for plants are caused by a lack of these nutrients. Nitrogen deficiency (see p.643) causes reduced growth, and potassium deficiency (see p.643) causes leaf discoloration. Phosphorus deficiency is less common. Manganese/iron deficiency (see p.643) causes leaves to brown and may be a problem if acidic soil-loving plants are grown in alkaline soil or watered with hard water.

Types of fertilizer

Deciding the amount and which type of fertilizer to apply can be complex. Understanding how each type works will make gardening more productive and even perhaps more environmentally friendly.

Bulky organic fertilizers

Weight for weight, bulky organic fertilizers supply fewer nutrients than inorganic fertilizers. For example, 0.98 tons (1 tonne) of manure typically contains 13.2lb (6kg) of nitrogen, 2.2lb (1kg) of phosphorus, and 8.8lb (4kg) of potassium; the equivalent amount of nutrients in a chemical form is provided by only 66lb (30kg) of inorganic fertilizer.

Manures are, however, integral to organic growing, because the fibrous organic matter that makes them so bulky provides greater benefits than a simple nutrient analysis would suggest. Manures normally contain high levels of micronutrients and are a long-term source of nitrogen. However, they may vary in quality, some batches having a poor nutrient content. Manures also provide the conditions in which worms thrive. Additions of manure improve the structure and water content of most soils (see p.614); since this encourages root growth, it increases the uptake of nutrients by plants.

Concentrated fertilizers

Commercial mixtures of blood, bone and other meals are good examples of concentrated organic fertilizers. They are easy to handle and contain fairly consistent proportions of nutrients but are relatively expensive for each unit of nutrient. Their slow release of nutrients is partly dependent on breakdown by soil organisms, so they may not be useful when these organisms are inactive, as in cold weather.

Soluble fertilizers

Soluble inorganic fertilizers contain high percentages of a given nutrient, weight for weight, and most are easy to carry, handle, and apply, although a few are unpleasant to handle. They are usually the cheapest source per unit of nutrient. They give a quick boost to plants deficient in nutrients, and they permit precise control over the timing of nutrient release. However, a large proportion of soluble fertilizer may be wasted on sandy soils because of leaching.

When using soluble inorganic fertilizers, be selective about which mineral ions are applied to the soil, since some may be damaging to particular plants. Redcurrants, for example, are sensitive to chloride salts, such as potassium chloride, so sulfates should be used instead. Large applications of some inorganic salts make the soil more saline and may harm beneficial soil organisms. Apply soluble inorganic fertilizers in split applications, sparingly but fairly frequently, rather than in a single, large dose.

Slow-release fertilizers

These are complex fertilizer formulations that are designed to release nutrients gradually. Some slowly degrade in the soil, while others absorb water until they swell and burst open. Many have membranes that gradually release nutrients from an internal store. By varying the thicknesses of these membranes, a mix is produced that will supply nutrients to plants over many months or even years in some cases.

Slow-release inorganic fertilizers are expensive, but they overcome many of the drawbacks of soluble fertilizers, such as the need for split applications and the loss of nutrients from the fertilizer by leaching. They make fertilizing container-grown plants much less time-consuming,

NUTRIENT CONTENT OF FERTILIZERS	% NITROGEN (N)	% PHOSPHORUS (P_2O_5)	% POTASSIUM (K_2O)
ORGANIC			
Animal manure	0.6	0.1	0.5
Compost	0.5	0.3	0.8
Bone meal	2	14	–
Tankage	7	10	–
Hoof and horn	14	2	–
Seaweed meal	2.8	0.2	2.5
Blood meal	12	–	–
Mushroom compost	0.7	0.3	0.3
Rock phosphate	–	26	12
Wood ash	0.1	0.3	1
Cocoa shells	3	1	3.2
INORGANIC			
Balanced fertilizers	available in various proportions		
Ammonium nitrate	35	–	–
Superphosphate	–	20	–
Muriate of potash	–	–	60
Potassium sulfate	–	–	49

COMPARING FERTILIZERS

COMPOST

MUSHROOM COMPOST

COCOA SHELLS

BONE MEAL

SOLUBLE INORGANIC FERTILIZER

These comparisons show the relative amounts of different types of fertilizer required to supply roughly the same quantity of nutrients.

SLOW-RELEASE FERTILIZERS

Water enters through pores   *Polymer coat*   *Three-quarter section of granule*

Dilute fertilizer is released

Water enters the fertilizer granules through pores in the polymer coat. Dissolved fertilizer is then released back through the coat..

since they remove the need to add fertilizer each time the plants are watered during the growing season. The nutrient release pattern of slow-release fertilizers may be difficult to predict, however, especially with long-term formulas, since the breakdown depends on the pH level of soil, as well as on the moisture content and temperature of the soil.

Green manures

These are plants that are grown purely to be dug back into the soil to improve fertility and add to the organic content. They are used on land that would otherwise be left fallow and can help prevent nutrients from being washed away, since fallow land is more prone to leaching. Do not use invasive plants as green manures, however.

Buckwheat, ryegrass, and oats are excellent green manures. Mixtures of fast-germinating annuals are also used. Plants such as peas, clovers, and alfalfa have nitrogen-fixing bacteria in root nodules that enable them to obtain nitrogen from air in the soil. The organic matter these plants provide may contribute as much nitrogen as would be added in a standard fertilizing schedule; it has a low carbon:nitrogen ratio and so breaks down rapidly, providing easily available nitrogen.

Applying fertilizers

Fertilizers may be scattered over the surface of the soil or placed around individual plants. Some fertilizers are also available in liquid form for application to the soil surface or as foliar fertilizers directly onto leaves.

When applying fertilizers, always use gloves and do not breathe in any of the dust or vapor arising from them. Use only the recommended quantities, since too much fertilizer could damage the plants.

Broadcast fertilization

Scattering fertilizer over the entire soil surface benefits the greatest area of soil and minimizes the risk of plant injury from overfertilizing. In dry weather, however, the uptake of some nutrients may be poor, particularly of immobile nutrients such as phosphorus, so, whenever possible, dig phosphates into the soil.

When broadcast fertilizing, do not allow any of the material to touch the leaves or stems of plants, since scorching may result.

Fertilizer placement

Applying fertilizer in a ring around the plant but not so that it touches the stem (see below, right) is an economical and efficient fertilizing method, because the fertilizer will be carried down into the root zone.

Liquid fertilizers

Dissolving fertilizer in water before application is a particularly efficient method of applying nutrients, especially if the soil is dry and if you are looking for quick results. Liquid fertilizers sprayed onto leaf surfaces are known as foliar fertilizers. They may be used to correct mineral deficiencies that are caused by certain soil conditions, such as high pH. For deep-rooted plants, such as fruit trees, foliar fertilizers may also be used to correct deficiencies of nutrients that are relatively insoluble. Do not apply foliar liquid fertilizers when rain is forecast, since the liquid may be washed away before it can be taken up by the leaves.

Liming

Liming or adding lime-rich material such as mushroom compost increases the alkalinity of the soil. This is sometimes desirable to improve yields from the vegetable garden but is seldom worthwhile for ornamental plants. It is usually preferable to choose ornamentals that are adapted to the existing conditions.

Types of lime

Ordinary lime (calcium carbonate) is usually the best choice because, although bulky, it is easy to handle and relatively safe to use. Quicklime (calcium oxide) is more efficient at raising pH, but since it is caustic it may scorch plant material; there is also a risk of overliming with quicklime. Slaked, also called hydrated, lime (calcium hydroxide) is made by treating quicklime with water; it is slightly less efficient than quicklime but is less caustic and easier to handle.

Applying lime

Lime may be spread on the soil at any time of year, but it should be applied as far in advance of planting as possible and preferably be well dug in. Choose a windless day, and always wear protective gloves and goggles. Do not routinely lime soil every year, because overliming will

LIMING

Using a spade, spread the lime over the surface of the soil, then distribute it evenly with a rake (see inset). Do not plant or sow for about a month.

contribute to nutrient deficiencies. Always take pH readings in several different parts of the area first, since any uneven rates of breakdown may cause temporary, localized problems, such as mineral deficiencies. The following table indicates the average amount of lime required (per oz/sq yd) for a particular type of soil of a given pH to achieve a pH level of 6.5 (see also "Optimum pH," p.611).

STARTING pH	SAND (oz/sq.yd)	LOAM (oz/sq.yd)	CLAY (oz/sq.yd)
4.5	6.7oz	10oz	14oz
5.0	5.5oz	8.3oz	11.6oz
5.5	4.6oz	6.7oz	9.2oz
6	4.2oz	5.5oz	7.6oz

To raise soil pH quickly, add lime during digging or other cultivation methods. If required for established plantings, lime may be applied as a top-dressing and watered in.

Do not apply lime at the same time as manure, because lime reacts with the nitrogen-rich manure, releasing nitrogen in the form of ammonia. This may damage plants, and it wastes nitrogen. If required, apply lime and manure in alternate years.

GREEN MANURING

Sow seed for green manures on fallow ground. Cut the plants to the ground when about 8in (20cm) tall, digging them in after a day or two.

HOW TO APPLY FERTILIZER

BROADCASTING
To apply fertilizer in accurate amounts over large areas, mark out the area into square yards or meters, using string or stakes. Fill a pot or bowl with the recommended quantity of fertilizer and sprinkle it evenly over each section of the area.

PLACEMENT
Sprinkle the fertilizer around the outer reach of the plant, making sure none touches leaves or stems.

Top-dressings and mulches

Top-dressings and mulches are materials that are applied to the surface of the soil. They are used to improve plant growth in some way, either by reducing weed competition, by increasing the organic or nutrient content, or by reducing water loss from the soil. They may also be used decoratively.

Top-dressings

The term top-dressing is used in two ways. First, it describes surface applications of soluble fertilizers around plants. Second, it refers to additives that are applied to the soil surface or to lawns. For example, a lawn may be top-dressed with sand or fine organic material, which will eventually be washed in by rain.

Gravel or grit is sometimes used as a top-dressing for plants in beds and containers to provide quick drainage away from the collars of plants that are sensitive to excess moisture. They also act as a mulch and discourage growth of mosses or lichens on the soil surface.

Plants may also be top-dressed with gravel or stone chips simply to achieve a decorative result.

Mulches

Mulches are available in organic and inorganic forms and improve plant growth in several ways: they regulate soil temperature, insulating

MATERIALS USED AS TOP-DRESSINGS

TOP-DRESSINGS AS ADDITIVES
Some top-dressings, such as bark and well-rotted compost, are added to the soil around plants to provide organic matter and a steady supply of nutrients. Sand, mixed with soil and peat, is used as a top-dressing on lawns to improve aeration.

SAND

DECORATIVE TOP-DRESSINGS
Materials such as gravel and grit are added to the soil-mix surface in containers or to the soil surface in a border or bed, particularly around low-growing plants such as alpines. These materials improve surface drainage as well as set off the plants.

GRAVEL

BARK

COMPOST

COARSE GRIT

CRUSHED STONE

plant roots from temperature extremes; they reduce water loss from the soil surface; and they help stop weed seeds from germinating by preventing light from reaching them.

Always remove all perennial weeds before mulching; otherwise, they benefit from the mulch to the detriment of your plants. A winter mulch, used to prevent plants from heaving during midwinter thaws, is best applied after the soil has cooled down or even frozen. It must be removed in the spring as soon as it thaws or it will keep the cold in the soil. After the soil has warmed up in the spring, apply a summer mulch, or the soil will remain too cool.

Organic mulches

To be effective, an organic mulch should be long-lasting and not easily dislodged by rain. It should also have a loose structure that allows water to pass through it quickly.

Coarse bark is one of the most useful organic mulches because it prevents weed seeds in the soil beneath from germinating, and weeds that do appear are easily removed.

Compost and peat are not quite as satisfactory, because they provide an ideal medium for the germination of weed seeds and are quickly mixed into the soil by worms, although this process does improve the texture of the soil as a result.

Inorganic mulches

Landscape fabrics are thin, woven materials that are widely available and easy to use. They prevent the growth of both weed seeds and perennial weed pieces. At the same time they allow rain and nutrients to pass through. Anchor them over the soil surface and cover with soil or mulch to retard breakdown. Make X-shaped slits for planting.

Plastic sheet mulches raise the soil temperature slightly and are particularly useful when growing crops such as melons. A disadvantage of sheet mulches is that, once they are in place, organic matter cannot be incorporated into the soil; it also decays more slowly underneath a sheet mulch. If required, extra nutrients may be added through holes punched in the plastic sheeting, and then watered in. Unless sheet mulches are perforated, almost no water evaporates from the soil, and rain cannot penetrate it. Therefore do not place a sheet mulch on dry soil or on soil that tends to be waterlogged or slow draining.

Floating row covers are sheets of light plastic or loosely woven fiber fleece that are used as covers – as the crop grows, the cover is raised by the plants. Floating covers are often perforated or permeable to allow rain and air through to the soil. Their main purpose is to increase soil temperature; they may also act as a barrier against pests and frost.

LANDSCAPE FABRIC

Landscape fabric controls weeds over a large area and should remain in good condition for several years. Anchor with pins, then cover with soil or mulch.

LOOSE MULCHES

APPLYING THE MULCH
A loose mulch regulates soil temperature, retains moisture, and discourages weeds. It should preferably be about 4–6in (10–15cm) deep.

AREA TO MULCH
For small to medium-sized plants, spread a mulch to the full extent of the foliage canopy.

Compost and soil mixes

Compost is decayed organic matter and is a valuable additive prized for its soil-improving properties. There are many kinds of soil mix, each made from precise combinations of (mainly) organic materials; they are used for growing plants in containers and for propagation.

Compost

The contribution of compost to the productivity of the garden can be enormous. It should be added to the soil when the rate of breakdown of the organic matter has leveled off; by this stage, it should be dark, crumbly, and sweet-smelling.

Making compost

To make a compost pile, build up a mixture of nitrogen-rich material (such as grass clippings) and carbon-rich material (such as bark and shredded paper), preferably in a proportion of 1:2. Almost any vegetable waste may be composted, but meat and cooked foods should not be used, since these attract vermin. Do not use thick layers of grass clippings: they inhibit air movement. Pruning clippings may be used, although any woody stems must be shredded first. Use only young weeds; those with seed, or about to set seed, should be discarded, as should all noxious perennial weeds.

Compost additives

Many materials compost satisfactorily, but additional nitrogen will speed up the process. The nitrogen may be provided as artificial fertilizer, commercial compost starter , or, preferably, as manure, which has the advantage of containing high levels of soil organisms. Add this, as necessary, to the compost pile so that there are alternate layers of organic material and manure.

If the material in the compost pile is too acidic, microorganisms will not work efficiently – adding lime will make it more alkaline.

The composting process

The process of making compost generates a high temperature, which encourages the natural breakdown of organic matter to operate quickly and also helps kill weed seeds and some pests and diseases. To heat up sufficiently, a compost pile should be at least 1 cubic yard (1 cubic meter) in size, but 2 cubic yards is preferable. Compost reaches its maximum temperature in two or three weeks and matures in about three months. Turning the pile speeds up the process and ensures complete breakdown. An ammonia odor indicates that the compost is too rich in nitrogen; a smell of rotten eggs means that the pile lacks air.

Slow composting

Composting may be undertaken in an unintensive way. Piles of moist leaves, for example, eventually rot down, even if they are not in a bin. No starter material is added, and the pile is not turned. There will, however, be some material that does not break down fully, and this will need to be composted again.

Soil mixes

Pot plants need a growing medium that is both well aerated and water-retentive, with a resilient structure that can withstand heavy watering. For best results, always use the most suitable type for the purpose.

The essential difference between the two most common mixes is that soil-based mixes contain real soil; soilless mixes, which are usually peat-based, do not. Although soilless mixes did not become popular until the 1960s, they are preferred today because they are cheaper, lighter, and more readily available.

Soil-based potting mixes

These should contain high-quality soil that is rich in organic matter. The soil is usually obtained by stacking sod for six months or more, and should be sterilized, either chemically or by heating the soil to a high temperature, to kill pests and weed seeds and eliminate diseases.

Soil-based mixes provide better conditions than soilless ones for long-term growth. They contain a steady supply of nutrients and are free-draining, with good aeration and structure. They do not dry out as rapidly as peat-based soil mixes and are less prone to waterlogging. Plants also grow on more readily when transplanted to garden soil.

Traditionally, gardeners have grown potted plants in a variety of soil-based potting mixes. The basic recipe is 1 part garden soil (a good loam, preferably sterilized and free of stones, sticks, and other foreign matter is ideal), 1 part peat moss, and 1 part perlite, vermiculite, turface, or clean, sharp sand. If the mix needs extra organic matter for a leafy tropical plant from the rain forest, such as many indoor foliage plants, add an extra part of well-rotted compost, leaf mold, or peat moss. If the mix needs extra drainage, perhaps for a cactus or other succulent, add an extra part of sand, turface, or perlite.

Soilless potting mixes

Widely used in commercial horticulture, soilless potting mixes are lightweight and clean to use. Many products that were previously available only to professionals are now available to home gardeners.

MAKING A COMPOST BIN

1 To make the first side, lay 2 4x4s (the uprights) on the ground at least 3ft (1m) apart. Nail boards across them, butting the joints together. Leave a 3in (8cm) gap as an air chimney at top and bottom.

2 Make the second side; nail scraps of wood across the top to hold the sides in place temporarily. Nail on the back boards.

3 Nail a 2x4 inside the front 4x4s (inset) for the front boards to slide between. Attach a piece of wood at the base as a stop.

4 Nail boards across the top and bottom of the front panel to stabilize the bin when the front boards are removed.

5 Check that the front boards slide easily between the uprights. If necessary, saw a little off the ends.

USING THE BIN

Place a thick layer of twiggy material at the base. Build up the pile in 6in (15cm) layers, sprinkling each layer with a little manure. Turn the pile occasionally to speed the composting process.

Manure

Garden and kitchen waste

Many soilless mixes are based on peat, which combines moisture retentiveness with good aeration and is relatively stable and long-lasting. Soilless peatlite (sphagnum moss, perlite, and vermiculite) may also be used. Soilless mixes are low in nutrients and do not hold them well compared with soil, so plants grown in these mixes need to be fertilized more often. Apply a balanced inorganic fertilizer, since many organic fertilizers are not suited to soilless culture. Soilless mixes dry out rapidly and are hard to rewet, and overwatering results in waterlogging, leading to root rot and other problems.

Plants grown in soilless potting mixes may adapt poorly when transplanted to garden soil. Teasing out the roots and shaking some of the mix from the root ball often stimulates the roots to grow into the soil. Most soilless potting mixes break down rapidly, so that the volume of mix shrinks and the remaining material loses much of its structure. Repot when the mix shrinks away from the pot, which allows water to run uselessly between the rootball and the pot, or when the surface of the mix becomes slimy or difficult to wet.

One of the most common soilless mixes is Cornell Peatlite Mix A. To make 1 bushel (0.36cu m) measure 4 gallons (18 liters) no.2 or no.3 grade horticultural vermiculite; 4 gallons (18 liters) shredded sphagnum moss; 2 tablespoons dolomitic limestone; and 2 tablespoons potassium nitrate or calcium nitrate.

Add 1 pint (600ml) of warm water to the sphagnum moss to moisten it. Put all ingredients into a large plastic bag, then shake to mix well.

Peat substitutes
The use of peat-based potting mixes poses environmental problems in countries where bogs are an endangered habitat. Alternative potting mixes, such as those based on coconut fiber and bark, are available in some areas and are becoming increasingly more available.

Propagation media

When sowing seed (particularly fine seed) and rooting cuttings, specifically formulated propagation media should be used.

Standard sowing media
Fine seed needs to have good contact with the medium in order to germinate and should be sown in a sowing medium that is fine-textured, moisture-retentive, and low in nutrients.

Standard sowing medium is made using 2 parts (by volume) sterilized soil, 1 part peat, and 1 part sand. To each cubic yard is added 2lb superphosphate of lime and 1lb ground limestone (1.2kg and 594g respectively for a cubic meter).

Standard rooting media
Freely draining rooting media may be based on bark, perlite, or coarse sand. Rooting media are low in nutrients, so fertilize cuttings once they have rooted.

A standard rooting medium typically contains equal parts of sand and peat. To each cubic yard (meter) is added 7½lb (4.4kg) dolomitic lime; 2½lb (1.5kg) each of bone meal or dried blood, superphosphate of lime, and calcium carbonate; and 4oz (148g) each of potassium nitrate and potassium sulfate. An absence of soil may mean that a specific micronutrient fertilizer should be added.

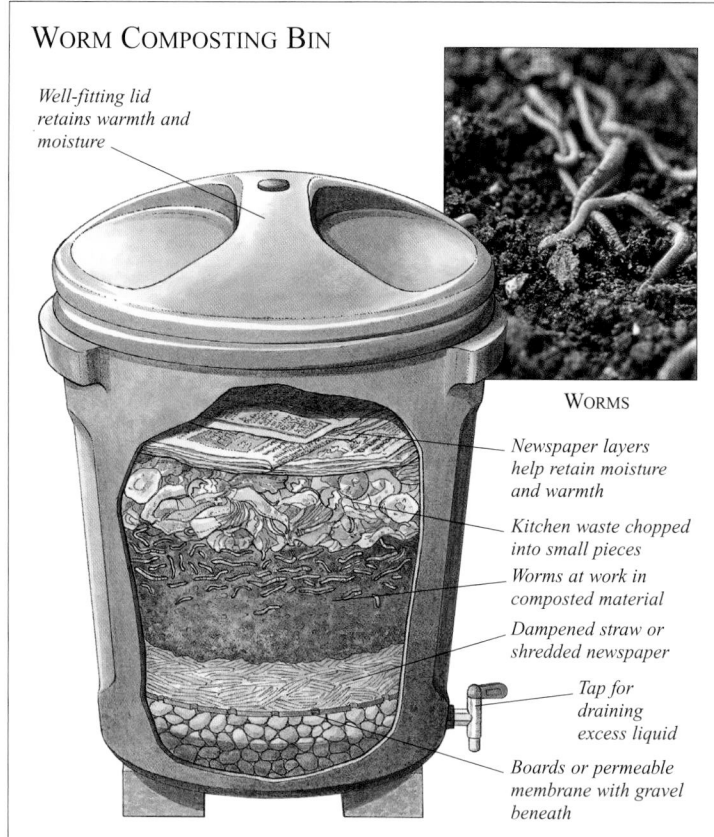

WORM COMPOSTING BIN

Well-fitting lid retains warmth and moisture

WORMS

Newspaper layers help retain moisture and warmth

Kitchen waste chopped into small pieces

Worms at work in composted material

Dampened straw or shredded newspaper

Tap for draining excess liquid

Boards or permeable membrane with gravel beneath

MAKING A LEAF MOLD BIN

1 Staple chicken wire to 2 wooden stakes of equal length. Then hammer the stakes 30cm (12in) into the ground.

2 Insert 2 more stakes into the ground and staple the wire to them, securing the 2 cut ends of wire to one of these stakes.

THE FINISHED BIN
A leaf mold bin should be broad and reasonably low to allow for easy access to the middle. You will need to compact the leaves after putting them in by walking on them or firming with a rake.

USING THE BIN
Leaf mold is an excellent soil conditioner and mulching material. It can also be used as an additive for potting mixes. It should not be removed from the bin until it has decomposed completely, which could take a year or more. Take from one bin while the other is rotting down.

6 PRINCIPLES OF PROPAGATION

Plant propagation is not difficult once the underlying principles are understood, and it is an inexpensive and satisfying way to increase the number of plants in your garden. In addition, it provides opportunities for exchanging plant material with other gardeners, and it thereby further increases the range of plants available in cultivation. To many people, the transition from a seed into a mature plant, the development of a seemingly lifeless hardwood cutting into a tree or shrub, or the formation of a young plant on a piece of leaf is a fascinating process. An understanding of the techniques outlined here should bring the rewards to be gained from successful plant propagation within the reach of every gardener.

Seeds

Seed is by far the most common way by which flowering plants reproduce in nature. It is a sexual method and, as such, always presents the possibility of a variety of genetic combinations. Such variation provides the basis by which plants adapt to their environment, and it enables the breeding and selection of cultivars with new combinations of characteristics. Seeds may more or less breed true but frequently vary considerably. In horticulture, variation is disadvantageous if the plants raised are to retain particular characteristics, but advantageous when new, improved traits are desired.

REPRODUCTIVE PARTS OF A ROSE FLOWER

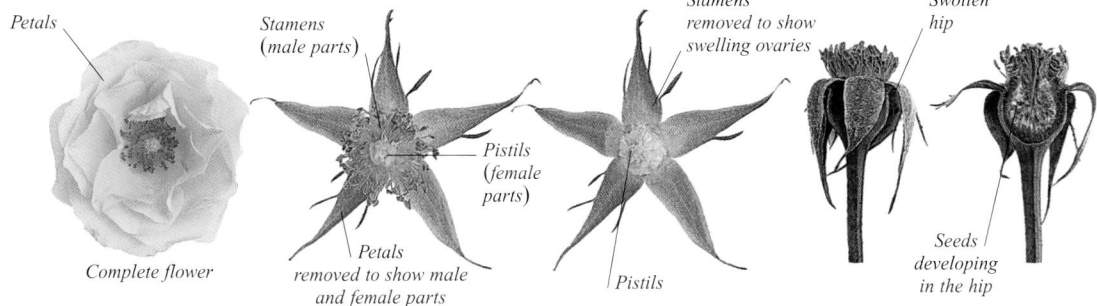

Petals

Complete flower

Stamens (male parts)

Petals removed to show male and female parts

Pistils (female parts)

Stamens removed to show swelling ovaries

Pistils

Swollen hip

Seeds developing in the hip

The parts of a flower needed for reproduction are the stamens (the male part, which bears the pollen) and the pistils (the female part, which consists of one or more stigmas, styles, and ovaries). The petals attract pollinators.

How a seed develops

Most plants are hermaphrodites – that is, each flower bears male and female parts. As the flower matures, pollen is transferred onto one or more stigmas of the same flower (self-pollination) or of a flower on another plant of the same species (cross-pollination) by insects, birds, water, or wind. The pollen grains then produce pollen tubes, which grow down the style toward the eggs in the ovary, and fertilization occurs when the male and female nuclei fuse. From these develop the embryos, which, nourished by adjacent storage tissue within a seed, are capable of forming complete new plants.

Gathering and storing seed

In general, seed should be gathered from a plant as soon as it is ripe and then stored in a dry, dark, airy place at 34–41°F (1–5°C) until it is used. Certain seeds, however, have special requirements. Some are viable for only short periods and should be sown as soon as possible. Others may be stored for very long periods at low temperatures without losing viability. Fleshy fruits should be soaked and softened in water, the seeds removed from the flesh, and then air-dried at 50–68°F (10–20°C).

Keep a close watch on fruits that split to release their seeds. As soon as a seed capsule splits, harvest it together with other capsules that are nearing maturity, even though they have not yet opened. Dry them in clean paper bags before separating out the seeds. When a few wind-distributed seeds blow away, gather the mature seed by covering the seed-bearing branches with fine muslin or paper bags, or cut one or two seed-bearing branches and place them in water indoors to mature.

Overcoming dormancy

The seeds of some plants have built-in mechanisms to assist in controlling the time of germination; for example, many seeds do not germinate in late fall, when conditions are unfavorable for seedling growth, but remain dormant until the temperature and other factors are more suitable. This dormancy is achieved by a variety of means including the presence of chemical inhibitors in the seed, by hardened seed coats that must rot or be breached before the seed can germinate, or by the need for the seed to experience alternating cold and warm periods. Several horticultural methods have been developed to overcome this natural dormancy so the seeds will germinate more quickly and are therefore less likely to fail.

Scarification

Here, the aim is to break down the hardened seed coat and allow water to enter, thereby speeding up (or in some cases, actually permitting) germination.

SCARIFICATION

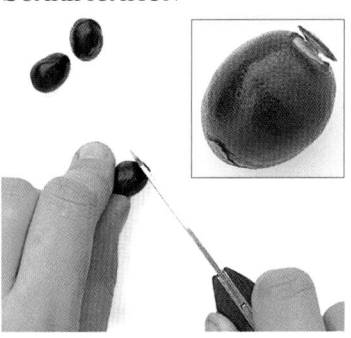

Before planting, carefully nick the hard coat on seeds such as Paeonia lutea *with a clean, sharp knife so that the seed can absorb moisture.*

Large, hard-coated seeds may be nicked with a knife. Smaller seeds may be shaken in a jar lined with sand-paper or one containing sharp gravel.

Warm stratification

This is used for hard-coated seeds of many woody species (see *Tree Seed Requiring Stratification*, p.79, and *Shrub Seed that Requires Special Treatment*, p.113). Place the seeds in a plastic bag in either an equal volume of sand and leaf mold, or an equal volume of slightly moist peat and sand, and store for four to 12 weeks at 68–77°F (20–25°C). This is usually followed by a period of cold stratification prior to the seeds being sown.

Cold stratification

Soak the seeds for up to 24 hours, then add them to a mix of moist peat and sand in a plastic bag or place them in an open dish with moist filter paper. Refrigerate the seeds at 34–41°F (1–5°C) for four to 12 weeks until germination starts. Or, place the seeds in a perforated can containing 1 part seed to 3 parts moist sand and bury the can outdoors for one or two winters. Periodically dig up the can and check for germination. Once this occurs, sow the seeds immediately.

SOAKING BEFORE COLD STRATIFICATION

Lupine seeds, soaked in water for 24 hours before cold stratification, will swell slightly.

Requirements for germination

In order to germinate, a seed needs water, air, warmth, and, for some species, light. The growing medium needs to be a fine mixture capable of drawing water up to seeds. To aid this capillary rise, the medium is firmed lightly. Without this firming, air pockets occur, and the water columns essential for capillary rise are broken. The medium, however, must not be compacted or so damp that air cannot penetrate; seeds will almost certainly fail in such an anaerobic medium, because they cannot obtain the oxygen vital for growth. Sowing media have only about a quarter of the fertilizer content of potting soil mixes and often contain a fungicide to prevent damping-off diseases (p.655).

For the most successful results, the temperature for germination of most seeds should be 68–86°F (20–30°C).

Light requirements vary during germination: some seeds need light (e.g. *Alyssum*, begonia, *Calceolaria*, and *Genista*), but others are inhibited by it (e.g. *Allium*, delphinium, *Nigella*, and phlox). There is no way of determining light needs by physical examination; if the requirement is unknown, initially keep the sown seed in the dark; if it fails to germinate after a period of some weeks, place it in the light.

Sowing and aftercare

After sowing the seed in containers or in open ground, do not allow the medium to dry out or become too waterlogged; cover the containers with glass or plastic and set in an appropriate place (see "The propagation environment," p.630). The first sign of germination is the emergence of the radicle (primary root) followed, in epigeal germination, by the cotyledons (seed leaves), which provide the initial food reserves. The true foliage leaves appear later and generally differ from the cotyledons.

HOW A SEED GERMINATES

In hypogeal germination (below), the cotyledons, or seed leaves, stay below soil level, whereas in epigeal germination (right), they appear above ground.

True leaves

True leaves

Cotyledon

Soil level

Radicle

Radicle

Cotyledon

SEEDLING GROWTH

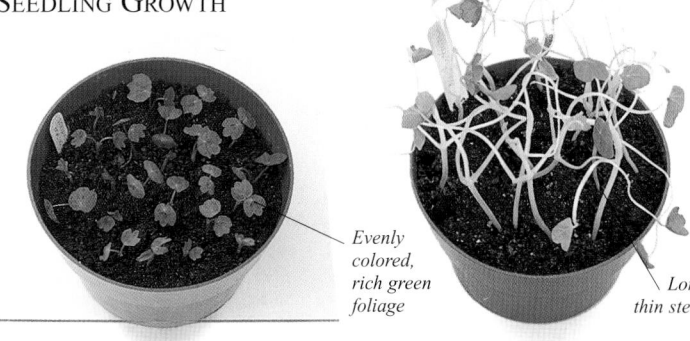

Evenly colored, rich green foliage

Long, thin stems

HEALTHY SEEDLINGS

Sturdy, well-spaced nasturtium (Tropaeolum) *seedlings flourishing under glass are ready to be pricked out.*

UNHEALTHY SEEDLINGS

If not pricked out early enough, the seedlings will become pale, crowded, and etiolated, and they may die.

As soon as the seedlings are large enough to handle, they should be pricked out (see ANNUALS AND BIENNIALS, "Pricking out," p.213). Failure to do so results in weak growth (and, in extreme cases, death), because the crowded seedlings compete for light and nutrients and readily succumb to fungal infection. Once transplanted, return the seedlings to the warm germination environment to reestablish; then gradually harden them off by placing the containers in cooler conditions (see "Hardening off," p.631).

TRUE LEAVES

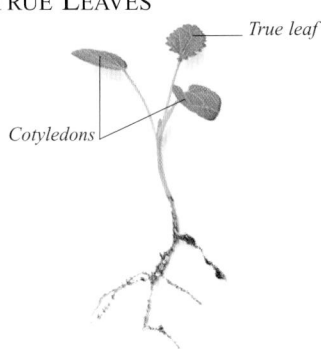

True leaf

Cotyledons

As the cotyledons (seed leaves) wither, the true leaves take over the process of photosynthesis.

Producing hybrid plants

When hybridizing plants, it is important to prevent self-pollination. For controlled cross-pollination, petals, sepals, and stamens are removed from the flowers on the proposed female parent and the denuded flowers protected from insects by paper or plastic bags until the stigmas on the female plant are sticky and receptive. Pollen, previously gathered from air-dried stamens, is then transferred to the stigmas, and the flowers are protected from insects once again until fertilization has occurred. Hybrid seed will then develop in the ovaries and should be gathered when ripe and sown according to its requirements (see also THE ROSE GARDEN, "Hybridizing," p.166).

F1 and F2 hybrids

For the gardener seeking uniformity , F1 and F2 hybrid seed is available for a limited range of plants, mostly annuals and vegetables. Such seed needs complex plant breeding techniques and is therefore more expensive for the seed companies to produce.

The first generation derived from crossing two carefully maintained, genetically inbred plants of the same species is termed a "first filial generation," or F1, hybrid. This process combines the benefits of greater uniformity that can result from inbreeding with the vigor that can flow from crossbreeding. F1 hybrids are usually more vigorous than their parents and give uniformity in flower characteristics such as color and form that seldom occurs with open-pollinated seed. Sometimes two controlled crosses from four selected lines are used to produce a "second filial generation," or F2, hybrid – retaining some of the vigor and uniformity of the F1 parents but often with other favored characteristics less evident in the F1s.

Layering

Layering is a natural form of propagation: roots are induced to develop by covering a stem with soil while it is still attached to the parent plant. The rooted portion of stem is then separated from the parent plant and grown on.

The stem to be layered is often cut, bark-ringed, or twisted. This partially interrupts the flow of hormones and carbohydrates, which, as they accumulate there, help promote root growth. Another important root stimulus is the exclusion of light from the stem: light-starved cells then become thin-walled and roots form more readily. In order to further stimulate rooting, use a rooting hormone at the point of layering.

Methods of layering

Layering methods are classified in three groups: those in which a stem is brought down to the soil (simple, serpentine, natural, and tip layering); those in which soil is mounded over a stem (mound layering, trench layering, and French layering); and air (or Chinese) layering, where the "soil" is brought up to the plant stem. The word "soil" is used loosely here to mean any growing medium such as garden soil, peat, sand, sawdust, or sphagnum moss.

Simple layering

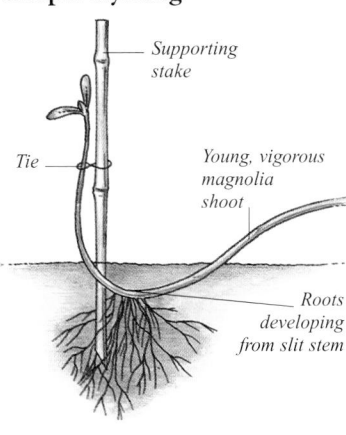

Supporting stake

Tie

Young, vigorous magnolia shoot

Roots developing from slit stem

This method is best carried out between fall and spring. The parent plant should be young and pruned the previous season to produce vigorous, flexible stems, which can be brought down to soil level. A slanting cut is made on the underside of the stem to be layered, which is pegged or secured at this point into the soil. The shoot tip is tied to a vertical stake inserted in the soil. Next fall, if the layer is well rooted, it can be cut from the parent (see also ORNAMENTAL SHRUBS, "Simple layering," p.114, and CLIMBING PLANTS, "Simple layering," p.143).

SERPENTINE LAYERING
Parent plant
Soil level
Peg holding clematis stem under mounded soil
Roots appearing between nodes

Serpentine layering
This modified form of simple layering is used for plants with pliable stems, such as clematis. Long, young stems are mounded with soil, leaving buds exposed to produce aerial shoots (see also CLIMBING PLANTS, "Propagation by serpentine layering," p.143).

Natural layering

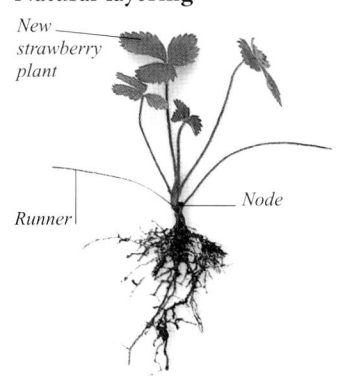
New strawberry plant
Node
Runner

Some plants such as strawberries reproduce naturally by sending out a series of runners. These then root at a node, forming a new plant. Once the new plant is fully established, sever it from the parent and grow on (see also "Strawberries: Propagation," p.464). This method is used for shrubs and

Tip layering

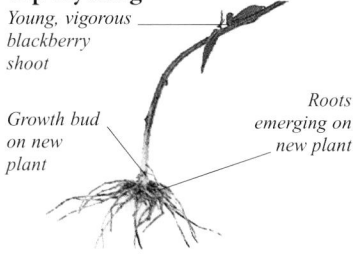
Young, vigorous blackberry shoot
Growth bud on new plant
Roots emerging on new plant

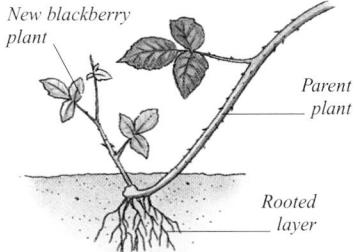
New blackberry plant
Parent plant
Rooted layer

climbers that produce roots from their shoot tips; one of the most common examples in nature is the blackberry. In summer, a young, vigorous shoot tip is buried in soil in a hole 3–4in (7–10cm) deep. A new shoot, having developed from the tip, appears a few

weeks later; the young plant may then be separated from its parent. Grow on the rooted layer *in situ*; transplant it the following spring, if required (see also "Blackberries: Tip Layering," p.465).

Although important for the com-

Mound layering

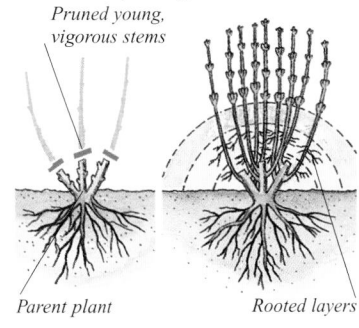
Pruned young, vigorous stems
Parent plant
Rooted layers

mercial production of rootstocks, mound layering, or stooling, is used by amateurs only for a few woody plants. The stems of a young parent plant are cut back in late winter or early spring to within 3in (8cm) of the ground. When the new shoots are about 6–8in (15–20cm) long, mound soil up over their bases, and again twice more until summer. With plants that root easily, such as thyme and sage, there is no need to cut the stems back before mounding. By fall the stems will have rooted; they are then separated from the parent plant and transplanted (see also THE HERB GARDEN, "Mound layering," p.408).

Trench layering
Trench, or etiolation, layering is primarily for fruit rootstocks, especially those that are hard to root. The parent plant is planted at an angle, to make it easier for its shoots to be pegged down in shallow trenches and covered with soil. The rooted shoots

French layering

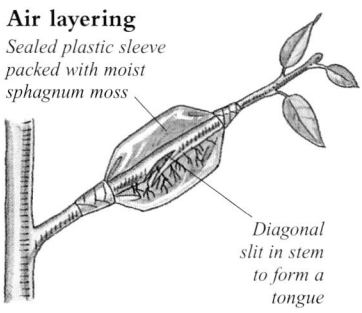
Soil mounded over shoot
Stem pegged down
Rooted layer

can be detached from the parent to form new plants.

French, or continuous, layering is a modified form of mound layering. In late winter, peg young shoots from the parent stem to the ground. Any new growths are gradually hilled up to a depth of 6in (15cm). These new shoots should have root-

Air layering
Sealed plastic sleeve packed with moist sphagnum moss
Diagonal slit in stem to form a tongue

ed by fall and after leaf drop may be separated and grown on (see also ORNAMENTAL SHRUBS, "French layering," p.115).

Use air, or Chinese, layering – also known as marcottage – on some trees (such as magnolias and hollies), shrubs such as rhododendrons and azaleas), and house plants (such as *Philodendron* and *Ficus*). In spring or summer (or, for an indoor plant, any time it is actively growing), slit an aerial shoot and pack the tongue with sphagnum moss; cover with plastic until roots develop (see *Air Layering a Shrub*, p.115, and THE INDOOR GARDEN, "Air layering," p.377). Rooting may take up to two years.

TRENCH LAYERING
Parent planted at 30–40° angle
Soil level
2in (5cm) deep trench
Young, vigorous shoots pinned in position

Cuttings

Propagation from cuttings is the most common vegetative method. There are three main types: stem, leaf, and root. Stem cuttings produce roots directly from the stem itself or from the mass of thin-walled, wound-healing tissue (callus) that develops at its base. These roots are called adventitious, which literally means added. Some large leaves can be used as cutting material and will develop adventitious roots from near their veins. Vigorous, young roots may also be used for cuttings – propagation by root cuttings is a simple and economical method neglected by most gardeners. Suitable species will produce both adventitious stem buds and roots on the root cutting.

How roots form

Adventitious roots most often develop from young cells produced by the cambium – a layer of cells that generates tissues involved in the thickening of stems. They are usually located close to food- and water-conducting tissues, which provide nourishment as they develop.

Adventitious root growth is also helped by natural hormones called auxins, which accumulate in the base of a cutting. Natural auxins can be supplemented by synthetic auxins, which are available as talc-based powders or as solutions. These aid rooting when applied to the base of a cutting and are recommended for all plants except those that root very easily. Use only a little hormone, however, because too much could harm immature tissue.

Rooting hormones can be bought with low concentrations of active ingredient for soft cuttings and higher concentrations for hardwood material; some contain a fungicide, which helps prevent infections entering the cuttings through the wounded tissues.

CALLUS PADS

Adventitious roots developing from the callus pad

Protective callus pad

Plants that are difficult to root (here Choisya ternata) *form a callus pad of wound-healing tissue at the base of a stem cutting, where they have been severed from the parent plant.*

SOFTWOOD CUTTINGS

Prepared cutting trimmed below the node

Rooted cutting

The soft, green stem on a softwood cutting (here Hydrangea macrophylla) *usually turns brown as it matures and develops its root system.*

Stem cuttings

Stem cuttings are often classified by the maturity of the stem tissue into softwood, greenwood, semiripe, and hardwood (or ripewood). The distinction is useful, though imprecise, because tissues develop continuously throughout the growing season.

Softwood cuttings
These are taken in spring, when the new shoots of the parent plant are almost fully developed and just beginning to harden. Such cuttings are generally made from the shoot tips (tip cuttings), but new, young basal shoots (basal cuttings) of herbaceous perennials are also used (see PERENNIALS, "Basal stem cuttings," p.198). Since young material roots most readily, softwood cuttings often provide the best chance of rooting species that are hard to propagate. However, they need a supportive environment, since they lose water and wilt quickly (see "The propagation environment," p.630).

Greenwood cuttings
These are taken from early to midsummer, from slightly more mature wood, when growth begins to slow. They root slightly less readily but survive better than softwood cuttings, although they still require a supportive environment in which to develop into new plants before being hardened off.

Semiripe cuttings
Taken in late summer, semiripe cuttings are less prone to wilting since the stem tissues are firmer and woody (see ORNAMENTAL SHRUBS, "Semiripe cuttings," p.110). Some genera with large leaves, for example *Ficus* and

camellia, may be propagated more economically by taking a short section from a semiripe stem just above and below a leaf bud, retaining a single leaf (see ORNAMENTAL SHRUBS, "Leaf-bud cuttings," p.111).

Hardwood cuttings
Fully mature, hardwood (or ripewood) cuttings are taken at the end of the growing season from fall through spring, when the tissues are fully ripened. They are the easiest to maintain in a healthy condition but are often slow to root. Hardwood cuttings fall into two categories: leafless deciduous and broad-leaved evergreen cuttings. Growth of many glossy-leaved evergreens, such as holly (*Ilex*) and rhododendron, wilts readily when young early in the season since their protective leaf waxes develop slowly; they are therefore best propagated by semiripe or hardwood cuttings (see also ORNAMENTAL TREES, "Hardwood cuttings," p.76; CLIMBING PLANTS, "Propagation from hardwood cuttings," p.141; and THE ROSE GARDEN, "Hardwood cuttings," p.163).

SEMIRIPE CUTTINGS

Stem with opposite buds cut below a node

New growth has developed from each node

The green stem (here Weigela) *has a darker and woodier base.*

LEAF-BUD CUTTINGS

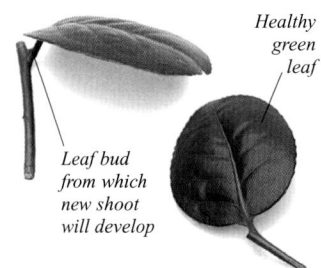

Healthy green leaf

Leaf bud from which new shoot will develop

A short piece of semiripe stem (here Camellia) *provides sufficient food reserves for a leaf-bud cutting, since it produces some food through its leaf.*

HARDWOOD CUTTINGS

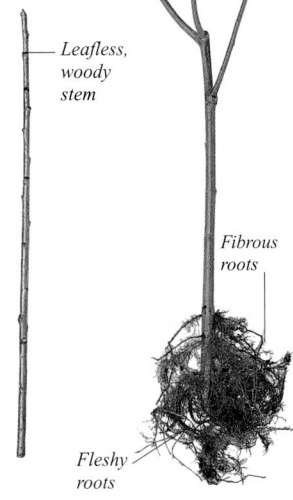

Leafless, woody stem

Fibrous roots

Fleshy roots

Hardwood cuttings (here Salix alba) *are the longest type of stem cutting, since they need large food reserves while their roots slowly develop.*

When to take stem cuttings

There are no hard and fast rules about when to take stem cuttings of a particular species, so if cuttings taken in spring fail to root, further cuttings can be taken later in the season and treated according to the relative maturity of the shoots.

Plants that are difficult to root are best propagated early so that the new plants have time to mature before winter. Because the action of root-producing hormones is suppressed by flower-initiating ones, use cuttings without flower buds wherever possible; if cuttings with flower buds must be used, remove these buds.

Preparing stem cuttings
Stem cuttings are normally prepared by trimming just below a node, or leaf joint, where the cambium (the layer of cells involved in stem thickening) is most active. A few easily rooting

NODAL CUTTING

Sharp, clean blade reduces the chances of infecting the cutting

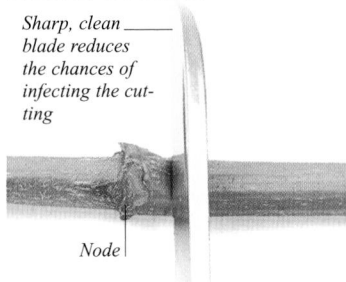

Node

Most cuttings (here Hydrangea paniculata) *root most satisfactorily at their nodes and so should be trimmed just below a node.*

INTERNODAL CUTTINGS

Internodal cuttings (here Clematis montana) *utilize scarce propagating material in an economical way.*

cuttings, for example willows (*Salix*), have preformed roots at the nodes, and these start to develop when the stem is cut from the parent plant. For these and for cuttings with densely crowded leaves on each stem, cut between nodes (internodal cutting).

The length of the cutting will depend on the species but is commonly 2–5in (5–12cm), or includes five or six nodes. The lower leaves are stripped to give a clean stem for insertion. To assist the cuttings in rooting, semiripe and hardwood cuttings are often wounded by removing a sliver of bark from the lowest 1in (2.5cm) of the cutting. This exposes a greater area of cambium and thereby stimulates roots to form. Some cuttings, especially semiripe ones, may be taken by pulling a sideshoot away from the main shoot with a small heel of bark still attached (see ORNAMENTAL SHRUBS, "Heel cuttings," p.111). A heel may provide added protection for a cutting until it has produced roots, although there is no satisfactory scientific explanation for this response.

With the exception of leafless, hardwood stem cuttings, which contain food reserves from the previous

WOUNDING

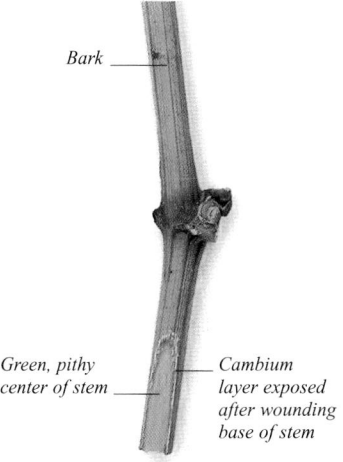

Bark

Green, pithy center of stem

Cambium layer exposed after wounding base of stem

*Use a very sharp, clean knife to make a shallow, angled, downward cut at the base of semiripe and hardwood cuttings such as grape (*Vitis*).*

PREPARING CUTTINGS

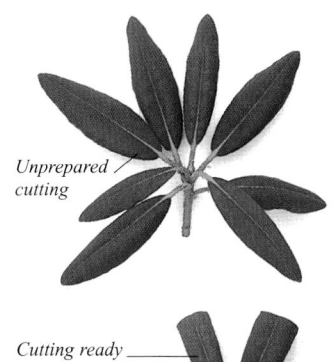

Unprepared cutting

Cutting ready for insertion

To reduce stress from water loss on leafy cuttings (here a rhododendron), remove some leaves, halve others.

growing season, few cuttings are able to produce roots and shoots without supplementing their food reserves through photosynthesis. However, active leaves lose water through their pores, which is not easily replaced, and excessive water loss will cause failure. To achieve a balance between retaining photosynthetic tissue and reducing water loss, trim away all but a few full-sized leaves, leaving any immature leaves. If the remaining leaves are large, as on many broad-leaved trees and large shrubs, reduce each by half to minimize water loss.

Leaf cuttings

For some plants, whole leaves (with or without leaf stalks) or sections of leaves may be taken as cuttings and inserted or secured onto the medium. With whole leaves laid flat, the veins should be nicked at intervals, since new plantlets form at the cut surfaces of large leaf veins. Propagate plants such as *Sinningia* and *Streptocarpus* from cut sections of fully expanded, undamaged leaves. African violets

LARGE LEAVES

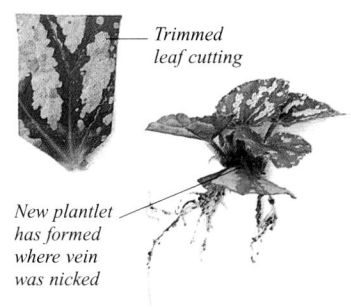

Trimmed leaf cutting

New plantlet has formed where vein was nicked

Large leaves of plants such as begonia may be divided into small pieces, each of which will form callus at a nicked vein, and then adventitious roots.

(Saintpaulia) and *Peperomia* may also be propagated from entire leaves with their stalks (see also THE INDOOR GARDEN, "Propagating from leaves," p.375).

Root cuttings

Root cuttings are taken in the dormant season from young, vigorous roots of about pencil thickness for most trees and shrubs, but the roots may be somewhat thinner for some herbaceous plants, such as phlox.

The length of the cutting

This is dependent on the environment in which the root cutting is to develop: the warmer the environment, the faster new shoots will appear and, therefore, shorter cuttings with smaller food reserves may be used successfully, although these should be at least 1in (2.5cm) in length. Root cuttings that are 1–2in (2.5–5cm) long are best grown on in a greenhouse, and those over 2in (5cm) long in a cold frame. For sumac (*Rhus*) and lilac (*Syringa*), which can be propagated in open ground, 4–6in (10–15cm) long root cuttings should be used.

Inserting root cuttings

It is important to insert root cuttings the correct way up, since the new roots always form at the distal end (that is, the end that was farther from the crown of the parent plant). Cuttings should be inserted vertically so that their other (proximal) ends are flush with the soil surface; herbaceous root cuttings, however, are frequently inserted horizontally (see also PERENNIALS, "Root cuttings," p.199).

The rooting medium

Cuttings need air (to obtain oxygen) and water in their rooting medium, but if the medium is too wet, the cuttings rot. Standard rooting medium must, therefore, have a more open structure than soil-based potting mix. The rooting medium should also be warm in

SMALL LEAVES

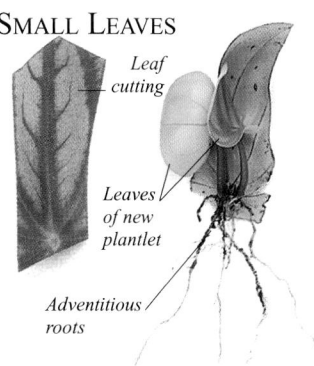

Leaf cutting

Leaves of new plantlet

Adventitious roots

To encourage callus to form and rooting to occur, small leaves such as Peperomia *may be trimmed at the edges.*

ROOT CUTTINGS

Straight cut at proximal end, nearest the crown of the parent plant

Shoots appearing just above roots

Roots appearing from the distal end

Slanted cut at distal end

To help distinguish the two ends when taking root cuttings (here Acanthus mollis), *make differently angled cuts.*

PROTECTIVE ENVIRONMENT

Leafy cuttings grow best in a humid environment, such as within a plastic bag secured over a container; keep the plastic away from the leaf surfaces.

order to speed up development of the roots: 64–77°F (18–25°C) is ideal for cool-temperate species, and up to 90°F (32°C) for those from warm climates. If necessary, use bottom heat (see p.630).

Caring for the cuttings

After insertion, keep leafy cuttings turgid in the humid atmosphere of a closed case, mist unit, propagator, or other similar environment. Leafless cuttings that have been planted outdoors, either directly into the soil or in a container, as appropriate, should be protected by either a clear plastic tunnel or a cold frame.

Every ten days, water the rooting medium lightly if required, and spray with a fungicide to help prevent disease; at the same time, lift the sashes or remove the plastic over the enclosed cuttings to enable air to circulate, for a 5–10 minute period.

Once rooted, cuttings should be potted up individually, and those growing under cover gradually hardened off (see p.631).

Storage organs

Storage organs have diverse structures, including bulbs, corms, rhizomes, and root and stem tubers. Most plants with storage organs will increase naturally by producing offsets, which should be lifted and divided to prevent overcrowding. Offsets will flower more quickly than seed-raised plants and will be identical to the parent, whereas seed-raised plants may be variable in character.

The main propagation methods apart from division are to cut the storage organs into sections and to stimulate them to produce offsets by wounding; these offsets or sections will form complete plants if provided with a warm, dark place and inspected occasionally for signs of trouble.

Bulbs

NONSCALY, OR TUNICATE, BULB

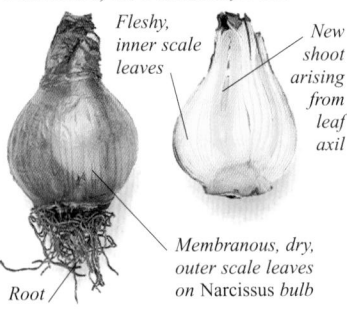

Fleshy, inner scale leaves

New shoot arising from leaf axil

Membranous, dry, outer scale leaves on Narcissus bulb

Root

SCALY BULB

New shoot

Fleshy scale leaves of lily bulb

Root

Bulbs may be propagated by chipping; division of offsets, bulbils, or bulblets; scaling or twin-scaling; and scooping or scoring. For lists of plants appropriate to each method, see BULBOUS PLANTS, "Propagation," pp.239–44.

Chipping

Nonscaly (tunicate) bulbs, such as snowdrops (Galanthus), that do not naturally increase quickly, may be multiplied rapidly by chipping. This method involves cutting each bulb into up to 20 pieces, depending on its size. Each piece, which generally consists of three or more scale leaves and a section of basal plate, is then soaked in or

CHIPPING

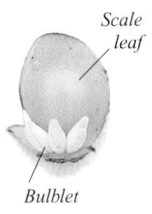

Scale leaf

Bulblet

Bulblets develop between the scale leaves on a chipped bulb such as snow-drop (Galanthus) in air temperatures that do not exceed 77°F (25°C).

dusted with a fungicide. The chips may be incubated (see "Chipping," p.243) or placed in a 1:1 mix of peat and sand or peat and perlite in a container in a cool place and left undisturbed for up to two years. Then separate the bulblets and repot or replant as required.

Division of offsets

Bulbs have wide, fleshy scale leaves that act as food storage organs. At their base are axillary buds, which may enlarge naturally to form offsets. When the bulbs are lifted at the end of the growing season, these may be separated and planted out individually (see "Dividing bulbs," p.239).

DIVISION OF OFFSETS

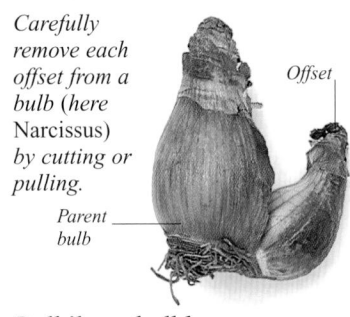

Offset

Parent bulb

Carefully remove each offset from a bulb (here Narcissus) by cutting or pulling.

Bulbils or bulblets

Bulbils are produced on flower heads or stems; bulblets develop on the bulb itself or on stem roots. Both may be detached and planted (see also LILIES, "Bulbils and bulblets," p.245).

Scaling

Scaling involves the removal of bulb scales, which are then induced to form bulblets. It is used for bulbs such as fritillaries (Fritillaria) and lilies

BULBILS AND BULBLETS

Some lilies (Lilium), for example L. lanci-folium, produce small, bulblike structures known as bulbils on their stems above the ground. Others, for example L. longiflo-rum, may develop similar bulblets on bulbs or stem roots in the soil.

Lily bulblets

Lily bulbils

Old stem, which has developed roots

SCALING

Scale leaf

Bulblets appear at the base of individual scale leaves of loose-scaled bulbs, here lily (Lilium).

New top-growth

Rooted bulblet

TWIN-SCALING

Two bud scales and a section of basal plate are used for nonscaly bulbs (here Narcissus).

Fleshy scale leaves

Bulblet

Basal plate

(Lilium) that are made up of fairly loose scales. Individual scales are pulled away from the basal plate and then left in a plastic bag of moist vermiculite or a peat and grit mix, in a warm, dark place. Bulblets appear at the scale bases. Grow on the scales in a container until the bulblets are large enough to be separated (see also "Scaling," p.242).

Twin-scaling

Nonscaly, or tunicate, bulbs such as daffodils and snowdrops may be twin-scaled. In this, the bulb is cut vertically into eight to ten sections, and each of these is divided into pairs of bud scales with a small section of basal plate. These are incubated and grown on in the same way as in scaling, above. (See also "Twin-scaling," p.242.)

Scooping and scoring

Some bulbs, such as hyacinths, can be propagated by either scooping or scoring the bulb. This causes callus tissue to develop, which encourages bulblets to form. For scooping, the basal plate of a mature bulb is scooped out at the center, leaving just the outer edge of

SCORING

Callus tissue

Bulblets developing inside cut

Basal plate

Shallowly cutting the basal plate of some bulbs (here hyacinth) stimulates the growth of bulblets.

the basal plate intact; for scoring, two shallow cuts at right angles are made into the basal plate. The bulb is then stored in a warm, dark place until bulblets have formed; these are then detached and grown on separately (see also "Simple cutting," p.244; "Scooping hyacinths," p.244; and "Scoring and scooping Trillium," p.244).

Corms

GLADIOLUS CORM

Food storage tissue

Thickened stem base

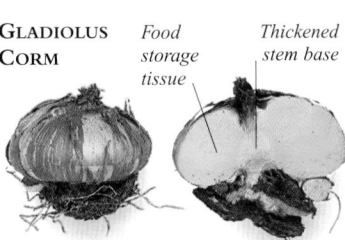

Corms are reduced, compact, underground stems with a solid internal structure. Most corms produce several buds near the apex; each bud naturally forms a new corm. Miniature corms, or cormels, are produced as offsets

New corm

RAISING CORMELS

In fall, separate the new corm and cormels from the parent and grow on.

Old corm

Cormels

DEVELOPMENT OF A CORMEL

Cormels may take up to 3 years to reach flowering size. This sequence shows their development in the first year.

between the old and new corms in the growing season (see also BULBOUS PLANTS, "Gladiolus cormels," p.239). Larger corms may be increased artificially by cutting them into pieces, each with a bud, just before the growing season. When planted, these cut sections will develop into new corms.

Rhizomes

IRIS RHIZOME

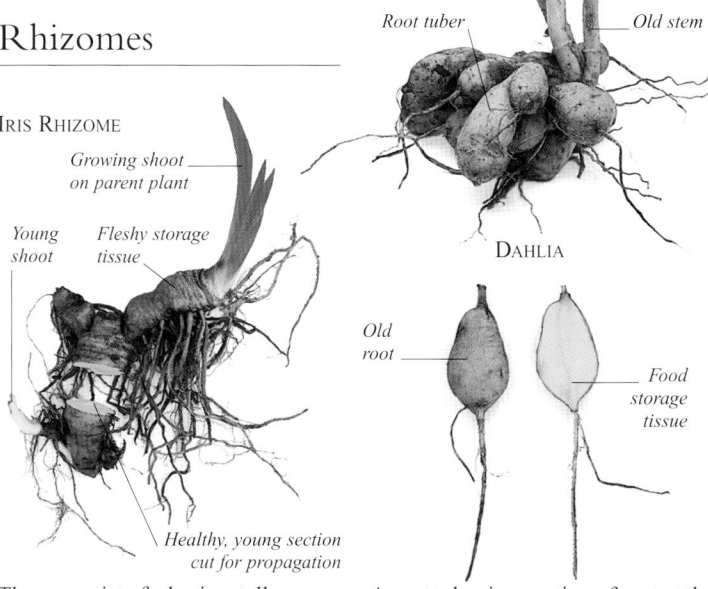

Growing shoot on parent plant

Young shoot

Fleshy storage tissue

DAHLIA

Healthy, young section cut for propagation

These consist of a horizontally growing shoot, usually beneath but sometimes on the soil surface. Cut the rhizome into healthy sections, each with one or more buds (see PERENNIALS,

"Division of rhizomatous plants," p.197; BULBOUS PLANTS, "Scoring and scooping *Trillium*," p.244; and ORCHIDS, "Division," p.363).

Root tubers

Root tuber — *Old stem*

Old root — *Food storage tissue*

A root tuber is a portion of root at the stem base that swells during summer and is modified into a storage organ, or tuber, as in dahlias. Such plants may be propagated in spring by

dividing a cluster of tubers into healthy pieces, each with a developing shoot (see also *Cutting Up Bulbs for Propagation*, p.243). Root tubers may also be propagated by basal cuttings of the young, emerging shoots in spring (see DAHLIAS, *How to Propagate by Basal Cuttings*, p.229).

Stem tubers

The stems of some plants are modified to produce tubers that act as storage organs. Tuberous begonias, for example, form tubers at the bases of their stems, which enlarge each year. In spring, these can be cut into pieces, each with a growth bud. Each piece will produce basal shoots, which can be used as basal cuttings (see DAHLIAS, *How to Propagate by Basal Cuttings*, p.229) or grown on to form a new tuber (see "Propagation of tuberous begonias," p.376).

JERUSALEM ARTICHOKE

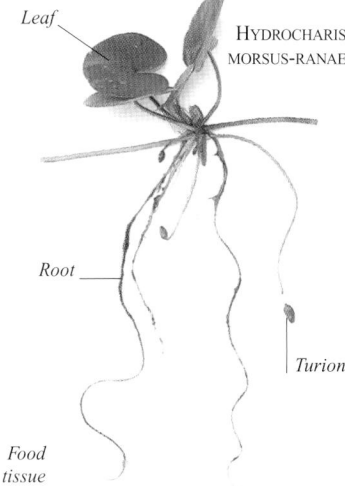

Old stem

Stem tuber

Bud

Food storage tissue

Other storage organs

Plants such as *Saxifraga granulata* and some *Kalanchoe* and *Asparagus* species develop round, bulblike buds at their shoot axils. These buds can be separated and grown on individually in the same way as bulblets or cormels (see opposite).

In some water plants, such as *Hydrocharis* and *Myriophyllum*, these relatively large bud structures are known as turions. When mature, they drop off the parent plant naturally, sink to the bottom of the water, and develop into new plants.

Leaf

HYDROCHARIS MORSUS-RANAE

Root

Turion

Grafting and budding

In a wide range of woody plants and a few herbaceous ones, a budded stem, or scion, is grafted onto a rootstock, or stock, of another species or cultivar, to achieve a composite plant with more desirable characteristics. The stock may be more resistant than the scion to root disease or more suited to a particular environment. Often, the stock is selected because it controls the growth of the scion to produce a dwarfed or a particularly vigorous plant. Sometimes, a cultivar that is difficult to increase from cuttings is grafted onto easily rooted stock. The rootstock also influences the age at which the tree bears fruit and its size and skin quality – dwarfing rootstocks generally conferring earlier fruit-bearing. Conversely, the rootstock's growing cycle may be affected by the scion cultivar, which in turn influences cold hardiness. Reactions to soil can also be affected by interactions between rootstock and scion. The scion may take the form of a single bud on a short portion of stem (usually known as budding) or it may be a multibudded length of stem.

When to graft

Most grafting is normally undertaken in late winter to early spring, when the cambium is particularly active; these warm conditions also favor the growth of callus cells. Hot weather later in the season may dry out the thin-walled cambial cells.

T-budding, on the other hand, is most often done in mid- to late summer, when well-developed scion buds are available and young stock material is of suitable diameter. For success, the stock plant needs to be growing actively, so that the bark can be lifted from the wood to allow the bud to be inserted – an action known as bark slipping. Chip-budding, however, may be undertaken over an extended season because the chip is positioned beside the stock.

How to graft

Because grafting cuts inevitably damage plant cells, and the thin-walled cells at the graft union are

vulnerable to fungi and bacteria, it is essential that knives are sterile and sharp, so that a single cut is sufficient. The propagation environment, prepared plant material, and ties must also be scrupulously clean.
Once stock and scion material have been selected and cut to shape, position the two pieces carefully so that there is maximum cambial contact. If the grafting materials are of different

CAMBIUM LAYER

Node

Bark

Cambium

Pithy center

For successful grafting, the scion cambium must be matched as closely as possible to that of the stock.

widths, be sure that cambium on at least one side of the graft is in contact. Central to the grafting process is the activity of the cambium – a narrow band of cells between the bark and the wood – which produces new cells. Within days of grafting, the region between the stock and scion should fill with callus cells. The cambial cells next to the callus then influence neighboring cells, so that a cambial bridge forms. Further divisions of this cambium produce water- and food-conducting tissue, which functionally joins the scion and stock.

Traditionally, grafts were bound with raffia and then coated with wax to prevent drying. However, waxing is used less often now that raffia has mainly been superseded by clear plastic tape, which seals the join better. Once grafted, potgrown stocks should be kept in a suitable protective environment (see "Greenhouses," p.630, and "Cold frames," p.631).

Regularly examine the graft, and remove the tape once the graft appears to have taken. The following growing season, cut back the stock plant just above the new shoot.

Chip-budding

A chip of mature wood is removed from the rootstock and replaced with a matching chip of similar size from the scion, or budstick, containing a bud (see THE FRUIT GARDEN, *Chip-budding*, p.426).

T-budding

In this technique, just the scion bud is grafted onto the rootstock by cutting a T in the stock bark and inserting the bud beneath (see THE ROSE GARDEN, "Bud-grafting," p.164).

Side-veneer grafting

A short, downward cut through the cambium layer of the stock is followed by a sloping cut down toward the base of the first cut. The chip is removed and replaced by the scion, which is shaped to match the stock (see ORNAMENTAL TREES, "Side-veneer grafting," p.80, and ORNAMENTAL SHRUBS, "Side-veneer grafting," p.116).

Side-wedge grafting

A downward, slightly inward cut is made into the side of the stock. The scion is then prepared by making two oblique cuts at the base. The scion's wedge-shaped base is inserted into the rootstock cut so that the cambium aligns and is bound in position.

Apical-wedge grafting

The stock is cut flat and a wedge-shaped chip is removed from the center, into which the scion is then inserted (see ORNAMENTAL SHRUBS, "Apical-wedge grafting," p.117).

Saddle grafting

The top of the stock is saddle-shaped, with upward sloping sides. The scion is shaped so that it fits closely over the top of the rootstock (see ORNAMENTAL SHRUBS, "Saddle grafting," p.116).

Basal-whip grafting

Cut back the stock at an oblique angle to 2–3in (5–8cm). Then prepare the scion to match. If the scion is thinner than the stock, first cut the stock horizontally, then obliquely to match.

Flat grafting

Both the stock top and scion base are cut horizontally and then joined (see CACTI AND OTHER SUCCULENTS, "Flat grafting," p.345).

Whip-and-tongue grafting

Make sloping cuts on the rootstock and scion, then cut shallow tongues along the cuts so that the scion meets the stock (see THE FRUIT GARDEN, "Whip-and-tongue grafting," p.427).

WHIP-AND-TONGUE GRAFT
The rootstock and scion gradually unite to function as one plant.

The propagation environment

During propagation, plants are at their most vulnerable and their environment is, therefore, vitally important. The choice of environment depends on which propagation method is chosen and on the relative maturity of the plant material itself. Propagation from leafy cuttings, for example, requires a more closely regulated environment than for leafless cuttings.

Greenhouses

It is essential that the greenhouse has adequate ventilation and, in the growing season, appropriate shading (see "Creating the right environment," p.567). For two months on either side of midsummer, a shading wash on the outside of the glass will ensure that propagated plants are not stressed unnecessarily by extreme weather conditions (see "Shading washes," p.570). Additional protective shading can be provided by mounting some shade cloth on wire runners across or along the length of the bench or greenhouse. The curtain can be opened during dull weather.

Protecting leafy cuttings

Because leafy cuttings initially have no roots and cannot easily take up water to replace that lost from the leaves, they must have further protection within the greenhouse.

Clear plastic sheeting or a plastic bag placed over a tray of cuttings and tucked underneath is perfectly satisfactory if appropriate shading is provided. Water vapor condensing on the inside of the plastic helps protect the cuttings against desiccation. Soft cuttings may succumb to disease if the plastic touches them; insert a framework of split stakes or wire in the medium to keep the plastic off the cuttings. In such closed systems, excessive air temperatures may build up in very hot conditions, so the containers of cuttings should be kept in a shaded place out of direct sunlight.

Rigid plastic propagators need shading similar to that needed by plastic sheeting and generally provide a drier environment, because water vapor may leak through their ventilation openings: these should be kept closed until the cuttings have rooted and are ready to be hardened off.

A mist unit provides the best system for summer propagation, but for winter and early- and late-season propagation it should be combined with bottom heat. Ideally, the mist unit should maintain a constant water film on the leaf surfaces; some water will still be lost from the leaves by transpiration, but this is amply replaced by water applied from the misting

RIGID-TOPPED PROPAGATOR
Because most of the moisture in a rigid-topped propagator is retained within the unit, cuttings remain turgid and so are more likely to root quickly and healthily.

process. Since the mist is applied in bursts, however, the greenhouse humidity fluctuates and so, inevitably, each leaf's water film is imperfect and some water loss occurs. Complete mist systems consist of supply pipes, water filter, nozzles, and a solenoid and sensor to regulate the misting frequency (see "Mist units," p.574).

For softwood cuttings, which wilt readily, the best system is to arrange a low, clear plastic tent just above the misting nozzles. This ensures a higher ambient humidity between mist bursts than does open mist. It is important to shade such a closed mist system in bright weather.

Bottom heat

Most biological processes are speeded up when temperatures are higher, and therefore raising the temperature of the medium usually increases the rapidity with which seeds germinate and cuttings root.

SHADING GREENHOUSES (Temperate climates)

To prevent the greenhouse from overheating when propagating, add one or more layers of shading, depending on the weather conditions and season. Greenhouses in open, sunny sites are particularly vulnerable to overheating.

		SPRING	SUMMER	FALL	WINTER
DULL DAYS	Whitewash		■	■	
BRIGHT DAYS	Layer of shade cloth	■	■	■	
	Additional shade cloth		■	■	
	Whitewash		■		

EFFECTS OF BOTTOM HEAT

CUTTING GROWN WITH HEAT

CUTTING GROWN WITHOUT HEAT

Poor, short roots

Long, strong, healthy roots

Cables or heating mats are most convenient for small greenhouses (see "Propagation aids," p.574). The temperature is controlled by a rod thermostat or electronic controller. If they are used in closed mist systems, excessive air temperatures may build up in bright conditions, during which the heating must be switched off.

Heated propagator units

These self-contained units are useful for extending the propagation season in minimally heated greenhouses (see "Heated propagators," p.574). Propagator units have heat loads that are well in excess of the 15 watts/sq ft (160 watts/sq m) recommended for mist systems, so they must be fitted with effective thermostats; otherwise, damagingly high temperatures may occur in sunny weather.

CIRCULATING AIR IN A COLD FRAME

Since cold air expands and rises as it heats up, the lid of a cold frame must be propped open in warm weather to allow some air to escape and the temperature to remain reasonably cool.

Cold frames

Cold frames provide a valuable increase in soil and air temperatures while maintaining high humidity and providing light for plants to grow successfully. They can be used to raise seedlings early in the season, protect grafts, and propagate leafless and leafy cuttings. They may also be fitted with bottom heat (see opposite).

Because such low structures have no great volume, they easily overheat in sunny conditions unless ventilated and shaded well (see "Cold frames," p.575). Conversely, when temperatures fall below 23°F (-5°C), frames must be insulated with thick layers of burlap, straw, or salt hay to avoid cold damage to the plant material.

Growing the propagated plant

Since most forms of propagation involve cutting various parts of the plants being increased, plant tissues are exposed to possible infection; it is therefore important to maintain hygienic conditions in the propagating area. Tools and benches should be regularly and thoroughly cleaned (using a mild disinfectant if necessary), and dead and damaged plant material removed. Media must always be fresh and sterile. Fungicidal solutions may also be applied to give protection to seedlings (such as captan) and leafy cuttings (such as captan or thiram), following the manufacturer's instructions fully.

When preparing pots or trays of medium for sowing seed, lightly firm the medium using a presser board, especially around the edges of the container. Water is drawn up through the medium by capillary action and, without this firming, air pockets occur and the water columns essential for capillary rise are broken. However, do not overly firm soil-based media: a medium filled with roots must be well aerated and have an open structure for optimum plant growth.

The media in which propagated plants are growing should be moist, but not wet, at all times. Too wet a medium will reduce the oxygen available, and the roots may die or succumb to disease. It is also important to maintain the correct environment until the young plants are sturdy enough to be hardened off (see "The propagation

FIRMING THE MEDIUM

Be sure seeds are germinated in evenly pressed, level medium so that capillary action and therefore seedling growth are not hindered by air pockets in the medium.

Continuous capillary action

Air holes

Broken capillary action

environment," opposite). Prick out seedlings to avoid overcrowding, since unless air is allowed to circulate freely around young plants, stagnant conditions may arise and cause damping off (p.655). Remove fallen leaves and dead matter immediately.

Most organic propagating media and soil mixes are acidic (with a pH value of less than 7), and the ideal range for an organic mix is pH 5–5.5. Test kits are available to measure the pH. A very alkaline medium reduces the amount of phosphorus, iron, boron, and manganese available to the plant, whereas too acidic a medium reduces the available calcium and magnesium. For fertilizing the plants, a commercial liquid fertilizer should be applied strictly in accordance with the manufacturer's instructions. It is generally recommended to use liquid fertilizers at half strength but twice as often as indicated on the package.

Hardening off

Hardening off, or acclimatizing the propagated plants to the outside conditions, must not be rushed since, over a period of days, the natural waxes coating the leaves undergo changes in

DAMPING OFF

Seedlings are more likely to damp off if they are overcrowded, especially if grown in damp, poorly ventilated conditions or if they are allowed to suffer cold damage.

form and thickness to reduce the rate of water loss. The stomatal pores on the leaf also need to adapt to a less supportive environment. Also, the plants must adapt to (normally) lower temperatures and higher levels of light, as well as wind and rain.

Turn off the heat, if appropriate, in the propagator or mist unit. Then, in the daytime, raise the covers for increasingly long periods. Finally, the covers may be removed for both day and night. This process also applies to plants grown under plastic bags. If the plant has been in the protective environment of a greenhouse and eventually needs to be planted outdoors, move it next into a cold frame. This, too, should be closed at first, then opened in stages. The hardening-off process takes one to three weeks.

Outdoor nursery beds

If propagating plants in any quantity, an outdoor nursery bed can provide the best conditions in which to grow on recently propagated plants and young seedlings in pots and other containers, once they have been hardened off. The nursery bed may be of any suitable size. First prepare a level site and then enclose it with 3in (8cm) high, wooden edging boards. There are two types of outdoor bed: water-permeable fabric beds and sand beds.

WATER-PERMEABLE FABRIC BED

Use edging boards to enclose the nursery bed and line with water-permeable fabric placed directly onto the soil.

Edging board 3in (8cm) above soil level

Water-permeable fabric

Two-way flow of water through the soil

Soil level

SAND BED

With this type of nursery bed, the containers are set directly onto the coarse sand topping.

Edging board 3in (8cm) above soil level

Sand

Two-way flow of water through the sand

Soil level

Plastic sheeting cut 1in (2.5cm) below the top of the edging boards

Place containers directly on the sand. The sand enclosed within the plastic liner provides a water reservoir, which reduces the frequency of watering needed and prevents media from drying out. Excess water drains away between the boards and the plastic sheeting. More complex sand bed designs incorporate drainage pipes and automatic watering systems.

Water-permeable fabric beds
In this, the simpler option, black polypropylene, woven fabric, or landscape fabric is laid over the prepared soil surface within the wooden edge boards. The fabric suppresses weeds and helps isolate plants set on its surface from soilborne diseases. Water-permeable fabric beds also enable containers to drain freely, yet give the

plants access to soil water through capillary action. If the soil is not well drained and sandy, or if the surface is uneven, level it with sand before laying the fabric.

Sand beds
A sand bed has the advantage over a water-permeable fabric bed of reducing the amount of watering necessary.

Lay an oversize plastic sheet that is folded double over the prepared soil and up over the edging boards. Cover the plastic with coarse, lime-free sand to within 1in (2.5cm) of the top of the edging boards. Then trim the plastic sheeting to the sand level. Fill in to the top of the edging boards with more sand and level off by drawing another board across the top.

Advanced techniques

Since the mid-20th century, many new propagation methods have been introduced commercially. These are, as yet, generally confined to nurseries using advanced technologies, but the results of their developments are affecting several branches of commercial and amateur horticulture.

Micropropagation

Micropropagation uses explants (tiny pieces of young plant material). Each explant is grown on in a glass or plastic container in a medium containing organic nutrients, mineral salts, hormones, and other elements needed for growth, and is placed in a closely controlled, sterile environment. The explant multiplies to form numerous shoots or complete plantlets, which are then rooted as microcuttings or, if

they have already rooted, weaned to greenhouse conditions. Sterile conditions are vital throughout, and transfer of the plant material from the culture to a greenhouse is especially difficult.

Micropropagation is used mainly for valuable plants, for example for the rapid introduction of new cultivars, for plants difficult to propagate by other means, and to produce disease-free stock.

Genetic engineering

It is now possible to identify and even extract particular genes from a plant's cells and to introduce these into another cell, not necessarily of the same species. Using such methods, resistance to certain fungi, viruses, and pests has been introduced into otherwise susceptible species. For example,

some lettuce, tomato, and pepper cultivars that are susceptible to cucumber mosaic virus can be given a gene that minimizes its effect. Petunias and tobacco plants can now also be made resistant to certain herbicides.

The potential for genetic engineering is vast, especially for the development of agricultural crops. Examples include special potatoes that do not suffer from low-temperature sweetening for chip manufacture; canola seed that has been altered so that it yields more oil; and tomatoes into which a gene has been inserted to allow them to be harvested while red and ripe (rather than while green and unripe), so that they are tastier but firmer and less prone to damage during transportation to market.

Advances in seed propagation

New methods have been developed to improve the speed and uniformity of seed germination. Seeds are soaked in solutions of salts, such as sodium chloride or potassium nitrate, or in polyethylene glycol solutions. They are thus primed for germination but are dried before the radicle emerges and are then packaged. The seeds can be sown conventionally as desired.
Fluid drilling and pelleted seed have been developed to make uniform sowing easier. In fluid drilling, seed primed for germination is contained within a

gel base, for example in a fungicide-free wallpaper paste, which is squeezed along a seed drill. In pelleted seed, primed seed is coated in an inert material that may contain fungicides, nutrients, and/or a dye. The seeds can then be handled individually and sown more evenly. Pelleted seed is made for bedding plants with small seeds and some vegetable crops.

Artificially produced seeds

Some flower tissues, when introduced into a special liquid culture medium, develop numerous embryos – each similar to the embryo within a seed. Artificial seed is produced by separating the embryos from the medium and giving them a synthetic coating. This process is known as somatic embryogenesis and may eventually lead to the manufacture of vast numbers of genetically uniform, so-called, seeds.

Hydroculture

Instead of in a medium, seeds and cuttings are propagated in a culture solution or an inert supporting medium, such as sand, gravel, clay granules, or rock wool, and bathed in nutrient solution (see THE INDOOR GARDEN, "Hydroculture," p.367). This technique is used in regions where a suitable medium is not easily obtainable.

MICROPROPAGATION

A microscopic portion of plant tissue is extracted under sterile conditions. This portion, or explant, is then divided (right) and grown on in test-tube conditions (far right). Once sufficiently large, these embryo plants may be further divided or grown on to form plantlets.

Embryo plant

Sterile, test-tube conditions

7
PLANT PROBLEMS

EVEN THE MOST experienced gardener may suffer problems caused by plant diseases and disorders, the ravages of pests, and the choking of plants by weeds. By following the principles of good cultivation and garden management, however, it should be possible to keep these problems to a minimum.

When problems do occur, it is important first to diagnose them correctly, before deciding upon the appropriate course of action required to remedy the situation. The choice of treatments now includes a wide and effective variety of organic and biological methods as well as the use of chemicals.

Pests, diseases, and physiological disorders

Most plant problem symptoms are easy to see. A tree, shrub, or plant may wilt or become discolored, or it may fail to come into leaf or to bloom at all. Insects, which may be the cause of the plant's poor health, may be seen on part or all of the plant. Sometimes an infestation or disease in the roots may be noticed first through symptoms in the leaves. This chapter gives detailed information on how to prevent and control the pests, diseases, and physiological disorders that can cause such problems.

What is a pest?

Pests are animals that cause damage to cultivated plants. Some, such as slugs, snails, and rabbits, are well known; most, however, are small invertebrates such as mites, nematodes, woodlice, and millipedes, which are less evidently plant pests. The largest group by far in this category are the insects. Pests may damage or destroy any part of a plant or, in some cases, even the whole plant. They feed in various ways – by sap sucking, leaf mining, defoliating, or tunneling through stems, roots, or fruits. Sometimes they cause abnormal growths known as galls. Some pests also indirectly damage plants by spreading viral or fungal diseases, while others coat plants with a sugary excrement that encourages the growth of sooty molds.

What is a disease?

A plant disease is any pathological condition caused by other organisms, such as bacteria, fungi, or viruses. Fungal diseases are commonest; bacterial diseases relatively rare. The symptoms that these organisms produce vary considerably in appearance and severity, but the growth or health of the plant is almost always affected and, in severe attacks, the plant may even be killed. The rate of infection is affected by factors such as weather and growing conditions. In some cases, the disease-causing organism (pathogen) is spread by a carrier, such as an aphid. The pathogen is sometimes visible as a discoloration on the plant, as with rusts. Symptoms such as discoloration, distortion, or wilting are typical signs of disease infection.

HOW TO DIAGNOSE PLANT SYMPTOMS

In a case where it is obvious that the leaves have been eaten away by some kind of pest, turn to the section on "Eaten leaves" to identify the cause.

When a plant shows several symptoms, look either in the section on the whole plant or in the part that deals with the worst aspect, here discolored leaves.

What is a disorder?

Plant disorders usually result from nutritional deficiencies or from unsuitable growing or storage conditions. An inappropriate temperature range, inadequate or erratic water or food supply, poor light, or unsatisfactory atmospheric conditions may all lead to physiological disorders. Problems may also be caused by deficiencies of the mineral salts that are essential for healthy plant growth.

Weather, cultural, or soil conditions may lead to a range of plants being affected. The problems become apparent through symptoms such as discolored leaves or stem wilt. A plant that lacks water, food, or the appropriate environmental conditions will not only appear unhealthy but will also be far less able to resist attack from either insect pests or diseases caused by fungi, viruses, or bacteria. Unless problems are correctly diagnosed and appropriately treated, in extreme circumstances affected plants may die.

How to use this chapter

This chapter is organized according to the site of symptoms (such as distorted flowers or discolored leaves), in sections covering leaves, stems, flowers, fruit, roots and tubers, bulbs, whole plant, and lawns. Within these, symptoms are grouped by type; for example, all yellow leaf spots will be found together.

To identify a problem, look in the appropriate section. If you cannot find it there, turn to the cross-references at the end of that section. Each entry lists the plants affected, the symptoms, the cause of the problem, and how to control it. Always check the label and any accompanying information on any pesticide container for specific uses, since not all commercial brands of any one chemical are always recommended for the same problems or the same plants.

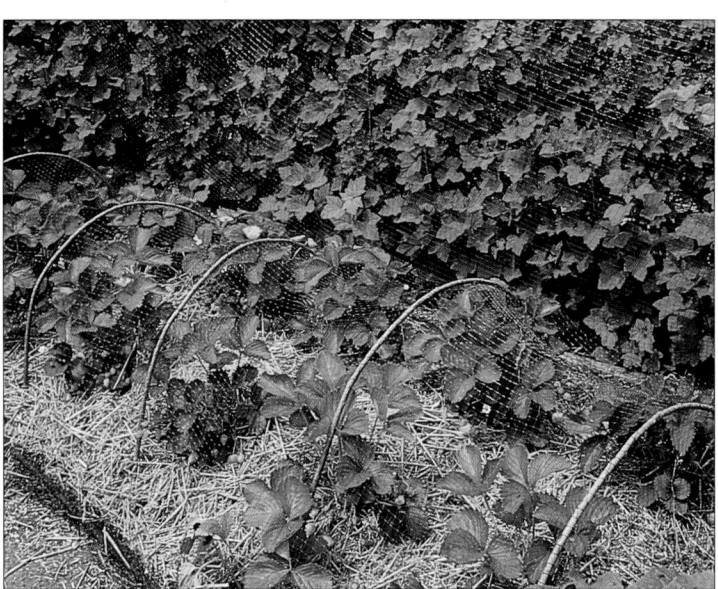

GUARDING AGAINST PROBLEMS
A combination of defenses protects these strawberry plants. Netting prevents depredations by birds, while a layer of straw maintains a clean, dry environment around the fruits, discouraging molds and rots.

Integrated pest management

The phrase "IPM" is used to describe what is widely agreed to be best practice in the limitation and management of pest and disease problems. It aims first to do everything possible to prevent problems from occurring, but then, should this be inadequate, to consider all the options for dealing with a problem – for example, using organic or biological controls – before resorting to chemicals. Gardeners practicing IPM combine the best aspects of organic and inorganic methods, always opting for the organic one first. They choose resistant plants and maintain high standards of garden hygiene, making sure plants are healthy and thus have the best chance of resisting attack; they also practice crop rotation. They seek to prevent pests from landing on plants by the use of traps, barriers, and repellents. Plants are inspected regularly to spot problems early, and care is taken to make an accurate diagnosis. Chemicals are used sensibly and correctly and only when warranted by serious pest or disease attack.

PREVENTING BUILDUP OF DISEASE

Practicing crop rotation prevents specific soil-borne problems from building up in the same patch of ground, for example clubroot of brassicas – here, plants are being removed after bearing.

Prevention of problems

Always buy strong, vigorous plants that look healthy. Do not purchase plants that are showing dieback or discolored stems, that have leaves that are an abnormal color for the time of year, or that are wilted or distorted. Do not buy plants showing significant pest infestations or disease. Check the root ball of container-grown trees and shrubs: do not buy them if they are either potbound or showing poor root development.

Check that the plant is suitable for its intended position, taking into account the type, texture, and pH of the soil, the exposure of the site, and whether the plant is prone to cold damage. Plant carefully, making sure that the ground is well prepared and that the roots are spread out. Follow the individual plant's requirements for watering, fertilizing, and, where appropriate, pruning.

Garden hygiene
Maintaining a neat and well-managed garden is one of the most important ways to reduce the risk of pest and disease attack. Examine plants regularly to identify any new problem as soon as possible, since a well-established infection or infestation is always far more difficult to deal with than one that is identified and treated early.

The regular removal and disposal of diseased parts of plants, and of some pests such as cabbage white caterpillars, may be laborious but certainly helps to control problems. Debris from infested or diseased plants should in all cases be discarded; otherwise, the pest or pathogen may survive, overwinter, and reinfect plants in spring.

If a plant is badly diseased or infested by pests, it may be impossible to revive it; these plants should be removed, especially if there is a risk that the trouble might spread to healthy plants nearby.

Crop rotation and replant problems
Rotating vegetable crops, usually on a three- or four-year basis, helps prevent soil-borne pests and diseases from building up to a damaging level. For further details on planning a crop rotation system, see GROWING VEGETABLES, "Crop rotation," p.492. Although a strict rotation plan is generally used for vegetables, it is also worth rotating annuals and bulbs where feasible, since this reduces the buildup of diseases such as tulip fire. Growing a particular kind of plant in the same ground for a number of years may also lead to problems. If a disease such as tulip fire becomes evident, remove all the plants and grow other botanically unrelated plants that are not susceptible on the site.

Resistant plants
Some plants are resistant to attack by pests or diseases. Plant breeders have been able to profit from this and have produced cultivars with a higher-than-average resistance to some pests or diseases. Cultivated plants resistant to pests include some butterhead lettuces, which are seldom affected by the lettuce root aphid. Plants resistant to disease include some tomato cultivars, which resist tomato leaf mold and a variety of other bacterial, fungal, and virus diseases as well as nematodes, and a number of roses that show some resistance to prevalent diseases such as powdery mildew, rusts, and blackspot.

In some cases, the resistance appears to be total, but even a resistant plant may succumb to a given disease if its growing conditions are poor, for example, or if other factors, such as the weather, weaken the plant. Before buying plants, check if there are disease- or pest-resistant cultivars readily available. The selection of resistant plants varies from year to year, so check catalogs annually for this type of information.

Correcting cultural disorders and deficiencies

Unsatisfactory growing conditions may result not only in poor general growth but also in some very specific symptoms that closely resemble those caused by pests and diseases. When problems manifest themselves and an obvious cause – such as pest infestation – is not immediately apparent, it is worth considering the plant's growing environment as a whole – recent weather conditions, for example, or the health of your soil, or indeed whether some aspect of plant care was not provided. At best, the plant may be restored to complete health by some simple measure – the addition of a mineral supplement, for example, or less frequent watering. At worst, you may need to accept plant losses caused by freak extremes of weather – or learn that certain plants simply are not suited to the conditions you are able to provide.

SYMPTOMS OF CULTURAL DISORDER

Bitter pit in apples, caused by a lack of calcium, may be triggered by dry conditions in soils that in fact do contain sufficient calcium levels.

FRIENDS AND FOES

FOE:
MILLIPEDE

FRIENDS:
CENTIPEDES

FRIEND: GARDEN SPIDER

FRIEND AND FOE:
SKUNK

*Flat
centipede*

*Snake
centipede*

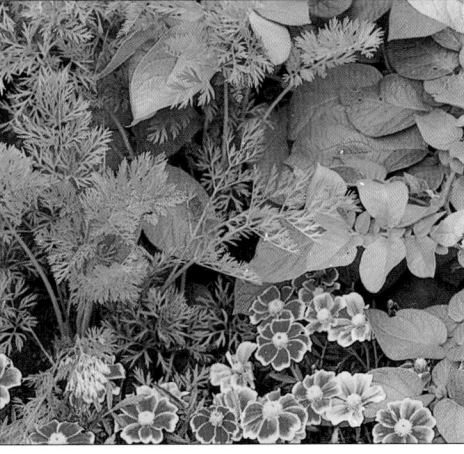

It is also worth remembering that the risk of certain pest and disease problems can be minimized by altering growing conditions. Liming in the vegetable garden (see p.619) is a classic example; by increasing the alkalinity of the soil, it reduces the risk of clubroot affecting brassica crops.

Organic controls

Organic control uses natural methods to help plants both resist and recover from attack by pests and diseases. Such methods have long played their part in gardening, but in recent years they have attracted an increasing level of interest, especially as some harmful organisms have become immune to chemicals that once controlled them. Gardeners have become increasingly aware of the damage that irresponsible use of chemicals can do to the environment, and especially to creatures that are the gardener's natural allies – those that are predatory on plant pests.

Attracting pest predators

Insects and other creatures found in gardens are by no means all destructive. Many are not only useful to the plant but actually essential for its survival; for example, a large number of fruits, vegetables, and flowers rely on pollinating insects, such as honey bees, to carry pollen from one flower to another to enable fertilization to take place. In other cases, some species of natural predator can help control certain types of pest and should therefore be encouraged to visit the garden. A natural balance between pests and predators may take a few years to accomplish but, once established, such a garden will be much healthier than one that relies on chemical remedies alone.

Areas of undisturbed land will attract beneficial animals, especially if planted with a wide range of native species. A stone or wood pile will attract toads and snakes, and a pond will bring dragonflies into your garden. Predators such as hoverflies and ladybugs can also be encouraged by the introduction of colorful flowers, especially if flat or open-centered in form, and so they, too, will help keep pests to a minimum.

Recognizing beneficial garden animals

Shrews, frogs, and toads feed on many ground-dwelling plant pests such as slugs and snails. Birds may be the cause of some damage in the garden, but this disadvantage is usually far outweighed by the enormous quantities of insect pests that many devour. Some invertebrates, for example centipedes, prey on soil-dwelling pests. It is possible to distinguish centipedes from the somewhat similar millipedes (which are often harmful) by the number of legs that are carried on each segment of their bodies: centipedes have only one pair per

body segment, whereas millipedes have two pairs (see also *Friends and Foes*, above).

Spiders are also useful allies as their webs trap countless insects. Certain insects, however, may be invaluable in the garden. Ladybugs are a familiar example nearly everywhere, and both the larvae and the adult beetles feed on destructive pests such as aphids. Lacewing larvae, too, have a voracious appetite for aphids, and they can be encouraged by planting flowers, such as pot marigolds (*Calendula*), and the provision of a nesting box in which they can overwinter. Ants and wasps, whose activities might damage some plants, may still help the gardener by preying on other insect pests. Ground beetles are voracious consumers of numerous pest species.

Companion planting

Certain companion plants grown in association with a crop may help to reduce pest attack. For example, some strong-smelling herbs such as mint and garlic may repel pests that are attracted to plants by smell, thereby keeping them away from nearby plants. Deliberate planting of host plants may deflect pests away from other plants or attract predators to feed on the pests: nasturtiums (*Tropaeolum*), for example, are susceptible to aphids, so plant French marigolds (*Tagetes patula*) nearby as these attract hoverflies, which have larvae that feed on the aphids.

Traps, barriers, and repellents

These work by preventing pests from getting near plants. Many are easily constructed from everyday items. Earwigs may be trapped in inverted flower

ORGANIC EARWIG TRAP

An inverted flower pot filled with dried grass and placed over a stake attracts earwigs (see p.638). Examine the pot and remove any earwigs daily.

COMPANION PLANTING
French marigolds (Tagetes patula) *attract hoverflies, which feed on aphids that may attack nearby plants.*

pots, and wireworms in old potatoes or carrots speared on a stick and buried. In the greenhouse, saucers of water under bench legs will foil ants and sowbugs – not in themselves pests of established plants but extremely destructive to delicate seedlings. Greenhouse whiteflies, which are attracted to the color yellow, may be caught on a piece of yellow cardboard smeared with grease. Place these near the top of the plants and move them up as the plants grow. Inspect these traps regularly and dispose of the pests. Consider introducing biological controls (see p.636) if the infestation is increasing.

Pheromone traps can be purchased from most garden centers and by mail order. They contain the chemicals used by specific insects, such as the codling moth, to attract a mate. The trap eliminates the males by luring them onto a sticky sheet, thereby also reducing the mating success of the remaining females. Such a trap also allows the gardener to monitor infestation levels and to determine whether further control methods are needed.

Traps and barriers can be used effectively against slugs and snails (see also "Controlling slugs and snails", p.636). Larger barriers, from horticultural row cover to fruit cages, can be erected around and over plants to deter winged insects such as carrot rust fly and cabbage whitefly, as well

CODLING MOTH TRAP

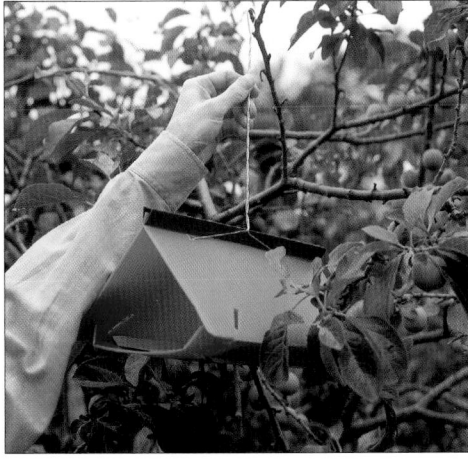

Hang a pheromone trap head high in apple and pear trees in spring. It will catch male codling moths and so reduce mating opportunities.

Controlling slugs and snails

There are many effective alternatives to slug pellets, which some gardeners prefer not to use. The value of hand-picking should not be underestimated, especially when several pairs of hands are available to help. Slugs and snails are most active at night and can be readily spotted by flashlight, especially on a damp evening. Gather up the pests and kill them by dropping in a strong salt solution.

There are a number of environmentally friendly traps and barriers, both commercial products and homemade. Some prevent the slugs from reaching the plants, while others attract them to more tempting fare nearby.
• Lure slugs and snails into a hollowed-out grapefruit or orange half that has been set, open side downward, on stones just above the ground. Slugs and snails, attracted by the citrus scent, will move under the fruit skin and are likely to remain there, until morning at least. The slugs can then be drowned in a strong salt solution.
• Partly fill a jar with beer or milk and almost sink it in the ground. The rim should be about ½in (1cm) above the surface so that useful predators such as ground beetles are prevented from toppling in. The smell of the beer or milk will attract slugs and snails, which should fall in and drown. Specially designed slug traps are available by mail order.
• Create a wide, physical barrier of a coarse material such as sand, grit, wood ash, soot, pine needles, diatomaceous earth, or finely ground eggshells around special plants. These will be either too dry or too scratchy for slugs and snails to be attracted to cross.
• Surround vulnerable seedlings and very small plants with individual tubes made from a plastic bottle with the top and bottom cut off. Press the plastic tube into the soil so it encircles a plant.
• Place a commercial porous mineral product as a barrier around plants that need protection. Such a barrier, however, is less effective under wet conditions, which is when slugs and snails are most active.

as birds, rabbits, and deer. Grease bands bar the way to pests climbing up trees and pots, and commercial brassica collars, or ones cut from carpet or padding, will prevent female cabbage root flies from laying their eggs around young brassica plants (see p.652).

Repellents, such as ultrasonic devices or humming tapes, are sometimes used to protect plants against moles, cats, and birds, which may be encouraged to move elsewhere in the vicinity. However, while bird-scaring devices and pet repellents may work initially, they often require changing frequently as the creatures become familiar with them.

Acceptable organic treatments
A few chemical preparations originate from natural sources; pyrethrum, for example, is derived from the pyrethrum daisy. Other organic treatments are rotenone dust, soft soap, vegetable oils, and sulfur dust. These may be obtained as ready-made powders or liquid sprays; copper-based ones are safe to use and spray damage is not a problem. They have short persistence, however, and act only on contact with the pest or disease, which necessitates regular and thorough applications. One disadvantage of organically "acceptable" insecticides is that most are nonspecific in action, harming all insect life, whereas some "unacceptable" chemical controls have been carefully formulated to target only the harmful pest and not other beneficial creatures such as pest predators. Such nonorganic treatments are arguably less environmentally damaging than organic alternatives.

Biological control

Some of the most troublesome pests, especially red spider mite, whiteflies, and vine weevil grubs, can be dealt with very effectively using the relatively recently developed technology of biological control. The term biological control describes the limiting of pest damage by the deliberate introduction of natural enemies, such as predators, parasites, or diseases. Biological controls are living organisms, usually nematodes or small predatory insects or mites, that have no detrimental effects on nontarget species. They are bred and supplied under controlled conditions; since they are alive, they must be introduced onto your plants or into

INDIVIDUAL COVER
Cut-down plastic bottles protect tender stems from voracious pests at ground level.

the soil as soon as they have been obtained. These tiny creatures may prey on their host or target pest during a specific stage of its development, or they may spread disease among them. For example, the microscopic pathogenic nematode *Heterorhabditis megidis* is watered into potting media or soil containing vine weevil grubs, which it infects with a fatal disease, while the predatory mite *Phytoseiulus persimilis* feeds on the eggs, nymphs, and mature forms of spider mite. Not all pests and diseases, however, can be countered by appropriate biological controls; other controls may be introduced as more research is carried out on insect and disease ecology.

Most of these organisms require daytime temperatures of at least 70°F (21°C) and good light intensity in order to breed faster than the pests. They can therefore be introduced into a heated greenhouse earlier than an unheated one or the

USING BIOLOGICAL CONTROLS

BIOLOGICAL CONTROL AT WORK
Minute Encarsia formosa *wasps attack and parasitize whitefly larvae, causing them to blacken and eventually die.*

YELLOW STICKY TRAP
A useful adjunct to biological controls, these can catch small numbers of pests and will alert the gardener if populations start to increase.

PEST	BIOLOGICAL CONTROL
Aphids	Fly larva predators (*Aphidoletes aphidimyza*)
Caterpillars	Bacterial disease (*Bacillus thuringiensis*)
Chafer grubs, leatherjackets	Pathogenic nematodes (*Heterorhabditis* and *Steinernema* spp.)
Fungus gnat larvae	Predatory mites (*Hypoaspis miles*)
Mealybugs	Ladybugs (*Cryptolaemus montrouzieri*)
Soft scale insects	Parasitic wasp *Metaphycus helvolus*
Spider mites	Predatory mites (*Phytoseiulus persimilis*)
Thrips	Predatory mites (*Amblyseius* spp.)
Underground slugs	Pathogenic nematode (*Phasmarhabditis hermaphrodita*)
Vine weevil grubs	Pathogenic nematode (*Heterorhabditis megidis*)
Whitefly	Parasitic wasp *Encarsia formosa*

open ground. Another key to successful use is to make sure that the pest has been correctly identified and therefore the appropriate specific control measures adopted. If you are not sure what pests you have, lure them onto a sticky yellow trap for easier identification.

Biological controls may be obtained from mail-order specialty suppliers. These generally advertise in the gardening press and on the internet. Good garden centers will also be able to provide advice on suitable controls and where to buy them if they do not carry them.

Greenhouse controls
Some biological controls are suitable for use only in the greenhouse or conservatory. Introduce the control before plants are heavily infested, since it may be a number of weeks before it becomes effective. Restrict the use of pesticides, since most are harmful to biological controls; the exceptions are primarily insecticidal soaps or vegetable oils, which control a range of small insects and mites.

Open-garden biological controls
Use of biological controls is less practical in the relatively uncontrolled conditions of the open garden, especially where pesticides are used, since pesticides often kill the controls as well as the pests. Of the controls listed in the table (facing page), only those for caterpillars, chafer grubs, leatherjackets, vine weevil, and underground slugs are suitable for use in the open garden, provided the soil temperature is suitably high.

Chemical control

Chemical control is the term used to describe the action of destroying plant pests and diseases by applying synthetic compounds to plants or soil. Although the emphasis on organic control is presently becoming stronger, the responsible and sparing use of chemicals still has a valuable role to play in pest and disease control. A sensible combination of the most suitable aspects of both methods may provide the best solution to these difficult and often recurrent problems.

Pesticides and fungicides
Most pesticides (which are used to kill insects, mites, and other pests) and fungicides (which are used to control diseases caused by fungi) either work by being brought into contact with the pest or disease organisms, or are systemic.

Contact pesticides kill pests when they crawl over a treated surface or when they are directly hit by the chemical (when sprayed, for example). Contact fungicides may kill germinating fungal spores and prevent further infection, but they have little effect on established fungal growths.

Systemic chemicals are absorbed into the plant tissues and are sometimes transported by the sap stream throughout the entire plant. Fungicides of this type kill fungi in the plant tissues. Systemic pesticides are predominantly used against certain sap-sucking pests, such as aphids, leafhoppers, and some scale insects, and may be less useful against foliage pests that have chewing mouthparts, such as caterpillars, beetles, and earwigs. Thorough spraying of affected plants, especially on the undersides of leaves, is essential if these pesticides are to work.

Pesticide-resistant strains may sometimes occur, particularly with persistent greenhouse pests such as whitefly, thrips, and spider mite. Fungi that are

THOROUGH APPLICATION
To avoid a wasted application, spray well into the center of plants and beneath foliage, especially with products that have a contact action.

SEPARATE EQUIPMENT
Keep watering cans, sprayers, and nozzles specifically for use with herbicides: residues in equipment can harm nontargeted garden plants.

frequently treated with systemic fungicides may also develop resistant strains. This problem can sometimes be overcome by using a different type of compound, but with greenhouse pests the use of biological control (where possible) is often a better alternative (see p.636).

Formulation of chemical preparations
The active ingredient of a chemical preparation kills the organism, and the way in which a preparation has been formulated determines its efficacy and use. Pesticides and fungicides are available as concentrated liquids, dusts, powders (with which a wetter may be incorporated to ensure thorough penetration of the active ingredient), smokes, baits, and ready-to-use dilute liquids. These are now formulated for maximum effectiveness and safety (for both gardeners and the environment), although in the past some environmentally harmful chemicals were available.

Phytotoxicity
Some plants are liable to suffer adverse reactions to fungicides and insecticides. This is known as phytotoxicity. The manufacturer's instructions often list those species that should not be treated. Such lists cannot, however, be complete, since the reaction of many ornamental plants to certain chemicals is as yet unknown. If in doubt about whether a certain chemical may be suitable, first test the fungicide or pesticide on a small area of the plant before undertaking treatment of the whole plant. Alternatively, where several plants of the same type are grown together, test the chemical on only one of them.

Various other factors, including the stage of growth and the environmental conditions surrounding the plant, can also increase the likelihood of a plant being damaged by chemical treatments. For example, young seedlings, cuttings, and flower petals are much more sensitive than is mature foliage to variations in the growing conditions and may therefore be adversely affected by the application of some chemical treatments. Similarly, plants that are suffering any stress should never be treated with chemicals.

In order to avoid problems with side-effects on mature plants, never spray them when they are in bright sunlight or when they are either dry around the roots or have been exposed to unusually high or low temperatures.

Using chemicals safely

If the instructions are followed precisely – that is, only in the way and for the purpose that the manufacturer describes – chemicals should prove effective with little risk to the user or to the environment. It is illegal for gardeners to use chemicals other than in accordance with the instructions provided. Always take the following precautions:

• think before you spray: is it really necessary, or could you use organic remedies or biological controls instead?
• choose the chemical carefully – make sure it is the right one for the job;
• apply the preparation at the rate and frequency stated on the label;
• never use any type of chemical on plants in ponds;
• never mix chemicals unless the manufacturer recommends this;
• always observe any suggested precautions;
• always spray when the wind is still, or almost still, to avoid damaging adjacent plants;
• always spray in the evening, when there are few bees and hoverflies around;
• do not spray on hot, sunny days, as such weather increases the risk of scorching plants;
• avoid contact with the skin and eyes by wearing goggles, rubber gloves, and long-sleeved clothing;
• do not inhale dusts, smokes, or sprays;
• make sure that the chemical does not drift into other people's gardens;
• keep pets and children away during treatment;
• never eat, drink, or smoke when applying a chemical;
• dispose of any excess carefully and wash out any apparatus thoroughly;
• do not use apparatus for anything other than chemicals;
• store chemicals out of reach of children and animals;
• store chemicals in their original containers, with their original labels, and keep any explanatory leaflets with them.

Leaf problems

Eaten leaves

Slugs and snails

Plants affected All seedlings, climbing plants, herbaceous perennials, hostas, small annuals, bulbous plants, vegetables, including potatoes (see also "Slugs," p.653), and strawberries.
Symptoms Holes appear in the foliage and stems may be stripped; silvery slime trails may be left on the leaves or the soil surface. Small holes are visible on the outside of bulbs and the underground part of their stems, leading to large cavities inside.

Slugs under leaves   *Holes in leaves*

Cause Slugs (e.g. *Milax, Limax,* and *Deroceras* spp.) and snails (e.g. *Helix aspersa*), slimy-bodied mollusks that feed mainly at night or after rain.
Control Cultivate regularly to expose eggs. Scatter slug pellets among plants, or place board or other traps; gather up and destroy regularly. (See "Controlling slugs and snails," p.636)

Earwigs

Plants affected Shrubs, perennials, and annuals, commonly dahlias, chrysanthemums, and clematis. Also apricots and peaches.
Symptoms Young leaves are eaten in summer. See p.649 for other symptoms.
Cause The earwig (*Forficula auricularia*), a 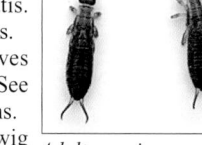 *Adult earwigs*
yellowish brown insect ¾in (2cm) long with a pair of curved pincers. Earwigs hide during the day and feed at night.
Control Loosely stuff pots with hay or straw and invert pots on stakes among susceptible plants (see p.634); earwigs use these traps as daytime shelters. Remove and destroy pests.

Sowbugs and pillbugs

Plants affected Seedlings and other soft growth, including strawberry fruits.
Symptoms Holes may appear in seedlings and in leaves near shoot tips, but sowbugs are not generally pests; they eat mainly decaying plant material
and are often found on plants that have already been damaged by other pests and diseases.

Cause Sowbugs (e.g. *Oniscus* spp.) and pillbugs, or roly-polys (*Cylisticus* spp). They are gray or brownish gray, sometimes with white or yellow markings, and up to ½in (1cm) long with hard, segmented bodies. They feed at night and hide during the day in dark shelters or under rocks or tree stumps. They sometimes occur in large numbers.
Control Always clear away plant debris and keep areas neat to reduce shelter.

Millipedes

Plants affected Seedlings and other soft growth, strawberry fruits, and potato tubers.
Symptoms Seedlings and soft growth are eaten; slug damage on potato tubers and bulbs is enlarged (see p.653). *Common millipedes*
Roots and stems may be eaten in dry periods. Damage is rarely serious.
Cause Millipedes (e.g. *Blaniulus, Orthomorpha,* and *Spirobolus* spp.), black, gray, brown, or creamy white animals that feed below or at soil level. They have hard, segmented bodies with two pairs of legs per segment (centipedes, which are beneficial predators, have only one pair per segment). The spotted snake millipede (*Blaniulus guttulatus*) is the most damaging species. Its slender, creamy white body is up to ¾in (2cm) long with a row of red dots along each side. Millipedes are encouraged by soils with a high organic content.
Control Millipedes, once present, are difficult to control. Cultivate the soil thoroughly and maintain good hygiene. Use inorganic rather than organic fertilizers in problem areas, especially where potatoes are being grown. Place board traps around plants; gather and destroy millipedes hiding by day.

Flea beetles

Plants affected The seedlings of brassicas, leafy vegetables, radishes, wallflowers (*Cheiranthus*), and stocks (*Matthiola*).
Symptoms Holes and pits appear on upper surface of leaves; plants may die if attack is severe.
Cause Small black or metallic blue beetles (e.g. *Phyllotreta* spp.), sometimes with a yellow stripe running down each wing case. They are usually 1/16in (2mm) long, with enlarged hind legs that enable them to leap off from plant surfaces when disturbed. They overwinter in plant debris.
Control Clear away plant debris, particularly in fall. Sow seed in warm soil and water seedlings regularly to help promote rapid growth through the vulnerable stages. Cover young plants with floating row cover.

Asparagus beetles

Plants affected Asparagus.
Symptoms Leaves are eaten; the epidermis is removed from stems, causing the upper growth to dry and turn brown. Damage occurs between late spring and early fall.
Cause Both the adult and larval asparagus beetle   *Adults   Larvae*
(*Crioceris asparagi*). The adult beetles are ¼in (6mm) long, with yellow and black wing cases and a reddish thorax. The larvae are grayish yellow.
Control Pick off light infestations by hand.

Black vine weevils

Plants affected Yews (*Taxus*) and many shrubs, such as rhododendrons, hydrangeas, *Euonymus,* and camellias; also grapes, strawberries, other herbaceous plants, and fuchsias.
Symptoms Notches appear in leaf margins, often near the ground, from late spring to midfall.   *Adult weevil*
Cause The adult black vine weevil (*Otiorhynchus sulcatus*), a grayish black beetle ⅜in (9mm) long, with a short snout and elbowed antennae; it emerges at night to feed. *Irregular holes in leaf margins*
Control Damage occurs over a long period and control is difficult, although good hygiene and the removal of plant debris reduce the number of hiding places. Check plants after dark with a flashlight; pick off and destroy any adults you find. Established plants can tolerate damage.
See also "Black vine weevil larvae," p.656.

Plant bugs

Plants affected Shrubs and perennials (especially chrysanthemums, asters, gladioli, zinnias, mint, and dahlias), annuals, vegetables (rarely), and fruits.
Symptoms The leaves at shoot tips are distorted with small holes. Damage occurs in summer. See p.649 for other symptoms.
Cause Tarnished plant bugs (*Lygus lineolaris*), brown insects ¼in (6mm) long. Fourlined plant bugs (*Poecilocapsus lineatus*) are greenish with four black wing stripes. Their toxic saliva kills plant tissues, causing leaves and flowers to wilt and die.
Control In winter, clear up plant debris. Keep garden areas free of weeds.

Leaf-cutting bees

Plants affected Mainly roses, but also trees and other shrubs.
Symptoms Lozenge-shaped or circular pieces of uniform size are removed from the margins of the leaf (see p.633).
Cause Leaf-cutting bees (*Megachile* spp.), which use the leaf pieces to build their nests. They are up to ½in (1cm) long and have orange hairs on the underside of their abdomen.
Control Leaf-cutting bees are of some benefit in the garden as pollinating insects and, unless plants are heavily damaged, control is not necessary. If they are a persistent nuisance, swat the bees as they return to the leaf to feed.

Sawfly larvae

Plants affected Trees, shrubs, perennials, bulbous plants, and fruits. Particularly affected are pines, willows (*Salix*), *Aruncus dioicus*, *Geum*, *Aquilegia*, Solomon's seal (*Polygonatum*), roses, gooseberries, and currants.
Symptoms Plants are defoliated.
Cause The larvae of various sawfly species (e.g. *Nematus*, *Pristiphora*, and *Diprion* spp.); caterpillar-like larvae that are up to 1¼in (3cm) long and generally green, sometimes with black spots. Bristly rose slug (*Cladius isomeris*), a serious pest in the East, is greenish white with stout spines. Most larvae grip the leaf edge and wave their bodies in an S shape when they are disturbed, but this does not occur with larvae that attack on *Geum* or Solomon's seal.
Control Where possible, remove by hand. Prune off infested terminals of pines. Note: *Bacillus thuringiensis* (Bt) is not effective.

Sawfly larvae eating

Colorado potato beetles

Plants affected Potatoes, tomatoes, eggplants, peppers, flowering tobacco (*Nicotiana*).
Symptoms Leaves are eaten, leaving only the main vein. Crop yield is greatly reduced.
Cause Larvae of the Colorado potato beetle (*Leptinotarsa decemlineata*), orange-red grubs up to ½in (1cm). More visible are the bright yellow and black striped adults, and the orange egg masses on the underside of the leaves.
Control Hand-pick adults and remove egg masses. Rotate crops. Spray small larvae with a beetle strain of *Bacillus thuringiensis*. Place cut potatoes around the garden to trap emerging adults in spring, then gather adults up and destroy.

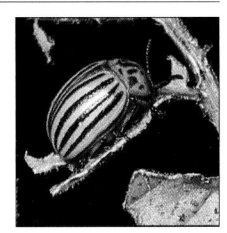

Cabbage caterpillars

Plants affected Mainly brassicas, including cabbages, cauliflowers, and Brussels sprouts. Some perennial and annual ornamentals, e.g. nasturtiums (*Tropaeolum*).
Symptoms Holes appear in the foliage between late spring and early fall, and caterpillars may be found in the hearts of brassicas and on leaves.
Cause Caterpillars of the small cabbage white butterfly (*Pieris rapae*), pale green with velvety hairs.
Control Pick off the young caterpillars by hand. For serious infestations, use the bacterial control *Bacillus thuringiensis*.

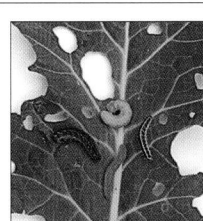

Gypsy moths

Plants affected Many deciduous trees and shrubs, especially apples (*Malus*), hawthorns (*Crataegus*), oaks (*Quercus*), and lindens (*Tilia*). Occasionally conifers such as spruce are affected.
Symptoms Leaves are eaten and plants may be defoliated. Repeated attacks will kill plants.

Cause Larvae of the gypsy moth (*Lymantria dispar*), which hatch from overwintering egg masses laid on the bark. While young, the larvae spin silken threads that act as parachutes and carry them from tree to tree. The larvae are black with two white lines down the back separating rows of spots, blue at the front and red at the rear. The caterpillars are covered with tufts of long hair. They grow to 2in (5cm) when mature and are voracious feeders that can defoliate an entire tree in 2–3 days.
Control Spray with *Bacillus thuringiensis* as soon as noticed. Watch for overwintering egg masses and scrape off. Wrap trunks with burlap bands to trap wandering caterpillars, or use sticky bands (but do not apply the adhesive directly to the tree).

Caterpillars

Plants affected Many garden plants.
Symptoms Leaves, and occasionally also flowers, are eaten away.
Cause Caterpillars of various species of butterfly and moth. The most common in gardens are cabbage caterpillars (see left), tent caterpillars (see p.640), and leaf tiers and rollers (see p.641).
Control Pick off caterpillars by hand, if possible. For serious infestations, spray with *Bacillus thuringiensis*.

Small animals

Plants affected Low-growing plants, young trees.
Symptoms Low-growing leaves are eaten, and the bark of young trees is gnawed away, especially during spells of cold weather.
Cause and control See p.656 for details.

See also "Tent caterpillars," p.640; "Leaf tiers and rollers," p.641; "Bacterial leaf spots and blotches," p.641; "Cut-worms," p.647; "Japanese beetles," p.649; and "Iris borers," p.652.

Discolored and wilted leaves

Aphids

Plants affected Woody plants, perennials, annuals, bulbous plants, vegetables, fruits, and indoor plants.
Symptoms Leaves are often sticky with honeydew (aphid excrement) or blackened by sooty molds; stems and buds may also be covered. See also p.644.

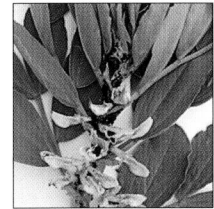
Black aphids on stem

Cause Aphids cluster, sometimes by the hundreds on stems and the undersides of leaves, sucking the sap; some attack roots. They are up to ¼in (6mm) long, either wingless or winged, and green, yellow, brown, pink, gray, or black; some, e.g. the woolly apple aphid, are covered in a fluffy white wax. Aphids may transmit viruses (see pp.642 and 651).
Control Aphids can be controlled by larva predators, such as ladybugs and *Aphidoletes aphidimyza*. Apply horticultural oil in winter to destroy aphid eggs on deciduous fruit trees and bushes. Spray severe infestations with insecticidal soap.

Whiteflies

Plants affected Both indoor and outdoor flowering plants, also some vegetables and fruits.
Symptoms Leaves are covered with sticky honeydew (whitefly excrement) and sooty mold. Small white insects fly off the plants when disturbed.

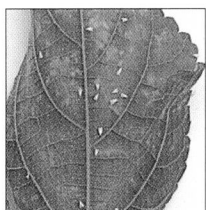
Adult whiteflies

Cause Whiteflies, active, white-winged insects $\frac{1}{16}$in (1.6mm) long that rest beneath young leaves; the immature, scalelike nymphs, which are immobile, whitish green (or black if dead), flat, and oval, are also found here. Several species occur, the most widespread of which is the greenhouse whitefly (*Trialeurodes vaporariorum*). Many plants are attacked by greenhouse whitefly and other species.
Control The parasitic wasp *Encarsia formosa* provides effective biological control in greenhouses from midspring to midfall, if introduced early. If you do choose to use pesticides, be aware that pesticide-resistant strains of greenhouse whitefly occur.

Mealybugs

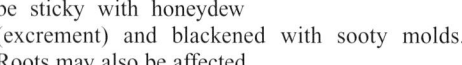

Plants affected Indoor and greenhouse plants, succulents, vegetables, grapes, some tender fruits, and *Citrus*.
Symptoms A fluffy white substance appears in leaf and stem axils. Plants may be sticky with honeydew (excrement) and blackened with sooty molds. Roots may also be affected.
Cause Various mealybugs (e.g. *Pseudococcus* and *Phenacoccus*); soft-bodied, grayish white, wingless insects up to $\frac{1}{4}$in (6mm) long, often with white, waxy filaments trailing from their bodies. Root damage is caused by root mealybugs.
Control Outside, ladybugs (*Cryptolaemus montrouzieri*) give biological control. Indoors, wipe with a swab dipped in a 50 percent rubbing alcohol solution. Discard heavily infested plants.

Lace bugs

Plants affected Rhododendrons, evergreen azaleas, *Andromeda*, *Kalmia*, *Platanus*, *Cotoneaster*.
Symptoms Pale green to yellow mottling on the upper leaf surface, with sticky spots on the undersurface, where feeding takes place.
Cause Nymphs of *Stephanitis pyroides* (mostly on azalea), *S. rhododendri*, and other species. Eggs are laid on the underside of the leaf or on twigs in fall and hatch in spring. There may be several generations each year.
Control Avoid growing susceptible plants in full sun. Wash lacebugs off with a strong stream of water directed under the leaves.

Powdery mildew

Plants affected Trees, shrubs, roses, perennials, annuals, bulbous plants, vegetables, fruits, and many indoor plants.
Symptoms A fungal growth, generally white and powdery, appears on the leaves; on rhododen-

drons it is buff-colored and felty. Usually found on the upper surface, it may appear on the lower side only or on both sides. A purple discoloration may develop. Leaves yellow and fall early. Flowers and fruits are also affected (see p.650).
Cause Various fungi, including species of *Sphaerotheca*, *Oidium*, and *Uncinula*, which thrive on plants in dry soil. Some have restricted host ranges; others attack widely. Spores are spread by wind and rain splash; fungus may overwinter on host plants.
Control Avoid growing susceptible plants on dry sites; water and mulch as necessary. Remove and discard affected areas promptly.

Spider mites

Plants affected Trees, shrubs, perennials, annuals, bulbous plants, cacti and other succulents, vegetables, and fruits. Beans, melons, apples, and plums are susceptible, as are indoor plants.
Symptoms The leaves become dull and increasingly yellowed as a fine, pale mottling develops on their upper surface. They fall prematurely, and a fine silk webbing may cover the plant.
Cause Spider mites, eight-legged animals less than $\frac{1}{16}$in (1.6mm) long. They are yellowish green, red, orange, or almost colorless. There are several species; the most common is the twospotted, or greenhouse, spider mite (*Tetranychus urticae*); this affects both garden and indoor plants in summer. Some species are beneficial predators (see p.635).
Control The rapid reproduction of the mites and the existence of pesticide-resistant strains make control difficult. Discourage those in greenhouses by spraying water underneath leaves and maintaining high humidity; predatory mites provide an effective biological control of *T. urticae* if introduced before heavy infestations develop.

Thrips

Plants affected A wide range of shrubs, perennials, annuals, bulbous plants, vegetables, fruits, and indoor and greenhouse plants. Gladioli, rhododendrons, dahlias, daylilies, peonies, ferns, *Citrus*, pears, peas, and onions are commonly attacked.
Symptoms A silver-white discoloration with tiny black dots appears on the upper leaf surface. See p.648 for other symptoms.
Cause Various species of thrips (e.g. *Thrips simplex*, *T. tabaci*, *Frankliniella occidentalis*, and *Heliothrips haemorrhoidalis*), brownish black insects with narrow bodies up to $\frac{1}{16}$in (1.6mm) long, sometimes crossed with pale bands. Immature nymphs are a pale yellow-orange but otherwise resemble the adults. Both adults and nymphs feed on the upper surface of the leaf. They thrive in hot, dry conditions.
Control Water plants regularly. Reduce the temperature in greenhouses with shading and ventilation. Predatory mites (*Amblyseius* spp.) are also available to control thrips.

Tent caterpillars

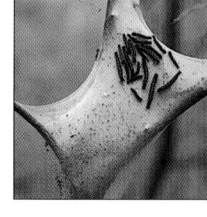

Plants affected Many deciduous trees, especially *Prunus* and *Malus*.
Symptoms Large white nests are spun in the forks of branches in spring. The larvae move out by day to feed on leaves, returning at night.
Cause Tent caterpillars that are black and hairy with a white line down the back and blue spots, of the eastern tent moth (*Malacosoma americanum*), or reddish brown with a blue line on either side of the California tent moth (*M. californicum*).
Control Look for shiny bands of eggs on small branches and prune out. Remove nests while young, if reachable, and destroy, or break open with a stick and spray with *Bacillus thuringiensis*. Alternatively, remove tents and caterpillars and, if legal in your area, burn well away from trees and houses. A species of fly (*Sarcophaga aldrichi*) may serve as a natural control; the fly lays its young in the caterpillar and eventually kills the host. Many birds feed on tent caterpillars.

Leafhoppers

Plants affected Trees, shrubs, perennials, annuals, vegetables, and fruits. Rhododendrons, roses, pelargoniums, primroses (*Primula*), and tomatoes are most vulnerable.

Spots on leaves

Symptoms A coarse, pale spotting appears on the upper leaf surface.
Cause Leafhoppers, such as the rose leafhopper (*Edwardsiana rosae*) and the aster or sixspotted leafhopper (*Macrosteles fascifrons*), green or yellow insects $\frac{1}{16}$–$\frac{1}{8}$in (1.6–3.2mm) long that leap from the plant when disturbed. Their bodies are widest just behind the head. The rhododendron leafhopper (*Graphocephala coccinea*) is pale blue and orange-red, and $\frac{1}{4}$in (6mm) in length. The creamy white, immature nymphs are less active.
Control Controlling leafhoppers will reduce the spread of aster yellows (see p.655), since leafhoppers are the carriers.

Psyllids

Plants affected Bay (*Laurus nobilis*), boxwood (*Buxus*), and pears.
Symptoms The leaf margins of bay are yellowed, thickened, and curled; boxwood leaves are stunted; pear leaves are sticky with honeydew (excrement) and blackened with sooty mold. Damage occurs throughout the spring and summer. See p.645 for other symptoms.
Cause Psyllids (e.g. the bay, *Trioza alacris*, the boxwood, *Cacopsylla buxi*, and the pear, *Psylla pyricola*), the flattened and

immature nymphs of small, aphidlike, winged insects. The nymphs are ¹⁄₁₆in (1.6mm) long and usually gray or green.
Control Prune out and destroy affected shoots.

Leaf and bud nematodes

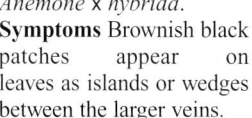

Dark Patches

Plants affected Annuals and most herbaceous perennials. Most commonly attacked are begonias, chrysanthemums, and *Anemone* x *hybrida*.
Symptoms Brownish black patches appear on leaves as islands or wedges between the larger veins.
Cause Microscopic nematodes (*Aphelenchoides*) that feed in large numbers inside infected leaves.
Control Discard all affected leaves or destroy the whole plant as soon as the infestation is noticed. For chrysanthemums, dip the dormant plants in clean, nematode-free water held at a constant temperature of 115°F (46°C) for at least five minutes to obtain clean cuttings.

Leaf miners

Linear blotching

Plants affected Trees, shrubs, perennials, and vegetables, especially birch (*Betula*), hollies (*Ilex*), apples, chrysanthemums, and *Aquilegia*.
Symptoms White or brown areas appear within the leaf, often of characteristic shape for the particular leaf miner, e.g. linear, circular, or irregular.
Cause Larvae of various flies, e.g. the columbine leaf miner (*Phytomyza aquilegivora*) and the chrysanthemum leaf miner (*Phytomyza syngenesiae*); moths, for example the arborvitae leaf miner (*Argyresthia thuiella*); beetles, such as the willow leaf mining weevil (*Rhynchaenus rufipes*); and sawflies, such as the birch leafminer (*Fenusa pusilla*).
Control Remove and destroy affected leaves if the plant is lightly infested. Some birch and holly cultivars are resistant.

Squash vine borers

Plants affected Summer and winter squashes, cucumbers, melons.
Symptoms Sudden wilting of leaves and stems and excrement around entry hole. Larvae may be visible nesting in stems.
Cause and control See p.645 for details.

Leaftiers and leafrollers

Plants affected Trees (ornamental and fruit), shrubs, perennials, annuals, and bulbous plants.
Symptoms Two leaves may be bound together with fine silk threads, or one leaf may be either similarly attached to a fruit or folded over on itself. Brown, dry, skeletal patches appear on the leaves.

Cause The caterpillars of moths such as *Archips argyrospila*, which feeds on apples, oaks, quinces, and roses, and *Pandemis limitata*, which attacks many trees and shrubs. They graze away the inner surfaces of leaves. They are up to ³⁄₄in (2cm) long, and are generally dark green or yellow with brown heads. The caterpillars wriggle backward rapidly when they are disturbed.
Control Squeeze bound-up leaves to crush the caterpillars or pupae that are inside.

Scale insects

Soft scale

Egg deposits

Plants affected Trees, shrubs, cacti and other succulents, fruits, and indoor and greenhouse plants.
Symptoms The foliage is sticky with honeydew (excrement) and blackened with sooty molds. Plant growth may be slow. White, egg-containing deposits may also appear. See also p.645.
Cause Scale insects such as brown soft scale (*Coccus hesperidum*), oystershell scale (*Lepidosaphes ulmi*), and San Jose scale (*Aspidiolus perniciosus*). They are yellow, brown, dark gray, or white, up to ¹⁄₄in (6mm) long, flat or raised, and circular, pear-shaped, or oval. They are found on lower leaf surfaces and stems.
Control Spray deciduous trees with dormant oil in winter, and other plants with highly refined horticultural oil (most effective when the newly hatched scale nymphs are present – all year on greenhouse plants, early to midsummer outside). *Metaphycus helvolus* is a biological control for soft scale insects.

Bacterial leaf spots and blotches

Spots   Yellowing

Plants affected Trees, shrubs, roses, perennials, annuals, bulbous plants, vegetables, fruits, and indoor plants.
Symptoms Various spots or patches develop. They may appear to be water-soaked, and are often angular with a yellow edge or halo ("halo blight"). As the spots merge, the entire leaf is killed. Black tarlike spots appear on delphinium leaves.

Cause *Pseudomonas* bacteria, spread by insects, rain splash, or windborne seeds.
Control Avoid wetting the foliage. Remove all affected leaves. Practice good sanitation in fall and spray woody plants with sulfur in winter.

Rusts

Small brown spores

Plants affected Trees, shrubs, perennials and annuals, bulbous plants, vegetables, fruits, and indoor plants; mints (*Mentha*), roses, raspberries, and blackberries are commonly attacked.
Symptoms Small bright orange or brown patches of spores develop on the lower leaf surface, each corresponding to a yellow discoloration on the upper surface. Spores may appear in concentric rings or pustules. Winter spores, dark brown or black, are sometimes also produced, and the leaves may fall early. Pustules may also develop either on, or apparently bursting from within, the stem. Some plants, e.g. junipers, develop gelatinous growths. In severe cases stems become extensively distorted and ruptured. Dieback may follow.
Cause Fungi, most often species of *Puccinia* and *Melampsora*. The spores are spread by rain splash and air currents and may overwinter on plant debris. A few rusts are systemic.
Control Most rusts have two generations per season, the first on apples, for example, the second on junipers. Troublesome rusts in North America alternate between apples or hawthorns and junipers or arborvitae, or between currants and pines. The removal of one host will give control.

Fungal leaf spots

Plants affected Trees, shrubs annuals, bulbous plants, vegetables, fruits, and many indoor plants.
Symptoms Discrete, concentrically zoned spots appear on the leaves; close inspection may reveal pinprick-sized, fungal fruiting bodies. Spots may be a range of colors but are frequently brown or slate-gray. In severe cases they merge, sometimes obscuring most of the leaf surface. Early leaf fall may occur, but in some instances there is little damage or effect on the overall vigor of the plant. Blackspot on roses is a fungal leaf spot.
Cause A wide range of fungi.
Control Remove all affected parts, and rake up and discard or burn any leaves that have already fallen.

Sooty mold

Plants affected Many plants, both outdoors and under cover, but especially birches (*Betula*), lindens (*Tilia*), oaks (*Quercus*), roses, *Citrus*, and plums.
Symptoms Black, sooty deposits cover the upper

surface of leaves. Mold may cover the leaves, blocking light to the point that the plant is unable to photosynthesize. Leaves fall prematurely.

Cause Fungi from genera such as *Aethaoderma*, *Morfea*, *Phragmocapnias*, and *Scorias*, which grow on the honeydew secreted by aphids (see p.639), whiteflies (p. 640) mealybugs (p.640), and some leafhoppers (p.640).

Control Prevent buildup of pest colonies by spraying with water as soon as noticed. On small plants, carefully wash leaves with a soft cloth or sponge and warm water with a little soap added. On trees, use a hose-end sprayer to wash off mold.

Scab

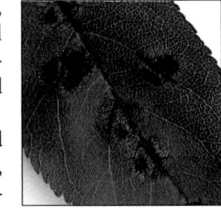

Plants affected *Malus*, including both ornamental and fruiting species, pyracanthas, pears, *Citrus*, and loquats.
Symptoms Dark and greenish brown patches, scabby and sometimes blistered, develop on the foliage; any affected leaves may fall early. See p.650 for other symptoms.

Dark blotches

Cause The fungi *Venturia inaequalis, V. pirina, Spilocaea pyracanthae*, and *S. pomi*, which thrive in warm, damp weather. They may overwinter on infected leaves or shoots; pear scab is especially likely to overwinter.
Control Plant resistant varieties. Keep the plant open-centered by pruning, remove any scabby shoots and fruits, and rake up and discard all fallen leaves. Do not store any affected fruits.

Viruses

Plants affected All plants.
Symptoms Leaves are undersized, distorted, or grouped in rosettes. Patterns of yellow discoloration (mosaics, ringspots, mottles) are common. See p.651 for other symptoms.
Cause A large number of viruses, some with very wide host ranges; others are very restricted to a given genus. Submicroscopic virus particles in the sap of infected plants may be transmitted to healthy tissues by sap-feeding pests such as aphids (p.639), by nematodes or other soil-borne pests, through handling, or on pruning or propagating tools; some are seedborne.

Yellowish streaks

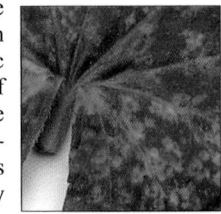

Ringspots

Control Buy certified (virus-free) plants where possible. Keep potential carriers, e.g. aphids (see p.639), under control, and make sure that the site is free of weeds since these may harbor viruses. Remove and discard affected plants as soon as possible; always handle suspect plants after those that appear healthy, and do not propagate from them. Use a new site for any replacement plants.

Clubroot

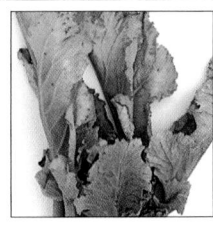

Plants affected The family Cruciferae, especially brassicas (e.g. cabbages, Brussels sprouts, rutabagas, and radishes). Also some ornamentals, such as stocks (*Matthiola*), candytufts (*Iberis*), and wallflowers (*Cheiranthus*).
Symptoms Plants are stunted and discolored with galls ("clubs") on roots; foliage wilts in hot weather. See also p.653.
Cause The slime mold *Plasmodiophora brassicae*, which thrives in poorly drained, acidic soils, and is also found on manure and plant debris. It is easily spread on boots and tools, and the spores are very resilient, remaining viable for 20 years or more, even in the absence of a host plant. Weeds that are susceptible to the disease (e.g. shepherd's purse and wild mustard) may be a source of infection.
Control Remove and destroy affected plants. Keep the area free of weeds, lime the soil, and improve drainage where feasible. Raise new plants in pots of soil-based potting mix so that their roots are well developed when planted out.

Tomato/potato late blight

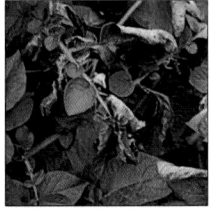

Plants affected Tomatoes (in the open and occasionally under cover), potatoes.
Symptoms Patches of brown discoloration develop on the leaf tips and edges; in damp conditions these may often be ringed with a white fungal growth. The leaf tissue is killed, and where the patches merge the entire affected leaflet may eventually die. See also "Tomato late blight," p.650, and "Potato late blight,".
Cause The fungus *Phytophthora infestans*, which thrives in warm, moist conditions. Spores produced on the foliage of tomato and potato plants, and on potato haulms, are carried from plant to plant by wind and rain, and these may be washed down into the soil to infect potato tubers.
Control Avoid overhead watering. Hill up potatoes deeply to provide a barrier that will help protect the tubers against falling spores, and choose resistant cultivars, for example 'Cherokee', 'Kennebec', 'Plymouth', and 'Essex'.

Fire blight

Plants affected Members of the family Rosaceae that bear pome fruits, mainly pears, apples, some *Sorbus*, cotoneasters, and hawthorns (*Crataegus*).
Symptoms The leaves generally turn blackish brown, shrivel, and die, and they remain clinging to the stem; those of some *Sorbus* and hawthorns may turn yellow and

fall. Oozing cankers appear on the branches, and the entire tree may eventually die. See p.653 for other symptoms.
Cause The bacterium *Erwinia amylovora*, which is produced from the cankers, attacks via blossoms. It is carried from plant to plant by wind, rain splash, insects, and pollen grains.
Control Remove the affected plants or prune out affected areas to at least 24in (60cm) past the damaged area; dip the saw in disinfectant between cuts and before using it on another tree. Inspect inner wood to make sure that no staining remains.

Fertilizer burn

Plants affected Ornamental plants growing in containers and hanging baskets, house plants, and lawns.
Symptoms Foliage develops discolored areas along the veins or around the leaf edges, often followed by severe wilting. Plants may die rapidly afterward. On lawns, dead areas may be in stripes or patches.
Cause Soluble fertilizer incorrectly dissolved so that solids are watered into the container or basket; or dry fertilizer applied at wrong rate. Manure that is applied too fresh may burn plants. Lawns may be burned if fertilizer is applied in overlapping stripes, or if a drop-type spreader is shut off incorrectly.
Control Take care when mixing and applying fertilizer. Fertilize tomatoes carefully; they react quickly to fertilizer overdose or toxic chemicals. In the case of accidental overdose, water repeatedly to dilute the fertilizer to safe levels.

Transplant shock

Plants affected Potentially all plants
Symptoms Soon after transplant, leaves droop and yellow, and plant wilts. Plants may die.
Cause Plant is stressed from improper handling during transplant or incorrect conditions.
Control Avoid shock by transplanting with care and providing appropriate cultural requirements.

Insecticide/fungicide damage

Plants affected Some indoor and garden plants.
Symptoms Discrete spots or patches, often bleached or scorched, appear on leaves, which may fall; the plant usually survives.
Cause Commonly, chemicals used at the wrong rate or interval, applied during hot, sunny weather, or when plants are under drought or other stress. Some plants are damaged by fungicides or insecticides applied correctly, and susceptible species should be noted on the packaging; check carefully before using.
Control Use commercial chemicals only, and always follow the manufacturer's instructions.

Contact weedkiller damage

Plants affected All plants.
Symptoms Pale, bleached spots appear on the contaminated foliage, sometimes turning brown, and

small bumps may appear on stems. Bulbs exposed to contact weedkillers before their foliage has died down show a very pale, almost white, leaf color the following season. In severe cases, vigor may be reduced and the plant may even die. Usually plants grow out of the symptoms.

Cause Spray drift during windy conditions, or from careless application. Poorly cleaned sprayers and watering cans may also lead to contamination.

Control Follow the manufacturer's instructions. Use a dribble-bar applicator or watering can in preference to a sprayer, and keep separate equipment for use with weedkillers.

Drought

Plants affected All plants, especially those that are young and container-grown, or in light, sandy soils.

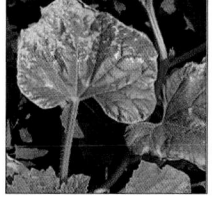

Symptoms Fall color develops early and defoliation may occur, sometimes followed by dieback. Plants wilt and growth is stunted. See pp.648, 655, and 657 for other symptoms.

Cause Prolonged or repeated water shortage due to dry soil, excessive water loss from leaves of plants on exposed sites, injured or restricted roots, or soil compaction. Plants in small containers are vulnerable in hot weather, since peat-based mixes allowed to dehydrate are hard to rewet.

Control Water plants regularly; check those growing in hot or sunny positions. Mulch, where appropriate, to improve moisture retention. It is easier to prevent drought than to treat it: plants exposed to prolonged water shortage are less likely to recover once adequate water is supplied or temperatures lowered than those suffering a sudden shortage.

High temperatures and scorch

Plants affected In particular, plants with fleshy leaves or flowers, those near glass, and seedlings; also trees, shrubs, perennials, annuals, bulbous plants, vegetables, fruits, and indoor plants.

Symptoms The leaves wilt, turn yellow or brown, become dry and crisp and may die; the tips and margins are often affected first. In extreme cases the stems die back. Scorching produces brown patches on the upper or exposed parts of the plant; foliage close to glass is very susceptible. Affected leaves may shrivel completely. Scorched petals turn brown and become dry and crisp. Roses may show "balling" (as the outer petals dry up they enclose the bud). Fruits are also affected (see p.650).

Cause Very high or fluctuating temperatures in a closed environment (e.g. a greenhouse); scorching is caused by bright, but not necessarily hot, sunlight. Scorch problems are increased by faults in the glass near plants, which magnify the sun's rays. Shade-loving plants (e.g. some *Impatiens*) scorch badly if planted in bright sunlight.

Control Where possible, shade greenhouses, provide adequate ventilation to keep temperatures down, and move plants away from any faults there may be in the glass. Locate shade-loving plants in a site with at least dappled shade.

Low temperatures

Plants affected Trees, shrubs, perennials, annuals, bulbous plants, vegetables, fruits, indoor plants; seedlings and young plants are most vulnerable.

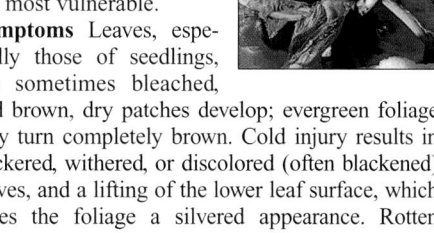

Symptoms Leaves, especially those of seedlings, are sometimes bleached, and brown, dry patches develop; evergreen foliage may turn completely brown. Cold injury results in puckered, withered, or discolored (often blackened) leaves, and a lifting of the lower leaf surface, which gives the foliage a silvered appearance. Rotten patches, brown and dry or dark and soft, develop on the petals, especially on exposed flower heads. Frost injury may leave petals withered or discolored and the whole flower may be killed. See pp.645 and 655 for other symptoms.

Cause Low temperatures or occasionally great fluctuations in temperature. Plants in exposed positions or frost pockets are likely to be affected.

Control Provide winter protection for young or tender plants, and those grown in exposed positions.

Nitrogen deficiency

Plants affected Trees, shrubs, perennials, annuals, bulbous plants, vegetables, fruits, and indoor plants.

Symptoms Pale green leaves are produced, and these sometimes develop either yellow or pink tints. Overall growth is reduced, and the whole plant may eventually become slightly spindly.

Cause Growing plants either in poor, light soils or in restricted surroundings such as hanging baskets, windowboxes, or other types of container.

Control Use green manures on affected areas, or apply a high-nitrogen fertilizer, e.g. nitrate of ammonia, dried blood, or soluble commercial fertilizer.

Potassium deficiency

Plants affected Edible and ornamental fruiting plants, mainly currants, apples, and pears.

Symptoms The foliage turns blue, yellow, or purple, with a brown discoloration either in blotches or on the leaf tips or margins. Some leaves may roll inward; they are fairly soft and therefore prone to attack by pathogens. Flowering, fruiting, and general growth of the whole plant may be reduced.

Cause Growing plants in soils either with a light texture or with a high lime or peat content.

Control Improve the soil texture. Dress with muriate of potash or a high-potassium fertilizer.

Phosphate deficiency

Plants affected Potentially all plants may suffer, but this particular deficiency is unlikely to be a problem in most gardens.

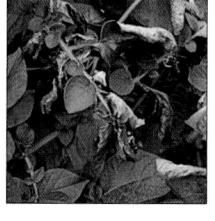

Symptoms Plant growth is slow, and the young foliage may appear dull or yellowed.

Cause The leaching out of phosphates in acidic soils and areas of high rainfall. Plants growing in heavy clay soils, in deep peat soils, or in soils with a high iron content are the most likely to be at risk from this condition.

Control Apply bone meal or superphosphate.

Manganese/iron deficiency

Plants affected Trees, shrubs, perennials, annuals, bulbous plants, vegetables, fruits, and indoor plants. Acidic soil-loving plants growing in alkaline soils are often affected.

Symptoms A yellowing or browning starts at the leaf margins and extends between the veins. The overall leaf color may also be rather yellow.

Cause The cultivation of plants in unsuitable soils or mixes; acidic soil-loving plants, in particular, are unable to absorb adequate trace elements from alkaline soils. Regular watering with very hard water, buried debris (e.g. builders' rubble), and rain runoff from mortar in walls are all possible causes of a locally raised soil pH.

Control Choose plants that are compatible with the soil type and clear the area of any builders' debris. Use rainwater, not tapwater, for susceptible plants. Acidify the soil before or after planting, and apply acidic mulches. Apply a chelated or fritted form of trace elements and chelated iron.

Magnesium deficiency

Plants affected A wide range of both outdoor and indoor plants; common in container-grown nursery stock. Tomatoes, roses, and chrysanthemums are most often affected.

Symptoms Distinct areas of discoloration, usually yellow but occasionally red or brown, develop between the leaf veins (interveinal chlorosis), and the affected leaves may fall early.

Cause Acidic soils; heavy watering or rainfall, both of which leach out magnesium; or high potassium levels, which make it unavailable. Plants given high-potassium fertilizers to encourage flowering or fruiting (e.g. tomatoes) are susceptible.

Control Treat plants and/or soil with Epsom salts in fall; add dry to the soil at a rate of 1oz/10sq ft (25g/sq m), or apply a foliar spray of 7½oz Epsom salts in 2¼ gallons of water (210g in 10 liters), adding a nondetergent dishwashing liquid.

Waterlogging

Plants affected Potentially all plants.
Symptoms Leaves turn yellow and the plants wilt.
Cause Too much water in the growing medium, owing to poor or degraded structure or slow drainage, or overwatering.
Control Improve soil structure and drainage. See also pp.651 and 655.

See also "Irregular water supply," "Edema," "Peach leaf curl," "Hormone weedkiller damage," "Mycoplasmas," all below; "Azalea galls," p.645; "*Verticillium* wilt," p.645; "*Cytospora* canker," p.646; "*Fusarium* wilt," p.646; "*Phytophthora* root rots," p.646; "Foot and root rots," p.646; "Etiolation," p.647; "Blossom wilt"; "Smuts," p.651; "Iris borers," p.652; "Carrot rust flies," p.652; "Narcissus nematodes"; "Iris soft rot," p.654; "Onion maggots," p.654; "Blackleg on potatoes"; "*Coryneum* canker,"; "Oak wilt," p.655; "Aster yellows," p.655; "Clematis wilt"; and "Anthracnose," p.656.

Distorted leaves

Irregular water supply

Plants affected All garden plants, especially container-grown ones.
Symptoms Leaves and flowers are distorted. Stems may split. See p.650 for other symptoms.
Cause An irregular supply of water leads to irregular growth. Sudden availability of water after a drought brings rapid swelling, rupturing stems and distorting the upper parts of the plant.
Control Provide a regular and adequate supply of water for plants, especially in hot or windy weather. Do not suddenly overwater plants after drought conditions. Apply a regular mulch around the plants, where appropriate, since this will help conserve the moisture in the soil.

Edema

Plants affected Potentially all plants, but particularly pelargoniums, camellias, eucalyptus, *Peperomia*, and succulents.
Symptoms Raised, warty patches appear on the foliage; they may extend across the whole leaf. The patches are of a color similar to that of the rest of the leaf, but later turn brown.
Cause Excessively high moisture levels in either the air or the growing medium, which give the plant cells an unusually high water content. As a result of this, small groups of cells swell, forming the outgrowths, and later burst, leaving brown patches on the leaves.
Control Improve air circulation around the plants by increasing ventilation, and by ensuring correct plant spacing. Decrease the amount of watering and try to improve drainage wherever possible. Although the damaged leaves will not recover, do not pick them off: new leaf growth will be normal.

Peach leaf curl

Plants affected Peaches, nectarines, almonds, and related ornamental *Prunus* species in the open.
Symptoms Leaves become distorted, blistered, and sometimes swollen, later turning a deep red; a white fungal growth then develops on the leaf sur-faces. The foliage falls, but a second flush of healthy leaves will be produced afterward.
Cause The fungus *Taphrina deformans*, which is encouraged by cool, wet conditions. Spores are carried by wind or rain to shoots, bud scales, and cracks in the bark, where they overwinter.
Control Pick off affected leaves before they turn white with fungal growth.

Hormone weedkiller damage

Plants affected Broad-leaved plants, mainly roses, tomatoes, grapes, and conifers.
Symptoms Leaves are small, narrow, often thickened, and with prominent veins. They may be cup-shaped and extremely distorted. The petioles become twisted. Small bumps may appear on stems. See p.650 for other symptoms.
Cause Contamination by a growth regulator or hormone-type weedkiller, often originally used a considerable distance away; minute quantities may cause extensive damage. Common sources of trouble are spray drift and the use of sprayers or watering cans that have previously been used for applying weedkillers.
Control Always apply weedkillers according to manufacturer's instructions, placing protective barriers around adjacent garden plants to prevent spray drift. Keep one sprayer or watering can for use with weedkillers only. Store weedkillers in their original containers, away from soil mixes, fertilizers, and plants. Affected plants usually outgrow the symptoms if damage is not extensive.

Aphids

Plants affected Trees, shrubs, climbing plants, roses, perennials, annuals, bulbous plants, vegetables, fruits, and indoor plants.
Symptoms Leaves are stunted and distorted.
Cause and control See p.639 for details.

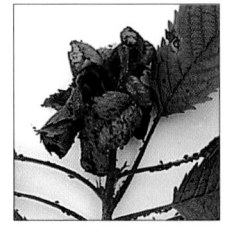

Psyllids

Plants affected Bay (*Laurus nobilis*), boxwood (*Buxus*), and pears.
Symptoms The leaf margins of bay are yellowed, thickened, and curled; boxwood has stunted stems and cupped, slightly distorted leaves. Damage occurs to boxwood in spring and to bay throughout the summer. See p.640 for symptoms on pears.
Cause and control See p.640 for details.

Mycoplasmas

Plants affected Trees, shrubs, perennials, annuals, bulbous plants, vegetables, fruits (especially strawberries), and indoor plants.
Symptoms Leaves may be undersized, distorted, and covered with patterns of discoloration. This condition on strawberry plants, which is known as green petal, produces young leaves that are small, irregularly shaped, and yellowed; in addition, the older foliage turns a distinctly red color when flowering has ceased. See p.648 for other symptoms.
Cause Mycoplasmas, which are believed to be related to bacteria. Mycoplasmas are spread from plant to plant by aphids (see p.639). Strawberry green petal is commonly transmitted by leafhoppers, which pick up the infection from clover plants suffering from phyllody disease. Mycoplasmas give rise to different symptoms in the different hosts.
Control Discard all affected plants, buy only certified fruit stock, and control aphids (see p.639) and leafhoppers (p.640). Remove weeds from neighboring areas because they may harbor the disease.

Gall mites

Plants affected Trees and shrubs, including plums, pears, walnuts, grapes (*Vitis*), maples (*Acer*), lindens (*Tilia*), elms (*Ulmus*), hawthorns (*Crataegus*), mountain ashes (*Sorbus aucuparia*), broom (*Cytisus/Genista*), beeches (*Fagus*), and ash (*Fraxinus*).

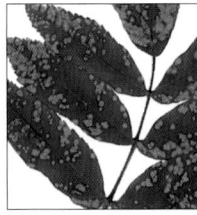
Pale leaf blotches

Symptoms These vary according to the species of mite, and include: whitish green or red pimples or spikes on foliage (maples, elms, lindens, and plums); creamy white or pink hairs on lower leaf surfaces (maples, lindens, and beeches); raised, blistered areas on upper leaf surfaces, with pale hairs underneath (walnuts and grapes); thick, curling leaf

margins (beeches and hawthorns); pale leaf blotches, later turning brownish black (mountain ashes and pears); and stunted leaves (broom). Plant vigor and overall appearance are not affected.
Cause Microscopic gall mites, or eriophyid mites, secreting chemicals that induce abnormal growth.
Control Remove affected leaves and shoots if desired. Apply horticultural oil in spring, just before bud break. Consult with an arborist.

Gall midges

Plants affected Many garden plants, especially violets (*Viola*), *Gleditsia*, and roses.
Symptoms Violet leaves thicken and fail to unfurl. *Gleditsia* leaflets swell and fold over to form podlike galls. Young shoots on roses become

deformed and die, and flower buds fail to open.
Cause Whitish orange maggots up to ¹⁄₁₆in (1.6mm) long that feed within the galled tissues; three or four generations may occur in a summer. These are the larvae of three types of midge: the honeylocust pod gall midge (*Dasineura gleditchiae*), the rose midge (*D. rhodophaga*), and the violet gall midge (*Phytophaga violicola*). The adults are tiny, grayish brown flies.
Control Remove and destroy affected leaves.

Gall wasps/cynipid wasps

Plants affected Oaks (*Quercus*) and roses.
Symptoms Symptoms on oaks include flat disks on the lower surface of leaves in fall; benign, spherical, woody growths (marble galls) or pithy oak apples on shoots in spring; wooly galls under leaves; and yellowish green, sticky "knopper" galls on acorns. Species rose stems and hybrid rose suckers develop swellings covered in yellowish pink, mosslike leaves (mossy rose galls or "Robin's pincushions") in late summer. Damage to the plant is minimal.

Cause The larvae of gall wasps, or cynipid wasps; they secrete chemicals as they feed.
Control Prune out and destroy galls when young. No other control is usually needed.

Azalea galls

Plants affected Rhododendrons and azaleas, especially *Rhododendron simsii* grown as an indoor plant.
Symptoms Fleshy, pale green swellings (galls) that develop on the foliage in spring, later turning white.
Cause The fungus *Exobasidium vaccinii*, which is encouraged by high humidity. The spores are insect- or airborne.
Control Remove and destroy the galls before they turn white. If the disease persists, spray the plants with a systemic fungicide.

> **See also** "Powdery mildew," p.640; "Leaf and bud nematodes," p.641; "Scab," p.642; "Viruses," p.642; "Smuts," p.651; and "Anthracnose," p.656.

Stem, branch, and leaf-bud problems
Stems discolored or with pests visible

Low temperatures

Plants affected All plants.
Symptoms Brown, dry patches develop on the stems. Stems may blacken, wither, or split, giving access to dieback organisms. The splits become enlarged if moisture freezes; the plant may die. See pp.643 and 655 for other symptoms.
Cause Low temperatures or occasionally great fluctuations in temperature. Plants growing in exposed positions are most likely to be affected.
Control Provide winter protection for young or tender plants, and those growing in exposed positions.

Verticillium wilt

Plants affected Many plants.
Symptoms Stained vascular system of stems and roots, creating longitudinal brown stripes. Woody plants deteriorate over several years, and may die.
Cause Several species of the fungus *Verticillium* present in the soil, plant remains, or new stock.
Control Remove any affected plants and soil near the roots. Clean pruning tools thoroughly after use on diseased or suspect plants. Keep weeds under strict control, and do not grow susceptible plants in the affected area.

Slime flux/wet wood

Plants affected Trees, shrubs, and woody perennials, especially plants already under stress from some other cause.
Symptoms The stem dies back and a pink, yellow, or off-white slime oozes from its base (often thick and pungent).
Cause Stem injury (often through cold or wounding) when sap pressure is high, just before the leaves break. The sap released from the wound has a high sugar content and is colonized by various microorganisms (in particular yeasts, bacteria, and fungi), which cause the thickening and discoloration.
Control Avoid injury to stems of susceptible plants. Remove affected stems, cutting back to healthy growth, below ground level if necessary. Given adequate nutrients and moisture, the plant should produce more shoots.

Scale insects

Plants affected Indoor and greenhouse plants, trees, shrubs, fruits, and cacti and other succulents.
Symptoms The stems are sticky with honeydew (excrement), and they appear blackened with sooty molds. Heavily infested plants may also show slow

Hemispherical scale (above) and mussel scale (right)

growth. White, waxy deposits containing eggs also occasionally appear on the stems.
Cause and control See p.641 for details.

Squash vine borers

Plants affected Summer and winter squashes, cucumbers, melons.
Symptoms Sudden wilting of stems and leaves; excrement around entry hole. Larvae nesting in stems.
Cause Larvae of *Melittia cucurbitae*, a red and black clearwing moth. The white larvae, which grow up to 1in (2.5cm) in length, feed inside the stem, causing foliage to wilt and eventually die.
Control Slit stem above entry point to find larvae and remove them. Heap soil over damaged part to aid in root formation.

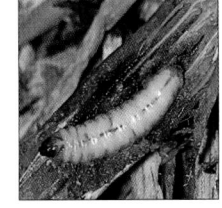

Stem borers

Plants affected Many trees and shrubs, including birches, pines, poplars, locusts, willows, lilacs, and peaches.
Symptoms Larvae, pupae, and a black gummy substance are found in holes in the trunk. Frass (chewed wood that looks like sawdust) may be seen at the base of the tree, in bark crevices, or at entry hole. Branches or the crown may die back. Branches become brittle.

Cause Larvae of various beetles and moths tunneling into the plant, particularly on trees under stress.
Control Cage or use row covers over young plants until moth activity period is over (normally by late spring). Prune larger plants below entry point.

Gray mold/*Botrytis*

Plants affected Trees, shrubs, perennials, annuals, bulbous plants, vegetables, fruits, and indoor plants. Soft-leaved plants are vulnerable.
Symptoms Dead and discolored patches develop on the stems and leaves. Rapid deterioration may occur, causing the upper parts of the stem to die. Fungal spores develop on decaying plant material. See pp.548, 650 for other symptoms.

Cause The fungi *Botrytis cinerea* and, on snowdrops (*Galanthus*), *B. galanthina*, which thrive in damp conditions and where air circulation is poor. Fungal spores are spread on air currents or by rain splash. Fruits may also become infected by contact with those already diseased. Hard, black, resilient sclerotia (fungal resting bodies), produced on plant remains, fall to the ground and may cause later infections.
Control Avoid injury to plants, clear up dead and dying plant material, and provide good air circulation. Remove affected areas.

Dutch elm disease

Plants affected Elms (*Ulmus*) and *Zelkova*.
Symptoms Notching appears in twig crotches, and young twigs may be crook-shaped. Longitudinal, dark brown streaks develop under the bark. Leaves in the crown wilt, yellow, and die. The tree may die within two years.

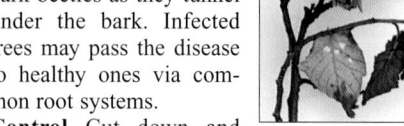

Cause *Ophiostoma ulmi*, a fungus often spread by elm bark beetles as they tunnel under the bark. Infected trees may pass the disease to healthy ones via common root systems.
Control Cut down and remove seriously affected trees and any which may have root grafted with them. Consult with a reliable arborist about possible chemical treatments for trees in the early stages of infection.

Woolly aphids

Plants affected Apples, cotoneasters, pyracanthas.
Symptoms A fluffy, white, moldlike substance appears on the bark in spring. Starting on the larger branches around old pruning cuts and in bark cracks, it later spreads to the new shoots where soft swellings may develop. Insects may be visible.

Cause The woolly apple aphid (*Eriosoma lanigerum*), a small, black insect, sucks sap from the bark and secretes white, waxy threads.
Control Spray with dormant oil in late winter.

Spittlebugs

Plants affected Trees, shrubs, perennials, annuals.
Symptoms Globules of white froth containing a small insect appear on stems and leaves in early summer. Where the pest feeds on shoot tips, growth may be distorted but damage is minimal.

Cause Spittlebugs, or froghopper nymphs (e.g. *Philaenus spumarius*), cream-colored sap-suckers that secrete a protective froth over themselves. The adults are darker in color, up to 1/8in (3mm) long, and live openly on the plant.
Control If treatment is necessary, remove nymphs by hand or spray with a strong jet of water.

Adelgids

Plants affected Conifers, particularly *Abies*, pines (*Pinus*), spruces (*Picea*), Douglas firs (*Pseudotsuga menziesii*), hemlocks (*Tsuga*), and larch (*Larix*).
Symptoms A fluffy, white, moldlike substance appears on the leaves and stems. Knobby swellings develop on *Abies*, conelike galls on young spruce shoots. Cottony masses and distorted needles develop on Douglas firs.

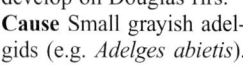

Cause Small grayish adelgids (e.g. *Adelges abietis*). Nymphs of *A. cooleyi* feed on spruces, causing the growth of a gall in which they live and pupate. Winged females migrate to Douglas firs to lay eggs.
Control Hand-pick galls. Keep spruces and Douglas firs separate. Apply horticultural oil in early spring.

Cytospora canker

Plants affected Spruces (*Picea*), pines (*Pinus*), *Abies balsamea*, Douglas firs (*Pseudotsuga menziesii*), hemlocks (*Tsuga*).
Symptoms Small cankers form. Needles turn brown; branches die. Resin drips from the cankers, crystallizing into white deposits.

Cause The fungus *Cytospora kunzei* on spruces, *C. k.* var. *superficialis* on pines, and *C. k.* var. *kunzei* on the other species. Disease is spread by rain splashes but enters the tree via a wound.
Control Avoid damaging the lower trunk. Sterilize pruning tools. Spray with Bordeaux mixture.

Fusarium wilt

Plants affected Perennials, annuals, vegetables, and fruits; most commonly affected are China asters (*Callistephus*), carnations (*Dianthus*), sweet peas (*Lathyrus odoratus*), beans, and peas.
Symptoms Black patches develop on the stems and the foliage; they are sometimes covered with a white or pale pink fungal growth. Roots turn black and die.
Cause Various species of the microscopic fungus *Fusarium*, which are present in the soil or on plant debris, or are sometimes seedborne; they may also be introduced on new stock. They will build up in the soil when the same type of plant is grown in the same site year after year.
Control There is no cure for affected plants. Remove them and the soil in their vicinity, and destroy the plants. Avoid growing susceptible plants in the area. Propagate only from healthy stock; if possible, grow resistant cultivars.

Phytophthora root rots

Plants affected Trees, shrubs, and woody perennials; maples (*Acer*), Lawson cypresses (*Chamaecyparis lawsoniana*), yews (*Taxus*), apples, rhododendrons, raspberries, and heathers are most commonly attacked.
Symptoms Patches of dead tissue may appear on the stem or the trunk with bluish black stains in the tissue beneath; the foliage is sparse and chlorotic. Dieback may follow, and plants may even be killed. See p.652 for other symptoms.

Cause Various species of the fungus *Phytophthora*, which is frequently found in wet or waterlogged soil. Roots are attacked by swimming spores that build up in the soil and in infected plant remains.
Control Always avoid heavy watering, and wherever possible improve soil drainage in the area. Do not overwater peat-based soil mixes. Dig up and destroy all affected plants. Buy only good-quality plants from reputable sources, and choose those that are tolerant or resistant to *Phytophthora*, such as *Tsuga heterophylla* and X *Cupressocyparis leylandii*.

Foot and root rots

Plants affected A wide range, especially petunias and other bedding plants, tomatoes, cucumbers, peas, beans, and young, container-grown plants.
Symptoms The stem bases discolor and shrink inward. This causes the upper parts of the plant to

wilt and die off; the lower leaves will usually show the symptoms first. The roots turn black and break or rot (see p.653).
Cause A range of soil- and water-borne fungi that flourish where growing conditions are not adequately hygienic. The fungi may be introduced through use of unsterilized soil mix and contaminated water, and build up in the soil, especially if susceptible plants are repeatedly grown on the same site.
Control Rotate susceptible plants. Maintain strict hygiene and only use fresh, sterilized soil mix and fresh water. Remove affected plants and the soil in the vicinity of their roots.

Southern blight

Plants affected Many vegetable crops grown in warm climates, including many perennials, annuals, and bulbs, beans, sweet potatoes, and tomatoes.
Symptoms Seedlings show symptoms of damping

off (see p.651). The collar or stem of older plants rots at soil level, and shoots may turn yellow, wilt, and eventually die.
Cause Invasion via the base of the plant by the fungus *Sclerotium rolfsii* (syn. *Corticium rolfsii*); nematode and insect wounds promote infection. Plants in light, sandy soils, well supplied with moisture, are most at risk.
Control Maintain crops well, remove diseased plants and debris, and avoid growing plants in contaminated areas; remove infected residues or bury them deeply.

Boron deficiency

Plants affected Carnations (*Dianthus*), lettuces, celery, root crops, tomatoes, all fruits. The condition is fairly rare.
Symptoms Growing tips die; plants become stunted and bushy. Celery stems develop transverse

cracks and the exposed tissues turn brown; lettuces fail to heart up. Pears become distorted and dimpled with brown, flecked flesh (very similar symptoms to those of the virus disease called stoney pit). Plums are misshapen and may show gumming (see "Pests and diseases" p.442). Strawberries are small and poorly colored. See p.653 for other symptoms.
Cause and control See p.653 for details.

> **See also** "Mealybugs," p.640; "Powdery mildew," p.640; "Rusts," p.641; ; "Contact weedkiller damage," p.642; "Irregular water supply," p.644; "Etiolation," p.647; "Fungal brackets," p.647; "Lightning," p.648; "Smuts," p.651; "Damping off," p.651; "*Armillaria* root rots," p.653; "Oak wilt," p.655; "Fire blight," p.656; "Anthracnose," p.656; "Black vine weevil larvae," p.656; and "Armyworms," p.656.

Stem distortion and abnormal growth

Etiolation

Plants affected Seedlings of all garden plants, and soft-stemmed plants.
Symptoms Stems are elongated and often pale, and the plant may grow toward the available light source, developing a lopsided habit. The leaves are chlorotic, and flowering is often reduced.
Cause Insufficient light, often owing to poor siting of the plant or shading from adjacent plants, buildings, and similar structures. Overcrowded plants are susceptible to the condition.
Control Choose and site plants carefully. Be sure that adequate light is provided for seedlings as soon as germination has occurred. Plants only slightly affected should recover if conditions are improved.

Cutworms

Plants affected Low-growing perennials, annuals, root vegetables, and lettuces.
Symptoms Stem bases and leaves of low-growing plants are visibly gnawed and roots may also be affected. Plants grow slowly, wilt, and may ultimately die.
Cause Caterpillars of various moths (e.g. *Peridroma* and *Agrotis* spp.), usually creamy brown in color and 1¾in (4.5cm) long. At night they feed above soil level.
Control Where damage is seen, search for and destroy the cutworms. Protect young plants with a paper or foil collar pushed into the soil. Keep the growing area free of weeds, which might attract egg-laying moths.

Hormone weedkiller damage

Plants affected Broad-leaved plants (mainly roses, tomatoes, and grapes), and conifers.
Symptoms Small bumps may appear on stems. Leaves are distorted and petioles twisted or spiraled. See pp.644 and 651 for other symptoms.
Cause Contamination by a growth regulator or hormone-type weedkiller, often from a great distance; even minute quantities may cause extensive damage. Sources of trouble are spray drift and the use of contaminated sprayers or watering cans.
Control Apply weedkillers according to the manufacturer's instructions, placing protective barriers around adjacent plants. Keep one sprayer or watering can for use with weedkillers only, or preferably use dribble bars. Store weedkillers away from soil mix, fertilizers, and plants. Plants that have been affected usually grow out of the symptoms.

Crown gall

Plants affected Trees, shrubs (most commonly cane fruits and roses), and woody perennials.
Symptoms Irregular, rounded, often woody swellings occur on or burst from the stem; plant vigor is not seriously affected. See also p.653.
Cause *Agrobacterium tumefaciens* bacteria, that are prevalent in wet soils, enter the plants via surface wounds and cause the cells to proliferate.
Control Avoid plant damage and improve soil drainage. Cut out and destroy all the affected stems.

Forsythia gall

Plants affected Forsythias.
Symptoms Rough, woody, rounded galls form on the stems. They persist from year to year but rarely have adverse effects.
Cause Unknown; possibly bacterial infection.
Control No action is strictly necessary, but the unsightly galled stems may be removed.

Black knot gall

Plants affected Plums, cherries, apricots; many other species.
Symptoms Large galls, generally sausage-shaped, develop on shoots. They may spread toward the crown. Initially brown, they turn black as fruiting bodies develop.
Cause The fungus *Apiosporina morbosa*, which attacks and eventually kills young shoots.
Control Inspect susceptible trees and shrubs each fall for new galls, and prune off. This prevents the formation of fruiting bodies.

Fungal brackets

Plants affected Trees, shrubs, woody perennials.
Symptoms Fungal fruiting bodies, often bracket-shaped, appear on the trunk, crown, or near branch

stubs or other wounds. Short-lived or perennial, they vary in appearance, often according to weather conditions. General growth is slow, and the tree may develop an excess of dead wood and a thin crown. See p.653 for other symptoms.

Cause and control See p.653 for details.

Witches' brooms

Plants affected Trees, mainly hornbeams (*Carpinus*) and birches (*Betula*); shrubs; woody perennials.

Symptoms Dense clusters of small shoots appear on otherwise normal branches. Leaves discolor early and remain small but vigor is not affected.

Cause Fungi (especially *Taphrina*) and mites (for example *Eriophyes*), which cause the mutations.

Control Cut branches back below the affected area.

Lightning

Plants affected Tall trees, especially those in isolation.

Symptoms Bark may be stripped, and a deep furrow may appear down one side, often following the spiral grain. The heartwood may be shattered, weakening the tree and leaving it susceptible to disease. Dead wood increases in the crown, and the upper crown may be killed.

Cause Lightning.

Control Lightning rods may be attached to valuable tall trees.

Mechanical wounding

Plants affected Potentially all plants.

Symptoms A neat-edged wound is visible on the stem or bark. Sap from the injured area may ferment into a slime flux (see "Slime flux/wet wood," p.645), and pathogens entering the wound cause dieback or even death. A healed wound may leave a raised area.

Cause Careless use of garden machinery and tools.

Control Remove severely damaged shoots or stems. Wounds on woody plants should be left alone.

Mice

Plants affected Shrubs and young trees.

Symptoms Bark is gnawed from stems and roots.

Cause Mice.

Control Traps are the most effective solution. See also "Mice, rats, and voles," p.653.

See also "Asparagus beetles," p.638; "Black vine weevils," p.638; "Tent caterpillars," p.640; "Rusts," p.641; "Irregular water supply," p.644; "Fasciation," p.648; "Squirrels," p.651; "Corn rootworms," p.652; "*Nectria* canker," p.655; "Aster yellows," p.655; "Anthracnose," p.656; "Small animals," p.656; and "Deer," p.656.

Flower problems
Discolored flowers

Gray mold/*Botrytis*

Plants affected Trees, shrubs, perennials, annuals, bulbous plants, vegetables, fruits, and indoor plants.

Symptoms A fuzzy, gray fungal growth appears on the flowers in patches, leading to total deterioration. This may later spread to the stems and body of the plant. See also pp.646, 650.

Cause The fungi *Botrytis cinerea* and *B. galanthina*.

Control Do not plant annuals too closely at first. Avoid injury to plants, clear up dead material, and provide good ventilation. Remove affected parts.

Thrips

Plants affected Perennials, often *Achimenes*, *Primula obconica*, *Sinningia*, *Streptocarpus*, African violets (*Saintpaulia*), chrysanthemums, roses, daylilies, peonies, cyclamens, *Pelargonium*, and gladioli.

Symptoms White flecks appear on the petals; loss of pigmentation can be severe. Heavy attacks prevent buds from opening. Leaves discolor to silver-white. Virus symptoms may be present.

Cause Various species of thrips, e.g. gladiolus thrips (*Thrips simplex*) and flower thrips (*Frankliniella tritici*) in gardens, and western flower thrips (*Frankliniella occidentalis*) in gardens and greenhouses. Adults are narrow-bodied, up to $^1/_{16}$in (1.6mm) long, and brown or black; immature nymphs are creamy yellow. They thrive in hot, dry conditions.

Control Water plants regularly and, in greenhouses, maintain a cool, humid atmosphere. Remove and destroy infested flowers. Discard heavily infested plants, especially those showing virus symptoms Predatory mites (*Amblyseius* spp.) are an effective control.

See also "Powdery mildew," p.640; "High temperatures and scorch," p.643; "Low temperatures," p.643; "Azalea galls," p.645; "Iris borers," p.652; "Aster yellows," p.655; and "Fire blight," p.656.

Distorted and eaten flowers

Drought

Plants affected All plants, especially those in light, sandy soils or in containers.

Symptoms The buds fail to develop fully, and the flowers are small and sparse. See also pp.643, 655.

Cause Prolonged or repeated water shortage. Plants in small containers are particularly vulnerable during hot weather, and peat-based soil mixes that are allowed to dry out too much are extremely difficult to rewet. Dry, brown buds on certain plants, e.g. camellias and rhododendrons, are the result of a water shortage the previous year.

Control Water plants regularly, and frequently check those in hot or sunny positions. Mulch, where appropriate, to improve moisture retention. Try to prevent drought rather than treat it: plants exposed to a chronic water shortage are far less likely to recover than those suffering a sudden shortage.

Fasciation

Plants affected All plants, most commonly delphiniums, forsythias, *Daphne*, and *Prunus subhirtella* 'Autumnalis'.

Symptoms Peculiar, broad, flattened flower stems develop. The main stems are also broad and flattened.
Cause In many instances, early damage to the growing point caused by insect, slug, or frost attack, or handling; it may also be due to bacterial infection or genetic malfunction.
Control Fasciation does no harm; affected areas may be either left on the plant or pruned out.

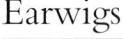

Proliferation

Plants affected Mainly roses, especially the older varieties, but occasionally other ornamentals and fruiting plants.
Symptoms The flower stem grows through the center of the existing flower, and a new flower may form above the first. In some cases several flower buds develop together, surrounded by one set of flower petals.
Cause Early damage to the growing point of the bud, often through frost or insect attack. Where the problem recurs, a virus (see opposite) may be the cause.
Control Severely and repeatedly affected plants, which may be virus infected, should be destroyed. In all other cases, treatment is unnecessary.

Earwigs

Plants affected Shrubs, perennials, and annuals, commonly chrysanthemums, dahlias, and clematis. Also apricot and peach trees.
Symptoms Petals are eaten in summer. See p.550 for other symptoms.
Cause The earwig (*Forficula auricularia*), which is a yellowish brown insect ¾in (2cm) long.
Control See p.638

Spotted cucumber beetles

Plants affected Many late-summer flowers, including *Calendula*, *Coreopsis*, *Cosmos*, *Impatiens*, sweet peas (*Lathyrus odoratus*), dahlias, zinnias, and many other plants.
Symptoms Holes appear in petals. In severe attacks, flower buds are damaged. Beetles may be seen.

Cause Spotted cucumber beetles (*Diabrotica undecimpunctata howardi*), ¼in (6mm) in length. West of the Rockies, the related species *D. u. undecimpunctata* feeds on almost everything except conifers.
Control Spray with insecticidal soaps if the infestation level is intolerable.

Rose chafers

Plants affected Species and hybrid roses. Cultivars of *Rosa rugosa* seem especially vulnerable. Peonies and hollyhocks are occasionally affected.
Symptoms Clusters of beetles are seen on flowers. Holes in petals appear; petals are eaten away; flower buds are eaten and may fail to open.

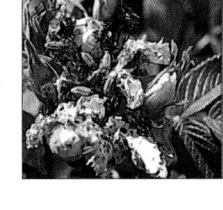

Cause Rose chafer beetles (*Macrodactylus subspinosus*). This grayish beetle, ½in (1cm) long, feeds for four weeks in midsummer. Larvae feed on grass roots and may be mistaken for white grubs of Japanese, June, and Asiatic garden beetles (see p.657).
Control Hand pick and destroy beetles when observed. Cover plants with cheesecloth or screening if pest numbers are high. Control larvae in lawns (see "White grubs," p.657).

Grasshoppers and crickets

Plants affected Many garden plants but mostly flowers on beans, squashes, and other cucurbits.
Symptoms Flowers have holes in petals; entire flowers may be missing.
Cause Daytime feeding of grasshoppers (e.g. *Melanoplus bivittatus*) and nocturnal feeding of crickets (e.g. *Acheta assimilis*).

Control Bait formulated for cutworms and earwigs generally keeps grasshopper and cricket damage to a minimum. Alternatively, pick grasshoppers and crickets off plants by hand.

Japanese beetles

Plants affected Many trees and shrubs, but especially roses and daylilies.
Symptoms Flowers are eaten by beetles, often in groups. Unopened buds are rarely attacked. See also "White grubs," p.652.
Cause Metallic green and brown beetles (*Popillia*

japonica). Beetles measure about ½in (1cm) long, with coppery brown wings and six patches of white hair under the edges of the wings. They feed in daylight. The larvae are a serious pest of lawns (see "White grubs," p.657).
Control Hand-pick beetles off plants and drown them in soapy water, if the numbers are few. Cover plants with screening during periods of intense activity. Traps baited with an attractant are available, but these may attract heavier infestations.

Plant bugs

Plants affected Shrubs and perennials (especially phlox, *Caryopteris*, dahlias, fuchsias, hydrangeas, and chrysanthemums, and asters).

Symptoms Flowers develop unevenly with undersized ray petals. Fuchsia flowers abort completely. Phlox blossoms may be deformed.
Cause In phlox, phlox plant bugs, orange bugs ¼in (6mm) long with red nymphs. See also p.638.
Control See p.638.

Pollen beetles

Plants affected Roses, daffodils, cauliflowers, sprouting broccoli, squashes, turnips, and other garden plants.
Symptoms Small black beetles are found in the flowers in the spring and mid- to late summer.

Cause Pollen beetles (*Meligethes* spp.), which are ¹⁄₁₆in (1.6mm) long and black. The beetles eat some pollen and may remain on cut flowers but otherwise cause little direct damage to the blooms.
Control Pollen beetles cannot be controlled, because vast numbers fly into gardens from canola oil fields, where they breed. It is not advisable to use insecticides – they can cause damage to the petals and harm useful pollinators, e.g. bees. Cut flowers can be freed of the beetles by placing the flowers in a shed or garage with one source of light (e.g. a lamp). The beetles will fly toward the light.

> **See also** "Caterpillars," p.639; "Low temperatures," p.643; "Irregular water supply," p.644; "Azalea galls," p.645; "Etiolation," p.647; "Thrips," p.648; "Birds," p.651; and "Small animals," p.656.

Fruit, berry, and seed problems

High temperatures and scorch

Plants affected Soft fruits, tree fruits, grapes, tomatoes, and apples, especially green-skinned cultivars.
Symptoms Discolored patches develop on the skin, particularly on the uppermost surfaces of fruits, or on the ones that are more highly exposed.
Cause and control See p.643 for details.

Gray mold/*Botrytis*

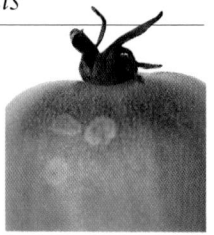

Plants affected Fruiting trees, shrubs, perennials, annuals, and indoor plants. Soft, thin-skinned fruits, e.g. strawberries, raspberries, grapes, and tomatoes, are vulnerable.
Symptoms Normally, a gray, fuzzy, fungal growth develops on a soft, brown rot. The damage spreads rapidly and the whole fruit may collapse. Unripe tomatoes may develop "ghost spot," where a pale green ring appears on the skin but the rest of the fruit colors normally and does not rot (the unaffected parts may be eaten). See also p.646.
Cause and control See p.646 for details.

Powdery mildew

Plants affected Most fruits, commonly grapes, peaches, and gooseberries.
Symptoms Whitish gray fungal patches appear on the skin, often turning brown as they mature. Grapes become hard and cracked, and may fail to swell fully; secondary fungi may invade the fruits. Cracking of gooseberries is uncommon and fungal growth can be rubbed off.
Cause and control Hop mildew (*Sphaerotheca macularis*) attacks fruits; grape mildew (*Uncinula necator*) attacks all parts of the plant. See p.640 for details.

Brown rot

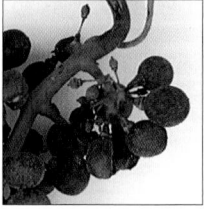

Plants affected Cultivated fruits, especially apples, plums, peaches, nectarines, and pears.
Symptoms Soft brown areas develop on the skin and penetrate throughout the flesh. Concentric rings of creamy white pustules then start to appear on the surface. Affected fruits either fall or may become dry and wizened and remain on the tree.
Cause The fungus *Sclerotinia* (*S. fructicola* and *S. laxa*). The pustules produce spores, and these are then carried by wind or insects to other fruits; infection occurs through wounds or blemishes on the surface of the fruit.
Control Prevent injury to fruits (e.g. that caused by pests), and pick off and destroy those affected.

Tomato late blight

Plants affected Tomatoes, mainly in the open but also in greenhouses.
Symptoms The fruits first develop a brown discoloration and then start to shrink and rot. Even fruits that may have appeared to be healthy when picked may begin to deteriorate rapidly within a few days.
Cause and control See p.642 for details.

Scab

Plants affected Pears, pyracanthas, *Citrus*, *Malus*, and loquats.
Symptoms Blackish brown, scabby patches develop on the skin; a severe attack will leave fruits small and distorted. In some cases cracks may develop, which will make the fruit vulnerable to secondary infections.
Cause and control See p.642 for details.

Calcium deficiency

Plants affected Apples (the condition known as bitter pit), and tomatoes, eggplants, and sweet peppers (referred to as blossom end rot).
Symptoms The flesh of apples is brown-flecked and tastes bitter; the skin is sometimes pitted. Bitter pit may affect fruits on the tree or in storage. Tomato, eggplant, and pepper fruits develop a sunken, brown discoloration at the flower end.
Cause A lack of calcium, possibly combined with other nutritional imbalances, resulting from an irregular or poor supply of moisture to the plant's roots, preventing adequate calcium uptake. Groups of cells that are deprived of calcium collapse and become discolored.
Control Avoid very acidic growing media. Apply lime according to soil test results. Water regularly and, where feasible, mulch plants. The foliage of tomato plants may be sprayed with a solution of calcium chloride every ten days from early summer until harvesting.

Plum curculio

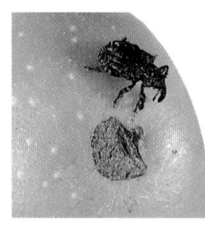

Plants affected All stone fruits; apples, pears, and quinces.
Symptoms Beetles are seen on fruit, leaves, or petals. Small crescent-shaped scars appear where the egg was laid earlier in the season by the female. Gray larvae with black heads may be visible within the fruit.
Cause Plum curculio (*Conotrachelus nenuphar*), a dark beetle 1/4in (6mm) long, with four bumps on its wings and a down-curved snout. Adults feed on fruit, leaves, and petals, leaving them open to attack by brown rot (see left).
Control Gather fruit as it drops. Shake branches over a sheet and gather weevils as they drop.

Shanking of grapes

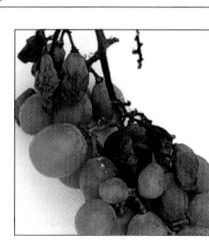

Plants affected Grapes.
Symptoms Berry stalks wither. Berries have a watery or sour taste; black varieties turn red, and white ones remain translucent. They may remain on the bunch but shrivel up and are vulnerable to disease, e.g. gray mold/*Botrytis* (see left).
Cause Heavy cropping, either over- or under-watering, or stagnant soil conditions.
Control Cut out withered berries, and regularly apply a foliar fertilizer. Decrease the crop for a few years and try to improve general soil conditions.

Irregular water supply

Plants affected Potentially all fruiting plants, but particularly noticeable on tomatoes and eggplants.
Symptoms Fruits are misshapen and undersized, and a sudden availability of water after a drought may cause their skin and flesh to crack, leaving them vulnerable to diseases that cause rotting. See p.644 for other symptoms.
Cause and control See p.644 for details.

Viruses

Plants affected Pears, cucumbers, melons, squashes, tomatoes, strawberries, and raspberries.
Symptoms Fruits may be undersized, distorted, discolored, or grouped in rosettes. Cucumber mosaic virus produces warty, distorted cucumber, melon, and squash fruits that are blotched dark green and yellow; pear stony pit virus produces distorted and pitted pear fruits with patches of dead, stony cells. See also p.642.
Cause and control See p.642 for details.

Hormone weedkiller damage

Plants affected All fruits, but commonly only tomatoes.
Symptoms Plum-shaped tomatoes form. Although they ripen normally and are safe to eat, they may taste unpleasant and be hollow. Fruits that have formed before contamination occurs are not usually affected. See p.644 for other symptoms.
Cause and control See p.644 for details.

Wasps

Plants affected Grapes, plums, pears, apples, and figs.
Symptoms Large cavities are eaten in ripe fruits in late summer; wasps may be seen feeding.
Cause Wasps, which are attracted to fruits initially damaged by birds.
Control Protect fruits by placing bags made of muslin or pantyhose over the clusters well before damage is likely to begin. Harvest ripening fruit promptly, and clean up fallen fruit. Many wasps serve a beneficial role as predators of other insects.

Birds

Plants affected Fruits, vegetables, and flowers.
Symptoms Peck marks leave ripe fruits susceptible to infection from brown rot (see p.650); soft fruits are often eaten. Vegetables, seedlings, flowers, and buds may be pecked.
Cause Blackbirds, starlings, and other birds.
Control Either net the plants at fruiting time or grow them in a permanent birdproof cage.

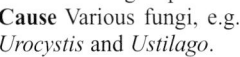

Codling moths

Plants affected Apples, pears, apricots, peaches, walnuts (*Juglans*).
Symptoms Holes are tunneled in ripe fruits.
Cause Caterpillars of the codling moth (*Cydia pomonella*), which feed in the core of fruit; when mature, each caterpillar makes a frass-filled tunnel to the outside of the fruit.
Control Hang pheromone traps from late spring to midsummer to catch males, reducing egg fertilization. Traps indicate when the males are flying, so that sprays may be timed to control the caterpillars as they hatch.

Apple maggots

Plants affected Apples, hawthorns.
Symptoms Brown tunnels wind through the fruit. The fruit center may become a soft, brown pulp. Larvae may be seen in or on fruit. The fruit surface is distorted and pitted. The fruit may fall early.
Cause Larvae of the apple maggot (*Rhagoletis pomonella*), a black fly 1/4in (6mm) long, with zig-zag black bands on its wings. The larvae emerge from the fallen fruit and pupate in the soil over winter, emerging as adults early the following summer.
Control Hang three red sticky sphere traps per tree from early to midsummer to trap the flies. Pick up and dispose of fallen fruit as soon as it is seen on the ground.

Smuts

Plants affected Sweet corn, *Anemone*, *Trollius*, and violets (*Viola*).
Symptoms Round or elliptical pale swellings develop and then rupture, releasing powdery black masses of fungal spores.
Cause Various fungi, e.g. *Urocystis* and *Ustilago*.
Control Destroy affected plants or plant parts; infection may recur. Grow resistant cultivars.

Squirrels

Plants affected Young trees.
Symptoms Bark, buds, ripening fruits, and nuts are eaten.
Cause Squirrels.
Control Traps work only if used over a wide area.

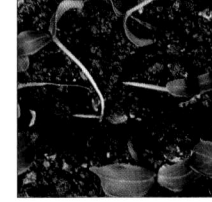

See also "Sowbugs," p.638; "Millipedes," p.638; "Leaf tiers and rollers," p.641; "Potassium deficiency," p.643; "Japanese beetles," p.649; "Corn rootworms," p.652; "Boron deficiency," p.653; "Drought," p.655; and "Small animals," p.656.

Root and tuber problems

Waterlogging

Plants affected Potentially all plants.
Symptoms Some roots may rot off completely. Those remaining are frequently blackened with a peeling outer surface. The first visible symptom is usually wilting leaves. See also pp.644 and 655.
Cause Excessive water levels in the growing medium, owing to factors such as poor soil structure, compaction, impeded drainage, or overwatering.

Control Where feasible, improve the structure and drainage of the soil and, if necessary, choose plants that are likely to survive in wet conditions. Check that drainage holes for container-grown plants are adequate and that flow through them is not impeded. Regular use of a foliar fertilizer during the growing season may help stimulate growth, replacing waterlogged roots.

Damping off

Plants affected The seedlings of all plants.
Symptoms Affected roots darken and rot off, causing the seedling to collapse and die. The disease often starts at one end of the seed tray, spreading rapidly to the other. A fluffy fungal growth may appear on the soil mix as well as on dead seedlings. See p.655 for other symptoms.
Cause Various fungi, such as *Pythium ultimum* and some *Phytophthora*, that are soil- or waterborne and attack seedlings via the roots or the base of the stem. They flourish in moist and unhygienic conditions.
Control There is no effective control once the disease is established, so it must be prevented.

Sow seed thinly, improve ventilation, maintain strict hygiene, and avoid overwatering. Use only sterilized media and clean trays and pots.

Root-knot nematodes

Plants affected Many garden plants, including fruit trees, vegetables, and ornamentals. Plants growing in greenhouses are also susceptible.
Symptoms Galls or swellings appear on the roots or tubers. Overall growth is stunted, and the plant may wilt, yellow, and sometimes even be killed.
Cause Root-knot nematodes (*Meloidogyne* spp.), which are thin, transparent, and only $^1/_{32}$in (0.5mm) long. The larvae penetrate the roots.
Control Destroy all affected plants. Rotate vegetable crops; choose resistant plants.

Black vine weevil larvae

Plants affected Shrubs, perennials, annuals, bulbous plants, and indoor plants; most commonly, begonias, cyclamens, fuchsias, *Impatiens*, primroses (*Primula*), *Sedum*, and strawberries. Yews (*Taxus*), rhododendrons, and container-grown plants are particularly vulnerable.
Symptoms The outer tissues of seedlings and cuttings are gnawed from the stem bases, and roots are chewed below ground level. Plants grow slowly, have a tendency to wilt, and then finally collapse and die.
Cause and control See p.656 for details.
See also p.656; and p.638 for information on damage caused to leaves by adult black vine weevils.

White grubs

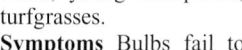

Plants affected Spring- and summer-flowering bulbs; young transplants; turfgrasses.
Symptoms Bulbs fail to grow, or shrivel and die; transplants wilt and die. Grubs are visible in soil and roots, especially when turf can be pulled up almost like a carpet.
Cause White grubs of several species of beetles, especially June beetles (*Phyllophaga* spp.), Japanese beetles (*Popillia japonica*), and chafer bugs (*Macrodactylus subspinosus*), about $^1/4$in (6mm) long, feeding on the roots; sometimes found on reclaimed lawn areas. See also p.657.
Control Drench the area with beneficial nematodes. See p.657 for related problems in lawns.

Cutworms

Plants affected Low-growing perennials, annuals, root vegetables, and lettuces.
Symptoms Cavities appear in root crops, and taproots may be severed, causing plants to wilt and die. See p.647 for other symptoms.
Cause The caterpillars of various moths (e.g. *Peridroma* and *Agrotis*), usually creamy brown in color and up to $1^3/4$in (4.5cm) in length. They eat roots and the outer tissues of stem bases.
Control Search for and destroy the cutworms. Keep garden beds free of weeds.

Iris borers

Plants affected Irises, particularly rhizomatous types such as tall bearded and *Iris tectorum*, but also *I. sibirica* and Louisiana irises.
Symptoms Destroyed rhizomes lead to collapsed plants. Sawtooth edges appear on leaves in late spring/early summer. As borers feed, foliage gradually yellows. Flowers in bud turn brown and watery.
Cause Larvae of a small, gray moth (*Macronoctua onusta*), which lays eggs on the old foliage in late summer. The following spring, they hatch and tunnel into the leaves a few inches above the ground. Fully grown borers are about $1^1/4$in (3cm) long, white with a reddish brown head. Their tunneling often introduces iris soft rot (see p.654).
Control Clean up in fall or early spring to remove eggs. Dig up and destroy infested rhizomes. Drench rhizomes with beneficial nematodes. Pinch fans to kill borers as they move down the leaves.

Carrot rust flies

Plants affected Members of the carrot family.
Symptoms Rusty brown tunnels are bored under the outer skin of mature roots. Small plants develop discolored foliage and may eventually die.
Cause Creamy yellow maggots, larvae of the carrot rust fly (*Psila rosae*), which feed in the surface tissues of the larger roots; in fall they may bore deeper. They are slender, legless, and up to $^1/2$in (1cm) long.
Control Enclose susceptible plants within a clear plastic fence at least 24in (60cm) high, to exclude the low-flying female flies. Sow seed after late spring to avoid early damage. Eliminate wild hosts nearby, such as Queen Anne's lace. Lift carrots for storage in fall to limit damage.

Cabbage root maggots

Plants affected Radishes and a wide range of brassicas (including broccoli, cabbages, cauliflowers, Brussels sprouts, turnips, and rutabagas).
Symptoms Plants grow slowly and wilt; seedlings and transplants die; tunnels appear in root crops.
Cause Root-feeding larvae of the fly *Delia radicum*, white, legless maggots up to $^3/8$in (9mm) long. Several generations occur between midspring and midfall, causing damage mainly to young plants.
Control Place collars of aluminum foil or half of a frozen juice can, about 5in (12cm) in diameter, around the base of transplanted brassicas to prevent the female flies from laying eggs in the soil. Both transplanted brassicas and seed rows can be protected with row cover during active periods

Corn rootworms

Plants affected Corn
Symptoms Poor growth, poor crops (if the attack is bad). Larvae may be visible eating the roots.

Cause The larvae of *Diabrotica*, threadlike, white, $^1/2$in (1cm) long worms that burrow through roots and leave brown tunnels. The eggs hatch in late spring, and the larvae feed on corn roots. The larvae pupate in midsummer and then emerge as beetles in late summer to feed on corn silks and pollen. After laying eggs in the soil of cornfields, the beetles die at first frost.
Control Rotate crops regularly to avoid growing corn in infested soil. Rotating corn crops with soy beans, alfalfa, or cereal crops may prove particularly effective.

Clubroot

Plants affected The family Cruciferae (cabbage family), especially certain brassicas (for example, cabbages, Brussels sprouts, and rutabagas and radishes), and some ornamentals, including candytufts (*Iberis*), wallflowers (*Cheiranthus*), and stocks (*Matthiola*).
Symptoms Roots are swollen and distorted; plants grow slowly and are often discolored; they wilt in hot weather. Plants will eventually die. See p.642 for other symptoms.
Cause The slime mold *Plasmodiophora brassicae*, which thrives in poorly drained, acidic soils, and may also be found on manure and plant debris. It is easily spread on boots and tools, and the spores remain viable for 20 years or more. Weeds susceptible to this disease (e.g. shepherd's purse and wild mustard) may be a source of infection.
Control Remove and discard affected plants. Keep the area free of weeds, improve drainage, and lime the soil. Raise new plants in soil-based media to encourage root development.

Phytophthora root rots

Plants affected Trees, shrubs, and woody perennials; commonly maples (*Acer*), yews (*Taxus*), Lawson cypresses (*Chamaecyparis lawsoniana*), apples, rhododendrons, raspberries, and heathers.
Symptoms The larger roots die back from the stem or trunk, although the fine roots may appear perfectly healthy; affected roots usually turn black. See pp.646 and 655 for other symptoms.
Cause Various species of the fungus *Phytophthora*, often found in wet or waterlogged soil. The roots of plants are attacked by swimming spores that build up both in the soil and within infected plant remains.
Control Avoid heavy watering and improve soil drainage. Dig up and destroy affected plants. Buy plants from reputable sources and choose those that are tolerant or resistant, e.g. *Tsuga heterophylla* and x *Cupressocyparis leylandii*.

Foot and root rots

Plants affected A wide range, especially petunias and other bedding plants, tomatoes, cucumbers, peas, beans, and young, container-grown plants.
Symptoms The roots turn black and break or rot. See p.646 for details of other symptoms.
Cause A range of soil- and water-borne fungi that flourish where growing conditions are unhygienic. The fungi are often introduced in unsterilized soil mix and standing water, and will build up in the soil over several years if susceptible plants are repeatedly grown on the same site.
Control Rotate susceptible plants. Maintain strict hygiene, and use only fresh, sterilized media and clean water. Remove affected plants and the soil in the vicinity of their roots.

Crown gall

Plants affected Trees and shrubs (most commonly cane fruits and roses).
Symptoms Irregular, often woody swellings develop on or burst from the roots, and occasionally the whole root system is distorted into a single large swelling. See p.647 for other symptoms.
Cause The bacterium *Agrobacterium tumefaciens*, prevalent in wet soils. The bacteria enter the plant through wounds made on the surface and cause cells to proliferate.
Control Avoid damaging plants and improve soil drainage. Cut out and destroy any affected stems in order to prevent secondary infection.

Armillaria root rots

Plants affected Trees, shrubs, climbers, and some woody perennials; most commonly affected are fruit and nut trees on the West Coast.
Symptoms A creamy-white mycelium develops under the bark at the base of the trunk or stem. Sometimes it also extends upward; tough black rhizomorphs (i.e. fungal strands) appear. In fall, fruiting bodies may develop in clusters on underground roots, at the base of the trunk, and occasionally at some height from the ground; they die back after the first frost. Resin exudes from cracks in the bark of conifers. Prolific flowering or fruiting may occur shortly before death.
Cause The fungus *Armillaria* (principally *A. mellea*) spread either by rhizomorph movement from an infected plant or stump, or through root contact.
Control Destroy affected plants, stumps, and as much of the root system as possible; if necessary, have the stump ground out. Avoid the more susceptible plants, choosing those showing resistance, e.g. yews (*Taxus*), *Cornus*, and beeches (*Fagus*).

Fungal brackets

Plants affected Mainly trees, and especially mature or overmature specimens, but also shrubs and woody perennials.
Symptoms Fungal fruiting bodies, often bracket-shaped, may appear above ground, following the line of the roots; they are attached to the roots by tiny fungal threads. They vary in appearance, often according to weather conditions. The roots may become hollow and eventually die, making the tree extremely unstable in the ground. Stems are also affected (see p.647).
Cause Various fungi, e.g. *Meripilus* or *Ganoderma*.
Control Seek professional advice, particularly if the tree poses a potential hazard. Removal of fruiting bodies will not prevent further internal decay, but it does reduce the chances of spread to other trees.

Verticillium wilt

Plants affected A large number of garden and greenhouse plants.
Symptoms The roots deteriorate and die, and if cut longitudinally in the early stages of degeneration they may show a central, vascular column of brown discoloration.
Cause and control See p.645 for details.

Fusarium wilt

Plants affected Perennials, annuals, vegetables, and fruits; most commonly affected are China asters (*Callistephus*), carnations (*Dianthus*), sweet pea (*Lathyrus odoratus*), beans, and peas.
Symptoms Roots turn black and die.
Cause and control See p.646 for details.

Mice, rats, and voles

Plants affected Shrubs, young trees, crocus corms, seedlings of peas and beans, seeds, vegetables, and fruits kept in storage.
Symptoms The outer layer of stems and roots is gnawed. Seeds, seedlings, corms, vegetables, and fruits are eaten.
Cause Mice, rats, and voles.
Control Traps provide the best solution.

Boron deficiency

Plants affected Roots of carrots, parsnips, rutabagas, turnips, and beets. The condition is fairly rare.
Symptoms The roots are of a poor shape and texture, and are grayish in color. They may split longitudinally and sometimes contain cavities. A brown discoloration known as brown heart may occur in the lower sections, often in concentric rings; it is found mainly in turnips and rutabagas and makes them fibrous, with poor taste. Beets show internal discoloration and may develop cankers. See p.647 for symptoms on stems.
Cause A lack of boron in the soil, or an inability of the plant to take up the trace element owing to unsuitable growing conditions. Most common on very alkaline or heavily limed soils, those that have been very dry, and those where the boron has been leached out. It rarely affects greenhouse plants.
Control Maintain correct soil moisture levels and avoid excessive liming. Before introducing a susceptible plant to a problem site, apply borax a1oz/20sq yd (35g/20sq m), mixing with horticultural sand for easy and accurate application. Apply trace elements.

See also "Aphids," p.639; "Mealybugs," p.640; "Slugs," "Wireworms," below; "Onion maggots," p.654; "Striped cucumber beetles," p.655, and "Fungus gnats or sciarid flies," p.656.

Potato tuber problems

Slugs

Plants affected Potatoes.
Symptoms Circular holes are bored in the outside of potato tubers, and extensive cavities appear in the interior, during late summer.
Cause Slugs, although white grubs and cutworms may cause very similar damage.
Control Scatter slug bait. Grow less susceptible cultivars; harvest tubers as soon as mature.
See also "Controlling slugs and snails," p.636.

Wireworms

Plants affected Potatoes and other root crops, seedlings, perennials, annuals, and bulbous plants.
Symptoms Tunnels up to ⅛in (3mm) in diameter, superficially similar to those made by slugs, are bored through root crops. Underground parts of other plants are damaged. Small plants wilt and die.
Cause The slender, stiff-bodied, yellowish orange larvae of click beetles (e.g. *Limonius* spp.), which feed on roots and stem

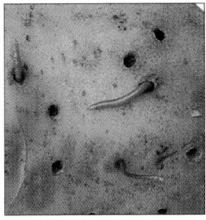

bases. They are up to 1in (2.5cm) long, with three pairs of short legs at the head end. The problem mainly occurs when grassland is brought into cultivation. **Control** Search for and destroy the wireworms. Lift root crops as soon as they are mature. The pest usually disappears once the ground has been cultivated for about five years.

Common potato scab

Plants affected Potatoes.
Symptoms Raised, scabby patches develop on the skin of the tubers, and these sometimes rupture.

Damage may be only superficial, but in some instances the affected tuber becomes extensively cracked and badly disfigured. The flesh of the potato is not generally damaged and may be safely consumed.
Cause *Streptomyces scabies*, a bacterium-like but mycelium-producing organism, common in soils that are sandy and light with a high lime content, and those only recently cultivated. Disease development is most common during hot, dry summers, and when soil moisture levels are low.

Control Improve soil texture and avoid liming; water regularly. Do not plant potatoes on soil that has recently been used for brassicas. Some varieties show a degree of resistance, such as 'Menominee', 'Ontario', 'Cayuga', and 'Seneca'.

> **See also** "Millipedes," p.638; "Colorado potato beetles," p.639; "Tomato/potato late blight," p.642.

Bulb, corm, and rhizome problems

Storage rots

Plants affected Bulbs and corms, especially if damaged or poorly stored.
Symptoms Discolored, sometimes sunken patches develop on the surface of the bulb, or beneath the outer scales or skin. A fungal growth may appear on the patches, spreading

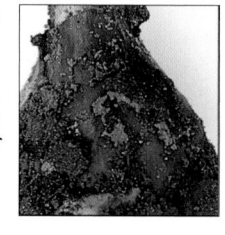

through bulb tissues, which become light and dry.
Cause A range of fungi. Infection is often restricted to a very few closely related bulbs or corms, and may affect both those in the ground and those in storage. Temperatures that are too low or too high, and overly damp conditions, encourage the disease.
Control Store and plant only healthy bulbs, and avoid injury to them. Store in suitable conditions, and immediately remove any that show signs of deterioration. Dusting them with sulfur may prevent attack.

Narcissus basal rot

Plants affected Daffodils.
Symptoms After about one month in storage, the basal plate of the bulb becomes soft and brown, then rots. The deterioration spreads to the inner scales, which turn dark brown, and a pale pink, fluffy, fungal growth may then appear between the scales and on the basal plate. The bulb gradually dries out and becomes mummified. Bulbs that become infected in the ground may, if not lifted, rot away in the soil. In some cases, foliage symptoms of yellowing and wilting occur first.

Cause The soilborne fungus *Fusarium oxysporium* f. *narcissi*, which infects bulbs through the basal plate; the fungus is encouraged by high soil temperatures. If the infected bulb is not lifted, it may infect adjacent bulbs. Stored bulbs that are infected but do not show symptoms also act as a source of infection when planted.
Control Check bulbs for signs of disease before storing, and discard any that are damaged.

Iris soft rot

Plants affected Irises.
Symptoms The base of outer leaves decays and the rot then spreads into the rhizome, attacking the youngest parts first. The infected area is reduced to a foul-smelling mass.
Cause The bacterium *Erwinia carotovora* var. *carotovora*, which thrives in waterlogged soil. The bacteria enter the rhizomes through wounds or other damaged areas.
Control Check all rhizomes for any kind of damage before planting, and be extra careful to avoid injuring them. Plant the rhizomes shallowly, and always in good, well-drained soil. Take steps to make sure that iris borers (see p.652), which may be the cause of injury to rhizomes, are kept under control. The prompt removal of any rotting tissue may help check the problem temporarily, but in the long term the entire rhizome is best discarded.

Onion white rot

Plants affected Onions, shallots, leeks, garlic.
Symptoms The base of the bulb and the roots are covered in a fluffy, white, fungal growth in which hard black sclerotia (fungal bodies) are embedded.

Cause The fungus *Sclerotium cepivorum*. Sclerotia in the soil will remain viable for at least seven years and, when stimulated by the presence of new host plant roots, they will germinate, causing infection again.
Control Dig up and discard affected plants as soon as possible. Do not grow susceptible crops on the affected site for at least eight years.

Onion maggots

Plants affected Onions; also shallots, garlic, leeks.
Symptoms Poor growth; the outer leaves turn yellow; maggots found in the bulb.
Cause The root- and bulb-feeding larvae of the onion fly (*Delia antiqua*), white maggots that are up to ³⁄₈in (9mm) long.
Control Carefully lift and discard infested plants. Seedlings are less tolerant of damage than sets. Clean up remains of plants in fall.

> **See also** "Slugs and snails," p.638; "Millipedes," p.638; "Squirrels," p.651; "Mice, rats, and voles," p.653; and "Small animals," p.656.

Whole-plant problems

Drought

Plants affected All plants, especially those that are young, container-grown, or in light, sandy soils.
Symptoms Fall coloration develops early and defoliation, followed by dieback, may occur. Plants wilt and growth is stunted. Flowering and fruit set may decrease markedly. Fruits may be small, sometimes distorted, and of a poor texture. See pp.643 and 648 for other symptoms.
Cause Prolonged or repeated drought due to inadequate or unavailable soil moisture; excessive water loss from the leaves of plants on exposed sites; injured or restricted roots; or soil compaction. Plants in small containers are vulnerable during hot weather, and peat-based soil mixes that dry out too much are extremely difficult to rewet. Dry brown buds on certain plants, such as camellias, rhododendrons, and azaleas are the result of a water shortage the previous year during the period of flower bud initiation.
Control Water plants regularly when in active growth, and frequently check those in hot or sunny positions. Mulch, where appropriate, to improve moisture retention. Drought is more easily prevented than treated; plants exposed to chronic water shortage are less likely to recover once adequate water is supplied or temperatures fall than those suffering acute (sudden) shortage.

Low temperatures

Plants affected Trees, shrubs, perennials, annuals, bulbous plants, vegetables, fruits, indoor plants; seedlings and young plants are especially vulnerable.
Symptoms The leaves are sometimes bleached, and brown, dry patches develop; evergreen foliage may turn brown and die. Brown, rotten patches develop on petals, especially on exposed flower heads. Frost injury causes leaves to pucker and petals to wither or discolor. In some cases, whole flowers may be killed. See pp.643 and 645 for other symptoms.
Cause and control See p.643 for details.

Waterlogging

Plants affected Potentially all plants, but especially those grown in containers.
Symptoms Leaves may turn yellow. Bark peels off smaller branches. Roots may rot off completely and plants tend to wilt. Remaining roots often partially blacken, and their outer surface peels away easily. See also pp. 644 and 651.
Cause Excessive water levels in the growing medium, owing to poor soil structure, compaction, impeded drainage, or overwatering.
Control Where feasible, improve the structure and drainage of the soil and, if necessary, choose plants that are most likely to survive in wet conditions. Check that container-grown plants have adequate flow through drainage holes. The regular application of a foliar fertilizer during the growing season may help stimulate growth, replacing waterlogged roots.

Damping off

Plants affected The seedlings of all plants are potential hosts.
Symptoms The seedlings collapse and die as their roots darken and rot off; the disease often attacks seedlings at one end of a seed tray, rapidly spreading to the 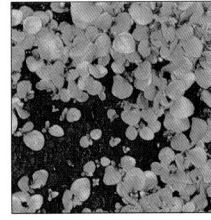 other. A fluffy fungal growth may appear both on the soil mix and on any dead seedlings. See p.566 for other symptoms.
Cause Various fungi, such as *Pythium ultimum* and some *Phytophthora*, that are soil- or waterborne and attack the seedlings via the roots or stem bases. They flourish in moist and unhygienic conditions.
Control There is no control once the disease is established, so it must be prevented. Sow seed thinly, improve ventilation around seedlings, maintain strict hygiene, and avoid overwatering. Always use sterilized media, clean water, and scrupulously clean seed trays and pots.

Nectria canker

Plants affected Woody perennials, shrubs, trees, especially apples, flowering and fruiting crabapples (*Malus*), beeches (*Fagus*), poplars (*Populus*), *Sorbus*, mulberries (*Morus*), and hawthorns (*Crataegus*).
Symptoms Small areas of bark, often close to a bud or wound, darken and sink inward; the bark cracks, forming loose, flaky, concentric rings. Enlarged cankers restrict nutrient and water flow and lead to stem and leaf deterioration. In extreme cases the entire shoot becomes ringed and dies back. White pustules appear in summer, red pustules in winter.
Cause Spores of the fungus *Nectria galligena* and *N. cinnabarina* attack and infect wounds caused by pruning, leaf fall, irregular growth patterns, frost and cold, scale insects, and woolly aphids.
Control Prune affected branches or, on larger limbs, remove the cankered area. Ensure good tree health by regular watering, fertilizing, and good pest and disease control.

Striped cucumber beetles

Plants affected Trees and shrubs; cucumber, melons, winter squashes.
Symptoms Leaf margins and roots are nibbled, holes appear in leaves and flowers. Vines may wilt, at first only during the day, later permanently.
Cause Yellow-and-black striped cucumber beetles (*Acalymma vittata*), ¼in (6mm) long, feed on pollen and petals of many flowers in spring, and later on leaves, flowers, and stems of cucurbits (e.g. melons and cucumbers). They may transmit bacterial wilt of cucurbits. Slender white larvae, ⅓in (8mm) long, feed on roots of cucurbits and sometimes on pumpkin and melon rinds lying directly on the soil.
Control Cover young plants with mesh-topped boxes or row covers until vines begin to run. Grow resistant cultivars.

Oak wilt

Plants affected Most species of oak, but especially those in the red oak group: black (*Quercus velutina*), red (*Q. rubra*), pin (*Q. palustris*), and scarlet (*Q. coccinea*).
Symptoms Leaves at the top of the tree become dull green and turn brown along the edges. They may also curl and wilt. The discoloration moves rapidly down the crown, and the tree may die in a single summer. Sapwood is usually stained black or brown.
Cause The fungus *Ceratocystis fagacearum*, spread by root grafts, borers, mites, and bark beetles.
Control Grow susceptible trees in isolation so root grafts cannot occur. Prune in late summer only. Sterilize pruning equipment between cuts. Grow oaks from the less-susceptible white oak group.

Phytophthora root rots

Plants affected Trees, shrubs, and woody perennials; all maples (*Acer*), Lawson cypress (*Chamaecyparis lawsoniana*), apples, yew (*Taxus*), rhododendrons, raspberries, and heathers.
Symptoms Patches of dead tissue may appear on the stem or the trunk with bluish black stains in the tissue beneath. Foliage is sparse. Dieback may follow, and plants may die. See pp.646 and 652 for other symptoms.
Cause Various species of the fungus *Phytophthora*, which is frequently found in wet soil. Roots are attacked by swimming spores.
Control Avoid heavy watering and improve soil drainage in affected areas. See also p.652.

Aster yellows

Plants affected China aster (*Callistephus chinensis*) is most affected, but a wide range of plants is attacked.
Symptoms Leaves turn pale yellow, plants become distorted, and flowers change color, often turning green, then brown. Aster leafhoppers may be seen on the underside of low-growing foliage. Plants do not die.
Cause A mycoplasma-like organism spread by the aster leafhopper (*Macrosteles quadrilineatus*) from infected plants. Aster leafhoppers, also called sixspotted leafhoppers, are greenish yellow with six black spots on the front of the head, and measure about ⅛in (3mm) long.
Control Pull up and dispose of infected plants as soon as seen.

Fire blight

Plants affected Members of the family Rosaceae that bear pome fruits, mainly pears, apples, cotoneasters, hawthorns (*Crataegus*), and some *Sorbus*.
Symptoms Blossoms wilt and adjacent stem areas discolor. The foliage turns blackish brown, shrivels, and dies, but remains on the stem. Dark greenish brown cankers then form on the branches, producing a bacterial ooze varying in color between yellowish brown and white, depending on the host. The inner surface of the bark and the wood beneath it may be stained brown. Affected limbs die and the tree is killed. See p.642 for other symptoms.
Cause The bacterium *Erwinia amylovora*, which is produced from the cankers and attacks via the blossoms. It is carried by wind, rain splash, insects, and pollen grains.
Control Remove affected plants or prune out affected areas 24in (60cm) past the damage; disinfect the saw between cuts and before using on another tree. Be sure that no staining remains on inner wood.

Anthracnose

Plants affected Maples (*Acer*), ashes (*Fraxinus*), elms (*Ulmus*), oaks (*Quercus*), sycamores (*Platanus*), walnuts (*Juglans*), and many other trees and shrubs.
Symptoms Small brown spots appear on the leaves enlarging into circular or irregular patches, often with a paler margin; leaves turn yellow, curl, and fall early; the patches may proceed along the veins. Shoots may develop brown sunken areas.
Cause A number of fungi (e.g. *Apiognomonia errabunda*, the maple anthracnose), all of which may be different forms of the same fungus.
Control Remove infected leaves in the fall. Spray with Bordeaux mix in spring.

Black vine weevil larvae

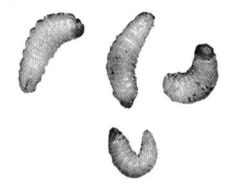

Plants affected Many shrubs, perennials, annuals, bulbous plants, and indoor plants; also, fuchsias, begonias, cyclamens, *Impatiens*, primroses (*Primula*), *Sedum*, and strawberries are commonly affected. Yews (*Taxus*), rhododendrons, and container-grown plants are particularly vulnerable.
Symptoms Plants grow slowly, wilt, collapse, and die. The outer tissues of seedlings and cuttings are gnawed from the stems below ground.
Cause The plump white larvae of the beetle *Otiorhynchus sulcatus*, which are up to ½in (1cm)

long and slightly curved, with brown heads and no legs. The brown-black adults, ⅓in (8mm) long, lay tiny white eggs in spring and summer, and the damage from the larvae occurs from fall to spring. Damage from adult weevils is minor.
Control Maintain good hygiene to avoid providing shelters for the adults. Drench the soil around infested plants with beneficial nematodes (*Heterorhabditis* spp.) in mid-and late summer. Use trap boards to attract the weevils, then gather and destroy hiding weevils.
See also "Black vine weevils," p.638.

Fungus gnats, or sciarid flies

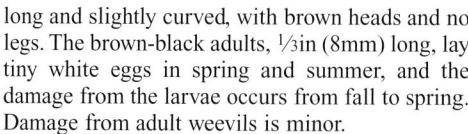

Plants affected Plants grown under cover. Seedlings and cuttings are more susceptible than established plants.
Symptoms Both seedlings and cuttings fail to grow; grayish brown flies run over the soil surface or fly among the plants. Larvae may be visible.
Cause The larvae of fungus gnats or sciarid flies (*Bradysia* spp.), which feed mainly on dead roots and leaves but may also attack young roots and stems. They are slender, white-bodied maggots up to ¼in (6mm) long with black heads. The adult flies are of a similar length. They do not cause any problems on healthy, established plants, but are a nuisance in the house.
Control Keep greenhouses neat, and remove dead leaves and flowers from the soil surface to avoid providing shelters for gnats and flies. Use sticky yellow traps suspended above plants to trap the adult flies. *Bacillus thuringiensis israeliensis* may be drenched onto infested soil to control the larvae.

Armyworms

Plants affected Most vegetables, but especially corn. This is chiefly a pest of farm crops but will eat almost any plant. Lawns can be severely damaged.
Symptoms Leaves and fruits are nibbled. The entire crop or lawn may be eaten by an army of caterpillars.
Cause Larvae of armyworm moths (*Pseudaletia unipuncta*), a green caterpillar, turning dark brown with stripes, up to 1½in (4cm) long. The adult is a brownish gray moth.
Control There are many natural predators, including skunks and toads. Apply *Bacillus thuringiensis* if required. Remove and destroy caterpillars if practical to do so.

Ants

Plants affected Most annuals and low-growing perennials and woody plants.
Symptoms Plants grow slowly and have a tendency to wilt. Heaps of soil may also appear, sometimes even burying some low-growing plants.
Cause Various species of black, yellow, or reddish

brown ants (e.g. *Lasius* and *Formica* spp.), which disturb the roots as they construct their nests. They do not usually feed on the plants but do spread aphids to uninfected plants.
Control Ants are often abundant and impossible to eliminate; as much as possible their presence should be tolerated, but set out traps containing boron if plants are being killed.

Small animals

Plants affected Many vegetables from seedlings to mature plants; trees and shrubs, bulbs, both dormant and in flower.
Symptoms Rows of seedlings, buds, branchlets are eaten and bark is stripped off, especially during cold weather. Bulbs are dug up and eaten, vegetables and fruit (especially tomatoes) have bites taken out of them, corn is partly stripped and eaten. Other low-growing plants may be grazed down to ground level.
Cause Woodchucks, raccoons, squirrels, rabbits.
Control Erect wire netting at least 3ft (1m) high and sunk another 12in (30cm) below ground level. Do not make it too tight or raccoons can climb over it. Alternatively, protect individual susceptible plants. Cover the base of trees with wire netting or spiral tree-guard collars. Do not feed squirrels in winter.

Deer

Plants affected Most plants, especially trees, shrubs (including roses), and herbaceous plants. Some plants are not normally eaten and are the subject of many localized publications.
Symptoms Shoots and leaves are eaten; tree bark is rubbed, frayed, and eaten.
Cause White-tailed and other species of deer, eating shoots, bark, and leaves. Bark is frayed when males mark trees with their scent glands or rub the velvet from their antlers.
Control Erect wire mesh fences at least 6ft (2m) high, or place wire netting around stems and trunks. Repellent sprays or scaring devices, such as hanging tin cans, provide only short-term protection.

See also "Clubroot," p.642; "Irregular water supply," p.644; "*Verticillium* wilt," p.645; "Slime flux/wet wood," p.645; "Gray mold/*Botrytis*," p.646; "Dutch elm disease," p.646; "*Fusarium* wilt," p.646; "*Phytophthora* root rots," p.646; "Foot and root rots," p.646; "Cutworms," p.647; "Crown gall," p.647; "Fungal brackets," p.647; "Lightning," p.648; "Mechanical wounding," p.648; "Grasshoppers and crickets," p.649; "Root-knot nematodes," p.652; "White grubs," p.652; "Carrot rust flies," p.652; "Cabbage root maggots," p.652; and "Wireworms," p.653.

Lawn problems

Cats and dogs

Plants affected Lawns, seedlings, garden plants.
Symptoms Lawns and other grassed areas are fouled with droppings; grass and foliage are scorched with urine; and newly planted areas are scratched up.
Cause Cats and dogs. Cats prefer dry soil and newly cultivated areas.
Control Where local dogs are a problem, site plants away from accessible parts of the garden or protect them with netting. Water regularly areas troubled by cats. Repellents and other irritating substances are available, but these often give only temporary protection.

Dollar spot

Plants affected Lawns, particularly those containing fine-leaved bents and creeping fescues.
Symptoms Small, pale, straw-colored patches 1–3in (2.5–7.5cm) in diameter start to develop in early fall but merge to form larger areas that darken with age.
Cause The fungus *Sclerotinia homeocarpa*, encouraged by compacted or heavy soils and by a high pH; alkaline or limed soils are vulnerable. The disease appears mainly in mild, damp weather.
Control Improve soil aeration and remove thatch.

Brown patch

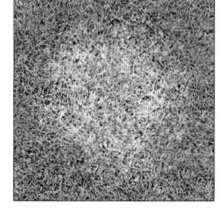

Plants affected Lawns.
Symptoms Brownish green patches appear, resembling chinch bug damage (see right).
Cause The soilborne fungus *Pellicularia filamentosa*. Excess nitrogen promotes soft growth. High temperatures encourage the fungus.
Control Brown patch rarely kills the roots, so plants do recover in time. Do not apply high-nitrogen fertilizer in late spring. Keep phosphorus and potassium levels high.

Snow mold

Plants affected Lawns, particularly those that contain a high proportion of annual bluegrass (*Poa annua*).
Symptoms Patches of grass become yellow and die, often merging to form large areas. In damp weather, a white fungal growth appears, causing the grass blades to stick together. It is most prevalent in late winter and early spring, especially on areas of grass that have been walked on while snow covered.
Cause Principally the fungus *Fusarium nivale*, which is encouraged by poor aeration and the overuse of nitrogen fertilizers.
Control Regularly aerate and scarify the lawn. Use winter-hardy grass species. Avoid using high-nitrogen fertilizers in late summer to early fall and rake thoroughly after mowing to prevent building up a water-holding mat. Cut grass short in late fall.

White grubs

Plants affected Lawns and other grassed areas.
Symptoms Brown patches appear and expand rapidly. Dead grass is loose and can be rolled up like a carpet. See also p.652.
Cause Larvae of June beetles (*Phyllophaga* spp.), Japanese beetles (*Popillia japonica*; see p.649), Asiatic garden beetles (*Maladera castanea*), Oriental beetles (*Exomala orientalis*), and rose chafers (*Macrodactylus subspinosus*; see p.649) are among the common species. Larvae are plump white grubs up to 1in (2.5cm) long with orange to brown heads. They feed on grass roots.
Control Milky disease and beneficial nematodes can be used where Japanese beetles are common.

Chinch bugs

Plants affected Lawns.
Symptoms Brown spots, often with a yellowish halo, appear on the lawn and expand slowly. Grass does not pull out. Bugs are visible on leaf blades.
Cause Chinch bugs (*Blissus* spp.), which feed on the crowns and leaf bases. Adults are ¹⁄₁₆in (1.6mm) long, black with red legs. Nymphs are even smaller and are orange to red.
Control To detect chinch bugs, part the grass and watch for movement, or push a bottomless can into the lawn and fill it with warm water; the bugs will float to the surface. Water lawns well during drought periods.

Melting out

Plants affected Lawns, especially those with a high proportion of Kentucky bluegrass (*Poa pratensis*).
Symptoms Small spots, consisting of oval areas with a pale brown center and dark margins, appear on the grass blades. The infection may spread to the crown; if it does, the plant will then die. The condition is sometimes mistaken for fertilizer burn, which it resembles.

Cause The fungus *Helminthosporum vagans*, which attacks closely mowed grass in cool, rainy weather, usually in early spring, but sometimes in late fall.
Control The Kentucky bluegrass cultivar 'Merion' is resistant to this disease. Do not mow the grass closer than 1¹⁄₂in (4cm).
See also "Fertilizer burn," p.642.

Toadstools

Plants affected Lawns and other grassed areas.
Symptoms Fungal fruiting bodies develop, sometimes in distinct circles (fairy rings), and often on buried woody material. Most cause little damage, but fairy rings are both harmful and disfiguring. Two circles of very lush green grass form, one within the other, sometimes several yards in diameter, and the grass in between them dies off; toadstools then emerge on the outer part of this middle zone. A white fungal growth permeates the soil in the area of the ring.
Cause Various fungi, including *Coprinus*, *Mycena*, and the ring-producing *Marasmius oreades*. They all have underground mycelia and are spread to new sites by windborne spores.
Control Brush off toadstools when they first appear, before their spores are produced. If the fungi are on buried wood, remove it.

Skunks

Plants affected Lawns and other grassed areas.
Symptoms Holes are dug in sod, leaving small piles of soil and divots of grass. Skunks may be seen in undergrowth.
Cause Skunks digging for white grubs, although they serve some beneficial purposes, since the grubs can be harmful. Skunk damage is most severe in fall when the grubs are growing large and feeding close to the surface.
Control Eliminate white grubs in lawn (see above). Push soil back into the holes and firm down. Grass will usually regrow.

Moles

Plants affected Lawns, seedlings, young plants.
Symptoms Heaps of soil (molehills) appear on the lawn and cultivated areas. Roots of young plants and seedlings are often disturbed.
Cause Burrowing moles.
Control Moles may be trapped, although they may be deterred by barriers cutting off their tunnels. Push metal sheets about 1ft (30cm) into the ground, through active tunnels.

Weeds

Weeds are plants that grow where they are unwanted and have common features: they are usually fast-growing and invasive, competing with cultivated plants for food and water; they are able to grow in a wide range of soils and sites; and they often show a marked resistance to control.

Cultivated plants may be considered weeds in certain circumstances: if they prove too invasive for their site and overwhelm their neighbors, or if they self-seed freely.

Categorizing weeds

Annual weeds complete their entire life cycle within one year. They set seed that germinates freely; occasionally, as in the case of groundsel (*Senecio vulgaris*), they may even produce several generations in one season. It is important, therefore, to remove annuals at the seedling stage, before they are able to produce seed.

Perennial weeds survive from year to year. Some grow readily from seed, but most persist by means of various storage organs such as rhizomes, bulbs, tubers, and taproots. Many perennials are able to proliferate because of poor cultivation techniques that leave small pieces in the soil when digging or rototilling.

Controlling weeds

Weeds may be controlled in two main ways: either they may be discouraged from growing by the use of good basic gardening techniques, or they may be removed by manual, mechanical, or chemical means.

The choice of how to remove different weeds depends on various factors: the habit of the plants themselves, the preference of the gardener, and the location of the weeds – whether in borders, lawns, paths, or neglected sites.

CULTIVATED PLANTS AS WEEDS

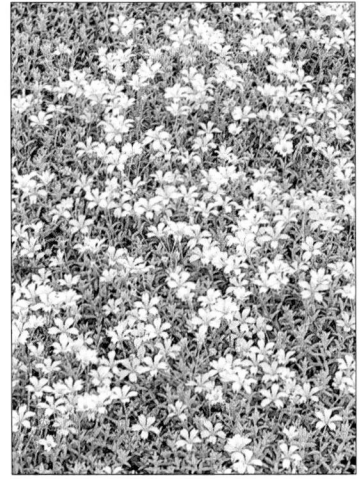

SNOW-IN-SUMMER
Any plant may become a weed if it dominates other garden plants. The dense growth and rapid spread of Cerastium tomentosum *may cause problems in a rock garden.*

RUSSIAN VINE
Although often planted to cover unsightly features rapidly, Fallopia baldschuanica *can easily overwhelm slower-growing and more delicate plants in its vicinity.*

Annual weeds

Annual weeds grow, flower, set seed, and die within one year. They occur most frequently in regularly cultivated areas, such as vegetable gardens or annual borders. Their rapid growth makes them troublesome among crops raised from seed *in situ*, because they smother slower-growing plants and compete for moisture, nutrients, and light.

The need for control

It is important to destroy annual weeds before they produce seeds, since many seeds are small, light, readily windborne, and quick to germinate. Quickly maturing species such as shepherd's purse (*Capsella bursa-pastoris*) may produce several generations in a single season. Common chickweed (*Stellaria media*) smothers nearby plants and is another weed that should be controlled at the seedling stage. Its seeds start to germinate in the fall and continue growing in mild winters to form dense mats.

Many seeds may be buried once they are shed, lying dormant for many years until they are brought to the surface during cultivation. The weeds then germinate and grow rapidly. If a site is heavily infested, it should be cultivated regularly to kill germinating seedlings.

Annual weeds may be controlled by hand, mechanical, or chemical means (see "Controlling weeds," p.660).

COMMON ANNUAL WEEDS

Shepherd's purse
(*Capsella bursa-pastoris*)

Hairy bittercress
(*Cardamine hirsuta*)

Annual bluegrass
(*Poa annua*)

Common chickweed (*Stellaria media*)

Annual nettle (*Urtica urens*)

Groundsel
(*Senecio vulgaris*)

Perennial weeds

Perennial weeds persist from year to year, surviving through winter cold and summer heat by storing food reserves in fleshy roots, bulbs, rhizomes, or tubers. They may be divided into two groups: herbaceous kinds and woody-stemmed kinds.

Herbaceous perennials

Most herbaceous perennials die back to the ground in fall. They survive the winter by storing food in their roots, then reappear in the spring. Examples are Canada thistle (*Cirsium arvense*), broad-leaved dock (*Rumex obtusifolius*), and field bindweed (*Convolvulus arvensis*). Also included in this group are the stemless herbaceous perennials that have leaves arising directly from their roots or rhizomes, for example dandelion (*Taraxacum officinale*) and goutweed (*Aegopodium podagraria*).

Kudzu vine (*Pueraria lobata)* is one of the most invasive climbers, particularly in the Southeast. In the West, *Cucurbita foetidissima* spreads rapidly in the area from Nebraska to California and Mexico; the plant develops long-running stems from the central root system and smothers more desirable plants.

Japanese knotweed (*Fallopia japonica*, syn. *Polygonum japonicum* and *P. cuspidatum*) dies back every year, but the tall, shrublike dead stems persist. New growth appears the following year.

Woody perennials

Woody-stemmed perennials survive the winter by storing food in their stems and branches. Some woody plants seed prolifically, with a high germination rate, producing unwanted seedlings throughout the garden. Among trees, *Acer platanoides, Ailanthus altissima,* and, especially in much of the South, *Broussonetia papyrifera* may be particularly troublesome.

Among shrubs, *Berberis thunbergii* and *Euonymus alatus* tend to produce large numbers of seedlings. Among the most invasive shrubs is *Rosa multiflora*, which by some estimates has spread across two-thirds of North America.

Several shrubby honeysuckles (*Lonicera*), including *L. maackii* and *L. tartarica,* may proliferate excessively. Both *L. japonica* and *L. j.* 'Halliana', vines with fragrant yellow and white blossoms, can be useful as groundcovers, but they can easily take over entire gardens. Similarly, *Campsis radicans* has attractive trumpet-shaped orange flowers, but it propagates by suckers that can spread very rapidly throughout the garden.

Rhus radicans, R. diversiloba in the West, and *R. vernix* spread quickly and contain a powerful skin irritant.

The need for control

Perennial weeds have fleshy roots, rhizomes, and other storage organs that are not easily controlled. Hoeing and digging, along with machine cultivation, break the roots and rhizomes into sections without killing them; many survive and increase the infestation. With most perennial weeds, weedkillers can be the most practical and effective control.

Preventing weeds

Both annual and perennial weeds may be prevented from establishing in various ways.

Working the soil

Before planting, clear the site of all weeds, either manually (by hand, with a hoe or similar tool, or with a rototiller or other cultivator), by covering the ground with plastic (this will take weeks or months to be effective), or with chemicals. Weeds are often difficult to eradicate from among established plants, which may need to be lifted and the weeds carefully extracted from the washed root system.

Conditioning very acidic soils with lime will deter some lawn weeds, especially many kinds of moss, which thrive where the pH if the soil is low.

Cultivating healthy plants

Vigorous, healthy plants are able to compete more effectively with weeds than are weak specimens. Plants with spreading foliage and habit, such as *Pachysandra*, provide a dark cover over the soil that discourages weeds.

Some vegetable crops, for example potatoes, compete well with annual weeds and may be grown to help maintain clean ground for a subsequent crop (see THE VEGETABLE GARDEN, "Rotation," p.492).

Groundcover plants

Some plants grow in dense carpets that suppress the germination of weed seeds. They are particularly useful for parts of the garden where, because of shade, or very wet or dry soil, weeds thrive. Choose groundcover plants carefully, since some are invasive and may quickly become weeds themselves (for more information, see GROUNDCOVERS, p.178).

Mulching

In early spring, apply a mulch 1–2in (2.5–5cm) thick of weed-free, organic material such as leaf mold or processed bark to help prevent weed seeds from germinating and to smother weed seedlings. Do not use compost or insufficiently rotted manure for this purpose, because these almost certainly contain weed seeds.

Established perennial weeds may grow through the mulch but, since they tend to root into the loose material, they are easy to remove.

PERENNIAL WEEDS
WEEDS WITH RHIZOMES AND STOLONS

Goutweed
(*Aegopodium podagraria*)

Hedge bindweed
(*Calystegia sepium*)

Canada thistle
(*Cirsium arvense*)

Quackgrass
(*Elymus repens*)

Willow herb
(*Epilobium* sp.)

Coltsfoot
(*Tussilago farfara*)

Horsetail
(*Equisetum arvense*)

Black plastic
Laid directly over the soil, black plastic prevents annual weeds from establishing. It can also be effective with perennial weeds: horsetail (*Equisetum arvense*) and field bindweed (*Convolvulus arvensis*) are both less likely to grow if the area is covered for at least two seasons. Cover the plastic with a bark mulch to improve its appearance. Black plastic is particularly useful in fruit and vegetable gardens; make slits in it through which the crops can grow.

Grassing down borders
Some persistent perennial weeds such as horsetail, *Oxalis corniculata*, and *O. stricta* may resist repeated diligent attempts to eradicate them with weedkiller or to dig them out. An alternative approach is to grass down heavily infested borders and maintain them as close-mown sod for several years. Given time, this treatment will clear the soil and usually eliminates most of the infestation.

Controlling weeds
Once weeds are present, they may be eradicated in one of three ways: hand-weeding, mechanical control, or chemical control. There are three different types of weedkiller: those

that act on the leaves, those that act on the soil (including preemergent weedkillers), and those that act on specific types of plant.

Hand-weeding and hoeing
Hand-weeding, hoeing, and forking are often the only practical ways of removing weeds in flowerbeds, the vegetable garden, and small patches of ground, where weedkillers cannot be used safely without risk of harming nearby garden or crop plants.

Small patches of perennial weeds, such as goutweed and quackgrass, may be forked out, but great care must be taken not to leave in the soil sections of rhizomes, roots, or bulbils that will grow again. Check a month or so later and remove any regrowth.

Hand-weed or hoe in dry weather, if possible, so that the weeds are easily loosened from the soil. In wet weather, remove uprooted weeds from the site to prevent them from rooting back into the soil. Hoe only lightly around cultivated plants to prevent their surface roots from being damaged.

Removing weeds mechanically
Market gardeners often use rotary cultivators (rototillers) with hoeing or cultivating attachments for annual weed control between rows of vegetables, but these machines are generally

unsuitable for most perennial weeds. They simply cut the rhizomes of weeds such as goutweed and quackgrass into many pieces that will continue to grow as new, vigorous plants. Wherever possible, use weedkillers to kill perennial weeds before digging or cultivating soil.

Foliage-acting weedkillers
Leaf-acting products, or postemergent weedkillers, enter the weeds through leaves or green stems and are applied with a sprayer or watering can and fine nozzle or dribble bar. There are two different types. The first acts by translocation, moving from the leaves to the roots, and so destroys both annual and perennial weeds. For maximum effect the weeds should be in vigorous growth. The second type works by contact, killing only by direct touch. They destroy annual weeds and the green leaves and stems of perennial weeds, although not the roots of perennials. Some weedkillers act through both leaves and roots.

Soil-acting weedkillers
These are applied to the soil and are absorbed into the roots of growing weeds. From there soil-acting weedkillers move to the parts of the plant above ground level, killing the weeds by interfering with their metabolism.

These chemicals kill established annual weeds and may also kill or suppress many established perennial weeds. When planning to use areas that have been treated with soil-acting weedkillers, check the package for details of residual activity, which may damage desirable plants.

Preemergent weedkillers are applied to bare soil or established lawns to kill weed seeds as they germinate. They can be used in shrub borders, between perennials, or on annual beds that will receive established transplants, but not where any plants will be grown from seed.

It is important to apply preemergents at the optimum time; that is, just before or as the weed seeds are germinating. For example, in much of the country, preemergents to control crabgrass are applied while forsythia is in bloom. Such timing allows the chemical to be incorporated into the soil and then absorbed by the crabgrass seeds as they germinate, thus killing the crabgrass.

Selective weedkillers
Most selective weedkillers kill broadleaved weeds and leave narrowleaved grasses unharmed, provided they are applied at the correct rate. They can just as easily kill your garden plants, so apply carefully.

WEEDS WITH TUBERS AND FLESHY ROOTS

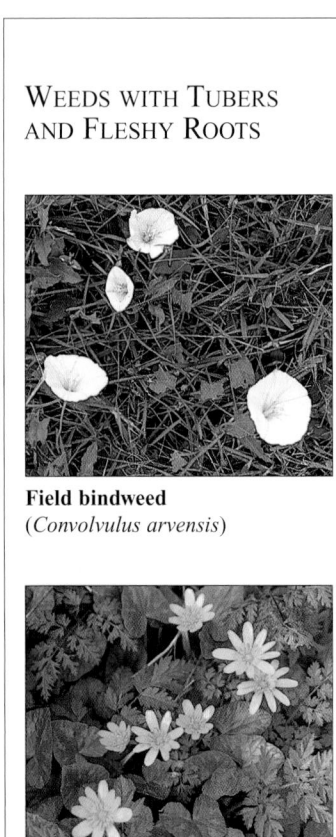

Field bindweed
(*Convolvulus arvensis*)

Lesser celandine
(*Ranunculus ficaria*)

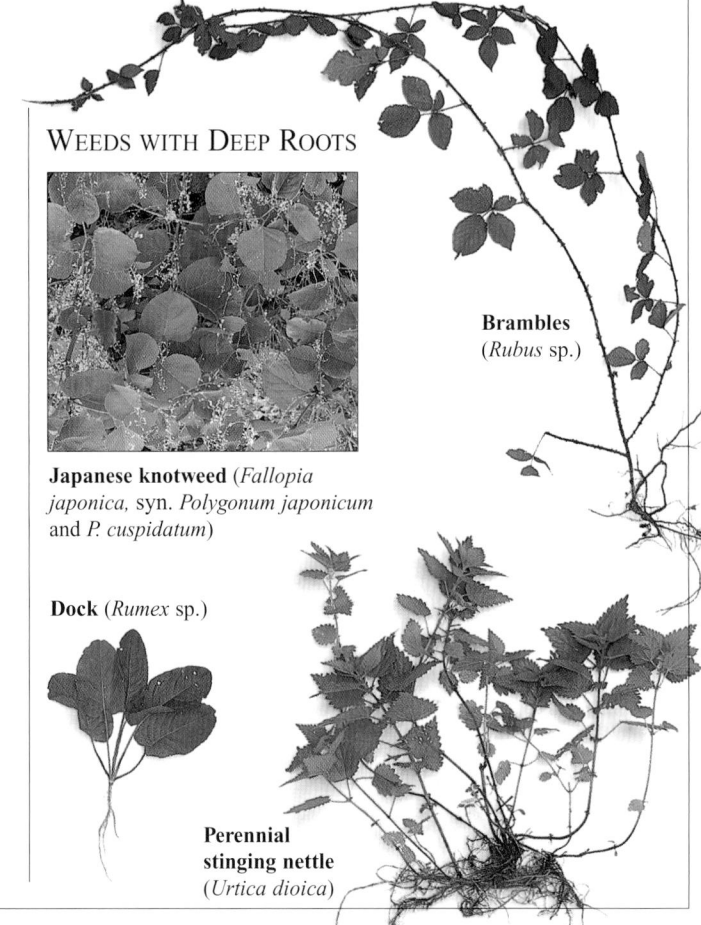

WEEDS WITH DEEP ROOTS

Japanese knotweed (*Fallopia japonica*, syn. *Polygonum japonicum* and *P. cuspidatum*)

Dock (*Rumex* sp.)

Brambles
(*Rubus* sp.)

Perennial stinging nettle
(*Urtica dioica*)

Using weedkillers safely
Care must always be taken when applying weedkillers:
• Wear protective clothing, for example rubber gloves and long pants and sleeves.
• Do not apply weedkillers in windy conditions when there is a risk of spray being blown across to nearby plants.
• Use only for appropriate purposes as recommended on the product label; for example, do not use a path weedkiller to keep down weeds in a rosebed.
• Always dilute soluble weedkillers according to the manufacturer's instructions.
• Always apply weedkillers at the recommended rates on the labels.
• Always keep in original containers, and make sure that the labels are well secured to the containers so that contents are known and no errors in usage occur.
• Never store diluted weedkillers for future use.
• Store away out of reach of children and animals, preferably in a securely locked cabinet in a frost-free workshop or shed.

Lawn weeds

Various perennial weeds can be troublesome in lawns. Their common survival factor is their ability to grow and thrive in the adverse conditions of short, regularly mowed grass. They usually originate from seeds carried by the wind or by birds. Once lawn weeds have germinated, most are then rapidly spread by the action of mowing, and early treatment is necessary if they are to be eradicated.

Among the most troublesome lawn weeds are annual bluegrass (*Poa annua*), crabgrass (*Digitaria sanguinalis*), dandelion (*Taraxacum officinale*), creeping Charlie (*Glechoma hederacea*), and plantains (*Plantago* spp.). Some do not respond to treatment by lawn weedkillers, so other forms of treatment will be required.

In lawns where the grass is too sparse to offer adequate competition, moss may also become a problem.

Preventing weeds and moss

Good lawn care is an effective preventive measure. The presence of numerous weeds in a lawn usually indicates that the grass is not growing sufficiently vigorously to prevent weeds from establishing. Lack of regular fertilizing and drought are among the most common reasons for poor growth. Soil compaction and mowing the grass too closely and too regularly may also lead to the spread of moss. For further details on lawn care, see THE LAWN, "Routine care," pp.389–94.

Coarser weed grasses, such as barnyard grass (*Echinochloa crusgalli*), may remain a problem, so clumps may need to be removed and the patch resodded or reseeded.

Raking to lift creeping stems before mowing may help check the spread of creeping weeds such as trefoils (*Trifolium* spp.) and creeping Charlie (*Glechoma hederacea*) if the grass is mowed immediately afterward.

Removing weeds

If weeds are already present in the lawn, there are two main ways of treating them, depending on the severity of the problem. Either they may be removed by hand if they are not too widespread, or they may be treated with an appropriate weedkiller.

Weeding by hand
Hand-weeding is an effective method of removing a few scattered rosetted weeds such as dandelion (*Taraxacum officinale*) and plantains (*Plantago* spp.). Use an asparagus knife or hand fork to lift the weeds, then firm back displaced sod.

Dealing with moss
Moss may be killed with moss preparations but is only a short-term solution: unless the conditions that encouraged moss are identified and corrected, the problem will recur.

Removing weeds with chemicals
Weedkillers intended specifically for use on lawns work by translocation (moving within the plant), and the weeds begin to distort and shrivel within a few days of application. The chemicals are selective and do not harm lawn grasses at normal dilution rates, but do not use them on lawns within six months of germination.

You should also avoid using lawn weedkillers on newly laid sod, sprigs, or plugs within a six-month period of laying or planting.

Buying weedkillers
Lawn weedkillers are usually sold as a concentrated liquid and therefore need to be suitably diluted. They may also be obtained in the form of soluble powder, ready-to-use spray, aerosol, wax bar, or in combination with liquid or granular lawn fertilizers.

Applying weedkillers
Apply weedkillers when grass and weeds are growing strongly. In spring, creeping lawn grasses soon colonize any bare patches left as weeds shrivel and die.

Hose-end sprayers can be used for large areas; a watering can with a fine nozzle or dribble bar is better for small lawns. Divide the lawn into strips using two garden lines to ensure that the grass has been given complete and uniform coverage.

If possible, wait for two or three days after mowing before applying the weedkiller so that the weeds have time to develop new leaf surfaces to absorb the chemical. Do not mow the grass for two or three days after spraying to allow time for the weedkiller to work its way down toward the roots.

How often to apply
Some weeds, such as dandelions and plantains, are killed by one or two applications; others, for example the trefoils, may need two or three applications at four- to six-week intervals. Some species, such as slender speedwell (*Veronica filiformis*) may survive several applications.

Where a weed shows no response to repeated applications of various weedkillers, the only solution is to remove it by hand.

LAWN WEEDS

Broad-leaved plantain
(*Plantago major*)

Common mouse-ear chickweed
(*Cerastium fontanum*, syn. *C. vulgatum*)

Dandelion
(*Taraxacum officinale*)

Nutsedge
(*Cyperus esculentus*)

Creeping Charlie
(*Glechoma hederacea*)

Yarrow (*Achillea millefolium*)

Common white clover
(*Trifolium repens*)

Sheep's sorrel (*Rumex acetosella*)

8
BASIC BOTANY

BOTANY – THE SCIENTIFIC study of plants – covers a number of disciplines. Familiarity with the basics helps the gardener understand the principles underlying many horticultural techniques and thus maintain plants in good health. The study of the internal plant structures (anatomy) and their external appearance (morphology) can explain how to graft successfully. Physiology, the study of plant metabolism, aids in the understanding of a plant's need for water and light, the role of nutrients, and the processes of photosynthesis, transpiration, and respiration. Taxonomy – the identification and classification of plants – can indicate close relationships between genera or species that have similar cultivation needs.

Plant diversity

There are more than 250,000 species of seed-bearing plant. They include annuals, which flower, seed, and die in a year or less; biennials, which grow from seed in their first year and then flower, seed, and die in the second season; and perennials, which live for several to many years, and include woody plants. The term "perennial" is commonly applied to herbaceous plants, while trees and shrubs are referred to as woody plants. Most garden plants have roots, stems, leaves, and fruits; these may be modified for particular purposes.

Roots

These anchor the plant in the soil and absorb water and mineral salts from which the plant manufactures its food. Fleshy taproots penetrate vertically downward, forming sparse lateral roots. Fibrous roots consist of a network of fine, threadlike roots that emerge from the base of the stem. The root tips bear fragile root hairs, which are in intimate contact with soil particles, from which water and mineral salts are absorbed. Roots are sometimes modified to form storage organs, such as the swollen taproots of carrots.

Stems

Plant stems provide the above-ground framework of the plant, supporting the leaves, flowers, and fruits. Some stem cells are specialized to conduct food, water, or nutrients from the leaves to all parts of the plant. Food is carried by phloem cells; water and mineral salts

BASIC PARTS OF A PLANT

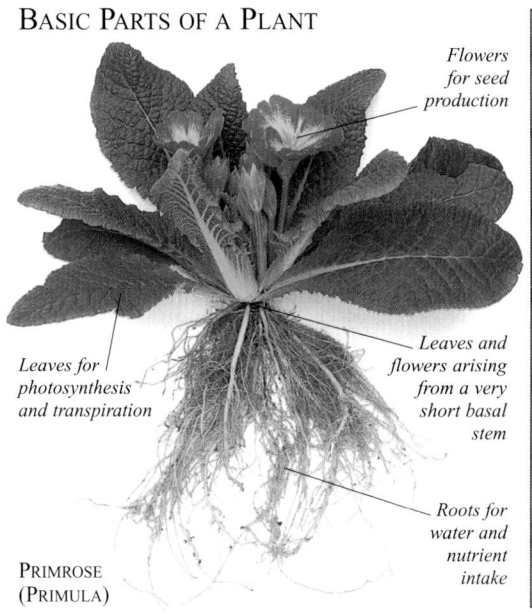

Flowers for seed production

Leaves and flowers arising from a very short basal stem

Leaves for photosynthesis and transpiration

Roots for water and nutrient intake

PRIMROSE (PRIMULA)

ROOT SYSTEMS

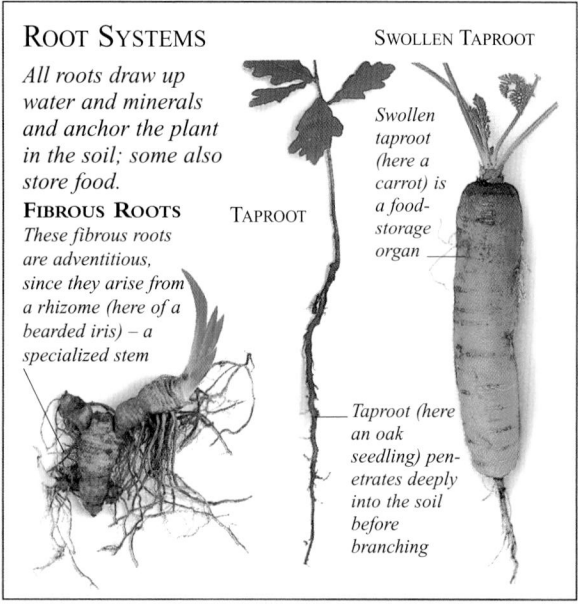

All roots draw up water and minerals and anchor the plant in the soil; some also store food.

FIBROUS ROOTS
These fibrous roots are adventitious, since they arise from a rhizome (here of a bearded iris) – a specialized stem.

SWOLLEN TAPROOT

Swollen taproot (here a carrot) is a food-storage organ

TAPROOT

Taproot (here an oak seedling) penetrates deeply into the soil before branching

TYPES OF STEM

HERBACEOUS STEMS
These are annual stems that die back in fall to a persistent, overwintering rootstock. Herbaceous stems (here Sedum spectabile*) are strengthened by thickened tissue, usually just below the epidermis (skin).*

Stem is supported by water pressure in the cells (turgor)

WOODY STEMS
The rigid outer structure of stems and branches of woody plants and trees (here an Acer*) is formed as a result of secondary thickening – a process that produces new conducting tissues containing lignin in the cells.*

A new protective layer, the bark, is formed at the epidermis (skin)

BULB
This modified stem serves as an underground food-storage organ so that the plant (here Narcissus*) can remain dormant while conditions for growth are unfavorable. A bulb consists of the basal plate and fleshy, modified leaves or leaf bases in the form of scales.*

An outer covering, or tunic, surrounds the bulb

LEAF FORMS

SCALELIKE LEAF (*Chamaecyparis obtusa* 'Nana Aurea')

PINNATE LEAF (Black locust, *Robinia pseudoacacia*)

BROADLY OVATE LEAF (*Camellia japonica*)

PINNATIFID LEAF (Swiss-cheese plant, *Monstera deliciosa*)

COMPOUND PINNATE FROND (Male fern, *Dryopteris filix-mas*)

DIGITATE LEAF (Horse chestnut, *Aesculus hippocastanum*)

LINEAR LEAVES (Annual bluegrass, *Poa annua*)

are conducted through xylem cells. Stems are often modified for other functions. Tubers, corms, and rhizomes are swollen stems that are modified for food storage; in cacti, the swollen stems contain water.

Leaves

Leaf form is extremely diverse and may be modified as spines, as in some cacti, or as tendrils, as in the garden pea. Whatever their form, leaves are the manufacturing centers of a plant. They contain the green pigment chlorophyll, which absorbs the energy of sunlight in order to convert carbon dioxide from the air and water from the soil into carbohydrates by the process known as photosynthesis. The by-product, oxygen, is essential to most forms of life. The energy required to drive the plant's metabolism is produced through respiration, which breaks down carbohydrates to release energy, carbon dioxide, and water.

Leaves present a relatively large surface so that they maximize absorption of light; they are thin enough for light to penetrate to the cells that contain chlorophyll, and to allow rapid

PHOTOSYNTHESIS

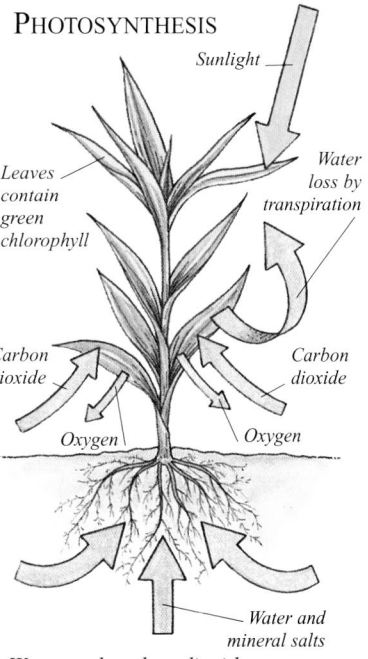

Sunlight

Leaves contain green chlorophyll

Water loss by transpiration

Carbon dioxide

Carbon dioxide

Oxygen

Oxygen

Water and mineral salts

Water and carbon dioxide are converted into carbohydrates and oxygen using the energy of sunlight, which is trapped by the chlorophyll in a plant's leaves.

movement of gases to all cells. Their surfaces contain numerous pores (stomata) through which oxygen and carbon dioxide pass in and out of the leaf. The stomata also control water losses through transpiration. A high evaporation of water vapor from the leaves and a lack of water entering through the plant roots are the cause of plants wilting in dry conditions.

Although only 1 percent of the fresh weight of a plant consists of minerals, they are essential. In solution they are directly concerned with the water balance of the cells and help regulate the

passage of substances between cells. They maintain the correct pH for biochemical reactions and are essential components of chlorophyll and all enzymes, the biological catalysts of the plant's internal chemistry.

Fruits and seeds

Seeds are a flowering plant's means of reproduction. Each seed develops from a single fertilized egg, and one or more seeds is contained in a fruit. The many types of fruit disperse their seeds in a variety of ways.

In some fruits, the seeds germinate rapidly with no special treatment; in others, it may be necessary for the seeds to undergo specific treatment in cultivation. For further information, see PRINCIPLES OF PROPAGATION, "How to overcome dormancy," p.623.

Pods and capsules are dehiscent fruits, splitting along a regular line or lines to release the seed, as in *Aquilegia* and violets (*Viola*). Indehiscent fruits do not split. Examples are hazelnuts (*Corylus*) and chestnuts (*Castanea*), in which a single seed is enclosed in a tough shell. These large seeds have a high moisture and fat content; they deteriorate quickly unless sown fresh or stored in cool, moist conditions. In roses, many small, indehiscent fruits, each containing one seed, are enclosed in a hollow receptacle, the hip. The individual fruits need to be extracted before sowing.

Succulent fruits, where the seed is enclosed in flesh, include berries (e.g. bananas, tomatoes, and grapes), which have many seeds; drupes (e.g. plums, cherries, and peaches), which typically have one seed in the form of a stone;

TRANSPIRATION

Stoma (pore) on lily leaf

Plant fluids

Water lost through open stomata (*pores*)

Guard cells controlling closing and opening of stomata

Water and minerals drawn up from roots

Evaporation of water from the leaf surfaces creates a constant flow of water and nutrients from the roots to the foliage; this is known as the transpiration stream.

FRUIT TYPES

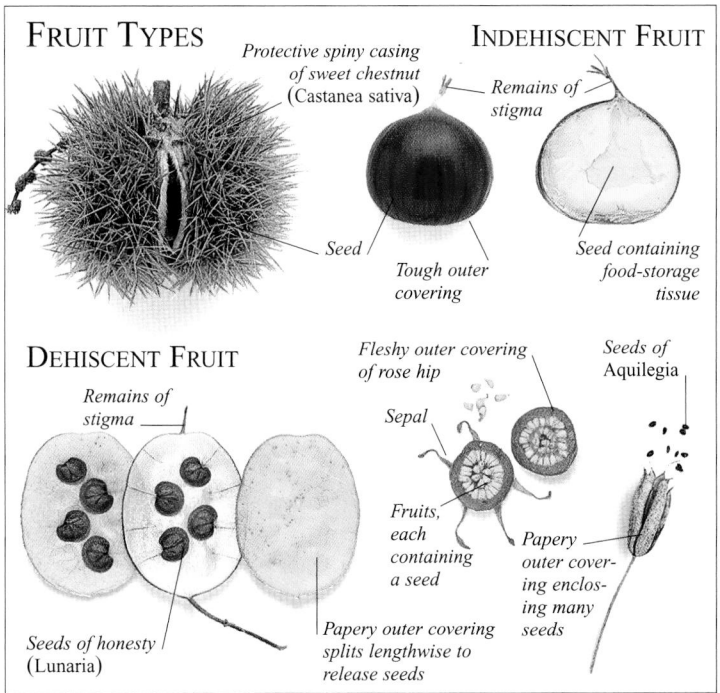

Protective spiny casing of sweet chestnut (*Castanea sativa*)

INDEHISCENT FRUIT

Remains of stigma

Seed

Tough outer covering

Seed containing food-storage tissue

DEHISCENT FRUIT

Remains of stigma

Fleshy outer covering of rose hip

Seeds of Aquilegia

Sepal

Fruits, each containing a seed

Papery outer covering enclosing many seeds

Seeds of honesty (Lunaria)

Papery outer covering splits lengthwise to release seeds

and pomes (e.g. apples, pears, and quinces), which develop from other parts of the flower besides the ovaries. In all these types of fruit, the seed should be removed from the mashed flesh and cleaned before being sown.

Flowers

Flowers show extraordinary diversity in color, scent, and form, with a wide range of adaptations to ensure that they fulfill their reproductive function. They may be borne as showy, individual flowers (*Hibiscus* and tulips) or in many-flowered spikes (*Kniphofia*), racemes (hyacinth), panicles (*Gypsophila*), umbels (*Agapanthus*), or in heads consisting of numerous florets, such as dahlias.

A flower has four main parts: petals or tepals, sepals, stamens (the male part), and one or more carpels (the female part), which are collectively known as the pistil. Most conspicuous are the petals, carried above a whorl of (usually) green sepals. The male reproductive nuclei are carried in pollen grains, enclosed in an anther attached to a stemlike filament; these vary greatly in number from three in crocuses to 30

PARTS OF A FLOWER

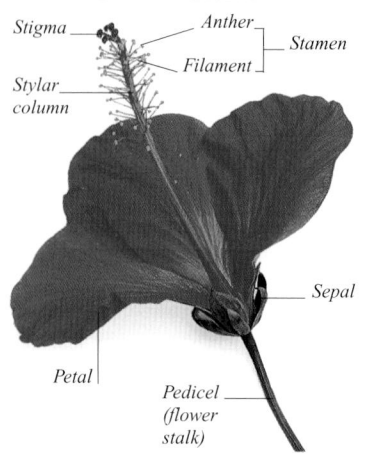

Stigma — *Anther* — *Stamen* — *Filament* — *Stylar column* — *Sepal* — *Petal* — *Pedicel (flower stalk)*

SEXUALITY IN FLOWERS

Dioecious plants – being either male or female – need a plant of each sex growing close to one another to set seed on the female. Monoecious plants bear separate male and female flowers on the same plant. Bisexual (hermaphroditic) flowers contain both male (stamens) and female (carpels) parts in the same flower.

FEMALE PLANT   **MALE PLANT**

DIOECIOUS
(*Skimmia japonica*)

MONOECIOUS
(*Begonia*)

Male flower (with stamens)

Female flower (with carpels)

BISEXUAL
(*Schlumbergera*)

Stigma (female part)

Stamens (male part)

or more in buttercups. The carpels enclose the female egg nuclei and have a projecting style with a stigma at its tip to receive pollen grains. Pollen grains germinate on the stigma and grow through the style tissue to fuse with the female nuclei (the process of fertilization), eventually forming seeds.

Many plants bear separate female and male (unisexual) flowers on the same plant. They are known as monoecious plants. Bisexual, or hermaphroditic, plants have both male and female parts in each flower. A few species bear unisexual and bisexual flowers and are known as polygamous plants. In dioecious plants all the flowers produced are of one sex only; examples are many holly

species (Ilex), *Aucuba*, and some *Skimmia*. Male and female plants must be grown together if they are to set seed; this is especially important where plants are grown for their ornamental berries.

Different but related species do not normally interbreed because they often occur in dissimilar habitats, flower at varying times, or possess minor variations in flower characters that prevent successful interbreeding. In cultivation, such barriers can sometimes be overcome, and hybrids are often created by design (see "Producing hybrid plants," p.624).

Flowering plants of the division Angiospermae produce seeds that are enclosed in an ovary. They differ from the Gymnospermae, which consist of nonflowering plants that bear naked seeds. Angiosperms are divided into monocotyledons and dicotyledons, based on whether there are one or two seed leaves (cotyledons) within the seed itself.

Monocotyledons have leaves with (usually) parallel veins, flower parts in threes, and often relatively slender, nonwoody stems. Dicotyledons have leaves with a branching network of veins; the petals and sepals are in multiples of two, four, or five; and the stems are thickened (and, in trees and shrubs, woody), originating from a special layer of cells within the stem called the cambium. Monocotyledon stems do not possess a cambium layer, so the plants are generally smaller.

CLASSES OF FLOWER

Flowering plants are grouped into two classes: monocotyledons and dicotyledons

Petals in multiples of two, four, or five

DICOTYLEDON
(*Ranunculus repens*)

Tepals in threes or multiples of three

Stamens in threes or multiples of three

Three-lobed stigma

MONOCOTYLEDON
(*Lilium*)

LEAF VEINS

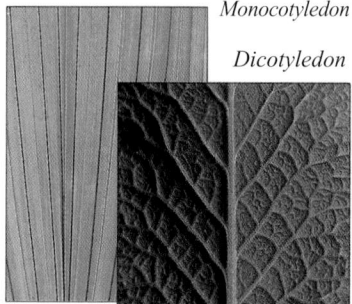

Monocotyledon

Dicotyledon

Leaf vein patterns in monocotyledons (here Curculigo recurvata*) are usually parallel; those in dicotyledons (here* Primula*) generally form a network.*

Taxonomy and nomenclature

Plants are referred to scientifically by two names, generally written in italics. The first name, which always has its initial letter capitalized, is that of the genus, the second is the species name: for example, *Rosa canina*. In nature, species often show minor variations; these are given a third name, prefixed by "subsp." (subspecies), "var." (varietas), or "f." (forma): thus *Rhododendron rex* subsp. *fictolacteum*. A cultivar (**culti**vated **var**iety) is one that has been selected either from the wild or from gardens, and whose characteristics are preserved by some means of controlled propagation. The name of such a plant is written in Roman type with an initial capital letter and in single quotation marks: thus *Choisya ternata* 'Sundance'.

Mutation

A mutation, also known as a sport, is a genetic change in a plant, either natural or induced, that may be exploited by propagating the mutated material to introduce a new cultivar. Mutations may occur in all parts of the plant, but those of horticultural interest are mainly color mutants or doubled flowers, plus variegated shoots that occur on a normally green-leaved plant.

Chrysanthemum cultivars often produce mutations; for example, one flower head in a spray of a different color from the parent.

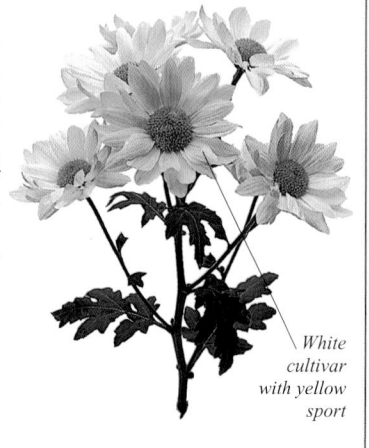

White cultivar with yellow sport

Seasonal reminders

THESE notes, distilled from Part One of this book, serve as reminders of important tasks to be done during the gardening year and the best times to do them. They should be taken only as a guide – in a cold region, you may need to delay some tasks; in a warm region, you may be able to start them earlier and finish later. Every garden is unique: its position and soil type affect the rate at which the plants grow and therefore the time when various activities are best undertaken. Whatever your conditions, prepare the soil and containers thoroughly before planting; do not plant in frozen, waterlogged, or very dry soil. Water plants well until established. Certain year-round operations are not covered here (such as controlling pests, diseases, and weeds, or potting cuttings). For full details of how to carry out the tasks mentioned, refer to the appropriate specific chapters.

Spring

Soil preparation and planting

Plant hardy plants in beds or containers, including container-grown annual vegetables (under covers, if necessary) and perennial vegetables. Start planting water garden plants. Sow half-hardy and hardy annuals indoors, and hardy biennials outdoors, in late spring. For a new lawn, sow seed or lay sod. Indoors, prepare greenhouse beds and soil benches; plant ornamentals, terrariums, bottle gardens, and hanging baskets.

Routine care

After flowering, plunge alpines, dwarf bulbs, and winter-flowering indoor plants outside, and re-cover bulb frames. Water established bulbs, cacti, and other succulents. Indoors, increase watering and mist-spray plants as needed. For epiphytes in bloom, keep soil moist.

Fertilize established plants except annuals; mulch mature trees, shrubs, climbers, perennials, fruits, and roses. In late spring, mulch vegetables.

Check stakes and ties; stake climbing and tall plants, if necessary. Erect supports for peas and climbing beans.

For trees and shrubs, cut out suckers and reverted shoots. Remove dead growth of perennials; cut back shrubby perennials and overly vigorous and straggly rock garden plants. Unless seed is needed, deadhead flowering shrubs, repeat-flowering climbers, bulbs, and indoor plants. Thin dense perennial shoots and pinch young perennials, annuals, biennials, and trailing indoor plants as needed. Top-dress or repot plants in containers (except spring-flowering climbers). If necessary, replenish top-dressing around outdoor rock garden plants. Transplant deciduous shrubs and perennials, if necessary. Protect any tender new growth on outdoor plants, and flowers on fruiting plants during late frosts.

In the water garden, clear blanketweed and thin oxygenating plants. Divide and replant or repot overcrowded aquatic and bog plants; overhaul neglected ponds and check on fish.

Roll lawns before starting mowing if sod has been lifted by frost; repair damaged areas. In mid- to late spring, lightly scarify the lawn and apply fertilizer. Cut grass around bulbs after flowering.

Harvest herb leaves as appropriate. In the vegetable garden, force rhubarb and chicory. Under cover, pollinate peach, nectarine, strawberry, and grape flowers; thin peach and nectarine fruitlets.

Pruning and training

Until midspring, give formative pruning, coppice, and pollard trees and prune deciduous trees that flower in late summer (except those that bleed heavily); renovate evergreen tree hedges. Root prune established trees as needed.

In early spring, prune shrubs that flower on new wood, and all hydrangeas; renovate deciduous shrubs. In midspring, give formative pruning and train shrubs; prune and renovate evergreen shrubs. Coppice and pollard shrubs grown for summer foliage or winter stems. In late spring, prune winter- or spring-flowering shrubs. Start clipping topiary. Root prune vigorous shrubs or those grown in containers.

In early spring, prune deciduous climbers that flower on new wood, evergreens, and, after flowering, those that flower on old wood. Give formative pruning to climbers. Prune Hybrid Teas, Grandifloras, Floribundas, miniatures, standards, Bourbons, Hybrid Perpetuals, and newly planted roses. Give formative pruning to species roses. Cut back roses on pillars.

In the rock garden, prune shrubs and woody perennials. Hard prune shrubby herbs. Pinch out and disbud new grape shoots; disbud and deshoot stone fruit fans under cover. Prune young stone fruit trees, blueberries, hazelnuts, figs, trained trees, and plum pyramids. Bark-ring overvigorous apple and pear trees.

In the indoor garden, cut back weak or damaged growth; prune shrubs and climbers that flower on old wood. In early spring, cut back shrubs and climbers that are in growth all year.

Propagation

Sow seed of hardy plants outside, and of tender plants under cover. Make successive sowings of regularly used annual and biennial herbs. From late spring, sow tender vegetables outdoors. Start sowing annual indoor plants. Gather ripe seed of early-flowering waterlilies.

In early spring, divide suckering shrubs, rooted suckers from roses on their own roots, fleshy-rooted perennials, mat- and clump-forming rock garden plants, and dahlias. In late spring, divide marginal plants and gather turions for replanting.

Take softwood cuttings of trees, shrubs, climbers, rock garden plants, oxygenating plants, herbs, and indoor plants. Take basal cuttings of perennials, rock garden plants, dahlias, and tuberous begonias. In late spring, take greenwood cuttings of shrubs. Start taking perennial stem tip cuttings. Take leaf cuttings, in early to midspring, of rock garden and indoor plants, and stem and leaf cuttings or sections of cacti, other succulents, and indoor plants.

Flat-graft and side-graft cacti and other succulents. Graft fruit trees. In early spring, layer trees, shrubs, and climbing plants, and tip layer and stool shrubs. Air layer ornamental trees and, in late spring, mound layer shrubby herbs.

Summer

Soil preparation and planting

Plant container-grown plants, including new strawberry runners and annual vegetables. In late summer, plant containers of shrubs and prepare soil for fall planting of shrubs. Plant winter brassicas, salad and tender vegetables, and, by late summer, fall-flowering bulbs. In the water garden, plant aquatic and marginal plants until midsummer, and deep-water plants until late summer. For lawns, lay sod and sow seed.

Routine care

Water established plants, fruit trees, and lawns as necessary. Regularly water and fertilize plants in containers and under cover. Mist-spray cacti, succulents, and indoor plants; hose down succulents in the garden or greenhouse. Fertilize fruit plants as required. After midsummer, apply fertilizer to roses. Mulch vegetables, fruit, and moisture-loving herbs.

Stake and tie tall or climbing plants and vegetables. Remove suckers (and blind shoots) from trees, shrubs, and roses.

Unless seed is needed, deadhead outdoor and indoor plants. In the rock garden, cut out dead rosettes and cut back spring-flowering plants. Continue to pinch perennial shoots, and pinch out growing tips of indoor plants if necessary. Repot cacti and other succulents; pot, repot, or renew top-dressing of indoor plants. Transplant rooted strawberry runners. Lift and heel in early-flowering bulbs. Ventilate, shade, and damp down greenhouses and alpine houses.

In the water garden, clear out any blanketweed from ponds and, in midsummer, fertilize waterlilies.

Mow lawns as appropriate, including grass around fruit trees, but stop mowing in areas with fall-flowering bulbs. Fertilize the lawn in early or midsummer; aerate lawn areas subject to heavy wear.

Harvest and store herbs, vegetables, and fruits. Hill up potatoes; lift and dry onions in late summer. Stake and tie tomatoes, and pinch them in late summer. In the fruit garden, thin fruitlets as needed; discard rotten fruits. Cut back summer-fruiting strawberries after picking.

Pruning and training

In early summer, prune spring-flowering trees; in midsummer, deciduous trees that bleed heavily and mature pleached trees; and in late summer, young pleached trees and deciduous tree hedges. Remove diseased or dead branches from evergreens. Clip topiary as necessary.

Prune shrubs that flower on old wood after flowering, mature shrub standards, informal shrub hedges, and deciduous shrubs that bleed heavily. For standards, pinch out sideshoots on shrubs. After flowering, prune climbers that flower on old wood. Tie in new shoots. Carry out the first pruning stage of *Wisteria*.

Prune ramblers and most old garden roses after flowering. Give renewal pruning to nonremontant shrub, species, and groundcover roses. Peg down Bourbons and Hybrid Perpetuals. Thin Gallica roses and train new shoots of climbing and rambling roses. In the herb garden, cut back herbaceous herbs after flowering, and start cutting back shrubby herbs in late summer.

In the fruit garden, pinch out and train shoots on stone fruit fans; pinch out new fig shoots. Break new sideshoots on hazelnuts. Prune sour cherries and fruiting raspberries; train new canes. Prune trained apples, pears, and pyramid plums.

Propagation

Sow seed of all annuals and biennials, including herbs, until midsummer. In late summer, sow hardy annuals and biennials in pots for fall planting. Sow seed of rock garden plants. Make successive sowings of summer vegetables; sow Oriental and winter vegetables and herbs for winter and spring crops. Gather and sow seed of perennials and water-garden plants (under cover); gather annual, biennial, and bulb seed.

In early summer, divide overcrowded bulb clumps, waterlilies, and offsets of clump-forming and some tuberous-rooted cacti and other succulents.

Take softwood cuttings of climbers and, in midsummer, of marginal and oxygenating water garden plants, and of herbs; take basal and greenwood cuttings of rock garden plants. In mid- to late summer, take semiripe cuttings of trees, shrubs, roses, rock garden and indoor plants, and herbs, and ripewood cuttings of rock garden plants. In mid- to late summer, take mallet cuttings of shrubs and leaf-bud cuttings of shrubs, hybrid berries, and blackberries. Take stem-tip cuttings of perennials, stem cuttings of herbs and indoor plants, and leaf and Irishman's cuttings of rock garden plants.

In midsummer, bud-graft ornamental and fruit trees. Graft cacti and other succulents. In late summer, chip-bud shrubs, side-graft deciduous shrubs, bud-graft, layer, and hybridize roses. Tip layer blackberries and hybrid berries. For bulbs, gather bulbils and remove bulblets (and pot them). In late summer, scale and twin-scale lilies and other bulbs.

Fall

Soil preparation and planting

Plant bare-root, balled-and-burlapped, and container-grown hardy plants, including overwintering bulb vegetables; in mild areas, plant out hardy annuals. Plant trees and spring-flowering bulbs in containers. In early fall, sow salad crops and plant winter salad vegetables and oriental brassicas under cover. In midfall, sow hardy, overwintering vegetables and start digging and manuring empty vegetable beds.

For the lawn, lay sod and sow seed. In early fall, lift, divide, and pot mature herb plants for winter use indoors; pot up strawberry runners for the greenhouse.

Routine care

Water plants as needed. Start watering bulbs that are dormant, under cover, and forced. Restrict watering of indoor plants, cacti, and other succulents after midfall; allow desert plants to dry out but keep epiphytes moist.

Fertilize cacti and succulents that start active growth in midfall; reduce fertilizing of indoor plants. Mulch trees, shrubs, climbers, and perennials. Check and renew stakes and ties as needed. Remove stakes from perennials after flowering.

Deadhead plants unless seed is required. Remove plant debris from around roses and perennials; clear dead annuals and cut out dead rosettes from rock garden plants. Clear fallen leaves from low-growing evergreen herbs. Cut back shrubby herbs in early fall, and tall roses in midfall; except in cold areas, cut down to the ground hardy perennials and those grown as biennials.

Repot or top-dress climbers in containers and winter-flowering indoor plants. Renew top-dressing around rock garden plants. In midfall, transplant established trees, shrubs, and fruit trees if necessary; begin transplanting mature perennials. Lift and store perennials, dahlias, and summer-flowering bulbs; lift and pot perennials grown as annuals.

In late fall, protect tender plants, including container-grown herbs. In cold areas, move shrubs and tender perennials in containers under cover. Protect tender, perennial, and root vegetables in the ground, and frost-tender crowns of water garden plants; move tender floating plants to a frost-free place. Protect plants in an unheated greenhouse from severe cold and raise heat in alpine houses to prevent plants from freezing. Scrub down and fumigate the greenhouse.

In the water garden in early fall, thin oxygenating plants; in mid- to late fall, cut back leaves of marginals and excess growth of submerged plants. Remove dead growth and seedpods of invasive plants; cover ponds with netting. Service and clean the water pump.

Mow lawns as appropriate and fertilize and water if needed. Control moss, aerate, then top-dress. Clear fallen leaves.

In the vegetable garden, in early fall, stake and hill up winter brassicas in windy areas. From midfall, lift plants for forcing. Harvest and store vegetables and fruits. Bring in winter-flowering indoor plants in early fall.

Pruning and training

Give formative pruning, renovate, and prune deciduous trees (unless they bleed heavily) and tree hedges. In early fall, prune mature pleached trees. In late fall, cut out dead, diseased, and damaged wood from shrubs. Give formative pruning to shrub hedges, and prune evergreen hedges. In windy sites, trim shoots of shrubs after flowering. Prune shrubs and woody perennials in the rock garden.

Prune Floribundas, Hybrid Teas, Grandifloras, climbers, miniatures, standards, and newly planted roses, and train new shoots of climbing roses.

Shorten pinched shoots on plum, apricot, and sweet cherry fans. Remove old canes from blackberries and hybrid berries; train young canes. Prune fan-trained peaches and nectarines after fruiting. In late fall, start to prune apples, pears, and bush fruits. Prune long shoots on indoor-grown shrubs and climbers, unless they bleed heavily.

Propagation

Sow seed of plants that overwinter outdoors, including alpine strawberries, and early-flowering indoor plants (under cover). Gather and sow seed of hardy shrubs, perennials, and roses (in late fall).

Divide shrubs, perennials with fibrous roots, mat- and clump-forming rock garden plants, established clumps of water garden marginals and bog plants (in early fall), and clump-forming and rhizomatous herbs. Chip bulbs.

In early fall, take stem-tip cuttings of perennials, basal cuttings of rock garden plants, and leaf-bud cuttings of shrubs. Take semiripe cuttings of trees (early to midfall), climbing plants, and herbs. Take hardwood cuttings of trees (late fall), shrubs (midfall), climbers, roses, rock garden plants, and herbs; plant hardwood cuttings of gooseberries and currants in open ground. Take root cuttings of rock garden plants.

Prepare rose rootstocks for budding. Layer shrubs and climbers; mound layer shrubby herbs. Divide rooted suckers of raspberries and hazelnuts. Indoors, store begonias for propagation in spring.

Winter

Soil preparation and planting

Plant container-grown, deciduous bare-root, and balled-and-burlapped hardy plants and tree, bush, cane, and vine fruits. In midwinter, check summer-flowering bulbs in storage. In the rock garden, build raised and scree beds when conditions permit. Prepare the site for a new lawn. In the vegetable garden, finish digging and manuring empty beds. Plant vegetables outdoors with protection, and set potatoes to sprout indoors.

Routine care

Water forced bulbs and bulbs under cover, if necessary. As epiphytes come into bud, keep soil moist. Water indoor plants less frequently; keep air around plants fairly dry. Fertilize fruit plants in late winter. When conditions permit, mulch trees, shrubs, and climbers. Check ties and supports. Remove supports and plant debris from perennials.

In late winter, repot or top-dress plants in containers. Top-dress rock garden plants and fruiting vine borders. Transplant deciduous trees, shrubs, and perennials, if necessary. Throughout the winter, protect plants outside from winter damage. In an unheated greenhouse, keep plants nearly dry; if necessary, protect plants from severe cold with plastic sheeting or similar material, or plunge small pots in sand. Periodically inspect alpine houses and raised ponds.

Mow established lawns only if necessary; clear fallen leaves. Service all equipment. Force chicory and rhubarb. Harvest and store vegetable crops. In the fruit garden, scrape old bark from grape vines; pollinate peaches under cover.

Pruning and training

Start coppicing and pollarding trees in late winter. Cut out dead, diseased, and damaged wood from trees and shrubs. Give formative pruning and renovate deciduous trees, shrubs, and hedges.

Give formative pruning and train climbing plants in late winter. Prune ornamental vines in early winter, deciduous climbers for shape, and, in late winter, hardy deciduous climbers that flower on new wood. In midwinter, carry out the second stage of pruning *Wisteria*.

Prune roses (in warmer climates) to induce an artificial rest period and give renewal pruning to remontant shrub roses.

Winter prune fruit trees, bushes, fall-fruiting raspberries and young tree roots. Tip-prune summer-fruiting raspberries, blackberries, and hybrid berries.

Propagation

Gather and sow seed of shrubs; sow perennial seed in containers, rose seed produced from hybridizing, seed of hardy rock garden plants, and vegetable seed indoors. In late winter, sow seed of water garden plants under cover.

From late winter, divide shrubs. Start dahlias into growth for division. Scoop rosette-forming rock garden plants.

Take cuttings from sprouting dahlia tubers. Take hardwood cuttings of trees, shrubs, and climbers in early winter. In late winter, plant hardwood cuttings of grapes in well-drained, open ground. Take root cuttings of climbing plants (in early winter), shrubs (in midwinter), perennials, and rock garden plants.

Carry out apical-wedge, side-veneer, and saddle grafting of trees and shrubs. Graft *Gypsophila* cultivars that do not root from cuttings. In late winter, cut back any budded rootstocks from roses.

Prepare trees in late winter for simple layering in spring, and carry out layering of shrubs and climbers. In the fruit garden, divide rooted suckers of raspberries and hazelnuts.

GLOSSARY OF TERMS

The glossary explains horticultural terms that are used in this book. Words in *italics* within a definition have a separate entry. Fuller explanations and illustrations may be found elsewhere by looking up the term in the index.

Acaricide. A *pesticide* used to control mites. (Cf. *Insecticide*; *Nematicide*.)
Acidic (of soil). With a *pH* value of less than 7. (Cf. *Alkaline*; *Neutral*.)
Adventitious. Arising from places where growths do not normally occur; for example, adventitious roots may arise from stems.
Adventitious bud. *See Bud.*
Aerate (of soil). Loosen by mechanical means in order to allow air (oxygen and carbon dioxide) to enter; for example, using a spiked roller to aerate a lawn.
Aerial root. A plant root growing above ground to provide anchorage and, on an *epiphyte*, to absorb atmospheric moisture.
Air layering. See *Layering*.
Alkaline (of soil). With a *pH* value of more than 7. (Cf. *Acidic*; *Neutral*.)
Alpine. A plant that grows above the tree line in mountainous regions; loosely applied to rock garden plants that may be grown at relatively low altitudes.
Alpine house. An unheated, well-ventilated greenhouse used for cultivating *alpine* and bulbous plants.
Alternate (of leaves). Occurring at different levels on opposite sides of a stem. (Cf. *Opposite*.)
Anemone-centered (of flowers). Flowers or flower heads in which the central petals or flowers (modified *stamens*) form a cushionlike mound and the outer rim of petals or ray florets are flat and spreading, as in some chrysanthemums.
Annual. A plant that completes its life cycle (*germination* / flowering / seeding / dying) in one growing season.
Anther. The part of a *stamen* that produces *pollen*; usually borne on a *filament*.
Apical. See *Terminal*.
Apical bud. See *Bud*.
Apical-wedge grafting. See *Grafting*.
Aquatic. Any plant that grows in water. It may be free-floating, totally submerged, or rooted on the pond bottom with leaves and flowers above the water surface.
Asclepiad. A member of the *family* Asclepiadaceae.
Asexual reproduction. A form of reproduction not involving *fertilization* and, in propagation, often involving mechanical methods (see *Vegetative propagation*).
Auxins. Naturally occurring or artificially synthesized plant growth substances controlling shoot growth, root formation, and other physiological processes in plants.

Awn. A sharp point or bristle, commonly found on a *glume* of a grass *inflorescence*.
Axil. The upper angle between a leaf and a stem, between a main stem and a lateral branch, or between a stem and a bract. (See also *Bud: Axillary bud*.)
Axillary bud. See *Bud*.
Back bulb (of orchids). A dormant, old *pseudobulb* without leaves.
Backfill. To fill in a planting hole around a plant's roots with soil.
Ball. See *Root ball*.
Balled. Of a flower that does not open and rots when still in bud.
Balled-and-burlapped. Of plants that have been lifted and had their *root ball* wrapped in burlap or other material to keep it intact during *transplanting*.
Bare-root. Of plants sold with their roots bare of soil.
Bark-ringing. The removal of a ring of bark from the trunk or branches of certain fruit trees to reduce vigorous growth and to encourage fruit bearing. Also known as "girdling."
Basal plate. A compressed *stem*, part of a *bulb*.
Basal stem cutting. See *Cutting*.
Basal-whip grafting. See *Grafting*.
Base dressing. An application of fertilizer or organic matter (manure, compost, etc.) applied to or dug into the soil prior to sowing or planting.
Basin irrigation. A form of irrigation whereby soil is scooped out from around the plant or made to form a ridge around it, creating a basin into which water is introduced.
Bastard trenching. See *Double digging*.
Bed system. A method of planting vegetable crops in closely spaced rows, often in blocks or narrow beds for easy access.
Bedding plants. Annuals and biennials (or plants grown as such) raised almost to maturity and then planted out ("bedded out"), often in large blocks for temporary display.
Biennial. A plant that flowers and dies in the second growing season after *germination*.
Biennial bearing. The production of a heavy fruit crop in alternate years, with little or no blossoms or fruit in the intervening years.
Blanch. To exclude light from developing leaves or stems in order to keep the plant tissue soft and palatable.
Bleed. To lose *sap* through a wound.
Blind. Of a plant that fails to produce flowers, or a stem with a growing point that has been damaged.
Bloom. 1) A flower or blossom. 2) A waxy, white or bluish white coating on a stem, leaf, or fruit.
Blown. Of flowers or hearted vegetables (see *Heart up*) that are past full maturity and fading.
Bog plant. A plant whose natural

habitat is soil that is permanently damp, or one that thrives in such conditions.
Bole. The *trunk* of a tree from ground level to the first major branch.
Bolt. To produce flowers and seed prematurely.
Bract. A modified, often protective leaf at the base of a flower or flower cluster. Bracts may resemble normal leaves, or be small and scalelike, or large and brightly colored.
Branch. A shoot arising from the main stem or trunk of a woody plant.
Brassica. A member of the cabbage *family*.
Break. A *shoot* growing from an *axillary bud*.
Broadcasting. Scattering seed or fertilizer evenly over the ground, rather than in furrows or *drills*.
Broad-leaved. Of trees or shrubs that bear broad, flat leaves rather than needlelike foliage.
Bromeliad. A member of the *family* Bromeliaceae.
Bud. A rudimentary or condensed shoot containing an embryonic leaf, leaf cluster, or flower. **Adventitious bud:** one produced abnormally, for example from the stem instead of from a leaf *axil*. **Apical** (or **terminal**) **bud:** the topmost bud on a stem. **Axillary bud:** one that occurs in an *axil*. **Crown bud:** a flower bud at the shoot tip, surrounded by other, usually smaller, flower buds. **Fruit bud:** one from which leaves and flowers (followed by fruits) develop. **Growth bud:** one from which only leaves or a shoot develop.
Bud union. The point at which the *scion* bud unites with the *rootstock*.
Budding. Bud-grafting, a form of *grafting*.
Budding tape. See *Grafting tape*.
Bud-grafting. See *Grafting*.
Budwood. A shoot cut from a tree to provide a scion for *bud-grafting*.
Bulb. A modified *stem* acting as a storage organ and consisting mainly of fleshy, more or less separate or tightly packed, scale leaves (a modified *bud*) on a much reduced stem (*basal plate*).
Bulb fiber. Undecomposed *sphagnum moss*, sometimes with charcoal, in which *bulbs* are grown in containers, often without drainage holes.
Bulbil. A small *bulb*-like organ, often borne in a leaf *axil*, occasionally on a stem or in a *flower head*. (Cf. *Bulblet*.)
Bulblet. A small developing *bulb* produced from the *basal plate* of a mature bulb outside the *tunic*. (Cf. *Bulbil and Offset*.)
Bush. 1) A small shrub. 2) An open-centered fruit tree with a *trunk* of 3ft (90cm) or less.
Bush fruit. Used of soft fruit bushes such as blackcurrants and gooseberries.
Cactus. A member of the *family* Cactaceae, characterized by fleshy,

water-storing tissue in the stems and areoles (specialized groups of cells) from which spines, flowers, and shoots develop.
Calcicole. *Lime*-loving; a plant that thrives in *alkaline* soil.
Calcifuge. *Lime*-hating; a plant that will not grow in *alkaline* soil.
Callus. Protective tissue formed by plants over a wounded surface, particularly in *woody* plants but also at the base of cuttings.
Calyx (pl. **calyces**). The collective name for the *sepals*, the outer *whorl* of segments, usually green, that enclose the flower in bud.
Cambium. A layer of meristematic tissue capable of producing new cells to increase the girth of stems and roots. (See also *Meristem*.)
Capillary matting. Matting made of synthetic fiber that is used to draw water upward by capillary action to irrigate pot plants on capillary beds or benches.
Capping. Formation of a crust that forms on the surface of soil damaged by compaction, heavy rain, or watering. (Cf. *Pan*.)
Capsule. A dry seed case that dehisces (splits open) when ripe to release its seeds.
Carpel. The female part of the flower of flowering plants that contains the *ovules*; several carpels in a flower are collectively known as the *pistil*.
Carpet bedding. The use of groups of closely planted, low-growing, colorful *bedding plants* in various patterns or designs.
Catkin. A racemose (see *Raceme*) flower spike, or a spikelike *inflorescence*, with conspicuous *bracts* and small, often unisexual flowers lacking petals.
Cell pack. Applied to various types of container, particularly those used in multiples for sowing seed and pricking out seedlings.
Central leader. The central, usually upright stem of a *tree*.
Certified stock. Plants certified by the US Department of Agriculture or Agriculture Canada as free from certain pests and diseases.
Chilling requirement. The requirement of plants for a specific period of dormancy below a particular temperature in order for them to initiate flowering.
Chinese layering. An alternative name for air layering; see *Layering*.
Chip-budding. See *Grafting*.
Chlorophyll. The green plant pigment that is mainly responsible for light absorption and hence *photosynthesis* in plants.
Clamp. A method for storing *root crops* outdoors. The crops are heaped up and protected against cold by layers of straw and soil. Often referred to as a "pile."

Climber. 1) A plant that climbs using other plants or objects as support: **self-clinging climbers** by supporting, *adventitious*, or *aerial roots*, or adhesive tendril tips; **tendril climbers** by coiling their leaf stalks, leaf *tendrils*, or modified *terminal* shoots; **twining climbers** by coiling their *stems*. **Scandent, scrambling, rambling**, and **trailing climbers** produce long, usually flexuous stems that grow over or through plants or other supports; they attach themselves only loosely, if at all, to the support. 2) A type of rose with long, rather flexible shoots.

Cloche. A small, usually portable structure made of clear plastic or glass, often in a metal framework; used to protect early crops on open ground and to warm the soil before planting. Often called a "cover."

Clone. 1) A group of genetically identical plants produced by *vegetative propagation or asexual reproduction.* 2) An individual plant in such a group.

Cold frame. A glazed, boxlike, unheated structure made from brick, wood, or glass, with a hinged or removable glass or clear plastic *sash*, used to protect plants from excessive cold.

Collar. 1) The part of a plant where the roots meet the stem; also known as the neck. 2) The part of a tree where a main branch meets the *trunk* (or a side branch meets a main branch).

Companion planting. Positioning plants together that are reputed to have a beneficial effect on neighboring plants by discouraging pests and diseases or improving growth.

Compositae. The daisy *family*.

Compost. A material, rich in *organic* matter, formed by decomposed plant remains and other organic matter, used as a soil improver or *mulch*.

Compound. Divided into two or more subsidiary parts, for example a leaf divided into two or more *leaflets*. (Cf. *Simple*.)

Cone. The densely clustered *bracts* and flowers of *conifers* and some flowering plants, often developing into a woody, seed-bearing structure, e.g. a pine cone.

Confused. Of petals, especially in roses, that have an overlapping, irregular arrangement.

Conifer. Gymnosperms, usually evergreen trees and shrubs, that are distinguished from flowering plants (Angiosperms) by the naked *ovules* that are not enclosed in an *ovary* but are often borne in *cones*.

Contact action. The action of a *pesticide* or weedkiller that kills or damages a pest or weed by direct contact.

Coppicing. The annual pruning back of trees or shrubs close to ground level to produce vigorous, usually decorative, *shoots*. (Cf. *Pollarding*.)

Cordon. A trained plant (usually a fruit tree) generally restricted to one main stem by rigorous pruning.

A **single cordon** has one main stem, a **double**, or **U, cordon** has two, and a **multiple cordon**, three or more stems.

Corm. A *bulb*-like, underground, swollen *stem* or stem base, often surrounded by a papery *tunic*. A corm is replaced annually by a new corm that develops from a *terminal*, or *lateral*, *bud*.

Cormel. A small *corm* developing around a mature corm, usually outside the main corm *tunic*, as in gladiolus.

Cormlet. A small *corm* arising at the base (and usually within the old *tunic*) of a mature corm. (See also *Offset*.)

Corolla. The interior *whorl* of the *perianth* of a flower, consisting of several free or fused *petals*.

Cotyledon. A seed leaf; the first leaf or leaves to emerge from the seed after *germination*, often markedly different from mature leaves. Flowering plants (Angiosperms) are classified into *monocotyledons* (one) and *dicotyledons* (two) depending on how many cotyledons are contained in the mature seed. In conifers (Gymnosperms) they are often produced in *whorls*.

Crest. A ridged outgrowth, often on *perianth segments*, as in orchids and some irises.

Cristate. Having exaggerated *cresting*, commonly seen in fern fronds and the *inflorescences* of cockscombs (*Celosia*) or the stems of cacti.

Crop rotation. A system in which vegetable crops are grown on different sections of a plot on a three- or four-year cycle to minimize the buildup of soilborne pests and diseases in one section.

Cross-fertilization. The *fertilization* of the *ovules* of a flower as a result of *cross-pollination*.

Cross-pollination. The transfer of pollen from the *anther* of a flower on one plant to the *stigma* of a flower on another plant; the term is often loosely applied to *cross-fertilization*. (Cf. *Self-pollination*.)

Crown. 1) The basal part at soil level of a *herbaceous* plant where roots and stems join and from where new shoots are produced. 2) The upper, branched part of a tree above the *bole*.

Crown bud. See *Bud*.

Culm. The usually hollow stem of a grass or bamboo.

Cultivar. A contraction of "*culti*vated *variety*" (abbreviated "cv"); a group (or one among such a group) of cultivated plants that has been selected either from the wild or from gardens and grown in cultivation, and whose characteristics are preserved by some means of controlled propagation. (Cf. *Variety*.)

Cupped. Usually of leaves or flowers, shaped like a cup.

Cutting. A portion of a plant (a leaf, shoot, root, or bud) that is cut off to be used for *propagation*. **Basal stem cutting:** one taken from the base of a (usually *herbaceous*) plant as it begins to grow in spring. **Greenwood cutting:** one taken from the soft tips of young growth after the spring

growth flush has slowed down; slightly harder and woodier stems than are used for softwood cuttings. **Hardwood cutting:** one taken from mature wood of both deciduous and evergreen plants at the end of the growing season. **Heel cutting:** one taken with a portion of the bark or mature wood at the base. **Internodal cutting:** one in which the basal cut is made between two *nodes* or growth buds. **Leaf cutting:** one taken from a detached leaf or part of a leaf. **Leaf-bud cutting:** one consisting of a short section of stem and a single or double pair of buds or leaves. **Nodal cutting:** one trimmed at the base just below a growth bud or *node*. **Ripewood cutting:** one taken from ripened wood, usually of evergreens, during the growing season. **Root cutting:** one taken from part of a semimature or mature root. **Semiripe cutting:** one taken from half-ripened wood during the growing season. **Softwood cutting:** one taken from young, immature growth during the growing season. **Stem cutting:** one taken from any portion of a plant stem. **Stem-tip cutting:** any cutting taken from the tip of a shoot; sometimes applied to softwood and greenwood cuttings.

Cyme. A usually flat-topped, *determinate inflorescence* in which the central or *terminal* flower opens first.

Damping down. Wetting greenhouse floors and staging with water to increase humidity, particularly in very hot and dry conditions.

Deadheading. The removal of *spent* flowers or *flower heads*.

Deciduous. Of plants that shed leaves at the end of the growing season and renew them at the beginning of the next; **semideciduous** plants lose only some of their leaves at the end of the growing season.

Degradable pot. A pot made from degradable material such as compressed peat or paper.

Dehiscence. Term used of *fruits* (usually *capsules*) and *anthers* to describe the process of opening at maturity to release their contents.

Dehiscent. Of a *fruit*, usually a *capsule*, or an *anther* that splits along definite lines to release seeds or pollen.

Determinate. 1) Used of *inflorescences* where the central or terminal flower opens first so that the main axis cannot extend further. (Cf. *Cyme*.) 2) Used of bushy or dwarf tomatoes. (Cf. *Indeterminate*; *Semideterminate*.)

Dibber (also dibble). A tool used for making holes in soil or potting mix into which seedlings or cuttings are inserted.

Dicotyledon. A flowering plant that usually has two *cotyledons* or seed leaves in the seed; it is also characterized by the (usually) net-veined leaves, the *petals* and *sepals* in multiples of two, four, or five, and by the presence of a *cambium*. (Cf. *Monocotyledon*.)

Dieback. The death of tips of shoots as a result of damage or disease.

Dioecious. Bearing male and female reproductive organs on separate plants. (Cf. *Monoecious*.)

Diploid. Having two basic sets of chromosomes. (Cf. *Triploid*.)

Disbudding. The removal of surplus *buds* to promote the production of high-quality flowers or fruits.

Distal end (of *cuttings*). The end that was originally farther from the *crown* of the parent plant. (Cf. *Proximal end*.)

Division. A method of increasing plants by dividing them into pieces, each with a root system and one or more shoots (or dormant *buds*).

Dormancy. The state of temporary cessation of growth and slowing down of other activities in whole plants, usually during the winter; **seed dormancy:** *non-germination* of seed (when placed in conditions suitable for germination) due to physical, chemical, or other factors inherent in the seed; **double** (seed) **dormancy:** nongermination of seeds due to two dormancy factors in the seed.

Double (of a flower). See *Flower*.

Double cordon. See *Cordon*.

Double digging. A cultivation technique in which the soil is worked to a depth of two *spits*. Also known as "trench digging" or "bastard trenching."

Drainage. The passage of excess water through soil; the term is also applied to systems used to remove excess water.

Drill. A narrow, straight furrow in the soil in which seeds are sown or seedlings planted.

Drupes. See *Stone fruits*.

Emasculation. The removal of the *anthers* before the pollen is shed to prevent *self-pollination* and hence *self-fertilization*.

Epicormic shoots. Shoots that develop from latent or *adventitious* buds on or from the *trunk* of a tree or shrub. (See also *Water shoots*.)

Epigeal. Type of seed *germination* in which the seed is pushed above soil level by elongation of the *hypocotyl*. (Cf. *Hypogeal*.)

Epiphyte. A plant that grows on another plant without being parasitic, obtaining moisture and nutrients from the atmosphere without rooting into the soil.

Ericaceous. 1) Term describing plants of the *family* Ericaceae, usually *lime*-hating and requiring soils of *pH* 6.5 or less (see also *Calcifuge*).

Espalier. A plant trained with the main stem vertical and (usually) three or more tiers of branches horizontally placed on either side in a single plane; often applied to fruit trees and other plants grown for attractive fruits and flowers.

Evergreen. Of plants that retain a substantial portion of their foliage for more than one growing season; **semi-evergreen** plants retain only a small proportion of their leaves for more than one season.

Explant. A tiny portion of a plant prepared and inserted in an aseptic growing medium for *micropropagation* purposes.

Eye. 1) A dormant or latent growth *bud*, such as the eye of a potato or dahlia tuber. 2) The center of a flower, especially if different in color from the petals.

F1 hybrids. First-generation plants obtained from crossing two selected pure-breeding parents to produce uniform, vigorous, and high-yielding offspring. Seed from F1 hybrids does not come *true*.

F2 hybrids. Plants that result from *self-* or *cross-fertilization of F1 hybrids*; they are less uniform than their parents.

Falls. The pendent or horizontally placed *tepals* or *petals* of irises and some related plants.

Family. A category in plant classification, a grouping together of related *genera*, for example the family Rosaceae includes the genera *Rosa, Sorbus, Rubus, Prunus*, and *Pyracantha*; the family Iridaceae includes the genera *Iris, Crocus, Dierama*, and *Crocosmia*.

Fastigiate. With the branches (usually of trees and shrubs) growing vertically and almost parallel with the main stem.

Feathered. Of *maiden* trees that have several *lateral* branches ("feathers").

Fertile (of plants). Producing viable seed; shoots bearing flowers are also said to be fertile shoots as opposed to nonflowering (sterile) shoots.

Fertilization. The fusion of a *pollen* grain nucleus (male) with an *ovule* (female) to form a fertile seed.

Fibrous. 1) Of roots, fine and often branching and dense. 2) Of soil, containing fiber derived from dead roots.

Filament. The *stalk* of the *stamen* which bears the *anther*.

Fimbriate. Of part of a plant that has a fringed edge. Plant organs with a fringe of hairs are said to be ciliate.

Flat. A shallow tray or container for seeds and cuttings.

Flat grafting. See *Grafting*.

Floating row cover (or simply "row cover"). Lightweight sheet, usually of woven polypropylene (fiber fleece), placed over a crop, which is lifted up by the plants as they grow. It provides some frost protection while allowing water and light penetration.

Floret. A (generally) small flower in a *flower head* consisting of many flowers.

Flower. The part of the plant containing the reproductive organs usually surrounded by *sepals* and *petals*. The basic flower forms are: **single**, with one row of usually four to six petals; **semidouble**, with two or three times the normal number of petals usually in two or three rows; **double**, with more than the normal number of petals in several rows with few or no *stamens* produced; **fully double**, flowers usually rounded in shape, with densely packed petals and with the stamens obscured or absent. (Cf. *Flower head*.)

Flower head. A mass of small *flowers* or *florets* that together appear to form a single flower, as in members of the family Compositae.

Flush. A distinct period of bloom.

Force. To induce plant growth, usually of flowers or fruit by control of the environment, normally by increasing the temperature.

Forma (f.). A variant within a *species*, usually distinguished only by minor characteristics: *Clematis montana* f. *grandiflora* is a larger-flowered, more vigorous form of *C. montana*. Also loosely used for any variant of a species.

Formative pruning. A method of pruning that is carried out on young trees and shrubs to develop the basic branch structure of the desired form or shape.

Foundation planting. The basic, usually permanent, plants complementing a structure and sometimes hiding its base.

Frame. See *Cold frame*.

Framework. The permanent branch structure of a tree or shrub; the main branches that determine its ultimate shape. **Framework plants**: the plants in a garden that form the basis or structure of the design.

Frame-working (of fruit trees). Pruning back all side growths to the main framework and grafting *scions* of a different *cultivar* onto each main framework branch.

French layering. See *Layering*.

Friable (of soil). Of a good, crumbly texture; capable of forming a *tilth* that can be worked easily.

Frond. 1) The *leaf*-like organ of a fern. Some ferns produce both *sterile* and *fertile* fronds, the latter bearing *spores*. 2) Loosely applied to large, usually *compound* leaves such as those of palms.

Frost pocket. A site, often a hollow, where cold air gathers, subject to severe and often prolonged frosts.

Frost tender. See *Tender*.

Fruit. The fertilized, ripe *ovary* of a plant containing one to many seeds, for example, berries, *hips, capsules*, and nuts; the term is also used of edible fruits.

Fruit bud. See *Bud*.

Fruit set. The successful development of fruits after *pollination* and *fertilization*.

Fully double. See *Flower*.

Fully reflexed. See *Reflexed*.

Fungicide. A chemical that kills fungi, especially those responsible for various plant diseases.

Genus (pl. **genera**). A category in plant classification ranked between *family* and *species*. A group of related species linked by a range of common characters; for example, all species of horse chestnut and buckeye are grouped under the genus *Aesculus*. (See also *Cultivar, Family, Forma, Hybrid, Species, Subspecies*, and *Variety*.)

Germination. The physical and chemical changes that take place as a seed starts to grow and develop into a plant.

Girdling. 1) The removal of bark all around a stem or branch caused by animal or physical damage or by a constricting tie that prevents the flow of water and *nutrients* to the upper part of the plant, eventually causing the death of all the tissue above the girdled trunk or branch. 2) See *Bark-ringing*.

Glaucous. With a blue-green, blue-gray, gray, or white bloom.

Glume. A chafflike, dry *bract* in the *inflorescences* of grasses and sedges.

Graft. To join artificially one or more plant parts to another.

Graft union. The point at which *scion* and *rootstock* are joined.

Grafting. A method of *propagation* by which an artificial union is made between the *scion* of one plant and the *rootstock* of another so that they eventually function as one plant. Methods include apical-wedge grafting; basal-whip (or splice) grafting; bud-grafting (including chip-budding and T-budding); flat grafting; saddle grafting; side grafting (see CACTI AND OTHER SUCCULENTS, "Side grafting," p.271); side-veneer grafting; side-wedge grafting; and whip-and-tongue grafting. (For details see PRINCIPLES OF PROPAGATION, "Grafting and budding," pp.543–4.)

Grafting tape. Tape used to protect a *graft union* during healing.

Green manure. A quickly maturing, leafy crop such as winter rye that is grown specifically to be dug back into, and thereby enrich, the soil.

Greenwood cutting. See *Cutting*.

Ground color. Main (background) color of petals.

Groundcover. Usually low-growing plants that quickly cover the soil surface and suppress weeds.

Growth bud. See *Bud*.

Half hardy. Used of an annual plant that will survive some cold but will not overwinter outdoors. The term generally implies an ability to withstand lower temperatures than *tender*.

Half standard. A tree or shrub that has a clear stem of 3–5ft (1–1.5m) between ground level and the lowest branches.

Hardening off. Gradually acclimatizing plants that have been raised under cover to cooler outdoor conditions.

Hardpan. See *Pan*.

Hardwood cutting. See *Cutting*.

Hardy. Able to withstand year-round climatic conditions, including cold, without protection.

Haulm. The top-growth of plants such as potatoes and legumes.

Head. 1) The part of a tree above a clear *trunk*. 2) A dense *inflorescence*.

Head back. To prune back the main branches of trees or shrubs by half or more.

Heading. See *Heart up*.

Heart up. The stage at which vegetables such as lettuces or cabbages begin to produce tight "hearts" or "heads" of inner leaves.

Heavy (of soil). Having a high proportion of clay.

Heel. A small piece or strip of bark or wood that is retained at the base of a *cutting* when it is pulled away from a main stem.

Heel cutting. See *Cutting*.

Heeling in. Temporary planting until a plant can be placed in its permanent position.

Herb. 1) A plant grown for its medicinal or flavoring properties or for its scented foliage. 2) Botanically, a *herbaceous* plant.

Herbaceous. A non-*woody* plant in which the upper parts die down to a rootstock at the end of the growing season. The term is chiefly applied to *perennials*, although botanically it also applies to *annuals* and *biennials*.

Herbicide. A chemical used to control or kill weeds.

Hilling up. Drawing up soil around the base of a plant to help prevent *wind rock*, to *blanch* the *stems*, or to encourage stem rooting.

Hip. The seed-bearing structure of a rose.

Hull. The outer casing of a nut.

Humus. The chemically complex, organic residue of decayed vegetable matter in soil. Often (incorrectly) used to describe partly decayed matter such as *leaf mold* or *compost*.

Hybrid. The offspring of genetically different parents usually of distinct taxa (see *Taxon*). Hybrids between *species* of the same *genus* are known as interspecific hybrids. Those between different but usually closely related *genera* are known as intergeneric hybrids. (See also *F1 hybrids; F2 hybrids*.)

Hybrid vigor. An improved growth and yield shown by some hybrids.

Hybridization. The process by which *hybrids* are formed.

Hydroculture. The cultivation of plants in nutrient-rich water, sometimes with sterile aggregates. (See also *Hydroponics*.)

Hydroponics. Growing plants in dilute solutions of nutrients. Applied loosely to any form of soilless culture.

Hypocotyl. The portion of a *seedling* just below the *cotyledons*.

Hypogeal. Type of seed *germination* in which the *cotyledons* remain below the soil surface while the young shoot (plumule) emerges above soil level.

Incurved. Applied to petals of flowers and *florets* that curve inward to form a compact, rounded shape. Incurving flower heads are less compact with more loosely arranged but still incurved florets.

Indehiscent. Of a *fruit* that does not split open to release its seeds. (Cf. *Dehiscent*.)

Indeterminate. 1) Used of an *inflorescence* not terminated by a single flower, in which the primary axis (stem) continues to develop as the lower flowers open (e.g. a *raceme* as in delphiniums). 2) Used of tall or staked tomatoes, which, in a suitable climate, can grow to an indefinite length. (Cf. *Determinate; Semideterminate*.)

Inflorescence. A group of flowers borne on a single axis (stem). *Racemes, panicles*, and *cymes* are all types of inflorescence.

Informal. Applied to some cultivars of chrysanthemums, dahlias, and others with irregular flower formation.

Inorganic. Of a chemical compound, one that does not contain carbon. Inorganic fertilizers are refined from naturally occurring chemicals or produced artificially. (Cf. *Organic*.)

Insecticide. A *pesticide* used to control or kill insects. (Cf. *Acaricide*; *Nematicide*.)

Insert. To place cuttings in a growing medium.

Intercropping. The growing of quick-maturing vegetable crops between slower-growing crops to make maximum use of the available space.

Intergeneric hybrid. See *Hybrid*.

Intermediate. 1) A term applied to chrysanthemums with flower heads intermediate in shape between *reflexed* and *incurved*. 2) A hybrid with characters intermediate between its two parents.

Internodal cutting. See *Cutting*.

Internode. The portion of stem between two *nodes*.

Interplanting. 1) The planting of fast-maturing plants between slower-growing plants to provide a display while they mature. 2) The planting of two or more types of plants together to provide a display of different colors or textures (e.g., tulips among wallflowers). Often used in relation to bedding.

Interspecific hybrid. See *Hybrid*.

Irrigation. 1) General term for watering. 2) The use of a system of basins, channels, or sprinklers to provide a controlled supply of water to plants.

Joint. See *Node*.

Knot garden. Beds laid out in a formal, often complex, pattern, formed from dwarf hedges or clipped herbs.

Laced. A term applied to some flowers (e.g., daylilies and irises) that have finely cut petal edges.

Lamina. The blade of a leaf, usually flattened, not including the petiole (leaf stalk).

Lateral. A side growth that arises from a shoot or root.

Layer planting. 1) A form of *interplanting* in which groups of plants planted closely together flower in succession. 2) A planting design such that the groups of plants form layers above each other.

Layering. A method of *propagation* by which a *shoot* is induced to *root* while still attached to the parent plant. The basic form is self-layering, which occurs naturally in some plants. Methods include: air layering (also known as Chinese layering or marcottage), French layering, mound layering (also known as stooling), serpentine, simple layering, tip layering, and trench layering. (For details, see PRINCIPLES OF PROPAGATION, "Layering," p.539.)

Leaching. The loss from the top soil of soluble *nutrients* by downward drainage.

Leader. 1) The main, usually central, stem of a plant. 2) The *terminal* shoot of a main branch.

Leaf. A plant organ, variable in shape and color but often flattened and green, borne on the stem, that performs the functions of *photosynthesis*, *respiration*, and *transpiration*.

Leaf cutting. See *Cutting*.

Leaf mold. Fibrous, flaky material derived from decomposed leaves, used in potting media and as a general soil improver.

Leaf-bud cutting. See *Cutting*.

Leaflet. One of the subdivisions of a *compound* leaf.

Legume. A one-chambered, *dehiscent fruit* splitting at maturity into two, belonging to the *family* Leguminosae.

Light. Of soil, with a high proportion of sand and little clay.

Lime. Loosely, a number of compounds of calcium; the amount of lime in soil determines whether it is *alkaline*, *acidic*, or *neutral*.

Line out. To plant out young plants or insert cuttings in lines in a nursery bed or frame.

Lithophyte. A plant naturally growing on rocks (or in very stony soil) and usually obtaining most of its nutrients and water from the atmosphere.

Loam. A term used for soil of medium texture, often easily worked, that contains more or less equal parts of sand, silt, and clay, and is usually rich in organic matter. If the proportion of one ingredient is high, the term may be qualified as silt-loam, clay-loam, or sandy loam.

Maiden. A *grafted* tree in its first year. (See also *Whip*.)

Maincrop (of vegetables). Those cultivars that produce crops throughout the main growing season, doing so over a longer period than either early or late cultivars.

Marcottage. An alternative name for air layering; see *Layering*.

Marginal water plant. A plant that grows partially submerged in shallow water or in constantly moist soil at the edge of a pond or stream.

Medium. 1) A *soil mix*, potting mixture, or other material in which plants may be propagated or grown. 2) Applied to those soils that are intermediate in character between *heavy* and *light*. (See also *Loam*.)

Mericlone. Genetically identical offspring produced by *meristem* culture.

Meristem. Plant tissue that is able to divide to produce new cells. Shoot or root tips contain meristematic tissue and may be used for *micropropagation*.

Micronutrients. Chemical elements essential to plants but needed only in very small quantities, also known as trace elements. (See also *Nutrients*.)

Micropropagation. Propagation of plants by *tissue culture*.

Midrib. The primary, usually central vein of a leaf or leaflet.

Monocarpic. Flowering and fruiting only once before dying; such plants may take several years to reach flowering size.

Monocotyledon. A flowering plant that has only one *cotyledon* or seed leaf in the seed; it is also characterized by narrow, parallel-veined *leaves*, and parts of the flower in threes or multiples of three.

Monoecious. Bearing separate male and female reproductive organs on the same plant. (Cf. *Dioecious*.)

Monopodial. Growing indefinitely from an apical or *terminal* bud on a stem. (Cf. *Sympodial*.)

Moss peat. See *Peat*.

Mound layering. See *Layering*.

Mulch. A material applied in a layer to the soil surface to suppress weeds, conserve moisture, and maintain a preferably uniform root temperature. In addition to organic materials (such as manure, bark, and compost), plastic, foil, and gravel may also be used. (See also *Floating row cover*.)

Multiple cordon. See *Cordon*.

Mutation. An induced or spontaneous genetic change, often resulting in shoots with variegated foliage or flowers of a different color from the parent plant. A mutation is also known as a sport.

Mycorrhizae. Soil fungi that live in beneficial association with plant roots.

Naturalize. To establish and grow as if in the wild.

Neck. See *Collar*.

Nectar. Sugary liquid secreted from a *nectary*; often attractive to pollinating insects.

Nectary. Glandular tissue usually found in the flower, but sometimes on the leaves or stems, that secretes *nectar*.

Nematicide. A *pesticide* used to control nematodes. (Cf. Acaricide; *Insecticide*.)

Neutral (of soil). With a *pH* value of 7, i.e., neither *acidic* nor *alkaline*.

Nodal cutting. See *Cutting*.

Node. The point on a stem from which one or more leaves, shoots, branches, or flowers arise. Also called a joint.

Nonremontant. Flowering or fruiting only once in a single *flush*. (Cf. *Remontant*.)

Nursery bed. An area used for germinating seeds or growing on young plants before planting them out in their permanent positions.

Nut. A one-seeded, *indehiscent* fruit with a tough or woody coat, for example, an acorn. Less specifically, all fruits and seeds with woody or leathery coats.

Nutrients. Minerals (mineral ions) used to develop proteins and other compounds required for plant growth.

Offset. A young plant that arises by natural, *vegetative* reproduction, usually at the base of the parent plant; in bulbs, offsets are initially formed within the bulb *tunic* but later separate out. Also known as offshoots.

Offshoot. See *Offset*.

Open-pollination. Natural pollination. (See also *Pollination*.)

Opposite. Term describing two leaves, or other plant organs, at the same level on opposite sides of a stem or other axis. (Cf. *Alternate*.)

Organic. 1) Chemically, referring to compounds containing carbon derived from plant or animal organisms. 2) Loosely, applied to mulches, fertilizers, or similar materials derived from plant matter. 3) Also applied to crop production and gardening without the use of synthetic or nonorganic materials.

Ovary. The basal part of the pistil of a flower, containing one or more *ovules*; it may develop into a *fruit* after *fertilization*. (See also *Carpel*.)

Ovule. The part of the *ovary* that develops into the *seed* after *pollination* and *fertilization*.

Oxygenator. Submerged aquatic plant that releases oxygen into the water.

Packs. Compartmented trays in which individual seeds or seedlings are grown.

Pan. 1) A shallow, earthenware or plastic pot that is much wider than it is deep. 2) A layer of soil that is impermeable to water and oxygen and impedes root growth and drainage. Some pans (hardpans) occur naturally on clay or iron-rich soils. Soils capped (see *Capping*) by heavy rain or excess watering, or by continuous use of cultivation machinery, are also known as pans or hardpans.

Panicle. An *indeterminate*, branched *inflorescence* often consisting of several racemose branches (see *Raceme*). The term is also loosely used to describe any type of branching inflorescence.

Parterre. A level area containing ornamental beds, often with low-growing plants and enclosed in dwarf hedges. (Cf. *Knot garden*.)

Parthenocarpic. The production of fruit without *fertilization* having taken place.

Pathogens. Microorganisms that cause disease.

Peasticks. Short, twiggy sticks used to support peas and, more commonly, bushy perennial plants.

Peat. Partially decayed, highly organic plant matter formed on the surface of waterlogged soils. **Moss** or **sphagnum peat** is largely derived from partially decayed *sphagnum* moss and is used in soil mixes. **Sedge peat** is derived from sedges, mosses, and heathers; it is coarser than moss peat and less suitable for soil mixes.

Peat bed. Beds usually constructed from *peat* blocks and filled with very peaty soil; used to grow acidic soil-loving plants, particularly in areas with soils of high *pH*.

Peat blocks. Blocks of peat cut from natural peat deposits.

Peduncle. The *stalk* of a *flower*.

Peltate (of leaves). A leaf with the stalk usually attached centrally beneath the leaf blade; sometimes the stalk may be off-center within the leaf margin.

Perennial. Strictly, any plant living for at least three seasons; commonly applied to *herbaceous* and *woody* plants (i.e. trees and shrubs).

Perianth. The collective term for the *calyx* and the *corolla*, particularly when they are very similar in form, as in many bulb flowers.

Perianth segment. One portion of a *perianth*, usually resembling a *petal* and sometimes known as a *tepal*.

Perlite. Small granules of expanded volcanic minerals added to growing media to improve aeration.

Perpetual. Of plants that bloom more or less continuously throughout the growing season or over long periods of time.

Pesticide. A chemical substance, usually manufactured, that is used to kill pests including insects (insecticide), mites (acaricide), and nematodes (nematicide).

Petal. A modified leaf, often brightly colored; one part of the *corolla* usually of a *dicotyledonous* flower. (Cf. *Tepal*.)

Petiole. The *stalk* of a *leaf*.

pH. A measure of alkalinity or acidity, used horticulturally to refer to soils. The scale measures from 1 to 14; *pH* 7 is neutral, above 7 is alkaline, and below 7 is acidic. (See also *Acidic*, *Alkaline*, and *Neutral*.)

Photosynthesis. The production of organic compounds required for growth in plants by a complex process involving *chlorophyll*, light energy, carbon dioxide, and water.

Picotee. A term for *petals* with a narrow margin of a contrasting color.

Pinching out. The removal of the growing tip of a plant (by finger and thumb) to induce the production of *sideshoots* or the formation of flower buds. Also known as "stopping."

Pistil. See *Carpel*.

Pith (of stems). The soft plant tissue in the central part of a stem.

Pleaching. A technique whereby branches from a row of trees are woven together and trained to form a wall or canopy of foliage.

Plumule. See *Hypogeal*.

Plunge. To sink a pot up to its rim in a bed of ashes, peat, sand, or soil to protect the roots of the plant or plants in the pot from extremes of temperature.

Pod. An loosely defined term generally applied to any dry, *dehiscent fruit*; it is particularly used for peas and beans.

Pollarding. The regular pruning back of the main branches of a tree to the main stem or trunk, or to a short branch framework, usually to a height of about 6ft (2m). (Cf. *Coppicing*.)

Pollen. The male cells of a plant, formed in the *anther*.

Pollination. The transfer of *pollen* from *anthers* to *stigmas*. (See also *Cross-pollination*, *Open-pollination*, and *Self-pollination*.)

Pollinator. 1) The agent or means by which *pollination* is carried out (e.g., by insects or wind). 2) Used in fruit growing to describe a *cultivar* required to ensure fruit set on another self- or partially *self-sterile* cultivar.

Polyembryonic. Containing more than one embryo in an *ovule* or *seed*.

Pome. A firm, fleshy *fruit* formed by the fusion of the *ovary* and the hypanthium (the fused base of *calyx* and *corolla*); for example an apple or pear.

Pompon. Usually small, almost globular *flower heads* made up of numerous *florets*.

Potting mix. A potting medium consisting of a mixture of soil, sand, *peat*, *leaf mold*, or other ingredients Also called soil mix.

Potting on. Transferring a plant from one pot to a larger one.

Potting up. Transferring seedlings or rooted cuttings into individual pots of soil mix.

Pricking out. The transferring of young seedlings from where they have germinated in beds or pots to positions where they have room to grow on.

Propagation. The increase of plants by *seed* (usually sexual) or *vegetative* (asexual) means.

Propagator. A structure that provides a humid atmosphere for raising seedlings, rooting cuttings, or other plants being propagated.

Proximal end (of *cuttings*). The end that was originally nearest to the *crown* of the parent plant. (Cf. *Distal end*.)

Pseudobulb. The thickened, *bulb*-like *stem* of a *sympodial* orchid arising from a (sometimes very short) *rhizome*.

Quartered rosette. A rosetted flower with the petals arranged in four sections of about the same size.

Raceme. An *indeterminate*, unbranched *inflorescence* with usually many stalked flowers borne on an elongated axis (stem).

Radicle. The embryonic root of a seedling.

Rain shadow. An area of ground next to a wall or fence that is sheltered from prevailing winds and therefore receives less rain than open ground.

Rambler. A trailing climbing rose.

Ray flower (or floret). Small flower with a flattened, elongated *corolla*, as borne in the outermost ring of a *Compositae* flower head.

Recurved. Applied to petals of flowers and florets that curve backward.

Reflexed. Applied to petals of flowers and florets that bend sharply backward at an angle of more than 90˚. They are sometimes called fully reflexed. Also loosely applied to any flower in which the petals or *perianth segments* are *recurved*.

Remontant. Of a plant that flowers more than once during the growing season (often applied to roses and strawberries). (Cf. *Nonremontant*.)

Renewal pruning. A system in which the *laterals* are constantly cut back to be replaced by young laterals stimulated by pruning.

Respiration. The release of energy from complex *organic* molecules as a result of chemical changes.

Revert. To return to an original state, for example when a variegated plant produces a plain green leaf.

Rhizome. A specialized, usually horizontally creeping, swollen or slender, underground *stem* that acts as a storage organ and produces aerial shoots at its apex and along its length.

Rind. The outer bark of a shrub or tree outside the *cambium* layer.

Ripewood cutting. See *Cutting*.

Root. The part of a plant, normally underground, that anchors it and through which water and nutrients are absorbed. (See also *Aerial root*.)

Root ball. The roots and accompanying soil or *soil mix* visible when a plant is removed from a container or lifted from the open ground.

Root crops. Vegetables such as carrots, parsnips, and radishes grown for their edible roots.

Root cutting. See *Cutting*.

Root run. The area of soil into which a plant's roots may extend.

Rooting. The production of roots, usually from cuttings.

Rooting hormone. A chemical compound synthesized in powder or liquid form and used at low concentrations to encourage root production.

Rootstock. A plant used to provide the root system for a *grafted* plant.

Rose (of a watering can). A perforated nozzle that diffuses and regulates the flow of water.

Rosette. 1) A cluster of leaves radiating from approximately the same point, often borne at ground level at the base of a very short stem. 2) A more or less circular arrangement of petals.

Rotation. See *Crop rotation*.

Rounded. Regularly curved, as in a circle.

Row cover. See *Floating row cover*.

Runner. A horizontally spreading, usually slender, stem that runs above ground and roots at the *nodes* to form new plants. Often confused with *stolon*.

Saddle grafting. See *Grafting*.

Sap. The juice of a plant contained in the cells and vascular tissue.

Sapling. A young tree or seedling before the wood hardens.

Sash. The movable, transparent cover of a *cold frame*.

Scandent. Ascending or loosely climbing. (See also *Climber*.)

Scarification. 1) Abrasion or chemical treatment of a seed coat to speed up water intake and induce *germination*. 2) Removing moss and thatch from a lawn using a scarifier or rake.

Scion. A *shoot* or *bud* cut from one plant to *graft* onto a *rootstock* (stock) of another.

Scrambling climber. See *Climber*.

Scree. A slope consisting of rock fragments formed by the weathering of rock faces: simulated in gardens as scree beds, in which high-altitude *alpines* that need excellent *drainage* may be grown.

Sedge peat. See *Peat*.

Seed. The ripened, fertilized *ovule* containing a dormant embryo capable of developing into an adult plant.

Seed dormancy. See *Dormancy*.

Seed leaf. See *Cotyledon*.

Seedhead. A dried cluster of ripe seeds.

Seedling. A young plant that has developed from a seed.

Selection. A plant selected for particular characteristics and usually propagated to retain the same characteristics.

Self-clinging climber. See *Climber*.

Self-fertile. Of a plant that produces viable *seed* when fertilized with its own *pollen*. (See also *Fertilization*, *Pollination*, *Self-pollination*, and *Self-sterile*.)

Self-incompatible. See *Self-sterile*.

Self-layering. See *Layering*.

Self-pollination. The transfer of *pollen* from the *anthers* to the *stigma* of the same *flower*, or alternatively to another flower on the same plant. (Cf. *Cross-pollination*.)

Self-seed. To shed fertile seeds that produce *seedlings* around the parent plant.

Self-sterile. A plant unable to produce viable *seed* after self-fertilization, and requiring a different *pollinator* in order for fertilization to occur. Also known as "self-incompatible" – incapable of self-fertilization.

Semideciduous. See *Deciduous*.

Semideterminate. Used of tall or staked tomatoes that will only grow to 3–4ft (1–1.2m) long. (Cf. *Determinate*; *Indeterminate*.)

Semidouble. See *Flower*.

Semievergreen. See *Evergreen*.

Semiripe cutting. See *Cutting*.

Sepal. The outer *whorl* of the *perianth* of a flower, usually small and green, but sometimes colored and *petal*-like.

Serpentine layering. See *Layering*.

Set. 1) A small onion, shallot bulb, or potato *tuber*, selected for planting. 2) A term describing flowers that have been successfully fertilized and have produced small *fruits*.

Sexual reproduction. A form of reproduction involving *fertilization*, giving rise to *seed* or *spores*.

Sheet mulch. A *mulch* using an artificially produced material (e.g. plastic).

Shoot. A branch, stem, or twig.

Shrub. A woody-stemmed plant, usually branched from or near the base, lacking a single *trunk*.

Side grafting. See *Grafting*.

Sideshoot. A stem that arises from the side of a main *shoot*.

Side-veneer grafting. See *Grafting*.

Side-wedge grafting. See *Grafting*.

Simple (mainly of leaves). Undivided. (Cf. *Compound*.)

Simple layering. See *Layering*.

Single. See *Flower*.

Single cordon. See *Cordon*.

Single digging. A method of digging in which only the topsoil is turned over to a depth of one *spit*.

Snag. A short stub or frayed end left after incorrect pruning.

Softwood cutting. See *Cutting*.

Soil mark. The usually noticeable point on a plant's stem that shows the original soil level before the plant was lifted.

Soil mix. A potting medium consisting of a mixture of soil, sand, *peat*, *leaf mold*, or other ingredients. Also called potting mix.

Soilless mix. A potting medium that contains *peat*, usually *perlite* or *vermiculite*, and, sometimes, fertilizer, but no soil. (Cf. *Potting mix*; *Soil mix*.)

Species. A category in plant classification, the lowest principal rank below *genus* containing closely related, similar individuals.

Specimen plant. A striking plant, usually a tree or shrub in prime condition, grown where it can be seen clearly.

Spent (of flowers). Dying or dead.

Sphagnum mosses. Mosses common to bogs; their moisture-retentive nature is valued when used as a component of growing media, for example in orchid cultivation.

Spike. A racemose (see *Raceme*) and hence *indeterminate inflorescence* that bears unstalked flowers along a common axis (stem).

Spikelet. A small spike, forming part of a compound *inflorescence*; often applied to grasses that have a flower head consisting of several flowers with basal *bracts*.

Spit. The depth of a spade's blade, usually 10–12in (25–30cm).

Splice grafting. An alternative name for basal-whip grafting (see *Grafting*).

Spoon-type. Applied to the *florets* of chrysanthemums (and some others) in which the quill-like florets expand to form a spoon shape at the tips.

Sporangium. A body that produces *spores* on a fern.

Spore. The minute reproductive structure of flowerless plants, such as ferns, fungi, and mosses.

Sport. See *Mutation*.

Spray. A group of *flowers* or *flower heads* on a single, branching stem, such as occurs on many chrysanthemums and roses.

Spur. 1) A hollow projection from a petal, often producing *nectar*. 2) A short branch or branchlet bearing flower buds, as on fruit trees.

Stalk. A general term describing the stem of a leaf or flower (e.g. petiole, peduncle).

Stamen. The male reproductive organ in a plant, consisting of the pollen-producing *anther* and usually its supporting *filament* or *stalk*.

Standard. 1) A tree with at least 6ft (2m) of stem below the first branches (see also *Half standard*). 2) A plant trained so that it has a clear length of stem below the branches (3–4ft/1–1.2m for roses). 3) One of the three inner and often erect *perianth segments* of the iris flower.

Station sow. To sow seed individually or in small groups at fixed intervals along a row or *drill*.

Stem. The main axis of a plant, usually above ground and supporting leaves, flowers, and fruits.

Stem cutting. See *Cutting*.

Stem tip cutting. See *Cutting*.

Sterile. 1) Not producing flowers or viable seed. (Cf. *Fertile*.) 2) Of flowers without functional *anthers* and pistils (see *Carpel*).

Stigma. The apical portion of a *carpel*, usually borne at the tip of a *style*, which receives *pollen* prior to *fertilization*.

Stock. See *Rootstock*.

Stock plant. A plant used to obtain propagating material, whether seed or vegetative material.

Stolon. A horizontally spreading or arching stem, usually above ground, which roots at its tip to produce a new plant. Often confused with *runner*.

Stone fruits. Fruits, also known as "drupes," with one or more seeds ("stones") surrounded by fleshy, usually edible tissue. They are common in the genus *Prunus* (e.g. apricots, plums, and cherries) and some other plants, such as mangoes, that produce *indehiscent*, woody fruits.

Stool. A number of shoots arising, more or less uniformly, from the base of an individual plant, for example

some shrubs cut back regularly to produce propagating material and also chrysanthemums.

Stooling. 1) An alternative term for *mound layering*. See *Layering*. 2) The routine pruning back of woody plants by *coppicing*.

Stopping. See *Pinching out*.

Strain. A loose, undefined term sometimes applied to races of seed-raised plants; not a term accepted under the International Code for the Nomenclature of Cultivated Plants because of its imprecise definition.

Stratification. Storage of seed in warm or cold conditions to overcome *dormancy* and aid *germination*.

Stylar column. A structure formed from joined *styles*.

Style. The usually elongated part of a *carpel* between the *ovary* and *stigma*, not always present.

Subfamily. A category in plant classification, a division within the *family*.

Sublateral. A side shoot originating from a *lateral* shoot or branch.

Subshrub. 1) A low-growing plant that is entirely *woody*. 2) A plant that is woody at the base but has soft, usually *herbaceous* growth above.

Subsoil. The layers of soil beneath the *topsoil*; these are usually less fertile and of poorer texture and structure than the topsoil.

Subspecies. A subdivision of a *species*, higher in rank than a *variety* or *forma*.

Succulent (of plants). A plant with thick, fleshy leaves and/or stems adapted to store water. All cacti are succulents.

Sucker. 1) A shoot that arises below ground from a plant's roots or underground stem. 2) On *grafted* plants, a sucker is any shoot that arises below the *graft union*. 3) A sideshoot of a tomato plant.

Sympodial. Definite growth of a *shoot* terminating in an *inflorescence* or dying; growth is continued by *lateral* buds. (Cf. *Monopodial*.)

Systemic. Term describing a *pesticide* or *fungicide* that is absorbed and distributed through a plant when applied to the soil or foliage.

Taproot. The primary, downward-growing *root* of a plant (especially a tree); also applied loosely to any strong, downward-growing root.

Taxon (pl. **taxa**). A group of living organisms at any rank; applied to groups of plants or entities that share distinct, defined characters.

T-budding. See *Grafting*.

Tender. Of a plant that is vulnerable to frost damage.

Tendril. A modified leaf, branch, or stem, usually filiform (long and slender) and capable of attaching itself to a support. (See also *Climber*.)

Tepal. A single segment of a perianth that cannot be distinguished either as a sepal or petal, as in *Crocus* or *Lilium*. (See also *Perianth segment*.)

Terminal. At the tip of a stem or branch; usually refers to a bud or flower.

Terminal bud. See *Bud*.

Terrarium. An enclosed container made of glass or plastic in which plants are grown.

Terrestrial. Growing in the soil; a land plant. (Cf. *Aquatic*; *Epiphyte*.)

Thatch. A layer of dead *organic* matter intermingled with living stems that accumulates on lawn soil surface.

Thin (of soil). Used loosely of poor soil, prone to *capping* and drought.

Thinning. The removal of seedlings, shoots, flowers, or fruit buds to improve the growth and quality of the remainder.

Tilth. A fine, crumbly, surface layer of soil produced by cultivation.

Tip layering. See *Layering*.

Tip prune. To cut back the growing tip of a shoot to encourage sideshoots or to remove damaged growth.

Tissue culture (of plants). The propagation of plants under sterile conditions from very small pieces of plant tissue.

Top-dressing. 1) An application of soluble fertilizers, fresh soil, or *compost* to the soil surface around a plant or to lawns to replenish nutrients. 2) A decorative dressing applied to the soil surface around a plant.

Topiary. The art of clipping and training trees and shrubs into often intricate geometric or free shapes.

Topsoil. The uppermost, normally fertile, layer of soil.

Trace element. See *Micronutrients*.

Trailing climber. See *Climber*.

Translocated (of dissolved nutrients or weedkillers). Moving within the vascular system (conducting tissues) of a plant.

Transpiration. The loss of water by evaporation from leaves and stems.

Transplanting. Moving a plant from one position to another.

Tree. A *woody* perennial plant usually with a well-defined *trunk* or stem with a *head* or *crown* of branches above.

Trench digging. See *Double digging*.

Trench layering. See *Layering*.

Triploid. Having three basic sets of chromosomes. Such plants are normally *sterile*. (Cf. *Diploid*.)

True (True-breeding). Of plants that when self-pollinated (see *Self-pollination*) give rise to offspring similar to their parents.

Trunk. The thickened, woody, main stem of a tree.

Tuber. A swollen, usually underground organ derived from a stem or root, used for food storage.

Tufa. Porous limestone rock that absorbs and retains moisture; used for cultivating alpine plants difficult to grow in garden soil.

Tunic. The fibrous membranes or papery outer skin of *bulbs* or *corms*.

Tunicate. Enclosed in a *tunic*.

Turion. 1) A detached, overwintering, usually fleshy *bud* produced by certain water plants. 2) A term sometimes applied to an *adventitious* shoot or sucker.

Twining climber. See *Climber*.

U cordon. A double *cordon*.

Underplanting. Low-growing plants planted beneath larger plants.

Union. See *Graft union*.

Upright. Term describing the habit of a plant with vertical or semi-vertical main branches. (Cf. *Fastigiate*.)

Urn-shaped (of flowers). Globose to cylindrical in shape with a somewhat constricted mouth; U-shaped.

Variable. Varying in character from the type; particularly of seed-raised plants that vary in character from the parent.

Variegated. Term describing a plant marked with various colors in an irregular pattern; particularly used for leaves patterned with white and yellow markings but not confined to these colors.

Variety. 1) Botanically, a naturally occurring variant (varietas, or var.) of a wild species, between the rank of *subspecies* and *forma*. 2) Also commonly but imprecisely used to describe any variant of a plant. (Cf. *Cultivar*.)

Vegetative growth. Nonflowering, usually leafy growth.

Vegetative propagation. The increase of plants by asexual methods normally resulting in genetically identical individuals.

Vermiculite. A lightweight, micalike mineral allowing good water retention and aeration when used in cuttings soil mix and other potting media.

Water shoots. Applied usually to *epicormic* shoots that frequently arise close to pruning wounds on tree trunks or branches.

Whip. A young seedling or grafted tree without *lateral* branches.

Whip-and-tongue grafting. See *Grafting*.

Whorl. The arrangement of three or more organs arising from the same point.

Widger. A spatula-shaped tool used for transplanting or *pricking out* seedlings.

Windbreak. Any structure but often a hedge, fence, or wall that shelters plants and filters strong winds.

Wind-rock. The destabilizing of a plant's roots by strong wind.

Woody. Ligneous; a term describing stems or trunks that are hard and thickened rather than soft and pliable. (Cf. *Herbaceous*.)

Wound. A cut or broken area in a plant.

Wound paint. A specialized paint that is applied to a cut surface of a plant after pruning.

CANADIAN HARDINESS ZONES

For each entry, the Canadian Hardiness Zone, Z, is given. The hardiness zone indicates the plant's cold tolerance. However, with perennial plants, hardiness is influenced by the depth and persistence of snow cover. T indicates tender plants. The zone map is on the endpapers.

Plant	Hardiness
Abelia floribunda	Z8
Abelia x grandiflora	Z5b
Abeliophyllum distichum	Z6
Abies grandis	Z6
Abies magnifica	Z7
Abies procera	Z5b
Acacia baileyana	T
Acacia dealbata	T
Acaena caesiiglauca syn. A. caerula	Z7
Acaena microphylla	Z7
Acantholimon glumaceum	Z5
Acanthus hungaricus	Z4
Acanthus mollis	Z5b
Acanthus spinosus	Z5b
Acer 'Silver Vein'	Z6b
Acer campestre	Z5
Acer capillipes	Z6
Acer cappadocicum	Z6b
Acer davidii	Z6
Acer griseum	Z6
Acer grosseri var. hersii	Z6b
Acer japonicum	Z5
Acer lobelii	Z7
Acer negundo	Z1b
Acer negundo 'Variegatum'	Z5
Acer palmatum	Z5b
Acer palmatum 'Dissectum Atropurpureum'	Z5b
Acer palmatum 'Senkaki'	Z6
Acer pensylvanicum	Z2b
Acer pensylvanicum 'Erythrocladum'	Z3
Acer platanoides	Z4b
Acer pseudoplatanus	Z5b
Acer rubrum	Z3
Acer saccharinum	Z2b
Achillea ageratifolia	Z3b
Achillea clavennae syn. A. argentea	Z3b
Achillea filipendulina 'Gold Plate'	Z3
Achillea x kellereri	Z5
Aconitum carmichaelii	Z3b
Aconitum napellus	Z3b
Acorus calamus	Z3
Acorus calamus 'Variegatus'	Z3

Plant	Hardiness
Acorus gramineus	Z6
Acorus gramineus 'Ogon'	Z6
Acorus gramineus 'Pusillus'	Z6
Acorus gramineus 'Variegatus'	Z6
Actinidia chinensis syn. A. deliciosa	Z7
Actinidia kolomikta	Z4
Adenium obesum	T
Adiantum raddianum syn. A. cuneatum	Z8
Adlumia fungosa	Z5b
Adonis amurensis	Z5
Adromischus cooperi syn. A. clavifolius	T
Adromischus festivus	T
Aechmea fasciata syn. Billbergia rhodocynea	T
Aeonium arboreum	T
Aeonium arboreum 'Zwartkop'	T
Aeonium nobile	T
Aesculus hippocastanum	Z4b
Aesculus parviflora	Z4
Aethionema 'Warley Rose'	Z5
Aethionema pulchellum	Z5
Agapetes macrantha syn. A. variegata var. macrantha, Pentapterygium macrantha	T
Agave americana	T
Agave americana 'Medio-picta'	T
Agave attenuata	T
Agave filifera	T
Agave lophantha	T
Agave parryi	T
Agave parviflora	T
Agave stricta	T
Agave utahensis	T
Agave victoriae-reginae	T
Agonis flexuosa	T
Agrostemma githago 'Milas'	Annual
Ailanthus altissima	Z6
Ajuga pyramidalis	Z3
Ajuga reptans	Z3
Akebia quinata	Z5b
Albuca humilis	T
Alcea rosea syn. Althaea rosea	Z4
Alchemilla alpina	Z4
Alchemilla ellenbeckii	Z7
Alchemilla mollis	Z4b
Alisma lanceolatum	Z6
Alisma parviflora	Z6
Alisma plantago-aquatica	Z5
Allamanda cathartica	T
Allamanda cathartica 'Hendersonii'	T
Allium christophii	Z5

Plant	Hardiness
Allium giganteum	Z3b
Allium sikkimense	Z7
Alnus cordata	Z5b
Alnus glutinosa	Z4
Alnus incana	Z4
Aloe arborescens	T
Aloe aristata	T
Aloe barbadensis syn. A. vera	T
Aloe brevifolia	T
Aloe ciliaris	T
Aloe distans	T
Aloe humilis	T
Aloe longistyla	T
Aloe rauhii	T
Aloe spinosissima	T
Aloe variegata syn. A. punctata	T
Aloysia triphylla syn. Lippia citriodora	Z8
Alternanthera ficoidea	T
Alternanthera philoxeroides	T
Alyssum montanum	Z4
Amaranthus caudatus	Annual
Amaranthus tricolor	Annual
Amaryllis belladonna	Z8
Amelanchier canadensis	Z3b
Amelanchier lamarckii	Z4
Ampelopsis brevipedunculata	Z4
Ampelopsis brevipedunculata var. maximowiczii	Z4
Anacyclus depressus A. pyrethrum var. depressus	Z5
Ananas bracteatus 'Tricolor' syn. A. b. 'Striatus'	T
Ananas comosus 'Variegatus' syn. A. c. var. variegatus	T
Anchusa caespitosa	Z3b
Androsace carnea subsp. laggeri	Z4b
Androsace chamaejasme	Z4
Androsace lanuginosa	Z5
Androsace sarmentosa	Z5
Androsace sempervivoides	Z5
Anemone apennina	Z6
Anemone blanda	Z5
Anemone coronaria	Z8
Anemone De Caen Series syn. A. coronaria De Caen	Z8
Anemone hupehensis	Z3
Anemone magellanica	Z3
Anemone nemorosa	Z5
Anemone ranunculoides	Z5
Anemone rivularis	Z7
Anemone St. Brigid Series syn. A. coronaria 'St. Bright'	Z8
Anemone x fulgens	Z8
Anemone x hybrida	Z4
Angelica archangelica	Z5

Plant	Hardiness
Anisodontea capensis	T
Anredera cordifolia	T
Antennaria dioica	Z3b
Antennaria dioica 'Minima'	Z3b
Anthriscus cerefolium	T
Antigonon leptopus	T
Antirrhinum glutinosum	Z8
Antirrhinum molle	T
Antirrhinum sempervirens	T
Aponogeton crispus	T
Aponogeton distachyos	T
Aponogeton madagascariensis	T
Aponogeton undulatus	T
Aporocactus flagelliformis	T
Aquilegia discolor	Z3
Aquilegia flabellata	Z8b
Aquilegia flabellata 'Nana'	Z8b
Aquilegia vulgaris	Z3
Arabis ferdinandi-coburgi 'Variegata'	Z5b
Aralia elata	Z5
Aralia elata 'Argenteovariegata'	Z5
Aralia elata 'Aureo-variegata'	Z5
Aralia elata 'Variegata'	Z5
Araujia sericifera	T
Arbutus menziesii	Z7
Arbutus unedo	Z8
Arbutus x andrachnoides	Z8
Archontophoenix alexandrae	T
Arctostaphylos alpina	Z2
Arctostaphylos uva-ursi	Z1
Arctotis stoechadifolia	T
Ardisia japonica	Z7
Arenaria montana	Z3
Arenaria purpurascens	Z4
Argemone mexicana	T
Aristolochia durior	Z5
Aristolochia elegans	T
Armeria juniperifolia	Z4
Armeria maritima	Z3
Aronia arbutifolia	Z4b
Artemisia absinthium	Z5
Artemisia glacialis	Z4
Artemisia lactiflora	Z5
Artemisia schmidtiana 'Nana'	Z3b
Arum italicum	Z5
Arum italicum 'Marmoratum'	Z5
Arum italicum 'Pictum'	Z5
Aruncus dioicus	Z3b
Aruncus dioicus 'Kneiffii'	Z3b
Aruncus sylvester	Z3b
Arundo donax	Z7
Arundo donax 'Macrophylla'	Z7b

Plant	Hardiness
Arundo donax 'Variegata'	Z7b
Asarina antirrhiniflora syn. Maurandella antirrhiniflora	T
Asarina erubescens	T
Asparagus densiflorus	T
Asparagus densiflorus 'Sprengeri'	T
Asperula suberosa	Z5
Asplenium nidus	T
Asplenium scolopendrium syn. Phyllitis scolopendrium, Scolopendrium vulgare	Z8
Astelia chathamica	Z8
Aster albescens	Z4
Aster novae-angliae	Z4
Asteranthera ovata	T
Astilbe chinensis	Z3
Astilbe simplicifolia	Z3b
Astilbe x arendsii	Z3b
Astilboides tabularis	Z6
Astrantia major	Z5
Astrophytum myriostigma syn. Echinocactus myriostigma	T
Astrophytum ornatum syn. Echinocactus ornatum	T
Atriplex halimus	Z8
Aubrieta deltoidea	Z4
Aucuba japonica	Z7
Aurinia saxatilis	Z3
Aurinia saxatilis 'Citrina'	Z3
Azolla caroliniana	Z8
Azolla filiculoides	Z8
Azorella trifurcata	Z8
Bacopa monnieri	T
Baldellia ranunculoides	Z6
Ballota pseudodictamnus	Z8
Banksia serrata	T
Beaumontia grandiflora	T
Begonia 'Non-stop'	T
Begonia 'Tiger Paws'	T
Begonia incana	T
Begonia prismatocarpa	T
Begonia prismatocarpa 'Variegata'	T
Begonia rex	T
Begonia rex hybrids	T
Begonia semperflorens	T
Begonia venosa	T
Belamcanda chinensis	Z6
Bellis perennis	Z5b
Bellis perennis Pomponette Series	Z5b
Berberidopsis corallina	T
Berberis buxifolia	Z5b
Berberis darwinii	Z7
Berberis empetrifolia	Z8
Berberis julianae	Z6
Berberis temolaica	Z7

Name	Zone
Berberis thunbergii	Z4b
Berberis verruculosa	Z4
Berberis x stenophylla 'Corallina Compacta'	Z6b
Bergenia 'Ballawley'	Z3b
Bergenia cordifolia	Z3b
Beschorneria yuccoides	T
Betula 'Jermyns'	Z6
Betula albosinensis var. septentrionalis	Z3
Betula ermanii	Z5
Betula nana	Z2
Betula nigra	Z4
Betula pendula	Z2
Betula pendula 'Dalecarlica'	Z2
Betula pubescens	Z6
Betula utilis var. jacquemontii	Z3
Bignonia capreolata	Z7
Billardiera longiflora	Z8
Billbergia nutans	T
Blechnum chilense	T
Bloomeria crocea	T
Bolax gummifera	Z6
Bomarea andimarcana	T
Bomarea caldasii	T
Bongardia chrysogonum	T
Borago officinalis	Z3
Brachyscome iberidifolia	T
Bracteantha bracteata	T
Brassica oleracea	Annual
Brassica oleracea 'Cabbage Cherry Sundae' (F1)	Annual
Brassica oleracea 'Kale Red and White Peacock' (F1)	Annual
Briza maxima	Annual
Briza minor	Annual
Bromelia balansae	T
Browallia speciosa	T
Brugmansia x candida	T
Brunfelsia pauciflora syn. B. calycina, B. eximia	T
Brunnera macrophylla	Z3b
Buddleja alternifolia	Z4b
Buddleja crispa	T
Buddleja davidii	Z5
Buddleja globosa	Z8
Bulbine frutescens	T
Bulbine latifolia	T
Bulbine mesembryanthemoides	T
Bulbocodium vernum	Z4
Bupleurum fruticosum	Z6
Butomus umbellatus	Z3
Buxus balearica	T
Buxus microphylla	Z6
Buxus sempervirens	Z6
Cabomba caroliniana	Z7
Caesalpinia pulcherrima syn. Poinciana pulcherrima	T
Calceolaria 'Sunshine'	Z8
Calceolaria integrifolia	Z8
Calceolaria pavonii	Z8
Calendula officinalis	Annual
Calla palustris	Z4
Callianthemum anemonoides	Z5
Callistemon citrinus 'Splendens'	T
Callitriche hermaphroditica syn. Callitriche autumnalis	Z6
Calluna vulgaris	Z5
Caltha leptosepala	Z5
Caltha palustris	Z3
Caltha palustris 'Alba'	Z3
Caltha palustris 'Flore Plena'	Z3
Calycanthus occidentalis	Z7
Camellia japonica	Z8
Camellia japonica 'Mathotiana'	Z8
Camellia reticulata	Z8
Camellia sasanqua	Z8
Camellia x williamsii 'Donation'	Z8
Campanula carpatica	Z4
Campanula cochleariifolia	Z3
Campanula garganica	Z4
Campanula isophyllaa	T
Campanula lactiflora	Z3
Campanula pilosa	Z5
Campanula piperi	Z8
Campanula portenschlagiana	Z3
Campanula poscharskyana	Z3
Campanula pyramidalis	Z7
Campanula raineri	Z5
Campanula zoysii	Z5
Campsis radicans	Z5
Campsis x tagliabuana	Z6
Campsis x tagliabuana 'Mme. Galen'	Z6
Capsicum quitoense	Z7
Caragana arborescens	Z2
Caragana arborescens 'Walker'	Z2
Caragana aurantiaca	Z2
Caralluma europaea syn. Stapelia europa	T
Cardamine pratensis	Z6
Cardiocrinum giganteum	Z7b
Carduncellus rhaponticoides	Z5b
Carex elata 'Aurea'	Z5
Carex pendula	Z4
Carex riparia	Z6b
Carlina acaulis	Z4
Carpinus betulus	Z5
Carpinus betulus 'Fastigiata'	Z5
Carpobrotus acinaciformis	T
Carpobrotus edulis	T
Carya ovata	Z4b
Caryopteris x clandonensis	Z6
Cassinia fulvida	T
Cassiope hypnoides	Z8
Castanea sativa	Z5b
Catalpa bignonioides	Z5
Catalpa bignonioides 'Aurea'	Z5
Catharanthus roseus	T
Cattleya bowringiana	T
Ceanothus 'Autumnal Blue'	T
Ceanothus 'Gloire de Versailles'	Z8
Ceanothus thyrsiflorus	Z8
Cedrus atlantica f. glauca	Z6
Cedrus libani	Z6
Celastrus orbiculatus	Z4
Celastrus scandens	Z3
Celmisia coriacea syn. C. semicordata	Z8
Celtis australis	Z7
Celtis occidentalis	Z2b
Centaurea cyanus	Annual
Centaurea dealbata	Z3
Centaurea hypoleuca	Z4
Centaurea macrocephala	Z4
Centaurea moschata	Annual
Centaurea pindicola	Z5
Centranthus ruber	Z4
Cephalanthus occidentalis	Z4
Cephalaria gigantea	Z4
Cephalocereus senilis	T
Ceratophyllum demersum	Z5
Ceratopteris cornuta	T
Ceratopteris pteroides	T
Ceratopteris thalictroides	T
Ceratostigma plumbaginoides	Z5
Ceratostigma willmottianum	Z7
Cercidiphyllum japonicum	Z5
Cercis canadensis 'Forest Pansy'	Z5b
Cercis siliquastrum	Z7
Cereus chalybaeus	T
Cereus forbesii syn. C. validus	T
Cereus jamacaru	T
Cereus peruvianus syn. C. uruguayanus	T
Ceropegia haygarthii syn. C. distincta subsp. haygarthii	T
Ceropegia sandersonii	T
Ceropegia woodii syn. C. lineans subsp. Woodii	T
Cestrum elegans	T
Chaenomeles japonica	Z5b
Chaenomeles speciosa	Z5b
Chaenomeles x 'Nicoline' syn. C. x superba 'Nicoline'	Z5b
Chaenomeles x superba	Z5b
Chamaecyparis lawoniana 'Ellwoodii'	Z5b
Chamaecyparis lawsoniana	Z5b
Chamaecyparis lawsoniana 'Lanei'	Z6
Chamaecyparis lawsoniana 'Stewartii'	Z5b
Chamaecyparis obtusa 'Intermedia'	Z5
Chamaecyparis obtusa 'Nana Aurea'	Z5b
Chamaecyparis obtusa 'Nana Pyramidalis'	Z5b
Chamaedorea elegans syn. Neanthe bella	T
Chamaerops humilis	T
Cheiranthus cheiri	Z4
Chiastophyllum oppositifolium	Z5
Chimonanthus praecox	Z7
Chionanthus retusus	Z6
Chlorophytum comosum syn. Chlorophytum capense	T
Choisya 'Aztec Pearl'	T
Choisya ternata	Z8
Choisya ternata 'Sundance'	Z8
Chrysanthemum carinatum	Annual
Chrysanthemum coronarium	Annual
Chrysanthemum hosmariense syn. Rhodanthemum hosmariense, Pyrethropsis hosmariense	T
Chrysanthemum segetum	Annual
Cimicifuga americana	Z3
Cimicifuga racemosa	Z3
Cissus antarctica	T
Cissus discolor	T
Cissus rhombifolia	T
Cistus x cyprius	T
Cistus x hybridus	Z7
Cistus x skanbergii	T
Citrus limon	T
Citrus limon 'Meyer'	T
Cladrastis lutea	Z4b
Cleistocactus straussii syn. Borzicactus straussii	T
Clematis 'Barbara Jackman'	Z3b
Clematis 'Carnaby'	Z4
Clematis 'Comtesse de Bouchaud'	Z3
Clematis 'Daniel Deronda'	Z4
Clematis 'Duchess of Albany'	Z2
Clematis 'Duchess of Edinburgh'	Z3b
Clematis 'Elsa Spath'	Z4b
Clematis 'Ernest Markham'	Z3b
Clematis 'General Sikorski'	Z4
Clematis 'Hagley Hybrid'	Z3
Clematis 'Henryi'	Z4
Clematis 'Jackmanii'	Z2
Clematis 'Lady Betty Balfour'	Z3b
Clematis 'Lasurstern'	Z4
Clematis 'Marie Boisselot' syn. C. 'Mme. Le Coultre'	Z4
Clematis 'Miss Bateman'	Z4
Clematis 'Mme. Le Coultre' see C. 'Marie Boisselot'	
Clematis 'Mrs. N. Thompson'	Z3b
Clematis 'Nelly Moser'	Z3b
Clematis 'Niobe'	Z4
Clematis 'Perle d'Azure'	Z3
Clematis 'Proteus'	Z4
Clematis 'The President'	Z3b
Clematis 'Ville de Lyon'	Z3b
Clematis 'Vyvan pennell'	Z3b
Clematis alpina	Z4
Clematis alpina 'Frances Rivis'	Z2
Clematis armandii	Z6
Clematis cirrhosa	Z5
Clematis florida	Z5
Clematis heracleifolia var. davidiana	Z5
Clematis integrifolia	Z5
Clematis macropetala	Z1
Clematis macropetala 'Markham's Pink'	Z1
Clematis montana	Z6
Clematis montana 'Tetrarose' syn. C. montana var. tetrarose	Z6
Clematis montana var. grandiflora syn. C. montana 'Grandiflora'	Z6
Clematis montana var. rubens	Z6
Clematis orientalis	Z3
Clematis paniculata	Z2
Clematis recta	Z5
Clematis rehderiana	Z5
Clematis tangutica	Z1b
Clematis viticella	Z3
Clematis viticella 'Abundance'	Z3
Clematis viticella 'Etoile Violette'	Z3
Clematis viticella 'Mme. Julia Correvan'	Z3
Clematis x cartmanii 'Joe'	Z6
Clematis x jouiniana	Z2b
Cleome hassleriana	Annual
Clerodendrum bungei	Z8
Clerodendrum splendens	T
Clerodendrum thomsoniae	T
Clethra alnifolia	Z4b
Clethra alnifolia 'Paniculata'	Z4b
Clianthus puniceus	Z8
Clitoria ternatea	Annual
Clytostoma callistegioides	T
Cobaea scandens	Annual
Codiaeum variegatum var. pictum	T
Codonopsis convolvulacea	Z5
Colletia armata 'Rosea'	Z7b
Colocasia esculenta	T
Combretum grandiflorum	T
Consolida ambigua syn. C. ajacis	Annual
Convallaria majalis	Z2
Convolvulus cneorum	Z8
Convolvulus sabatius	Z8
Convolvulus tricolor	Annual
Cordyline australis syn. Dracaena australis	T
Cordyline australis 'Purpurea'	T
Coreopsis, Early Sunrise Series	Annual
Cornus 'Eddie's White Wonder'	Z7
Cornus alba	Z2
Cornus alba 'Aurea'	Z2

Plant	Zone
Cornus alba 'Elegantissima'	Z2
Cornus alba see C. stolonifera 'Flaviramea'	
Cornus alba 'Kesselringii'	Z2
Cornus alba 'Sibirica'	Z2
Cornus alba 'Spaethii'	Z2
Cornus alba 'Variegata' syn. C. alba 'Elegantissima Variegata'	Z2
Cornus alternifolia 'Argentea'	Z4
Cornus canadensis	Z2
Cornus controversa	Z5
Cornus florida	Z7
Cornus kousa	Z6
Cornus kousa var. chinensis	Z6
Cornus mas 'Variegata'	Z4b
Cornus nuttallii	Z7
Cornus sanguinea 'Winter Flame' syn. C. s. 'Winter Beauty'	Z4b
Cornus stolonifera	Z2
Cornus stolonifera 'Flaviramea'	Z1b
Correa pulchella	T
Cortaderia selloana	Z7
Corydalis cashmeriana	Z6b
Corydalis flexuosa	Z5
Corylus avellana 'Contorta'	Z5
Corylus colurna	Z5
Corylus maxima 'Purpurea'	Z5
Cosmos atrosanguineus	Z8
Cotinus 'Grace'	Z4b
Cotinus coggygria	Z5
Cotinus coggygria 'Flame'	Z5
Cotoneaster 'Hybridus Pendulus'	Z7
Cotoneaster conspicuus	Z7
Cotoneaster dammeri	Z4
Cotoneaster divaricatus	Z5
Cotoneaster horizontalis	Z5
Cotoneaster x watereri	Z8
Cotula coronopifolia	Z8
Cotyledon ladismithiensis	T
Cotyledon teretifolia	T
Cotyledon undulata syn. C. orbiculata var. oblonga	T
Crambe cordifolia	Z5
Crassula falcata syn. C. perfoliata var. minor	T
Crassula ovata syn. C. argentea, C. portulacea	T
Crassula perfoliata	T
Crassula rupestris	T
Crassula sarcocaulis	T
Crassula sarmentosa	T
Crassula socialis	T
Crataegus laevigata	Z6
Crataegus laevigata 'Paul's Scarlet'	Z6
Crataegus monogyna	Z4b
Crataegus x lavallei	Z5
Crataegus x lavallei 'Carrierei'	Z5
Crepis incana	Z5
Crinum x powellii	Z8
Crocosmia 'Lucifer'	Z5b
Crocus laevigatus 'Fontenayi'	Z3
Cryptanthus bivittatus	T
Cryptocereus anthonyanus	T
Cryptocoryne ciliata	T
Cryptomeria japonica 'Vilmoriniana'	Z6
Cuphea hyssopifolia	T
Cupressus glabra	Z7
Cupressus glabra 'Pyramidalis' syn. C. arizonica 'Pyramidalis'	Z7
Cupressus macrocarpa 'Goldcrest'	Z8
Cupressus sempervirens	Z8
Cycas revoluta	T
Cyclamen coum	Z5
Cyclamen hederifolium	Z5
Cyclamen purpurascens	Z6
Cyclmen repandum	Z8
Cymbidium Strath Kanaid	T
Cynara cardunculus	Z8
Cynara scolymus	T
Cyperus haspan	T
Cyperus involucratus	T
Cyperus longus	Z5
Cyperus papyrus	T
Cyperus papyrus 'Nanus' syn. Cyperus papyrus viviparus	T
Cytisus battandieri	Z7b
Cytisus scoparius	Z7
Cytisus x beanii	Z5
Dahlia imperialis	T
Dahlia x coccinea syn. Dahlia coccinea	T
Damasonium alisma	Z8
Danäe racemosa	Z7
Daphne arbuscula	Z6
Daphne bholua	Z8
Daphne blagayana	Z8
Daphne cneorum	Z2b
Daphne jasminea	7b
Daphne laureola	Z8
Daphne petraea	Z7
Daphne petraea 'Grandiflora'	Z7
Daphne retusa	Z8
Daphne sericea	Z8
Daphne x burkwoodii 'Somerset'	Z5
Decumaria sinensis	T
Dendrobium 'Happiness'	T
Dendrobium nobile	T
Dendromecon rigida	T
Deschampsia cespitosa	Z5
Deutzia longifolia	Z7b
Deutzia scabra	Z6
Deutzia x elegantissima 'Rosealind'	Z5b
Deutzia x rosea	Z6
Dianthus 'Bombardier'	Z6b
Dianthus 'Brympton Red'	Z6b
Dianthus 'Old Clove Red'	Z6b
Dianthus alpinus	Z4
Dianthus anatolicus	Z6
Dianthus barbatus	Z3
Dianthus carthusianorum	Z4
Dianthus chinensis	T
Dianthus deltoides	Z3
Dianthus echinacea syn. D. erinaceus	Z4
Dianthus freynii	Z4
Dianthus glacialis	Z4
Dianthus haematocalyx	Z4
Dianthus Chabaud Series	Z7
Dianthus Giant Chabaud Series	Z7
Dianthus Knight Series syn. D. caryophyllus Knight series	Z6b
Diascia 'Ruby Field' syn. D. barberae 'Ruby Field'	Z7
Diascia cordata	Z7
Dicentra eximia syn. D. formosa	Z4
Dicentra spectabilis 'Alba'	Z3
Dicksonia antarctica	T
Dictamnus albus	Z3
Diervilla lonicera	Z2
Digitalis grandiflora	Z3
Digitalis lutea	Z3
Digitalis purpurea	Z4
Dionysia aretioides	Z6
Dioscorea discolor	T
Dipelta yunnanensis	Z8
Distictis buccinatoria	T
Distylium racemosum	T
Dizygotheca elegantissima	T
Dorycnium hirsutum	Z7b
Draba bryoides	Z4
Draba mollissima	Z4
Draba polytricha	Z4
Dracaena deremensis 'Souvenir de Schriever' syn. D. fragrans Deremis Group 'Warneckei'	T
Dracaena reflexa	T
Dracaena sanderiana	T
Dracocephalum moldavicum syn. D. moldavica	Z4
Drimys winteri	T
Dryas octopetala	Z3
Dryas octopetala 'Minor'	Z3
Dudleya ingens	T
Dudleya rigida	T
Eccremocarpus scaber	T
Echeveria agavoides	T
Echeveria cuspidata	T
Echeveria derenbergii	T
Echeveria elegans	T
Echeveria gibbiflora	T
Echeveria pilosa	T
Echeveria pubescens	T
Echinocactus grusonii	T
Echinocereus blanckii	T
Echinocereus chloranthus	T
Echinocereus engelmannii	T
Echinocereus enneacanthus	T
Echinocereus pentalophus syn. E. procumbens	T
Echinocereus triglochidiatus	T
Echinocereus viereckii	T
Echinocereus viridiflorus	T
Echinodorus bleheri	T
Echinodorus maior	T
Echinops bannaticus	Z5
Echinops ritro	Z3
Echinopsis aurea syn. Lobivia aurea, L. cylindrica, Pseudolobivia aurea	T
Echinopsis chamaecereus syn. Chamaecereus silvestrii, Lobivia silvestrii	T
Echinopsis eyriesii syn. Echinocactus eyriesii	T
Echinopsis kermesina	T
Echinopsis multiplex syn. E. oxygona	T
Echium candicans	T
Echium pininana	T
Echium vulgare	Z4
Edraianthus dinaricus syn. E. dalmaticus	Z5
Edraianthus graminifolius	Z5
Edraianthus pumilio	Z5
Egeria densa syn. Anacharis densa, Elodea densa	Z6
Eichhornia azurea	T
Eichhornia crassipes	T
Elaeagnus angustifolius	Z2b
Elaeagnus commutata	Z2
Elaeagnus pungens	Z7
Elaeagnus x ebbingei 'Gilt Edge'	Z7
Eleocharis acicularis	T
Elodea canadensis	Z5
Embothrium coccineum	T
Ensete ventricosum	T
Epigaea gaultherioides syn. Orphanidesia gaultherioides	T
Epigaea repens	Z3
Epiphyllum cartagense	T
Epiphyllum oxypetalum	T
Epipremnum aureum	T
Eranthis hyemalis	Z4
Ercilla volubilis	T
Erica arborea var. alpina syn. E. arborea 'Alpina'	Z8
Erica carnea	Z4
Erica cinerea	Z6
Erica lusitanica	Z8
Erica x williamsii 'P.D. Williams' syn. E. x williamsii	Z5
Erigeron karvinskianus syn. E. mucronatus	Z6
Erinacea anthyllis	Z8
Erinus alpinus	Z3b
Erinus alpinus 'Dr. Hähnle'	Z3b
Eriobotrya japonica	T
Eriocereus bonplandii	Z6
Eriogonum ovalifolium	Z4
Eriophorum angustifolium	Z6
Eriophorum latifolium	Z5b
Eriophyllum lanatum syn. Bahia lanata	Z6
Erodium chamaedryoides	T
Erodium guttatum	Z5
Eryngium agavifolium	Z6b
Eryngium variifolium	Z5
Erysimum cheiri	Z6
Erysimum helveticum syn. E. pumilum	Z6b
Escallonia 'Donard Seedling'	Z8
Escallonia 'Langleyensis'	Z8
Espostoa lanata	T
Espostoa melanostele	T
Eucalyptus coccifera	T
Eucalyptus dalrympleana	T
Eucalyptus gunnii	T
Eucalyptus pauciflora	T
Eucryphia glutinosa	T
Eucryphia lucida	T
Eucryphia milliganii	T
Eucryphia x nymansensis	Z8
Eucryphia x nymansensis 'Nymansay'	Z8
Euonymous fortunei 'Emerald Gaiety'	Z5
Euonymus alatus	Z4
Euonymus alatus Compactus	Z3
Euonymus fortunei	Z5
Euonymus fortunei 'Emerald'n'Gold'	Z5
Euonymus fortunei 'Silver Queen'	Z5
Euonymus japonicus	Z5b
Eupatorium purpureum	Z3
Euphorbia amygdaloides	Z6
Euphorbia amygdaloides subsp. robbiae	Z6
Euphorbia characias	Z8
Euphorbia cotinifolia	Z5
Euphorbia fulgens	T
Euphorbia mellifera	T
Euphorbia milii	T
Euphorbia myrsinites	Z4
Euphorbia obesa	T
Euphorbia palustris	Z8
Euphorbia pulcherrima	T
Euryale ferox	T
Euryops acraeus	T
Euryops pectinatus	T
Exacum affine	Annual
Fagus grandifolia	Z4
Fagus sylvatica	Z5b
Fagus sylvatica 'Dawyck Gold'	Z6
Fallopia baldschuanica syn. P. aubertii	Z5b
Fargesia murielae	Z6
Fargesia nitida	Z6
Fascicularia bicolor	T

Fatsia japonica	Z7b	Gasteria verrucosa		Hakonechloa macra	Z5	Hosta sieboldiana var. elegans	
Faucaria felina	T	syn. G. carinata		Hakonechloa macra		syn. Hosta 'Elegans'	Z4
Felicia amelloides		var. verrucosa	T	'Aureola'	Z5	Hottonia palustris	Z6
syn. Aster capensis	Annual	Gaultheria forrestii	Z8	Halimodendron halodendron	Z5	Houttuynia cordata	Z4
Felicia bergeriana	Annual	Gaultheria shallon	Z6	Hamamelis mollis 'Pallida'	Z6	Houttuynia cordata	
Fenestraria aurantiaca	T	Gelsemium sempervirens	Z7	Hamamelis vernalis	Z5b	'Chamaeleon'	
Ferocactus acanthodes		Genista delphinensis	Z8	Hamamelis virginiana	Z4b	syn. H. c.'Variegata',	
syn. F. cylindraceus	T	Genista lydia	Z3b	Hamamelis x intermedia		H. c. 'Plena'	Z5
Ferocactus latispinus	T	Genista sagittalis	Z5	'Diane'	Z6b	Hoya australis syn. H. daminii	T
Ferula communis	Z8	Genista tinctoria	Z3	Hardenbergia comptoniana	T	Hoya bella	
Festuca glauca	Z3b	Gentiana acaulis	Z3	Harrisia gracilis	T	syn. H. lanceolata	
Ficus benjamina	T	Gentiana asclepiadea	Z4	Hatiora salicornioides		subsp. Bella	T
Ficus benjamina 'Reginald'	T	Gentiana lutea	Z5	syn. Rhipsalis salicornioides	T	Hoya carnosa	T
Ficus benjamina 'Variegata'	T	Gentiana saxosa	Z4	Haworthia attenuata	T	Hoya linearis	T
Ficus carica	Z6	Gentiana sino-ornata	Z5	Haworthia cooperi	T	Hoya polyneura	T
Ficus deltoidea	T	Gentiana verna	Z4	Haworthia limifolia	T	Humea elegans	
Ficus elastica	T	Gentiana verna var. angulosa		Haworthia planifolia	T	syn. Calomeria	
Ficus lyrata	T	syn. G. verna 'Angulosa'	Z4	Haworthia reinwardtii	T	amaranthoides	Annual
Ficus pumila		Geranium endressii	Z4	Hebe buchananii 'Minor'	Z8	Humulus lupulus	Z4
syn. F. repens	T	Geranium farreri	Z4	Hebe pinguifolia 'Pagei'	Z7	Humulus lupulus 'Aureus'	Z4
Ficus pumila 'Variegata'	T	Geranium sanguineum	Z3b	Hedera helix	Z5b	Hutchinsia alpina	
Filipendula rubra	Z3b	Geranium sanguineum		Hedera helix 'Buttercup'	Z6	syn. Pritzelago alpino	Z5
Filipendula ulmaria	Z3	var. striatum	Z3b	Hedera helix 'Eva'	Z5b	Hyacinthoides non-scripta	Z4
Fittonia argyroneura		Gilia capitata	Annual	Hedera helix 'Goldheart'		Hydrangea anomala	Z5
syn. F. albivenis		Ginkgo biloba	Z3	syn. H. helix 'Gold Heart'	Z6	Hydrangea anomala	
Argyroneura group	T	Glaucidium palmatum	Z7	Hedera helix 'Ivalace'	Z5b	subsp. petiolaris	Z5
Fittonia verschaffeltii		Glaucium flavum	Z7	Hedera helix		Hydrangea arborescens	Z2b
syn. F. albivenis		Glechoma hederacea		'Parsley Crested'	Z6	Hydrangea aspera	Z6
Verschaffeltii group	T	'Variegata'	Z4	Hedera helix 'Pedata'	Z6	Hydrangea macrophylla	Z6
Foeniculum vulgare	Z4	Gleditsia triacanthos	Z4	Helianthemum oelandicum	Z6	Hydrangea paniculata	Z3b
Fontinalis antipyretica	Z7	Gleditsia triacanthos		Helianthus annuus	Annual	Hydrangea paniculata	
Forsythia ovata 'Ottawa'	Z4	'Sunburst'	Z4	Helianthus		'Floribunda'	Z3b
Fragaria 'Baron Solemacher'	Z5	Gleditsia triacanthos		Color Fashion Series	Annual	Hydrangea paniculata	
Fraxinus americana	Z3b	var. inermis	Z4	Helichrysum coralloides	Z8	'Grandiflora'	Z3b
Fraxinus excelsior	Z4b	Globularia cordifolia	Z5	Helichrysum milfordiae		Hydrangea paniculata	
Fraxinus excelsior		Globularia meridionalis	Z5	syn. H. marginatum	T	'Unique'	Z3b
'Pendula'	Z4b	Gloriosa superba	T	Helichrysum petiolare	T	Hydrangea quercifolia	Z5b
Fraxinus ornus	Z6	Glottiphyllum linguiforme	T	Helichrysum selago syn.		Hydrangea quercifolia	
Fraxinus oxycarpa		Glyceria maxima 'Variegata'	Z4	Ozothamnus selago	T	'Snowflake'	Z5b
'Raywood'	Z6	Gomphrena globosa	Annual	Heliocereus speciosus		Hydrocharis morsus-ranae	Z5
Fritillaria camschatcensis	Z4	Graptopetalum amethystinum	T	var. superbus	T	Hydrocleys nymphoides	T
Fritillaria cirrhosa	Z6	Grevillea robusta	T	Heliotropium arborescens	T	Hygrophila polysperma	T
Fritillaria imperialis	Z5	Gunnera chilensis		Helleborus argutifolius	Z5b	Hylocereus ocamponis	T
Fritillaria imperialis		syn. G. tinctoria	T	Helleborus foetidus	Z6	Hylomecon japonicum	Z6
'Maxima Lutea'		Gunnera manicata	Z6	Helleborus niger	Z4	Hypericum calycinum	Z5b
syn. F. i. 'Lutea Maxima'	Z5	Gunnera tinctoria		Helleborus orientalis	Z4b	Hypericum x moserianum	Z5b
Fritillaria persica	Z5	syn. G. chilensis	T	Hemerocallis 'Stella de Oro'	Z3	Hypoestes phyllostachya	
Fritillaria roylei	Z6	Guzmania lingulata	T	Hepatica nobilis	Z5b	syn. H. sanguinolenta	Annual
Fritillaria uvavulpis	Z5	Guzmania lingulata var. minor	T	Hepatica transsilvanica	Z6	Hypoestes phyllostachya	
Fuchsia magellanica	T	Gymnocalycium baldianum	T	Heuchera micrantha var.		'Purpuriana'	Annual
Fuschia 'Lady Thumb'	T	Gymnocalycium bruchii	T	diversifolia 'Palace Purple'	Z4	Hypoestes phyllostachya	
Gaillardia pulchella	Annual	Gymnocalycium gibbosum	T	Hibbertia scandens	T	'Splash'	Annual
Galanthus nivalis	Z3	Gymnocalycium mihanovichii	T	Hibiscus rosa-sinensis	T	Hyssopus officinalis	Z5
Galax aphylla	Z6	Gynandriris sisyrinchium	T	Hibiscus syriacus	Z5b	Iberis amara	T
Galega x hartlandii	Z6	Gynura aurantiaca	T	Hibiscus syriacus		Iberis saxatilis	Z5
Galium odoratum	Z5	Gypsophila aretioides	Z5	'Red Heart'	Z5b	Iberis umbellata	Annual
Gardenia jasminoides		Gypsophila dubia	Z5	Himalayacalamus falconeri		Ilex aquifolium	Z7
syn. G. augusta, G. florida,		Gypsophila elegans	Z5	syn. Arundinaria falconeri,		Ilex aquifolium	
G. grandiflora	T	Gypsophila repens	Z4	Drepanostachyum falconeri,		'Golden Milkboy'	Z7
Garrya elliptica	Z8	Haageocereus acranthus	T	Thamnocalamus falconeri	T	Ilex aquifolium	
Gasteria angulata	T	Haageocereus setosus	T	Hippeastrum advenum	T	'Madame Briot'	Z7
Gasteria batesiana	T	Haageocereus versicolor	T	Hippophäe rhamnoides	Z2b	Ilex crenata 'Mariesii'	Z6b
Gasteria distichia	T	Haberlea rhodopensis	Z5	Hoheria lyallii	T	Ilex x altaclerensis	Z8
Gasteria liliputana		Hakea lissosperma	T	Hordeum jubatum	Z4	Ilex x altaclerensis	
syn. G. bicolor				Hosta plantaginea		'Golden King'	Z8
var. liliputana	T			var. grandiflora	Z4	Impatiens tinctoria	T
						Impatiens walleriana	Annual

Imperata cylindrica 'Rubra'	Z5
Indocalamus tessellatus	Z8
Ipheion uniflorum	Z5
Ipomoea batatas	T
Ipomoea hederacea	T
Ipomoea horsfalliae	T
Ipomoea tricolor	Annual
Iris cristata	Z4
Iris ensata	Z3
Iris foetidissima	Z7
Iris foetidissima 'Variegata'	Z7
Iris graminea	Z4
Iris laevigata	Z4
Iris laevigata 'Variegata'	Z4
Iris pseudacorus	Z3
Iris reticulata	Z5
Iris sibirica	Z3
Iris unguicularis	Z6b
Iris versicolor	Z3
Iris Dutch Hybrids	Z6
Itea ilicifolia	Z7
Itea virginica	Z6
Ixora coccinea	T
Jacaranda mimosifolia	T
Jasminum beesianum	T
Jasminum humile	Z8
Jasminum mesnyi	
syn. J. primulinum	Z8
Jasminum nudiflorum	Z7b
Jasminum officinale	Z8
Jasminum polyanthum	Z8
Jatropha podagrica	T
Juglans nigra	Z3
Juncus effusus	Z4
Juncus effusus 'Vittatus'	Z4
Juncus effusus f. spiralis	Z5
Juncus ensifolius	Z6b
Juniperus chinensis 'Aurea'	Z5
Juniperus communis	
'Compressa'	Z4
Juniperis communis	
'Sentinel'	Z3
Juniperus horizontalis	Z2
Juniperus procumbens	
'Nana'	Z4
Juniperus scopulorum	
'Skyrocket'	Z3
Juniperus squamata	
'Blue Carpet'	Z5
Juniperus squamata	
'Blue Star'	Z3
Kadsura japonica	T
Kalanchoe beharensis	T
Kalanchoe blossfeldiana	T
Kalanchoe jongsmanii	T
Kalanchoe manginii	T
Kalanchoe marmorata	T
Kalanchoe pumila	T
Kalanchoe tomentosa	T
Kalanchoe tubiflora	
syn. K. delagoensis	T
Kalmia angustifolia	Z3
Kalmia latifolia	Z5b
Kalmia polifolia	
'Microphylla'	Z2

Kennedia rubicunda	T
Kirengeshoma palmata	Z5
Knautia macedonia	Z4
Kniphofia caulescens	Z6b
Kniphofia uvaria	Z5
Kochia scoparia f. trichophylla syn. Bassia scoparia f. trichophylla	Annual
Koelreuteria paniculata	Z6
Lablab purpureus	Annual
Laburnum x watereri 'Vossii'	Z6
Lagarosiphon major syn. Elodea crispa	T
Lagerstroemia indica	Z7b
Lagurus ovatus	Annual
Lamium maculatum	Z3
Lamium maculatum 'Chequers'	Z3
Lampranthus falcatus	T
Lampranthus multiradiatus syn. L. roseus, L. mesembryanthemum, L. multiradiatum	T
Lapageria rosea	T
Lardizabala biternata	T
Larix decidua	Z2b
Lathyrus grandiflorus	Z6
Lathyrus latifolius	Z4
Lathyrus odoratus	Annual
Laurus nobilis	Z8
Lavandula stoechas	Z8
Lavatera cachemiriana	Z4
Lavatera maritima	T
Lavatera thuringiaca	Z5
Lavatera trimestris	T
Leiophyllum buxifolium	Z6
Lemna trisulca	Z4
Lenophyllum pusillum	T
Leontopodium alpinum	Z4
Leontopodium nivale	Z4
Leptospermum scoparium	T
Leucanthemum x superbum	Z4
Leucojum vernum	Z4
Leucojum aestivum	Z4
Leucopogon fraseri	T
Leucothoë keiskei	Z7
Lewisia leeana	Z4
Lewisia tweedyi	Z4
Lewisia, Cotyledon Hybrids	Z4
Libertia grandiflora	T
Ligularia clivorum syn. L. dentata	Z4
Ligularia dentata 'Othello'	Z4
Ligularia przewalskii	Z5
Ligularia stenocephala	Z4
Ligustrum japonicum	Z8
Ligustrum lucidum	Z8
Ligustrum ovalifolium	Z7
Limnobium spongia	Z7
Limnobium stoloniferum	Z7
Limonium bellidifolium	Z7b
Limonium latifolium	Z4
Limonium sinuatum	Annual
Linaria alpina	Z4

Linnaea borealis	Z2
Linum arboreum	T
Linum grandiflorum	Annual
Linum suffruticosum	Z7b
Linum suffruticosum subsp. salsoloides 'Nanum' syn. L. salsoloides 'Grace Ward'	Z7b
Liquidambar styraciflua	Z6
Liriodendron tulipifera	Z5b
Liriope muscari 'Variegata'	Z6
Lithodora diffusa syn. Lithospermum diffusum	Z6
Lithops bella syn. L. karasmontana subsp. Bella	T
Lithops dorotheae	T
Lithops pseudotruncatella var. pulmonuncula	T
Lobelia cardinalis	Z2
Lobelia erinus	Annual
Lobelia fulgens	T
Lobelia paludosa	Z5b
Lobivia densispina	T
Lobivia famatimensis	T
Lobivia jajoiana	T
Lobivia pentlandii syn. Echinopsis pentlandii	T
Lobivia silvestrii syn. Echinopsis chamaecereus	T
Lobularia maritima	Annual
Lonicera japonica var. halliana	Z6
Lonicera korolkowii	Z4
Lonicera nitida	Z7
Lonicera periclymenum	Z4b
Lonicera periclymenum 'Graham Thomas'	Z5
Lonicera periclymenum 'Serotina'	Z5
Lonicera pileata	Z7
Lonicera sempervirens	Z4b
Lonicera standishii	Z7
Lonicera x americana	Z7
Lonicera x brownii	Z3
Lonicera x heckrottii	Z4
Lonicera x purpusii	Z7
Lonicera x purpusii 'Winter Beauty'	Z7
Lonicera x tellmanniana	Z6
Lotus berthelotii	T
Lotus maculatus	T
Ludwigia arcuata	Z8
Lunaria annua	Z4
Lunaria rediviva	Z7
Luronium natans	Z6
Luzula sylvatica 'Marginata'	Z4
Lysichiton americanus	Z6
Lysichiton camtschatcensis	Z4
Lysimachia nummularia 'Aurea'	Z4
Macfadyena unguis-cati	T
Macleaya cordata	Z4
Magnolia 'Elizabeth'	Z6b
Magnolia acuminata	Z5
Magnolia campbellii	T

Magnolia campbellii 'Charles Raffill'	T
Magnolia campbellii var. mollicomata	T
Magnolia grandiflora	Z8
Magnolia salicifolia	Z6
Magnolia sieboldii	Z7
Magnolia stellata	Z5
Magnolia virginiana	Z6
Magnolia x loebneri 'Merrill'	Z5
Magnolia x soulangiana	Z5
Magnolia x thompsoniana	Z6
Mahonia aquifolium	Z4
Mahonia bealei	Z7
Mahonia japonica	Z7
Mahonia repens	Z4
Mahonia x media group	Z8
Maihuenia poeppigii	T
Malus 'Dartmouth'	Z2b
Malus 'Golden Hornet'	Z4b
Malus 'Magdeburgensis'	Z4
Malus 'Red Jade' syn. M. x schiedeckerii 'Red Jade'	Z5
Malus floribunda	Z5b
Malus tschonoskii	Z6
Malva alcea var. fastigiata syn. M. alcea 'Fastigiata'	Z4
Malva moschata	Z4
Malva sylvestris	Z4
Mammillaria blossfeldiana	T
Mammillaria bocasana	T
Mammillaria compress	T
Mammillaria gracilis	T
Mammillaria hahniana	T
Mammillaria microcarpa	T
Mammillaria muehlenpfordtii	T
Mammillaria mystax	T
Mammillaria nana	T
Mammillaria polythelle	T
Mammillaria rhodantha	T
Mammillaria spinosissima	T
Mammillaria zeilmanniana	T
Mandevilla splendens syn. Dipladenia splendens	T
Manettia cordifolia	T
Manettia inflata	T
Manihot esculenta 'Variegata'	T
Maranta leuconeura	T
Marsilea quadrifolia	T
Matteuccia struthiopteris	Z3
Matthiola bicornis syn. Matthiola longipetala	Annual
Matthiola Brompton Series	Annual
Matthiola East Lothian Series	Annual
Matthiola incana	Z6b
Matthiola Ten-week Series	Annual
Matucana aureiflora syn. Oreocereus aureiflora	T
Meconopsis cambrica	Z5
Meconopsis delavayi	Z7
Melia azedarach	T
Melianthus major	T

Mentha aquatica	Z5b
Mentha requienii	Z5
Menyanthes trifoliata	Z4
Menziesia ciliicalyx	Z7
Merremia tuberosa	T
Metasequoia glyptostroboides	Z5b
Metrosideros excelsa	T
Metrosideros robusta	T
Metrosideros umbellata	T
Mikania scandens	T
Miltonia candida var. grandiflora	T
Mimulus cardinalis	Z7
Mimulus cupreus	T
Mimulus guttatus	Z7
Mimulus hybrids syn. Mimulus x hybridus	Annual
Mimulus ringens	Z5b
Mimulus Calypso Series	Annual
Mimulus Malibu Series	Annual
Mirabilis jalapa	Annual
Miscanthus sinensis	Z5
Mitchella repens	Z4
Mitraria coccinea	T
Moluccella laevis	Annual
Monstera deliciosa	T
Moraea spathulata	T
Morisia monanthos syn. M. hypogaea	Z8
Morus nigra	Z7b
Musa basjoo	T
Mutisia decurrens	T
Mutisia oligodon	T
Myosotis rupicola	Z5
Myosotis scorpioides	Z5
Myosotis scorpoides 'Mermaid'	Z5
Myosotis sylvatica	Z4
Myriophyllum aquaticum syn. M. proserpinacoides	T
Myriophyllum hippuroides	T
Myriophyllum verticillatum	Z3
Myrtus communis var. tarentina	Z8
Myrtus luma	T
Narcissus cyclamineus	Z4
Narcissus triandrus	Z4
Narcissus watieri	Z4
Neillia thibetica	Z6
Nelumbo 'Pygmaea Alba'	Z6
Nelumbo lutea	Z6
Nelumbo nucifera	Z6
Nelumbo nucifera 'Alba Grandiflora'	Z6
Nelumbo nucifera 'Alba Striata'	Z6
Nelumbo nucifera 'Rosa Plena' syn. N. nucifera 'Roseum Plenum'	Z6
Neoregelia carolinae f. tricolor	T
Nephrolepsis exaltata	T
Nerine bowdenii	T
Nerium oleander	T

Nertera granadensis syn. N. depressa	T
Nicotiana alata	Annual
Nicotiana x sanderae	Annual
Nierembergia hippomanica var. violacea 'Purple Robe' syn. N. caerula	Annual
Nierembergia rivularis	Z8
Nigella damascena	Annual
Nopalxochia phyllanthoides	T
Nothofagus dombeyi	Z8
Nothofagus obliqua	Z8
Nothofagus procera	Z8
Nuphar advena	Z7
Nuphar lutea	Z3
Nuphar pumila	Z4
Nymphaea 'American Star'	T
Nymphaea 'Attraction'	Z3
Nymphaea 'Aurora'	T
Nymphaea 'Blue Beauty'	T
Nymphaea 'Carnea'	T
Nymphaea 'Chromatella'	Z3
Nymphaea 'Ellisiana'	Z4
Nymphaea 'Escarboucle'	Z3
Nymphaea 'Fire Crest'	Z3
Nymphaea 'Laydekeri Purpurata'	Z4
Nymphaea 'Laydekeri Rosea Prolifera'	Z4
Nymphaea 'Pygmaea Helvola' syn. N. tetragona 'Helvola'	Z3
Nymphaea 'Virginalis'	Z3
Nymphaea alba	T
Nymphaea candida	Z3
Nymphaea odorata	T
Nymphaea odorata var. minor	T
Nymphaea tetragona	Z3
Nymphaea tuberosa	Z3
Nymphoides aquatica	T
Nymphoides humboldtiana	T
Nymphoides indica	T
Nymphoides peltata	Z7
Nyssa sylvatica	Z5b
Oenothera biennis	Z4
Oenothera odorata	Z5b
Olea europaea	T
Omphalodes luciliae	Z6b
Onopordum acanthium	Z5
Onosma albo-roseum syn. O. albo rosea	T
Onosma echioides	T
Onosma taurica	T
Ophiopogon planiscapus 'Nigrescens'	Z6
Opuntia compressa syn. O. humifusa	T
Opuntia exaltata	T
Opuntia fragilis	Z4
Opuntia hystricina	T
Opuntia lanceolata	T
Opuntia microdasys	T
Opuntia paraguayensis	T
Opuntia polycantha	Z4
Opuntia rastera	T

Opuntia robusta	T
Opuntia subulata	T
Orbea variegata syn. Stapelia variegata	T
Origanum amanum	T
Origanum rotundifolium	T
Orontium aquaticum	Z6
Orostachys chanetii	T
Orostachys spinosus	T
Oroya neoperuviana syn. O. peruviana, Oreocereus neoperuviana	T
Osmanthus delavayi	Z8
Osmanthus fragrans	T
Osmanthus x burkwoodii syn. Osmarea burkwoodii	Z7
Osmunda regalis	Z4
Osteospermum 'Starshine' (and other seed selections)	Annual
Ostrya carpinifolia	Z6
Othonna dentata	T
Ourisia 'Loch Ewe'	T
Ourisia caespitosa	T
Ourisia coccinea	T
Oxalis 'Ione Hecker'	T
Oxalis adenophylla	Z5
Oxalis enneaphylla	Z6
Oxydendrum arboreum	Z6
Pachycereus pringlei	T
Pachyphytum oviferum	T
Pachyphytum viride	T
Pachypodium geayi	T
Pachypodium lamerei	T
Paeonia lactiflora	Z2
Paeonia suffruticosa	Z4
Panicum violaceum	Annual
Panicum virgatum	Z5
Papaver burseri	Z5
Papaver lateritium	Z8
Papaver miyabeanum	Z5
Papaver nudicaule	Z2
Papaver orientale	Z4
Papaver rhaeticum	Z5
Papaver rhoeas	Annual
Papaver somniferum	Annual
Papaver Summer Breeze Series	Annual
Paphiopedilum callosum	T
Parahebe catarractae	T
Paraquilegia anemonoides syn. P. grandiflora	Z6
Paraquilegia anemonoides	Z6
Paris polyphylla	Z6
Parnassia palustris	Z4
Parodia aselbergii syn. Notocactus aselbergii	T
Parodia brevihamata syn. Notocactus brevihamata	T
Parodia chrysacanthion syn. Notocactus chrysacanthion	T
Parodia graessneri syn. Notocactus graessneri	T
Parodia leninghausii syn. Notocactus leninghausii	T
Parodia mammulosa syn. Notocactus mammulosa	T
Parodia mutabilis syn. Notocactus mutabilis	T
Parrotia persica	Z6
Parthenocissus quinquefolia	Z2b
Parthenocissus tricuspidata	Z5b
Parthenocissus tricuspidata 'Lowii'	Z5b
Passiflora caerulea	Z6
Pelargonium 'Breakaway'	Annual
Pelargonium 'Copthorne'	T
Pelargonium 'Lady Plymouth'	T
Pelargonium 'Mini Cascade'	Annual
Pelargonium 'Multibloom'	Annual
Pelargonium 'Sensation'	Annual
Pelargonium 'Summer Showers'	Annual
Pelargonium (all F1 and F2 seed selections)	Annual
Pelargonium (F1 and F2 hybrids)	Annual
Pelargonium acetosum	T
Pelargonium echinatum	T
Pelargonium tetragonum	T
Pellaea rotundifolia	T
Pellionia daveauana syn. Elatostema daveauana	T
Peltandra alba	Z7
Peltiphyllum peltatum syn. Darmia peltata	Z5
Pennisetum alopecuroides	Z5
Pennisetum villosum	Annual
Penstemon newberryi	Z6
Penstemon newberryi f. humilior	Z6
Pentas lanceolata syn. P. carnea	T
Peperomia caperata	T
Peperomia dolabriformis	T
Pernettya mucronata 'Seashell' syn. Gaultheria mucronata 'Seashell'	Z7
Pernettya mucronata 'Wintertime' syn. Gaultheria mucronata 'Wintertime'	Z7
Persicaria affinis 'Donald Lowndes'	Z3
Persicaria amphibia	Z3
Persicaria amplexicaule	Z3
Persicaria bistorta	Z3b
Persicaria bistorta 'Superba'	Z3b
Persicaria campanulata	Z6
Petasites fragrans	Z4
Petrea volubilis	T
Petrophytum hendersonii	Z6
Petroselinum crispum	Z5
Phalaris arundinacea	Z4
Phalaris arundinacea 'Picta'	Z4
Phaseolus coccineus	Annual
Phillyrea latifolia	T
Philodendron scandens	T
Phlebodium aureuma syn. Polypodium aureuma	T
Phlomis chrysophylla	T
Phlomis russeliana	Z5
Phlox 'Chatahoochee' P. divaricata subsp. laphamii 'Chatahoochee'	Z5
Phlox bifida	Z4
Phlox mesoleuca	Z7
Phlox paniculata	Z3
Phlox stolonifera	Z4
Phlox subulata	Z4
Phoenix canariensis	T
Phoenix dactyliferad	T
Phormium cookianum	T
Phormium tenax	Z8
Photinia villosa	Z5b
Phragmites australis	Z6
Phragmites australis 'Variegata'	Z6
Phragmites communis	Z6
Phyllanthus fluitans syn. Breynia fluitans	T
Phyllodoce caerulea syn. P. taxifolia	Z2
Phyllodoce glanduliflora	Z3
Phyllodoce nipponica	Z3
Phyllostachys aurea	Z7
Phyllostachys flexuosa	Z8
Phyllostachys nigra	Z7
Physalis alkekengi	Z4
Physocarpus opulifolius	Z2b
Physoplexis comosa	Z5
Picea abies	Z2b
Picea abies 'Clanbrassiliana'	Z3
Picea abies 'Gregoryana'	Z3
Picea abies 'Nidiformis'	Z2b
Picea breweriana	Z5b
Picea glauca var. albertiana 'Conica'	Z3
Picea mariana 'Nana'	Z2b
Picea omorika	Z3b
Picea pungens 'Montgomery'	Z2
Picea pungens var. glauca syn. P. p. f. glauca	Z2
Picea sitchensis	Z2
Pieris 'Forest Flame'	Z5b
Pieris nana	Z4
Pilea 'Norfolk'	T
Pilea cadierei	T
Pilea involucrata syn. P. mollis	T
Pilea spruceana	T
Pileostegia viburnoides	T
Pinus bungeana	Z6
Pinus contorta	Z4
Pinus halepensis	T
Pinus mugo	Z2b
Pinus nigra	Z4
Pinus pinaster	T
Pinus radiata	Z8
Pinus strobus	Z3
Pinus sylvestris	Z2
Pinus sylvestris 'Gold Coin'	Z3
Pinus thunbergii	Z4b
Pinus wallichiana	Z6
Pistia stratiotes	T
Pittosporum eugenioides 'Variegatum'	T
Pittosporum tobira	T
Platanus x hispanica	Z5b
Plectranthus oertendahlii	T
Pleioblastus auricomus	Z5
Pleioblastus variegatus	Z5
Plumbago auriculata	T
Plumeria rubra var. acutifolia	T
Polemonium pulcherrimum	Z4
Polygala calcarea 'Bulley's Form'	T
Polygala chamaebuxus	Z7b
Polygala myrtifolia 'Grandiflora' syn. P. x dalmaisiana	T
Polygala vayredae	T
Pontederia cordata	Z4
Pontederia lanceolata	Z8
Populus alba	Z3
Populus candicans 'Aurora' syn. Populus x jackii 'Aurora'	Z4
Populus nigra 'Italica'	Z4
Populus x canadensis 'Serotina Aurea'	Z2b
Portulaca grandiflora	Annual
Potamogeton crispus	T
Potentilla 'Elizabeth'	Z3
Potentilla 'Nana Argentea'	Z3
Potentilla fruticosa	Z2
Potentilla nitida	Z2
Pratia pedunculata	Z7
Primula allionii	Z4
Primula alpicola	Z4
Primula auricula	Z3
Primula boothii	Z5
Primula bulleyana	Z3
Primula denticulata	Z2
Primula edgeworthii syn. P. nana	Z4
Primula farinosa	Z4
Primula florindae	Z3
Primula gracilipes	Z6b
Primula helodoxa	Z3
Primula japonica	Z4
Primula malacoides	T
Primula marginata	Z4
Primula obconica	T
Primula Polyanthus Group syn. Primula x polyantha	Z4
Primula pulverulenta	Z3
Primula rosea	Z3b
Primula scotica	Z4
Primula secundiflora	Z4
Primula sikkimensis	Z4
Primula sinensis	T
Primula sonchifolia	Z5
Primula vulgaris	Z4
Primula vulgaris 'Double Sulfur'	Z4
Primula vulgaris 'Miss Indigo'	Z4
Primula x kewensis	T
Prostanthera rotundifolia	T
Prunus 'Amanogawa'	Z6
Prunus 'Kanzan'	Z6
Prunus 'Kiku-shidare' syn. Prunus 'Kiku-shidare-zakura'	Z6
Prunus 'Okame'	Z7b
Prunus 'Pandora'	Z7
Prunus 'Spire'	Z7
Prunus americana	Z2b
Prunus avium 'Plena'	Z4b
Prunus glandulosa	Z5
Prunus laurocerasus	Z7
Prunus laurocerasus 'Otto Luyken'	Z7
Prunus laurocerasus 'Schipkaensis'	Z7
Prunus lusitanica	Z7b
Prunus maackii 'Amber Beauty'	Z2b
Prunus mume	Z5b
Prunus mume 'Beni-shi-dare' syn. Prunus mume 'Beni-shidori'	Z5b
Prunus sargentii	Z5b
Prunus serrula	Z7
Prunus spinosa	Z5b
Prunus subhirtella	Z6
Prunus subhirtella 'Autumnalis'	Z7
Prunus tomentosa	Z2
Prunus triloba	Z2b
Prunus x yedoensis	Z7
Pseudolarix amabilis	Z5b
Pseudotsuga menziesii var. glauca	Z5
Psylliostachys suworowii	Annual
Pteris cretica	T
Pterocarya fraxinifolia	Z6
Pterocephalus perennis	Z6
Pueraria lobata	Z7
Punica granatum 'Nana'	T
Puya alpestris	T
Pyracantha 'Golden Charmer'	Z7
Pyracantha 'Mohave'	Z7
Pyrola rotundifolia	Z5
Pyrostegia venusta	T
Pyrus calleryana 'Chanticleer'	Z5b
Pyrus salicifolia 'Pendula'	Z5
Quercus ilex	Z8
Quercus myrsinifoliae	Z7b
Quercus palustris	Z4
Quercus robur	Z5
Quercus rubra	Z3
Quercus virginiana	Z8
Quercus x hispanica	Z8
Quercus x turneri	Z7b
Quisqualis indica	T
Ramonda myconi	Z4
Ranunculus asiaticus	Z7b
Ranunculus ficaria	Z4
Ranunculus lingua	Z4
Ranunculus lingua 'Grandiflora'	Z4

Species	Zone
Raoulia australis	Z8
Rebutia albiflora	T
Rebutia aureiflora	T
Rebutia fiebrigii syn. R. musculata	T
Rebutia heliosa	T
Rebutia marsoneri	T
Rebutia minuscula syn. R. violaciflora	T
Rebutia senilis	T
Rehmannia elata syn. R. angulata	T
Reseda odorata	Annual
Rhamnus alaternus	Z7b
Rheum alexandrae	Z8
Rheum palmatum	Z3
Rheum palmatum 'Atrosanguineum'	Z3
Rhipsalidopsis gaetneri syn. Hatiora gaetneri	T
Rhipsalidopsis rosea	T
Rhipsalis cereuscula	T
Rhipsalis mesembryanthemoides	T
Rhipsalis pachyptera	T
Rhodanthe manglesii	T
Rhodiola crassipes	T
Rhodochiton atrosanguineus	T
Rhododendron 'Fragrantissima'	T
Rhododendron 'Hinodegiri'	Z7
Rhododendron 'Homebush'	Z5
Rhododendron 'Polar Bear'	Z7
Rhododendron augustinii	Z8
Rhododendron auriculatum	Z7
Rhododendron edgeworthii	T
Rhododendron indicum 'Hakurei'	Z7
Rhododendron luteum	Z4
Rhododendron maddenii	T
Rhododendron occidentale	Z6
Rhododendron ponticum	Z7b
Rhododendron Subsection Triflora	Z7b
Rhododendron vireya	T
Rhododendron viscosum	Z4
Rhododendron wardii	Z7b
Rhododendron yakushimanum	Z5
Rhododendron Ghent Hybrids	Z6
Rhododendron Loderi Group syn. R. x loderi	Z7
Rhododendron Rustica Hybrids	Z6
Rhodoleia championii	T
Rhoicissus capensis	T
Rhus typhina	Z3
Ribes odoratum	Z2
Ribes sanguineum	Z6b
Riccia fluitans	T
Ricinus communis	Annual
Robinia pseudoacacia 'Frisia'	Z4
Rodgersia aesculifolia	Z5
Rodgersia pinnata	Z3
Rodgersia podophylla	Z5
Romneya coulteri	T
Rosa 'Champlain'	Z3
Rosa 'Frau Dagmar Hartopp'	Z4b
Rosa 'Fryminicot'	Z6
Rosa 'Fryministar'	Z6
Rosa 'Jaclover'	Z6
Rosa 'Meitonje'	Z6
Rosa 'Nevada'	Z5
Rosa 'Poulbells' syn. R. 'Pink Bells'	Z6
Rosa 'Poullen'	Z6
Rosa 'Roseraie de l'Haÿ'	Z2
Rosa 'Surrey'	Z6
Rosa filipes 'Kiftsgate'	Z6
Rosa moyesii 'Geranium'	Z6
Rosa pimpinellifolia	Z3
Rosa rugosa	Z2b
Roscoea cautleoyoides	Z7
Rosmarinus officinalis	Z7
Rosularia modesta	Z7b
Rubus 'Tridel'	Z6
Rubus biflorus	T
Rubus cockburnianus	Z7
Rubus deliciosus	Z6
Rubus thibetanus	Z4b
Rudbeckia hirta	Z3b
Rudbeckia laciniata 'Goldquelle'	Z3
Ruscus aculeatus	Z7b
Ruta graveolens	Z5
Sagina procumbens	Z4
Sagina subulata 'Aurea'	Z4
Sagittaria graminea	T
Sagittaria latifolia	Z3
Sagittaria sagittifolia	Z3
Sagittaria sagittifolia 'Flore Pleno'	Z3
Salicornia europaea	Z5b
Salix acutifolia 'Blue Streak'	Z3
Salix alba	Z2
Salix alba 'Britzensis'	Z2
Salix alba var. sericea	Z2
Salix alba var. vitellina	Z2
Salix babylonica	Z6
Salix caprea	Z4b
Salix caprea 'Kilmarnock'	Z5
Salix daphnoides	Z2b
Salix daphnoides 'Aglaia'	Z3
Salix fragilis	Z3b
Salix irrorata	Z6
Salix matsudana 'Tortuosa'	Z5
Salix melanostachys S. gracilistyla var. melanostachys	Z4b
Salix x boydii	Z7
Salix x erythroflexuosa	Z5
Salix x sepulcralis syn. S. sepulcralis var. chrysocoma	Z4b
Salix x sepulcralis 'Chrysocoma'	Z4b
Salix x sepulcralis 'Erythroflexuosa'	Z5
Salvia coccinea	Annual
Salvia confertiflora	T
Salvia discolor	T
Salvia elegans 'Scarlet Pineapple'	T
Salvia farinacea	Annual
Salvia horminum syn. S. viridis	Annual
Salvia patens	Z8
Salvia sclarea var. turkestanica	Z5
Salvia splendens	Annual
Salvia uliginosa	Z6b
Salvia viridis syn. S. horminum	Annual
Salvinia auriculata	T
Salvinia natans	T
Sambucus racemosa 'Plumosa Aurea'	Z3
Sanguinaria canadensis	Z3
Sansevieria trifasciata	T
Sansevieria trifasciata 'Hahnii'	T
Sansevieria trifasciata 'Laurentii'	T
Santolina chamaecyparissus	Z7
Saponaria ocymoides	Z3
Sarcococca confusa	Z7b
Sarcococca humilis	Z7b
Sasa veitchii syn. S. albomarginata	Z8
Saururus cernuus	Z6
Saxifraga 'Tumbling Waters'	Z6b
Saxifraga callosa	Z7b
Saxifraga cochlearis	Z7b
Saxifraga cotyledon	Z4
Saxifraga longifolia	Z7
Saxifraga paniculata	Z2
Saxifraga stolonifera 'Tricolor' syn. S. sarmentosa	Z7b
Saxifraga umbrosa	Z3
Saxifraga x urbium	Z6b
Scabiosa graminifolia	Z5
Scaevola aemula	Annual
Schefflera actinophylla	T
Schefflera arboricola 'Gold Capella'	T
Schinus molle	T
Schizanthus pinnatus	Annual
Schizophragma hydrangeoides	Z5
Schizophragma integrifolium	Z7b
Schizostylis coccinea	Z7
Schlumbergera bridgesii syn. S. x buckleyi	T
Schlumbergera truncata syn. Zygocactus truncatus	T
Schlumbergera truncata var. delicata	T
Sciadopitys verticillata	Z6
Scilla bifolia	Z3
Scilla peruviana	T
Scirpus lacustris syn. Schoenoplectus lacustris	Z5
Scirpus lacustris subsp. tabernaemontani 'Albescens' syn. Schoenoplectus lacustris	Z5
Scirpus lacustris subsp. tabernaemontani 'Zebrinus'	Z5
Scrophularia auriculata 'Variegata'	Z6
Sedum anglicum	Z6
Sedum cauticola	Z4
Sedum cyaneum	Z4
Sedum dasyphyllum	Z7b
Sedum formosanum	Z6
Sedum hintonii	Z5b
Sedum hispanicum	Z6
Sedum lanceolatum	Z6
Sedum montanum	Z5
Sedum morganianum	T
Sedum rosulatum	Z7
Sedum rupestre syn. S. reflexum	Z6
Sedum sediforme	Z6
Sedum sempervivoides	Z5
Sedum spathulifolium 'Cape Blanco'	Z6
Sedum spectabile	Z3b
Sedum spectabile 'Brilliant'	Z3b
Sedum spurium	Z3b
Sedum telephium syn. Hylotelephium telephium	Z3b
Sedum ternatum	Z6
Sedum villosum	Z5
Selaginella kraussiana	T
Selaginella kraussania 'Aurea'	T
Selaginella martensii	T
Selenicereus grandiflorus	T
Selinicereus macdonaldiae	T
Sempervivum arachnoideum	Z4
Sempervivum montanum	Z4
Sempervivum ruthenicum	Z4
Senecio cineraria	Annual
Senecio confusus	T
Senecio fulgens	T
Senecio haworthii	T
Senecio jacobsenii	T
Senecio macroglossus	T
Senecio macroglossus 'Variegatus'	T
Senecio maritima syn. S. cineraria	Annual
Senecio mikanioides syn. Delairea odorata	T
Senecio smithii	T
Senecio tamoides	T
Senecio x hybridus	T
Sequoiadendron giganteum	Z6b
Serissa foetida syn. S. japonica	T
Setaria glauca	T
Setaria palmifolia 'Rubra'	T
Setiechinopsis mirabilis	T
Shibataea kumasasa	Z7
Shortia soldanelloides	Z6
Shortia uniflora	Z6
Silene acaulis	Z3
Silene schafta	Z3b
Silene vulgaris subsp. maritima	Z4
Silene vulgaris subsp. maritima 'Flore Pleno'	Z4
Silphium perfoliatum	Z5
Silybum marianum	Z5
Sinningia pusilla	T
Sinningia speciosa syn. Gloxinia speciosa	T
Sisyrinchium striatum	T
Skimmia japonica	T
Smilacina racemosa	T
Solandra maxima	T
Solanum capsicastrum	T
Solanum crispum	T
Solanum crispum 'Glasnevin'	T
Solanum jasminoides	Z8
Solanum pseudocapsicum	T
Solanum rantonnei syn. Lycianthes rantonneti	T
Solanum wendlandii	T
Soldanella alpina	Z4
Soldanella montana	Z4
Soldanella villosa	Z4
Soleirolia soleirolii syn. Helxine soleirolii	T
Solidago canadensis	Z4
Sonerila margaritacea	T
Sophora japonica	Z5b
Sorbus aria	Z4
Sorbus aria 'Lutescens'	Z4
Sorbus aucuparia	Z3
Sorbus cashmiriana	Z5
Sorbus commixta 'Embley'	Z6
Sorbus intermedia	Z4
Sorbus reducta	Z4b
Sorbus vilmorinii	Z3
Sparganium erectum syn. S. ramosum	Z6b
Sparganium minimum	Z6b
Spartium junceum	Z7b
Spiraea x bumalda 'Gold Flame'	Z2b
Spiraea douglasii	Z5b
Spiraea japonica	Z5
Spiraea prunifolia	Z4
Spiraea thunbergii	Z3
Spiraea x arguta syn. S. 'Arguta'	Z2b
Stachys byzantina	Z4
Stachys byzantina 'Silver Carpet'	Z4
Stanhopea tigrina	T
Stephanotis floribunda	T
Sternbergia lutea	Z7
Sternbergia sicula	Z6
Stewartia pseudocamellia	Z6
Stigmaphyllon ciliatum	T
Stipa gigantea	Z7
Stipa pennata	Z7
Stratiotes aloides	T
Streptocarpus 'Heidi'	T
Streptocarpus saxorum	T

Streptosolen jamesonii	T			
Strombocactus disciformis	T			
Strongylodon macrobotrys	T			
Stylophorum diphyllum	Z6			
Styrax japonicus	Z5b			
Sulcorebutia glomeriseta	T			
Sulcorebutia steinbachii	T			
Symphytum grandiflorum	T			
Syngonium hoffmannii	T			
Syngonium podophyllum	T			
Syringa meyeri var. spontanea 'Palibin' syn. *S. palibiniana, S. velutina*	Z2b			
Syringa microphylla 'Superba'	Z3			
Tabebuia chrysotricha	T			
Tagetes signata syn. *T. tenuifolia*	Annual			
Tamarix ramosissima	Z3			
Tanakaea radicans	Z7			
Taxodium distichum	Z5			
Taxus baccata	Z6			
Taxus baccata 'Aurea' syn. *T. b.* Aurea Group	Z6			
Taxus baccata 'Standishii'	Z6			
Taxus x media	Z5			
Tellima grandiflora	Z4			
Tellima grandiflora 'Purpurea'	Z4			
Tetrastigma voinierianum	T			
Thalia dealbata	Z7			
Thalia geniculata	T			
Thalictrum flavum	Z4			
Thelocactus bicolor	T			
Thelocactus nidulans	T			
Thelocactus setispinus syn. *Ferocactus setispinus, Hamatocactus setispinus*	T			
Thompsonella platyphylla	T			
Thuja occidentalis	Z3			

Thuja occidentalis 'Caespitosa'	Z3			
Thuja orientalis 'Aurea Nana' syn. *Platycladus orientalis*	Z7			
Thunbergia alata	Annual			
Thunbergia gregorii	T			
Thymophylla tenuiloba	Annual			
Thymus caespititius syn. *T. azoricus, T. micans*	Z4			
Thymus membranaceus	Z5			
Thymus praecox	Z5			
Thymus serpyllum	Z4			
Thymus serpyllum 'Minus'	Z4			
Thymus vulgaris	Z4			
Tiarella polyphylla	Z7			
Tibouchina urvilleana	T			
Tilia 'Euchlora' syn. *Tilia x euchlora*	Z3			
Tilia platyphyllos	Z5			
Tilia tomentosa	Z4b			
Tilia tomentosa 'Petiolaris'	Z4b			
Tilia x euchlora	Z3			
Tilia x europaea	Z4			
Tillandsia caput-medusae	T			
Tillandsia ionantha	T			
Tillandsia latifolia	T			
Tillandsia stricta	T			
Tillandsia tectorum	T			
Tillandsia usneoides	T			
Tolmiea menziesii	Z7			
Toona sinensis 'Flamingo'	Z6			
Torenia fournieri	Annual			
Trachelium caeruleum	T			
Trachelospermum jasminoides	T			
Trachycarpus fortunei	T			
Trachymene coerulea syn. *Didiscus coeruleus*	Annual			
Tradescantia cerinthoides syn. *T. blossfeldian*	T			
Tradescantia fluminensis	T			

Tradescantia spathacea syn. *Rhoeodiscolor spathacea*	T			
Tradescantia zebrina	T			
Trapa natans	T			
Trichocereus fulvilanus	T			
Trichocereus pachanoi	T			
Trichocereus pasacana	T			
Trichocereus spachianus syn. *Echinopsis spachiana*	T			
Trichocereus terscheckii	T			
Trillium grandiflorum	Z4			
Trillium sessile	Z4			
Trochodendron aralioidese	T			
Trollius europaeus	Z4			
Trollius ledebourii syn. *T. chinensis*	Z4			
Trollius x cultorum	Z3b			
Tropaeolum majus	Annual			
Tropaeolum majus 'Empress of India'	Annual			
Tropaeolum majus Gleam Series	Annual			
Tropaeolum majus Whirlybird Series	Annual			
Tropaeolum peregrinum	Annual			
Tropaeolum speciosum	Z8			
Tropaeolum tricolorum	Annual			
Tropaeolum tuberosum	Z8			
Tsuga heterophylla	Z7			
Tsuga mertensiana f. argentea	Z6			
Tulipa sylvestris	Z4			
Typha angustifolia	Z2			
Typha latifolia	Z2			
Typha latifolia 'Variegata'	Z2			
Typha minima	Z3			
Typha stenophylla syn. *Typha laxmannii*	Z3			
Ulex europaeus	Z7			
Ulmus parvifolia 'Geisha'	Z5			
Umbilicus chloranthus	T			

Umbilicus intermedius	T			
Umbilicus rupestris	T			
Utricularia exoleta	T			
Utricularia minor	T			
Utricularia vulgaris	T			
Vaccaria hispanica	Annual			
Vaccinium corymbosum	Z4			
Vaccinium delavayi	Z7			
Vaccinium myrtillus	Z6			
Vaccinium parvifolium	Z6			
Vaccinium uliginosum	Z7b			
Vallisneria gigantea	T			
Vanda rothschildiana	T			
Veratrum nigrum	Z7			
Verbascum 'Letitia'	Z5			
Verbascum bombyciferum	Z5			
Verbascum densiflorum	Z5			
Verbena bonariensis	Annual			
Verbena x hybrida	Annual			
Veronica beccabunga	Z6			
Veronica gentianoides	Z4			
Veronica peduncularis	Z7			
Veronica spicata	Z3			
Viburnum davidii	Z7b			
Viburnum dentatum 'Blue Muffin'	Z3			
Viburnum dilatatum	Z5			
Viburnum dilatatum 'Xanthocarpum'	Z5			
Viburnum opulus	Z3			
Viburnum plicatum	Z6			
Viburnum tinus	Z7b			
Viburnum x bodnantense	Z7			
Victoria amazonica	T			
Victoria regia	T			
Vigna caracalla syn. *Phaseous caracalla*	Annual			
Vinca minor	Z3			
Viola cazorlensis	T			
Viola cornuta 'Minor'	Z5			

Viola jooi	Z6			
Viola labradorica	Z2			
Viola odorata	Z5			
Viola odorata 'Czar'	Z5			
Viola x wittrockiana	Z5			
Viola x wittrockiana Universal series	Z5			
Vitaliana primuliflora	Z5			
Vitex agnus-castus	Z7			
Vitis coignetiae	Z5			
Vitis vinifera	Z5			
Vitis vinifera 'Purpurea'	Z6			
Waldsteinia ternata	Z4			
Wisteria sinensis	Z6			
Wisteria sinensis 'Alba'	Z6b			
Wolffia arrhiza	T			
x *Citrofortunella microcarpa* syn. *Citrus mitis*	T			
x *Cupressocyparis leylandii*	Z7			
x *Cupressocyparis leylandii* 'Castlewellan Gold'	Z7			
x *Fatshedera lizei*	Z7			
Xanthorhiza simplicissima	Z5			
Xeranthemum annuum	Annual			
Yucca filamentosa	Z4			
Yucca flaccida syn. *Y. filamentosa*	Z4			
Yucca gloriosa	Z7			
Zantedeschia aethiopica 'Crowborough'	T			
Zea mays 'Gracillima Variegata'	Annual			
Zea mays 'Japonica Multicolor'	Annual			
Zelkova carpinifolia	Z7			
Zenobia pulverulenta	Z6			
Zephyranthes candida	Z7b			
Zizania aquatica	Z6			
Zygopetalum mackayi syn. *Z. mackaii*	T			

INDEX

691

XY

Z

Abbreviations

C	centigrade	ml	milliliter(s)
cf	compare	mm	millimeter(s)
cm	centimeter	oz	ounce(s)
cv(s)	cultivar(s)	p(p)	page(s)
f.	forma	pl.	plural
fl oz	fluid ounce(s)	sp.	species
ft	foot, feet	spp.	species(pl)
g	gram(s)	sq	square
in	inch(es)	subsp.	subspecies
kg	kilogram(s)	syn.	synonyms
lb	pound(s)	var.	varietas
m	meter(s)	yd	yard(s)

Note: The generic and species names of plants are abbreviated to their initial letters after their first full mention in a sentence or a list.

ACKNOWLEDGMENTS

Photography credits

The position on the page is given from top to bottom and across the page from left to right. The photographs in plant portrait boxes are numbered sequentially from left to right across the rows and from the top row to the bottom row. Where the picture is in a step-by-step sequence it is given the number of its caption.

ADAS Crown ©: 615 bottom 1–6, 651 bottom right

A. W. Ambler: 661 bottom row first left

Peter Anderson: 30 center top

Heather Angel: 633 bottom left

Jane Aspden: 90 bottom, 332, 333 top left

A-Z Collection: 478 center left, 482 center left

Harry Baker: 414 bottom, 482 bottom left and right

Dan Barton: 368 top left

B & B Photographs: 562 center right

Gillian Beckett: 226 portrait box 1 and 8

Birmingham Botanical Gardens: 476 left

Boys Syndication: 123 top left, 489 bottom left

Ken Brate: 648 top left

John M. Burnley: 639 top right

W. Atlee Burpee & Co.: 526 bottom right

Nigel Cattlin ©: 661 top row far right

Prof. Chin: 516 bottom right, 517 top left, 524 center left, bottom right, and inset, 473 center right, inset, and bottom left, 480 bottom, 481 top left, center, and bottom left

Jack K. Clark: 656 bottom center

Bruce Coleman: 649 bottom right

Comstock: 657 center

Eric Crichton: 62 top, 83 top, 91 bottom left and right, 124 bottom right, 149 bottom right, 156 top and bottom right, 151 bottom, 171, 172 top right, 173 top left, 193 bottom left, 206 bottom, 248, 252 top, 220, 221 box 3, 222 bottom left, 226 top left and right, 227 top left and right, 228 portrait box 2, 381 top right, 382 bottom, 383 top, 398, 489 top, 592 top right

Geoff Dann: 252 bottom

Jack Elliott: 249 top, 223 bottom left

R. J. Erwin: 651 top right

Raymond Evison: 125 top, 136 portrait box 7, 137 bottom left

Roger Foley: 45 top, 50 top left and right,

Forestry Commission: 645 bottom center, 648 top center

Michael P. Gadomski: 661 top center second right

Garden Picture Library: 150 bottom left, 206 top left and top right, 207 top, 251 top, 221 box 4, 277 top right and bottom, 334 bottom left, 351 top right

John Glover: 92 bottom left, 123 bottom right, 276, 560, 561 top

Paul Goff: 368 center left, center right, bottom left, bottom center and bottom right, 369 top, center left, top center right, top right, center and center right

Gilbert Grant: 639 top center

Jerry Harpur: 2 courtesy of Chris Grey-Wilson, 55 top left, 58 top and bottom left, 122, 124 top, 149 bottom left, 180 bottom, 251 bottom, 348, 380, 486, 487 top, 412, 416 bottom, 417 bottom, 587 top

Grant Hellman: 646 top left, 650 top right, 652 top center

Holt Studios International: 642 bottom right, 643 bottom left, center bottom and top right, 650 top left, 652 top right, 655 top center, 656 top left, 657 center and center bottom left, 658 bottom left, 661 top center left

Horticulture Research International, Kirton: 242 top sequence 3, 643 top center, 647 bottom right, 653 top left

ICI Agrochemicals: 642 top right

Jacqui Hurst: 21 top right

Anne Hyde: 30 center below

Clive Innes: 334 top

Andrew Lawson: 55 top right, 119 top left, 149 top, 151 top left, 172 top left, 181 bottom left, 186 top right, 221 bottom, 223 top left and bottom right, 278 bottom right, 304 bottom, 352 top

George D. Lepp: 649 bottom left

Elvin McDonald: 334 bottom right, 525 center left and inset, 532 center right, 452 bottom

S. E. Marshall: 176 bottom right

Silvia Martin: 585 bottom

Tania Midgley: 415 top

Graeme Moore: 381 top left

Patti Murray: 649 bottom right

J. Nicholas: 632 bottom

Oxford Scientific Films: 124 bottom left, 657 top right

Park Seeds: 526 bottom left and right

Stephen P. Parker: 640 top right

Richard Parker: 640 center left below

Photos Horticultural: 417 top, 651 bottom left

Harry Rogers: 645 below right

Royal Botanic Gardens, Kew: 477 center

Royal Horticultural Society, Wisley: 488 bottom, 642 bottom center, 645 top right, 646 center left, center above and below, center right, 651 top right and center right below, 653 right, 654 bottom right, 656 center left, top right

Harry Smith Horticultural Photographic Collection: 58 bottom right, 82 bottom left, 205 top left, 335, 352 bottom, 474 top, 477 top left, 478 center right, 483 center, 517 center left, 657 top left

Lauren Springer: 55 portrait box 1

Prof. H.D. Tindall: 509 center left and bottom right, 537 bottom, 539 center, 461 bottom, 474 bottom, 475 top, 477 top right and bottom, 480 top left and right

Mathew Ward: 19 top left, 305 top

Elizabeth Whiting Associates: 54, 57 bottom, 89 top, 249 bottom, 277 top left, 400 bottom left

Steve Wooster: 1, 2, 4/5, 10, 11, 14, 20 right, 28 bottom left, 30 top and bottom, 33 bottom right, 34 top, 42 right, 88 bottom left, 118 top, 126 bottom left, 146, 173 top right, 174 top, 192 top, 578, 587 bottom left, 589 bottom left, 600

Tom Wright: 125 bottom, 207 bottom

Additional photography by:

Jane Burton, Peter Chadwick, Trevor Cole, Eric Crichton, Geoff Dann, John Glover, Jerry Harpur, Neil Holmes, Jacqui Hurst, Dave King, Elvin McDonald, Andrew McRobb, Andrew Lawson, Andrew de Lory, Tim Ridley, Karl Shone, and Gerry Young

Dorling Kindersley would like to thank the following for:

Expert advice

Mr. Ted Andrews (sweet peas); Darrell Apps (daylilies); Peter and Fiona Bainbridge (landscape design and construction); Harry Baker (fruit); Kenneth Bauman (nuts); Don Birkholz (peaches, nectarines); John Bunker (plums, gages); Douglas Burns (pears); Richard Campbell (limes); Brenda Cole (vegetables); Marie-Jose de Saint Victor (pest controls); Phillip Dukes (sweet potatoes); Dr. Bob Ellis (vegetable cultivar lists); Mark Freeman (olives); Dennis Gobbee (rose hybridizing); Richard Goetze (pest controls); Patrick Goldsworthy, British Agrochemical Association (chemical controls); Paul Goodspeed (pest controls); Ken Grapes, Royal National Rose Society; Dale Hellegers (pests and diseases); Roy Klehm (peonies); John Kreutziger (grapes); Harbey Lisle (quinces); George Martin (olives); Ed Mashburn (Ribes); Jim Matsuka (cherries); Kenny Maxfield (persimmons); Michael McConkey (figs); Peter Orme (rock garden design and construction); Paul M. Otten (brambles); Ken Paddock (potatoes); Michael Pilarski (kiwis); Terence and Judy Read (grape cultivar lists); David Ronninger (potatoes); Prof. S. Sansavini (fruit cultivar lists); Pat Sawyer (rare fruit); Arty Gordon Schronce (vegetables); Ed Seligman (apricots); Steve Sibbert (olives); Bud Slemmer (lilies); Bryan Smith (strawberries); Carol Spiers (roses); Lee Strassburger (vegetables); Gerald Swaley (weeds); Pham van Tha (fruit cultivar lists); John Warren (apples); James Watson (orchids); Joe Williamson (structures and surfaces).

Providing plants or locations for photographs

Joy Bishop; Brickwall House School, Northiam; Brinkman Brothers Ltd, Walton Farm Nurseries, Bosham; Denbies Wine Estate, Dorking; Mrs. Donnithorne; Martin Double; J. W. Elliott & Sons (West End) Limited, Fenns Lane Nursery, Woking; Elsoms Seeds Ltd, Spalding; Mrs. Randi Evans; Adrian Hall Ltd, Putney Garden Centre, London; Mr. & Mrs. R.D. Hendriksen, Hill Park Nurseries, Surbiton; The Herb and Heather Centre, West Haddlesey; Hilliers Nurseries (Winchester) Ltd, Romsey; Holly Gate International Ltd, Ashington; John Humphries, Sutton Place Foundation, Guildford; Iden Croft Herbs, Staplehurst; Mr. de Jager; Nicolette John; David Knuckey, Burncoose Nursery; Mr. & Mrs. John Land; Sarah Martin; Frank P. Matthews Ltd, Tenbury Wells; Mr. & Mrs. Mead; Anthony Noel, Fulham Park Gardens, London; Andrew Norfield; Notcutts Garden Centre, Bagshot; Bridget Quest-Ritson; Royal Botanic Gardens, Kew; Royal Horticultural Society Enterprises; Lynn and Danny Reynolds, Mrs. Rudd, Surrey Water Gardens, West Clandon; Rolawn, Elvington; Miss. Skilton; Carole Starr; Mr. & Mrs. Wagstaff; Mrs. Wye.

Tools for demonstration photographs

Spear and Jackson Products Ltd, Wednesbury, West Midlands; Ed Jenson of Carl's Equipment, Patchogue, NY; Felco pruners supplied by Burton McCall Group, Leicester.

Supplying equipment

Agralan, Ashton Keynes; Bob Andrews Ltd, Bracknell; Black and Decker Europe, Slough; Blagdon Water Garden Products PLC, Highbridge; Bloomingdales Garden Centre, Laleham; Bulldog Tools Ltd, Wigan; Butterley Brick Ltd, London; CEKA Works Ltd, Pwllheli; Challenge Fencing, Cobham; Anthony Cieri; J. B. Corrie & Co Ltd, Petersfield; Dalfords (London) Ltd, Staines; Diplex Ltd, Watford; Direct Wire Ties Ltd, Hull; Robert Dyas (Ltd), Guildford; Fishtique, Sunbury-on-Thames; Fluid Drilling Ltd, Stratford-upon-Avon; Gardena UK Ltd, Letchworth Garden City; Gloucesters Wholesales Ltd, Woking; Harcros, Walton-on-Thames; Haws Elliott Ltd, Warley; Honda UK Ltd, London; Hozelock Ltd, Birmingham; ICI Garden Products, Haslemere; LBS Polythene, Colne; Merck Ltd, Poole; Neal Street East, London; Parkers, Worcester Park; Pinks Hill Landscape Merchants Ltd, Guildford; Qualcast Garden Products, Stowmarket; Rapitest, Corwen; Seymours, Ewell; Shoosmith & Lee Ltd, Cobham; SISIS Equipment Ltd, Macclesfield; Thermoforce Ltd, Maldon. Tracmaster Ltd, Burgess Hill; Two Wests and Elliot, Chesterfield; Wilkinson Sword, Fiskars UK Limited, Bridgend; Wolf Tools Ltd, Ross-on-Wye.

Additional assistance

Diana Craig, Trent Duffy, Eleanor Hoffman, Caroline Macy, Louise McConnell, K. Selody.

PACIFIC OCEAN

U.S.A. (ALASKA)

YUKON

Whitehorse

Mackenzie

Great Bear Lake

NORTHWEST TERRITORIES

NUNAVUT

Coppermine

Liard

Yellowknife

Great Slave Lake

0a

Dubawnt

BRITISH COLUMBIA

Williston Lake

Slave

Nueltin Lake

Prince Rupert

Terrace
Kitimat

C

Fort St.John

Dawson Creek

Peace

Lake Athabasca

N

A

Grande Prairie

Prince George

A

Fort McMurray

0b

Wollaston Lake

Kazan

Reindeer Lake

7a
6b

Williams Lake

ALBERTA

Athabasca

Fraser

1a

Churchill

Nelson

6a

Campbell River

Powell River

Courtenay

Port Alberni

Nanaimo

Richmond

Esquimalt

7b

Squamish

Vancouver

Victoria

Kamloops

Vernon

Kelowna

Penticton

8a

Chilliwack

7a 6b

St.Albert   Fort Saskatchewan

Leduc   Edmonton

Wetaskiwin   Camrose

Red Deer

Airdrie

Calgary

3a

3b

Lethbridge

Medicine Hat

4a

5a/5b

Cranbrook

1b

2a

Saskatchewan

SASKATCHEWAN

North Battleford

2b

Saskatoon

Prince Albert

Swift Current

Moose Jaw

Regina

Weyburn

Estevan

MANITOBA

Thompson

1a

Cedar Lake

Lake Winnipegosis

Lake Winnipeg

Lake Manitoba

Yorkton

Brandon

Portage la Prairie

Selkirk

Winnipeg

1b

2a

2b

3a

UNITED STATES OF AMERICA

Based on the Plant Hardiness Zones of Canada 2000 map developed by Natural Resources Canada and Agriculture and Agri-Food Canada, this map indicates the different zones in Canada where various types of trees, shrubs, and flowers will most likely survive. Ranging from 0 (the harshest) to 8 (the mildest), there are 9 major zones split into 17 subzones.

Reproduced with the permission of the Minister of Public Works and Government Services Canada, 2003.